Asian Security Practice

Asian Security Practice

Material and Ideational Influences

Edited by

MUTHIAH ALAGAPPA

STANFORD UNIVERSITY PRESS
STANFORD, CALIFORNIA
1998

Stanford University Press
Stanford, California

©1998 by the Board of Regents of the
Leland Stanford Junior University

Printed in the United States of America

CIP data appear at the end of the book

Contents

◇

Preface

Asia is now in the post-postcolonial era. Though Asian states were liberated from colonial rule and foreign domination some four to five decades ago, much of the international politics of Asia in the post–World War II period continued to be dominated by external powers—especially the rivalry between the United States and the Soviet Union. Now that this dominating overlay has been removed, Asian states are interacting more autonomously with each other. This is not, however, a return to history. Asia is an integral part of the global international system, and the Western nations, especially the United States, continue to be important actors in Asia. Nevertheless, for the first time in a long while, Asian states have greater freedom and control over their interests, goals, and destiny. Concurrently, Asia, notwithstanding the financial crisis in 1997, has been economically vibrant; many states have already modernized themselves or are rapidly so doing. Their leaders seek to take advantage of this opportunity not only to protect and enhance the security and welfare of their states, but also to actively participate in the writing of the rules of the game in the political, economic, and security arenas. It is thus both opportune and imperative to investigate the thinking and behavior of Asian elites in these areas.

This study investigates the security thinking and behavior—termed *security practice* in this book—of Asian elites as well as that of other segments of society that challenge the elites' conception of security. Specifically, it identifies the critical security problems and approaches, and the factors that underlie or shape them, for each of the sixteen selected countries. The study also identifies and explains the key common features that characterize security practice in most if not all Asian states, as well as conceptualize security on the basis of the Asian experience. Its purpose is not to provide time-sensitive guidance for policy makers on immediate issues such as the situation across the Taiwan Straits, the confrontation on the Korean peninsula, the Indo-Pakistani conflict, the conflicts in the South China Sea, nuclear proliferation, or the many domestic conflicts in Asian states. Rather, the intention is to illuminate the sources and nature of such internal and international security concerns of Asian elites and to explain their behavior at the domestic, regional, and global levels. Such an understanding will facilitate analysis and may contribute to policy making in the long term. It may also enable analysts and policy makers to make more accurate judgments about the future of the region as well as helping them to shape initiatives to promote peace and security in Asia and the Pacific.

The study, which has a long horizon in time and substantial historical content, identifies the following five features as common to the practice of security in most, perhaps all, Asian states: (1) The nation-state is the primary security referent, but it is also deeply problematic in many countries; (2) both the domestic and international arenas are sources of insecurity for Asian states; (3) political survival, defined broadly, constitutes the core of the security concerns of Asian elites, but it does not exhaust their security agendas; (4) self-help strategies have been dominant in the Asian approach to security, but increasingly cooperation is also becoming significant; and finally, (5) Asian security practices have been dynamic, and more change is in the offing. Although this is by no means an exhaustive list, collectively these elements describe much of the security practice in Asian states. These features are not unique to Asia. The specific content of certain of them are distinctive, but in a temporal and developmental sense rather than in cultural terms.

The security practice in Asian states is often a product of the interplay of ideas, interests, and power. No single international relations theory or paradigm can effectively capture and explain the various features. The realist paradigm continues to be salient, but it has to be supplemented with insights from other international relations theories as well as from theories that deal with state-society interaction. To this end, the study advances two propositions. First, the nature of the political units and state-society interaction is as important as international structure in influencing the security behavior of Asian states. Explanations of Asian security practice must therefore draw upon and, where necessary, integrate factors at the intrastate, unit, and international levels. Arbitrary emphasis on a specific level—as, for example, in weak state analysis or in neorealism, which privilege the intrastate and international levels, respectively—will by definition preclude certain crucial aspects of Asian security practice or minimize their consequences, and thus distort analysis. Second, it is argued that only a combination of material and ideational (social) factors can explain the full range of the security concerns and behavior of Asian states. The argument is not that material factors are unimportant, only that by themselves they have limited explanatory power. The inclusion of social factors—such as political identity of the state, national self-conceptions, political legitimacy, and the national and international historical-cultural-institutional context— as well as other considerations like geography and level of development adds to material structural explanations in at least three ways: by influencing the determination of social reality and hence the definition and urgency of the security problem; by extending the causal chain and thus providing a more complete explanation of the problems and behavior; and by explaining variations in behavior across states as well as changes over time in the behavior of individual states. Social factors also help to explain behavior that may not make sense in the context of material explanations.

Based on the Asian and other experiences, it is argued that the conceptualization of security, though it must include and build on the realist definition, should extend to concerns beyond the international military threat to political survival. It must be capable of accommodating a multiplicity of referents, both internal and international challenges to political survival, a more comprehensive interpretation of political survival and the inclusion of a range of related values, and an array of approaches including not only self-help strategies but also cooperation and community building. The study advances a conceptualization of security based on several levels of abstraction. At the generic level, security is defined as *the protection and enhancement of values that the authoritative decision makers deem vital for the survival and well-being of a community*. This inclusive definition identifies the essence of security and the criteria for classification of an issue as a security concern, but it is of limited analytical usefulness. However, by descending the ladder of generality we can derive analytically relevant concepts from it. Such a hierarchic conception of security has both more internal coherence and greater external relevance, and, in many ways, as demonstrated by the proliferation of security adjectives, it is already common practice.

As with my earlier project, *Political Legitimacy in Southeast Asia*, I decided to invite mostly younger scholars to write the country chapters and to involve more established scholars—international relations theorists, regional and country specialists on Asian security—in an advisory capacity to review, discuss, and comment on their work. In addition to concentrating some of the best minds on the subject, I believe that the inclusion of leading theorists and regional specialists and the facilitation of their interaction with younger scholars fosters the development of theoretically informed study of Asian security, especially among younger Asians. It has also helped in the development of new networks within and among all three groups, and, I hope, has also increased the interest of the international relations theorists in Asian security. The authors and the senior scholars—drawn from twenty countries in East, South, Southeast, and Central Asia, the United States, the United Kingdom, France, Israel, and Australia—met in two stimulating and productive workshops: first in August 1995 in Honolulu and then in Singapore in March 1996.

Covering sixteen countries, involving 17 contributors, 39 senior scholars, and 17 readers, and spanning three years, the study turned out to be a major undertaking, much larger and intellectually more challenging and complicated than I had anticipated. Miles Kahler characterized it as the "Angkor Wat of security studies," and Peter Katzenstein termed it as "wrestling with an elephant." The more deeply we, the contributors, probed, the less sure were we of our understanding of the subject matter. At times our analysis and findings looked good; at other times they appeared commonplace. The experience, at least for me, has been truly humbling but also very rewarding. The other contributors and I hope that the readers will find the book useful and as stimulating as writing it has been for us. We consider our work not the final word, but one among few comparative studies that seek not only to provide substantial analysis but also to elevate the study of Asian security from mere description of contemporary issues and articulation of policy options to inquiries that are conceptually and theoretically informed. Several of our findings require further investigation, refinement, and development; some perhaps warrant reformulation as well. We strongly commend others, especially Asians, to undertake such inquiries. I have come to realize in the course of the last decade or so—and especially during my search for contributors to this book—that very few Asian scholars are trained and willing to engage in this kind of scholarship. I hope that the foundations and others who promote the study of Asian security will in the future be more supportive of scholarship that focuses on concept development and theoretically informed inquiry.

Many people have helped in this undertaking. Vinod Aggarwal, David Elliott, Peter Katzenstein, Stephen Krasner, Michael Leifer, Richard Little, Andrew Mack, S. D. Muni, John Ruggie, and Yang Jiemian as members of the advisory committee and Yoshihide Soeya as co-collaborator gave generously of their time and expertise. Participating in both workshops, they read and reread several chapters, and some commented on the penultimate drafts. Many of their comments and insights have been incorporated into the conceptual and country chapters. Thomas Christensen, Wimal Dissanayake, James Dorian, Mehrdad Haghayeghi, Manuel Montes, Charles Morrison, Darini Rajasingham, Terry Rambo, Johan Saravanamuttu, Akio Watanabe, Geoffrey White, Robert Wirsing, Zakaria Haji Ahmad, Suchit Bungbongkarn, Chan Heng Chee, Chin Kin Wah, Soedjati Djiwandono, François Godement, Ha Young-Sun, Miles Kahler, Bruce Koppel, Kwa Chong Guan, Lee Lai To, Jonathan Pollack, Akihiko Tanaka, Yaacov Vertzberger, Jianwei Wang, and Tom Wingfield attended one of the two workshops and commented on one or more chapters. James Cotton, Harry Harding, Dwight King, Ron May, Andrew Nathan, Denny Roy, Stephen Cohen, Donald Emmerson, Cho Oon Khong, Andrew MacIntyre, Mike Mochizuki, Michel Oksenberg, David Steinberg, Richard Stubbs, William Turley, David Wurfel, and Raju Thomas read one or more of the penultimate draft chapters. Robert Scalapino and Sheldon Simon read and commented on the entire manuscript. To all these scholars I would like to express my deep appreciation and thanks. They made an enormous contribution to the project, and it has been my privilege—professionally and on a personal basis—to interact with them. Russ Phillips, Peter Geithner, Christine Wing, Kimberley Ashizawa, and Jun'etsu Komatsu, although they were not direct participants, provided strong support for the project.

I would also like to thank the contributors to the book. Their knowledge—not only of the countries of their specialization but also of the broader region—is remarkable, and their willingness to ground their inquiry in a common conceptual framework and to rework their contributions several times is admirable. Our reading one another's chapters at the various stages and interacting not only during the workshops but also after them has contributed to the book's coherence and facilitated better understanding of different perspectives. The synergy thus created has added value to the project in several other ways as well. From my own perspective, it has contributed immensely to my understanding of Asian security. The contributors are a talented and diligent group of scholars. I greatly value the opportunity I have had to work with them. I would like to thank Chung-In Moon and K. S. Nathan for stepping in at a late stage to write the chapters on South Korea and Malaysia.

Thanks are also due to the Rockefeller Brothers Fund, the Ford Foundation, the Center for Global Partnership, and the East-West Center for providing funding support; the Institute of Southeast Asian Studies for cohosting the second workshop in Singapore; Michel Oksenberg, Bruce Koppel, Kenji Sumida, Lee Jay Cho, and Charles

Morrison of the East-West Center for their support; Don Yoder for his copyediting; Christopher Collier and Rosevelt Dela Cruz, who served as my research interns during the latter part of the project; Jeanne Hamasaki for so ably organizing the two workshops; Ann Takayesu for so efficiently word-processing the entire manuscript as well as providing excellent secretarial support throughout the project; and Catherine Blickos and Marilu Khudari for their secretarial assistance during its various stages.

Finally, I would like to express my deepest appreciation for my wife, Kalyani. Without her love, forbearance, and support, I could not have devoted as much time and effort as I have to this book. My children—Radha, Shanthi, and Padmaja—have contributed in their own ways. Through their teens, college years, and now as they begin their own professional careers, they have been a source of joy, pleasure, pride, and strength.

MUTHIAH ALAGAPPA

Contributors

SAMINA AHMED is a senior research analyst at the Institute of Regional Studies, Islamabad, Pakistan. She received her Ph.D. from the Department of Political Science at the Australian National University. Her research interests include South and Southwest Asian politics with special emphasis on civil-military relations, and defense and strategic analysis.

MUTHIAH ALAGAPPA is senior fellow and director of the Center for Politics and Security at the East-West Center in Honolulu. He has a Ph.D. from the Fletcher School of Law and Diplomacy, Tufts University. His research interests include international relations theory, international politics of the Asia-Pacific region, government and politics in Southeast Asia, and the interaction of the United Nations with regional institutions.

DEWI FORTUNA ANWAR is currently head of the Regional and International Affairs Division at the Center for Political and Regional Studies, the Indonesia Institute of Sciences (PPW-LIPI). Concurrently, she holds the position of research executive at the Center for Information and Development Studies. She received her Ph.D. from Monash University, Australia. Her primary research interests are Indonesian foreign and defense policies and ASEAN political and security cooperation.

KANTI BAJPAI is associate professor in the Centre for International Politics, Organization, and Disarmament, School of International Studies, Jawaharlal Nehru University, New Delhi. He received his Ph.D. from the University of Illinois, Urbana-Champaign. His areas of research interest are strategic studies, models of regional security and cooperation, and South Asian government and politics.

ROGER CLIFF is a political scientist at the Rand Corporation. He received his Ph.D. from Princeton University's Woodrow Wilson School of Public and International Affairs. His research interests include Asian security and Chinese and Taiwanese politics and foreign policy.

CHRISTOPHER COLLIER received his Ph.D. from the University of Hawaii at Manoa. He was a research fellow at the University of the Philippines and the Ateneo de Davao University in 1990–92, and head of research for the Philippines, Malaysia, and Singapore at Amnesty International's International Secretariat in 1995.

NARAYANAN GANESAN is senior lecturer in political science at the National University of Singapore. He also teaches at the Southeast Asian Studies Programme at that university. He received his Ph.D. in Political Science from Northern Illinois University. His research interests are Southeast Asian politics and foreign policy.

IFTEKHARUZZAMAN is presently the executive director of the Regional Centre for Strategic Studies, Colombo. He is permanently employed as research director of the Bangladesh Institute of International and Strategic Studies, Dhaka. He received his Ph.D. from the Central School of Planning and Statistics, Warsaw. His research interests include politics, security, and interstate relations in South Asia.

DAVID KANG is assistant professor of government at Dartmouth College, and adjunct assistant professor of business administration, Tuck School of Business, Dartmouth College. He received his Ph.D. in political science from the University of California at Berkeley. His research interests include political economy, Asian development, and international relations of Asia.

CHUNG-IN MOON is professor of political science and associate dean of the Graduate School of International Studies, Yonsei University. He received his Ph.D. from the University of Maryland, College Park. He is completing a book-length manuscript on national security, economy, and defense industry in South Korea.

NOEL M. MORADA is assistant professor in the Department of Political Science, University of the Philippines, Diliman, Quezon City, and a fellow at the Institute for Strategic and Development Studies (ISDS), Manila. He is also a Ph.D. candidate in political science at Northern Illinois University. His research interests include Southeast Asian security and comparative political economy, ASEAN external relations, and democratization issues in Asia.

K. S. NATHAN is professor of international relations, Department of History, University of Malaya. He received his Ph.D. in international relations from Claremont Graduate School in California. His research interests include strategic studies, big power relations in the Asia-Pacific region, ASEAN regionalism, and Malaysian security and foreign policy.

KIM NINH is the program officer of the Program on State and Society at the Asia Foundation. She received her Ph.D. from the Department of Political Science, Yale University. Her research interests include political culture and social change, with an emphasis on Southeast Asia, particularly Vietnam.

YOSHIHIDE SOEYA is professor of political science in the Faculty of Law, Keio University. He received his Ph.D. from the Department of Political Science, University of Michigan. His research interests include politics and security in the Asia-Pacific region and Japanese diplomacy.

TIN MAUNG MAUNG THAN is a fellow at the Institute of Southeast Asian Studies, Singapore, and coordinator of its Regional Strategic and Political Studies Programme. He is also a Ph.D. candidate in the Department of Politics, School of Oriental and African Studies, University of London. His research interests include democratization, political economy, and security issues in the Third World. He is a specialist on Myanmar.

PANITAN WATTANAYAGORN is lecturer and director of the Defense Studies Program at the Institute of Security and International Studies at Chulalongkorn University. He received his Ph.D. from Northern Illinois University. His research interests include foreign, security, and defense policies of Thailand, and Southeast Asian regional security.

NIRA WICKRAMASINGHE is a senior lecturer in the Department of History and Political Science, University of Colombo. She received her Ph.D. in modern history from the University of Oxford. Her research interests include ethnic conflict, social theory, and global civil society.

WU XINBO is an associate professor at the Center for American Studies, Fudan University. He received his Ph.D. from the Department of History, Fudan University. His research interests include China's foreign and security policies, Sino-American relations, and Asia-Pacific political and security issues.

Asian Security Practice

Introduction

MUTHIAH ALAGAPPA

Despite and in some ways because of the end of the Cold War, security in Asia continues to be a major concern both in and outside of the continent. In the decades since World War II, Asia has been the scene of several interstate wars: the Korean War (1950–53), the First (1946–54) and Second (1959–75) Indochina Wars, the Cambodian conflict (1978–91), the Sino-Vietnamese war (1979), the three Indo-Pakistani wars (1948, 1965, and 1971), the Sino-Indian border war (1962), and the Afghanistan conflict (1979–89). Asia has also been beset by many internal conflicts, including communist insurgencies, regional rebellions, ethnic and religious clashes, and contests over political legitimacy that have led to political upheavals and revolutions. Although only a few of these wars and conflicts had their origins in the Cold War, nearly all of them were influenced by it in varying degrees. With the termination of the Cold War, some of the conflicts have ended. Others persist, although they have become much more localized. The tensions in the Taiwan Straits, in the Korean peninsula, and between India and Pakistan are dramatic manifestations of the continuing conflicts.

New apprehensions, rivalries, and tensions are also surfacing, due in large part to uncertainty about the future positions and behavior of China, Japan, the United States, Russia, and India and about the state of relations among these countries. The rapid increase in China's economic power is perhaps the most significant factor contributing to long-range apprehensions in Japan, some Southeast Asian countries, and India. It is unclear whether China as a great power will be benign or will seek to dominate its neighbors. Meanwhile, China and the two Koreas are

1

concerned that Japan may seek to develop military capabilities and become a "normal" power, while Japan worries about a rising China, a nuclear-armed Korea, and a nationalist Russia. India worries about the growing power of China, and the other South Asian countries fear that economic reforms may further increase Indian power and domination of the subregion. All these concerns are informed not just by ongoing and anticipated changes in the distribution of power, but also by perceived ambitions and aspirations—for example, the desires on the part of China, Japan, and India for "great power" status—as well as deep-rooted historical experiences, rivalries, and suspicions. The Chinese and the Koreans harbor deep suspicions of the Japanese, the Japanese mistrust the Russians and Chinese, the Vietnamese and Indians have suspicions about the Chinese, and the Indians and the other South Asian peoples mistrust each other. In such an environment, even minor incidents assume great significance, easily escalating tensions in the bilateral relations of many of these countries. The fears and concerns, particularly in Northeast Asia and to a lesser degree in Southeast Asia, also reflect uncertainty over the future role of the United States in the security of the region and the U.S.–Japan security relationship. If the United States should withdraw abruptly from Northeast Asia, or if U.S.–Japanese relations should turn sour, then it is assumed that Tokyo will most likely rearm, setting off a strategic competition among indigenous powers. Although most Asian nations take a positive view of the U.S. security role, there is also a desire in the region, particularly in China, to avoid American hegemony as well as American-led containment of China. The concern over American hegemony and distrust of Japan underlie, in part, Beijing's opposition to the revised guidelines for U.S.–Japan defense cooperation issued in September 1997.

The uncertainties and concerns just outlined are exacerbated by domestic unknowns in several key countries. China, Russia, India, Indonesia, Vietnam, and Pakistan all are undergoing or are likely to undergo fundamental economic or political transitions, the outcomes of which are by no means certain. It is probable that in the course of their transitions these countries will be confronted with major political and socioeconomic challenges that could lead to internal tensions and conflict. There could be international ramifications as well. Even more consequential would be the emergence of xenophobic nationalism in any of the major countries, including Japan, which itself is the midst of a political transition. More immediately, there is the possibility of turmoil or even collapse in North Korea, which could transform the situation in Northeast Asia. These internal transitions and their international repercussions are likely to be prolonged.

The foregoing uncertainties and the resulting unpredictability in the international politics of Asia are intensified by the irrelevance of familiar strategic frameworks, such as bipolarity, the strategic triangle (U.S.–USSR–PRC) and nonalignment, that previously guided state policies. An additional complication is the collapse, termination, or redefinition of alliances, alignments, and agreements centered on Moscow (Soviet-Vietnamese, Soviet-Indian, Soviet–North Korean) and Washington (Sino-American, U.S.–Philippines Base Agreement, U.S.–Japan security treaty), which had underpinned security and stability in Asia. There is a quest in the region for new analytical and policy frameworks, as well as for a new architecture for regional security. Thus, despite the prevailing relative peace, security and stability remain a major focus of concern in Asia.

An Emerging Asian Regional System

The term *Asia* originated with the early Greeks, who used it as a synonym for the Persian Empire (Toynbee 1957: 238–40). Later, on the basis of a mariners' chart, all lands east of the Urals in the Eurasian landmass progressively became designated as Asia. Notwithstanding its Greek origin and accidental delimitation, and despite the fact that Asia, unlike Europe, lacks cultural and civilizational unity,[1] the concept of Asia has become entrenched both in the West and in Asia. It has also acquired an indigenous quality in Asia. The continent of Asia is usually depicted in maps as stretching from Iran to Japan, including the Indian subcontinent and Southeast Asia. There is, however, little agreement on the exact meaning of *Asia* as a concept. The name has been used in several ways, both in Asia and in the West.[2] In the 1950s and 1960s, the use of *Asia*, for example in the pan-Asian movements formed in the context of the struggle against colonial rule, conformed fairly closely to the cartographic delimitation. More recently, *Asia* has been appropriated by some in the West as well as in Northeast and Southeast Asia to refer to the group of countries in the latter two subregions. This has been the case, for example, in the Asian versus Western values debate (over such issues as the content of human rights and the applicability of democracy to Asia) and in the determination of membership in such regional institutions as the forum for Asia-Pacific Economic Cooperation (APEC), the ASEAN Regional Forum (ARF), and the Asia-Europe Meeting (ASEM). Other countries including Australia have in recent years laid claim to the label of Asia as well.

In this study, *Asia* is used to refer to the collective of countries in Northeast, Southeast, and South Asia.[3] This essentially geopolitical delimitation is based on the geographical location of these countries in the continent of Asia and on their security interdependence. China is the interconnecting core of this security region. It has security interests in all three subregions, and most countries in those subregions have security concerns that are focused on or call for interaction with China in one or more ways. The adjacent subregional systems and the dominant actors in them—China, Japan, Russia, India, Indonesia—are becoming increasingly more interdependent and interactive—some more than others. Japanese economic power and the projection of American military and economic power also lend credence to the idea of Asia as a security region composed of several interacting subsystems with Northeast Asia as its core for the present and foreseeable future.

The end of the Cold War has contributed to the regionalization of international politics (Alagappa 1991b; Friedberg 1993–94). Security in Europe, Asia, the Middle East, or Africa can now be investigated independently of developments in other regions. During the Cold War, Asian regional security was closely linked to—and in many ways subordinated to, if not subsumed by—the Soviet-American confrontation and the associated Sino-Soviet conflict. Attempts by Asian countries to escape the dynamics of superpower competition through movements and strategies such as nonalignment, neutrality, and peace zones were only partially successful. In Japan, initial sentiments for neutrality gave way to a security alliance with the United States. Indonesia under Suharto tilted toward the West. India's nonalignment was compromised by its treaty with the Soviet Union. And the proposals by the Association of Southeast Asian Nations (ASEAN) for a Zone of Peace, Freedom, and Neutrality (ZOPFAN) and a Southeast Asia Nuclear Weapons Free Zone (SEANWFZ) remained unrealized (Alagappa 1991c, 1987b).

In the post–Cold War era, however, there is no comparable overarching global dynamic. Local and regional dynamics are becoming more salient, and states appear to have greater latitude in shaping their immediate environments. Unlike the economic domain, where the Asian economies and their regional activities are becoming integrated into the global economy, the security domain seems to be witnessing the development of a much more independent regional system.

Asia is now entering a new era that may be characterized as postpostcolonial. In the 1940s and 1950s, Asia, though freed from a long period of colonial rule and foreign domination, emerged only as a subordinate system, subject to the dynamics of the global ideological conflict.[4] In the 1990s Asia is emerging as a more autonomous system, the dynamics of which are likely to be determined much more by indigenous actors than by extraregional powers. The development of this system is likely to be gradual, however, and its configuration may not become firm for some time to come. Indigenous powers will become progressively more consequential in the structure and dynamics of the system, although the United States will continue to play a critical role. U.S. influence, however, is likely to gradually lessen. The emergence of an Asian regional system has generated interest among political analysts with regard to its likely structure and dynamics, as well as the question of whether Asia will be a zone of peace or a zone of conflict.

Analysts have depicted the emerging situation in Asia as a five-power balance of power system (Dibb 1995), as "ripe for rivalry" (Friedberg 1993–94), and as heading for instability (Betts 1993–94). It has been said that "Europe's past could well be the future of Asia" (Friedberg 1993–94: 7), and that Asia "may well become the most important zone of conflict in the twenty-first century" (Buzan and Segal 1994: 20). The persistence of historical antagonisms, the absence or weakness of institutions (and the belief that this situation is unlikely to improve dramatically), the weakness of the Asian countries as modern states and the diversity of their political and economic structures, the existence of an incipient arms race and the potential for its further escalation, and the belief that war is still a cost-effective instrument of policy in Asia: these are among the reasons why such analysts privilege the realist lens and forecast a "back to the future" scenario for Asia.[5]

Although concerned with many of the same factors and developments, other analysts, primarily Asian specialists and policy makers, are less pessimistic about the future of Asia.[6] Many reject the relevance of Western paradigms and the analogy with Europe. Among the arguments advanced in support of this position are that the situation in Asia is radically different from that of Europe, that Asian countries attach greater weight to economic matters than do their European counterparts, and that Asian countries conceive of security in a broad or comprehensive manner.[7] In this view, Asian countries are quite capable of charting an independent course, the future can be shaped, and the current period presents a rare window of opportunity that must be used to create the necessary structures for peace and security and to foster a benign atmosphere conducive to economic growth and modernization (Koh 1995; P. Ho 1995).

The latter view is not rooted in any clear-cut theoretical framework; rather, it rests on beliefs and aspirations and is policy oriented. It is possible, however, to construct this viewpoint in conceptual terms as one that seeks the development of a functionally based international society.[8] The argument would run like this. Although Asian states may be competitive and have a history of antagonistic relations, they now have a mutual interest in pursuing economic modernization, which requires international stability and the avoidance of war. This mutual interest, coupled with increasing economic and social interaction, will gradually give rise to a functionally rooted international society. Through multilateral forums, such as Asia-Pacific Economic Cooperation (APEC) and the ASEAN Regional Forum (ARF), Asian states will gradually seek to limit the use of force, provide for sanctity of contracts, and arrange for assignment and recognition of property rights. Asian cultures, such as Confucianism in East Asia, may also be deployed as a civilizational basis for such a society. A group identity might also be developed through the interaction of various groups, such as the East Asian Economic Caucus, with similar organizations in North America and Europe.

The foregoing scenarios—both of the pessimistic and optimistic varieties—may or may not be fulfilled. The concern of the contributors to this book is not to validate such predictions about the future security situation in the region or to offer other predictions. Rather, the aim is to lay the groundwork for an in-depth understanding of Asian security by investigating conceptions of security in sixteen Asian countries.

In this book we undertake an ethnographic, country-by-country study of how Asian states conceive of their security. For each country, we investigate its security problematic and how it has changed over time as well as the policies deployed by the central decision makers. We also seek to explain the construction of security in these countries. This inside-out or bottom-up approach facilitates identification of similarities and differences in the security thinking and behavior of Asian countries and exploration of their consequences. The crucial insights into the dynamics of international security in the region provided by this approach can then form the basis for further inquiry, including debates about the future of the region. How Asian nations, particularly the larger countries, conceive of security will have a significant bearing on conflict and cooperation, and also on the management of international affairs at the subregional, regional, and global levels. For this reason, it is essential to have a good understanding of their security thinking and behavior— termed *security practice* in this book.

Asian Security and Its Broader Relevance

As Asia becomes more powerful and consequential in international economics and politics, security in Asia becomes an issue of concern to other countries and regions as well, particularly the United States and Western Europe. The contemporary rise of Asian countries has been labeled by some as the dawn of an Asian or Pacific century, while others have called it an Asian Renaissance and a "return to history," when Asia was a cradle of major civilizations and an important arena for international trade (see, for example, Commission for a New Asia 1994). Whether or not one agrees with such claims, it is a fact that Asia, particularly East Asia, is emerging as a crucial power center in the world. At present this is most evident in the economic domain. In 1993 Asia accounted for 25.9 percent of the world gross domestic product (GDP), compared to about 4 percent in 1960. In 1993 the U.S. share of the world GDP amounted to 26.3 percent, while that of Europe amounted to 30.5 percent.[9] Although it may be difficult to replicate the impressive growth rates of recent years, it is likely that the East Asian share of world GDP will continue to increase, in spite of some occasional setbacks like the 1997 currency crisis in several Southeast Asian countries.[10] The ongoing economic crisis is generally viewed not as the end of the Asian economic "miracle" but as a setback. Growth is expected to resume in two to four years. The economies of South Asia, particularly that of India, are also picking up speed. During the 1980–95 period these economies grew at an average annual rate of 5.25 percent.[11] If this growth rate is sustained and even marginally improved upon, then the collective economic weight of Asia will further increase.

On the basis of purchasing power parity, in 1995 Asia had three of the ten largest economies in the world (China, Japan, and India). In 1994 Asia collectively accounted for 27.2 percent of global exports, 26.2 percent of global imports, and 37.5 percent of global reserves.[12] Clearly, Asia is a crucial part of the global economy, and East Asia is now one of three key economic regions of the world, along with North America and Western Europe. Economic growth and industrialization continue to rank high among the priorities of nearly every Asian government. For this reason, among others, the already substantial market, capital, and technological power and influence of Asia are likely to expand.

Asian governments, with the exception of Japan, have little or no inhibition about translating growing economic strength into political and military power and influence.[13] China and India clearly aspire to regional and global positions of greater power, prestige, and influence, which they seek to realize as their economic might grows. Even Japan, despite many domestic and international inhibitions, has publicly articulated its goal to seek an "honored place in international society," and there is growing domestic support for Tokyo to play a larger political role commensurate with its economic power. For example, Japan has formally stated its desire to become a member of the U.N. Security Council. These countries, particularly Japan and China, may in the next three to four decades be in a position to challenge the predominant position currently enjoyed by the United States in the Asia-Pacific region. Several other Asian countries have the potential to develop into middle-rank powers that will rival, if not surpass, countries like Canada and Australia. Some of these states, such as Indonesia, South Korea, Thailand, and Pakistan, already seek to play regional and international roles. The realization of these potentials for power will dramatically alter the political and security landscape of the Asia-Pacific region and, by extension, the world.

An investigation of Asian security assumes even greater urgency in light of the growing assertiveness of Asian countries with regard to the management of regional and global affairs. The broadening and deepening of ASEAN, the enlargement of the ASEAN Post-Ministerial Conference (ASEAN PMC), the launching of the ARF, the active role of the ASEAN countries and Japan in seeking to influence the direction of APEC, the attempt to create an East Asian Economic Caucus (EAEC), and the Asian initiative in launching the Asia-Europe Meeting (ASEM): all these developments are illustrative of the desire of Asian nations to be masters in their own homes and to shape their strategic environments.

The proactive stance of Asian governments in attempting to shape their regional environment can be traced to several developments: growing self-confidence, arising primarily from economic achievements; recovery of and pride in their long histories and civilizations (some East Asians, for example, attribute their economic successes to cultural values); desire to avoid the foreign domination to which they were subjected in the past; and recognition of the need to maintain a stable and peaceful environment to facilitate further economic growth.

The Asian countries, individually and collectively, have sought and will continue to seek to influence the rules of the political, economic, and security games in a changing world. In the area of human rights and democracy, for example, some Asian governments have challenged the projection of Western values as universal and have sought to provide an alternative framework for discourse on human rights and governance.[14] Truly universal values, it is claimed, can emerge only from the interaction and fusion of the values of the West and the East (Lee Kuan Yew 1993; Mahbubani 1995). At the 1993 World Conference on Human Rights in Vienna, the West was compelled to accept basic economic and social rights and the right to development as part of human rights, while the Asian governments had to accept the existence of basic civil and political rights that are not entirely matters of domestic jurisdiction (Boyle 1995: 80).

The claim by some prominent Asian leaders and officials that Asia has a distinct value system, different from that of the West, further underscores the need to study Asian security practice. Political and sociocultural values not only shape domestic structures of domination but also inform worldviews. They shape identities, interests, and policies, and affect outcomes. Thus, uniquely Asian values, if they do exist, can be expected to influence security practice as well.[15] The implications merit inquiry. The claim to distinctive Asian values has already been deployed in "West versus the rest" debates over sovereignty, democratic governance, and human rights.[16] Samuel Huntington has argued that in the post–Cold War era, "the great divisions among humankind and the dominating source of conflict will be cultural" (Huntington 1993: 22). He posits a Confucian-Islamic alliance that will challenge the dominant position of the West and seek to shape the world in non-Western ways. Former French prime minister Edouard Balladur, in arguing for protectionist policies on the part of Europe, stated that "the question now is how to organize or protect ourselves from countries whose different values enable them to undercut us."[17]

From an academic perspective, the study of Asian security will broaden the empirical base of international relations and security studies. Until now, European regional politics has been presented as international politics. Concept and theory formulation and testing in these subfields of political science have been grounded essentially in the experiences of the North Atlantic countries, thereby contributing to inadvertent Eurocentrism, as pointed out by Ken Booth (1979). Asia is fertile ground to debate, test, and develop many of these concepts and competing theories, and to counteract the ethnocentric bias. For example, the status of Japan, once described by Prime Minister Keiichi Miyazawa as an "economic superpower but political pygmy," has been an issue of contention among the competing theories of international relations. Neorealists, viewing the hybrid state as an anomaly, claim that Japan will eventually emerge as a normal power (Waltz 1993; Layne 1993). Kenneth Waltz asserts that Japan will be the next great power and that it will be forced to acquire greater military capabilities, including a nuclear capability (1993).[18] Constructivists, on the other hand, do not necessarily see the current position and orientation of Japan as an anomaly. Building on the case made by John Ruggie (1983) for the possibility of functional differentiation of units in the international system, they argue the case for the coexistence of different kinds of states, including a trading state like Japan (Jepperson, Wendt, and Katzenstein, 1996). They deploy historical and cultural legacies to explain the current position of Japan (Katzenstein 1993). Chalmers Johnson claims that Japan is a problem for international relations theories, particularly neorealism (Johnson 1993). His explanation stresses the historical continuity of the Japanese tradition, in particular the continuity of the essential role of the state. In his view, the trading state and capitalist developmental state theories provide a more accurate, if incomplete, framework for studying the international behavior of Japan.

Many other issues of contention in the theory of international relations, such as systemic versus unit-level explanations and ideational versus material interests in explaining state behavior, can be investigated or tested in the context of Asian experiences. Theories relating to balancing behavior, the behavior of ascending and declining powers, power transition and stability, interdependence and security, and the emergence, development, and effectiveness of international institutions can also be tested based on the Asian experience. Because of its long history and rich cultural traditions, Asia can provide many cases for the study of strategic culture and its impact on the international behavior of states. There have already been some good introductory works on the strategic cultures of China, India, and Japan (Johnston 1995; Tanham 1992; Gordon 1992; Rosen 1995; Berger 1993). In addition to broadening the base for international relations and security studies, theoretically informed investigations will introduce much-needed rigor to the study of Asian security, which until now has been predominantly empirical and issue oriented.[19] Theoretically informed inquiries of Asian security have been few and far in between, and often fragmentary. Further, the analysis of Asian security has explicitly or implicitly tended to privilege realism or neorealism (for example, Friedberg 1993–94; Betts 1993–94; Dibb 1995; Buzan and Segal 1994). The relevance of other paradigms has been little explored. A more comprehensive theoretically informed research program is required.

Finally, Asia is representative of the wider world in several ways. As in many other parts of the world, nation-states in Asia are still problematic and, in several cases, subject to contestation. Asian states share with many others several trends and experiences including transitions to market economy, political liberalization and democratization (in some countries) or resistance to political change (in others), a colonial history, generational changes in leadership, and changes in state capabilities. Asia comprises strong and weak states with a wide variety of political systems and cultural traditions, in different stages of political and economic development. It experiences not only a relatively high incidence of political-military conflict but in some subregions also a high degree of economic interdependence and cooperation. Thus, Asia can be said to be more broadly representative of the world than either North America or Western Europe. The study of Asian security can provide insights applicable to many other countries and regions. It may therefore be a more suitable base for articulation of security and its elements—the second central purpose of this book.

Defining Security

Security continues to rank high on national agendas worldwide. It commands enormous resources, including the sacrifice of life, liberty, and property, the protection of which justifies the state in the first place. The end of the Cold War has not altered these facts. The anticipated peace dividend has materialized in only a few countries.[20] Very large amounts of resources continue to be devoted to defense in most countries—especially in Asia. Termination of the Cold War, however, has contributed to a rethinking of security, especially on the part of the major protagonists in that ideological conflict.[21] Receding concern over a general nuclear war, the growing salience of regional security issues, concern with "new" referents, dimensions, and threats, and more generally the complex post–Cold War situation have stimulated interest in the redefinition of security. Policy makers' interest in broadening the scope of security has further stimulated the controversy within the academic community over how security should be defined. Since the early 1980s quite a few scholars have argued for a broader definition.[22] Others have argued the contrary (see, for example, Walt 1991; Morgan 1992; and Dorff 1994); at most they accept only limited broadening of the concept, preferring to keep it within the parameters of realism, the reigning paradigm for this subject area, especially during the Cold War.

The debate over the redefinition of security is a welcome development, but it has been largely abstract, lacking roots in empirical investigation. In some respects it has also been a dialogue without listeners. With a few exceptions, participants have been talking past one another, more interested in expounding the merits of their own paradigms and definitions and elaborating upon the shortcomings of alternatives than in building on the strengths of competing expositions. There is no shared understanding of security (Lynn-Jones 1991: 53–54), and there has been little interest in developing such an understanding. This situation has led to a proliferation of neologisms. *Security* is now used with more than 30 different adjectives. See Figure 3 (Chapter 20) for a listing and classification of these terms.

Definitions and discussions of security often privilege selected elements or certain instruments or, worse, confuse the different elements, adding to the bewilderment that characterizes the subject. Stephen Walt's (1991: 212) definition of security studies as "the study of the threat, use, and control of military force," for example, focuses exclusively on one instrument—force. In a similar vein, Richard Shultz, Roy Godson, and Ted Greenwood (1993: 2–3), in designing a curriculum for security studies in the 1990s, state that they do not oppose expansion of the field, yet choose to "concentrate on the traditional and historical essence of the subject: the threat, use and management of military force, and closely related topics." These and other such formulations not only restrict the concept of security to one instrument, but also ignore (or make assumptions about) crucial elements of security, such as who or what is to be secured and what aspects or values relating to that entity are to be secured. Further, they encourage a narrow, technocratic approach to security. There is a clear need to rethink the concept of security. But some of the attempts to formulate alternative conceptions (discussed in Chapter 1) broaden the concept indiscriminately, making it an analytically useless grab bag.

A further problem has been loose interpretation of such concepts as collective security, collective self-defense, common security, and cooperative security, and a tendency to stretch their meanings.[23] David Dewitt (1994), for example, in his eagerness to depict cooperative security (a Canadian-sponsored initiative) as the most suitable concept for the Asia-Pacific region, seeks to subsume the competitive approach to security (including balance of power and alliances) under the label of cooperative security (which properly connotes the pursuit of security through international arrangements that regulate or even preclude independent national use of force).[24] He also seeks to broaden this concept to encompass comprehensive security, the primary concern of which is to indicate the breadth and depth of what is to be secured. Although deployment of concepts in this manner may have utility as a political project, the conceptual stretching that ensues reduces the analytical utility of the concept of cooperative security.

The current unsatisfactory state of affairs may be attributed, in part, to the nature of the concept itself, which has been variously described as elusive, ambiguous, amorphous, difficult, and essentially contested (see, for example, Wolfers 1962c: 147–65; Buzan 1991: 7). But this is the case with most core concepts in the social sciences—power, justice, the state, and culture, for example—and it has not prevented their conceptual flowering. Security is no more difficult or contested than these other core concepts. With sustained, rigorous, and concerted effort, analysis and development of the concept of security should make at least some headway. Because concepts constitute the basic "units of thought" and in large measure inform, if not define, discourse and theorizing, explication and elaboration of security and a shared understanding of the concept are crucial for the development of the security studies subfield.[25] This book seeks to make a modest contribution to that effort. Drawing upon the social practice of security in selected Asian countries, as well as the ongoing debate within the academic community, it seeks to explicate and elaborate the concept of security.

About This Book

This study has a threefold purpose. One is investigation of security practice in sixteen Asian countries to develop an in-depth understanding of and to explain security thinking and behavior in those countries. The second purpose is to ascertain whether there are common features among the various security practices and to advance possible explanations for them. The third purpose is to contribute to the conceptual development of security, by drawing upon the findings of this empirical investigation and upon the ongoing debate in the academic community. Specifically, this study explores the following sets of questions:

1. How is security conceived and executed by the central decision makers (CDMs) in the selected Asian countries?[26] Are their security practices contested? Why? Have security practices changed over time? If so, how and why?

2. What are the similarities and differences among security practices in Asian countries? What accounts for them? Is there anything distinctively Asian about security practices in Asia? If so, to what can this be attributed?

3. Is the security thinking and behavior in Asian countries best explained by systemic or unit-level factors—or by a combination of both? In each case, which is more salient, material interests or ideational variables? Which paradigms best explain the practice of security in Asia?

4. What are the implications of the Asian cases for conceptualizing security? How should security be defined?

This study departs from the more common approach in international relations of positing and testing one or more hypotheses. The intention here is not to prove or disprove any hypothesis, but rather, on the basis of comparative inquiry, to arrive at propositions about security practice in Asia and to conceptualize security. The research method and strategy have been tailored accordingly.

Method

As noted earlier, the debate over defining security has been conducted primarily at an abstract level, including minimal and usually selective reference to actual practice. Security and its pursuit are defined by analysts in a logical-deductive manner. The assumptions and logic of a paradigm, rather than practice, are believed to determine security goals and behavior. Realist definitions, for example, based on the assumption of anarchy and a certain logic of it, assert that survival—defined in terms of political independence and territorial integrity—is the core security objective and that self-help is the basic principle governing state action. Those who contest such definitions do so largely by challenging the imputed logic of anarchy, suggesting that security can be achieved through cooperation as well as competition, or by challenging the assumption of anarchy itself.

Although capable of providing powerful insights, the logical-deductive approach has serious limitations.[27] Political survival, for example, while important, is not always at issue, and political independence and territorial integrity may not be the only concerns. Survival may be defined, especially by the major powers, in terms of national self-extension goals, such as "making the world safe for democracy." The content of such milieu goals cannot be ascertained by the logical-deductive method.[28] Further, security behavior may be affected by unit-level attributes, such as the normative context and domestic state structure, and these in turn will be influenced by political-strategic culture and historical legacies. The impact of these variables—which may vary over time and across states—cannot be discerned and explained deductively. For example, explanations of the differences in the security behavior of pre- and post–World War II Japan, as well as the differences between the security behavior of contemporary Japan and that of Germany or the United States, have to draw heavily on the differences in those countries' state structures and normative contexts, both of which have been shaped by different historical legacies.[29] Security behavior that is linked to norms, identity, and domestic political structure can only be investigated empirically in specific historical settings.

Empirical investigation may also be helpful in getting around the problem of evaluating competing definitions of security that are based on different assumptions. Security in the empirical-inductive approach is not formulated a priori but is developed on the basis of comparative study of the articulations and behavior of the CDMs.[30] Unless actors are perceived as "judgmental dopes" or as self-serving manipulators of public interest, one should accept that each, knowing a great deal about the society of which he or she is a member, is articulating the security concerns of that society.[31] Adopting this approach requires that security be framed and evaluated in the context of a society's "mutual knowledge."[32] The specific content of security is determined by the legitimate decision makers. The task of the observer is to interpret and evaluate on the basis of the rules of the society without imposing arbitrary rules or definitions. Concepts, as observed by Anthony Giddens, must necessarily draw upon social practice and are adequate only when they master and build on notions that "are already embedded in the contexts of use of ordinary language," including, in this case, policy language (Giddens 1979: 246–48).

Thus, while abstraction and internal coherence are important in concept formulation, so is external relevance. Concepts and theories, to be meaningful, must be grounded in reality and must be able to accommodate contextual and historical variations. Artificial bounding of a concept in the interest of theoretical elegance and analytical utility will divorce theory and analysis from reality, making them less useful if not irrelevant and possibly misleading. The concept, however, must be sufficiently abstract without becoming a grab bag. The challenge, then, is to conceptualize security in a way that is both analytically useful and empirically relevant.

Research Strategy

To provide a common departure point and to allow for comparison across countries, this study employs a statist approach that focuses on the security conceptions of central decision makers. Despite its shortcomings, the nation-state is still the dominant expression of political community, and governments continue to be the central actors in domestic and international politics. They are the primary agent of security as well as the paramount problem for security. The focus on CDMs, however, does not imply that the state is being privileged and that competing conceptions of security are not to be explored. On the contrary, the contributors to this study take the position that it is important to problematize the state both as a political community and as a legitimate actor, and to investigate contestations of it, as well as competing conceptions of security. There are at least three reasons for this position.

First, the nation-state, the political system, and the incumbent government are contested entities in many countries. Identities and ideological preferences are the focal points of contestation. In these situations, incumbent governments may view such contestations as threats to "national" security, and it is likely that security as constructed by the CDMs does not encompass the concerns of some segments of society and may even threaten their security. Instead of being viewed as a provider, the incumbent government in such situations could be perceived as the principal source of insecurity for those groups. Security in such countries will be highly contested, making it imperative that competing conceptions be explored.

Second, even where the state is not politically contested, it may be unable to provide equal security for all its citizens or may not have a monopoly over the security function. In these situations, other entities at the individual, group, societal, regional, and global levels may well become the referents or providers with regard to one or more aspects of security. Consequently, the construction of security by all such entities requires examination.

Third, contestations make explicit the assumptions and interests of the various agents, thereby providing an important focus for research on the meaning of security. To keep the exercise manageable, however, discussion of competing conceptions will be limited to those that bear upon and affect the security behavior of CDMs.

As it examines practices of security, the inquiry addresses four questions. First, who or which entity is to be secured? That entity is the *referent* of security. Second, what *core values* or aspects associated with the referent must be protected or enhanced to ensure its security? The concern here is with the goals and values that decision makers of the community in question consider vital and seek to protect under the label of security. Third, what are the *types of threats*—political, military, sociocultural, economic, or environmental—against which these core values have to be protected? And what is the *nature of the security problem* in each case? Is the security problem zero-sum and distributional (relative gains) in nature, or is it one of political market failure?[33] The second and third questions may be grouped under the heading of scope or domain. The fourth and final question is, How is security to be achieved? Is the *approach* to security (that is, coping strategies) competitive, cooperative, designed to build community, or some combination of them? These four key interrelated elements—referent, core values, threats and nature of the security problem, and approach to security— constitute the *structure of security*. They also constitute the dominant terms of security discourse and inform the investigations in this study (see Table 1).

It is possible to identify a hierarchy among these four elements. The referent is fundamental. It has a crucial bearing in determining both the level of analysis and the values to be protected. Political autonomy and territorial integrity, for example, are critical values when the state is the referent, but may be less important for referents at the individual, group,

TABLE 1
Structure and Terms of Security Discourse

Element of Security		Illustration
Referent (Who?)		Communal, religious, or other group, society, regime, nation-state, state, regional community, world/planet
Scope/Domain (What?)	Core Values	Political independence and territorial integrity; social harmony, internal order, political stability, national unity; sociocultural essence of nation; economic security (safeguarding prosperity, promoting economic growth and modernization, international competitiveness, distributive justice, etc.); safe environment
	Types of Threats	Political, military, economic, sociocultural, environmental
	Nature of Problem	Zero-sum, distributional, political, market failure
Approach (How?)		Competitive (self-help), cooperative security; community security

or global level. These values and the type and nature of threats will in turn influence the coping strategies and instruments deployed to achieve security. Although these elements can be separated for analytical purposes, in theory as well as in practice they are interconnected and must be considered together, particularly in conceptual discussions of security.

A meaningful discussion of the four elements of security also requires investigation of the domestic and international political environment. That environment will have a significant, if not defining, impact on the collective and national identity of states, as well as on the sources of insecurity, the nature of the security problems, the types of threats, and the approaches adopted. Discussions of security thus should be embedded in the general theoretical discourse on the nature of domestic and international politics.[34] According to Oran Young, "only in this way can security studies escape static assumptions of international [and domestic] society and avoid devolving into a technocratic exercise."[35] The impact of the political environment is mediated, however, by its interpretation by the CDMs. The beliefs they hold set "bounds within which interpretations are accepted or rejected" (Vertzberger 1990: 123; see also Goldstein and Keohane 1993). Such beliefs play a crucial role in diagnosis and policy prescription and may have a significant impact on security behavior. Thus, the cultural-institutional context in which CDMs operate must be investigated as well (Katzenstein 1995).

To discern how security is constructed and practiced by CDMs, it is useful to begin with formal articulations in public documents and pronouncements, as well as interviews with political leaders and officials. When making use of such sources, however, one must be careful to distinguish between rhetoric and actual behavior, particularly in the priority ranking of referents, core values, and approaches. This is best done through the investigation of hard cases, wherein the actors must make choices between competing referents, values, and approaches. It is essential, therefore, to go beyond formal articulation to explore what CDMs actually do—that is, how they operationalize security—and assess whether their behavior is in keeping with formal articulations and is consistent over time.

To explain security practice, two related questions must be explored. First, Is the security behavior of the CDMs driven by systemic or unit-level considerations, or by a combination of them? (And if by a combination, how are the different levels linked?) Second, Which factors—material or ideational—are more salient in explicating behavior? The first question focuses on the explanatory level, whereas the second focuses on the explanatory variable. Ideational and material factors are relevant to both systemic and unit-level explanations. The relevant theories and their principal claims are sketched out here; for a further discussion, see Chapter 1.

There are four system-level theories that attempt to explain international politics and, by implication, state behavior. Of these, neorealism and constructivism may be viewed as the two main contending theories; neoliberalism and commercial liberalism as falling between them. Based on anarchy as the ordering principle of the international system, neorealism asserts that international politics is competitive and conflictual; that state survival is problematic and the highest end of states; and that self-help is the basic principle of action (Waltz 1979). Neorealism is skeptical of cooperative security strategies. Although it accepts that state behavior may be conditioned by attributes and interaction at the unit level, it privileges the international material structure in explaining state behavior. State behavior is seen as a set of rational responses to the pressures created by the international material structure—principally changes in the distribution of power. The key predictions of neorealism are that states will engage in balancing and that because of the competitive nature of the system, states will be driven to become like units and to behave in a similar manner.

The acultural and ahistorical bases of neorealism and its claim to universality are challenged by constructivism. This theory contests the imputed logic of anarchy as well as the privileging of material capabilities. It argues that the structure of the international system is intersubjectively constituted. Anarchy is what states make of it (Wendt 1992). The neorealist logic of anarchy, in this view, is socially constructed and can be transformed. John Ruggie's (1983) key insight that international anarchy need not preclude functional differentiation of units is developed to substantiate this argument and to make the case that different units can coexist in anarchy. Further, constructivism posits that the international structure is social, comprising shared knowledge, material capabilities, and state practices (Wendt 1995: 73). Material capabilities in and of themselves have no meaning. Their meaning is derived instead from shared knowledge. Shared knowledge, often principles and norms, which may be constitutive or regulatory, shape state identities and interests as well as interstate normative structures (Jepperson, Wendt, Katzenstein, 1996). Constructivism holds that state practices and structure are mutually constitutive (see Giddens 1979). It is claimed that constructivism can at least equal, if not better, neorealism in explaining international politics and state behavior.

Neoliberalism accepts the key premises of neorealism. Its main contention is directed at the neorealist claim that cooperation is difficult to sustain and that institutions matter only on the margins. Neoliberalism posits that a higher degree of cooperation is possible under anarchy than is allowed for in neorealism and that institutions can alter conceptions of self-interest, reduce uncertainty, and stabilize expectations (Keohane 1984). State behavior can be constrained through the operation of rules. Institutions can facilitate peaceful change and have done so.

Commercial liberalism, for its part, contends that growing trade and economic interdependence will minimize the negative effects of anarchy and gradually transform the nature of international politics and international relations, moving it in the direction of a "trading world." In this world, considerations of interdependence, rather than insecurity born of anarchy, affect the international disposition and behavior of states (Rosecrance 1986).

Neoliberalism and commercial liberalism can be incorporated into a constructivist explanation. In the view of constructivists, neorealism also can be explained as a social construction. Neorealists, of course, would dispute such a claim. If systemic considerations are deemed critical in explaining state security behavior, then it is necessary to explore which of these competing theories has the most power in explaining the security practice of Asian states.

It is generally recognized that unit-level and domestic factors play an important role in conditioning the international behavior of states and must therefore be taken into account in any attempt to explain state behavior. The case of the Soviet Union, where internal developments (leading eventually to its collapse) had dramatic implications for its international behavior, is frequently cited in support of the proposition that internal factors must be taken into account in explaining the security behavior of states (for example, see Kolodziej 1992a, 1992b). Waltz has all along accepted that state behavior is rooted in a conjunction of external and internal factors (1959, 1979, 1986), and Robert Keohane has stated that the "next major step forward in understanding international cooperation will have to incorporate domestic politics fully into the analysis—not on a mere ad hoc basis but systematically" (1989: 30).

The problem is that a plethora of unit-level theories have been deployed to explain state behavior, all of them emphasizing the importance of unit-level and domestic factors. Unfortunately, no attempt has been made to link those factors in any systematic fashion. Richard Rosecrance and Arthur Stein (1993: 5), for example, argue that domestic bases "play an important, indeed a pivotal, role in the selection of grand strategy and, therefore, in the prospects for international cooperation and conflict." Yet they do not seek to provide a grand theory of domestic factors, but instead simply list some: domestic groups, social ideas, the character of constitutions, economic constraints, historical social tendencies, and domestic political pressure groups. Similarly, it is beyond the scope of this book to formulate an overarching theory of unit-level variables. Instead, the study is limited to four sets of theories and factors that appear most relevant: realpolitik or political realism, which emphasizes raison d'être and material strength; domestic constructivism, which emphasizes ideas, norms, history, and culture; regime type theories that link state behavior to the type of political system or the dominant functional imperative of the state; and state-society interaction focused on national identity and regime survival.

Realpolitik, the basis for neorealism, resembles it in some ways but differs from it in others. The key differences lie in the level and concerns of analysis. Neorealism is essentially a theory of international politics, but one that can be used to explain the behavior of states in terms of systemic (structural) constraints.[36] Realpolitik, on the other hand, is a theory of foreign policy that seeks to explain the international behavior of states deploying a power rationale. The key element of political realism is its assumption that CDMs think and act in terms of interest defined as power, and this assumption is claimed to be universally valid (Morgenthau 1978: 5, 8). National interests rather than ideas dominate the behavior of CDMs, although the content of such interests will be informed by the political and cultural contexts of the particular historical period. The ultimate goals of states may vary (freedom, security, prosperity), but power, as the means to achieve them, is always the immediate goal. Consequently, as Morgenthau (1978: 27–92) argues, states will struggle for power to preserve the status quo (that is, to maintain the present distribution of power), to engage in imperialism (to seek a favorable change in the distribution of power), or to pursue a policy of prestige (to demonstrate or increase its own power). This aspiration to power necessarily leads to balancing behavior. Although the elements of power are defined broadly, military power is privileged because it is believed to be the ultima ratio in international politics (Morgenthau 1978: 31; Carr 1964: 109). War is posited as a common instrument of policy among states actively engaged in international politics, although the advent of nuclear weapons has radically transformed this situation. For the states that possess nuclear weapons, diplomacy has a crucial role in creating and maintaining new institutions for the pursuit of common security.

Constructivism, at the domestic level as at the international level, seeks to explain state behavior by drawing upon the power of ideas and norms. Similarly, historical experiences, such as colonialism, and politically defining moments, such as national liberation and dramatic political change through revolutionary struggle, can have lasting impact on state identity, interests, and behavior.[37] Like ideas, they can influence the state's interpretation of the world, shape policy agendas, and affect outcomes. Strategic culture, a subset of ideas relating more specifically to the use of force, has also been deployed to explain state behavior. The argument is that strategic choices of states are conditioned by historical experiences and historically rooted strategic preferences, rather than being determined by changes in the objective strategic environment (Johnston 1995).

Concerning the link between regime type and international behavior, some analysts have claimed that a particular type of regime, the liberal democracy, is less prone to war than others (Rummel 1983) and that liberal democracies will not go to war with each other (Doyle 1989;

Russett 1993). In this view, authoritarian leaders will be more likely to resort to aggressive international behavior. Others have argued that the transitional nature of certain regimes, rather than regime type, is the critical factor in explaining the propensity of states to go to war. Edward Mansfield and Jack Snyder argue that during the transitional phase of democratization, states become "more aggressive and war prone, and they do fight wars with democratic states" (1995: 5). Still others, among them Stanislav Andreski (1980: 3), argue that the emergence and existence of military dictatorships "have little connection with...the waging, or preparation, for war" and that military dictators "have been notably pacific in external relations." The impact of regime transitions and the international behavior of authoritarian regimes are particularly relevant in Asia, which is still home to several authoritarian governments and where several countries are undergoing major economic and political changes.

The functional imperative theory rests on a distinction between political-military states and trading states. Unlike political-military states, it is argued, trading states "accept equality of status on the basis of differentiation in functions. Their objectives...do not require preventing other states from achieving such goals" (Rosecrance 1986: 28). Considerations of interdependence, and not insecurity born of anarchy, affect the disposition and behavior of states. Although states may try to improve their relative positions, they do so in the context of interdependence. Cooperation, rather than competition and conflict, is the more rational approach to security in these circumstances. Chalmers Johnson introduces the idea of the capitalist developmental state, which, like the mercantilist state, is imperial in its international behavior (Johnson 1993: 222–23). There are many other types of states—corporatist, nationalist, revolutionary, bureaucratic-authoritarian—with varying dispositions and behaviors. The objective here, however, is not to determine the validity of these various claims but rather to assess whether and how regime type and functional imperative can explain the security behavior of Asian countries.

When national identity and regime survival are at stake, explanatory power shifts to domestic politics, and specifically to the interaction of state and society. Where nation and state are not coterminous, and if there is contestation over the constitution and identity of the political community, such conflict (usually along ethnic or religious lines), depending on its severity, may have a deep impact on the domestic and international behavior of the CDMs. Similarly, security thinking and behavior may be driven by concerns of regime survival in countries where the legitimacy of the political system and the incumbent power holders is at issue. In both these situations, the identity and legitimacy of the security referent are likely to be the object of contestation and a principal source of the state's security problem. Such contestation is also likely to inform the international behavior of CDMs in the affected states. The kinds of international regimes in which membership is sought and the alliances and alignments that are entered into, for example, may be explained with reference to the identity and survival concerns of the incumbent governments (David 1991; Acharya 1992a). Given that nation-states are imagined communities (Anderson 1992) and that ideological preferences are constructed, the impact of these variables on security thinking and behavior can be folded into a constructivist explanation.

It may be the case that several of the factors discussed here are at work simultaneously. It then becomes necessary to trace their interconnections as well as to disentangle and assess the significance of each factor. Similarly, systemic and unit-level factors may operate simultaneously, so that here too the interactions and salience of each level and factor will have to be considered. If structural-materialist theories emerge dominant in explaining Asian security behavior, then Asian security practice cannot be considered distinct. To lay claim to distinctiveness, at a minimum, constructivism and nonmaterial unit-level theories would have to be more pertinent in explaining Asian security practice. If this is the case, Asian practice will then have to be compared with those in other regions to determine whether it is indeed distinctive.

The method of research outlined here illuminated for the authors what areas needed to be investigated and suggested how some of those issues might be explored. The authors, however, had wide latitude to expand and enrich this core approach in a manner they considered appropriate to their respective countries.

Structure of the Book

The study is organized in three parts. Part I critically reviews and appraises the debate on defining security, and provides a historical overview of international politics in Asia. It sets the context for the country-specific chapters that follow. Part II investigates practices of security in sixteen Asian countries. The countries were selected and grouped on the basis of security interdependence. Political, economic, and strategic weight, as well as each country's significance for regional security, also influenced the composition of the clusters. Thus, China, India, and Japan constitute one cluster. The other countries were grouped on a subregional basis: Northeast Asia (North Korea, South Korea, Taiwan), continental Southeast Asia (Thailand, Vietnam, Burma), maritime Southeast Asia (Indonesia, Malaysia, Singapore, the Philippines), and South Asia (Pakistan, Bangladesh, and Sri Lanka). Using a common framework, the country chapters seek to discern and explain the construction of security as well as its contestation and changes over time. The common framework ensures that the questions raised are examined in a systematic and substantive manner, and it facilitates comparison. Based on the findings of the country studies and drawing on other published works, Part III seeks to compare the national practices, with a view to identifying and explaining key characteristics of Asian practice of security. It also attempts to conceptualize security on the basis of the Asian experiences.

PART I

Conceptual and Historical Perspectives

Rethinking Security
A Critical Review and Appraisal of the Debate

MUTHIAH ALAGAPPA

> The main focus of security studies…is the phenomenon of war.… Accordingly security studies may be defined as the study of the threat, use, and control of military force.
>
> STEPHEN M. WALT, 1991

> It is important to confine the concept of security to physical safety from deliberate physical harm inflicted internationally, i.e., across national boundaries.
>
> PATRICK MORGAN, 1992

> [Security is] primarily about the fate of human collectivities…about the pursuit of freedom from threat. [The] bottom line is about survival, but it also includes a substantial range of concerns about the conditions of existence.… Security…is affected by factors in five major sectors: military, political, economic, societal, and environmental.
>
> BARRY BUZAN, 1991

> The key concept in talking about security is emancipation. Emancipation means freeing people from those constraints that stop them carrying out what freely they would choose to do, of which war, poverty, oppression and poor education are a few.
>
> KEN BOOTH, 1991

> *Security needs to encompass the interests of the people rather than just states, in gaining access to food, shelter, basic human rights, health care, and the environmental conditions that allow these things to be provided into the long-term future.*
>
> SIMON DALBY, 1992

> *I do not disagree…that these problems are serious and should be of concern to us all. What I disagree [with] is that all of these policy problems (domestic, regional, and international) should be subsumed under security studies. There is no conceptual thread…that holds them all together except that they are "problems."*
>
> ROBERT H. DORFF, 1994

*S*ecurity is a sharply contested concept, as the epigraphs to this chapter illustrate. Contestation encompasses all four of its constituent elements: the referent, the composition of core values, the type and nature of threats, and the approach to security. Stephen Walt and Patrick Morgan take it for granted that the state is the referent of security, but Ken Booth and Simon Dalby argue that the referent should be people instead. For Barry Buzan, the referent is human collectivities, and the specific referent varies with the level of analysis. At the international level, he posits the state and society as the referents of security. Morgan, Walt, and Robert Dorff would limit security to the international level and focus on deliberate threats (primarily, if not exclusively, of a military nature) to physical safety. Booth and Dalby view security as encompassing all issues (at the domestic, international, and global levels) that affect the emancipation or interests of the people. Concerning threats to security and how security is to be achieved, Walt, Morgan, and Dorff appear to emphasize international competition and conflict, positing military force as both the principal threat and the principal means to achieve security. Booth and Dalby would go beyond the military threat to encompass a wide range of threats and dangers affecting the conditions of existence. According to Buzan, the security of human collectivities, which includes not only survival but also a range of conditions of existence, is affected by military, political, economic, societal, and environmental factors. The articulations of Walt, Morgan, and Dorff are essentially in the realist tradition. Buzan's position has its roots in neorealism but permits variations in the referent and broadens the scope of security. The articulations of Booth and Dalby are more in the liberal tradition.

These differences point to the lack of a shared understanding of the meaning of "security," which has led to a debate among analysts over rethinking the concept of security. Often this debate is characterized as one between the advocates of "limited" (or "bounded") and "broad" (or "expanded") definitions of security. But that characterization is inadequate, for it draws attention only to the differences over the scope (the second and third elements) of the concept and misses the disagreements over the referent and approaches to security. In fact, rethinking security must begin with the referent, which is the fundamental element and which has consequences for the other three elements of security as well as for the nature of the domestic and international environment.

This chapter critically reviews and appraises the key features of the debate over the rethinking of security, with a view to developing some guidelines for conceptualizing security, a task that is undertaken in Chapter 20. The review and appraisal of the competing conceptions of security are organized under the headings of referent, scope, approach, and explanation of security. Each section begins with an elaboration of the core assumptions and claims of realism, which was and continues to be the hegemonic discourse on international politics. Realism, as the term is used here, comprises political realism and especially its prominent contemporary version, neorealism.[1] Security is the central concern and the home turf of neorealism; most of those who argue against any substantial rethinking of security are neorealists. Neorealism is also the starting point for some competing expositions of security[2] and the point of comparison and departure for others. Elaboration of the neorealist claims is followed in each section by a critique of them and a discussion of the core assumptions, claims, and problems associated with alternative conceptions. The chapter concludes with the observation that, although it continues to be relevant, the neorealist articulation is inadequate, and that security must be conceptualized to go beyond it. Some guidelines for the conceptualization of security are also identified. We begin with a review of the debate over the security referent.

Referent of Security: State or People?

The state is the dominant form of political organization (Gilpin 1981: 116–23). Internally, it defines and protects the life, liberty, and property of individuals and groups through the creation of political and socioeconomic order. Externally, it protects the rights of its citizens from the harmful actions of other states and nonstate entities. The state also fulfills a crucial identity function and a welfare role that has progressively become more significant. The sovereign state is deemed to separate the inside from outside, order from struggle, and "us" from "them." In essence, it represents an "in group" with a defined territory and ultimate authority. In the realist view, despite the proliferation of other actors and the erosion of its authority in several domains, the state will continue to be the principal actor in the domestic and international arenas until other actors rival and surpass it (Waltz 1979: 85; Gilpin 1981: 116–23; Thompson and Krasner 1989). For as long as the state remains the primary political community and actor, it will also be the primary agent and provider of, and therefore the referent of security.

This realist claim has been challenged on at least three counts. One is the claim that the capacity of the state to discharge its primary functions of identity, physical security, material welfare, and habitable environment is declining (James Rosenau 1989, Ken Booth 1991a, 1991b). The general argument here is that the state is too large to satisfy human needs and too small to cope with problems that are increasingly regional and global in nature. People have multiple and overlapping identities, and the claim of the state in this respect is narrowing. In addition to national identity, regional and local identities are also becoming important. Because the strategy of nuclear deterrence risks the lives of the very people the state is supposed to protect, the state is no longer seen as an effective provider of external defense. International specialization and the development of a global economy and transnational networks limit the autonomy of the state and thereby diminish its role and effectiveness in discharging its socioeconomic welfare function. Environmental problems are mostly global in scope and cannot be addressed at the level of the state. Thus, although it will not disappear, the state has become much less relevant. It now has to share authority with other actors; it no longer provides an effective handle to understand the agendas of politics, economics, defense, and environment, which are increasingly set by popular social movements and not by governments.

A second argument is based on a suspicion of the state or even outright hostility to it. This argument posits the state as an oppressor and a producer of insecurity. It is in part rooted in classical liberalism (which views civil society as the fount of all virtues and government as a necessary evil that must be limited and checked) and Marxism (which views the state as the agent of a certain class), both of which, for different reasons, are society centered and depict government as self-serving and predisposed toward international conflict. Domestically, the rhetoric of "national" security, according to this argument, may be deployed by governments to maintain a certain identity and impose an order that privileges some segments while threatening others (Dalby 1992). The poor, women, minorities, and children are often victims of structural violence. Instead of providing security, states can and in many cases do threaten the security of some of their citizens. For dissidents, so-called national security becomes a threat to their own individual and group security. In such situations there is usually more than one referent of security, often competing and at times irreconcilable. It becomes crucial to distinguish between individual, group, and national security and to identify the tensions among them.

A final argument holds that the state must be viewed as a means to protect the life and liberty of people and to advance their material well-being, and not as an end in itself. Protection of people, and not of the state, should therefore be the ultimate goal of security (Booth 1991a; Dalby 1992). Making the state the referent can lead to abuse, particularly in countries where the legitimacy of the nation-state, regime, or government is contested. For these reasons, people rather than the state should be the referent of security. A variant of this argument claims that the state is not the only referent: there are others, such as society and humanity, that may be more salient in certain situations and domains.

These arguments, particularly the one that holds that security is about people, have considerable merit. Political institutions like the nation-state and government gain their legitimacy by fulfilling the safety, identity, and welfare needs of people. Without the consent and support of people, they have no legitimacy. Similarly, unless occupied or claimed by a group of people, territory in itself has no value. Threats make sense only in terms of the physical and moral injury they can inflict upon people and their livelihood. A hole in the ozone layer is of concern because of the harm it can cause people. This is belaboring the obvious, but the point must be firmly registered that security is fundamentally about people. All too often political constructs become reified in security analysis and policy, obscuring the fact that they are a means and not an end. Consequently, "the people" are relegated to the status of one among several elements of the state—on a par with other elements, such as territory—or worse, put at risk or sacrificed in the pursuit of "national" interest.[3] Putting people at the center of security analysis will help to keep ends and means in perspective and to highlight contradictions, such as the strategy of nuclear deterrence.

As a concept and referent, however, "the people" is just as ambiguous and diverse as "the state," if not even more so. Does "the people" mean the whole of humankind, or some part of it? If the latter, then on what basis do the people define themselves? Who defines their interests? How are interests aggregated? Who speaks for the people? Clearly, some form of political organization is required. And in this regard, despite its many shortcomings, the state is still the most relevant object of political identity and allegiance and the most effective agent of the security and welfare functions. Humankind is too vast for us to easily comprehend and identify with; the nation-state—even though it may be imagined (Anderson 1991)—is more concrete. It is a useful mediation between the local and global levels. Thus, despite the trend toward an increasingly globalized world, the state will remain of central importance (Calhoun 1994).

The relevance and effectiveness of the state as a political community has been questioned periodically, and its "withering away" has been forecast for about the last hundred years. But, as noted by David Strang (1991), states are robust organizations that have edged out many competitors. International social practice naturalizes this principle, leading analysts such as Robert Jackson and Carl Rosberg (1982) to argue that there is strong world cultural support for the principle and practice of sovereign statehood. Stephen Krasner (1995–96: 123) points out that assertions claiming a basic transformation of the international system because "sovereignty seems so much at risk" are not well founded. It appears that the state will continue to be the principal form of political organization and the principal actor in the domestic and international realms. This is not to proclaim an eternal life for the state. It may be, as Ruggie (1993c) has suggested, that the activities of the contemporary "medieval trade fair" will challenge and eventually bring about the demise of the state; but, as he himself notes, for the foreseeable future states will continue to be "the most powerful form of political organization."[4] Even in Western Europe, where integration is most advanced and where it has to share authority with other regional, local, and nongovernmental actors, the state continues to be resilient (Taylor 1991; Hoffmann 1991).[5]

In some developing countries, particularly in Asia, identification of the people with the state and state capabilities (including penetration, extraction, appropriation, and application) has strengthened.[6] The existence of secessionist movements, though reflective of the weakness of the constitution of specific countries, is not indicative of the obsolescence of the idea of the nation-state as the basis of political community. On the contrary, such movements are a vindication of its continued vitality. The goal of the secessionist movements is to create new nation-states in which the fit between ethnic or religious nation and state is closer and in which the movement's ethnic or religious group becomes the Staatsvolk, the dominant ethnic group that controls state power.

There is as yet no political alternative to the state. As noted by Walker (1990), "the state" is a political category in a way that "the world," "the planet," the "globe," or "humanity" is not. Because the meaning of security is tied to historically specific forms of political community and because "other forms of political community have been rendered unthinkable," the understanding of security continues to involve primarily the concerns of state security (Walker 1990: 5–6). This is an elementary point that is missed by some critics of the state.

To make the case for the continued relevance of the state as the basis for political community, however, is not the same as to accept the state as the sole referent or to equate security with national security. As noted earlier, the state suffers limitations as a provider of security and, in some cases, its legitimacy may be contested. In the latter situation, the state could well be a threat to the security of some segments of its body politic. Even when the state is not contested, security as defined by the government may differ from the security of the society or of groups within it.[7] Therefore, the state should not be uncritically accepted as the sole referent of security.

Further, states in the real world are not all like units, varying only in terms of power capabilities, as is claimed by realists. They vary widely on many other counts as well, including the capacity for self-government, monopoly over the legitimate use of force and internal pacification, cohesiveness as a political community, capacity for international inter-action, and participation in the regional and global economies. Georg Sorenson (forthcoming) posits that the international system is populated by three types of states: the postcolonial, modern, and postmodern. The security referent and the sources of insecurity will vary by type of state. In states closer to the postcolonial ideal type—in most of sub-Saharan Africa and the former Soviet states, and in some parts of Asia and Latin America—the state may not command the loyalty of all people living within "national" territorial boundaries. Some segments may view the state as a threat to their survival and well-being. In this situation alterna-tive security referents—based on religious, ethnic, or economic consid-erations—are likely to emerge. In states closer to the postmodern ideal type—in Western Europe—state identity will be informed and tempered by the larger regional identity, and society's interests may differ from those of the state (Waever et al. 1993; Waever 1995). In this situation a regional entity, such as the European Union, and other nonstate entities, such as society, may become additional security referents.

Consequently, although still dominant, "states form a part of a complex network of authority patterns pertaining to different levels of governance" and coexist with a host of other important actors at the subnational, regional, and global levels (Holm and Sorenson 1995: 189). For several reasons, any one or more of the units at these levels can become the referent of security in both the postcolonial and postmodern states. The relationships among these different referents and the priorities accorded to them will vary with the context and cannot be predetermined. The referent of security may also change over time and therefore cannot be assumed. Instead, it must be problematized and investigated.

Scope of Security: Internal or International? Narrow or Broad?

The debate over the scope of security has several dimensions. We address three of them in this section. First, should security be defined to include the intrastate level? Second, are the "traditional" concern of security with international survival and the emphasis on military power still relevant? And third, should the scope of security be expanded to include problems and threats in economic, environmental, demographic, sociocultural, and other nonconventional sectors?

Intrastate Security

Internal security is not a focus of realist theories. Neorealists, though aware of the prevalence and intensity of violence at the domestic level, build on the key assumption of a unitary (coherent and cohesive) sovereign state that acts rationally. This assumption is justified on the basis that there is "an effective government [that] has a monopoly on the legitimate use of force" and that the national system is therefore not one of self-help (Waltz 1979: 102–4). National politics, characterized as a realm "of authority, of administration, and of law" (Waltz 1979: 113), is sharply differentiated from the realm of international politics, which is characterized in Hobbesian terms. The assumption of unitary, cohesive, sovereign state by definition excludes consideration of intrastate security. To the extent that the intrastate level figures in realist analysis, the concern is with how variables at that level (such as nationalism and revolution) affect the international behavior of states.[8]

Some analysts have challenged the binary distinction between national and international politics (Milner 1993: 153–62). Stephen Krasner (1995–96) has argued that sovereignty (the hook for the binary distinction) is better viewed as a convention or reference point than as an analytic assumption. Even if a sharp distinction is necessary for the purpose of constructing a theory of international politics, it should not be the basis for security analysis. The state should not necessarily be treated as a cohesive and legitimate actor. As noted earlier, states vary widely in terms of the attributes of a modern nation-state. In a large number of countries, including some major ones such as Russia, China and India, the very constitution of the state is problematic. Not all peoples living within existing national boundaries identify with the state as constituted, and governments do not necessarily have monopoly over the legitimate use of force. Thus, the state is not in all cases the agent and provider of security. For some inhabitants the state may well be the primary source of insecurity.

Governments in many such countries, for their part, are confronted with internal challenges to the integrity of national territory and political institutions that, in some respects, are far more severe than external ones. These challenges are labeled and addressed by these groups and governments as concerns of group or national security. Some internal conflicts have significant international ramifications and fuse with international conflicts, blurring the distinction between domestic and international politics. In some cases the domestic realm may be as Hobbesian as the international realm, if not more so. The term *failed states* has been coined to describe such states. These states present security problems—conflict and war, genocide, mass exodus of refugees, external intervention and rivalry—not only for their own people but also for neighboring states and the international community. Treating the state as a unitary actor and the domestic realm as one of authority, law, and order closes off these crucial dimensions and ignores issues that may affect group, national, and international security.

The intrastate security problematic has been addressed by analysts studying the security of developing countries (Buzan 1983, chaps. 1–3; Thomas 1987; Alagappa 1987a; Azar and Moon 1988; Job 1992a; Ayoob 1995).[9] Some parts of the problematic have also been addressed by analysts interested in ethnic identity and conflicts (Horowitz 1985; Smith 1986, 1991; Montville 1990; Romanucci-Ross and De Vos 1995). With the rise in the number and intensity of ethnoreligious conflicts in post–Cold War Eastern Europe, the former Soviet Republics, and Africa, the causes and consequences of internal (especially ethnic) conflicts have commanded the attention of a broader spectrum of analysts. Some have sought to explain internal conflicts in terms of the realist theory: imperial collapse leading to a situation of anarchy, the consequent concern with survival and the struggle for power, and the resulting internal security dilemma (Posen 1993). Others have sought to explain internal conflicts in terms of underlying and proximate causes influenced by structural, political, economic or social, and cultural or perceptual factors. Of the proximate causes, "bad leaders" are identified as "the biggest problem" (Brown 1996: 575). The literature on the causes of internal conflict, especially ethnic conflict, is too vast and too diverse to be classified and subjected here to systematic appraisal. Instead, we limit our discussion to three key, interrelated issues—national identity (the ideational basis for delineating political community as well as the political organization of that community), political legitimacy or the title to rule, and distributive justice—that in large part have been the source of internal conflicts.

Though national identity has several components,[10] two are important from the perspective of this study: the identity of the nation (the nation has become the accepted basis for political community) and the political ideology of the state.[11] The identity of the nation defines the basis for the collective self as well as the national purpose, heritage, symbols, and character, whereas the political-legal organizing ideology of the state (democratic, socialist, secular, theocratic, and so on) defines the structure of political domination. Together they—the identity of the nation and the identity of the state—establish a hierarchy among the political, sociocultural, and economic beliefs of the state and order the positions and worth of individuals and groups in society (Verdery 1993: 40; Smith 1991: 17). They assign "subject positions in the modern state" and "[legitimate] numerous social actions and movements" (Verdery 1993: 38). Internationally, national identity distinguishes the nation-state in question from the rest of the international community, with significant consequences for its international orientation and its definition of national interest. National identity is a powerful symbol and basis for classification that commands deep passion, extending to the sacrifice of lives. It is, however, not a given. National identity is a conscious construction, and the process of identity creation has in some cases been productive of intense conflict.

The second issue—title to rule—can be an object of contention because of ideational and material considerations. The ideational component relates to contestation over the normative framework for acquiring and exercising political power. Such conflict, when it exists, will be over the "correct" organizing ideology—communism, authoritarianism, or democracy—and here convictions can run deep. In situations where the exercise of state power is not rooted in moral authority, the legitimacy of the regime, as well as that of the incumbent government, is likely to be contested by rival claimants to power. Without accepted mechanisms and procedures to manage them, such challenges are likely to translate into extralegal and violent means, such as coups d'état, rebellion, and revolution. The material component relates to the actual control and exercise of state power. Here the conflict may be one of a pure struggle for power among competing elites. The two components are intimately connected, but one cannot always be reduced to the other. Similarly, although identity may be deployed in the service of elite competition for power, such mobilization is conditional upon the projected identity having appeal in the target group. In other words, it must have a history—be built up over time and space. Identity cannot be manufactured at will, although it can be manipulated.

Finally, conflict may issue from grievances over distributive justice. Socioeconomic grievances can fuel ethnic, religious, and caste strife and peasant rebellions or protests and strikes by farmers and industrial workers. Still, their consequences are likely to be limited unless they feed into the conflicts over political identity or legitimacy. Often there is an overlap. Less developed regions provide fertile ground for the development and support of separatist movements or political organizations that challenge the legitimacy of incumbent governments on the basis of competing ideologies or promises of better performance.

These issues—identity, legitimacy, and distributive justice—are not always of concern, and even when they are, they need not always lead to violent conflict. Hence it is important to investigate why, how, and under what circumstances these issues become of concern and when they can lead to violent conflict. In the case of identity concerns rooted in ethnic considerations, for example, it is necessary to investigate why, how, and when group differentiation (the idea as well as act of political imagination) occurs, what alienations and resentments trigger and sustain ethnic tensions, and what conditions permit and impel the resort to violence.[12]

Challenges rooted in the problem of national identity affect the political and territorial integrity of the state. In the former Yugoslavia, for example, war conducted in the name of ethnic solidarity has destroyed the state and resulted in hundreds of thousands of casualties and millions of refugees. At present, ethnic conflicts are challenging the territorial integrity of many states. Challenges rooted in the legitimacy problem and socioeconomic grievances may affect the integrity of political institutions as well as law and order and, more generally, political stability. The international behavior of countries thus affected and their conception of national security are heavily influenced by tensions and conflicts at the intrastate level. But the sharp distinction between domestic and international politics, and the focus on insecurity issuing from international anarchy, divert attention from the security problems at the domestic level. With a few exceptions, domestic issues have been viewed as peripheral concerns and excluded from mainstream security analysis. Mainstream analysts maintain that the proper concern of security studies is international security (Morgan 1992). A further justification for this exclusion rests on the claim that the nature of the problems (identity, legitimacy, socioeconomic grievances) and the expertise required to address them are radically different for domestic than for international security problems. Such arguments, as will be shown later, are not tenable. Although it is important to distinguish between the problems of different groups of states—a process in accord with the rationale underlying this study—it is equally important not to exclude by definition the security concerns of a very large number of countries from the general conception of security and treat them as peripheral or marginal. Moreover, developed countries—the United Kingdom, for example—are not totally immune to internal security challenges. In rethinking the national security of the United States, Peter Peterson (1992: 59) has argued that domestic problems may have a greater direct impact on American institutions and values than do the traditional threats from abroad. We must therefore conceptualize security in such a way as to permit the investigation not only of international challenges but also of domestic challenges, where appropriate, and of the interconnection between the domestic and international sources of insecurity.

International Political Survival

Realists depict international politics as a realm of "power, struggle, and of accommodation" (Waltz 1979: 113). This pessimistic view flows from another of neorealism's core assumptions—anarchy—and the logic that it is deemed to imply.[13] In the neorealist view, the international system, populated by sovereign states, must necessarily be decentralized and anarchic. In the absence of a central authority, each state retains the right to judge "its grievances and ambitions according to its own dictates or desire" and to decide on the use of force (Waltz 1959: 159). The risk of conflict and war in such a decentralized system is high, because there is a constant possibility that governments may resort to the use of force at any time. Survival is precarious and highly contingent, and securing it is posited as the basic goal of states in an anarchic system (Waltz 1979: 91–93, 126). Security in the neorealist articulation is a scarce value. One state's gain in security usually comes at the expense of others, therefore zero-sum and distributional calculations inform security practice.

Some realists recognized early on that, in the atomic era, one nation's security cannot be "purchased...at the expense of another nation" (Morgenthau 1978: 553). National survival requires that all (nuclear) nations be made secure. This idea may be seen as the precursor of the concept of *common security*. In the view of neorealists, however, acceptance of a stable nuclear deterrence situation does not qualify as a commitment to common security, for it still rests on a threat of mutual destruction. *Common security* is defined by the Palme Commission (1982: xiii) as the achievement of security "not against the adversary but together with him" through a noncompetitive and nonconfrontational commitment to joint survival. The idea of common security has not been accepted by neorealists, who have argued that it is untenable because states are not likely to equate their own security with that of others (Elman and Elman 1995: 187). Neorealists continue to posit national survival as the basic goal in anarchy, maintaining that states have to look out for their own security and well-being.

National survival is defined essentially in political terms. For Kenneth Waltz, survival means the preservation of the political autonomy of states—that is, their preservation as independent political entities (Waltz 1979: 91–92). For Hans Morgenthau, national survival, equated with national interest, encompasses "the integrity of the nation's territory, of its political institutions, and of its culture" (Morgenthau 1952: 988; see also Morgenthau 1978: 553). The minimum national "core values," according to Arnold Wolfers, are national independence and territorial integrity. But beyond this, Wolfers asserts that some states may seek to acquire and protect other values, such as "rank, respect, material possessions, and special privileges," while other states may deem that national self-preservation requires national self-extension (Wolfers 1962c: 154–55).[14] Realists recognize that the goals of states may vary endlessly but argue that political survival is most important and a prerequisite to the achievement of other goals, such as "tranquility, profit and power" (Waltz 1979: 126). In other words, there is a hierarchy of values, and political survival is at the top of the list. In terms of threats to national survival, the realist concern is with capabilities and not with intentions, which are deemed to be more difficult to discern and in any case subject to rapid change. Although neorealists recognize the many elements of power, military power is privileged. They see force as both the principal threat to security and the principal means to secure political survival. It is not only the ultima ratio, but "indeed the first and constant [possibility]" (Waltz 1979: 113). Hence the emphasis on military force and war in realist definitions of security.

This realist concern with international political survival and the emphasis on military force have been critiqued on different grounds. The first set of criticisms issues predominantly from international relations scholars termed as neoliberal institutionalists. Neoliberalism, which accepts several of the key premises of neorealism,[15] asserts that the negative effects of anarchy posited by neorealism can be mitigated by international institutions and that political survival need not be as precarious as neorealism contends. In this view, a relatively high degree of international governance and order is possible (Keohane 1986a: 194). Neoliberal institutionalism merges with the English school on the issue of international society, which, according to Buzan (1993a), is the necessary condition for the development of international regimes.[16] He argues that international society, like the balance of power, is a natural product of international relations in anarchy.

A related contention is that anarchy has been overemphasized at the expense of interdependence, an equally important structural feature (Milner 1993: 162–63). Interdependence and its presumed consequences form the core of commercial liberalism, which contends that growing trade and economic interdependence will minimize the negative effects of anarchy and gradually transform the nature of international politics.[17] Although the military-security component will continue to be important, commercial liberalism holds that the growing and inextricable connection between national economic well-being and the global economy will reduce the importance of political independence and territorial integrity. Individual states may still try to improve their relative positions, but they will do so in the context of interdependence. The international disposition and behavior of states in a "trading world" will be influenced by considerations of interdependence rather than by insecurity born of anarchy.

A third thesis is that war among Western nations has become subrationally unthinkable (Mueller 1989). Peace has become addictive. Not only is war not rational, but also, because of its ineffectiveness and undesirability, it is no longer even an option. Major war among these countries has become obsolete. Finally, the democratic peace theory contends that regime type, and not international material structure, is the determining factor and that a world of democratic states is inherently peaceful. This thesis holds that democracies do not go to war with each other, or at least that relations among them are more peaceful than relations among nondemocracies or between democracies and non-democracies (Doyle 1989; Oren 1996; Russett 1993). Belief in the institutional constraints (the weight of public opinion and the checks and balances in a democratic system) and the transferability of democratic norms (compromise and peaceful resolution of conflicts) from the domestic to the international realm underlies this logic.

These various but interrelated theses have been deployed to contest the neorealist prediction of the future of international politics in Western Europe. Neorealists claim that the anarchic structure and the distribution of power are still the critical determinants of war and peace, and that with the termination of the Cold War, the prospects for major crises and war in Europe are likely to increase markedly (Mearsheimer 1990). The others argue that Europe will not go "back to the future" and that change has been and will continue to be peaceful (Keohane, Nye, Hoffmann 1993). Robert Jervis has argued that "time's arrow" predominates in Western Europe and that international politics among developed countries constitutes unmapped territory; it will be different in the future than it was in the past (Jervis 1991–92). Material structure, it is argued, is no longer a guide to the behavior of states. Peace among Western European countries—because of the increase in the cost of war, its decreasing benefits, growing economic interdependence and the benefits of trade, and the strength of democratic institutions and values—is "overdetermined." Because these changes are deep and mutually reinforcing, they cannot easily be reversed.[18] Consequently, the traditional concern with political survival and military threats is seen as no longer applicable to these states.

Realist predictions of an unstable, multipolar system in Western Europe have yet to materialize. Change in that region thus far has been peaceful. Although the institutional, commercial liberal, and democratic peace arguments appear plausible, they suffer limitations as well.[19] It may still be too soon to arrive at any firm conclusion, and in any case these propositions apply only to a small group of countries in one region of the world. It is pertinent to note that most of the scholars who argue that the future of the developed world will be different following the end of the Cold War at the same time recognize the continued salience of the political survival problem and accept the focus on military threats with respect to the so-called periphery. There, the future is expected to resemble the past. In fact, they expect more rather than less conflict in the Third World (Jervis 1991–92: 58–61).

A second set of criticisms issue from scholars of Third World security. Although they are not engaged in a direct debate with neorealists, some of their claims rest on premises that go against the grain of realism. For example, many of these analysts tend to stress the domestic challenges and to skew security analysis in favor of the intrastate level. Although they acknowledge the existence of international security concerns, those issues are more often treated as extensions of internal vulnerabilities. This attempt to explain the security behavior of Third World states, including major ones like China and India, in terms of domestic factors runs against realist analysis, which privileges international material structure. Some analysts (Job 1992; Jackson and Rosberg 1982) go even further, arguing that the international security dilemma does not apply to Third World states because they "are preoccupied with internal rather than external security, and weak states have a guaranteed existence" due to the force of international norms that support sovereignty and territorial boundaries. It is claimed, therefore, that "the assumptions of the traditional security dilemma metaphor are violated" (Job 1992a: 18). This extreme position, like that which would seek to limit security to international concerns, is untenable. International norms of sovereignty and territorial integrity have not prevented territorial disputes or encroachments. Such disputes and violations are in fact very common among the so-called Third World states. Further, these states, certainly those in Asia, are as much concerned with the international security dilemma as are those in the West—in some cases, even more so. The balance between internal and international concerns will vary by country and region. Care should be taken not to arbitrarily privilege one category or the other. At the conceptual level, provision must be made for the study of security at both levels as well as of the interconnection between them.

The final critique does not contest the relevance of the problem of international political survival as a security concern. It is directed at the subordination of the political and sociocultural dimensions to the military one. The security of human collectivities—group, nation, and state—can be endangered not only by force but also by ideas and policies short of force. In some cases, political threats may be more potent and consequential than the threat of military force—as demonstrated, for example, by the social and political revolutions in Iran, the Philippines, South Korea, the Soviet Union, and several Eastern European countries. At the international level, the present government in China and to a lesser degree that of Vietnam consider the threat of "peaceful evolution" (a euphemism for Western advocacy of democracy and human rights as universal values) posed by the United States and Western Europe more serious than a military threat to their national security. According to some analysts, neglect of this political and sociocultural dimension has led to the militarization of international relations and of security. It is hard to deny that some core values, especially those relating to identity, are essentially political and sociocultural and may be threatened at least as much by ideas as by force. It is important to recognize the salience of these dimensions and to factor them into security analysis.

These criticisms have merit, but they do not negate the continued importance of the problems of international political survival and military threat for a large number of countries. Although the nature and urgency of those problems may vary across countries and over time, they must continue to feature in the conceptualization of security. A more fundamental challenge to the realist articulation of security is posed by analysts who attempt to broaden the scope of security to include problems and dangers in nonconventional sectors.

Nonconventional Dimensions

Since about the mid- to late 1970s there have been growing calls to redefine security to include economic, environmental, and other nonmilitary dimensions. The case for inclusion of these concerns has been argued more vigorously since the end of the Cold War; it should be noted here, however, that a broad view of security was common among certain Asian countries even during the Cold War era. Since the termination of the Cold War, such a comprehensive view of security has met with greater acceptance among some policy makers in the West as well. Their receptiveness can be traced to a number of developments, including the complexity of post–Cold War international politics and the attempt to gain a handle on it; the growing concern with domestic issues in many Western states; the continuing weaknesses of many states as modern nation-states; the eagerness of Asian states to modernize rapidly; a perception in the United States and Western Europe that the character and scale of economic change was undermining American and Western dominance of the international political economy; increasing awareness of and concern over issues like population explosion, climatic change, and other related problems; globalization and its perceived negative effects in some countries on state autonomy and national values; and the rise of ethnonational conflicts.

Some policy makers and academics argue that the "highest stakes" are now in the economic realm, and that the outcome of competition in that area will ordain the future relative power positions of states in the international system and determine the welfare of their people (Sandholtz et al. 1992). Thus "[it] is impossible to speak of national security without speaking about economics. It is now an accepted truth that there is an essential economic dimension cutting across the more familiar political and military aspects of our [U.S.] overall national security strategy" (Kimmit 1991: 398). A new era has begun, in which "security issues are often submerged and hidden by market relations, and conversely market relations can be distorted to appear as security questions" (Zysman 1991: 105). In this new era, "the struggle and threat [will be] economic, not military" (Sorenson 1990). National economic well-being, cast increasingly as economic security, has been depicted as a core objective of governments.[20]

The case for including environmental concerns and problems stresses the threat to the physical survival of humankind that supposedly arises from environmental degradation.[21] In the words of U.S. vice president Al Gore, "this process [environmental degradation] threatens not only the quality of life but life itself. The global environment has thus become an issue of national security" (Gore 1990: 60). Changes in the climate pattern and sea levels induced by global warming, increased exposure to dangerous ultraviolet radiation resulting from depletion of the ozone layer, the decimation of biodiversity as a consequence of indiscriminate deforestation, and the hazards of toxic waste disposal and pollution are all presented as threats to the quality of life, if not to life itself, on a massive scale. Among the examples put forward are these:

- The welfare of some 400 million people living in the lowland plains of India, Pakistan, and Bangladesh has been affected by upland deforestation (Hassan 1991).

- Land and water degradation have created millions of environmental refugees worldwide, leading to large-scale domestic and international population flows with destabilizing consequences (Jacobson 1988; see also Ek and Karadawi 1991).

- A sea-level rise of 1.5–2.0 meters would flood 20 percent of Bangladesh, inundate most of the Maldives, and threaten nearly half the population and production of Thailand (Oerlemans 1989; Vellinga and Leatherman 1989).

- Global warming will increase the probability of severe drought in the agricultural heartlands of Australia, Europe, North America, and the former Soviet Union.

Such severe consequences are depicted as comparable to or even greater than those of military conflict. The environment is said to be in a state of crisis that requires urgent action. Because "the environment" is common and indivisible, some have argued that human and planetary survival rather than national survival should be the primary concern of states.

It has also been argued that environmental degradation could fuel violent conflicts among human groups. The environment is already a major domestic political issue and will become an issue of high politics at the international level (MacNeill, Winsemius, and Yakushiji 1991: 52). Environmental concerns and ecological power, independently or in conjunction with other elements, will figure prominently in defining the international behavior of states.[22] Political discourse is replacing scientific and technical consideration of matters relating to the environment. Whereas environmental threats were once viewed in the context of the struggle of man against nature, expansion in knowledge has made cause and effect more readily identifiable and attributable to the actions of human collectivities (Buzan 1991: 131). Thus, environment-induced stress, which has always been present, will now take on a more explicitly political dimension with the potential to fuel conflict. Developing

countries, because of their lesser ability to mitigate the negative consequences, are viewed as particularly vulnerable to such conflict. Social
consequences of environmental degradation, such as reduced agricultural production, economic decline, population displacement, and
disruption of social relations, may fuel domestic (relating to group
identity and relative deprivation) or interstate conflicts (Homer-Dixon
1991, 1994).

There is also a tactical component to the case for broadening the
scope of security. Because of the emotive character of national security
and the enormous sacrifices that it commands, the association of
environmental concerns with national security may be an attempt to
elevate further the profile of environmental issues and to secure greater
funding for related programs. The attempt to link environment and
security may also be aimed at demonstrating the futility of spending vast
amounts of money on armaments that only breed mutual insecurity
when there are many other crucial issues to be addressed. Highlighting
environmental concerns could also be a way of justifying an environmental role, and funding, for the military establishment in the post–
Cold War period.[23]

Some aspects of these new dimensions are not really new and can
readily be accommodated by the realist paradigm. Economic strength has
always been considered an important component of national power and
security (Morgenthau 1978; Knorr 1975). The development and sustenance of military power and the relative positions of states in the
international system have depended on their economic health and
ranking. Politically motivated disruptions in the flow of strategic
supplies, such as oil in 1973, and explicit economic sanctions, including
blockades and denial of markets, have been viewed and dealt with as
security issues. On some occasions governments have resorted to the
threat or use of force in dealing with such situations. Economic power
has also been deployed in the form of inducements or sanctions—access
to or denial of aid, resources, or markets—in the service of foreign and
security policy.[24] These economic aspects—the relative power and
position of states, politically motivated threats, and the deployment of
economic power as an instrument of state policy—fit into the neorealist
construction of security and are not contested.

Similarly, environmental degradation as a source of domestic or international conflict does not pose a problem for the realist paradigm.
Environmental problems that can be a source of political conflict and
contribute to violence within and among states are considered by realists
as falling within the domain of security (Lynn-Jones and Miller 1995: 5,
Critchley and Terriff 1993). Some have argued that the causal connec-

tion between environmental degradation and violent conflict is not warranted. There are multiple mediating factors, so that the linkage is open to varying interpretations. At best, environmental degradation is a proximate rather than an underlying cause of conflict. Because they fail to recognize the distinction between environmental migrants and refugees, the push-pull factors at work, the long gestation period and the gradualism that characterizes migration and refugee flows, the advocates of environmental security inflate the number of refugees, their power, the urgency of the situation, and the potential for environmental disputes to cause open conflict (Suhrke 1992). One study concludes that "insofar as it causes displacement of people, [environmental degradation] is more likely to generate long-term social tension or exploitation than acute conflict" (Suhrke 1992). Similarly, resource wars are held to be less likely in the contemporary era because of a robust world trading system that provides access to resources without the need for territorial control, the difficulty of exploiting resources through conquest, and the availability of substitute sources and materials (Deudney 1990). The merits of these criticisms notwithstanding, the linkage between environmental degradation and violent conflict and such like other linkages are not antithetical to the realist paradigm. As pointed out by Quincy Wright (1964) more than five decades ago, the causes of war can be numerous and wide-ranging.

The broadening of the concept of security to include concerns like revitalization of the economy or a safe environment that do not involve violent conflict is, however, controversial. Some analysts label the linking of nonconventional sectors like the environment and security as "muddled thinking" (Deudney 1990; see also Levy 1995). The critique has several strands. First, there is the problem of defining what constitutes economic or environmental security. These can be, and have been, defined in many ways. Economic security, for example, may be defined variously as "acceptable levels of welfare,"[25] unrestricted access to resources of production and markets for goods and services, the capacity to maintain international comparative advantage, or the maintenance of a healthy international economic system. In the case of environmental security, there is no agreed-upon definition of "the environment" or of what would constitute a secure environment. In the period immediately following World War II, the term *environment* came to mean "the *natural* influences surrounding people including flora, fauna, climate, water and soil" (Worster 1977; italics in original), and a unified theory of ecology emerged. But over time that consensus broke down, giving rise to competing definitions. There is also no agreement on the defining quality of nature, although some argue for equilibrium. Controversies surround the issues of stability and change and the determination of what constitutes a damaged or healthy environment. There is no clear, compelling norm (Worster 1977: chap. 16, 342–33). Ecologists appear divided among themselves as to how society should be advised to act in relation to the earth.

Second, even if economic and environmental security can be adequately defined, the next problem is to identify threats to them. With the exception of a narrow range of politically motivated actions, threats to national economic well-being are difficult to identify. A whole spectrum of economic activities are rooted in the market economy and its pluralist management—changes in prices, interest rates, and exchange rates; differences in patterns of saving and investment; differences in innovative capacity, management methods, marketing techniques, distribution system, and financial system—that can negatively affect the health of a national economy. It would be difficult and possibly meaningless to classify them as security threats. Not only will the precise source of threat be difficult to locate, but the consequences will be unclear. The consequences of economic or related developments are often indirect and do not become apparent until long after their occurrence. Similarly, there is no agreement on what constitutes the greatest threat to the environment: population growth, the bourgeois lifestyle, and industrial pollution have all been named. A related criticism is rooted in the inconclusiveness of scientific evidence. Critics question the basis and evidence for the posited environmental changes. Is global warming really taking place? Even if that point is conceded, the rate of warming and its consequences cannot be ascertained with any degree of certainty. Given the ambiguous nature of the evidence and the enormous cost involved in addressing such problems, governments will be unable to act decisively, especially in the face of other pressing claims on resources.

Third, "securitizing" economic and environmental problems is counterproductive and carries the risk of militarizing economic and environmental relations. A security-oriented management of the economy might argue for greater self-reliance to reduce exposure to circumstances and conditions beyond national control in order to minimize vulnerability. Whatever the merits of such an approach, it also opens the door to economic nationalism and fuels protectionism. Sectors and groups unable or unwilling to make the necessary adjustment, or a government unwilling to incur the political cost associated with implementing unpopular welfare-reducing policies, may seek refuge in national security and attempt to force the burden of adjustment onto other countries. Protectionist policies, regardless of rationale and origin, almost always have costs and, despite short-term gains, imply loss of efficiency with negative consequences for long-term welfare. Similarly, it is argued that linking environment and security to raise environmental awareness is counterproductive (Deudney 1990). Subsuming them under the label of security nationalizes and militarizes environmental issues, making their resolution even more difficult. Further, the label of national security deprives environmental issues of the long-term attention they deserve. Environmental issues are important but are better addressed separately on their own merits, not under the label of security, which has a specific meaning and an urgent character.

Finally, and perhaps most important, critics argue that economic and environmental problems and their solutions have little in common with the traditional focus on the pursuit of security from organized violence. The two differ in crucial ways: the nature of the problem, the source of threats, the degree of intentionality, the levels at which the related problems have to be addressed, and the instruments involved in ameliorating or resolving them are all vastly different. The expertise and mindset required to address economic and environmental issues are not the same as those needed to resolve security issues. Although the concept of common security has been in vogue, it has not been widely accepted outside progressive circles. National rather than common security is still the focus of mainstream thinking and practice. Simply labeling economic and environmental issues as security concerns does not alter their nature or change the way they will be dealt with. Nothing is gained by attaching the security label to them, and doing so could well have negative consequences by militarizing economic and environmental relations and possibly reducing material welfare. Thus, there is no conceptual, analytical, or policy value in making the linkage. If all forces and events that threaten life are treated as threats to national security, then the term will cease to have any analytical value. According to this line of thinking, the linkage between the nonconventional sectors and security is relevant only as a possible cause of interstate conflict or as a factor to be considered in assessing the impact of war (see Critchley and Terriff 1993).

These criticisms have considerable merit, but they are also flawed in several respects. First, the differences between the nonconventional dimensions (economic and environmental) and the so-called traditional focus of security are overdrawn. Admittedly, economic and environmental threats are diffuse and their consequences difficult to predict in time, space, and magnitude; they can issue from within and without state borders; they are largely unintentional; force is irrelevant; and their resolution, for the most part, depends on international cooperation. However, with the exceptions of intentionality and the use of force, the other problems or features are not unique to the economic and environmental dimensions, but apply to the political-military dimension as well. Political and cultural threats that bear upon political identity and autonomy are seldom clear-cut and often have a long gestation period; even the deployment of force in what has been described as low-intensity conflict or insurgency is less precise than that presumed in traditional definitions of security. Political and military threats to territorial integrity and political institutions, as noted earlier, can arise from domestic as well as international sources. International cooperation and institutions are not irrelevant to the mitigation and resolution of political-military security problems. Further, common security is not popular just in "progressive" circles and is not necessarily a competing alternative to national security. With growing limitations on the effectiveness and roles of the state, increasing benefits from international specialization, and the increasing destructiveness of war, common security is gaining prominence.

A second shortcoming of the argument concerns its definition of security in terms of a specific instrument (organized violence). It is fallacious to argue that issues that do not involve force are not security concerns. Organized violence is only one means by which even the traditional core values can be threatened or protected; other means can also be deployed to threaten or secure political survival. Thus, to define security in terms of a single instrument, however important it may be, is unnecessarily restrictive and misleading. Further, the threat, use, and control of organized violence is more aptly addressed under the label of defense, which is a component of security.

A third shortcoming of these criticisms is their limitation of security to the nation-state level. As noted earlier, although the nation-state is still dominant, there can also be other referents of security, and security can be pursued at different levels. Once this is acknowledged, the fact that political survival issues are addressed primarily at the national level whereas some economic and environmental issues must be addressed at the regional and global levels, ceases to be a fundamental problem. Admittedly, there may be tensions between the approaches at the different levels and between the different issue areas. Action to enhance the health of the world trading system may in certain situations undermine national economic security; action to enhance resource security may conflict with action to promote environmental security. But such tensions are inevitable and will have to be managed. Management will require making hard choices, but that would be true even if the problems were considered separately and addressed by different groups or agencies of government.

Fourth, the meaning of words and concepts evolves over time and varies across space. As circumstances change, so will the content of "security." To insist that because something has been so in the past, it must be so now and in the future—to foreclose reconstruction and even modification, despite changing circumstances—can drain a concept of its practical relevance. In any case, the construction of security that has been labeled as traditional, conventional, or classic is not as old or as universal as it is made out to be. David Baldwin (1995) points out that the primary concern during the interwar years was the elimination of war. Democracy, international law, national self-determination, disarmament, and collective security were viewed as the most important ways to promote international peace and security. National security became predominant only after World War II. Further, in the early postwar period, analysts such as Harold Lasswell and Arnold Wolfers emphasized both military and nonmilitary means, warning against overreliance on armaments to ensure national security (Baldwin 1995). They also linked security to domestic affairs, including economic matters, civil liberty, and the democratic political process. The U.S. National Security Council was established in 1947 as a forum to integrate domestic, foreign, and military policies related to national security (Peterson 1992). Only later, during the Cold War, did international military issues dominate and become the focus of security thinking.

Going farther back in history, Ernest May (1992) argues that American security thinking has evolved in four stages. In the first stage (1790s–1870s), the concerns were preservation of the Union and safe borders; in the second stage (1880s–1930s), social order at home and hemispheric independence; in the third stage (1945–1960s), prosperity at home and the independence of the "free world"; and in the fourth stage (1970s onward), stability and economic growth. This historical perspective illustrates that the scope of national security is broad and variable over time. What is needed is a more flexible and dynamic conception of security that can accommodate diversity and change.

Finally, the argument that the analysis and solution of environmental and economic problems require radically different expertise and that for this reason they should not be considered security issues is not tenable. It assumes that an expert must be knowledgeable on all aspects of security. This is not the case even with regard to so-called traditional security. There are experts on nuclear strategies, conventional wars, unconventional wars, disarmament and arms control, regional conflicts, and so forth. No one person has equal expertise in all areas. As Lasswell (1950: 55–66) observed, "there are no experts on national security. There are only experts on different aspects of the problem." Admittedly, the expertise required for addressing economic and environmental problems is substantially different from the kind of knowledge required to deal with "traditional" security issues. But this fact argues for an interdisciplinary approach to the study of security, not for defining the domain on the basis of the expertise of the analyst. Expertise is properly defined in terms of subject matter and not the other way around.

There is still the difficult problem of how to define and delimit the scope of security. As correctly argued by those advocating a limited conception, without specific criteria all manner of things can be labeled as security concerns, so that the concept and the subfield will cease to have coherence. For this reason, criteria such as similarity in the nature of problem, political motivation or intentionality, and the role of force are appealing. But such criteria are invariably bound to specific paradigms, and they will include or exclude various issues by definition. To depend on them is not an objective way of evaluating contending conceptions rooted in different worldviews. The requirement is for criteria independent of specific worldviews. The issue of independent criteria for classification is discussed further in the final chapter of this study.

Approach to Security: Competition or Cooperation?

The neorealist claims that security is a scarce value, that its pursuit must necessarily be competitive and based on self-help, and that military power must play a crucial role are contested by neoliberalism and commercial liberalism. The latter contend that security in anarchy can be achieved through cooperation as well as through competition, and that cooperation may be the more rational approach in certain circumstances.

The Case for Self-Help

Because there is no higher authority to guarantee survival, neo-realists argue that each state has to be responsible for its own security. This logic places a premium on self-help, which is equated with unilateral and competitive policies, and the buildup of national capabilities (Waltz 1979: 105–7, 111). Neorealists recognize that the buildup of capabilities to ensure national survival can intensify security competition and establish a vicious circle, but this is accepted as an inevitable feature. The resulting security dilemma cannot be solved as long as anarchy persists;[26] it can only be managed, and thus only relative security is possible. "Peace, if one defines that concept as a state of tranquility or mutual concord, is not likely to break out in the world" (Mearsheimer 1995a: 12).

If national capabilities are available in sufficient quantity and quality, then self-reliance is the most reliable and efficient strategy to ensure survival. Self-help, however, does not rule out seeking assistance from others. Alliances and alignments are viewed as ways of enhancing national power and spreading costs. An alliance is formed in response to an imbalance in power (Waltz 1979: 123–31) or as a "balance against threats" (Walt 1987: 5). Alliance is viewed as a temporary arrangement. Because alliance is an "outer directed" arrangement, based on calculations of national interest and the distribution of power, realists do not consider it an institution in the mode of liberal institutionalism (Mearsheimer 1995b: 83).[27] Similarly, a concert, because it is a great-power condominium reflecting the distribution of power among them and does not violate their self-interest, is considered largely consistent with realism (Mearsheimer 1995a: 35).

Collective security, on the other hand, is considered to be sharply at variance with neorealism. Although collective security is concerned with the management of power, the emphasis is on across-the-board application of norms and rules that may entail the subordination of national interests to that of the community.[28] This strategy is believed to be deeply flawed and untenable as a national security strategy (Mearsheimer 1995a: 36–37).

Neorealists are skeptical about cooperative security strategies. While accepting that cooperation does occur, they argue that it is difficult to achieve and even more difficult to sustain. Concern over cheating and relative gains and over the enormous cost of failing to develop national capabilities inhibits and limits cooperation, particularly in the security domain (Grieco 1993).[29] Similarly, institutions are not viewed as significant in matters of war and peace (Mearsheimer 1995a: 13–14). Seen basically as a reflection of the distribution of power and the calculation of national interest, particularly that of the great powers, institutions are believed to have no independent effect on state behavior and to be of consequence only on the margins.[30]

Realists also argue that international politics cannot be transformed by abstract ideals and reason; it can be managed only by "manipulating the perennial forces that have shaped the past as they will the future" (Morgenthau 1979: 10). Peace can be achieved only through accommodation. Diplomacy has a crucial role in the mitigation and minimization of political conflicts, especially among nuclear states. Neorealists and, to a much higher degree, the earlier realists attach great importance to diplomacy as an element of national power and an instrument of statecraft (Morgenthau 1979: 529).

The Case for Cooperation

Neoliberalism's challenge is directed primarily at the neorealist claims that cooperation is difficult to achieve and sustain and that institutions matter only on the margins. It posits that anarchy permits a variety of interactions among states and that a higher degree of cooperation is possible under anarchy than neorealism would acknowledge. Where and when mutual interests exist (that is, in situations where potential gains can be derived from coordination and collaboration), states will engage in cooperation. Relative gains are important, but only when "gains in one period alter power relations in another, and where there is some likelihood that subsequent advantage in power may be used against oneself" (Keohane 1993: 275). Both the economic and security realms are seen as characterized by opportunities for cooperation, although the security realm is more impoverished in this regard (Lipson 1993; see also Jervis 1983). The difference between the security and economic realms is attributed to the high cost of betrayal, the difficulties of monitoring, and a tendency to perceive security in zero-sum terms.[31] Nevertheless, cooperation in the security realm is not totally absent even among adversaries, for example, between the United States and the Soviet Union during the Cold War.[32]

Concerning institutions, the demand for which is seen as increasing with rising interdependence, the claim of institutionalism is threefold: first, institutions are constitutive (can help define interests); second, through rules and conventions they can regulate state behavior by affecting incentives; and third, by altering conceptions of self-interest, reducing uncertainty, and stabilizing expectations, they can facilitate peaceful change (Keohane 1984, 1989, 1993). The peaceful adaptation to the changed structure of the international system after the dramatic developments during the 1989–91 period and the continued relevance of international institutions in the post–Cold War strategies of the major powers are advanced in support of the third claim (Keohane 1993; Keohane, Nye, and Hoffmann 1993; Ruggie 1993a).

As noted earlier, commercial liberalism contends that the negative effects of anarchy can be overcome through growing economic interdependence. The relatively low cost of trade and its increasing benefits, the growing cost of force and its diminishing returns, and the social learning that will occur, it is argued, can move international relations in the direction of a "trading world" characterized by interdependence based on differentiation in functions and on reciprocity.[33] Incentive to wage war will dissipate because war disrupts trade and other economic interactions. In these circumstances, cooperation rather than competition is the more rational approach to national security (Rosecrance 1986: ix). The reasoning of commercial liberalism is in some ways similar to the expansive logic of neofunctionalism (Haas 1968; Lindberg 1967), which asserts that economic integration, as it begins to embrace more issues and groups, will gradually spill over and affect areas of high politics. The process will make war less likely and even eliminate it altogether among the affected group of states, leading to the establishment of a pluralistic security community (Deutsch 1957: 5–7).

A Continuum of Systems

Although the various approaches to security are usually presented as fundamentally different and competing, it is possible to view them as part of a continuum of security systems. This proposition is underpinned by the constructivist claim (elaborated in the next section) that security systems are social constructions and that anarchy permits self-help as well as other-help systems. Based on this proposition, self-help, cooperative security, and community security may be constructed as three ideal types of security systems on a continuum, with relational identity as the key determining variable.[34] In a self-help system the relational identity is negative. States, fearing each other, formulate their security in zero-sum and distributional terms. The emphasis in such a system will be on the development of national capabilities and, where applicable, on collective self-defense arrangements.

In a cooperative security system, relational identity is not negative, or is only minimally so, and it may even be positive. States may be somewhat suspicious and mistrustful of each other, but there is no perception of an immediate threat. In this situation countries accept the status quo or at least are not bent on radically altering it. They are likely to conceive of their security in limited terms. The central security concern stems from the uncertainty and potential for misperception inherent in anarchy. States oriented toward the status quo have a mutual interest in avoiding least preferred outcomes through coordination and in promoting common interest through collaboration (Stein 1990: chap. 2).

In such a situation there is incentive to cooperate for mutual gain, and international regimes seem well placed to play a direct role in reducing or eliminating uncertainty and ameliorating the security dilemma. They may do so through the codification of principles, rules, and procedures to govern international relations (including the use of force) among participating states; through regulation, including limitation, of arms acquisition and deployment; and by mechanisms for dispute settlement. These measures will help lift the fog of suspicion, enable a more accurate reading of the intentions of other states, and prevent misperception and unintended escalation of tension and conflict. Instead of planning for worst-case scenarios, a practice that can become self-fulfilling, states interested in preserving the status quo and assured that others have a similar commitment can follow a moderate course, one that emphasizes security through defense rather than offense.[35] Strategic doctrines, force structure, acquisition of weapons systems, planning and training, and alignments and alliances can all be tailored accordingly. This is the thrust of the strategic principle of cooperative engagement and cooperative security advocated by Ashton B. Carter, William J. Perry, and John D. Steinbruner (1992), and by Janne E. Nolan (1994).

The improved climate resulting from the implementation of assurance and deterrence strategies can foster higher levels of cooperation in other areas—for example, economic cooperation or collective action with regard to external actors or global issues. The benefits of such cooperation may spur even more cooperation and spill over into other issue areas. Such cumulative cooperation strengthens the web of interdependence and raises the cost of resorting to force, while reducing the utility of force; in general, it alters the cost-benefit calculus in favor of peaceful resolution of political disputes. Cooperation to reduce uncertainty, increase the cost of resorting to force, and decrease the risks of war through restraints is rooted essentially in the rational calculation of self-interest and reciprocity on the part of participating states.

Community security, the third ideal type, is rooted in the constructivist claim that identity and interests are embedded in the cultural-institutional context. It is potentially more enduring than cooperative security and has the potential to prevent the emergence of new power struggles. In a community security system, national identity and national interest become fused with those of a larger community of states. The problem of political survival has been overcome, and security is not a scarce value. Each state has an interest in the security of the others. There is no expectation that force will be used to resolve disputes. Force becomes illegitimate as an instrument of policy in the international politics among the states that form the community.

The three systems as just described (summarized in Table 2) are pure or ideal types. In practice, elements of different systems may coexist and overlap. A competitive system does not preclude cooperation, but any cooperation that takes place will be designed to regulate competition and to avoid mutually undesired outcomes (such as mutual annihilation) rather than to eliminate competition. Such was the basis of cooperation and arms control agreements between the two superpowers during the Cold War. The perceived destructiveness of war may also create demands for common security. The Palme Commission, which articulated the common security alternative to mutual deterrence, based its recom-

TABLE 2
Identity Relations and Security Systems

Identity Relation	Interest Formulation	Security System
Negative	Zero-sum, distributional	Competitive, self-help
Indifferent	Mutual interest, absolute gains	Cooperative security
Positive	Internationalization of national identity and interest	Community security

mendations on the premise that there will be no victors in a nuclear war. Security must therefore be achieved "not against the adversary but together with him. International security must rest on a commitment to joint survival rather than on a threat of mutual destruction" (Palme Commission 1982: xiii). The commission recommended a positive approach to security that essentially seeks to curb and manage the competitive pursuit of security. Similarly, competition is not ruled out in a cooperative system, but it is conducted within an overall framework that values cooperation as being in the national interests of the participating states. "Cooperative security is a model of interstate relations in which disputes are expected to occur, but they are expected to do so within the limits of agreed-upon norms and established procedures" (Nolan 1994: 5).

The significance of the different approaches and the manner in which they combine are not predetermined but depend on the international political context. In situations that approximate the neorealist worldview, competitive strategies and military power may be critical; in situations that may be characterized as "mature anarchy,"[36] cooperative strategies would be more relevant. In the case of complex interdependence, both competitive and cooperative strategies may have to be deployed.[37] If the security agenda is broadened to include the economic and environmental dimensions, then cooperative and community security may become even more salient.

Over time there may also be movement from one security system to another. For example, cooperative security may lead to community security. By providing an environment in which socialization and learning can occur, regimes can contribute to the internalization of "new understandings of self and other, of acquiring new role identities," which over the long term helps transform identity, interest, and power politics (Wendt 1992: 417; Caparaso 1993: 66–81). In addition to legitimating the international order, the shared norms and values forged and consolidated through the process strengthen international society and could lead to the development of a pluralistic security community in which force is no longer an option in resolving disputes. But such "progress" is not inevitable. There is no necessary linear progression from competitive through cooperative to community security. Movement can proceed in both directions.

Explaining Security: Material or Ideational?

Neorealists explain the security problem and the approach to security in terms of a certain logic of anarchy, which, they argue, cannot be transformed as long as the ordering principle is anarchy. Its consequences can only be managed, and thus considerations of power and diplomacy are critical. State behavior is explained largely if not exclusively on the basis of the international material structure. The constructivists hold that there is nothing inevitable and immutable about the realist logic of anarchy that has produced the survival problem and the associated system of self-help. Rather, they are the product of a set of historically rooted, intersubjective understandings among states. A change in intersubjective understanding can alleviate or transform the security problem. Constructivism argues that material factors have no meaning in and of themselves; they derive their meaning from shared understandings and state practices, and ideational factors and perspectives are as important as material ones in explaining security behavior. This section reviews and appraises the claims of the neorealist and constructivist perspectives.

Neorealist Explanation of State Behavior

Neorealism seeks to explain state behavior as conditioned largely by the material structure of the international system, both deep and distributional, and the placement of the state in that system.[38] Because the deep structure is static (anarchy will be the ordering principle for so long as the key actors remain sovereign states) and the intermediate level relating to functional differentiation of units drops out because states are like units, states respond primarily to changes in the distribution of power. Considerations of power, and not ideas and institutions (except those grounded in the realities of power), will inform state behavior. The privileging of structure in neorealism, however, does not equal structural determinism, as is often claimed by critics (Buzan, Jones, and

Little 1993: 22–23). Waltz recognizes that first- and second-image variables can and do influence state behavior and may in fact be the immediate or most efficient cause of decisions relating to war and peace (Waltz 1959: 232). He explicitly states that a conjunction of system- and unit-level variables will have to be deployed to explain individual state behavior (1979: 87, 122, 174) and that a "bothersome limitation" of systems theories arises from the difficulty of weighting unit-level and structural causes (1986: 343). Further, he acknowledges that unit-level variables may cause a state to behave differently from the behavior predicted by neorealism.

Despite these qualifications, Waltz asserts that the competitive pressures of the international system and the survival imperative will compel weak powers to imitate the systems, structure, and policies of the stronger ones. Further, competitive pressures will compel nonconforming countries to be socialized into the system. Consequently, differences will disappear over time, and states will display similar characteristics. In other words, the system will not tolerate functionally differentiated units. Based on this prediction, neorealists have argued, for example, that Japan will eventually emerge as a "normal" power. It has also been argued that competitive pressure and the survival imperative will compel states to behave in a like manner. A state that repeatedly behaves differently will "lay itself open to danger, will suffer" (Waltz 1979: 118). The structure, therefore, is privileged, and state behavior is expected to vary more commonly with "differences of power than with differences of ideology, in internal structure of property relations, or in governmental form" (Waltz 1986: 329). Waltz has argued that in spite of differences in ideology, strategic culture, and political system, the United States and the Soviet Union showed striking similarities in their behavior during the Cold War because of their similar power placement in the international system (Waltz 1993). Others, such as Mearsheimer (1990), accord even greater weight to material structure and move closer to structural determinism.

A second prediction of neorealism is that states operating in an anarchical system and interested in ensuring their survival will engage in balancing behavior, because their first goal is to maintain their position, not to maximize their power (Waltz 1979: 121, 126, 128).[39] A weaker power will seek to balance a stronger one, and the tendency is to restore a balance that has been disrupted. Balancing can take many forms, depending on the distribution of power in the system. In a bipolar system, internal balancing and arms racing will be important, whereas in a multipolar setting, alliances will be more significant. The focus of neorealism is on major powers, particularly the distribution of capabilities among them, and it has little to say about the behavior of smaller powers. Secondary states, according to Waltz, will tend to balance rather than bandwagon (1979: 127), because it is the stronger state that threatens them. Stephen Walt holds that considerations of threat rather than of power condition state behavior and that, although the system encourages balancing, weak powers will tend to bandwagon rather than balance, because they "add little to the strength of a defensive coalition but incur the wrath of the more threatening states nonetheless" (Walt 1987: 29). It has been argued that weak powers may also resort to hiding, free-riding, and accommodation, and that these strategies are consistent with neorealism because their choice is based on a rational calculation of gains and losses (Elman and Elman 1995: 186–88). This last claim implies that only irrational behavior is inconsistent with neorealism (Schroeder 1995: 194).

Constructivism's Challenge

There are moderate and radical critiques of the neorealist logic. The moderate version (presented by neoliberalism and commercial liberalism) asserts that the negative effects of anarchy, posited by neorealism as essential features, can be mitigated if not overcome. These claims have been explored earlier and will not be repeated here except to note that rather than claiming that power relations do not matter, institutionalists hold that power relations alone cannot explain variations in the patterns of international interactions. The structure of the international system must include institutions, and the relevance of material capabilities in explaining state behavior will vary inversely with the degree of institutionalization (Keohane 1989: 8–9, 1993: 287–89). Where there is a high level of institutionalization, as in Western Europe, power will be much less relevant in explaining state behavior than in other, less institutionalized regions. Institutions are held to be as fundamental as capabilities in explaining state behavior (Keohane 1989: 8–9).

A more radical challenge builds on Ruggie's (1983) contention that there is not just one anarchy (defined as a segmented realm); rather, different principles of differentiation (for example, heteronomy in medieval Europe, sovereignty in the contemporary world) will yield different types of anarchy. Whether or not unlike units can coexist depends on the principle of differentiation. Buzan (1993b: 39–41) extends this argument to open up the possibility of a deep structure in which the ordering principle of anarchy does not preclude the coexistence of unlike units. Alexander Wendt and Daniel Friedheim's (1995) constructivist explanation of informal empire may be interpreted as lending weight to the possibility of this type of structure even in the contemporary period. Hierarchy and unlike units can exist (among a group of states) even when the de jure principle is sovereignty and the structure of the international system is anarchic. The logic of anarchy among such a group of countries will be quite different from that of a group in which, through competition and socialization, units are driven to be alike. If unlike units attract and become "strongly glued together because they depend on one another's different abilities and skills" (Waltz 1986: 325), then survival among the group of states concerned may not be problematic—provided, of course, that the hierarchy is considered legitimate by the audiences concerned.

An even bolder and more far-reaching challenge to neorealism issues from constructivism,[40] which contends that the cultural-institutional context is important and has as much explanatory power as the materialist or choice-theoretic perspectives (Jepperson, Wendt, and Katzenstein, 1996). Constructivism makes three basic claims. One is that the structure of the international system is social and comprises not just material resources but also shared knowledge and state practices (Wendt 1995: 73). Material capabilities in and of themselves have no meaning; their significance derives from shared understanding and practices. Institutions, in an intersubjective sense, are therefore a crucial part of the structure. Second, the cultural-institutional context affects not only the incentives for behavior, as argued by neoliberalism, but also identities (Jepperson, Wendt, and Katzenstein, 1996). Identities and interests are socially contingent and not intrinsic to states. Variations in identities are held to affect national interests and policies; changes in the configuration of identities are said to affect interstate normative structures, such as regimes and communities. Third, state practices matter: they inform and are informed by structure, which is both "medium and outcome" and can be transformed by actions of "capable and knowledgeable"[41] agents. Structure and agent are mutually constitutive, and state practice "is the core of constructivist resolution of the agent-structure problem" (Wendt 1992). A crucial question for constructivism is how to bring about change. Here it rests its hopes on ideas and institutions (Wendt 1992: 410–22, 1995: 80). As identities and interests change, they can transform international politics and increase the possibility for peaceful change (Wendt 1995: 71–72). Thus "anarchy is what states make of it."

From the perspective of constructivism, the causal logic of realism is not a necessary consequence of anarchy or of the distribution of capabilities, but rather flows from a certain set of intersubjective understandings. Process, not material structure, has produced the present self-help system. If the intersubjective understanding can be changed, so can the realist logic of anarchy. Prospects for survival are thus contingent on the shared understanding among the society of states. For example, despite the weakness of African states, international survival has not been a severe problem for them because of the international recognition of their juridical sovereignty (Jackson and Rosberg 1982). Similarly, lines of amity and enmity and the role of force are socially contingent. North Korea and Vietnam, for example, are not far different in terms of their power relationship with China, and both have common land borders with that country. Yet North Korea, though suspicious of China, does not view it as an enemy. Vietnam, however, fears Chinese hegemony and has frequently viewed China as an enemy. Material capabilities by themselves cannot explain the differences in the international relations among these countries. An investigation of their histories and the intersubjective understandings to which they give rise will be much more telling.

A Case for Synthesis

The various systemic theories (neorealism, neoliberalism, commercial liberalism, and constructivism) have often been presented as competing and incompatible paradigms. Proponents have argued over which is of the most utility in explaining international politics and predicting state behavior.[42] Although they serve important intellectual and professional functions, such debates also tend to have a certain sterile and unreal quality. The reality of international politics is complex and changing, and it is not uniform throughout the world. No single existing theory can adequately capture and generalize about all of reality. Even Waltz (1986: 331) admits that "realist theory can by itself handle some, but not all, of the problems that concern us."

Despite the claims of some neorealists, it is difficult to deny that certain regions of the world are characterized by a high degree of economic and other forms of interdependence and are already in or are moving toward a situation of complex interdependence or a pluralistic security community.[43] Expectations of the state and the norms that govern interaction among states in those regions are informed by the high degree of institutionalization that characterizes their environment. Although anarchy is still the ordering principle, its consequences are not those posited by neorealism, so that other theories become relevant in explaining regional politics and security. However, although they are useful in highlighting the flaws of neorealism, the competing theories themselves have some serious shortcomings and are inherently limited in their applicability. The thesis that there can be more than one logic to anarchy is quite persuasive and useful in explaining variations in behavior across regions and states, but at the same time anarchy is not infinitely malleable. Nor can constructivism predict when and why a discourse will become dominant or what the new hegemonic discourse will be.[44] In its present form, constructivism, though useful in terms of explanation, does not provide a general theory of action. Neoliberalism has focused mainly on political-economic cooperation in the advanced industrial world, and commercial liberalism's relevance is limited to trading states with market economies. These categories cover relatively few states.

Understanding contemporary international politics requires complex theories of a kind that do not yet exist. Rather than engaging in a sterile argument as to which theory is better, a more productive exercise will be to recognize and deploy the strengths of the contending theories to enhance the understanding of international politics.[45] Although the theories rest on some fundamentally different assumptions and compete on many dimensions, they are not incompatible. Neoliberalism, as noted by Grieco, can be helpful in understanding the politics of cooperation (1993: 335). Constructivism does not disregard material capabilities but seeks to highlight the salience of the cultural-institutional context in explaining the meanings attached to them. Although the position is not stated explicitly, some realists, such as Waltz and Walt, come close to accepting a constructivist viewpoint on some key features of realism, such as the creation of like units through competition and socialization, and the depiction of threats rather than imbalance in power as the basis of alliance. Regional variations imply that no one theory may be adequate. Different theories may have to be deployed to explain variations across regions and states—for example, the development of regional integration and pluralistic security communities in some regions, that of competitive security and self-help in others, and the coexistence of both in yet other regions.

The analysis and explanation of security cannot therefore be limited to any single paradigm. It can, however, begin with neorealism, because that is the only theory to articulate a security problem. Neoliberalism is concerned only with mitigating the problem raised by the realist logic of anarchy. Constructivism, though it holds that there can be more than one logic, does not specify which will prevail. Moreover, some of the core theoretical assumptions (state is the central actor; anarchy is the ordering principle) of neorealism, though not their imputed consequences, have gained acceptance by policy makers. For this reason as well, the realist paradigm provides a good starting point for analysis. But it must not be limiting; in crucial ways, analysis and explanation must be modified by insights provided by the other theories. This augmentation may not appeal to purists, but the social practice of security is not limited by any specific theory.

Observations

It is clear from the discussion in this chapter that the so-called traditional definitions of security, which confine the concept to the threat, use, or control of military force at the international level, are unduly restrictive and misleading; they exclude critical dimensions relating even to the core concern of political survival. It is also clear that matters relating directly to the threat, use, and control of force are better dealt with under the label of defense or strategic studies. Security is a broader concept that includes defense but is not limited to it. Security must therefore be conceptualized in a way that goes beyond the concern with force. But this must not be done indiscriminately, because it carries the risk of making the concept a grab bag and further increasing its potential for political and intellectual abuse. The analytical utility of the concept will also be undermined. The need to conceptualize security to allow for variations in referent, scope, and approach, while preserving its analytical utility, presents a formidable challenge that will be taken up in the final chapter of this study.

The critical review and appraisal in this chapter of the debate over rethinking security suggests that the conceptualization of security must be informed by the following considerations:

1. There can be multiple and often competing referents of security. The specific referent will vary with the level of analysis and the sociopolitical context. As the most attractive and most powerful form of political organization, the state will continue to be the primary referent of security. It is important, however, to recognize that it coexists with or competes with other referents at the subnational and international levels. Because of their potential to provide the rationale for alternative political communities, referents at the subnational level may take priority over the state, especially when the identity and legitimacy of the state are contested. This is much less likely to be the case with entities at the international level, which have a more utilitarian and augmenting function. Their effect, at least for the foreseeable future, will be to temper sovereignty and modify international interactions, not to supplant the state. A partial exception may be the European Union.

2. The bottom line for all referents is survival. Survival, however, need not always be problematic. Whether it is so depends on the distribution of material capabilities, on intersubjective understandings, and on social practice. From the perspective of the

state, political survival—defined in terms of political and territorial integrity—is a minimum requirement. Political survival
may also be defined, especially by the major powers, to include
milieu goals. Political survival can be endangered not only by
military means but also, and in some cases even more critically,
by political and sociocultural threats.

3. Challenges to political survival need not issue only from other
states; they can also come from within the state. For many states
and for many communities within them, internal challenges
may pose as grave a threat as external ones. Their conception of
security will be heavily conditioned by such domestic considerations. It is therefore crucial to integrate the international and
intrastate security problematics.

4. The scope of security should be broadened but not indiscriminately. The attempt to broaden the scope of security to go
beyond political survival and encompass economic, environmental, or other nonconventional problems and dangers is
complicated and presents some fundamental challenges. To the
extent that issues or problems in these areas are political and
have zero-sum or distributional characteristics—for example,
the goal of maintaining or increasing the position of the state
through economic growth and modernization—they can be accommodated by the realist conception with little or no modification. But the inclusion of other problems poses grave difficulties for the realist conception. These difficulties do not imply
that such issues cannot be considered as security concerns.
Rather, they must be included in such a way that security does
not encompass everything. Certain criteria must be established.

5. Competition, cooperation, and community building are all relevant in the pursuit of security. Cooperative strategies can be
useful in mitigating the international security dilemma under
certain conditions and possibly even overcoming it, leading to
the formation of pluralistic security communities. Cooperative
strategies will be even more relevant in the economic and environmental issue areas. But self-help is still important. Often a
combination of approaches and instruments will have to be deployed, even with respect to a single core value. This is the case,
for example, in dealing with security at the intrastate level,
where a wide array of political, sociocultural, economic, and
military measures—some competitive, others cooperative and
accommodative, yet others designed to build a community—
may have to be deployed.

International Politics in Asia

The Historical Context

M UTHIAH A LAGAPPA

T his chapter provides an overview of international politics in Asia from about the third century B.C. to the end of the Cold War. The choice of the starting point is deliberate: in the third century B.C., for the first time, all but the southern part of modern-day India came under one imperial authority during the rule of King Asoka (274–232) of the Maurya dynasty (322 B.C.–A.D. 183) and China was unified under the Qin (221–206) and Han (202 B.C.–A.D. 220) dynasties. Similarly, the choice of end point is deliberate: the end of the Cold War marked the end of the domination of Asia and its international politics by Western powers and the emergence of a more autonomous Asian regional system.

Tracing the origins and interactions of Asian "states" over a period of 2,000 years highlights the long histories of several Asian countries and their interactions. The security thinking and behavior of some contemporary Asian leaders is informed in part by their reading of history. As Western influence recedes, there is some indication that earlier, precolonial "national" self-conceptions, principles, and patterns of interaction, as well as lines of amity and enmity, may reassert themselves, though in modified form. For these reasons, a good historical understanding is useful in contextualizing contemporary problems and practices of security and avoiding the pitfalls of ahistorical analysis and policy. At the same time, however, one must be careful not to read too much into history or to submit to the tyranny of history. A good grasp of the changes and continuities in the underlying principles, structures, and dynamics of the historical Asian interstate systems and of their transformations over time will aid our understanding of the emerging post–Cold War Asian regional system. Discussion of the Asian interstate systems also provides a useful comparative perspective for students of international politics who have been trained essentially in the Western tradition. In addition to enriching knowledge and broadening perspectives, a comparative approach leads to a more enlightened interpretation of non-Western statecraft and facilitates explanation of similarities and differences among Asian systems and practices, as well as between Asian systems and those of the West.

The approach used in this chapter is historical narrative, informed by the idea of the "system," in which the interactions of member states are contingent upon each other. The organizing theme is transition and transformation of Asian interstate systems. To cover 2,000 years of history of a large number of countries in the space of one chapter is a difficult—some would say an impossible—undertaking. The presentation is necessarily one of broad strokes, limited to critical aspects and developments. The task is complicated by the fact that histories are complex and nuanced, so that some "facts" and interpretations may be contested among policy makers as well as among scholars. This account aims not to establish the authenticity of a certain factual account but to provide a sense of history by tracing the broad temporal and geopolitical context within which Asian international politics has evolved.

Historical Asian Interstate Systems: Subregional and Autonomous

Historically there were two distinct interstate systems in Asia: the Sinic system in East Asia and the Indic system in South Asia. The states in Southeast Asia, with the exception of Vietnam, adhered to some form of Hindu-Buddhist notions of political authority, and their interstate relations paralleled those of the Indic system. But they also participated, though only peripherally, in the Sinic interstate system.

The Sinic Interstate System

The origins of China can be traced to the Xia dynasty (2205–1766 B.C.), although the country was not unified until the Qin and Han dynasties. After consolidating his rule in the Chinese cultural area (modern-day northern China), the first emperor embarked on a southward expansion, incorporating the "barbarians" of present-day southern China down to Guangzhou (Canton) and the northern part of present-day Vietnam (Fairbank, Reischauer, and Craig 1978: 56–57). He also sought to secure the northern border against the nomadic barbarians through the construction of a single defense system based on the Great Wall. After this period, various dynasties centered in the northern heartland of modern-day China held sway in East Asia until the mid-nineteenth century. At their height, the power and influence of some dynasties reached into Southeast and Central Asia and touched parts of South Asia.

The philosophical doctrines and institutional framework of the Chinese political system were codified in the works of Confucius (sixth to fifth centuries B.C.) and his disciples. According to Confucianism, there is a preordained natural order, in which heaven is the source of all authority and all men are subject to the will of heaven (Nelson 1965: 32–41). In theory, the emperor, who receives his authority from heaven and is the supreme executive, has absolute power. In practice, however, the exercise of power is constrained by the requirement of virtuosity as well as "by tradition, precedent, factionalism, and simple bureaucratic inertia" (Richard Smith 1994: 47). Because the natural order is a hierarchic one, inequality is a fundamental feature of a society structured on the basis of five fundamental relationships (Nelson 1965). Peace and order will prevail when these relationships are fulfilled. Confucian society functions by example and instruction, not on the basis of "lifeless" laws or the use of coercion. Rule of law was practiced in the third and fourth centuries B.C. but was discredited because of its tyrannical use by rulers, resulting in its replacement by government of virtuous men. Use of force is incompatible with Confucian theory, which requires the "conquest" of people through the display of civic culture and virtue, not through coercion.

The same theory was applied to the international domain. The world was viewed as a single unit, with China as the *Chung-kuo* or central country and the emperor exercising authority over all people under heaven (Fairbank 1968b: 1–11). Belief in the superiority of China's culture and the claim to universal kingship provided the ideological basis of this Sinocentric international system (Schwartz 1968: 276–90). Those who lived outside the Chinese cultural area were considered "barbarians," which meant that intergovernmental relations could not exist. As the barbarians became "civilized," however, the Confucian system was extended to them. As in the domestic realm, inequality was a fundamental feature in the international realm among the Confucian family of nations. China presented itself as a superior nation and as the model for others to emulate, while the non-Chinese units accepted tributary status (Fairbank 1968b). The non-Chinese units were grouped into three concentric zones: the Sinic Zone, comprising Korea, Annam (Vietnam), the Ryukyu (Okinawa) Islands, and, for a brief period, Japan; the Inner Asian Zone, comprising Tibet and some of the units constituted by the nomadic and seminomadic peoples of modern-day Central Asia; and the Outer Zone, comprising those peoples farther away in parts of modern-day Southeast and South Asia, and eventually Japan and the West.

Because of the inbuilt inequality among states and the abhorrence of law at the domestic level, there was no role for international cooperation or law in the Chinese interstate system. The use of force was not ruled out, but force was to be used primarily to secure the recognition of the authority of a new dynasty or to chastise a state that had strayed from the proper rules of conduct (Nelson 1965). Interaction between China and the other units took place through the system of tribute. The tributary relationship, which had cultural, economic, and political dimensions, was a complex one; it rested not on formal treaties between units but on implicit personal understanding of obligation between rulers, which was not transferable. The tributaries recognized the superiority of China, and in return China recognized their independence, did not interfere in their internal affairs, and had an obligation to render assistance in times of need. China retained the right to intervene, however, on the basis that heaven separated the territories but not the people and that the emperor as the son of heaven had responsibility for all people under heaven (Lam 1968: 178–79). The deep structure of this system may be characterized as anarchic, for each unit had its own separate territory and government, and the tributaries were not under the direct political control of China. This anarchy, however, permitted hierarchic relations among the units based on the ideas of universal kingship and higher culture.

As noted by Fairbank (1968b: 11–14) and others, the Sinocentric interstate system elaborated here is an ideal. In practice, the conduct of Chinese foreign relations varied greatly. Yang Lien-sheng argues that the Sinocentric world order was "a myth backed up at different times by realities of varying degrees, sometime approaching nil" (Yang 1968: 20). Rossabi (1983) argues that when the dynasties were united and strong, the pattern of relations described by the Sinocentric world order appears to have been the effective practice. During such periods, the dynasties were expansive, insisting on hierarchy in relations with their neighbors, rewarding compliant behavior, and punishing "rogue" units. At other times, when the dynasties were weak or disintegrating (that is, in the "yin" or descending phase)—for example, during the late Tang (751–907) and Song (960–1279) dynasties—despite the formal rhetoric, greater equality characterized the relations among the units in East Asia (Ledyard 1983; Rossabi 1983). At such times the Chinese dynasties became more flexible and pragmatic, accepting others as equals.

Adda Bozeman contends that although the idea of war was accepted by all Chinese schools of thought as a supplement to rule by benevolence, in practice "the principle of righteous war usually served as a moral cloak for open acts of aggression" (Bozeman 1993: lvii). War was crucial in bringing about the unification of China, and the military dimension of statecraft was perfected over the centuries. The realist writings of Sun Tzu, Lord Shang, and Han Fei Tzu, according to Bozeman, convey the "uncompromising recognition that war and organization for war are the mainstays of the government" (Bozeman 1993: lvii). In a similar vein, Alastair Johnston (1995: x) asserts that there is evidence of two Chinese strategic cultures: a symbolic or idealized set of assumptions and an operational set. The latter, he argues, reflects "hard realpolitik" strategic culture and had a "nontrivial impact on strategic choices in the Ming Period." The symbolic set, according to Johnston, "is, for the most part, disconnected from the programmatic decision rules governing strategy, and appears mostly in the habitual discourse designed, in part, to justify behavior in culturally acceptable terms."

It appears that China's relations with other states were based on both "majesty and power" (Wang 1968: 61–62). The idea of a Sinocentric world did inform the thinking, if not the behavior, of various dynasties until the nineteenth century (Schwartz 1968), and a Chinese world order of sorts did operate during certain periods and was accepted as legitimate by some, if not all, units. But force was also used with regularity, and China's relations with its neighbors varied greatly, as illustrated by the cases of Korea and Vietnam, both of which were tributary states that borrowed heavily (culturally and politically) from China.

Korea, whose origins can be traced to the second century B.C. (Fairbank, Reischauer, and Craig 1978: 278), was subject to periodic invasions from China and, much later, Japan, making for strong nationalism and extreme distrust of foreigners and of dependence on external powers (Koh 1984: 235). Nonetheless, Korea, though suspicious of China, has generally had a positive orientation toward it. Korean tributary relations with China during the Ming (1368–1644) and Qing (1644–1911) dynasties have been described as the model preferred by China (Chun 1968). This relationship was of considerable political benefit to Korea. It ensured that China did not interfere in Korean internal affairs, and it also helped the Korean rulers and upper class to preserve status and power. Ming China helped Korea in its fight against Japanese invasion in the late sixteenth century. Also significant was

Korean respect for Confucianism, which carried over from the Ming into the Qing period. At base, the tributary relationship served the interests of the rulers of both China and Korea.

Vietnam, whose origins date to about the third century B.C., is a different case, for several reasons. First, unlike Korea, which was occupied by China for a relatively short period (108 B.C.–A.D. 313), Vietnam was annexed and made part of the Chinese empire for nearly a thousand years (111 B.C.–A.D. 939). After a long struggle it reemerged as an independent state. Even afterward, Chinese dynasties made several attempts to reimpose their rule, but those efforts were never successful for long. Tired of the military cost, the Chinese dynasties accepted a tribute relationship, which became the norm. Second, unlike Korea, which occupies a peninsula and has a language belonging to the Altaic family, Vietnam was less distinct from China in terms of geography and language. It thus had a greater need for, and more difficulty in establishing, a separate identity and its independence. Third, and again unlike Korea, which was geographically close to the capitals of the Chinese dynasties and had no room for territorial expansion, Vietnam lay considerably farther away and continually expanded southward, making contacts with Southeast Asian empires. Vietnam was able to assert a higher degree of autonomy than Korea (Fairbank, Reischauer, and Craig 1978: 266–67). Finally, although Vietnamese rulers accepted the tribute relationship, later rulers viewed themselves as "great" and set up their own dynasty (Le dynasty, 1428–1789). The constant struggle to maintain independence in the face of persistent attempts by various dynasties to reimpose Chinese rule, and the Chinese perception of Vietnam as a noncompliant, rebellious tributary state, helped shape the legacy of Vietnam. In some periods, such as the reign of Nguyen Van Hue (1788–92), Vietnamese rulers enjoyed close ceremonial relations with Chinese rulers; but this did not prevent the Vietnamese rulers from pursuing an independent policy to further the interest of Vietnam, even when doing so antagonized the Chinese rulers (Lam 1968: 176–77).

Japan was part of the Sinic Zone for only a brief period. It self-consciously borrowed heavily from Chinese culture, especially during the ninth century. But the political and social systems that developed in Japan were quite different from those of China (Fairbank, Reischauer, and Craig 1978: 324–91). Some Japanese rulers sent tribute to China; however, Japan, separated from China by the Tsushima Straits, was never under Chinese political control. Interaction between the two countries was minimal, due in part to the long periods of self-imposed isolation in both countries. Nevertheless, Japan acknowledged its enormous cultural debt to China, while China tended to view Japan as a junior member of the Chinese cultural area (Barnett 1977: 90). The Sinocentric interstate system in East Asia lasted until the nineteenth century, when it was penetrated and eventually destroyed by the Western powers, as well as by an imperial Japan.

The Indic Interstate System

India, like China, has a very old cultural tradition that has been preserved without a break to the present. The origin of the Indian state, however, is complicated. In its present form, India is a new state, the legacy of British colonial rule. But British rule was preceded by several Indian empires rooted in the Indo-Gangetic heartland: the Maurya (322 B.C.–A.D. 183), Gupta (320–540), Khaljis (1290–1320), Tughluks (1320–94), and Mughal (1556–1707). At their heights, these empires controlled much of the Indian subcontinent and at times—for example, during the rule of Asoka—went beyond them (Allan, Haig, and Dodwell 1934: chap. 4). Only the three south Indian kingdoms of Chola, Pandya, and Chera (the predecessors of present-day Tamilnadu and Kerala), which had continuous existence until the fourteenth century, were not under the political control of the empires.

Unlike China's heartland, which expanded over time by absorbing outlying provinces, the heartland of the Indian empires was effectively limited to the Indo-Gangetic plains. Regional kingdoms, after being subdued, were treated as tributaries (Allan, Haig, and Dodwell 1934: 89). Kingdoms at the frontiers acknowledged the power of the *Rajadhiraja* (the great king, or king of kings) and paid homage. Those immediately outside the frontier also felt and acknowledged the power of the great king. Because of this system of tributary rule, as well as the presence of several strong regional kingdoms (Andhras, Kalingas, Marathas, and Gujaras, for example), the empires never fully digested the outlying regions. Consequently, as the empires weakened, they were subject to dismemberment. Each collapse gave rise to numerous independent kingdoms, many of which were racially based, had long histories of their own, were quite strong, and at various times established their own regional empires for appreciable periods. The limited expansion of the Indian heartland and the successive collapse of empires have been attributed to, among other factors, the Hindu-Buddhist idea of righteous conquest that forbade annexation, the martial tradition of Indian states, the lack of an integrated and competent bureaucracy, and geography (Basham 1954: 123–26).

Because of this pattern and the long periods of foreign domination, initially by Muslims and then by the British, it is possible to think of each Indian empire as distinct and to divide Indian history into Hindu,

Muslim, and British periods. However, as Hugh Tinker notes, these empires and periods blend and blur and are better viewed as ebbs and flows in a grand cycle (Tinker 1990: xvii). Like the Mongol and Manchu conquerors of China, the conquerors of India, except for the British, were often themselves conquered and in due course became Indianized. Further, despite the racial, religious, and regional fault lines, over time a cultural and civilizational unity developed throughout the subcontinent. According to Jawaharlal Nehru, Indian history is better understood as "some ancient palimpsest on which layer upon layer of thought and reveries had been inscribed, and yet no succeeding layer had completely hidden or erased what has been written previously. All of them exist together in our conscious and subconscious selves, though we may not be aware of them, and they have gone to build up the complete, mysterious personality of India" (Nehru 1994: 59). He continues: "Though outwardly there was diversity and infinite variety among our people, everywhere there was that tremendous impress of oneness, which had held all of us together for ages past, whatever political fate or misfortune had befallen us."

Absorption and synthesis characterize the history of India. The postindependence Indian leaders certainly saw themselves as successors to the empires, including the British Raj. This accounted, in part, for the rejection by the Hindu and some Muslim leaders of the theory of two nations (insisted upon by the Muslim leaders who later formed Pakistan) and their reluctance to accept the partitioning of British India. Some leaders, like those of the Hindu Bharatia Janata Party (BJP), seek an Indian identity rooted even more deeply in history. Thus, it is not only possible but necessary to view India both as the successor to a series of earlier empires and as a nation-state still in the process of formation. India, like China, is still transforming itself from an empire into a nation-state. The enormous differences that set these two countries apart from others are sometimes obscured when all countries are treated as formally equal. The security conceptions of China and India are in some ways more those of empires than of nation-states.

A historical view may contribute to an understanding of Indian national self-conceptions as well as some aspects of Indian foreign and security policies. Indian aspiration to great-power status, for example, is rooted in part in the perceived greatness of the earlier Indian empires, especially that of Asoka. According to Tinker and Basham, the Asoka empire was one of the greatest of the world in its time (Basham 1954: 50–57; Tinker 1990: 7–8), and beginning with it Indian philosophical, cultural, and economic influence spread to many parts of Asia. This view of Indian aspiration contrasts sharply with the popular external view of

India as a poverty-stricken developing country overreaching itself for great-power status. Some contemporary Indian security concerns (relating to Afghanistan and Central Asia and to naval activities by external powers in the vicinity of India) may also be traced to earlier historical periods. Similarly, inspiration from the past may be a factor in India's foreign relations. In the words of Nehru, who was virtually the sole architect of Indian foreign policy until his death, "the most important thing about our foreign policy is that it is part of our great historical tradition" (quoted in Larus 1965: 13). Some analysts have argued the relevance of earlier traditions in analyzing contemporary Indian policy (Panikkar 1960: 29), while others have disagreed with this view. Norman Palmer (1962: 3), for example, argues that there is no continuity between ancient Hindu political thought and the political ideas that move modern India.

In the Indic (Hindu-Buddhist) conception, the state was not viewed as "an organism transcending its component parts," but as an extension of the king (Basham 1954: 88). Kautilya, for example, assumes the king to embody the six other constituent elements of the state (verses 6.1.1. and 8.2.1. in Rangarajan 1992: 119 and 141 respectively). The exposition of his theory of foreign policy is thus grounded in the interests and interaction of kings. Further, the divinely ordered society transcended and was independent of the state, although the king had the duty to protect and regulate society as well as to supervise the economic life of the realm. The right to rule was derived through heredity and divination. Divinity, however, did not rule out challenges from rival contenders for political power. In theory, the ruler had absolute power. In practice, however, the exercise of power was constrained by the sense of accountability stemming from ethical codes governing the conduct of kings and the sacred laws that governed society. That a king must be just and rule according to *dharma* is emphasized in nearly all Indian treatises dealing with government. And the people had the right to rebel against oppressive and unjust rule. The counsel of ministers and public opinion also constrained the exercise of power (Basham 1954: 87–88). Thus, although the concentration of power could have made for harsh autocratic rule, in practice, beneficent rule was the norm. The Indic ideal is peace, tranquility, and "energetic beneficence" (Basham 1954: 89–90).

The peaceful ideal did not, however, carry over to the international arena. The ideas of a higher culture and a claim to universal kingship that underpinned the hierarchic Sinocentric system were not applicable to the Indian subcontinent. The cultural unity of the Indian subcontinent made gradations on the basis of culture irrelevant. The ideal of a universal emperor ruling prosperously and righteously did exist in the Indian tradition, though it was seldom realized (Basham 1954: 83). Kautilya posits the eventual objective of the would-be conqueror-king to be *chakravartikshetram*—the conquest of all of *Bharatavarsha* (i.e., the Indian subcontinent) and its rule in accordance with *dharma*. As a goal, this made for constant struggle between states bent on expansion and those seeking self-preservation. There was no middle way. Status quo was difficult to maintain. War and conquest became the norm (Scharfe 1989: 203). Power was paramount in asserting authority over other states. This explains in part the lack of permanence of the tributary relationships in the Indic system. An idealist tradition in Indian thought, exemplified by Asoka, abhorred international wars, but more commonly war was accepted as a normal activity of the state. Even the principle of nonviolence was not deemed to forbid war (Basham 1954: 123), which could be waged for wealth and power or for glory. Acceptance of war, however, did not preclude peace. One of the seven principles of foreign policy advocated by Kautilya was that peace is to be preferred to war. (Rangarajan 1992: 546).

The geographical area of the Indic system extended from the "Himalayas in the North to the seas in the South and a thousand *yojanas* wide from the east to the west" (Kautilya, quoted in Rangarajan 1992: 543). For several reasons—geographic, religious, and administrative—conquest of territories beyond the subcontinent was considered not feasible and not desirable. It is pertinent here that Indian influence beyond the subcontinent has been predominantly cultural and economic rather than political. The structure of the Indic system was anarchic; in it, relative power played a central role in interstate relations. The political realist tradition in Indian thought was articulated in several texts, including the well-known *Arthashastra* and *Mahabharata*. The "mandala doctrine," a key idea in the management of interstate affairs, is based on the *vijigisu* (conquest-seeking prince). It exhorts the *vijigisu* to seek "strength and prosperity," to be concerned about relative power, and to become the center of a universal system (then defined in terms of the subcontinent). Neighbors are posited as enemies, and the enemy's enemy as a friend and ally. Considerations of relative power made power balancing (internal and external) a critical concern of Indian rulers. Alliances, always temporary, were forged to defeat a common enemy. Although the *Mahabharata* is an account of war among feuding families and not states, it is representative of the Indian realist tradition. It states: "There is no natural enemy or friend; friends and enemies are born out of application of political interests" (quoted in Scharfe 1989: 204).

The Indic interstate system allowed for confidence and security building among kings, but within the realist tradition. Kautilya posits the peace treaty, the policy of nonintervention, and the practice of hostage taking and giving as instruments to be deployed to build confidence among kings (verse 7.17.1,2 Rangarajan: 581). Like the Sinic system but for different reasons, the Indic system did not allow for the concept of international law; however, rules of war, including treatment of the defeated, were articulated in the *Mahabharata, Arthashastra, Thirukural,* and other texts. International cooperation was also not a feature of the Indic system.

The Indic system may have ceased to function with the advent of Muslim rule in India, and it certainly died out with the advent of British rule. Except for Nepal and Bhutan, the states that interacted with the Indian heartland have now either become part of India or ceased to exist. The ancient kingdom of Nepal had extensive religious, cultural, and economic interaction with Indian empires but remained a separate kingdom, although it acknowledged the suzerainty of Indian emperors and kings at various times—for example, during the rule of Samudra-gupta (A.D. 335–75). Nepal was a vassal state of the Chalukya kingdom in the eleventh century (Allan, Haig, and Dodwell 1934: 116–18).

Like Nepal, Sri Lanka had a precolonial existence. Although it em-braced Buddhism during the visit of the brother of King Asoka in the second century B.C., Sri Lanka had no political interaction with the Indian empires. It did, however, interact continuously for about two thousand years with the Tamil kingdoms in southern India. The other large South Asian states—Pakistan and Bangladesh—are postcolonial Islamic states; the dynamics of their interaction with India are of recent vintage.

Although the Indic system ceased to function several centuries ago, contemporary international politics in South Asia is not far different from that articulated in the *Arthashastra,* despite the addition of several new actors, the recent origins of the causes of conflict, and the involve-ment of external actors. Suspicion and enmity characterize the bilateral relations of nearly all neighboring countries in the region. Struggle, competition, and power balancing have been common. War is accepted as an instrument of state policy. Peaceful coexistence and cooperation have been rare. Moreover, abstracted from the specific actors and dynamics, the Indic system seems more congruent with the contempo-rary anarchic international system than does the hierarchic Sinic system. The Indic system is of intellectual interest, and its study can sensitize the student of international politics to an early Asian counterpart of Western political realism.

International Politics in Southeast Asia

The precolonial states in Southeast Asia were modeled essentially on the Indian tradition, and their international politics was in many ways similar to that of the Indic system. International politics in Southeast Asia that is of contemporary relevance dates from about the tenth century. There were earlier kingdoms (Coedes 1971: 1–80), but data about them and their interactions are rather sketchy, and contemporary Southeast Asian states do not trace their origins to those kingdoms. During the tenth to fourteenth centuries, mainland and island Southeast Asia became more distinct from each other. A key factor contributing to this distinction was the southward migration of the Vietnamese, Thai, and Burman peoples (which began much earlier but accelerated during that period) and their eventual domination of mainland Southeast Asia (Tate 1971).[1] Island Southeast Asia was not affected by the migration. Its population remained predominantly of the Malay stock, and Hindu-Buddhist cultural influences held sway until the arrival of Islam in the fourteenth and fifteenth centuries. Further, the mainland kingdoms were primarily agricultural and continental, whereas those in island Southeast Asia were both land and sea powers for whose prosperity seaborne commerce was vital.

Continental Southeast Asia

The international politics of mainland Southeast Asia until the arrival of Western colonial powers was rooted in the formation, expansion, and struggle for domination of the Vietnamese, Thai, and Burmese kingdoms, which took place largely at the expense of the Khmer (Cambodian) empire (Silverman 1974: 54–59). From its founding in 802 to the thirteenth century, the Khmer empire was the mightiest and wealthiest state in Southeast Asia. Beginning in the fourteenth century, however, the Khmer empire was challenged in the West by the ascending Thai kingdom in Ayuthia. To counterbalance the Thais, the Khmers at first welcomed the Vietnamese, who were embarked on a southward expansion (Tate 1971: 437). Continued Vietnamese expansion, however, became a threat to Cambodia. Vietnam eventually absorbed large parts of eastern Cambodia (much of modern-day South Vietnam, which Cambodians call Khmer Krom), arousing deep hatred and fear on the part of the Khmers toward the Vietnamese. Since the early eighteenth century the primary problem for Cambodian rulers has been maintaining their independence and indeed survival in the face of persistent Thai and Vietnamese encroachments on their territory and the struggle between those two countries for overlordship of Cambodia. But for the

French intervention, Cambodia would most likely have suffered further losses and might even have ceased to exist.

Although formed much later by the southward migration of the Thai people, Laos suffered a similar fate. The initial Laotian kingdom at Lang Chang (Luang Prahbang) eventually embraced all of present-day Laos. Beginning in the eighteenth century the kingdom disintegrated, opening the way for influence by its powerful neighbors, Siam (Thailand) and Vietnam. Like Cambodia, Laos became a buffer and a target of competition for overlordship between Vietnam and Thailand. Again like Cambodia, Laos was saved by French intervention from further losses and possibly from extinction.

The Thai kingdom in Ayuthia, like Vietnam, was expansionist from its founding in 1350. In addition to bringing the other Thai kingdoms under its vassalage, the Ayuthia kingdom reached eastward to conquer the Khmer capital of Angkor in 1432 and expanded southward to reach the shores of the Malay peninsula. This southward expansion was checked by the Chinese protection offered to the Malacca sultanate in the early fifteenth century. In the West, the Ayuthia kingdom was engaged in a bloody struggle with the Burmese for almost three centuries, eventually defeating them in 1785. Thereafter, the Burmese competition receded, and it disappeared altogether with the British occupation of Tenasserim. Like the Vietnamese and the Thais, the Burmese, as they migrated south, came into conflict with the Mon Kingdom in the lower part of Burma and with the Shans (Thai-Chinese people) in the northeast, who had risen to power after the fall of Pagan to a Mongol army in 1287. The Burmese defeated the Shans in the 1550s and eventually emerged victorious over the Mons in 1755. That victory led to the establishment of the Konbaung dynasty, which lasted until its annexation by Britain in 1885.

The international politics of mainland Southeast Asia of this early period has left some enduring features. One relates to the security dynamic that links Thailand, Cambodia, Laos, and Vietnam, which form the geopolitical core of mainland Southeast Asia (Alagappa 1991a: 13–16). Thailand and Vietnam, as the two dominant states, view each other as rivals and compete for power and influence in this subregion. Cambodia and Laos, as weak powers and the targets of competition, have become preoccupied with survival. Deep resentment and distrust characterizes relations among all these countries. French colonization of Vietnam, Laos, and Cambodia halted this dynamic, but only temporarily. With the granting of independence to Cambodia and Laos, and the liberation and unification of Vietnam, the old security dynamic resurfaced.

Second, although the Thai-Burmese rivalry in the west is much less relevant today than in the past, deep mistrust continues to characterize the bilateral relations of the two countries. The relationship is further complicated by the presence in Burma, close to the border with Thailand, of several Thai-Chinese minority groups (e.g., Shans, Karens) who have been at war with Rangoon for much of the postindependence period. Bangkok has supported these minority groups at various times, both for their value as a buffer and to bring pressure to bear upon Rangoon.

Third, the pattern of migration, domination, and displacement has produced, in nearly every state, several indigenous minorities that either can lay historical claim to separateness or have affinities to populations in neighboring countries. This is true even though each mainland Southeast Asian state is controlled by a dominant population group. This situation heightens the tensions and conflicts that complicate the domestic and international politics of these countries.

Fourth, competition and conflict to achieve domination and to demonstrate superiority—as in the Indic system—appears to have been the predominant mode of interaction among the three key states, each of which has tried to expand its own power and influence. In the process they either annexed or established hierarchic relations with kingdoms in their immediate vicinity, while engaging in competition with other dominant powers in areas where their interests conflicted. Alliances among them or with external powers were not a feature of the interaction among the dominant states during this period, although they allied with the smaller states to secure control over those states and to prevent their domination by other powers. The smaller states of Cambodia and Laos appear to have engaged in the practice of alliances to ensure their survival. There were no international institutions for mutual recognition, coexistence, or cooperation.

Maritime Southeast Asia

Unlike their counterparts on the mainland, island Southeast Asian states have little historical continuity as political entities. The predecessors of Indonesia and, to a lesser degree, Malaysia were the central political actors. Although a large number of kingdoms existed in the different islands, only those rooted in Sumatra and particularly in Java were able to control significant parts of contemporary Indonesia. The Sri Vijaya empire, based in Sumatra, appears to have been dominant from about the eighth to the twelfth century. It was essentially a maritime commercial power with control over the critical Straits of Malacca. At its height, Sri Vijaya's power extended from the Isthmus of Kra to central

Java. It eventually gave way to the Javanese empire of Majapahit, itself the successor to a series of earlier Javanese kingdoms—Sailendra, Mataram, Kediri, Singasari—dating to the seventh century.

Majapahit, unlike Sri Vijaya, was a land and sea power with a strong agricultural foundation. It was a center of culture and civilization as well. Majapahit began to decline during the fifteenth century. Its decay, unlike the quick collapse of Sri Vijaya, was gradual, lasting more than a century. Majapahit was succeeded by the state of Mataram and subsequently by the states of Surakarta and Jogjakarta, which survived as separate entities until the last days of Dutch rule. The royal house of Jogjakarta played an important role in the struggle for Indonesian independence from Dutch rule. For these and other reasons, the kingdoms and empires located in Java, which has always been the most populous island of the area, may be seen as the predecessors of the modern Indonesian state. The Javanese heritage appears to have a bearing on the national self-conception of contemporary Indonesia. The kingdoms located in Sumatra may be viewed as having played a secondary and ephemeral role in the evolution of the Indonesian state.

The only other empire to have arisen in the maritime subregion was that of the Malacca sultanate, founded in 1403. It was a commercial empire, in many ways similar to the earlier Sri Vijaya. The decline of Majapahit, the resurgence of Chinese influence under the Ming dynasty and the Ming rulers' interest in protecting the trade routes through the Southeast Asian straits, and Malacca's location in the critical Straits of Malacca all facilitated the growth of Malacca from a small fishing village to the largest port in Southeast Asia with several vassal states. Although some Malay states in peninsular Malaysia can lay claim to longer existence, none rose to the prominence of Malacca or the Johor-Riau empire that succeeded Malacca upon its conquest by the Portuguese in 1511. Malay leaders view the Malacca sultanate as the classical period of their culture and civilization, much as the kingdom of Sukothai is viewed by the Thais.

The other three states—Singapore, the Philippines, and Brunei—were nonexistent or else peripheral to the international politics of maritime Southeast Asia. Singapore has no historical record as a separate kingdom. Except in the south, there is no record of any major kingdom in the history of the Philippines. It was constructed as a state by Spanish and later American imperialism. Brunei, unlike Singapore and the Philippines, can trace its political history to the fifteenth century, when it emerged as a flourishing sultanate, reaching its zenith after the fall of Malacca. At its height Brunei controlled all of present-day East Malaysia, and its influence extended to the Sulu archipelago, now part of the

Philippines. The sultanate then declined and lost control over Sarawak, Labuan, and British North Borneo. Fearing further loss and possible extinction, Brunei became a British protectorate in 1888.

Because of the lack of historical continuity, little of the precolonial international politics of the maritime subregion has contemporary relevance. Many of the kingdoms that interacted with the Javanese kingdoms and empires have disappeared or become part of Indonesia. Consequently, the traditional competition between land-based Javanese kingdoms and sea-based Malay kingdoms in Sumatra, for example, appears now to have more impact on the internal politics of Indonesia than on the international politics of the region. It may, however, be possible to link some aspects of the international behavior of contemporary Indonesia and Malaysia and the tensions in their bilateral relations to the historical rivalries and tensions between Javanese (Majapahit) and Malay (Malacca, Sri Vijaya) kingdoms and the attempt by the former to control the latter and, more generally, to be the dominant power in the subregion.

External Powers and Southeast Asia

Situated astride critical waterways as well as overland routes between China and India (and later the Middle East), Southeast Asia has always been exposed to outside influences (McCloud 1995). But it was never passive and was not colonized until the arrival of the Western powers. Kingdoms and empires in both India and China engaged in trade with the region and were concerned at various times with the safety of navigation in the Southeast Asian straits.

Indian influence in Southeast Asia was largely philosophical, cultural, and economic. Political influence spread through Southeast Asian borrowings of ideas and political and legal systems, and sometimes through marriage. Except for the Cholas in the eleventh century, no Indian kingdom exerted direct political or military influence in Southeast Asia. But Southeast Asian kingdoms such as Sri Vijaya saw the value of cultivating good relations with the Indian (Chola) kingdoms; the conversion of the ruler of Malacca to Islam was intended in part to preserve the trade with Indian (Gujerati) traders, who by then had become Muslims.

Chinese influence in Southeast Asia was not so much cultural (except for Vietnam) as economic and to some degree also political. But the degree of political influence must not be exaggerated. Except for Vietnam, the Southeast Asian states did not belong to the Sinic Zone. Many Southeast Asian kingdoms sent tribute to China, but tribute meant neither acceptance of the Chinese moral order nor subordination to China (McCloud 1995: 94). Often, tribute was simply expedient, serving the domestic political interests of Southeast Asian rulers against rival claimants to power, or economically beneficial. But there were occasions when tribute to China did aid local rulers against Chinese invasion (Ayuthia's regular tributes, for example, saved it from being destroyed during the Kublai Khan invasion) or provide relief from foreign pressure (as in the case when the Malacca sultan confronted Thai pressure). But such instances were few and far between. Tributary relations between Southeast Asian countries (except Vietnam) and China did not carry the same meaning and obligations as those between China and the states in the Sinic Zone. The long interaction of China and India with Southeast Asia was brought to a halt by the arrival of the Western colonial powers.

The Colonial Interregnum: Transition and Transformation of Asian States and Interstate Systems

Western intrusion into Asia began in the early sixteenth century. By 1896 all of South and Southeast Asia, except for Nepal and Thailand, was under European colonial rule. Western political intrusion into East Asia began in the early nineteenth century. In the course of the next hundred years, China lost control over its tributary states and suffered political, commercial, and territorial encroachments by the Western powers and Japan. By the early twentieth century it was reduced to semicolonial status and Manchuria, Korea, and Taiwan were colonized by Japan. Western political penetration and domination had three major consequences. First, it ended the autonomous subregional interstate system in East Asia (the Indic system having ended earlier). Second, it contributed to the rise of Japan and to the deep-rooted suspicions and enmities that characterize the subregion dominated by Japan. Finally, it transformed the nature of Asian political units and integrated them into the global international system dominated by the West.

End of the Chinese World Order

The two crucial bases of the Chinese world order—claim to higher culture and universal kingship—were substantially undermined by the nonacceptance by the Western powers of the cultural superiority of China, the rise of Japan as a great power, and, internally, the weakness of the Qing dynasty.

Initially the Western powers sought to cooperate with China by drawing it into a multistate system. Their demands were limited to diplomatic equality and commercial opportunity (Fairbank, Reischauer, and Craig 1978: 454). But as the power of the Qing dynasty weakened, the Western powers engaged in imperial acquisitions. The uncertain boundaries of China and its vague claims to suzerainty made its tributaries (Ryukyu Islands, Taiwan, Vietnam, Korea, and areas in Central Asia) fair game for competition and acquisition. Russia encroached upon Chinese territories and tributaries in Central Asia, France colonized Vietnam, and Korea became the object of competition among China, Japan, and Russia that led eventually to its annexation by Japan. The Japanese defeat of the Chinese navy in 1894 resulted in Taiwan being handed over to Japan. More significantly, it inspired a new round of competition and imperial ambitions on the part of Western powers, this time at the expense of China itself. All the Western powers, and later Japan, acquired "spheres of influence" in China that became quasi-colonial, threatening the Qing dynasty with extinction. The inability of the Qing dynasty to respond effectively to Western pressure, to defend Chinese interests in the tributary states, or to quell regionalism within China compelled it not only to concede equality to the Western powers but in fact to submit to an inferior status.

The rise of Japan and its attempt to create under its domination a Greater East Asia Co-prosperity Sphere challenged the centrality of China in East Asia. For several reasons, Japan was better able than China to cope with the Western powers, and rose quickly from "semi-colonial status under the unequal treaties to become a great power and ally of Britain" (Fairbank, Reischauer, and Craig 1978: 648). Further, in the latter capacity, Japan sat on the victorious side of the Versailles Conference and picked up German colonial possessions in East Asia and the Pacific. Through the Washington Conference in 1921–22, Japan sought to preserve its status, its territorial gains, and the military status quo in the Pacific. Rising Japan posed a graver challenge for China than did the Western powers. Unlike them, Japan was indigenous to the region, and in the Chinese view it was a subordinate state. Japan, however, not only sought equality with the Western powers but also attempted to replace China as the central power in East Asia. Despite its eventual failure in this attempt, the rise of Japan as a great power implied that uncontested Chinese domination of East Asia was no longer tenable.

Unable to cope with Western and Japanese imperial designs, and confronted with acute internal problems, the Qing dynasty collapsed, bringing about the end of the Chinese world order and plunging China into warlordism and civil war. China and the rest of East Asia were irretrievably drawn into an international system dominated by Western norms. The integration of East Asia into the international system was furthered by the rise of Japan and its membership in the club of Western great powers. China was compelled to behave internationally as one among equals. It has been argued that the Nationalist and Communist governments that followed the Qing dynasty acted on the basis of a system of nation-states (Schwartz 1968: 284–88) and that, for the most part, their goal was a strong Chinese nation rather than the restoration of a Chinese world order. Others, however, citing Mao Zedong, contend that a China-centered world order persists in the thinking of Chinese leaders. Benjamin Schwartz (1968: 284) is extremely skeptical of such claims, arguing that the traditional Chinese notions of world order have been fundamentally undermined. Our own view is that China, for the present, has come to accept a global international system in which it is one of the great powers. With regard to Asia, the traditional Chinese worldview persists, but in a modified form and alongside the formal egalitarian system. Beijing seeks to become the crucial power in the management of Asian affairs. It cannot be doubted that Mao and his successors have sought to recover the greatness of China and to establish its "proper" place in East Asia and the world (Funabashi, Oksenberg, and Weiss 1994).

The unequal treaties that were forced upon China during the 1842–1943 period and the accompanying scramble among the Western powers (Britain, France, Germany, Russia, and the United States) for spheres of influence in China, as well as the Japanese ambitions that threatened China's political and territorial integrity, have left a deep imprint on Chinese leaders. Mao wrote in 1939: "In defeating China in war, the imperialist states have taken away many Chinese dependent states and a part of her territory. Japan took away Korea, Taiwan and Ryukyu islands, the Pescadores, Port Arthur; England seized Burma, Bhutan, Nepal and Hong Kong; France occupied Annam and even an insignificant country like Portugal took Macao" (quoted in Jain 1959: 106–7). China, therefore, is not satisfied with the territorial and political status quo and is extremely sensitive to norms and actions that may infringe on its territorial integrity and political autonomy. Developments during the "century of humiliation" contributed to a deep fear and hatred of imperialism, and to the rise of Chinese nationalism. Subjection and humiliation, coupled with the internal weakness and disunity that prevailed during this period, underlie the emphasis of Chinese leaders on a united and strong Chinese nation.

Finally, Japan, like China (but for different reasons), had difficulty in conducting international relations with other Asian countries on the basis of equality. According to Maruyama, an awareness of equality in international affairs was totally absent and Japanese leaders viewed international relations in terms of the premises of national hierarchy.

"Consequently when the premises of national hierarchy were transferred horizontally into the international sphere, international problems were reduced to a single alternative: conquer or be conquered. In the absence of any higher normative standard with which to gauge international relations, power politics (became) the rule" (Maruyama 1963: 140). A hierarchic worldview underscored Japan's effort to dominate East Asia. The Chinese belief in superiority, as noted earlier, was rooted in the ideas of universal kingship and a higher culture, and backed by material power. The East Asian order under Chinese domination, when it existed, was at least in part a moral one. This, as well as the absence of contending powers, may account for its persistence over some two thousand years. Japan, on the other hand, while desirous of becoming the dominant power in East Asia, could not articulate a satisfactory ideology for its domination of the region. Several rationales—continentalism, pan-Asianism—were advanced to justify Japanese imperial policy in Asia, but none had broad appeal domestically or in the target countries (Iriye 1967; Mayo 1967). Further, Japan, unlike China, was not economically self-contained. The lack of primary resources was a key factor in the Japanese imperial drive that led to the colonization of Manchuria, Korea, and Taiwan. Japanese colonization differed from that of the West in that it sought to turn the colonies into sources of industrial strength, whereas Western nations sought to perpetuate underdevelopment. Japan's domination of East Asia was short-lived. Nevertheless, it implied that China could no longer expect to be the uncontested hegemon in the subregion and that a hierarchic order with a single center of power and authority was no longer tenable in East Asia. China and Japan would have to come to terms with each other. This continues to represent a tremendous challenge, because the two states have no history of coexistence as great powers. The situation is complicated by Japan's history of aggressive behavior during its great-power period.

Imperial Japan and Animosities in East Asia

Japan's concerns at the outset of Western intrusion were security from the Western powers and acceptance by them as an equal. Imperialism and domination were later goals, which came to be viewed as essential to its great-power status. Japanese security (defined to include economic security) was held to require control over Korea and Formosa (Taiwan). Tokyo's attempt to open up Korea and draw it away from China in 1867 led to Sino-Japanese rivalry in Korea and eventually to the military defeat of China in 1895. Under the Treaty of Shimonoseki, China ceded to Japan Taiwan, the Pescadore Islands, and the Kwantung peninsula in Manchuria; recognized the independence of Korea; and negotiated a commercial treaty with Japan that gave Japan the same privileges enjoyed by the Western powers in China.

Japan's triumph alarmed Russia, which also had designs on Korea and Manchuria. With the backing of France and Germany, Russia forced Japan to give up the Kwantung peninsula, which Russia appropriated for itself in 1898 under a 25-year lease. A later Russian attempt to take over all of Manchuria provoked mutual suspicion and enmity between Japan and Russia, erupting in the Russo-Japanese War, in which Japan routed Russia on land and at sea. The Treaty of Portsmouth, signed in 1905, recognized Japan's paramount interest in Korea, restored Chinese sovereignty and administration in Manchuria, and gave the Russian lease on the Kwantung peninsula to Japan. Free of all foreign competitors, Japan made Korea a protectorate in 1905. Five years later, following a vigorous suppression of widespread nationalism, Japan annexed Korea. Japanese colonial rule, which lasted 40 years, decapitated the Korean political and social order and was a bitter experience for the Koreans.

Japan's victories over China and Russia enhanced its prestige among the Western powers, which began to show a decidedly pro-Japanese attitude, embodied in the revision of the unequal treaties. By the early 1920s Japan had achieved its twin goals of security and equality. But the interconnected developments of the Great Depression and the rise of militarism set Japan on an imperialist course, beginning with an initially successful but eventually terrible and costly war in China. The refusal of the Chinese nationalist government to recognize the special importance of the northern Chinese provinces for the security of Japan's continental empire led eventually to the Sino-Japanese war and the setting up of a pro-Japanese puppet government in Nanjing in 1940. This development and the wanton slaughter in Nanjing created deep resentment and apprehension in China about Japan, especially as a great power.

Japan's policy in China violated the agreement reached at the 1921–22 Washington Naval Conference.[2] Its quest for a Greater East Asia Co-prosperity Sphere through the capture of the colonial possessions of Britain, Holland, and France upset the balance of power in East Asia and conflicted with the interests and policies of the United States and Britain. Japan's alliance with Germany, the principal problem country for the United States and Britain, aggravated the situation. The Japanese attack on Pearl Harbor brought a declaration of war from the United States and eventually resulted in Japan's defeat by the Allies.

Several effects of Japanese behavior during the first half of the twentieth century have relevance today. First, it created deep resentment and apprehension of Japan in China and Korea, sentiments that strongly condition contemporary attitudes of these countries toward Japan.

Second, the competition among China, Japan, and Russia for control over the Korean peninsula reinforced Korean nationalism and xenophobia. Third, Russo-Japanese competition for power and influence in Northeast Asia during this period contributed to those two countries' negative perceptions of each other and accounts in part for the slowness of improvement in their bilateral relations despite the end of the Cold War. Fourth, Japan's attempt to dominate East Asia and its attack on Pearl Harbor left a strong imprint on the U.S. attitude toward Japan. Although Japan is a close ally, the U.S.–Japan alliance is touted as the most important pillar of American strategy for regional security, and Washington supports and encourages a bigger political and security role for Tokyo, the United States will not willingly accept Japan as an independent great power. Fifth, Japan's defeat and the severe suffering of its people, particularly from the atomic bombings of Hiroshima and Nagasaki, deeply marked Japanese society—particularly attitudes toward the Japanese state, militarism, and war—contributing to strong pacifism.

Taken together, these consequences have severely curtailed the international orientation and role of post–World War II Japan, and they also affect the conduct of international politics in Northeast Asia. The Japanese interregnum also gave an unintended boost to the liberation of Southeast Asian and South Asian countries from Western colonial rule.

Transformation of Political Units

International politics in South and Southeast Asia during the colonial era, with a few minor exceptions, was an affair of the colonial governments, which took their directives from the metropolitan capitals in Europe. As such it is of little contemporary relevance. Colonial rule and its liquidation, however, left some enduring legacies. Foremost among them is the transformation of the political units from kingdoms and empires into modern nation-states. Precolonial states in Asia— despite differences between Sinic and Indian versions, as described above—were in essence extensions of kings and emperors who derived their right to govern from heaven or heredity, rather than from the people. Power in these states tended to radiate outward from the palace and capital, waning with distance so that it was subject to contestation at the frontiers by local kings and chieftains as well as by other centers of power. Boundaries were not clearly demarcated. Physical barriers (mountain ranges, seas, deserts, wilderness) marked off territories and in some cases isolated one center of power from another. Monopoly of force and sovereign jurisdiction over the entire kingdom were not common, especially in South and Southeast Asia. Interstate relations were a matter of relations between individual rulers.

Colonial rule and the struggle against it contributed to the rise of the norms of nation, nation-state, and sovereignty in Asia. These Western norms have taken root among the postcolonial "national" political elites. Although the ideological and territorial bases of states, as well as the legitimacy of regimes and incumbent governments, are the objects of contestation in several countries, the nation-state has become the unit of *international* relations in Asia. Sovereignty and egalitarianism have become key principles in the conduct of international relations. The experiences of the colonial period—domination and exploitation by colonial powers, treatment as inferior people in their own lands, perceived obstruction by Western powers of their struggle for independence—also strengthen their attachment to the principles of sovereignty, territorial integrity, and noninterference in domestic affairs.

The specific political units that exist today and their boundaries are another legacy of colonial rule. Several of these units are new states (Pakistan, Malaysia, the Philippines, Singapore) that had no earlier existence as separate political entities. Several others (Cambodia, Laos, Brunei) owe their continued existence to colonial rule. Although the Indian and Indonesian heritages include earlier empires, the present construction of those states is largely a product of British and Dutch colonial rule, respectively. Similarly, the boundaries of such states as Nepal, Bangladesh, Vietnam, Cambodia, Laos, Thailand, and Burma are a product of colonialism.

By privileging certain existing units and imposing arbitrary boundaries, colonial rule contributed to the ethnic and racial diversity, and hence the artificiality, of many states. Admittedly, much of the diversity is a product of earlier migration, but just as colonial rule terminated such unregulated movements, it also froze the existing population patterns. Similarly, colonial rule halted the cycle of rise, fall, renewal, and succession of kingdoms. Thus, several kingdoms and peoples (the Tamils in Sri Lanka, outlying regional kingdoms in India, the Pattani in southern Thailand, the Moros in southern Philippines, outer island kingdoms in Indonesia, and the many minorities in Burma) were "permanently" trapped as parts of other nation-states. Colonial rule encouraged new migration from India and China to Sri Lanka, Burma, Malaysia, Singapore, and Indonesia, and from Vietnam to Laos and Cambodia. These movements further complicated the racial makeup of the receiving countries.

Finally, by ending the autonomous subregional Asian interstate systems and transforming the political units, colonial rule paved the way for the integration of the Asian states into the global international system. Although an Asia-wide regional system could not and did not emerge under colonial rule, such rule, and especially the nationalist struggles against it, did contribute to notions of Asian identity and solidarity. The actual emergence of an Asia-wide system was due primarily to the global ideological-military rivalry between the two superpowers and its manifestation in Asia.

The Cold War: Emergence of an Asia-wide Regional Security System

An Asia-wide regional security system emerged, for the first time in history, during the Cold War. The intense zero-sum competition between the two superpowers created connections among the Asian subregional systems that emerged after the end of colonial rule. The new Asia-wide system was rather loose and clearly subordinate to competition at the global level. The dynamics of this regional system were driven by three distinct but interconnected sets of rivalries and conflicts. One was the global rivalry between the United States and the Soviet Union that provided the strategic framework and integrating dynamic for much of the international politics in Asia. The rivalries and conflicts involving the two superpowers and the three major Asian powers—principally the Sino-American, Sino-Soviet, and Sino-Indian conflicts—constituted the second layer. The third dynamic consisted of the competition, conflict, and cooperation among the local powers at the subregional level in Northeast, Southeast, and South Asia, overlaid by the rivalries among the major powers.

Superpower Competition: The Strategic Overlay

The origins of the Cold War in Europe and its extension to Asia are well documented (Gaddis 1982; Iriye 1974; Reynolds 1994) and will be recounted here only briefly. By 1947–48, the United States and the Soviet Union had begun to perceive each other as the principal security threat. The United States, which emerged from World War II as the global hegemon with the greatest power to influence the strategic environment in Asia, viewed the "loss" of China, the conclusion of the Sino-Soviet alliance in early 1950, and Chinese intervention in the Korean War with Soviet material support as confirmation, despite some contrary evidence, of the thesis of a Soviet-led monolithic communist movement intent on world domination. In the U.S. view, the Soviet Union was the principal enemy and China, believed to be under Soviet control, was the principal communist threat in Asia. The outbreak of the Korean War appeared to confirm several conclusions of the National Security Council Memorandum 68: that interests are indivisible, so that all interests are vital, and that any further shift in the balance of power in any part of the world could upset the entire structure of postwar international relations (Gaddis 1982: 109–10). Expansion of Soviet power must therefore be blocked by all means short of direct war, and effort must be made to induce a retraction of Soviet control and influence. With the outbreak of the Korean war, the Truman administration extended to Asia this zero-sum strategy of containment with emphasis on military power.

Japan, which until then had been the primary enemy, came to be viewed as the cornerstone of the American strategy to contain the Soviet Union and China in Asia. The creation of a stable, friendly, and economically powerful Japan that was clearly subordinate to and dependent on the United States became a key American goal (Cumings 1993: 41–52). Following the signing in San Francisco of the Japanese Peace Treaty in September 1951, the United States and Japan concluded a bilateral security treaty. Reversing the earlier policy that had called for the demilitarization of Japan, the treaty required Tokyo to assume greater responsibility for its own defense. America's new Japan policy had the implicit goal of containing Japan as well. To block communist expansion, the United States sought to draw as many Asian states as possible into alliances. It contracted security treaties with the Philippines (1951), South Korea (1953), Taiwan (1955), Thailand and Pakistan (through the Southeast Asia Treaty Organization [SEATO], 1954), and Iran (1959). Further, the United States unilaterally extended protection to South Vietnam, Cambodia, and Laos after the 1954 Geneva agreements. The U.S. "defense perimeter" in Asia stretched from Japan through Southeast Asia and around India to the Persian Gulf; it was described at the time as the "Grand Crescent."

The goal of blocking and rolling back communism was uppermost in the Asia policy of the United States. All other concerns, such as facilitating national self-determination, were subordinated to that goal. Thus, the United States intervened on behalf of or gave moral and material support to noncommunist factions in the civil wars that raged in China, the Korean peninsula, Vietnam, Laos, the Philippines, Indonesia, Burma, and Pakistan (Wilcox 1972: 247–72). Similarly, the United States supported noncommunist states in local and regional conflicts. The United States was initially hostile to neutral and nonaligned states on the ground that their neutrality was immoral and short-sighted (Martin 1962: xvii–xix). That stance, however, was subsequently softened. By the time of the Kennedy administration the United States no longer viewed a policy of independence and nonalignment as inimical to American interests, although it by no means approved.

The Soviet Union, for its part, renewed its ideological hostility against the capitalist West in the immediate postwar period (Daniels 1984: 120–45). At the founding conference of the Communist Information Bureau (Cominform) in 1947, the Soviet Union framed the world situation as a bitter contest between two camps: the "socialist camp" and "American imperialism" (Daniels 1984: 145–48). Asia did not figure in this Soviet worldview until 1947, when an aggressive line replaced the notion of peaceful coexistence. Frustration with the lack of progress in Europe and a desire to capitalize on revolutionary struggles in China, Vietnam, and Indonesia intensified the Soviet attention to Asia (McLane 1966: 367–71). But several years passed before Moscow actually followed through on its formal articulations. In any case, interest in Asia did not match the Soviet focus on Europe throughout the Stalin era.

Soviet policy in Asia under Stalin was driven primarily by realpolitik considerations and limited largely to Northeast Asia. In return for entering the war against Japan, Stalin, in a secret agreement with Roosevelt and Churchill in Yalta, had extracted several concessions in the Far East. They included the preservation of the status quo in outer Mongolia, the cession to the Soviet Union of the Kuril Islands, and restoration of the Russian rights in China lost to Japan after the Russo-Japanese War.[3] Immediately after World War II, following a Soviet-sponsored plebiscite in 1945, Mongolia became an independent country and entered into a ten-year pact of mutual assistance with Moscow (Lach and Wehrle 1975: 22–23). In Korea, in accord with an understanding reached with the United States, the Soviet Union occupied the northern half of the peninsula in 1945. In 1948 it created the Democratic People's Republic of Korea (DPRK) under the leadership of the Russian-trained Kim Il Sung, who brought North Korea into line with Soviet policy.

Soviet policy toward China was less clear. Unlike the United States, which had sponsored Nationalist China in the international community and accepted it as one of the four big powers, the Soviet Union was reluctant to concede such status to China. Its policy toward the ongoing civil war in China was designed to fulfill Soviet political and economic goals. Ideology was not a consideration. Throughout the civil war, the Soviets displayed ambivalence toward the Chinese Communists (Lach and Wehrle 1975: 46–49). But communist victory in China changed their attitude. In the Soviet view, that victory enhanced the prospects for communist success elsewhere in Asia. Further, an alliance with China as the junior partner would ensure continued Soviet leadership of the international communist movement in Asia (McLane 1966: 369–70). It would also help secure the treaty rights that the Soviet Union had won from the Chinese Nationalist government and prevent Chinese demands for boundary revision. Finally, it would strengthen the Soviet defense of its eastern flank from the threat posed by the United States, which was now firmly entrenched in Japan. For these reasons of ideology and realpolitik, Moscow entered into a 30-year treaty with Beijing.

In South and Southeast Asia, the Soviet Union expressed support for communist parties and for the ongoing struggles in Indochina and Indonesia, but it was not actively engaged in these regions. The Soviet attitude toward countries like India and Burma that opted for a non-aligned policy was decidedly negative and hostile, on the ground that these countries "slandered" the USSR by equating it with U.S. imperialism (McLane 1966: 355–56).

The Soviet Union's Asia policy changed substantially under Khrushchev. Unlike Stalin, Khrushchev wanted détente with the United States at the global level, but he also wanted to increase Soviet influence in Asia by reducing Western and Chinese influence. He thus adopted a more active stance in Asia by participating in the 1954 Geneva conference and providing material support for the socialist struggle in Vietnam. Under Khrushchev, the earlier hostile policy toward neutral and nonaligned countries was reversed; those states were actually wooed, making for improved relations with India, Burma, Afghanistan, and, briefly, Indonesia. These policies were continued and strengthened under Kosygin and Brezhnev. Over time, in addition to its interest in Northeast Asia, the Soviet Union became more active in South and Southeast Asia.

Although the Soviet-American competition waxed and waned in the course of the next four decades, the basic features of the competition remained unchanged and provided the framework, or strategic overlay, for much of the international politics in Asia.

Major-Power Interaction: Shifting Alliances and Alignments

In the early stage of the Cold War, the United States and Japan allied against the Soviet Union and China, while India opted for a nonaligned policy. As noted earlier, the United States reversed its Japan policy and concluded a bilateral security treaty with Tokyo. For a number of reasons—including the strong antimilitarist and antinuclear bias among the Japanese body politic and the desire to concentrate on economic development—Tokyo accepted and indeed welcomed the security relationship with the United States. The Japanese, however, viewed the rights granted to the United States under the 1952 treaty as unequal and an outgrowth of the American occupation (Sneider 1982: 26–27).[4] The United States, for its part, wanted to maintain its military bases in Japan but recognized that such presence must be for mutual benefit and on terms acceptable to Japan. The Japanese and American concerns at the intergovernmental level were addressed through several compromises that were later codified in the 1960 U.S.–Japan Treaty of Mutual Cooperation and Security and the 1969 treaty that reverted Okinawa to Japan but allowed the continued operation of U.S. bases.

The idea of the Japanese state as the agent and provider of security was opposed by several strong groups in the Japanese body politic, particularly the socialists and the left. These groups also opposed the 1952 security treaty. Their opposition had several bases: the claim that the Japanese state was a continuation of the prewar political and bureaucratic elite that had led Japan on the path of militarism and war, the strong pacifism in Japanese society, and the political and legal barriers imposed by the peace constitution. These groups argued for internationalism and neutralism. The tensions between the Japanese government and the public over Japan's defense effort, its security relationship with the United States, and the continued stationing of American troops in Japan grew more vehement after the conclusion of the 1960 treaty and continued into the mid-1960s. Such domestic opposition caused the government to tread carefully on issues of security. Nonetheless the Japanese government was comfortable with the security arrangements that in effect enshrined Japanese security dependence on the United States and committed the United States to defend Japan but not vice versa. Tokyo came to see the bilateral treaty as the cornerstone of its security and foreign policy.[5] By the mid-1960s the treaty was accepted as a given on both sides of the Pacific.

In the case of the Sino-Soviet alliance, the initiative was taken by Beijing. Weak and vulnerable, the People's Republic of China (PRC) in its early years was mainly concerned with regime and national security (Barnett 1977: 20–32). The U.S. policy of containing international communism, the virtual American nuclear monopoly, and U.S. interventions in Korea, the Taiwan Straits, and later Indochina were viewed as threatening the Chinese Communist regime and preventing the unification of China. The United States was therefore viewed as the principal threat.[6] Further, Mao shared the ideology and worldview of Stalin. Endorsing the two-camp thesis, Beijing accepted the ideological and military leadership of the Soviet Union in international affairs and emulated its developmental model. The Soviet Union provided much-needed economic and technological aid. For these reasons, China decided to "lean" toward the Soviet Union. The Sino-Soviet alliance was the mainstay of Chinese foreign policy for about a decade.

Beginning in the mid- to late 1950s the Sino-Soviet relationship encountered tensions (Zagoria 1962), and the alliance became a dead letter by about 1962–63. From that point until its alignment with the United

States in the early 1970s, China followed an independent course. Differences in ideological and strategic outlook accounted for the Sino-Soviet rift, whose beginnings are usually traced to 1956. Concern with nuclear conflict led Khrushchev to advocate peaceful coexistence with the United States. The Soviet Union argued that war was no longer inevitable and that the transition to socialism could be peaceful. Mao opposed this "revisionist" line and argued for a more militant worldwide struggle. China was concerned that the softer approach of the USSR would compromise the Chinese Communist regime as well as national goals like the recovery of Taiwan. The bilateral relationship was strained further by the Chinese perception that the Soviets failed to support them and betrayed China's national interests in the 1958 offshore island crisis and in the border dispute with India that became public in 1959. Soviet backtracking on assistance in the development of Chinese nuclear weapons and the drying up of Soviet economic aid added to the strain. At the same time the Soviet Union was concerned about irrational behavior by China that might lead to war with the United States. It saw Chinese tensions with India as undermining Soviet Third World policy. China's abandonment of the Soviet developmental model also caused resentment in the USSR, contributing to the cutback in Soviet economic aid.

From about 1962 the Soviet Union and China engaged in hostile competition to secure the allegiance of communist parties and communist states in all parts of the world. When the war in Vietnam intensified and there was a real danger of U.S. intervention on a large scale, China did not heed the Soviet call for united action. Despite the fear of a military clash with the United States, China decided to follow an independent course in supporting North Vietnam. From about the mid- to late 1960s China was at odds with the Soviet Union, the United States, India, and Japan. This was the period of Cultural Revolution, intense domestic power struggle, and "angry isolationism."

Of even greater consequence for Sino-Soviet relations was the border tension that surfaced in the early 1960s and became a dispute contributing to military buildup along the long Sino-Soviet border. Chinese fears mounted as the Soviet Union's enormous military power gave it the option of initiating a major action. The Soviet occupation of Czechoslovakia in 1968 and the Brezhnev doctrine of limited sovereignty alarmed the Chinese. Two serious military clashes occurred in 1969, and the Soviets hinted at the possibility of a nuclear strike. By 1969 each country had begun to view the other as a crucial threat. For China, the Soviet Union replaced the United States as the principal security threat. China then sought alignment with the United States to balance the Soviet Union, while the Soviet Union took measures within and outside of Asia to isolate China. These steps included the 1969 Soviet proposal for an Asian collective security scheme (clearly directed against China) and the 1971 treaty with India.

Unlike the PRC, which chose to "lean to one side," India opted for nonalignment. The policy of nonalignment was grounded in idealism as well as considerations of power (Subrahmanyam 1976: 104–7). Nehru had a distaste for power politics, which he saw as productive of tension and conflict (Nanda 1976a). But he was aware that power is a key factor in international politics, although it may be true that in practice (as opposed to formal statements) he did not accord it sufficient weight. Nonalignment was based also on the belief that India had the potential to become a great power, together with the recognition that it was not one as yet. India was too big to become a satellite, so it would have to preserve autonomy in foreign policy and decide each issue on the merits. Despite the Indo-Pakistani war in 1947, India did not perceive any immediate external threat to its national security.

Based on these considerations, India sought to cooperate with the United States, the Soviet Union, and China on the basis of equality, without entering into any alliance. But this approach was spurned by all three major powers. All, for reasons mentioned earlier, were hostile to the policy of nonalignment at the outset of the Cold War. India's refusal to participate in the containment policy contributed to poor Indo-American relations during the 1947–60 period, as did U.S. support for Pakistan. Indo-American relations improved during the Kennedy administration, and the United States provided much-needed assistance during the 1962 border war with China.[7] For reasons including India's persistence with nonalignment and U.S. pressure to negotiate on the issue of Kashmir, the improvement was not sustained.

Some have argued that Nehru had apprehensions about Communist China (Subrahmanyam 1976: 107–8). In practice he emphasized cooperative relations to "disarm [China's] fears and suspicions" in the hope that China would become a peaceful neighbor. Bilateral relations appear to have been fairly cordial until 1954, when the two countries signed an agreement that proclaimed the "Panchsheel doctrine." The Chinese occupation of Tibet, and especially the border dispute that became public in 1959, caused strains in the bilateral relationship. But even after 1959, Nehru ruled out the possibility of a Chinese invasion of India.

The 1962 border war resulting in India's defeat was a turning point, leaving a deep imprint on the Indian political psyche and shaping India's international politics. The idealist strain in nonalignment, though still maintained in form, yielded in practice to power politics. China became

India's principal security concern. There were several dimensions to the Indian perception of the Chinese threat. One was military, focused on the border dispute. A second aspect was concern over Chinese support for Pakistan. In addition to providing political and massive military support for Pakistan, China threatened India with war on a second front, particularly in 1965 (Barnds 1972: 183–208). Third, China exploited and, in the Indian view, aggravated tensions between India and its other neighbors. Fourth, Chinese inroads into South Asia undermined the Indian quest for preeminence in the subregion and abroad. Finally, China incited revolts within India and lent support to border tribes in northeastern India (Barnds 1972: 220). These concerns contributed to a substantial military buildup. Chinese nuclear tests precipitated the quest for an Indian nuclear force. From the perspective of China, apart from the border dispute, Indian alignment with the Soviet Union magnified the Soviet threat. Competition for influence in several neighboring states and the longer-term prospect of an Asian strategic rival also played a role.

Mutual concern with China was a critical factor in the dramatic improvement in Indo-Soviet relations, which strengthened steadily from 1954 onward. From the perspective of the Soviet Union, improved bilateral relations facilitated its attempt to become a key player in South Asia (the Tashkent Agreement of 1965 between India and Pakistan, for example, was brokered by the USSR). For India, this relationship, while helping to counter the Chinese threat, did not seriously affect the autonomy of its foreign policy. Indo-Soviet relations were strained at times during the 1965–69 period, when India on several occasions failed to support Soviet initiatives (for example, the Soviet proposal for an Asian collective security scheme). Still, improved relations culminated in the 1971 Treaty of Friendship and Cooperation.

Between 1968 and 1971 international politics in Asia entered a new phase. Global bipolarity and Soviet-American competition continued to remain fundamental features, and Japan continued to ally with the United States. But China and India changed their policies and alignments, the former tilting toward the United States to address the threat from its former ally, the Soviet Union, and India turning to the Soviet Union to counter the Chinese threat. The Sino-Soviet conflict and, in a more limited way, the Sino-Indian conflict became defining features of Asian international politics. Although détente characterized the bilateral relations of the two superpowers at the global level, this was less true in Asia. In several respects, the positions in Asia of the United States and the Soviet Union were reversed in this new phase. The United States, no longer perceiving a monolithic communist threat and facing strong domestic opposition to the Vietnam War, was intent on reducing its commitments in Asia. It decided to "Vietnamize" the war in Vietnam, not to become involved in ground combat elsewhere in Asia, and to encourage Asian countries to assume greater responsibility for their own defense. These new directions were articulated in the 1969 Guam doctrine. As it reduced its own direct role, the United States came to view China as an important strategic ally in the containment of the Soviet Union.

At the same time the USSR was engaged in enhancing its position and role in Asia, in competition with China. A key element in Soviet strategy was further strengthening relations with India. Building on the 1971 treaty, the two countries continued to improve their bilateral relations in spite of change of government in India. In Southeast Asia the Soviet Union underwrote the Vietnamese invasion and occupation of Cambodia (1978) as well as the subsequent Vietnamese attempt to dominate all of Indochina. The following year the Soviet Union invaded and occupied Afghanistan. Combined with the Soviet military buildup in the Pacific (Solomon and Kosaka 1986), these developments intensified Soviet-American competition, putting an end to détente. For its part, China viewed the Soviet policies in Asia as tightening the encirclement of China, which heightened the Sino-Soviet conflict. To contain the Soviet threat, China, in addition to aligning with the United States, provided support for opposing groups and states involved in the Cambodian and Afghan conflicts. China also supported Pakistan, undertook a punitive war against Vietnam, and emphasized the development of its strategic nuclear forces. Soviet policies and actions contributed to a common apprehension among China, the United States, and Japan that deepened Sino-American relations as the United States and Japan provided much-needed assistance for the Chinese modernization program that had begun in 1979.

The 1969 Guam doctrine and the Nixon *shokkus* (shocks: his visit to China and elimination of the gold standard in 1971) were perceived by Japan as reflecting the decline of the Pax Americana; these events introduced a credibility gap with regard to U.S. commitment to the security of Japan. The erosion of the IMF-GATT system and the 1973–74 oil crisis (OPEC *shokku*) also increased Japanese concern over economic security (Akao 1983: 1–14). Together, these various developments compelled Japan to reassess its security policy. The treaty with the United States continued to be critical, and Japan took several measures to strengthen the bilateral security relationship. These steps included increasing its contribution to U.S. forces stationed in Japan, facilitating American access to Japanese dual-use technology, deploying Japanese official development assistance (ODA) to serve American strategic interests, and enhancing U.S.–Japanese defense cooperation under the 1978 guidelines for Japan–U.S. cooperation (*Defence Bulletin* 1986: 43). In addition, Japan began to increase its own defense capability under the 1976 National Defense Program Outline. In 1981, under U.S. pressure, it extended its defense responsibility to protect sea lanes out to 1,000 nautical miles. These measures were primarily designed to fill gaps and complement American policy in an effort to strengthen U.S.–Japan security relations, rather than to make Japan independent of the U.S. security umbrella. Japanese prime minister Yasuhiro Nakasone exemplified this approach when he attempted to depict Japan as an integral part of the Western alliance system.

Thus, from the early 1970s to the end of the Cold War, Japan and China were allied or aligned with the United States against the Soviet Union, while India was aligned with the USSR. But these "blocs" were quite loose, and threat perceptions varied from state to state. Although they disapproved of India's Soviet alignment, the United States and Japan did not consider India a threat, and the reverse was also the case. The principal security concern of the United States and Japan was the Soviet Union, whereas India focused on the threat posed by China. Each "bloc" also suffered internal tensions and contradictions that were temporarily subordinated to the principal security concerns of the time. India's quest for autonomy did not jibe with dependence on the Soviet Union. Although India endorsed the Vietnamese invasion of Cambodia in 1978—and in the process alienated the ASEAN countries—it did not support the Soviet invasion of Afghanistan; rather, it called for the withdrawal of all forces from Afghanistan, including the Soviet forces. Beginning in 1982 Indira Gandhi and later Rajiv Gandhi sought to improve relations with the United States, Britain, France, and China in an attempt to diversify India's foreign relations. Nonetheless, the Soviet Union remained a key strategic partner.

China was not happy with its junior-partner status in the alignment with the United States but accepted it because of the need to counter the Soviet threat. Beginning in 1982, China moved toward a more independent foreign policy—the result of unhappiness with the Reagan administration's strong anticommunist rhetoric and support for Taiwan, combined with China's own reassessment of the Soviet threat (Zhu 1989: 42–44). The goal of reunification, specifically the issue of Taiwan, and China's aspiration to equality with the United States became more significant with the termination of the Cold War.

China's deep, historically informed animosity toward and distrust of Japan was subordinated during the Cold War to concerns over the Soviet threat and the desire to secure Japanese assistance for China's modernization program. Further, Japan's security dependence on the United States reduced its prospects as an independent power. From the Japanese perspective, a rising China aligned with the United States against the Soviet Union was more acceptable than a rising China that might seek to dominate the region. The end of the Cold War, the continuing rapid growth of China, and Japan's quest for a larger political and security role brought the fears of both countries to the fore.

The development of Japan, first as a major economic power and then as an economic superpower, undermined several key premises of the U.S.–Japan security treaty.[8] Japan sought greater equality in the relationship, which the United States conceded at the level of rhetoric while in practice continuing to treat Japan as a junior partner. Japan, however, was now required to bear a higher share of the "burden" of security. Further, bilateral economic relations in the 1970s and 1980s were acrimonious. The meteoric economic rise of Japan and the American public perception that it had occurred at the expense of the United States contributed to public animosity and the identification, though only briefly, of Japan as a greater threat than the Soviet Union. These difficulties, however, were managed in the context of the overriding goal of containing the Soviet threat. The end of the Cold War and the disappearance of the Soviet threat (although Japan continued to view Russia with suspicion) compelled both the United States and Japan to reappraise and redefine their bilateral security relationship. Although Japan has attempted to broaden its options, particularly by engaging in global and regional multilateral forums such as the United Nations, the forum for Asia-Pacific Economic Cooperation, and the ASEAN Regional Forum, the security treaty with the United States continues to be the cornerstone of Japanese security policy. Growing apprehension with regard to China and the dynamism of the American economy have in fact made for a strengthening of bilateral security ties. Both countries reaffirmed their commitment to the treaty in April 1996 and have adopted revised guidelines for defense cooperation that increase the profile of Japan in maintaining regional security.

To sum up, during the Cold War none of the Asian powers could stand on its own.[9] India's initial attempt to do so was unsuccessful. All three of the major Asian powers chose alliance or alignment with one of the two superpowers. The inability of the Asian powers to stand on their own, as well as the predominant postwar position of the United States and its containment policy, contributed to the deep penetration and domination of Asian international politics by global bipolarity and the dynamics of the superpower competition. Still, the increasing geostrategic weight of China contributed to the development of a strategic triangle in Northeast and Southeast Asia, and a strategic quadrangle in South Asia. Despite the enormous increase in the economic and technological power of Japan, that country did not become an independent strategic player and so had little effect on the strategic situation except to boost the position of the United States.

The interaction of the two superpowers with the Asian powers interconnected the subregional systems in Northeast, continental Southeast, and South Asia in that order of priority, contributing to the emergence of an Asia-wide regional security system. Maritime Southeast Asia was much less affected by the conflict between the two superpowers. One effect of the interpenetration of the security dynamics at the various levels was the transformation of the dynamics of subregional security systems and the escalation of local and subregional conflicts. This was most evident in Northeast and continental Southeast Asia.

Northeast Asia: Conflicts Among Divided States

As the interests of four major powers (the United States, USSR, China, and Japan) intersected in Northeast Asia, the security dynamics of the subregion reflected the competition and conflict among those powers. These larger issues were superimposed on the local conflicts between the divided states in the Korean peninsula and across the Taiwan Straits.

The Korean problem was in many ways the central concern in Northeast Asia throughout the Cold War. Implementation of the agreement reached at the 1945 Moscow Conference to create a free and independent Korea was disrupted by the onset of the Cold War and the subsequent establishment of the Republic of Korea (ROK) in South Korea, backed by the United States, and the communist Democratic People's Republic of Korea (DPRK) in North Korea, backed by the Soviet Union. With the outbreak of the Korean War in 1950, the United States intervened militarily on behalf of South Korea. This intervention by American forces was perceived as a threat to the national security of China, causing it to intervene in support of North Korea. The war was suspended in 1953, but Korea remained divided.

Strongly nationalistic, the two Koreas have been committed to unification, but only on their respective terms. Since 1953 they have engaged in intense ideological, economic, military, and diplomatic competition. Inter-Korean dialogue began in the early 1970s, and several bilateral declarations and agreements have been signed. Dramatic changes have taken place in the two Koreas' domestic politics (from authoritarian to democratic rule in South Korea and generational leadership change in North Korea). There have also been changes in their economic and military capabilities: for South Korea, from economic basket case to membership in the Organization for Economic Cooperation and Development (OECD); for North Korea, considerable weakening, possibly bordering on collapse. These developments, however, have not altered the deep mutual distrust and competition that continues to characterize relations between the two Koreas.

International involvement in the conflict, however, has changed greatly in the last decade. Until the mid-1980s the probability of major-power involvement in a war in the Korean peninsula was high. The USSR and China provided strong political, economic, and military backing for the DPRK. South Korea was strongly backed by the United States and became a U.S. ward. Growth in economic and military strength, as well as democratic change, made the ROK a much more independent actor, but it continued to rely on the United States for its security. Beginning in the late 1970s the ROK engaged in what has been described as a Northern Policy (or nordpolitik) aimed at preventing war in the Korean peninsula by normalizing relations with the Soviet Union and China (Park 1993: 218–44).[10] Nordpolitik was given a boost by Gorbachev's rise to power in the Soviet Union, leading to normalization of Soviet-ROK relations in 1990. Normalization of Sino-ROK relations was slower but did eventually occur in 1992.

These changes, reinforced by the end of the Cold War, have reduced the conflict essentially to the inter-Korean level. The potential for escalation involving the competitive military engagement of the United States, China, Russia, and possibly Japan has been considerably reduced compared to the Cold War period. Despite intermittent credibility gaps—for example, during the Carter administration—the U.S. commitment to the security of South Korea remained strong. But the same cannot be said of the Soviet or even the Chinese commitment to North Korea. A net effect has been the isolation of North Korea, which has become more militant and has threatened to exercise a nuclear option. In spite of its localization, however, the Korean conflict continues to engage the interests of the United States, Japan, China, and Russia.

The Taiwan conflict had its origins in the Chinese civil war but became enmeshed in the Cold War. Since 1949 both the PRC and the Kuomintang (KMT) have claimed to be the legitimate government of China, including the province of Taiwan. The PRC was committed to liberating Taiwan, while the KMT, at least in its rhetoric, was intent on recovering the mainland. Tension has characterized the relationship across the Taiwan Straits since then, leading to periodic crises (1953, 1955, and 1958). Initially the Chinese threat was to the KMT regime, but with democratization in Taiwan and the passage of political power to native Taiwanese, the Chinese threat has been transformed into a national security concern for Taiwan. The PRC views the conflict as an issue of territorial integrity and national dignity, and considers it a domestic concern of China. The PRC's attempt to use force to liberate Taiwan was forestalled when the United States decided to back Taiwan and signed a mutual defense treaty with it in 1954. Since then the PRC and Taiwan have engaged in diplomatic competition to gain international recognition. That competition was eventually won by the PRC in the early 1970s, when the United States decided to improve relations with the PRC and when the PRC acquired the Chinese seat at the United Nations.

Under the 1972 Shanghai Communiqué, the United States did not challenge the view that Taiwan is part of China but held firmly to the view that unification was to be achieved peacefully. Despite the formal downgrading of diplomatic and security relations between the United States and Taiwan, the U.S. factor continued to be critical. Under the 1979 Taiwan Relations Act the United States continued to sell arms to Taiwan, and U.S. support for Taiwan increased under the Reagan administration. China, for its part, although it dropped the term "liberation," reserved the right to use force under certain circumstances (Lai To Lee 1988: 188). There have been several proposals for unification (Lai To Lee 1988: 167–74), and bilateral economic relations between the PRC and Taiwan have improved dramatically. But the underlying dispute remains unresolved and has become more complicated with democratic transition in Taiwan and generational leadership change in Beijing. This conflict, more than the Korean issue, may still have the potential to engage China and the United States in a competitive manner.

Continental Southeast Asia: Struggle Against Colonial Rule and the Revival of Historical Animosities

Like Northeast Asia, mainland Southeast Asia was witness to competitive engagement of the major powers from 1945 onward, resulting in three Indochinese wars (1945–54, 1959–75, and 1978–91). Vietnam's struggle for independence and unification lay at the heart of the first two conflicts.

In the first war the protagonists were the communist Viet Minh and France, which was seeking to reimpose its colonial rule after World War II. With the extension of the Cold War to Asia, the United States backed France. The Soviet Union did not initially support the Viet Minh. In fact, the Democratic Republic of Vietnam (DRV), which was proclaimed in 1945, was not recognized by the USSR until January 31, 1950. Even after recognition, Stalin did not publicly support the DRV, although after the Korean war the Soviet Union did provide covert military aid through China. The First Indochina War was brought to a conclusion by the 1954 Geneva agreements, which terminated French colonial rule and recognized the sovereignty of Laos, Cambodia, and Vietnam. The agreements, however, were implemented only with respect to Cambodia. Competition among rival factions caused political fragmentation and conflict in Laos. An international agreement in 1962 to neutralize Laos was not successful, and that country became enmeshed in the Second Indochina War. The U.S.–backed South Vietnamese government refused to comply with the provision in the 1954 agreement to hold national elections to determine the future of Vietnam, a decision that transformed the provisional division of Vietnam along the seventeenth parallel into de facto statehood for South Vietnam.

The DRV then committed itself to the goals of liberating South Vietnam and uniting Vietnam under communist rule. Still aiming to contain international communism and believing in the domino theory, the United States provided political, military, and economic assistance to the South Vietnamese government and later intervened directly. The Soviet Union and China, to counter the U.S. intervention and to compete with each other, supported North Vietnam. China viewed the U.S. intervention in Indochina as a threat to its own national security. As the Sino-Soviet conflict intensified, North Vietnam tried initially to mediate and then stayed clear of the conflict. Eventually it moved closer to the Soviet Union, in part because of the historically rooted belief that China would seek hegemony and therefore would not want to see a unified Vietnam (Pike 1987: 87–89). Communist victories in Vietnam, Cambodia, and Laos brought the Second Indochina War to a conclusion in 1975. Vietnam was unified in 1976.

These victories did not end the conflicts in Indochina; in fact, they reignited historically rooted hostilities and ambitions. Cambodia's radical nationalism and Vietnam's desire for dominance in Laos and Cambodia intensified border disputes between Vietnam and Cambodia, leading to the Vietnamese invasion of Cambodia in December 1978 and the installation of a pro-Vietnam puppet government in that country. This action and Vietnam's earlier treaty with the Soviet Union angered China, which undertook a punitive war in February–March 1979. China later supported Thailand as well as rival factions in Cambodia. Vietnamese domination of Laos and Cambodia effectively eliminated the traditional buffers, and Soviet-backed Vietnamese military presence in those two countries was viewed by Thailand as dramatically altering the local balance of power in favor of Vietnam and constituting a threat to

Thai national security (Alagappa 1987a: 78–147). To counter that threat, Thailand reinforced its alignment with China, which had begun in 1975, and sought to reinvigorate its security relationship with the United States as well as to harness ASEAN to its cause. Thus the historical Sino-Vietnamese hostility and Thai-Vietnamese rivalry became engaged in the Vietnamese-Khmer conflict. Soviet support for Vietnam further increased China's anxiety, thus adding the Sino-Soviet dimension to the conflict. American concern over the Soviet military buildup in the Pacific and growing Soviet influence in Asia, as well as concern for Thai security, added the Soviet-American dimension to the conflict. Thus, a local conflict with deep historical roots became engulfed in broader regional and global conflicts.

Change in Soviet policy beginning with Gorbachev (Alagappa 1990b: 321–50) led to the easing of the Soviet-American and Sino-Soviet conflicts, permitting an end to the Cambodian stalemate that had lasted almost a decade (Alagappa 1990a: 266–71). These developments put pressure on Vietnam and the Cambodian factions to move toward a settlement. Changes in the policies of Cambodian leader Sihanouk in 1987 and of Thailand in 1988, combined with the pressure of the U.N. Security Council, eventually brought the thirteen-year-old conflict to a settlement in a U.N.–sponsored peace conference in October 1991. This, however, was a settlement, not a resolution of the many deep-seated suspicions and fears that linger in the subregion (Alagappa 1993: 466–67).

South Asia: An Indocentric Subsystem

The liquidation of British rule in South Asia gave birth to a system that, by virtue of history, geography, and disparities in size and power, was Indocentric. That characteristic became even more pronounced with the collapse and truncation of Pakistan in 1971, leading to the creation of Bangladesh. Formally the South Asian system is egalitarian, but in practice there are huge disparities in almost every dimension. This asymmetry is a crucial factor in the international politics of South Asia. India's quest for leadership—even hegemony—and the refusal of the smaller states (with the support of some external actors) to acknowledge its dominant position, as well as their fear of domination, intensified the many bilateral conflicts in the region. This made for a zero-sum situation in which balancing rather than bandwagoning or accommodation became the norm. The only country that could have engaged in limited internal balancing was Pakistan, but after its break-up in 1971 no country in the region could individually balance India. Even acting collectively— and there were numerous hurdles, some insurmountable—the other countries in South Asia could not balance India. This made balancing through alliance with external powers the only option, opening the way for the involvement of China, the Soviet Union, and the United States and connecting South Asia to the larger Asian regional and global systems.

The conflict between India and Pakistan is the central feature of the South Asian subsystem. From its inception Pakistan's primary concerns were regime and national security, the liberation of Kashmir, and equality with India (Barnds 1972: 68–82). India was determined to hold onto Kashmir and did not accept Pakistan as an equal. Further, some Indian leaders thought that Pakistan would not survive long as a nation. Thus, from the start, India became the primary concern for Pakistan, the issue to which all other matters were subordinated. For India, although Pakistan was a concern, it was not critical until Pakistan's alliance with the United States in 1954 and later its alignment with China. The disputes between India and Pakistan led to three wars (1947, 1965, and 1971). There have been intermittent dialogues between the two, leading to several bilateral accords.[11] The basic issues in dispute, however, remain unresolved. Bilateral relations continue to be dispute-ridden and conflict prone, although war has been averted during the last 25 years.

Pakistan has followed a security-through-strength approach ever since independence. Unable to match India on its own, Pakistan sought to redress the imbalance though alliance with external powers. Uneasy about the Soviet push toward the Persian Gulf and disenchanted with India's nonaligned policy, the United States came to view Pakistan as critical to the Western defense of the Middle East. This led to Pakistan's membership in SEATO (1954) and the Central Treaty Organization (CENTO) or the Baghdad Pact (1955). Pakistan, however, deployed U.S. arms and aid to compete with India. The souring of Sino-Indian relations and U.S. assistance to India during and after the 1962 border war provided the pull and push for a long-lasting Sino-Pakistani alignment, the origins of which can be traced to 1956. The Sino-Indian conflict and Sino-Pakistani alignment accelerated the improvement in Indo-Soviet relations.

Following its dismemberment after the disastrous 1971 war, Pakistan's security worries became acute and it's government also became deeply committed to the liberation of Kashmir. As U.S. support became more limited and conditional, Pakistan moved closer to China. With the Soviet invasion of Afghanistan, Pakistan regained its strategic importance for the United States and once again became the recipient of U.S. arms and aid. But with the end of the Cold War, the United States began to adopt a more balanced approach, treating India as a regional power.

Sino-Indian relations also improved, although the substantive issues remained unresolved. These developments raised fears in Pakistan, accelerating its nuclear program. Pakistan also sought to solidify its relations with China, while trying simultaneously to improve relations with the United States.

Like Pakistan, although to a much lesser degree and much less successfully, Nepal has sought to balance India by involving China in its affairs. India has sought a special relationship with Nepal, as embodied in the 1950 security treaty between the two countries. But successive Nepali governments have sought to emphasize equality rather than the special relationship preferred by India. To counter India, Nepal improved relations with China and opted for what it calls an equidistance policy. In India's view, the Nepali connection to China has the potential to undermine India's security. Issues of contention in Indo-Nepali relations include the 1950 security treaty, Nepal's peace zone proposal, and mass migration in both directions (Tiwari 1989: 129–39).

Postindependence Indo–Sri Lankan relations were relatively cordial, although from time to time Sri Lanka perceived India as a security threat. Since the early 1980s the perception of this threat has been focused on Indian support for and possible intervention on behalf of the Sri Lankan Tamils. The Liberation Tigers of Tamil Eelam (LTTE) have been engaged in armed struggle for an independent homeland in the north and east since 1981. Despite its many attempts to attract international attention and support, Sri Lanka has not been successful in its attempt to balance India and consequently has accommodated Indian concerns by implicitly acknowledging Indian predominance. Following the failure of Indian mediation and peacekeeping efforts, the two countries signed a bilateral agreement in 1987 in which India agreed not to allow its soil to be used for terrorist activities against Sri Lanka, while Sri Lanka agreed to consult with India before employing foreign military-intelligence personnel and not to allow Sri Lankan ports to be used to the detriment of Indian security (Tiwari 1989: 139–43).

Maritime Southeast Asia: An Indonesia-centric Subsystem

The liquidation of colonial rule in maritime Southeast Asia resulted in a subsystem centered on Indonesia. The huge disparity in size between Indonesia and its smaller neighbors (Malaysia, Singapore, and Brunei), its national self-conception as a major state and its quest for a commensurate position in subregional and regional affairs, and the apprehension these created in the other states influenced the security dynamics of the subregion in the postcolonial period (Alagappa 1991a: 17–22). Indonesia under Sukarno viewed the formation of Malaysia (comprising Malaya, British North Borneo [Sabah], Sarawak, and Singapore) as a neoimperial plot, which it sought to "crush" in a confrontation with Malaysia that lasted from 1963 to 1965.

A second, related security dynamic stemmed from the survival concerns of tiny Singapore and Brunei, both much smaller than either Indonesia or Malaysia. Singapore, which became part of Malaysia in 1963, separated and became independent in 1965. The process of separation was bitter and colored bilateral relations for about two decades. Singapore's primary international concern in the early post-independence phase was ensuring survival in a Malay world that was hostile to it. Although Brunei is a Malay-Muslim country, it too feared for its national and regime survival in a nonmonarchic Malay world.

The Philippines, for the most part, stood at the periphery of the maritime Southeast Asian subsystem. The Sulu Sultanate, which was not brought under the control of Manila until the period of U.S. rule, did for a period exercise control over parts of what became known first as British North Borneo and then as Sabah. That history underlies the Philippine claim to Sabah, which brought the country into conflict with Malaysia.

Extraregional powers were involved in the many postindependence conflicts in this subregion. Malaysia relied on the Anglo-Malaysia Defense Agreement to counter the Indonesian challenge. Singapore followed a global strategy to enhance its survival prospects. It also supported the U.S. military presence in the region, not only to balance other extraregional powers but also to balance Indonesia and Malaysia. In the wake of the closing of U.S. military bases in the Philippines in 1992, Singapore offered to host facilities for the United States. Malaysia and Singapore continue to be members of the Five Power Defence Arrangements. They also engage in naval exercises with the American navy and provide it some minimal bunkering and service facilities. Despite these and other interactions, the involvement of major powers in maritime Southeast Asia is small compared with their participation in the affairs of the other three subregions. Further, tensions and conflicts in maritime Southeast Asia have moderated considerably since the change of regime in Indonesia in 1965, which opened the way for subregional cooperation.

Regional Cooperation

The conflictual nature of major-power relations and the interpenetration of the security dynamics at the various levels prevented the development of regional cooperation among Asian countries. In the early post–World War II period there were several attempts to involve Asian countries in regional cooperation (SEATO and Economic Cooperation in Asia and the Far East [ECAFE], for example), but all were initiated by external powers. The first Asian initiative was that of India, which convened the Asian Relations Conference in 1947. This eventually led to the Colombo Powers (India, Burma, Ceylon, Indonesia, and Pakistan) meeting in 1954, which in turn paved the way for the Asian-African Conference in Bandung, Indonesia, in 1955. The purposes of these meetings were to provide an alternative to alignment with the two superpower-dominated blocs and to draw attention to the developmental needs of the Third World countries. The Indian initiatives and the Bandung Conference laid the foundations for the Nonaligned Movement, but it did not translate into a regional forum or organization for Asia.

The first indigenous efforts toward Asian regional cooperation took shape in maritime Southeast Asia. As noted earlier, that subregion, though subject to civil and international strife in the 1950s and 1960s, was not the scene of intense competition among the major powers. Malaya (now Malaysia), the Philippines, and Thailand formed the Association of Southeast Asia (ASA) in 1961. However, the Philippine claim to Sabah and the Indonesian confrontation with Malaysia halted the development of ASA from about 1963 until 1967, when it was succeeded by the Association of Southeast Asian Nations (ASEAN, composed of Indonesia, Malaysia, the Philippines, Singapore, and Thailand (Jorgensen-Dahl 1982). Several reasons lay behind the formation of ASEAN: fear of internal and international communism, reduced faith in or mistrust of external powers, Indonesia's decision to pursue its "active and independent" foreign policy through regional cooperation, the desire on the part of Malaysia and Singapore to constrain Indonesia and bring it into a more cooperative framework, considerations of regime consolidation in nearly all member states, and the desire to concentrate on economic development. Although the formally articulated purpose of ASEAN was economic and sociocultural cooperation, security was a key concern from its inception. The development of ASEAN has been linked to and stimulated by several political-military developments in the region. The 1969 Guam doctrine and the British decision to withdraw from the east of Suez by 1971 were important factors leading to the 1971 Kuala Lumpur Declaration to make Southeast Asia a Zone of Peace, Freedom, and Neutrality (ZOPFAN). Communist victories in 1975 in Laos, Cambodia, and Vietnam prompted the second summit meeting, the Declaration of ASEAN Concord, and the Treaty of Amity and Cooperation in 1976. Vietnam's invasion and occupation of Cambodia, and ASEAN's opposition to that act, was a milestone in the development of the association.

ASEAN confronted several problems in its early years—the Philippine claim to Sabah and tensions in Malaysia-Singapore and Singapore-Indonesia relations. It survived the early problems and gradually became stronger. ASEAN has had several successes in promoting peace and security in Southeast Asia (Leifer 1989; Alagappa 1991d: 297–300). It helped create trust, goodwill, and confidence among member states. In the process it transformed the normative structure and eased the political survival problems of member states. ASEAN facilitated the transformation of a subregion of turmoil into a more stable and predictable area in which the role of force has been minimized, though not eliminated. International political stability in turn facilitated economic growth and development. ASEAN's cohesion, regional identity, and growing international stature enabled it to take collective political and diplomatic action, most effectively with regard to Cambodia. ASEAN has also been relatively successful in its dialogue with the major powers. Over the years it has become an important force in the international politics of Southeast Asia. The end of the Cold War has seen the broadening and deepening of ASEAN. Vietnam became a member in 1995, and Burma, Cambodia, and Laos secured admission in 1997. ASEAN has committed itself to creating a free trade area by 2003.[12] It also took the lead in creating the ASEAN Regional Forum (ARF) and has been active in charting the future of the Asia-Pacific Economic Cooperation (APEC) forum.

ASEAN also suffered limitations. The conflict-settlement mechanisms specified in the 1976 treaty remain largely unused, and most disputes among member states are unresolved. The association's diplomatic success with regard to the Cambodian conflict would not have been possible without the support of the United States, China, and Japan (Alagappa 1993). Despite its many efforts, ASEAN was unable to end the Cambodian conflict: that development had to await changes in the interests and policies of the major powers. The ZOPFAN proposal and the Southeast Asia a Nuclear Weapons Free Zone (SEANWFZ) proposal could not be realized. ASEAN did not make much headway in economic cooperation. Until the early 1990s cooperation among ASEAN members remained largely political and diplomatic, and the organization's support base was limited to a relatively small group of political leaders and bureaucrats. These limitations, although significant, do not negate the organization's achievements.

The success of ASEAN subregional cooperation served as an example, contributing to the formation of the South Asian Association for Regional Cooperation (SAARC) in 1983.[13] Like ASEAN, SAARC did not explicitly focus on security, and an understanding was reached to avoid dealing with contentious bilateral issues. Nevertheless, the regular meetings among heads of governments have provided the opportunity to discuss difficult bilateral issues, even during periods of tension. On occasion, such meetings have led to agreements, such as the bilateral agreement between India and Pakistan not to attack each other's nuclear facilities. SAARC, however, has not been able to modify the security thinking and behavior of the South Asian countries—at least not thus far.

The focus of SAARC from its inception was on social, economic, and technical issues. The 1983 Declaration on South Asian Cooperation called for collective self-reliance through economic growth, social progress, and cultural development. The Integrated Program of Action (IPA) endorsed regional cooperation in nine areas (Tiwari 1989: 47–61). But deep-seated bilateral problems, concern about security, and pre-occupation with relative gain permitted only modest progress even in areas other than political security. More recently, however, there have been some encouraging signs. An agreement on a SAARC Preferential Trade Arrangement (SAPTA) was concluded and entered into force in December 1995. Settlement of some of the bilateral disputes that complicated Indo-Nepali and Indo-Bangladeshi relations was reached in 1996, and changes in government in India and Pakistan in 1997 appear to have introduced a thaw in their bilateral relations. These winds of change—still very tenuous—appear to have led to an improved atmosphere at the ninth SAARC summit, held in May 1997. At that meeting the heads of government decided to accelerate the formation of a free trade area in the region, advancing the target date to 2001.

The intersection of the competitive interests of the four major powers, as well as the zero-sum nature of the Korea and Taiwan conflicts, prevented the development of regional cooperation in Northeast Asia. The absence of formal organizations, however, did not prevent the emergence of multilateral economic and, to a lesser degree, political interactions in the subregion, a phenomenon called "soft regionalism" (Scalapino 1988: 3).

Conclusions

This broad overview of the history of international politics in Asia over a period of two thousand years suggests several observations. First, despite the considerable cultural and economic interaction among the Asian countries, historically there was no sustained pattern of political interaction that embraced all Asian countries. Patterned political relations did develop at the subregional level, and such relations were almost entirely autonomous, especially in Northeast and South Asia. Colonization by

European powers put an end to these autonomous subregional systems, contributing to the integration of Asian states into a global system that was dominated by European powers and their rivalries. Although an Asian system could not emerge under colonial rule, colonial rule and the nationalist struggles against it contributed to the development of a concept of Asian identity.

During the Cold War, for the first time in history, an Asia-wide regional security system evolved. It was rather loose and remained subordinate to and dominated by the global rivalry between the United States and the Soviet Union. This subordinate Asian system included five interconnected security clusters. At the broad regional level was the cluster composed of the United States, the Soviet Union, China, India, and Japan. Its dynamics were driven by the Soviet-American, Sino-American, Sino-Soviet, and Sino-Indian conflicts, in that order. This cluster had a deep impact on and interconnected the other four clusters in Northeast, South, continental Southeast, and maritime Southeast Asia. The security dynamics of the Northeast Asia cluster were in many ways the same as those of the broad regional cluster. The other clusters had their own local dynamics, but those dynamics were penetrated and—in the case of Northeast and continental Southeast Asia—dominated by the rivalries and conflicts among the major powers.

Second, the historical interstate systems in Asia were structurally anarchic but permitted hierarchic relations. In East Asia the hierarchy was based on the ideas of higher civilization and universal kingship, as well as power. In South and Southeast Asia, hierarchy rested largely on gradations of power and was subject to more frequent challenges. Systems with imperial centers and tributary or vassal states that maintained a relatively high degree of autonomy operated in all subregions. In the postcolonial phase, an international system based on the notion of sovereign, egalitarian nation-states has taken root in Asia, but traces of the earlier hierarchic systems remain visible. The huge disparity between countries like China, India, and Indonesia, on the one hand, and other Asian nations, on the other, as well as dissatisfaction with their current status, informs the desire of those former imperial centers for leadership and respect, if not dominance and hegemony. Notions of deference and accommodation attest to the informal operation of hierarchy. But at base there is a tension between the two systems. Because of the availability of countervailing power from regional and extraregional powers, as well as the prevailing international norms that support equality among states, the weaker powers, which in earlier eras would have acquiesced to an inferior status, now resist and contest claims by others to positions of leadership and dominance.

Third, there is a strong tradition of power politics in Asia. This was explicit in the Indic system and also formed part of the Chinese strategic culture. Conflict was endemic in Asian systems, and power balancing was common when feasible. The quest for hierarchy and universal domination by imperial centers left little scope for coexistence and cooperation, and international law was not a feature of Asian systems. The Cold War, with its emphasis on military power, alliances, and alignment, reinforced this tradition and worked against regional cooperation in Asia. Nevertheless, regional cooperation did flower in one subregion—maritime Southeast Asia—and now appears to be making some limited headway in South Asia and the broader Asia-Pacific region. These developments, especially that in Southeast Asia, lend support to the constructivist proposition that the logic of anarchy is a social construction and that the realist logic can be transformed.

Fourth, the nature of the political unit in Asia was transformed by the colonial experience. The nation-state became the principal actor in Asia. However, as nation-states the Asian countries are still new, and several have no prior existence as separate political units. Nearly all suffer weaknesses and confront internal and external challenges. The process of consolidation may take decades, if not centuries, and success is not guaranteed, although so far there has been only one case of dismemberment. Consequently, in the conduct of their international relations these nation-states attach great significance to the principles of sovereignty, territorial integrity, and noninterference in domestic affairs. Finally, this chapter highlights the historical underpinnings of national self-conceptions (particularly those of China and India), the historical roots of the identity dilemma confronting contemporary Japan, and the deep distrust that characterizes many bilateral relations (Sino-Vietnamese, Sino-Japanese, Japanese-Korean, Japanese-Russian, Thai-Vietnamese, Vietnamese-Khmer, Khmer-Thai, Sino-Indian, Indo-Pakistani, and Indo–Sri Lankan). Power differentials have reinforced some of these lines of enmity, but they did not produce them in the first place. Considerations of history and identity must figure prominently in the analysis of Asian security.

PART II

Security Practice: Country Studies

China
Security Practice of a Modernizing and Ascending Power

WU XINBO

> The Chinese have always been a great, courageous, and industrious
> nation; it is only in modern times that they have fallen behind. And that was
> due entirely to oppression and exploitation by foreign imperialism and domestic
> reactionary governments....Ours will no longer be a nation subject to insult
> and humiliation. We have stood up.
>
> MAO ZEDONG, SEPTEMBER 21, 1949

For Mao and the Chinese Communist Party (CCP), the founding of the People's Republic of China (PRC) not only marked the end of the era of foreign aggression and internal chaos but also introduced the prospect of building a strong, prosperous, and respected China. Both the political leadership and the Chinese public believe that, given its vast territory and large population, its long unbroken history, its contribution to the progress of civilization, and its historic position in the Sinocentric world order, China must regain major-power status. This has been a central goal of the PRC since its founding. But Chinese security thinking and behavior in the first several decades of communist rule were also shaped by a sense of vulnerability, issuing both from the "century of humiliation" and from the combination of China's weakness in material strength and technological capability, its unfavorable position in the global balance of power, and direct external military threats, initially from the United States and later from the Soviet Union.

Although Chinese security thinking and behavior during this period were largely in the realist tradition, they also bore some features of idealism. The international environment was seen as inherently hostile; the nation-state and the regime were the crucial referents of security; political survival (of regime and nation) topped the security agenda; and security through power (national power, alignment, and alliance) and diplomacy was the dominant approach. Meanwhile, some aspects of Chinese security policy (such as the rift with the Soviet Union and support for international revolutionary movements) were obviously affected by ideological and moral considerations. Since the early 1980s, Chinese security thinking has changed substantially. The international environment is perceived as less hostile, even benign and beneficial; economic modernization tops the national agenda; and the value of international cooperation to national survival, strength, and status is increasingly recognized. These developments, however, do not imply that Chinese security thinking has become liberal and internationalist; they indicate only that the hard realpolitik of the early Cold War period has moderated. As China modernizes and becomes more of a status quo power, its conception of security is likely to change further. In the near term, however, Chinese notions of security will continue to be shaped by realist elements.

Security Thinking During the Cold War

A deep sense of vulnerability pervaded Chinese security thinking following the founding of the PRC. The feeling was rooted in China's relatively recent experiences with the Western powers and Japan. Before 1840 the Middle Kingdom had been very successful in managing its foreign relations, which were conducted mostly with "barbarians" from within the tributary system. After the First Opium War (1839–42), however, China suffered one blow after another in dealing with industrialized powers. Unequal treaties, war indemnities, concessions, extraterritoriality, and territorial cession all turned the Middle Kingdom into a semicolony. Almost all the nineteenth-century major powers joined in to take advantage of China's weakness. This "century of humiliation" left a bitter memory, creating a belief among the Chinese that China would always be the target of the sinister motives of other countries, especially the major powers, because of its great market potential, huge amount of cheap labor, rich resources, and strategically important location.

The sense of vulnerability was aggravated by China's material weakness. The founders of the PRC held that although China is a large country in both territory and population, it is a weak power in terms of economic and technological capability (Mao 1994: 175, 193). This reality severely limited the resources China could draw upon to enhance its national security and put it at a disadvantage with regard to the major powers. As Mao Zedong said in 1954, "We are now weak industrially, agriculturally, culturally and militarily, and the imperialists, calculating that we have only that much strength, come to bully us" (Mao 1993: 359).

The security thinking of PRC leaders has been marked by a consistently strong concern over the balance of power in the global context and China's position within it. When the PRC was founded, the status quo was far from satisfactory. The international system was dominated by two superpowers, neither of which the PRC was capable of challenging. The Western world, headed by the United States, adopted a hostile attitude toward the newly born republic, while the socialist camp, to which China belonged, stood in a weak position with regard to the capitalist camp. Within the socialist camp, the PRC was dependent on the USSR and was unable to exert any independent influence.

In late 1957 Mao suggested that the balance of power between East and the West had reached a turning point, marked by the launching of two satellites by the USSR. In Mao's words, "the East Wind prevails over the West Wind" (Mao 1994: 291). His optimism, however, was short-lived. The rupture of the Sino-Soviet alliance and the détente between the USSR and the United States in the early 1960s brought the PRC under the combined pressure of both superpowers. The 1960s turned out to be the harshest years for China. In the late 1960s, when the global competition between the United States and the Soviet Union intensified and the United States readjusted its Asian strategy, China saw an opportunity. The Sino-American rapprochement in 1972 greatly improved the PRC's position in the strategic triangle, as well as in the international community. Although the global distribution of power was far from encouraging, China had greatly improved its position vis-à-vis the superpowers.

Challenges to Security

Direct military threats were a key factor in the PRC leadership's security thinking from the 1950s through the early 1980s. From its founding, the PRC had faced U.S. economic sanctions, diplomatic isolation, and military pressure. Hostility between the two countries soon led to direct military conflict on the Korean peninsula. The end of the Korean War brought no improvement in China's security environment: China faced the U.S.-led "crescent" encirclement from Northeast to Southeast Asia. During the 1950s what concerned the PRC leaders most was U.S. involvement in the Taiwan issue and not the possibility of a major war between China and the United States. In the 1950s Mao assumed that although there was the possibility of a third world war, such a war could be prevented from breaking out (Mao 1994: 136). This thinking continued through 1960 when he stated that the relationship between the socialist and capitalist camps was characterized not by "hot war" or "peaceful coexistence," but by "cold war coexistence" (Mao 1994: 422).

The full-scale intervention in Vietnam by the United States beginning in 1964, however, aggravated the PRC leadership's concern over the U.S. military threat. China worried about the escalation of the war in Vietnam and its possible spillover into southern China. The apprehension was so strong that Zhou Enlai sent a warning to President Lyndon B. Johnson through Pakistan, in an effort to prevent another Sino-American military confrontation (Zhou 1990: 460–61). Nationwide mobilization was ordered, and the People's Liberation Army (PLA) was prepared for "an early war, a major war and a nuclear war" (Foundation for International and Strategic Studies 1993: 249). While the U.S. military threat still lingered, the Sino-Soviet border conflict in 1969 generated even greater alarm within the PRC leadership. That confrontation was viewed as the most serious external military threat to China since the Korean War. The crisis caused Mao to reassess the international strategic situation and to reach the conclusion that the world war was not only inevitable but also imminent (Xu 1991: 539). This point of view dominated China's security thinking until the early 1980s.

Responses

From the 1950s to the 1970s China's responses to various security challenges were shaped by considerations linked to traditional realism, ideology, and moralism, and comprised a combination of diplomatic and military approaches. One component of the diplomatic approach was alignment with the superpowers. The underlying rationale was that to oppose the more dangerous of the two superpowers, China should exploit common ground with the other, more friendly or less threatening superpower. The first attempt of this kind was the Sino-Soviet alliance against the United States. Because the United States had taken the side of the Nationalists against the CCP in China's Liberation War (1946–49), Mao declared even before the founding of the PRC that China would "lean to one side"—that is, toward the Soviet Union, with which China shared ideological and strategic interests. The Sino-Soviet alliance forged in February 1950 helped offset the U.S. strategic pressure on China throughout the 1950s. In the early 1960s, ideological differences began to strain ties between Beijing and Moscow. The PRC leaders, unhappy with Khrushchev's internal policy of criticizing Stalin and his external policy of seeking "peaceful coexistence" with the United States, asserted that the Soviet leadership had betrayed orthodox Marxism-Leninism and adopted a "revisionist" line. Although the Soviet "great-nation chauvinism" also contributed to Beijing's ill feeling toward Moscow, it was the ideological conflict between China and the Soviet Union that fatally undermined the bilateral alliance. Even though the United States was still viewed as the major threat to China's national security, Mao decided to break with the Soviet Union. At this juncture, China's realism was challenged and temporarily superseded by Mao's strong idealism. After the 1969 border conflict, with the Soviet Union now identified by China as its most dangerous enemy and the United States under President Richard M. Nixon seeking rapprochement with the PRC, China's alignment strategy was revitalized. The pattern of Sino-American cooperation against Soviet expansion characterized the strategic triangle well into the 1980s.

The other component of the diplomatic approach was the "united front" strategy, aimed at mobilizing all possible forces against the immediate enemy. The strategy had its origins in the CCP's experiences in the Anti-Japanese War and the Liberation War. The united-front strategy had three stages, corresponding to the 1950s, the 1960s, and the 1970s.

In the 1950s, Mao identified three forces on the world political landscape: socialists, nationalists, and imperialists. Although the major task of opposing imperialism belonged to the socialist camp, the nationalists in the newly independent Asian and African countries, to the extent that they struggled for national independence and against colonialism and imperialism, were the forces with which the socialist countries should unite (Mao 1994: 337, 342). Based on that assumption, China entered into close relations with India and Indonesia, both of which were very influential among the newly independent, nonsocialist countries. Development of relations with those Third World countries not only served the purpose of opposing imperialism but also enhanced China's international stature and reduced its dependence on the Soviet Union (Garver 1993: 49). During this period, the united-front strategy was not primarily ideological; rather, it was driven by considerations of national security.

In the 1960s, as a result of détente between the USSR and the United States and the collapse of the Sino-Soviet bloc, Mao could no longer count on the Soviet Union and its Eastern European comrades to fight against imperialism. He thus turned to the intermediate zone (those countries besides the United States and the USSR) for help. At this stage the united-front strategy had a strong ideological component. Displeased with the Soviet Union's efforts to secure détente with the United States, Mao began to take a militant attitude with regard to the United States. His rhetoric became extremely radical during this period, as he openly called for the defeat and elimination of imperialism. The PRC pursued so-called "revolutionary diplomacy," extending support to communists in Southeast Asia and to national liberation movements in Africa. Mao calculated that the success of communist revolution and wars of national liberation in those parts of the world would serve to weaken the global strategic position of the United States and thereby distract it from pressuring China.

Another aspect of the united-front strategy in this stage was the growth of the anti-imperialist camp. Mao proposed in 1961 that "we should expand the scope of unity, [we] should unite all the Asian, African and Latin American nations as well as over 90 percent of people all over the world except imperialists and counterrevolutionaries of various nations" (Mao 1994: 482). To that end, he suggested that the intermediate zone should be composed of two parts: Asia, Africa, and Latin America on the one hand, and Western Europe and Japan on the other. Mao believed that Japan and the countries of Western Europe were unhappy with U.S. control and U.S. imperialism, therefore he saw them as potential allies against Washington. As such, Mao conceived of forming a wide united front against U.S. imperialism that would extend from London and Paris to Beijing and Tokyo (Mao 1994: 506-7, 509, 514, 522).

The 1970s witnessed significant adjustments in the united-front strategy. In 1974 Mao put forward his theory of the three worlds, which envisioned the two superpowers as the first world, other developed capitalist countries such as Japan and the nations of Western Europe as the second, and the rest of the globe as the third world (Mao 1994: 600).[1] The theory of the three worlds, which identified the Soviet Union as a hegemonic power, was deployed by Beijing to challenge Soviet leadership of the Socialist bloc and to forge an anti-Soviet united front, which comprised part of the third world, the entire second world, and the United States. Beijing downplayed its anti-imperialist rhetoric, and became much less enthusiastic about "world revolution."

The united front strategy conformed to the realist tradition to the extent that it sought to address the imbalance in the distribution of power. However, it also reflected other concerns and displayed other features. China's massive military and economic assistance and political support to some socialist countries and to national liberation movements in the Third World, for example, reflected a strong sense of the "proletarian internationalist obligation," which can be characterized as "revolutionary moralism." Further, the expectation of "world revolution" and the intent to form the widest possible anti-imperialist camp render China's security approaches radical and idealist.

Notwithstanding such diplomatic maneuvers, military might was viewed as the ultima ratio in international politics and was considered crucial in assuring national security. In view of the constant external military threat to China from the 1950s to the 1970s, the PRC maintained the world's largest army; but its weapons systems, force structure, and military doctrine were all defense oriented. The doctrine of "people's war," developed during the early 1950s, took into account the inferiority of the PLA in firepower and mobility. According to the doctrine, if China were attacked by either of the superpowers, PLA troops would not engage the enemy in border or coastal areas but instead would retreat to the interior. Once the aggressor's troops followed, they would find themselves dispersed in China's vast territory, isolated and surrounded by its large standing army and militia. Under such circumstances, the invaders would soon lose access to supplies and information. When the enemy had been exhausted by a long war of attrition, the PLA would counterattack. In addition to formulating the "people's war" doctrine, the PRC in 1955 decided to develop its nuclear capability in response to the U.S. nuclear threat. China conducted its first nuclear explosion in 1964 and tested a hydrogen bomb in 1967. Beijing declared from the outset that its purpose in possessing nuclear bombs was to deter a nuclear attack and that it would never use nuclear weapons first. As such, "no first use" and "second strike" policies have been characteristic tenets of China's nuclear doctrine.

From 1950 to 1979 China's international use of military force fell into three categories, based on motivation: to deter a perceived superpower attack (e.g., involvement in the Korean War), to defend China's territory from encroachment or to recover territories to which it laid claim (e.g., the Sino-Indian border war and the Sino-Soviet border clash), and to maintain the regional balance of power (e.g., the 1979 Sino-Vietnam border war).[2] These three motivations were not mutually exclusive; sometimes the decision to use force involved all three considerations. In at least one case—the Sino-Soviet border clash—the use of force was strongly influenced by domestic political factors.[3] Subscribers to Clausewitz's axiom that war is the continuation of politics, the PRC leaders of Mao's generation were willing to use force to serve China's security and, more broadly, foreign policy goals whenever necessary. However, in most cases China sent strong warnings and protests or engaged in negotiation before applying the ultima ratio. Such conduct was a legacy of China's cultural tradition, which advocated "trying peaceful means before resorting to force" (*Xian li hou bing*) in resolving disputes.

Reappraisal of Security

Beginning in the early 1980s, several developments led to the reappraisal of security in the PRC. Foremost among them was the high priority accorded to national development. During the Mao era, the first priority in domestic affairs had been to ensure regime security. To that end, Beijing had adopted the principle of "taking class struggle as the key link" and had launched political campaigns one after another, aimed at liquidating all sorts of class enemies and solidifying socialism and the proletarian regime. Deng Xiaoping, though also concerned about regime security, did not see serious danger to the CCP's leadership. What worried him most was China's weakness as a nation, especially its backward economy. Deng also believed that the best way to promote regime security was through improvement of public welfare, not political suppression. For this reason, in the late 1970s, the CCP decided to adopt the "Four Modernizations"—modernization of agriculture, industry, national defense, and science and technology—as the highest priority on the national agenda. To promote modernization, Beijing adopted a "reform and open door" policy. This change in focus engendered a broader view of and new approaches to national security.

Change in the domestic agenda called for a reassessment of the international situation. Deng Xiaoping, after scrutinizing the international situation, came to the conclusion that world war could be averted for some time to come and that the preservation of peace was likely. With the recession of war and revolution from the international agenda, Deng argued, peace and development had become the central themes of international relations (Deng 1993: 104–6, 127). Although Deng still shared Mao's opinion that the international system is anarchic and chaotic, and that individual nations within it compete for their respective national power and interests, Deng differed from Mao on two points: he saw the international system as a source of more opportunity than danger, and he was more inclined toward cooperation than confrontation in pursuing national interests.

The third development was the amelioration of the PRC's immediate security environment. To create a favorable external atmosphere for China's modernization program, Beijing decided in 1982 to seek to moderate the confrontation with Moscow. In the mid-1980s, as China and the Soviet Union moved to improve bilateral relations, the possibility of a major military conflict between them gradually receded. For the first time since 1949, PRC leaders did not have to worry about direct external military threats. As a result, the military element, both as a security concern and as an approach to security goals, was downplayed.

In spite of these developments, the central theme of the PRC's security thinking remained unchanged. In 1980 Deng set three priorities for China's national agenda throughout the 1980s: economic development, national unification, and opposition to hegemonism (Deng 1994: 239–40). Intended respectively to increase China's material strength, remove the vestiges of the humiliating past, and promote China's position on the world arena as a major power, these aims all served a central goal: to turn China into a great power.

Deng's reappraisal of security represents a refinement rather than an abandonment of Mao's construction of security. Deng agreed with Mao about the nature of the international system. He also believed in the need to transform China into a great power. Deng, like Mao, believed in the primacy of the nation-state and the regime as security referents; he differed from Mao, however, on the scope of and approaches to security. Mao defined security narrowly, limiting it to the political and military dimensions. Deng broadened the concept and brought social, economic, scientific, and technological elements to the security agenda. Mao's approaches tended to be confrontational, whereas Deng sought cooperation and conciliation. Deng also emphasized the role of economics and was to a certain extent willing to make use of international institutions and regimes.

State and Regime: Key Referents of Security

In China, the state is the paramount referent of security on both the domestic and international levels, and regime security is usually considered an element of national security. There are several reasons for this view. Historically, the state has been thought of as the protector, rather than the oppressor, of the people. The Chinese term *guojia* (country) is composed of two characters, *guo* (state) and *jia* (family)—the two fundamental units within which people live. The state is also regarded as the protector of other referents of security, such as *zhong* (race) and *jiao* (religion or, broadly defined, culture). This notion finds expression in such idioms as *guo po jia wang* (the country is defeated and home lost), *bao jia wei guo* (to protect our homes and defend our country), *wang guo mie zhong* (national subjugation and genocide), and *bao guo bao jiao* (to defend our country and protect our religion). The fact that in modern times China has never generated a mature civil society vis-à-vis the state is a contributing factor to the hegemony of the state and to the people's acceptance of it. Another contributing factor is the CCP's approach to China's domestic politics. Ever since the founding of the PRC, the CCP has taken every measure to create a unified and purified social-political order and a highly centralized political structure, thus ensuring the paramount position of the state. Because the CCP is the only ruling party, the party, government, and state are fused. Regime concerns are usually mixed with those of the nation-state and clothed in the language of national security.

The state and regime, however, face several internal challenges. First, ethnic groups have long been strong competitors. The Chinese nation is composed of 55 national minorities. Although most get along well as part of the "great family of nationalities," separatist influences exist in some ethnic minority areas, notably Tibet, Xinjiang, and Inner Mongolia. The Tibetans are mainly concerned with the preservation of their political, religious, and cultural identity. The Uigurs of Xinjiang and the Inner Mongolians are more interested in uniting with their ethnic and religious counterparts across the borders than in being part of the Chinese "great family."

Some ethnic groups do not identify with the state and the regime. For them their ethnic group is the paramount referent of security. Their security goals clash with those of the government. For example, they view secession from the PRC as their major security objective, while the PRC views secession as a threat to its territorial integrity and thus to national security. Central government policies that tighten control over minority areas are perceived by these groups as threats to their political autonomy and cultural tradition; the central government, for its part, views some of these groups' activities as threats to national unity.

In recent years economic growth has also created competing referent units. Since the 1980s the expansion of a market economy in the PRC has been accompanied by the decentralization of economic and political power. Local governments have obtained more authority than ever before as they direct indigenous economic development. The weakening of central power and the rise of localism have created some tension between the central government and local units. For example, local leaders in China's coastal areas may be more concerned with foreign economic linkage than with national security goals such as unification or the expansion of international influence. Even more significant, the economic boom has fostered the growth of a middle class, which is likely to pose an even greater challenge to regime security.

Still, the challenges posed by economic growth are less obvious and severe than those issuing from minority ethnic groups. So far the CCP and the central government have maintained an effective monopoly of political and military power, as well as partial control of economic power. At present no existing group or organization can seriously compete with the party and the political center, although the long-term impact of economic growth is difficult to predict.

Broadening the Scope of Security

Since the late 1980s a combination of internal and external developments has had a dramatic effect on the PRC security agenda. These events include the student movement in the PRC and the Western world's strong response to the Tiananmen Square incident, the end of the Cold War, the failure of socialism in Eastern Europe and the former Soviet Union, the Persian Gulf War, and the implosion of the USSR, almost none of which were anticipated by the PRC leaders.

Policy makers in the PRC see both opportunity and challenges arising from the drastic changes in the international situation. On the positive side is the perception that since the end of the Cold War the international situation has become less confrontational and hostile, with disputes increasingly being settled through negotiation. The relatively peaceful international environment is believed likely to endure, virtually eliminating the threat of a new world war. The collapse of the bipolar system put an end to the manipulation of international affairs by the two superpowers, and the world is moving toward multipolarity. Economics is more and more important in international relations. Peace and development remain the central themes of international relations (Jiang 1992: 26; Li 1995: xv).

Such developments have created favorable conditions for China. First, the comparatively stable and peaceful international environment enables China to focus on internal development. Second, under the influence of a trend toward multipolarity, the vast number of developing countries, including China, are playing an active role in international affairs. Third, the rapid economic growth and expanding economic cooperation in the Asia-Pacific region provides China with an opportunity to ride on the regional "economic express." Finally, China's fast-growing domestic market is increasingly attractive to the world, especially the developed countries. That circumstance grants Beijing more leeway in the international arena by enabling it to play the "market card."

At the same time, the PRC leaders have some negative perceptions of the current scene. With the end of the Cold War, China lost its strategic leverage vis-à-vis the two superpowers, especially the United States. Its strategic importance declined drastically in the eyes of Washington. The post–Cold War international power structure features "one superpower plus several major powers,"[4] and the United States, as the only remaining superpower, exercises overwhelming influence on international affairs and is trying to build a "new world order" of its own conception. In some ways China, as the only remaining major socialist country, has to bear even greater political and strategic pressure from the United States and its allies. And although a major war can be averted in the foreseeable future, the world is still far from tranquil: ethnic conflicts, territorial disputes, and religious conflicts have surfaced, resulting in bloodshed and local wars. For this reason, China must be prepared for contingencies on its periphery that may result from ethnic and territorial disputes.[5] As international economic competition has become increasingly intense, China has had to make even greater efforts to widen its access to foreign markets, capital, and technology. The Gulf War that occurred after the end of the Cold War had several implications for the PRC. First, in the post–Cold War era, the PLA should be well prepared for a limited, high-tech war. Second, the PLA lags far behind its Western counterparts in its ability to conduct modern warfare. Third, control over oil resources should occupy a special position on the national security agenda.

The Tiananmen Square incident and the collapse of socialism in Eastern Europe and the USSR alarmed PRC leaders, who believe that the legitimacy of the CCP regime has been seriously undermined by those events. Furthermore, Beijing has asserted that because Washington and its Western allies no longer need to play the "China card" against Moscow, they will regard China, the only remaining major communist country, as the prime target of their "peaceful evolution" strategy.[6] At the same time, Beijing suspects that hostile internal forces, encouraged by developments in the former Soviet bloc, will work in concert with external anticommunist forces in an attempt to topple the CCP regime. As a result, regime security could become a matter of grave concern.

Since 1988 great changes have taken place in relations across the Taiwan Straits and on the island itself. The expansion of cross-straits exchanges in social, economic, and cultural areas has greatly improved the atmosphere across the strait and raised the prospects of peaceful unification. At the same time, however, political democratization and the rise of the secessionist influence on the island are pushing cross-straits relations the other way. As Beijing perceives an ever-growing momentum on the island for its breakaway from China, the Taiwan issue moves up on the PRC's list of security concerns.

All these considerations and recent developments inform the PRC leaders' perception of threats to national security in the post–Cold War era. Although a long list can be compiled, five security goals appear to be prominent at present: sustaining economic growth, preserving territorial integrity, consolidating regime security, maintaining a favorable strategic balance, and expanding international influence.

Economic Security

Economic security is both a means to and a goal of national security. In China it means preserving elements crucial to national economic, scientific, and technological development strategy while promoting national interests and gaining an advantageous position in both international competition and economic cooperation. Special emphasis is placed on protecting the domestic market and opening international markets (Ho Fang 1995: 5).

Although economic growth has been the top priority on China's national agenda since the late 1970s, its significance to national security was not fully understood until the late 1980s and early 1990s. Chinese leaders drew a lesson from the disintegration of the USSR and recognized economic competition as the essence of the post–Cold War international game. That recognition deepened their conviction that national security depends more upon overall national strength, based on a solid economy, than on military might. According to the report of the Fourteenth Congress of the Communist Party, "modern Chinese history and the realities of the present-day world show that so long as a country is economically backward, it will be in a passive position, subject to manipulation by others. Nowadays the competition among the various countries is, in essence, a competition of overall national strength based on economic, scientific and technological capabilities" (Jiang 1992: 16). Observing the collapse of socialism in the former Soviet bloc, PRC leaders also learned that economic development can have a direct impact on regime survival. President Jiang Zemin warned the CCP, "If we fail to develop our economy rapidly, it will be very difficult for us to consolidate the Socialist system and maintain long-term social stability" (Jiang 1992: 16). Thus a strong economy is believed to be the key to a strong defense capability, a stable political system, and sustained social harmony. Threats to economic security come from many directions, both internal and external. A few are identified in the paragraphs that follow.

Growing Protectionism in World Trade

Since 1979 the PRC has made remarkable progress in integrating into the world economic system. Exports and imports as a percentage of its gross domestic product grew from about 10 percent in 1978 to around 45 percent in 1994 (*Beijing Review* 1995b). Consequently, the PRC's economic growth has depended heavily on the expansion of its share in the international market. However, it seems to Beijing that regional cooperation and regional protectionism have developed in tandem since the end of the Cold War. The passage of the North American Free Trade Agreement and the establishment of a unified European economic community were viewed by China as obvious signs of the pursuit of protectionism by the industrialized states, with which China conducts most of its foreign trade. Some of China's major trading partners, such as the United States, Japan, the European Community, and South Korea, have imposed so-called antidumping taxes and quota limitations on certain types of commodities imported from the PRC, and their actions have adversely affected the development of related industries in China.

Politicization of Economic Issues

Since 1990 the PRC has been obsessed with the maintenance of most favored nation (MFN) trading status in the United States. In response to the Tiananmen Square incident, the United States linked the annual renewal of MFN status for China to its concessions on human rights, nonproliferation of weapons of mass destruction, and other issues. This put the PRC in an awkward position. On the one hand, it has been unwilling to lose MFN status, which is indispensable to its thriving export-oriented industries; on the other, it is difficult for China to meet all the conditions imposed by the Americans. It is an area where economic security is shadowed by political controversy. A similar problem confounds China's entry into the General Agreement on Tariffs and Trade (GATT) and the World Trade Organization (WTO).

Since 1986 China has been endeavoring to resume its membership in GATT and, more recently, to join the newly established WTO. However, there are serious differences between the PRC and the developed countries, especially the United States, over the price of admission. China requests that it be treated basically as a developing country and accepts only conditions commensurate with that status. The developed nations, however, in view of the already remarkable scale of China's economy and its strong momentum of growth, insist that the PRC should enter WTO as a more competent economy, bearing the corresponding obligations. In Beijing's opinion, such a demand is excessive and driven by political motives, implying that some developed nations are unwilling to see a stronger China.

The International Economic Intelligence War

Since the end of the Cold War, the intelligence agencies of the major states have shifted their priorities from obtaining political and military information to seeking economic, financial, and technological information. As one of the world's fastest-growing economies, the PRC believes that it has been selected by foreign intelligence agencies as an important target of operations. These agencies collect information on topics ranging from China's macroeconomic policy to plans for the import and export of specific commodities. The success of the PRC's efforts in fighting international economic espionage will help determine whether China can protect its domestic and overseas markets, how fast it can narrow the technological gap with the industrialized countries, and how effectively it can protect the economic benefits of its technological inventions (Yan 1993: 7).

Challenges to China's Maritime Rights and Interests

China boasts 3 million square kilometers of territorial sea rich in fish, petroleum, and natural gas. As the national economy continues to grow and the country's available land resources can hardly support the huge population, the exploitation of those marine resources becomes a matter of increasing strategic importance. The fact that China has become a net importer of oil since 1993 makes the protection of its marine resources even more crucial. Oil exploitation activities by other countries (Vietnam, for example) in some parts of the South China Sea where the PRC claims sovereignty pose a threat to the PRC's oil supply and to its sustained economic development.

Territorial Integrity

China's position on territorial integrity is shaped by its cultural and historical legacy. Since the Qin dynasty (221–206 B.C.), when China was first unified, there has been a cultural tradition of "great national unity" (*da yi tong*), which holds that unity is better than division and that division is temporary and abnormal whereas unity is permanent. Therefore, in the eyes of the PRC elites and the populace, the effort to recover territories that China has lost in its modern history is part of nation-building; only by resuming the exercise of sovereignty over Taiwan, Hong Kong, and Macao can China call itself a unified nation. Further, because the problems of Taiwan, Hong Kong, and Macao were created by foreign aggression, only by resolving those issues can China remove the last vestige of the "century of humiliation" and become a true great power.

The key threats to the PRC's territorial integrity are the national minority separatist movements in Tibet and Xinjiang, and the pro-independence forces in Taiwan.

Tibet

Tibet is a special entity in almost every respect. Located on the Qingzang plateau, the southwesternmost part of China, Tibet has only a difficult overland connection with the principal part of China. Culturally, the people of Tibet speak languages and practice religions different from those of China's majority Han population. Demographically, according to China's official 1982 census, 95 percent of Tibet's residents are ethnic Tibetans. Tibet was "peacefully" liberated by the PLA in the spring of 1951 and became an integral part of the PRC. Ever since, separatist forces have been trying to break away from China. In 1959 separatist groups launched revolts; when the rebellions were put down, the Dalai Lama—the spiritual leader of Tibet—and his followers fled to India. In October 1987 and March 1989, Tibetan secessionists organized demonstrations and riots in Lhasa, the capital city of Tibet, and openly called for Tibetan independence. The PRC authorities have been able to deal with such open revolts and riots. The real problem is the influence of the Dalai Lama in Tibet and the separatist activities of his followers in exile. So long as the exiled Tibetan community exists, Tibetan separatism will remain a major concern for PRC leaders.

Xinjiang

In Xinjiang, the impetus for secession comes partly from ethnic and cultural differences between the Han and the local peoples, and partly from the ethnic and religious ties between Uigurs and Uzbeks on both sides of the border. In the early 1960s, when Sino-Soviet relations soured, there occurred a Soviet-instigated emigration of Xinjiang Uigurs and Tajiks from China to Soviet Central Asia. The PRC's attempt to clamp down on emigration finally led to widespread demonstrations, riots, and other disturbances (Garver 1993: 273). During the period of Sino-Soviet confrontation, the PRC had been extremely sensitive to the Soviet influence in Xinjiang and resentful of its exploitation of the exiled Uigurs in the Soviet Union to incite anti-Chinese uprising. The implosion of the USSR at the end of 1991 and the resulting independence of the Central Asian republics—especially Kazakhstan, Kyrgyzstan, and Tajikistan, which border on China—further complicated the situation in Xinjiang. The separatist groups, encouraged by the disintegration of the Soviet Union and the national independence gained by their ethnic and religious counterparts across the border, have become ever more active; meanwhile, the emergence of relatively unstable Islamic states on China's Central Asian borders to some extent facilitates Islamic fundamentalist infiltration into Xinjiang.

Taiwan

The Taiwan issue is gaining greater salience on the PRC's security agenda. In addition to the historical and cultural factors already mentioned, other considerations influence the PRC's stance on Taiwan. If Taiwan breaks away, Xinjiang, Tibet, and Inner Mongolia might follow. Strategically, China would lose control of its door to the western Pacific. Furthermore, to offset the strategic superiority of the mainland nation, an independent Taiwan would seek alliance with other major powers, perhaps the United States and Japan, thus adversely affecting China's security environment.[7] Politically, especially with the recovery of Hong Kong and the scheduled return of Macao to Chinese control, it would be very hard for Beijing to explain to the populace why Taiwan should be left out. No mainland Chinese government can hope to survive an independent Taiwan.

A further concern is the tremendous difference between the political systems of the PRC and Taiwan. Taiwan has completed its political transformation and established a Western-style democracy; the PRC still adheres to its socialist political system. The huge economic gap between the two sides is another obstacle to unification. Taiwan's per capita income is about 20 times that in the PRC. As a result, the Taiwanese fear that their prosperous island will be submerged in a sea of poverty once unification takes place.

Political developments in Taiwan have changed the attitude of the Taiwanese elite toward unification. During the era of Chiang Kai-shek and his son Chiang Ching-kuo, Taiwan was controlled by mainlanders—people who had fled to the island after the Nationalists lost their war to the Communists on the mainland. Since that time more and more native Taiwanese have taken the place of the mainlanders in the political arena, so that the political leadership has become "Taiwanized." This new-generation political elite, lacking historical and personal links to the mainland, would prefer independence to unification.

At present, the international environment seems favorable to Taiwan's independence. Taiwan's economic prosperity and political democratization have won it considerable sympathy in the world community. In recent years national splits in the former USSR and the former Yugoslavia have fed secessionist sentiment in Taiwan. In addition, Taiwan is trying to exploit the principle of national self-determination, generally endorsed by the international community, to justify its desire for independence.

A final dimension of PRC leaders' concern over Taiwan is the U.S. factor. Given the history of relations between the United States and Taiwan, the PRC is extremely sensitive to any U.S. actions that might directly or indirectly encourage Taiwan's attempt to gain independence. The PRC leaders believe that the United States has never wished to see Taiwan's unification with the PRC, and that at a time when China is emerging as a world power, the United States, unwilling to accept such status for China, is trying to thwart its growth. In Beijing's opinion, to play the "Taiwan card" and prevent unification is part of the U.S. "soft containment" strategy toward China. Promoting U.S.–Taiwan relations, expanding the sale of weapons to Taiwan, and granting a visa to Taiwanese leader Lee Teng-hui: all these actions are viewed as part of the U.S. scheme to facilitate Taiwan's independence.

Regime Survival

As noted earlier, the Tiananmen Square incident and the collapse of communist regimes in Eastern Europe and the Soviet Union alarmed the PRC leaders, who believe that regime survival is now threatened by a combination of internal and external challenges. Overall, the PRC elite identifies three sources of threat to its regime security: the "peaceful evolution" strategy of the Western world, the influence of "bourgeois liberalism"[8] within China, and social instability.

Peaceful Evolution

The PRC leadership believes that ever since the 1950s the Western world has been employing a dual strategy to subvert socialist systems: military containment and peaceful evolution. In the closing years of the Cold War the Western countries, faced with the common threat from Moscow, supported the PRC's economic development and political stability. With the end of the Cold War and the disappearance of the Soviet threat, however, some Western countries have changed their conciliatory and collaborative attitudes toward China and have begun to view China as a major target of the peaceful evolution strategy. In Beijing's opinion, this strategy involves using economic aid and trade as means to exercise political influence, gaining ideological and cultural penetration through various channels, stirring up antigovernment sentiment in China, supporting political dissidents, and nurturing pro-Western forces (Lin 1991: 156). Since 1994, the PRC leadership has described Western political schemes against China as "Westernization" and "splitting" (Xinhua News Agency 1995).

Bourgeois Liberalism

The internal challenge to regime security is much more complicated than the external one. Since the 1980s the ideologies of Marxism-Leninism and Maoism have gradually lost their appeal in China. At the same time some segments of the populace, influenced by Western democratic values, have begun to embrace Western-style multiparty politics and to question the CCP's monopoly of power. As the revolutionary generation dies off, the legitimacy of the present regime is increasingly challenged. A by-product of the "reform and open door policy" is that most of the people in China are finding the Western economic system more efficient and productive. They have lost confidence in the socialist economic system and are highly skeptical of the CCP's ability to manage China's economy. Finally, social and economic developments in the post-Mao era have given rise to entrepreneurs and self-employed professionals, and a middle class is burgeoning in China. Once this new social force has fully emerged, it will pose serious challenges to the economic, social, and political foundations of the Communist regime.

In the view of PRC leaders, the greatest danger to the regime exists when there is collaboration between internal and external hostile forces. The Tiananmen Square incident is a typical example. Beijing believes that student protest in China was initially incited by the international anticommunist influence. Then the internal hostile forces issued two fundamental calls: to overthrow the CCP and to topple the socialist system. Their ultimate purpose, in the eyes of the CCP, is to make China abandon the socialist system and to establish a capitalist republic that will be a vassal to the Western world (Deng 1993: 303, 331).

Social Instability

In addition to political forces, social instability is seen as a challenge to regime security. From the 1950s to the 1970s China successfully established a unified and tightly controlled social order. Social stability was not seriously challenged, even though state actors considered it a major concern. Since the late 1970s, however, the adoption of economic reform and opening has caused several social problems. One is the loss of social control. China's attempt to transform its centrally planned economy into a market economy was accompanied by relaxation of political control over the society. This change was especially evident in the countryside, where the rural economy was decollectivized and the "people's commune" dissolved. As a result, the government lost its most effective means to maintain political control over huge rural areas. Today in some regions, law and order is seriously challenged and chaos prevails, presenting a direct threat to regime stability.

Another social problem is the corruption that is rampant throughout the bureaucracy. Although China's centrally planned economy is gradually giving way to a market economy, the government still plays an important role in economic and social activities. In a period when communist ideology has lost its influence on people's behavior but the system of rule by law is not yet well established, those who hold power can easily become corrupt. At present, corruption ranks among the top concerns of the populace. To some extent, it has smeared the CCP's image and undermined people's confidence in the government.

A third social ill is economic inequality. Although economic reform has led to remarkable prosperity throughout China, not everyone has benefited equally. Growing unemployment in cities and in the country-side, uneven economic development between the coast and the interior, and income disparity between urban and rural residents and between people from different walks of life are all factors that have combined to produce widespread dissatisfaction with the CCP and the government.

A final major source of social instability is organized crime. As a result of the increased openness to the outside world and the internal loosening of social control, there has been increasing infiltration of outside criminal organizations into China and a rise in crimes committed by Chinese gangs. Drug-related activities are of special concern to the PRC leaders. In the early years of the twentieth century, opium addiction was a major problem in China: out of a population of 400 million, as many as 20 million (5 percent) were drug users and more than 300,000 made their living in the drug trade (Hong 1995: 15). After the founding of the PRC, the government tackled the problem reso-lutely and in three years largely eliminated the blight of opium that had affected China for more than a century. Beginning in the early 1980s, however, international drug traffickers took advantage of China's opening policy to transport drugs from the "Golden Triangle" via the Chinese mainland to Hong Kong and Macao, from whence the drugs entered the international market. As time went on, more and more drugs began to circulate within China, resulting in a growing number of drug addicts. Because drug addiction not only drains a state's wealth but also leads to the spread of disease and an increased crime rate, it is commonly regarded as a serious threat to social stability. The bitter memory of the Opium Wars that unleashed the "century of humiliation" upon China fuels the government's concern over the consequences of drug addiction for national security.

Strategic Concerns

Strategic concerns did not disappear from the PRC's security agenda with the end of the Cold War. Continuing strategic worries involve the possibility of a limited war and the balance of power among the major powers.

The PRC leadership and strategists recognize that with the end of the Cold War, the prospect of a large-scale war in the foreseeable future has become remote; a more likely possibility is a limited war on China's periphery. China has more immediate neighbors than any other state in the world. Ethnic rivalries and unresolved territorial disputes could, under certain circumstances, trigger armed conflicts. In addition, if Taiwan ventures to declare its independence, the PRC is very likely to resort to force, and some foreign powers, especially the United States, might intervene militarily. The PLA might find itself hard-pressed to cope with such eventualities. Although military modernization has been under way since the early 1980s, the PLA's existing force structure, operational doctrine, training, deployment, and equipment would give it little chance of winning a limited, high-tech war.

As a regional power, China is very sensitive to any shift in the East Asian balance of power and seeks to maintain a strategic position in the region that is not inferior to that of any of the other major powers. The United States, with forward deployment and bilateral security alliances in the region, is in a position to significantly affect China's security environment. The adjustments in U.S. East Asian security strategy under President Clinton—including the maintenance of about 100,000 troops deployed in the Western Pacific and the reaffirmation of the U.S.–Japan security alliance—have caused much concern in China. Some strategists see these adjustments as indicative that growing concern over a rising China has driven the United States to increase its strategic constraint on Beijing. If necessary, the U.S. forward military presence and its bilateral security alliances could become part of a U.S. containment strategy against China.[9]

As early as the 1970s the PRC leadership suggested that Japan, after transforming itself into a major economic power, would seek to become a major political and military power as well. For historical reasons, China is very sensitive to any signs that Japan is moving in that direction. The PRC leaders believe that since the 1980s Japan has been endeavoring to secure a political status commensurate with its economic might. In fact, Japan has considerably increased its defense budget; today Japan possesses an army equipped with the most advanced weapons, and its Self-Defense Force (SDF) personnel have been dispatched overseas several times. In Beijing's view, the redefinition of the U.S.–Japan alliance is designed to enable Japan to play a larger role in regional security affairs. The PRC policy community is concerned about how far Japan would go. Although in the short term the United States constitutes China's principal strategic concern, some Chinese strategists suggest that in the long run Japan will replace it as the greatest threat to China.[10]

At present Russia is not a major strategic concern for China. However, given the troubled history of bilateral relations and the long common border, the PRC leadership must always keep in mind the Russian factor. No matter how the Russian situation evolves—whether the country falls apart or emerges as a revived power—Russia will inevitably have a great impact on China's security environment. Strategic analysts in the PRC tend to believe that after overcoming its internal chaos, Russia will rapidly recover its vigor and once again loom large on China's northern border. Therefore, Beijing should carefully manage its relations with Moscow before that day arrives.

Since the end of the Cold War, the Association of Southeast Asian Nations (ASEAN) has gained prominence as an independent strategic actor. It is of strategic concern to China for two reasons. First, the PRC watches closely to see in what directions the ASEAN countries, as the motor of the ASEAN Regional Forum (ARF), will move that budding regional security organization and how it will affect China's security interests. The PRC fears that the ARF may somehow fall under U.S. control and become another instrument of U.S. strategic pressure on China. Another concern, particularly since Vietnam has become a member of the association, is the possibility that ASEAN countries may form a united front against China on the South China Sea issue.

Promoting International Influence

As a regional major power and a prospective global power, China is not content to limit its influence to the region but also seeks to expand its influence globally. On the regional level, it would like to see a more Asia-oriented political-strategic landscape. In the view of PRC leaders, Asian affairs should be managed mainly by Asians themselves, with external influence kept to a minimum, and China should play a role commensurate with its status. Globally, the PRC leadership welcomes further multipolarization of the international structure and holds that the superpower's excessive influence on international affairs should be cut down, while other states, especially regional powers, should have a louder voice at the decision-making table.

The PRC perceives challenges to its international influence predominantly from the United States and its Western allies. Beijing frequently complains about the pressure it continually has to bear from hegemonism and power politics, by which it refers to attempts by the United States and its allies to manipulate international affairs while denying the voice of other states, including the PRC. For instance, the United States is nearly always able to mobilize majority support within the U.N. Security Council, setting its agenda and manipulating the outcome of the votes, whereas China is generally unable to take any initiative that is not welcomed by the United States. Sometimes PRC leaders also view the G-7 summit as a manifestation of hegemonism and power politics because it often makes significant political and economic decisions without consulting those likely to be affected (Deng 1993: 345). Overall, the power imbalance between China and the United States and its allies makes Beijing feel greatly constricted in the world arena.

Prioritizing Security Concerns

Although the security concerns discussed so far are all closely related, they are not equally important. Regime survival is a paramount internal security issue; territorial integrity is the key concern in the external dimension. Other security concerns, such as economic growth or international influence, can be sacrificed for the sake of those two goals. Nevertheless, given the growing importance attached to economic well-being, some compromise of regime security may be deemed acceptable to advance important economic interests. This approach has been exemplified by China's release of some political dissidents in an effort to obtain MFN trading status with the United States in the years following the Tiananmen Square incident.

The relative salience of various security concerns changes from time to time. At present, economic development is the PRC's central task; consequently, economic threats draw the most attention from the PRC leadership. Political threats to regime survival were regarded as a pressing issue in the wake of the Tiananmen Square incident in 1989; however, after the normalization of relations between China and most Western countries and the restoration and consolidation of internal political control, Beijing began to view both the peaceful evolution strategy and bourgeois liberalism as long-range challenges rather than immediate threats. Social instability has received more attention as the PRC's economic reform and political succession enter a crucial period. Hegemonism and power politics are regarded as long-term threats to China's sovereignty and international influence and are managed accordingly, with the exception of a few situations that may call for immediate responses. Strategic challenges are potential rather than actual: there are no immediate antagonists, and the balance of power in East Asia is still evolving. Since 1994 the PRC has been increasingly concerned over Taiwan's possible separation, and the Taiwan issue could become even more prominent in the future.

Some tensions exist between the various security concerns. For instance, to speed up economic growth, China should close or reorganize many state-owned enterprises that have incurred heavy losses due to poor management and administration. Such reform, however, would aggravate the already widespread unemployment and seriously endanger social stability as well as regime security. Because social and political stability is the overriding concern, reform of the state-owned enterprises has been postponed. Similarly, there is tension between the goals of economic growth and unification. If the PRC uses force to address the Taiwan issue, its economic development will suffer tremendously; however, if Taiwan declares independence, the PRC leaders will have no choice but to resort to force. The PRC leadership seems resolved that in such an event, economics should give way to territorial integrity.

Security threats can be divided into two groups according to their nature and perceived consequences. Challenges to the PRC's sovereignty, territorial integrity, and regime security endanger the state's identity and values and thus have primary importance; these threats are generally assessed in zero-sum terms and are not regarded as subject to compromise, although minimal concessions could be made under certain circumstances. Other security threats are viewed as less fundamental and to a certain extent negotiable.

The broad articulation of security in the PRC not only exists at the level of rhetoric but also is embodied in the state's policy and practice. China's centralized political structure enables the government to pursue an integrated approach to various security issues. On the operational level, various government branches such as the ministries of defense, foreign affairs, national security, public security, and foreign trade and economic cooperation play their respective roles in dealing with different aspects of national security. They analyze the sources and consequences of threats and plan and implement policies. On the decision-making level, the members of the CCP's Politbureau—especially the Central Military Commission, the Central Leading Small Group on Politics and Law, and the Central Leading Small Group on Foreign Affairs—are responsible for formulating overall national security strategy and coordinating the efforts of various branches.

Within the established political structure, the military is emerging as an independent and crucial actor in the state's security policy making process. From the 1950s to the 1980s, the top CCP and state leaders were also the founders of the PLA. When they projected China's security policy on behalf of the CCP and the government, they naturally represented the military as well. The PLA had no notion of the need to make its voice heard in the decision-making circle. Now the situation is different. The present top leaders do not have the background that would allow them to exercise absolute authority over the army. The military finds it difficult to identify with civilian leaders and to be receptive to whatever major decisions they make. The PLA now seeks to argue strongly for its own interests and views. In fact, there are signs in recent years that the military takes a tougher stance than the government on some issues, including Sino-American relations, Taiwan, and the South China Sea disputes.

Approaches to National Security

During dynastic times, China accumulated rich experience in dealing with threats posed by the surrounding barbarians. "Strategies of coping with barbarians" (*zhi yi zhi dao*) included

- maintaining internal stability and thereby leaving outsiders no opportunities to exploit

- maintaining moral and cultural superiority to the barbarians so as to draw their admiration, respect, and loyalty

- engaging in skillful diplomatic maneuvers, such as "playing barbarians against barbarians" (*yi yi zhi yi*) and "associating with those in the distance while attacking those in the vicinity" (*yuan jiao jin gong*)

- applying the carrot and stick judiciously (*en wei bing shi*) so as to deter barbarians from attempting to invade.

These and other such strategies still have lingering effects on the PRC's security thinking.

China's security strategy is made up of three interrelated and mutually reinforcing components. The first is the maintenance of internal stability. Internal stability is in itself a paramount security goal, and it is also a prerequisite for the advancement of other security objectives, such as economic development and international influence.

The second component is building China's "comprehensive national strength." As of the late 1980s China had developed the notion of comprehensive national strength, which holds that the optimal approach to national security is to strengthen all the dimensions of national power—economic, technological, political, social, and military. By increasing its overall national strength, China will be able to achieve domestic cohesion and maintain internal stability, improve its security position with regard to other powers, and be better equipped to deal with external threats.

The third aspect of China's security strategy consists of diplomatic maneuvers. Skillful engagement with other countries, international institutions, and regimes is supposed to create a more favorable external environment that will promote internal stability and economic growth, enhance China's international status, and enhance its influence in the world arena.

Maintaining Internal Stability

The approach to internal stability comprises three dimensions: ensuring regime survival, maintaining social stability, and preserving territorial integrity.

As noted earlier, regime survival is a key security concern. Measures adopted in this regard include political and legal suppression, education, and accommodation. According to the PRC Criminal Law, people involved in attempts to overthrow the present regime and the socialist system would be held guilty of "counterrevolution" and subject to severe punishment.[11] For instance, the Tiananmen Square student protest in the summer of 1989 was labeled and suppressed as a "counterrevolutionary riot." Subsequently, the CCP and the government placed greater emphasis on ideological education and political propaganda with the goal of deepening the public's faith in the CCP's leadership. Most significant, in order to ameliorate the economic and political grievances of the populace, the PRC is speeding up the tempo of its economic development as well as the promotion of "socialist democracy." China's legislature, the People's Congress, for example, has since the mid-1980s been vested with greater power to supervise the work of the government. In China's countryside, village and town councils are now formed through election rather than appointment.

The response to the Tiananmen Square incident is typical of the PRC's approach to regime security. When the students began to take to the streets, the government set the propaganda machine in motion. Beijing asserted that a handful of people with ulterior motives were instigating students to create chaos and to challenge the leadership of the CCP, and vowed to stand firm against the uprising. Such psychological warfare was designed to deter students from escalating their protest. When the students' protest spread and drew wide support from other sectors of the body politic, Beijing attempted to appease and accommodate them by agreeing to enter into a dialogue with the students and to entertain some of their "reasonable" demands. However, once the student movement had reached such a scale as to directly threaten regime stability, the CCP resorted to force: troops were called in to impose martial law and dispel the protesters from Tiananmen Square. After the incident, Beijing once again set its propaganda machine in full motion to educate the people, especially the students, on how the internal and external hostile forces had plotted and collaborated to manipulate student protest and incite riots with the aim of toppling the CCP and creating chaos to weaken China and turn it into a vassal of the West.

To deal with the problem of social instability, the PRC has adopted a series of measures. By reorganizing administrative and political organizations at the village and town levels, Beijing has attempted to improve its social control. By establishing the anticorruption division within the procuratorial organs at various levels and by launching a nationwide anticorruption campaign, the government endeavors to hold back corruption and mitigate the public's anger. Because economic inequality has become a critical issue, the central government has formulated a set of social and economic policies to boost the development of the poor areas. "Aid-the-poor" projects are under way to help the backward rural areas to shake off poverty as soon as possible. From 1996 to 2000, the state government plans to grant more preferential economic treatment and more resources to the underdeveloped areas. Aimed at regulating personal income gaps and alleviating the contradictions arising from the great disparity between high and low income levels, efforts have been made to reform the personal tax system. A new individual income tax law went into effect as of January 1994. According to the new taxation system, personal income tax is levied on high-income earners, while medium- and low-income earners are granted reduced rates or exempted from personal income taxes (Li 1994).

The PRC has formed an effective law enforcement network to fight organized crime. A number of laws have been introduced against smuggling and drug-related crimes. The Ministry of Public Security has also set up an anti–organized crime division to oversee the fight against gangs. At the same time, to make such efforts more effective, China maintains close cooperation with other countries through Interpol and the judicial assistance system. The State Council established the National Narcotics Control Commission (NNCC) in 1990 to push forward the national antidrug campaign. One of China's key measures to crack down on drug crimes is a system of strict checks on drug traffickers in transit. Public security organs and customs officials in all localities have effectively coordinated their efforts to reduce the menace of drugs (Hong 1995; *Beijing Review* 1992, 1994a).

A combination of suppression and appeasement has been used to address threats posed by ethnic minority separatist movements. According to the PRC's Criminal Law, persons involved in separatist activities can be imprisoned for a period of ten years to life. In 1989, when separatist riots broke out in Lhasa, the central government enforced martial law in the city; instigators and chief participants of the riots were arrested and put on trial. In Xinjiang and Inner Mongolia, local public security organs make relentless efforts to eliminate any separatist activities and organizations.

On the other hand, Beijing views political, social, and economic appeasement as an indispensable part of the strategy to manage separatism. For instance, Beijing has been calling for negotiations with the exiled Tibetans headed by the Dalai Lama. Beijing declares that provided the Dalai Lama recognizes Tibet as an inseparable part of China, completely abandons his idea of Tibetan independence, and stops engaging in separatist activities, the central government will accept an end to his exile and welcome his return to China (*Beijing Review* 1994b). To eliminate conditions that are considered conducive to separatism, the PRC formulated the Law on Regional National Autonomy, which guarantees the right of the national minorities to self-government. A variety of preferential policies have been put in place for the national minority areas. For instance, the minority people are not required to abide by the national birth-control policy, which is strictly carried out among the Han. The state government provides financial and other assistance for the preservation and development of minority religions and cultures. Most important, the central government has been paying greater attention to improving the welfare of the minority people and to accelerating social and economic progress in ethnic minority regions. As President Jiang Zemin pointed out, "To strengthen national unity, consolidate frontier defence and promote economic development nationwide, it is extremely important to bring about faster development in areas inhabited by people of minority nationalities" (Jiang 1992: 22). To further this objective, the state government tilts toward the minority regions in the distribution of resources. Beginning with the Eighth Five-Year Plan for National Economic and Social Development (1990–95), more allocations have been directed to promoting minority economic prosperity. Meanwhile, economically developed regions are encouraged to help the minority economies through investment, technology transfer, and training of workers. In addition, Beijing has pursued a policy of encouraging Han people to settle in ethnic minority regions, especially Xinjiang, not only to guard against the separatist influence but also to promote the development of the border areas.

Augmenting Comprehensive National Strength

Central to comprehensive national strength are economic and military power, an idea reflected in a slogan put forward by PRC leaders in the early 1990s: *fu guo qiang bing* (rich country and strong army).

Rich Country

Economic growth, as the key to the development of overall national strength, has become the top priority on the national agenda. The PRC leaders have formulated a "three-step strategy" for China's national economic development. The first step (1981–2000) is to make China's gross national product in year 2000 quadruple that of 1981; the second step (2001–2010) will try to secure a 100 percent increase in China's GNP within ten years; the third step (2011 to around 2050) will be aimed at turning China into a moderately developed country by the middle of the twenty-first century.

To accomplish these goals, Beijing attaches special importance to the creation of a favorable environment for economic growth. Responses to external challenges to economic security include enhancing regional and global economic cooperation, diversifying China's external economic links, playing the "market card" to prevent the politicization of economic issues, fighting economic espionage, and protecting its maritime resources.

The trend toward regional grouping in world economic development has impelled the PRC to formulate new strategies and policies for foreign trade. The opening of China's economy, originally confined to the coastal areas, has extended to border and inland areas. An omni-directional opening pattern has been established to promote economic ties with other nations in the region. Currently, the Asia-Pacific markets account for 70 percent of China's imports and exports, and 85 percent of its foreign investment comes from within the region (Gao 1995: 19). Beijing is actively involved in the activities of Asia-Pacific Economic Cooperation (APEC) and other regional economic organizations, and has called for intensification of regional economic interactions. The PRC supports the proposal put forward by Malaysia to establish an East Asian Economic Caucus (EAEC), anticipating the positive role of such a group in promoting economic cooperation among its East Asian members to counterbalance rising protectionism in other regions. In addition, China seeks to participate in a comprehensive multilateral trade system and has participated in and signed the Final Act of the Uruguay Round of multilateral trade negotiations. Now the PRC is bargaining hard for admission to the World Trade Organization.

China's efforts to resist protectionism and promote regional integration face some problems. While advocating a more open and liberal world trade system so as to enable the steady expansion of its overseas markets, the PRC as a developing economy considers it necessary to protect its national industries. Such inconsistency in the country's trade policies will not disappear in the near future. Growing economic interdependence naturally calls for more cooperation and compromise on political and security issues, thus posing a challenge to the PRC's conception of sovereignty as well as to its usual practice with respect to political and security affairs.

Confronted with the U.S. policy of seeking "free and fair" trade and of linking economic and political issues, the PRC has adopted a plural market strategy to diversify its foreign economic links. China tries to reduce its dependence on the U.S. market and expand its economic interaction with Japan, South Korea, ASEAN, and the European Union, while at the same time skillfully playing its market card. For example, every year the United States has to decide whether or not to extend China's MFN status. Before the decision is made, China sends a large "purchasing delegation" to the United States to spend as much as several billion U.S. dollars. To force the United States to soften its position on China's entry into the WTO as a developing country, Premier Li Peng, during his trip to Europe in April 1996, made a $1.9 billion deal with the European Air Bus Company—a contract that could have gone to Boeing—and the move proved to be successful.

In the face of the intensifying international intelligence war, the PRC promulgated its first patent law in 1985 and its first national security law in 1993. The national security apparatus has been devoting considerable manpower and resources to the fight against foreign economic espionage. Because most Chinese people think of security only in terms of the military, territorial integrity, and regime survival dimensions—neglecting the economic dimension—the government must continue to remind the public to maintain economic and technological secrecy. However, the PRC has long adopted excessively high and wide secrecy standards, which tends to blur people's concept of secrecy and make it difficult to keep real secrets. Further, China lacks sophisticated technology and the necessary funds to fight economic espionage effectively. Therefore, the PRC has still a long way to go before it can fully guarantee its economic security (Fang 1993: 17–19; Yan 1993: 9).

Since the late 1980s and especially after the Persian Gulf War, the PRC has attached greater importance to preserving its maritime resources. As a high-ranking PLA navy officer emphasized in April 1992, "it is high time for China to readjust its marine strategy and make more efforts to recover the oil and gas resources in the South China Sea" (Gao 1992). In early 1996 the National People's Congress passed the Laws of Territorial Waters and Contiguous Zones, reaffirming China's sovereignty over the Nansha Islands.[12] In May 1996 the National People's Congress ratified the U.N. Convention on the Law of the Sea, which provides a legal basis for China's claim to a 200-nautical-mile Exclusive Economic Zone. Beijing has also accelerated the development of its maritime resources in recent years. For instance, since 1992 China has been cooperating with a U.S. oil company, Crestone Energy Corporation, to explore oil and natural gas in the South China Sea. According to the Ninth Five-Year Plan for National Economic and Social Development (1996–2000), marine output is expected to reach 5 percent of the gross domestic product. To protect its maritime rights and interests, the PRC now grants a higher priority to the modernization of its navy. The PLA has abandoned its long-held "coastal defense strategy" and adopted the "green water defense strategy," thus expanding China's strategic frontier to cover the various maritime territories claimed by Beijing.

Strong Military

Although in the early 1980s Deng Xiaoping had come to the conclusion that a world war could be averted for the foreseeable future, the PRC's defense doctrine remained unchanged. With the goal of being prepared for "fighting a people's war under modern conditions," military reform, as part of the overall defense modernization drive, focused on reducing military personnel, streamlining and reorganizing the force structure, establishing army groups and special troops, and raising the caliber of both professional soldiers and regular army troops. The rationale for the reform was the need to prepare the PLA for fighting a major anti-aggression war on Chinese territory. The "people's war" theory—which stresses manpower rather than weapons and technology, and embraces such tactics as "luring the enemy in deep" (*you di shen ru*), "protracted war of attrition" (*chi jiu zhan*), and "entire nation in arms" (*quan min jie bing*)—was regarded as still relevant and in need of only some adjustment and supplementation.

During the late 1980s this defense doctrine was challenged by some security analysts who suggested that of the three kinds of war that the defense strategy envisioned—a world war, a large-scale war of aggression against China, and border conflicts or limited war—the first two were unlikely to occur and the third would be China's major defense concern. This argument called for a fundamental revision of China's defense doctrine as well as a series of reforms in the PLA's force structure, training, operational doctrine, and weapons systems (Chu 1994: 186–88).

The end of the Cold War and especially the outbreak of the Persian Gulf War prompted the PLA leadership to turn to the school of limited warfare. A new defense doctrine was developed that emphasized the following points:

1. What China will probably encounter in the future is limited, local war on its periphery. Such conflict is likely to be of low intensity and short duration, emphasizing the joint operation of air and naval power, and the use of high-tech weapons systems and the most advanced military technology.

2. Given the nature of the warfare and the necessity of protecting China's economic centers in the coastal areas, the PLA should do its best to engage the enemy on the periphery and thus to minimize the economic damage that would be inflicted by the extension of war into the interior.

3. The ability to fight such a war successfully entails the creation of a smaller, highly trained and motivated, technologically advanced, and well-coordinated military force operating under a modern combined arms tactical operations doctrine utilizing sophisticated Command, Control, Communication and Intelligence (C^3I) systems (Swaine 1996: 203).

The new defense doctrine of "limited local war under modern conditions" requires readjustment of the PLA's force structure. The order of priority in the traditional force structure was ground, air, and naval forces, with the ground forces constituting a vast majority. The new doctrine changed the order of priority to naval, air, and ground forces. The navy and air force have high priority in the modernization drive, while in the modernization of ground forces, the emphasis is on technical arms (Liu 1993: 2). To develop the PLA's rapid reaction capability, efforts have been made to build some well-equipped "first units."

The major problem the PLA would face in fighting a high-tech limited war is its outdated weaponry and its poor C^3I system. Therefore, military reform stresses the development of air and naval electronic warfare systems, improved missile and aircraft guidance systems, precision-guided missiles, communications and early-warning satellites, and in-flight refueling technology (Swaine 1996: 203–4). While mobilizing its military research and development capability, China also has purchased from Russia a variety of advanced weapons, including Su-27 fighters, S-300 surface-to-air missiles, and Kilo-class conventional submarines. Other weapons are reported to be on the shopping list: MiG-31 fighters, Tu-22M bombers, Il-76 airborne warning and control system aircraft, and an airborne early-warning system (Sutter and Kan 1994: 11).

After a decade of relative decline, the PRC's defense budget has experienced double-digit growth since 1989,[13] partly to offset the impact of high inflation and partly to upgrade military equipment. Official figures show that in 1994 China's expenditure on national defense totaled 55.071 billion RMB yuan, of which 34.09 percent was spent on living expenses, 34.22 percent on maintenance of activities, and 31.69 percent on equipment (Information Office of the State Council of the PRC 1995: 14). This means that less than one-third of the PRC's military expenditure was devoted to updating the PLA's weapons inventory. However, some foreign observers believe that the actual defense spending and allocations for weapons development are much higher than the official figures, though they differ on the exact amount.[14]

PRC leaders recognize that it will not be possible to rapidly narrow the technological gap between the PLA and its counterparts in the developed nations. Partly for this reason and, more important, to secure a reliable balance of power among the major powers, the PRC works hard to modernize its strategic weaponry. Efforts have focused on the qualitative improvement of intercontinental and intermediate-range ballistic missile capabilities and the creation of a more potent, though small, tactical nuclear arsenal for possible use in local war scenarios (Swaine 1996: 204). These efforts explain why China continued to conduct nuclear tests until 1996 even though the United States, Russia, and Britain had declared a moratorium on nuclear tests.

In this connection some have suggested that Chinese nuclear doctrine is in the midst of change. Alastair Johnston, for example, suggests that since the late 1980s, the PRC strategists have developed a concept of "limited deterrence" to describe the kind of deterrent China *ought* to have (Johnston 1996). Limited deterrence rests on a limited war-fighting capability aimed at communicating China's ability to inflict costly damage on the adversary at every rung on the escalation ladder and thus to deny the adversary victory in a nuclear war. Given that China does not presently have the operational capabilities to implement this vision of limited deterrence, Johnston argues that over the next decade or so Beijing will gradually seek to shift from a minimum strike-back assured destruction posture toward one of limited war-fighting. Johnston admits that his analysis of the nature and implications of limited deterrence thinking requires additional testing. Meanwhile, other studies suggest that although Beijing is clearly committed to modernizing and perfecting its strategic nuclear forces, China's long-term thinking about the use of nuclear weapons will combine with constraints on scarce resources to limit Beijing to a second-strike, countervalue nuclear doctrine (Institute for National Strategic Studies, U.S. National Defense University 1997: 50).

Diplomatic Maneuvering: Struggle and Cooperation

To bolster its major-power status and to create a favorable international environment for its domestic economic development, the PRC, drawing upon its profound diplomatic tradition, has developed a set of sophisticated strategies.

The first is freedom of action. The PRC leaders believe that an independent diplomatic posture enables China to exploit every possible opportunity in international relations and thus maximizes its weight. As Deng Xiaoping put it, "China is in itself a poor country, [so] why do people talk about China–U.S.–USSR 'great triangle'? It's just because we act independently and keep the initiative in our own hands" (Deng 1993: 311). China once entered into an alliance with the Soviet Union, and in the late 1970s it approached the United States to form an anti-Soviet united front. In the early 1980s, however, the PRC leaders decided that China should abstain from forming an alliance with any country or group of countries, and from joining any military bloc, because alliances and tight alignments limit freedom of maneuver (Xue and Pei 1988: 340).

The second approach, which is deeply rooted in China's strategic tradition, is to create or maintain a favorable balance of power in the world arena. Currently, the PRC leaders believe that the United States, as the only remaining superpower, constitutes the primary constraint on China's international maneuvering. China, therefore, seeks the following:

- To divert U.S. pressure by developing close political or strategic relations with real and potential adversaries of the United States, such as Russia, India, and Iran

- To isolate the United States by exploring contradictions among its allies—for instance, using economic incentives to lure Japan and the Western European countries to pursue China policies different from that of the United States

- To balance U.S. influence by forging strong ties with the Third World states through economic aid and efforts to defend their rights and interests internationally

• To undermine the dominant role of the United States in world affairs by encouraging multipolarity in the post–Cold War power structure

The third approach is to deal with other nations, as much as possible, in bilateral settings. Beijing dislikes and lacks confidence in its ability to manage complex multilateral relations, preferring the simplicity of bilateral interactions. At the same time, bilateralism allows China to exploit its relative superiority over a weaker adversary. When the PRC is confronted with a stronger power, such as the United States, bilateral dealings prevent the strong rival from mobilizing the support of other countries and international organizations.[15] So far China has been involved in bilateral negotiations over border disputes or in diplomatic or security dialogues with Vietnam, India, the United States, Japan, and ASEAN. Following this approach, Beijing rejects the idea of discussing the South China Sea sovereignty dispute in the ARF and insists on negotiating in bilateral settings with other parties to the dispute. (Because Beijing claims sovereignty over the entire Spratlys, multilateral discussion could cause Beijing to be confronted with a united front formed by other disputants, thus putting it in a disadvantageous position.)

A final approach is to pursue omnidirectional diplomacy. To create a favorable international environment, the PRC leadership manages its foreign relations pragmatically. As Deng Xiaoping emphasized in the wake of the Tiananmen Square incident, "In spite of troubles in Eastern Europe and the Soviet Union, in spite of the G-7 sanctions against us, we stick to one principle: to continue to deal with the Soviet Union and manage well relations with it; to continue to deal with the United States and manage well relations with it; to continue to deal with Japan and Europe and manage well relations with them" (Deng 1993: 359).

The practice of omnidirectional diplomacy does not mean that China weighs equally each of its bilateral ties. Instead, there are two focal points: relations with the developed nations, particularly the United States (essential to China's access to international markets, capital, and technology), and relations with surrounding countries (indispensable for securing long-term tranquility on China's periphery and for reducing external assistance to and support for the ethnic minority separatists).

One of the most conspicuous features of China's foreign policy since the 1980s has been the shift in its attitude toward the international system. Before the 1980s the PRC leadership harbored deep suspicion of the international system. There are three main reasons for this attitude, all with historical roots. First, from the 1840s to the 1940s China's record of engaging the modern world-system—vastly different from the

Sinocentric world order—was basically a failure, and after 1949 the PRC was isolated from the international community for almost thirty years. Such experiences inevitably weakened China's confidence in dealing with global society. Second, China's strong sense of vulnerability caused Beijing to believe that the Western-dominated international society was full of "traps and tricks," so that China could become an easy victim. Such distrust was exacerbated by the fact that China was not writing the rules of the game. Finally, China's domestic politics, its level of socio-economic development, and its very limited connection with the outside world caused the PRC leaders to adopt a traditional concept of sovereignty. In their opinion, the best way to protect China's sovereignty from being violated was to shun international institutions and regimes.

Much has changed since China opened its doors to the outside world. State actors seem more flexible than before in dealing with international competitors. The extent to which China would be willing to share sovereignty with them depends on how such sharing would affect its own political and material interests, and on whether China would have a role in framing the rules. The most difficult thing would be for Beijing to give any external actor a voice in China's internal politics. To yield on that issue, PRC leaders believe, would not only violate China's core value of sovereignty but also undermine the legitimacy of the regime and its political control.

In the military-security arena, China has been willing to make some compromises on certain issues after deliberately weighing gains and losses. For example, China consented to abide by the Missile Technology Control Regime in exchange for some trade-offs with the United States. But, because China is not a formal party to the treaty and has no voice in setting the rules, its compliance is reluctant and controversial. In 1995 the PRC published its first defense white paper. Although others have been critical of the paper, given China's military tradition of secrecy its publication was a notable event. The act was intended to dispel the notion of the "China threat" and to respond to the consensus reached within the ARF, of which China is a member.

On the economic front, as China endeavors to merge its own economy with the global economy, Chinese leaders are well aware of the necessity to play by the rules of the international game. Beijing has gradually become accustomed to adjusting its trade policy and practice to the international standard; this is especially obvious in China's efforts to join the GATT and the WTO. In the environmental sector, China recognizes that environmental problems sometimes transcend national and regional boundaries and that a global approach is in the interest of all countries and regions. In this regard, China has committed to certain international requirements and cooperated with international actors. But Beijing insists that each country enjoys sovereign rights over its national resources and biological species and has the right to draw up and carry out its own strategies for environmental protection and development in light of national conditions (Li 1992: 8).

The PRC understands that the best way to defend its interests in the international political, economic, and security realms is to make its own voice heard in the rule-making process. For example, when the United States and its allies tried to pass a resolution at the annual session of the U.N. Commission on Human Rights condemning China's human rights record, Beijing proposed that the commission be reformed in order to end unequal application of human rights standards, to prevent abuse of the supervision mechanism, and to stop trampling on the U.N. charter, which stipulates the principle of noninterference in other countries' internal affairs. The PRC also suggested that the commission should prohibit a few big powers from imposing their ideological values on others, should give priority to addressing large-scale violations of human rights such as racism and foreign invasions, and should pay more attention to the right of development (*Beijing Review* 1995a). In the case of nuclear nonproliferation, Beijing has advocated an international convention specifying no first use of nuclear weapons, as well as an international legal instrument to safeguard nonnuclear states and nuclear-weapons-free zones against the use or threat of use of nuclear weapons (*China Daily* 1995).

The PRC's efforts to enhance its international influence have encountered some problems. As China merges into the international system, it has to show respect for and commitment to international practices and standards, and it must become responsive to international consensus. That necessity inevitably limits the PRC's opportunity for independent action. The issue of nuclear testing is a typical example. Although China may need to conduct more tests to upgrade its nuclear weaponry, it had to respond to international pressure after the negotiation of the Comprehensive Nuclear Test Ban Treaty by declaring a moratorium on nuclear testing in July 1996.

The growth of multilateralism in the post–Cold War era has challenged the PRC's preference for bilateralism. Like it or not, China has had to participate in the ARF and discuss regional security issues in a multilateral framework. As the role of ideology in Chinese foreign policy has declined, ties between China and other Third World countries have loosened, and the international resources that China can draw upon are decreasing. As the PLA's modernization drive proceeds and China's rapid economic growth raises the prospect of its becoming a world power, the concern over a China threat grows in neighboring countries, thus straining the PRC's good-neighbor policy.

Preserving Territorial Integrity: The Case of Taiwan

The Taiwan issue stands as a prototype of the PRC's use of multiple means to deal with a vital security concern. Beijing's strategy consists of three elements: international pressure, military deterrence, and political and economic inducements. Beijing holds to the "one China" principle in its foreign relations: "There is but one China and Taiwan is a part of China; the government of the People's Republic of China is the only legitimate government of China." The PRC insists that any country that has diplomatic ties with Beijing should not establish official relations with Taipei. It endeavors to frustrate every effort on the part of Taiwan to join international organizations as a separate sovereign state and seeks—through diplomatic pressures and economic aid—to reduce Taiwan's international recognition so as to isolate it in the world arena.

The PRC has always kept military pressure on Taiwan to prevent it from separating. Beijing declares that it will use every possible means, including military force, to preserve national territorial integrity. While indicating that it will do its best to resolve the Taiwan issue peacefully, the PRC refuses to reject the use of force. For instance, Beijing saw the visit to Cornell University by Taiwanese leader Lee Teng-hui in June 1995 as an overt effort to create "two Chinas" or "one China, one Taiwan." In response, the PLA conducted a series of military exercises in the Taiwan Straits to send a warning to Taipei. Before Taiwan's first presidential election in March 1996, the PLA launched missiles in waters adjacent to Taiwan in an attempt to prevent the Taiwanese from voting for the secessionists. Although such actions have created some tensions in the Taiwan Straits, military measures are believed to be the most effective means of deterring Taiwan from seeking de jure independence.

At the same time Beijing has used political and economic measures in an attempt to draw Taiwan closer to the mainland. In the early 1980s Deng Xiaoping created the formula "one country, two systems" as a way to achieve national reunification. According to this idea, Taiwan would retain its present political system and its own army after reunification. Since the early 1990s two nongovernmental bodies, the Beijing-based Association for Relations across the Taiwan Straits (ARATS) and the Taiwan-based Straits Exchange Foundation (SEF), have held several rounds of talks on issues such as the repatriation of airplane hijackers, illegal immigration, and the settlement of fishing disputes. On January 30, 1995, President Jiang Zemin made an eight-point proposal on the development of relations between the two sides of the Taiwan Straits and the peaceful reunification of China. In his speech, Jiang stressed that "Chinese should not fight their compatriots," making explicit the PRC's stance on the use of force against Taiwan (*Beijing Review* 1995c).[16]

Special attention has been paid to enhancing cross-straits economic interaction. In Beijing's calculus, increased commerce will lead Taiwan to depend heavily for its economic growth on the relatively cheap labor, huge market, and rich resources of the mainland, thus creating a great stake for Taiwan in reunification with the mainland. To this end, since the late 1970s the PRC has been appealing for and encouraging direct commercial, communication, and transportation links between the two sides of the straits. PRC leaders have formulated a series of preferential policies to attract Taiwanese investment to the mainland. Beijing's "market attraction strategy" has been partly successful. By the end of 1996, Taiwan's total investment in the mainland exceeded $20 billion, and investment in the mainland accounted for 80 percent of total external investment by Taiwanese industry. Cross-straits trade in 1996 totaled $22.2 billion; the mainland had become Taiwan's biggest export market and the number-one source of trade surplus (Tamura 1996; Central News Agency 1997).[17]

The PRC's policy toward Taiwan has met with both successes and problems. So far Beijing has been quite successful in preventing the international community from recognizing Taiwan as a sovereign state. Cross-straits economic, cultural, and social links have expanded significantly since the late 1980s. Because Hong Kong has been returned to China, direct commercial, communication, and transportation between Taiwan and the mainland will be inevitable and will greatly advance Beijing's objective of seeking unification through integrating Taiwan into a web of wide links with the mainland. Further, China believes that its military exercises in the Taiwan Straits in 1995 and early 1996 demonstrated to the world, especially the United States, its determination to prevent Taiwan from breaking away. On the other hand, the PRC's Taiwan policy has been challenged by the growing influence of the Democratic Progressive Party and its supporters on the island. In the near term, it appears that Beijing will be unable to compel Taiwan to accept its "one China" policy and discuss unification. Although it is unlikely that Taiwan will risk declaring independence in the foreseeable future, the prospect of unification is still remote. It is largely dependent on social, economic, and political developments on the mainland as well as the flexibility of the PRC's policy toward Taiwan.

✧   ✧   ✧

In sum, the broad definition of security and the changing nature of security threats in the post–Cold War era have led to diversification of approaches to security in China. In comparison with the Cold War era, when China relied heavily on military and diplomatic means to enhance national security, in recent years the PRC has introduced a wide range of political, economic, and social measures for that purpose. Diplomatic and economic means are used most frequently, while military means have become less relevant. For instance, from the 1950s to the 1970s the buildup of military power was the top priority on China's national security agenda. Since the 1980s, however, the PRC leadership has made it clear that defense modernization should proceed at a moderate pace and should not be pursued at the expense of social and economic development.

Changes in the domestic agenda and in international politics have caused state actors in the PRC to develop a more positive attitude toward international economic and political institutions with a view to promoting China's security interests. This is especially evident on economic front. During the Mao era, China embraced autarky and had only very limited connections with the outside world. Deng's "open-door" policy, however, was aimed at integrating China into the international economy and making full use of foreign capital, technology, and markets. At the same time, PRC leaders believe that China should also exploit the international political institutions—especially the United Nations—to increase its influence in the world arena. For instance, since the adjustments of its foreign policy in 1982, China has become more and more actively involved in multilateral diplomacy within the United Nations.

Shifts in domestic priorities and the relaxation of the international situation, especially the end of the Cold War, have also caused Beijing to adopt a less confrontational approach to its security interests. Dialogue, negotiation, compromise, and cooperation have come to characterize a more rational code of conduct in the PRC's handling of world affairs. PRC leaders admit that cooperation stands as a prominent feature of post–Cold War international relations. In their calculus, the adoption of a cooperative posture not only demonstrates that China can behave as a responsible power but also best serves China's national interests by avoiding the potential political and material costs of confrontation or noncooperation. China's changing role within the ARF—from passive to active—for example, indicates that Beijing has begun to embrace the notion of cooperative security.

Since the late 1980s, the influence of both ideology and geostrategic thinking on China's foreign policy has markedly declined, and the PRC's international behavior appears to be more flexible, balanced, and rational. China's contribution to the political settlement of the Cambodian issue (including withholding support for its long-term ideological ally, the Khmer Rouge), and its help in brokering the U.S.–North Korean agreement on Pyongyang's nuclear program suggest that pragmatism figures prominently in China's foreign and security policies in the post–Cold War era.

Conclusion

China's security thinking and behavior are informed by a wide array of factors. Beijing's view of the nature of international politics has grown out of China's experiences during the "century of humiliation," its peripheral position in the international system, and Marxist-Leninist theory, which stresses contradictions, conflicts, and the predatory nature of capitalism and imperialism. The role of the state was defined by the interaction of China's cultural tradition and its domestic sociopolitical structure, in which the state was installed as a hegemon with regard to the society, the individual, and the subnational unit. Security goals are largely determined by a country's stage of socioeconomic development, its stage of nation-building, and its domestic priorities and concerns. In comparison with the developed nations, China remains committed to building a modern nation-state, and consequently its security practice coincides with the expectations of the realist paradigm. Finally, these variables—the PRC leaders' view of international politics, the role of the state, and China's stage of nation-building—combine to make self-help the foremost principle governing state action in the pursuit of security.

Realism, however, is not adequate to explain several features of China's security thinking and practice. The first one is the strong influence of ideational factors. China's humiliating experience in its modern history, its profound cultural tradition, and the Marxist-Leninist ideology together exerted a great impact on China's worldview and security behavior. The second feature is the broadening of the scope of security. Following adjustments in China's domestic priorities and changes in international relations, the notion of "comprehensive security" has been adopted. In the security equation, the socioeconomic dimension has become more prominent vis-à-vis the political-military dimension. The third feature is the salience of internal concerns. The disappearance of major external military threats, the end of the Cold War, the growing awareness of the relevance of economics to overall national strength, and rising concern with regime security, social stability, and national unification have all combined to prompt the PRC leadership to turn inward. The fourth feature is that pursuit of national security through international cooperation—a neoliberal approach—has gained some sway among the PRC political elites. Though they still harbor suspicion of international institutions, the PRC leaders are increasingly aware of the reality of growing interdependence and can hardly resist the temptation of benefits issuing from international cooperation—not only in economic and environmental areas but also on some security issues. Therefore, although the realist model is still critical in explaining China's security behavior, explanations of Chinese security practice must also recognize elements of neoliberalism and constructivism.

Among the factors that contribute to the PRC's construction of security, some (such as cultural tradition and historical experiences) are relatively stable, whereas others (such as stage of socioeconomic development, stage of nation-building, domestic sociopolitical structures, and international environment) are variable. Changes in the domestic and international contexts will inevitably lead to reconstruction of China's conception of security. As China's modernization progresses and as it becomes a stronger power with a greater vested interest in international stability, its security thinking and behavior will undergo further change. It is thus important to take an evolutionary rather than a static view of China's security practice.

India
Modified Structuralism

KANTI BAJPAI

India is a major actor in Asia and the world as a function of its geostrategic location, the size of its population, its large and growing economy, its indigenous technological capability, and its army, which is the fourth largest in the world. With the termination of the Cold War and the ongoing reforms in the Indian economy, many Indian and international observers believe that in the next two or three decades India could emerge as a great power whose reach extends well beyond South Asia. How India conceives of its security, therefore, is of international interest. In keeping with the general thrust of this book, the present chapter seeks first to explain how and why India's central decision makers think and act in the security domain as they do, and second to discuss India's behavior in terms of the various theories that have been advanced to explain the behavior of states in this regard.

I argue that India's security practice is close to what Stephen Krasner calls "modified structuralism." In the modified structuralist view, decision makers operate in "a world of sovereign states seeking to maximize their interest and power" but under certain conditions choose to transcend "individualistic calculations of interest" (Krasner 1983b: 7). In a world of sovereign states, Indian decision makers are primarily concerned with protecting the two major attributes of sovereignty: territory and independence of foreign policy. To do so, they understand that their country must be powerful. Their comprehension of national power is a broad one that includes three key elements—military strength, economic development, and internal order. But India's approach to security also goes beyond this classical conception. Its decision makers are willing to resort to methods that involve concessions to rival interests, both external and internal. With external rivals, these methods include negotiation, regular summitry, promotion of economic and cultural links between societies, confidence-building measures, nonalignment, and regional cooperation. With internal rivals, too, India has negotiated (for example, reaching peace accords with various ethnic separatists). It has also attempted to use economic incentives and rewards to end militant struggles. Most important, it has granted collective rights to dissatisfied communities and tried to decentralize power within a federal system of government.

The reason for India's modified structuralism in security affairs, I argue, is twofold: expediency, arising from deficiencies in national power; and conviction, based on the existence or evolution of norms against the untrammeled pursuit of power and exercise of coercion. Thus, India's conception of security can be understood in terms of material as well as ideational factors. Over time, our analysis suggests, India has shifted perceptibly from a modified structuralism based on conviction and ideational factors to one based on expediency and material factors. However, with economic growth, India may move toward cooperative security and a modified structuralism once again based on conviction.

To substantiate this argument as well as to elucidate Indian security thinking and behavior, this chapter is organized in four parts. The first part delineates India's historic conception of security in terms of the nationalist interpretation of Indian history, which was vital to the "operational code" of decision makers through the 1950s. The second part reviews the conceptualizations of security held by Indian strategic thinkers of the postcolonial period. Once we have abstracted India's core values from these conceptualizations, the third part discusses the threats to these values and the responses by India's central decision makers. The fourth part advances an explanation of India's conception of security.

Interpreting Indian History

Present-day ideas about national security bear the mark of history. The influence of the past on the present is not a simple one: it is not merely a residue, some essential characteristic that inheres in the present. Nor is the past infinitely malleable. Rather, historical legacies are interpreted, recovered, and constituted within the limits set by contemporary interests and constraints. India's conceptions of security since independence, in this sense, owe much to the past. Its leaders have invested the past with a certain significance that bears upon contemporary notions of security.

India's security conceptions after independence were informed by British India's strategic ideas but were not identical to them. For Britain, India was the linchpin of its empire. Control of India gave Britain prestige and material power on a world scale. British policies rested on the postulate that India is vitally located at the juncture of several regions in Asia and at the top of the Indian Ocean. On the Asian landmass, it resides between the Middle East, Russia, Central Asia, China, and Southeast Asia. In the Indian Ocean, it was Britain's key to controlling an area that extended from the Suez to the Strait of Malacca. The threats to British control of India were perceived to derive from the Asian landmass and, subsidiarily, from the ocean. On land the principal threats were from Russia and China. To protect India from them, the British constructed a system of "ring fences" comprising an "inner ring" of Himalayan kingdoms and the tribal areas of northeastern India and an "outer ring" of the Persian Gulf, Iran, Afghanistan, and Thailand. The inner ring would be defended by military power; control of the outer ring would be denied to outside powers by diplomacy and force (Kavic 1967: 9). By sea, the threats initially came from other European powers, although by the late nineteenth century there was little prospect of any real challenge there. The British navy was the key instrument for the defense of India from seaborne threats and for the projection of British power from the Cape of Good Hope to the Strait of Malacca (Kavic 1967: 9).

The view of India as a strategic linchpin was internalized by Indian nationalists. Indian governments saw great powers and other outsiders coveting India for geopolitical reasons (Kavic 1967: 20–21). British policy stressed "forward defense" and ocean control. Independent India shifted the emphasis. Jawaharlal Nehru had less faith in military instruments, though he did not ignore them.[1] Instead he stressed diplomacy—nonalignment and *panchashila* (literally "five virtues" or five principles of moral and proper conduct)[2]—and the importance of internal political stability in dissuading outsiders from threatening India (Kavic 1967: 40).

In addition to British conceptions, postindependence governments also drew on more indigenous visions, even if they were refracted through colonial lenses. In particular, they drew on an image of Indian history through the ages and a narrative of successive political invasions and internal integrations and disintegrations (Nehru 1981: 237–38). The British had helped shape that narrative in order to justify their rule. In the British narrative, imperial rule was a deliverance for Indians—a liberation from invasion and internal collapse. India was depicted as having constantly been prey to invasions. The Indian narrative, however, stressed periods of Indian glory, casting the British in the role of one among a long line of invaders. Most of the invasions, according to the nationalist narrative, came through the northwest passes via present-day Afghanistan and Pakistan. The Europeans were exceptional in that they came from the sea. These invasions succeeded because Indians were internally disunited and because they were backward—not only in terms of military hardware but also in the art of war. The incursions of the Europeans were more subtle; they came posing as traders but stayed to consolidate their commercial niches. They carved out larger and larger enclaves as they exploited internal differences between Indians (Nehru 1981: 276–81). India's suspicion of foreign investment, multinational corporations, and a globalized economic order can be traced to this reading of colonial history.

India had handled earlier invaders via social integration, but the Europeans stayed aloof. What marked the Europeans off from the others—and made them more powerful—was not just their technology but their entire social system, which, in its insistence on rationalism and a relatively egalitarian and competitive civic life, was superior to that of other conquerors and indeed to India's. Thus Nehru wrote: "The recent causes of [India's]...decay are obvious enough. She fell behind in the march of technique, and Europe, which had long been backward in many matters, took the lead in technical progress. Behind this technical progress was the spirit of science and a bubbling life and spirit....New techniques gave military strength to the countries of western Europe, and it was easy for them to spread out and dominate the East" (Nehru 1981: 54).

For Nehru and other Indian nationalists, India's history was marked not just by external threats and relative backwardness on a world scale but also, significantly, by long and recurring periods of internal disorder. Golden periods when India was united, well governed, socially tolerant, culturally and scientifically advanced were succeeded by dark periods of disunity, tyranny, intolerance, and cultural and scientific stagnation (Panikkar 1960: 235). For the nationalists, the chaos at the end of the Mughal Empire and the long period of British rule signified the torpor into which India had fallen. Beneath the torpor, though, there was a vitality and an immanent sense of unity in India, and the nationalist movement had begun to rediscover and release it. India could be a great force once again if its internal structure were refurbished.

The past influenced Indian thinking in another way. The precolonial past and colonial rule combined to produce a political culture that had an impact on conceptions of security. Ancient Hindu thought and practice were marked by tension between a deep involvement in social and political life, on the one hand, and a desire for detachment from the phenomenal world on the other. Thus Indian elites in the ancient past seem to have feared that involvement in social and political life would lead to disorder and violence. Their response was to withdraw from the world of phenomena and entrust order to those with the power to coerce—either through naked force or through a highly structured social system such as caste. The problem was that these social forces in turn would, by their excessive reliance on coercion, bring on the very collapse that haunted Indians. Thus India traditionally seems to have lacked an ability to produce mediating institutions capable of sustaining social order without excessive coercion. Nor did the medieval period with its various Muslim empires produce such institutions.

British liberalism provided a way out from the attachment–detachment dichotomy. It showed how mediating political institutions could be built and operated. For postcolonial India, entering a society of nation-states, this new political culture translated into a predilection for institutions that promised order without an overreliance on force. Nehru, who led India into this international society, was therefore predisposed, broadly speaking, to a liberal institutional view—one that recognized the realities of a nation-state system but also recognized that without mediating institutions that system must eventually fall prey to the disorder and violence it sought to avoid (Rana 1976: chaps. 7–8).

Apart from such conceptual influences, three key developments in international relations and domestic politics seemed to confirm and reconfirm the nationalist reading of India's history: the Cold War, hostilities between India and Pakistan, and the Communist victory in China. First, by 1948 the Cold War had begun. Nehru, as early as 1944, had understood that the United States and the Soviet Union would be the leading powers and would engage in global competition.[3] Like the colonial powers who had played Indian rulers off against one another, the superpowers would approach lesser powers all over the world with the promise of military and economic aid and then use them for their own ends. India must therefore resist being drawn into the competition. Second, the postpartition war between India and Pakistan over Kashmir meant that the division of the subcontinent had not solved the basic quarrel in South Asia; indeed it had added a layer of hostility. The postcolonial conflict between India and Pakistan can be related to the theme of internal weakness and disunity in the nationalist narrative. As India historically had been internally divided, now South Asia was internally divided between India and Pakistan, two sovereign and potentially rival states. As Hindus and Muslims had been manipulated by the colonial power, so India and Pakistan could be manipulated by "neocolonial" powers who wished to divide South Asia. And third, the Communist victory in China meant that India would have to rethink its relations with the Middle Kingdom. Nehru and the Congress had developed close links with the Chinese Nationalists under Chiang Kaishek. After 1949, India had to reckon with a new regime in Beijing. New Delhi could see that, depending on how the relationship evolved, India could be faced with two hostile neighbors: Pakistan and China. The new China also fitted into the nationalist narrative: as a great power that could be turned against India, thus dividing resurgent Asia against itself, but also as a potential fraternal partner in continental affairs.

Four strands were therefore central in Indian security thinking in these first moments after independence. First, India was a strategic and economic prize and would one day be a great nation. It must be vigilant in protecting its territory and its independence from external powers and forces who coveted it, wanted to dominate it, even wished to destroy it. In particular, India had to be on guard against the superpowers, Pakistan, China, and, not least, foreign capital. Second, vigilance must be backed by power. India could not expect to preserve its borders and independence if it once again lagged behind other countries. Third, India had to be stable internally. Without internal resilience and progress, Indian unity and independence could be undermined by internal and external forces, either separately or in combination. A strong state was essential if such disintegration was to be avoided. Fourth, mediating institutions were necessary in both the international and domestic spheres. Any system, external or internal, equilibrated purely by coercive power was prone to collapse. Norms and institutions at the international and domestic levels were viewed as vital to check "power politics" and to prevent collapse in the long run.

This cognitive map or operational code, it should be emphasized, has been abstracted from the ideas of Indian leaders as well as the material conditions facing India at independence, which reinforced those ideas. A more systematic statement of Indian security conceptions would have to wait until the 1960s and 1970s and beyond.

Defining India's Security in the Postcolonial Period

From the vantage point of the present, there is a tendency to think that India neglected security and defense in the immediate postcolonial period at both the conceptual and material levels. There are at least three reasons for this view. First, after independence the term *security* was rarely used. The preferred term was *defense*. This usage reflected the relative currencies of the two terms in the Anglo-American world. British usage favored the term *defense*, and even in the United States, which has done so much to popularize the term *security*, its use was not as widespread as it would become by the 1950s and 1960s. Second, with regard to "defense," the extent of public debate in India was minimal. This relative silence reflected the British inheritance, which stressed secrecy in colonial military matters; it also reflected Nehru's worries about "militarism" in India. Third, India's defeat at the hands of China in 1962, never thoroughly probed, was attributed to political and administrative oversight and lapses—hence the charge that security and defense were ignored.

A more nuanced retrospective view of the period reveals, however, that although security (or defense) was neglected by the Indian National Congress prior to independence, it was an important area of postindependence endeavor, and that the oversight and lapses were more of a conceptual than material nature. Nehru himself, his defense minister and trusted lieutenant, Krishna Menon, the historian and diplomat K. M. Panikkar, the jurist H. N. Kunzru, as well as an additional group of officials (e.g., H. M. Patel, H. C. Sarin, P. V. R. Rao), all were attentive to security/defense, especially in material terms. Nehru and his team attempted to evolve a new decision-making system for security/defense, they invested in an indigenous defense and nuclear industry, and they bought major weapons systems from abroad when necessary (Chris Smith 1994: 44–73). Indeed, "Indian decision-makers were more ambitious than they were cautious [in defense], especially on the procurement side" (Chris Smith 1994: 42).

India's war experiences, in 1962 with China and in 1965 and 1971 with Pakistan, were important milestones in the development of a more self-conscious discourse that attempted to explicitly define the nature of security/defense. With each war, there grew a realization that, materially, Indian security/defense had been and probably was more or less adequate. What was lacking was integrated decision making, technical expertise, and sufficient attention to the long-term assessment of threats, instruments, and strategies.

From the 1970s onward, therefore, a discourse based on the term *security* increasingly came to be articulated, not so much within the state apparatus as by a growing and vocal policy community, located in New Delhi, consisting of diplomats, bureaucrats, politicians, soldiers, journalists, and academics. That community increasingly resorted to the word *security* and began a conceptual delineation of the term.

Thus K. Subrahmanyam, perhaps the leading member of India's strategic community and a former Defense Ministry official, cites the *Encyclopedia of the Social Sciences* definition of security, the "ability of a nation to protect its internal values from external threat." He also approvingly quotes Walter Lippman's famous definition: "A nation has security when it does not have to sacrifice its legitimate interests to avoid war and is able, if challenged, to maintain them by war" (Subrahmanyam 1972: 67; D. Singh n.d.: 126–27). Similarly, H. C. Sarin, a former Indian defense secretary, suggests that "for a nation, security is a state of mind when it is able to apply its resources to activities it considers germane to its national purpose without having to be unduly concerned about extraneous considerations" (Sarin 1979: 9).

Subrahmanyam argues that national security goes beyond "threats to our territorial integrity and sovereignty" to encompass "economic development plans" and "communal harmony" (Subrahmanyam 1972: 68). This broader conception has been articulated by others as well. A major seminar in New Delhi, attended by virtually the entire Indian security community, held that

> in the contemporary world threats to security were not limited to threats of military action or occupation of territory....In defining 'security' it was felt that too narrow a view—one which looked at it purely in terms of prevention of military invasions and loss of terri- tory—should be avoided. 'Security,' properly understood, was a far wider concept covering to a lesser degree or greater degree almost all aspects of the domestic situation in a nation, as well as its military pre- paredness and foreign policy. (U. S. Bajpai 1983: 9)

Govind Narain, another former defense secretary, writes that national security "is much wider and much more comprehensive [than territorial integrity]. It extends virtually to all the freedoms that we cherish and wish to enjoy and to uninterrupted and uninterfered imple- mentation of all that we plan, intend or wish to do for our country" (Narain 1986: 16). Finally, a knowledgeable and articulate former defense minister, K. C. Pant, argues: "National Security is a broad con- cept, which covers political stability, which covers economic growth, economic strength of the country, and obviously it covers defense pre- paredness. These are well recognized aspects of National Security, and they are in very many ways interdependent" (Pant 1988: 4).

At the heart of these definitions is, first, the idea that the state is the referent of security, the entity that must be protected. This is not particularly surprising. That the state is the primary referent is a classical formulation: in the Indian *Arthashastra* tradition as in Aristotle, a secure state is regarded as a necessary, though not sufficient, condition for the security of other social entities and individual citizens (Rana 1976: 149).

Second is the idea that security lies in the protection of a set of interdependent values: territorial integrity, foreign policy autonomy, military strength (referred to as "defense preparedness"), economic development ("economic growth," "economic strength"), and internal order ("communal harmony," "domestic situation," "political stability"). Indian decision makers and analysts do not regard this list of values as being particularly controversial: a survey of official documents and pronouncements shows widespread agreement on them. Third, although there is no clear statement of priorities among the five core values, we can infer that territorial integrity and political autonomy are primary, for they are intrinsic to the notion of sovereignty. The other values—military strength, economic development, and internal order—can be regarded as secondary or instrumental values in that they are necessary for the fullest attainment of sovereignty. In other words, control of one's territory and the freedom to choose one's enemies and friends depends on military, economic, and domestic political resilience—a classical national security formulation.

Threats to Core Security Values and India's Responses

A national security conceptualization is incomplete without an assessment of threats to core values and strategies to contain or eliminate those threats. As we will see in the following sections, the threats to virtually every core value are simultaneously external and internal, with the two levels interacting in ways that exacerbate India's security problems. The Indian state's strategies for coping with this complex environment of threats are correspondingly varied, exhibiting a reliance on force and coercion but also more institutional, noncoercive, and indirect measures.

Territorial Integrity

Three territorial issues have been of concern to India's decision makers. First, there was the problem of integrating the various units of the British Empire—the states of British India plus the Princely States—as well as the French and Portuguese colonial possessions. Second, there were external threats to India's territorial integrity. And third, territorial integrity was threatened from within by secessionists aided and abetted by external foes.

The first challenge was dealt with almost immediately by the integration of the Princely States into the Indian Union. Most of the princes quickly acceded to either India or Pakistan, but a few hoped to stay independent or chose sides that went against the demographic composition of their states. Hyderabad and Junagadh were the most important cases. Indian military action in 1948 ended their independence. Kashmir was the other key state. When tribal invaders backed by Pakistani forces attempted to incorporate the state into Pakistan, India resisted with force. Most of Kashmir was saved and gradually became integrated into the Indian Union. With regard to the colonial territories of Pondicherry and Goa, France quickly signed over Pondicherry, and India argued that Goa, too, must be returned by Portugal because colonial enclaves were unacceptable on the Indian landmass. Nehru negotiated, but when the Portuguese proved intransigent India took Goa by force in 1961.

The second and third challenges to India's territorial integrity persist. The principal external threats issue from Pakistan and China. The threat from Pakistan relates primarily to Kashmir; the Chinese threat concerns the demarcation of the Sino-Indian border.

Kashmir is the subject of the most important quarrel between India and Pakistan. Since 1948, when Pakistan questioned the accession of the Princely State of Kashmir to the Indian Union, it has stood at the center of their troubled relationship. As a result of the 1948 war, the Kashmiri state was divided between the two countries. Neither accepts the partition. For India, Kashmir accounts for only about 4 per cent of its national territory (and only 1 per cent of its total population), but its presence in the Union represents much more than territorial completeness. As long as Kashmiris stay within the Union, they affirm India's secular credentials—and, by extension, falsify Pakistan's claim that Muslims need a separate homeland in the subcontinent. Thus Kashmir is vital to India's construction of its national identity.

Since the end of the "long peace" of 1972–89, Kashmir has become the critical issue in Indo-Pakistani relations. New Delhi is convinced that Pakistan instigated the present troubles in Kashmir and that it continues to provide refuge, training, money, and arms to the militants.[4] India fears that this proxy war could again escalate to full-fledged combat as in 1948 and 1965. If the situation in Kashmir deteriorates and Pakistan perceives a weak or distracted government in India, it might choose to attack.

The territorial conflict with China dates to 1954. At issue are the Aksai Chin area in the west and the Northeast Frontier Agency (NEFA) in the east (Steven Hoffman 1990: 9). It appears that China was willing to swap Aksai Chin for its claims in NEFA (Steven Hoffman 1990: 86–87). If, as Nehru noted, Aksai Chin was a wasteland without "a blade of grass" (Steven Hoffman 1990: 73–74), that should have been an attractive offer. However, India opposed the idea of a swap for a number of reasons. First, Nehru saw China as an expansionist power: a strong stand was necessary in order to check it. Second, Nehru faced strong internal pressures not to swap.[5] Third, he calculated that, in the end, with Soviet and U.S. sympathies on his side, the correlation of forces was against China. Finally, India's borders were not simply artifacts of colonial rule, as claimed by the Chinese: they were of precolonial origin and intimately bound up with an Indian identity that had existed, subconsciously if not consciously, for hundreds of years (Steven Hoffman 1990: 24–28).

The border war of 1962 was followed by an uneasy but "long peace" between India and China. China annexed the Aksai Chin and then withdrew substantially from all other territories it had occupied during the hostilities. Public opinion in India, in reaction to the humiliation of defeat, put a stop to any serious negotiations with China for nearly twenty years, but the earlier hysteria over the border ended. Except for occasional border skirmishes, the Line of Control has remained stable since the war.

Apart from the overland challenges from Pakistan and China, India fears intrusions into its territorial waters and its massive exclusive economic zone. From their colonial past, Indians have learned that great-power navies can be harbingers of domination. Since the early 1970s, India has been particularly anxious about the growing presence of superpower navies in the Indian Ocean. In addition, in the 1980s it has watched the growth of the Chinese navy and the development of its capacity to sail the Indian Ocean on a regular basis. Beijing's deepening relationship with Burma has added to Indian fears. New Delhi has seen China develop Burmese ports and is worried that the Chinese navy may make use of the Hanggyi Islands. Finally, India recognizes that in case of war Pakistan could attack vital oil-producing areas near Mumbai.

India faces internal threats to territory as well. In Kashmir, Punjab, and the northeastern states, India has been challenged by a number of secessionist groups that have been supported by outside powers, most notably Pakistan and China. Kashmir, since 1989, has become the country's major internal security problem. Sikh militancy in the Punjab was a separatist threat from the early 1980s until 1993. Sikh dissidents found their way to Pakistan and obtained refuge, training, arms, and money from their hosts. By 1993, India had brought the militancy under control and the Punjab had reverted to near normalcy. The seven northeastern states have almost constantly been at war with New Delhi. The uprisings have been instigated or sustained by external support— mostly by China (until the mid-1970s) but also by various groups or state agencies in Burma, Bangladesh, and Pakistan. The northeast's integrity is also under threat from illegal migration from Bangladesh.[6]

Some regard Dhaka as having encouraged migration; others see it as indifferent. Migration threatens territory in two ways: it feeds separatist feelings, and it may produce Muslim majorities in those states, leading to "new Pakistans."[7]

This review suggests that the internal threats to territory are at least as significant as the external threats and, moreover, that the internal and external are deeply enmeshed. Pakistan and China present ongoing military threats to border areas, but the internal threats in Kashmir, Punjab, and the northeast, compounded by external involvement, have been the most troubling.

India has relied on a combination of force, negotiations, and indirect strategies to deal with threats to its territorial integrity. We will see this in the case of Pakistan and China but also in India's approach to its ocean territories and to secessionism.

The 1948 war put paid to the hope that partition would pacify South Asia. Lord Louis Mountbatten had hoped that India and Pakistan would combine against external threats and contribute to British and Commonwealth strategic defense. Indeed, he had persuaded the two sides to agree to a joint defense council that in the postpartition period would help coordinate defense policies (Hodson 1985: 507–16). When the Kashmir war broke out, the idea of joint defense collapsed. Henceforth the Indian army's primary orientation was against Pakistan. Most of India's land forces were deployed in Kashmir and along the western border with Pakistan, not on the northern border with China. This remains India's posture.

Border defense has been supplemented by an interest in confidence-building measures. Thus, India offered Pakistan a no-war declaration in 1949, 1953, 1956, 1959, 1968, and 1969. Pakistan responded that the issue of Kashmir must be resolved before a no-war pact could be signed. Islamabad advanced its own proposals for joint defense in 1953 and 1959; New Delhi, fearing it would be sucked into the Cold War, rejected them. Since the early 1980s India has emphasized confidence-building measures, and the two sides have agreed to the following: prohibition of attack on nuclear installations and facilities; advance notification of exercises, maneuvers, and troop movements; prevention of airspace violations and permission for overflights and landings by military aircraft; a joint declaration on the prohibition of chemical weapons; and a hot line between the armed forces.

Confidence-building is intended to stabilize a military situation; it is not intended to bring about a resolution of the fundamental dispute. From time to time, India has made efforts to solve the Kashmir problem and other territorial disputes with Pakistan through bilateral and multilateral negotiations. In October 1954, the prime ministers of the two countries attempted to resolve the Kashmir dispute bilaterally; by 1955 there were glimmerings of a settlement based on a plebiscite and a partition of the state. Two years later, agreement was reached on the border between India and East Pakistan and on the future of each country's enclaves in the other's territories. In 1960, the two countries settled five disputed claims along the West Pakistan–India border. After the 1962 war with China, the United States and Britain persuaded India to resume talks on Kashmir. In 1972, after the Bangladesh war, India and Pakistan agreed in the Simla Agreement to deal peacefully with their disputes, including Kashmir. India claims that at Simla, Pakistan agreed to accept a partition of Kashmir along the Line of Control. Despite its reservations, India also went along with various U.N.–led efforts to solve the Kashmir problem. These included the Nimitz and McNaughton mediations, the plebiscite negotiations (1950), the Dixon plan (1951), and the Graham efforts (1953–58). The key to most of these interventions was the idea of a plebiscite in Kashmir. Given its suspicions of Pakistan and of Anglo-American involvement in the issue,[8] India was doubtful about the possibility of a free and fair plebiscite, and in the end the U.N.'s interventions came to naught.

In addition to force and negotiations, India has tried to engineer less direct methods of settling disputes. Since the 1965 war, it has argued for the "normalization" of relations with Pakistan. India envisions a dense network of government-to-government and society-to-society links that would enmesh Pakistan and lead Pakistanis to a reevaluation of basic interests. An issue such as Kashmir, like other territorial disputes, would in time be superseded. In 1969, in 1972, in 1979 after the Soviets invaded Afghanistan, and repeatedly thereafter, India has argued for easing restrictions on trade, travel, and communications and for the normalization of diplomatic and cultural interactions.

New Delhi's approach to the border dispute with China has also featured a combination of force, negotiations, and indirection. In 1950 India embarked on a border defense plan that included building roads and check posts, increasing intelligence activity and patrolling, and creating border police forces (Kavic 1967: 40). In the late 1950s, in the key western sector, India pursued the "forward policy," a program of establishing small, isolated check posts in disputed areas. These posts and patrols were intended to block intrusive Chinese forces more aggressively, subvert Chinese control, and threaten communications and supply lines (Kavic 1967: 169). The policy led to a heightening of tensions. In 1959, Indian army units were ordered to evict intruding Chinese forces, and contingency plans were drawn up for major clashes (Kavic 1967: 86–89).

After the 1962 border war, India built up its forces rapidly, eventually deploying ten divisions along the front and equipping them with modern weaponry that outstripped Chinese capabilities. In 1974, India's nuclear test was a signal that New Delhi would harden its defense posture. By the early 1980s, India was militarily confident. When Indian and then Chinese units established a presence in the Sumdurong Chu Valley in 1986–87, India responded aggressively in the ensuing confrontation.[9] Later in 1987, the Indian military held a massive exercise—once again demonstrating that it was prepared to meet force with force.[10]

While building up its defense forces along the Sino-Indian border, India also resorted to confidence-building measures in an effort to avoid border clashes. In May 1980, India and China issued a joint communiqué on the need to avoid border clashes. The initial list of formal measures included hot lines between local army commanders, face-to-face meetings between commanders, and prior notification of army exercises. In September 1993, additional measures were instituted: pledges to respect the Line of Actual Control (LOAC); force reductions along the LOAC; limits on military exercises and prior notification; consultations between border personnel in a crisis; measures to prevent air intrusions across the LOAC, with possible restrictions on air exercises near the line; and expert groups to help resolve differences over the LOAC.[11] During President Venkatraman's visit to China, a joint statement noted that confidence-building measures were intended to improve relations and lead to "an early, fair, reasonable, and mutually acceptable settlement" of the border problem (Ganguly and Greenwood 1996: 226–27). President Jiang Zemin's return visit in 1996 furthered the confidence-building process. The 1993 measures were amplified. Most important, the two sides agreed to reduce forces to "minimal" levels in mutually defined zones, to scale down "major" categories of armaments in border areas, to eventually replace military with paramilitary and police forces along the Line of Actual Control, to stop firing and blasting within 2 kilometers of the Line of Actual Control, and to increase transparency in military matters.

Concurrently with conventional defense and confidence-building measures, India has at various times sought to resolve the Chinese border problem through bilateral negotiations. New Delhi first raised the border issue with the PRC in 1954. Zhou Enlai assured India that the problem lay in the "reproduction of the old preliberation maps" and said that those maps would be revised (Kavic 1967: 63). Subsequently, New Delhi conceded China's "liberation" of Tibet, gave up its Tibetan rights in 1954, and signed the "Panchashila" agreement with Beijing that committed both sides to nonaggression (Kavic 1967: 44). In the late

1950s, Nehru tried to get China to agree to the MacMahon Line as the border, but Beijing brusquely refused. In January 1960, Zhou suggested setting up a joint border commission, but India rejected the idea, contending that the frontier required only minor adjustments. When New Delhi proposed that officials meet to consider the documentary evidence, China agreed, but viewed the meeting as a way of setting up a joint-survey team. The subsequent meetings of officials charged with resolving the boundary question failed to achieve much (Steven Hoffman 1990: 88–89). In general, India favored a legalistic, sector-by-sector approach based on some general principles to delineate the border, whereas China preferred a more political approach consisting of concessions and compromise across sectors.

After the impasse of 1960–61, negotiations ended and were resumed only in the 1980s. In June 1981, both sides made procedural concessions. China dropped its insistence on a package deal that stressed the linkage of adjustments in one sector of the border to adjustments in other sectors. India, for its part, abandoned its commitment not to discuss substantive issues until China withdrew from "Indian" territory occupied in 1962 (Ganguly 1989: 1126). Border talks have continued through the 1990s.

Since the 1980s, India and China have agreed to various indirect strategies aimed at improving the climate for negotiations. The two sides have pursued a process of normalization. Trade, cultural, scientific, and political exchanges to some extent have been delinked from the ups and downs of the border talks and other strategic disagreements. Bilateral trade in particular has responded to normalization, rising from $200 million in 1991 to $670 million in 1993 and to $1.02 billion in 1995. With both economies growing and with encouragement from the two governments, these figures are expected to increase further. A process of summitry has been initiated. Thus the foreign ministers met in New York before the sixth round of border talks. Prime Minister Rajiv Gandhi and Premier Zhao Ziyang held a brief summit, also in New York, in October 1985. The foreign ministers conferred again after the seventh round of border talks. Finally, Rajiv Gandhi made a state visit in December 1988, as did the Indian president in 1992 and Prime Minister Narasimha Rao in 1993. Premier Li Peng came to India in 1991, and President Jiang Zemin in 1996. This brings to six the number of high-level visits in the past eleven years. In short, beginning in 1980 the two sides entered a phase of relatively normal diplomacy. Although this process has had its limits, it has been seen as an essential complement to negotiations over the border conflict.

The combination of force, negotiations, and indirection can also be observed with respect to India's ocean territories. Since the early 1970s New Delhi has built up its naval forces to counter not only the great-power navies but also those of Pakistan and China. It has tried negotiating. In the 1960s and 1970s, India labored hard in the United Nations to develop the idea of the Indian Ocean as a zone of peace where the activities of nonregional navies would be restricted (Marwah 1987: 299–317). It is now trying indirect measures. India has become part of a fourteen-member group called the Indian Ocean Rim Association for Regional Cooperation (IOR-ARC) that will focus on economic, environmental, and technical issues. By fostering cooperation among the major countries, IOR-ARC will, New Delhi hopes, make the ocean more secure.[12]

In essence, the same combination of approaches has been applied to separatist struggles too. The Kashmiri militancy—like the Sikh militancy before it—is being fought by the massive use of the regular army, paramilitary forces, and local police. India is defending the northeast using a similar combination of means. When the government senses that the militants are fatigued, it holds out the possibility of negotiations. Meanwhile it deploys a strategy of indirection toward the society: the military engages in local health and relief work; economic and other developmental activities are increased; eventually, an amnesty releases militants captured during counterinsurgency operations, new elections are held in the state, the separatist organization is brought in from the cold, often to govern the state, and a peace accord is signed wherein the government makes concessions relating to major grievances.[13]

India's approach to territorial security relies on military force and confidence-building, on the one hand, and negotiations and indirect strategies on the other. That is, it combines coercive approaches that seek to advance India's interests with measures that demonstrate readiness to concede something to the other side. The mix of approaches is not necessarily a conscious and carefully calibrated policy of sticks and carrots. Idiosyncratic decisions, the attitudes and actions of adversaries, and domestic politics and public opinion influence India's stance at any given time. But at a deeper level, policy is shaped by an equilibrating tendency in Indian political thought. There is, as suggested earlier, an understanding that power-based, coercive approaches by themselves cannot bring peace and stability in the long term and must be tempered by conciliatory, noncoercive methods and instruments. This understanding rests on both material and ideational factors, a point we will return to later. Suffice it to say here that Indian policy on territorial security is complex and cannot be reduced to any single approach.

Foreign Policy Autonomy

At independence, Jawaharlal Nehru said in a famous remark (1983b: 241): "What does independence consist of? It consists fundamentally and basically of foreign relations. That is the test of independence. All else is local autonomy." India values foreign policy autonomy, and, for the most part, New Delhi has steered its own course. This does not mean that India has not tilted toward one great power or another at various times. It has always maintained the right to do so in its own interest. But, as the following episodes reveal, it has at key junctures maintained its own line of policy:

- At independence, despite British pressures, India refused to enter into an alliance. When the United States wanted India to join in the containment of the Soviet Union, India declined, even though it was clear that this position might incur U.S. wrath and that Pakistan would profit by enlisting in the Western alliance system (Heimsath and Mansingh 1971: 343–62). British and American sympathies for Pakistan's case on Kashmir did not cause India to recant or to shun relations with the two communist giants. Indeed, India established close relations with both.

- In 1962, when China was winning the war against India, New Delhi was vulnerable. It needed British and U.S. military aid and even sought outright military intervention. Yet Nehru was greatly exercised over the implications for Indian nonalignment, even though Washington did not insist on public expressions of solidarity with the West (Kux 1993: 204–6).

- In a last-minute attempt to join the nuclear Nonproliferation Treaty (NPT), Indira Gandhi asked for a nuclear umbrella (Mirchandani 1968: 156–67). Here was a moment when India was prepared to give up a measure of its foreign policy autonomy. When it did not get a security guarantee, India refused to sign the NPT and reverted to a policy of nuclear autonomy that it has maintained ever since.

- During the Johnson presidency, India–U.S. relations became especially strained over Vietnam. When India was hit by massive food shortages, Lyndon Johnson, annoyed by Indira Gandhi's outspokenness, slowed U.S. grain shipments to India in his famous "short tether" policy. Even so, India's stance on the Vietnam War did not appreciably change (Ganguly 1993: 87).

- India also resisted Soviet pressures when necessary. In 1969, New Delhi refused to join Moscow's anti-China "Asian Collective Security" system. The Soviet Union was India's biggest arms supplier and also a major economic partner. With Nixon in the White House and not sympathetic to Indian concerns, India depended also on Soviet diplomatic support. Yet India made it quite clear that it would not join the proposed system (S. N. Singh 1986: 46–52, 76–79).

- Ten years later, India was to display a good deal of autonomy over Afghanistan. Although New Delhi was about to sign the largest arms deal ever with the Soviets, India's initial reactions to the Soviet invasion were condemnatory. They soon moderated, but India continued to indicate that it did not approve of the Soviet action. An American specialist on Indo-Soviet relations concludes that it was the coincidence of interests that accounted for India's relative softness on the Soviets, not Moscow's ability to influence Indian choices (Horn 1982: 180–90).

During the Cold War, India's foreign policy autonomy was threatened by the bipolar confrontation: as early as 1944, Nehru had understood that the United States and the Soviet Union would be dominant and competitive and there would be pressure on the rest of the world to choose sides (Nehru 1981: 536–48). Forty-five years later, the threats to autonomy have changed: a bipolar Cold War no longer exists, but in India's estimation there are other powers and forces that seek to subvert Indian independence. Thus, in September 1994, on his state visit to Singapore, Narasimha Rao (1994: 10–11) told his audience that "the Non-aligned Movement is fully relevant today....Its principles have not really been diluted by the recent strategic changes—we continue with the determination to decide our own destiny."

Since 1991, New Delhi has seen as the major threat to its autonomy a concert of the United States and the industrial countries, primarily Japan and the European Union.[14] The post–Cold War order is perceived as unipolar as well as multipolar. It is unipolar because the United States will be dominant for some time to come in terms of military and economic power. But the international system is also incipiently multipolar, because China, the European Union, and Japan are emerging power centers whose interests will diverge from those of the United States. Further, while the United States is the premier military power, economic power is more widely distributed, beyond even Japan and the European Union: China, the East Asian newly industrializing countries, and the ASEAN countries are emerging centers. Economically, therefore, the world is multipolar.[15] Yet New Delhi recognizes that, these contradictions notwithstanding, in the transition to a genuine multipolarity the United States leads a coalition of states from East Asia and Southeast Asia, North America, and Western Europe.

The second threat to foreign policy autonomy, from New Delhi's perspective, is "the new institutionalism," once again led by the United States. India fears that a range of organizations and regimes, strengthened since the end of the Cold War, will reduce its room for diplomatic maneuver (Dixit 1994: 932–33). A revitalized United Nations and the World Bank and International Monetary Fund (IMF), under U.S. leadership, could impose constraints on Indian foreign policy options. The United Nations could resurrect its role in the Kashmir issue. The World Bank and the IMF have already warned India that its defense expenditures are too high, and loans could be made conditional on the scaling down of military outlays (Gupta 1995: 5). These institutions could become more intrusive with respect to issues such as India's relations with Pakistan and the rest of the region. In addition to those organizations, a variety of U.S.–brokered and U.S.–led regimes are seen as inimical to the conduct of an independent foreign policy. The capacity to choose one's enemies and friends and to take a stand on issues depends, in the end, on military power. The nonproliferation regime, in particular, is seen as a curb on Indian military power. The NPT, the Nuclear Suppliers' Group, the Missile Technology Control Regime, and now the Comprehensive Test Ban Treaty are seen as denying India weapons and technological capabilities essential for its military preparedness.[16]

The third threat to foreign policy autonomy, in India's calculus, is economic globalization. India has always been suspicious of what it regards as a global capitalist system, represented by multinational corporations and foreign investment, that could ensnare it in a neo-colonial order. During much of the Cold War, India looked on the activities of such companies with suspicion—they were agents not just of capitalism as a productive system but of capitalist powers, especially the United States. Although India has moderated its views, suspicion of the system itself and of multinationals and foreign investors prevails in certain sections of the bureaucracy, in older Indian business houses, and in the leftist and rightist political formations, including parties, trade unions, and intellectual circles. The government increasingly wants to integrate India with the global capitalist system, and it recognizes that foreign business is often outside the control of foreign governments. However, especially among elements of the political left and right, there continue to be concerns about the pace and extent of integration with a system that revolves about the members of the Organization for Economic Cooperation and Development (OECD), and those concerns are reinforced by doubts about the autonomy of multinational corporations.[17]

In sum, New Delhi sees the major threat to Indian foreign policy autonomy as being constituted by the U.S.–led concert of Western powers. The concert can operate directly on India but also works through various international institutions, regimes, and a globalized economic order. These entities could punish India diplomatically (in the United Nations, for example, on an issue like Kashmir), militarily (by denying it key technologies), and economically by withholding multi-lateral funding (from the World Bank or IMF) or impeding private investment flows. The U.S.–led concert could also threaten India somewhat more indirectly. One of the greatest fears of Indian decision makers since 1947 has been that powerful outsiders will intervene in regional affairs as a way of constraining India. That fear has waxed and waned. Since the mid-1980s, Indian anxieties have lessened. Washington was quietly supportive of the India–Sri Lanka accord of 1987 and backed Indian intervention in the Maldives coup. New Delhi recognizes, though, that the great powers could always hurt India by supporting one or more of its neighbors against it. Given that all the bilateral quarrels in South Asia are between India and the smaller states, there are many potential pressure points.

In its relations with greater powers, a state can choose among several strategies: bandwagoning, balancing, nonalignment, even "hiding."[18] In the bipolar world, India chose nonalignment. In the unipolar (or multipolar) world after 1991, India's strategy for autonomy has been one of bandwagoning with balance. Over the long term, though, New Delhi's ambition is what I will refer to as internal balancing.

India's conception of nonalignment was a distinct contribution to the norms and institutions of international society. While affirming the essentially Westphalic conventions of the "society of states"—the primacy of states and national interest, the inviolability of territory, peace among nations, the honoring of agreements, international law, diplomacy—it added several elements.[19] Nonalignment represented a refusal to become permanently attached to any great power and a desire to establish a zone free of great-power competition. It was an insistence that relatively weak powers could choose to stay aloof from great-power rivalries. This did not mean that they should always forsake great-power support or refuse to choose sides if either national interest or morality warranted such a choice. Nonalignment, in the Indian conception, was therefore perfectly realist, but also idealist: Nehru never tired of repeating that he was free to choose sides so long as he avoided permanent attachments; he was committed, he said, to a positive ethical stance in the sense of being obliged to commend and condemn the actions of other states, including the great powers. Nonalignment was also a positive program that promoted international cooperation across ideological lines and mediated between the Eastern and Western blocs (Damodaran 1995: 190–205).

In the Cold War period, nonalignment appeared to Indian leaders as a perfectly rational response to the pressures and pulls of the East-West conflict. Since the end of the Cold War, the shine of nonalignment has dulled—although some contend that great-power pressures on weaker states continue, that great-power rivalries are not altogether over (e.g., the United States versus Russia), that new rivalries are in the making (e.g., the United States versus China), and that nonalignment as a basic refusal to be permanently identified with any big power is therefore still essential. Yet the insistence on standing apart from the big powers has clearly softened. In the post–Cold War period, Indian decision makers see the United States as the greatest power, and bandwagoning seems to be a rational response. On a variety of issues related to the Persian Gulf War and nuclear proliferation, New Delhi has apparently gone along with Washington or softened its stand. It allowed U.S. air force flights to refuel in India during the Gulf War. It voted with the U.S.–led United Nations resolutions against Iraq, a country with which it had had close relations over a considerable part of the Cold War period. On nuclear matters, India joined the United States in sponsoring two key U.N. resolutions supporting a Comprehensive Test Ban Treaty (CTBT) and a fissile materials cutoff (FMC), even though these measures would limit its own nuclear capabilities. India also restrained itself during the NPT extension process and held off criticizing the extension, when for years it had decried the NPT.[20]

For three reasons, though, the long-term trend in Indian policy is to seek balance. First, if there is a second and third tier of states that combine military and economic power, a coalition with them creates a counterbalance against U.S. diktats. Second, seeking balance is an insurance policy: when the world moves toward a genuine multipolar structure, India will have the advantage of having cultivated three or four alternative power centers. Third, balancing is necessary for domestic reasons: Indian decision makers can continue to claim that India is "nonaligned" and has not yielded to pressure.

Thus, even as India has bandwagoned with the United States, it has intermittently projected a more independent diplomatic stand. In August 1996, India blocked consensus on the CTBT. According to New Delhi, the CTBT was not truly comprehensive—it did not cover nonexplosive testing—and therefore it was not in India's interest to join. The deeper reason has been a desire to "stand up" to the United States, which was seen as leading the CTBT charge (Mohan 1996). India's attitude toward the FMC is likely to be just as negative. In short, although India has recently been less stringent about autonomy, it continues to resist being identified too closely with any great power.

India has also sought balance through a number of informal coalitions. At various times, it has signaled an interest in a triangular Iran–China–India relationship.[21] Commentators have perceived other triangles: Russia–China–India; Australia–South Africa–India in the Indian Ocean rim; Israel–Southeast Asia–India; even an Asian triad of China, Japan, and India.[22] In addition, India is exploring membership in regional organizations. It is trying to energize the South Asian Association for Regional Cooperation (SAARC) by pushing for the SAARC Preferential Tariff Arrangement (SAPTA), with a free trade area and full-fledged economic community to follow. It has become a member of the ASEAN Regional Forum (ARF), would like to be part of Asia-Pacific Economic Cooperation (APEC), and has been central in constructing an Indian Ocean Rim grouping. With Brazil and a group of other developing countries, it launched the "G-15." It remains part of the Nonaligned Movement and continues to propound that movement's importance.

Bandwagoning with balance is for India an interim strategy. In the end, India would prefer "internal balancing": it would like to be militarily strong enough to shed such entanglements. It continues, therefore, not only to import major weapons systems but also to build its basic military design and production capacities. Much effort has gone into the nuclear and missile programs. No one knows what India's nuclear capabilities are, but estimates place it at roughly 60 bombs at short notice (Perkovich 1993). India is close to intermediate-range ballistic missile capability with its "Agni" systems, and ICBM capability is not inconceivable. The real constraints in the nuclear arena are financial and therefore also diplomatic. India is under pressure from the United States and others to halt its missile program. Financial commitments through the IMF and the World Bank may be at risk, and unilateral sanctions are also a threat. Key technologies, some of them relevant to the nuclear and missile programs, are being denied until India stops the programs. Nevertheless, all indications suggest that India will continue to pursue a strong indigenous military capability.[23] Indeed, in the wake of the CTBT negotiations in Geneva in 1996, the debate over going nuclear has sharpened.

In addition to India's general desire for balance is a regional policy that seeks to exclude the great powers from South Asian affairs. In this regard Indian policy displays a good deal of consistency. Indian decision makers are aware that the smaller states in South Asia perceive three basic threats to their security—threats posed by extraregional powers including the great powers; internal subversion; and India itself—any of which may cause them to turn to outside powers for assistance. India has in turn fashioned three basic responses by which it tries to reduce the insecurity of the small states and their incentive to woo nonregional powers. The first response is to forge bilateral defense agreements with the smaller states. These agreements give India a role in those states' external security and obviate the need for nonregional protectors: thus India has treaty arrangements with Bhutan, Bangladesh, and Nepal.[24] The second response is to insist that, in the event of internal instabilities that require external military help and other forms of assistance, India should be consulted and used as a first resort: commentators in South Asia have called this "the India Doctrine."[25] The third response has been to forge regional organizations that will reassure the smaller states with respect to Indian motives and actions: SAARC is the most recent example, but India's attempts to bring South Asians into a regional arrangement date back to the Asian Relations Conference held in Delhi in March 1947.[26]

India's strategy for foreign policy autonomy is a mix of two broad approaches. While it accepts a certain degree of bandwagoning with the United States in the short term, its search for strategic balance, its long-term concern with internal balancing through indigenous arms production, and its regional policy of defense agreements and Indian-led collective security ("the India Doctrine")—all these reveal that New Delhi seeks to marshal power and force against threats to India's autonomy. At the same time, India seeks to protect its autonomy through more institutional and noncoercive practices. Nonalignment and regional cooperation in South Asia represent this alternative track.

National Power

If India is to defend its territory and become a truly autonomous actor in the international system, it must be powerful. Indian leaders have had different notions of national power. For Nehru (1947—64), power included military capacity. India's first prime minister, it should be remembered, laid the basis for India's defense industry and its nuclear program. But power was also economic strength, technological capacity, and social and political stability. In addition, power lay not so much in coercive as in mediatory diplomacy and had "cosmopolitan" ends.[27] Such diplomacy would serve Indian interests but also the interests of international society as a whole. India would be powerful to the extent that it had the ability to persuade and reassure others rather than coerce them (Rana 1976).

With Indira Gandhi (1966–77, 1980–84), India's view of power came closer to the realpolitik notion of military and other coercive instrumentalities (Mansingh 1984: 1–2, 32–40). Moreover, whereas Nehru saw Indian security in a global environment, Mrs. Gandhi focused on the region, the near region, and domestic politics, a policy focus that was even more central to the security conception of the successor Janata government (1977–79). In Mrs. Gandhi's second term there was a shift from *machtpolitik* focused on the region and on domestic politics to an enlarged view of power. This enlarged view encompassed greater attention to the nonmilitary components of power and a realization that Indian power had more cosmopolitan responsibilities. Thus, for instance, Mrs. Gandhi led the way in reestablishing an economic and technological partnership with the United States (Kux 1993: 386–99). She also began the economic reform process, which would be enlarged by Rajiv Gandhi and then Narasimha Rao. In this period, India returned to global disarmament issues. It was a key member of the four "Six Nation–Five Continent Peace Initiatives" involving Argentina, Mexico, Greece, Sweden, Tanzania, and India. The first initiative was a joint public statement urging nuclear disarmament, reform of the United Nations, and the transfer of resources from arms to development. It was issued on May 22, 1984, just months before Mrs. Gandhi's death.[28]

With Rajiv Gandhi (1984–89) and Narasimha Rao (1991–96), Indian conceptions of power continued to change in the direction Mrs. Gandhi had begun to chart in her second term. Rajiv deepened the economic reforms and adhered to the more cosmopolitan vision of power. Economic liberalization represented a major policy shift under Rajiv, and India–U.S. links in economics, technology, and defense were strengthened. India's continuing involvement in the Six Nation–Five Continent initiatives (in 1985, 1986, and 1988) and the Rajiv Gandhi Action Plan for disarmament (presented at the United Nations in June 1988) were part of the larger ambition for Indian power. Rajiv, like his mother, brandished Indian power in the region. Indian forces went to Sri Lanka in 1987 to help the government solve the Tamil separatist problem.[29] In 1988, Indian forces stopped a coup in the Maldives. They also carried out two massive military exercises—one near the Pakistani border (1987) and the other near the Chinese border (1988)—at least in part to signal India's military strength and confidence.[30] Finally, recognizing that domestic order must be achieved if India was to become a great power, Rajiv energetically set about forging various internal peace agreements with separatists, as in the Punjab and Assam.

Narasimha Rao, after the Cold War, maintained the Rajiv Gandhi program in substantial measure but, even more than his predecessor, cast

Indian power in economic terms. At least in part as a result, India's strategic gaze swung away from South Asia. It focused instead on the United States and, in what was called the "Look East policy," on East Asia and Southeast Asia.

This review of Indian visions of power suggests that national power, whether it is cosmopolitan or more inward-looking, rests on three components: military strength, economic development, and internal order. These in turn become secondary values of a security conception. As we shall see, these secondary values are also vulnerable to external and internal threats or limitations. India's strategies for managing its vulnerabilities have been partially successful. New Delhi has built up conventional and nuclear weapons capabilities to an impressive level. Given its size and highly diverse society, it has maintained a fair degree of internal order. Its greatest failure has been in the realm of economic development. India's promarket reforms since 1991, though, may bring about a turnaround.

Military Strength

Military strength is a key component of India's conception of power. Indian decision makers want enough military capacity for deterrence—and for defense should deterrence break down—against both Pakistan and China. Some have suggested that India also needs a general deterrent in the Indian Ocean against great-power navies. This requirement, they argue, has grown since the U.S.–led war against Iraq.[31] In addition, there are situations that require compulsion, mostly in the region or near-region. Indian leaders want enough extra force to be able to project power in the neighborhood, whether as a "peacekeeping force" in Sri Lanka or as an interventionary force on an Indian Ocean island or even in the Persian Gulf, where India gets most of its oil.

India's ability to deter and defend against Chinese and Pakistani attacks rests on its conventional and nuclear preparedness. India's armed forces, numbering 1.265 million (down from a peak of about 1.5 million) and 200,000 reservists, are the fourth largest in the world (J. Singh 1992: 72–73). The major increase in forces came after 1962, when India had about half a million men under arms (Kavic 1967: 97). The defense budget has grown from an average of 2 percent of gross domestic product in the 1950s, to 3.4 percent in the 1960s, to 3.6 percent in the 1970s and 1980s. The 1990s show a downward trend, with the budget closer to 3 percent of GDP (J. Singh 1992: 54–55).

Indian conventional forces—heavily reliant on external sourcing for high technology and combat systems—are vulnerable to foreign suppliers. The arms relationship with the Soviet Union brought stability to

Indian sourcing during much of the Cold War. Since 1991 and the collapse of the Soviet economy, supplies have been erratic. Although the situation has improved, there remain serious concerns over the preparedness of the Indian forces. India has bought systems from other suppliers, but their terms and reliability are suspect. New Delhi is keen to buy from the United States. U.S. suspicions of the Soviet-supplied Indian forces linger, however, and Indian decision makers fear that Washington might cut off supplies at a critical moment or use an arms relationship as political leverage.

Internally, a host of problems exist. The most serious relate to the ability of India's defense industry to produce combat systems and subsystems that meet the armed forces' changing requirements in a technologically sophisticated and fast-changing world, to do so in timely fashion, to maintain quality control, and to remain within cost specifications. The progress of the Main Battle Tank (MBT), Light Combat Aircraft (LCA), and Advanced Jet Trainer (AJT) projects has not been encouraging. The missile program has performed well, but the MBT, LCA, AJT, and other programs have disappointed. Indian decision makers have not been able to fathom why some sectors excel and others do not, apart from idiosyncratic reasons such as the quality of administrative leadership.[32]

There are also budgetary constraints to defense production. Since 1987–88, the defense budget has declined or stagnated in real terms (Joshi 1992: 83). This decline has cramped the missile program and postponed the acquisition of key items including deep-penetration strike aircraft, a light combat aircraft, an advanced jet trainer, corvettes, frigates, destroyers, submarines, and carriers.[33] The situation has been made worse by the Hank Brown Amendment in the U.S. Congress, which has allowed Pakistan to purchase U.S. equipment in recompense for the F-16s it was refused.

India's nuclear deterrent, too, is vulnerable to pressures from external powers. Whereas the basic nuclear technologies have been mastered indigenously, there are concerns about a fully operational deterrent. India has continued to refine the design of its nuclear device but would need to test further to establish confidence in its reliability. If it is to miniaturize the device, that too will require a testing program. But testing could bring economic and other sanctions, from the Western powers in particular, especially after passage of a CTBT. World public opinion, if not official opinion, turned against France in 1995, and India may confront a similar situation. Indian experts estimate that sanctions will indeed slow the country's progress on its nuclear program, including the crucial missile subprogram, although they will not stop it.[34]

The nuclear program has its internal problems as well. Two are critical. First of all, a series of safety and maintenance lapses have come to light. The former head of the Atomic Energy Regulatory Board (AERB), Dr. A. Gopalakrishnan, has recently gone public with these lapses. They present a worrying picture: problems at Tarapur, Kaiga, Narora, Kalpakkam, and the Rajasthan Atomic Power Station (RAPS) reactors over the past five years or so have tarnished the nuclear estate's image (Prasad 1995). Second, the Narasimha Rao government curtailed funding to the nuclear program. Whether this was an act of economic austerity or a response to the program's growing troubles is unclear.[35] The point is that the Indian nuclear program is in the financial doldrums. Although funding may be restored, the operational problems of the reactors and massive cost overruns have seriously harmed the program. Not surprisingly, India is signaling an interest in nuclear cooperation—with Canada, Russia, and the United States. It is also keen to sell nuclear technology (e.g., to Iran). The problem is that buying and selling nuclear technology make India vulnerable once again to external pressures.

A host of external and internal problems thus curtail India's capacity to maintain its military strength.

Since independence, India has been aware of its vulnerability to external suppliers of military equipment. The Blackett Report of 1948 recommended that India deal with the problem by embarking on a process of indigenization. Thus India has invested in a large defense production base that is intended to make the country self-sufficient. It presently has 39 ordnance factories (OFs) and 8 defense public-sector undertakings (DPSUs). These installations produce ammunition, battle tanks, armored vehicles, aircraft, warships, missiles, electronic and communications equipment, engines, alloys, and specialized components and spares. Indian investment in the OFs and DPSUs in 1994 was $920 million (Basu 1996: 14).

The Indian defense industry, though, has failed to indigenize the production of key combat systems and subsystems, including such key items as aircraft, armor and artillery, carriers and submarines, engines, and electronics. To correct for this deficiency, Indian strategy has been to increase research and development allocations, to enter into licensing and coproduction relationships, and to increase privatization.[36] Increasing R and D funding has not worked, however, except in missile technology and some electronics and alloys. The Main Battle Tank is being delivered to the army, but controversy surrounds its quality. Licensed production (such as that of MiG-21s) has been successful to a considerable extent. India has avoided coproduction because it would again reduce national control over a military project. Thus the LCA project has a coproduction component but, not surprisingly, has been stalled. Most recently, New Delhi has tried to infuse some dynamism into defense production by privatizing. The idea seems to be to reduce the burden on the public sector so that it can focus on key items and to improve efficiency through private involvement. Traditionally the private sector has been restricted to producing "nonlethal" items. This restriction will continue; but under a new policy, private business will enlarge its role in defense production. The Department of Defense Production, in a recent move, set up ten technical committees to determine the scope of "indigenization" of defense production. The committees envisage that in terms of the total value of items, 67 percent will come from the private sector (Basu 1996: 56).

Since the nuclear test of 1974, New Delhi has intermittently made statements encouraging the view that it has a nuclear weapons capability that could be operationalized at very short notice. Although the government denies having a nuclear arsenal, it has made clear that India could put together a deliverable weapon quickly. These Indian statements have usually been made in the context of a nuclear crisis with Pakistan. India's covert nuclear posture has been called "ambiguity," "nonweaponized deterrence," "recessed deterrence," and "opaque."[37] The posture's premise is that nuclear deterrence rests not necessarily on the certainty of retaliation but even on the mere possibility of it. Given the destructive potential of nuclear weapons, anyone contemplating military action against India will have to reckon that New Delhi can retaliate massively with just a few strikes. Indian decision makers hope that in the calculus of aggressors this will rule out the use of force: no rational political goals would be served by the nuclear destruction of key towns and cities.

India's posture has skeptics both at home and abroad. While the logic of deterrence by ambiguity is persuasive, there are questions about its stability. One doubt is that in a crisis ambiguity may not be sufficient: that is, the posture may be "deterrence stable" but not "crisis stable." Thus, over time, Indian decision makers will be forced to seek a more transparent, classical posture. Part of this argument is sociological. Indian decision makers at the highest level—politicians, officials, generals—may simply not accept ambiguity as a strategic doctrine. Social organizations such as the state and its agencies are invented to reduce the role of uncertainty in collective life. To rely on uncertainty in an area of public policy vital to national survival surely goes against their raison d'être.

While Indian politicians and officials have been reticent about expressing themselves on this subject in public, senior members of the armed forces have been outspoken in various semipublic settings. At various seminars in New Delhi, they have repeated that although they must obey the decisions of civil authorities, deterrence by uncertainty is not a strategic posture they like. A testing program; clear doctrinal guidelines on deployment, targeting, and use; a survivable command and control system—all the classic components of nuclear deterrence are essential if India is to have a credible posture. This attitude does not reflect a lack of understanding of the logic of deterrence, as some Indian critics of the armed forces aver; rather it reflects the organizational culture of the armed forces. The armed forces do not necessarily want "a baroque arsenal"—a large deterrent with all the refinements prized by the nuclear powers. A minimal deterrent would suffice. Nor do they necessarily dream of "war fighting" and elaborate doctrines. But they do want a bomb that they can see, smell, touch, taste, and hear.

Despite some skepticism, India's commitment to a "neither-confirm-nor-deny" posture has been maintained. In the prelude to India's decision to reject the CTBT and then block the consensus, a segment of the strategic community called for a program of testing and weaponization. A vigorous debate on India's nuclear option ensued, of the kind not seen since 1964–66. Yet India's nuclear middle road prevailed.

Why successive governments have stuck to the middle ground remains unclear. A number of considerations are likely at work. First, nuclear weapons could adversely affect the balance of civil and military power.[38] Second, rivalry within the forces—between the army, air force, and navy—over who will control nuclear weapons may be a factor (K. P. Bajpai 1996: 25). That the weapons might be entrusted to an entirely new force is a disquieting possibility for the three services, but one they must countenance if they urge nuclearization. Third, and more important, the geopolitical wisdom of going nuclear remains in doubt. An India armed with nuclear weapons might very well become a nuclear target. India must worry about the chances of a preemptive strike and the long-term danger of having a place on the permanent targeting plans of the nuclear powers (K. P. Bajpai 1996: 42). Fourth, the economic costs of weaponization are a cause for restraint. Though India may have already borne most of the costs of R and D and infrastructure building, the ongoing costs could be daunting. Critics disagree, citing apparently modest figures for a minimal deterrent. But there is the fear that an arms race mentality will prevail, that a maximalist posture will result, and that the real costs, including those of testing, command and control, environmental safety, and health, will be much greater than current projections.[39] Fifth, there is a moral barrier to weaponizing. Mahatma Gandhi and Nehru expressed revulsion at the bomb. India has for fifty years argued that possession and use of nuclear weapons is abhorrent and that deterrence is ethically dubious. Most recently, India argued in the International Court of Justice that nuclear weapons are illegal. Although it may be easy to dismiss Indian statements as hypocritical or tactical, there is moral doubt, at least over going nuclear outright.[40] Sixth, public opinion, to the extent that it has truly been gauged on a national scale, seems to support the middle road (Cortright and Mattoo 1996: 11).

In sum, India has devoted considerable resources to building up the country as a military power, primarily against China and Pakistan. Self-sufficiency in conventional and nuclear forces is the country's ambition, and it has gone a long way toward achieving that goal. Deficiencies still exist, however, particularly in the major conventional weapons systems. Those deficits, due to both external and internal circumstances, will continue to constrain India's military power in the years to come.

Economic Development

Ever since independence, India has held to the vision that economic development is a key security value. An economically backward India would be prey to external and internal foes. Economic weakness would hurt India's defense, keep it technologically backward, and promote internal instability. The country's enemies, both external and internal, would find fertile soil for subversion.

This logic was exemplified in a speech Nehru gave in 1948 in which he warned: "If we do not ultimately solve the basic problems of our country—the problems of food, clothing, housing, and so on,…we shall be swept away" (Nehru 1983b: 140–41). Economic productivity was a vital national objective. It was necessary for the achievement of other national goals: "The ultimate peril is the slow drying-up of the capacity of the nation to produce. That affects us politically, economically and in every other way, and gradually our strength goes down to resist these very perils that face us" (Nehru 1983b: 95). Four decades later, the logic of economy and national strength was echoed in Defense Minister Pant's argument that "you need political stability in order to have well planned economic growth. You need economic growth and proper distribution of the fruits of economic growth in order to have social stability which is the bedrock of political stability. You need both in order to have the right environment in a democracy for defense preparedness in depth, and defense preparedness obviously is a priority area for both the other areas" (Pant 1988: 4).

From Nehru's time to the last years of Mrs. Gandhi's second term in office, development meant a steady but not necessarily high rate of economic growth, equitably distributed, and a self-sufficient economy.

Self-sufficiency was perhaps considered even more important than "growth with equity." Thus Indian socialism stressed the construction of basic infrastructure—heavy industry, power, transportation, roads, communications—and, particularly after Nehru, the capacity to feed the country's own population. In general, it looked upon consumer satisfaction and choice as a luxury; indeed, consumerism was seen as derogating from investment in infrastructure and agriculture.

From Rajiv Gandhi's period onward, development has been inflected differently. It has come to be equated, as never before, with high rates of growth (6 or 7 percent annually). "The fundamental objective of economic reform," the Narasimha Rao government wrote, "is to bring about rapid and sustained improvement in the quality of life....Central to this goal is the rapid growth in incomes and productive employment" (Ministry of Finance n.d.: 1). While there remains a commitment to a "middle way" of growth with equity, that goal is more rhetorical than real. Self-sufficiency continues to animate Indian development ambitions, but the need to "catch up" has substantially moderated the earlier orthodoxy. Thus in the Ministry of Finance's discussion paper on the post-1991 economic reforms, a key paragraph relates to the comparative advance of East and Southeast Asia, and to India's stagnation: "Within a generation, the countries of East Asia have transformed themselves. China, Indonesia, Korea, Thailand and Malaysia today have living standards much above ours....What they have achieved we must strive for" (Ministry of Finance n.d.: 2).

Now that economic development has come to be equated with high rates of economic growth, a number of constraints stand in its way. Disagreement within India is perhaps sharpest on the issue of those constraints. For the Narasimha Rao government they were primarily internal, whereas for domestic critics they are mostly external. The defeat of Narasimha Rao in 1996 wrought some changes but not substantial ones. The leftist coalition in power under Prime Minister Deve Gowda and I. K. Gujral is more attentive to equity goals but is still committed to the same general policy.

For the Narasimha Rao government and its successors, the biggest constraint facing the growth agenda stems from "old habits of thinking and working" within India. The most important of these habits is the expectation that the state rather than the market must play the leading role in structuring production, consumption, investment, and trade. That expectation is widespread in Indian society, but in addition, "powerful sectional interests" sustain such expectations and oppose reform (Ministry of Finance n.d.: 1). Thus a second constraint is the role of various special interests. A third constraint on the growth agenda is the negative view Indians take of foreign involvement in the Indian economy. The older business houses—particularly the so-called Bombay Group—and sections of the intelligentsia, political classes, and the general public resent the presence of "the multinationals."

In the face of these limitations, India's strategy for "development as growth" has two components. First, the state must lead a "revolution from above" to overcome the old habits of thinking and working and the resistance of special interests—a revolution Narasimha Rao called "a certain Market Plus."[41] The state must foster an "economic environment" that "combines the discipline of competitive markets with efficient provision of key public services such as primary education, primary health care, transport and communication and, of course, law and order." This effort will require reforms not just of "broad policy" but also "of laws, rules and procedure." (See Ministry of Finance n.d.: 1–2.)

The second component of the new developmentalism consists of reassuring external investors that India wants and can handle foreign investment. The government has therefore launched a massive publicity campaign stressing the size of the market (a middle class of 150 million whose buying power equals that of France), the nature and irreversibility of the reforms, the vitality of the Indian legal system, a long-standing stock market, English as the language of business and administration, and the stability of Indian politics (Gupta 1995: 65). While India has been slow to allow investments in some sectors (for example, consumer products), it has offered special concessions in others (particularly in infrastructure).

Overall, India's strategy is one of state-led internal reforms in the pursuit of rapid economic growth. The state, according to Ikenberry, Lake, and Mastanduno (1988: 10), may be viewed in two ways: as an organizational structure—laws and institutional arrangements shaped by previous events—and as an actor. In the latter conception, they suggest, the "primary emphasis is on the goal-oriented behavior of politicians and civil servants as they respond to internal and external constraints." The actions of central decision makers are "distinct from the parochial concerns of either societal groups or particular governmental institutions, and are tied to conceptions of the 'national interest' or the maximization of some social welfare function" (p. 10).

Our analysis of Indian economic strategy reveals an *étatiste* conception in the sense of a relatively autonomous state pursuing the "national interest." The Indian state appears as an activist and interventionary mechanism, as in the past, but one committed now to securing high rates of growth by bringing about a change in values, overcoming the resistance of special interests, providing public goods and a promarket regime of norms and rules, and attracting foreign investors in the name of "national development."

Internal Order

India's decision makers understand that however strong India may be in terms of military and economic capabilities, the country is vulnerable as long as it is internally unstable. Given the heterogeneity of Indian society and the economic backwardness of various groups, Indian governments have always expected to deal with challenges to internal order. Their concerns about order have grown since the relatively calm years of the Nehru period. A series of threats exist, mostly homegrown but aided and abetted by external actors, particularly Pakistan and China.

In Nehru's time, internal disruption was limited. The early years saw the "police actions" in Hyderabad and Junagadh, the Kashmiri problems, the liberation of Goa from the Portuguese (1961), trouble in Punjab (1954), the threat of communism, and of course religious violence at the time of partition and after. Since Nehru's time, the tide of internal troubles has risen steadily, bringing the northeastern rebellions from the 1960s to the present, the language riots in Tamil Nadu in the 1960s, increasing Hindu-Muslim violence in the 1970s and 1980s, the Sikh militancy of the 1980s, and the Kashmir insurrection of the 1990s.

Not surprisingly, the government's concern about internal order has heightened. For the first time since independence, in the Narasimha Rao government India had a Minister of State for Internal Security. The National Security Council (NSC), created in 1990, was chartered to deal with both external and internal security matters. On his visits to the United States and Russia in 1994, Narasimha Rao repeatedly drew attention to a shared commitment to social pluralism, in the interest of international stability but also of *internal* order. He frequently argued that economic reforms, though necessary and desirable, must be crafted with an eye to domestic stability.[42] The Ministry of Defense's annual report for 1994–95 concludes its opening paragraph with the judgment that "it is not so much inter-state wars as intra-state violence, international terrorism and proxy wars by external powers that characterize the global security environment." The report makes several other references to internal troubles (Ministry of Defense 1995: 1).

The growth of paramilitary forces is another indication of the increasing inwardness of security concerns. The paramilitaries grew sixfold in the late 1960s and early 1970s (Misra 1980: 376–77). In roughly the same period, the Indian military grew threefold (Kavic 1967: 97; J. Singh 1992: 72–73). The paramilitaries increased their numbers by 50 percent between 1985 and 1993 (Ministry of Home Affairs 1994: 39).

In that period, the military actually declined somewhat in size (J. Singh 1992: 72–73). Expenditure on the Border Security Force (BSF) and the Central Reserve Police (CRP) increased more than threefold between 1968–69 and 1976–77 (Misra 1980: 376–77). Between 1985–86 and 1992–93, expenditure on the major paramilitaries increased by a factor of 3.5 (Ministry of Home Affairs 1994: 40). The central government's expenditure on what is termed "police" increased by a factor of 37 between 1951 and 1984–85 (Rajgopal 1988: 20).

The threats to internal order arise from four sources: separatism, illegal migration, religious conflict, and caste tensions. Although the roots are domestic, Indian decision makers see external involvement, or opportunities for external involvement, in virtually every case.

Separatism and migration are seen as long-term threats to territory, but in an everyday sense they are threats to internal order. Separatism involves large-scale, organized violence between the rebelling ethnic group and the state as well as other ethnic groups. The unrest is abetted, as noted earlier, by external actors. Violence of a secondary nature occurs outside the main theaters. Terrorist groups from Punjab and Kashmir have operated in other parts of the country, including Delhi.

Illegal migration, though less immediately and less visibly disruptive, also upsets internal order. The migrants affect local ethnic and religious balances in areas that have a precarious social structure. Indian decision makers see Bangladeshi migrants as the most dangerous influx. There is a widespread perception that they are filtering into West Bengal and the northeastern states in large numbers and moving on to the big Indian cities in the north. As Bengalis, they exacerbate anti-Bengali feeling in Assam. As Muslims, they worsen communal relations in West Bengal, the northeast, and the major urban centers. Even though the impetus to migrate is a personal one and generally stems from broad socioeconomic conditions, Bangladesh is regarded as either actively encouraging the movement of people or not doing enough to stop it.

With respect to religious conflict, the government remains worried about Hindu-Muslim violence above all. The rise of "Muslim fundamentalism" and the growth of an unabashed "political Hinduism" are both the causes and effects of a heightened religious consciousness.[43] The government is particularly concerned about Muslim communalism, which it sees as part of an upsurge of Islamic feeling globally and which it believes is fueled by Iran, Pakistan, and Saudi Arabia. The wave of bombings in Mumbai in 1993 following the destruction of the Babri Masjid mosque was attributed to Pakistani instigation of local Muslim gangs and provocateurs. Although Hindu fundamentalism has its own external component—Indians studying and settled abroad, for example—the government has not shown any great anxiety over the majority community's foreign links.

Hindu-Muslim religious differences are paralleled by caste tensions in northern India: caste Hindus versus the scheduled castes and tribes; "other backward classes" (OBCs) versus the upper and middle castes; OBCs versus the lower castes. Though caste rivalries are not new, what is new is the large-scale political mobilization according to caste in the huge northern states. The most dangerous aspect of this mobilization is the formation of private militias. Rivalry between the militias has led to an "undeclared war," particularly in the state of Bihar but also in eastern Uttar Pradesh (Narayanan 1994: 37–38).

These developments point to the most worrying aspect of religious and caste tensions, namely, their militarization. Underlying the growth of violence is the proliferation of small arms. Estimates vary on the numbers of small arms available and on the sources—Afghanistan, Burma, Pakistan, Southeast Asia—but Indian analysts see their prevalence as a serious threat. Operationally, the critical problem is the nexus between small arms smugglers, drug trafficking mafias, and ethnic dissidents, a nexus that is transnational in scope.

The threats to internal order, then, are both internal and external. Except in the case of separatism, the Indian government does not regard these threats as involving the large-scale use of organized violence directed against state authority. Religious and caste violence can be extensive and claim a high toll. These traumas too are planned rather than spontaneous. But the groups organized to produce violence are evanescent: they tend to disappear after bouts of violence. They are not in any case very large groups. Although the number of *senas* (militias, private armies) is growing, these groups are not trained and skilled perpetrators of violence. And they are not, in the end, primarily dedicated to fighting the state but rather are members of other religious or caste communities. The greatest dangers on this front, in New Delhi's estimation, are the spread of small arms and the increase in drug trafficking and mafia activity, which in the long run could thoroughly militarize Indian society and undermine state authority.

India's approach to these various internal threats has been twofold. It has used force or the threat of force against militant groups and their external supporters. But it has also conceded rights to minority groups and decentralized power to create an increasingly layered federal structure.

New Delhi has responded with force to internal violence over nearly fifty years. It has used the army extensively. Indeed, the incidence of "aid to civil" has risen steeply over the last two decades. In response to criticism from the public and from the army itself, New Delhi has built up an array of paramilitary and police forces to deal with internal violence.[44] India has also threatened force against external provocateurs. Whereas the Chinese abandoned their support of the northeastern separatists in the late 1970s, Pakistani support has been active since the early 1980s, first in Punjab, then in Kashmir, and now, reportedly, as far away as the northeast. Indian leaders have publicly warned Pakistan of the possibility of a punitive war. These warnings have been seen as intemperate outbursts, but they must also be regarded as exercises in coercive diplomacy. On at least two occasions—in 1987 and 1990—Indian mobilizations led to crises.[45] Pakistan is not the only country that has been the object of Indian warnings. Bangladesh has also been suspected of interfering, mostly in the northeast. Police and military clashes along the border have resulted.

The general response to the demands of minority groups, though, has been to concede various types of group rights, including linguistically organized states, religious and vernacular schools, separate civil codes, and caste and tribal reservations in education, government employment, and political representation. These measures have been aimed mostly at linguistic, religious, and caste and tribal groups.

For ethnic separatists, the favored solution has been decentralization of power. From Nehru's time, while the central government has remained enormously powerful, it has also created exceptions to the general division of responsibilities between the central government and the states. The most prominent exception, of course, is Kashmir, which is governed by Article 370 of the constitution. Kashmir is by no means the only exception. Responsibility has also been increasingly layered, though it remains to be seen how effectively. Thus, in addition to the division of authority between the center and the states or union territories, there are regional councils (consisting of groups of states), autonomous district councils, and *panchayats* (elected councils at the local, usually village, level). In short, group rights plus a multilayered federalism make up the Indian formula for internal order.

Conceding group rights and instituting multilayered federalism has not diminished central government control. Even as special rights and provisions are conceded, central authorities remain supreme. The authorities maintain a skewed distribution of power, for the means of violence are substantially under their control as is also the power of the purse. Any group that attempts to accumulate the means of violence or to extract resources from the populace (through "taxes," for example), such as insurgents or various communitarian groups, becomes for the authorities "antinational." Such organizations are eliminated by force or brought into the political process after a campaign of military attrition has rendered them amenable to "normal" politics. Although this approach has had success in managing internal order, there are challenges ahead for which India has not yet evolved a coherent approach. The militarization, even criminalization, of caste and religious confrontations is the most serious of these.

Explaining Security

The Indian conception of security appears at first glance to bear out the classical conception of national security. In the classical formulation, the state is bound to protect two primary values that are intrinsic to the enjoyment of sovereignty—territorial integrity and foreign policy autonomy—and to cultivate if not maximize power in order to protect those values. Our review of India's security has shown that the Indian state is clearly the referent of security; that security strategies seek to protect three primary values—territorial integrity, foreign policy autonomy, and national power; that national power in turn is a function of three secondary values—military strength, economic development, and internal order; and that national power is vital to the protection of India's territorial integrity and foreign policy autonomy.

On further reflection, the Indian conception of security appears more complex. India's strategies for coping with threats and vulnerabilities appear diverse and numerous. New Delhi perceives a structure of external and internal threats and, more often than not, of external actors working with internal actors to harm India. Externally, the major threats to India are China, Pakistan, and, subsidiarily but not insubstantially, a U.S.–led concert of mostly Western industrial countries. China and Pakistan constitute military threats; the U.S.–led concert is a diplomatic and political threat. Internally, the major threats are ethnic separatists whose rebellions furnish opportunities for outside meddling, principally from China and Pakistan but also potentially from the West. Religious and caste rivalries are also a destabilizing factor, especially with the spread of small arms. With respect to military strength and economic growth, internal institutions and attitudes present vulnerabilities.

India's policies with respect to the threats to and vulnerabilities of its core values are multifarious. New Delhi has resorted to force to defend core values. It has done so to protect its borders and territory from external and internal threats. It has also built up an indigenous capacity to produce arms, both conventional and nuclear. In addition, it has imported major weapons systems. These give it the ability to defend its borders and territory, but they also give it a reputation for power, which is vital for foreign policy autonomy and for its self-conception as a major power.

However, in addition to force, New Delhi has used a variety of institutional mechanisms and noncoercive measures to protect core values. These include negotiations (e.g., with China and Pakistan and with ethnic separatists), nonalignment (with respect to the great powers), and group rights and decentralization (to deal with internal ethnic, religious, and caste disaffection). New Delhi has also turned to strategies that it hopes will improve the diplomatic environment with rivals and lead to a reconceptualization of its adversaries' interests. These strategies include diplomatic normalization (with China and Pakistan), summitry (primarily with China but also with Pakistan whenever possible), and economic and cultural cooperation (bilaterally with China and Pakistan, multilaterally within SAARC). India hopes that its economic opening to the West, especially the United States, will ease American pressures on it in issue areas such as nonproliferation and human rights. Internally, India's concern with economic development rests in part on a view that material well-being will buy off dissent.

India's mix of strategies—power and coercion but also institutional and noncoercive measures—belies the picture of a classical conception of national security. Indian decision makers do see their country as a major if not a great power. They seek power in terms of military strength, economic development, and internal order as a way of protecting national sovereignty. But, in contrast to the classical conception of security, they do not appear relentlessly preoccupied with power and its deployment. Indeed, they repeatedly turn to other resources and methods.

India stands revealed, therefore, as a modified structuralist state in security matters, to use Stephen Krasner's term. National interests as articulated by the state, national power, and the ability to coerce are very much a part of India's security conception, but so, broadly, are institutional and noncoercive measures that aim to accommodate or change through peaceful means the views of enemies and rivals, both external and internal.

Two interpretations of India's modified structuralism can be advanced. In the first interpretation, modified structuralism arises from expediency. Given the magnitude of the external threats facing India and its internal vulnerabilities—in the areas of military strength, economic development, and internal order—the country must combine coercive with accommodative strategies as a way of compensating for its weaknesses. As India's power grows, it will rely less on strategies of accommodation and peaceful change; until then, a modified structuralist approach is apt.

In the second interpretation, modified structuralism is a function of conviction. Power is India's ambition; but Indian decision makers understand that power-seeking provokes power-seeking, force begets force. Beyond a certain point, then, power approaches are self-defeating: they may provoke the very outcome that one seeks to avoid, namely, large-scale violence. In addition, large-scale violence, even if it is visited on an adversary, is unacceptable. The pursuit of power without supple-mentary strategies designed to accommodate others or to change their attitudes could end in physical or moral disaster. The urge to power must therefore be moderated.

In the first interpretation Indian security choices are explained by material factors. The deficiencies in Indian military and economic power as well as internal order simply cannot sustain a pure power approach. In the second interpretation, by contrast, a deep-seated norm against a power approach exists or evolves. Such a norm may arise from "egoistic self-interest," which holds that it is rational to try to avoid a mutually undesirable outcome such as massive violence between two or more states. Thus, India's first prime minister wrote: "Self interest itself should drive every nation to...wider co-operation in order to escape disaster....The self interest of the 'realist' is far too limited" (Nehru 1981: 540). The norm against pure power approaches may also arise from other "norms and principles, habit and custom, and knowledge," as Krasner has argued with regard to regime development (Krasner 1983b: 10–20). Thus, Gandhian norms and principles of nonviolence have imbued India with an aversion to a pure power approach. The role of knowledge in generating this norm can be illustrated by Nehru's understanding of European history in terms of a security dilemma engendered by balance of power politics: "Germany, nursing dreams of world conquest, was obsessed by fears of encirclement. Soviet Russia feared a combination of her enemies. England's national policy has long been based on a balance of power in Europe....Always there has been fear of others, and that fear has led to aggression." Referring to Spyk-man's geopolitical ideas, Nehru noted: "All this looks very clever and realistic and yet it is supremely foolish, for it is based on the old policy of expansion and empire and the balance of power, which inevitably leads to conflict and war" (Nehru 1981: 539–40).

Thus India's modified structuralism in national security affairs is a function of both expediency and conviction, of material deficiencies and of ideational legacies and configurations. It is not purely one or the other. Different sets of decision makers in India, at different times, have been and are influenced more by one set of factors than the other. In Nehru's days, the ideational factors were probably the more important source of India's modified structuralism. This interpretation is reflected in the common judgment that the first prime minister was an idealist and a moralist.

Since Nehru, the pendulum has swung toward material factors as the primary cause of India's policy of modified structuralism. India's security posture and behavior, many have argued, appears incoherent. Most recently, Sandy Gordon has ascribed this inconsistency to India's being a "weak-strong" state—weak internally, economically, and in some respects militarily; strong in terms of its overall size, resources, and ambitions (Gordon 1995). Our analysis suggests a somewhat different interpretation of Indian security policies. India's policies are not particularly incoherent: modified structuralism has been and is central. What looks like incoherence is the ebb and flow in the policy-making process between currents that favor modified structuralist postures based on expediency (material factors) or on conviction (ideational factors), the former inclining toward a "power" approach, the latter toward an "institutional" one. On the whole, Indian policy is a tempered, combinatorial one, susceptible to modulation and correction, rarely extreme in any direction.

Does India's policy work? Only a sketchy and brief answer to that question is possible here. On balance, India's policy has served it well. It has lost wars (1962) and won wars (1971), but above all it has not been involved in a major war and its casualties in all its wars combined have been relatively few. It lost some territory to China—the Aksai Chin, essentially—and some to Pakistan in Kashmir in 1948, but no more. Notwithstanding intermittent tensions, it has sustained at least a cold peace with both neighbors since 1971. India has maintained a foreign policy distance from the great powers. It has slowly—admittedly, more slowly than it would like—built up its military and economic strength; it is now a military power that can defend itself against its major rivals and something more, and with recent reforms it is poised to push ahead economically. Its internal politics have been marked by upheavals and violence, but given India's size and diversity it has managed to preserve both stability and democracy. That India's approach to security has not brought about a lasting peace with the country's major rivals or with internal dissidents has been its greatest limitation.

Conclusion

If India's modified structuralist posture has increasingly been informed by material deficiencies rather than normative conviction, what is the future of its security conception? Assuming that material deficiencies are substantially reduced, what will be crucial is whether military or economic deficiencies are remedied first. If Indian military deficiencies are corrected before the economic ones, it is likely that a move toward power and coercive approaches will ensue. If, on the other hand, the economic deficiencies are dealt with before the military, then we may see a swing back toward softer Nehruvian conceptions of security. In such a scenario India would increasingly participate in cooperative security arrangements with its neighbors, with the near regions such as the Persian Gulf, Southeast Asia, and the Asia-Pacific, and with the great powers. New Delhi's more concessionary stance with regard to its neighbors since 1996 (which has already produced major river water agreements with Bangladesh and Nepal), Indian membership in the ARF, and joint military exercises with Southeast Asian countries and the United States presage just such a development.

Since 1991, the signs indicate that the economic deficiencies of India are being treated as the higher priority. In 1991, the financial crisis unleashed India's economic reforms, which have already raised Indian growth rates from between 1.5 and 3 percent to 5 percent a year, brought in foreign investment, and increased India's imports and exports. The economic crisis and the collapse of the Soviet Union, which was India's main military supplier, set off a decline in defense allocations and purchases. In addition, the problems plaguing indigenous arms production and the nuclear program remain largely unresolved. Defense allocations and purchases are already, in 1997, showing signs of increasing once again, but indigenous arms production and the nuclear program will require a considerable effort.

India seems to have chosen butter over guns for the time being. It appears to have set its sights on an economic reform process that will increasingly tie it into a globalizing economy. Growing interdependence promises to move India in the direction of a more cooperative notion of security. Involvement in cooperative security arrangements is vital, because sustained economic growth can lead to a resurgence of defense spending, as is apparently the case in Southeast Asia. With high rates of economic growth and membership in cooperative security structures, India will remain a modified structuralist state—for the sake of conviction rather than expediency—to the benefit of international peace and stability in the twenty-first century.

Japan
Normative Constraints Versus Structural Imperatives

Yoshihide Soeya

Throughout the postwar years, many studies have interpreted the evolution of Japan's security policy as signifying that the country was on the verge of reemerging as a great power in its own right. Although that prediction has not come true, preoccupation with the prospect has never weakened. In fact, it has heightened in the post–Cold War era and is becoming a dominant feature of the discourse on Japan's position in the region and the world, as well as on its security policy. This view of Japan's future, typically articulated by neorealists, reflects an inaccurate understanding of contemporary Japan, but its appeal lies in the belief that, because of systemic pressures from the structure of international politics, an economic superpower cannot remain a political pygmy. Kenneth Waltz argues: "Some countries may strive to become great powers; others may wish to avoid doing so. The choice, however, is a constrained one. Because of the extent of their interests, larger units existing in a contentious arena tend to take on systemwide tasks" (Waltz 1993: 55).

In contrast to neorealists, constructivists seek to explain Japan's actual behavior throughout the postwar years.[1] Reflecting the legacy of Japan's militaristic behavior as a great power, postwar Japanese society has developed a strong antimilitarist norm that has become deeply knit into constitutional and legal institutions, political culture, public opinion, the party system, and the decision-making process. Sporadic challenges to the norm by traditional nationalists have often been frustrated by the tenacity of those social and political elements. In short, Japan in the postwar years has chosen not to become an independent great power in global and regional politics.

Although this constructivist perspective explains much about the postwar realities of Japan's security behavior and its impact on the regional security environment, it does not fully capture the realpolitik considerations that also inform Japanese security thinking. Japan's geographical location, its limited physical endowments, and the complex fabric of the Asia-Pacific security environment ensure that traditional security concerns remain salient. Japan is a close neighbor of Russia and China, as well as the United States across the Pacific Ocean, and is adjacent to the Korean peninsula, traditionally a hotbed of major-power conflict in Northeast Asia. Moreover, Japan is a maritime state and lacks critical natural resources. Secure sea lanes, therefore, continue to be vital to Japan's survival. Thus the standard realist components of security can never be ignored.

This chapter argues that both realism and constructivism are relevant in explaining Japan's security thinking and behavior. Japan has traditional security concerns, but a historical legacy of military expansionism has prevented it from behaving as an independent great power in the usual sense. As we shall see, this tension between Japan's security needs and the normative constraints within which it operates continues into the post–Cold War era. The question this chapter addresses, therefore, is not whether Japan will reassert its identity as an independent military power, but how Japan has coped with this tension and how its coping has evolved over the years. Although there is always the possibility that unpredictable developments may trigger a major shift in Japan's security conception and policy, discussion of such possibilities would be extremely speculative and beyond the scope of this analysis.

In the postwar years, Japanese governments have sought to manage national security needs by limiting the scope of Japan's self-help efforts strictly to self-defense in order to conform to the pacifist clause of Article 9 of the postwar constitution, but compensating for this limitation by relying heavily on the security treaty with the United States.[2] That posture constitutes the essence of Japan's "postwar realism," which is based on the dual identity of postwar Japan. In short, Japan has been a major actor in international politics but has chosen not to act independently in the security arena. What has allowed this apparently contradictory condition to continue is none other than the U.S.–Japan security arrangement (Soeya 1996).

The U.S.–Japan security relationship thus remains central to Japan's security conception and policy. Not only has it enabled the Japanese government to take care of traditional security needs despite the dominant culture of antimilitarism, but it has influenced the way Japanese governments have conceptualized and approached nontraditional security concerns. Despite changing domestic and international developments, the basic tenets of postwar realism and dual identity continue to inform Japanese security thinking and behavior. To substantiate this argument, we begin with a discussion of the referent, the scope and approach to security, and the changes that have taken place. The second part of the chapter develops the argument further from the above analytical perspectives.

The Japanese State

In postwar Japan, the state has not been challenged in its authority to look after political stability and national welfare. During the Cold War, however, as a referent and provider of national security the state was constantly challenged by an influential grouping of pacifists and opposition parties. They viewed the Japanese state as the main provenance of prewar militarism, whose basic elements, they believed, continued into the postwar regime, symbolized by the survival of the emperor system, the institution of the Self-Defense Force (SDF), and the U.S.–Japan security treaty. The opposing political forces inclined toward a neutral internationalism based on the universal appeal of antiwar pacifism (Iwanaga 1985). Although resistance to involvement in military affairs is still strong among the general public, ideological attacks against the political authority gradually declined toward the late 1960s as Japanese society achieved affluence under the government controlled by the Liberal Democratic Party (LDP). More recently, the social-democratic ideology of internationalism as an antithesis to statism has lost its appeal, and its influence in the security debate has considerably weakened with the decline of the Cold War.

The latter development has had two consequences. First, the state as a provider of security is no longer controversial. Security policy making by the government is unlikely to develop into harsh political fighting in the domestic arena so long as the government remains within the constitutional constraints. Consequently, one of the two key elements of Japanese postwar realism—the government's interpretation of the constitutionality of the SDF and the U.S.–Japan security treaty—has become much less controversial in domestic politics. In fact, it has now become possible to debate the scope of the constitutional constraints, including the right of collective self-defense. The second consequence is a corollary of the first: the Japanese government has begun to consolidate the external dimensions of its postwar realism. Tokyo is making a concerted effort to solidify and build on the U.S.–Japan security treaty, particularly with regard to Article 6, which stipulates the legality of U.S. military presence in Japan to promote peace and stability in the Far East.

Scope of Security

During the Cold War, the Soviet threat and instability on the Korean peninsula were major security concerns. They provided a fundamental rationale for the U.S.–Japan security relationship. But, as a consequence of the massive capability of the United States and its determination to meet the Soviet challenge without a direct military contribution from Japan, the Japanese public was shielded from these security threats despite their importance in the eyes of the central decision makers. The public did not necessarily regard the traditional security threats as posing imminent danger to the survival of Japan or to its territorial integrity. As far as the pacifist forces were concerned, threats from the Soviet Union were directed against the United States. Thus Japan would be safer if the U.S.–Japan security ties were terminated. In the context of this popular sentiment and under the effective protection of the United States, the Japanese government did not make specific references to traditional security threats in its articulation of official security policy throughout much of the postwar period. Even in the 1970s, when the Japanese government began to discuss U.S.–Japan military cooperation, a deliberate effort was made to deemphasize traditional security threats.

Traditional Security

The government's articulation of security issues, however, has begun to change significantly in the 1990s as Japanese policy makers have come to discuss traditional security concerns openly. The Diplomatic Bluebook of 1995, for example, states: "The Asia-Pacific region...faces a host of unresolved problems and elements of instability, including heightened military tensions between the North and the South on the Korean peninsula, North Korea's suspected development of nuclear weapons, and the dispute over the territorial claims to the Spratly Islands." The "National Defense Program Outline in and After FY 1996" (*New Taiko*), adopted by the Security Council and the Cabinet on November 28, 1995, summarized the new regional situation as follows:

"While the possibility of a global armed conflict has become remote, complicated and diverse regional conflicts are taking place in the Asia-Pacific and new kinds of dangers such as the proliferation of weapons of mass destruction are on the increase. In the areas surrounding Japan, the possibility of a situation which could seriously affect the security of Japan cannot be excluded." *New Taiko* made specific reference to Russia's large-scale military capabilities (including nuclear arsenals), to the military expansion and modernization of other countries in the region, to various unresolved territorial issues, and to uncertainty on the Korean peninsula.

One underlying feature in these articulations of security concerns is that they refer mainly to sources of instability for the Asia-Pacific region, which then would have security implications for Japan. This indicates that the Japanese government is primarily concerned about the uncertainty in the regional security environment and has not yet ascertained how such unpredictability would affect Japan's security. Most of the expressed concerns indeed focus on Japan's immediate neighbors: Russia, China, and the Korean peninsula.

Russia

Japanese security policy makers continue to be bothered by lingering problems with Russia (among them the issue of the Northern Territories), its military capability, the safety of its nuclear power industry, and the uncertainty in Russian domestic politics and its implications for Moscow's external behavior (Ministry of Foreign Affairs [MOFA] of Japan 1996). The Defense Agency perhaps takes the most alarmist stance in this respect. While acknowledging that "Russian forces in the Far East continue to show the tendency toward quantitative reduction, and their military activity is low key, and their state of readiness is considered lower than before," the Defense White Paper of 1994 points out that "they still constitute enormous military strength and are still being modernized through the relocation of new equipment from the European theater. The presence of such Russian forces in the Far East, coupled with the unpredictability of the Russian forces establishment, constitute a de-stabilizing factor for the security of the Asia-Pacific region" (Defense Agency 1995a: 5).

Instability and fluidity in both Russia's and Japan's domestic politics, though different in character and magnitude, have contributed to the stalemate in the negotiations over the Northern Territories. In particular, Russian attitudes toward the territorial dispute are becoming increasingly hard-line, contributing to the intensification of Japan's long-standing uneasiness with its northern neighbor. Although the Japanese government has helped Russia to stabilize and democratize in cooperation with the international community, it is no secret that skepticism about the effectiveness of these measures has been a dominant feature of Japanese attitudes. Moreover, suspicion toward Russia is not seriously contested by any significant group of Japanese.

The Japanese government will continue to remain vigilant about Russia's security posture and military capability as well as its overall policy toward Japan. How and why those factors might pose a threat for Japan, however, is not seriously examined by Japan's central decision makers. Russia is simply regarded as a source of instability for the Asia-Pacific region.

China

In general, the idea of China as a security threat is alien to the Japanese government and its people. Until the Sino-American rapprochement in the early 1970s, the Japanese government found "containing China" to be the most troublesome aspect of the U.S. Cold War strategy in Asia. From their long history of contact with China, the Japanese knew that China is a "small universe" unto itself. China, therefore, did not figure as a security threat in Japan's postwar realism.

When Shigeru Yoshida decided to sign the security treaty with the United States and thus to subordinate Japan's traditional security concerns to those of the United States, he tried in vain to resist U.S. pressure to recognize the regime in Taiwan. Chinese communism was different from that of the Soviet Union, Yoshida argued, and Japan's role should be to keep China as an independent entity rather than to contain it. Maintaining some form of economic relations with China at the height of the Cold War did not represent a contradiction for Japan; it was a natural development because Japan conceptualized relations with China outside the logic of the Cold War. For the Japanese government as well as its people, the most significant consequence of Sino-Japanese diplomatic normalization in 1972 was that Sino-Japanese relations and the U.S.–Japan relationship finally became compatible. It was the new logic of the Sino-American strategic alignment that made this possible, but the Japanese government and its people refused to see themselves as a factor in that strategic configuration (Soeya 1995).

A central goal in Japan's China policy since then has been to support China's modernization programs, its economic development, and its domestic stability. That aim has not changed fundamentally despite the Tiananmen incident in June 1989. Japan was not pleased with the international sanctions against China, and in August 1991 Japanese Prime Minister Toshiki Kaifu became the first G-7 leader to visit China since the Tiananmen Square incident. Since Kaifu's symbolic visit, Japan even began to add a new dimension to its China policy and a new rationale for its commitment to China. In his policy speech in Beijing, Kaifu used the phrase "Japan-China relations in the world" for the first time in a Japanese policy pronouncement, arguing that a stable Sino-Japanese relationship is important for the stability and prosperity of the Asia–Pacific region and the world (Ishii 1995). The approach was consolidated by the official visit of General-Secretary Jiang Zemin to Japan in April 1992 and by the first-ever visit to China by the Japanese emperor in October of the same year.

A series of new developments since 1992, however, have begun to change Japan's perceptions of China in a significant way. The emphasis on maintaining good relations with China and supporting its modernization efforts continues to inform the official articulation of Japan's China policy. But there are unmistakable signs that the Japanese people in general and some of the central decision makers have become increasingly concerned about new challenges, if not a threat, posed by China. The central challenge, in essence, is that of coping with a new China that appears to be interested in extending its universe beyond the confines that were accepted during the Cold War.

The Chinese proclamation of a territorial law in February 1992 that included the disputed Senkaku Islands (as well as the entire Spratly Islands group in the South China Sea) within Chinese waters, for instance, rang an alarm bell for security policy makers. Japan has claimed sovereignty over the Senkaku Islands since 1895. China disputed that claim in 1971 when the agreement to return the administrative rights of Okinawa (and the Senkakus) to Japan was about to be formally signed. When Chinese fishing boats intruded into the Senkaku waters in the midst of negotiations over the peace and friendship treaty in 1978 and Japan protested, the Chinese government decided to shelve the issue. The Japanese perceived the proclamation of the Chinese territorial law in 1992 as an important departure from that earlier Chinese position, and the Japanese have begun to worry about Chinese territorial ambitions.

Strong Chinese resistance at the first ASEAN regional forum to discuss the territorial issues in the South China Sea clearly aggravated Japanese suspicion about Chinese ambitions. Against this backdrop, China's seizure of the Mischief Reef, well within the exclusive economic zone of the Philippines, in February 1995 was not perceived as an isolated incident. The use of military exercises to intimidate the Taiwanese movement toward democracy in the spring of 1996 in the midst of its first presidential election was enough to stimulate a deep concern in Japan over China's propensity to use military force for political purposes.

In August 1995, the Japanese government decided for the first time in its history to suspend grant assistance as a protest against continued nuclear testing by Beijing. It is symbolic that the decision was made by a socialist prime minister, Tomiichi Murayama. Traditionally, Japanese progressive forces and opinion leaders were sympathetic to the Chinese nuclear program, arguing that it was for self-defense and peaceful purposes. Indeed, many of them relied on that logic to support China's nuclear development in the 1960s while denouncing the U.S.-Japan security treaty; but now they recognize the necessity of the U.S.-Japan security treaty and denounce Chinese nuclear testing.

In October 1995, Foreign Minister Yohei Kono of the Murayama cabinet stated in the National Diet that the China factor "is quite significant from the viewpoints of Japanese security, the U.S.-Japan security regime, and the future of Asia."[3] This statement indicates that the Japanese government has begun to be concerned about the long-term implications of an increased Chinese influence for Japanese and regional security. The China factor has not yet been designated as an explicit threat, nor has Japan begun to think in terms of "containing" China, but the change in perception is unmistakable.

How these changing perceptions will affect Japan's China policy is still not clear, but China's new assertiveness "has cast a new light on its rapid economic growth and seeming inability to move beyond nine-teenth-century concepts of state sovereignty" (Green and Self 1996: 36). In Japanese academic circles, which have not traditionally been alarmist about China, there is an emerging consensus that China's external behavior is a case of classic power politics (Okabe 1996).

A long-term assessment of China's future still involves a scenario of economic stagnation and political disruption, which in fact used to be the predominant source of Japanese concern. Since 1992, however, the wind has shifted toward discussion of the self-assertiveness of the new China, suggested by rising Chinese nationalism and proactive military behavior that appears in the eyes of the Japanese to be sustained by long-term strategic thinking. As a direct reflection of this development, sympathy in Japan for Taiwan appears to have increased. The new feeling toward Taiwan has certainly been influenced by Taiwan's remarkable progress in development and democracy, but it also has much to do with China's overbearing behavior.

The new developments discussed here are of concern but are not yet major determinants of Japanese security policy. Even today, there are strong pro-China elements in Japan who do not subscribe to the notion of a "China threat" even as a remote possibility. If China's overbearing attitudes toward the region are modified and softened in the future or if China's domestic problems and instability become greater concerns than its external behaviors, there is still an excellent chance that Japan's traditional attitude of seeking Chinese stability and development could once again become the central element in Japanese thinking.

Korean Peninsula

Much of Japan's security concern with respect to the Korean peninsula involves two elements of the North Korean question: instability in the peninsula, initiated either by North Korea's government or by its domestic instability, and suspected North Korean nuclear development. Regarding the former, the sources of threat discussed by security experts, if not articulated in public documents, include inflow of refugees, intrusion of terrorists, domestic instability instigated by those among the Korean minority in Japan who are sympathetic to Pyongyang, and possible military attacks against U.S. bases in Japan and Japanese supporting forces.

Concern over North Korea's nuclear program and missile development has become serious in the Japanese government, particularly since North Korea refused to allow the return of the inspection team of the International Atomic Energy Agency in February 1993 and announced its withdrawal from the Nonproliferation Treaty in March 1993. The 1993 Diplomatic Bluebook stated: "This issue is particularly a grave one bearing on the security of Northeast Asia" (MOFA Japan 1994: 17). The 1994 Defense White Paper was more alarmist: "Particularly, North Korea's suspected nuclear development is not only a problem that affects the security of North East Asia, including Japan, but also a serious problem for the international community....Furthermore, a combination of nuclear arms development and missile development could create a more dangerous situation" (Defense Agency 1995a: 5).

Given the volatile situation on the Korean peninsula and the unpredictability of North Korea's intentions and behavior, the combination of the suspected North Korean nuclear program and the development of medium-range missiles poses a direct military threat to Japan. Moreover, the Japanese government worries that North Korea's nuclear program has the potential to encourage nuclear proliferation on the Korean peninsula as well as elsewhere in the world, undermining the international nonproliferation regime.

In the longer term, some Japanese security experts, if only privately, perceive two other potential sources of security concern from the Korean peninsula. The first is an instability inherent in the unification process if indeed the process begins; the second is the potential new security policy of a united Korea, for which anti-Japanese nationalism might become an important driving force. With regard to the latter concern, the dispute over Takeshima has always had the potential to ignite Korean anti-Japanese nationalism. The Takeshima Islands, claimed by Japan since 1905, were placed under South Korea's physical control in 1952. Since then, Japan has reasserted its claim of sovereignty whenever necessary—most recently in February 1996 when both Tokyo and Seoul declared exclusive economic zones of 200 nautical miles according to the Law of the Sea Convention. Although the declaration was a legal procedure and was understood as such between the two administrations, the public, the mass media, and many politicians in Korea reacted highly emotionally. The Japanese reaction was calm, in general, but the episode was a reminder that the Takeshima issue will continue to be a source of mutual emotional recriminations, heightening Japanese caution about Korean nationalism.

Economic Security

After Japan's devastating defeat in World War II, reconstruction of the national economy became a top priority for the Japanese governments. It affected the most fundamental aspect of national security, the survival of the people. Their economic well-being was also considered crucial to prevent the infiltration and expansion of communism among the Japanese people as well as in domestic politics. In the early postwar period, the United States regarded Japan's economic problems as incompatible with its own Asian strategy and therefore provided massive economic assistance along with effective security protection. That situation allowed the Japanese policy makers to devote their attention to economic development while taking advantage of the benefits of the Pax Americana.

The basis for this mentality and the attendant greenhouse effect that discouraged the Japanese from taking traditional security seriously, however, began to be shaken with the weakening of the Pax Americana at the end of the 1960s under the Nixon administration. The shift led Japanese security experts and decision makers to undertake a serious reconceptualization of Japan's security needs, which culminated in the concept of comprehensive security. The idea of comprehensive security, formalized by security experts and presented to Prime Minister Masayoshi Ohira in 1980, is often seen as tantamount to a preoccupation with economic security alone that permitted Japan to disregard military security issues under the protection of the United States. The reasoning behind the concept, however, was quite the opposite: it was the perception of declining American hegemony, not the predominance of the United States, that propelled the idea of comprehensive security, of which economic security was an important part. With the decline of U.S. economic hegemony and the rising temptation to engage in economic protectionism, it became harder to maintain a liberal international economic system. Moreover, the management of economic friction with the United States became an important agendum as the United States began to readjust its own economic policies and to regard its own economic security as increasingly important.

The two oil shocks in the 1970s reminded Japan that its postwar economic success was fragile. The striking features of the Japanese economy at the time were a major dependence on crude oil, which accounted for 77.6 percent of the country's energy requirements, and dependence on the Middle East for 77.4 percent of its oil supply (Orr 1993: 291). The shocks made the Japanese government recognize not only its near-total dependence on imported energy resources but also its lack of effective policies to cope with such a fragile situation. Under these circumstances, differences with the United States over the management of economic problems were an added burden to the Japanese government—not necessarily because the U.S. demands were perceived as damaging to Japan's economic well-being (in fact, the dominant perception not only of the Americans but also of many Japanese was quite the opposite), but because the economic differences could spill over into the security relationship and undermine the basis of Japan's postwar realism.

Japanese economic nationalists, such as those in the Ministry of International Trade and Industry (MITI), were generally interested in protecting Japan's domestic interests, including their own bureaucratic control over the Japanese economy. Security and political experts, however, tended to argue for the paramount importance of preserving a healthy overall relationship with the United States. While the Foreign Ministry was leading the economic negotiations with the United States, therefore, Japan repeatedly made concessions in the end, albeit grudgingly.

That situation continued into the early 1990s, when MITI began to lead economic negotiations with the United States. The symbolic turning point came in February 1994 when Prime Minister Morihiro Hosokawa, accepting the argument of MITI officials, said no to President Bill Clinton, rejecting the U.S. insistence on "numerical targets" in the automobile negotiations. It was the first time that economic negotiations had broken up a summit meeting between the United States and Japan in the postwar years. At this juncture, however, the Japanese economy began to slip rapidly, and—as already discussed—new traditional security concerns began to emerge, calling eventually for the "reaffirmation" of the U.S.–Japan security alliance in April 1996. Now, the Japanese government perceives economic problems such as sluggish growth and the hollowing out of manufacturing industries, as well as those associated with the rapidly aging society, as threats to the well-being of the nation. Increasingly the causes are considered to lie in the domestic structure, and the solutions to require a fundamental reconfiguration of the postwar political and economic system. Consequently, the high tensions that have long characterized U.S.–Japan economic relations have begun to subside.

Milieu Goals

In the post–Cold War era, the Japanese government regards the management of fluidity in international relations and power transition after the demise of the Cold War structure as an important security goal. The Diplomatic Bluebook of 1995, for example, defined Japan's "active diplomatic efforts to secure international peace and security" as one of the three main pillars of Japan's security policy along with "firmly maintaining the U.S.–Japan security arrangements and securing Japan's own appropriate defense capability" (MOFA Japan 1995).

In the Japanese government's recent enunciations of security concerns, such milieu goals are increasingly taking a prominent place alongside the solidification of the U.S.–Japan alliance. This phenomenon has several implications. First, Japan's status requires it to assume "systemwide tasks" (i.e., to manage international security issues), but those functions must be performed in a way that does not contradict the premises of Japan's postwar realism, and in particular its commitment to military self-restraint. Second, to the extent that Japan's contribution to traditional security continues to be constrained by the framework of postwar realism, the Japanese government considers it important to play a role in other security areas. In other words, contributing to security in nontraditional domains is not only considered a rational goal in itself in the post–Cold War context but is also thought to be necessary to preserve the basic framework of postwar realism.

These milieu goals involve both global and regional issues. Global issues often discussed in government documents include environmental conservation, human rights and humanitarian issues, population and health problems, and proliferation of weapons of mass destruction. Regional issues include, apart from the global issues, the lack of confidence among Asian neighbors, divergent and ambiguous perceptions about the regional roles of the United States and other major powers, and the growing military buildup by countries in the region.

Domestic Security

In the early postwar years, social uprisings by leftists and challenges by pacifists to the government's conservative, pro–United States policies were major sources of domestic instability. Soon after the war, amid Japan's economic devastation, popular dissatisfaction with the economy was easily linked with antiestablishment political movements. This situation compelled the U.S. and Japanese governments to include a stipulation in the 1951 security treaty to the effect that the U.S. forces in Japan could be used to "put down large-scale internal riots and disturbances in Japan." However, as Japanese society became affluent toward the end of the 1960s and the 1970s, the dissident political movements gradually came to be seen as less threatening to domestic security.

Under those circumstances, contingencies such as a major earthquake came to occupy the minds of Japanese policy makers and experts. The "Comprehensive Security Strategy Report" of 1980, for instance, warned that because Japan's political, economic, and cultural functions are concentrated in large cities that are vulnerable to severe earthquakes, effective measures to prepare for and cope with such occurrences are a matter of comprehensive national security. *New Taiko* of 1995 also cited "large-scale disasters" as an issue of domestic security.

Recently, in a volatile post–Cold War security environment, the Japanese government has begun to see the danger of terrorist insurgency as a serious threat to national security. According to a draft plan of *New Taiko* reported in the *Asahi Shinbun* in May 1995, Japan should be prepared for a variety of dangers rather than for a military invasion alone—including (in addition to obstruction of sea lanes, encroachment on the territorial sky, and partial occupation of national land) various terrorist activities and intrusion by armed refugees. As noted earlier, many of these contingencies are associated with instability and conflict in North Korea and the Korean peninsula, even though the association is not explicitly stated in any government document.

Approaches to Security

Such a broad range of security concerns naturally call for a variety of means to cope with them. Japan combines traditional means of self-help and alliance to meet traditional security challenges with diplomatic and economic means to cope with nontraditional issues. The actual mix of these measures is significantly affected by Japan's dual identity and the premises of its postwar realism.

Approaches to Traditional Security

In postwar Japan, a balance-of-power approach to traditional security concerns has been officially taboo; such an approach would imply that Japan's involvement in power politics had gone beyond provision for its self-defense. Postwar Japanese security policy pronouncements, therefore, have never referred to the concept in justifying Japanese approaches to security. Indeed, the tendency has been to deny publicly any Japanese involvement in balance-of-power politics. In reality, however, balance of power has been an important component of Japanese security thinking and behavior. Prime Minister Shigeru Yoshida's choice in 1951 was to conclude the U.S.–Japan security treaty, which in fact subordinated Japan's traditional security concerns to those of the United States in the balance-of-power game. In the tradition of Japan's postwar realism, Japan's own efforts at self-help have been justified only as means of self-defense. This approach to traditional security has been affirmed repeatedly through a series of central governmental policy documents and Japan's actual behavior.

Self-Help

Before the 1976 "National Defense Program Outline" (*Taiko*) was developed, Japan's defense policy was articulated in a series of four defense programs respectively adopted in 1957, 1961, 1966, and 1972. The guiding principles for those programs were stated in the "Basic Policy for National Defense" (*Kokubo no Kihon Hoshin*) adopted in 1957. That document did not state how the U.S.–Japan security ties and Japan's own defense were related. It simply said that the U.S.–Japan security system is the "basis" of defense efforts against foreign aggression and asserted that Japan's acquisition of an effective defense capability should be a "gradual" one "commensurate with its national power and conditions and within the limits necessary for self-defense."

A serious attempt to establish an organic linkage between Japan's self-help efforts and the U.S.–Japan security ties was triggered by a new U.S. policy articulated in the 1969 Nixon Doctrine, which called for increasing its Asian allies' participation in their own defense and development. The link eventually materialized in the form of *Taiko*, adopted in October 1976 (Tanaka 1996). *Taiko* dismissed the likelihood of full-scale aggression against Japan and recognized only the possibility of limited military conflict in Japan's neighborhood. Based on that view, *Taiko* called for the establishment of the "Standard Defense Force" to ensure "the maintenance of a full surveillance posture in peacetime and the ability to cope effectively with situations up to the point of limited and small-scale aggression." In this context it is significant that the government's decision to set the defense budget ceiling at 1 percent of gross national product was made in November 1976, one month after the adoption of *Taiko*, and thus apparently was an important element of the *Taiko* regime. Any contingency beyond "limited and small-scale aggression" would be met through the U.S.–Japan security arrangements.

When the concept of comprehensive security was formalized by Japanese security experts and presented to Prime Minister Masayoshi Ohira in 1980, the significance of Japanese self-help efforts was reaffirmed using a similar logic. The "Comprehensive Security Strategy Report" argued that the new U.S. security policy based on the Nixon Doctrine augmented the importance of military security issues for Japan. Therefore, "for the first time in the postwar years, Japan has to think seriously about its own efforts toward [military] self-help" (Sogo-anzenhosho Kenkyu-group 1980: 33). The report thus justified Japan's defense capability as a "denial capability," which should be effective in deterring a small-scale and limited aggression. National defense based on such a capability would be sufficient, it argued, under the aegis of the sustained U.S.–Japan security system, which should be effective for the defense of Japan and for maintaining a military balance vis-à-vis the Soviet Union (Sogo-anzenhosho Kenkyu-group 1980: 50–53). In other words, Japan's own defense efforts were justified within the confines of constitutional constraints and as an integral component of the overall scheme of the U.S.–Japan security arrangements, which meant the reaffirmation of Japan's postwar realism under new circumstances, based on its dual identity.

In the post–Cold War environment, the "National Defense Program Outline in and After FY 1996" (*New Taiko*), which was officially adopted on November 28, 1995, discussed the role of Japan's defense capabilities in three areas: national defense; response to large-scale disasters and various other situations, including a situation in the areas surrounding Japan "which will have an important influence on national peace and stability"; and contribution to the creation of a more stable security environment, including participation in international peacekeeping activities, promotion of security dialogues and exchanges among defense authorities, and cooperation on arms control and disarmament. Accordingly, it dropped a reference to "limited and small-scale aggression" as a target of Japan's defense preparedness, although it continued to employ the concept of a Standard Defense Force.

The signs are unmistakable that the SDF's role has now expanded beyond the traditional role of national defense into two new areas: "various situations including a situation in the areas surrounding Japan" and the creation of a stable security environment. The first role implies that the SDF will be coping with terrorist activities and inflows of refugees and supporting U.S. military operations in Japan's vicinity based on the stipulations of the security treaty and the peace constitution. The second role implies that the SDF will be supporting Japan's overall efforts to pursue the milieu goal of creating a stable security environment through noncombative measures. The adoption of these new roles is a reflection of Japan's new perceptions of security concerns in the post–Cold War era.

The U.S.–Japan security relationship is still considered the fundamental and indispensable basis for these new dimensions of Japan's self-help efforts. As such the fundamental premises of Japan's postwar realism are still central to it's approach to traditional security.

U.S.–Japan Security Ties

Traditional security concerns originally provided the fundamental rationale for the U.S.–Japan security relationship. Moreover, the security relationship allowed the Japanese government to live up to the peace constitution, which prohibited Japan from becoming involved in "international disputes." The U.S.–Japan security setup has thus allowed postwar Japan to maintain its dual identity—as a major actor coping with traditional security issues and as a pacifist nation committed to a nonthreatening security posture.

In the 1970s, reacting to their perception that the Pax Americana was declining, Japanese policy makers began their first serious attempt to establish a linkage between Japan's defense efforts and the mission of the U.S.–Japan security arrangements. The consolidation of the *Taiko* regime, therefore, proceeded alongside a search for institutionalized defense cooperation between Japan and the United States. A concrete outcome was the adoption of the "Guidelines for U.S.–Japan Defense Cooperation" in November 1978.

The guidelines defined the broad responsibilities of each side and called for joint studies on operational issues in three areas: prevention of aggression against Japan, responses to military attacks on Japan, and U.S.–Japan cooperation in case of a conflict in the Far East. Two sets of studies were conducted on joint defense planning as stipulated in the guidelines: one presupposing an attack on Japan, the other envisioning an emergency in the Far East. The latter studies, because of the constitutional and political constraints on Japan's regional security role, were not very productive. The former, however, resulted in an important development after the May 1981 meeting between Prime Minister Zenko Suzuki and President Ronald Reagan, at which Suzuki agreed to make efforts to protect 1,000 nautical miles west of Guam and north of the Philippines. Thereafter, defense of sea lanes became an important component of U.S.–Japan joint defense planning, the study of which was completed in December 1986. In addition, Japan has cooperated with the United States by extending host-nation support for U.S. forces in Japan and by supplying military technology. In recent years, Japan's expenditures for support of U.S. forces in Japan have accounted for about 10 percent of its total annual defense budget, which makes Japan the most generous supporter of U.S. forces abroad. The Japanese government also decided in January 1983 to supply military technology to the United States, making an exception to its ban on arms exports.[4]

New Taiko recognized three functions of the U.S.–Japan security relationship: it is indispensable to "Japan's security"; it will continue to play a key role in achieving "peace and stability in the surrounding region of Japan" and establishing "a more stable security environment"; and it facilitates Japanese efforts for "peace and stability of the international community, including promotion of regional multilateral security dialogues and cooperation, as well as support for various United Nations activities."

The most important of these functions in the post–Cold War context amounts to a new role for the U.S.–Japan security relationship in maintaining regional stability. That function, however, does not necessarily derive from particular stipulations of the security treaty, nor is it directed against any particular country. Rather, it would become apparent only in the long-term dynamics of shifting great-power relations. This role of stabilizing changing regional security environments could be called an implicit function of the U.S.–Japan alliance. The "U.S.–Japan Joint Declaration on Security," signed by Prime Minister Ryutaro Hashimoto and President Bill Clinton in April 1996, reaffirmed this logic. The Declaration states that "the Japan–U.S. security relationship, based on the Treaty of Mutual Cooperation and Security between Japan and the United States of America, remains the cornerstone for achieving common security objectives, and for maintaining a stable and prosperous environment for the Asia-Pacific region as we enter the twenty-first century."

The U.S.–Japan alliance also has had the explicit function of dealing with potential short-term regional conflict such as the situation on the

Korean peninsula. This function derives from Article 6 of the bilateral security treaty, which states: "For the purpose of contributing to the security of Japan and the maintenance of international peace and security in the Far East, the United States of America is granted the use by its land, air and naval forces of facilities and areas in Japan." The 1996 Joint Declaration elaborated the explicit function of the alliance by listing five areas where efforts should be undertaken to advance cooperation: (1) continued close consultation on defense policies and military postures, as well as exchange of information and views on the international situation; (2) a review of the 1978 guidelines for Japan–U.S. defense cooperation, including studies on bilateral cooperation in dealing with situations that may emerge in the areas surrounding Japan and would influence the peace and security of Japan; (3) promotion of the bilateral cooperative relationship through the Acquisition and Cross-Servicing Agreement (ACSA) signed on April 15, 1996; (4) promotion of mutual exchange of technology and equipment; and (5) prevention of the proliferation of weapons of mass destruction and their means of delivery, as well as cooperation in the ongoing study of ballistic missile defense. The contact between the Japanese and U.S. defense establishments to promote this new logic is expanding rapidly. The central decision makers' aim is to accomplish this explicit role of the alliance without major changes in the current political arrangement, including the constitution.

Two concrete measures agreed to during Clinton's 1996 state visit are the ACSA and a revision of the "Guidelines for Defense Cooperation Between Japan and the United States." The ACSA defines ways and means of U.S.–Japan cooperation in such areas as joint military exercises, U.N. peacekeeping operations, and international humanitarian relief activities. The revised Guidelines for U.S.–Japan Defense Cooperation were completed in September 1997. Categories of U.S.–Japan security cooperation to cope with "situations in areas surrounding Japan" listed in the new guidelines are relief activities and measures to deal with refugees; search and rescue; noncombatant evacuation operations; activities for ensuring the effectiveness of economic sanctions; use of Japanese facilities by the U.S. military; rear-area support (supply, transportation, maintenance of equipment, medical services, security of U.S. bases in Japan, communications, etc.); surveillance; minesweeping; and sea and air space management. The new guidelines listed 40 concrete items of cooperation as examples.

Regarding a potential nuclear threat from North Korea, Japan will continue to rely on its security cooperation with the United States. A newly emerging case of such cooperation is in theater missile defense

(TMD). The first administrative working group meeting on TMD was held in December 1993, followed by a second meeting in May 1994 and a third in October 1994, for purposes of information exchange and joint research planning (Defense Agency 1995b). Nothing concrete, however, has evolved yet.

China is not an explicit target of the efforts to strengthen the U.S.–Japan security alliance. The "reaffirmed" U.S.–Japan alliance, however, has an implicit purpose of maintaining a balance in regional security in general if not against a specific country. Whether this implicit aspect of the alliance will develop into explicit security planning against China, therefore, will depend on Chinese actions over the long run and on the perceptions of decision makers in Tokyo and Washington.

Approaches to Economic Security

As long as the Bretton Woods system was stable under strong U.S. leadership, Japan's economic vulnerabilities did not present themselves as imminent security concerns for the Japanese decision makers. But as the Bretton Woods system began to weaken in the early 1970s, Japanese governments began to perceive an acute need to cope with economic security concerns. The U.S. inclination since the Nixon administration has been to redefine its approach to international economic issues in terms of protecting and promoting national interests; that tendency has given rise to chronic structural economic friction between Japan and the United States. As the United States increasingly viewed economic relations with Japan as having significant implications for its own national security, coping with the economic friction began to have security implications for Japan—not necessarily because of its effects on Japan's economic prosperity but because of its potential to spill over into the security relationship.

Resource Diplomacy

The import of natural resources and the export of manufactured products were two crucial pillars of Japan's postwar economic development. When the prospect of a China market was shattered in 1950 by the outbreak of the Korean War and the subsequent U.S. decision to "contain" China, the United States decided to nurture a Southeast Asian market for Japan's growth. In this overall strategy, the Japanese government would use war reparations to strengthen its economic ties with Southeast Asia, and particularly to establish a pattern of trade that exchanged natural resources from Southeast Asia for manufactured products from Japan. Later, Japan's official developmental assistance

(ODA) to Southeast Asia was deployed for the same purposes. Japanese investment in Southeast Asia also grew as an integral part of the overall development of economic ties.

The oil shock of 1973—which caused a reduced oil supply and a sharp hike in the oil price (from about $3 to $12 per barrel) and had a hyperinflationary impact on the domestic economy—was a sobering event that made the Japanese recognize a fundamental vulnerability of their nation. The Japanese government responded to the crisis with straightforward resource diplomacy toward the Arab countries, even at the risk of contradicting the U.S. pro-Israel policy. Concurrently, Tokyo supported the overall U.S. policy in the Middle East wherever possible, because support for U.S. policy was considered crucial for the stability of the Middle East and thus for Japan's economic security as well as for the stability of the U.S.–Japan security relationship.

The sense of crisis during the 1973 oil shock was so acute that Prime Minister Kakuei Tanaka dispatched an entourage led by Takeo Miki, an LDP leader who would succeed Tanaka a year later, with a major aid package of $3 billion including $1 billion each to Iran and Iraq. This move was a clear deviation from Japan's usual approach of request-based aid giving. Accordingly, Japan's ODA to the Middle East increased sharply as a proportion of Japan's total ODA, from 1.4 percent in 1973 to 10.6 percent in 1975 to 24.5 percent in 1977 (Orr 1993: 291–92). This and other pro-Arab policies, particularly the government's announcement in November 1973 indicating that it might reconsider its policy toward Israel, were not welcomed by the U.S. administration. Nonetheless, placating oil-supplying countries proved effective. In December 1973, OPEC decided to designate Japan as a "friendly" nation whose oil supply would not be reduced.

To the extent that these efforts at resource diplomacy proved effective, the other logical approach was to support U.S. policy in the Middle East as much as possible. The new ODA after the first oil shock, therefore, included a political consideration to promote the overall U.S. objectives in the Middle East. During the Ford and the Carter administrations, for example, Japan increased its assistance to Egypt, which chose to lean away from the Soviet Union toward the United States. Between 1977 and 1980 Egypt received $441.64 million in Japanese ODA, and through the mid-1980s it enjoyed the highest amount of yen credit increases of any recipient (Orr 1990: 94). Japan's strategic aid to support the overall U.S. policy in the 1980s was a natural development emerging from the political use of ODA initially deployed in support of its resource diplomacy.

Energy Security

The oil crisis in 1973 made Japan realize the urgent need to stabilize the supply of energy resources. The Japanese approach to the energy situation was twofold: to diversify its supply countries and to diversify its energy resources. This policy was formally endorsed by a cabinet decision in December 1975. Accordingly, the government set the target figure for the oil share among all energy sources in 1980 as 68.9 percent, compared with the actual figure of 77.6 percent in 1973. The policy proved effective; the oil share in 1980 actually dropped to 66.4 percent.

In 1992, Japan depended on imports for 83.6 percent of its energy resources. In the same year, 58.2 percent of energy came from oil, 16.1 percent from coal, 10.6 percent from natural gas, 10.0 percent from nuclear energy, and the rest from hydroelectric power and other sources (Genshiryoku Iinkai 1995: 28, 30). Japanese oil imports, however, still come mostly from the Middle East, indicating that the policy to diversify supply countries has not been very successful. Japan is trying to fill the gap by lowering the share of oil and compensating with an increase in the share of nuclear energy. The government projects that the share of oil among energy resources will be reduced to 47.7 percent by the year 2010, for example, whereas the share of nuclear energy will be increased to 16.9 percent (Genshiryoku Iinkai 1995: 30). As the world's largest importer of energy, Japan is weary of the unpredictable international energy situation—hence its quest to produce nuclear energy (Donnelly 1993).

With regard to Japan's energy reserve, the Petroleum Reserve Law enacted in 1975 demands that petroleum-related private companies together hold the total of a 90-day reserve. That goal was achieved in 1981. The government itself began to hold oil reserves in 1978, and by 1988 it had achieved its initial goal of a 50-day reserve. Since then, under the new policy adopted in 1987 to increase the government's share with a commensurate cut in private reserves, Japan has maintained approximately a 140-day oil reserve in all (Nihon Enerugi Keizai Kenkyu-jo 1993: 82).

Managing Tensions in U.S.–Japan Economic Relations

The economic and political implications of recurring tensions in U.S.–Japan economic relations are both enormous and diverse. A full examination of those consequences, therefore, is beyond the scope of this analysis. Of central concern here is the potentially devastating impact of those tensions on the central premise of Japan's postwar realism: the U.S.–Japan security relationship. Some of the outcomes of conflict—for instance, the sharp rise in the value of the yen—have affected Japan's economic interests adversely. But even then, maintaining a good overall relationship with the United States was considered crucial to Japan's basic interests. Therefore the pattern of Japan's response has been to make concessions to the demands of the United States in the end, albeit grudgingly, for the sake of healthy overall relations.[5]

The first significant case of friction was the textile dispute during the Nixon administration; in that case Japan conceded by agreeing to restrict Japanese exports. In the quarrels over steel and color televisions in the late 1970s, disputes were settled by orderly marketing agreements that constituted de facto voluntary export restraints. In the automobile dispute in the early 1980s, Japan adopted unilateral voluntary export restraints. Since then the focus of U.S. demands has shifted from Japanese exports to the U.S. market to U.S. exports to the Japanese market, and contentious issues have included products in the agricultural and high-technology sectors, where the United States has enjoyed comparative advantage. The U.S. demands to liberalize beef and citrus markets, originally made in 1981, finally prevailed in 1988. The semiconductor agreement, setting a numerical target of a 20 percent share of foreign products in the Japanese market, was concluded in 1986.

Since the late 1980s, reciprocity and Japan's domestic impediments to import and foreign investment have become central concerns for the United States. That concern was reflected in the Super 301 provision of the Omnibus Trade and Competitiveness Act of 1988, which justified U.S. retaliations against trading partners that would not "open" their markets to U.S. products. It was no secret that Japan was the primary target. The items subject to negotiation with Japan according to the Super 301 provision were supercomputers, satellites, and wood products; by 1990, Japan had accepted the U.S. demands. Then came the structural impediments initiative (SII) talks in 1989–90, which attempted to rectify Japanese structural barriers in pricing, public investment, distribution, the use of land, and more.

The dominant perception among Japanese decision makers and the Japanese public regarding these negotiations is that they are constantly making concessions to the United States. That this ever-growing negative perception has not had a backlash effect on the security dimension of the relationship indicates that the concession approach has been effective and that the centrality of the U.S.–Japan security relationship for Japanese postwar realism is accepted by the majority of the Japanese policy makers and the public. In other words, it is the strength of Japanese postwar realism that has motivated the Japanese to survive this series of conflicts with the United States. Those who are tough on the United States tend to be "nationalists" both in economic and general terms.

Approaches to Milieu Goals

To the extent that Japan's postwar realism limits its approach to traditional security concerns, the relative importance of nontraditional security in the policy agenda is augmented. In other words, the Japanese government considers it crucial to promote security in nontraditional domains in order to preserve the basic premises of Japanese postwar realism. Also, in the post–Cold War context, where fluidity and uncertainty are typical and a fundamental shift in security environments is under way, the milieu goals of managing a stable transition and maintaining peace and stability in a volatile security environment are important in themselves. This post–Cold War reality further contributes to Japan's energetic pursuit of milieu goals.

United Nations

In the mainstream thinking of the Japanese government, eagerness to participate in the management of a new international order is the central driving force in its bid for permanent membership in the U.N. Security Council. According to Hisashi Owada, a senior official of the Foreign Ministry and a chief promoter of the policy, its purpose is to show Japan's determination "to assume a due responsibility in the U.N. scheme to realize peace and prosperity in the post–Cold War world" (Owada 1996: 97). According to another senior Foreign Ministry official, a country like Japan that bears a huge financial burden should have a permanent voice in U.N. decision making.

There are two notable arguments in Japan opposing the pursuit of permanent membership in the U.N. Security Council. One position argues that Japan should not volunteer for the post but should wait until it is invited to become a member. The other contends that Japan should not seek membership because it would mean assuming responsibilities in the area of collective security, which is prohibited by the Japanese constitution. In these domestic debates, the Foreign Ministry's position is not necessarily a majority view and there is no domestic consensus.

The Gulf Crisis and the Gulf War in 1990–91 became a turning point in Japan's approach to U.N. peacekeeping operations. Japanese efforts to contribute to the U.N.'s peacekeeping operations through manpower (i.e., SDF participation) were sparked when Japan's financial contribution of $13 billion did not receive due credit in the international community (Inoguchi 1991; Purrington 1992). The Japanese government's policy on peacekeeping operations has been determined by two opposing factors: the government's aspiration to discharge its responsibility for international peace and stability through an active contribution of manpower, on the one hand, and various political, legal, and social constraints on its expanded security profile, on the other.

Japan's Law Concerning Cooperation for United Nations Peacekeeping Operations and Other Operations (commonly referred to as the International Peace Cooperation Law), enacted in June 1992, was illustrative of the policy shift. Under the law Japan may participate in peacekeeping operations and humanitarian international relief, including cease-fire monitoring, election monitoring, police monitoring, medical care, assistance for disaster victims, transport, and construction. Japan's participation in peacekeeping operations, however, is bound by five conditions: agreement to a cease-fire among conflicting parties should be in place; consent to the deployment of peacekeeping operations and to Japan's participation should be given by conflicting parties and concerned territorial states; impartiality of the peacekeeping operations should be maintained; upon violation of any of the preceding three requirements Japanese activities should be suspended and Japanese troops should be withdrawn; and use of weapons should be limited to actions necessary to protect people's lives. The law also stipulates a freeze on the SDF's participation in peacekeeping forces (as distinguished from peacekeeping operations), which are defined to include cease-fire operations, demobilization, and stationing and patrolling in buffer zones between conflicting parties.

Cases of Japanese participation in peacekeeping operations since the adoption of the International Peace Cooperation Law include the United Nations Angola Verification Mission II (UNAVEMII) in 1992, the United Nations Transitional Authority in Cambodia (UNTAC) in 1992–93, the United Nations Operation in Mozambique (ONUMOZ) in 1993–95, the United Nations Observer Mission in El Salvador (ONUSAL) in 1994, Rwanda refugee relief activities in 1994, and the United Nations Disengagement Observer Force (UNDOF) in the Golan Heights in 1995–96.

Multilateral and Bilateral Security Dialogue

In its policy toward regional political talks and security dialogue, the Japanese government's initial thinking emphasized the flexible application of "multiplex" mechanisms involving effective use of existing relationships and institutions for regional cooperation (MOFA Japan 1992: 71–73). Out of this multiplex thinking developed a two-track approach whose official version was enunciated by Prime Minister Kiichi

Miyazawa in 1992: on the one hand would be Japanese efforts toward "the promotion of subregional cooperation to settle disputes and conflicts"; on the other would be "regionwide political dialogue to enhance the sense of mutual reassurance." The Japanese government's initiative for "political dialogue" was first articulated by Foreign Minister Taro Nakayama in July 1991 at the ASEAN Post-Ministerial Conference (PMC) in Kuala Lumpur. Nakayama expressed Japan's willingness to participate in "political dialogue aiming at enhancing a feeling of reassurance [*anshin-kan*] with each other" and proposed to use the ASEAN PMC as a forum for the dialogue.

Behind Japan's interest in multilateral security dialogue was a mixed motive of coping with the legacies of the past and taking part in the creation of a stable security environment in the region. This balancing element was manifest in Nakayama's proposal in 1991: in proposing political dialogue at the ASEAN PMC, he referred to regional fears about not only Japan's increasing political role but also its possible military role in the future, thus hinting that widely held concerns about Japan's regional role could be placed on the agenda of regional political dialogue. Japan's interest in the Asia-Pacific multilateral security dialogue was sustained also by its concerns about the future roles of the United States and China. The 1993 Diplomatic Bluebook stated that behind the region's increasing interest in political and security dialogue were "common concerns about the U.S. military presence and engagement in the future and the future roles of Japan and China" (MOFA Japan 1994: 61). In sum, in the initial conception of an approach emphasizing multilateral security dialogue by the Japanese government, the central intention was twofold: to create a forum for dispelling mutual distrust among nations in the Asia-Pacific and to reengage major powers constructively in the transitional process taking place in the regional security environment.

The United States was initially wary of Japanese intentions and their possibly adverse impact on the U.S.–Japan security relationship. There was fear that Japan might drift away from the United States. The ASEAN countries, naturally cautious about external powers taking a regional initiative, were also cool to the Japanese initiative. Subsequently the idea of political dialogue was promoted by ASEAN as an ASEAN initiative, culminating in the first ASEAN Regional Forum convened in Bangkok in July 1994. The Japanese approach was then readjusted: it now emphasized the importance of a regional security dialogue as a supplement to the U.S.–Japan security relationship. Today the Japanese government expects the regional forum to function also as a mechanism for regional confidence-building, pushing in particular for increased transparency in the security policies of the region's countries.

In parallel with a multilateral dialogue, bilateral confidence-building measures have been promoted by the Japanese government: personal exchanges such as high-level state visits and official policy dialogues; troop exchanges including port calls and exchanges of military observers; and other activities including information exchanges to increase military transparency and agreements to prevent incidents. Japan's primary targets of bilateral confidence-building in recent years have been Russia, China, and South Korea.[6] Through these efforts the Japanese authorities expect to increase the military transparency of those countries, grasp their political and military trends, enhance their understanding of Japanese defense policy, exchange mutual perceptions on regional security environments, and stabilize bilateral relations.

Aside from semigovernmental exchanges such as contacts between defense researchers, Japan and Russia held security policy planning talks in June 1992, February 1994, and July 1995, sponsored by the two foreign ministries and attended by the defense authorities. In May 1993, an Agreement on the Prevention of Incidents at Sea was signed at the occasion of Boris Yeltsin's visit to Tokyo. The agreement provided for annual meetings among policy planners to oversee its implementation. In April 1996, the director general of Japan's Defense Agency (JDA), Hideo Usui, visited Russia for the first time as head of JDA, agreeing with the Russian minister of defense to promote security dialogue and defense exchanges as confidence-building measures. In August 1996, Japan's Maritime SDF paid a port call to Vladivostok for the first time.

As for Japan and China, the first bilateral security dialogue was held in December 1993 between the two foreign ministries. That exchange was followed by a security dialogue between the two defense authorities in March 1994. The third security dialogue, held in January 1995, was attended jointly by the ministries of foreign affairs and defense; it was followed by a fourth security dialogue in January 1996.

The director general of JDA visited South Korea in 1979, 1990, and 1995; South Korea's defense minister visited Japan in 1994 and 1996. Annual policy planning talks between the two countries began in November 1994, followed by a second round of talks in June 1995. South Korea's navy paid a port call to Japan for the first time in December 1994, a visit returned by Japan's Maritime SDF in September 1996.

Political Use of Official Development Assistance

The first explicit use of official development assistance for strategic purposes took the form of grants to Pakistan and Turkey after the Soviet invasion of Afghanistan in December 1979. Those grants have been referred to as "strategic aid" (Yasutomo 1986). In 1980, the Japanese government decided to double its assistance to Pakistan and to extend a major aid package to Turkey (Orr 1990: 111). Although these policies were carried out at the encouragement of the United States, Japan did in fact embark on a new ODA policy for the purpose of stabilizing the security environment. Moreover, justifying the use of ODA for strategic purposes shared with the United States meant that ODA had now become a tool for consolidating the alliance with the United States.

The new Southeast Asian policy announced in August 1977 by Prime Minister Takeo Fukuda, which came to be known as the Fukuda Doctrine, was an earlier instance of a Japanese attempt to use economic assistance in support of political and security objectives. The focus in this case was Southeast Asia; the stated policy objective was to serve as a bridge between ASEAN and Indochina and thus to bring about greater stability in Southeast Asia by encouraging peaceful coexistence between the two. Southeast Asia was regarded as an important region: not only did its geographical location render it capable of threatening Japan's vital sea lanes, but it was an important supplier of natural resources as well as an import and export market (Soeya 1997). Of course, the use of ODA was bound to become ineffective wherever military conflict came to the fore. The Fukuda Doctrine, therefore, was frustrated when Vietnam invaded Cambodia in late 1978. The thinking that informed the Fukuda Doctrine, however, has been reinvigorated in the post–Cold War era. The end of the Cambodian conflict with the Paris Peace Accords of October 1991 led Prime Minister Kiichi Miyazawa, in January 1993, to call for the establishment of a "Forum for Comprehensive Development of Indochina" as a concrete step to implement the Fukuda Doctrine.[7]

In the post–Cold War era, ODA came to be regarded as an effective means to cope with global issues. The ODA Charter, adopted in 1992, represents some of the principles promoting the pursuit of such goals: development and environmental conservation should be pursued in tandem; any use of ODA for military purposes or for aggravation of international conflicts should be avoided; full attention should be paid to trends in recipient countries' military expenditures, their development and production of weapons of mass destruction and missiles, and their export and import of arms; full attention should be paid to recipient countries' efforts to promote democratization and a market-oriented economy as well as to secure basic human rights and freedom for their citizens (MOFA Japan 1994: 94). The objective of using ODA for such political and security purposes is "positive linkage"—encouraging and rewarding the positive records of recipient countries—rather than the "negative linkage" of punishing negative records.

Among those global issues, the Japanese government now devotes most attention to the world environment: in 1992 Japan committed to spend 900 billion to 1 trillion yen on environment-related ODA over five years beginning in 1992; it dispensed 500 billion yen over the two-year period from 1992 to 1993. Environmental conservation is now a central consideration in Japan's ODA to China, where 15 of the 40 projects adopted for the first three years (fiscal 1996–98) of the fourth yen loan to China were devoted to environmental conservation (Hirabayashi 1995). With respect to other terms of the ODA Charter, the effects are harder to ascertain, although the Japanese government has stated its determination to uphold the charter's principles.

Approaches to Domestic Security

In the absence of imminent threats and amid lingering skepticism about government power in postwar Japan, for a long time domestic security was the most neglected area of national security. The Comprehensive Security Strategy Report of 1980 was the first serious attempt to address the question of domestic security. It recommended a comprehensive approach to severe earthquakes, addressing such areas as prediction techniques, city planning, transportation policy, community policy, and the crisis management capacity of the national and local governments (Sogo-anzenhosho Kenkyu-group 1980: 79–83). Since then there has been an increasing awareness of the issue, and central and local governments have begun preparations such as stockpiling emergency food and holding regular drills.

The 1995 Hanshin earthquake, however, exposed serious shortcomings in the government's disaster plans. The prefectural government of Hyogo, for example, had not prepared a manual or conducted exercises regarding cooperation with the SDF in disaster relief. Indeed, many local governments, including that of Hyogo prefecture, in the dominant public spirit of pacifism, have been extremely reluctant to establish a working relationship with the SDF. The 1995 earthquake, which claimed the lives of more than 6,000 citizens, also brought into relief several major defects in the Japanese crisis management system, including the process of gathering and assimilating information in a crisis and the question of political leadership.

Accordingly, *New Taiko*, adopted in November 1995, emphasized the necessity of preparation for "large-scale disasters which can have a significant impact on our highly developed and diversified society" and called for a larger role for the SDF. *New Taiko* also emphasized the need to prepare for "disasters caused by acts of terrorism or other events which require the protection of lives or assets." As an approach to these new security concerns, it states that "Japan's defense capability [should] be reconstructed, both in scale and function, by streamlining, making it more efficient and compact, as well as enhancing necessary functions and making qualitative improvements to be able to effectively respond to a variety of situations."

Explaining Japanese Security

We have seen that since the end of World War II Japan has ceased to seek the status of a traditional great power. Its mercantilist economic behavior, which concerns neorealists such as Kenneth Waltz, was basically the product of a catch-up mentality and a deep sense of economic vulnerability, not an indication that Japan sought to control the world economy. Waltz says that a national choice is constrained by systemic and structural factors, however, and predicts that Japan might even go nuclear because of the structural pressures. In the 1970s, when such structural pressures became real because of the decline in U.S. hegemony, the deep sense of vulnerability and the need to function in an increasingly interdependent world became even greater concerns in the minds of Japanese policy makers. No responsible decision maker in postwar Japan has ever attempted to convert accumulated economic wealth into military might.

The Impact of Systemic Imperatives

The nature of Japan as a power in the structure of international politics is closer to a "civilian power" than to a nuclear Japan. Hanns Maull argues that "international relations are not just undergoing a reshuffling of power hierarchies, but a sea change affecting both the structure and substance of international politics." He believes that Japan, like Germany, is a prototype of a "civilian power" in the world of interdependence (Maull 1990–91: 92). In the same vein, Yoichi Funabashi contends that Japan's unorthodox power portfolio "presents Japan with the opportunity to define its own power and role in the radically changing world ahead. Emergence of a more internationalist and actively engaged Japanese pacifism could play a constructive role in making Japan a global civilian power" (Funabashi 1991–92: 65). Both Maull and Funabashi see the importance of the U.S.–Japan relationship for Japan's status as a successful civilian power. The image of a civilian power is one that better suits Japanese postwar realism, given Japan's commitment to the U.S.–Japan alliance and to military self-restraint.

The neorealist prediction that Japan will reemerge as an independent military power is tantamount to the prediction that the U.S.–Japan security alliance will be terminated as a result of structural pressures. As the foregoing analysis has shown, however, there is no sign that either the Japanese government or the U.S. administration wishes to end the relationship. Moreover, conscious wishes aside, a new structural pressure in Asia—the emergence of China as a structural pole in a new regional system—may move the United States and Japan even closer to each other. There is no indication that Japan is likely to emerge as an independent structural pole comparable to China. The only viable alternative for Japan, even if China becomes a threat, continues to be the alliance with the United States.

From the standpoint of U.S. interests, too, "there is no need to assume that international pressures inevitably dictate that Japanese leaders must become military realists." Even if an independent Japan were to behave within the confines of the U.S. strategy, "it is difficult to think of a U.S. interest in the balance of power that would be served, unless Washington withdraws from the region and relies on Tokyo as its proxy" (Betts 1993–94: 57). Whether Japan's nonnuclear principles will survive the structural pressures that Waltz discusses may also depend on the fate of the U.S.–Japan security alliance. The strength of Japan's norm of pacifism, however, suggests that Japan will continue to rely on the United States for a nuclear umbrella—a policy that is reassuring for the entire region, including China, as well as for the United States.

These arguments, however, do not necessarily suggest that the U.S.–Japan security alliance is certain to be maintained in the coming years. It is commonly understood among experts today that the future of the alliance will depend as much on the intentions of the United States as on those of Japan (Tsuchiyama 1993: 70–71). This raises a central question: Are U.S. intentions a product of structural imperatives or a result of domestic and identity factors including isolationist legacies? U.S. responses that grow out of its domestic and identity factors—which many fear will occur—are beyond anyone's control and moreover do not fit with the realist theory. The U.S.–Japan alliance is certainly not immune to the structural pressures of a changing international order, but Tokyo and Washington are still in full agreement that the alliance will contribute to stability in a shifting world order in which the United States is expected to function as primary leader. Inoguchi (1988–89), pointing to this same expectation, argues that "Pax Americana II" will continue for the short-term future if not forever.

In summary, there are strong indications that the impact of systemic imperatives on Japan's security conception and policy has not weakened the basis of Japanese postwar realism; those imperatives have instead impelled Japanese decision makers to consolidate the U.S.–Japan alliance while seeking a new international role in nontraditional security domains that will not require major modification of Japan's policy of military self-restraint.

Domestic and Identity Factors

Japan's conception of security is fundamentally affected by domestic constraints and identity factors. In this regard the application of a constructivist perspective to Japanese security policy offers useful insights (Katzenstein and Okawara 1993). In the post–Cold War context there are important questions to be explored: how are such internal factors changing, and what impact will they have on Japanese security thinking and behavior in the future?

Domestic Constraints

Domestic political and other constraints on Japan's security policy in the conventional military realm have been strong throughout the postwar years. These constraints operate at three levels: constitutional and legal constraints; public opinion; and the polarization and immobility of domestic politics over the issue of military security. These constraints are all reinforced by the social norm of pacifism and the political culture of antimilitarism.

The culture of antimilitarism is a reflection of how the Japanese in general regarded the war experience: the majority of Japanese felt victimized by their own military. The central theme in the Japanese discourse on the causes of the war, therefore, has been how the military came to power in an "irresponsible" domestic political system where there were no effective checks and balances against the military. According to Thomas Berger (1993: 137), "The negative view of the military is shared all along the political spectrum in postwar Japan. Where these groups differ, however, is in how they propose to prevent the military from becoming a danger again." Under the 1955 regime—which was characterized by an LDP monopoly of power and by the constant failure of the oppositions to form a government—the opposition parties, the national teachers union, and major newspapers and journals became strong supporters of the antimilitarist spirit. Their efforts to prevent the "remilitarization" of Japan were concentrated mainly on staying strictly true to the intent of Article 9 of the constitution. These constraints were important factors in determining the scope of Japan's military security and the country's approach to it. First, the scope of military security in Japan became restricted to areas relevant for self-defense. The Japanese government stipulated three conditions that would permit the use of self-defense: the existence of an imminent and wrongful aggression against Japan; the lack of other means to dispel it; and the minimum use of force if justified according to those two conditions.[8]

The mission of the U.S.–Japan security relationship was also understood to be limited to "the security of Japan and the maintenance of international peace and security in the Far East."[9] The Japanese government's interpretation has been that Japan can contribute to the maintenance of international peace and security in the Far East to the extent that it has a bearing on Japan's self-defense.[10] Still, the effective management of the U.S.–Japan security arrangements has to address the question of collective defense. The current government's interpretation of the constitutional constraints, however, does not recognize the right of collective defense. The Japanese government's official stance on collective defense, clarified in May 1981, is as follows: "It is natural that Japan, being a sovereign state, should have this right of collective defense from the standpoint of international law. The government, however, interprets that the right of self-defense permitted under Article 9 of the constitution should be used within the minimum range of need to defend Japan, and believes that the exercise of the right of collective defense exceeds the range and thus is not allowed constitutionally" (*Boei Handbook* 1995: 417–18). Legally speaking, therefore, joint military actions between the United States and Japan are allowed only in situations where armed attacks or threats are interpreted to justify Japan's self-defense.

It was in this context that the cabinet secretary issued a statement upon the release of *New Taiko* emphasizing that "there is no change in the previous interpretation of the government on items prohibited by the constitution such as the right of collective defense" and stating that the expression "in achieving peace and stability in the surrounding region of Japan" in the section on U.S.–Japan security arrangements does not entail a change in the government's understanding on the range of the "Far East" stipulated in the treaty. In sum, then, the revision of *Taiko* and the "reaffirmation" of the U.S.–Japan alliance were attempts to broaden the scope of Japan's security and define Japan's new approaches at a time of uncertain transition without violating the constitutional constraints or contradicting the previous security and defense policies of the Japanese government. This new "activism" of the Japanese government, therefore, was the direct result of compromise over domestic constraints and identity factors.

New Domestic Developments

In recent years there have been signs that the domestic tension over traditional security has begun to ease and that a new set of questions is emerging. The Socialist Party (formally the Social Democratic Party, SDP), the largest opposition under the 1955 regime, reversed its stance on basic security policy with the ascendance of its leader, Tomiichi Murayama, to prime minister in June 1994. The party's current position is that the SDF is constitutional, and it supports the U.S.–Japan security treaty. The SDP also supports Japan's participation in the U.N.'s peacekeeping operations, a policy it vehemently opposed in 1992 when the peacekeeping bill was passed in the Diet. It is, however, still against Japan's taking part in the U.N.'s Peacekeeping Force (PKF), which could use force in carrying out its mission.

Indeed, the most important development among the recent political changes is the absolute decline of the SDP's influence in the Japanese political process and system.[11] The coalition between the LDP and SDP—archrivals during the Cold War—in June 1994 was a marriage of convenience between two losers in the summer 1993 elections in a desperate attempt to survive this period of massive political transition. Further reshuffling within and among political parties is likely in the coming years. These developments have made it possible to talk about reviewing the peace constitution—a subject that was politically taboo when the SDP was a strong opposition party. That review will have a significant impact on Japan's security conception and policy in coming years.

Reflecting the more tolerant mood, the *Yomiuri Shinbun* (Japan's most widely read newspaper, with a circulation of ten million) has begun to advocate revision of the peace constitution. On November 3, 1994, it devoted four full pages to its own proposed revision.[12] Like the current constitution, the *Yomiuri* proposal does not recognize "the threat or use of force as means of settling international disputes." It does, however, clarify the constitutionality of the SDF by clearly stating that "Japan shall form an organization for self-defense to secure its peace and independence and to maintain its safety." Further, the proposal states that "in case of need, it may dispatch public officials and provide a part of its self-defense organization for the maintenance and promotion of peace and for humanitarian support activities." The central rationale for this proposed revision of the constitution was clearly to remove sources of unproductive domestic conflict in order to allow the SDF's active participation in the maintenance of international peace within the confines of Japanese postwar realism. This basic motive is also increasingly shared by the general public.

According to the *Yomiuri* polls since 1986, the percentage of those in favor of the revision more than doubled from 22.6 percent in 1986 to 50.4 percent in 1995. Conversely, the percentage of those who oppose the revision dropped from 56.6 percent to 30.9 percent in the same period.[13] Regarding the reasons for supporting the revision, "[the current constitution] hinders [Japan's] international contribution" was selected by 56.9 percent of those in favor of the revision in the 1995 poll.

It was in this tolerant atmosphere that the revision of *Taiko* was debated in late 1995. The LDP proposed to reconsider the question of collective security and defense. In its counterproposal to the draft revision of *Taiko*, it asserted that "the argument should be deepened concerning collective security at the United Nations and the right of collective defense" (Policy Affairs Research Council 1995). Nonetheless, domestic resistance from the SDP and other "progressive" politicians and the mass media was not insignificant: they voiced a typical concern about a possible expansion of the regional range of the Far East as covered by Article 6 of the U.S.–Japan security treaty. In the foreseeable future, therefore, the expansion of Japan's security role will probably occur only through reinterpretations of the constitutional constraints. Although the more tolerant public mood suggests that the range of reinterpretation will widen, the fundamental strength of resistance suggests that any attempt at substantive change will continue to be politically controversial.

The Evolution of Postwar Realism

The Japanese conception of security shows that domestic factors complicate the impact of the international security structure. This does not mean that elements of realism and neorealism are not important; it does suggest that they do not necessarily affect security in the way an abstract theory would predict. The domestic factors that shaped Japan's postwar security conception and policy are a direct result of the Japanese prewar experiences. Indeed, the central decision makers of postwar Japan have made that history a central reference point in their articulation of security issues. Consequently, Japan has a dual identity with respect to security: that of a potential great power capable of affecting the international security structure, and that of a self-restraining state. The U.S.–Japan security treaty has been the primary mechanism through which Japan has reconciled its traditional security concerns with the predominant social norm of pacifism and the political culture of antimilitarism. To live with both realities has been the government's choice—and that choice, I have argued, constitutes Japanese realism in the postwar context.

The development of Japan's postwar realism can be summarized roughly in terms of three time periods. In the first period, at the height of the Cold War in the 1950s and 1960s, Yoshida's decision to sign the U.S.–Japan security treaty and to refrain from rearmament beyond the minimum needed for self-defense, known as the Yoshida Doctrine, proved highly effective in securing a favorable environment for economic recovery, the top national priority at the time. Hayato Ikeda's policy of keeping a low political profile and concentrating on economic development in the early 1960s also proved conducive to double-digit growth throughout the 1960s. Under these circumstances, Japan's security was treated primarily as a matter of domestic politics. The dominant Pax Americana obscured the direct link between Japanese security and regional security. The relevance of the U.S.–Japan security arrangements (as well as of the SDF) was debated almost exclusively from the viewpoint of their constitutionality and in terms of whether the security relationship would involve Japan in international military conflict.

The decline of the Pax Americana, foreshadowed in the new diplomacy of U.S. President Richard Nixon in the early 1970s, however, shook the basis of Japan's postwar realism. Japan's fundamental wish at that juncture was to preserve the premises of its postwar realism under the new circumstances. Its efforts to do so evolved in two dimensions. First, the Japanese government began, for the first time in the postwar years, to conceptualize an organic relationship between Japan's self-defense efforts and the mission of the U.S.–Japan security relationship. Increased self-defense efforts by Japan, for example, came to be regarded as important not only as evidence of its willingness to share the security burden with the United States but also as a demonstration of Japan's determination to sustain the U.S.–Japan security relationship. Second, in the eyes of Japanese policy makers, the decline of the Pax Americana augmented the importance of economic security. A stable international economic system was no longer a given. Moreover, the economic tensions made the management of the U.S.–Japan relationship a sensitive issue with significant implications for the security alliance and thus for the viability of Japan's postwar realism. Japan's repeated concessions to U.S. economic demands, however reluctant, were testimony to the government's ultimate determination to protect its postwar realism based on its dual identity.

In the post–Cold War period, the scope of Japan's security has expanded even further. Today it includes the goal of maintaining international peace and stability as well as global issues such as the environment and the proliferation of weapons of mass destruction. To the extent that the Japanese government is bound by a postwar realism that constrains it from assuming an independent role in the handling of traditional security needs, the importance of nontraditional milieu goals for international peace and stability is augmented in two respects. First, these nontraditional security issues are becoming significant in their own right in a new post–Cold War security environment, and it is politically easier for the Japanese government to devote resources to these new security goals than to more traditional ones. Second, devotion to nontraditional security is considered important for protecting the premises of postwar realism: such devotion functions as a compensation for self-restraint in traditional security and is expected to address the "free ride" criticism often directed against Japan.

At the same time, new traditional security needs are emerging in the post–Cold War context. Emphasis on the importance of the U.S.–Japan alliance is thus increasing in the post–Cold War era, and the government has not attempted to revise Article 9 of the constitution. When constitutional revisions have been proposed, such as the one advanced by the *Yomiuri Shinbun* in 1994, their predominant aim has been to lay the domestic political groundwork for the promotion of Japan's active participation in the maintenance of international peace and stability. But even this type of constitutional revision continues to be regarded as politically unfeasible.

It is likely, therefore, that domestic and identity factors, reinforced by the reaffirmed U.S.–Japan alliance, will continue to compel the Japanese to seek a higher international profile in nontraditional aspects of security in the post–Cold War era. The strengthening of Japan's security posture is likely to take the form of an expansion of the framework of Japanese postwar realism—and both the reaffirmed U.S.–Japan security alliance and Japan's commitment to security goals outside the domain of that alliance will continue to be integral parts of that framework.

North Korea
Deterrence Through Danger

DAVID KANG

> *War can only be prevented if you will fight and keep a strong stance. If a bully sees you preparing for a fight by running and working out, he will think differently. You must prepare for war in order to gain peace.*
>
> CHUN DOO HWAN

> *We will destroy Seoul in a sea of fire, like a rabid dog barking at the sky, unaware of the fate about to befall it.*
>
> PARK YONG-SU, quoted in *Vantage Point* 17, no. 3 (1994): 13

In the past few years, as the nuclear "crisis" on the peninsula has intensified, the major policy debates in South Korea (the ROK) and the West have focused on whether to appease or contain North Korean (the DPRK) (Park 1994–95; Bracken 1993; Bailey 1994).[1] Yet this debate, carried on with great vigor by proponents of both camps, presupposes a prior condition: that we understand what drives North Korea's foreign policy. Questions over whether the North will attack the South, whether the North Koreans can be expected to live up to their international agreements, whether it is possible to negotiate with them—all depend upon assumptions about North Korea's conception of security and about how North Korea pursues its foreign policy goals.

The generally accepted view regards the North Koreans as intractable, dangerous, bent on destruction and invasion. In this view North

Korean foreign policy is dominated by personality and perception and can be erratic, violent, and irrational.[2] Scholars with such views write that North Korean foreign policy is "erratic and periodically violent" (Taylor and Mazarr 1992: 152), "logic-defying" (Koh 1988: 384), and prone to "inexplicable spasms of violence" (Perry 1990: 186). Yet almost all theories of war in the literature on international relations conclude that a stronger power is more threatening than a weaker power. Similarly, theories of deterrence and stability point out that the stronger a nation, the more likely it is to deter a weaker power. Even the underlying logic in "preponderance-of-power" theories of stability relies on the notion that the stronger power will not need to fight and the weaker power will not want to fight.

This juxtaposition of theories of international relations with our conception of North Korea leads to a puzzle: these theories would lead one to believe that not only should North Korea be deterred from attacking South Korea, but in fact it should fear an attack by the South. Yet our dominant conception of North Korea is that of an aggressive, dangerous state that wants to attack the South, which is on the defensive. Are our theories of international relations wrong? Can they not account for the behavior of an "outlier" country? Or is the general wisdom on North Korea in need of updating? In this chapter I argue that theories of international relations—with modifications—can easily explain the North Korean case. I will show that North Korea's actions, when viewed through a methodological lens that focuses on consistency of argument and the search for contrary evidence, are consistent with our general conception of international relations.

Essentially, both North and South Korea are mired in a zero-sum battle for the Korean nation. An almost total absence of linguistic, ethnic, and religious cleavages leaves no simple way to "divide the pie" on the Korean peninsula, and the relatively constricted geographic situation, lacking natural barriers to inhibit conflict, intensifies an already acute security dilemma between the two sides. The result is unsurprising: each side views the other as a dangerous and illegitimate state with which compromise is tantamount to surrender.[3] The ongoing contest has far-reaching political, economic, and social consequences.

The most important question for determining North Korea's conception of security is whether or not the North has genuine external security concerns. If North Korea truly has no basis for fear, then either its foreign policies are terribly misguided, through some sort of irrationality or paranoia, or it is pursuing some internal strategy through the cynical and cunning creation of a false external threat. In either case, if there is no genuine external security concern then North Korea's true conception of security must be something other than defensive. If the North does have a genuine fear of South Korea or of the United States, however, its actions become comprehensible.

The underlying theoretical question is how to assess the inherent disposition and goals of a nation. One way of going about this is to ask how nations assess their security. Here I begin the preliminary work of such a task by asking three main questions. First, how does a nation assess its external situation and when does it feel threatened? Second, is North Korea's conception of security offensive or defensive? Finally, does North Korea's policy derive from its external situation, or is it driven by considerations of internal domestic control?

I contend that North Korea's foreign policy is based on a mixture of fear and opportunism and that North Korea's conception of security is overwhelmingly concentrated on its external relations, in particular with South Korea. More important than underlying notions of a country's fixed intentions is an understanding of how intentions change with altered circumstances. Dividing the history of North Korea's foreign policy into three broad eras—predominance, decline, and poverty—I argue that although North Korea invaded the South 45 years ago, it is highly unlikely that North Korea currently retains such aggressive intentions in any serious way. I will also show that although North Korea is an outlier state in a fairly unique situation, its foreign policy responses have been relatively predictable. Because of North Korea's position in the world, it is not surprising that North Korea does not behave like Belgium or like Mexico. North Korea is in an extreme international position: situated on the front lines of the Cold War, at the intersection of the interests of four major powers (China, Russia, Japan, and the United States), North Korea has existed in a more tense situation than most nations. Even today North Korea remains in the same structural position. Thus it should not be surprising that North Korea's international behavior has been different than that of "normal" countries far from the front lines of geopolitical struggle.

This chapter is divided into five sections. The first section examines theories in international relations that try to explain the sources of external threats and draws out implications for the study of North Korea. In the second section I divide North Korean history into three periods—predominance, decline, and poverty—and trace how this structural shift has affected North Korean foreign policy. The third section focuses on the Kim dynasty and foreign policy. The fourth section discusses "observational equivalence" and military doctrine. In the final section I discuss North Korea's security preferences.

Sources of External Threats

In this section I derive hypotheses from general theories of international relations that might illuminate how North Korea assesses its external security situation. In so doing I examine two central questions in international relations: war initiation and stability.

I begin my review of the literature with neorealist, or structural, theories of international relations. Structural theory begins with the standard assumptions: states are unitary actors concerned with survival; the international arena is ordered on the principle of anarchy and is hence a self-help system (Waltz 1979; Mearsheimer 1990; Walt 1985; Morgenthau 1967). Structural realist approaches do not peer into the domestic decision-making structure; the locus of explanation resides in the power positions of states in the international system. Yet within these approaches there is disagreement over whether a balance of power is more stable than a preponderance of power.

For Kenneth Waltz the source of threats is clear: power is threatening. Waltz (1993: 74) writes: "Balance of power theory leads one to expect that states, if they are free to do so, will flock to the weaker side. The stronger, not the weaker side, threatens them....Even if the powerful state's intentions are wholly benign, less powerful states will...interpret events differently." Because states are concerned primarily with their own survival, as well as their relative power, there always exists the possibility that a strong nation may decide to begin hostilities with a weaker nation. In other words, "parity preserves peace" (Paul 1994: 5). Thus a potential aggressor will not initiate a conflict if it cannot win. In this sense threats arise by the mere presence of capabilities, and thus intentions can always change for the worse (Niou and Ordeshook 1984; Layne 1993). As Robert Jervis (1978: 105) writes, "minds can be changed, new leaders can come to power, values can shift, new opportunities and dangers can arise." Even if a nation was peaceful when it was weak, changes in power can bring changes in goals. Examining great powers, Robert Gilpin (1981: 95) writes that "rising power leads to increasing ambition. Rising powers seek to enhance their security by increasing their capabilities and their control over the external environment." In this sense neorealism does not take intentions as fixed but allows that they respond to changes in capabilities. The obverse of Gilpin's argument is that as a nation's capabilities fall behind, as it grows relatively weaker, its fears about the external environment will increase, its ambitions will lessen, and its perception of external threat will rise.

But another school of thought argues that preponderant capabilities in one country will lead to stability. In such a case the stronger power will not need to fight, and the weaker country will not consider it. As A. F. K. Organski (1968: 294) argues, "a preponderance of power... increases the chances of peace, for the greatly stronger side need not fight at all to get what it wants, while the weaker side would be plainly foolish to attempt battle for what it wants." Thus structural theories lead to three clear predictions:

- Hypothesis 1: Preponderant capabilities make a state appear threatening to weaker nations regardless of intentions.

- Hypothesis 2: Intentions are not fixed, but follow changes in capabilities.

- Hypothesis 3: Only the stronger state threatens stability.

The Security Dilemma

The security dilemma occurs because even if state A knows that it is a pacifist state, because of the anarchic international order A can never be sure that B is also peaceful. Therefore A must prepare for war even while professing peace. State B in response must arm against A's behavior, and the security dilemma results. Without examining the internal attributes of nations, we expect that two countries locked in a high-threat situation will each perceive the other side as the aggressor and accordingly worry about the relative power of the opposing state (Grieco 1988; Snidal 1991; Powell 1991; Waltz 1979). This theory can be extended to include variables to which I have previously alluded: whether the offense or the defense has the advantage and whether an offensive posture is distinguishable from a defensive posture. Robert Jervis (1978: 211) argues that when the offense has the advantage and offensive postures are indistinguishable from defensive ones, "there is no way to get security without menacing others, and security through defense is terribly difficult to obtain. Status-quo states acquire the same kind of arms that are sought by aggressors...and attacking is the best route to defending what you have....Arms races are likely [and] cooperation will be extremely hard to achieve."

The security dilemma thus predicts an action-reaction effect whereby North and South Korea are caught in a circular web of responding to the other side. We expect that both the North and the South will be extremely concerned with the other state and will react accordingly. In such a zero-sum environment even minor actions will be magnified, provoking a response from the other side. This effect is summarized in a fourth hypothesis.

* Hypothesis 4: When the offense has the advantage and mistrust is high, nations will appear threatening to each other.

Domestic Politics and Internal Threats

Recently there has been a spate of work dealing with internal threats and Third World security (David 1991; Ayoob 1991). Positing that states will at times undertake foreign policies designed to counter internal threats, these studies have called for recognition that the "search for security" in Third World countries may be focused on both external and internal threats. Manufacturing a false external threat provides many benefits for the leaders. First, they can mobilize public support for the regime against the external threat. This is the well-known "rally around the flag" phenomenon (Levy 1988). Second, an external threat can be used to legitimize domestic authoritarian measures such as abrogation of civil rights and repression. Justified in the name of "national security," such measures can strengthen a weak regime against domestic uprisings. Finally, an external threat justifies the elimination of domestic political rivals. By linking domestic competitors with an external threat, a regime can harass or even destroy its domestic opposition. The problem is that the domestic sources of a manipulated threat can coexist with the external reality of a threat, thus making it difficult to distinguish between ultimate causes.

* Hypothesis 5: The less the internal cohesion, the more likely the ruler will create and use a perceived threat to bolster the regime's domestic control.

Beginning with these five hypotheses we can examine the situation on the Korean peninsula.

A Note on Methodology

As I will show later in this chapter, many of the empirical situations on the peninsula are observationally equivalent—that is, North Korean actions in those situations would be the same whether their fundamental goals were offensive or defensive. If this is the case, there is little value in producing a list of reasons why those behaviors are offensive or defensive. The analyst must therefore produce alternative hypotheses that will point to different empirical observations.

Given that deriving testable propositions about the "true" nature of external threats from a structural view is less than helpful, the next logical step is to pursue the creation of alternative propositions that will eventually result in a dichotomous prediction in the dependent variable. That is, if both an offensive and defensive North Korea will deploy its troops forward, search for allies, and pursue a divisive strategy toward the South, it is not possible on the basis of these observations to conclude that North Korea's internal posture is either offensive or defensive. We must therefore look for demonstrations of intent that will provide us with some clues. Under what circumstances will the manifestations of an offensive and a defensive orientation differ?

Moreover, explanations for North Korea's actions, or surmises about its intentions, cannot be made in isolation. Scholars often attempt to explain one course of action without explaining why other alternatives were not chosen. This tendency truncates the dependent variable and makes causal inference more difficult. That is, if we want to explain why a nation seeks allies to strengthen its security, we are also explaining, implicitly or explicitly, why that nation *did not* choose to pursue unilateral attempts to increase its power, take colonies as buffer states, or go to war. A thorough explanation must examine the full range of strategies available and present convincing evidence why one path was chosen over the others (Morrow 1993; Lake 1996).

Finally, it is significant to point out the options that North Korea *did not* choose during the last 40 years. One can imagine three broad strategies the North could have pursued: invasion of South Korea; a "holding pattern" with minimal change in foreign policy but without provocation of war; and reform. North Korea has generally followed the second of these three options, while making limited moves to open its economy to the outside. Thus those who argue that North Korea's underlying goal is to communize the South must explain how those intentions have led to actions that seem antithetical to such a purpose.

Overview of the Situation

The zero-sum contest for the "Korean nation," broadly defined, makes it inevitable that each side perceives the other as the aggressor, as destabilizing, and as illegitimate. Thus, although the North may have been preeminent in the early years after the war, as the South caught up and passed the North we could expect to see its security become more and more threatened. North Korea's history after the division can be divided into roughly three periods: predominance, decline, and poverty.

The situation on the Korean peninsula is a result of external forces dividing the peninsula. Both North and South Korea have fought a battle for legitimacy for the last 45 years. That contest and each side's concern about the other side's potential capabilities have spurred economic development on both sides of the border, altered the political landscape of both countries, and affected their relations with external powers (Koh 1992; Yang et al. 1990; Foot 1985; Acheson 1969; Cumings 1990; Goncharov, Lewis, and Litai 1993; Suh 1968, 1988). Table 3 shows estimates of GNP growth in North and South Korea since the signing of the armistice in 1953. Between 1953 and 1960, North Korea's GNP actually closed the gap with the South; in per capita income, the North remained ahead of the South into the 1970s.

Neorealist or structural views of North Korea point clearly to the conclusion that its situation will be defensive. Even if at one time North Korea was in a position of strength and may have considered a more aggressive strategy relative to the South, today the North is unambiguously weak. The previous decade has evinced broad changes in North Korea's international position: attempts at rapprochement with Japan, admission to the United Nations, the loss of powerful patrons, and the nuclear weapons crisis of the early 1990s.

TABLE 3

North and South Korea's Gross National Product
and Per Capita Gross National Product

Year	GNP (billions of U.S. dollars)		GNP per capita (U.S. dollars)	
	North	South	North	South
1953	0.44	1.35	58	76
1960	1.52	1.95	137	94
1965	2.30	4.78	192	165
1970	3.98	7.99	286	248
1975	9.35	20.85	579	591
1980	13.5	60.3	758	1,589
1985	15.14	83.4	765	2,047
1990	23.1	237.9	1,064	5,569
1993	20.50	328.7	904	7,466
1994	21.3	508.3	923	9,980

SOURCES: *Vantage Point* 19, no. 3 (July 1995): 18; National Unification Board 1988: 30.

Predominance

After the Korean War, the North began to rebuild its economy and Kim Il Sung moved to consolidate his internal position. While rebuilding a decimated party membership, Kim also conducted purges of opposing factions and began a period of intense indoctrination of the North Korean populace (Koh 1991: 94). Even as Kim focused on domestic consolidation, North Korea's external relations with its patron states were at their warmest, although it would be simplistic to view those relations as directed mainly to help the North to take over the South. Although many scholars have asserted that North Korea believed during the Cold War that China and the Soviet Union might support Northern military moves against the South, there is considerable evidence to the contrary. Powerful patrons are usually demanding sponsors, not indulgent supporters.

North Korea took many steps to increase its independence vis-à-vis the Chinese and the Soviets. North Korea's ability to remain outside the formal strictures of the Council on Mutual Economic Cooperation (COMECON) and the Soviet bloc, for example, derived from the presence of another friendly superpower, China. Unlike the Eastern European states—which depended on the Soviet Union for both their existence and their security—North Korea could balance two major powers against each other. North Korea did not have to choose which superpower it would have as its primary patron, since each "friendly" superpower was potentially willing to move closer to North Korea to take advantage of North Korea's differences with the other (Kim 1986; Hunter 1983). But having more room to maneuver than puppet states did not mean that North Korea was the "tail wagging the dog."

Relations between the two communist superpowers and North Korea have never been steady or equal. After Khruschev's renunciation of Stalin in 1956, Kim Il Sung directly criticized the Soviets and leaned toward China, going so far as to emulate Mao's "Great Leap Forward" with a North Korean variant, the Chollima, or "Flying Horse," movement of 1958. In 1961 both China and the Soviet Union signed mutual defense treaties with North Korea, loaned or granted financial support to rebuild its economy, and generally supported North Korean rhetoric toward the West. Beginning with the Sino-Soviet split in the early 1960s, North Korean reliance on the PRC and the USSR was increasingly complemented by internal balancing and a search for other sympathetic states with which North Korea could ally. As a result of the diminished military and economic aid given to North Korea by the two feuding nations, North Korea embarked on its own military buildup. What has been seen by analysts as a relentless drive toward military dominance may well have been a response to shrinking security guarantees from China and the Soviet Union (Park 1983).

For the first decade after the armistice in 1953, North Korea began to gain an advantage over the South in economic growth and political stability. While the South was mired in political factionalism and uneven economic growth, the North managed to proceed apace at recovery and then development. Well into the 1960s North Korea still had a basis for confidence relative to South Korea.

Decline

As late as the mid-1970s, North Korea's economic and military strength was roughly equivalent to that of the South. The early 1980s, however, brought both the continued rise of South Korea's economy and the beginning of economic stagnation in the North. This trend led to further disparities in the quality of their respective military establishments: as maintenance and improvement in the North became more costly, the South was able to buy and produce more advanced hardware than ever before. Most analysts agree that South Korea's per capita GNP in 1994 was about ten times that of the North, while their military establishments remained in rough parity (Masaki 1995; Lho 1988; Ha 1989; Eberstadt and Bannister 1991).

It was during this time of relative equality between the two states that North Korea began to plan for the succession of Kim Il Sung by his son, Kim Jong Il. This was also the time when détente in Asia began to loosen the tight bond between China and North Korea. Both North and South Korea felt the pressure of changing superpower relations, which resulted in the July 4, 1972, joint communiqué between North and South Korea. Although both sides pledged to work toward peaceful unification, both sides promptly fell back into the familiar pattern of mutual recrimination and allegations.

The effect of changing superpower relations becomes particularly evident when one considers that the North, far from desiring intimate relations with its two patrons, must consider two potential problems with such involvement. First, to rely too heavily on a patron diminishes the client's independence. In international relations, nations breach treaties and break promises with regularity. To depend on a superpower for one's defense is to invite vulnerability and dependence. North Korea had reason to believe that neither the Soviet Union nor China would intervene on its behalf, because both have proved unreliable to another communist state, Vietnam. Kenneth Waltz (1981: 23) writes that "early in the [1970s], Pyongyang watched Moscow welcome President Nixon while the United States was bombing Haiphong. Late in the decade, Pyongyang watched China invade Vietnam while the Soviet Union failed to protect its client state." Second, any interference by a superpower on North Korea's behalf would not be for North Korea's sake, but in pursuit of the superpower's interests, and as such it would diminish North Korea's independence. Far from being in a position to play the Soviet Union and China against each other in order to gain an advantage over South Korea, North Korea faced the challenge of maintaining its independence from the more powerful states that surrounded it. Such balancing could occur because the two friendly powers, China and the Soviet Union, faced two rival powers, the United States and Japan. Seen in this context, North Korea's foreign policy relative to China and the Soviet Union during the 1970s and beyond appears both defensive and reactive.

Poverty

By the mid-1980s North Korea had fallen far behind the South according to almost every indicator. A structural view of North Korea leads to the conclusion that it should be experiencing fear. The intensity of the security dilemma, the loss of allies, the tremendous economic growth in South Korea—all are signs that North Korea's external situation has severely worsened. There have been three major developments since the mid-1980s that have exacerbated an already weak situation for North Korea. First, North Korea's two major patrons, China and the Soviet Union, have significantly reduced the level and intensity of their ties with North Korea—for example, Soviet aid to North Korea fell from $260 million in 1980 to no aid at all in 1990 (see Table 4). Second, North Korea's autarkic economy has begun to grind to a halt and has even contracted in the past few years. And third, Kim Il Sung, North Korea's paramount leader since 1945, died in 1994, leaving the country with a murky and potentially volatile internal situation (see Table 5). In response to these three developments, North Korean foreign policy in the late 1980s revolved around three major elements: attempts to reverse the economic slide, cautious efforts at rapprochement with the United States and Japan, and a campaign to develop nuclear weapons.

By the late 1980s, certainly by 1991, North Korea faced the real possibility of losing material and rhetorical support from both China and the Soviet Union. Indeed by 1992 both China and the Soviet Union had officially recognized South Korea and established formal diplomatic relations with Seoul, leaving North Korea without any partisan allies (Sanford 1990). At the same time, North Korea began falling far behind the South in terms of economic development and faced slow and even declining growth.[4] One result was that North Korea began to actively yet cautiously approach both the United States and Japan in an attempt to relieve both the military and the economic problems it faced. In 1991 Shin Kanemaru, one of Japan's most powerful politicians, traveled to Pyongyang and held talks with Kim Il Sung regarding normalization of relations and reparations by Japan. But the emergence of the nuclear issue made it politically impossible for Japan to continue talks with North Korea. Similarly, North Korea's recent desire to improve communications with the United States is a sign of the North's recognition that it must alter its geopolitical relationships, even if nuclear weapons remain an impediment.

TABLE 4
Aid to North Korea from the Soviet Union
(millions of U.S. dollars)

1980	1981	1982	1983	1984	1985
260	145	130	40	55	93

1986	1987	1988	1989	1990	
6	–33	–41	–16	0	

SOURCE: Noland 1996: 149.

TABLE 5
North Korea Compared with Its Neighbors and the United States:
Population and Gross Domestic Product, 1992

	1992 population (millions)	1992 GDP (billions of U.S. dollars)	Ratio of GDP to that of North Korea
North Korea	22	21	—
South Korea	43	296	14:1
Japan	124	3,666	174:1
China	1,184	434	20:1
Russia	150	450	21:1
United States	257	5,945	283:1

SOURCE: International Institute for Strategic Studies 1995.

Indeed, even South Korean observers note that North Korea's doctrine has undergone a period of extensive rethinking. Hak-joon Kim (1995: 88) writes:

> North Korea believes that the military balance on the peninsula has changed, in the direction of being very disadvantageous for it....North Korea harbors apprehensions that the United States may be acting to bring about the collapse of North Korea by playing upon its weaknesses. North Korea has minutely evaluated the cause of the Soviet Union's ruin, and has concluded that the Soviet Union was induced into excessive military spending by the USA which resulted in domestic economic failure, which in turn led to the inevitable collapse. This makes North Korea's political elite profoundly paranoid over U.S. military activity in South Korea.

In sum, then, while the North is undeniably opportunistic and aggressive, the important point is that North Korea has not challenged the central balance of power on the peninsula. Far from being in a position of power, North Korea has found itself obliged to keep pace with the South and manage its alliance relationships with China and the Soviet Union while retaining its own independence. The reciprocal and zero-sum nature of peninsula relations has heightened both South and North Korea's feelings of insecurity. Regardless of the history on the peninsula, however, the situation for North Korea has changed dramatically in the last five years. North Korea has been forced to forge a new foreign policy strategy under deteriorating internal and external conditions.

Foreign Policy and the Kim Dynasty

Much of North Korea's foreign policy is said to be the result of personality or leadership by the Kim dynasty—either the former ruler, Kim Il Sung, or his anointed successor, Kim Jong Il. The conventional wisdom has focused on Kim Il Sung and his attitudes and attributes. Some critics may argue that my analysis ignores precisely the central aspect of North Korea's foreign policy—the personalities of the North Korean leaders, in particular that of the late Kim Il Sung. They may further argue that certainly North Korea's foreign policy will be affected by the tenuous future of his son, Kim Jong Il.

The problem with this criticism is that by resorting to the personality of an irrational demagogue as an explanatory variable, analysts are creating a deus ex machina by which any North Korean action can be explained. We have less information about the internal workings of the

North Korean state than we do about almost any other nation. Even if we grant that Kim Il Sung's attitudes were important, we must ask how Kim's value system and attitudes explain North Korean behavior. This question rests on another: if Kim's attitudes and rationality were important in explaining North Korean foreign policy, would a different North Korean leader have produced a different set of outcomes? What a focus on personality ignores is that we cannot predict actions based on attributes if the situation itself matters. Kenneth Waltz (1979: 61) writes: "Just as peacemakers may fail to make peace, so troublemakers may fail to make trouble. From attributes one cannot predict outcomes if outcomes depend on the situations of the actors as well as on their attributes." Given the Cold War, the circumstances that led to the division of the peninsula, and the Sino-Soviet split of the late 1950s, it is hard to imagine an outcome in which North Korea is not an authoritarian communist regime or one in which North and South are not locked in competition.

This point is worth emphasizing. To my knowledge, only one scholar has mentioned a counterfactual: James Cotton (1992: 521) makes a one-sentence remark that had Pak Hon Yong—a communist who remained in Seoul after liberation—become North Korea's leader, perhaps North Korea would have been different. Cotton does not, however, go on to specify how North Korea would have been different. I agree that leaders have idiosyncratic styles and that certain domestic situations would probably have been different had North Korea ended up with a different dictator. The relevant question for my analysis remains whether foreign policy would have differed markedly. Given that we have so little information about Kim Il Sung, Kim Jong Il, or decision making in North Korea, it seems plausible to begin with a systematic evaluation of North Korea's observable behavior and to see how that behavior conforms to broad theories of international relations.

Much has been made of the "dynasty" being implemented in North Korea (Oh 1991; Park 1982; Kim 1983; Yu 1982; Rhee 1987). But dynastic succession is not as singular as it may appear. In small or developing countries with significant institutional or political weaknesses, "anointing" a son or close relative may be one way to ensure both continuity and a smooth transfer of power. Chiang Kai-shek's son, Chiang Ching-Kuo, took power, after his father's death, as president of Taiwan and head of the Kuomintang (KMT). In Singapore, Lee Kwan Yew's son, Lee Hsien-loong, is a general, first deputy prime minister, and minister for trade and industry; he also was head of the youth wing of the ruling People's Action Party. It is also extremely common in China to place sons and daughters in influential positions either in state enterprises or in the Communist Party (Lewis, Di, and Xue 1991). In this context, Kim Jong Il's rise to power, although it has provoked intense scrutiny of the prospects for successful succession, is not as anomalous as it may appear at first glance.

Succession Politics

The more important question for this study is whether or not domestic succession politics have had an effect on North Korea's foreign policy and its conception of security. Succession politics certainly did not play a large role in determining North Korea's foreign policy before the early 1980s, and I would submit that such concerns have not unduly influenced North Korea's foreign policy since that time either. The fundamental North Korean actions in the last decade—attempts to gain nuclear weapons, continuing confusion regarding relations with China and the Soviet Union, and cautious efforts at rapprochement with the United States and Japan—do not seem to have been unduly influenced by succession dynamics. The concerns that inform those actions derive from changes in the international system and represent efforts to survive as a political entity; thus they make sense within the framework of neorealism.

More relevant for our analysis, however, are the "rationality" and personality of Kim Jong Il, the son and successor of Kim Il Sung. Intense speculation has surrounded Kim Jong Il, and various anecdotes (virtually none extant in published works) call him either an effete playboy, a terrorist mastermind, or a deranged and sickly individual.[5] This issue is problematic: any explanation of North Korean foreign policy based on the leader's personal attributes requires two causal connections to be made. First, we need conclusive evidence of the leader's personality. Second, and more important, we also require evidence that these personality traits affect his decisions regarding foreign policy. For example, a popular perception of Kim Jong Il cites a penchant for Western movies and Swedish starlets. But how does this reputed interest translate into foreign policy decisions? Will a taste for Western cinema make Kim Jong Il more sympathetic to the West—or less? Will knowing actresses make Kim more likely to open the economic doors to the West—or less? The scanty amount of knowledge regarding Kim Jong Il should make any analyst cautious about such inferences.

Although there is no question that North Korea is a highly authoritarian state and is currently grappling with a myriad of domestic problems, it would be unwise to assume that North Korea has never been able to manage its domestic affairs or that today's problems are insurmountable. In fact, North Korea has a record of skillful domestic management. According to Nicholas Eberstadt (1995: 132), "Because North Korea presents such an unattractive—even freakish—face to the outside world, it has often been misjudged. In important respects the regime has been underestimated. Fanatical or surreal as this 'red dynasty' may appear, many of its policies have been practical and effective. Of all Asia's communist states (including the USSR), only North Korea avoided famine in the course of its collectivization of agriculture."

Again, the reciprocal nature of peninsular relations is important. South Koreans and Americans focus on North Korea's recent effusive thanks to Japan for sending rice aid—and its pointed refusal to thank South Korea for its support. That rebuff has prompted the South Koreans to declare that they will not provide further aid to North Korea until it responds appropriately. Yet the South declined to acknowledge the death of Kim Il Sung, refused to let South Koreans attend the funeral, and began a crackdown on students and campuses reminiscent of the Chun era. Without assessing the merit of any of these actions, the evidence is fairly clear that both North and South Korea engage in petty diplomatic squabbling to the detriment of larger and more important negotiations.

The worldviews of leaders are indeed important, especially when one is assessing a nation's conception of its security. In these few pages I have attempted to show that North Korea, despite its singular domestic leadership, is not entirely different from other nations in terms of its choice of leaders or their actions. Although the Kim dynasty is undoubtedly concerned with the stability of its own regime, it is hard to imagine any North Korean ruler acting substantially differently toward the South or toward the United States. Regardless of internal politics, North Korean leaders of any sort will be concerned with preserving regime and state and deterring the South.

Internal Politics

Domestic politics in North Korea remains tightly controlled, and there is mixed evidence as to whether internal decay is occurring. In 1995, only 36 North Koreans defected to the South—compared to more than 39,000 defectors from East Germany to West Germany in 1988, the year before the opening of the Berlin Wall. Many of these "North Korean" defectors came through China and were in fact Siberian lumberjacks from the northern regions. What is startling about this number is the dearth of defectors. There are only two explanations: that political control from the center—even at the fringes of North Korean society—remains robust; or that North Koreans are genuinely satisfied and do not wish to leave the country. I place very little stock in the latter hypothesis. I conclude that North Korea's political control is likely to remain firm. Indeed, other analysts have made similar points (Kim 1995: 84). This brief discussion of North Korean internal politics raises two implications for the study of North Korea. First, scholars know very little about what happens in North Korea. Second, most of the evidence about North Korea's achievements with regard to gross domestic product and quality of life is quite mixed. The high-level defection of Hwang Jong Yop in early 1997, along with a stagnant economy, raised anew questions of North Korea's stability and long-run viability.

Another potential source of instability that does not involve civil unrest is division within the elite. Although there have been rumors of palace intrigue among members of the Kim family, they appear to be no more than rumors. Kim Pyong Il—widely reported to be the most ambitious and capable of the half-brothers of Kim Jong Il—made clear in Helsinki in 1994 that Kim Jong Il is the only legitimate successor to his father. Additionally, as Hak-joon Kim writes,

> The members of the new generation who function in a leadership role, without regard to their original stations in life, are working-level officials....Kim Jong-il's advisors are drawn from a wide variety of fields—from politics, diplomacy, the military, economics, the sciences, ideology and the arts. The change in the composition of those who serve Kim Jong-il appears to be because, with the installation of the junior Kim as successor, North Korean society also entered a period of stability. (Kim 1995: 79)

Thus, although there is considerable potential for domestic strife in North Korea, the evidence to date reveals little active protest.

Observational Equivalence and Military Doctrine

There exists a general perception that North Korea's military is poised for conflict and intends to start a major war, but a closer examination reveals that this is not necessarily the case. A major question is whether North Korea's military doctrine is offensive or defensive. Any discussion of North Korea's conception of security, whether revisionist or status quo, must begin by laying out the range of possible military deployments, force structures, and doctrines that North Korea might have pursued. These range from a deployment north of Pyongyang (militarily unrealistic), to building a Maginot Line along the demilitarized zone (DMZ), to deploying only around Pyongyang and Wonsan and basically ceding the bulk of North Korean territory to the South in the event of a war.

Many analysts have used forward deployment as an indicator of North Korean intentions. Yet with Pyongyang and Seoul separated by less than 250 kilometers, no deployment could be considered purely defensive. The geographic proximity of the two armies exacerbates an already acute security dilemma. In the event of a conflict, neither side can afford a strategy of "trading space for time" as Stalin did in World War II. There are three reasons why offensive and defensive intentions are observationally equivalent on the Korean peninsula—that is, why observable behaviors based on either offensive or defensive intentions would be identical. First, forward deployment is the unsurprising result of the strategic situation on the peninsula. Second, the North has not taken other actions that might enhance an offensive tactical doctrine. Third, the U.S.–ROK forces too have an offensive doctrine and forward deployment—yet they believe they have peaceful intentions.

The million-man army in the North is composed of four front-line corps, four mechanized corps, an armored corps, and an artillery corps, with five other corps-sized units deployed throughout the DPRK. The U.S. Defense Intelligence Agency reports that 65 percent of those troops are deployed within 100 kilometers of the DMZ (Defense Intelligence Agency 1991: 9). Yet it is important to remember that Pyongyang is only 125 kilometers from Panmunjom in the DMZ. Thus it might be more accurate to say that 65 percent of the North Korean troops are deployed in front of their capital. This is hardly surprising. It would be far more surprising if the DPRK were to deploy its troops in the north, far from where conflict is likely to occur, or behind the capital. Thus a fruitful discussion of "forward deployment" in the Korean context is far more difficult than it might initially appear.

Moreover, military analysts have argued that the North has forward-deployed its munitions, stockpiling weapons and material close to the border. They argue that this demonstrates that North Korea is preparing for a sudden strike. Yet there are equally compelling explanations for this behavior. Certainly the logistical situation in North Korea—never good—has deteriorated over the past decades. Although a great deal of effort has been put into transport facilities leading to the DMZ, many roads remain unpaved and much reinforcement is needed on the 75 percent of North Korea's railroads that are electrified (Von Hippel and Hayes 1995). Thus North Korea's transportation grid is vulnerable to air interdiction. Given an already acute energy crisis in the North and the likelihood of U.S.–ROK air superiority if not dominance, front-line units cannot expect to be resupplied from rear areas. Thus it makes sense to stockpile munitions as close to the units as possible. This forward deployment, however, creates offensive problems as well. Offensive movement is far more difficult from fixed munitions positions—lacking adequate logistical support, North Korean military units will face serious problems if they leave their stockpiles to advance or retreat.

North Korea might have taken other steps to increase its ability to advance, but those steps have not been taken. The one lesson North Korea should have learned from the Korean War is that it is extremely vulnerable to naval interdiction. Indeed, the Inchon landing of 1950 threatened to wipe out the North Korean forces south of Seoul. More-over, an enemy's ability to bypass the Alpha-Feba line through am-phibious landings would appear to be critical. Yet North Korea's naval forces remain overwhelmingly of the coastal defense variety—small ships incapable of moving large units south or of foiling U.S. naval actions.

General Robert Riscassi, commander of the U.S. forces in Korea, provided some insight in his testimony before the House of Representa-tives in 1992.

> North Korea has prioritized its force structure...so some force elements are not presently at peak readiness. Employing its vast armed forces in a limited notice attack would be a difficult undertaking for even the most highly trained military force, so we assume some current level of degra-dation. Prior to an offensive, however, we would expect enhanced training activity to improve their prospects of success. Also, a number of North Korea's military systems are based on old technologies, updated with product improvement programs, but still limited in capability due to vintage.[6]

Table 6 compares the quality and quantity of selected aircraft and armor for North and South Korea.

Moreover, armies are designed to fight. Taking soldiers and putting them on "100-day campaigns" to build bridges or bring in rice crops seriously degrades their fighting performance. Not only does morale suffer but cohesion and training—essential for a functioning army—are neglected. Large numbers of soldiers do not make a high-quality army; more important is the quality of the forces. Because it is impossible to keep an army at peak readiness at all times, troops lose their edge if "war fever" is continuous. If troops are held at battle readiness too long, their performance deteriorates.

Finally, the U.S.–ROK forces, though they identify themselves as nonthreatening to the North, also operate under an offensive doctrine and use forward deployment. U.S.–ROK doctrine calls for "American forces and their South Korean counterparts to assume the offensive and strike deep into the rear echelons of the attacking forces" in the event of a North Korean invasion (Tow 1991: 179). This is perhaps the most revealing argument for observational equivalence. There are sound strategic reasons for the U.S.–ROK forces to be forward-deployed in front of Seoul, not the least of which is defense of the capital. Such defensive preparations, regardless of the conditions under which they are made, can appear offensive to the other side. The lack of geographic space and the need to gain momentum make forward deployment a sound choice for both sides.

TABLE 6
Comparison of North and South Korea's Military Hardware

	North Korea	South Korea	Comments
Main battle tanks	3,700: T-34; T-54/55; T-62; Type 59	1,800: 400 M-47; 950 M-48; 450 Type 88	T-34 are WWII vintage; T-55 introduced in 1957. M-47 are WWII vintage; M-48 from 1952.
Fighter aircraft	640 MiG-17 360 MiG-19 160 MiG-21 46 MiG-23 14 MiG-29 14 Su-7 36 Su-25	132 F-4D/E 206 F-5 96 F-16	MiG-17, MiG-19 and MiG-21 all introduced before 1956; MiG-29 in 1983. F-4 introduced in 1963; F-5 in 1972; F-16 in 1980. U.S. has 72 F-16s in South Korea.
Bombers	240 H-5	—	
Amphibious equipment	24 LCM 7 LCU 100 LCVP	7 LST (200 troops, 16 tanks) 7 LSM (50 troops, 4 tanks)	

SOURCES: International Institute for Strategic Studies 1995; Dunigan 1983.

Adding to the North's security fears, the annual U.S.–ROK joint military exercises known as "Team Spirit" regularly include amphibious assault and airborne exercises. Team Spirit, the largest U.S. military exercise anywhere in the world, involves nuclear-capable aircraft, aircraft carriers, and units brought in from around Asia. What the North fears, as Team Spirit occurs year after year, is that at some point the U.S.–ROK forces will actually attack the North, having dulled its wariness through repeated yearly exercises. For the U.S.–ROK forces, Team Spirit is an opportunity to assess battle readiness as well as to practice and integrate the latest weapons systems. For the United States, therefore, Team Spirit serves many purposes. But each time the exercises are held, activity in the North comes to a virtual standstill as the nation prepares for a surprise attack. It should be noted, however, that the United States has canceled Team Spirit in the past few years as a sign of good faith toward North Korea.

I am not arguing that South Korea is the aggressor on the peninsula. My point, rather, is that a zero-sum contest for supremacy and constricted space have fairly straightforward implications: each side's conception of security is oriented primarily to the other side; each side is dependent on the other for survival; and each side can destroy the other. Thus both sides will concentrate on deterring the other side as the perceived aggressor. One would hardly expect the North not to be concerned about South Korea's intentions.

Given that deriving testable propositions about the "true" nature of external threats from a structural view is not possible, the next step in our analysis is to create alternative propositions that will eventually result in a prediction that will show some change in the dependent variable. We must look for extensions of their intentions that will provide us with some clues.

The Real Question: North Korean Preferences

What is really in dispute is the theory of preference formation, not actual capabilities or even doctrines. The standard explanation is that North Korea wants to invade the South. Even the most informal of rationalist approaches shows that this is an overly simple way of thinking about preferences. Generally a researcher posits that hierarchic goals are pursued in relation to their expected utility. Decisions about competing goals are then undertaken with an eye toward which action will best maximize overall utility. That is, without evaluating probabilities and alternative actions, merely having a goal does not fully specify the decision tree. Thus any argument about North Korean preferences must also include the costs, the benefits, and the chances of success. A decision to invade the South involves three separate calculations: the value and costs of achieving the goal, the likelihood of success, and the efficacy of other possible actions. Although North Korea may value the goal of communizing the South, the analyst must also show that in the North's perception the benefits outweigh the costs, the probability of success is positive, and other actions are less desired.

Moreover, the analyst must be very clear about the range of the variables under analysis. Thus any discussion of why North Korea took the policies it did toward South Korea and the world must explain why other potential choices were not made. Certainly North Korea as a nation may have a variety of goals: deterring invasion from the South, unifying with the South, maintaining the regime's stability, maximizing the benefits it receives from the international system while minimizing the costs, and many others. Much of the work on North Korea, however, seems to ignore this range of goals, choosing to focus only on what has happened or what North Korea wants to happen. In short, any argument about North Korea's decision to invade or not to invade the South must also incorporate a discussion about other potential North Korean choices regarding North-South relations (see Figure 1). Because of the Korean War, many analysts have focused on the idea that North Korea wants to invade. But any argument that North Korea would invade must also explain why it would not choose other options. From Figure 1 it is fairly clear that, given the alternatives, North Korea's actual choices of armistice and small-scale violence are not that surprising. And, as I will show, such choices fit easily within an explanation of North Korea's actions that focuses on its security concerns and instrumental behavior.

We need to understand North Korea's foreign policy toward other nations, as well. Much rhetoric has surrounded North Korea's bellicose stance against the West, leading to the conclusion that this must be a nation of cult-worshipping deadheads. Yet the range of choices available

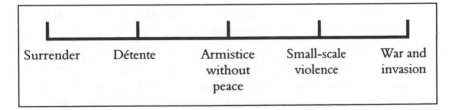

FIGURE 1
North Korea's Policy Options Toward South Korea

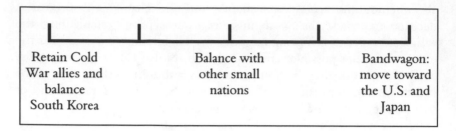

FIGURE 2
North Korea's Options for International Relations

to North Korea was severely limited until the early 1990s, and even since then the range has not changed dramatically (see Figure 2.) After all, North Korea has not invaded the South for more than 45 years. Its "revealed preferences" have been for armistice, not war. Yet we have seen a series of post hoc rationalizations arguing that North Korea must still be revisionist, including discussions of terrorism and nuclear weapons.

The notion that North Korea might indeed have genuine security fears is generally scoffed at in South Korea and in the United States. Yet there is good evidence that the South Koreans have at times desired to invade the North. Certainly North Korea was increasingly aggressive during the 1960s, especially in 1968 when a team of North Korean commandos infiltrated the South with the goal of assassinating Park Chung Hee. The commandos were stopped within a mile or so of the Blue House, the Korean presidential mansion. Events along the DMZ led to increased firefights. In response, Park urged preemptive strikes against the North (Cho 1969), but U.S. help was not forthcoming. The United States had operational control of the South Korean military and was virtually immobilized by the U.S. involvement in Vietnam. The Tet offensive began a week after the North Koreans captured the USS *Pueblo* and paralyzed U.S. responses in Korea. Indicative of the situation is this exchange between Congress and the U.S. ambassador to South Korea:

> MR. FRASER: How did the Korean Government perceive these events in relation to its ongoing concern about its security?

> MR. PORTER: With great concern. It was a very severe shock. Both items were very severe shocks for the president, the Cabinet, and the people as a whole. President Park was quite intent on striking back. He told me he could be in Pyongyang within 2 days' time, and I had to tell him that if he tried that he would have to do it alone.[7]

The South, too, would like to see the unification of the peninsula on its terms. But while South Korea may cherish that goal, the South also realizes that the costs of such an action would be too severe. Tensions on the peninsula also prompted the South to begin a search for nuclear weapons in the early 1970s. Although the program was eventually dropped because of extensive U.S. pressure, it is likely that the effort increased North Korean fears of the South (Meyer 1978; Spector 1984; Gillette 1978; Hayes 1991). In the 1990s, South Korea's increasing confidence based on economic development has occasionally led to a more militant posture toward the North. In one widely quoted statement, a senior South Korean official called for military strikes against the North Korean nuclear plant at Yongbyon in late 1993. North Korea is in no position to move beyond the basic realist goals of survival and deterrence, because its own survival in the world is by no means assured.

Terrorism as a Cheap Coup

Perhaps the most compelling evidence that North Korea is in some sense "irrational," and its conception of security revisionist, derives from its use of terrorism as a tool of foreign policy. North Korea has been described as a nation of "paranoid survivalists" (Olsen 1986: 852) and "a renegade state" (Spector and Smith 1991: 8). Typical of this perspective is a statement by John Perry (1990: 188): "Rhetorical style and financial irresponsibility pale beside the impact on international public opinion of the inexplicable spasms of violence perpetuated by North Korea. Much can be said against the erratic ferocity of such behavior." North Korea has indeed pursued a fairly consistent policy of terrorism against South Korea. From the 1968 attack on the South Korean presidential mansion, to the attempted assassination of South Korean president Park Chung Hee in 1974, to the bombing of the Chun cabinet in Rangoon in 1983, to the destruction of a KAL airliner in 1987, North Korea has consistently shown that it is willing to use terror as a means of foreign policy. The analyst's task is to make sense out of the terrorism. For some, terrorism is proof that North Korea is both irrational and undeterrable— a nation so bent on pursuing the overthrow of the South that it takes actions that are counterproductive to its own goals.

Terrorism, however, occurs for political reasons. The analyst must answer two questions: Why terrorism? And why a certain type of terrorism? An extensive literature has distinguished between two types of terrorism: antistate and antisociety (Gurr 1970; Ford 1985; Chai 1993; DeNardo 1985; Taylor 1988). Antistate terrorism (sometimes referred to as guerrilla warfare) involves some group attempting to make the costs of governance so high that the state chooses either to capitulate or to bargain with the group. Examples include the Jewish use of terror in Palestine while attempting to drive out the British in 1945–48 and, more recently, the Intifada in Palestine by which the Palestinians attempted to drive out the Israelis. The second type of terrorism occurs against society itself. Its aim is to make life so difficult for the people that they pressure the state to take action. Examples include the "troubles" in Northern Ireland and Arab terrorism against Israel.[8]

Why Terrorism?

In a previous section I have shown that North Korea is unlikely to invade the South. Given the South's overwhelming economic, military, and political advantage, it would in fact be irrational for the North to invade. Although most analysts cite terrorist activities as evidence of aggressive intentions, a nation may pursue terrorist activities to avoid threatening the central strategic balance. Given the evidence, one can argue that precisely because the North does not wish to challenge the status quo on the peninsula, it pursues peripheral actions (Hayes 1991: 158). There is a distinction between reckless behavior and aggressive behavior. I am not arguing that North Korea is satisfied with the status quo; I am arguing that North Korea is well aware of the risks of challenging the central balance of power.

This point is controversial. Let me emphasize that although neither South Korea nor North Korea is a status quo state that is satisfied with the current division on the peninsula, the North has not been reckless. Terrorist activities have been undertaken when the risk was essentially low, and the North has never come close to actually threatening war on the DMZ. Consider the "tree-cutting" incident of 1976, when two U.S. soldiers were killed in the DMZ by North Koreans. In response, on August 20, 1976, nuclear-capable B-52 bombers flew from Guam to Korea and up toward the DMZ, veering off only at the last moment. A U.S. analyst who monitored North Korean communications during the flights said: "They didn't know what was in them and we scared the living shit out of them" (Hayes 1991: 89). Within a few weeks Kim Il Sung had publicly called for a reduction of tensions. Thereafter North Korea began pursuing warmer relations with the Carter administration. Indeed, Kim Il Sung went so far as to call President Carter "a man of great justice." The point is that although North Korea has chosen to pursue terrorist activities when the risks were low, it has not risked direct confrontation on the peninsula. When tensions have escalated, the North has backed away.

Why Antistate Terrorism?

The form of terrorism pursued by the North is consistent with the idea that North Korea clearly assesses the international environment. Given that the North desires the overthrow of the South Korean government but also wants the support of the people, North Korea pursues antistate activities while explicitly avoiding attacking the population of South Korea itself. North Korean terrorists could detonate bombs in downtown Seoul on a daily basis if that were their goal. But the goal of the North Korean regime is not to turn the entire Southern population against the North, but rather the opposite—to destabilize the South Korean regime in the hope that a coup or insurgency will result in a government more favorable to the North.

There is, in fact, sufficient evidence that the South has been so unstable that the North might reasonably hope to topple the South Korean regime with just a small shove. Student riots overthrew the Syngman Rhee administration in 1960 (the famous April 19 movement). In the early 1970s, civilian unrest forced Park Chung Hee to close the universities and declare martial law. In a thoroughly manipulated 1971 presidential election, Park barely won with 51 percent of the vote. In 1979, an assassination and a coup led to huge protests in the city of Kwangju that were violently suppressed by the South Korean military—official estimates are 200 killed and 2,000 injured. This record of unstable and repressive regimes in the South has been a lure to the North. In light of such obvious discontent among a large portion of the South Korean populace, the North's hopes that attacking the South Korean leadership might result in chaos or collapse were certainly justified.

Terrorist attacks against the people themselves, however, would have unified the South Korean populace against the North. And so, not surprisingly, the North has attacked not the population of the South but the leaders. That policy is consistent with the idea that North Korea is not willing to risk a direct military attack on the South and also with the notion that North Korea has specific goals in mind when it uses terrorism. This argument implying rational choice leads to some clear predictions. First, North Korea will not use terrorism against the people of the South Korea.[9] Second, as the South Korean government becomes more legitimate through the use of democratically elected officials and the redress of past crimes by its political leaders, the North will come to realize that the utility of terrorism is receding. Thus, the more legitimate the South Korean government, the less likely North Korea will use terrorism. Such an analysis allows for fairly specific predictions and focuses the discussion of North Korean foreign policy.

Nuclear Weapons and Military Effects

North Korea already has the functional equivalent of a nuclear deterrent: its threats to destroy Seoul "like a rabid dog barking at the sky" are taken seriously in Asia and in the West, leading South Korean and U.S. leaders to deal cautiously with North Korea. Because Seoul is vulnerable to air attack and is the center of South Korean life, the South Korean military is reluctant to escalate tensions too quickly. Rather than saying that the North is in a position to invade the South, it would be more accurate to describe the peninsular situation as a standoff. Neither side wishes to provoke a war, because both sides know the destruction it would bring.

Much of the discussion surrounding proliferation of nuclear weapons to small states has focused on unit-level analyses, debating the reliability of command and control, technical barriers, and systems vulnerability (Davis and Frankel 1993; Dunn 1982; Rosen 1977; Subrahmanyam 1984; Ilke 1973; Spector 1984). It seems clear that any state with an intense security dilemma should wish to procure or develop nuclear weapons. In the face of declining superpower support, a small state must secure its own defense. One highly effective way of doing this is to develop a nuclear weapons capability—especially if the other side has nuclear weapons. North Korea's statements, although equivocal, reveal its acute awareness of its own vulnerability.[10]

What little evidence we have about North Korean nuclear weapons development is circumstantial and limited at best. Whether the goal is to gain a bargaining chip or to attain an effective deterrent, the pursuit of nuclear weapons by North Korea should come as no surprise. As Andrew Mack (1991: 93) notes, "From the North Korean perspective, the reasons for not going nuclear may be outweighed by the perception of a growing strategic need for nuclear weapons." North Korea's allies are deserting it. Its economic infrastructure is stagnant. The South appears threatening. Why then did North Korea wait until the 1980s to begin developing a nuclear weapon? Surely it could have begun much earlier. After all, China first detonated a nuclear weapon in the early 1960s, and the Soviets had developed bombs in the 1950s (Cumings 1992).

It was not until South Korea began to overtake and surpass North Korea in the late 1970s that the North's security was threatened seriously enough for it to attempt to develop such a weapon. During the 1970s South Korea tried to procure nuclear weapons, prompting strong reactions from both the United States and North Korea. The North Koreans acknowledge that they are searching for security. The North

Korean press has quoted Kim Yong Nam, the foreign minister, as saying that détente between the Soviet Union and South Korea "will leave us no other choice but to take measures to provide us...some weapons for which we have so far relied on the Soviet Union" (Spector and Smith 1991: 13). Even though the United States officially removed its land-based nuclear warheads from the peninsula in 1991, the nuclear deterrent remains quite strong: the Seventh Fleet has nuclear-capable weaponry and is assigned to the Pacific region; the annual Team Spirit exercises include nuclear simulations; the United States retains nuclear-capable aircraft at bases in Korea.

Such factors have no doubt exacerbated the North's concern over possible aggression from the South. The South's stunning growth, along with the North's frequently cool relations with both the Soviet Union and China, have combined to make North Korea feel that it must provide for its own security without expecting help from others. The general consensus among Western policy makers is that nuclear weapons in the North would result in an aggressive North acting irrationally and dangerously (Song 1991). But we must remember two facts about tensions in Korea. First, two or three crude nuclear weapons provide no offensive capability and would not significantly alter the military balance on the peninsula, although the diplomatic context might change. North Korea is no more likely to win a war with nuclear weapons than without them. North Korea, knowing that the stakes would be even greater and that the United States could respond with nuclear weapons, might even be less likely to launch a war. Second, robust deterrence on the Korean peninsula has resulted from a steadfast U.S. commitment to the South. Less important to deterrence than actual American troops stationed on the peninsula is the potential for U.S. involvement: North Korea cannot hope to win a war against the United States. Thus stability is maintained by the U.S. military commitment to the South, whether nuclear or conventional. While that commitment remains strong, the likelihood of war on the peninsula is slight.

Moreover, nuclear weapons confer no offensive capability. Surprisingly, many specialists regard North Korea's acquisition of nuclear weapons as potentially offensive and believe that it increases the likelihood that North Korea will initiate war. Yet nuclear weapons are too large and powerful to confer militarily useful offensive capability. Nuclear weapons do not "fight" anything; they merely destroy. Thus they offer little offensive or defensive capability. What nuclear weapons do best is deter, for they allow the loser of a war to kill the winner (Waltz 1990). Some scholars have argued that North Korea is developing the bomb because it wants to invade South Korea under a nuclear umbrella that will ensure that a conventional war is fought. Along these lines is William Tow's statement that "the immediate effect of a North Korean nuclear force would be to complicate American escalation control options in response to [a] DPRK blitzkrieg invasion (1991: 198)." If that is the case, the peninsula will continue to be stable as long as the U.S. conventional deterrent remains solid. As offensive weapons, nuclear weapons hold little value; but if North Korea were to develop the bomb, it would have a robust deterrent.

Nuclear weapons are political, not military, instruments. Here are four possible scenarios under which North Korea might use a nuclear device. First, without actual military hostilities, a nuclear device could be hidden away in Seoul to blackmail the South Korean regime into capitulation. Second, the nuclear weapon could be a deterrent to the South after North Korea made a limited invasion and took Seoul. Third, nuclear weapons could deter U.S. escalation of hostilities by threatening a port city such as Pusan, where major U.S. reinforcements would arrive. Finally, a nuclear device could be used against front-line troops. These scenarios, though frightening, are far from likely. It is important to remember that a nuclear weapon, like terrorism, is used for political effect. Random use of nuclear weapons is improbable. In this sense, nuclear weapons are much more valuable unused than used. If North Korea has a tiny stockpile of weapons (one or two), those weapons would be capable of virtually nothing that conventional weapons cannot already do. North Korea already has the conventional capability to destroy Seoul. North Korea can already target the Japanese islands with its SCUD missiles.

There is only one difference in outcome that would result from the use of a nuclear weapon—and that difference would be unambiguously negative for North Korea. The use of nuclear weapons would remove any barriers constraining the United States and South Korea to a limited war. There would be no limit to the escalation the United States could mount. Any domestic pressure in the United States against the use of nuclear weapons or overwhelming force would be likely to vanish, and the result would undoubtedly be the destruction of the North Korean regime.

The point of this section has been to show that the pursuit of a nuclear capability in North Korea—even the suspicion that such a program exists—is useful to North Korea's long-term strategy of contest with the South. Nuclear weapons constitute just one of a series of military and diplomatic strategies that North Korea has pursued in an effort to unify the peninsula. North Korea's ability to portray itself as a dangerous nation that must be taken seriously works to its long-term advantage.

That image is particularly important when the economic reality in North Korea is increasingly one of stagnation, decay, and impotence.

Conclusion: Deterrence Through Danger

North Korea's conception of security, then, is essentially defensive and realist in orientation. The theories of international relations cited at the beginning of the chapter do in fact explain the North Korean conception of security fairly accurately: a small power facing a rising power and losing its allies will experience more fear. Yet North Korea remains opportunistic as well. Resilient and resourceful, the North may well decide on a policy that will allow it to survive into the near future.

While much of North Korea's domestic politics remains shrouded in mystery, its foreign policy actions point to a consistent goal of deterrence through danger. Caught in a zero-sum battle for legitimacy and supremacy on the peninsula, North and South Korea are interdependent as each pursues its own security—neither can ignore the other, both can destroy the other. The implications are straightforward: North Korea's conception of security remains overwhelmingly realist in orientation and external in focus. Domestic considerations of economic development and quality of life are subordinated to the goal of survival for the regime.

South Korea
Recasting Security Paradigms

CHUNG-IN MOON

Geopolitical destiny has burdened the Korean peninsula with a historical legacy of humiliation and suffering. Frequent Chinese invasion, Japanese colonial domination, a forced division of the Korean nation, and the lingering memory of the Korean War have instilled in Koreans a fatalistic sense of insecurity and resignation. Security issues still haunt South Koreans. Military threats from the North are real and acute. Despite the facade of strategic stability buttressed by the bipolarity of the Cold War era, South Koreans have been captives of a self-imposed image of international, regional, and peninsular anarchy. In a world of anarchy, ensuring the survival of South Korea (the ROK) as a sovereign state has become a national mandate, even an obsession. For the preservation of the South Korean state, realist prescriptions have prevailed: military self-help through the maximization of physical power, effective mobilization of human and material resources, and assertive pursuit of an alliance with the United States. South Korea's security practices during the Cold War era can be best described as a fortified realism.

Since the late 1980s, however, South Korea has undergone major internal and external transformations that have profoundly affected its traditional conception of security. While the demise of authoritarian rule and the transition to democratic governance have facilitated the transformation of the ideological and institutional foundations of security, the end of the Cold War international system has altered regional and peninsular strategic parameters as well as perceptions of threat. Growing economic, social, and ecological interdependence and the diffusion of globalization into new policy arenas have also fostered new discourses on the referents and practice of security in South Korea (see Moon 1995; Moon and S. Lee 1995: 99–115; Steinberg 1995; Choi and Lim 1993; Hahm 1992).

The concept and practice of security do not exist in a vacuum; they vary according to context. South Korea is no exception. Democratization, the advent of a posthegemonic world order, and globalization have indeed precipitated contextual changes that have altered the dominant security paradigm in South Korea. Against the backdrop of those changes, this chapter explores the shifting nature of security discourses and practices in South Korea. The first section examines South Korea's dominant security paradigm along four analytical dimensions: metastructure, institutional foundation, external management, and security agenda. The second unravels the metastructural foundation of the country's security practices by looking into the dynamic interplay of perception, ideology, and identity. The third section analyzes changes in the domestic institutional foundation by elucidating the impact of democratization on state structure. The fourth addresses the external dimensions of security practice, including the politics of alliance management and the recent policy tilt toward regional and multilateral security cooperation regimes. The chapter concludes by recasting the scope of South Korea's security agenda in the light of domestic and international changes.

Unraveling the Dominant Security Paradigm

The concept of security is largely subjective and even elusive (Wolfers 1962a; Knorr and Trager 1977; Buzan 1983; Azar and Moon 1988). As Muthiah Alagappa has explained in Chapter 1 of this volume, its interpretation and practice can vary in terms of referents or according to epistemological positions taken by central decision makers. The concept of security and its application to national and international politics can be approached from four salient angles: metastructure, institutional foundation, external management, and scope of security agenda.

Metastructure shapes the cognitive map that guides central decision makers as they assess threats, formulate policy, and implement overall security. It is the software of a security management system. Metastructure comprises three dimensions: historical context of threat perception, ideology, and identity. Historical context informs threat perception by identifying sources and types of outstanding and potential threats; ideology provides a set of norms, beliefs, and value orientations that shape society's understanding of the security concerns; identity is important because it offers a critical referent for defining the contents and scope of the security in question. In a world of complex interdependence and multiple actors, security cannot be limited simply to national or state security. Depending on the context from which the security problem arises, it can involve diverse meanings and identities.[1]

The *institutional foundation* refers to the domestic structure and process of decision making about and implementation of security policy. It is significant not only because it defines the rules of the game related to security practice, but also because it determines the effectiveness of the domestic security coping mechanism. The institutional foundation is largely a reflection of the underlying political structure, which comprises three interrelated factors: the degree of executive dominance, bureaucratic unity and fragmentation, and the extent to which security policy making is insulated from contending social and political pressures (Krasner 1978; Katzenstein 1978; Rockeman and Weaver 1993). Articulation and enforcement of security policies, as well as mobilization and allocation of resources, usually depend on the institutional arrangements that govern security practice.

The patterns of *external management* can condition the nature and direction of security practice as well. External management is largely contingent on the perception of the security environment. If it is perceived as being anarchic—that is, an environment in which stability is assured only through the logic of balance of power and military deterrence—alliance will be the most compelling choice for external management. If the security environment is less hostile or no viable alliance is available, however, multilateral or regional security cooperation regimes might be favored. Whether one should apply realist or liberal institutionalist prescriptions to the external management of the security dilemma is determined largely by the context.

Finally, the *scope of security* matters. The concept of security has been traditionally confined to the physical protection of a nation-state's territorial and political integrity from external military attack. That thinking narrowly defines *security* as military security. In reality, however, the scope of the security agenda cannot be so circumscribed. For some countries, military security may be of vital importance; in other countries, nonmilitary issues may be just as pressing, perhaps even more so. Economic security involving competitiveness, stability, and welfare (Knorr and Trager 1977; Sandholtz et al. 1992); survival of the national population through ecological integrity (Brown 1977; Pirages 1978; Myers 1989); prevention of the nation-state's disintegration by ensuring communal harmony (Horowitz 1985; Azar 1990; Gurr 1994); and preservation of social stability by coping with transnational penetration of organized crime, drug trafficking, and terrorism could be of greater national importance than military security.

According to these analytical guidelines, South Korea's dominant security paradigm could be called a developmental realism that combines realism with developmental statism. Whereas its scope, metastructure, and external management reveal the predominance of realism (Min 1973; Baek 1985; Rhee 1986; Min-yong Lee 1996), the domestic institutional foundation is embedded in developmental statism (Haggard and Moon 1990; Moon and Prasad 1994; Evans 1995). Developmental realism has guided South Korea's security practices in the Cold War period.

Central decision makers and the general public in South Korea have understood its security environment to be anarchic and hostile. For them, international politics is governed more by force than by international law and morality. In the world of the strong the weak are not spared. Koreans learned the iron law of survival of the fittest through painful historical experiences: annexation under Japanese colonial rule, national division by the Yalta agreement, and the outbreak of the Korean War and its settlement through an unwanted truce agreement. For them, North Korea's vow to liberate the southern part of the peninsula by force and to implant a communist ideology was real. Indeed, it was perceived as a threat to the very survival of South Korea as a sovereign state—not only because of the bitter memory of the Korean War and a series of military provocations by the North, but also because of the North's formidable patrons: China joined the Korean War as North Korea's ally; the Soviet Union patronized the North throughout the entire period of Cold War confrontation. China and the Soviet Union, then, were South Korea's explicit enemies (Moon 1996a: chap. 3).

The conflict that threatened the security of South Korea was not limited to the military domain. Beneath the military confrontation lay the clash of ideology (Moon 1996a: chap. 5). North Korea had adopted communism as its guiding ideology and attempted to communize the South by force with the support of China and the Soviet Union. Central decision makers in the South responded to threats of communist expansion by devising their own security ideology of *chongryok anbo* (total security). The new security ideology was anchored in a combination of anticommunism, nationalism, and *buguk gangbyong* ("rich nation, strong army") (Min 1973: 353–72). While anticommunism served as an ideological guide for security practice, nationalism was instrumental in mobilizing the general populace in the name of the supremacy of the nation-state over individuals. The idea of *buguk gangbyong* was used to promote the program of military self-help through economic growth and modernization.[2] It was through this overarching ideology that the sacrifice of social, economic, and political values was justified. Civil society was reorganized, indoctrinated, and mobilized for security. A rigid ideological template prevailed in the management of security concerns.

South Korea's insecurity arose from the contest between two states and two regimes for one nation. The contest for legitimacy has led to a complex definition of security. Because North Korea has always posed an acute threat to the South's sovereignty, the state itself has been the primary referent of security. State security (*kukga anbo*) was the ultimate goal in the South.[3] In actuality, however, state security was often equated with regime security. Regime security occasionally overrode state security—that is, threats to the ruling regime were considered threats to state security per se. In the name of state security, domestic stability and unity were emphasized, political opposition was prohibited, and civil liberties were repressed. The National Security Law, which has governed the basic mode of security discourse and practice, made the regime's security identical with the state's security (Sohn 1989; Yoon 1990).

The metastructure of security practice in South Korea can thus be epitomized in the following terms: a perception of international anarchy; the state as the central referent of security; and the ideology of total security. This is realism par excellence. One caveat is in order, however. The rigid anticommunism and misuse of the label of security for domestic political purposes undermined the realist nature of Korean security practice. The emphasis on regime security—as opposed to just national security—reduced the effectiveness and flexibility of the security posture and also clouded the vision of a peaceful resolution of the Korean conflict.

The institutional foundation of South Korea's security practice during the Cold War era can be best understood in terms of developmental statism, a theory designed to account for institutional determinants of economic growth in East Asia including South Korea. (See Haggard and Moon 1990; Amsden 1989; Wade 1990.) Its proponents attribute the East Asian "economic miracle" to the region's peculiar state structure, characterized by executive dominance, bureaucratic unity, availability of policy instruments and resources and their strategic allocation, and insulation of economic policy making from contending social and political pressures. Developmental statism offers useful insights into the dynamics of the domestic institutional arrangements that underlie security practices in South Korea. Indeed, in the South Korean context the idea of developmental statism was initially conceived to describe the security arena and then applied to the management of economic development (Jones and Sakong 1980; Kim 1992).

The most salient aspect of developmental statism is executive dominance and bureaucratic unity. Security decision making during the Cold War period was centralized in the hands of a few political elites such as the president, the presidential staff, the Ministry of National Defense, and the Agency for National Security Planning (ANSP, formerly KCIA). Legislative intervention, bureaucratic fragmentation, and politicization of security practice were virtually blocked. The National Assembly was neutralized and the ruling political party was subjugated to the state. The primacy of military security in the hierarchy of national values left no terrain for interagency rivalry and bureaucratic infighting. The military and the security and intelligence organizations encountered no challenges from other agencies in managing security affairs. The executive dominance was a result of several factors: the constitutional arrangement (a presidential system), an authoritarian mode of governance, and the monopoly of information and expertise that lay in the hands of the executive branch (Moon 1989; Moon and S. Lee 1995).

Another important feature is the strategic position of the security sector in resource allocation. During the Cold War period, the military was the largest beneficiary of the government's resources. More than 30 percent of the national budget was annually diverted to defense during the 1960s and 1970s. Even the economic development strategy was realigned to facilitate military self-help. In the mid-1970s, the South Korean government initiated heavy-chemical defense industrialization despite internal and external opposition and skepticism. The big push toward heavy-chemical industrialization was designed not only to cope with changing comparative advantage, but also to produce forward and backward linkages to the defense industrial sector (Moon 1991; Kim 1992). As a result of resource mobilization, South Korea was able to accelerate the modernization and improvement of its defense forces.

Security affairs had long been considered a sacred domain. Security policy making was thoroughly shielded from political and civil society. Threat perception and assessment were left solely to central decision makers; strategic doctrines were formulated and implemented without public debate. Weapons decisions, resource mobilization, and the articulation of defense and foreign policies were subject to neither legislative oversight nor public screening. Dissenting views on security were not tolerated, and public accountability and transparency imposed few constraints on security practice. While the National Security Law and the Anticommunist Law offered legal and institutional protection against political and societal interference, the Military Secrecy Act blocked public access to information on security affairs. It was the airtight insulation of security practice that enabled the speedy, flexible, and effective formulation and implementation of security policies by the South Korean government. The strong, autonomous developmental state not only nurtured economic performance; it was also essential to security practice.

If South Korea was to survive in the tough security environment, effective external management was as critical as military self-help because of the country's inherent military weakness. Its external security management consisted mainly of maintaining and strengthening its alliance with the United States. In a bipolar setting where the other pole was backing the North, South Korea could not help but rely on the United States. Within the framework of the U.S.–ROK Mutual Defense Treaty, the United States indeed offered the most credible deterrence against North Korean aggression. The U.S. security commitment was more than a symbolic edifice. The United States forward-deployed sizable combat forces composed of the Second Infantry Division, the Seventh Air Force, and extensive networks of communication and intelligence in South Korea, and exercised command and control over the South Korean military. The U.S.–South Korean military ties became further integrated with the creation of the ROK–U.S. Combined Forces Command (McLaurin and Moon 1989: chap. 7; Manwoo Lee, McLaurin, and Moon 1988: chap. 3). Given North Korea's military superiority and the unfailing support it received from Beijing and Moscow, effective management of the alliance with the United States was simply indispensable: any reduction or withdrawal of U.S. forces would endanger South Korea's security. Military deterrence through the alliance with the United States, therefore, was the backbone of South Korea's external security management during the Cold War, limiting the utility of other alternatives.

The dominant security paradigm in South Korea limited the scope of security to the military dimension. Other security issues were to a great extent downplayed. Central decision makers and the general public alike shared a belief that military threats from the North were real and dangerous. History and the behavior of North Korea supported that perception. Apart from the lingering memory of the Korean War, covert and overt military provocations such as skirmishes over the demilitarized zone, the commando raid on the presidential mansion in January 1968, and frequent guerrilla infiltration made military insecurity a fact of life for South Koreans (Seok-soo Lee 1993). For all its growing importance, economic security did not draw public attention because the South Korean economy was not so deeply integrated into the international division of labor that its people felt vulnerable to the transmission of external turbulence. Furthermore, extensive mercantile practices minimized the public's fear of economic insecurity. As in most developing countries, a preoccupation with economic growth diverted policy makers' attention away from ecological issues including environmental integrity. Occasional food shortages and the domestic economic backlash from oil crises reminded South Koreans of the urgency of ecological security, but such troubles did not overshadow military security. Because of the lack of transnational intercourse, such issues as organized crime, drug trafficking, and terrorism did not emerge as prominent security concerns either.

In sum, then, the traditional security paradigm in South Korea evolved during the 1960s and 1970s out of a confluence of realism and developmental statism. The developmental realist paradigm seems quite plausible given the structure of bipolar confrontation, formidable military threats from the North, and a series of repressive authoritarian regimes. Yet its viability and desirability have been increasingly questioned. Domestic, regional, and international environments have undergone a profound transformation since the mid-1980s. The advent of a post–Cold War order, democratic opening and reforms, the irreversible trends of globalization—all have entailed new constraints and opportunities, signaling changes in the dominant security paradigm.

Metastructure: Between Inertia and New Thinking

Have international systemic changes, democratic reforms, and globalization brought about any changes in the metastructural foundation of South Korea's security practice? The effects have been mixed. Threat perception and the formation of a security identity have undergone changes, but the ideological template remains intact.

Table 7 summarizes the new threat perception shared by defense planners in South Korea (Ministry of National Defense [MND] 1995: 2–53). Central decision makers and military planners in South Korea still consider North Korea the primary source of threats to its security, but the threat no longer appears monolithic. It now depends on the status of inter-Korean relations. The Ministry of National Defense (MND) postulates three possible scenarios of inter-Korean relations: confrontation, coexistence, and unification. As long as the confrontation persists, the North is perceived as the primary source of threats. China and Russia are no longer regarded as actual or potential threats—a payoff of a new regional order and the end of the Cold War system. South Korea has been able to normalize its diplomatic ties with Russia and China

TABLE 7
South Korean Perception of Future Threats
on the Korean Peninsula

Inter-Korean developments	Nature of threats
Confrontation	• Explicit military threats from North Korea • Conflict of national interests among regional actors (China, Japan, Russia)
Coexistence	• Continuation of North Korean military threats despite progress in inter-Korean confidence-building measures and arms control; problematic transparency in North Korea's will and capability • Regional actors could hinder inter-Korean unification; increased interference by regional actors expected (China, Japan, Russia)
Unification	• Advent of unspecified threats • Possibility of civil war with residual forces of North Korea • Potential territorial conflicts with regional powers (China, Japan)

SOURCE: Ministry of National Defense 1995: 31.

since 1987 and has cultivated a broad range of exchanges and political, economic, cultural, and even military cooperation. Conflict of interest among regional actors is a source of serious security concerns, but it does not seem to be insurmountable.

Under the scenario of coexistence, South Korea's insecurity could be reduced because confidence-building measures and arms control will enhance transparency, certainty, and stability. But South Korea's defense planners appear to be less optimistic. They believe, with history as a guide, that North Korea will fail to demonstrate its transparency and accountability, destabilizing the Korean peninsula. Regional actors will not pose any direct and immediate threats to South Korea, but their interference in inter-Korean relations could undermine the process of reunification.

Surprisingly, South Korea's defense planners do not believe that peninsular reunification will resolve its security dilemma. They envision two potential threats to a unified Korea. One is internal, the other regional. Korean unification is likely to follow the German formula— that is, the South will absorb the North through the latter's internal collapse. But South Korea could not expect a smooth takeover of the North, such as occurred in Germany, because North Korean ruling elites might resist by forming an exile government in northern China or engaging in guerrilla warfare from within. Thus the possibility of a transitional civil war cannot be ruled out. Although South Korea's defense planners have been working on plans to deal with contingencies, such developments could seriously jeopardize the security and stability of a unified Korea (Song 1996; Moon and Rhyoo 1996; Samsung Economic Research Institute 1996).[4]

The regional security environment could develop into a much worse situation (Chun 1996; MND 1995: chaps. 1–2). Long-standing territorial disputes (over Tok Do with Japan, over the northern border with China) could abruptly escalate into military conflicts with regional actors. More critical is the structure of finite deterrence in the East Asian region that is likely to emerge in the posthegemonic era (Moon 1996a: chap. 4). The advent of the post–Cold War era will foster U.S. disengagement from the region in the medium to long run, leaving East Asia with a power vacuum in which Japan and China will compete for regional hegemony. Japan's remilitarization, China's ascension to regional hegemony, and the resulting regional instability will produce a precarious security environment for a unified Korea because of its defensive nationalism, which emanates from the bitter memory of Japan's colonial domination and China's military invasions. Korea, whether divided or unified—will not be free from insecurity. Its geopolitical destiny has reduced the value of the peace dividends promised by the end of Cold War. Lifting the Cold War overlay from the East Asian theater is the equivalent of opening Pandora's box, amplifying the scope of Korea's insecurity (Moon and J. Lee 1995).[5]

Democratic transition and consolidation put an end to the ideology of total security (*chongryok anbo*). Delegitimized and even discarded by a growing number among the older and younger generations, it no longer works as a deus ex machina. Democratic changes have widened the spectrum of ideological diversity. Anticommunism, ultra-right-wing nationalism, and the slogan of "rich nation, strong army," all of which embodied the dominant security ideology during the Cold War era, have been under increasing attack. A progressive intellectual has summed up the changing ideological mood: "The Roh regime is Janus-faced. It has shown a procommunist face by actively seeking an open door policy with communist countries while retaining an anticommunist face for its own people....Now it is time for a change. Our people's political consciousness has become mature, and there is no need to be afraid of communist and socialist ideology. The government should allow people to have access to it for study" (Hong 1988: 200–201).

The ideological offensive from the left-wing camp has intensified (Cho and Kim 1989; Hong 1988; Hahm 1992). It has called for extensive institutional reforms in security practice, including the abrogation of the National Security Law, the Anticommunist Law, and the Military Secrecy Act. The Agency for National Security Planning and other state security agencies have become primary targets of liberal attacks. Liberals have branded these security organizations as anti–peaceful unification forces and have demanded their immediate dismantling. Major policy realignments are called for as well: a more conciliatory posture on North Korea, the withdrawal of U.S. forces from the South, and the replacement of the Armistice Agreement by a North Korea–U.S. peace treaty. These demands are almost identical to those of North Korea. They defy the old security ideology, calling it an instrument by which the military, the technocrats, and the capitalist class have sought hegemonic domination.

A more dramatic turn came with the inauguration of the Kim Young Sam government in 1993. The Kim government appointed Han Wansang, a leading liberal intellectual, as deputy prime minister for national unification. Han's appointment was touted as a triumph for the liberal cause. Despite a myriad of unresolved issues with the North, he pushed for resuming inter-Korean dialogues and presented a variety of incentives and concessions (*Shin Donga*, June 1993, pp. 74–79). North Korea responded positively to South Korean proposals, including one for the exchange of special envoys to make a breakthrough in inter-Korean relations. But the breakthrough was soon aborted. The conservative camp, which had remained dormant during the initial period of democratic opening, staged a counteroffensive. It criticized the progressive camp of being full of pro–North Korean sympathizers and argued that North Korea has not abandoned its ambition of communizing the South by force. Conservatives charged that it was premature and even presumptuous of them to tolerate socialist and communist ideology in the South. North Korea is not East Germany, they said, and its *juche* (self-reliance) ideology has not shown any sign of changing. Therefore, they continued, anticommunism should not be compromised. Such compromise would endanger the very foundation of national security, liberal democracy, and capitalism (Chul-seung Lee 1988: 210–21). Hard-line bureaucratic agencies took advantage of this resurgence of conservative ideology. The ANSP, the MND, the Ministry of Foreign Affairs (MOFA), and even the presidential staff were not happy with the liberal, progressive forces and formed a tacit coalition to deter their growing influence on national security affairs (*Mal*, June 1993, pp. 74–79). Under mounting pressure, Han was forced to step down.[6] The old security ideology had prevailed, once again closing the window of opportunity for liberal ideology.

There has been an important change, however, in the referent of security. National security (*minjok anbo*) has emerged as a new security identity comparable to state security (*kukga anbo*). In his inaugural address on February 25, 1993, President Kim Young Sam stated that "no allies can be better than the [Korean] nation. We are ready to meet [North Koreans] any time and any place." (*Donga Ilbo*, Feb. 26, 1993). In the following month President Kim stated further, in his speech delivered at the commencement ceremony of the Korea Military Academy, that the "new government has set its security objective as embracing North Korea as a member of the same nation and opening the new era with the entire nation" (*Donga Ilbo*, Mar. 5, 1993). The Ministry of National Defense immediately redefined its security policy by expanding the scope of security from the physical protection of South Korea to the preservation of the political and territorial integrity of the entire Korean nation including North and South Korea as well as overseas Koreans (MND 1995: 38). The change is predicated, of course, on the realization of Korean reunification. Still, it suggests a profound shift in the security discourse in that it deviates from the earlier preoccupation with the realist referent of state security.

Democratic changes have not, however, severed the symbiotic links between state security and regime security. Whereas Park Chung Hee and Chun Doo Hwan seized political power through military coups and justified their authoritarian rule in the name of state security, governments under democratic rule have used "state security" as a tool for domestic political manipulation. The Roh Tae Woo government skillfully exploited security issues such as nordpolitik and rapprochement with North Korea to ensure its domestic political legitimacy and popularity. Despite its earlier pledge not to politicize security issues in general and inter-Korean relations in particular, the Kim Young Sam government has become increasingly sensitive to the domestic social and political mood in steering security practice. Kim's continuing slide into a hard-line position can be attributed partly to North Korea's provocative behavior and partly to his domestic political calculus. Seoul's tough responses have invited similar reactions from the North, resulting in troublesome amplification of action-reaction and quasi-crisis situations. At times of crisis, voters tend to be conservative, favoring the ruling party. Getting tough on the North has proved to be a safe bet in electoral campaigns.[7] Ironically, then, democratic transition and consolidation have furthered the politicization of security issues.

Democratization and the new post–Cold War order have not greatly altered the metastructural terrain of security practice. Central decision makers believe that South Korea has become more vulnerable than ever, not only because of outstanding military threats from North Korea, but also because of the broader insecurity emanating from the newly emerging structure of finite deterrence in the region. The security ideology is also trapped in the conservative closet. A dramatic surge of liberal, progressive ideology following the democratic opening did not last long, and the ideological pendulum has swung back to the hard-line, conservative side. Unless North Korea demonstrates convincing changes in its own security practice, the conservative ideology will continue to dictate South Korea's approach to security. Establishing national security (*minjok anbo*) as a new security objective, however, signals a positive development. As Korean unification approaches, such a conceptual shift seems desirable. The demarcation between state security and regime security, however, is still blurred. Democratic reforms have not severed the links between the two. The metastructural foundation is caught between the old inertia and new thinking (Moon and S. Lee 1995).

Recasting the Institutional Foundation

South Korea has been singled out as one of the most successful countries in terms of security management as well as economic performance (Azar and Moon 1988; Bobrow and Chan 1986). That success has often been attributed to South Korea's developmental statism: the state enjoys a great degree of strength and autonomy, which facilitates the efficient, coherent, and consistent formulation of policy and its effective and flexible implementation (Haggard and Moon 1990; Moon and Prasad 1994). How have democratization, the rise of the post–Cold War order, and globalization affected the state's institutional foundation?

Executive dominance is still alive and well. The president and his staff command enormous power over the formulation and implementation of security policy. Despite the growing power of political parties and the legislative branch, the chief executive is in full control of the state's security machinery. In addition to the inertia stemming from the imperial presidency of the past, the institutional arrangement framed around the presidential system reinforces the concentration of power in the hands of the president and his staff. One caveat should not be ignored, however. Although the president still holds a tight grip over the ruling New Korea Party, his control over the bureaucracy seems to be waning. Democratic reforms have fostered the delegation of power to bureaucratic agencies, creating a classic principal-agent dilemma of coordinating policy between the Blue House and bureaucratic agencies. The president's lack of commitment to, and lack of expertise concerning, security affairs appears to aggravate further the dilemma of security policy coordination (Chun and Chung 1994; Song 1995; Choi 1996; M. Lee 1996).

A loose vertical control over bureaucracy has in turn intensified a horizontal competition among bureaucratic agencies, precipitating an artificial compartmentalization within the government and a fragmentation of bureaucratic consensus. Bureaucratic politics existed even under the Park and Chun regimes. But since the democratic transition it has become much worse, resulting in an erratic, inconsistent, and unpredictable security posture. Division between hard-liners and soft-liners has never been more pronounced than under the Roh and Kim governments. Although bureaucratic cleavages and subsequent political dynamics vary from issue to issue, the National Unification Board (NUB) and the Ministry of Foreign Affairs (MOFA) are generally the soft-liners, while the ANSP and the MND form the core of the hard-line camp. The interagency rivalry is shaped by the dynamic interplay of bureaucratic interests, ideological orientation, and competition for loyalty (Song 1995: 259–61; Moon 1996a: chap. 5).

Intensified bureaucratic infighting has defied the old myth of the developmental state and bureaucratic unity. The NUB generally favors a conciliatory posture on North Korea and calls for resumption of inter-Korean dialogue. Management of inter-Korean interactions is its raison d'être; without it, the NUB would not have any power and influence. The MOFA's position is more variable than the NUB's, but it has shown a tilt toward the soft-line posture. Its primary concern is policy coordination with allies, especially the United States, and thus its policy line is often influenced by the American position. When the United States took a hard-line position linking North Korea's compliance with international inspections to activation of inter-Korean relations, the MOFA advocated the linkage option. As the United States has favored a soft-landing policy on North Korea—that is, stabilization of the situation in North Korea followed by gradual, negotiated unification—since the signing of the Geneva Agreed Framework, the MOFA has softened its hard-line rhetoric. Meanwhile, the ANSP and the MND have consistently taken a hard-line posture. They argue that South Korea should not seek reconciliation until the North shows signs of a genuine change toward peaceful coexistence. This diversity of bureaucratic positions has not only fragmented internal unity; it has also sent conflicting signals to the domestic audience, the United States, and even North Korea.[8]

Several institutional mechanisms have been devised to reduce the bureaucratic fragmentation and enhance interagency coordination: an interministerial conference on unification policy coordination and a consultative council on security policy, both headed by the deputy prime minister for national unification; a high-level strategic conference headed by the prime minister; and an interministerial conference on national security headed by the president. These institutional arrangements have not, however, resolved the problem of policy coordination. Concentration of power in the Blue House, the president's personalized style of security management, and the overlapping boundaries of power and authority among cabinet ministers have significantly undermined the process of consensus building and policy coordination (Song 1995).

Since the democratic opening in 1987, the security sector has become an apparent victim of resource allocation and mobilization. As Table 8 illustrates, defense expenditure accounted for 5.95 percent of gross national product and 35.95 percent of government expenditure in 1980. Since 1990, however, reduction of the resource allocation to the defense sector has been pronounced. In absolute terms, the size of the defense budget has increased, but it has shown a rapid decline in relative terms. The defense budget's share of GNP declined from 5.3 percent in 1985 to 4.35 percent in 1990 and to 3.26 percent in 1995. Its share of government expenditure has also decreased: from 30.05 percent in 1985 to 29.3 percent in 1990 and 22.1 percent in 1995.

The defense sector can no longer be viewed as the primary beneficiary of resource allocation. The relative decline of the defense sector is apparent in less direct ways as well. During the 1970s and 1980s, the defense tax was one of the major sources of finance for modernizing and improving the armed forces. The contribution of the defense tax was equivalent to 2 percent of GNP on average during the period. But the tax was abolished in 1990. More important, the defense industrial sector has been encountering hard times. In the 1970s, that sector had nearly unlimited access to financial, material, human, and administrative resources. The entire strategy of heavy-chemical industrialization was initiated to facilitate defense industrialization. Government procurement was virtually guaranteed. Since the mid-1980s, however, the defense

TABLE 8
Changing Patterns of Defense Spending in South Korea
(selected years)

Year	Defense Budget (in hundreds of millions of won)	Percentage of increase over previous year	Percentage of GNP	Percentage of total budget
1980	20,865	(37.61)	5.95	35.95
1985	36,892	(11.59)	5.30	30.05
1990	66,378	(10.40)	4.35	29.30
1992	84,100	(12.5)	3.72	25.30
1994	100,753	(9.3)	3.48	23.30
1995	110,744	(9.9)	3.26	22.10

SOURCE: Ministry of National Defense, *Defense White Paper* (various issues).

industry has become a sunset industry with an average capacity utilization rate hovering below 55 percent. Domestic market saturation, regulation of third-country arms sales by the United States, and declining domestic acquisition have been phasing out the defense industrial sector. The government has not undertaken any serious efforts to bail it out (Moon 1991).

Moreover, waning insulation of security policy making from contending social and political pressures reveals the passage of time. Electoral accountability, public opinion, and overall social and political mood have become the new barometers for measuring the direction of security practice. The mass media now constitute the single most important factor in dictating security policy. Legislative and bureaucratic intervention has also been on the rise. Although the ruling New Korea Party maintains a majority in the National Assembly, increased legislative oversight with the revival of the national audit system has set new terms of engagement with the executive branch. The defense sector has become vulnerable to other bureaucratic agencies, as well, especially the Ministry of Finance and Economy (MOFE). In 1990, for example, the MOFE, not the National Assembly, cut the MND's defense budget request by 9.2 percent (677 billion out of 7.37 trillion won). The margin of budget cuts varies from year to year, but it indicates that the previous pattern of insulation no longer exists (MND 1995: 146).

The changing status of the military underscores a key aspect of the domestic institutional transformation. The military has constituted the mainstay of the South Korean security machinery and has occupied a privileged and strategic position in politics and society. The South Korean military intervened in civil politics and ruled for more than 25 years. Nevertheless, democratic reforms have been successful in ensuring civilian control of security machinery by depoliticizing the military. Kim Young Sam's reform politics overhauled the entire military institution, removing intramilitary factionalism through the purge of Hanahoi, the dominant military faction, undertaking a sweeping anticorruption campaign within the military, and preventing military interference in civil politics. The arrest of two former generals-turned-president, Chun Doo Hwan and Roh Tae Woo, on charges of treason and corruption has also sent shock waves through the military, creating a formidable deterrent to future military intervention in politics (Moon and Kang 1995). Democratic consolidation has indeed civilianized the military and placed the security machinery under civilian control.

In sum, the institutional foundation has undergone sweeping changes. Democratization has realigned the developmental statism that has governed domestic management of security in South Korea. Autonomy and strength no longer characterize the state's institutional configuration. Bureaucratic fragmentation, shrinking resource allocation, and cracks in the protective shield of the security management system have led to a new institutional contour. Although the realist underpinning of its metastructure remains reasonably intact, the domestic institutional foundation of the developmental state has rapidly eroded. The mismatch between continuing realism and weakening developmental statism necessitates a new security paradigm in South Korea.

Between Alliance and Multilateralism: Managing External Relations

The demise of the Cold War system has not meant the end of history. On the contrary, it begins the journey into an uncertain future for South Korea. In their efforts to cope with two layers of external threats—persistent military threats from North Korea, and the unspecified threats that could result from a future regional order based on finite deterrence—South Korea's central decision makers are dwelling on two possible options. One is the strengthening of the bilateral alliance with the United States; the other is multilateral management through the formation of East Asian security cooperation regimes. The alliance option has been the cornerstone of South Korea's traditional security practice; multilateral security cooperation is a relatively new venue. Although the two options appear incompatible, a close examination reveals that there are some complementary features.

Central decision makers still believe in the primacy of an alliance with the United States in South Korea's management of its external relations (MND 1995–96). The ROK–U.S. alliance is well structured and credible. Despite an emerging asymmetry of threat perceptions between the two nations, strategic interdependence still exists. The United States has repeated its pledge to continue its security commitment to South Korea (Department of Defense 1995; Moon and Moon 1995; Kaufman 1996). Although defense planners in South Korea do not see any immediate changes that might impair the bilateral alliance, they have become increasingly concerned about recent difficulties in policy coordination with regard to North Korea's nuclear problem.

From the beginning, the United States defined the North Korean nuclear quagmire as a global issue closely related to overall nuclear proliferation. The North's possession of nuclear weapons was more than an inter-Korean or regional security concern. It could have jeopardized the Nonproliferation Treaty regime itself. To induce North Korea's compliance with safeguard requirements of the International Atomic Energy Agency as well as to prevent its possession of nuclear weapons, the United States has considered a wide variety of policy measures ranging from surgical strikes to political, economic, and diplomatic incentives. After a series of tough negotiations, the United States and North Korea finally reached a compromise through the Geneva Agreed Framework in late 1994. As a result, the Korea Energy Development Organization was instituted to assist the development of nuclear power as an alternative energy source in the North. The United States has also taken a conciliatory posture toward the North not only by rendering tacit support of North Korea's soft landing but also by allowing expanded social and economic exchanges with the North (Bayer 1995; Cotton 1995; Moon 1996a: chap. 2).

By riding the crest of these new developments, North Korea has taken a diplomatic offensive. In return for compliance with American demands on the nuclear issue, North Korea has actively pushed for a liaison office, the signing of a peace treaty, the promotion of economic assistance and cooperation, and eventually full diplomatic normalization with the United States. The North is aware, of course, that its wish list cannot be easily realized. But it has taken some daring tactical moves. To justify the signing of a peace treaty with the United States, the North has unilaterally abrogated the existing armistice agreement. That move was predicated on the assumption that nullification of the armistice agreement will oblige the United States to sign a peace treaty with the North. South Korea has been totally excluded on the ground that it is not a signatory to the armistice agreement. For all its implausibility, the North is pushing for the treaty on two accounts. First, treaty negotiations could serve as a critical pretext for public debates on the reduction and withdrawal of American forces in the South. Second, it might lead to a sense of South Korea's diplomatic defeat and isolation (Moon 1996c).

The new development has heightened Seoul's anxiety. The South has always wanted to contain the North Korea–U.S. rapprochement within the bounds of inter-Korean relations. Failure to do so could pose a serious liability to its domestic political maneuvering as well as its foreign policy undertaking. But Washington has been seeking a more independent posture in dealing with Pyongyang—not only because of it places priority on management of the North Korean nuclear crisis, but also because of Seoul's erratic and inconsistent policy behavior toward the North. Policy coordination between South Korea and the United States has been rare since the inception of the North Korean nuclear crisis. When the United States was deliberating on punitive military options toward the North in June 1994, South Korea was desperate to block it. Since the Geneva Agreed Framework, the United States has been tilting toward a soft-line posture favoring the North's soft landing and increased bilateral exchanges and cooperation.[9] South Korea has been almost hysterically critical of the U.S. stance. To quiet the growing policy discord, Seoul and Washington have recently proposed a four-party talk (South and North Korea, the United States, and China) to discuss the peaceful settlement of the Korean conflict and have attempted to place North Korea–U.S. relations within the framework of such a talk. However, the proposal has stagnated because of North Korea's rejection and China's lukewarm attitude. North Korea's recent submarine incursion in the northeastern part of South Korea has further complicated the diplomatic entanglement, straining ties between Seoul and Washington. Although such developments will not critically damage the military alliance, they do cloud the future of bilateral relations.

Another source of concern is potential discord over the issue of defense cost sharing in the intermediate term. The Clinton administration has pledged its security commitment to the East Asian region through the continuing pursuit of engagement and enlargement. The U.S. commitment to South Korea can be understood in the same context. Nevertheless, that commitment is contingent upon defense cost sharing with U.S. allies in East Asia (Department of Defense 1995). Like

Japan, for domestic political reasons South Korea will find it difficult to assume increased defense cost sharing. A tradition of free-riding in the security domain, coupled with rising public expectations for welfare and quality of life, will pose major barriers to sharing defense costs in a way acceptable to the United States.

More critical are the long-term implications of the end' of the Cold War. Despite its explicit pledge, South Korea's defense planners do not believe that the United States will be able to sustain its role as hegemonic stabilizer in the East Asian region. Evaporation of the principal U.S. enemy, mounting domestic pressure for social welfare spending, and a rapidly diminishing defense budget are likely to prevent the United States from continuing the current level of security commitment to East Asia. The reduction and withdrawal of U.S. forces in South Korea are coming to be viewed as simply a matter of time. Regional instability followed by American disengagement could considerably complicate South Korea's security environment in the twenty-first century. It is in this context that some South Korean defense planners advocate the continuing presence of U.S. forces even after national unification. But finding a justification for that will not be easy.

Emerging fears of a new regional anarchy as well as the influx of new ideas have induced South Korea's central decision makers to look into multilateralism as an alternative for external security management. In the past, South Korea's quest for multilateral security cooperation was confined to the resolution of the Korean conflict through the involvement of regional powers. Seoul's favorable responses to earlier proposals—in the early 1970s, Henry Kissinger's four-party talks and cross-recognition; in the mid-1980s, James Baker's "two plus four" formula—exemplify such a trend. Since 1987, however, South Korea has gone beyond the Korean issue by giving more attention to collective management of East Asian peace and security. In October 1989 in his address at the United Nations, President Roh Tae Woo proposed the establishment of a six-country consultative body for East Asian peace. In May 1993, President Kim Young Sam emphasized the importance of a multilateral security dialogue in the region in his speech at the Asia-Pacific Economic Cooperation (APEC) summit meeting. And in July 1994, Han Sung Joo, then minister of foreign affairs, proposed the launching of a Northeast Asian multilateral security dialogue in tandem with the ASEAN Regional Forum (Han 1995; Min-yong Lee 1996: chap. 9).

All of these proposals represent South Korea's growing effort to resolve the Korean dispute and regional conflicts through security cooperation regimes as well as to depart from sole diplomatic reliance on the United States. South Korea wants to take its own initiative in forming a new multilateral security cooperation regime similar to the Conference on Security Cooperation in Europe. Accordingly it has proposed several measures for regional military confidence-building measures designed to enhance transparency, certainty, and strategic stability among regional actors. Those measures include the exchange of defense white papers, registration of conventional weapons at the United Nations, regularized contacts among defense planners, exchanges of military personnel and naval vessels, mutual cooperation on nonmilitary matters, and active participation in U.N. peacekeeping efforts (MOFA Korea 1995; Min-yong Lee 1996: chap. 9). Simultaneously the South Korean government has been encouraging civilian participation in multilateral security dialogues to develop an epistemic community of multilateralism.[10]

South Korea's external management reveals two seemingly conflicting approaches. On the one hand, it still relies on the United States as its ultimate ally and partner. On the other, South Korea is gradually shifting toward multilateral solutions in resolving the Korean conflict as well as the regional security dilemma. This can be seen partly as a fallback strategy in light of the waning security guarantee provided by the United States. But it can also be interpreted as a result of the transmission of new ideas on multilateral security cooperation. In fact, a community of experts on comprehensive security and multilateral security cooperation regimes is gradually being formed in South Korea (Moon 1996a: chap. 5). That in itself represents a significant shift in South Korea's security discourse.

Exploring the New Security Agenda

Military security still tops the security agenda in South Korea (Han 1996). President Kim Young Sam himself made this clear by stating that so long as military threats from North Korea do not disappear, physical protection of its political and territorial integrity should remain the South's number-one priority (*Donga Ilbo*, Apr. 20, 1996). Democratization, the advent of a post–Cold War order, and globalization have not changed the scope of security in a significant way. Nevertheless, changes are taking place. As people's perception of the security agenda changes, so too does the perception of central decision makers (S. Lee 1995: 53–80). A nationwide public opinion poll conducted in 1989 by the National Defense University shows that the largest segment of respondents (38.6 percent) cited social stability as the top security concern, followed by national defense (26.5 percent) and political stability (18.9 percent). In another survey undertaken by the same institution in 1995, some 24 percent of respondents said that trade conflicts with advanced industrial countries are the most serious threat to security while 24 percent cited the lack of international negotiation capability as another source of insecurity. Only 23.5 percent felt that military threats from North Korea were the top security concern (National Defense University 1989, 1996). In a more recent survey, 52 percent cited enhancing international competitiveness as the number-one security concern, whereas 33 percent said that improving the quality of life should be given top priority. Military self-help through increased military power ended up a distant third (14.6 percent) in that survey (Mok 1996).

Evidence of the shifting priorities in national policy is not limited to expression of public perception. The government's resource allocation has shown a similar tendency. During the third and fourth five-year plans (1972–81), military self-help was given the top priority for resource allocation, far exceeding economic development and heavy industrialization. Since 1982, however, the defense sector has been relegated to fourth and fifth place. Price stability and social development were the number-one policy priority. During the seventh five-year plan (1992–96), the top priority was given to efficiency maximization of government expenditure, and limiting the growth of the defense budget was singled out as a primary goal of budgetary adjustment. Expansion of social infrastructure, promotion of the rural sector, technology development, and social welfare and housing were cited as important areas for resource allocation (Economic Planning Board 1991).

Central decision makers have also begun to pay more attention to the nonmilitary security agenda. President Kim Young Sam has set economic security as a new area of policy emphasis. In the era of globalization and infinite competition, strengthening international competitiveness has become a new national mandate. Driven by democratic forces, Kim has also elevated improvement of the quality of life to a status comparable to military and economic security. Recently he also declared himself an "environmental president" and pledged to concentrate his policy efforts on the preservation of environmental integrity (Environmental Protection Agency 1996).

Equally important are the ANSP's changing priorities in the area of intelligence collection. The ANSP, the epitome of the national security machinery in South Korea, has traditionally defined its primary mission as early warning of North Korea's military attack through the collection of political and military intelligence. But recently the agency has radically expanded the scope of its activities. The ANSP now engages in monitoring environmental conditions by using its own equipment, including on-site and aerial inspections. It has also set up new bureaus to handle organized crime, drug trafficking, terrorism, and computer hacking. Economic security has emerged as one of its primary concerns. The ANSP has not engaged in the collection of overseas economic, industrial, and technological intelligence, but it has been collaborating with the private sector on industrial counterespionage (Moon 1996b).

South Korea's experience shows that the security agenda is not fixed. As national values change, depending on internal and external conditions, the security agenda too is subject to variation. Facing acute threats from the North, the South's military security still occupies an important position in its security agenda. But it is no longer monopolistic. Other nonmilitary security concerns are now appreciated. Democratization, post–Cold War changes, and globalization have entailed cascading security concerns, making the management of South Korea's future security all the more difficult.

Concluding Observations

Our examination of South Korea's security practices suggests several interesting implications. The state's stalled metastructure implies that international and regional anarchy could be a self-contrived image rather than an objective reality. No objection can be raised to South Korea's perception of the North as a threat, but the way it portrays the future regional order reminds us of the power of the realist paradigm. No wonder the demise of the Cold War international system has not brought about an end to realist thinking. Pursuit of power cannot be justified without corresponding external threats, whether real or contrived. South Korea presents a classic example in this regard. So too does its ideology. Still, a positive development can be detected. South Koreans are beginning to recognize that state security is not the only definition of security. Growing public attention to the issue of national security (*minjok anbo*), whether Korea is unified or divided, could offer a valuable clue to the complex security dilemma on the Korean peninsula. Finally, the type of regime does not matter. Regardless of the regime, state security and regime security are destined to be intertwined. Despite management backlash, however, a democratic mode of governance is better. Although it might not be able to sever the complex ties between state and regime, the democratic regime will increase public accountability and the transparency of security practice. It is simply a matter of distinguishing between short-term losses and long-term gains.

The myth of developmental statism is shattered. While external threats are amplified, the domestic institutional foundation is shrinking and deforming. Bureaucratic fragmentation has undermined the coherence of security policy; failure to mobilize material and human resources has weakened the capacity of security management. Moreover, legislative intervention, penetration by diverse political and social interests, and mass media sensationalism have virtually crippled the security enterprise in South Korea. Executive dominance alone cannot assure the formulation of efficient, coherent, and consistent security policies and their effective and flexible implementation. The political leadership's commitment, informed knowledge and expertise, and sensible utilization of the presidential staff will be essential if the waning institutional foundation is to be renewed.

If the realist logic of anarchy is assumed, security becomes a national imperative. According to this line of reasoning, effective alliance management with the United States should remain the primary concern for the external management of South Korea's security. No other alternative can be considered. But if cooperation is feasible, a blind obsession with the alliance could become a hindrance to peace and security. In this sense, South Korea's quest for multilateral security cooperation is a welcome development. One caveat is in order, however. Regional security cooperation should be sought as an end in itself, not as an instrument to reach other ends. Otherwise, such a move will engender negative boomerang effects.

The South Korean case teaches us a valuable lesson. The existence of military tensions does not necessarily justify the primacy of military security. Military threats are always prominent.[11] But economic, ecological, and social security concerns can be just as pressing and vital as the military issue. In the new age of globalization, a country's security performance cannot be judged solely in terms of its military capability. Threats are manifold and diverse, and they may endanger security in a synergistic manner. Depending on military power alone is tantamount to committing the fallacy of misplaced concreteness. Resilience, flexibility, and the capacity to handle multiple threats are the new national virtues. If South Korea has not yet fully arrived at such a realization, it is prudently moving in that direction. The election of Kim Dae-jung as president in December 1997 and the initiation of his political and economic reforms to address the severe financial crisis that has engulfed the country since October 1977 will further move South Korean security practice in the direction argued in this chapter.

Taiwan
In the Dragon's Shadow

ROGER CLIFF

> *Without national security, we have nothing....Only with security*
> *can our prosperity be guaranteed.*
>
> LEE TENG-HUI

For the last fifty years, Taiwan's conceptions of security have been defined by its relationship with mainland China. Given its size and proximity, it is not surprising that China should dominate Taiwan's concerns about external military threats, but even more important than the physical juxtaposition of the two are their ethnic, cultural, and historical ties. This relationship underlies not only questions about external military threats to Taiwan but concerns about internal security and nonmilitary threats as well. Only by understanding the nature of Taiwan's relationship with mainland China can we hope to comprehend Taiwanese conceptions of security.

Taiwan's association with China has long been ambiguous. The original inhabitants of Taiwan were primarily Malayo-Polynesians (who still make up about 1.7 percent of Taiwan's population [Government Information Office 1993: 8–9]), and it was not until the thirteenth century that significant numbers of Chinese settlers began to arrive (Long 1991: 5). As late as the early seventeenth century, when European powers attempted to establish settlements there, Taiwan was still not formally administered by China and only about 25,000 Chinese were living on the island (Long 1991: 8–9; Copper 1990: 18–19). In 1662 the Ming loyalist Zheng Chenggong (Coxinga) drove out the last remaining

European settlers and attempted to use Taiwan as a base for resistance against the Qing dynasty. This led to a Qing invasion and the island's incorporation into the Chinese empire as part of Fujian province in 1683 (Long 1991: 11–13; Copper 1990: 19–20). Taiwan remained a frontier region of China, however, and as late as the middle of the nine teenth century only about half of its population was Chinese (Copper 1990: 21).

In 1895 Taiwan was ceded to Japan as part of the Treaty of Shimonoseki, which ended the Sino-Japanese War. Japanese rule was harsh and oppressive but resulted in considerable economic development and modernization: indeed, by the time Taiwan was recovered by the Chinese government at the end of World War II, educational levels and standards of living were much higher in Taiwan than in mainland China (Clough 1991: 815–17). A desire for independence had existed in Taiwan even before the end of World War II, but the exploitive nature of mainland Chinese rule after the island was recovered in 1945 did much to increase those feelings, which culminated in the uprising of February 1947. The Nationalist government violently suppressed the rebellion, driving the movement underground but further strengthening resentment of mainlander rule and the desire for independence (Lai, Myers, and Wei 1991).

The question of Taiwan's national identity was further complicated when the defeated Nationalist government led by Chiang Kai-shek fled there in 1949. The Nationalist regime continued to call itself the Republic of China (ROC) and claimed to be the legitimate government of all China, including both Taiwan and the mainland. For its part, the communist People's Republic of China (PRC) claimed that Taiwan was part of its territory and was preparing an invasion of the island in 1950. American intervention prevented the PRC from occupying Taiwan, however, and allowed the Republic of China to survive. As a result, two rival Chinese governments have existed simultaneously, each claiming to be the sole legal government of their combined territory (Clough 1991: 819–25).

As a consequence of this history, conceptions of security in Taiwan have centered on the question of national identity and on Taiwan's relationship with mainland China. The mainland government's continued effort to assert sovereignty over the island means that Taiwan's foreign policy concerns are dominated by the threat of occupation by the PRC. Indeed, for some Taiwanese the fact that the ROC itself was originally a government of mainlanders has meant that Taiwan is already under occupation by an alien regime. Conversely, for the ROC government the existence of a domestic opposition movement based on

Taiwanese self-determination has meant that threats to its security have been internal as well as external.

Other aspects of Taiwan's relationship with mainland China have affected Taiwan's security as well. Ethnic and linguistic similarities between the two have facilitated the rapid growth of economic and social interactions in recent years. Coupled with the mainland's geographic proximity these connections have resulted in a level of interdependence that poses a variety of additional threats to the security of life in Taiwan. In addition to potential overt actions by the PRC government in the form of economic warfare or subversion, these threats include the effects of social problems on the mainland such as crime or drug trafficking. Thus Taiwan's relationship with mainland China dominates not only the traditional security questions of military attack or internal subversion, but even those issues included under much broader definitions of security.

Taiwan's Political Transformation

After the Nationalist government fled to Taiwan, Chiang Kai-shek and the Kuomintang (KMT) were able to maintain an unchallenged monopoly on political power despite the Republic of China's nominally democratic constitution. This monopoly was legitimized through two devices. The first was a set of "temporary provisions" enacted by the National Assembly in 1948 that gave the president (Chiang) sweeping powers and exempted him and his vice president from the two-term reelection limit (Sung and Ho 1986: 115). The second was the Republic of China's continuing claim to be the government of all China. This meant that national elective bodies, particularly the National Assembly (responsible for electing the president and amending the constitution) and the Legislative Yuan (responsible for enacting laws), continued to be filled by representatives of all regions of China. Because the mainland was under Communist control, however, representatives from districts on the mainland were not subject to reelection and were able to maintain their seats indefinitely. These delegates were all loyal to Chiang and the KMT; thus their presence guaranteed that Chiang (and later his son, Chiang Ching-kuo) would be reelected regularly regardless of popular support in Taiwan, and also that all legislation proposed by the KMT leadership would automatically be enacted.

The KMT government used its emergency powers to exercise strict censorship over the media and publishing and thus had a monopoly not just on political power but also on the articulation of security conceptions. As a result, prior to the 1980s a very narrow conception of security prevailed in Taiwan. The regime's primary concern was simple: maintaining its position as the ruler of Taiwan. For propaganda reasons, however, and because the security of its territory was a prerequisite for the security of the regime, Taiwan's leaders spoke of security in terms of the *national* security of the Republic of China. But, because most of China was under Communist control, in practice the "Republic of China" consisted only of Taiwan and a few small islands. The identification of national security with that of the regime limited the scope of security to the political-military dimension. Two major threats to the regime were perceived: external invasion and internal subversion. The one significant external threat was the PRC, which maintained its goal of "liberating" Taiwan; the regime was also concerned about internal threats in the form of the self-determination movement or communist subversion.

The KMT's approach to defense against external attack by the PRC consisted of maintaining a high level of military preparedness and a formal defense alliance with the United States. Taiwan's indigenous defense capabilities were sufficient to ensure that the island could not easily be conquered; the alliance with the United States ensured that an attack on Taiwan would involve the PRC in a war with the United States. Internal security was maintained on the one hand by tight political control and on the other by efforts to increase the legitimacy of KMT rule. The former included a ban on contact with the mainland, restrictions on political activity, and intense surveillance of the population. The latter included a land reform program that forced landlords to trade their landholdings for stock in government-owned industries (giving them a stake in Taiwan's economic development while defusing resentment of unequal landownership), a relatively high degree of freedom in economic matters, and a program of recruiting potential opposition leaders into the KMT (Clough 1991: 827–49).

By the late 1970s, however, new challenges to Taiwan's security were emerging as the utility of these policies began to diminish. Internally, rising income levels had resulted in a better-educated and more assertive population who had time for concerns other than day-to-day subsistence. Demands for democracy and self-determination grew stronger, resulting in riots in Chungli and Kaohsiung in 1977 and 1979. Although the initial response was a tightening of political control, it was clear that domestic opposition could be contained only by ever more repressive measures (Clough 1991: 857, 869–71; Tien 1989: 95–98). Externally, meanwhile, Taiwan was becoming increasingly isolated. When the People's Republic was first established, most nonsocialist countries refused to establish relations with Beijing and continued to recognize the ROC as China's government (Clough 1991: 826). As late as 1970, more countries recognized the ROC than recognized the PRC and Taipei continued to occupy the "China seat" in the U.N. General Assembly and Security Council. By 1971, however, the PRC had finally acquired enough support in the United Nations to replace the ROC as the representative of China, and the change signaled a rapid downward slide in Taiwan's international status. By 1978 only 22 countries still maintained diplomatic relations with Taipei and Taiwan belonged to only a handful of intergovernmental organizations (Kim 1994: 151, 160).

Most significant, at the end of 1978 Taiwan's chief protector, the United States, announced that it was normalizing relations with the PRC and terminating its mutual defense treaty with Taiwan. Although the U.S. Congress subsequently passed a "Taiwan Relations Act" that declared a continuing U.S. interest in Taiwan's security, the commitments the act contained were less binding than those in the previous Mutual Defense Treaty (U.S. Public Law 96-8, 1979). Whether the United States would actually come to Taiwan's defense in the future would be contingent on such factors as the geostrategic circumstances and public opinion in the United States. At the same time as it normalized relations with the United States, however, the PRC initiated a program of economic reform on the mainland, creating an image of a China that was rapidly liberalizing and westernizing—in contrast to a rigid, unchanging Taiwan. As a result, by the mid-1980s it was unclear which way public sympathies in the United States would lie in the event of a conflict between Taiwan and the mainland. That question was further highlighted when, in 1982, the United States signed a communiqué with the PRC in which the United States announced that it would begin reducing its arms sales to Taiwan (*Beijing Review* 1982: 14–15).

Concurrent with the deterioration of U.S. security guarantees was a renewed political offensive by the PRC. At the same time as they were normalizing relations with the United States and launching their reform program, China's leaders dropped their earlier rhetoric about "liberating" Taiwan and announced instead that their goal was "peaceful unification." Under an arrangement termed "one country, two systems," PRC leaders declared that after reunification Taiwan would become a highly autonomous "special administrative region" of China and would be allowed to continue to practice its capitalist economic and social systems. According to this formula Taiwan would be permitted to maintain economic, cultural, and social ties with other countries, but not formal diplomatic relations (Ye 1981: 1; Deng 1986: 25–26). Because at that point Taiwan had official relations with only 22, mostly insignificant, countries (the major exceptions being South Korea, Saudi

Arabia, and South Africa), the "one country, two systems" proposal appeared to be well on its way to becoming a reality, and there was reason to be concerned that Taiwan would eventually no longer be recognized as an independent entity in the international system.

The KMT leadership's initial response to these internal and external developments was to tighten internal political controls and explore alternatives to dependence on U.S. military protection (Lai To Lee 1991). But no substitute for the United States existed, and it was unclear for how long domestic opposition could be suppressed (Clough 1991: 871). As a result, by the mid-1980s serious threats were emerging to Taiwan's ability to remain an independent state and to the KMT's ability to remain the ruler of that state. Although the threats had not yet reached crisis proportions, there was reason to be concerned about the long-term future.

Two additional developments around the same time added to the pressures created by Taiwan's international isolation and rising domestic opposition. The first was the changing composition of the ruling KMT party. Although originally it had been almost exclusively a party of mainlanders, by the 1980s the same recruitment programs that had been used to increase the KMT's legitimacy and co-opt potential opposition leaders had resulted in a party whose membership was predominantly native Taiwanese. But that predominance was not reflected in power sharing: the highest positions in the party and government, including the presidency, continued to be controlled by mainlanders (Tien 1989: 37). Thus by the 1980s a significant imbalance had emerged between party membership and political power within the KMT, and a new generation of leaders were pushing for reforms that would allow them to take advantage of their local political bases and popular appeal.

A second development that helped trigger changes that ultimately affected conceptions of security in Taiwan was the sudden appreciation of Taiwan's currency. In the early 1960s a fixed exchange rate had been established for the new Taiwan dollar (NTD) that favored Taiwan's export-oriented development strategy. By the 1980s, however, that exchange rate was producing persistent annual trade surpluses, particularly with the United States, that reached more than $10 billion by 1985 (Council for Economic Planning and Development 1995: 4, 192, 198). Consequently the United States began pressuring the government to reduce the surpluses (Lin Tung-hsiung 1987: 57–58; Tien 1989: 21–22). Taiwan's dependence on American goodwill for protection against the PRC meant that it had little choice in the matter, and the NTD was allowed to appreciate by some 40 percent from the end of 1985 to the end of 1987 (Council for Economic Planning and Development 1995:

4). This sudden appreciation, however, caused Taiwan's exports to become markedly more expensive almost overnight. For those labor-intensive industries whose competitive advantage was based on cost and which were already under pressure from rising wages in Taiwan, this meant it was necessary to relocate operations to a less expensive production site. The logical choice—for reasons of geographic proximity, cultural and linguistic similarity, and the family connections that are central to the Chinese way of doing business—was mainland China. As a result, by the mid-1980s Taiwanese businesses were lobbying the government to lift its ban on commerce with mainland China (*Independence Evening Post* 1987: 2; Southerland 1988: A19).

In response to this combination of internal and external pressures, in March 1986 the leadership of the KMT, led by President Chiang Ching-kuo, decided to initiate a process of political reform that began with lifting martial law and legalizing opposition parties in July 1987, and ending the ban on travel to mainland China in November 1987 (Nathan and Ho 1993: 31–61; Yang 1987: 2; Tien 1989: 13–14, 111–12). These changes had far-ranging implications for conceptions of security in Taiwan. Their initial motivation, however, was simply to preserve the security of the regime. Externally they were expected to strengthen Taiwan's security against the PRC threat by improving Taiwan's image abroad, broadening support for the regime in the United States, and increasing sympathy for its claim to an independent existence in the international community. Internally the moves were expected to improve the regime's security by defusing domestic opposition and reducing resentment of the KMT's political monopoly. By allowing the opposition to participate in the political process, the KMT diminished the likelihood of a violent confrontation at some point in the future (Nathan and Ho 1993: 40–44).

Lifting the prohibition on visits to mainland China was closely related to the decision to implement political reforms. Continuing the ban would have been inconsistent with the general easing of social controls that the KMT leadership hoped to use to appease domestic opposition and improve Taiwan's image abroad. Moreover, having embarked on the path toward democracy, Taiwan's leaders knew that if they were to maintain the security of their position in power they would have to be more responsive to popular demands. The ban on mainland travel was widely unpopular and was an important point of attack for the opposition (Huang 1987: 3).

Aside from the arguments against maintaining the prohibition, however, there were also reasons why allowing people to travel to mainland China would contribute positively to the security of the regime. By 1986 the KMT knew that living conditions in Taiwan were vastly superior to those on the mainland. Allowing Taiwanese to see for themselves how much better off they were under KMT rule was expected to reflect well on the party, boosting its prestige and justifying its past authoritarianism. In the competitive elections it would face in the future, the KMT's record of success in governing Taiwan would help it to maintain its position as the ruling party (Mooney 1987: 30–31).

Lifting the ban on mainland travel was expected to contribute to the security of the ruling party in another way. After 38 years of enforced separation, the vast majority of Taiwan's population had never been to mainland China and had little sense of identity with their mainland counterparts. Because the KMT's position in power was based on its claim that Taiwan was part of China (in contrast to the nativist opposition, which argued that Taiwan was an independent nation), such a sense of identity was vital if the party was to have the popular support needed to win competitive elections. Party leaders hoped that allowing people to visit mainland China would reinforce for Taiwanese their identity as Chinese, not just Taiwanese, and thus strengthen the party's base of support (Huang 1987: 3).

Although lifting the prohibition on travel to mainland China contributed to the regime's security in a number of ways, it also had important symbolic implications. Allowing people to travel to mainland China tended to suggest that a state of emergency vis-à-vis the Communists no longer existed, and thus undermined the legitimacy of the "temporary provisions" and mainland delegates in Taiwan's elective bodies by which the regime ensured its monopoly on power. It was for this reason that the domestic opposition movement was particularly vocal in its criticism of the ban, but it meant that the capable younger generation of KMT leaders, who stood to benefit from a more representative political system, had reason to support the lifting of the travel ban as well (*Independence Evening Post* 1987: 2).

The legalization of opposition parties and the lifting of martial law in 1987, although intended to increase the security of the regime by improving Taiwan's image abroad and defusing one of the political weapons of the Taiwanese nationalists, allowed the opposition to increase the intensity of its attacks on the KMT as an undemocratic clique of outsiders. If the KMT were to continue to enjoy the benefits of its concessions, therefore, it had to respond to those attacks by implementing further reforms that would transform the KMT into a party whose leaders had local bases of popularity.

The first major step in this direction occurred with the death of Chiang Ching-kuo in January 1988, which provided the opportunity for ascension to the presidency by a native Taiwanese, Vice President Lee Teng-hui. Once Lee Teng-hui's native Taiwanese faction had secured its position within the KMT, he was able to repeal the temporary provisions and announce the retirement of the mainland deputies in Taiwan's elective bodies (Lam 1991: 1).[1] These devices had been used by the KMT's mainland leaders to justify their monopoly on power, but they had become a liability for the party and they were not needed by the party's native Taiwanese.

Thus the ultimate result of the mid-1980s regime's efforts to maintain its security was clear: while the KMT preserved its position as the ruling party of Taiwan, the government and its relationship to the rest of the nation were radically transformed. Once a highly autonomous regime with interests distinct from those of the nation as a whole, the KMT has become a locally based government much more directly accountable to its people. This transformation has had a profound effect on conceptions of security in Taiwan.

New Conceptions of Security

Democratization has had two important effects on Taiwanese conceptions of security. First, the legalization of opposition parties and the lifting of martial law meant that for the first time alternative voices can be heard, breaking the ruling party's monopoly on the articulation of security conceptions. Second, democratization has forced the ruling party itself to become more responsive to popular demands, and in doing so the party has altered its own definitions of security. These changes have resulted in broader and more openly contested conceptions of security.

Referent of Security

Both changes are evident with regard to the referent unit of security. It is clear from the publications of the Taiwanese government that for central decision makers the primary referent unit of security is still the nation-state, the Republic of China (National Defense Report Editorial Group (NDREG) 1994: 59–66). Others, however, argue that alternative referent units of security may also be valid. One example can be seen in the concept of "international security," which is said to apply when the security of one country is interdependent with that of others. Such a referent unit is said to be more appropriate when states are members of alliances or international organizations (Taiwan Research Fund 1989: 21). Observers writing in Taiwan also recognize the existence of dangers that threaten the security of "all nations or even all of humanity." These problems are said to be "true" international security problems. They include the proliferation of nuclear weapons, international terrorism, economic crises, environmental destruction, and the spread of epidemic diseases. These are described as global problems that are beyond the ability of a single nation to solve but that "universally threaten the security of every nation and even every person" and thus require international cooperation for their elimination or reduction (Taiwan Research Fund 1989: 21–22). This wording suggests a concept of *global* security in which the entire world (or "all of humanity") is the referent unit, rather than the nation-state.

In general, however, few question the government's assumption that the nation is the fundamental referent unit for security. Instead, debate centers on the *identity* of the nation, which again involves the issue of Taiwan's relationship with mainland China. Despite the termination of the state of emergency with the Communists and the reconstitution of Taiwan's elective bodies, Taiwan's government still calls itself the Republic of China and the nation's territory is still said to consist of not just Taiwan but also mainland China (Government Information Office 1993: 3).[2] Even more broadly, the Chinese nation is conceived of as embracing all people of ethnic Chinese descent throughout the world and Chinese political culture requires that national leaders claim to be acting for the good of the entire Chinese people. Even after the reform of Taiwan's elective bodies, about 5 percent of the seats in the National Assembly and Legislative Yuan are reserved for representatives of overseas Chinese (Government Information Office 1993: 65).

This broad conception of the nation is strongly disputed by Taiwanese nationalists, who argue that the nation consists solely of Taiwan and the other small islands under the control of Taiwan's government. For them Taiwan's separation from mainland China for all but four of the last hundred or so years has created a distinct national identity that is unique to Taiwan and not shared with mainland China. Mainland China is regarded as a foreign country outside the boundaries of the Taiwanese nation (DPP Central Headquarters Election Strategy Committee 1995: 34–40).[3]

Emphasizing Taiwan's distinctness from mainland China is not an argument for a conceptualization of security in terms of ethnicity, however. The primary ethnic division in Taiwan is that between "native Taiwanese" (*benshengren*)—people whose ancestors arrived from China prior to the Japanese occupation in 1895—and "mainlanders" (*waishengren*)—those who arrived after the recovery of Taiwan in 1945 and their offspring.[4] Although *benshengren* are primarily southern Fujianese in origin and often distinguish themselves from *waishengren* by the use of the *Minnan* dialect, *benshengren* also include a significant minority of Hakka[5] and generally do not consider themselves to share an identity with other southern Fujianese (or Hakka) populations in mainland China or elsewhere. (Fujianese and Hakka are strongly represented in the overseas Chinese communities of Southeast Asia.) Although some extreme Taiwanese nationalists might wish to expel the *waishengren* (Yang 1987: 2; Jeff Hoffman 1990: 1) most advocates of independence argue that Taiwan's separation from mainland China for the last half century has resulted in a distinct cultural and national identity that is shared by all of Taiwan's residents, regardless of ethnicity (DPP Central Headquarters Election Strategy Committee 1995: 1).

Similarly, *waishengren*, if they do not describe themselves as Taiwanese, will invariably identify themselves as Chinese, rather than in terms of a particular sub-Chinese ethnic group that includes only part of the populations of both Taiwan and mainland China. Thus, although ethnic differences divide Taiwan internally, the division has not resulted in the advocation of transnational or subnational ethnic groups as the proper referent unit for security. The dispute centers solely on the issue of whether the "Taiwan" or "China" is the proper identity of the nation.

In practice, of course, the area under the control of the ROC government is still limited to Taiwan and a few small islands and, despite its rhetoric, since 1949 the ROC has rarely pursued policies intended to protect the security of parts of China not under its control.[6] Hence the debate about the identity of the nation is primarily symbolic. The advent of democracy, however, has forced the government to be more sensitive to the views of those who consider their primary identity to be Taiwanese. Thus Taiwan's government now claims that, though it strives for the good of all 1.2 billion Chinese, the interests of the 21 million residents of Taiwan take precedence (Mainland Affairs Council 1994: 25–26).

Taiwan's democratization has affected the referent unit of security in another way, however, by altering the relationship between the regime's security and national security. Prior to the 1980s the fundamental goal of KMT policies was regime security, not national security. National security was a prerequisite for regime security, but the regime also pursued policies, such as suppression of opposition, whose goal was to protect the regime, not the nation (although such policies were always justified in terms of national security).[7] With democratization, "national security" can no longer be used as a code word for regime security, but in practice the two are more closely coincident: the accountability that democracy requires places a regime that is seen as putting its own security ahead of national security at risk of being voted out of office. If it wishes to remain in power, the ruling party must be seen as giving national security the highest priority. Thus the principal referent unit of security in Taiwan today is now the nation, not the regime.

Scope of and Threats to Security

Democratization and the replacement of regime security by national security have also affected the scope of security in Taiwan. When security is defined in terms of the government's ability to perpetuate itself as the ruler of a state, security conceptions naturally accord priority to the political-military dimension. Once the referent unit is expanded to include the entire nation, however, other dimensions may be recognized. Moreover, democratization means that the people of a nation are able to articulate the specific values that they wish to have protected. This has occurred in Taiwan. One independent treatise, for example, describes the primary goal of national security as "protecting the national interests of survival, freedom, and economic prosperity" (Taiwan Research Fund 1989: 17–18). Similarly, along with more traditional missions such as "preventing or defeating an enemy attack" and "ensuring territorial integrity and the exercise of sovereignty," the government's National Defense Report lists the goals of national defense as including the maintenance of economic prosperity and social stability (NDREG 1994: 61).

Nonetheless, the political-military security of the state is seen as a prerequisite for the achievement of other security goals. For example, the same work that asserted that the fundamental goals of security are survival, freedom, and prosperity also argues that "the traditionally understood interpretation of national defense is the basis and bottom line for national security" (Taiwan Research Fund 1989: 19). Similarly, the National Defense Report lists preventing or defeating an enemy invasion as the "most important goal" of national defense, while maintaining economic prosperity, social stability, and so forth are listed as "other" goals (NDREG 1994: 61).

The obvious reason for this hierarchy is the existence of an eminent military threat to Taiwan. Mainland Chinese leaders have repeatedly declared that their long-term goal is the "recovery" of Taiwan, and they have explicitly stated that they do not rule out the possibility of using force to achieve this goal (*People's Daily* 1979: 1). Most Taiwanese have little confidence in the PRC's promises of local autonomy and believe they would lose their prosperity, freedom, and personal security under PRC rule (Mainland Affairs Council 1994: 4–5). If anything, Taiwan's democratization has increased the severity of this threat by giving Taiwanese an even greater stake in preserving their present way of life.

As a result, the maintenance of Taiwan's existence as an independent nation is seen as essential to the achievement of other security goals. In this sense the traditional realist conception of the state as guarantor of the welfare of its citizens appears to be an accurate description of perceptions in Taiwan (Morgenthau 1985). And with one of the world's largest armed forces separated from Taiwan by a mere 90 miles of water, the military threat to the state is very real.

Even if it were unable to take control of Taiwan through military means, mainland China is seen as threatening to Taiwan's security in a number of other ways. Even an unsuccessful attempt to invade the island would put the personal and economic security of its inhabitants at risk—not only as a direct result of the destruction but also because most of Taiwan's financial and intellectual capital would likely flee at the first sign of hostilities. Indeed, the PRC could use military force in forms other than an invasion attempt, such as missile attacks or a blockade, in an effort to force Taiwan to accept political unification (NDREG 1994: 63). Regardless of whether such efforts were successful, the loss of life and the economic damage could be enormous. As a result, the possibility of armed attack by the PRC is considered the primary threat to Taiwan's security (NDREG 1994: 59–61).

The perception in Taiwan is that the PRC is also using other means in pursuit of its goal of political unification with the island. These include "dividing and subverting Taiwan internally," "diminishing Taiwan's international status," "weakening Taiwan's economic power," and "breaking down the psychological defenses of Taiwan's military and civilians" (NDREG 1994: 63). Although these measures are intended to reduce Taiwan's ability to resist the PRC's political and military pressure to accept unification, they threaten aspects of Taiwan's security even if they do not succeed in bringing about that result. In the area of "dividing and subverting Taiwan internally," for example, the PRC is believed to have several thousand secret agents operating in Taiwan (Luo 1993: 4; Lu 1993: 2). Although their main purpose is believed to be sabotage and sowing panic in the event of a crisis, they have also been accused of encouraging Taiwanese separatism (Lu 1994: 4).[8] In addition to making Taiwan vulnerable to external attack, such actions threaten Taiwan's social order and increase the threat to the security of the state posed by internal conflict.

"Diminishing Taiwan's international status" refers to the PRC's efforts to prevent states and intergovernmental organizations from recognizing Taiwan. This is part of Beijing's campaign to enforce its legal claim that Taiwan is part of the territory of the PRC and to prevent Taiwan from forming alliances or joining collective security organizations that could protect it from military attack, but it affects Taiwan's security in other ways as well. For example, Taiwan's inability to participate in international organizations such as the World Bank, International Monetary Fund, Interpol, World Health Organization, or the Montreal Convention on Chlorofluorocarbons (CFCs) works to the detriment of the economic, environmental, and personal security of its citizens. Similarly, PRC efforts at "weakening Taiwan's economic power" would obviously affect Taiwan's economic security. "Breaking down the psychological defenses of Taiwan's military and civilians," by undermining confidence in the future, could affect Taiwan's social stability and economic security as well.

Another PRC effort that affects Taiwan's nonmilitary security consists of attempts to promote the economic and social integration of Taiwan and mainland China. Since 1979 the PRC government has implemented various policies designed to encourage commercial and other interactions between Taiwan and the mainland. These have included tariff exemptions for Taiwanese imports, tax holidays for Taiwanese investors, and concessionary lodging and transportation rates for Taiwanese tourists (Zhuang 1991: 84–101; Mainland Affairs Council 1992a: 1–5, 23–25, 31–33, 95–99, 116–48; *South China Morning Post* 1988: 8). Although one aim of such policies is to increase Taiwan's interdependence with the mainland and heighten the sense of identification with China on the part of Taiwan's residents, they also have the effect of making Taiwan more vulnerable to potential economic warfare by the mainland.

In this last regard, however, even more profound than the effect of PRC policies has been that of Taiwan's legalization of travel to the mainland, which vastly accelerated the growth of interdependence between Taiwan and mainland China. The mainland has now become Taiwan's second-largest export market (after the United States), taking nearly a fifth of Taiwan's exports, and Taiwanese businesses have at least $11 billion (by some estimates more than $25 billion) of direct investment in mainland China.[9] By contrast, mainland China depends on Taiwan for only about 2 percent of its export earnings and has no direct investment in Taiwan (*Liang'an jingji tongji yuebao* 1995: 44, 56). Thus an embargo or seizure of assets by the PRC would be much more damaging to Taiwan (at least in the short run) than any actions Taiwan could take against the mainland.

Economic reforms in China and democratization in Taiwan also mean that because of its size, proximity, and economic backwardness, mainland China poses threats to Taiwan's nonmilitary security for reasons other than the deliberate designs of the PRC government. One concern is that Taiwan will be overwhelmed by a flood of economic migrants from the mainland, where per capita incomes are roughly one-twentieth of those in Taiwan. Such migrants threaten both Taiwan's economic prosperity and its social order (Central News Agency 1987: V1).[10] The mainland is also seen as the source of much of Taiwan's growing crime and drug problems: the majority of illegal narcotics reaching Taiwan are said to arrive from mainland China; most automobiles stolen in Taiwan are believed to wind up on the mainland.[11] In addition to the direct consequences of these crimes, the cross-straits criminal organizations that have arisen in response to new smuggling opportunities are themselves a threat to public safety and social order.

All of these problems have increased dramatically since the changes of 1987 (*United Daily News* 1989: 3). The number of illegal immigrants from mainland China apprehended each year, for example, increased from 762 in 1987 to 5,626 by 1990 and has averaged more than 4,000 per year since then (*Liang'an jingji tongji yuebao* 1995: 41). To some extent the migration is due to the ongoing breakdown of social controls in mainland China, but it is primarily a result of Taiwan's democratization and opening to the mainland. Frequent contact with Taiwanese visitors since Taiwan's opening to the mainland has enabled people in mainland China to acquire a much better idea of the employment opportunities available for them in Taiwan (and perhaps has provided Taiwanese businesspeople and gangsters an opportunity to actively recruit mainland labor), while Taiwan's democratization has meant that the government's control and monitoring of society have diminished radically, making it far easier for illegal immigrants to operate without detection. Thus, by altering Taiwan's relationship with mainland China, Taiwan's democratization and opening to the mainland have broadened the nature of the mainland's security threat to Taiwan as well.

Aside from mainland China, the other two main threats to Taiwan's security are considered to be "territorial separation" and regional conflict (NDREG 1994: 59). Although it is primarily internal in origin, territorial separation (which refers to the Taiwan independence movement) is also an aspect of Taiwan's relationship with mainland China. If the opposition party were to take control of the government, for example, and issue a declaration of independence, in addition to possibly provoking military or economic attacks by the PRC it might also result in a violent reaction from those in Taiwan who strongly believe that the island is part of China (NDREG 1994: 62). Serious domestic upheaval would affect the personal safety, economic prosperity, and political freedom of Taiwan's populace and threaten the security of the state as a whole.[12] In addition, of course, it would weaken Taiwan's ability to resist external military attack (Voice of Free China 1991: 71).

Not all threats to Taiwan's security are perceived as related to mainland China, however. The possibility of other conflicts in the region affecting Taiwan is also a concern (NDREG 1994: 59–61). Potential scenarios could include military action on the Korean peninsula or a clash over competing claims in the South China Sea. Such conflicts could involve Taiwan simply because of the island's geographic proximity to the fighting or because Taiwan is perceived as supporting one of the combatants. Or, in the case of the South China Sea, it could even involve a deliberate attempt by one of the claimants to seize territory controlled (or claimed) by Taiwan. Perhaps even more important than the military threat represented by regional conflict, however, would be the threat to Taiwan's economic security. As a country dependent on seaborne trade for almost 40 percent of its gross national product, Taiwan is extremely vulnerable to any disruption of shipping in the region—which could occur with conflict either in the South China Sea or on the Korean peninsula (Council for Economic Planning and Development 1995: 1, 3).

Approaches to Security in the 1990s

Writings on security in Taiwan emphasize its relative nature—that is, the impossibility of being absolutely secure against all possible threats. All nations represent some degree of threat to each other. Even if no dangers existed at a particular moment, events such as advances in military technology or regime changes in another country could occur at any time. Thus the best that can be hoped for is to minimize the severity of the various threats against a nation (Taiwan Research Fund 1989: 18–20). That security is relative can mean something else, however—namely, that measures taken to enhance one type of security may put another at risk. When a unidimensional conception of security—say a regime's political-military security—is adopted, this problem does not occur. But when multidimensional conceptions are employed, the task of determining which security policies are optimal becomes more complex.

Taiwan's approaches to security in the 1990s reflect the changes in Taiwan's politics and relationship with mainland China that have occurred since 1987. Approaches to security in Taiwan are now based on the nation, rather than the ruling regime, as the primary referent of security; they acknowledge economic prosperity and social stability, not just military-political security, as goals of security policy; and they recognize the new threats represented by mainland China and other states as a result of these changed definitions and Taiwan's transformed relationship with the mainland. At the same time, changes in Taiwan's politics and relationship with the mainland have led to new approaches to securing its redefined goals.

Although the scope of security has been broadened to include economic and social dimensions, the nation's military-political security continues to be regarded as the prerequisite for security in those other dimensions. And because the principal threat to political-military security remains armed attack by the PRC, military defense remains the central goal of Taiwan's security policy. The two primary means for achieving that goal remain unchanged. The first pillar of Taiwan's defense strategy is a strong indigenous defense capability. Taiwan's armed forces consist of nearly 400,000 active duty personnel and 1.7 million reserves, out of a total population of 21 million. Representing more than 70 percent of the adult male population between the ages of 18 and 32, armed forces of such a size can be maintained only through universal conscription: all physically able males 18 or older are expected to provide two years of active military service and to maintain reserve availability until the age of 30 (International Institute for Strategic Studies 1995: 192; Government Information Office 1993: 51). Taiwan's defense expenditures are correspondingly high, amounting to more than $11 billion in 1994. That figure represented 4.7 percent of Taiwan's gross domestic product, a greater proportion than most countries in the region devoted to defense (International Institute for Strategic Studies 1995: 192).[13]

The second pillar of Taiwan's defense strategy has been its security relationship with the United States. Taiwan's forces alone are probably incapable of fending off the PRC military indefinitely in the event of a protracted effort by the mainland,[14] and the PRC could inflict great harm on Taiwan even without invading the island. The potential responses of other countries, therefore, are an important part of Taiwan's ability to deter such attacks. In addition, Taiwan's military depends on purchases of advanced armaments from abroad to maintain its technological edge over the PRC. Because it is the only nation with the power and commitment to protect Taiwan's security, the United States plays a central role in both these areas.

Because the Taiwan Relations Act contains no unambiguous guarantees, however, maintaining good relations with the United States is essential to ensuring American protection. The traditional means for achieving good relations with the United States have been a close economic relationship,[15] careful cultivation of key opinion makers and members of Congress, appeals to anticommunist sentiments in the

United States, and submissiveness to U.S. demands in matters such as trade policy, protection of intellectual property rights, and trafficking in endangered species (Sciolino 1996). Indeed, U.S. pressure to allow Taiwan's currency to appreciate was partly responsible for the government's decision to open to mainland China.[16]

To these traditional approaches to cultivating relations with the United States must now be added Taiwan's democratization. That Taiwan is now a more or less fully democratic country has significantly increased sympathy in the United States for its plight (Sciolino 1996). Whereas it is unclear whether the U.S. public would have supported military intervention on Taiwan's behalf in the mid-1980s, there is little doubt which side U.S. public opinion would favor today. Taiwan's carefully publicized democratization, along with the more negative images of the PRC that have prevailed since the Tiananmen massacre of 1989, has resulted in a marked transformation of how the two countries are perceived in the United States.[17]

Even though the United States is the only country likely to intervene militarily in the event of an attack by the PRC, Taiwan's relations with other countries are also important to its security against such an attack. The reduction of U.S. arms sales to Taiwan as a result of the 1982 agreement between the United States and PRC, for one thing, means that Taiwan is constantly seeking alternative sources for armaments.[18] Even more important, however, are the potential economic and diplomatic responses by various Asian and Western countries to an attack by the PRC. Although these countries would not themselves intervene militarily in such an event, their attitude and support would influence the likelihood of the United States taking military action (NDREG 1994: 64–65). Moreover, other nations could themselves apply a variety of diplomatic or economic sanctions against the PRC. Japan, for example, has reportedly indicated to China that it would cut off economic aid and impose a trade embargo against the mainland if Taiwan were to be invaded (*Economic Daily News* 1988: 1). Taiwan's leaders believe that Western European nations would contemplate similar sanctions against China (NDREG 1994: 65).

The degree of international support for Taiwan against the PRC would depend on the extent to which individual national interests were affected, as well as on public opinion in Asia and the West. Aside from its strategic location in the region, Taiwan's primary importance to Asian and Western countries is economic. Taiwan is Japan's third-largest trading partner and export market, for example, and had $29 billion in trade with Europe in 1994. Together Japan and Europe had nearly $10 billion in investments in Taiwan by the end of 1994 (Council for

Economic Planning and Development 1995: 207, 248). For Southeast Asia, Taiwan is both an important trading partner and a vital source of foreign investment.[19] The currently high degree of interdependence with Asia and the rest of the world is a direct result of Taiwan's open economic policies. Although those policies are in place primarily for economic reasons, they have also given the world a significant economic interest in Taiwan's security.

In addition to its economic links with Asia and the West, since the political reforms and redefinition of its relationship with mainland China in the late 1980s Taiwan has been engaged in an active campaign to increase its diplomatic and political involvement in the international system. In 1986 Taiwan had official diplomatic relations with only 23 countries and belonged to only one significant intergovernmental organization, the Asian Development Bank (Kim 1994: 151; Yearbook of International Organization 1986: L3344). The reason for Taiwan's relative isolation was that both the PRC and the ROC insisted on exclusive recognition. Countries that established relations with the PRC were required to sever relations with Taiwan (and vice versa), and neither would participate in an intergovernmental organization if the other was a member. Given the PRC's greater size and importance, the eventual result was Taiwan's exclusion from most bilateral and multilateral relationships.

Beginning in 1988, however, Taiwan began to change its position on dual recognition. The first instance was the Asian Development Bank (ADB), which the PRC had joined in 1986 without being able to force Taiwan's expulsion (Kim 1994: 160). Initially Taiwan had refused to participate in ADB activities as part of its policy of having no contacts with the PRC, but in 1988 Taiwan's leaders decided to send a delegation to the annual meeting in Manila (Yang 1988: 69–71). This marked the beginning of a new campaign of "flexible diplomacy" (tanxing waijiao) under which Taiwan dropped its objection to dual recognition of the PRC and ROC by nations or intergovernmental organizations (Yin 1990: 1).

Coupled with increased efforts at improving Taiwan's international status, flexible diplomacy has contributed to Taiwan's security in three ways. First, it has resulted in a modest increase (to about 30) in the number of countries that maintain official diplomatic relations with Taiwan. Although the new additions are all small, uninfluential countries, they nevertheless strengthen Taiwan's legal claim to statehood. PRC leaders are unlikely to feel constrained by arguments about Taiwan's status that rely on international law, but the fact that Taiwan is recognized as an independent state could influence public opinion in other countries, particularly Western democracies (even those that do not themselves recognize Taiwan), and make them more likely to support Taiwan's position in the event of conflict with the PRC. Second, the willingness to participate in international organizations of which the PRC is also a member (under a name acceptable to Beijing such as "China, Taipei") has enabled Taiwan to continue to participate in the Asian Development Bank and avoid PRC opposition to its joining two more important intergovernmental organizations: Asia-Pacific Economic Cooperation (APEC) and the World Trade Organization (WTO).[20] Although it participates in those organizations as an "economic region," not as a sovereign state, doing so allows Taiwan to increase its economic interdependence with Asian and Western nations and to strengthen its unofficial political ties with them. Third, flexible diplomacy has enabled Taiwan to take the offensive in lobbying for membership in other intergovernmental organizations, particularly the United Nations. Even unsuccessful efforts to join such organizations call attention to Taiwan's existence as a de facto independent state, increasing the likelihood that international public opinion will favor Taiwan in the event of conflict with the PRC.

Taiwan's ability to pursue flexible diplomacy is the result of the redefinition of its relationship with mainland China in the late 1980s. As long as the regime's monopoly on power was premised on its claim to be a government of all China that had "temporarily" lost control of portions of the country to Communist rebels, Taiwan could not pursue a foreign policy based on acceptance of the Communist regime's equal claim to being a government of China. Once the ROC ended its pretense of being representative of all China, however, and acknowledged that it controlled only the Taiwan area, it was no longer necessary to deny the existence of the "mainland authorities" as a regime of equal status, and a more practical diplomatic stance could be employed.

Despite its successes in reducing Taiwan's diplomatic isolation, the flexible diplomacy policy has been strongly criticized by the Taiwanese opposition. The opposition argues that Taiwan's efforts to establish diplomatic relations with other nations and intergovernmental organizations are unsuccessful because of the government's "one China" policy, under which, although it permits dual recognition, the ROC continues to claim to be a government of China. Not only does this make other nations less likely to recognize Taiwan, it also amounts to tacit admission of the PRC's claim that Taiwan is China's internal affair, legitimizing its possible use of military force. The opposition argues that Taiwan's efforts to improve its diplomatic standing would be more successful if they were conducted in the name of Taiwan, rather than the Republic of China (DPP Central Headquarters Election Strategy Committee 1995: 32–45).

Another important new weapon in Taiwan's efforts to increase international support has been its democratization. As in the United States, Taiwan's democratization means that public opinion in other democracies is now much more likely to favor Taiwan in the event of conflict with the PRC. Although for economic and geostrategic reasons most governments continue to maintain relations with the PRC in preference to Taiwan, if the PRC were to attack Taiwan the general publics of Western democracies would likely put pressure on their governments to apply economic and diplomatic sanctions against the mainland (NDREG 1994: 65).

Aside from military force, of course, the PRC could also use economic warfare against Taiwan. Possible actions include seizure of Taiwanese assets on the mainland or a trade embargo against the island. Originally the potential impact of such actions was limited by the ban on contacts with the mainland. The 1987 decision to allow family visits, however, initiated an easing of controls on interactions with the mainland that has made Taiwan much more vulnerable to economic warfare by the PRC. Nonetheless, significant restrictions on commerce with the mainland remain, the most important of which is the ban on direct shipping and air links between Taiwan and mainland China. The prohibition is partly for military reasons—heavy cross-straits traffic would reduce the warning time available in case of a surprise attack—but it is also intended to limit Taiwan's economic dependence on the mainland (DPP Central Headquarters Election Strategy Committee 1995: 47).[21] Restrictions also exist on the types of mainland industries in which Taiwanese businesses can invest (although they are difficult to enforce) and on the mainland products that may be imported. These policies are partly for economic reasons—to avoid promoting industries that compete with Taiwan's own manufacturing—but are motivated also by concerns about strengthening a potential enemy or becoming dependent on the mainland for vital imports (Shaw 1989: 5; Yang Li-yu 1990: 6). Another government policy has been to encourage Taiwanese businesses to direct their investment away from the mainland and toward Southeast Asia (Huang 1993: 2).

Some might argue that an increased level of interaction with mainland China actually contributes to Taiwan's security: the closer the links between Taiwan and the mainland, the greater the cost to the mainland of any military or economic action against the island. After all, Taiwan is now mainland China's second most important source of direct foreign investment and its fourth-largest trading partner (*Liang'an jingji tongji yuebao* 1995: 44–46). Thus, although Taiwan has become more vulnerable to economic warfare by the PRC, the potential cost to mainland China has also increased significantly. Few, however, doubt that the PRC would be willing to pay such a price. But allowing greater interaction with the mainland may benefit Taiwan's security in another way. When the ban on visits to the mainland was first lifted, Taiwan's leadership justified the move as a "political counteroffensive" against the Chinese Communists (*United Daily News* 1987: 2; Lin Hung-lung 1987: 2; Southerland 1987: A1; *China Times* 1988: 2; *United Daily News* 1988). Allowing people on both sides of the Taiwan Straits to see how much better life was in Taiwan, they argued, would bring about the collapse of communism in mainland China. Although this rhetoric was primarily a way of justifying a change in policy that was made for other reasons, in light of the events in Eastern Europe in 1989 the role of capitalist cultural influences in undermining socialism should not be dismissed. Taiwan is just one of the external influences on mainland China; but as a self-governing, democratic, Chinese state it plays a unique role in demonstrating the types of political organization that are possible within Chinese culture. Thus, although greater contact since 1987 has made Taiwan more vulnerable to economic coercion by the PRC, those contacts may in the long run contribute to China's transformation to a more democratic society that would be less likely to use force against Taiwan (Doyle 1995: 97, 1983).

Taiwan's government has also made efforts to limit the other types of threats the mainland represents to Taiwan, particularly the threat to its social stability. The ban on direct shipping and air traffic, in addition to its other purposes, has the effect of limiting the impact of the mainland's crime and drug trafficking on Taiwan. Similarly, the government has so far opposed the importation of mainland laborers, preferring instead to permit the contracting of workers from the Philippines or Thailand, even though linguistic and cultural similarities suggest that mainland workers could be more efficiently employed. This policy is pursued not only because such laborers might include Communist agents sent to subvert Taiwan, but also because the cultural and linguistic similarities of the mainland workers would enable them to escape from their work sites and blend into the local population, where their illegal status would make them more likely to become involved in crime (Mainland Affairs Council 1992b; Tsai 1993: 1).

Aside from actions by mainland China, the other factors considered to be significant threats to Taiwan's security are territorial separatism and regional conflict (NDREG 1994: 59–61). The principal strategy for preventing separatism has been democratization. Providing the opposition with the opportunity to compete with the ruling party on an equal basis and allowing the question of national identity to be debated openly have greatly reduced the possibility of internal conflict over the issue. Although Taiwan's population remains divided over the issue of national identity, the existence of a democratic process does much to ensure that a consensus may someday be reached in a peaceful and rational way.

With regard to regional conflict, the same military preparations that Taiwan undertakes to prevent attack by the PRC also defend it against attack by other nations. Taiwan's ability to prevent regional conflicts that could affect it would also be improved by participation in regional security organizations such as the ASEAN Regional Forum (ARF) or the Council on Security Cooperation in the Asia-Pacific (CSCAP), and Taiwan's leaders have expressed a desire to join such organizations (Central News Agency 1992: 56, 1993: 75). The PRC's objection, however, has restricted Taiwan's membership in these forums.[22]

Beyond the Realist Paradigm

Taiwan's relationship with mainland China is central to the political changes that have occurred since 1986 and remains fundamental to current conceptions of security in Taiwan. For example, one of the strongest pressures that contributed to the leadership's 1986 decision to implement political reforms—Taiwan's diplomatic isolation—was due to the efforts of the mainland government, which claims that both Taiwan and the mainland are part of the People's Republic of China. A similar claim by the ROC government that it is the government of all China gave rise to internal pressure from the opposition. That opposition stemmed partly from a belief that Taiwan is *not* a part of China—and therefore the ROC government was a regime of foreign intruders—but also simply from resentment of the unrepresentative and undemocratic government that was legitimized by the claim that Taiwan is part of a greater China.

Recognition of this latter sentiment was the reason for the KMT's policy of recruiting local leaders into the party, which became another source of pressure for political change in the 1980s. A final pressure for political change came from the desire of Taiwanese businesses to have closer economic ties with mainland China. That desire, in turn, was an indirect product of Taiwan's need for U.S. protection against invasion from the mainland. Such considerations compelled Taiwan's leaders to give in to U.S. pressure and allow Taiwan's currency to appreciate. The desire for closer economic relations was also a product of Taiwan's cultural and linguistic ties to mainland China.[23]

The political changes that have taken place since 1986 have fundamentally altered conceptions of security in Taiwan, but the relationship with mainland China continues to be central to the new conceptions. The prominence of that relationship is evident in disputes within Taiwan over the identity of the nation-state, which is taken to be the primary referent of security. The government behaves as if the nation consists only of Taiwan and other ROC-held islands, but it continues to claim that it represents all of China. The opposition, by contrast, argues that the nation is limited solely to Taiwan. Taiwan's relationship with the mainland is also the primary reason for the consensus on the nation-state as the principal referent of security. Beijing's claim that Taiwan is part of the PRC represents a universal threat to all of Taiwan. Given this common threat, the survival of the nation-state is crucial for protecting the Taiwanese way of life. For the same reason, although threats to other aspects of Taiwan's security exist, military-political security is considered more fundamental than the economic or social dimensions.

Taiwan's relationship with mainland China features in virtually every security threat to Taiwan. The PRC leadership's ideas about the proper relationship between Taiwan and mainland China create the constant threat that the mainland might invade or otherwise use force against the island. The PRC could also use economic warfare to enforce its claim, and the potency of that weapon is increased because of the close ties that have arisen as a result of the cultural, linguistic, and familial relationships between Taiwan and the mainland. Those relationships (along with the close geographic proximity) also mean that potential threats to Taiwan's security from the mainland have origins other than the deliberate acts of the PRC government—for example, cross-straits crime, drug trafficking, and illegal immigration.

Similarly, many of Taiwan's efforts to protect its security center on the relationship with the mainland. The policy of flexible diplomacy, for example, is based on the idea that although Taiwan and the mainland are both part of a single Chinese nation, the two separate parts are under the jurisdiction of different governments. This represents a break from the earlier claim that all of China was under the jurisdiction of Taiwan's government. Likewise, efforts to protect Taiwan's economic security consist of policies to limit its economic relationship with the mainland. At the same time, increasing interactions with the mainland are seen as contributing to Taiwan's security in the long run by hastening the transformation of the mainland polity into something that more closely resembles Taiwan. Finally, Taiwan's democratization has contributed to its security by modifying the government's claimed relationship to mainland China and permitting debate about what that relationship should be.

The fact that Taiwan's conceptions of security center on its relationship with mainland China does not make them easy to define. The relationship has both material and ideational aspects: the former include geographic proximity and the huge difference in power between Taiwan and the mainland; the latter involve the question of national identity. Perhaps because both material and ideational aspects are involved, it is difficult to explain Taiwan's security conceptions in terms of a single paradigm, whether realist, liberal, or constructivist. Rather, they reveal features of all three. For example, much of Taiwan's behavior is consistent with a classic realist perspective. Faced with a major military threat, Taiwanese regard the nation-state as the basic referent unit of security and regard political-military security as more fundamental than other types. Similarly, the principal approaches to security are the traditional policies of defense preparation and alliance-building. More broadly, Taiwan's growing diplomatic isolation in the 1970s can also be explained in (structural) realist terms as being the result of the Soviet Union's achievement of strategic parity with the United States and consequent U.S. overtures to China to balance the Soviet threat.

The means Taiwan has used to maintain its close relations with the United States, however, cannot readily be explained in terms of realism. Once the Soviet Union achieved strategic parity, the United States should have completely abandoned Taiwan for the benefit of better relations with mainland China. Instead the United States continued to support Taiwan even after it had normalized relations with the PRC. Taiwan's close relations with the United States may originally have been based on military considerations—the island was MacArthur's "unsinkable aircraft carrier"—but later they came to depend on ideology: first a common anticommunism and now a shared commitment to democracy.

Nor does the realist perspective explain Taiwan's approach to improving its relations with other Asian and Western nations. Although Taiwan's economic links with those nations give them a greater interest in preserving the island's autonomy, according to the realist perspective Taiwan's democratization and efforts to establish its claim to statehood under international law should be irrelevant to the likelihood of other countries taking action on Taiwan's behalf. Most significant, the actions Taiwan's leadership expects these states would take are primarily nonmilitary (NDREG 1994:64–65). The implicit assumption that the PRC's involvement in the world trading system limits its ability to use force against Taiwan fits better with theories of complex interdependence under which the use of force is subordinated to other instruments of international relations (Keohane and Nye 1977).

Taiwan's own economic relationship with mainland China is also inconsistent with a purely realist perspective. The appreciation of Taiwan's currency that helped precipitate the 1987 decision to open to the mainland was a result of Taiwan's dependence on the United States for military security; but according to neorealists such as Kenneth Waltz, states should seek to minimize their interdependence with countries that are potentially threatening (Waltz 1979). Instead Taiwan's government has allowed economic ties with the mainland to expand dramatically. Although Taipei recognized the dangers of such a policy, the decision was made anyway, because of pressure from business and the general public. The choice of a policy that is detrimental to a state's security as a result of competing interests within the state contradicts the realist assumption of states as unitary, rational actors and is more consistent with liberal theories of international relations. Moreover, Taiwan's government has justified its decision to open to the mainland by claiming that increased trade and other interactions with Taiwan will lead to the transformation of the mainland Chinese state into a more pluralist form. This notion, contrary to realism, is consistent with liberal ideas about the democratizing effects of trade and the unlikelihood of warfare between liberal democracies (Doyle 1995, 1983).

The threats to Taiwan's security, too, are difficult to explain in purely realist terms. Now that the KMT no longer represents a significant security threat to the Communist regime, the mainland government's efforts to extend its control to Taiwan cannot be justified as an attempt to protect its own security. An alternative explanation might be Robert Gilpin's theory of hegemonic expansion (Gilpin 1981: 106–55). But although cultural and linguistic similarities mean that Taiwan could be more easily controlled than other small countries on China's periphery, and the ambiguity about Taiwan's status means that the international community would be more likely to accept the PRC's dominion over Taiwan, the PRC's efforts to recover Taiwan seem to go beyond a simple attempt to maximize power and wealth. The PRC's quest to unify with Taiwan cannot be explained without reference to Chinese ideas about the importance of political unity and the restoration of an empire that was dismembered by foreign powers (MacFarquhar 1991: 875–81; Garver 1993: 2–28).

Conversely, note that Japan is not currently considered a threat to Taiwan despite its possession of an air force and navy comparable in capabilities to the PRC's and economic and technological capacities that far exceed mainland China's. From a realist perspective that focuses on capabilities, there should be little difference in the degree to which China and Japan are regarded as security threats to Taiwan. Taiwan's defense preparations are aimed solely at mainland China, however, and Japan is not viewed as a current security concern. This attitude can be explained only in terms of ideational factors such as Japan's current aversion to using military force and its lack of a territorial claim on Taiwan.[24]

Ideational factors must also be invoked to explain the internal threat to Taiwan's security. Few in Taiwan wish to unify with the PRC regime on the mainland, and there is little practical difference (other than potential PRC reactions) between a de facto independent Taiwan that claims to be part of a greater Chinese nation and one that does not. The national identity question, therefore, is essentially a symbolic issue. But the potential for internal conflict over the issue is nonetheless very real, as is the possibility of a PRC attack provoked by a purely symbolic change in Taiwan's status.

Consequently, although they contain certain features that resemble the realist model, Taiwan's conceptions of security cannot be adequately explained by the realist paradigm. Indeed, the very feature that is most responsible for the "realist" aspects of Taiwan's conceptions of security—the PRC threat—results not from realist mechanisms such as the security dilemma or hegemonic expansion but from purely constructed ideas about Taiwan's proper relationship to mainland China. Similarly, Taiwan's approach to security is also based on constructed identities—in this case Taiwan's identity with the Western world as a democratic, capitalist nation. The way Taiwan conceives of its security, therefore, cannot be fully explained by theories that refer only to objective conditions such as the distribution of power in the international system. Taiwan's conceptions of security can only be understood in terms of subjective ideas about the identity of the nation and its relationship to mainland China.

Bangladesh
A Weak State and Power

IFTEKHARUZZAMAN

> *We don't want to wage war against anyone. We are a peace-aspiring nation that wants to establish friendship with every other nation. But we must also have the capability to defend ourselves. We believe in peaceful coexistence and in global peace. We demand that instead of spending on arms, the rich nations of the world should invest resources in people so that the scourge of poverty is eliminated from the world....But our own imperative is to become self-reliant.*
>
> SHEIKH MUJIBUR RAHMAN

The epigraph, a quotation from the founder of the nation, illustrates the comprehensive and multidimensional definition of security in Bangladesh.[1] The weakness of Bangladesh as a state and its many domestic and international vulnerabilities account for Sheikh Mujibur Rahman's (hereafter called Mujib) emphasis on peaceful coexistence, noninterference by outsiders in the country's internal affairs, elimination of poverty, and economic emancipation as the paths to national security. The same spirit is reflected in Article 25 of the Bangladesh Constitution, which stresses "the principles of respect for national sovereignty and equality, noninterference in the internal affairs of other countries, and respect for international law and the principles enunciated in the United Nations Charter."[2] Article 25 also declares that Bangladesh will "strive for the renunciation of the use of force in international relations," a policy that essentially seeks to enhance the country's security with the support of the international system. It further upholds the right of all peoples to determine and build up their own social, economic, and political systems by means of free choice. This provision reflects the country's historical experience as a neocolonial state and at the same time affirms its commitment to reject constraints on ideological choices in postindependence Bangladesh. This conception of security has prevailed since independence with some minor modifications to accommodate changes in the geopolitical context, national imperatives, and regional and international developments.

This chapter delineates Bangladesh's conception of security, focusing mainly on security as perceived by the central decision makers of the state. It also analyzes the response of those decision makers to the security demands of subnational groups. In discerning the conception and approach to security, the analysis focuses on the nexus between internal and external threats and examines the geopolitical context of the country. After considering the main sources of insecurity, the chapter explores Bangladesh's approaches to security. Throughout I have tried to highlight the enduring as well as the changing elements by reference to specific issues and developments.

Sources of Insecurity

Threats to the national security of Bangladesh fall into three broad categories: geopolitical threats, the weakness of the state, and external factors.

Geopolitical Threats

Apart from its border of 283 kilometers with Myanmar (Burma) in the southeast, Bangladesh is bordered on three sides—north, east, and west—by India. Its opening to the Bay of Bengal (a coastline of about 414 km) is also virtually cordoned by India. That concave seacoast is also responsible to a great extent for the disputes with India and Myanmar arising from overlapping claims in the sea. Indeed, demarcation of borders remains one of Bangladesh's outstanding problems. Disputes with India include the ownership claims to the newly surfaced island of South Talpatty / New Moore / Purbasha in the estuary of the border river Hariabhanga.

Two other aspects of Bangladesh's geopolitical dependence on India are important. First, Bangladesh constitutes the lower riparian region of as many as 54 rivers, many of which originate in the eastern Himalayan basin and flow through India. Because of its position as the upper riparian state, India holds the key to managing, sharing, controlling, and augmenting the water resources of all these rivers. Second, the Chittagong Hill Tracts in the southeastern part of Bangladesh, where the failure of successive governments to accommodate the aspirations of ethnic minorities has led to insurgency, also border India. Geography gives India an advantage in abetting the insurgency movement, and hence its resolution is dependent on the goodwill of India.

Bangladesh's proximity to the politically unstable and turmoil-ridden northeast Indian states of Assam, Manipur, Nagaland, and Tripura is another source of concern. Continuing insurgencies in those states have long been a matter of concern for the central government of India, but in recent years Bangladesh has been accused of abetting Pakistan's alleged intelligence activities to step up militancy in the subregion. Whatever the accuracy of these allegations, the continued instability across the border is a major source of insecurity for Bangladesh. And when China's role is considered, the geostrategic importance of Bangladesh in the region becomes apparent. In the event of a major Sino-Indian military conflict, the small Indian corridor that separates Bangladesh from Nepal could turn out to be of tremendous strategic importance. Because the corridor is India's only land access to the otherwise volatile northeast region, Bangladesh believes that its friendship is of strategic value to India.

Bangladesh's geographic location also dictates the country's vulnerability to natural disasters and environmental degradation. The flat alluvial land has an average elevation of only 10 meters. Most of the mighty rivers originating in the Himalayas, principally the Ganges, Jamuna, and Meghna, pass through Bangladesh before emptying to the Bay of Bengal. As we shall see, the erratic water supply from these rivers—too much in the monsoon, too little in the dry season—makes Bangladesh dependent on the vagaries of nature to an extent matched in few other countries of the world. Moreover, the concave shape of Bangladesh's coastline renders the country extremely vulnerable to natural phenomena originating in the Bay of Bengal. Disasters of catastrophic proportions wrought by floods, cyclones, tornadoes, and tidal waves, which cause numerous deaths and enormous damage in this overpopulated and impoverished country, often more than once a year, constitute a constant threat to Bangladesh.

Weakness of the State

Bangladesh is a weak state with fragile institutions. In terms of sociopolitical cohesion its weakness is evident. As far as conceptions of the state are concerned, there is a clear-cut divide between the two main political parties with respect to "core values." At independence, the new constitution enshrined four principles—secularism, Bengali nationalism, democracy, and socialism—that may be considered core values.

With the change in government following the assassination of Mujib, however, secularism was replaced in the constitution by "faith in Almighty Allah."[3] This change has been a divisive factor in Bangladeshi politics. The conflict is not over whether the state should be secular or Islamic, but rather over whether it is advantageous to uphold the religious aspect of national identity. At the core of the political movement that led to the country's independence struggle was the rejection of the use of religion in politics by the Pakistani ruling elite. Therefore, the commitment to secularism is not only a state principle but also a deeply ingrained value of the people of Bangladesh. The subsequent addition of the religious dimension to Bengaliness was perceived as necessary to distinguish the people of Bangladesh from Bengalis in the Indian state of West Bengal, most of whom are not Muslims. The deletion of the term "secularism" from the constitution in no way represented a rejection of secular values in Bangladeshi politics; similarly, the insertion of Islam was not based on any genuine evidence that the national ethos of Bangladesh had turned to religion as the basis of statecraft. The stated objective of the change was to promote friendly relations with Muslim countries that were reluctant to recognize a newly emergent country that had broken away from the Islamic state of Pakistan. Beyond that, the change was also intended to distance the state from the influence of India, with which its relations had already deteriorated. Accordingly, the military-backed post-Mujib political forces that controlled state power favored the newly formulated national identity expressed as *Bangladeshi*, mainly to gain political advantage by capitalizing on anti-India as well as pro-Islamic sentiments. Meanwhile the followers of Mujib's Awami League continued to insist on *Bengali* nationalism, stressing the secular aspect.

That a country like Bangladesh with a nearly homogeneous society in ethnic, linguistic, and cultural terms would experience any controversy over national identity was hardly expected before independence. The dispute over the question of identity, however, has contributed to a sharp polarization of politics in Bangladesh. Indeed, Bangladesh's failure to create a domestic political and social consensus has led to instability in the nation's political and economic life. The degree of dissension is such that no ideas or institutions have managed to achieve a national status. As a result, the state has failed to offer a clear referent of national security. Because of continuing political fragmentation, domestic challenges to the government are often labeled as threats to national security. Domestic security problems are entangled with external threats, as well, which renders the state chronically insecure. The linkage of domestic factors with external problems is further complicated by the country's dependence on external economic assistance—a situation that is compounded by the outstanding disputes with Bangladesh's immediate neighbor.

Bangladesh emerged independent in the wake of a massive political upsurge, but it inherited a fragile base for political institutions: more than half of its life as part of Pakistan had been spent under military rule. Although the new country started off with elaborate paraphernalia for a Westminster-style democratic political system, democracy was quickly undermined. Instead, in the name of strong leadership and effective governance, power was concentrated in the ruling party and its charismatic leader, Mujib. The need for strong leadership was viewed as sufficient justification to suppress political opposition, curb the freedom of the press, curtail the power of the legislative and judicial branches of government, and enhance that of the executive bodies. Threats to the stability and security of the regime were called threats to national security. In February 1974, the Special Powers Act (SPA) was passed to provide for preventive detention. Ironically, the SPA was formulated in line with East Pakistan's Public Safety Ordinance, which had been used by the central government of Pakistan to suppress the political and economic assertion of the people of what now constituted Bangladesh. Under the provisions of the SPA any person could be detained if the government believed such detention was necessary to prevent that person from committing any act "prejudicial" to the interest of the state.

Although the SPA was apparently designed to deal with "antisocial" offenses, the all-embracing measure turned out to be a legal instrument to suppress political opposition to the government. The law has been protested by every political organization as long as it has remained in opposition. On assuming state power, however, the same organizations have used the law widely and quite conveniently against their political opponents. The other striking aspect of the SPA is its equation of national sovereignty, territorial defense, and national security with domestic law and order, public order, and the political and economic interest of the state. National security issues are therefore explicitly enmeshed with issues of regime security and political stability.

The democratic process in Bangladesh has suffered other setbacks over the years. Concentration of power in the executive has been at the expense of the legislature and judiciary. The parliament has been rendered virtually ineffective and transformed into an instrument to justify the excesses carried out by the executive. The independence of the judiciary has been severely curtailed, and the rule of law has been rendered practically impossible. Rigging of elections and widespread instances of malpractice, manipulation, force, and violence have destroyed the electoral process in Bangladesh. The press and the media have been heavily censored. The constitution and the constitutional process have been the primary casualty of these practices. Orderly change of government has not been practiced. Force has become the instrument for political change. Moreover, few of the numerous political parties operating in the country have a strong organization down to the grassroots level. They have no clear policies or programs. Instead, personalities, patronage, and prestige drive political behavior. Leadership of political parties is either inherited or usurped. Hardly any of the parties practice democracy in their own operations.

Military intervention in politics is common, and the military remains outside civilian control. Two of the main opposition parties in the current seventh parliament—the Bangladesh Nationalist Party (BNP) of Khaleda Zia and the Jatiyo Party (JP) of General Ershad—owe their origin to the army and thrive on its support. The Awami League, the party with the deepest political roots, has been the worst victim of military intervention in politics. Now that it is in power, the Awami League appears to have decided that the best way to retain power is to keep the army in "good humor."[4] In any case, the military is an important part of the state elite, and its own perception of security, both internal and external, continues to be a determining factor in Bangladeshi politics, adding to the weakness of democratic institutions. As a result, the state elite is too divided and polarized to create a national consensus.

Bangladesh is known for its chronic political instability.[5] Strikes and nationwide work stoppages, traditionally used in Bangladesh as instruments of political activism, have paralyzed the polity, putting a severe drag on efforts to improve production, trade, and investment. The boycott of parliament by all opposition members for nearly two years—and then their mass resignation to press their demand for a neutral caretaker government—created a debilitating stalemate in the political life of the country.[6] By one estimate, during the year preceding the June 1996 elections some 54 working days were lost because of general strikes that shut down all economic activity. The cost of strikes in 1993–94 was estimated to be $241 million,[7] which is more than 1 percent of the country's annual gross domestic product. Despite positive movement, signified by the formation of a new government as a result of the nationally and internationally recognized free and fair elections of 1996, the tradition of confrontational politics and the lack of mutual accommodation mean that there is no assurance of political stability. In a country that has for the greater part of its independent history experienced direct or indirect military intervention in politics, the continued failure to achieve political stability remains a potential threat to the democratic future, which is one of the core constitutional values.

Socioeconomic Issues

Bangladesh faces nearly every conceivable challenge that can confront a developing country. It has one of the highest population densities in the world. Poverty, malnutrition, and illiteracy are pervasive. It has inherited a poor infrastructural base. It suffers from economic, industrial, and technological deficiencies. Administrative and managerial inexperience, coupled with political mismanagement, have aggravated sociopolitical instability in the country, further disrupting economic development.

Poverty on a massive scale, dependence on foreign aid, and vulnerability to disaster[8] together pose a formidable threat to the sheer survival of the people of the country. At independence, roughly half the population lived below the poverty line.[9] By 1977–78 the poverty ratio had reached nearly 80 percent. The preindependence level was regained in 1985, but poverty remains alarming. With about 56 percent of the urban and 51 percent of the rural population below the poverty line in 1990, Bangladesh is in a much worse situation than most of its South Asian neighbors.[10] The infant mortality rate in Bangladesh is 108 per 1,000 live births compared to 82 in India, 91 in Pakistan, and 18 in Sri Lanka.[11] Bangladesh also ranks very low in the U.N. Development Program ranking on the Human Development Index—146th among 174 listed countries.[12]

Bangladesh's critical dependence on external aid has, according to expert opinion, denied it the prospect of self-reliance (Sobhan 1991; Rizvi 1993: 126–32). The result of that dependence is an expanding network of the aid-sustained elite while the poor continue to grow poorer and more numerous. The power elite of Bangladesh maintains its exclusive position literally by trading on poverty—the main justification for continuing dependence on foreign aid from which the elite have benefited more than the poor. The interplay of all these factors has created pervasive frustration, lack of accommodative attitude, growing tension, and uncertainty, all of which contribute to national vulnerability.

The Tribal Insurgency Movement

Central to Bangladesh's domestic concerns is an unresolved problem of national integration. More than 98 percent of the population is Bengali. Of the 2 percent ethnic minorities, about 60 percent live in the

Chittagong Hill Tracts (CHT) in the southeastern part of the country. All the ethnic minorities are Buddhists of Mongoloid origin who belong to three major ethnic groups: Arakani, Tripuri, and Kuki. The largest tribal group, known as Chakmas, constitutes about 60 percent of those living in the CHT. Although they speak the dominant Bengali language, they have their own distinct dialects, and some also have separate scripts, now rarely used.

Instead of making best use of its overwhelming ethnoreligious homogeneity in nation-building, Bangladesh quickly developed the typical majoritarian state syndrome. What began as a problem of sociocultural and political-economic grievances among the minority tribal community has turned into a major problem of national integration that constitutes a threat to territorial integrity. The irony is that similar experiences of cultural oppression perpetrated by Pakistan led to the assertion of political and economic rights and eventually to the national liberation of Bangladesh.[13] But when the turn came for Bangladesh itself to accommodate the grievances of its own minority community, the response lacked vision and ignored the lessons of history.

Compared to other parts of Bangladesh the CHT is rich in resources and natural beauty, but the region's inhospitable topography insulated it from large-scale contact with the outside until about the fifteenth century. Settlement by Bengali people from the plains began in the late seventeenth century. But when the movement of Bengalis gathered momentum in the nineteenth century, the local tribal peoples feared domination because the Bengalis were more vigorous, active, and socially assertive (Shelley 1992: 74). The movement of nontribals to the region was restricted by the Indian Limitation Act of 1877 (Regulation XV). During colonial times the tribal peoples were left to themselves, except for the purpose of revenue collection, under a regulation of 1900 that protected their exclusive social and cultural rights. At the time of partition, some elements of the CHT desired to become part of India rather than Pakistan on the ground that they were not Muslims, but their petition was rejected by the Radcliffe Commission. Ultimately the tribals capitulated to reality, but their discontent remained. They had economic grievances as well, including the Karnaphuli hydropower project that converted 54,000 acres of settled and cultivated land into a huge lake and affected some 100,000 people, whose traditional lifestyle was destroyed (Bose 1996: 108–9).

After independence, a tribal delegation met the head of the government, Sheikh Mujibur Rahman, in early 1972 with a list of demands. The timing of the meeting was important: the government was busy preparing a new constitution for the country. The demands were expressed in terms of the tribal peoples' long-standing concerns: autonomy for the CHT and the establishment of a special legislative body; retention of the 1900 regulation in the new constitution; continuation of the offices of the tribal chiefs; and a constitutional provision restricting the amendment of the regulation of 1900 and imposing a ban on Bengali settlement in the CHT (Shelley 1992: 110). Mujib rejected their demands on the ground that they were contrary to national interests (Hassan 1993: 248).

The reasons behind Mujib's sharp reaction are not clear. Considering the enormous problems facing the newly emergent country—problems that demanded national unity—perhaps he considered the plight of the small minority community to be secondary. Perhaps, in the realist tradition, he viewed the tribals as competitors for power. Perhaps the ruling elite was unwilling to accommodate social and ethnic diversity and offer a democratic space to the minority community. In any case, Mujib's demand that tribals forget their ethnic identity failed to persuade them. The new constitution was adopted without any specific safeguards of tribal interests. After a bill was passed in January 1974 declaring Bangladesh a unicultural and unilingual nation-state, the tribals found it futile to pursue their demands through constitutional means. The Shanti Bahini ("peace force"), the armed wing of the tribal political organization, launched insurgency operations and took refuge across the border in India where they received support and, Bangladesh claimed, training and arms.

The armed phase of the dispute is believed to have started in early 1975 when the Mujib government was still in power. Following his assassination, the Shanti Bahini attacks began to intensify. The government's counterinsurgency measures were stepped up in the hands of Mujib's successors, Zia and Ershad, both of whom emphasized military solutions and repression. Nonetheless, the tribals not only continued their armed struggle but expanded their demands to include self-determination with a separate legislature, restoration of the fundamental rights of the tribal people, constitutional arrangements to ensure preservation of tribal identity, and a total ban on further settlements plus transfer of current landownership to the tribal people. The gradual demographic transformation of the area—presently the main concern of the tribals—is viewed as a deliberate strategy on the part of the central government to dilute their strength. According to one estimate the proportion of tribal peoples in the area fell from 90.9 percent in 1951 to 88.4 percent in 1974 and 67.1 percent in 1980 (Larma 1980). The government's main response is that people's movement within the various regions of the country cannot be restricted. Despite recent positive developments—such as the cease-fire following government initiatives to repatriate the tribal refugees from India—the problem persists as a low-intensity conflict that impedes national integration. And with the involvement of India in the problem, its security implications become even more complex.

Flight and Plight of Refugees

Another security concern is that Bangladesh is at both the sending and receiving end of refugee migrations. Political, economic, and, in recent times, environmental forces account for emigration out of the densely populated country. The influx into Bangladesh can be traced to political factors. Indeed, Bangladesh emerged independent to a great extent as a result of the flight and plight of refugees to India from what was then East Pakistan. The ten million refugees who fled into India to escape Pakistani atrocities not only imposed a heavy burden on India but so destabilized that country, socially and demographically, that India was able to portray itself as faced with a genuine security threat justifying a rightful role in support of Bangladesh's liberation struggle. The refugee dimension of the Bangladesh crisis of 1971 was indeed a catalyst in the Indo-Pakistan war that resulted in the independence of Bangladesh. The overwhelming majority of the refugees returned. But a large number of them (according to some estimates, one million) did not return, leading to problems in Indo-Bangladeshi relations that persist to this day (Ahmed 1996: 129).

The flow of Bangladeshis to India has continued, this time impelled by economic and environmental factors. Out-migration from postindependence Bangladesh—and the outflow is not limited to India—is associated with the country's economic underdevelopment on the one hand and with natural disasters on the other. Given its geographic proximity and a porous border that renders such movements of population almost uncontrollable, India receives the largest number of Bangladeshis. The migrants are a major source of dispute between the two countries and a security concern for both. A similar problem exists between Pakistan and Bangladesh over the status of people of Bangladeshi origin who have stayed in Pakistan. Most of these people stayed in Pakistan after independence; others may have migrated illegally for economic reasons. Bangladesh denies that its nationals are moving illegally into Pakistan, claiming that Bengali-speaking people have been settled in Pakistan for decades. As in the case of the refugees in India, the possibility of these people being forcibly sent to Bangladesh in large numbers threatens the sociopolitical stability of the country.[14]

Another refugee problem confronting Bangladesh involves the

community of Urdu-speakers stranded in Bangladesh who retained their allegiance to Pakistan after independence and opted to be repatriated. Commonly known as Biharis, these people sought refuge in post-1947 East Pakistan to escape persecution by extremist Hindus and Sikhs in their Indian homeland. Many of them subsequently moved to West Pakistan. After the independence of Bangladesh, 260,000 of them living in refugee camps in various parts of the country including Dhaka, Chittagong, Rangpur, and Syedpur wanted to be repatriated to Pakistan, which they now consider their homeland. After prolonged negotiations, Pakistan ultimately agreed to repatriate. Only a few thousand have so far been repatriated, however, and the problem remains a thorny issue between Bangladesh and Pakistan. Otherwise, relations between the two transformed significantly within a few years after the independence of Bangladesh and have remained friendly during most of the post-1971 period, mainly thanks to their shared perception of India as a threat. It is not clear, however, whether friendly relations have helped them to contain the Indian threat. Moreover the collusion has not become deeply rooted, and the failure to settle the issue of repatriation underscores the ongoing differences between the two. Because the Biharis have always rejected allegiance to Bangladesh and because their repatriation to Pakistan is far from complete, their status will continue to be a source of social and political instability for Bangladesh.

Yet another problem is the influx of Rohingya refugees into Bangladesh from Myanmar. This in-migration—which has occurred twice since independence, first in 1978 and again in 1991—has become a major national security concern for Bangladesh. The Rohingyas are an ethnic minority Muslim community living in the Arakan (Rakhaine) region of Myanmar close to the Bangladeshi border. Faced with political suppression by the Myanmar military regime, Rohingya people on both occasions crossed in large numbers—170,000 in 1978 and 250,000 in 1991—into Bangladeshi territory. During the second influx, some 6,000 refugees crossed the Naaf River daily to escape the reign of terror in Myanmar; they were sheltered in makeshift camps in the southeastern Cox's Bazar and Bandarban districts of Bangladesh. The exodus of refugees was associated with Myanmar's massive military mobilization in the border areas, and thus presented a direct security threat. In one incident on December 21, 1991, an outpost of the Bangladesh Rifles paramilitary force in the Bandarban district was attacked. From Bangladesh's point of view, the influx is a source of national insecurity in addition to an excessive economic and administrative burden. The problem is complicated by the insurgency factor: militant Rohingyas have reportedly taken up arms to fight for an independent homeland in the Arakan. The crux of the problem lies in the fact that whereas most of the 1978 refugees returned to Myanmar, their more recent counterparts are increasingly reluctant to return for fear of persecution. Without a democratic transformation in Myanmar, Bangladesh is likely to continue to face this refugee problem.

External Factors

Because of the geopolitical factors discussed earlier, the external security concerns of Bangladesh are dominated by India. A typical Bangladeshi outlook regards India as the main threat to national security because of Bangladesh's geopolitically "India-locked" situation. India-bashing is common. According to the mind-set of the Bangladeshi political elite as well as the public in general, India is deliberately putting pressure on its smaller and weaker neighbor (Hossain 1991: 47). Two critical issues in Indo-Bangladeshi relations that have security implications are the Ganges water dispute and India's support for the ethnic insurgency movement in the CHT. The previous section discussed the problem of ethnic insurgency, which is essentially a domestic problem of Bangladesh but which poses an external security threat because of India's involvement. This section addresses the Ganges water dispute. Though essentially a problem created in India, it has implications for the security and survival of Bangladesh.

The Ganges, originating on the southern slope of the Himalayas, spreads over China, Nepal, India, and Bangladesh. Its flows are highly seasonal, with heavy and often devastating floods during the monsoon and acute scarcity during the dry season. Because about 80 percent of the annual rainfall on the Ganges plain occurs during the monsoon (June to September), the flow of water is highest at that time of the year, reaching about 2.5 million cubic feet per second at Farakka; during the dry season the flow is reduced to 55,000 to 65,000 cubic feet per second. The erratic flow of the Ganges makes it difficult for the basin states to devise an equitable water-sharing arrangement. Yet Bangladesh's dependence on river water is enormous: 86 percent of the total land area depends on three major river systems—the Ganges, Brahmaputra, and Meghna. The Ganges basin accounts for nearly 32 percent of the land. Aside from the country's historical and cultural attachment to the river, Bangladesh is crucially dependent on the Ganges as the source of its agroecological system, production structure, fisheries, forestry, industry, navigation, and environmental balance. The livelihoods of more than 40 million people depend directly on the river.

The Ganges water dispute centers on the barrage and feeder canal constructed by India at Farakka, 18 kilometers upstream from Bangladesh, designed to divert part of the river's dry-season flow through the Bhagirathi-Hoogli River to flush the silt from the port of Calcutta. It is designed for the "preservation and maintenance of Calcutta port by improving the regime and navigability of the Bhagirathi-Hoogli river system."[15] In October 1951, when information on the planned barrage first appeared in newspaper reports, concern began to grow in Bangladesh (then known as East Pakistan) regarding the potential adverse affect of the barrage on the river's downstream flow and therefore the economy and ecology of the lower riparian state, Bangladesh. India, however, went ahead with construction. The project was commissioned after the independence of Bangladesh, belying expectations that the issue could be resolved in the context of the cordial relations that existed between the two states at that stage.

The impact of the Ganges water issue on the society, polity, and economy of Bangladesh is enormous and multidimensional.[16] As a result of systematic diversion of water upstream, the dry-season flow of Ganges water in Bangladesh has fallen alarmingly—to a record low level of about 10,000 cubic feet per second compared to a historical average of nearly 65,000 cubic feet per second at this time of year—causing havoc to the ecosystem of Bangladesh. The hydrologic system has been extensively damaged, and the country's agriculture, fishery, forestry, navigation, industry, and every other productive sector has been exposed to disastrous consequences. The navigability of more than 320 kilometers of large and medium waterways in the region has become a thing of the past. Excessive upstream withdrawal at Farakka has drastically weakened the upland flow within Bangladesh as well, resulting in unprecedented intrusion of salinity in the coastal areas.

The social impact, too, has been pervasive. Its worst manifestation has been widespread unemployment in the immediately affected sectors, particularly agriculture, navigation, and fisheries. Crop losses and shrinking employment opportunities in the directly affected regions are causing massive economic migration to other parts of the country, particularly to the capital city, adding to the sociopolitical instability. Moreover, recent years have witnessed a greater intensity and frequency of floods in Bangladesh, commonly attributed to the release of excess water upstream at Farakka during the monsoon season. According to one report, Bangladesh claims that its growing food deficit, which reached 4 million tons in 1995–96, is the direct outcome of crop losses associated with devastating floods that hit the sixteen northern districts of the country three times during the monsoon of the previous year.[17] The failure to resolve the water dispute remains a major impediment to realization of the full potential of trade and economic relations between the two countries.

The political implications of the water-sharing issue have been significant. Indeed, it has galvanized anti-Indian sentiment in Bangladesh. In Bangladeshi eyes, the country can no longer be sure of India's intentions and motives (Hassan and Khan 1989: 89). The irony for the people of Bangladesh is that a similar dispute between India and Pakistan was settled by the Indus Water Treaty of 1960, a pact that withstood the strains of full-scale armed conflict between the two, but the Ganges dispute has persisted even though Bangladesh gained independence through a liberation struggle in which India played a significant role.[18] Bangladesh's frustration is linked to the fact that, as the lower riparian state and a weak power, Bangladesh is unable to affect the situation substantially. The Ganges issue is a popular theme in public debate in the country and a recurrent topic in the domestic politics of Bangladesh. All political parties condemn India's intransigence. The opposition political parties, besides condemning India, criticize the government of Bangladesh for pursuing a weak foreign policy and failing to force India to give Bangladesh its due share.[19] The dispute, moreover, is an issue in the electoral politics of Bangladesh.[20] India's disregard for Bangladesh's concern, as noted earlier, has exacerbated anti-Indianism in Bangladesh.

Apart from the issue of sharing the flow at Farakka, from the long-term perspective the crux of the problem is the failure of Bangladesh and India to agree on a strategy for augmentation of water. The augmentation problem dates back to August 1974 when the two parties examined each other's proposals to augment the dry-season flows of the Ganges. Bangladesh proposed that several storage dams be built on the Nepalese tributaries of the Ganges in the foothills of the Himalayas to store the surplus monsoon flow, which could then be released in the lean season. India, however, proposed that the flow could be augmented by diverting water from the Brahmaputra by connecting it with the Ganges with the help of a 320-kilometer-long link canal, 120 kilometers of which would run through Bangladesh. Each party rejected the other's proposal, and two decades have passed without progress.

Bangladesh's proposal is based on its concern for the control of water in both the dry and the monsoon seasons. The scheme would not only augment the flow, it is argued, but also control downstream flooding in the monsoon. In addition, the projects would generate vast amounts of hydroelectricity for the use of the whole region. India rejected the idea on the ground that the problem is a bilateral issue in which a third party (Nepal) has no role.[21] India's proposal is based on the idea that the three river basins—Ganges, Brahmaputra, and Meghna—

constitute one single system. Because the flow of the Ganges is inadequate and the Brahmaputra has untapped surplus flow during the dry season, the resources of the two could be combined. Bangladesh, however, argues that the dry-season flow of the Brahmaputra is not adequate to meet the full requirements of the basin.

Bangladesh is also concerned that the link canal would displace millions of people from their land, homes, and livelihoods. For a country already overpopulated and short of cultivable land, the loss of another half million hectares of fertile land would be a nightmare. Besides, the canal would add to the country's communications problems by creating another large river bisecting its northwestern region (Hassan 1991: 52). In addition, the security implications of a link canal with both ends in Indian territory make Bangladesh apprehensive, particularly with respect to the possibility of troop movement through such a canal, which would be 0.8 kilometers in width and a minimum of 9 meters in depth, involving earthworks equivalent to seven Suez Canals, and would require several decades to complete.

Sharing and augmenting the Ganges water is only one of the water problems that Bangladesh confronts with India.[22] The two countries share 54 rivers. India has already started to unilaterally construct barrages and other works on the major rivers to divert or impede their natural flow (Hassan 1991: 35). Bangladesh fears, therefore, that there may be many more Farakkas soon.[23] India's position of bilateralism in dealing with such issues as water sharing and augmentation—which are fundamentally regional problems—is a source of major concern for Bangladesh. India's resistance to a regional approach makes unlikely any long-term resolution of the problem and adds to the perception of vulnerability in Bangladesh.

Approaches to Security

It was Mujib's aspiration to build Bangladesh as the "Switzerland of Asia" (Maniruzzaman 1982: 26). As the founder of a weak nation attempting to isolate itself from superpower influences and overcome the disadvantages arising from the dictates of geography, the expression appealed to him. But Mujib quickly realized that Swiss-type neutrality was more easily desired than achieved. Within a few months of independence he signed a 25-year Treaty of Friendship, Cooperation, and Peace with India.[24] The thinking behind the treaty, however, remains far from clear (Hassan 1987: 119). Some have suggested that it was the price for the withdrawal of the Indian army from Bangladesh. With a number of countries, especially China and the oil-rich Muslim states, still withholding recognition of Bangladesh, a quick withdrawal of the foreign troops was considered essential. Others have suggested that Mujib and Indira Gandhi may have considered the treaty to be in their respective national interests. For Mujib the treaty could be taken as evidence of Bangladesh's sovereign and independent status while at the same time providing insurance from the friendly neighbor against external threats as well as domestic political upheaval (Hossain 1984: 35). Mrs. Gandhi, for her part, may have needed the treaty to show her people what India had achieved in return for all it had done for Bangladesh. This notion lends credence to the other interpretation—namely, that Mujib may have viewed the treaty as an obliging gesture to India and its prime minister. Mujib may also have hoped that the treaty would obviate the necessity of maintaining a sizable defense force. With India as the "guarantor," Bangladesh could limit its defense spending and devote more resources to much-needed socioeconomic development.

From Alliance to Diversification

Whatever the rationale for the treaty, Bangladesh soon realized the political and economic consequences of dependence on India and, by extension, the Indo-Soviet axis. Domestically the treaty was portrayed by its opponents as a surrender of independence. Article 8 of the treaty, which required each country to abstain from entering or participating in any military alliance directed against the other, and Article 9, which required mutual consultations in order to take appropriate steps to eliminate threats to either country, were viewed as restricting Bangladesh's security options. The treaty was therefore viewed, on the one hand, as preventing Bangladesh from seeking a security arrangement in the event of a possible Indian threat and, on the other hand, as permitting India to use Bangladeshi territory in case of a Sino-Indian war. The growing frustration with India also contributed to widespread suspicion in Bangladesh. Internationally, the treaty was viewed not as an instrument institutionalizing friendship between two neighbors, but as an instrument to keep Bangladesh free from the influence of outside powers, particularly China (Maniruzzaman 1982: 48). As a result, recognition of Bangladesh by China and by Muslim countries (which backed Pakistan) was further delayed.[25]

It was not lost on Bangladesh that India and the Soviet Union had only limited economic and financial resources. Mujib quickly realized that the inflow of credit and other forms of assistance were a sine qua non for "economic emancipation" and self-sufficiency. In addition, the constraints imposed by the devastated economic infrastructure that the country had inherited prompted Bangladesh to move quickly to develop cordial relations with the West. The result was a gradual policy shift. The government moved to build a consortium of aid donors. Bangladesh joined the Organization of the Islamic Conference, and Mujib participated in its Lahore summit in 1974. Stronger efforts were made to gain Chinese and Western recognition. The initiatives undertaken under Mujib opened up new opportunities, but he did not survive to see Western aid flow to Bangladesh and the country's integration with the international community.

Under the Zia regime, Bangladesh moved further away from the Indo-Soviet axis. Although no formal security arrangements were developed, it moved closer to the West and the Islamic world and developed stronger ties with China. Particularly notable was the tilt toward the Islamic world, which was viewed as a substitute for the development of close relations with India—a psychological prop, that is, in an environment of deteriorating relations with India. Whether or not this policy enhanced Bangladesh's security is not clear. But the shift occurred within a decade of independence and had obvious implications for Bangladesh's foreign policy and national security. The new orientation was more diversified than before, and the country's security concerns would henceforth be approached at four main levels: national, bilateral, regional, and international.

Bangladesh's security issues are addressed from a classic realist perspective. The emphasis is on national strength and self-reliance—and hence on the building of a strong and vibrant national economy and polity. This approach is complemented by a well-integrated military establishment capable of defending national independence and territorial integrity until international support can be mobilized.

Limits of the Bilateral Approach

Bilateral negotiation has been Bangladesh's main instrument for improving its relations with India. Not much has been achieved, however, on most of the outstanding issues except for the transfer of the Tin Bigha corridor to Bangladesh in 1992 in exchange for Berubari, which was transferred to India in 1974. Bangladesh's relationship with India began cordially. Indian assistance to the millions of Bengali refugees who flooded into India in 1971 to escape the reign of terror unleashed by Pakistan's military junta laid the foundation for friendly relations between the two. India provided the lifeblood for the provisional government of Bangladesh, too, and contributed organizational, logistic, and diplomatic support to the liberation struggle. But Bangladesh's independence also served the long-term strategic objectives of India: while the enormous burden of refugees created favorable international opinion toward India, the Pakistani blunder of open attack gave India an opportunity to retaliate in full strength, cutting an unfriendly neighbor down to size and emerging as the unchallenged regional power in South Asia. Although India's military intervention expedited Bangladesh's independence, certain actions of the Indian army prior to its withdrawal—actions mounting to "wholesale plunder of Bangladesh's material resources"—sowed the seeds of distrust in Bangladesh.[26] Nevertheless, relations between Bangladesh and India developed smoothly in the immediate postliberation period. Indeed, the euphoric heights were signaled by pronouncements that the friendship between Bangladesh and India was "everlasting" and that "no power on earth will be able to make any crack in this friendship."[27]

The reality, however, turned out to be different. Cracks soon surfaced. The Ganges water issue was a key factor. Mujib raised the issue during his talk with Mrs. Gandhi in May 1974. The communiqué signed at the end of the meeting stated that the Ganges water problem should be resolved "with understanding so that the interests of both countries are recognized and the difficulties removed in a spirit of friendship and cooperation" (Ghosh 1989: 86–87)—a clear indication by both sides at the highest political level that difficulties did exist and that they would have to be removed. An interim agreement was worked out to withdraw the water at Farakka,[28] and India commissioned the barrage pending a mutually acceptable solution. Bangladesh, however, felt deceived by this interim agreement and was further agitated when India continued to run the feeder canal after May 31 (Verghese 1990: 261). This "short-term agreement" has been viewed as one of the reasons for the assassination of Mujib (Swain 1993: 8). Although his assassination by a group of disgruntled army officers cannot be directly linked with his failure to resolve the Farakka issue, the growing tide of anti-Indianism in Bangladesh, symbolized by disapproval of the commissioning of the Farakka barrage, turned out to be one of the easily projected justifications for the killing.[29] In any event, the Ganges water issue contributed to growing anti-Indianism in Bangladesh.

India's unresponsiveness and continued withdrawal of water during the dry season caused serious damage to Bangladesh. In its first attempt to draw global attention to the problem, Bangladesh took the issue to the Colombo summit of the Nonaligned Movement, later to the Islamic Foreign Ministers' Conference in Istanbul, and finally to the United Nations. As a result of several rounds of bilateral negotiations, in September 1977 India and Bangladesh reached an agreement for sharing the dry-season flow at Farakka for a five-year period (1978–82).[30] Bangladesh paid a considerable price for the agreement: it had to agree to almost a doubling of India's withdrawal authority.[31] Except for a memorandum of understanding signed in 1985 and renewed for 1986–88 that further curtailed Bangladesh's entitlement, no subsequent agreement existed between the two countries until December 1996 when they signed an accord on sharing of the water of Ganges under a formula that appeared satisfactory to both sides. A changed atmosphere of understanding between newly elected governments in Dhaka and New Delhi provided the impetus, and the water treaty was considered a signal of a promising new beginning, though far from a resolution of the complex problem.[32] It was also seen as having opened possibilities of resolving other issues of dispute, including the CHT problem discussed earlier. Much would, however, depend on the actual implementation of the treaty, two key provisions of which remain of great concern in Bangladesh: commitment to work out agreements with regard to the other—more than fifty—common rivers, and to devise mutually agreeable ways of augmenting the flows of the Ganges during the dry season. These are difficult objectives to achieve, and more important ones from a long-term point of view. The agreement makes no provision for arbitration in case of the failure of either side to honor its obligations, nor does it address the long-standing question of involving the other riparian state, Nepal, in working out a long-term solution of the problem.

Drawing international attention to its predicament became a major plank of Bangladesh policy on the Ganges water issue. Apart from the United Nations, Bangladesh has tried other multilateral forums such as the Commonwealth.[33] Given India's resistance to introducing any third party to the resolution of what it considers a bilateral dispute, the main objective of Bangladesh's approach has been to create international public awareness of the challenges it faces as a result of unilateral withdrawal of water from an international river by an upper riparian state with absolute disregard for the adverse effects upon the lower riparian state.

Regional and International Cooperation

Bangladesh's initiative to foster regional cooperation in South Asia, which resulted in the establishment of the South Asian Association for Regional Cooperation (SAARC), was aimed primarily at creating conditions conducive to peace and stability in the region. Cooperation on noncontroversial socioeconomic issues was expected to reduce regional tensions. Formally SAARC precludes the discussion of "bilateral and contentious" issues. But one of the main considerations of President Ziaur Rahman, who launched the initiative, was to enhance the security of Bangladesh by bringing the kind of collective pressure to bear on India that could not be exerted bilaterally. India was not enthusiastic about the idea of SAARC, of course, mainly because it feared that smaller countries would "gang up" against it. Apart from the Gordian knot of Indo-Pakistani rivalry, this is the main reason that SAARC could be established only with a clear constitutional prohibition on raising contentious issues in its deliberations. To that extent, Bangladesh's attempt to use regionalism as a way of responding to security concerns was not successful. Nevertheless, SAARC has made limited progress in several areas including trade, development financing, and the relief of poverty. Bangladesh has in fact used the forum, successfully or not, in negotiating with its fellow members on such contentious bilateral issues as (with India) the Ganges water and CHT problems and (with Pakistan) repatriation of Biharis and settlement of the issue of assets and liabilities. The forum has also been used by other member countries, in some instances successfully, to diffuse tension in the region.[34] And many believe that SAARC can contribute, even if indirectly, to regional peace and understanding by removing mutual suspicion and fear, thereby enhancing the security of member states.

Internationally Bangladesh seeks close relations with great powers and plays an active role in the United Nations and other forums, including the AL-Quds Committee, the Group of 77, and the Non-aligned Movement. More recently Bangladesh was among the first countries to join the U.S.–led international military force during the Gulf War. Although it had very close relations with Iraq prior to the war, Bangladesh readily joined the force and sent its troops. Subsequently, it stepped up its contributions to international peacekeeping and became one of the few countries to have its forces or observers in nearly every U.N. peacekeeping mission. Indeed, Bangladesh is the fourth-largest contributor of troops and observers to the U.N. peacekeeping operations. This activism in the international arena is also thought to generate support, even if only moral and political, that strengthens the security of Bangladesh within the global system. Bangladesh's activism is designed to compensate for its weak status and to enhance its security through adherence to international norms. The country has also used its international relations—both bilateral and multilateral—in addressing many of the crucial issues affecting national security, including the Ganges dispute and the problems of Rohingya and Bihari refugees. Even on issues of a strictly domestic nature Bangladesh has sought external mediation. For example, in 1994 a representative of the Commonwealth secretary general joined the diplomatic community in Dhaka to explore a workable formula for holding elections under a caretaker government.

Economic factors, particularly trade and aid relations, have prompted Bangladesh to develop close ties with major economic powers such as the United States, Japan, Canada, Australia, and European Union countries. Apart from economic considerations, however, through these relations Bangladesh seeks to attract powerful patrons who can provide at least moral and political support against potential adversaries. China, for example, is not only a source of moral and political support but also a major supplier of arms for Bangladesh and hence an important balancing factor for Indo-phobic Bangladesh. One of the main objectives of Bangladesh's efforts to establish close links with Pakistan, the Islamic states, the United States, and China was to escape from alleged Indian hegemony (Rizvi 1993: 150).

Joining the Global Trend

By a historic coincidence, the renewed wave of democracy that followed the triumph over communism found resonance in Bangladesh. To be sure, the political transition in Bangladesh in 1990–91 was more an outcome of internal political dynamics than a response to external events. The coincidence was nevertheless notable—as were the recurrent, often traumatic, setbacks. Like many other developing states, Bangladesh is struggling to establish democracy and strengthen its institutions.

In the economic domain, liberalization and the free market system are taking root. Major policy changes have been introduced that, despite the political instability, are resulting in higher rates of growth, greater macroeconomic stability, and a surge in direct foreign investment. Caught up in the worldwide economic trends, Bangladesh has embarked in a big way on the process of privatization and promotion of free enterprise. Basic reforms have been introduced to make currency convertible, to ease restrictions on foreign investment, and to eliminate import controls. Efforts have been made to deepen and broaden earlier reforms aimed at achieving self-reliance through greater internal resource mobilization, reduction of public expenditures and subsidies, and promotion of the public sector's efficiency. "Economic diplomacy," though not a precisely defined expression, has become a key word in the corridors of government. The idea is to promote trade and foreign investment and thereby strengthen the country's interface with the international economy.

Lessons

Bangladesh's conception of security is essentially that of a weak state. Not only are the ideas and institutions of the state weak and fragile, but there is little internal sociopolitical cohesion. Indeed, the failure to create a domestic political and social consensus has led to continuing instability in the political and economic life of the nation. The degree of dissension is such that the constitutional core values have failed to achieve national status. Hence there is considerable ambiguity regarding *what* is to be secured. Given the political fragmentation and the weakness of the state, internal threats to the survival of the government are often proclaimed to be issues of national security. Although it is ethnically, religiously, and linguistically homogeneous, the country suffers from the usual difficulties associated with nation-building and national integration.

Domestic security problems are aggravated by the country's geopolitical situation, economic underdevelopment, and external dependence. Bangladesh does not have the political, economic, and military capabilities to influence its external environment, nor is it capable of facing many of its domestic challenges without external support. The internal and external threats to Bangladesh's security interact with each other and are closely linked to the geopolitical realities of the country. The internal threats are related to basic issues of nation-building. The failure of successive ruling elites to accommodate social and ethnic diversity by ensuring a democratic space for the small minority community accounts for the centrifugal tendencies. Forces impeding the fulfillment of national aspirations—both economic and political—also contribute to Bangladesh's perception of insecurity.

External threats are both structural and behavioral, real and perceived, and are to a great extent Indocentric. The approach adopted by Bangladesh to ensure its security can be characterized as based in the realist tradition but with an active use of neoliberal instruments. It began with a vision of neutrality and progressed to an alliance with India. Disillusionment with that arrangement then prompted Bangladesh to search for diversification and balance. As the weaker partner in their mutual relations, Bangladesh approaches its perceived security threats from India with a queer combination of deference and distraction. For geopolitical, historical, ecological, and economic reasons Bangladesh depends on India for its survival and development. But in response to what is viewed as Indian indifference to its smaller neighbor's vulnerable position—as well as in fear of domination—Bangladesh seeks to improve its relations with other countries. Those efforts have been complemented by activism in regional and multilateral institutions. Bangladesh's initiative to set up the South Asian Association for Regional Cooperation, despite the forum's well-known limitations, is clear evidence of the country's reliance on regionalism to offset its weakness and vulnerability. Domestically the country's efforts to build a self-reliant and strong society, polity, and economy also depend on external support. Collaboration with regional and international institutions complements bilateral negotiations on contentious issues. With respect to the problem of national integration, the adopted strategy is a typical combination of majoritarian fear and force: fear of challenges to its monopoly of power and force as the instrument of response. From a state-centric perspective, therefore, the Chittagong Hill Tracts problem continues to be approached more as a separatist threat than a problem of nation-building. In that case, the government's policy combines political accommodation and various means of suppression.

Pakistan
The Crisis Within

SAMINA AHMED

A s Pakistan approaches the twenty-first century, it faces a changed security environment, both domestically and internationally. Internally Pakistan is in the midst of a transition from military to democratic rule. The transition is occurring at a time when long-standing, unresolved disputes (social, economic, and political) among internal forces have become more acute and now pose severe challenges to the state. Internal challenges include ethnic and sectarian violence and an overall atmosphere of acute political polarization. The state also appears less and less capable of protecting its citizens against threats posed by political and criminal elements, especially in the urban centers.[1] In fact, the policies and priorities of the state are aggravating the crisis of insecurity in Pakistan. The overemphasis on defense has skewed government priorities at a very high socioeconomic cost.

The internal socioeconomic insecurities have been further exacerbated, at least in the short term, by the demands of international institutions such as the International Monetary Fund (IMF) and the World Bank. Aid-dependent Pakistan's overreliance on these international economic institutions[2] is forcing it to follow their prescriptions for economic transformation—including an increase in taxaton, a reduction of state subsidies, and increased unemployment as a result of privatization—that exacerbate feelings of alienation among the poorest sections of society in a deteriorating economic climate.[3] As the state adopts free market policies, the increasing gap between rich and poor is intensifying the socioeconomic tensions in civil society.

In terms of external threats, India continues to be the defining concern of Pakistan. A long history of distrust and hostility, which encompasses three wars and has yielded no progress toward even a limited rapprochement, means that Pakistani perceptions of threat still center on India, its regional rival and most powerful neighbor. (Cheema and Cheema 1994). Regional power imbalances have played a major role in defining the South Asian geopolitical environment. India's size, population, and economic and military strength, combined with its aspirations for a commensurate regional and global role, have led to feelings of insecurity in Pakistan (Tellis 1995: 288). At the same time, these asymmetries and Pakistan's conception of its own national role have led to consistent Pakistani attempts to challenge India in its neighborhood, taking advantage of opportunities presented by Pakistan's strategic location at the crossroads of South, Southwest, and Central Asia with sea lanes to the oil-rich Persian Gulf region. The end of the Cold War has reduced the strategic importance of Pakistan, however, posing new security challenges for its central decision makers.

Challenges in the Post-Cold War World

Although the end of the Cold War has contributed to the resolution of several long-standing disputes, the two major actors in South Asia, Pakistan and India, remain deeply divided. In fact, in the 1990s the Kashmir dispute, both a symptom and a cause of conflict between the two states, has once again gained salience, leading to a further deterioration in Indo-Pakistani relations. Pakistani resentment and fear of India have led to continued attempts to counter perceived threats from India and to project Pakistan as a credible regional rival through the adoption of security policies that focus on the acquisition of military power, including a nuclear capability. These policies, in turn, contribute to the ongoing arms race in South Asia, further accentuating regional tensions and instability.

Regional Tensions and External Challenges

Pakistan has also endeavored to acquire a regional standing of its own through policies of alignment with regional powers such as China and extraregional powers such as the United States. But changes in the global power balance in the post–Cold War years have placed new constraints on Pakistan's ability to maneuver (Hussain 1988). The end of the Cold War and demise of the Soviet Union have not only reduced South Asia's significance in U.S. strategic perceptions, but have also virtually nullified its need for alliance with states such as Pakistan.

Although the importance of the United States has not declined for Pakistan, which is especially keen on reviving the military relationship, bilateral relations between the two former allies are strained over such issues as Pakistan's acquisition of a nuclear capability.

During the Cold War years, Pakistan's policy makers made effective use of the opportunities presented by Sino-Soviet and Sino-Indian tensions to establish close ties with China, as well, with the dual aim of counterbalancing India's power and increasing Pakistan's leverage with its main external ally, the United States. Close links with the PRC did provide Pakistan a measure of security in its dealings with India—demonstrated by Chinese pressure on India during the 1965 Indo-Pakistan conflict (Syed 1974: 114–15) and by China's extension of arms assistance, sales, and related technology to Pakistan. Pakistan's role as an intermediary in bringing about a U.S.–PRC détente in the 1970s also helped to strengthen its links with the United States. During the late 1970s and 1980s, Pakistan and China collaborated closely on political and military matters.

But in the context of the disintegration of the Soviet Union, an easing of tensions between the PRC and Russia, and an improvement of Sino-Indian relations, Pakistani policy makers can no longer depend on unequivocal Chinese support vis-à-vis India. Though Sino-Pakistani defense cooperation continues to be critical, especially with respect to Pakistani acquisition of nuclear technology and hardware,[4] there are clear limits to the scale and level of military technology China can transfer to Pakistan, and there is little likelihood of Chinese physical intervention to assist Pakistan in the event of conflict (Tellis 1995: 291, 298). Moreover, new Sino-Pakistani tensions are emerging as a result of Chinese perceptions of threat from religious separatist elements in Xinjiang province, because the activities of Pakistani religious parties and extremists extend beyond the state's borders (Baum 1992: 502).

Now that the rationale for security relationships forged during the Cold War is no longer tenable—or at least is far less relevant—Pakistani policy makers are faced with the need to reformulate their strategic policies to meet their India-centered objectives of state security. At the same time, other developments in Pakistan's immediate neighborhood affect its security. An escalation in the ongoing Afghan civil war, in particular, bears direct repercussions for Pakistani security due to its geographic proximity.

Regional Developments and Internal Security

The Afghan crisis underscores the close relationship between Pakistan's internal and external security environments. For example, not only does the existence of a large Afghan refugee population mean that Pakistani territory continues to be used as a sanctuary and a base for rival Afghan contenders, but the Afghan civil war and the refugee presence have had their own impact on internal Pakistani politics and security. The issue of narcotics production, use, and trade in Pakistan is closely linked to the absence of an effective state authority in Afghanistan—as is the flow of sophisticated arms across the Pakistani-Afghan border, which undermines the security of Pakistan's citizens, deprives the state of its control over the means of violence, and promotes the criminalization of politics.[5]

These detrimental effects on Pakistan's internal security are particularly visible in Sindh province. While state policies have led to an intensification of state-ethnic, interethnic, and intraethnic tensions in Sindh, ethnic dissidents have used sophisticated arms, obtained from the cross-border arms trade, to violently confront security forces and each other in Sindh's provincial capital, Karachi—the country's industrial and financial heart and its sole major port, providing nearly two-thirds of all central revenue.[6] There have been frequent rocket attacks on government offices and personnel, such as the attack on the Sindh Secretariat in July 1995.

The Afghan refugee presence also places a substantial economic burden on the state as the international community continues to reduce its funding in light of the ongoing civil war. The refugee presence has resulted in widespread environmental degradation in the North West Frontier Province (NWFP) and Baluchistan, the two Pakistani provinces bordering Afghanistan. Moreover, the influx of Afghan Pakhtuns has upset the delicate demographic balance between ethnic Baluch and Pakhtuns in the province of Baluchistan.[7] The buildup of ethnic tensions increases the potential for interethnic violence and heightens Baluch alienation toward the center (Zulfikar 1993: 132).

Another issue of particular relevance for Pakistan's internal and external security is the intensification of sectarian strife, especially in urban centers where violence is already endemic. Sectarian tensions between militant Shia and Sunni organizations create new security considerations, as well, because they make Pakistan more vulnerable to external intervention. Tensions with neighboring Iran could conceivably lead to Iranian intervention, given that Iran has maintained a close relationship with the minority Shia community in Pakistan (Lodhi 1994a). Sunni militants, for their part, have the moral and material support of countries such as Saudi Arabia.

The rise of Islamic extremism is in large measure a consequence of the political manipulation of religion by incumbent governments and by all political parties. Until the dismemberment of Pakistan in 1971, religion was used by Islamist parties in a bid to broaden their narrow support base and by state authorities as a nation-building tool to justify, for example, the formation of Pakistan on the basis of the two-nation theory.[8] Yet central decision makers made no systematic effort to institutionalize religion as a legitimizing tool. When a majority of Pakistan's Muslim Bengali population opted for secession, the two-nation theory became increasingly redundant. Political bargaining and the quest for identity then focused primarily on regional and ethnic competition.[9]

The Pakistan People's Party (PPP) government of Prime Minister Zulfikar Ali Bhutto, therefore, relied on populist rhetoric to counter perceived threats to centralized power posed by demands for regional autonomy from the peripheral federating units. Following the coup d'état of 1977, however, the new military rulers, having deposed an elected government and executed a prime minister, faced a crisis of legitimacy. Consistent efforts were therefore made to legitimize military rule through the institutionalized use of religion. As part of their legitimizing strategy, the new rulers provided state patronage to Islamic extremist groups and parties as a counterweight against the political opposition (Ziring 1988: 807). At the same time, the Pakistani military and external powers such as the United States patronized Afghan religious factions in their fight against the Afghan government and its Soviet allies. Pakistani fundamentalist parties, too, were encouraged to play an active role in the Afghan crisis.[10] As a result, Islamic extremists in Pakistan and their Afghan counterparts are well organized and equipped to confront perceived threats to their interests in a far less sympathetic domestic, regional, and global environment.

New Imperatives

The domestic compulsions of Pakistani policy makers have therefore had their impact on the present directions of Pakistani security practice, as have their strategic perceptions. In the Indian case, for example, both internal and external forces have contributed to Pakistan's adoption of a hostile stand. Though there is indeed a deep distrust in Pakistan of its more powerful and ambitious neighbor, the Indian "threat" has also been used by unrepresentative regimes as an expedient tool to attain domestic ascendancy, to control the state's resources, and to defuse internal opposition (Harrison 1992). But such confrontational policies, in turn, increase regional tensions and instability.

Internal instability, historical animosities, the unavoidable facts of geography, and ambitious policies aimed at expanding Pakistan's regional role—all intertwine to determine the directions of Pakistan's security policy. Global, regional, and internal developments such as the spread of Islamic fundamentalism and an unsympathetic international economic order have equally significant impacts on the security of the Pakistani state. Because these developments are taking place at a time when the role of Pakistan's former allies, such as the United States and China, is changing in South Asia, one might reasonably expect Pakistan to be undertaking a major reappraisal of its security imperatives. Is the Pakistani leadership reordering its priorities to deal with new internal, regional, and global challenges? Are new Pakistani conceptions of security evolving, placing a greater stress on political and socioeconomic dimensions, or do strategic and defense concerns still dominate security policy making? Have new strategies been devised to meet such reordered goals? These are some of the questions this chapter seeks to answer.

Directions of National Security Policy

A look at Pakistan's contemporary security thinking and behavior provides ample evidence that continuity, rather than change, characterizes its perceptions and policies. No serious attempt has been made, beyond the rhetorical, to formulate and implement alternative concepts of security that would incorporate all levels and dimensions of threat.

Continuity in Core Values

Although Pakistan has no formal security doctrine, official definitions of security can be ascertained through the speeches, statements, and writings of its central decision makers. Their pronouncements reveal a continued focus on military security. The core values of national security are identified primarily as the protection of the state's territorial integrity, independence, and sovereignty. Articulated perceptions of threat, moreover, concentrate on external threats, although internal threats have assumed a greater significance in official appraisals of late. The consistency of this conception of security can be traced from the declarations of the first Pakistani prime minister, Liaquat Ali Khan, who stressed that "the defense of the state is our foremost consideration," to those of the last military ruler, President and Army Chief of Staff General Zia-ul-Haq, who emphasized that the country's very future—social, political, and economic—"depended on its capability to defend its geographic frontiers" (Rizvi 1988: 17).

To a considerable extent, this propensity to concentrate on the external threat continues to rest on Pakistani perceptions of threat from India. The deep-rooted belief in an ever-present Indian threat is evident in the declarations, over the decades, of Pakistani policy makers. In the 1960s, for example, as India armed itself following the Sino-Indian conflict, the president of Pakistan, Field Marshal Ayub Khan, warned that "India is planning to raise two armies, one with which to face China and the other to use against Pakistan and other smaller neighbors in pursuance of her expansionist ambitions" (Khan 1964: 204–5), and his foreign minister and later prime minister of Pakistan, Zulfikar Ali Bhutto, claimed that India's augmentation of its military strength had led to fears that "these weapons will be turned against...the people of Pakistan. This is a genuine fear. It is also a natural fear" (Bhutto 1964: 5). More than twenty years later, a former Pakistani ambassador to India provides a representative picture of official perceptions of India: "For us in Pakistan...we perceive that the Indian leadership and a sizable segment of its following continue to regard the formation of Pakistan as an historical error forced on India, that given the opportunity, they would like in some way to redress the situation." Pakistan, he states, is "hemmed in by the very real apprehension that at best India will not be satisfied with anything less than a client-state status for its neighbors, of whom, for India, we are the most recalcitrant and important. This fear about Indian hegemony is very real" (Hyder 1987: 74–75).

State Building, Regime Legitimacy, and National Security

The realist conception of security that such statements reflect is also the outcome of Pakistan's political history. Because the Pakistani military has been the dominant domestic force during most of the country's existence, its perceptions, value system, and institutional interests have dominated the state's approach to security issues. Hence both the military's hostility toward India and its need to justify the disproportionately large expenditure on defense by citing the danger of an external enemy influence Pakistan's security discourse. President Zia-ul-Haq, for example, justified military expenditure on the ground that "Pakistan cannot afford any cut or freeze in defense expenditure since you cannot freeze threats to Pakistan's security";[11] and his vice chief of army staff, General Mirza Aslam Beg, claimed that the existence of neighbors as powerful as India determines Pakistan's "security environment and therefore the need for Pakistan to maintain a very large armed forces, larger than what we can support. This is a fundamental truth and this is the price that we have to pay to retain our national security and territorial integrity of the country."[12]

As a consequence, security policy focuses primarily on maintaining a balance of power with India. In the 1960s, for example, General Ayub's foreign minister, Z. A. Bhutto, emphasized that Pakistan had been forced to arm itself: "We have made our poor people take less than what was their share, we have deprived them of their basic minimum requirements, in order to maintain a precarious military balance with India....[Peace can] only be maintained when there is a balance of power...in the subcontinent" (Bhutto 1964: 7–8). In the 1990s, Prime Minister Benazir Bhutto's chief of naval staff, Admiral Saeed M. Khan, stated that any "system in which power imbalances exist is inherently unstable....Vast disparities in the size and power potential of states in the region seriously complicate the task of establishing a stable security regime in this area."[13] Her foreign minister, Sardar Assef Ali, stressed that Pakistan is "fully prepared" to deal with any potential threats posed by the ongoing Indian arms race.[14]

Decision makers in multiethnic Pakistan, moreover, consistently uphold the myth of the nation-state. They believe that the state's security demands that every citizen's loyalty must be to the state, overriding ethnic, linguistic, territorial, and economic interests, which one military official calls the "cancer of provincialism."[15] According to former president Ghulam Ishaq Khan, not only does Pakistan's geopolitical situation mean that its very survival depends on building and maintaining a credible defense capability, but internal unity is a prerequisite for external defense. "We must have the moral courage," he adds, "to rise above short-term political expediency [and] narrow parochial considerations."[16]

The military-strategic conception of security in the external sphere is applied in the internal context as well. Policy makers have consistently created a body of legislation that has strengthened the state's coercive capacity to counter perceived threats to the political order.[17] The imperatives of an unstable political system have led to a change in rhetoric, however, and a new emphasis is being placed in public announcements on the physical and material well-being of citizens. Articulating her government's priorities after winning the 1993 election, Prime Minister Benazir Bhutto declared that, in line with the reordered priorities of her government, "in four years, there will be sustainable levels of inflation and unemployment"; health care would be provided as well, and education and major development projects would be implemented.[18] Pointing to the link between interstate conflict and internal development, Prime Minister Nawaz Sharif has stressed that Pakistan and India "have wasted enough time...due to heavy spending on non-development expenditures we are stuck and are running 50 years behind" the rest of the world.[19]

But, in practice, domestic goals and concerns remain subordinate to military and strategic objectives in the formulation and implementation of security policies.[20] Meanwhile, official articulations tend to link the internal to the external threat. It is claimed, for example, that political instability is both a result of external intervention in Pakistan's internal affairs and a weakness that can be exploited by external rivals to undermine the Pakistani state. In 1986, facing political and ethnic dissent, the military's nominee for prime minister, Junejo, claimed that India was arming "antigovernment subversives" who then "manage their entry into Pakistan for subversive activities, especially in Sindh."[21] Even Prime Minister Bhutto, perceived as a political threat after her dismissal from office by the military in 1989, was declared a "security risk" by military intelligence, allegedly due to her close ties with Indian Prime Minister Rajiv Gandhi.[22]

Although this focus on military power and the external threat reflects the inclinations of Pakistan's security decision makers, there are many other actors within the state whose definitions of security do not necessarily coincide with those of the central decision makers. It is therefore necessary, in any discussion of Pakistani conceptions of security, to examine those other actors and assess their impact on security policy.

The Many Faces of Pakistani Security

Because the Pakistani state, like any other state, is neither an abstract concept nor a solitary actor, its definitions of security and its ranking of defense priorities are the product of internal decisions. Those decisions, in turn, are determined by the perceptions, domestic interests, and goals of the dominant political actors. They decide on various security options, which determine whose security is upheld and whose is undermined (Hussain 1988: 3).

The civil and military bureaucracies remain the dominant actors, but others who influence policy include the political leadership both within the government and in the opposition. Nongovernmental organizations and various social, economic, and political interest groups have yet to acquire a voice in policy formulation. But international actors, including such organizations as the United Nations, the IMF, and the World Bank, do play a role, albeit limited and indirect, in determining the direction of Pakistan's security policy.

Decision Makers and Security Policy

The military's dominant political role has enabled it to shape security policy according to its own perceptions and gear it toward the promotion of its own goals. Thus, the military's perceptions of hostile interstate relations have led to the adoption of security policies that emphasize the need for military security against the external (mainly defined as the Indian) threat to the sovereignty and territorial integrity of the state. The same threats have also been used to legitimize Pakistan's disproportionately large defense spending and its continuous expansion of the military establishment, helping to ward off challenges from competing actors such as the political leadership.

Although there has been a transition from authoritarian to democratic rule in Pakistan, no radical transformation in civil-military relations has occurred. The military's political role and its ability to intervene at will have not changed. The military's decision to transfer power to civilian hands following General Zia-ul-Haq's abrupt death in a plane crash in August 1988 was itself a tactical withdrawal, motivated by concern that continued military rule could lead to a strong civil challenge and would not be looked on favorably in the new international environment. The transfer of power was, in fact, undertaken in such a way as to ensure the military's continued political dominance and the protection of its interests. Hence the newly elected prime minister, Benazir Bhutto, was allowed to form a government only after agreeing to a continuation of the army's defense and foreign policies and pledging to respect its institutional autonomy.[23] The prime minister later admitted that her government's autonomy was restricted institutionally, economically, politically, and structurally by the Army High Command (Rizvi 1991: 40).

When the civilian government was perceived as challenging the military's authority, it was replaced by a caretaker military government. Steps were taken to ensure that the party of the military's chosen candidate, Nawaz Sharif, would emerge victorious in the 1990 elections (Lodhi and Hussain 1990b). But the government of Nawaz Sharif was itself dismissed after its relations with the military deteriorated. In the 1993 elections, the PPP once again emerged victorious. As in the past, the present elected leadership had limited room to maneuver because military officials made it clear that the army would continue to provide "guidance and advice," especially in sensitive areas such as defense and security policies, foreign affairs, and internal security (Lodhi 1994b: 298).

In November 1996, the Bhutto government was dismissed by the President in an "army-backed" constitutional coup. (Hussain 1996: 25). Once again, a shadow military government took steps to ensure that the army's chosen candidate, Nawaz Sharif, heading the Muslim League, would win the general elections scheduled for February 1997. An aggressive media campaign was launched against the PPP. Its leaders were arrested and the Bhutto government was accused of economic mismanagement, large-scale corruption, and human rights violations, including extrajudicial killings in Karachi. Anti-PPP figures were installed in key positions, including that of the prime minister and the governors and chief ministers of all four provinces.

In January 1997, a few weeks prior to the polls, President Leghari announced the formation of the Council for Defense and National Security (CDNS), to be chaired by the president and composed of the prime minister, the chairman, of the Joint Chiefs of Staff Committee, the three service chiefs and key ministers. Supposedly an advisory body, the CDNS was an indicator of the military's desire to formalize its dominant role over policy making in sensitive areas such as defense, foreign policy, the economy, and internal security (Rashid 1997: 20; Hussain 1997: 28–29).

In the February elections, the Muslim League won a two-thirds majority in the federal parliament. The Muslim League then formed independent or coalition governments in the provinces of the Punjab, the NWFP, and Sindh. On April 1, 1997, the federal parliament adopted the Thirteenth Amendment bill, removing the president's powers of dissolving the national and provincial legislatures, which had been used to dismiss the past three elected governments. Yet Prime Minister Sharif remains dependent on the military's continued support to complete his full term of office. That support, in turn, will depend on his willingness to follow the military's policy directives, particularly in the realm of internal and external security.

Because the military remains the dominant domestic actor, the traditional emphasis on the attainment of military power to ward off external threats remains in place. Military spending continues to be justified on the grounds of the "national interest" as defined by the military in line with its perceptions and institutional interests. According to a senior military official, "given the geopolitical situation in the region...security has been and will remain the prime concern" of Pakistan, and the defense expenditure will not be reduced if it means "diminishing the level of security."[24] Another official observes that although "maintaining a large standing army is very costly, we at the same time cannot be oblivious to the threats to our integrity and solidarity."[25]

The continuation of the political status quo is most clearly reflected in the direction of the state's economic policies. Following the coup d'état of 1977, an effort was made to redefine economic priorities in line with changed circumstances. As allocations for the military and civil bureaucracies continued to increase, straining the economic resources of the state, policies of deregulation and privatization were adopted, concentrating on a disinvestment of state assets in order to fund such nondevelopmental expenditure. These policies, which were institutionalized by the 1990s, include the sale of key assets and utilities to both domestic and foreign investors.

By the 1980s the gradual reduction of funding from external sources, which had been used for both developmental and nondevelopmental purposes, had led to a greater reliance on foreign loans. As a result, debt service has become a major portion of the annual budget.[26] At the same time, direct and indirect taxation has been used to meet the budget deficit. In the 1996–97 budget, for example, out of a total outlay of 500 billion rupees (Rs.), 131.4 billion was allocated for defense, an increase of 14 percent over the previous fiscal year;[27] Rs. 186 billion was allocated for debt servicing, and Rs. 40 billion was to be raised by additional taxation to help meet the budget deficit of Rs. 60.8 billion. Tax exemptions and state subsidies for food and social services have been reduced as well, adversely affecting the poorest sections of society as a result of soaring inflation and a higher cost of living (Mian 1996: 39; Zia 1996: 34–35).

Disputation and Discord

In a system of democratic rule, an elected political leadership cannot completely ignore the demands of its varied constituencies for socioeconomic development. Yet in Pakistan, where the political transformation has been incremental and political leadership is weak, it has been impossible to transfer funds from defense to development or to bring about the structural changes required to remedy long-standing grievances and alleviate the sense of alienation, especially among domestic elements who believe they have been excluded from decision-making circles and deprived of their due share of the state's resources. Nor are elected governments in a position to challenge the domestic aspects of the military's approach to security. Even after the assumption of power by an elected leadership, the military has continued to use force to suppress political dissent without the government's foreknowledge or approval. In its military operations in urban Sindh in July 1992, for example, the military high command took unilateral action against a major partner of the governing party in the center. The military justified its actions on the ground that "we sincerely want to help the administration to restore law and order in the province, but the civilian government is not cooperating with us."[28]

The military's position as the dominant decision-making unit, and its continued use of coercion in domestic affairs, have their own implications for Pakistani security. Indeed, the legitimacy of the state's norms and actions is being questioned by a growing number of domestic entities. Prominent among these are various ethnic groups and parties who do not identify with the nation-state as constructed by the central government. In multiethnic Pakistan the concept of the nation-state is becoming increasingly irrelevant, partly because of deeply rooted and distinct historical, territorial, linguistic, and social identities. The assertion of ethnic, regional, tribal, and even sectarian identities is also a product of the authoritarian nature of the state, where overcentralized structures of control have been continually expanded and force used to curb dissent (Rashid and Shaheed 1993). The absence of representative institutions and the forcible suppression of political dissent have led to perceptions of threat from the state itself on the part of ethnic movements and minorities who have been targets of coercion by the state apparatus. For those minorities, security is therefore defined as protection from the coercive forces of the state and assurance of physical safety through the acquisition of political, economic, and social autonomy.[29] For the dominant ethnic group—those who control the state apparatus and hence policy making in the state—security means the consolidation of the political, economic, and social status quo.

Internal instability and endemic violence have led many nongovernmental agencies, including such human rights organizations as the Human Rights Commission of Pakistan (HRCP) and the Women's Action Forum (WAF), to emphasize the need for reprioritizing state policies to protect citizens against such threats.[30] Their impact on actual policy making, however, remains minimal. As the state gradually loses control over its population and territory, especially in urban centers such as Karachi, and as its authority and autonomy are contested by parties engaged in criminal activities such as drug trafficking and the illegal arms trade (Hanif 1989b), the legitimacy of the political system and the policies of the state's managers are increasingly disputed by alienated domestic political actors. Although these trends indicate the existence of more serious threats to security emanating from internal rather than external sources, the government's national security policy remains largely unaffected. The continued emphasis on external security and on the acquisition of military power reflects the internal division of power among the various domestic actors.

External Influences

The state of Pakistan's economy could, however, affect the priorities of its national security policy. In an increasingly interdependent world, Pakistan's economic vulnerability has increased the influence of international institutions such as the IMF and the World Bank.[31] That dependence could lead to a change in national security policy, because those institutions are pressing for a diversion of state expenditure from defense to developmental goals.[32] Major bilateral aid donors and investors such as Japan are also pressuring Pakistan to abandon its nuclear program and support nonproliferation measures for South Asia.[33]

Yet the state's decision-making units are still in a position to accept or reject international and domestic pressures. Modifications in policy, or even just in rhetoric, are made only to the extent that the institutional interests of those units are not adversely affected. Security concepts still depend, therefore, on the imperatives of the internal political processes in the state.

Paths to Security

Because Pakistan's long history of conflict with India has created a "cold war" mind-set, the security thinking of its principal decision makers remains centered on India.[34] They believe that the primary objective of policy making must rest on ways of "guarding Pakistan from India" (Hyder n.d.: 12) and of providing it with the ability to protect itself from "the dangerous and hegemonistic designs of India."[35] In President Zia's words, "We will not allow India to bully us" (Hussain 1988: 1). The consistency of such thinking can be seen in the discourse of military personnel over the years. In the mid-1960s, for example, Pakistani army officers claimed that ever since Pakistan's independence, India "has employed every conceivable tactic to destroy Pakistan and coerce her into subjugation." Hence the size and shape of Pakistan's defense forces are "mainly based against a threat from India."[36] In the late 1980s and 1990s, India's objectives are thought to remain unchanged: to keep Pakistan "weak, militarily, politically, and economically, so that it does not stand in the way of Indian aims and objectives in South Asia."[37]

Arms and Security

Conditioned by their values and training, the Pakistan armed forces also believe that the Indian threat cannot be met through dialogue and negotiation; it can be countered only through the acquisition of military power, mainly conventional but also nuclear. Pakistan, it is stressed, must be "prepared in all respects to defend its territorial integrity at all costs and with all available resources."[38] What remains unsaid, however, is that military power is also used to legitimize the military's disproportionate claims on the nation's economic resources and even its internal political dominance (Table 9).

TABLE 9
Pakistan's Military Expenditure and Size of Armed Forces, 1981–91

	Annual military expenditure (millions of U.S. dollars)	Armed forces (thousands of persons)	Military expenditure as percentage of GNP
1981	873	560	5.5
1982	1,033	588	5.8
1983	1,349	588	6.2
1984	1,401	588	5.9
1985	1,650	647	6.3
1986	1,833	645	6.5
1987	1,989	645	6.5
1988	2,185	645	6.5
1989	2,387	684	6.5
1990	2,829	790	7.1
1991	2,672	803	6.1

SOURCE: *World Military Expenditures and Arms Transfers 1991–1992.* Washington, D.C.: U.S. Arms Control and Disarmament Agency, 1994.

NOTE: Any figures on Pakistani military expenditure must be taken as approximate because expenses are hidden under several budgetary and extrabudgetary headings.

Pakistan's objective of achieving a conventional military balance has been difficult to attain because of regional asymmetries in capability and resources. Following India's "peaceful nuclear explosion" in mid-1974, Pakistan too adopted a nuclear program, which officials claim is primarily a defensive response to the Indian threat. According to Pakistani leaders and senior officials, Pakistan "is surrounded by nuclear powers ....Only China is a confirmed friend....India is a confirmed enemy" (Chishti 1989: 5). Pakistan must therefore have a bomb to "ensure security, to create a deterrent."[39]

For Pakistani decision makers, the strategy of nuclear deterrence appears to be a cost-effective option, with the added advantages of prestige and the acquisition of a regional standing comparable to

India's.[40] The country's nuclear doctrine is based on creating strategic ambiguity. Official statements stress, for example, that Pakistan has the "capacity to make one [nuclear weapon] within a reasonable period of time" but has decided against a weapons-oriented program, intending "to keep ourselves at this stage because it provides us with an effective deterrent."[41] They also claim that Pakistan is prevented from following a nonproliferation regime in the absence of "reciprocal reduction on the part of neighboring countries."

Moreover, an effort is made to link the nuclear issue with the Indo-Pakistani dispute over Kashmir by stressing that the nonresolution of such long-standing differences forces an insecure Pakistan to retain its nuclear program, which remains the "only potent deterrent against aggression from India."[42] The Pakistani stand on the Comprehensive Test Ban Treaty (CTBT) reflects this position. Officials have stressed that "the CTB will bring no dividends to South Asia if India is not on board";[43] that Pakistan will not sign the treaty if India abstains; and that the Kashmir dispute remains "the key to the problems of South Asia."[44]

Alignment and Security

Aware of the imbalances in Indo-Pakistani conventional and nuclear capabilities, Pakistani policy makers have also consistently, over the decades, attempted to acquire access to reliable external sources of arms and assistance, with special emphasis on the establishment of a security relationship with the United States. Thus in the Cold War years of the 1950s and again during the 1980s, Pakistan's military regimes skillfully manipulated anticommunist sentiments in the West, through formal and informal alliances, to attain their multiple goals of security against India, strengthening of their domestic position through external assistance, and expansion of Pakistan's influence in South and Southwest Asia.[45]

The flow of U.S. military and economic aid has, however, come to a halt as Pakistan's strategic significance has declined with the collapse of the bipolar world order and the disintegration of the Soviet Union. Moreover, Pakistan's nuclear program has once again come to the fore in U.S.–Pakistan relations.[46] Since imposing an embargo in October 1990 on the supply and sale of weaponry to Pakistan, the United States has continued to pressure Pakistan to abandon its nuclear program. Pakistani governments, for their part, are attempting to persuade the United States to revise its ban on the sale and supply of military equipment and are hoping to counterbalance India's power through the reestablishment of special ties with the United States (Lodhi 1994a).

In their discussions with U.S. officials on the nuclear issue, Pakistani authorities have continued to emphasize Pakistani perceptions of threat from India and the need for a regional approach that encompasses the nuclear programs of both India and Pakistan.[47] In her address to the U.S. Congress in mid-1989, for example, Prime Minister Bhutto stated that Pakistan did not possess or intend to make a bomb and would be willing to accept any safeguards or verification measures provided they were applied on a regional and nondiscriminatory basis.[48] Caretaker Prime Minister Moeen Qureshi, during his visit to the United States, reiterated that Pakistan "cannot commit suicide by accepting unilateral restrictions on its nuclear program."[49] Pakistani policy makers have also attempted to use the nuclear card to bargain for concessions by asking the United States to recognize Pakistan's restraint in capping its nuclear program and calling on the United States to help Pakistan avoid depending solely on its nuclear capability to deal with the Indian threat by helping it to build up its conventional strength.[50] These requests are accompanied by calls for a greater U.S. role in South Asia.

Global and regional changes have heightened Pakistani perceptions of vulnerability since economic factors have assumed greater importance in an emerging multipolar system. It is now feared that India's rising importance, economic and political, will further erode Pakistan's position in the strategic perceptions of its former American ally.[51] There is also apprehension that Pakistan's close ties with China—partly the result of Cold War imperatives and partly the product of mutual differences with India—might lose their relevance in the wake of the dissolution of the Soviet Union and the ongoing Sino-Indian rapprochement. For Pakistani policy makers, the Chinese continue to play an important role in helping Pakistan to improve its military balance vis-à-vis India. Chinese assistance has included the help extended to Pakistan to launch its two indigenous ballistic missiles, Hatf I and II, and reportedly includes the delivery of Chinese-built M-11 missiles to Pakistan.[52] However, the post–Cold War security environment and U.S. pressures to curb the transfer of sensitive technologies, together with new sources of threat arising out of Islamic fundamentalism, could weaken the Sino-Pakistani relationship. Moreover, a continuous easing of Sino-Indian tensions could further limit Pakistan's utility for China.

Regional Influence and Intervention

In the context of these changing circumstances, alongside the policy of trying to reestablish or consolidate alliances, Pakistani decision makers are continuing to follow a decades-old strategy of enhancing Pakistan's regional prestige as well as its bargaining power with regional and extraregional actors by extending the country's influence over neighboring states such as Afghanistan.

The communist takeover in Afghanistan in 1978 and the Soviet intervention that followed gave General Zia-ul-Haq's military regime an opportunity to gain international recognition and domestic ascendancy as Pakistan became a major recipient of Western (in particular U.S.) as well as Middle Eastern and Chinese military and economic assistance. Zia's successor, Army Chief of Staff General Aslam, also saw the Afghan situation as an opportunity to attain "strategic depth" and to create a zone of Pakistani interest (Rubin 1989–90: 164). Although attempting to improve Pakistan's strategic environment by expanding its influence over Afghanistan remains an attractive option for the military, the Soviet withdrawal and the subsequent decline of Afghanistan's importance for the West have halted the flow of assistance. Meanwhile the continuation of the Afghan civil war is contributing to Pakistani perceptions of threat based on the presence of contending Afghan factions and a substantial refugee population on Pakistani soil, the involvement of Pakistani domestic factions in Afghan politics, and the existence of similar ethnic communities on both sides of the Pakistani-Afghan border.

The perceptions of threat are compounded by the knowledge that Pakistan's internal security environment has been adversely affected by terrorism as well as by a cross-border drug trade, arms trafficking, and other criminal activities that involve both Pakistani and Afghan elements. Those problems are to some extent a side effect of outside involvement in the Afghan war: two-thirds of the thousands of tons of American weapons transferred to Afghanistan via Pakistan were siphoned off at various points along the way,[53] and the production of opium and its refinement into heroin remains a major source of income for Afghan and Pakistani political groups and criminals (Siddiqi 1988; Hussain and Hussain 1993). Pakistani policy makers are therefore pursuing strategies aimed at containing hostile Afghan activity on Pakistani soil while retaining a dominant role in Afghan politics to enhance Pakistan's regional influence and acquire sufficient geostrategic importance to balance that of India. Effective influence over Afghanistan, it is believed, will not only give Pakistan greater leverage in its dealings with foreign powers but also give it political and economic access to the newly independent Central Asian republics (Naqvi 1994: 13–16).

Pakistani strategies have continued to focus in particular on the use of surrogate forces in Afghanistan; such policies were adopted in the early 1970s and rigorously implemented after the overthrow of the Daud regime by the People's Democratic Party of Afghanistan (PDPA) in 1978. The ultimate goal of this strategy, in the current context, is to install a "suitable" government in Kabul.[54] Pakistan was, for example, instrumental in creating an Afghan Interim Government even before the ouster of the PDPA government in 1992 (Weinbaum 1991). Pakistani-dictated "peace formulas" have included the Peshawar accord of April 1992, which set up an interim government in Kabul, and the Islamabad accord of March 1993, which instituted a power-sharing formula. These accords have failed to resolve internecine Afghan hostilities, however, while tensions have heightened between Islamabad and the Afghan factions opposing the Taliban Islamic Student Militia, a loosely organized group that surfaced for the first time in October 1994 (Zulfikar 1994b) and has now gained control over the Afghan capital and 22 of Afghanistan's 32 provinces.[55] Although Pakistan denies supporting the Taliban, most were recruited from Pakistani soil, and many Pakistani politicians and observers claim that Pakistan's military intelligence has close links with the Taliban.[56]

Aware of the dangers arising from an escalation of tensions with contending Afghan factions, Pakistani strategists have also made use of diplomacy and bargaining through both open and closed channels. Channels of communication, for example, have consistently been kept open with less favored but influential Afghan politicians, such as General Dostum, whose party controls much of Afghanistan's northern belt that borders the Central Asian states of Uzbekistan and Tajikistan. The Pakistani objective is to acquire the support of Afghan factions for a power-sharing formula that would best suit Pakistan's political, strategic, and economic interests.

Intervention and Diplomacy

A similar Pakistani strategy of using surrogate actors has been used against India. Limited support, for example, was extended to Indian insurgents in the Khalistan movement. Since the late 1980s, Pakistani authorities have tacitly provided various levels of moral and material support to anti-Indian elements in the disputed territory of Jammu and Kashmir, mainly through fundamentalist Pakistani and Afghan parties and activists.[57] According to Prime Minister Mian Nawaz Sharif, for example, during his first term of office he provided central government funds to the Jamaat-i-Islami, an extremist Islamic party and a member of his governing coalition, to assist anti-Indian elements in Jammu and Kashmir.[58] This indirect use of force has been accompanied by a sustained effort to acquire external support for Pakistan's stand on the Kashmir issue, highlighting, in particular, human rights abuses in Indian-held Kashmir and using the forums of international organizations such as the U.N. Security Council and General Assembly. Pakistani use of multilateral diplomacy also extends to regional organizations such as the South Asian Association for Regional Cooperation (SAARC).

Set up originally with the objective of increasing sociocultural, economic, and environmental cooperation in the hope of reducing tensions in South Asia,[59] SAARC has made little progress because of interstate differences and mistrust. For Pakistani policy makers, SAARC's usefulness lies partly in its potential for exploiting fears of India's hegemonic designs with respect to smaller states such as Sri Lanka, Bangladesh, and to a lesser degree Nepal, while projecting Pakistan as a counterweight to offset India's power in the region. At the same time, this international alliance-building has been accompanied by preventive diplomacy to avoid an outbreak of conflict, in view of Pakistan's military weakness in comparison to India. At times of high levels of tension— during Exercise Brasstacks in 1987,[60] for example—and more recently to defuse tensions arising from the Kashmir dispute, secret diplomacy and top-level contacts have been used as crisis management tools.

This strategy of negotiating is primarily aimed not at resolving disputes but at managing conflict. The interests of Pakistan's dominant decision-making unit, the military, would not in fact be served by a comprehensive resolution of Indo-Pakistan differences, because its demands for a substantial percentage of the state's economic resources are based on the ground of the Indian threat.

Internal Conflict and State Control

Pakistan's strategies to counter internal threats emphasize coercion and intervention with the purpose of reasserting state control. In its rhetoric, the military's continued political intervention is ostensibly intended to prevent an internally divided and irresponsible political leadership from threatening the state's autonomy and security. The dismissal of the PPP government in 1990, for example, was partly justified by Army Chief of Staff General Beg on the ground that "the army would not allow" the conflict between the government and its Islami Jamhoori Ittehad (IJI; the Islamic Democratic Alliance) opponents "to tear the nation apart."[61]

Because it is the military that decides whether a civilian government will remain in office, political leaders are aware that the main threat to their retention of power comes from within the state apparatus itself, not from domestic discontent. As a result, their overriding concern is to obtain the military's approval by accepting its policies in all sensitive areas, including the allocation of the state's resources and the formulation of internal and external security policies. As a sophisticated system of checks and balances limits the autonomy of the civilian leadership, civil society remains weak while the military's corporate interests are advanced.

In the absence of structural change, human rights advocates are pressing for a transformation of this semiauthoritarian system into a functioning democracy.[62] As violence with criminal and political roots increases throughout the society, these advocates stress the need to find remedies that will, for example, institute state-imposed sanctions on the perpetrators of such violence.[63]

But the central decision makers are not averse to providing rewards, if necessary, to attain their ultimate goal of reasserting the state's control. In Malakand division in 1994, for example, when fundamentalist groups violently opposed state authority, law enforcement agencies used force to contain the uprising, but they also attempted to cajole the disputing parties through a partial enforcement of Islamic legislation.[64] Faced by renewed Islamist violence in mid-June 1995, the NWFP government again sought to appease the agitators by promising the appointment of qualified Islamic judges for the Malakand division (Yusufzai 1996).

Ethnic and Sectarian Violence

Pakistani governments of the day appear unable or unwilling to guarantee the security of minority communities against violence perpetrated by extremist parties and groups belonging to the majority Sunni denomination. Minorities such as the Christians, Hindus, and Ahmediyas are either too weak economically and politically or too small numerically to challenge the various threats posed by discriminatory state legislation,[65] government inaction, and Sunni fundamentalism. Elements of the minority Shia sect, however, have opted to protect themselves through violent means. Militant factions such as the Sipah-e-Mohammed Pakistan (Soldiers of Mohammed) target Sunni fundamentalist groups and supporters, especially the Anjuman-Sipah-e-Sahaba Pakistan (Soldiers of the Sahaba: the companions and political heirs of Mohammed), the most active in anti-Shia violence.[66]

Ethnic conflict poses an even more pervasive threat to state control. To counter such threats, as in the external domain, the state has adopted coercive strategies, accompanied by negotiation, when domestic tensions have been seen as presenting serious challenges to state control. Yet state policies have themselves contributed to political polarization and ethnic conflict. Aside from authoritarian and centralized structures of governance and the use of force to stifle ethnic dissent, the military's political role and its ethnic policies have played a significant role in promoting ethnic divisions. The capture of state power by an ethnically skewed (Punjabi-dominated) military, its subsequent policies of excluding "unreliable" ethnic groups from its ranks, the economic exploitation of the state's resources to meet the military's corporate interests, the absence of representative institutions, and the forcible suppression of political opposition led the majority Bengali population of the eastern wing to opt for secession in 1971, which led in turn to the dismemberment of Pakistan and the creation of Bangladesh.

In post-1971 Pakistan, the Punjabi-dominated military still identifies itself with the nation-state.[67] It perceives ethnic demands for autonomy and a restructuring of centralized governing structures as threats to the legitimacy and autonomy of that state, and it frequently resorts to manipulation and force to retain control.[68] As a result, ethnic-state, interethnic, and intraethnic tensions have grown. Because the incumbent power holders are perceived to be partisan ethnic actors, the state's legitimacy is gradually eroding, especially in the province of Sindh (Ahmed 1995).

Ethnic Conflict in Sindh

During the 1980s and the early 1990s, ethnic Sindhis resisting military rule were subjected to systematic suppression, and Muhajirs (migrants and their descendants from northern India), represented by their party, the Muhajir Qaumi Movement (MQM), were used by the military as a counterweight to Sindhi dissent. Inevitably, the policy led to an intensification of Sindhi-Muhajir tensions (Ahmed 1988: 33). The military's subsequent creation of factions within the MQM, such as the Haqiqis, to control an increasingly ambitious Muhajir leadership under Altaf Hussain led to violent intraethnic clashes.[69] In 1995 alone, more than 1,950 people were killed in intraethnic violence, in clashes with law enforcement agencies, or in judicial custody, including 222 members of law enforcement agencies in Karachi (Sindh's provincial capital).[70]

Aside from engaging in coercive tactics, state authorities have also attempted to justify their ethnic management strategies and contain ethnic violence by laying the blame on the external threat. Throughout the military operations in rural Sindh, for example, the military claimed that Sindhi political dissent was inspired by India (Mujtaba 1991; Mirza 1991). When military operations were shifted to urban Sindh, it was claimed that Altaf Hussain's MQM, which had earlier been called a "strong shield against anti-Pakistan forces" by the head of Inter-Services Intelligence, was a party of Indian-trained terrorists.[71] As intraethnic violence escalates between the two factions of the MQM, military officials claim that "whenever the situation in Kashmir worsens, we see a rise of violence in Sindh" (Hanif 1995: 31).

The political leadership is equally prone to use the Indian "threat" to gain domestic support, weaken its opponents, and divert attention from pressing internal problems. Faced by MQM violence, the Bhutto government claimed that the violence was Indian-inspired. According to then foreign minister Sardar Assef Ali, there was "evidence that the Indians are behind the Sindh situation. They use Karachi as a launching pad for various sabotage activities. They want to weaken Pakistan and that's why they encourage criminal gangs there."[72] In the wake of violence in Karachi, the Indian consulate there was closed. As violence in Karachi continued, so too did Pakistani accusations of Indian and even Afghan intervention in Sindh.[73]

Political leaders as well as the military have resorted to co-optive and divide-and-rule strategies in Sindh. Both the Bhutto and Sharif governments, during their first terms of office, entered into alliances with the MQM to offset their political opposition, and later acquiesced to military-directed operations against the MQM. The military, for its part, has either opposed or supported Muhajir and Sindhi ethnonationalist groups and parties to advance its perceived corporate interests. Mir Murtaza Bhutto, for example, had been declared a terrorist by military courts but was allowed by the military to form his party and to contest elections in a bid to divide the PPP vote bank in Sindh. PPP leaders now claim that PPP (Shaheed Bhutto), the splinter party led by his widow, Ghinwa Bhutto, has the support of the security apparatus.[74]

Strategies based on co-optation and divide-and-rule have been used, in Sindh and elsewhere, with several goals in mind: containment of political dissent; maintenance of the social, economic, and political status quo; and promotion and protection of the interests of dominant state actors, including the armed forces, against perceived internal challenges and threats. But it is the unresponsive internal order and the shrinking pool of economic resources that continue to promote political violence, posing threats to the security interests, internal and external, of Pakistan's central decision makers.

Whither Pakistani Security?

As Pakistan approaches the twenty-first century, it finds itself at a crossroads. The path its decision makers take will determine the future shape of the state and the destiny of its people. Although there has been no radical departure from past thinking—security is still defined as narrowly as it has been over the last five decades—there could well be a change in the present direction of the state as a result of internal and external pressures.

The present state-centered conception of national security will, however, remain in place should the ongoing democratic process fail to lead to the gradual reassertion of civilian control over the military. In the absence of structural change that would allow for an opening of the political system, internal tensions are likely to intensify even further and could assume threatening proportions. The state's failure to contain urban conflict in Sindh is one indicator of the serious nature of internal threats to national security. Another sign is the inability of law enforcement agencies to protect the citizenry against widespread politically and criminally motivated violence.

Domestic extremism, overpopulation, environmental degradation, drug trafficking, an illegal trade in arms, a substantial refugee presence, a deteriorating economy, the absence of an institutionalized democratic framework, strategies based on coercion and manipulation—all combine to erode the state's ability to assert effective control over its territory and its population. It appears, however, that Pakistan's decision makers either are underestimating the urgency of these threats or believe that their present strategies can contain them.

An external enemy is needed to buttress internal security by diverting attention from politically divisive issues and creating a national consensus based on the external threat; therefore the present strategies of military deterrence and military power are unlikely to be replaced by diplomatic bargaining. Pakistan's continuing to depend on military power, both conventional and nuclear, and to ignore the geostrategic reality of its neighborhood could bring serious repercussions, for Pakistan has a history of conflict with India and the balance of power obviously favors its much larger neighbor.

Although policy makers believe that an immediate physical threat can be averted through a policy based on nuclear deterrence, the continuation of Indo-Pakistani tensions not only will retard the growth of South Asian regionalism but also will increase the dangers of conflict, which need not encompass the nuclear dimension. At the same time, civil society and its institutions will further weaken because a politicized military will be legitimized as the ultimate shield against the external threat. Domestically, moreover, excessive defense spending at the cost of socioeconomic development will gradually erode the legitimacy of government as it fails to meet the pressing needs of a vast majority of its citizens.

Pakistan's strategy of conducting a surrogate war in the disputed territory of Kashmir could also undermine its security (Lodhi 1993: 28c). An accidental war could result from a spillover of the conflict across the Line of Actual Control,[75] or even from the domestic compulsions of an Indian central government attempting to divert attention from the conflict by embarking on a limited war. Given that an exercise of the nuclear option in a limited conflict is highly unlikely, the conventional arms imbalance between the two states would work to Pakistan's disadvantage.

Alliance-Building, External Assistance, and Military Power

Pakistan's dependence on strategies of formal or informal alliance-building will not successfully address its security concerns if Indo-Pakistan tensions continue to rise. Effective use of the SAARC forum to settle interstate scores will be hampered by the economic interdependence and political constraints of the smaller states imposed by their relations with India. Nor is Pakistan likely to be any more successful in its attempts to gain access to U.S. military power to counterbalance its regional rival.

Pakistan's projection of an Indian threat and its drive to acquire conventional weapons, which would allow it to restrain its nuclear program, could bear fruit in the foreseeable future in the form of a removal of the U.S. ban on the sale of spare parts and even arms. Furthermore, Pakistan can still offer tangible incentives for a renewed, but limited, security relationship by supporting U.S. goals in the Middle East and by playing a role in containing terrorist threats to U.S. security emanating from its unstable Asian neighborhood.[76] Pakistani authorities have already demonstrated their willingness to assist the Americans in these areas, offering troops during the Gulf War and extraditing suspected terrorists and drug traffickers to the United States.[77] Should the need arise, Pakistan would also be willing to promote U.S. objectives in other sensitive areas of its immediate neighborhood, such as the Central Asian republics.

After former Prime Minister Bhutto's visit to the United States in April 1995, it appeared that Pakistan's potential assets and its continued overtures had borne fruit: the U.S. Senate approved a one-time waiver of the Pressler Amendment in September, permitting the supply to Pakistan of $368 million worth of military equipment that had been embargoed since 1990, along with the removal of economic and nonmilitary sanctions imposed by the amendment. Justifying this shift in U.S. policy, administration figures such as Defense Secretary William Perry have argued that it is in America's interest to improve relations with Pakistan, a "moderate Islamic democracy in a troubled region," warning that the ability of the United States "to work with Pakistan to achieve non-proliferation goals is eroding" because the "status quo...offers few incentives."[78] Though Prime Minister Bhutto called the passage of the Brown Amendment a "great moral victory,"[79] a drastic change in U.S. policy toward Pakistan is unlikely as long as Pakistan retains its nuclear option.

Under pressure from other key countries such as Japan—Pakistan's largest donor of overseas assistance and a major source of private investment—Pakistani leaders make repeated pledges that they would pursue the nonnuclear path if the Indian threat were to recede. During her visit to Japan in January 1996, for example, Prime Minister Bhutto stressed that the "world understands Japan's special sensitivity to the issue of nuclear proliferation." Although Pakistan "strongly endorses the commitment to nonproliferation in our region," she continued, it has no choice but to retain its nuclear option because "we live in a rough neighborhood and we are determined not to be bullied."[80] As in the case of the United States, however, Pakistan's nuclear policies will continue to create strains in its relations with an important source of funding. And Pakistan's defense spending, for both its conventional and its nuclear programs, is likely to become a major obstacle in its future dealings with other influential institutions such as the World Bank and the IMF.

Regional Expansionism and National Security

Pakistan's strategies of expanding its regional influence and strategic depth vis-à-vis India by playing a dominant, interventionist role in Afghan affairs are equally likely to have an adverse impact on its national security. In the external sphere, Pakistani support for the Taliban brought its relations with the anti-Taliban alliance to a new low. As the relationship continues to deteriorate, General Dostum's spokesman, for example, accuses the Taliban of being "the puppets of Pakistan," incapable of taking "independent decisions."[81]

As a result of Pakistan's Afghan policy, its relations with Iran have deteriorated as well. Since the capture of Afghanistan's western provinces, bordering on Iran, by the Sunni fundamentalist Taliban, Iran has adopted an interventionist stance to safeguard its interests and those of the Afghan Shia minority by supporting the Rabbani-Wahdat-Dostum alliance against the Taliban. High-level talks have been held between the Pakistani and Iranian governments on the Afghan issue,[82] yet Pakistan acknowledges that there is a "major difference in perception" on the Afghan issue.[83]

This rivalry between Iran and Pakistan in the Afghan context is closely linked with their competition for access to the resource-rich Central Asian republics via neighboring Afghanistan. While Iran has established a rail link with Turkmenistan, opening its ports for Central Asian trade, Pakistan has consistently made efforts to acquire economic and political access to Central Asia through Afghan territory. Indeed, it was the difficulty of opening a trade route via Peshawar, due to differences with the Kabul regime, that led Pakistan to back the Taliban offensive. Pakistan's ultimate aim is to gain control over an alternate route, via Pakistani Baluchistan, to the western Afghan provinces of Kandahar and Herat and hence to Turkmenistan.[84]

The Taliban now control 26 of Afghanistan's 32 provinces. In the last week of May 1997, Taliban forces, in alliance with defecting commanders including Uzbek General Abdul Malik, captured three provinces in northern Afghanistan and entered Dostum's capital of Mazar-i-Sharif. Soon after, Pakistan extended formal recognition to the Taliban government in Kabul, urging the international community to follow suit.[85] The Taliban advance was accompanied by Iranian accusations of Pakistani interference in Afghan affairs as President Rabbani and the Hizb-i-Islami chief, Hekmatyar, went into exile in Iran and the Taliban confronted Shia Wahdat forces in Bamiyan province. General Dostum and his Central Asian allies, including Uzbek President Islam Karimov also accused Pakistan of intervening on the side of the Taliban.[86] Even as all countries bordering on Afghanistan, with Pakistan's exception, were expressing concern at the Taliban advance to the north,[87] there was a reversal of Taliban fortunes when Malik's forces switched their allegiance once again, forcing the Taliban to retreat from Mazar and other northern provinces in the wake of hundreds of Taliban casualties.[88] Although the Pakistan government stresses that its recognition of the Taliban government is "based on objective realities,"[89] there is no guarantee that its Taliban allies will succeed in stabilizing their precarious control over the territories they govern.

Pakistan's stand on Afghanistan has adversely affected its relations with important regional and extraregional actors, including Iran, Uzbekistan, and Russia. The Central Asian republics are concerned about the spread of Islamic fundamentalism from across the Afghan border. It is that fear of Islamic resurgence, which has already contributed substantially to political instability within Tajikistan, that has led the Uzbek government to extend support to General Dostum's army (Fange 1995: 23). The Taliban advance has also created differences between Pakistan and Russia: the latter provides support to the Rabbani-Wahdat-Dostum alliance against the upsurge of Sunni fundamentalism—represented by the Taliban—that threatens Russian security in its hinterland (Quinn-Judge 1997).

Aside from the potentially adverse repercussions of its Afghan policy in the external context, Pakistan's internal security could be seriously affected even if it were to succeed in its efforts to install a "suitable" government in Afghanistan through continued manipulation of the Afghan political process. Afghan groups, contesting the legitimacy of any such future setup, could extend their intraparty struggle across the border into Pakistani territory. There are already indications of the negative consequences of Pakistan's interventionist strategy in Afghan politics. The close links established between Pakistani religious parties and their Afghan counterparts are beginning to pose a threat to both Pakistani civil society and the state, as was witnessed during the Malakand armed uprising of 1994 (Mehdi 1994: 36).

The continued presence of Afghan refugees is another potential threat. Apart from the ecological destruction caused by the refugee presence in Baluchistan and the NWFP, tensions between locals and refugees could assume more dangerous proportions in the future and could even erupt into conflict as ethnic and socioeconomic competition intensifies. At the same time, a perpetuation of the civil war in Afghanistan through external intervention will provide disgruntled Pakistani factions, such as MQM militants in Sindh, with continued access to sophisticated weapons for use in their armed conflict with the authorities of the state.

The Crisis Within

Ultimately it is the policies adopted to deal with internal instability that will determine the security of the Pakistani state. So far, a reliance on coercion, co-optation, and manipulation has enabled Pakistan's dominant military to combat the immediate internal challenges. The political leadership within the major parties appears to have internalized the military's superiority: politicians are hesitant to challenge the corporate interests of the armed forces and the civil bureaucracy, and violence, ethnic and sectarian, has not broken the control of the state over most of the country. Yet the very use of these strategies by the military threatens the state's security because their objective is not to resolve political differences but merely to contain violence, which is the product and not the source of domestic challenges to the state. In the absence of a sustained effort to negotiate internal disputes through democratic institutions, incidents of politically motivated violence will inevitably increase and could take on more serious dimensions in the future.

The security implications of the state's internal strategies—fostering a sense of national identity and loyalty to the state by externalizing domestic disputes—will continue to spill over into the external domain and hinder the resolution of interstate disputes. The use of official propaganda in both domestic and international forums to create hostility toward India, for example, could make it extremely difficult to resort to diplomatic bargaining, even if such a course should become desirable for

Pakistan's overall security. It is becoming apparent that the directions of state policy in Pakistan are in fact creating new categories of threat, both internal and external, while they fail to address the present security risks to the Pakistani citizenry and the state. Although the physical contours of Pakistan are unlikely to change, as they did when a majority of its citizens opted for secession in 1971,[90] there will be a gradual and inevitable erosion of the state's authority. As a result, there will be, in the long term, neither security for the state nor security for its citizens.

Sri Lanka
The Many Faces of Security

NIRA WICKRAMASINGHE

> *If we have to live as minorities, we might as well live in a place that*
> *promises security to the children.*
>
> KAMALA, a victim of the 1983 riots

> *Over two hundred thousand people have been liberated by the security*
> *forces. Over one thousand families have been cleared so far by the security*
> *forces to return to Vallikaman division. Security forces captured a van*
> *transporting terrorists. All terrorists were killed on the spot.*
>
> GOVERNMENT COMMUNIQUÉ, Operation Riviresa II, April 1996

As we try to understand the state's conception of security in Sri Lanka, it is important to recognize that there are a multiplicity of voices speaking about national security. Some of these challenge or even contest the state's conception of security.[1] Security, it appears, is not a static phenomenon but a changing, wavering perception. Borrowing from Ashis Nandy's formulation, I would liken it to an "amoeba" word that can take any shape and convey any meaning (Nandy 1994: 1) This chapter starts with the premise that security per se does not exist. There are only *conceptions* of security—and hence of national security—that vary from agent to agent, from consciousness to consciousness, along lines of community, class, and gender, and over time. Conceptions of security can be understood only in the context of the discourse, conventions of argument, habits, customs, and political actions that produce them. Thus my focus is both on national security as it has been defined by the state at different periods and on the challenges put forward by groups that contest the state's definition. Above all, I wish to address perceptions or narratives of security that are not usually given a voice in academic studies. Although marginalized, such perceptions inform the conscious-ness of many Sri Lankans. But do these muted voices count? To what extent do they pose a challenge to the state's perception of security? Do they in any way influence power?

In Sri Lanka, it is possible to distinguish at least three different con-ceptions of state security. The first is the state's definition of security as national security, a conception rooted in the notion of territoriality and infused with the idea that the security of the whole equals the security of its components. In this view, the primary threat to security is external. This conception has dominated state thinking and behavior since independence. Since the Janata Vimukti Peramuna (JVP) insurrection in 1971 and the wars in the north and east in the 1980s, however, internal concerns have begun to dominate. This second notion of state security, with its emphasis on internal threats, is now being displaced at the state level, under the new government of Chandrika Bandaranaike Kumara-tunge, by a third conception. The new government, which has close links with human rights groups and the nongovernmental sector on the whole, has proposed a concept of national security that encompasses human values as well. The limitations of this third conception of security, however, are evidenced by the violent secessionist challenge the state faces from the Liberation Tigers of Tamil Eelam (LTTE) and the military option it has been compelled to adopt after the collapse of negotiations between the state and the LTTE.

The first part of this chapter examines the state's three conceptions of national security. The second investigates the nongovernmental approach to security and its impact on the state approach. The final part examines other challenges to the state's conception of security that stem from antisystemic groups such as the Janata Vimukti Peramuna, which on two occasions has tried through violent means to capture power, and also from the Buddhist Sangha (order of Buddhist monks). We will then assess the importance of their voices in the national context.

National Security as State Security: Evolution from External to Internal Considerations

For the person on the street, security has many meanings—from "safety as in job security" to "the country and the people living free of troubles."[2] In a way these meanings reflect the perception of many scholars today who concede that security is not confined to military security, which can be defined as the absence of threat or conflict. Security does have its intrinsic positive elements—presence of values, satisfaction of needs, a sense of feeling secure and striving unhindered for growth and development—but the concept also implies subtle threats to economic, social, and cultural independence. Until recently, however, academics and diplomats in Sri Lanka rarely accepted a maximalist definition of security such as that of James N. Rosenau, who defines security both in the personal sense of securing a meaningful identity and in the collective sense of maintaining territorial integrity, political stability, and economic well-being (Rosenau 1994). When speaking of security, state officials and international relations specialists still tend to focus on the security of the state. Let us begin by examining the state discourse on security, which is mirrored in mainstream academic writings on security, while noting that the understanding of security has changed over the years. Since independence it is fairly safe to say that the state rhetoric of security in Sri Lanka has been primarily about national security rather than people's security. Like most rhetoric encouraged by the state and the major mass media, the language of national security is not innocent. The noble cause of safeguarding the nation is used to confer legitimacy on other, perhaps less noble, causes and acts.

To analyze the state's conceptions of security one has to rely, if cautiously, on selected documents of the state, such as the speeches of officials, to get at the dynamics below the surface. One must also be aware that those officials do not usually base their actions on carefully formulated sets of objectives. Many government transactions are unplanned; important decisions are often made in response to urgent pressures rather than as part of a coherent and farsighted policy. It is also useful to distinguish between the "declaratory" and the "operational" objectives of policy makers.

Official definitions of security lean toward a realist approach—that is, security is defined primarily from the military-strategic perspective and the focus is on protecting the state from physical attacks from within and without. The object of national security is to preserve the state or, in Aristotelian terms, to achieve "the good for the state." In this sense the good of the individual is considered secondary by Sri Lanka's policy makers, who indeed could have cited Aristotle: "Though it is worthwhile to attain the end merely for one man, it is finer and more godlike to attain it for a nation or for city-states" (Sen 1990: 4). But again, is it correct to speak of a state approach without differentiating between the governments that have ruled the country since independence? How did the state's policy makers understand security in the 1950s and 1960s? Did they actually think in the same terms?

The Foreign Policy Approach: External Threats to Security

My purpose here is not to give a chronological account of the security problems during a certain period but to show how the framework of discourse has shifted from the external to the internal. According to mainstream thinking, both official and academic, the major security problems for most of the countries in South Asia have to do with their relationship with India. As Shelton U. Kodikara has observed, the "security dilemma" that confronts the South Asian states arises from the fact that the region is militarily Indocentric. The fundamental security problem, he says, is one in which the states peripheral to India seek a maximization of security vis-à-vis India while India itself seeks to regionalize security within a subcontinental framework (Kodikara 1993: 8). Most studies of Sri Lanka's security adopt a regional outlook: Sri Lanka can be understood only as part of South Asia or the world system.

Gamini Keerawella stresses that fear of Big Brother was one of the main elements of the defense-oriented perspective of the first United National Party (UNP) government of 1948–56. Even in the 1970s during Sirimavo Bandaranaike's premiership, Indo–Sri Lankan relations were characterized by suspicion. The demarcation of the maritime boundary between the two countries in the Palk Strait and the Gulf of Mannar was a high priority (Keerawella 1990: 180). In the 1970s and 1980s, the development of the Indian Ocean as a zone of peace was perceived as central to Sri Lanka's security. The conference on the Indian Ocean due to be held in 1981 never materialized, however, and the U.N. Declaration of the Indian Ocean as a Peace Zone has yet to be implemented (Kodikara 1990). Thus in the state's conception, Sri Lanka's security could be maintained by a sort of cordon sanitaire wrapped around its coastline. In the writings of Sri Lankan analysts one finds that the notion of a secure boundary and territorial protection is at the core of the state's appreciation of security. The regime in power is irrelevant. Thus, for all intents and purposes, security is equated with national security whether in the language of diplomats or mainstream academics. Until the mid-1950s, threats to national security were perceived as coming from outside.

After the emergence of a militant Tamil separatist movement in Sri Lanka, the state's apprehension sharpened and was long focused on the possibility of Indian military intervention in support of Tamil militants in the northern province. The state has what is often called a minority complex vis-à-vis the subcontinent, where 65 million Tamils live. Not only has Sri Lanka never integrated with the mainland economies on the subcontinent, it has in fact made overtures for membership in the

Association of Southeast Asian Nations (ASEAN) in 1981 and 1984. This policy was guided by Colombo's interest in attracting ASEAN capital to the free industrial zones under preferential terms. But security too played an important part. Sri Lanka was interested in obtaining support from the informal ASEAN security system because of its apprehension over the external threat posed by the possibility of Indian intervention. Due to these preoccupations, Colombo's commitment to the South Asian Association for Regional Cooperation (SAARC) was somewhat questionable at the outset. It was during the UNP era, in 1987, that an Indian peacekeeping force landed in the northeast of Sri Lanka to disarm the Tamil militants—thus, in the common perception, threatening the sovereignty of the state of Sri Lanka. Not surprisingly, after this event the fear of an Indian invasion of the island—and of Indian interference in the general affairs of the country—remained the central security issue. But the 1987 intervention by the Indian peacekeeping force also broke the psychological barrier. The Indians had indeed come, but they left in 1989. P. R. Chari questions the Indian hegemony thesis. First, he argues, the approach ignores the superpower's role in exacerbating subcontinental tensions. And second, it ignores subregional tensions (Chari 1987: 50–60). In the case of the Tamil militant movement in Sri Lanka, it is obvious that ethnopolitical issues spilled across national boundaries.

Violence and the Internal Dimension

Two events led to a change in the state's perception of security as a predominantly external concern. The first was the JVP revolt in 1971. The second was the escalation of the armed struggle of the LTTE in the northern and eastern provinces in the early 1980s.

The Janata Vimukti Peramuna Insurrections: Security as Order

In 1971 the JVP, a violent political movement, tried to topple the leftist government of Sirimavo Bandaranaike but failed. It resumed the effort in the late 1980s in an even more violent manner using murder, torture, and intimidation. The trigger for this resurgence was the 1987 Indo–Sri Lankan Accord, which sanctioned the use of Indian troops in Sri Lanka to quell the LTTE in the north and east. The JVP movement nearly succeeded in destroying the state institutions but was crushed by the Sri Lankan security forces working with death squads.

In social and ideological terms, the JVP is made up of radical Sinhalese Buddhists who are both anti-Tamil and anti-Indian. Many of its members are political and social reformers drawn from the educated unemployed youth of the south. In 1971, the JVP sought to "save" the country from eastern imperialism and Indian expansionist designs. In 1987–89, it again sought to "save" the country from an unholy trinity of American imperialism, Indian imperialism, and Tamil expansionism. The JVP became a security issue: for the first time the state had to face serious internal threats. The JVP insurrection was first analyzed by state officials and mainstream academics as an antistate movement that would have to be crushed by the security forces to safeguard the legitimate state. There is at the core of Sri Lanka's state ideology the notion of its responsibility to ensure a *dharmista samajaya*, a just society. The state and its security forces see the "*dharmista* society" as one where social justice prevails but can be achieved only through political stability. The ruler and his agents undertake to govern righteously, to provide for all citizens according to their merits and virtues, and to bring about material benefits for the ruled. In return, the ruled are expected to accept the status quo and to confine their dissent within the bounds of the political order. Crushing the JVP insurrection was a security imperative, therefore, that the state and the security forces took upon themselves to undertake.

In 1971 and 1988–89, national security was not all-inclusive: it meant, in effect, protecting the legitimacy of the ruling classes, which were threatened by a political revolt of disadvantaged youth who were attempting to capture state power. The JVP's activities were described in the state media as subversive threats to the state that could be dealt with only through the use of the Public Security Act. In 1971, when officials defined the political threat posed by the insurgents as a security problem, security was understood as "order" or as preservation of the status quo. There were plans to "tighten security all over Ceylon," and Mrs. Bandaranaike proclaimed she was "ready for any threat to the peace."[3]

Although the 1971 insurrection and the JVP's resurgence in the 1980s were explained by officials as a security threat to the state, and thereby used as a rationale for the state's authoritarian tendencies, those two events were not described as security problems by political analysts until the late 1980s. In political science works dealing with developments in Sri Lanka and in specific studies of the JVP—where, interestingly, the term *security* is invisible[4]—the analytical framework was different. It is only since the late 1980s, and in studies specifically pertaining to security, that the concept of security is used to analyze political threats from within such as the JVP (Werake and Jayasekera 1995). It is no coincidence that the inclusion of security as an analytical concept to appraise internal threats to the state was adopted at the time Tamil militancy began to pose a serious threat to the state.

Ethnic Conflict and Security of the South

The ethnic conflict became a security problem for the state only in the 1980s when the Sri Lankan police and military were incapable of suppressing the increasingly violent LTTE struggle in the northern and eastern provinces and Colombo was under threat from terrorist attacks and bombs. When the ethnic conflict began to affect the majority community, it became a security issue.

The Sri Lanka Tamils—or Ceylon Tamils, as they were called until the 1970s—constitute 12.6 percent of the total population; the Up-Country Tamils, whose antecedents were brought from southern India by the British in the nineteenth century to work as laborers in the new plantation sector, constitute 5.5 percent. The Sri Lanka Tamils live mainly in the northern and eastern parts of the island, whereas the Up-Country Tamils live in the central highlands where the tea plantations are located.

The demand for a separate state for the Tamil people arose from the failure of repeated attempts to meet Sri Lanka Tamil aspirations. This failure, together with growing economic problems and rising unemployment, contributed to the rise of assertive and aggressive Tamil militancy.

There was a difference in degree between the nonviolent methods used by the Federal Party and the Tamil United Liberation Front to push for their separatist demands and the later use of terrorist methods, particularly suicide bombers, against civilians in the south by the LTTE.

There was first a "communal problem." At the time of independence, the Ceylon Tamils held a disproportionately high number of jobs in the prestigious Ceylon Civil Service and places in the most important higher education faculties (Wickramasinghe 1995). To combat the advantages enjoyed by Tamils after independence, the Sinhalese majority adopted two policies that are the source of much of the subsequent discontent of the Tamils: a "Sinhala only" language policy and a quota system based on race and residence (referred to as "standardization") for admission to university. When the Sinhala Only Act was adopted in 1956, a proposal to include a clause on the use of Tamil was dropped because of pressure from extremist Buddhist groups. Tamil protests led in 1956 to the Bandaranaike-Chelvanayakam Pact, which provided for the use of Tamil in Tamil areas and would have established regional councils with powers to enact agriculture, education, and colonization schemes. The pact was never implemented—again because of strong objections by Buddhist elements—and in 1958 the first major outbreak of communal violence occurred.

In the 1950s with the resurgence of Sinhalese nationalism and the emergence of the Federal Party, which pressed for a Tamil homeland, officials came to look upon national security not only as an interstate problem but also as an internal issue: protecting the unity of the state. "We must find a formula to preserve the unity and maintain the unity of Ceylon," said S. Corea, minister of commerce, trade, and fisheries, to his Chilaw electorate in 1956.[5] The term *security*, however, was still not commonly coupled with *internal*. The crisis facing the country in the mid-1950s was described as a communal problem rather than a security issue.

In 1958 a rumor that a Tamil had killed a Sinhalese sparked off nationwide communal riots. Hundreds of people, mostly Tamils, died. A dusk-to-dawn curfew was declared throughout the country, press censorship was enforced, and the Federal Party was banned. The governor general, Sir Oliver Goonetilleke, declared a state of emergency on the island "in the interests of public security, the preservation of public order, and the maintenance of supplies and services essential to the life of the community."[6] After 1958, national security took on a wider meaning that encompassed not only preserving the integrity and unity of the state but also protecting the people. Security of the people gradually began to mean security of the majority community, the southern people who faced threats from aliens.

A watershed in the "Sinhalization" of the state came in May 1972 with the passage of the republican constitution, which asserted Sinhalese Buddhist cultural forms and contained weaker protection for minorities. For many Tamils the 1972 constitutional provisions on religion and language confirmed their feeling of being second-class citizens. Their sense of alienation was further reinforced by the United Front government's policies on university entrance, which brought down dramatically the proportion of Tamils entering the university.

The Tamil response was first civil disobedience and then separatism. In 1976 the Tamil United Liberation Front demanded the formation of a separate state of Tamil Eelam in the areas that were considered the Tamil homelands in the north and east. Those areas accounted for two-thirds of the coastline and one-third of the country. This demand paved the way for militants, who began by assassinating Tamils associated with the ruling party and then started attacking state targets (Nissan 1996).

Tensions between Tamils and Sinhalese increased during the Sri Lanka Freedom Party (SLFP) rule of Mrs. Bandaranaike, and a major outbreak of violence occurred in August 1977, only a few months after the election of the Jayawardene-led United National Party (UNP) government. The third major outbreak of communal violence occurred in August 1981. Mutual fear and anger had developed as terrorist attacks against police in the north increased, accompanied by the detention of Tamil youths incommunicado and by arson and looting by police in Jaffna. Their burning of the Jaffna Public Library, a Tamil cultural center, was particularly resented and is still referred to as an early example of the lawlessness of the security forces.

Once the LTTE began to retaliate by sending suicide squads to the capital to destroy army or business establishments—in the process killing civilians in the south—the state's definition of security gained a further complexity. The new understanding privileges the security of the south, because its institutions and people are under threat from terrorist attacks. Although national security has assumed a new dimension—the security of the south is now given higher priority than that of any other region—the notion of territorial integrity remains at the core. Every night the state television news broadcast updates the "security situation" by giving a head count of the number of soldiers and terrorists killed in the northeast, an account of any terrorist attack perpetrated in the south, and measures taken to ensure the safety of the capital. The emphasis, however, is on the square footage of territory captured by the army in its various operations, not on the lives and deaths of human beings.

For the Sri Lankan state, internal security still entails protecting the boundaries of the state against secessionist movements—thus avoiding the dilution of state sovereignty and safeguarding it from external intervention. The notion of territoriality, therefore, still predominates in the state's perception of security. The concept of territory is crucial, too, in the state's understanding of nationalism and the nation-state. A nation-state is perceived as a spatial unit lying between borders that it must defend. Territory, as Louis Dumont defines it, is a continuous tract of country that symbolizes the unity of individuals who own parts of the country. If the nation is "a collection of individuals and their properties," territory is the total of the properties belonging to that collection of individuals, known as the nation (Dumont 1970: 108). Writing about the Indo–Sri Lankan Accord of 1987, Jayadeva Uyangoda points out that the primary aspect of the crisis was the prospect of territorial breakup and the disintegration of the Sri Lankan state. The theoretical possibility of a territorial split gained momentum with the outbreak of violence in the north and east and with the Tamil guerrilla campaigns (Uyangoda 1989).

A certain consensus seems to have emerged on the necessity of military action against the LTTE. In the view of the UNP government in the early 1990s, only a military takeover of the north and the east could assure the security of the south. For the UNP, now in the opposition, military action has been found to be the only option. While he was prime minister, Ranil Wickremesinghe said, "In the absence of any other option at the moment, security forces would continue their efforts to bring more areas in the North under the government's control."[7] The government of Chandrika Bandaranaike Kumaratunge eventually adopted the military option because everything else had failed. She initiated a peace process, but after about four months of cease-fire the LTTE broke the truce by destroying two navy boats and firing heat-seeking missiles at two aircraft. The LTTE has subsequently tried to explain its breaking of the truce. It claims that the stance of the government expressed in the president's letter to the LTTE leader, Vellupillai Prabakharan, was that "enough concessions and privileges had already been given to the Tamils and that further giving of anything would endanger the national security."[8] By April 1996 the government forces had recaptured the Jaffna peninsula, pushed the Tigers into the jungles of the Wanni, and given protection to its civilian population, which had been reduced to the status of refugees in LTTE-controlled areas. There are signs that the state is evolving a concept of security that combines security of the south from terrorist attacks, security of the north from guerrilla/military clashes, and protection of the sacrosanct boundaries of the nation-state from secessionist tendencies.

The State and Violence: From Army to Security Forces

Anthony Giddens has defined the nation-state as "a set of institutional forms of governance maintaining an administrative monopoly over a territory with demarcated boundaries (borders), its rule being sanctioned by law and direct control of the means of internal and external violence" (Giddens 1985: 121). He points out that a feature of the nation-state is its monopoly of the means of violence. Sri Lanka's situation demonstrates that when other groups in society—armed groups or insurgent movements—threaten that monopoly, the state is compelled to strengthen the instruments of internal pacification by transforming its army into a modern and technically advanced outfit that it calls its "security forces." The army played a ceremonial role during the first decades of independence and functioned in a limited capacity in assisting the police force to maintain law and order. The term then in vogue was "law and order," which paradoxically has a much more authoritarian resonance than "security." It is as though, at some point, a reversal of meanings took place. During the decades of relative "law and order" (1947 to the early 1980s), the political culture of the state and the army—whose officer corps was recruited from the upper classes and trained at Sandhurst—was above all democratic. Since the end of the

1970s, when Tamil groups took arms against the state, the Sri Lankan army has had to face real war for the first time.

The term *security* entered the vocabulary of the state at the end of this era of innocence—as though the predictable excesses of the armed forces would need to be semantically exorcised by use of the word *security*, which connotes protection and comfort rather than violence. *Security* and *forces* were thus coupled in an oxymoronic fashion. The "internal security of the state" became a familiar phrase in the political jargon of the 1980s, and the army was rebaptized as the "security forces." It was a less confrontational way of making civil society accept the realities of war and violence under the guise of a discourse on "security."

The worsening of the ethnic conflict and the consequent expansion of the armed forces in the 1980s contributed to the creation of a "security"-oriented state. The process of militarization and the special role assigned to the security forces resulted in several changes in the structure of the state, which in the last decade, according to some analysts, has begun to slide toward political authoritarianism (Warnapala 1994). As Michel Foucault reminds us, "politics has been conceived as a continuation, if not exactly and directly of war, at least of the military model as a fundamental means of preventing civil disorder." What he suggests in fact is that politics, as a technique of internal peace and order, attempts to implement the mechanism of the perfect army and to a certain extent succeeds in training people to be disciplined and docile bodies (Rabinow 1984: 185). The militarization of the state in the 1980s even influenced many Sri Lankans into uncritical admiration for a ruler such as Singapore's Lee Kuan Yew. It is not uncommon to hear people openly aver that what the country needs is ten years of military rule, proper discipline, or a benevolent dictatorship.

The late 1970s and 1980s were a period of torture and deaths in custody, extrajudicial killings, and reprisal massacres. Arbitrary arrests and detention for long periods were common. Except for a period of five months, Sri Lanka has been in a state of emergency since 1983. In 1994, the new leftist government of Chandrika Kumaratunge lifted the emergency decree in the south. In the north and the east, the security forces are still invested with extraordinary powers under the emergency regulations and the Prevention of Terrorism Act (PTA).[9] Indeed, since the outbreak of civil war the security forces have been invested by the state with a sort of semi-divine aura. Under the UNP government it was considered a crime against the state to criticize the security forces even if they had committed excesses. The UNP Manifesto of the 1994 elections offered a eulogy of the armed forces:

> Sri Lanka is proud of the heroism and dedication of its Security Forces. Despite being involved in violent and painful conflict with terrorism, our Security Forces have performed magnificently and with courage against every threat. Whereas increasing militarization in many countries brings about public hatred and contempt for their security forces, we have widespread sympathy and affection for the men and women who serve their motherland in our army, navy, airforce, and police.[10]

The security forces were the protectors of "national security," modern-day heroes who fought courageously for the good of the country, the motherland. This feeling, encouraged by the state, seeped down to the Singhalese people. Indeed, their widespread sympathy for the security forces was obvious during the late 1980s when the leftist and violence-prone JVP was gaining much ground among the poorer classes. The JVP's crucial mistake was to threaten the families of the security forces in its struggle against the state. That policy led to a major reversal in sympathy that helped the government to crush the JVP militarily. Initially the Chandrika government was ambivalent about the security forces. Although it started a campaign to bring to justice some of the military men involved in massacres, this effort has recently slowed. With the recent capture of Jaffna city, despite the obvious instances of violence, bribery, and corruption in the higher command, the security forces are once again hailed as the saviors of the nation.

Despite the changes in the state's conception of security, in the mainstream view security means protection of the boundaries of the sovereign state of Sri Lanka from encroachments—first on the part of India, then by unlawful sons of the soil. Very few studies offer an epistemological reflection on security. Security itself is a given. The core values to be protected are territorial integrity and political independence. The only shift in emphasis in Sri Lanka has been that national security in recent years has come to mean, more and more, defending the sovereignty of the state against enemies from within.

Human Security: The Nongovernmental Approach

Among members of majority and minority communities alike there is a sense that the state is incapable of ensuring their security. In the minds of the Sinhalese people, terrorist acts of the LTTE constitute the main threat to their own security and that of the country.[11] The fear is amplified by an impression of the state's helplessness. In November 1995, for example, all schools were closed for two months after the LTTE threatened to target schoolchildren. Eventually it was the Central Bank of Sri Lanka, in the heart of the business district of Colombo, that was blown to pieces in January 1996 by a suicide bomber, causing nearly 100 deaths and millions of rupees worth of damages.

For the minority community, the threat comes from the state institutions. Tamil civilians are frequently detained indiscriminately after guerrilla or terrorist attacks or during army operations. "Security," according to a female Tamil undergraduate, "is when you feel protected by the law. Security means protection of life. As a Tamil in the present day, the biggest threat is the security forces—having to produce identification." Her words summarize the perception of the members of the Tamil community who were interviewed for this study. Unlike most Sinhalese, who when asked to define security said it meant to live "without problems," Tamil men and women had a very precise understanding of the concept. The state's failure to protect all its citizens was highlighted. "Being a Tamil, my name, my birthplace, is a source of suspicion. I am not accepted as a citizen of Sri Lanka. I don't have the same freedom as a man from the majority community," complained a Tamil teacher.[12]

Most people's conceptions of security share an important feature with the state's conception: both give a primary rank to the notion of territory. For the state, we noted that security is attached to the land and protection of the land or nation-state. For most individuals, the home constitutes the last bastion of security once the state fails its citizens. The events that took place in 1983 in Sri Lanka put the entire issue in perspective. After the deaths of thirteen soldiers in Jaffna, the center of the separatist struggle, anti-Tamil riots broke out in Colombo. The mob targeted all Tamils. In this situation the recognized institutions of the state—the police and the armed forces whose duty it was to help the victims and control the violence—were seen as manifestly failing to do their duty, whereas the Christian church offered help and sympathy. For the victims it was the informal network of friends and neighbors and the Christian church organizations that provided the means for reformulating their lives. It is not surprising, then, that they should have felt betrayed by the state. The circle of security, therefore, has become smaller. As Kamala, a victim of the violence, recalls: "I could not stand outside exposed to the violence. So I took my family and ran into the house. I suppose at that moment instinct makes us run into the security of our home" (Kanapatipillai 1990: 334). For many victims, not even the home was secure.

Thus when the state breaks its contract to protect all its citizens, people are left to create their own security. For many in Sri Lanka this meant leaving the country altogether. Kamala's family felt that the future of Sri Lanka had no place for them and decided to migrate to New

Zealand: "If we have to live as minorities," she said, "we might as well live in a place that promises security to the children" (Kanapatipillai 1990: 334). Security means life.

Thus the individual's security is very much contingent on events. In the space of a few hours the state had changed its role from purveyor of security to prime threat and even oppressor. Another feature of individual security is that it is precisely when their security is threatened (by a bomb blast or riot) that people consciously reflect on their security needs. In situations of violence, therefore, security is not only contextual and malleable, it is also fundamentally reactive. Moreover, the feeling of threat persists. Many victims of violence, uprooted in different countries and more than ten years after the events, still see crowds as hostile mobs. Former residents of Jaffna now in London or Toronto, who for years lived in fear of aerial bombing, still listen with apprehension to the sound of planes or helicopters. As Valli Kanapatipillai puts it, "The violence did not just 'erupt' and then disappear. Perhaps the difference between the threats from natural disasters, and violence coming from human agencies, is that the latter is experienced as continuous violence. It is not contained in time; like waves created by throwing a stone in the river, it has repercussions which far exceed the moment of its occurrence" (Kanapatipillai 1990: 343).

Security as a Human Value

In 1994, the United National Party lost the elections to the People's Alliance, a conglomeration of left, left-of-center, and minority parties. In contrast to previous governments for which security was mainly envisioned as national security, the present government's definition encompasses human values, too, at least at the declaratory level.

The Election Manifesto of the People's Alliance in the parliamentary elections of 1994 contained in its very title a notion of security at variance with the UNP approach: "For a secure prosperous society where human values reign, devoid of corruption and terror." In this formulation, it is society and not the state that has to be secure. Compared to the previous government, the emphasis had shifted from the state and a dominant concern for national security to a focus on civil society. In the manifesto, the three main aims of the People's Alliance underlined a "liberal democratic" approach to rights and suggested the vital national values that must be protected: freedom to live in a humane society; a free and democratic society with law and order; and rapid and sustainable economic development.[13] After the People's Alliance captured power and formed a government, its leader, Chandrika Bandaranaike Kumararunge, won the presidential elections. Since then, the new government has been eager to introduce liberal-democratic ideas into society through constitutional means as well as through efforts to involve civil society in governance.

Constitutional Responses

Sri Lanka's 1978 Constitution is in the process of being transformed into a liberal-democratic constitution that protects the freedom of the individual. Security is not, however, the main concern of the constitution makers, who, like John Rawls, claim that freedom is the highest good and that a rational social order dedicated to principles of justice must strive to realize them (Rawls 1971). That men and women can aspire to freedom only to the extent that their basic needs are met is not sufficiently taken into consideration. Those basic needs encompass the social goods that are essential to human subsistence—food, clothing, housing, medical care, schooling. Basic human needs imply the duty of government to satisfy the welfare requirements, taking into account the constraints of limited resources and the vagaries of natural disasters such as drought and floods.[14]

The right to life, liberty, and security of person was expressly stated in Chapter 6 of the 1972 Constitution, but there is no comparable provision in the 1978 Constitution. In the current constitution the various fundamental rights are not treated as absolute but are subject to the limitations stated in Article 15. National security, racial and religious harmony, parliamentary privilege, contempt of court, defamation, public health, and morality are among the recognized grounds for imposing restrictions on fundamental rights (Goonesekere 1988).

In the recently released draft constitution the Chandrika government has rectified a number of deficiencies of the present constitution. The right to life is an important departure from the 1978 Constitution. Although security is conspicuously absent as a fundamental right, the draft constitution, which strengthens democratic institutions and provides an enhanced protection of fundamental rights and freedoms, implicitly acknowledges the importance of security.[15] Concurrent with the constitutional measures have been attempts by the Chandrika government to forge closer links with the dynamic nongovernmental organization (NGO) sector as a way of filling gaps left by the state.

Nongovernmental Organizations and Security

There is evidence to suggest that the NGO sector has had an impact on government thinking about security. Indeed, the last twenty years have seen a rapid growth of indigenous NGOs in Sri Lanka.[16] The new emphasis on the NGO sector can be placed in the intellectual framework of wider changes in macroeconomic policy, privatization, and the reduced role of the state in all aspects of the economy and provision of services. In the political realm, too, organizations that find inspiration in the values embedded in the Declaration of Human Rights and the International Covenant on Civil and Political Rights have emerged since the 1970s. Among the most active and influential are the following: the International Center for Ethnic Studies, the Institute of Policy Studies, the Social Scientists' Association, the Movement for Inter-Racial Justice and Equality, the Center for Society and Religion, and Colombo University's Center for Policy Research and Analysis.

Until recently, governments have kept NGOs at a distance because they tend to critique the human rights record of the state. The change of government, however, saw a important change in the position of NGOs vis-à-vis the state. This change is due to the president's personal ties with intellectuals and human rights proponents, a bond that stems from her own intellectual interests. Unlike her predecessors, who were known for being anti-intellectual, Chandrika has close links with the left-liberal intellectuals in Sri Lanka. Her political philosophy has evolved from socialism and a dependency-theory approach to world economics to a carefully modulated brand of liberalism with a human face. In drafting her political program prior to the elections of 1994, she relied on a think tank composed of university lecturers, journalists, and human rights activists who, like her, had started their journey in the left movement.[17] This group of advisers constitutes an important human rights lobby within the government, and they have undoubtedly influenced the government's approach to security.

The political package for devolution of power—a plan that entails the division of the country into seven regions—was drafted as a political solution to the ethnic conflict by G. L. Peiris, former professor of law and former vice chancellor of the University of Colombo, and Dr. Neelan Tiruchelvam, the director of the International Center for Ethnic Studies. Both men are committed to the values of human rights and promote a human rights discourse that goes a considerable distance beyond the liberal-freedom discourse that was in vogue in the 1980s. The president's close advisers speak a humanist language of human rights, which acknowledges the basic need for security as well as for freedom and which links the two basic value claims within theories of social and international justice. In Sri Lanka, the postliberal struggle for human rights is linked more and more with the struggle for peace and economic-political development.

The NGOs' intervention in security matters invariably revolves around the notion of peace in the country as a precondition to the security of all its citizens. Middle-class elements such as the radical intelligentsia who work in the NGO sector and the progressive human rights community adhere to Western-style rationalist doctrines of equality but also uphold the individual's right to liberty and life. They see this as a necessary element of a peaceful society, a *sama samajaya*. Thousands of peace and human rights activists, representatives of more than 40 nonparty formations and NGOs, staged a mass peace rally on December 9, 1994—the eve of International Human Rights Day. The procession was accompanied by street theater artists who sang, danced, and portrayed the horrors of war and the joys of peace. The crowds were kept absorbed by speeches on various themes pertaining to peace, democracy, and human rights. The peace rally ended with the lighting of torches and the formal adoption of two appeals, one to the government and the other to the LTTE.[18]

Today most NGOs concerned with human rights support the devolution of power to regions suggested by the government as a long-term solution to the ethnic conflict, while advising the government to refrain from military action that could harm the civilian population in Jaffna. But on other fronts, dissatisfaction is brewing. Two years after the change of government there is a clear discrepancy between, on the one hand, people's expectations for a state that will protect them and, on the other, the liberal free-market approach adopted by the new regime in its dealings with labor problems.

Critiques of the State's Approach

The state's approach to security is challenged on many fronts. It is criticized specifically for its failure to include cultural and economic elements in its conception of security. Those outside the government are concerned with threats of a nonmilitary character—external domination of the country's economy, dependence on other countries for scientific research and technology, and the unrestricted penetration of Western values through the media resulting in an erosion and eventual loss of national identity. For a sizable group of people, security cannot refer simply to the preservation of the state's independence and territorial integrity.

Insurgent groups such as the JVP list a range of problems, including the threat posed by capitalism to the culture and traditions of the Sinhalese people and the government's submissive attitude to the dictates of lending institutions. Other pressure groups such as trade unions argue that the state has sold out to international capitalism and failed to protect its children from want. Religious groupings such as the powerful Buddhist Sangha criticize the state's approach for subordinating culture and religion to economic and political concerns. Do these voices influence the state's conception of security?

The Context: Liberalization and Privatization

In 1977 Sri Lanka opened up its economy after more than a decade of import control. Chandrika came to power with a promise to the financial world that her government would not reverse the liberalization and privatization program of the previous government. The People's Alliance's political program, however, was more ambivalent about the privatization issue. Although it clearly accepted the inevitability of a market economy, it stated that "public utilities which are essential for day-to-day life must function under government control, but with adequate autonomy for efficient management."[19] Thus although the People's Alliance maintained its commitment to the privatization program begun in the previous regime, its manifesto emphasized a people-oriented approach to social and political reforms. People, the manifesto argued, matter more than reasons of state. In its election manifesto the government had stated that health, education, water, electricity, highways and railway, airports, irrigation, main state banks, and public-sector insurance establishments must function under government control.[20] But in February 1996 it was revealed that the government was considering the privatization of no fewer than 70 state institutions. Among the enterprises earmarked for divestment of shares were the State Mortgage and Investment Bank, the Independent Television Network, the Ceylon Shipping Corporation, and Air Lanka.[21] The government's inability or refusal to keep its electoral promises has led to challenges from labor and to a growing feeling that the government has duped its supporters.

Security as Social Justice

Paradoxically, the JVP insurrection of 1987–89 started in the name of national security defined in a manner very similar to the state's conception. Its manifesto proposed that "a new foreign policy will be adopted to ensure the national independence and territorial integrity of Sri Lanka." The JVP's approach was in fact a combination of two perceptions of security. On the one hand, it claimed to be the savior of a nation that was then enduring external threats and internal conflict. This vision of national security was in no way different from that of the diplomats and mainstream academics. On the other hand, the JVP articulated a conception of security whereby the state would protect and look after the people.

In 1988, the JVP Action Center issued a communiqué calling the masses to protest against the J. R. Jayawardena–Rajiv Gandhi accord, which brought about provincial councils and devolution of power. The rhetoric was one of justice and equality rather than rights: "We shall not keep quiet when the patriots in the South who fight for equality and justice are massacred by mercenaries. We shall not wait patiently when the reasonable struggle by the students—our future generation—for justice and equality is repressed brutally" (Gunaratna 1990: 291). The idea that basic needs are contained in the concept of security is reflected in the notion of rights embodied in the JVP vision of a *sadharanaya lokaya* ("equitable world") where the poor are not discriminated against and social justice prevails. In 1987–89, a primary component of its vision of social justice was the notion of mass universal education as a basic human right. In the economic field, foreign trade, internal wholesale trade, and heavy industry would be maintained as state monopolies. Foreign banks and financial institutions would be nationalized. A radical land reform would be implemented. The ethnic problem would be dealt with by ensuring that equality prevailed among all races in education and land distribution.

The JVP took it upon itself to secure social justice among the Sinhalese by taking up arms against what it saw as an oppressive state. It argued that the Sri Lankan state since independence had been committed to welfarism—that is, to safeguard the basic needs of its citizens. After 1977, however, the economy was opened and industrial growth based on foreign investment was encouraged. A necessary concomitant to such an export-led strategy was the World Bank and International Monetary Fund's "structural adjustment policies," which demanded a shifting of public resources away from social welfare into investment. The JVP opposed the system of private property on the grounds that a society based on humanistic principles can never be built on a capitalist framework. The socialization of property relations was firmly defended. The JVP claimed that Sri Lanka had a neocolonial economy completely subservient to the imperialists. In this view capitalism, which has led to neocolonial domination and an erosion of traditional mores and values, is the main enemy (Gunaratna 1990: 259–66). One of the primary global threats, according to the radical nationalists, is the involvement of lending institutions such as the World Bank and the IMF in running the country, especially in light of their demands for "good governance" (Lipset 1960: 403).

Significance of the JVP Alternative

Until recently, governments have ignored these voices from below. But after two insurrections and thousands of dead, the problems of the poor unemployed youth of the south can no longer be ignored. Although the JVP movement was violently crushed in the late 1980s, its ideas remain popular in certain circles such as the student movement and some trade unions. Militant Sinhala groups such as the Jathika Chintanaya (National Ideology), student movements such as the Janata Mithuro (Friends of the People), and trade unions have offered their own definition of security—a definition that involves a critique of the state in Sri Lanka as a component of global capitalism. Many young men and women interviewed for this study expressed, if not allegiance to the JVP, at least an intellectual affinity with its ideas. A well-known social critic, Gunadasa Ameresekere, has put forward the concept of *jathika arthikaya*, a national or indigenous economy. His vision idealizes the village and rural culture and castigates the open economy without clearly advocating an alternative model of development. The Janata Mithuro envisages an environment-friendly regime that would control the pernicious effects of modernization—tourism, pollution, urbanization. These approaches reflect the need for security from "imperialist/global threats" and the turning inward turn to focus on indigenous culture rather than international conceptions of human rights.

Clearly, then, the state's approach to security has not been influenced by the JVP/antisystemic critique, which challenges the foundation of society itself and the belief that Western-style economic and political liberalism represents "the good society" (Lipset 1960: 403). No government will agree to reverse the ongoing process of liberalization in order to appease the JVP or its supporters. But under pressure from these anticapitalist forces, the state can be forced to change its policy on certain issues. Thus one could say that the JVP/antisystemic ideology, when used in a limited manner, may have some impact—as in the recent Ceylon Electricity Board strike. In that case the state had to compromise in order to assure workers that privatization would not take place at the expense of their interests. Here one can say that the voice of antisystemic groups did have an impact on the state's approach to security. Through strikes, pickets, and representations, these groups act as watchdogs that now and then remind the government of its commitment to human security.

The Sangha's Critique

According to Sinhala-Buddhist tradition, fashioned largely by the Ancient Chronicles of the island, Sri Lanka is the Dharmadvipa (island of the faith) consecrated by the Buddha himself as the land in which his teachings would flourish. One such Chronicle, *Mahavamsa*, states that on the very day of the Buddha's death, Vijaya, the founder of the Sinhala race, landed in Sri Lanka as if to bear witness to the Buddha's prediction (Geiger 1950). The king was traditionally the protector of Buddhism, and after independence the new nation-state took over this function. Every constitution of the country since 1972 has stressed the special place given to Buddhism, the religion of more than 70 percent of the population. Buddhism is in Sri Lanka a legitimizing, integrative, and moral force that governments and politicians must take into account. Although Buddhism is protected by the state and practiced by the vast majority of people, many of its proponents present it as a religion under threat. The threat has been portrayed as coming from various places at different times. In the 1950s, Buddhist leaders complained of the influence of "Catholic action" and spearheaded the SLFP campaign, taking over denominational schools, evicting Catholic nursing nuns, giving Buddhist preachers more time over national radio, and securing employment for Buddhists in the higher echelons of the administration and armed services. This was in fact a process of rectifying perceived colonial favoritism to Catholics.

Since independence, political monks organized in pressure groups have taken positions on crucial issues, and they influence people by virtue of their moral prestige. When the UNP came to power and liberalized the economy, monks protested against the growing consumerism. The same groups protested against the signing of the Indo–Sri Lankan Accord in 1987, claiming that the agreement betrayed the Sinhala people by conceding too much to the Tamils and allowing Indians to enter the island as a peacekeeping force. The rhetoric of betrayal, and of the need to protect the land, are ever-present elements in the Sinhala nationalist discourse where Sinhalese and Buddhist identities are merged into one. The threat is identified as coming from the West, Christianity, and capitalism.

The phenomenon of religious influence was particularly apparent a few years ago when a book published by Stanley Tambiah, *Buddhism Betrayed? Religion, Politics and Violence in Sri Lanka* (1992), became the center of a controversy. It was alleged in the Sinhala press that with the publication of the book an international conspiracy had been launched: the co-conspirators included the World Institute for Development Economic Research (WIDER), its former director, and the United Nations organizations; the chief beneficiary of the plot was the LTTE. This controversy, and the response of the reading public in Sri Lanka, showed that quite a few people believe that American imperialism is behind most of the evils of the world and that a number of traitors in Sri Lanka have sold out to the West. A few months later the government, bowing to the pressure of the Sangha, imposed a ban on the import and sale of the book.

The Buddhist Sangha plays an important role in fostering such ideas, because many Buddhists look to the leaders among the sects of Buddhist monks in Sri Lanka as moral guides even on temporal matters. The condemnation by many influential monks of the devolution package—a proposal offered to the Tamil people by Chandrika Bandaranaike Kumaratunge's government—as a threat to the unitary character of the state seems to have dampened the initial enthusiasm of its promoters. On March 5, 1996, a vast gathering of the Buddhist order, numbering more than 2,000 members, assembled to denounce the government's proposals to defuse the ethnic problem. A prominent scholar-monk, the Venerable Dr. Walpola Rahula, made the following statement: "These devolution proposals could only cause chaos and doom to the country and hence the package should be rejected in toto."[22] When the Sangha believes the state is failing to protect the majority culture, language, and religion of the land or is endangering the sovereignty of the country, it voices its opinion in the media. The state is then obliged to take the Sangha's view into account even if it does not always reflect the view of the majority.

Lessons

The definitions of security in Sri Lanka surveyed in this chapter draw attention to certain features of the concept: the plurality of conceptions of security and the relativity of the core values that must be protected as one moves from the state's perception of security to the perceptions of others. Globalization is a security concern of antisystemic groups as well as of influential segments of the population such as the Sangha.

For the state, security means the protection of the boundaries of the sovereign state of Sri Lanka from external and internal aggression. Recently, the state's concept of security has been broadened to include a concern for the human side of security by focusing on the people who live within the boundaries of the state. The state's realist approach to security is contested in the name of social justice by groups such as the LTTE and the JVP. But the People's Alliance too is challenged when it attempts to backtrack on its promises and seemingly fails to protect the boundaries of the sovereign state. Thus in both its incarnations—as human security and as state security—the definition of security is contested. It has many faces. This is perhaps the most important conclusion one can draw about security in Sri Lanka.

Sri Lanka's conception of security is due not only to its location or weakness in power but also to the nature of the state, its ruling elites, and the incidence of ethnic conflict. These factors explain the diverse conceptions of security. The perception of a threat from the capitalist West, for instance, stems from the deep wounds inflicted by colonialism—a feeling shared with all former colonies whether Asian or African. In the same way the communal nature of people's conception of security is shared in many other settings where majority and minority peoples coexist in other parts of the world.

What about Sri Lanka today? After the LTTE broke the truce and resumed fighting, the state once again outlined its conception of security: protecting the sovereignty of the state (territory) in the north and east and protecting the people in the south from terrorist acts by using the services of the security forces. For the people of Jaffna, however, security means security from the state bombing their homes. For the Tamils in Colombo, some of whom are arbitrarily arrested in anticipation of terrorist activities, there is no security from the counterinsurgent state. For the Sinhalese patriots, who have begun to accuse the state of weakness and of playing into the hands of the LTTE and the foreign hegemonic forces that support it, the notion of security is subsumed in a global critique of capitalism and a naive antiforeign rhetoric. More than ever, security is a complex concept with a multiplicity of faces.

Myanmar

Preoccupation with Regime Survival, National Unity, and Stability

TIN MAUNG MAUNG THAN

> *Our Three Main National Causes: non-disintegration of the Union;*
> *non-disintegration of national solidarity; perpetuation of sovereignty.*
> *We reject any scheme to break up the Tatmadaw [Burmese armed forces].*
> *No matter who tries to divide us, we will always remain united. Anyone*
> *who tries to break up the Tatmadaw is our enemy.*
>
> GOVERNMENT SLOGAN

Myanmar's[1] conception of security is overwhelmingly domestic, focused primarily on survival of the regime, national unity, and law and order. The "state" has been the primary referent of security since January 1948 when Myanmar, then known as Burma, gained independence from Britain. But the state and regime have been fused since the military coup of 1962. This has become even truer since the military coup of 1988 that led to the creation of the State Law and Order Restoration Council (SLORC)—the military junta that now controls Myanmar.[2] The state has been the object of contestation by minority groups since Myanmar gained independence. The regime also has been contested periodically since 1962, and the contestation has escalated since 1988. In its rhetoric, the government has hailed sovereignty and territorial integrity as its primary security concerns. The threats to these realist values, however, have been internal rather than international. In fact, Myanmar's geopolitical horizon did not extend beyond its immediate neighbors until the advent of the SLORC.

Historical reasons account for the predominance of internal concerns in Myanmar's conception of security. After gaining independence from Britain in 1948, Myanmar had a succession of governments that were opposed by a variety of local insurgent groups (Taylor 1987: 217). Moreover, bitter historical experience (Mongol and Chinese invasions, rivalry with Thailand, and the British annexation) dating back to the thirteenth century has impressed on Myanmar leaders the imperative of safeguarding the territorial integrity and the sovereignty of the state from external aggression.

Security Thinking: The Preserve of a Small Elite

All Myanmar governments have regarded security as the preserve of state leaders. The "security elite" in Myanmar has usually consisted of a very small inner core of top political and military leaders. In fact, the discourse on security has been monopolized by the defense establishment. Intellectual analysis, media coverage, and public debate of security issues are virtually absent. All along, the polity has accepted its own exclusion as well as the inexorable logic of state security, which has subsumed societal interests. The gaps between individual, group, and national security have never been acknowledged by the state, and the public has generally acquiesced to the state's hegemony in the name of order and stability.[3] Thus, the scope and structure of security in Myanmar from the beginning of sovereign statehood to the 1990s have essentially been determined by a small elite who, for all practical purposes, seem to be insulated from societal influences.

After the military coup of 1962, state leadership took the form of a "single apex structure" with General Ne Win at the apex (Kaung 1995). The "security consciousness" of leader Ne Win became that of the state. For the SLORC, although there is no comparable single leader, the structural configuration is not dissimilar. Despite a generational change from a "founding father" type of leadership to a "military-bureaucratic" type (Cohen 1989: 36–40), the existence of a tightly knit decision-making system within SLORC gives the top military leadership an opportunity to dominate the conception of state security. As for the translation of the leadership's security concerns into specific policies and their subsequent implementation, in the absence of documentary evidence one has to look for clues in the behavior of the central decision makers as well as in the institutional structures that undergird state security.

Traditionally, there has been a compartmentalization of state security agencies into those geared toward external defense and counterinsurgency operations (the Ministry of Defense and its operational units) and those responsible for law enforcement (the Home Ministry and the police force). Before the advent of the SLORC these agencies were coordinated at the cabinet level, whereas intelligence organizations were coordinated, since the mid-1970s, by the National Intelligence Bureau (NIB) under the purview of the prime minister.

Under the SLORC, the formal organizational division has been maintained, but the military, as the single dominating institution in state affairs, has become an almost monolithic hierarchical structure for dealing with national security affairs. The SLORC has an absolute monopoly in defining the state security agenda and differs dramatically from the previous trilateral power configuration in which the Burma Socialist Programme Party (BSPP), the state executive, and the military shared lineage, power, and responsibilities (Than 1993: 39–42). The Security and Management Committee of SLORC is presumably the focal point for dealing with security matters at the state level. In the field of intelligence, the NIB is believed to have been superseded by the Office of Strategic Studies headed by SLORC secretary-1, Lieutenant General Khin Nyunt.

Although specific leaders and the organization of the security infrastructure have changed over time, there is continuity in some of the factors that influence the construction of Myanmar's security. History, geography, geopolitics, and resource availability not only provide continuity in security thinking but also impose constraints and offer opportunities for Myanmar's security managers in their management of national security.

History, Geography, Geopolitics, Society, and Resources

History is one important factor that shapes central decision makers' conception of security. The historical developments that inform Myanmar's security conception include the almost continual struggle to establish an autonomous Bamar nation;[4] the incessant wars fought among the various "nations" of the proto-Myanmar state and conflicts with neighboring states over eight centuries of dynastic cycles; the ignominy of being colonized by the British for over a century; the subsequent struggle for national self-determination; the Japanese invasion during World War II; the "anti-fascist revolution"; the intense efforts to achieve national unity in confronting the British to regain political independence; the postindependence civil war and subsequent ideological and ethnic insurgencies; and the Kuomintang (KMT) aggression during the height of the Cold War.

Geographically, Myanmar shares more than 6,100 kilometers of contiguous land frontiers with five states and possesses a coastline stretching more than 2,800 kilometers. Hemmed in between the two most populous states on earth (nearly 1.3 billion Chinese and 950 million Indians), Myanmar's 45 million inhabitants (as of 1996) are outnumbered by its other neighbors as well except for Laos. Myanmar has prominent natural barriers in the form of "montane zones" in the northwest, north, and east, and rivers in the west and southeast. But those barriers did not prevent military invasions in the past (Lim 1984: 1–3, 59–65). For the last four decades, the frontier zones have been, more often than not, contested areas where drug traffickers, warlords, and insurgent groups have challenged the authority of the central state.

Geopolitical ramifications for the modern Myanmar state have been overwhelmingly determined by bilateral relations with China, which date back to the early Pyu kingdoms of the ninth century (Han 1988: 16–17; *Working People's Daily* [hereafter *WPD*], Dec. 11, 1992).[5] Post-independence Myanmar has, all along, accommodated China as its "senior" in a *paukphaw* (sibling) relationship, taking great pains to avoid incurring China's wrath (Han 1988: 16–18).[6] During the Cold War, Myanmar kept out of harm's way by eschewing military alliances and pursuing a strictly neutral foreign policy.

Myanmar has remained a multicultural, multiethnic, and multi-religious society. Because of topography and differing political econo-mies and sociocultural practices, substantial assimilation of other major indigenous groups such as Kachin, Chin, Kayin (Karen), Mon, and Shan into a supraethnic Myanmar nationality has not occurred. The existence of enclaves along ethnic lines and the colonial ascriptive notion of lowlanders and highlanders persisted well into the twentieth century (Taylor 1982). Growing urbanization and the concerted drive for national unity by the vanguard leaders of the independence movement somewhat attenuated the sense of alienation and mistrust, and the communalist tendencies engendered by ethnic divisions. However, the minorities' perception of majority dominance (Bamars constitute about 68 percent of the total population) in ethnic relations has been a most contentious political issue in independent Myanmar with far-reaching security implications (Yaungwe 1987; Silverstein 1980).[7] The ethnic dimension is a critical factor in the predominance of internal security issues in Myanmar.

In terms of physical resources, Myanmar has been more than self-sufficient in food and is well endowed with water, land, forests, min-erals, and other resources commensurate with its population and level of consumption. It seems that most Myanmars have subscribed to the long-cherished but somewhat vague notion of an inexhaustible natural resource base with immense potential for wealth creation (Steinberg 1982: 14–15). As such, the apparent ability of Myanmar's natural resources to provide physical sustenance for its population perhaps has reinforced the country's affinity for a self-sufficiency doctrine that, at times, has bordered on isolationism. Yet the economic development of Myanmar during the four decades after independence, in which the state played a dominant role, was poor, resulting in a very low per capita gross national product of some U.S.$200 in 1986. Even after SLORC opened up the economy its size was extremely modest, though economic growth was quite rapid after 1990.[8] Thus, the government's ability to expend financial resources for security was constrained by budget deficits and foreign exchange shortages up to the early 1990s (International Monetary Fund 1988; World Bank 1972).

Security Referents: State, Regime, and Military

The unitary Burmese state, usually referred to as the *naing-ngan-daw* (literally, royal state) or Union, has been the primary referent for "national" security since independence. The current state leadership apparently sees no clear distinction between the state, regime, and the incumbent government. This has led to a reification of the state and its conflation with the regime as well as with the military, which claims to be the guardian of the state.[9]

Because the country is governed by a military junta that exercises absolute power under martial law, alternative conceptions of security are rejected by the government and in fact are viewed as a threat. There is virtually no space for public discourse on the referent of security. Nevertheless, in addition to the armed minority groups, several societal actors and expatriate groups are openly challenging SLORC's right to govern as well as the very idea of a unitary state. Lawfully constituted political parties and "accredited" national groups tread carefully to avoid contravening existing laws and voice their concerns in a muted manner within the bounds of the constitution-drafting process initiated by SLORC in January 1993. Others have either gone underground or taken up residence abroad to confront SLORC. Those groups, which have been outlawed by SLORC, include dissident students, lay activists, dissident monks, some representatives who were elected in the May 1990 elections but not allowed to take their seats, and expatriate activists. Twenty-two groups formed an anti-SLORC united front called the Democratic Alliance of Burma (DAB), and some dissident-elected representatives formed a government-in-exile called the National Coalition Government of the Union of Burma (NCGUB). A shadow parliament in the form of the National Council of the Union of Burma (NCUB) also was established.[10] The common aim of these contenders to SLORC's legitimacy was to install a democratically elected civilian government that would seek a federal solution to satisfy the ethnic groups' demands for greater autonomy.

The ethnic groups find SLORC's conception of state security a threat to their individual well-being as well as to communal interests. There have been allegations of cultural and communal destruction, religious persecution, forced labor, porterage, forced relocation, wanton destruction, discriminatory repression, and collateral damage as manifestations of the state's attempt to enforce security at the expense of nonstate actors and institutions (Rajah 1994: 6–8, 11–12).[11] Moreover, ethnic dissidents identify the military leadership with the majority Bamar, and this, in turn, raises suspicions that a hidden agenda for perpetuating ethnic hegemony is part of SLORC's conception of security wherein the state, the regime, and the military are practically interchangeable (Yaungwe 1990).

SLORC is, nevertheless, determined to press home its interpretation of state security, rejecting the alternative vision of its detractors as not only inimical to its own existence but also detrimental to the perpetuation of Myanmar as a sovereign state. SLORC envisages a "strong" state in which "unity, economic and military strength" are essential elements (*New Light of Myanmar* [hereafter, *NLM*], Apr. 10, 1995). To that end, SLORC's vision of a unitary state is nonnegotiable. The identities of the state, the regime, and the military all seem to have been amalgamated to form a seamless web in which the security interests of one institution cannot be considered apart from those of another.

Security Goals and Perceived Threats

SLORC has enunciated its national objectives in terms of upholding the "Three Main National Causes": nondisintegration of the union, non-disintegration of national solidarity, and perpetuation of sovereignty. According to SLORC these causes are inseparable.

> For perpetuation of the Union [the first aim], unity among our national brethren is essential....
>
> The second aim....National solidarity is essential for non-disintegration of the Union....
>
> Perpetuation of sovereignty, the third aim, is also based on non-disintegration of the Union and non-disintegration of national solidarity. If there is no national unity, the Union will disintegrate and if the Union disintegrates, independence will be lost. These aims are correlated and cannot be separated.[12]

The state's security goals may be identified as an interdependent dyad comprising national unity and state sovereignty. Threats to those goals are deemed to issue from within the state as well as from international sources. Actually, the internal and external dimensions are seen as interrelated, and the principal international security concern is not interstate conflict but external interference in domestic contestation or conflict. The specter that haunts Myanmar's current security elites is "the dangerous mixture of domestic vulnerability and external meddling" (Cohen 1989: 31).

Strict adherence to very narrow notions of sovereignty and independence are sometimes relaxed and trade-offs accepted in the economic dimension. Because the long-standing (1962–88) near-autarkic, inward-looking economic policy was found wanting, SLORC abandoned it in favor of a more open policy soon after coming to power. SLORC has been willing to relax Myanmar's long-cherished notion of territorial sanctity, allowing border trading and tolerating a daily influx of foreigners across the borders with Yunnan and Thailand. It also has given logging and fishing concessions to foreign companies and allowed foreign direct investment to the extent of 100 percent foreign ownership. The agreement signed with Thailand and a multinational consortium in September 1994 for the development of Myanmar's offshore natural gas field and the export of the gas through a pipeline across the border, and the agreement with a Singapore–People's Republic of China consortium to develop a vital port facility near Yangon on an unprecedented BOT (build, operate, transfer) basis, are examples of SLORC's willingness to allow economics to override Myanmar's time-honored practice of conserving its natural resources for own use and maintaining national control of strategic facilities (*Bangkok Post*, Sept. 10, 1994; *Business Times* [Singapore], June 29, 1995). All these steps arise mainly from the need for economic growth to underpin state and regime security. Yet as it opens the state's borders to multinationals, foreign businessmen, and tourists, SLORC seeks to set the rules of the game and reserves the right to change them as it sees fit in the interests of the state in general and its own security in particular.[13]

Domestic Threats

Domestic threats usually are seen by state leaders as closely related to the problem of national unity, whose root causes are attributed to colonial machinations. To understand this perception one must look at Myanmar's historical experience before independence. The separation of "Burma proper" from frontier areas (designated as "Scheduled Areas," populated by non-Bamar ethnic groups) in the administration of the

British colonial state had far-reaching implications for the subsequent creation of an independent Myanmar state. Tantamount to an institutionalized political and sociocultural divide, the separation became a bone of contention for Myanmar nationalists (the majority being Bamar), who accused the British of pursuing a divide-and-rule policy.[14] To the advocates of a unitary state, it seems to have denied the opportunity for the indigenous nationalities of Myanmar to develop a sense of belonging and bonding that would culminate in an "imagined community" of sorts able to forge a modern nation-state out of disparate ethnic "nations" (Anderson 1991).

World War II also highlighted the problem of ethnic tensions between Bamars and indigenous minorities: some minorities loyal to the British crown found themselves at odds with Bamar nationalists who were allies of the Japanese. Heavy-handed behavior by inexperienced nationalist commanders added insult to injury and fostered resentment among communities such as the Kayins of lower Myanmar (Cady 1965: 443–44). Such experiences under Japanese occupation "revived and intensified" the minorities' ancient antagonisms against Bamars for their perceived hegemony. Moreover, such antipathy was "encouraged by the Allies" as part of the war effort (Selth 1986: 495).[15] The antifascist resistance movement also had differential impacts on different ethnic communities, and the differences led to problems in majority-minority relations (Taylor 1982: 14; Selth 1986: 505). A substantial number of ethnic irregulars were recruited by the retreating British, and these Kachin, Kayin, and Chin levies continued their clandestine resistance in the border regions and in their communal base areas. Apparently, "the British government, or at least some of its representatives, were prepared to use [them]...even to the point of deliberately misleading them as to their rewards after the fighting was over" (Selth 1986: 502). As such, a sense of "betrayal" by the British authorities who allowed the postwar decolonization process to be controlled by the Bamar-dominated Anti-Fascist People's Freedom League (AFPFL) was engendered among these "loyal" subjects of the crown—especially the Kayins—thereby aggravating the national unity problem of independent Myanmar (Brown 1994: 59–63).

The solidarity among the national races achieved on the eve of independence was mainly attributed to the stature and charisma of Aung San and did not last very long after his assassination in July 1947. Myanmar's inability to attain the elusive goal of national unity during the first four decades of independence was exemplified by the incessant armed conflict between the central government and a variety of insurgent groups fighting for separation, for autonomy, or to establish a communist state. These insurgencies intensified after the 1962 coup.

Such was the structure of disunity and conflict among the national races that SLORC inherited. Following the 1988 upheaval, it also encountered opposition in the central heartland of Myanmar. Thus, SLORC is challenged on two fronts: the political and social threats in the center and the military insurgency threat on the periphery.

Political Threats

On the political front, the legitimacy of SLORC is being contested, and there also is opposition to the direction and pace of the political change sought by SLORC. Though dismissed as an aberration exploited by communists, power-crazy political aspirants, neocolonialist stooges, anarchists, and criminal elements, the upheaval witnessed in Myanmar during August and September 1988 apparently left an indelible imprint on the military leaders' perceptions of state and regime security and on the nature of state-society relations.[16]

Referred to as the "disturbance" or "affair" by state authorities and the "democratic revolution" by opposition groups, the turbulent episode of 1988 exposed previously unrecognized vulnerabilities of the incumbent regime and, by extension, the state, which found itself confronted by the previously latent opposition—that is, the very subjects who were supposed to be beholden to the state for their own security (Lintner 1990a). Moreover, the upheaval spawned a horde of dissident activists (mainly urban youth) who reacted forcefully to the state's attempt to instill order and compliance during and after the upheaval. Many of these activists are determined to carry on the struggle against SLORC by whatever means available. Most significant, it led to the emergence of Aung San Suu Kyi as an immensely popular champion of liberal democracy and human rights as well as the preeminent leader of the National League for Democracy (NLD), the most popular of the political parties formed after the 1988 upheaval. Suu Kyi is the charismatic daughter of Aung San, founding father of the armed forces and the widely acclaimed savior of modern Myanmar. As it confronted the polity, the military found itself in a situation akin to "protracted social conflict"; its corporate solidarity was threatened and the long-nurtured image of the patriotic "peoples' armed forces" had been tarnished (Rajah 1994: 3–8). As such, the military's "legitimacy as a social institution," which in the past had been "maintained through an emotionally determined public loyalty," seems to have suffered, thereby heightening the military's sense of vulnerability (Harries-Jenkins and van Doorn 1976: 4).

The political opposition, encouraged by the defection of some military personnel at the height of the 1988 upheaval, later made overtures to sway the military rank and file in their favor. At the same time they dropped hints about possible retribution against the top leaders, which raised the possibility of a divided military that could lead to civil war. These overtures were accompanied by many attempts to defy and obstruct the military's activities.[17] Given the historical experience of military units joining the communist rebellion as well as the mutiny by Kayin troops during the Kayin separatist insurrection, the fear of divided loyalties leading to the dismemberment of the military still remains extremely credible to SLORC. Thus, for the military leadership the quest for national unity begins in the barracks, and the maintenance of cohesion and solidarity within the Tatmadaw is the paramount—perhaps the overriding—security concern. In all probability, this is the perspective from which SLORC views and assesses all domestic threats.

After some 26 years of depoliticization of Myanmar society, the political awakening triggered by the 1988 upheaval liberated vast pent-up emotions and energy sympathetic to the regime's opponents, who used democracy as a catch-all term to challenge SLORC's legitimacy.[18] Consequently, the mobilization of the polity by the politicians and the tremendous surge of political activity following the relative widening of the political space were accompanied by sharp criticisms of the military's conduct in the 1988 upheaval and of its subsequent role in administering the state. Meanwhile, the Western press, nongovernmental organizations (NGOs), expatriate dissident groups, and even governments continually condemned and criticized the military over a wide spectrum of issues ranging from logging to human rights, while praising and lionizing the opposing dissidents. Moreover, international interest in the ethnic insurgencies was rekindled by widespread media coverage, which shifted from urban Myanmar to the border enclaves of the armed opposition groups in the aftermath of the 1988 upheaval. The military suddenly found itself in an unaccustomed role, as insurgent groups were depicted as freedom fighters and allies of democracy. Consequently, the security discourse of the central decision makers took on a new theme: legitimate the central role of the military in politics and governance to safeguard the state. Typically, the refrain has gone like this:

> The Tatmadaw [armed forces], since 1988 has been giving priority to implementing the tasks...to bring peace and tranquillity and to ensure rule of law in the country and [political] stability....Our Tatmadaw has laid stress on national reconciliation for restoring perpetual peace....A duty to build our nation anew for its advancement and prosperity devolves on us. So, in essence the Tatmadaw should be able to participate...in the national political leadership role of the future Myanmar.[19]

Social Threats

A particular threat, identified by successive Myanmar governments since the early 1970s, is the drug problem. The BSPP government declared that the proliferation of narcotic drugs (especially heroin) was a national scourge and took measures to mobilize the entire population in the fight against trafficking and use. Drugs have been regarded as a threat to national security because of their dissipative impact on the nation's human resources. The narcotics problem, especially in the form of the armed drug-trafficking groups, is both a social threat and a major source of instability in the border regions. Many of the regime's detractors have accused the military of colluding with the ex-insurgent groups, which had peace pacts with the government, in sustaining the drug trade. All this being said, the narcotics problem in all likelihood remains high on the lists of threats confronting the Myanmar state.[20]

There is also the problem of illegal immigration. Despite Myanmar's strict immigration laws, migrants from China (Yunnan) and Bangladesh (previously East Pakistan) have continued to stream into the country over the last four decades. Stemming mainly from population pressures and the pull of family ties, as well as perceived economic benefits, this phenomenon has been viewed by successive governments as an internal security and law enforcement problem. During the Cold War and at the height of the communist and Muslim separatist insurgencies, it also was seen as an aspect of the military security problem, in that the migrants could have been prone to irredentist tendencies or could have become a fifth column for their homeland. Since the late 1970s, however, illegal migration has been looked upon more as a social and religiocultural threat against national identity. In the 1990s there have been growing concerns about migration from Yunnan; especially in light of the perceived economic clout of the migrant Chinese (Maung 1994). Conscious of the negative socioeconomic impact of migration from India during the colonial period, Myanmar's present leaders are beginning to take the threat seriously.[21]

Military Insurgency Threats

As noted earlier, the paramount security concern in the first decade of independence was national survival in the face of multiple insurgencies (Government of Burma 1949a, 1949b, 1952; Nu 1958). The military government that came to power through the March 1962 coup claimed that it had to intervene and take political power to prevent the dismemberment of the state by ethnic minorities who were taking advantage of the disunity among the ruling political elites (Than 1989: 41). The insurgency threat was viewed as the principal security problem, and its complete annihilation by military means was the goal (BSPP 1985: 29–30). The military threat posed by the insurgencies escalated in the aftermath of the 1988 upheaval as a consequence of the alliance between student groups and ethnic insurgents as well as the material and moral support garnered by the Democratic Alliance of Burma. But over the years this threat has declined greatly.

The militarily most powerful communist insurgency ceased to be a threat to the government after the ethnic rank and file revolted against the aging leadership in April 1989 and sought a truce with SLORC. The top leadership escaped to China, where they were given refuge on humanitarian grounds (Lintner 1990b: 44–46, 51–54). The dismembered armed units of the Burma Communist Party (BCP), however, still have not been demobilized; they have been maintained as local militia who could some day resort to armed struggle if their demands for local autonomy are not satisfied. In fact, this is true of many armed ethnic groups who have entered into cease-fire arrangements with SLORC (Kyi 1994: 227–28).

As a result of opening up the economy and the greatly improved relations between the Myanmar and Thai militaries, the Thais appear to have discarded their previous policy of regarding the ethnic groups along the border as a security buffer. The lack of Thai support has severely constrained communications and logistics for those groups. There also has been a change in SLORC's conflict management strategy, which now allows a two-pronged approach of exerting military pressure while offering peace negotiations. Consequently, beginning with the erstwhile communists, sixteen armed groups—including the Kachin, who were the most potent military adversary, the tenacious Mon, whose territory covered important trading routes in southern Myanmar, and the Mong-Tai Army (MTA), which under the drug lord Khun Sa reputedly controlled much of the opium and heroin output of the infamous Golden Triangle (Myanmar-Thailand-Laos)—have accepted the government's peace offer extended on a bilateral basis.[22] The armed student groups formed from the scattered remnants of the 1988 uprising also are affected by factional struggle and by attrition due to disease and to re-patriation and refugee settlement programs. These factors have reduced the number of insurgent groups by some 60 percent and their combined armed strength by more than 80 percent.[23]

The oldest ethnic insurgency, waged by the powerful Kayin minority, which attracted the most media attention as the military backbone of the DAB, NCUB, and the NCGUB, has all but disintegrated since its central headquarters at Manerplaw fell to a rebel faction in early 1995.

This was a double blow for anti-SLORC forces, because the symbolically important headquarters of the DAB, NCUB, and NCGUB was no more. The subsequent political humiliation of losing the liberated zone and the seat of the provisional government turned out to be a death knell for the grand alliance of democratic activists and ethnic dissidents. The internal revolt by Buddhist Kayins against a mainly Christian Kayin leadership was brought about by a confluence of war fatigue, the religious insensitivity of the inept leadership, and the government peace overture. That conflict effectively neutralized the Kayin "revolution." The losing faction, having lost perhaps three-quarters of its armed strength and now denied its territorial reach, vowed to carry on the fight through guerrilla tactics, but its heyday as a quasi-provisional government controlling territorial enclaves in the regions bordering Thailand is over.

There are a smattering of other marginal insurgents representing dissident Muslims and the Rakhine, Wa, Dawei, Chin, and Naga groups. They have very little political clout and are capable of only small-scale guerrilla action, harassment, and sabotage.

External Threats

In the 1990s Myanmar does not have to face any adversarial state or a militarily hostile external environment. It does not have any serious dispute with its neighbors, nor is it involved in any regional disagreements. Myanmar has, since the early 1950s, astutely used its neutral foreign policy and friendly relations with virtually all states in the international system to avoid involvement in the Cold War or in regional rivalries (Han 1988: 18–20; Taylor 1983: 102–4).

Nevertheless, Myanmar leaders always have been mindful that contiguous land borders with Bangladesh, India, China, Thailand, and Laos are potential sources of conflict and contention. Given the current level of amity between Myanmar and China, the latter is seen more as a powerful ally than a threat per se, though the sheer size of such a powerful neighbor, which is rapidly developing into an economic giant, must be rather disconcerting for Myanmar's leaders. The economic ties between China and Myanmar are still developing at a fast pace, and the interests of the two states are likely to overlap considerably in the foreseeable future. The high point of China-Myanmar ties was symbolized by the visit of Chinese premier Li Peng to Yangon in December 1994, which was reciprocated by Senior General Than Shwe, the SLORC chairman, in January 1996. Although there have been regional concerns over speculations of closer strategic ties between the two countries, there is no hard evidence to suggest that any such relationship has developed (Richardson 1995).

Relations with India, which had been rather cool because of its offer of refuge to anti-SLORC dissidents and its pro-opposition stance, have improved considerably since 1992 when New Delhi decided to accommodate the military government. Since the opening of the border trade, the reestablishment of air links between the two countries, and the reported cooperative interdiction of Mizo insurgents by the two armies, there seems to be no basis for viewing India as a threat despite India's concern that Myanmar might become a client state of China (*Straits Times*, June 5, 1995; Selth 1995). Nevertheless, Sino-Indian rivalry could become a security issue for Myanmar in the years to come (Malik 1994).

Similarly, after having amicably settled the Rohingya refugee problem of 1991 with Bangladesh, Myanmar apparently has no reason to view its weak western neighbor as a serious threat.[24] The subnational threat of illegal migration remains a problem, but it could be seen as a domestic issue rather than an external security one.

Laos was the first country whose head of government visited Myanmar after SLORC assumed power. It always has been a benign neighbor, and the landlocked state is seen more as a friendly partner in curbing the Golden Triangle narcotics trade and developing the Mekong River Basin than as a viable threat (*NLM*, Feb. 10, 1994).

Thailand is probably the most problematic among Myanmar's neighbors in security terms. Historically, Myanmar and Thailand have been rivals. And Thailand's long-standing practice of utilizing "buffer zones" occupied by anti-Yangon rebels as part of its border security policy has been a source of irritation for Myanmar (see Lintner 1995a: 46–49). But after Thailand initiated the "constructive engagement" policy toward Myanmar in the wake of the latter's more open economic policy, bilateral relations improved rapidly. The military establishments in both countries have repeatedly emphasized the fraternal relationship between them.[25] The visit of the Thai prime minister Banharn Silpa-archa to Myanmar in March 1996 heralded the renewal of close ties between the two countries; those ties had been under threat for some time from tensions brought about by disputes and disagreements over border security, the territorial boundary, and resource extractions. Such tensions reached a climax in May 1995 when speculation about possible armed confrontation between the two sides appeared in the Thai press, but they were later defused through bilateral military interactions.[26]

Despite some hiccups, Thailand has become a major investor in Myanmar—the third biggest, in fact, behind Singapore and Britain as of the end of October 1996. The Thai business lobby is a powerful advocate of improving bilateral relations. Nonetheless, recurring problems associated with illegal logging, black-market trade, fish poaching, and contentious territorial claims will continue to have serious security implications.

As of now, Myanmar does not perceive external threats in the form of hostile states bent on conflict and conquest. Yangon's primary concern is with external actors who seek to intervene in the internal affairs of the state to influence the way in which Yangon deals with its domestic problems.[27] Two examples of external threats perceived by Myanmar are international support for anti-SLORC opposition in general and for Aung San Suu Kyi in particular, and the Western imposition of universal norms for human rights and democracy, environmental protection, and utilization of labor.[28] Myanmar leaders see the clamoring for the release of "political prisoners" and for "dialogue" with Aung San Suu Kyi, as well as calls for handing power over to the elected representatives who won the 1990 elections, as attempts by Western governments, legislators, lobbying groups, and NGOs to destabilize the state and undermine governmental authority. Condemnations of military porterage, "voluntary labor" for public works, relocation of urban dwellers, exploitation of natural resources, and the constitution-drafting process also are perceived as attacks on the government's "laudable" social, economic, and political development policies (Lintner 1991; Amnesty International 1992; Weller 1993: 263–442).

> Such attempts by external actors to influence SLORC's behavior are regarded as unwarranted interferences that aggravate the problem of domestic threats by imparting external pressure against the government and simultaneously giving sustenance to the regime's opponents. Thus, the military leadership's refrain has been that the former colonial powers sought to maintain some sort of hold in one way or the other....There are still signs of trying to maintain their influence through machinations which are quite transparent....
>
> With all these threats...leaders here and in all the former colonies have to be on the lookout for any act of encroachment on sovereignty or threat to national security. ("Perspectives," *NLM*, Jan. 23, 1995)[29]

Approaches to Security

The current leadership seems to be driven by nationalism and notions of self-reliance, as well as by a distrust of aliens and of the West in particular. Myanmar's approach to security concerns, focused overwhelmingly at the national level, embodies both competitive and cooperative strategies. At the domestic level, SLORC's strategy employs massive force in conjunction with some forms of dialogue and accommodation to handle the insurgency threat. In its efforts to neutralize political threats to the regime, SLORC seems to be banking on rapid economic development, coercion, and firm military control over the political process. At the international level, the traditional strategies of bilateralism and nonalignment are now supplemented by regional cooperation through the Association of Southeast Asian Nations (ASEAN). But the realist approach to security through military strength has not been neglected, although the current expansion of the military has to do more with domestic political control and military corporate solidarity than with external defense. The leitmotif of Myanmar's approaches to resolving or alleviating problems of state security seems to be an emphasis on self-reliance stemming from both necessity (in the light of a Western-inspired moratorium on official aid and trade) and choice.

Managing Political Challenges to the Regime

As a result of the military's praetorian tendency, reinforced by its politicized roots in a national liberation movement, the military has assumed a dual role in both civil and military affairs. In short, the military culture is now the dominant political culture in Myanmar. The current crop of military leaders is not prepared to leave the fate of the future Myanmar state in the hands of political parties and is pushing for the adoption of a constitution that allows the emergence of a strong state led by an autonomous military. Completely free from civilian political control, the military is assuming a symbiotic relationship with the state, a relationship it seeks to institutionalize under the new constitution. That would exclude political parties from a role in defining the national interest and setting the policy agenda. This purpose is evident in the Armed Forces Day address given by Senior General Than Shwe on March 27, 1995, in which he stated. "In accord with the emerging Constitution, the duty to build our nation anew for its advancement and prosperity devolves on us. So, in essence, Tatmadaw should be able to participate, with genuine goodwill, in the national political leadership role of the future Myanmar" (*NLM*, Mar. 28, 1995).

To that end, the military has steered the national convention entrusted with the task of drafting a new constitution toward entrenching the dominant political role of the military in that document.[30] Among the 104 "fundamental principles" underlying the prospective constitution, there are provisions to reserve one-quarter of all seats in the legislature for military representatives nominated by the armed forces commander in chief. Furthermore, the military will enjoy complete autonomy with its commander in chief designated as the supreme commander. Ministerial portfolios in the central government for defense, security / home affairs, and border areas are reserved for military personnel nominated by the commander in chief, who will also nominate the deputy ministers. Furthermore, coordination with the commander in chief is required to appoint military personnel to any other ministerial or deputy ministerial post. The assignment of military personnel to leading governing bodies of self-administered areas is also the commander in chief's prerogative. Moreover, there will be a provision for the supreme commander to assume state power in a national emergency.

Another guiding principle for the drafting of the new constitution states that the executive president must be elected by an electoral college and should be "well acquainted with the affairs of State such as political administrative, economics and military affairs." Given this requirement, it is extremely likely that the future president will be recruited from those with a military background. Between them, the president and the commander in chief of the armed forces will wield considerable executive authority according to these guiding principles. In this configuration, which effectively insulates state power from political competition and representation, the military will retain its control over national security policies and practices as well as those concerning all important national issues.

In the process of managing the political transition from the previous one-party socialist system to a military-controlled, multiparty electoral system, Myanmar's leaders are prepared to use force and the full coercive power of the state against those who challenge SLORC's authority and legitimacy. Thus, SLORC deals with those who defy existing laws or contravene martial law provisions mainly by sentencing them to long prison terms or taking them into protective custody under the Law Protecting the State from Dangers of Disruptive Elements. For example, opposition leader Aung San Suu Kyi was placed under house arrest on July 20, 1989, for "repeated infringements of the [above] law; especially activities which threaten the safety of the state" and for attempting "to sow discord between the people and the Tatmadaw" (SLORC Information Committee 1990: 5).[31]

As spelled out by Senior General Than Shwe, SLORC justifies its uncompromising stance by positing that

> this transitional period is fraught with danger. You will have seen the disintegration of some countries in the period of transition from the old system to the new. There are instances where even some big nations ran into difficulties for having used carbon copies of democracy and human rights. In this connection, what we have accepted is that the most basic human right is right to food, clothing and shelter. (*NLM*, Apr. 8, 1995)

To institutionalize its grip on society, SLORC established in September 1993 the Union Solidarity and Development Association (USDA). The aims of USDA are to promote and vitalize national pride and the "emergence of a prosperous, peaceful and modern Union" (*NLM*, Aug. 2, 1994). Though registered as a private social organization, USDA is regarded by the regime's critics as an institutionalized patronage system to support the current regime (Diller 1996: 18–19). Others point out that it resembles Indonesia's Golkar and that it is meant to sustain military's political influence (Steinberg 1996: 14; Sundhaussen 1995: 777).

In response to the onslaught of Western media, SLORC set up an information committee that held more than 100 news conferences between September 1988 and July 1990. Entry visas for foreign reporters, academics, and even some critics—except those who were blacklisted—were issued, in contrast to an almost total ban on foreign reporters and analysts during the socialist era. SLORC also set up a committee to produce Myanmar's postindependence history, and another series on the history of the armed forces is being published. The government's information agencies produce an astonishingly high number of books, magazines, articles, news bulletins, and audio-visual materials in an apparent attempt to counter the negative portrayal by the dissident groups and the regime's detractors.[32] Apart from state control of radio, television, and newspapers, extensive control of private printing and audio-video output is enforced through elaborate rules and regulations on registration, monitoring, and censorship (Allot 1993).

In the past, the governing elites of Myanmar employed reproduction of the traditional concepts of power, authority, culture, and religion for the purpose of nation-building and the legitimation of their regimes (Myint 1994; Steinberg 1992: 223, 228–29; Wiant 1981: 60–66). Since the nation gained independence, successive regimes have constructed a Myanmar national identity, based on Bamar values, for the multiethnic and multireligious indigenous communities. Those constructions have tended to appeal to the spirit of cooperation and racial harmony reputedly achieved during the national liberation struggle, which culminated in the 1949 Panlong Agreement wherein some non-Bamar ethnic groups decided to throw their lot in with the Bamar in a united effort to gain independence and statehood.

The military tradition of the monarchic period recently has become the focus of much attention as an exemplar for a strong national identity. Portrayed as the legacy of Myanmar's liberation movement, the military has long been portrayed as a model for national unity and hailed as the embodiment of the patriotic and altruistic spirit of a "true Myanmar." In this vein, the glorious legends of Myanmar warrior kings and military heroes of the past have been revived in all forms of mass media and joined with the exploits of the national liberation struggle, together with the more recent "victories" of the armed forces against the enemies of the state. Although war and conflict per se have never been glorified and militarism as such has not been advocated, the military profession in the context of the noble duty of safeguarding the state and protecting its citizens has been much acclaimed (Wiant 1981: 67; Sarpay 1992; Media Group 1994).

Nationalism and self-reliance, recurring themes since independence, are being reiterated with the slogan "Our strength lies within our country." Resistance to the encroachment of alien ways and values is advocated, and depictions of the negative aspects of "decadent" Western societies are presented through the state-controlled media, apparently to rally the public around the military's endeavor to develop national values, indigenous literature and culture, and a Buddhist ethos. The Buddhist polity is presented with the military leadership's pious promotion of the *sangha* (order of monks and novices) and *sasana* (the legacy of Buddha by word and deed).[33]

In its attempt to instill patriotism, unity, and self-reliance in the polity, the leadership's constant refrain has been:

> The Union of Myanmar had stood tall among the nations of the world as a sovereign and independent nation with its own monarchy and leaders for thousands of years....At present neo-colonialists are waiting for an opportunity to influence Myanmar again and interfere in its internal affairs....[They] are trying to harm unity of national races and cause disintegration of the Union with the use of traitors in the country through crooked means....It is of utmost importance to vitalize patriotism and nationalist fervour....It is necessary to cleanse ourselves of inclinations to think highly of foreign nations, to imitate foreign cultures and to be swayed by external instigations and internal persuasions.[34]

All in all, the military portrays itself "not simply as a defender but as the core of [Myanmar] society" (Steinberg 1993: 163). This propagation of the military ethos and the reproduction of traditions, in the name of unity, harmony, and cultural integrity, provides a rationale for the military to play a leading role in the political and sociocultural life of Myanmar. The assumption, of course, is that such a portrayal would enhance regime security and safeguard the traditional way of life, as interpreted by the ruling elites, against the uncertainties of modernity.

Other SLORC tactics include accommodation and coercion. More than 2,000 political detainees have been released since April 1992, including ex-general Tin Oo and the NLD chairman Kyi Maung, both of whom had been serving long prison sentences for sedition and contravention of the Official Secrets Act. In January 1993 the sentences (ranging from ten years to death) of citizens convicted since the military came to power were commuted.[35] The government managed to confound and surprise its critics by initially engaging in a dialogue with Aung San Suu Kyi and later releasing her unconditionally on July 10, 1995. In releasing its arch foe, who apparently was no longer considered a serious security threat, SLORC exhibited its high confidence in its ability to manage the political transition. Thus far, it appears to have been a low-cost, high-benefit measure. SLORC received international acclaim without any detrimental consequences to regime security, demonstrating that SLORC is capable of utilizing conciliatory measures to its advantage.[36]

The government, however, is not averse to using its coercive powers when it judges a situation threatening enough to warrant punitive actions. A case in point was its response to Aung San Suu Kyi's attempt in May 1996 to call a meeting at her residence of party representatives who were elected in May 1990. This act of defiance, apparently timed to coincide with the sixth anniversary of the general elections in which the NLD won more than 80 percent of the seats, was seen by the government as a serious provocation that challenged the legitimacy and authority of the ruling military junta. In a preemptive move, the authorities detained more than 200 elected representatives of the NLD for "questioning." With more than 90 percent of the delegates absent, Aung San Suu Kyi then upped the ante by transforming the meeting into a party congress. The Western media and governments entered the fray and soundly condemned the government for its actions while encouraging the NLD leaders. During the course of the congress, the state-sponsored national constitutional convention was harshly criticized and a resolution was passed entrusting the party's central executive committee to draw up the NLD version of the state constitution. That action prompted the military leadership to launch a vitriolic media blitz against both the NLD leadership and its foreign sympathizers. Organized mass rallies sprang up all over the country, wherein the NLD leadership was denounced for its unpatriotic and self-serving acts and the progress on all fronts under the present government was solemnly reaffirmed. The rallies were followed by a nationwide poster campaign against "neo-colonialists, foreign stooges and destructionists." Moreover, a new law entitled "The Law Protecting the Peaceful and Systematic Transfer of State Responsibility and the Successful Performance of the Functions of the National Convention Against Disturbances and Oppositions" was enacted on June 7, 1996. This law imposes tough penalties for infringements: harsh jail sentences for individuals and a variety of punishments for organizations that include deregistration, suspension, confiscation of assets, and banning.

Managing Relations with Ethnic Minorities

SLORC has been quite successful in dealing with the insurgent threat. Until 1989, peace negotiations between the government and the rebels had not been particularly successful, and several amnesties had not been enough to win over the majority of rebels. The armed opposition always insisted on political recognition, the right to retain their military organization, and territorial rights as conditions for conflict resolution—terms that the government of the day could not concede to.

Under Senior General Than Shwe's leadership, circumstances and (more or less self-imposed) constraints on both sides have changed considerably, with remarkable results. First, weakened by internal dissent the communist rebel organization disintegrated in 1989. Breaking the ideological mold, the various units reorganized themselves into ethnic-based groups and made peace with the government. Subsequently, in a radical departure from the past, SLORC instituted a new modus vivendi for armed opposition groups wishing to "come to the light." This approach allows the ex-rebel groups to function as indigenous ethnic organizations with their own militia and recognizes their leaders' authority over their base areas. These indigenous group leaders are accorded a say in the development of their respective regions and also may take part in the ongoing constitutional process. Meanwhile, military pressure is kept up on the more intransigent groups, punctuated by gestures of goodwill such as the unilateral moratorium on offensive operations in the Kayin state that was announced in April 1992.

To alleviate the problem of the developmental gap between central Myanmar and the outlying regions, SLORC formed a high-level border area development committee in 1989 and initiated the Ministry for Progress of Border Areas and National Races and Development Affairs in January 1994. These groups are seeking to foster national solidarity through the socioeconomic development of areas where the ethnic minorities reside and rebel enclaves have been situated. The government envisages a multisector border area development scheme covering sixteen target areas in Myanmar's western, northern, and eastern border regions, encompassing nearly 59,000 square miles (19 percent of the state's total area) and 3.5 million inhabitants. To be implemented over the eleven years from 1993 to 2004, the scheme includes infrastructure and human resources development, social welfare enhancement, and economic activities in agriculture, forestry, livestock breeding, trade, energy generation, and mineral exploration and exploitation. Despite the detractors' contention that the plan is a ploy to extend state hegemony over the ethnic minorities and that forced labor is being used for infrastructure development, the plan's impact on the local populations, combined with the economic opportunities created by border trade, seems to have reinforced the government's claim that it will uphold the interests of indigenous races. The armed rebel groups responded by accepting the truce on the terms offered by the government, which are similar to those given to the ex-communists.

These agreements do not imply, however, that the problems of ethnic minorities have been overcome. In the short to medium term, violent guerrilla action by intransigent elements can be quite damaging to the fragile peace, and development projects are especially vulnerable to such attacks. Moreover, it would be fanciful to expect that tensions arising out of alienation, misperception, mistrust, enmity, and insecurity, exacerbated by decades of traumatic confrontation, could be removed overnight.[37] After the initial step of achieving a truce, the more complex and difficult tasks of reconciling different views and aspirations with regard to regional autonomy, ethnic relations, resource allocations, and other divisive issues remain to be tackled.

International Strategies: Toward Regionalism

Myanmar's "independent foreign policy," presumably guided by the five principles of peaceful coexistence, has been consciously dictated by the country's "geographical position and perceptions of what constitutes its own security" (Han 1988: 69).[38] Foreign policy has been intertwined with the security policy aimed at preserving independence, ensuring the perpetuation of the unitary nature of the Myanmar state, and safeguarding its territorial integrity through national unity and internal strength. Strict neutrality and nonalignment, combined with low-key bilateral relations, have been the means employed to achieve these goals. Myanmar's political and military leaders have always been sensitive to regional and extraregional developments and have constantly taken great pains to avoid situations that would give outsiders the slightest excuse for aggression or intervention in Myanmar's domestic affairs.

SLORC is now actively pursuing a policy of developing close bilateral relations with its regional neighbors by utilizing economic ties. China, which has extended assistance in the economic and military spheres, has become a staunch ally. The ASEAN states have adopted a "constructive engagement" policy and have become major investors in Myanmar. Moreover, Yangon is relying increasingly on ASEAN's support to counter Western attacks and boycotts (Than 1994). Myanmar has been steadily drawn into the ASEAN community. Thailand invited Foreign Minister Ohn Gyaw to the 1994 ASEAN Ministerial Meeting in Bangkok. In March 1995, Ohn Gyaw, who was accompanying Senior General Than Shwe on his official visit to Vietnam, publicly expressed Myanmar's interest in joining ASEAN (*Straits Times*, Mar. 12, 1995). In July of that year Myanmar acceded to the ASEAN Treaty of Amity and Cooperation. Brunei extended to Ohn Gyaw the privilege of attending the 1995 ASEAN Ministerial Meeting, where Myanmar formally presented the instrument of accession to the treaty. Myanmar's junta leader, Senior General Than Shwe, was subsequently invited to attend the Bangkok summit of leaders from the "Southeast Asian ten" in December 1995 (*Straits Times*, Dec. 13, 1995). Myanmar's desire to embrace ASEAN is further exemplified by its unprecedented move in signing the Southeast Asia Nuclear Weapons Free Zone (SEANWFZ) treaty at the Bangkok summit. The ASEAN attitude toward Myanmar generally has been favorable, and Myanmar was granted observer status at the 1996 ASEAN foreign ministers' meeting in Jakarta and became a full-fledged member in July 1997.

Thus, Myanmar—which has diligently pursued its neutrality to the extent of leaving the Nonaligned Movement in 1979—has broken significant new ground. After eschewing participation in regional groups and relying on friendly bilateral relations with all nations, Myanmar's foreign policy has come full circle since the country's endorsement of the spirit of regional cooperation during the 1955 Bandung Conference. ASEAN's attraction to Myanmar lies in the association's "constructive engagement" policy. Constructive engagement emphasizes confidence-building measures predicated on noninterference in internal affairs, demonstration effect, gentle persuasion, and quiet diplomacy, thereby enhancing mutual trust and goodwill. SLORC, which has perceived itself as under siege from Western powers, can gain legitimacy (both within and outside the country) by being part of the internationally respected regional group. It seems that both economic and political (domestic as well as international) imperatives are behind Myanmar's move to integrate itself with the region via ASEAN (Sukhumbhand 1996: 6).

Myanmar also secured membership in the ASEAN Regional Forum (ARF) and participated in the ARF meeting that immediately followed the ASEAN Ministerial Meeting of July 1996. Myanmar's acceptance into ASEAN's foremost forum for multilateral security discussion may be seen as another significant success for the country's central decision makers' efforts to gain legitimacy and employ the cooperative approach in the area of regional security.

Myanmar also has been a strong participant in multilateral forums such as the U.N. General Assembly and other U.N.–sponsored conferences, where it has staunchly defended its position on human rights, democracy, and development and emphasized its achievements in economic growth, privatization, border areas development, drug eradication, and national reconciliation.[39]

In essence, Myanmar leaders have employed bilateral diplomacy within the framework of strict neutralism to establish friendly relations with all countries, particularly regional states. That policy was supplemented in the 1990s by attempts to enter into regional cooperation through ASEAN institutions. In addition to improving Myanmar's external security environment, diplomacy also serves as an adjunct to domestic security measures in shoring up the regime against threats from within.

The Military Dimension

As we have seen, the paramount concern of the present military leadership has been the perpetuation of unity and corporate solidarity in the armed forces. Dire warnings about the catastrophic consequences of disunity and cleavage in the military have been enunciated repeatedly by its leaders. The rank and file are reminded constantly of the threats posed by an array of hostile elements such as communists, ethnic insurgents, so-called "treasonous minions" of left- and right-wing interventionists, neoimperialists and neocolonials, the irresponsible Western media, self-serving expatriates and maligned lobbies, hypocritical proponents of human rights and democracy, and a hostile world order.

In response to the perceived threats to corporate solidarity posed by the political opposition, the military closed ranks amid the fear of individual retribution and divisive factionalism. This sentiment is exemplified by the statement made by General Saw Maung at the 44th Anniversary Armed Forces Day parade on March 27, 1989:

> Our State has been able to stand firm and united because our Tatmadaw, from its very inception has been standing firm unitedly, loyally and valiantly....You have witnessed the unity and solidarity of our Tatmadaw in the recent incidence [the 1988 upheaval]. However much the unscrupulous persons tried to sow discord among us, we rallied around the Tatmadaw we loved...adhering to the principle that our Tatmadaw is our father and our mother. (Government of Myanmar 1991: 101–2)

Attempts have been made to raise the professional capability of the armed forces through reorganization, expansion, and procurement of modern weapons. After 1988 the number of regional commands were increased from nine to ten and the number of combat divisions from nine to ten. Three new regional control commands with respective combat units were established for border regions where cease-fires are in force. Air force, navy, and infantry combat arms such as armor and artillery, air defense, and signals were expanded through the formation of additional units equipped with materiel purchased from abroad (Selth 1996: 174–89). Upgrading of senior ranks has been instituted across the board, ostensibly to bring command and staff positions in line with the rank structure practiced internationally. The total strength of the armed forces reportedly was increased from some 180,000 in 1987 to 286,000 in 1995 (International Institute for Strategic Studies 1987, 1995).[40]

Arms, ammunition, and equipment with a market value of about U.S.$2 billion reportedly have been purchased.[41] The procurement included small arms ammunition, automatic rifles, machine guns, rocket-propelled grenade launchers, mortars and mortar bombs, recoilless rifles, aerial ordnance, trucks and other vehicles, Yugoslav and Chinese supersonic jet fighters, Chinese military transports, Polish helicopters, Chinese-made light and main battle tanks and tracked armored vehicles, air defense radar, surface-to-air missiles, antiaircraft and long-range artillery, multiple rocket launchers, Hainan-class patrol boats, Jianghu-class missile-armed frigates, Yugoslav coastal patrol crafts and a variety of surveillance and communication equipment. However, whether these weapons and equipment can be effectively utilized and maintained remains questionable.

According to a knowledgeable observer, despite the massive expansion program and the modernization of its military inventory, Myanmar "still does not possess any real power-projection capability" (Selth 1996: 148, 152). It seems that SLORC has undertaken this expansion and modernization for "purely domestic political reasons" and out of the "fear that it might lose its monopoly of political power" (Selth 1996: 154). It can also be seen as a measure taken to satisfy the demands within the military for more professionalism and to uplift the morale of the combat services—especially the navy and the air force—which have been saddled with obsolescent equipment for a long time. As such, the military expansion does not contradict the domestic orientation of Myanmar's security conception, even though taken at face value it creates the impression of a classic realist attempt to enhance the country's military capability to counter external aggression.

Conclusion

In the Myanmar conception, the security of the state, regime, and military are conflated. A threat to any one institution is seen as a threat to all. The primary security concerns—national unity and regime security—are internal and lie in the political dimension. Ethnic separatism, which has threatened Myanmar's unity from within since independence, is currently contained. But contestation of the regime has become more acute since 1988 and is currently the chief concern of SLORC. The economic dimension is viewed essentially in terms of enhancing regime legitimacy and making available the resources to build military power and solidarity. At the international level the concern is with state sovereignty and territorial integrity. In the post-1988 period, Myanmar's government has become concerned with external, primarily Western, attempts to undermine its authority by supporting human rights and democratic activists in Myanmar.

In summary, the values included under the label of security are the unity of the military and its dominant political role; domestic order and stability; national unity; and the territorial integrity of the state. They are all assumed to be interdependent and no clear rank ordering can be ascertained, although at the moment regime security appears to have the highest priority. The approaches deployed by the central decision makers over the last four decades embrace both competitive and cooperative strategies. Military force was the primary means used to deal with the threat posed by ethnic minorities until SLORC came to power. Since then, accommodation has yielded successful results—at least for now. As for the political threats to incumbent regimes, the strategy used during the socialist era from 1962 to 1988 was again a mixture of coercion and co-optation. In the mid-1990s, however, SLORC has become intolerant of political opposition and the strategy has become much more coercive. In external relations, Myanmar pursued a cooperative strategy based on strict neutrality up to 1962 and then retreated to isolation during 1963–72 period. Thereafter, a broad neutralist orientation stressing bilateralism was evident. Under strong attack and criticism from the West, SLORC in the 1990s appears to be moving toward regional cooperation via ASEAN.

SLORC believes that a firm grip by the military on the social, political, and economic dimensions of the state is necessary to achieve national security. Economic prosperity through foreign direct investment and state-regulated private initiatives also is viewed as a necessary ingredient of the security matrix to ease management of political transition, promote national reconciliation, and enhance military strength. Since independence, overt security challenges to the Myanmar state have been internal. Naturally, then, forty years of incessant internal conflict have produced a bias toward domestic security concerns. The fixation on national unity and regime security as the pivotal elements of the national security problematic has led to a preference for order and conformity over pluralism and diversity. The state is continually portrayed as under attack from enemies labeled "economic insurgents," "black marketeers," "extremists," "destructionists," "saboteurs," "axe handles of foreign powers," "neocolonialists," and "cultural imperialists." The concept of internal security often has been manipulated to serve the interests of incumbent governments.

The state's conception of security is contested. The regime's detractors point out that the very notion of state security divorced from concerns for "human security" has resulted in a "security psychosis" that has led to the present predicament of domestic opposition and Western reproach (Booth and Vale 1995: 295). In this respect, the state's conception of national security is seen as a "euphemism for the ambitions and self-image" of the ruling elites (Cohen 1989: 50). In fact, the contention is that "in its usage, the concept has degenerated into a labelling device" and its "specification…in turn depends on the presumably self-serving interpretation given it by the national leadership" (Khong 1991: 14).

The security problematic of Myanmar is thus enmeshed in the problems of political legitimacy and national unity that accompany the process of state-making along the lines of a modern majoritarian state (Ayoob 1993). In the domestic context, the current conception of state security held by the military leadership is highly state-centric and of a zero-sum nature. Moreover, it is conflated with regime security. It will have to be modified to incorporate societal elements if the goals of national solidarity and political stability are to be achieved. At the regional and international levels, it remains to be seen whether the cautious steps taken thus far to incorporate regionalism into the traditional neutralism are sufficient to keep up with the dynamic regional and international developments that impinge upon state security. All in all, one can safely say that the past and present fixation on domestic security in Myanmar will remain well into the next century.

Thailand
The Elite's Shifting Conceptions of Security

PANITAN WATTANAYAGORN

Thailand's national security practice, like that of many other countries, has been dominated by its elite.[1] The elite have essentially controlled the government institutions, defined national security, implemented their ideas through a hierarchical structure, and mobilized support using cooperative or even suppressive measures.[2] The dominance of a select group in the Bangkok area began in 1782 when the first Chakri king (Rama I) founded the new capital and has continued to this day. This situation allows only a few individuals in society to exert a significant impact on Thailand's conception of security.

The composition of the elite group is, however, far from static. For more than a century, various groups have competed with each other for the domination of Thai society. The main challenge to those in power often comes from another elite group or from different factions within the ruling elite itself (Sinsawasdi 1986, 1996). Moreover, the base of the elite group has broadened over the years. New individuals and groups have begun to participate in the central decision-making process over the past several decades, particularly in the 1980s (Tongdhamachart et al. 1983: 4; Alagappa 1987a: 32). And as the elite's domination waxes and wanes, so does its influence on the conception of national security.

The Beginning of "National" Security

In the mid-nineteenth century, the king and the aristocracy were predominant in building and securing the foundations of the absolutist Siamese state. Creating and defending a territorially defined state, constructing a centralized administration, and implementing a national ideology were among the main tasks of the elite group. King Chulalongkorn the Great (Rama V) (1868–1910), in particular, systematically established the centralized civilian bureaucracy, which "ran the provinces, kept the peace, collected taxes, and educated the children" (Phongpaichit and Baker 1995: 235). King Chulalongkorn created, reorganized, and centralized institutions such as the army, police force, and ministries of finance, interior, justice, and others, using a European bureaucratic model, with specific objectives in mind.[3] Above all, he wished to exert his authority against the powerful aristocrats who dominated the economy of the state. Indeed, the great aristocrats had dominated the state's economy to such an extent that the king had to borrow money from them for his royal expenses.[4] A further purpose was to unite the country to cope with the expansive colonial ambitions of the West. In particular, the British were pressing forward from Burma and from Singapore through the Malay states, and the French were rapidly stretching their control in Indochina toward Siam. In the mid-nineteenth century, therefore, the elite's concept of security concentrated on the establishment of a decisive authority as well as on the defense of its loosely defined territory.[5] Indeed, Thailand's modern conception of security originated in the competition for power among the elites, the establishment of the state's centralized authority, and the state's determination to remain an independent nation.

After King Chulalongkorn and the royal aristocrats succeeded in establishing control over the old aristocrats through the new bureaucracy, the new ruling group turned to new objectives: creating a national ideology and centralizing the religious establishments. The elite's aim was to further unify the new nation and consolidate its power. Hence the idea that all the people in Siam—the Mon, Burmese, Shan, Vietnamese, Khmer, Lao, and Chinese—were in some way "Thai" under one king began to appear. As the king proclaimed: "The Thai, the Lao, and the Shan all consider themselves peoples of the same race. They all respect me as their supreme sovereign, the protector of their well-being."[6] Given the immediate threats from the colonial powers, the introduction of the concept of "Thainess" under the institution of the monarchy was a rational strategy for organizing the people. Organizing the people as one unified nation was seen as vital for the well-being of the new state; it was also important for the consolidation of the power of the new ruling elite. Accordingly, the notion of *chart Thai* (the Thai nation) as a single community began to take root for the new absolutist Siam by the early twentieth century.

With the powerful bureaucracy as its tool, the elite group also exerted more control over Buddhism. The control of religious practice was seen as another urgent task of the elite. At that time, most people were educated at the *wat* (temple) using a variety of languages and scripts. Moreover, there were different sects of Buddhism, and religious practice varied widely. Through control of religious behavior, the two components perceived to be important in preserving a homogeneous community—standardization of the education and the language of the people — could now be achieved. The early Chakri kings such as Rama IV (Mongkut) had begun to reform the Buddhist doctrine for the Siamese during the mid-nineteenth century. At the turn of the century, all monastic institutions were reorganized into a hierarchical structure during the reign of King Chulalongkorn. King Chulalongkorn's brother Wachirayan was appointed as the person in charge of drafting a Sangha Act. The 1902 act imposed a high degree of central control by arranging all monastic institutions in a pyramidal hierarchy (Phongpaichit and Baker 1995: 231). The king and the supreme patriarch were placed at the apex of the central religious administrative structure; the provincial and local temples were at the middle and bottom levels. The new centralized religious administration utilized one language, one syllabus, and one concept of Buddhism at every temple. Thus the elite's notion of one single nation with one religion was institutionalized at the turn of the century.

With the two core values—nation and religion—clearly established, the last pillar of the new absolutist state—the institution of kingship— was conclusively addressed by the elite. Specifically, King Vajiravudh (Rama VI) demonstrated the intent with this proclamation: "The king is the one who possesses the power of the group and he uses this power for the benefit and happiness of everyone. Therefore, respecting or admiring the king is respecting and admiring the power of the group....Being loyal to the king is the same as loving oneself because the king has the duty of protecting the nation."[7] The notion of a nation under a king is deeply rooted in the religious ideology and political practice of Siam (Alagappa 1987a: 40–43). In the mid-nineteenth century, however, the Thai elite began to elaborate the historical roots of the monarchy, primarily for the support of the monarchy's legitimacy. It was King Vajiravudh who openly brought the concepts of nation and religion together with the institution of kingship. He believed in the need to unify all the different peoples in Siam under a common set of "core values." The people, he contended, were not bound together by common values—a condition seen as a potential threat to the well-being of the Thai nation and its monarchy. His effort was also directed toward uniting the Thai nation against the Chinese minorities, who played a significant role in the economy.

King Vajiravudh formally advocated three core values to be preserved for Siam: the "Thai" nation, the Buddhist religion, and the Thai monarchy. A person with "Thai" values was broadly defined as anyone who was born in Siam, spoke Thai, and was committed to Buddhism and the Thai monarchy. Commitment to the three institutions was seen as essential to the stability of *prathetchart* (nation-state), the unified concept adopted by the elite to organize the people under the same core values within a defined geographic space. King Vajiravudh understood the state's limited capacity to impose the elite's concept of the *prathetchart*, however. More important, he foresaw the consequences that could arise if the elite's core values were to be imposed forcefully upon the different ethnic groups. Therefore, his efforts to unify the Thai nation-state were mostly rhetorical and did not result in repressive measures against groups deemed not to have "Thai" values. Nevertheless, it was during the reign of King Vajiravudh that *chart* (the nation), *satsana* (religion), and *phra mahakasat* (the monarchy) emerged formally for the first time as a powerful and integrated concept.

"National" Security Under the Military

When political power shifted from the monarchy to the military in 1932,[8] the three basic core values of national security remained unaltered. Initially the concepts of one nation and one religion were firmly supported by the new elite group. Moreover, the new elite's objectives in pursuing national security were the same: to gain decisive authority over other competing groups and to counter internal and external aggression. The difference now was that the military was the new leader, and it managed to forge an alliance with leading civilian bureaucrats. Since that alliance in 1932, Thailand's conception of security has been directly under the influence of two bureaucratic groups, the military and the bureaucracy.[9]

Only a few years after the 1932 revolution, significant changes occurred in the ways the traditional core values were interpreted and imposed. On May 8, 1939, Field Marshal Phibul Songkram's cabinet reportedly took ten minutes to decide to change the country's name from Siam to Thailand.[10] From that moment on, the means for building a unified "Thai" state consisted principally of military-authoritarian measures. Numerous institutions were established to support the military elite's interpretation of "Thainess"[11]—for example, there were orders for "proper" Thai language, new national dress, a new official new year's day, and new legislation to protect "Thai" society. Among these new measures were a series of "anticommunist" orders and legislation such as the Communist Act of 1932, the Anticommunist Activities Acts of 1952, 1969, and 1979, Order 78 of the junta of 1972, and the Order of the National Reform Council of 1976, which gave the military enormous powers to define security, set up its apparatus, and implement its expanded policies. Under these measures a person deemed not to be "Thai" can easily be prosecuted as a communist traitor.

For almost fifty years, the military elite's focus on national security was militaristic and authoritarian (Samudavanija 1982: 6–24; Settabut 1987; Santasombat 1989: 90–97). It emphasized unity, stability, order, and discipline. More important, the military often used force to impose its values through a "cult of personality." Military leaders such as Phibul, Sarit, Thanom, Prapat, and Narong were among the cult personalities who used their positions to impose their personal ideas on the people in the name of the Thai state. "Believe in the leader, our nation will be saved" was one of their slogans (Samudavanija 1990: 106). In this regard, the three core values under the heading of national security were modified by the elite to suit the purposes of military statism.

Field Marshal Phibul Songkhram, in particular, imposed his idea of national security with extremism. Phibul's series of cultural edicts called "Rattha Niyom" in Thai, for example, instructed the public in a range of "do's" and "don'ts" for good, cultured behavior ranging from personal hygiene, health, and diets to a national dress code (Wright 1991: 98–100). Moreover, Phibul's restriction of the rights of Chinese immigrants was another of his strategies to build a secure nation free from foreign economic domination. Phibul's idea of national security also included recovering territory that had earlier belonged to or been claimed by Thailand. The lands along the Mekong in Laos and Cambodia were Phibul's target. In 1941, Phibun's military clashed with the French troops in the disputed areas in Cambodia. With Japan as mediator, Phibun's government gained three Cambodian provinces and a small territory of Laos. Because he was successful in imposing his ideas of nationalism, patriotism, militarism, and irredentism in the name of national security, Phibun's political power was subsequently secured for several years before a new domestic political crisis would erupt within the ruling elite.

In the late 1950s, the elite's concept of national security extended to include another dimension: development.[12] The concept involved the modernity, progress, wealth, and efficiency of the state. The elite began to realize that their ideas of security could not be imposed forcefully—and certainly not without economic development. Regime opponents at that time were generally from the rural areas and had been born in poverty. To help carry out the military's developmental tasks, various bureaucratic institutions and military agencies were established.[13] Among the key organizations were the National Security Council (NSC), the Central Security Operation Command of the Supreme Commander's Office, the Accelerated Rural Development Agency, the Internal Security Operation Command (ISOC—formerly known as the Communist Suppression Operations Command), the Capital Security Command, and the Army's Directorate for Civil Affairs. Some of these agencies, such as the ISOC, were directly responsible for defense-oriented mass mobilization programs including the National Defense Volunteers, the Volunteer Development and Self-Defense Villages, and the Military Reservists for National Security. Other agencies including the NSC were responsible for coordinating projects such as the Strategic Development for Security in Specific Areas, which aimed to control and develop villages in the communist-infested areas.[14]

Government orders and legislation provided the military with a special role in managing national security affairs. There was the Government Order 298/2519 (1976), for example, which stipulated that the army has a special role in national development. There was the Commander of the Capital Security and Order Act of 1979, which gave the supreme commander control over activities such as peacekeeping, crime suppression, and other security-related operations in the Bangkok area. Among the most significant orders, however, were those that were part of the new strategy to fight communism under the Prime Minister's Office: Orders 66/2523 (1980) and 65/2525 (1982) (Samudavanija, Snitwongse, and Bunbongkarn 1990: apps. II–III). Those two orders allowed the military to use the country's resources more freely in fighting the communists. It also allowed the government to grant amnesty to the communist insurgents, who had begun fighting actively against the state in 1946. In the end the two new prime minister's orders, combined with international developments—especially the change in the PRC's policy toward supporting communist insurrection in other countries—enabled the military to defeat communism in 1982.

A few years before the defeat of communism, however, the elite's militaristic concept of national security began to change—due largely to the leadership change that took place in the mid-1970s. In 1973, the military regime that had ruled the country for several decades was overthrown by the student movement. The aftermath was one of the most violent periods in Thai history. For nearly three years, radical groups of students and their right-wing opponents fought one another almost daily over the ideology and direction of the country. The student movement believed that the old elite—the military and the bureaucracy with their capitalist ideology and support of the United States—should be replaced by a new group of leaders. Moreover, some radical thinkers argued that the institution of the monarchy was simply the "big land-lord" and that revolution was needed to turn the country around.[15] But the military crushed the student-led movement on October 6, 1976—leaving many people dead and injured—and regained control over society.[16]

After the October 6 incident, several thousand people, mostly students, fled to the jungle, joined the Communist Party of Thailand (CPT), and mounted attacks on the government. In addition to this active opposition from within, the military regime faced intensified conflict with the neighboring countries in Indochina. Faced with imminent threats beyond the military's capability to handle, the elite then changed tactics. In response to the internal aggression, the elite used the two prime minister's orders to grant amnesty and allow more participation by other groups in society. To counter the external threats, the elite sought support from the international community in general and from China in particular to oppose Vietnam in the Cambodian conflict.[17] Therefore, other civilian elements—particularly the leading academics and foreign affairs experts—were allowed to participate in the making and implementing of national security policy for the first time since 1932. Consequently the traditional core values were modified and reinterpreted to include new concepts such as democracy, territorial integrity, political independence, and a favorable regional environment.[18] Nevertheless, the military kept tight control over civilian participation in national security issues. The conflict in the late 1980s between Prime Minister Chartchai Choonhavan's foreign policy advisers and the military over the development of policy toward the former Indochina countries is a case in point.[19] Eventually the military demanded that the prime minister dismiss one of his key advisers, largely because of the adviser's criticism of the military establishment. The military's demand was accommodated.

In Thailand, as in many developing countries, the military have historically considered themselves to be the protectors or defenders of national security as well as the developers or modernizers of society. Even at the end of the twentieth century, this traditional perception still prevails in the thinking of military leaders: "In accordance with the Constitution, the Royal Thai Armed Forces has the responsibility of safeguarding the sovereignty, security, and national interest of the State, conducting armed conflict or war, acting as a deterrent in order to protect the Institution of the Monarchy, and suppressing and deterring rebellion and anarchy in order to maintain the security of the State and to develop the country."[20] More than three decades ago, one scholar had already observed the effect of such thinking: "Since the kingdom became a constitutional regime in 1932 the military has ruled, led the ruling groups, dominated the institutions of government, and set the style of Thai politics" (Wilson 1962: 253). Through decades of domination over the governmental institutions responsible for formulating and implementing security policies, therefore, the Thai military elite has continued to define security for the country and to enforce its own definitions through authoritarian structures, with support from the bureaucracy.

The dominance of the military elite, however, has not gone unchallenged. In fact, its attempts to rule and to shape national ideology have been challenged again and again by various competing groups, including factions within the military itself (Dhiravegin 1986; Samudavanija 1982; Settabut 1987). Thai politics, one scholar observes, "has been dominated by intense conflict among and within competing forces as the traditional consensus over values and actions was challenged" (Samudavanija 1982: 67). Indeed, the contestation among the elites over power and authority to rule the society is a historic theme. And no contestation has been more intense, perhaps, than the competition for control over the issues deemed vital to national security.

The Contest over Security

In Thai society, it has been observed that the domination of one elite group is naturally contested by other elite groups. Specifically there has been "a pattern of rhythmic alternation between elites who either proposed political and social innovations or who resisted change preferring to maintain order and stability" (Wright 1991: 11). In the 1930s, the contest was mainly between the royalists and the opposition elite. For almost 60 years after the 1932 revolution, the contests were concentrated among the military, the bureaucracy, and the civilian elites. In the latest round of contestation in the 1990s, the struggle is largely among the bureaucracy, the politicians, and the mass groups that have emerged in the 1990s. Although the contests have involved several issues, most have concentrated on the interpretation of such concepts as nation and state, regime legitimacy, and the authority of the elite.

In the early twentieth century, only 22 years after the reign of King Chulalongkorn, an intense struggle for power erupted among the elite groups. Essentially the contest was between the monarchy and the antiroyalists, led by young civilian, military, and bureaucracy figures (see Mektrairat 1992). This conflict focused on three issues: first, who should control the enormous wealth generated by the expanding economy; second, the rule of law that should be exercised by the bureaucrats; third, and most important, the concept of *chart* (the nation). The conflict over the *chart* issue emerged from a new sense of nationalism that had been growing for over two decades. The absolute monarchy was perceived as no longer pertinent for the development of the new nation-state. Rather, the opponents of royal absolutism believed, there should be three new core values—nation, religion, and state.[21] The final outcome of the contest was the bloodless revolution of June 24, 1932, which forced King Prajadhiphok (Rama VII) to abdicate. Although power and authority were now transferred to the new elite group, the new rulers accommodated the institution of kingship by placing it under the constitution. It was clear that the conflicting values among the elites had played a significant role in the revolution.

From the 1940s through the early 1990s, contestation among the elites in Thai society occurred more frequently—and several times with more violent consequences (Dhiravegin 1996; Samudavanija 1995). The contests mainly involved the same issue: the legitimacy of whichever elite group was defining the values of the nation. Between 1940 and 1960, military statism was contested by the opposition, led largely by a group of the civilian elites. The principal contested issues were how the country should develop economically and politically, and what its position should be in the conflict with communism. Between 1960 and 1970, as the ruling elite intensified its effort to impose military-oriented concepts of national security, intense contestation erupted with violent consequences—for instance, struggles increased between the government and the Communist Party of Thailand (CPT) and the Muslim separatists in the south.[22] By 1967 some 6,600 people had joined the CPT; in 1957 there had been only 1,900 members. Moreover, communism had spread to 38 of the 71 provinces in 1971—a dramatic increase from only a few villages in the 1960s. And when Southeast Asia became a battleground of the Cold War, external powers—the United States and later China—became involved inadvertently in the contest among the competing forces in Thai society (Jain 1984; Muscat 1990).

From the late 1960s to the late 1970s, students and other citizen groups joined the contestation over the legitimacy of the ruling elite and its values. Indeed, the student movement posed the greatest challenge to military dominance, and in 1973 it effectively toppled the military dictatorship. The student-led movement, which attempted to set new ideals for society with the support of politicians and civilians, lasted less than three years. The new ideas were mainly the left-wing ideologies the student leaders had brought back from their overseas studies. In their eyes, bureaucratic malpractice and corruption, labor problems, alliance with foreign countries such as the United States, and social injustices stemming from capitalism threatened the survival of Thai society. A sweeping change was demanded. Demonstrations became a daily event.

By late 1976, conservative forces within the military and the bureaucracy mounted a counterattack. The contest was primarily between radical leftists and the conservative group over the type of society, the system of government, and the legitimacy of the regime. When the military-led right-wing group crushed the student movement on October 6, 1976, it effectively placed the country under an extreme conservative regime. Thousands of students and activists, as noted earlier, then escaped the crackdown and joined the CPT in the jungle. The 1976 coup, however, could not turn the clock back to the 1950s. Anti-communism and ultraconservative ideology were not a sufficient basis for political legitimation in light of the rapid social and economic changes that had transpired. Moreover, the government could not cope with the powerful threat from the Communist Party of Thailand. Nor could it gain the support of the intellectuals, the middle class, the business community, the workers, or even the military. In October 1977 the same military group that had staged the 1976 coup dislodged the ultra-conservative government and installed a less conservative government, first under the leadership of General Kriangsak Chomanan and later under General Prem Tinsulononda. This quasi-democratic period was relatively more stable and lasted through 1988.

In the early 1990s, however, the character of contestation began to change significantly. In earlier conflicts, the focus had been on a few core values and the contest was largely confined to a select group of traditional elites—namely the royalists, the military, the bureaucracy, and later the intellectuals, the armed separatists, the communist insurgents, and the student-led movement. By the beginning of the 1990s, the Thai state had developed its economy and the number of urban middle-class people had increased significantly. More important, the urban middle class felt it had little control over how the country was being managed (Laothamatas 1993: 76–83). Furthermore, middle-class people believed that the state was not responding to their needs, and thus they demanded more participation in the state's ruling process. What the middle class wanted, in fact, was to control the state and its elite through participation in its political institutions (Samudavanija 1994: 29). This was a new situation for Thailand. Now a large number of people demanded to participate in a ruling process that had been reserved for small groups of the chosen.

As the state's economy became more developed, so too did the influence of the middle class. Prosperity, equality, liberty, and justice were among its most important demands (Kriengsak 1996: 125–69). With their specific focus on decentralization, political and bureaucratic reforms, and environmental and distributional issues, those demands were far more complicated than any the governments had faced in the past. The ruling military elite simply could not accept such a radical change in society. In an effort to retain its influence, the military sized power from the elected civilian government in February 1991. As in many successful coups in Thailand, the military abrogated the constitution, dissolved the National Assembly, prohibited political activity, imposed martial law, and appointed a ruling junta. This time the junta was named the National Peace-Keeping Council (NPKC). The junta justified its actions by concluding that the public was thoroughly frustrated with corrupt politicians. That, however, was not the problem. When it became apparent that the military junta wanted direct and prolonged control of Thai politics, the public began to protest in May 1992.[23] Mass demonstrations in many urban centers were then organized and led by, among others, a former Bangkok governor. The protesters, mostly from the urban middle class, centered their efforts on the army strongman, General Suchinda Kraprayoon, who had just accepted the premiership.

The contest took on a violent edge when more than 100,000 protesters clashed with police commandos and armed military forces. It took a direct appeal from the king to end the confrontation. Some 52 protesters had been killed, and 697 protesters and 284 police and military officers injured.[24] Damage to property and loss of wages were reported at 1.79 billion baht during the four days of turbulence (Theeravit 1993: 102). Related damage to industry, trade, services, construction, and the like was estimated at 31.1 billion baht.[25] The military leader, General Suchinda, retired from politics.

Since 1946, despite all the contestation, one institution has managed to remain largely intact: the monarchy has been able to stay above all competition. King Bhumibol ascended to the throne only after his elder brother, King Ananda (Rama VIII), died from a mysterious gunshot wound in 1946. At that time, the role of the monarchy under the constitution was not well defined. It was the military strongman, Sarit, who systematically built up the role of the monarch as symbolic leader of the nation (Chaloemtiarana 1979). Throughout the years, the monarch has become institutionalized through a close relationship with the military elite, through an active role in religious practice, and through the monarchy's own conduct, which is formally separated from the role of governing.

Although the aftermath of the latest contestation between the ruling elite and the urban middle class has not yet fully unfolded, the event does reflect the intensity of the contest over central issues. Since 1932, there have been 17 military coups, 15 constitutions, and 21 prime ministers in Thailand. The latest contest reveals how much Thai society has changed over the past decades. The fundamental threats to the survival of Thailand are no longer the communist insurgency or the armed separatists. Moreover, the external threat posed by Thailand's communist neighbors has diminished. The country is, in fact, moving progressively toward becoming an industrialized economy. The middle class, in particular, is increasingly gaining influence in Thai society. In this new security environment, most urban middle-class people do not consider the traditional elites—the military, the bureaucracy, the politicians—as the only important forces in leading the nation. Indeed, they no longer consider the elites' monopoly of power and authority as appropriate for a changing Thai society. Although the Thai nation, its religion, and the institution of kingship have been firmly established, today the people, particularly the urban middle class, demand much more say in defining the meaning and content of security.

Changing Concepts of Security

As a new century approaches, most observers agree that Thai society has been in the midst of a fundamental transformation. Significant changes have occurred in its political and economic affairs. Beginning in the early 1980s, the country's political stability was reinforced with the defeat of communist subversion. By the late 1980s, political stability had been further enhanced by the continued leadership of Prime Minister Prem Tinsulanond. For eight consecutive years (1980–88), several major development programs were able to proceed without significant inter-ruption. Moreover, the administration provided opportunities for the parliamentary system to evolve. In 1988, a parliamentary democracy was established with an elected premier for the first time in twelve years. Although the elected government was challenged by the military elite in 1991 by way of a coup, parliamentary democracy was restored quickly and decisively by emerging new forces: the urban middle class, civilian politicians, and other interest groups, including nongovernmental organizations.

The Thai economy was transformed as well, as the country continued to experience high economic growth rates. In fact, the real gross domestic product (GDP) has increased by an average of 7 percent per year since 1985 (National Economic and Social Development Board 1995). In 1988, Thailand's GDP increased at an unprecedented rate of 13.2 percent—the highest ever for the country and highest in the world for that year. In 1995, the country's GDP was $144 billion, up from $86 billion in 1990. Growth in nonagricultural sectors—particularly in export-oriented industries—continued to be strong, while inflation was kept to 3 to 5 percent. Increases in private-sector investment were particularly significant in the late 1980s as the production bases moved from Japan and other countries to Thailand. Recently, however, the country has begun to experience economic slowdown. Rising labor costs, infrastructure problems, and inappropriate finance policies are among the obstacles that require major policy adjustments. Nevertheless, Thailand, by and large, has begun to transform itself from an agrarian society into a newly industrializing economy.

These political and economic changes have altered the dominant role of the military elite in defining Thai concepts of national security. They have also led to the institutionalization of civilian control. Moreover, the traditional security conceptions have been broadened to include such issues as economic development, equality, liberty, and justice with a specific focus on political reform, decentralization of the bureaucracy, human rights, and environmental issues (Samudavanija and Snitwongse 1992; Kriengsak 1996: 194–211; Piriyarangsan and Phongpaichit 1996: 15–26; Samudavanija 1995). In this new environment, the new elite has begun to articulate its concepts of security more openly and formally.

Changes from Military Domination

In the 1990s, the Thai military elite, once a dominant power in Thai politics, is no longer able to set the agenda in the creation and implementation of national security policy. After the May 1992 incident, the National Assembly immediately passed constitutional amendments allowing only an elected member of parliament to become prime minister—thus preventing military leaders from stepping directly into politics. The new charter also designates the Speaker of the House of Representatives, instead of the Speaker of the Senate, as president of parliament. Furthermore, new amendments limit the power of the appointed senators to initiate a general debate against the government and to vote on no-confidence motions. These new conditions were designed to prevent the military elite, which usually has influence over the senators, from gaining control over parliament.[26] Finally, the Internal

Peace-Keeping Command Act, which gave excessive power to the military, has been repealed and the military's use of force in domestic affairs now requires cabinet approval. Thus an era of strong military domination in Thai politics is coming to an end.

The May 1992 incident enabled the civilian government to become significantly involved in military appointments for the first time. While the new amendment was awaiting the king's signature, Anand Panyarachun was appointed caretaker prime minister. Anand then went on to do what many critics had considered impossible: he removed the high-ranking military officers involved in the May incident from their command. The commander-in-chief of the army, for example, the most influential military officer in the country, was "promoted" to deputy permanent secretary, a position with much less power. The supreme commander was transferred to the post of inspector general. The First Army Region commander—the most powerful commander among the three armed forces—was transferred to become commander of the Institute of the Army Academy. Then a number of career officers were promoted to command posts. This sweeping replacement of the top military positions spurred the Thai military toward more professionalism for the first time in Thailand's modern history.

From these incidents it is apparent that the role of the military elite has changed significantly. Several "professional" officers at several important posts appear not to be highly motivated by their own political agenda or by personal gain, as compared to the earlier generation of military leaders. Moreover, the military's influence in general has been declining for some time. The most conclusive evidence of the decline can be seen in the change in the military's share of the total government budget. Traditionally the military had a huge share of the budget. During 1982–84, for example, the Thai military had the largest portion of the budget (Table 10). In the subsequent six years (1985–90), its share dropped below that of the Finance Ministry for the first time. In 1990, the military budget slipped into third place. Not only has the military budget declined in its ranking, but it has fallen as well in terms of percentage of total government expenditure. Its share, for example, went steadily down from 18.3 percent in 1982 to 15.6 percent in 1989 and then to an all-time low of 11.9 percent in 1996. Moreover, despite Thailand's impressive growth rate in the past decade, the military budget has not kept up with the economic growth. In fact, the military budget tends to lag behind—for example, its share as a percentage of GDP dropped from a high of 3.4–4.1 percent between 1982 and 1987 to a low of 2.4–2.9 percent in 1988–94. Based on these budgetary figures, it appears that the military's strong domination of governmental affairs has ended.

TABLE 10
The Thai Military Budget: 1982–97

Fiscal year	Defense budget (in millions of baht)	Percentage of GDP	Percentage of total budget	Rate of increase (%)	Rank of military's share
1982	29,384.5	4.1	18.3	—	1
1983	33,055.6	3.8	18.7	12.4	1
1984	35,926.7	3.9	18.7	8.7	1
1985	38,308.6	4.3	18.5	6.6	2
1986	38,866.2	3.8	18.3	1.5	2
1987	39,155.2	3.4	17.2	0.7	2
1988	41,170.7	2.9	16.9	5.2	2
1989	44,484.1	2.6	15.6	8.0	2
1990	52,632.5	2.4	15.7	18.3	3
1991	60,575.2	2.4	15.6	15.0	2
1992	69,272.9	2.5	13.2	14.3	2
1993	78,625.3	2.5	12.4	13.5	3
1994	85,423.9	2.4	12.6	8.6	3
1995	91,638.7	2.2	12.0	7.3	3
1996	100,603.0	2.2	11.9	9.8	3
1997	108,573.6	—	11.0	7.0	3

SOURCES: Thai Bureau of the Budget, *Budget Summary for 1982–91;* Thai Government House, *Annual Budget Legislation, 1985–97;* Satha-Anan 1995; Ball 1995: 9.

NOTE: 1982–90 from Ball 1995, based on U.S. dollars; 1991–97 from NESDB 1995, based on Thai baht.

Toward Civilian Control

With the end of military domination, the civilian government has increasingly been able to exert control over the activities previously reserved for the military. In 1992, Prime Minister Anand's cabinet approved a new plan for defense called the "National Preparedness Plan." It marked the beginning of a systematic approach by the civilian government to deal effectively and comprehensively with security problems. In the past, the military was primarily responsible for virtually every issue deemed important to national security. The civilian bureaucracy, for its part, was responsible for all the economic and social problems left by the military. There was no single comprehensive plan that addressed all the important national security issues. Coordination among the various agencies implementing different security policies was clearly minimal.

The adoption of the National Preparedness Plan changed that arrangement. The plan outlines the overall objectives, scope, and rules for all government agencies in coping with the country's security problems. Under the established guidelines, all agencies must fulfill their specified obligations as related to the security conditions of the state. They are to collaborate their efforts with the Ministry of Defense but are also required to collaborate with the private sector, if necessary, to achieve their objectives. The new plan also incorporates two other major plans already in place for dealing with issues deemed vital to the nation's well-being: the military's National Defense Policy and the government's National Economic and Social Development Plan. The National Defense Policy outlines general objectives in defending the country, describes potential threats, and specifies measures to counter the threats. The National Economic and Social Development Plan deals with economic and social issues but also undertakes special projects in areas determined to be sensitive to subversion and aggression. By integrating the two plans into a single master plan for defense, the civilian government is now able to set and implement national security policy for the first time.

A Comprehensive Concept of Security

There has also been a shift in how security is conceptualized and articulated by the elite. Although the concept of security has been articulated by a number of specific Thai elites in the past, namely the top military and civilian leaders, it was not done openly and formally. Moreover, the emphasis would shift between the internal and external dimensions, depending on the prevailing situation. When the elite was faced with competition from other groups, for example, the emphasis was placed on internal authority and control. When the country was faced with communist subversion, the main focus was on countering the communist threat by all means available. When the invasion of Cambodia took place in 1979, the Thai leaders shifted emphasis to the external threat from Vietnam. More important, the conceptualization of security was a product of the immediate interests of small elite groups in the military, the foreign affairs office, the intellectual circle, or the political parties. In many instances, their concepts of security were in conflict with one another. In other cases, ideas of the group in power were simply accepted by rival groups for a short period of time. The military conceptualization of security in the 1940s to 1960s, developed and promulgated without any significant contribution from others, is a good example. Another example is the way security was defined by the Chatichai government in dealing with the Cambodian problem in the late 1980s, also without much input from others. In both cases the results were disastrous. What has clearly been lacking among the Thai elite is a durable, long-term consensus.

In 1994, however, came a change in how the elite articulated the concept of security. The elite's notion of security was articulated formally in the country's first defense white paper, entitled *The Defence of Thailand 1994*. Most significant was that in this document the diverse but elite group of 100 asserted that the country had four national interests: maintenance of the state with independence, sovereignty, and territorial integrity; the happiness and well-being of the people; the growth and advancement of the nation as a whole, both in economic and social terms, and the existence of an administrative system that benefits the people; and honor and prestige in the international community. The group of 100 leading professionals from the military, the civil services, the business community, and other private organizations were together for the first time, attempting to develop a formal concept of security for the nation. In that formal articulation, therefore, they attempted to include all the security concerns and to encompass all segments of society and all aspects of political, economic, and sociocultural issues. In many ways this comprehensive concept of security represents the elite's response to the rising demands of various emerging groups in a changing society. Although the term *national security* refers to the traditional need to defend the nation's independence, sovereignty, territorial integrity, and status in the international arena, it concerns domestic factors as well—in particular, it concerns the "happiness and well-being of the people," the "growth and advancement of the nation," and the need to have "an administrative system that benefits the people."

In this context, the elite's concept of security has been broadly perceived and loosely defined. But that tendency is, in fact, rooted in the nature of the Thai people. The Thais usually consider their country to be unique in one important aspect: it is the only country in Southeast Asia that was able to maintain its independence throughout the colonial period. The fact that Thai society has continued to evolve, for more than 700 years, without foreign values being imposed upon it has a significant influence on the Thai people. As a result, the Thais are generally conscious of their independence, and the elite, in particular, are wary about any threat to the country's independence. Issues regarded as important to the security of the Thai society have, therefore, been broadly perceived and loosely defined.

Nevertheless, the elite attempted to sharpen the concept of security by focusing on five specific domains: political security, economic security, social and psychological security, military security, and scientific and technological security.[27] With respect to political security, the elite considers a democratic form of government under a parliamentary system with the king as head of state to be fundamental. Although this concept is typical, continued efforts to make the system more democratic and responsive are important new elements. In the elite's view of economic security, sustainable economic development is vital. In particular, implementation of the National Economic and Social Development Plan is seen as essential to the development of the Thai economy. The elite also states that the emphasis must now be placed on flexibility, freedom, and choosing the right approaches in dealing with domestic and international economic conditions to ensure that the economy remains competitive in the international market. Furthermore, the elite believes in looking for new markets, particularly in neighboring countries. Among the economic issues perceived to be affecting the country's well-being are rural poverty, unequal income distribution, disparity among regions, a shortage in skilled labor, and environmental harm caused by economic development.

This elite is also concerned with the effect of economic development, urbanization, and rapid globalization on traditional Thai values. Several Thai cultural values may be affected: *kiatiphum* (a deep sense of independence, pride, and dignity); *kreng jai* (being considerate); *bun khun* (being grateful); *raksa nam jai* (polite personality); *alum aluay* (flexibility); *wasana* (accepting fate and religious beliefs); esteem of education; *sanuk* (enjoyment); and esteem of achievement (Komin 1995: 3). How Thailand can maintain these values while incorporating other foreign values and without causing significant conflicts in society is a key concern.

With respect to military security, the elite now believes in self-defense but regards the use of military power as the last resort for the protection of national security.[28] Alliances or alignments with major powers are believed to be less essential in the post–Cold War period. In particular, links with the United States or China are not perceived to be vitally important. The elite also thinks that significant changes in the domestic, regional, and global security environment require the Thai military to be more competent, better trained, and well equipped.

Professionalization of the military is therefore a must in responding to the changing environment.

Finally, the current elite considers science and technology to be critical in the nation's development. Appropriate knowledge and technology must therefore be sought through importation or indigenous development. Specific concerns in the realm of science and technology include human resource development, information technology, hardware technology, and organizational management. The elite also thinks that the development of human resources and information technology should be given high priority. The short-term goals are to create skilled labor for industries and to use information technology more effectively. In the long run, development based on science and technology is expected to enhance the country's competitiveness.

It is apparent from these new conceptions that the current elite is trying to respond to challenges from other emerging groups. The elite's thinking about national security is more systematic and comprehensive now than in the past. Moreover, it articulates its concept of security formally and openly. The elite has also initiated new measures in its effort to operationalize its ideas. Reorganization of policy making and streamlining of the decision-making apparatus with the goal of institutionalizing civilian control are among its main tasks. Whether or not this comprehensive approach to national security issues will be fully accepted remains to be seen. Perhaps the reinterpretation of security will ignite yet another round of intense contestation. In any case, process by which national security policy is made and implemented in Thailand has already changed significantly.

Post Cold War: Growing Concern with International Security

In Thailand, the elite's ideology often dictates the direction and process of nation-building. Consequently, concepts such as security or development depend on how the elite interprets and implements them. Even in the midst of contestation the Thai elite has managed to create a certain social consensus. Since the reign of King Chulalongkorn, the elite has been most successful in establishing three national values: the *chart Thai* (Thai nation), *satsana Bhuddh* (Buddhist religion), and *phra mahakasat* (the monarchy). Also, an emphasis on development and political participation has been emerging since the 1960s. Consequently, the Thai state cannot be classified as a "weak state" as defined by Buzan (1983: 67).

The Thai ruling elite, however, has been less successful in establishing the authority necessary to govern the state effectively. In other words, the government's power is constantly challenged by various competing groups. Under this prevailing condition, the ruling elite is inherently weak and often concerned about the regime's security. In constructing the concept of security, therefore, the central decision makers are primarily driven by domestic considerations. When faced with imminent threats from outside, however, the competing forces in Thai society often rally to the defense of the state. The elite, in particular, claims that the survival of the state is the ultimate goal. There have been several examples of this conduct throughout modern Thai history, particularly during the colonial period, the two world wars, and the Indochina conflicts. At such times the state exhibits the behavior of a unitary state in an anarchical international environment: constantly concerned about survival, looking for alliances, balancing relations, and seeking to gain more from others.

Thus the thinking and behavior of the central decision makers in Thailand can be explained in some instances by systemic factors according to the neorealist paradigm and in others by domestic factors related to regime security. Neither paradigm, however, offers an adequate explanation of the conception of security in Thailand over the years. The state and its ruling elite have been faced with different threats from within and without, creating a distinctive situation for a country like Thailand.

There has been a significant change, however, in the central decision makers' behavior since the end of the Cold War, and in particular since the end of the conflict in Cambodia. Today, external military threats to Thailand's survival are remote. Nor is there an active threat from communist or minority insurgencies. Nevertheless, the elite is evincing concern about the external security environment. The elite's increasing concern about Thailand's border issues, maritime claims, and resources is obvious. Concern over military power and political influence is also discernible.

Territorial and Regional Security Concerns

For the Thai elite, maintaining independence, sovereignty, and territorial integrity is considered the central security objective. Given Thailand's area of 514,000 square kilometers located mostly in the central plains of Southeast Asia, the elite often considers the country to be vulnerable to land-based aggression. This fear, in fact, has had a historical basis since the thirteenth century (Paribatra 1984: 28–46). During the Ayudhaya period (1349–1767), for example, the Thai capital was raided twice by Burmese warriors. In the post–World War II period, Communist Vietnam and the wars in Indochina were considered threats to Thailand's independence and sovereignty. When Vietnam invaded Cambodia in late 1978 and subsequently clashed with Thai troops along the Thai-Cambodian border in 1980, the incidents validated the Thai leaders' belief that Thailand's survival is directly challenged by Vietnam (Chinwanno 1993: 3; Eiland 1983: 50–52). Moreover, with Bangkok only 300 kilometers from the Cambodian border, Thai elites in Bangkok are very sensitive to any changes in Cambodia. Thus, the historical behavior of the Thai elite in countering these threats from the western and eastern frontiers can be understood from a realist perspective.

The threat from the western border, however, has not been considered seriously by Thai leaders since the Chakri dynasty (1782–present). And since the end of the Cambodian conflict in the late 1980s, the threat from the eastern frontier has not been treated as serious either. Nevertheless, the Thai elite is still concerned with unresolved border issues between Thailand and its neighbors. The defense white paper, for example, specifically states that "it is certain that Thailand will face problems in the future concerning unclear borders" (*Defence of Thailand* 1994: 16–17). The elite's concern is due largely to the geostrategic fact that Thailand has some 5,000 kilometers of borders—2,401 kilometers with Myanmar, 1,745 kilometers with Laos, 789 kilometers with Cambodia, and 552 kilometers with Malaysia—and some of these boundary lines have not been demarcated clearly. With the end of the Cold War confrontation in the region, the elite believes that unresolved border issues among these countries may resurface. In fact, Thailand has already quarreled with all of its neighbors in recent years over border issues. With Laos, for example, the disputed areas include five villages in the two northeastern provinces and a small island in the middle of the Mekong River. Thai security forces clashed with Laotian troops several times in these areas in the late 1980s.[29] Thailand and Cambodia contest areas in three eastern provinces and in the exclusive economic zone. Moreover, Thailand disputes the five northern and central provinces with Myanmar. In the south, there are four disputed areas that have not been resolved between Thailand and Malaysia. Skirmishes have erupted occasionally along all these contested borders except in the south, and some of the clashes have been intense.

The boundary problems between Thailand and its neighbors have been exacerbated by a number of border incidents involving illegal entry, cross-border smuggling, trade in weapons, drug trafficking, and prostitution.[30] These activities concentrate mostly on the eastern, northeastern, and western borders. On the western borders, illegal entry is mostly related to the fighting in Myanmar. The armed confrontation between the Karen nationalists (KNU) and the State Law and Order Restoration

Council (SLORC) troops, for example, has pushed an estimated 60,000 people into Thailand over the years (*Report on National Interests and Threats on the Border Areas* 1995). Moreover, drug trafficking in the border areas by figures such as the warlord Khun Sa has further complicated Thailand's relations with Myanmar and other countries.

On the eastern border, the elite is increasingly concerned about the Khmer Rouge, which still controls a number of areas along the Thai-Cambodian border. Fighting between the Cambodian troops and the Khmer Rouge breaks out periodically. Given the Thai government's close ties with the Khmer Rouge over the years, the relationship between Thailand and Cambodia is beset with mistrust and suspicion. Moreover, border issues such as illegal weapons trade and labor migration create further problems for Thailand. The illegal entry of workers from Laos is another cause for concern. Drug trafficking and ethnic conflicts on the Thai-Laos border create further problems for Thailand.

On the southern border, religious differences in the five southern provinces are less important in the thinking of the Thai elite today than in earlier times. Now that communist activity has been terminated, complications between Thailand and Malaysia have lessened substantially. The Thai authorities in the area also appear to be more sensitive toward Muslim minorities. But economic prosperity in the Thai border towns has brought new concerns to the ruling elite: prostitution, drug trafficking, and illegal trading activities have increased. Some of the elite think that these problems will eventually affect the relationship between Thailand and Malaysia. In recent years, such border activities have indeed increased. In the elite's view, they do not threaten the survival of Thailand but they do complicate its relationship with others. Cross-border smuggling, drug trafficking, and prostitution have damaged the country's image. Therefore, Thai leaders believe that, in the long term, threats to Thailand will come primarily from the border areas.

The Thai elite is also becoming attentive to the competition for offshore resources and the conflicting maritime claims in the Asia-Pacific region. Thai leaders fear that conflicts may arise from these situations (*Document on Submarine Procurement Program* 1995: 1–2). This was not the case in the 1980s when the Cambodian conflict was the main concern for the Thai elite (Paribatra 1988b: 140–58). Now that 95 percent of the country's trading activity depends on sea-lanes and the country's economy increasingly depends on international trade,[31] threats to the sea-lanes of communication have received more attention. As a result, the government has initiated several new security policies. The main policies are the National Preparedness Plan of 2535[32] (1993), the National Defense Policy of 2535–2538 (1993–95), and the Development for Added Security Plan of 2536 (1993). More important, the Thai military has intensified its efforts to modernize the armed forces that must deal with these border concerns. All these new developments indicate that the elite has been responding to the changing external security environment.

Centralization of Border Development

To deal more effectively with border problems, the civilian elite has focused on creating a central institution for coordinating and integrating development in the border areas. The institution devoted to that purpose is the National Security Council (NSC). The NSC was first established during the reign of King Rama VI (1910–27) under the name of the Council for Defense of the Kingdom. Although its main objective was to ensure the effectiveness of the Thai military in defending the country, it was also charged with advising the king on military matters. Under the National War Council Act of 1932, during the reign of King Rama VII, the council's name was changed to the National War Council. The new council was granted authority in managing not only military affairs but also economic and political affairs. During 1932–48, its name was changed to the National Defense Council. Finally, the National Defense Council was succeeded by the NSC under the National Security Act in 1959. The NSC, under the Office of the Prime Minister, advises the cabinet on national security policy. Its activities, in fact, cover a wide range including politics, military affairs, economics, social affairs, science and technology, and energy and environment.

In the past, however, when the military was dominant, the NSC did not play a significant role in formulating and implementing security policy. Its role consisted largely of articulating an official concept of national security in accordance with the military's thinking. The cabinet's decision on February 4, 1992, however, changed all that: the cabinet specified that the NSC is to coordinate all development projects related to security, including those programs directed by the military in the border areas. The NSC is also required to make all security-related development programs concur with the National Economic and Social Development Plan. This means that the NSC must work closely with the National Economic and Social Development Board (NESDB). In addition, the cabinet's decision now requires the NSC to coordinate its efforts with the private sector. Finally, the NSC is to evaluate all these projects for the cabinet.

Although the cabinet's decision certainly increased the NSC's effectiveness, the most significant change to the NSC occurred in 1993. On December 29, 1993, the NESDB called for a coordinated plan for security-related programs and other economic development projects in all 30 provinces on the borders. All of the projects' budget allocations, including those for the military, are now to be coordinated through the NESDB. The NESDB, in turn, works closely with the NSC under the National Coordinating Center for Preparedness. This change in the budget process gives the NSC the power to integrate all domestic programs for security. In short, the elite's intention to deal with the border problems more effectively is clear. More important, it is a systematic approach that institutionalizes civilian control and streamlines the decision-making apparatus. In addition, the elite has given the central agency, the NSC, a much-needed tool—control over budgets and support from experts—with which to attack the problems. Whether or not the council's performance will match these intentions remains to be seen.

Development of Military Capabilities

The elite's response to uncertainty in the sea-lanes of communication is even more apparent. In particular, the military initiated a new defense policy aimed at comprehensive improvement of the capability of the armed forces. The objectives of the new defense policy are as follows:

1. Restructure the armed forces so that they are more compact and have professional personnel with modern weapons and equipment, thus enabling them to guarantee the country's independence, sovereignty, and national interests.

2. Improve the reserve and conscription systems so that they are more suitable for the new conditions. At the same time, increase cooperation with allies.

3. Revise the curricula of all military educational institutions so that they take into account the economic, social, and political changes occurring in the country.

4. Promote the role of the armed forces in the country's development, including the protection of economic interests both on land and at sea.

5. Raise the morale of lower-ranking personnel by improving welfare and providing more vocational training so that they are able to earn a livelihood after demobilization (*Defence of Thailand* 1994: 20).

Not only does the new defense policy aim to deal more effectively with the external environment; it also shifts the Thai military's focus from counterinsurgency to a conventional warfare capability. The first priority is to develop a more compact and effective armed forces with modern military equipment; then attention will focus on improvements in the reserve and conscription systems, education, and welfare.

The main emphasis, however, is on modern equipment.[33] The Royal Thai Army (RTA), for example, aims to be "compact in size, light, and have destructive power." This will enable it to respond quickly to various contingencies, particularly in the border areas. The RTA's new weapons include more main battle tanks and light tanks such as M-48A5s and M-60A3s from the United States. Self-propelled guns with a greater range, such as the M-109 (155 mm), are currently being imported. The RTA is also improving its battlefield surveillance and night operations equipment. All these weapons are considered important to meet the country's new security needs.

As for the Royal Thai Navy (RTN), its modernization programs emphasize developing greater capabilities to protect territorial waters, maritime natural resources, industrial energy sources, and the sea-lanes of communications. More modern surface warships and a small fleet of submarines are being given serious consideration.[34] New *Naresuan*-class and *Knox*-class frigates will be commissioned within a few years in addition to the four Chinese-built *Chao Phraya*–class frigates and two *Kramronsin*-class corvettes. More capable missiles and air defense systems such as the Sea Sparrow ship-to-air missiles and the LW-108 and STIR radar systems are being acquired. The most significant addition to the RTN's capability is the 11,400-ton *Chakkrinareubet* light aircraft and helicopter carrier commissioned in 1997. This carrier will essentially transform the RTN from a coastal navy into a maritime navy with significant striking power.[35] The RTN also seeks to acquire a submarine capability. The initial proposal was for two small diesel-powered submarines at an estimated cost of $560–$680 million. Although the RTN deferred the proposal just before it was to be submitted to the cabinet in 1995,[36] it is quite likely to make the request in the future.

The Royal Thai Air Force (RTAF) emphasizes its modern fighter aircraft inventory: additional jets with higher performance capability such as the new F-16s and F/A-18s will be acquired.[37] The acquisition of airborne early warning systems such as the E-2 Hawkeyes is also planned. The RTAF is also upgrading its air defense systems and electronic surveillance.

In short, the Thai elite has responded to the uncertainties of the regional environment in a typical way—by building up its military capabilities. And, in general, the military capabilities it has been acquiring are fairly impressive, especially the new acquisitions of the Royal Thai Navy. The Thai military's past performance in warfare, however, particularly with neighboring countries, is far less impressive. Whether the military can fully utilize its new capability is still a big question. In the end, the Thai military elite realizes that it can never develop a truly powerful military force. The country imposes too many constraints: a declining military budget, weak support from the civilian government and the general public, and, more important, the lack of specific objectives among the military elite. The severe financial crisis that struck Thailand in 1997 has resulted in substantial cutbacks in defense expenditures. Many procurement plans have been shelved. Even otherwise, domestic and international constraints have compelled Thailand to cooperate with other nations in solving regional security concerns.

Regional and International Cooperation

In the post–Cold War era, the Thai elite has begun to place serious emphasis on good relations with neighboring states and other regional countries. Today the government places greater importance on relations with China and on economic cooperation. There have also been increased efforts to promote economic relations with India and Russia. But the most serious emphasis has been on promoting good relations with Vietnam, Laos, Cambodia, and Myanmar for the first time in decades. In the past, the Thai military elite pushed the idea of "Suwanaphum" (golden land), which implied an imperialistic attitude toward Indochina (Wood and Wheeler 1990: 18–19). Nevertheless, that idea mainly reflected the thinking of certain leaders and was motivated mostly by their desire for personal economic gain. Today more emphasis is placed on economic cooperation with and investment activities in these former Indochina countries. The campaign began officially with the policy of the Chatichai government to "turn battlefields into marketplaces." In recent years, as we have seen, Thai officials have also increased their efforts to solve border-related issues with neighbors.

In accord with the new interest in regional and international cooperation, more consideration has been given to international and regional organizations. In 1993, Thailand became a member of the Nonaligned Movement. The official reason given was that Thailand can benefit in its dealings with other countries by being a member of the movement. In subsequent years, it has become involved in hosting the first ASEAN Regional Forum (ARF) in 1994, the Fifth ASEAN Summit in 1995, and the first Asia-Europe Meeting (ASEM) in 1996. Moreover, Thailand has given high priority to cooperation within ASEAN, particularly since the Cambodia conflict.

Changes in Thailand's alliances with superpowers such as the United States are also evident. Alignments and alliances have always been an important element in the elite's approach to security. Now that the conflicts with neighboring countries have ended, the elite believes it will not gain significantly from being heavily reliant upon major powers such as the United States and China. Although the elite still intends to continue its alliance with certain powers, Thailand will not be as accommodating in those relations as before. Thailand's criticism of the United States over the missile attack on Baghdad in July 1993 and Thailand's 1995 decision to reject a U.S. request to station supply ships in the Gulf of Thailand reflect this new thinking (Snitwongse 1994: 151).

Conclusion: New Forces, New Definitions

The process of making and implementing Thailand's national security policies has historically been dominated by a small elite. The Thai core values, under the label of national security, began to take root in the mid-nineteenth century when the king and the aristocracy established the concept of nation, religion, and kingship. Under the domination of the military and the bureaucracy, the Thai conception of security was highly influenced by militaristic-authoritarian ideology for almost 60 years. In the 1990s, however, there has been a significant change in Thai national security practice. Although the three core values remain largely intact, security has become multidimensional: increasingly the notion incorporates socioeconomic issues, as demanded by the emerging new forces in society.

The elite's conception of security has often been challenged by competing groups in Thai society, occasionally with violent consequences. The competition has largely been among the traditional elite groups: the royalists, the aristocracy, the military, the bureaucracy. In recent times, however, new forces—including the civilian politicians, the intellectuals, the urban middle class, and various interest groups—have joined in the contestation. Today the contest centers on the interpretation and implementation of key concepts such as the Thai nation, the system of government, the authority of a particular group, and the regime's legitimacy.

When faced with an immediate threat from inside, the thinking and behavior of the Thai elite are driven by domestic factors relating to political authority and regime stability. When faced with an imminent threat from outside, however, the competing forces in society often rally to the defense of the state. Then, the goals of a unitary state—survival, alliance, and cooperation according to a commonly defined national interest—can be invoked to explain the elite's concept of security. At the present time, in the absence of both internal subversion and immediate external aggression, the central decision makers are concerned about the state's border problems and regional security. Thus they have strengthened military self-defense by modernizing the armed forces, while adjusting alliances and initiating new approaches to regional cooperation. Although it would not be entirely correct to use systemic factors to explain the Thai elite's thinking and behavior at the present time, it appears that the Thai state is becoming more responsive to regional conditions and, perhaps, to the international environment. To what degree this is so, however, remains to be seen when the next round of contestation over the concept of security arises in Thai domestic politics. Predicting who will emerge as the leaders in Thai politics has proved to be, as some scholars put it "the most problematic" for most observers (Neher and Marlay 1995: 45). It seems clear, therefore, that the conception of Thai security cannot be explained by a single theoretical approach.

Vietnam
Struggle and Cooperation

KIM NINH

> At present our advance is gaining momentum, at the same time we have
> also come under pressure from many directions....Unlike in past times, today
> the hostile forces have many means by which to influence our country with the
> aim of driving us onto the capitalist road or steering us into their orbit, thus
> making us dependent on them. For this reason, external relations activities
> should hold fast to the two aspects of cooperation and struggle in order to
> develop and protect the economy, to defend national security, and to preserve
> and develop the national cultural traditions and characteristics.
>
> LE QUANG THANH, 1994

L e Quang Thanh's analysis of Vietnam's security situation, which appeared in the *Communist Review*, the official journal of the Vietnamese Communist Party (VCP), underlines the dramatic changes that have enveloped the country in the last decade and focuses on the dilemmas facing the Vietnamese Communist leaders today. Since the adoption of the strategy of *doi moi* (renovation) in 1986, Vietnam has withdrawn from Cambodia, mended relations with China and the United States, and become a member of the Association of Southeast Asian Nations (ASEAN) in 1995. These developments have returned Vietnam fully to the fold of the international community, allowing it to concentrate on economic development, which has become a primary national goal. The country's continued steady economic growth, rising foreign investment, and controlled level of inflation have led to noticeable improvements in the standard of living for many Vietnamese. The difference between 1986 and 1996 is indeed remarkable, but such a dramatic turnaround can obscure the extent to which one of the oldest and most cohesive communist parties in the world had to undergo elemental change and, in the process, reconceptualize several of its key beliefs, goals, and policies, including those in the area of security.

Dramatic changes in the international environment, its own policy of renovation, growing concern with regime legitimacy, and a host of domestic problems associated with economic liberalization are compelling Vietnam to rethink its security. A new construction of security is emerging, but there also are elements of continuity. The ethnonationally constructed Vietnamese state continues to be the referent of security. There is little or no significant contestation of the nation-state, although its socialist identity is becoming increasingly untenable, forcing the VCP to reconceptualize socialism and to become more concerned with the defense of the "socialist fatherland." Vietnam has long been accustomed to viewing its immediate regional and global environment as a hostile place; to perceiving its survival as being continually threatened; and in the final analysis, to relying on itself to ensure its survival. Socialism, the threat from the United States, and the historical threat from China provided the ideological framework and the substantive context for this worldview, which is close to realism. That realist interpretation of the world and Vietnam's place in it, however, is now increasingly tempered by an acceptance of an interdependent region and world and an acknowledgment of the benefits of participation in regional and global cooperative arrangements. That in turn has led to the elaboration of a new "struggle-cooperation" strategy—a more flexible approach to ensuring Vietnam's security and prosperity in a changing era.

Political survival continues to be of concern, but economic growth is also accorded high priority. The latter is viewed as vital to ensure the security of Vietnam and its position in Southeast Asia as well as to legitimate the VCP's monopoly of political power and satisfy the economic aspirations of the people. However, liberalization of the Vietnamese national economy and its integration into the global capitalist system—both deemed necessary to promote economic growth—pose several new challenges to the Vietnamese state and society. The tension between the VCP's commitment to continuing its monopoly of political power and the demands and consequences of economic renovation has given rise to internal security concerns focused on regime survival, challenges to the identity of the state, and socioeconomic grievances issuing in large measure from the growing disparity in income distribution, especially between the urban and rural areas. The effort of the United States and the West to propagate democracy and human rights as universal values and the attempt to attach political conditions to economic intercourse have heightened Vietnam's concern with regime survival, connecting its internal and international security concerns.

As it investigates the changing conception of security in Vietnam, this chapter will document the changes as well as the reasons for them. Because history weighs heavily on the thinking of Vietnamese leaders, it begins with a discussion of the impact of history on the practice of security in Vietnam.

The Legacy of History

The defining characteristic of Vietnamese politics has long been a sense of having to construct a nation-state in hostile surroundings. To survive the geopolitical accident of being the small neighbor of the overwhelming cultural, political, and military force to the north in the form of China, Vietnam through the centuries has responded with a mix of strategies in its efforts to maintain independence. Vietnam's ability to adopt and indigenize sophisticated Chinese institutions and practices ensured its survival, but the preservation of a distinct state and Vietnamese national identity required constant rebellion against Chinese domination, particularly during the numerous times that China occupied Vietnam and sought to turn it into an integral part of the Chinese empire. This complex love-hate, dependent-independent relationship with China was a fundamental factor in the Vietnamese conception of security.

The struggle against China was part of a broader condition of having to survive in a hostile environment and against great odds. Vietnam's southward expansion was a response to the northern Chinese threat as well as a consequence of an aggressively expanding state throughout its history. In the process, the powerful Cham state that once inhabited central Vietnam ultimately disappeared; Vietnam gained its southern territory from the Khmers as late as the nineteenth century. In short, the legacy of history and geopolitics left Vietnam with the view that it would be able to maintain its existence and independence only with hard work and sheer force of will. The strong sense of self, however, was accompanied by deep ambivalence about the adoption of foreign ways that had been necessary for the construction of the nation-state. The experience of French colonialism contributed to this ambivalence, which was evident in the spirited intellectual debate in the 1930s and 1940s over what constituted national identity and culture (Pham Van Tho 1994: 52).

By the early 1940s, the pathetic remains of imperial power, waning French colonialism, and brutal Japanese occupation had all combined to underline the weakness of the Vietnamese nation and the nonexistence of what could be termed a Vietnamese state. Marxism-Leninism appealed to so many Vietnamese during this period precisely because it offered a worldview that eased the sense of national weakness by imputing a larger global force at work and, more important, by providing a model for party organization and for a new state. The search for community, for an organized structure, was feverish in Vietnam because, as the historian Alexander Woodside has suggested, the colonial system had exposed so starkly the weakness of the traditional structure of organization (Woodside 1976).[1] In the Vietnamese case, therefore, the construction of the state was seen as the key to maintaining the national essence, which had always needed protection and which was particularly vulnerable in the years before the August Revolution.

Vietnam's struggle for survival did not end with the conclusion of World War II. France's adamant demand in 1945 for the return of its colonies in Indochina, and American support for its European ally, taught Vietnam a bitter lesson. Even with military victory over the French in 1954, the Vietnamese Communists, under pressure from both the Soviet Union and China, who wanted to placate the United States, were forced to accept the division of their country. In the end, big-power politics always took precedence. Vietnam's small size meant that it had always to be flexible to survive, and the lesson was that no one could be trusted to guarantee Vietnam's survival—not the Western statesmen who proclaimed new political ideals in a new world and not the communists who promised international brotherhood. The realist paradigm captured Vietnam's situation well. In an essentially anarchic world where the big powers had the capability to define the international system for the smaller states and were much more willing to come to terms among themselves than to be guided by notions of equality and fair play, small states such as Vietnam had do all they could to ensure their own survival, from diplomacy to balancing and engaging in military struggle.

Pre-'doi moi' Security Views

In the Vietnamese Communist Party's struggle for power throughout the 1930s and the 1940s, it confronted not only repressive colonial authorities but also other Vietnamese nationalist parties with very different views of how an independent Vietnamese state should be constructed. The beginning of the anti-French struggle in 1946 threw the society into chaos, allowing the VCP to pursue a brutally systematic elimination of its domestic rivals without having to resort to political maneuvering. In response to the contentious internal and external environment in which the party managed to achieve its dominant position and the need to prepare for the eventual establishment of a socialist state, the VCP's policies in key areas such as culture and land reform became increasingly restrictive and orthodox during the nine years of the anti-French struggle. The emphasis on an explicitly socialist ideology and centralizing, authoritarian institutions were deemed necessary to ensure adequate material support for the war effort, to engender a new nationalist culture for the new socialist state, and to contain opposition to the VCP's agenda.[2]

Under the VCP's leadership, North Vietnam officially became a socialist state in 1954. The socialist organization of the state and the move toward a centralized economy quickly generated a gap between the VCP and a significant number of intellectuals who had come of age in the chaotic but intellectually inquisitive atmosphere of the 1930s and 1940s. Though they also believed in the central importance of the state and in firm rule, these intellectuals held different views about the nature of the Vietnamese state and about how invasive state control should be. When the VCP suppressed this brief but intense moment of intellectual questioning in 1958, it effectively ended the inclusive tendency of the Vietnamese revolution and forced the intellectual movement underground.[3]

The subsequent two decades of warfare that turned Vietnam into a battleground for the opposing worldviews of the United States and the Soviet Union bolstered the socialist framework. The U.S.–backed South Vietnam presented the VCP with a formidable domestic rival, underlining the need for organizational control and firm leadership. In support of the U.S. effort to combat communism, many countries in the region also sent troops to Vietnam. Even in instances involving leading members of the socialist bloc whose common ideology should have guaranteed Vietnam's interests, Vietnamese Communist leaders have found themselves subdued by the demands of big-power politics. The division of the country in half in 1954 was but one example. In this context, the development of a strong us-versus-them mentality within the VCP was hardly surprising.

Given its weak position in the East-West struggle and within the socialist bloc itself, Hanoi sought to manipulate the struggle to its best advantage externally while maintaining firm control over its population through a dense state structure fully under the VCP's command. Over the years, this gave rise to the belief that although skillful and flexible politics was key to Vietnam's survival and eventual achievement of national unification, the country must above all safeguard its own interests and maintain a high level of vigilance. Despite the internationalist tone adopted by the VCP throughout the Vietnam War, suspicion permeated its dealings with the outside world, including its relations with other socialist countries. To ensure that Vietnam was ready at all times for any exigency, the government adopted a comprehensive strategy requiring that the society itself always be on the alert and always be under close observation. External security threats and the need to control society were tightly interwoven.

Suspicion and vigilance were further heightened by military conflicts with Cambodia and China in the late 1970s and through the 1980s, as well as by the U.S. trade embargo and ASEAN's effort to force Vietnam to rescind its position in Cambodia. A statement by the minister of interior in 1982, typical of the period, echoed Vietnam's apprehensions:

> After the failure in the war to invade our country at the southwestern and northern borders, the expanding, hegemonic China colludes even more with imperialist United States and other reactionary forces. On the one hand, they continue to move military forces to the northern border of our country, generating military conflict in many areas in order to encroach on more land, maintain the usual anxiety at the border, and create the danger that a war of invasion can occur in different forms; on the other hand, they strive to destroy our people's effort to build socialism, keenly driving our country's destruction on many fronts, from many angles, through many forms and many means extremely dangerous and conniving in order to destabilize our country's political, economic and social situation, making us weak so as to generate chaos and when there is an opportunity, they will move to invade our country. (Pham Hung 1982: 24–25)

From the premise that its enemies were powerful and that they sought to destroy Vietnam by any means available, the Vietnamese socialist state extended its definition of national security to encompass virtually all nooks and crannies not only of its international relations but also of the society itself. Social vices, economic mishaps, mismanagement, and dissenting voices among the intelligentsia and the rank and file of the party were construed as the work of the external enemies. The Khmer Rouge in Cambodia, the large number of overseas Vietnamese, and the ethnic insurgency represented by FULRO (Front Unifié de Libération des Races Opprimées) also were considered threats to Vietnamese security because in many cases they were viewed as being proxies in American and Chinese efforts to destroy Vietnam. During this period, the media constantly referred to "reactionaries disguised as priests," and the intellectuals in the south as well as in the overseas Vietnamese community were castigated for being "agents of the U.S. Central Intelligence Agency" who were plotting to destabilize the revolution (Amnesty International 1990: 20, 22). A number of prominent southern writers also were arrested.

Into the 1980s, therefore, Vietnam's view of security remained externally oriented toward a hostile international environment. For the

VCP, the regime *was* the state whose survival was threatened, and in this context, domestic politics was mobilized to react to the external situation. The fury of the security pronouncements were at their highest in the early 1980s, as if to compensate for the slackened vigilance evident after national reunification. Firm control was reiterated, and demands similar to those occurring during the wars against France and the United States were made on the population.

There were, however, significant differences between the situation during the Vietnam War and that after unification in 1975. For one thing, during the Vietnam War total mobilization of the population, encapsulated in the brilliant military tactician General Vo Nguyen Giap's strategy of a "people's war," was possible because the physical and spiritual threats to the population were so immediate. The "people's war" was not simply a military strategy but an abbreviated description of the total psychological impact of living through a time when wartime hardships were the norm rather than the exception. The military conflicts with Cambodia and China in the late 1970s and early 1980s simply did not have the same urgency and consequence for the whole population. Thus, in the mid-1980s Vietnam's security situation was uneasily defined this way: "The country does not face a large-scale war now [but it] does not have complete peace [either]....[It] is now in a situation in which there are both war and peace in certain proportions" (Vo Nhan Tri 1988: 340).

Also significantly different in the mid-1980s was the fact that a unified socialist Vietnam had to contend with a still-capitalist south. Ideas and practices far removed from the clearly defined socialist framework exerted their influence over the north, undermining the notion that the party's way was the only option. Meanwhile, the Communist government's harsh treatment of the south quickly ended the euphoria that had greeted the convoys of northern soldiers entering Saigon in 1975. Even in the face of firm socialist authority, the southern characteristic of blunt speaking did much to emphasize the gap between the two halves of the country structurally, ideologically, and culturally. Over time, this southern view began to find echoes in the more moderate and inclusive segment of the revolution in the north that had been driven underground in late 1950s and that now helped to temper the state's more radical and explicitly socialist policies.

'Doi moi' and Changing Security Views

A decade after the attainment of the long-cherished goal of national unification, the Vietnamese Communist leadership found the fruits of national unification to be elusive. The economy was sliding toward chaos, exacerbated by an unfortunate string of natural disasters. Military engagement in Cambodia and border skirmishes with China further drained Vietnam's meager resources. The U.S. trade embargo and international isolation forced Vietnam to rely mostly on other socialist states for aid and trade, but those states were increasingly preoccupied with their own dramatic domestic upheavals. When other socialist countries' attempts at structural reform failed, the eventual result was the disintegration of socialism and of the states constructed in its name in East Germany, the Soviet Union, and Eastern Europe. China, having experienced tremendous growth after a decade of economic reform, faced a severe reminder of unresolved social and political fissures in the 1989 student demonstrations at Tiananmen Square. The Chinese government's bloody crackdown was disturbing to the Vietnamese leadership. Meanwhile, the ASEAN states' stable and high rates of growth increasingly forced Vietnam to confront an alternative model of development much closer to home.

Faced with the stark reality of failure and cognizant of the fact that socialist states elsewhere also were finding it necessary to undergo changes, the VCP moved to adopt the strategy of *doi moi*, or renovation, at the Sixth Party Congress in 1986. The desperate need for change was clear; top party leader Truong Chinh referred to *doi moi* as a life-and-death requirement. Yet what would *doi moi* really mean to a system that had long seen itself as the repository of the national essence and a loyal adherent of socialism? What was the right mix of economic and socio-political reforms, in light of the stark difference between the Chinese and the Soviet examples?

To overcome its developmental impasse, Vietnam had to harness the domestic potential fully while aggressively pursuing crucial foreign investment. In particular, the agricultural sector had to be able to stand on its own. Toward this end, state control over cooperatives and land use was eased, resulting in the spectacular rise of Vietnam in early 1990s as the world's third-largest rice exporter. Private commercial activities flourished, and foreign investment began to arrive. All these developments, however, were accompanied by intense ideological discussions that revealed fear and ambivalence as well as hope and the desire for openness.[4] For so long, constant vigilance had been required for the state under siege to guarantee its physical survival as well as its own sense of cohesiveness. That vigilant stance had to be relaxed in order for Vietnam to begin the process of integration into the regional and international community.

However, internal developments continue to be firmly linked to the external situation. Historical distrust of foreign influences in Vietnamese affairs is evident in the obsession with notions of "beyond containment" (*vuot tren ngan chan*) and "peaceful evolution" (*dien bien hoa binh*), which are seen as attempts by the capitalist world to undermine the existence and growth of the remaining socialist states like Vietnam through a wide range of political, economic, cultural, and ideological measures. The American penchant for linking aid with human rights and democratic reforms is a vivid example of such a strategy in Vietnamese eyes (Quang Loi 1990: 82–84). This seemingly strident view of security, however, acknowledges the absence of an imminent military threat and the need to respond to the challenges posed by liberal political, economic, social, and cultural threats. Moreover, it recognizes the need to examine the nature of communist parties and the problems generated by the process of renovation in order to understand the reasons for the collapse of socialist states elsewhere (Tran Trong 1990: 108). The Vietnamese assessment of communist parties in Eastern Europe, for example, is particularly frank in noting their abuses of power and their failure to accommodate popular grievances.[5]

Reconceptualizing Socialism

The recognition of serious problems with the old socialist model is evident in the recent many and diverse attempts to reconceptualize the international situation, Vietnam's foreign relations, and even the fundamental tenets of Marxism-Leninism in an effort to go beyond the dogmatic ideological framework that guided Vietnamese development for so long. Reconceptualization also strives to provide theoretical legitimacy to the increasingly market-oriented economic development and the aggressive foreign investment strategy being pursued by the VCP while the party continues to insist that it is leading the country resolutely down the socialist path. Even Ho Chi Minh's thoughts have been resurrected in support of the development of a unique Vietnamese brand of socialism. At the Seventh Party Congress in July 1991, the party's platform and regulations for the first time enshrined the idea that "the Party takes Marxism-Leninism and Ho Chi Minh Thought to be the ideological base and the compass for its actions" (as quoted in Song Thanh 1992: 8). In a world in which the first country of socialism no longer existed and China could not lead Vietnam because of the difficult and complex relations between the two countries, "Ho Chi Minh Thought" was the VCP's attempt, in the words of the director of the Ho Chi Minh Institute, to "assert the maturity in independent thinking and self-mastery of our party, [and to] affirm the value of Ho Chi Minh Thought in the struggle for peace, for national independence, and for democracy and socialism in the contemporary era (Song Thanh 1992: 8).

Rejecting the road mistakenly taken in other socialist states, proponents of an independent ideological course in Vietnam argue that the final form of socialism itself is unclear and still under formation. Therefore, although "moving toward socialism is an objective necessity," the official ideological stance recognizes that a much longer period of transition to socialism is needed for an underdeveloped country such as Vietnam—a period in which a certain amount of national capitalistic development is required (Truong Mau 1995: 63). The vagueness of this ideological position on socialism, coupled with the emphasis on flexibility, practicality, and creativity in responding to what is seen as Vietnam's rare opportunity to catch up with the rest of Southeast Asia, provides the party with the wide latitude it needs to focus on national construction without abandoning the claim to socialist purity. The Vietnamese continue to have enormous genuine respect for Ho Chi Minh, and the ideology of a dead but revered father of the nation is always much easier to defend and to utilize creatively than the discredited ideology of a world that no longer exists.[6]

The emphasis on Ho Chi Minh Thought also is intended to address the rising discontent among prominent intellectuals and party members. Party purification, the need to separate the party apparatus from the state structure, and high regard for intellectuals, for example, are claimed to have been issues of concern for Ho Chi Minh (Tran Dinh Huynh 1993). Thus by coming back to Ho Chi Minh, the party is justifying its right to rule by recalling the mythical moral universe of the August Revolution and the more specific and emotion-charged appeal of nationalist construction.[7] The official elevation of Ho Chi Minh Thought to the pantheon of orthodox socialist ideology is, in fact, a claim that Vietnamese nationalist socialism is derived from a source untainted by the extremes of socialist development elsewhere.

Regional Cooperation

As noted earlier, Vietnam's desire to overcome its developmental impasse led to a dramatic reorientation of its economic, political, and social agendas. Vietnam is increasingly following the model of one-party, state-controlled capitalist development that has been deployed successfully in post–World War II Asia. The most noteworthy shift in Vietnam's conduct of external relations and its views of security in the past decade has been the reorientation from its intense preoccupation with big powers, particularly China, to a more balanced position in which regional cooperation with other Southeast Asian states plays a significant role.

Long forced to play on the international stage a role far larger than its size, power, or importance would warrant, Vietnam is finally coming face to face with its true position in Asia. The turn toward Southeast Asia is fortuitous for Vietnam in many respects: the region is one of the most economically dynamic in the world and is politically stable. Vietnam can certainly benefit from the technological know-how and the regional surplus of capital for investment, and it can emulate the one-party systems employed by several Southeast Asian countries. For all the weaknesses inherent in the organization of ASEAN, at the very least it is a viable institution bringing the Southeast Asian states together so that they are in a better position to balance the other more dominant powers in Asia, namely Japan and China. Diversification of its economic and political relations is the purpose underlying Vietnam's participation in a number of other multilateral institutions as well, such as APEC (Asian-Pacific Economic Cooperation). Clearly, regional cooperation serves several purposes from the Vietnamese perspective.

Finally, Vietnam's reorientation toward Southeast Asia has an identity component. What has long been dominant in the Vietnamese self-assessment is the extent to which it is not Chinese (and to a lesser extent not French), but now Vietnamese intellectuals are beginning to rediscover the nation's roots in other terms.[8] Although much of the interest in ASEAN continues to focus on the economic dimension, there is a growing desire to explore historical, cultural, ethnic, and religious connections with Southeast Asia.[9] That desire is suggestive of the attempt to construct a more meaningful and balanced Vietnamese identity—one in which a relativist rather than an essentialist view of culture is dominant and one in which influences other than Chinese or French can be given their proper places. As such, it can be argued that Vietnamese receptiveness to constraints associated with regional institution-building go beyond a purely instrumental motive and also reflect a deeper desire to establish linkages with the region in more emotional terms. Given that the Southeast Asian states also emphasize strong state control and noninterference in each other's internal affairs, it is relatively simple for Vietnam to accept the regional imperatives at the moment while it continues to pursue stable growth and a more confident definition of nation and state.

Current Security Thinking

Although still seemingly strident and ideologically orthodox, both the dire warnings of "peaceful evolution" and the emergence of Ho Chi Minh Thought are aspects of the new security thinking in Vietnam. This new thinking takes into account the global trend emphasizing economic progress over strictly military concerns and argues that Vietnam must establish an independent course in both ideology and developmental policy in the aftermath of the collapse of socialism.

The threat of "peaceful evolution" is often articulated in the army's newspaper and journal. Those articulating this threat argue that although global military conflicts are less likely, insidious efforts by Vietnam's enemies to destroy the country from within through quietly destructive means such as human rights, "multipartyism," depoliticization of the army, and religious and ethnic revivalism have become more significant. The Foreign Ministry, however, paints a more benign view of the international environment. As Deputy Foreign Minister Nguyen Dy Nien put it in 1990, the world is now seeing "a primary interest in economic development" and "the strength of a country is measured mainly by its economic strength and cultural values." Therefore, "war is no longer an effective way to settle conflicts in international relations. Of course, at times countries still resort to military force to achieve definite objectives and schemes. However, a country always has to pay for such an action and must carefully calculate to avoid a war that might bankrupt its development plan and make it inferior to other nations" (Pham Van Tho 1994: 52). The remark certainly conjures up the bitter lesson of Vietnamese military involvement in Cambodia, but what is more important here is that the larger linkage between the political and economic realms and between internal and external dimensions is viewed in the context of global interdependence.

These two different approaches to international developments led to some conflict in the early years of Vietnam's effort at renovation. Given the official strategy of renovation, the army feared that its role might be diminished not only by the primary status of diplomacy but also by a different and possibly conflicting assessment of the international situation and national defense.[10]

Whatever discord might have existed between the army's views and the Foreign Ministry's approach to international relations and national defense seems to have been resolved, however. As the first half of the 1990s unfolded, the party reiterated the connection between foreign relations and national defense. As General Secretary Do Muoi stated in his delivery of the Seventh Party Central Committee's political report at the Midterm National Party Conference (on January 20, 1994),

> While concentrating our efforts on national construction, we must not neglect even for a moment the task of defending the fatherland; safe-guarding national independence, sovereignty, territorial integrity, and security; firmly maintaining sociopolitical stability and the socialist orientation of development....We must continue to promote the imple-

mentation of an independent, sovereign, open, diversified, and multilateralized foreign policy, maximize similarities, and limit differences, thereby creating favorable conditions for national construction and defense. (Dinh Nho Liem 1994: 70)

A more unified view of national security is emerging to consolidate the dramatic gains that the VCP has managed to achieve in the international and domestic arenas in the last decade. The common starting point is that the world has truly entered a phase in which the dominant concern is economic development, and, given that Vietnam is fortunate enough to be located in the most dynamic region of the world, that this is indeed a golden opportunity for Vietnam to break out of its own developmental impasse. Such a chance is rare, and the urgency of the task is embodied in the oft-repeated phrase "combining the strength of the nation with the strength of the era in the new period."

The relationship between national security and foreign relations is becoming more coordinated. After years of carefully cultivating an image of a friendly and cooperative Vietnam in the international arena, resulting in normalized relations with all of its former enemies and in memberships in regional and international organizations, Vietnam is now more confident of stating its national interests in less accommodating ways. In a 1994 article written for the army's monthly publication, Deputy Foreign Minister Dinh Nho Liem emphasized that "independence with sovereignty and territorial integrity is an important objective of the diplomatic struggle combined with national defense." He further elaborated: "We should not give up Vietnam's sovereignty and sacred territory for the sake of improving relations, economic interests, and friendship. The important thing is that we must have clever ways of doing things and seek a formula of talks that both sides could agree upon" (Dinh Nho Liem 1994: 71). The reference to China is unmistakable. Despite Liem's stress on "clever ways" of diplomacy to iron out the differences between the two countries, this is a considerably harder line against China than was taken in previous years. Vietnamese protestations against China's oil exploration grant to the American company Crestone in 1994 bluntly stated that it was a violation of Vietnamese territorial integrity.

The Ministry of Foreign Affairs also is firm when it comes to the issue of human rights and routinely rejects any linkage between foreign aid and human rights. Vietnam insists that human rights are part of its own internal affairs and are inherently connected with the country's history, culture, traditions, and socioeconomic conditions.[11] The Foreign Ministry's strategy on a number of issues such as that of human rights is to take part in all the relevant international forums, thereby indicating its interest in participating in the larger discourse, while at the same time firmly maintaining Vietnam's own views. This so-called cooperation-struggle strategy aims at a flexible approach to obtain the best possible outcome. In the words of Hong Ha, the secretary of the Central Committee and the head of the party's External Relations Committee,

> [In international relations] depending on the opposite side, on the issue and at a different point in time, the cooperative side or the struggle side may be more prominent. One-way cooperation or one-way conflict both lead to a losing and unfavorable situation. We push for cooperation but we still have to struggle in a form and at a pace appropriate to each opponent in order to safeguard our people's interest, establish equal relations that are mutually beneficial and maintain peace. But we struggle in order to push forward cooperation, avoiding the weak spots that would push us into a corner and generate provocation. (Hong Ha 1992: 13)

It is not a zero-sum view of security, but the elaboration of a cooperation-struggle strategy reveals a strong attachment to national independence and a perception that even though the current trend is toward economic interdependence and cooperation, Vietnam must not be lulled into thinking that this will always be the case. Power can be utilized in conjunction with cooperation, depending on the particular situation, to garner the best possible outcome. It is a view of power and international relations from the perspective of a small state, aware of its limitations but also determined to maximize its possibilities. Given Vietnam's success in both external relations and fostering economic development in recent years, the state is finally at a point where it can begin to put the cooperation-struggle strategy to use through a skillful and confident Foreign Ministry.[12]

Despite its growing salience, however, diplomacy has not usurped the army's special position. After all, the first generation of military leaders of the People's Army of Vietnam (PAVN) was simply an extension of party leadership. Intimately connected with the struggle for national independence and the construction of the socialist state, the army has always had a strong political role, in marked contrast to the customary division between civil and military affairs in other countries (Thayer 1994a). The insistence on a political role for the army has ensured that a wider view of economic and social development—rather than the army's own interests—is dominant in national policy, along the lines shaped by the VCP (Pike 1986). The fusion of civilian and military leadership has eased over the years, especially with the recognition of the need for a more professional army. Given the PAVN's unique origin and experience and its exceptional record of internal unity, however, William Turley, a longtime observer of the PAVN, concluded in 1988 that direct conflict between the party and the army is "virtually unimaginable at present" and that "the military will not exceed the limits of its legitimate political participation" (Turley 1988: 209).

Withdrawal from Cambodia and relative peace led to the demobilization of troops and the rise of a new generation of officers in a streamlined but efficient army. The spirit of being Uncle Ho's soldiers must be preserved, but the PAVN wants to inject greater professionalism in order to maintain discipline and morale. The army has sought to modernize and to expand its foreign military relations. Simultaneously, it has focused on political and ideological education and ensured an adequate standard of living for the soldiers (Thayer 1994a). Vietnam's small gross domestic product and pressing development needs will hamper the effort at modernization, but a strong army is an integral part of Vietnam's security strategy. As one analyst has noted, "the increase in the proportion of military spending in national income from 6.6 to 8.4 percent of gross domestic product in 1993 put Vietnam at a level of defense spending well above the ASEAN average" (Turley 1996: 187). Rising state revenues have allowed increases in defense spending, largely to strengthen Vietnam's defense in the South China Sea (Thayer 1994a: 41). It has been further reported that the army's budget has risen every year since 1992, and its growing business activities are generating funds for the modernization effort and ensuring a higher level of loyalty and prestige among the rank and file (Mydans 1996).

Overall, there is no indication that Turley's 1988 assessment of party-army relations and the army's role in the political structure needs to be revised, although the growing involvement of the PAVN in economic activities may become a source of real tension in the future. For now, the army's strong organizational structure and its general reputation for being the least corrupted institution have been attractive selling points to foreign companies contemplating new joint ventures. Continued economic success may mean a better standard of living for the soldiers, new weaponry, and a more realistic opportunity for some version of a national defense industry. However, the infusion of large amounts of money into the army may also introduce corruption and a divergence between the party's agenda and that of the army. It is not inconceivable that in such a situation the PAVN's remarkable internal cohesion may suffer greatly as private motives at different levels override the organization's ideals and interests. The massive amount of smuggling that goes on at the borders from China to Cambodia, which many Vietnam-watchers believe could be conducted only with the active involvement of military, customs, and police officials, may be an example of such breakdown (Schwarz 1996b).

External Security Threats

Although they acknowledge that the common trend in the world is peace and development, the Vietnamese Communist Party's assessments of the current situation maintain that new regional alliances do not lead to the end of regional conflicts, especially those with a historical dimension. At the moment, the two main external security threats to Vietnam are China and Cambodia.

China

China looms large in the Vietnamese mind because so much of what defines Vietnam historically is the extent to which Vietnam is not Chinese. China's physical existence at Vietnam's northern border serves as a constant reminder of Vietnam's difficult and complex relationship with the Middle Kingdom. Even after the normalization of relations with China in 1991, Vietnam has remained extremely wary of China's intentions, especially in the post-Tiananmen period as Chinese nationalism has been promoted by the state to overcome the ideological gap between a still self-proclaimed socialist China and the world, and between the government and its people (Chanda and Huus 1995). With a booming economy, an army loaded with new weaponry, and growing influence in foreign affairs, the rising China is causing anxiety in Vietnam.

The most complicated and dangerous conflict between Vietnam and China is in the South China Sea. The locus of the conflict is the Spratly Islands and adjacent waters, all or parts of which are claimed not only by Vietnam but also by China, the Philippines, Malaysia, Taiwan, and Brunei. The area's rich potential in mineral, fishing, oil, and other natural resources is naturally attractive to Vietnam, but the more immediate concern is security. Given that Vietnam's coastline facing the South China Sea is more than 3,000 kilometers long and contains all of its major ports, how to defend the country in this area has always been a major concern. The following is a common Vietnamese assessment of the South China Sea (Eastern Sea, from the Vietnamese perspective) security situation: "Many wars of aggression by reactionary and imperialist forces against our people have come from this direction. The threat of their blockades against our country from this sea direction has never been reduced. Penetrations to steal intelligence information, conduct sabotage, establish connections, and plant reactionary agents have also come from this Eastern sea zone" (Nguyen Thanh Lieng 1990: 54).

Some Vietnamese believe that "[the Chinese aim] is to gradually occupy the entire eastern coastal zone. In the name of implementing the agreements, [the Chinese] will use their naval forces to perform defense tasks and regularly maintain strong naval forces in this zone with the aim of creating tension and turmoil throughout it" (Le Ke Lam 1994: 70).

From the Vietnamese perspective, therefore, the dispute with China over the control of the islands in the South China Sea has a strong security component. In addition, the dispute has the potential to become even more dangerous because of claims of oil and natural gas deposits in the area. Both China and Vietnam have been awarding exploration rights to foreign companies as a way to shore up their territorial claims. In 1992, Beijing signed an agreement with the small American firm Crestone Energy Corporation to explore an area west of the Spratly Islands, and in April 1996, Vietnam leased two exploration blocks in the same waters to the American oil firm Conoco, whose parent company is DuPont. The diplomatic exchanges between China and Vietnam have become more hard-line, with both sides asserting indisputable sovereignty (Schwarz and Forney 1996).

Vietnam's concern with China also extends to economic interaction along the northern border. Since the opening of the border between the two countries in late 1988, border trade has grown enormously, and the balance of trade has been in China's favor. The trade has eased the serious shortage of ordinary consumer goods in northern Vietnam in particular, but the large inflow of Chinese goods has serious consequences for Vietnam's domestic production (Womack 1994: 507–8). Nevertheless, Vietnam's general success in obtaining capitalist foreign investment may ease this dilemma, and such intense competition may spur the Vietnamese domestic industrial sector to transform itself. More problematic for Vietnam is the smuggling and corruption that accompany the intense border trade, affecting not only the state budget but also the effort to revamp the administrative and legal structures. Although the border trade has transformed the isolated provinces on both sides of the border, the much more impoverished Vietnamese border areas have become a market for arms as well, drawing large numbers of criminals of all types, including heavily armed bandits (Chapon 1991). This domestic security concern is overlaid with fear of Chinese intentions. A Vietnamese military source asserts that "the constant and massive smuggling of Chinese goods from China is a form of economic sabotage"; other Vietnamese experts are convinced that the smuggling is part of a plan by Beijing to destabilize Vietnam's domestic market and damage its industries (Bekaert 1993: 56). Although the amount of trade with Vietnam is minuscule for China, the fact that Vietnam serves as a dumping ground for cheap Chinese products stokes the latent historical fear that China wants to keep Vietnam from achieving a high level of prosperity and independence. The view of China as a looming threat is one that is shared by much of the population.[13]

China, therefore, remains the biggest external security threat to Vietnam. Having normalized relations with China in 1991, Vietnam is doing its best to cultivate friendly bilateral relations and is engaging in talks over a number of contentious issues between the two countries. Nevertheless, the cooperation-struggle view of security also means preparing for possible conflict. To this end, Vietnam has stepped up its defense line in the coastal areas, incorporating the local population in the expansion of fishing activities and habitation of the islands as a way to increase its meager naval capability. The increases in the defense budget since 1992 as a response to the South China Sea issue have been noted, and Vietnam's utilization of foreign companies in the exploration of oil and gas in the contested waters is also a strategy to shore up its territorial claims.

Vietnam's effort at improving relations with the United States also is aimed at countering the Chinese influence in the region. Industry sources, for example, argue that it is no coincidence that Hanoi awarded the latest exploration concession to a giant American oil company. They believe that it is part of Vietnam's strategy to engage the United States, the world's greatest sea power, in sharing economic interests in the highly contested area (Schwarz and Forney 1996). Membership in ASEAN and other multilateral institutions is another way that Vietnam tries to balance and constrain China. Being vastly inferior to China in military capability, and specifically naval power, Vietnam cannot hope to confront China alone on a large scale over the island dispute. Vietnam's efforts to maintain and increase the current rate of foreign investment and its war-weary population are additional constraints to any dramatic military venture.

Diplomacy is therefore Vietnam's best hope for restraining Chinese action and improving its own position. For a long time, ASEAN has been reluctant to make a concerted response to China's behavior in the South China Sea, preferring to leave the discussion at the bilateral level. Nevertheless, there are signs that that reluctant mood may be changing. For one thing, China's incursion into what was considered to be Philippine waters in February 1995 irked the Philippines considerably and helped to push through the Philippine Congress a U.S.$2 billion armed forces modernization program (Tasker 1995). As one of the original members of ASEAN, the Philippines' concern regarding China's intention cannot go unnoticed by ASEAN itself, which is always sensitive to Chinese dominance. ASEAN has begun developing a dialogue with China to express the member states' concerns, particularly on security issues. In such a dialogue meeting with China in April 1995, the ASEAN states took Beijing by surprise by condemning the Chinese action toward the Philippines and criticizing China's claim of sovereignty in the South China Sea (Vatikiotis et al. 1997).

Vietnam seeks to capitalize on these new developments to bolster its own situation. In March 1997, a Chinese exploration vessel drilled for gas about 65 nautical miles off the coast of central Vietnam in waters claimed by Hanoi, opening up a new geographic area of dispute with Vietnam. Although the area is not claimed by other ASEAN states, Vietnam has called for ASEAN support. One senior ASEAN official was quoted as saying, "We don't recognize any Chinese rights to Vietnam's continental shelf, nor do we recognize the right of the Chinese to do what they did. Now we're all in this together" (Vatikiotis et al. 1997). ASEAN's position is far from clear, though many observers view this as a possible test case for ASEAN in terms of its relations with China as well as its credibility as a regional organization. For its part, just to make sure that China is listening, Vietnam opened the discussions with the ASEAN ambassadors in March 1997 by mentioning a possible military relationship with the United States. It is pertinent to observe here the visit of Admiral Joseph Prueher, commander in chief of the U.S. Pacific Command, to Vietnam during the same month (Vatikiotis et al. 1997). As one Vietnamese official maintained, "the fear of China is a new glue in Asia" (as quoted in Chanda and Huus 1995), and China's rise as a new global power is certainly watched with great concern by the ASEAN states and the United States.

Cambodia

Vietnam's second major external concern is Cambodia. Vietnam no longer espouses the concept of the "special relationship" that bound the three communist states in Indochina together in the past, although its relations with Laos continue to be close. Vietnam's current relationship with Cambodia is described by a longtime observer as one of "a neutral and non-aligned state," but potential sources of friction exist between them. These include border demarcation disputes, conflicting maritime territorial claims, and the status of ethnic Vietnamese residents in Cambodia (Thayer 1994a: 67). Such a list, however, does not reveal the fierce anti-Vietnamese sentiment in Cambodia. In 1978 the visceral Khmer hatred for Vietnamese spurred the Khmer Rouge's attacks on Vietnamese border villages, leading to the retaliation by the Vietnamese military and to Vietnamese occupation of Cambodia. The anti-Vietnam sentiment is regularly exploited by Cambodian political parties.

Vietnam has stated time and again that it has no desire to return to Cambodia in military terms; the ten-year military involvement in Cambodia was costly. There is no reason to doubt that statement, and Vietnam has scrupulously tried to maintain a neutral stance. Hanoi, for example, rejected a recent Cambodian request for weapons parts and ammunition to replenish its dwindling stocks in the war against the Khmer Rouge (*Bangkok Post* 1994). Nevertheless, because Vietnam cannot count on Cambodia to behave in the same manner, it does what it can to maintain control at the border and to prepare for the possible eruption of civil war in Cambodia. Territorial disputes will continue to be a problem. For one thing, the land issue looms large in the Cambodian psyche, which is permeated by the old fear of being swallowed up by Vietnam. The Khmer Rouge exploited this issue during the 1970s with its demands for a reexamination of historical territory lost to Vietnam during the nineteenth century, including large areas of southern Vietnam and even Ho Chi Minh City itself. In more stable times, Vietnam and Cambodia under different regimes have explored how best to resolve their disputes over the land border mapped out by the French colonial authorities. Though the relationship between Vietnam and the current Cambodian government has been fairly calm, the constant Cambodian accusations that Vietnamese farmers are encroaching into Cambodian territory along the border areas with official support reflects both the continuing latent distrust of Vietnam as well as the use of anti-Vietnamese sentiments to boost Cambodian politicians' popularity (Schwarz 1996a). Security concern with disputed borders aside, the problem is also an economic one from Hanoi's point of view. A massive volume of smuggled goods cross the border into Vietnam, resulting in a serious loss of tax revenues for the state (Schwarz 1996a).

Finally, the Khmer Rouge's continuing attacks on ethnic Vietnamese living in Cambodia have led to a stream of Vietnamese crossing the border back to Vietnam. The promulgation of the Cambodian immigration law on August 26, 1994, by the Cambodian government—a law seen by foreign observers as targeting the Vietnamese community in Cambodia—is certainly viewed by Vietnam as a play of the race card that grants the Khmer Rouge an additional measure of credibility for its already virulent anti-Vietnamese message.[14]

Internal Security Threats

Since the collapse of socialism in the Soviet Union and the Eastern European countries, "defending the socialist fatherland" has become a crucial security goal for the VCP. A key element of this goal is the maintenance of firm control over society. The argument is that internal political stability is a crucial condition for development—a lesson, according to one commentator, learned from "the failure of restructuring in the Soviet Union and Eastern Europe, from the experience of reform in China, and from the realities of renovation in our country over the past seven years" (Le Huu Nghia 1994: 52). This rationale for the need to maintain tight control in the domestic arena is common in East and Southeast Asian states and has been deployed to counter international and domestic pressures for further political liberalization. Given its fear of being undermined by peaceful means, the government's view of internal security is particularly broad. According to the Ministry of Interior, "national security is not only political security, but also economic security, cultural security, ideological security and social security" (Bui Thien Ngo 1992: 5). The contention that *"all forms of ideological and economic sabotage originate from political demands and lead to political sabotage"* presents the image of a state that is constantly on guard, ready to quell any sign of unapproved development in any arena of social and economic activity for fear that it might undermine the state itself (Bui Thien Ngo 1992: 5; emphasis in the original). There is no doubt that the overdeveloped Vietnamese security apparatus takes itself seriously and has the power to project its purposes through a vast network of police officers and informants.

Concern with internal security always has been strong in communist states like Vietnam, but what constitutes a threat has changed substantially since 1986. Some of the earlier internal threats are no longer salient or are much less significant. Listening to foreign broadcast programs, such as those of the Voice of America or the British Broadcasting Corporation, and selling produce from one's backyard were previously construed by the Ministry of Interior as antistate activities. But in the era of *doi moi* such activities are no longer viewed as security concerns. The dramatic transformation of economic and social values since the adoption of renovation has had a profound effect on the state's definition of antistate political activities.

In this connection, a number of issues previously high on the security agenda are no longer viewed with the same degree of concern. The overseas Vietnamese community, for example, is now much less of a security concern. In fact it is being actively wooed for investment and technological know-how. With time and a more open policy in Vietnam, the overseas community also has largely dropped its anticommunist tone and, consequently, has decreased its financial support for anti-Vietnam ventures. Many expatriates also have chosen to come back to Vietnam to invest in small-business activities. Thus, the threat to the state from the overseas Vietnamese remains primarily ideological, and the state habitually rails against overseas reactionary organizations, intellectuals, journals, and magazines that call for democratization and the party's demise. Nevertheless, armed activities against the state supported by an overseas Vietnamese connection continue to be troublesome. One of the most serious overseas Vietnamese efforts to wage an armed uprising against the state was discovered in Ho Chi Minh City itself. Residents woke up one morning in March 1993 to find the city swarming with military tanks. It later was reported that a group of repatriated Vietnamese, armed with guns, grenades, and explosives and under the leadership of an overseas Vietnamese, planned to occupy the state radio and television stations and the offices of the party's newspaper *Nhan Dan* (*Kyodo* 1993: 56).

Ethnic problems do not trouble Vietnam as much as they do other states. The population is largely homogeneous, with a small number of Chinese and a host of ethnic minority groups scattered in the highlands. Almost all of the small but economically important Chinese population was driven out of the country after the 1979 border war with China, but there are signs that the liberal economic atmosphere is drawing them back. The number of ethnic Chinese in Vietnam is currently too small to present a problem, and the government is actively wooing them for investment and for their connection to the world's overseas Chinese community. As for the ethnic minority groups, the insurgency movement among them is essentially under control. They do live in the border areas, however, and the possibility of their exploitation by foreign enemies is a sensitive issue for the Vietnamese leadership. Thus there is a constant effort to ensure that the basic needs of the ethnic minority villages are accommodated and that the army pays special attention to the units based there.

If a number of previous domestic security concerns have fallen by the wayside with *doi moi*, political and economic changes have brought about new and difficult challenges to the state. Increasingly, concerns are being expressed about the depletion of natural resources, the dramatic growth of prostitution and related diseases such as AIDS, the rapid decline of the health care and education systems, the developmental gap between the cities and the countryside, the rising rates of corruption and smuggling, and the inadequacy of the legal system, among other issues. The more serious among these problems for the state can be grouped under two related categories: state-society tensions and the growing urban-rural gap. Feeding on one another, these issues cut to the core of the dilemma facing the state: how to balance continued growth while maintaining political stability in which the VCP can continue to play its leading role. Furthermore, although currently there is no viable political opposition to the VCP, growing critical voices have to be accommodated in ways that will not undercut the regime's legitimacy.

State-Society Tensions

The VCP's penchant for organization has led to the development of a state structure that is far too unwieldy for its size, encumbered by layers of overlapping institutions. The overlapping nature of party and state institutions also has created a situation in which power can easily be used for personal gain and responsibility is difficult to discern. As Vietnam makes the transition to a market-oriented society, the current state machinery and legal system are simply not equipped to deal with the vast array of changes in economic, administrative, social, and legal matters the transition entails. Corruption and smuggling have become difficult problems for the state. The escalating flow of money and goods into an impoverished country and the money-making fervor of the open-door period have meant opportunities for many who otherwise would languish, but at the same time corruption is being pushed to a new height and taking increasingly sophisticated forms. Government estimates of corruption and smuggling, generally underreported to begin with, show that they are rising and involving increasingly large losses to the state (Le Quang Thanh 1994). The economic crimes also spell political troubles. Highly visible cases of corruption by top party members in key government posts have greatly damaged the prestige of the party and the state apparatus.[15] Moreover, the very mechanism to safeguard against corruption and smuggling often has succumbed to the same vices, and the opportunities of an open economy have presented new temptations to those in positions of authority.

The system is simultaneously being challenged by new developments. Tourism, for example, has fostered the creation of new golf courses near major cities such as Hanoi and Dalat, and people who must relocate to make room for these projects are not giving up their homes without a fight, at the very least for appropriate compensation from foreign companies that are acting with state approval. In another instance, the state is finding that it is ill equipped to deal with mistreatment of Vietnamese workers in joint ventures and foreign-owned companies. The number of strikes is increasing. Official figures list more than 200 strikes since 1990, but union officials indicate that the number of unofficial work stoppages and wildcat strikes is substantially higher (Schwarz 1996a: 63). The list of complaints includes a much lower wage than what is stipulated by the government, long working hours, and physical abuse. Trade union organizations, long an integrated part of the administration of state-owned enterprises, have little capability to organize the workers in a foreign-owned enterprise, and in fact are present in only 15 to 20 percent of the joint ventures with foreign countries (Xuan Hai and Dang Ngoc Chien 1994). This is an area in which the state is being criticized for not protecting its own people against the deleterious effects of foreign investment.

Fraud committed by foreign companies, international drug smuggling through Vietnam, use of Vietnam as a dumping ground for other countries' waste—these are new issues for Vietnam to understand and to handle. In this complex period of change, the state is being criticized by intellectuals and the general population alike for being both too weak to resolve key social issues and too overpowering in its control. A more assertive intellectual community also is causing problems for the leadership. The younger generation of intellectuals, who came of age during or since the Vietnam War and who are much less affected by the moral universe of the August Revolution and the anti-French struggle, are becoming impatient with the heavy weight of the socialist state and with their own poverty and isolation. They demand quick action to rectify past mistakes.

A more open atmosphere has allowed other social grievances to surface. Religious conflict is one example. Catholicism is a legacy of French colonialism, and Vietnam, although predominantly Buddhist, has the second-largest number of Catholics in Asia, after the Philippines.[16] The Vietnamese Catholic Church has been very successful in quietly negotiating for the return of church land and buildings in Hanoi and elsewhere, the reopening of seminaries, and the renovation of crumbling churches and offices after years of neglect. Nevertheless, there is constant conflict with the Vatican, particularly over the selections for top clerical posts and the Vatican's refusal to acknowledge state-organized religious organizations such as the Solidary Committee of Patriotic Catholics.[17]

Although the relationship between the state and the Catholic community remains cool, ironically it is easier for the state to deal with the Catholic community than with certain Buddhist groups. Buddhism permeates many aspects of Vietnamese society and culture, but Vietnamese Buddhism is amorphous, resulting in many Buddhist organizations with emphasis on different aspects of the faith. In 1981 the Vietnamese government consolidated some nine Buddhist organizations into the state-sponsored Buddhist Church of Vietnam (BCV); the Unified Buddhist Church of Vietnam (UBCV), under the leadership of the monk Thich Huyen Quang, was the lone dissident. Since then, there has been constant conflict between the state and the supporters of the UBCV, particularly in 1994 and 1995.

The difficult relationship between the state and the UBCV is further underlined by the fact that the UBCV maintains strong connections with members of the overseas Vietnamese community in France and Australia. The high international profile maintained by the UBCV through its supporters in the overseas Vietnamese community and the involvement of international human rights groups in the UBCV cause put the government on the defensive, stoking the familiar charges of foreign enemies and their Vietnamese agents whipping up "a campaign to criticize and distort the truth about our party and state's religious policy. Worse still, they have cooked up many stories to falsely accuse our state of religious repression and of human rights violations" (Phan Hai Nam 1993: 55). In addition, the UBCV's tactics whereby monks burn themselves, engage in sit-in protests, and vocally denounce the state-sponsored Buddhist organization do not give the state much leeway for negotiation. In late 1994 the UBCV led large public demonstrations in Hue and Ho Chi Minh City calling for religious freedom and for a boycott against the activities of the state-sponsored Buddhist organization (Agence France Presse 1994b: 54, 1994c: 55). The large number of people involved in these demonstrations apparently caught the authorities by surprise, and participation on such a large scale does raise the possibility that the grievances will coalesce and erupt in some kind of organized protest. While being careful to contain public reaction by emphasizing the difference between religious and civil matters, the state moved firmly against the UBCV by arresting its top officials in 1995 (Agence France Presse 1995: 72).

In response to the opening up of the economy and the growing presence of Western and overseas Vietnamese, the Vietnamese state has stepped up its warnings against social and cultural pollution. There is a nativist reaction against the breathtaking changes in society, especially in light of the younger generation's fascination with Western culture and material gains. The 1996 campaign against "social evils" is one example of such reaction. The Vietnamese government fears the inroads of Western culture and has, like the other Southeast Asian countries, sought to define a specifically Asian approach to political, economic, and cultural development. Moreover, as David Elliott (1993) has noted, generations socialized in communitarian values and traditional cultures in the Soviet Union, China, and Vietnam make it difficult for the population as a whole to accept the rise of social stratification and vast differentiated levels of wealth. Elliott, therefore, cautions against outside observers' tendencies to equate the backlash against the disruptive aspects of reform as simply the hardliners' reactions and argues that the state's seemingly moralistic pronouncements against individualism, anarchism, and the like actually resonate with many because they accord with deeply rooted traditional norms (Elliott 1993: 57).

The state's dilemma, therefore, is twofold. On the one hand, it must seek to contain old and new sources of discontent from within that have emerged because of liberalization. On the other hand, it must maintain the firm apparatus of state power if it is to deal with the myriad new challenges coming from the flood of foreign investment in a recently decentralized socialist economic and political system. The state has continually emphasized that it seeks to ensure further economic development along with the firm maintenance of order and security, and that one requires the other. The VCP certainly understands that order and security in an open economy mean something different, requiring people's voluntary participation more than ever. In this regard, top party leaders have moved to institutionalize some administrative reforms. One method has been to revive the National Assembly as a forum for frank exchanges rather than simply a body to rubber-stamp the party's directives. Another has been to streamline the administrative apparatus, consolidating the activities of the various ministries and disentangling the party structure from that of the state. Yet another measure has been to purify and invigorate the party apparatus by weeding out bad cadres and tightening up the recruitment process.

Viewed in relative terms, the party has achieved some success, although the bureaucracy as a whole remains very unwieldy and unresponsive. The rising rate of corruption and smuggling testifies to the entrenchment of the system. The state is trying to effect change through the attempt to transform the legal system, but unless a serious overhaul of the whole legal system is contemplated, the level of administrative injustice and corruption will continue to grow, reinforcing the general disdain for the state apparatus and the widely held belief that corruption and bribes are not only endemic but are tactics to be learned and executed skillfully if one wants to get ahead. Continued growth and distributive justice, issues of both economic and political concern, will be greatly hampered if the state cannot find ways to narrow the gap between a society reaching chaotically for material gains any way it can and one in which the rule of law can be an impartial and just alternative source of authority. Nevertheless, the system that the VCP has constructed over some 40 years is a formidable one, and there is no credible alternative opposition in sight. The party's contention that without it there would be anarchy and chaos is a powerful argument for many Vietnamese. But the party, as we have noted, also faces many challenges. Turley's assessment of the current situation is apt: "The greatest challenge to the regime lies not in any imminent danger of collapse but in the long-term task of institutionalization in the absence of a proven model" (Turley 1993: 343).

Urban-Rural Gap

One of the biggest changes in policy Vietnam has pursued since the adoption of the renovation strategy is the effort to free the productive potential of agriculture. The state began the process by validating a number of spontaneous local economic practices being used in the struggle against the decline of the agricultural sectors (Kerkvliet and Porter 1994; Fforde and de Vylder 1996). In 1988 the party essentially abandoned inefficient cooperatives and began to return land to private hands. Although the move resulted in the dramatic rise of Vietnam from a rice-importing country to the third-largest rice exporter in the world in 1989 and the appearance of abundant farm produce in markets, real farm incomes have fallen sharply. In 1992 food prices dropped 15 percent while the cost of nonfood items rose by 20 percent, according to the government (Hiebert 1993b: 60). Plots of land in the Red River Delta around Hanoi are very small because of overcrowding, and many farmers are forced to go to Hanoi and other cities to find work during the off-season. The rise of urban wages has led to some noticeable movement of population from rural areas into the cities, exacerbating the high rates of unemployment, crime, housing shortage, and urban pollution.

In July 1993 the state eased the peasants' situation through its land-mark decision to grant them long-term land-use rights for a period of twenty years. Landholdings remain small at less than three hectares, but the peasants can now transfer, exchange, lease, and inherit land (Hiebert 1993a). A number of villages have seen substantial increases in their standards of living, but they are successful generally because they are located near a city like Hanoi that provides easy access to market or because they have managed to revive a traditional handicraft. Village life is better for many, but poverty continues to be the norm for the bulk of the rural population, many of whom cannot adjust quickly enough to the rapid marketization of social and economic activities. By the government's own estimates, nearly 10 percent of the urban population and about half of the rural workforce are unemployed, leading to higher crime rates and the growth of such societal problems as prostitution and drug addiction (Vu Oanh 1994: 71–72).

The astounding 50 percent unemployment rate among the rural workforce points to another problem, less immediate than the urban situation but potentially more devastating. Foreign observers have noted the growing differentiation of development between urban and rural areas, and data from studies done by various government offices and research institutes in Vietnam all agree. Although the urban population makes up only 20 percent of the total population, preliminary results from a 1994 government survey of 4,800 households show that nine-tenths of the most impoverished live in the countryside while two-thirds of wealthiest live in the cities (Hiebert 1994: 71). Other Vietnamese statistics show some 64 percent of the rural population in the poorest categories compared to some 16 percent of urban population.[18] These numbers show the extraordinary level of poverty in the countryside and the wide difference between urban and rural standards of living. The wide urban-rural gap also has exacerbated the country's historical regional disparities. A 1992 study by the General Statistics Office revealed that per capita income in Ho Chi Minh City and its surrounding provinces is 2.7 times higher than the national average, followed by Hanoi and the Mekong Delta with an income of 116 to 126 percent of the national average (Hiebert 1994: 71). Though the per capita income of the Red River Delta in the north is only half that of the Mekong Delta in the south, it is the northern mountains, the central highlands, and the central coast that lag farthest behind the rest of the country with incomes of less than half the national average.

The sharply rising rates of homelessness, drug addiction, prostitution, teenage marriages, and juvenile delinquency are direct consequences of the country's uneven development. The increasing references in the public press to the explosive rural situation indicate growing state concern. The seriousness of the rural situation is further underlined by the use of the term "hot spot," defined as "a place where a major or even fierce struggle is going on among the people over some issue in a particular sphere…which cannot be resolved on the spot and requires intervention on the part of the party committee echelons, the authorities, and judicial organizations from the primary level on up" (Nhi Le 1994: 71). A hot spot, therefore, is a place where conflict beyond the capability of the local political structure to handle has flared up. The general relaxation of government control on agriculture and village life has lifted the lid off simmering grievances in a number of the rural localities, far removed from the fast pace of development in Hanoi and other cities.[19] Land reform and collectivization, the taking of land for administrative offices, and the numerous consolidations and divisions of provinces have resulted in complicated land disputes that involve not only individual families but whole villages. Land disputes, which account for 54 percent of the hot spots in Thanh Hoa province, for example, can escalate to include a large number of people, pitting one village against another and thereby entailing wider police involvement.[20]

Another characteristic of these disputes has to do with the state structure itself, in particular the problems of corruption and abuse of power.[21] Peasants' numerous complaints often go unresolved, and it is not surprising that "in some places, the masses suspect that the district is covering up the mistakes of the primary-level cadres, which has made the situation even more complex and tense" (Pham Van Tho 1994: 52). The seriousness of the people's grievances can be seen in the extreme acts to which the people of Thanh Hoa resort in order to publicize their complaints and to force appropriate official responses. These acts range from lawsuits to public reprimands of corrupt cadres and party members to taking a number of them hostage. The intense level of popular anger demands in turn responses not only from the primary- and district-level leadership organizations but also from "the internal affairs, public security, control, and inspection sectors" (Pham Van Tho 1994: 52). Far from presenting a picture of firm authoritarian control, the study of Thanh Hoa's hot spots provides a rare glimpse of the countryside in turmoil where security and order are not guaranteed, not even among the components of the state charged with maintaining law and order (Nhi Le 1994: 72).

The state is trying to ease the tension by streamlining administrative practices and party apparatus and by channeling investment into these troubled, impoverished areas, but so far with little success. The gap between the party machinery and the people has never seemed so great, and it is further troubling that the VCP central leadership does not seem to be able to control the party apparatus in some regions. In those regions, which are far from central control and also removed from the economic rush that is happening elsewhere in the country, provincial party leaders rule with an iron hand and are often dismissive of central directives. Abuses of power frequently result. The center-periphery problem goes deeper than that, however. The easing of state control has allowed for the return of the self-contained world of village Vietnam, and in many localities what matters is local law, not national law. The growth of this center-periphery gap will cause enormous problems for continued economic development and for the cohesiveness of the state.

Conclusion

A decade after the official adoption of the *doi moi* strategy, Vietnamese prime minister Vo Van Kiet can state that the country is now "walking with both feet," meaning that Vietnam has managed to establish and consolidate regional relations while diversifying its international relations with the big powers (Nguyen Ngoc Truong 1994: 63). The image is one of a Vietnam feeling more secure within its immediate geographic space and more confident as an active member of the larger international community. Neither an isolated Vietnam alone in its struggle for survival nor a deeply polarized world is depicted in the Prime Minister's discussion of Vietnam's foreign policy in the renovation period.

The current situation in Vietnam is dramatically different from the one a mere ten years ago, and it represents a significant transformation of the mind-set of the Vietnamese Communist leaders. The Vietnamese worldview is shifting from a pure realist one to one of complex interdependence. The state remains the primary unit in both international relations and domestic politics, but whereas security once was externally oriented, it is increasingly focused on the internal dimension. If international survival of the state was previously the central security problem that subsumed all other considerations, national unification and the collapse of socialism have modified the almost exclusive focus on the political-military dimension to include a much greater awareness of and concern with socioeconomic grievances and political stability.

The survival of the regime became an issue after reunification in 1975, and *doi moi* was a response to the loss of political legitimacy. The recognition that economic prosperity is crucial to regime legitimacy and that societal voices must be given room for expression is generating an increasingly complex response. The world is, therefore, viewed through a much less hostile lens than a decade ago, and the give-and-take nature of an economically and politically interdependent international system is increasingly being accepted as a fundamental guiding factor for strategies of economic development and international relations. Furthermore, the end of the Cold War coincided with a period in which Asia, and more specifically Southeast Asia, was being heralded as the most dynamic region of the world. The methodical moves of withdrawing from Cambodia, normalizing relations with China and the United States, and achieving membership in ASEAN clearly pointed to Vietnam's recognition that the region is currently enjoying an unprecedented period of development, one in which the risk of conflict and war is relatively low while the potential gain from investment and technological transfer for Vietnam is quite high.

For the moment, however, although the VCP's formulation of a socialist state has been greatly undermined since 1975 and critical voices are being heard, there is so far no coherent alternative framework to challenge what is already in place. The general disdain for the party is very high, and yet there is no consensus as to what can replace it. Tradition, fear of chaos, and decades of existence as a socialist state have all contributed to make Vietnamese society a conservative one, desiring of law and order. In fact, the central issue the state is grappling with currently is not whether less control over society is warranted but what state control should entail and how it can be made more effective. Since the official endorsement of liberal economic practices, people have protested less about the oppressive weight of the state than about the state's lack of effectiveness in resolving key social issues.

Fear of chaos and a tortuous history of trying to erect a cohesive state to safeguard the national essence also mean the acceptance of the dominant position of the state in the Vietnamese political culture. Moreover, there is a heady sense of discovery as Vietnam begins to open itself to the larger world. A younger generation of Vietnamese, however, also is trying to recover the past. There is a burgeoning interest in the literature and intellectual currents of the 1930s and 1940s, the period of greatest development of the modern Vietnamese culture, long censored by the VCP. Southern works, banned after 1975, also are being reprinted. The VCP is uneasy with all these developments, but it is a process the party cannot fully control. Members of this younger generation, less encumbered by the legacy of the revolution or even of the anti-American war and more confident about their place in the world, will pose a great challenge to the party and its views of state and society in the future. Furthermore, national pride is emerging after the years of poverty and underdevelopment and the psychological exhaustion of the war.

Vietnam's embrace of regionalism is easily understood given Southeast Asia's economic growth and political stability, but this chapter has argued that a more confident Vietnamese identity is also emerging which allows for a more balanced appraisal of Vietnam's own Chinese-inspired classical past as well as for a discovery of historical linkages with other Southeast Asian states. Fierce independence coupled with a more confident and assertive national identity are important whenever Vietnam looks outward, and external threats such as China (and to a lesser extent Cambodia) that impinge on the Vietnamese state will arouse great resistance among the Vietnamese population, which can easily be stimulated to feel the threat to the nation itself. Vietnam has shown in the past that, in spite of its small size, it is capable of and ready to use military force when necessary.

Nevertheless, with general peace in the region and Vietnam undergoing a period of intense changes, it is the internal dimension that poses more immediate challenges to the state. Economic prosperity, social harmony, and issues of distributive justice are domestic concerns that demand a restructuring of the state in terms of its organizing ideology and its administrative and legal systems. In particular, the problems of the countryside, if not soon alleviated, could prove to be explosive, combining as they do the issues of uneven development, the growing gap between the center and the periphery, and the lack of an adequate social safety net and channels for redress. The level of intense unrest in Thai Binh province in the north and Dong Nai province in the south in late 1997, for example, pointed to a long list of grievances that included land disputes, treatment of Catholics by local authorities, uneven wealth distribution, and corruption by officials. The economic crisis that affected Asia in the second half of 1997 should also give the Vietnamese government pause in pushing single-mindedly for economic growth capitalist style without giving sufficient attention to the social and political implications of these new developments.

In short, with the arrival of peace, a certain measure of economic success, and a coherent state structure, the question of national identity is emerging once again—but this time in the context of a more judicious and balanced view of the past and the nature of "Vietnamese-ness." Fierce nationalism and the conviction that struggle is endemic in international relations are constants in this view, which still emphasizes vigilance, but a new sense of national confidence clearly acknowledges the need for and the advantages of cooperation. In practical terms, this new confidence means that Vietnam's current concerns are converging with those of the ASEAN states and focusing on economic growth, friendly external relations, and noninterference in what are considered to be a country's internal affairs. State-managed economic and social development in a one-party state and the insistence on sovereignty and national cultural values when it comes to issues such as human rights and political change are powerful core elements linking Vietnam to the other countries of Asia.

Socialism, as it is increasingly being expressed by Vietnam, resembles more and more the successful model of the one-party authoritarian state so prominent in Asia, liberal in economic growth but conservative in political and social change, insistent on an independent national organizing ideology. Given Vietnam's much more realistic appraisal of its own position in the regional context and in the international arena, coupled with the understanding that this is a global age, it appears likely that the changing construction of security outlined in this chapter will endure. Cautious and gradual change will be the VCP's preferred mode of action in the foreseeable future, and the skillful practice of the struggle-cooperation strategy will allow Vietnam to maintain its position and maximize its potential. The process will include its share of backward steps, but the emphasis on moving forward is one that is valued by virtually all Vietnamese.

Indonesia
*Domestic Priorities Define
National Security*

DEWI FORTUNA ANWAR

> *We today stand firmly upright in the mighty ranks of the new emerging
> forces, and we are now storming the last bulwarks of imperialism. There is
> no power in the world that can prevent the peoples of Asia, Africa, Latin
> America from emancipating themselves.*
>
> PRESIDENT SUKARNO, 1965

> *I feel that the national resilience concept is the only answer to the challenges
> posed by a world still dominated by tension. National resilience encompasses
> ideological resilience based on a nation's own identity which receives the full
> support of the entire nation, economic resilience capable of meeting the nation's
> own basic needs, social resilience which ensures the feeling of solidarity and
> harmony among the peoples, and an appropriate military resilience to face
> aggression from outside. Without national resilience we shall always be afraid.*
>
> PRESIDENT SUHARTO, 1970

Indonesian national security under the New Order is defined primarily, though not exclusively, by domestic priorities. Since the military-led New Order government under President Suharto came to power in 1966, the articulation of security goals, the perception of threats, and the approaches to security have overwhelmingly been framed in terms of internal political and economic needs. The emphasis on domestic priorities stems from the general belief, particularly among the military elite, that the greatest threats to Indonesian national security come from within the country itself—secessionist movements, religious radicalism, challenges to Pancasila,[1] and activities that promote class conflicts. The consequences of these threats are perceived to be wide-ranging, from fragmentation of national unity and integrity to social disorder that could disrupt economic activities.

In the view of the New Order, Indonesia is relatively secure from conventional external threats. Envisaged external threats take the form of infiltration and subversion designed to exploit existing internal conflicts or exacerbate societal differences. Such a view stands in sharp contrast to that espoused by President Sukarno, the first president of the republic (1949–67). Sukarno believed that Indonesia's independence and national unity were directly threatened by foreign powers, in particular by the former colonial and imperialistic states, which continued to maintain their military presence in the neighboring countries.

The New Order's emphasis on the internal sources of insecurity has led to the development of a comprehensive and largely, though not exclusively, inward-looking security strategy. Security is not primarily regarded as a solely or even primarily military problem; rather, it is seen as a political, economic, and social concern connected to nation- and state-building. The fundamental insecurity of Indonesia stems from the fact that it is a newly independent country with a highly heterogeneous population, most of whom are still poor and barely educated, living in an equally fragmented territory. Indonesia unilaterally declared its independence on August 17, 1945, but the Dutch only transferred sovereignty to the new republic in the last days of December 1949 as agreed at the Round Table Conference in the Hague (Kahin 1970: 433–45). These basic weaknesses are compounded by the fact that the new unitary republic has no real historical antecedents,[2] so that commitment to the Indonesian national identity has not spread equally throughout the archipelago and can never be taken for granted. At the same time the political system is still fragile, and the government has limited economic capability to govern effectively and gain the allegiance of the people.

The Suharto government has devoted most of its energy to overcoming these basic national weaknesses and developing "national resilience." The concept of "national resilience" is defined as "the dynamic condition of a nation which includes tenacity, sturdiness, and toughness, which enables her to develop national strength to cope with all threats and challenges coming from within as well as from without, which would directly or indirectly endanger national life and the struggle for national objectives" (Suryohadiprojo 1987: 20–29). National resilience is all-embracing, including national identity, national economy, and society as well as military capability.

It is difficult to discuss Indonesian national security as a distinct topic, separate from the other aspects of national life. Security considerations are paramount in almost every action taken by the government: the New Order's raison d'être is the restoration of political stability and the improvement of the peoples' living standard. The political structure of the New Order, which reaffirms the dual functions—sociopolitical and defense—of the military, and the limitations placed on political activities in general have all been designed as parts of the comprehensive security policy. Economic development is regarded as an equally crucial security strategy. The goal of economic development is not simply to remove most of the root causes of social and political opposition to the government by increasing prosperity, but also to unify the country and make government control more effective through the building of modern communication infrastructures.

Given this overwhelming emphasis on domestic priorities, Indonesian national security conceptions and approaches have tended to downplay external threats. Although Indonesian nationalism still harbors suspicions of the outside world, particularly where relations with the major powers are concerned, the New Order government has for the most part tried to neutralize possible threats from outside through regional cooperation and diplomacy. The government's objective is to ensure a friendly and stable regional environment so that it can devote most of its energy and resources to resolving internal political and economic problems. Although the military has played a predominant role since the establishment of the New Order, building a credible conventional defense capability has not been accorded high priority. This is the result of both limited funding and the recognition that economic development should come first.

Nevertheless, the end of the Cold War, which led to decline in U.S. military presence and the prospect of increasing competition among major regional powers, has produced new regional uncertainties that are forcing Indonesia to pay much more attention to its external environment than ever before. So far, however, no new doctrines have emerged to indicate a major shift in the country's security outlook, though piecemeal attempts are being made to improve Indonesia's conventional defense capability, such as through the purchase of fighter aircraft and frigates (Dupont 1996: 275–97). Limited funding, however, has continued to constrain the modernization of the navy and the air force. Rather than building a credible defense capability, the Indonesian government has continued to put a much greater emphasis on the development of bilateral security relations with neighboring countries as well as on various modes of regional cooperation, including multilateral security dialogues.

Changing Worldviews and Their Consequences

The present-day Indonesian conception of security that emphasizes domestic concerns and challenges stands in sharp contrast to that of the earlier Guided Democracy period under Sukarno. Sukarno saw the most immediate threats to Indonesian security as coming from external forces, especially from Western colonial and imperialistic powers that wished to continue their presence and influence in the region by other means. Sukarno was convinced that Indonesia was surrounded by hostile forces bent on subverting its independence.

These differing worldviews manifested themselves in sharply different policies. Sukarno's view led him to launch a confrontation against the West, and in particular against the new Malaysian Federation, which he considered to be a plot to encircle Indonesia. In contrast, Suharto's New Order has befriended the West and established close bilateral and regional cooperation with its noncommunist neighbors.

The first two decades of the republic of Indonesia were marked by political, social, and economic turbulence. The new nation faced a multitude of internal challenges, ranging from violent disputes about the ideological foundation of the state to regional rebellions and secessionist movements in various parts of the archipelago. Many of these challenges, including an armed uprising by the Partai Komunis Indonesia (PKI, or the Indonesian Communist Party) in 1948, had to be put down militarily. Simultaneously, Indonesia was engaged in an increasingly acrimonious conflict with the Netherlands over West Irian, which was not included in the transfer of sovereignty from the Dutch colonial power to the Republic of Indonesia in December 1949.

Debates about whether the government should give priority to internal political consolidation and economic rehabilitation or to the liberation of West Irian divided the political elite between the so-called "administrators" and the "solidarity makers" (Feith 1962). The "administrators," led by Vice President Mohammad Hatta, were primarily concerned with governance and with developing the national economy. In their view, the revolution had ended with the transfer of sovereignty from the Dutch. They opposed actions that diverted national attention from the business of establishing an orderly process of government and restoring the national economy. This group of leaders supported a negotiated settlement of the West Irian issue. The "administrators" advocated close cooperation with the West. For the "solidarity makers," led by President Sukarno, the revolution was not yet over because West Irian had not been returned to the republic. This group stressed independence and advocated a confrontation against all forms of colonialism and imperialism, even if this meant allowing the Indonesian economy to suffer. Sukarno's fervent anticolonialism received the support of the nationalist and the communist parties. Although the army leadership shared Sukarno's belief in the need to secure West Irian by any means necessary, including force, its outlook on the importance of maintaining internal stability and promoting economic development was much closer to that of the "administrators."

The division within the postindependence political leadership was a legacy of its revolutionary experience. Unlike Malaysia or the Philippines, Indonesia had to fight for its independence from the Dutch, in a struggle that culminated in a revolutionary war between 1945 and 1949. That revolutionary experience promoted an ambivalent worldview: the outside world was hostile, replete with forces constantly threatening Indonesia's independence and integrity and seeking to exploit its natural wealth and strategic location; but at the same time the outside world represented a source of aid and support.

The failure of the negotiations on West Irian between Indonesia and the Netherlands, which took place throughout the 1950s, and Indonesia's defeat at the United Nations General Assembly vote in 1957, strengthened the position of the "solidarity makers." Sukarno's obsession with the West Irian dispute and his militant anticolonialism led him to view the world not in terms of the global ideological conflict between the "free" and communist worlds, but in terms of the nationalist struggle the world over against colonialism and imperialism. It was the struggle of the "newly emerging forces" (NEFOs: the new states of Asia and Africa plus the socialist countries) against the "old established forces" (OLDEFOs: the imperialist powers of the West). In keeping with this view, the Indonesian government opposed the presence of the British bases in Malaya, Singapore, and British North Borneo as well as the U.S. bases in the Philippines, which Sukarno felt were actually aimed at containing Indonesia. That suspicion was strengthened by the covert help given by the British and the Americans to the PRRI/PERMESTA regional rebellions that took place in Sumatra and Sulawesi in 1958.[3] PRRI stands for Pemerintah Revolusioner Republic Indonesia, or the Revolutionary Government of the Republic of Indonesia; and PERMESTA stands for Perjuangan Rakyat Semesta, or Universal People's Struggle. The two rebellious movements, led by local military commanders, the former based in West Sumatra and the latter in North Sulawesi, joined forces to set up an alternative government in opposition to the Java-based central government, which was perceived to be leaning to the left. The regional rebels were joined by a number of prominent Jakarta-based politicians from the Muslim Party, Masyumi, and the

Socialist Party, PSI, who were opposed to Sukarno and the Indonesian Communist Party (PKI). The PRRI/PERMESTA rebellion was quickly crushed by the military loyal to the central government.

The importance attached by Sukarno to the process of decolonization and the strategies adopted to achieve it have attracted a great deal of scholarly analysis. One observer argued that the course of Indonesian foreign policy during this period was mainly determined by President Sukarno's psychological impulses as a "fervent nationalist" (Bunnell 1966). Another maintained that the emphasis on anticolonialism was mainly a continuing attempt by an "emerging" nation to forge its national integration (Reinhardt 1971). In yet another view, the sense of constant movement and crisis that the anticolonial struggle engendered was specially created by Sukarno as an integral part of his "mechanic" of government" (Legge 1972).

There is no doubt that Sukarno's anticolonialism was genuine, but clearly he used the struggle against an external enemy as a rallying point to unite the polarized national elites and to keep himself in power. From the very beginning the "solidarity makers" opposed the development programs espoused by the "administrators" because such programs would weaken their political position, which thrived on tensions and rapid politicization. The campaign to liberate West Irian and the subsequent confrontation against Malaysia left little room for those who wanted to focus on internal stability and economic rehabilitation. Equally important, the mass mobilization and constant political agitation ensured that the initiative did not slip from Sukarno's hand to the army. Instead, the army's growing power—particularly after the massive arms purchases intended for the West Irian campaign—was effectively counterbalanced by the PKI. The PKI in turn was totally dependent on the president, who protected the party from the army, which all along had sought to ban it (Feith 1963).

While Sukarno's political balancing kept him in power, the rapid politicization and mass mobilization deeply polarized Indonesian society, particularly between the anticommunist forces (the army and Muslim groups) and the PKI. The growing political tension was exacerbated by Indonesia's economic crises, caused by the confrontation against Malaysia and the drying up of Western economic aid and investment. The political and economic crisis reached its climax in the abortive communist coup of September 30, 1965, by soldiers close to the PKI. The army under General Suharto put down the attempt. In the counteroffensive the PKI was disbanded and declared illegal, and PKI members and sympathizers were either killed or imprisoned. President Sukarno was impeached and Suharto was appointed president in his place.

The New Order government under Suharto was dominated by the military in partnership with civilian technocrats. In almost every aspect the new government was the antithesis of Sukarno's earlier Guided Democracy. Unlike Sukarno, who could maintain his power only through mass mobilization and political radicalism both at home and abroad, the military's political control in fact entailed severe restriction of political activities. This meant that militant anticolonial struggles such as the confrontation against Malaysia, which radicalized and mobilized the population, were not acceptable to the New Order leaders.

Similarly, the New Order's concerns about domestic unrest in general and its violent communism led to a shift in priorities from anticolonial struggles to internal political stability and economic development. In the view of the New Order elite, the greatest danger to Indonesia, and to Southeast Asia as a whole, was not external military threats but rather economic underdevelopment and backwardness (Prawirasoebrata 1989). In their view, poverty provided a fertile ground for communist ideas to flourish, and it exacerbated other social and political grievances against the government. Therefore, the New Order adopted economic development as the *panglima* (commanding priority) rather than politics, the *panglima* during Sukarno's era. Thus, since 1966 participatory politics has been sidelined in order to give the government maximum political control to allow it to achieve its interrelated objectives of political stability and economic growth. This ideological outlook and shift in priorities pushed Indonesia closer to the West as the primary source of finance and technology necessary for economic development. Indonesia's anticommunism also pushed it closer to its noncommunist neighbors, including Malaysia.

The rise of the New Order did not transform Indonesia's ambivalent view of the world, however. Although it now saw the outside world, particularly the major Western powers, as an important source of aid and support, Indonesia still considered the major powers as potential sources of external threats. But these potential external threats were no longer viewed in terms of direct invasion, occupation, and annexation that threatened Indonesia's existence and integrity as a sovereign and independent state. Rather, the danger was external interference in the domestic as well as regional affairs of the nations of Southeast Asia as they pursued their own interests in the context of the Cold War and the Sino-Soviet conflict. Such external interference, however, would be made possible by domestic as well as regional conflicts and instability. For this reason the New Order has emphasized the importance of achieving domestic as well as regional peace and stability through the development of national and regional resilience. Regional resilience is based on the national resilience of individual countries in the region and on harmonious relations among them (Anwar 1992: 13–14).

Security Goals

Indonesia's defense and security doctrine states that the ideal of the national struggle is to realize a unitary Republic of Indonesia that is independent, united, sovereign, just, and prosperous based on Pancasila and the 1945 Constitution. The struggle is aimed at transforming the Indonesian national condition from that of a colonized and backward people into an independent and successful nation, freed from exploitation, poverty, ignorance, backwardness, and other forms of suffering (Departemen Pertahanan 1991: 14–15). Within these general national ideals one can distinguish several distinctive but closely related security goals: sovereignty, unity and integrity, stability, economic development, and regime security.

Sovereignty

At the top of the list is the need to maintain Indonesia as an independent and sovereign state. This is regarded as sacrosanct and not subject to compromise. This national commitment is clearly reflected in the country's defense and security principle that "the Indonesian nation loves peace, but it loves independence and sovereignty even more" (Departemen Pertahanan 1991: 27–28). Without independence and sovereignty the Indonesian nation cannot achieve any of the other national goals.

As a country that suffered colonialism and foreign exploitation for centuries and that obtained its independence only after a bloody revolutionary war, Indonesia is understandably zealous with regard to its independence and sovereignty. As a result it is generally opposed to any activities or associations that may impinge on its sovereignty. Indonesia is a member of many regional and international organizations such as ASEAN (Association of Southeast Asian Nations), APEC (Asia-Pacific Economic Cooperation), and the Nonaligned Movement. All of these organizations, however, are fairly loose in nature, emphasizing deliberation and consensus in decision making. Membership in such organizations is generally seen as a means to enhance the country's independence and economic development.

National sensitivity over sovereignty is very pronounced in the political and defense arenas. Indonesia's violent opposition to defense alliances during the Cold War period was due to the fear that such alliances would subordinate Indonesia's interests to those of the major military powers that usually dominated them. Indonesia's adoption of and continuing adherence to a "free and active" foreign policy doctrine and its membership in the Nonaligned Movement are clear testimonies to its unwillingness to share sovereignty in the fields of politics and security. Even after the New Order came to power and Indonesia developed close relations with Western countries, including relations in security areas, Indonesia has refused to take part in defense alliances.[4] This stance, however, seems to have softened in recent years, clearly as a consequence of the end of the Cold War and the emergence of new security challenges and threats in the wider Asia-Pacific region. In December 1995 Indonesia signed a "Framework Security Agreement" with Australia, the first such agreement that Jakarta has ever signed, though officials in Jakarta have strenuously denied that the agreement constitutes a defense alliance between Indonesia and Australia. That agreement will be discussed later in the chapter.

It has been difficult for the government to maintain autonomy in areas outside the political-security arena, such as the economic sector. Indonesia's developing economy requires the infusion of foreign capital and technological know-how. Sukarno's radical nationalism and violent opposition to Western political and economic interests led him to advocate *berdikari*, or "standing on one's own feet," in the economic field. The experiment in autarky was disastrous, bringing the Indonesian economy to a standstill and leading to a popular uprising against President Sukarno. The New Order government under President Suharto from its very early days looked to the Western industrialized countries and Japan for assistance in stabilizing and developing the Indonesian economy. In 1966 the Intergovernmental Group on Indonesia (IGGI), a consortium of donor countries and international financial institutions, was set up under the chairmanship of the Dutch Minister for Cooperation and Development.

In spite of Indonesia's great dependence on external capital, technology, and markets, Jakarta is very sensitive to any attempt to link economic arrangements to political conditions. It refuses to accept any economic or technological assistance if there are political strings attached. President Suharto unilaterally dissolved the IGGI in 1992 because its chairman, Jan Pronk, the Dutch Minister for Cooperation and Development, was critical of Indonesia's policy in East Timor after soldiers fired at demonstrators in Dili in November 1991. Within a year, however, Indonesia was able to persuade the World Bank to form and chair another aid consortium for Indonesia, called the Consultative Group on Indonesia (CGI), from which the Netherlands has been excluded.[5]

Unity and Integrity

Equal to independence and sovereignty is the goal of maintaining national unity and integrity. This objective in fact contains several elements. The first is the unity among the peoples and the unity of the territories, as elaborated in the national idea of *Wawasan Nusantara*, or Archipelagic Outlook. This national doctrine conceives of Indonesia as a single political, social, economic, and defense unit. All of the islands and the seas in between are regarded as forming one indivisible entity, reflecting Indonesia's conception of the "motherland" as *Tanah Air* or "Place of Land and Water."

The concept of national unity also involves a commitment to maintain a unitary form of government based on Pancasila and the 1945 Constitution. This commitment is a reaction to the Dutch-sponsored federated system, the Republic of the United States of Indonesia (R.U.S.I.) introduced immediately after the transfer of sovereignty in December 1949. Indonesian nationalist leaders viewed the federal system as an attempt to preserve Dutch influence and weaken Jakarta's control of the archipelago. The unitary system of government that soon replaced R.U.S.I. ensured a much more centralized system of government, under which the provinces depended politically and economically on the central administration.

Adherence to Pancasila and the 1945 Constitution is considered to be the prerequisite for a united Republic of Indonesia. Pancasila, as the only state ideology that so far has been capable of uniting the many ethnic groups and competing religious faiths under one political system, is firmly believed to be indispensable to national unity. Indonesians see Pancasila as uniquely Indonesian, blending universal and indigenous values, stressing religious tolerance as well as balance and harmony in all aspects of life. Nationwide acceptance of Pancasila as the sole foundation of the state and other sociopolitical organizations is regarded as a primary security goal by the government, especially the military.

Stability

Second only to concerns about national integrity is the government's obsession with maintaining political stability. Political disturbances of any kind, including overt criticisms of government policy, are usually not tolerated because of the constant fear that they might undermine the government's authority. There is also a general fear that political instability in one area would be regarded as a sign of weakening government control and thus would lead to trouble in other parts of the country, weakening national integration. Political instability could also be exploited by antigovernment forces within the country as well as by hostile foreign interests through infiltration and subversion. The state's obsession with maintaining political stability is related to the conviction that it is essential to economic development.

Maintenance of political stability under the New Order cannot be separated from adherence to the 1945 Constitution, which gives enormous power to the executive. During the liberal democracy period (1950–58) the 1945 Constitution was replaced by a provisional constitution while a new one was being drafted. President Sukarno and the military leaders had little patience for either the provisional constitution or the one being drafted by the civilian politicians. Under those constitutions the president was only a titular head of the state, and the military would be firmly under civilian control. Further, Sukarno and his circle blamed the liberal democratic system for political instability during this period and for the outbreak of regional rebellions. One and a half years after the rebellions started, President Sukarno, supported by the armed forces' central commanders, issued a decree on July 5, 1959, that dissolved the Parliament and returned the country to the 1945 Constitution (Feith 1962; Nasution 1992).

The New Order government obviously has an interest in maintaining loyalty to the 1945 Constitution, for that constitution enables the government to accumulate and centralize power. Earlier experiments with constitutional democracy, the search for a more balanced distribution of power, and the promotion of civil liberties in the 1950s are now seen as deviations from the ideals of the 1945 Constitution that had negative consequences for the state. Upholding the 1945 Constitution alongside Pancasila is regarded as a primary security goal, and it is firmly stated in the armed forces' oath of allegiance. In the government's view, political stability entails a strong executive control.

Economic Development

The New Order government has elevated economic development to central importance. Economic development is seen by the political elite not only as an end in itself to increase prosperity and social welfare—a key aim of the independence struggle—but, equally important, as a prerequisite for political stability. Many of the earlier insurgencies and grievances against the central government had their roots in economic dissatisfaction. Further, the government's claim to legitimacy rests to a considerable extent on its economic performance.

Because uneven economic development or disparities in the enjoyment of the benefits development can breed ethnic and class conflicts and undermine political stability and national unity,[6] the New Order government has in principle pursued the "development trilogy": political stability, economic growth, and equitable distribution of development benefits. During the first decades of the New Order, political stability was the first priority, followed by a high rate of economic growth and social equity. Since 1978, however, equal distribution of development opportunities and benefits has been at the top, followed by a relatively high economic growth rate and a healthy and dynamic political stability, as can be seen from the successive Guidelines of State Policy (GBHN, or Garis-Garis Besar Haluan Negara) (Lemhanas 1982). Despite such formal commitment, however, and the numerous measures adopted to eradicate poverty, the lack of political transparency and accountability has led to corruption, collusion, and monopolistic practices privileging a small number of Chinese conglomerates and members of the president's family.

Regime Security

A final security goal of the government is clearly the maintenance of its own power, authority, and legitimacy (Pabottingi 1995b). The security of the state and that of the government are usually portrayed as one and indivisible, so that challenges to government authority are construed as challenges to the state. In other words, criticisms of government policy or officials are usually regarded by the government as attacks against the state itself and as evidence of disloyalty to Pancasila and the 1945 Constitution. Public officials and military leaders often argue that without the existing political system and form of government Indonesia would fall back into chaos, probably resulting in the disintegration of the unitary republic and the destruction of whatever economic development has been achieved. For obvious reasons, regime maintenance as a security goal is not usually articulated in official documents. The New Order, however, has closely identified itself with Pancasila and the 1945 Constitution, two increasingly sacrosanct principles. The maintenance of the New Order government is thus presented as synonymous with the preservation of national security.

The security goals described here have been encapsulated in a comprehensive security doctrine known as *ketahanan nasional*, or "national resilience." As noted earlier, it does not emphasize military strength alone; rather, it refers to a balanced resilience in all aspects of national life—ideological, political, social, economic—as well as in the defense and security fields. Economic development is the foundation for all the other components of national resilience. Indonesian leaders believe that to ensure national resilience, the country must avoid involvement in ideological confrontation and bloc politics, whether military, ethnic, or religious (Anwar 1992: 14).

Indonesia's internal security goals are seen as directly dependent on global peace and especially on regional peace and stability in South east Asia. Although Indonesia's security conception has tended to emphasize the domestic and nonmilitary aspects of security, Indonesian leaders have always been very conscious of the direct link between national security and international conditions. As one New Order official pointed out,

> To Indonesia, South East Asia represents her main interest, not meant for domination as feared by some countries, but through which Indonesia honestly sees her own survival. This can be understood from the fact that Indonesia is a territory richly endowed with potential wealth and large population, forming an archipelago with the longest coastline which is exposed to infiltrations and very difficult to control. The sea no longer represents a barrier, but instead has become a highway in the communications of nations. Therefore, any threat to Indonesia's security and its internal stability has to come through neighboring countries. (Soenarso 1970: 1–2)

As a corollary to the concept of national resilience, therefore, Indonesia under the New Order has also attached great importance to the development of regional resilience.

Perceived Threats to Security

The Indonesian defense establishment defines as a threat anything that can negatively affect the attainment of the national objectives and survival, arising from outside or within the country. Potential threats range from acts of crime, sabotage, terrorism, and subversion to crises such as armed rebellions, limited warfare, and open warfare. They cover the political, economic, sociocultural, and military dimensions. As noted earlier, in the view of the New Order leaders the greatest dangers to Indonesian national security come from within the country itself.

Internal Threats

The obsession with internal sources of insecurity is clearly the product of the first two decades of independence, during which the central government, particularly the army, had to deal with a multitude of domestic challenges including regional rebellions, Islamic insurgencies, and attempted communist coups d'état. This political turbulence was mainly due to the lack of a national consensus among the postindependence national elites regarding the form—that is, the state structure and political system—that the new republic should take. Another factor was the growing regional differences with the central government. Differing political orientations, which during much of this early period were shaped by the so-called *aliran*, or "streams" (such as Islam, secular nationalism, traditional Javanism, socialism, and communism) resulted in considerable tensions. Each *aliran* had its own ideals of what the Indonesian state should be and its own notion of the most serious threats to that ideal. In many cases, the presence of an opposed sociopolitical group was regarded as the greatest danger to national and group security. This was the situation between the Muslim parties—especially the modernist Muslim party, *Masjumi*—and the PKI, the two most antagonistic groups in Indonesian politics in the 1950s.

Civil-military divisions were also major sources of national tensions, producing different perceptions of security. To the military the multitude of political parties, none of which drew enough support to form a viable government, and their sharp political differences presented a major source of national instability. The military also viewed the liberal democratic system of government, which subordinated the military to civilian political leaders, as a direct threat to its own corporate identity and solidarity, because the politicians often tried to use the military for their own political ends. For their part, civilian leaders regarded the military's impatience with democratic processes and its intervention in politics as threats to the fragile democratic system of government and contributors to its instability.

A primary objective of the New Order when it came to power was to eradicate the competing referent units of security in the name of maintaining order and stability. The nation-state was posited as the only legitimate referent of security. The New Order has identified three key internal threats to security: first, the threat to the ideological foundation of the state from the extreme left (communist) or extreme right (Muslim fundamentalist) groups; second, the ideological threat posed by democratic movements; third, the threat of separatist movements or rebellions that endanger the unity and territorial integrity of the state.

Ideological Threats from Communism and Islam

The New Order regards communism as the most dangerous ideology. The communists earned the undying enmity of the army when the former staged an armed rebellion to seize control of the national leadership in September 1948, while the Indonesian Republic was still fighting for its survival against the returning Dutch power. The army's hatred of the communists reached a new peak when the PKI master-minded the abortive coup in September 1965 in which several senior army generals were murdered. Although the PKI was banned within days of the abortive coup, the New Order continues to believe that undetected communist members and sympathizers are still active, waiting for opportunities to undermine the government's authority through the so-called unformed organizations.[7] The government's suspicions about the possibility of a leftist subversion have not disappeared with the end of the Cold War. The government usually sees the hands of underground communist sympathizers in many of the activities of radical NGOs, in student demonstrations, and in labor strikes.

The New Order government also continues to harbor suspicions of political Islam. Although the vast majority of Indonesians are Muslims, the New Order government has been strongly opposed to political Islamic organizations. There is a deep-seated suspicion, especially within the military establishment, that Islamic organizations still have reservations about Pancasila, even though it was accepted as the sole ideological basis of the state by all political groups and mass organizations in 1985. This attitude on the part of the military also has origins in the 1950s when the army had to put down several armed revolts by radical Islamic groups that rejected Pancasila as the ideological foundation of the Indonesian Republic and wished to set up an Islamic state. Those Islamic movements, which spread to many parts of the archipelago and lasted until the 1960s, were popularly known as the DI/TII (Darul Islam / Tentara Islam Indonesia or the World of Islam / Indonesian Islamic Army).

Just as the Indonesian government restricted Indonesian interactions with the communist world during the Cold War period, it took similar measures with respect to what it regarded as radical Muslim countries in the Middle East. Indonesia, therefore, has not played a very active role in the Organization of the Islamic Conference (OIC); indeed, until recently was only an observer in the OIC. In the past few years, however, the government's antagonism toward the nonreligious aspect of Islam has diminished. This is evidenced by the increasing rapprochement between President Suharto and the Islamic community, particularly his support for the Indonesian Muslim Intellectual Association, founded in 1990. The government has also increased its involvement in the OIC and promoted closer relations between Indonesia and other Muslim countries. Those efforts are primarily aimed at diversifying Indonesia's export markets and promoting South-South cooperation to reduce dependence on the West. Indonesia is a founding member of the so-called D-8 (the *D* stands for developing countries) which was launched in Istanbul, Turkey, on June 15, 1997. The D-8 groups eight Muslim countries with the aim of promoting closer economic and technical cooperation among the members, analogous to the G-7, the group of major economic powers.[8] Nevertheless, Islam as a political ideology still remains anathema to the government.

The Democratic Threat

The global march toward democratization and greater concern for human rights has found echoes in Indonesia, particularly among Western-educated intellectuals, nongovernmental organizations active in community development work, and people's empowerment projects, as well as among independent journalists and university students. These groups and individuals increasingly challenge the authoritarian system of government and demand a more open, pluralistic, and accountable political system. Demands for a more democratic system of government are also directly linked to criticisms of cronyism in the economic sector. The critics charge that cronyism has led to monopolistic and oligopolistic economic practices involving top-ranking officials and their families in collaboration with a few Chinese conglomerates.

In the post–Cold War period the government views these prodemocracy groups and human rights activists as its most immediate threat, for they question the legitimacy of the government and seek to undermine the basis of power of the New Order government. Government distrust of prodemocracy activities is not new. As we have seen, the army had little sympathy for the liberal democracy experiment in the 1950s, which it largely blamed for the political instability during that period.

Political stability and economic development are perceived to be linked together in an endless chain of cause and effect. Threats to political stability from any source would hinder the smooth process of development by distracting the government's attention and resources from development efforts. Conversely, obstacles put in the way of economic development projects are seen as a direct threat to political stability. Examples include opposition from people dispossessed of their land to make way for a major dam project to supply much-needed electricity, and the actions of environmental groups protesting industrial pollution or deforestation. In the same way the government sees workers' strikes to demand higher wages or better working conditions as politically subversive activities, while those who question the propriety of certain government policies are accused of being antidevelopment.

The Secessionist Threat

In the past three decades Indonesia has not faced any serious threats of regional rebellions like those that engulfed the country in civil wars in the 1950s. There are, however, three small secessionist movements active in Aceh, West Irian, and East Timor. Publicly the government refers to these regional secessionist movements as Gerombolan Pengacau Keamanan (GPK, or Security Disturbance Bandit Groups), a pejorative term that denies their legitimacy as political groups. Although the three provinces account for only a very small percentage of Indonesia's population and territory, the government views secessionism as a threat to the idea of the Indonesian nation-state as well as to its territorial integrity. It has therefore acted vigorously to confront and contain them with the eventual goal of eliminating them.

Aceh, one of the most volatile provinces in Indonesia because of the independent and warlike nature of its people, was one of the earliest supporters of the republic of Indonesia. But because of political mishandling by Jakarta, the province soon turned against the central government. Trouble began when the central government incorporated Aceh into the province of North Sumatra, reducing its status from a province to a district or regency in early 1953. The Acehnese protest was interpreted by Jakarta as a revolt. Government military action pushed the province into an open revolt led by Daud Beureuh, who launched an armed struggle to establish an Acehnese Islamic state (DI/TII) in 1953. The rebellion lasted until 1959, when the central government promised to give the province a special status with autonomy in religious and customary laws.

Although Daud Beureuh and most of his followers returned to the fold of the Indonesian republic, a few, such as Hasan Tiro, continued the struggle to set up an independent Acehnese state (*Aceh Merdeka*) and from time to time take up arms against the government. Although the separatist movement has dwindled into insignificance, Aceh is still occasionally engulfed in violence, mostly due to religious and socio-economic grievances. As hosts of the country's largest liquefied natural gas (LNG) plant, the Acehnese feel that they should have benefited more from this natural wealth. Instead, the industry is owned and controlled by the central government because the 1945 Constitution clearly stipulates that all the country's natural resources belong to the state. The most serious recent disturbance took place in 1990 and lasted several months. Order was restored only after the government launched a major military offensive spearheaded by the elite Special Force Command (*Tempo* 1990: 22–31).

Although there are many similarities between them, the West Irian problem is many ways much more intractable than that of Aceh. The trouble dates back to 1962 when West Irian was finally made part of Indonesia. The Dutch had supported West Papuan nationalism in an attempt to abort Indonesia's takeover of West Irian. In 1965 Permenas Ferry Awom, a sergeant major in the Dutch-created Papuan Volunteer Army, started an armed rebellion for the independence of Western Papua. The Indonesian government dubbed the movement Organisasi Papua Merdeka (OPM, or Free Papua Movement). On July 1, 1971, the OPM proclaimed the establishment of the Government of Western Papua under the presidency of General Seth J. Rumkorem. Between 1971 and 1984 there were at least seventeen major OPM offensives. The OPM also carries out international campaigns from its basis in the Netherlands.

The OPM resistance is much more difficult to eradicate than the Aceh problem because of the intractable differences that separate the Irianese from other Indonesians. Whereas the majority of Indonesians are ethnic Malays, the Irianese are Melanesians. Islam, the majority religion, has not had much influence among the Irianese, most of whom still adhere to their traditional beliefs or have been converted to Christianity. These differences, however, do not really constitute major stumbling blocks to the West Irianese integration with the rest of Indonesian society; Indonesia comprises more than 300 different ethnic groups and five recognized religions. Although Melanesian solidarity has pushed the West Papuan nationalists to forge closer links with other Melanesian states in the South Pacific, there are in fact more Melanesians living in eastern Indonesia than in the Pacific islands.

The fundamental problems relating to West Irian arise from the huge gap in the level of development between the local economy (most of the Irianese depend for their livelihood on hunting and gathering) and the rest of Indonesia, as well as from the government's socioeconomic policies. To relieve the population pressure in other parts of Indonesia, particularly in Java, the government has encouraged migration to West Irian, which is sparsely populated. The government has also sought to exploit West Irian's natural resources, especially copper, with little benefit to the local population. The central government's policies on migration and resource exploitation underscore the political unrest that has periodically erupted in West Irian. The intrusion of the modern economic sector into Indonesia's most undeveloped province has clearly disrupted the traditional mode of living of the Irianese, stimulating support for the separatist movement.

More than Aceh and West Irian, the question of East Timor has proved to be the most difficult security and diplomatic problem for Jakarta. The incorporation of East Timor into Indonesia has continued to meet with internal resistance and external criticism. When the nation's founders fought for Indonesian independence, they claimed only the territory controlled by the Netherlands East Indies. The nationalist leaders ignored East Timor, a tiny Portuguese colonial backwater. East Timor was thrust to the forefront of Indonesian national concerns in 1974 when the new leftist and anticolonial government in Portugal gave East Timor three options: to continue its association with Portugal, to become independent, or to integrate with Indonesia. Three major political parties emerged in East Timor: the Fretilin, which demanded independence for East Timor; the Apodeti, which wanted to integrate with Indonesia; and the UDT, which advocated continuing the association with Portugal.[9]

Civil war broke out in August 1975 when the UDT launched a coup d'état against the Fretilin, which had seized control after the Portuguese left. Apodeti later joined forces with the UDT. At their request, Indonesia sent "volunteers" to help them in the battle against Fretilin, which was supported by the Portuguese government. On November 28, 1975, Fretilin declared an independent East Timor state, but this unilateral declaration was rejected by both Indonesia and Portugal. On November 30, 1975, the UDT, Apodeti, and two smaller parties, Kota and Trabalhista, proclaimed East Timor to be part of Indonesia. At their request, on July 16, 1976, the Indonesian House of Representatives passed a bill on the integration of East Timor into the country. President Suharto signed the bill the next day, officially making East Timor Indonesia's 27th province (Bilveer Singh 1995; Saldanha 1994). About 200,000 people were reportedly killed during the brief civil war.

The United Nations and most members of the international community have not recognized Indonesian sovereignty over East Timor. Portugal and several other Western countries have accused Jakarta of forcibly annexing the former Portuguese colony. The Fretilin, moreover, has continued its struggle for independence, both from within the territory and from bases overseas. The integration of East Timorese into Indonesian society has been made more difficult by the traditional independence of the local Catholic Church, which is under the direct administration of the Vatican, separate from the Indonesian Council of Churches. The East Timorese Catholic Church has often been openly critical of the military, and it is sometimes suspected by Jakarta of encouraging dissent among the East Timorese youths.

Many young Timorese have become supporters of the Fretilin, and recently a small number of them have left the country for Portugal, because of the military's heavy-handed approach to the East Timor problem. In November 1991 soldiers fired at demonstrators, killing a great many (the official number was much lower than that reported by foreign media). The incident served to alienate the East Timorese further, and Western criticisms of Indonesia over the issue has intensified. Now, although the military strength of the Fretilin has become relatively insignificant, the social, political, and economic problems of East Timor still loom large because popular resentment against the central government has made it increasingly difficult to maintain the status quo in the region.

Equally important, the East Timor issue is beginning to strain Indonesia's relations with Western countries because of the importance attached to human rights in the West in the post–Cold War era. Support from Portugal and various Western organizations for the Fretilin has made East Timor a diplomatic burden for the Indonesian government, harming the New Order's traditionally close relations with the United States and Western European countries. In fact, the internal threat to security from the secessionist movement in East Timor is much less serious than the possible threats of economic or military-related sanctions from the West.[10]

External Threats

Indonesia's external security concerns under the New Order are mostly related to indirect threats, such as subversion, that can weaken Indonesian society from within. Those threats can take many forms, such as challenges to the ideological basis of the nation-state or the political system, weakening of the Indonesian economy, or activities that can lead to the disintegration of the unitary republic. Such external challenges, however, can be effective only if there are preexisting internal problems to exploit. At present the Indonesian government does not fear any immediate external threat to Indonesian security from foreign military aggression, but Jakarta has always been conscious of the importance of a stable and friendly regional environment to its well-being.

The Major Powers

During the Sukarno period the presence of foreign military bases (British and American) in Southeast Asia was regarded as a threat to Indonesia. With the advent of the New Order government, Jakarta's policy changed dramatically. The Western military bases were viewed as beneficial in some ways, for they afforded Indonesia a measure of security against communist threats from China and the Soviet Union. Nevertheless, Indonesia continues to be ambivalent toward foreign military bases. Although some leaders privately admitted that the U.S. bases in the Philippines gave Indonesia a sense of security, the official line continued to oppose the bases. For Indonesia, security must rest upon national and regional resilience rather than protection by foreign military patrons. The presence of foreign military interests in the region is viewed as an obstacle to the development of national and regional resilience.

With the closure of the U.S. bases in the Philippines, the Indonesian government believes that the way is open for the ASEAN members to develop an indigenous and autonomous regional order, as formulated in the concept of the Zone of Peace, Freedom, and Neutrality (ZOPFAN). However, new threats are on the horizon. Though most Indonesians do not adhere to the theory of a regional vacuum—it is a matter of national pride to state that Indonesia's security depends on its own efforts—they are increasingly concerned about a possible American departure and the intentions of other regional powers. Although the end of the Cold War has greatly reduced global tension and increased the salience of political and economic issues, there is still the possibility of conflict among the smaller and medium powers (Suryohadiprojo 1989).[11] Questions have been raised in Jakarta about the expanding military capability of Japan and India, but Japan is not perceived as a serious threat because of its heavy involvement in mutually beneficial economic relationships with Southeast Asian countries, and India has never been regarded as an enemy. Nevertheless, Indonesia views those nations' military outreach with concern because such activity could hinder the realization of ZOPFAN.

The most serious perceived threat to regional security is that emanating from the People's Republic of China. The New Order government has long been suspicious of China because of the PRC's earlier close tie with the PKI and its suspected involvement in the abortive communist coup. One of the first acts of the Suharto government was to freeze Indonesia's diplomatic relations with China. Relations were not normalized until August 1990. Throughout this period the Indonesian government tried to insulate the nation from any contacts with China, even banning the use of Chinese characters for fear that they might contain subversive messages.

Since the normalization of diplomatic ties between Jakarta and Beijing, relations between the two countries have improved, particularly in the economic arena. Nevertheless, the Indonesian government, and especially the military, still suspects China's intentions in Southeast Asia. Those suspicions have been compounded by China's claims in the South China Sea and its aggressive behavior in enforcing them, particularly with regard to the Spratly Islands. Although Indonesia is not a claimant in the Spratly dispute, it has a special interest in its peaceful settlement because conflicts in the South China Sea can affect the security of the Indonesian island of Natuna, where major LNG production is taking place. Indonesian concerns have been exacerbated by the publication of a Chinese map that includes part of the Natuna waters under China's patrimony, and by China's military buildup aimed at developing its capability for power projection (Anwar 1992, 1994a).

Concerns have also been expressed domestically about the political and economic implications of the increasingly powerful overseas Chinese communities in Indonesia and other Southeast Asian countries and their possible relations with Beijing. China's call for the overseas Chinese to participate in its economic development is seen as a threat not only to Indonesia's national integration but also to its economic well-being. The government tends to view any investment made by Indonesian Chinese in their ancestral land as capital flight; most Indonesians see it as a sign of disloyalty.

Economic and Political Changes

In recent years another external challenge has appeared in the form of economic protectionism among the major industrialized countries that constitute Indonesia's traditional export markets. That protectionism has an added dimension in the post–Cold War period because of the tendency among the Western governments to link economic concessions with political conditions, such as democratization, protection of human rights, improvement of workers' conditions, and environmental protection. The Indonesian government regards such attempts to impose political conditions on economic interactions as a threat to its national sovereignty. It sees Western countries' promotion of democracy and human rights—now very much part of the former's foreign policy agenda—as disguised economic protectionism as well as a new form of cultural imperialism that tries to impose "Western values" on Indonesian society.

The Indonesian government also sees a threat in the activities of international human rights organizations, such as Amnesty International and Asia Watch. These two organizations have often published reports on the Indonesian government's abuses of power and violation of human rights, particularly in the case of East Timor. Such reports have embarrassed the Indonesian government and set Western public opinion against Indonesia, thus affecting those countries' policies toward Jakarta. As noted earlier, the East Timor issue has become a primary area of contention between Indonesia and the West. The Indonesian government sees a growing danger in the efforts of Western governments and international organizations to promote universal acceptance of democratic and human rights principles. Such notions are dangerously attractive to the intellectual community and nongovernmental organizations at home, and thus present a political challenge to the authoritarian political system.

Approaches to Security

The policies and strategies the Indonesian government deploys to attain its articulated security goals and to address perceived threats clearly reflect its comprehensive conception of security, which emphasizes the domestic dimension. They are aimed at ensuring national unity and political stability, combating internal sources of insecurity, and protecting Indonesia from external threats of all kinds. These strategies are necessarily multidimensional, encompassing economic, political, and social as well as military approaches.

Strategies to counter internal threats include management of ideological conformity, tight sociopolitical control of society, and economic development. Internationally, the strategies include seeking international recognition of Indonesia's archipelagic outlook, developing a limited conventional weapons capability, establishing good bilateral relations with neighboring countries, and cooperating in regional affairs. Further, Indonesia recently signed a security agreement with Australia, breaking a long-held taboo about entering into security alliances. In facing external threats, Indonesia's security approach has emphasized liberal institutionalism in an attempt to transform international relations from a zero-sum to a positive-sum game.

Internal Strategies

One of the most important strategies for internal control is to ensure ideological conformity, which means to enforce the total acceptance of Pancasila, the state ideology. Pancasila is to be the only ideological basis of political parties and social organizations. This policy has been successful insofar as Pancasila was formally accepted by the political parties and social organizations as the sole ideology in 1985. Interpretations of Pancasila, however, continue to be contested. The government, therefore, has made continuous attempts to promote a uniform understanding of what Pancasila really stands for. This ideological conformity is enforced through "Penataran P-4" training to enhance national understanding and devotion to Pancasila at all levels of society. (P-4 is *Penataran Pemahaman dan Pengamalan Pancasila*, or training on understanding and the implementation of Pancasila.) For government employees this *Penataran* is compulsory. According to the ideals of the Pancasila Democracy, which has been actively promoted by the New Order government, the republic of Indonesia is an "integralistic" state, meaning it does not recognize the distinction between state and people or between military and civilians. The government acts as the father of the people in one large, happy family. Within this political construct opposition to the government is considered to be illegitimate and, therefore, intolerable. The concept of "loyal opposition" that exists in liberal democracies is considered alien to Indonesia's political traditions. Opposition to the government challenges Pancasila Democracy and the state itself (Vatikiotis 1993).

As noted earlier, the New Order has emphasized the need to maintain political stability as a prerequisite for economic development, which in turn is regarded as indispensable for preserving internal peace and stability. The threats to national unity, the endemic political instability, and the economic problems faced by Indonesia before the New Order came to power were blamed by the military on too much politicization and division among the political elite. Consequently, the New Order has tried to limit popular political participation, but at the same time to mobilize the people to support development activities through various corporatist organizations led by the military and the bureaucracy.

The New Order keeps political control of society through depoliticization and the concept of the floating mass. This approach is a reaction to the frantic politicization and resulting sociopolitical polarizations that characterized the pre-1966 period. Under the New Order, political parties cannot operate below the district level so that the villagers will not be "confused" or "misled" by political parties. The government's political organ, Golkar, however, is allowed to campaign down to the village level. The requirement that all civil servants, including district heads and village functionaries, become members of Golkar ensures that the government's own political party will win the majority of the seats contested at every election. At the same time the legislative and judicial branches of the government are firmly under the control of the executive (Liddle 1978).

Political freedom has also been severely curtailed through various regulations. For instance, the mass media can operate only after obtaining a special permit, which can be revoked any time if the government feels that a certain publication has stepped out of line. The Indonesian government also continues to enforce the Dutch colonial law that required large gatherings of people for other than social purposes to obtain special permits from the police. Until 1996 a permit was needed to conduct a seminar or workshop. The police often stopped such activities in midstream if they felt that the meetings were too critical of the government or if some of the speakers were known to have voiced opposition to the government. These laws have now been relaxed so that anyone planning a large gathering has only to notify the police of the planned event, without having to wait for a permit.

The activities of nongovernmental organizations and the labor unions are also subject to tight control. Until recently strikes and demonstrations were regarded as subversive activities punishable by imprisonment. Most social, political, and economic organizations sanctioned by the government are in reality extensions of the executive arm, designed to simultaneously control the populace and mobilize it for development purposes. Besides the threat of imprisonment, critics of the government may be prevented from traveling overseas (a restriction known as *cekal*). Similarly, foreign critics are often regarded as persona non grata, forbidden to remain in or enter the country (*tangkal*).

The government justifies all these controls and regulations that proscribe civic freedom in general, and political activities in particular, in the name of development. Because the government has succeeded in developing the economy and improving the general standard of living, it has been able to forestall serious challenges to its authority. Except for the educated elite—whose numbers, though small, are growing—the majority of the population seems to be relatively content to trade political liberties for economic growth. Discontents surface, however, when the government seems only to favor certain well-connected individuals and big Chinese businesses over the rest. The sporadic violence that rocked various parts of Indonesia in 1996 and 1997, however, reveals a disturbing increase in dissatisfaction with government political and economic policies. During the violence, rioters' attacks targeted mostly government buildings and Chinese-owned properties.

The *Hankamrata* (Total People's Defense System), designed with external aggression in mind, also enables the government to control society. This doctrine envisions the military, acting as a core, and the whole population rising in unison against an invading force. The Hankamrata doctrine was a product of the revolutionary war against the returning Dutch colonial forces. The poorly armed and trained Indonesian militia was able to wear down the professional Dutch military forces because the militia received the full support of the population in the long, drawn-out guerrilla warfare. This led to the belief Indonesia's defense must rely on solidarity between the armed forces and the civilian population. In any war the military would only act as a nucleus, mobilizing the entire population against the enemy.

Although the Hankamrata doctrine was initially a response to external aggression, its later applications have usually been related to internal sources of security. The Hankamrata doctrine led to the development of the territorial defense system, which reaches down to the district level. The idea is that each local command can mobilize, train, and arm the local population to defend the country against enemy attacks through territorial defense. Because most of Indonesia's security concerns come from within the country itself, the presence of army personnel down to the district level, paralleling local governments' apparatus, is clearly not designed to prepare the populace against an external enemy. Rather, it points to a basic distrust of the population. Thus, in spite of the ideal of Hankamrata, the military has been reluctant to give the general populace military training, let alone to provide villagers with weapons. The official explanation is that such universal military training would be costly and unnecessary, given the fact that Indonesia does not face any immediate external threat. In practice, the territorial defense concept has served as an effective tool for sociopolitical control, allowing the army to monitor the people down to the local level and thereby neutralize potential opposition to the government before it becomes unmanageable.

The government's sociopolitical control over the population has been strengthened further by the military's so-called Dwi-Fungsi, or "dual function role," which gives the military sociopolitical rights and responsibilities alongside its purely defense role. Through the dual-functions doctrine, military personnel are allotted seats in the parliament. They also can occupy various non-defense-related positions in government bureaucracies and in state-controlled social and economic organizations from the highest to the lowest level, while they are still in active service or after retirement. The current president and the last vice president of Indonesia are retired generals. Military officers have served as cabinet ministers, ambassadors, provincial governors, district chiefs, directors of state banks and state enterprises, and heads of various national sports organizations (Crouch 1978; Sundhaussen 1982).

The military's involvement in politics is aimed at ensuring political stability so that economic development can take place. Economic development, in turn, is expected to ensure popular acceptance of the government and give further legitimacy to the military's dual functions. Political stability is achieved by the imposition of tight political control to strengthen the state and correspondingly weaken the civil society.

Another major internal threat comes from the various secessionist forces. Coercion and economic development have been the dominant themes in the government's approach to secessionist threats. Political solutions have not been explored, because the government believes that giving in to the political demands of the secessionist groups could threaten Indonesia's national unity and integrity. Further, as noted earlier, maintaining a unitary system of government in which the provinces are mostly dependent on the central government has long been a primary security goal of the republic of Indonesia. In the past few years attempts have been made to introduce more regional autonomy at the district level (below the province). The government, however, is strongly opposed to giving regional autonomy at the provincial level, fearing that it may pave the way toward federalism, a concept that is still anathema to the ruling elite.

The New Order believes that secessionist efforts are mostly the result of economic grievances. The government, therefore, has paid special attention to the economic development of such trouble spots as Aceh, West Irian, and East Timor, allocating large sums of money to provide physical and social infrastructures such as roads, electricity, schools, and hospitals. The government clearly hopes that with improved living standards the people in these provinces will become loyal citizens and will no longer support secessionist activities. If such activities continue to take place, however, the military will try to wipe them out. The government has also maintained a more visible military presence in these areas, particularly in West Irian and East Timor.

East Timor provides the best case study of Indonesia's efforts to counter secessionism. In the past two decades the Indonesian government has poured no less than 1.9 trillion rupiahs (U.S.$832 million) into development projects—mostly consisting of physical infrastructure—to bring East Timor to the level of the rest of Indonesia. The Portuguese had neglected the territory, so that in 1975 East Timor had only 20 kilometers of paved roads, 47 elementary schools, 2 junior high schools, and 1 senior high school. By 1996, East Timor had more than 2,683 kilometers of paved roads, 715 elementary schools, 114 junior high schools, 58 senior high schools, and 4 tertiary institutions (a university and colleges). Today, every school-age East Timorese attends school (*Jakarta Post*, July 14, 1997).

This economic strategy to win over loyalties, however, has not always been successful. Although Indonesia no longer faces any serious secessionist threats, anti-integration activities still occasionally disturb political stability in East Timor, West Irian, and Aceh. In most cases, the regional military commands are able to deal with the threats. But when the regional military commands cannot deal with a particular security emergency, such as the armed rising in Aceh and the hostage-taking in West Irian, the Special Force or Kopasus (Komando Pasukan Khusus) based in Jakarta is deployed until the crisis is over.

The East Timor case shows, however, that by confining its anti-secessionist strategy to economic development and coercion alone, the Indonesian government cannot resolve the political situations in the long run. Indiscriminate use of force to quell secessionist threats only produces more grievances against the government. Further, economic development has also created new problems, such as the emergence of a new educated class whose rising expectations the government cannot always satisfy. Recent antigovernment demonstrations in East Timor were led by university students and graduates. It seems that in the future the government will have to think about possible political solutions if it is to overcome the secessionist threats once and for all without weakening national unity and integrity.

International Strategies

Despite its preoccupation with internal security problems and domestic issues, the Indonesian government also pays considerable attention to the immediate regional and international environment. Experience in the late 1950s showed that Indonesia's internal security and stability were closely linked to the stability of the Southeast Asian region as a whole, as well as to Indonesia's relations with its close neighbors and with the major powers that have interests in the region. To protect Indonesia from external threats, the government has pursued several strategies that include attempts to insulate the archipelago from external intrusion and interference, improving Indonesia's defense capability by modernizing the military, fostering regional cooperation with neighboring Southeast Asian countries, and promoting confidence-building measures with regard to security issues in the wider Asia-Pacific region.

Recognition of Archipelagic Status

Indonesia's "archipelagic principle" was first declared by Prime Minister Djuanda in December 1957. It received international recognition at the Third Law of the Sea Convention in Jamaica on December 10, 1982. In all, 144 members of the United Nations signed that convention, while 41 countries, including the United States, Turkey, and Greece, refused. The Indonesian parliament ratified the Law of the Sea Convention (LOSC) through Law Number 17 in 1985 (Djelani 1993).

Called Wawasan Nusantara, or Archipelagic Outlook, the doctrine is aimed at ensuring the geographical unity of the archipelago as well as achieving the ideal unity of its peoples. It was introduced in response to regional rebellions and the Dutch claim on West Irian (Djiwandono 1986). In 1966 it was applied to unifying the armed forces, which until that time had a fragmented security doctrine based on their respective areas of specialization (Dino Patti Djalal 1996: 63–67).[12]

Wawasan Nusantara is also designed to keep foreign powers from intruding into Indonesian territorial waters. Before it was introduced, Indonesia had been fragmented by the international regulation that gave each island only a limited amount of territorial waters, while the rest were considered part of the high seas. This rule clearly placed island countries at a disadvantage and made it difficult for the Indonesian government to enforce its sovereignty over the entire archipelago: foreign vessels of all kinds were free to move between the islands, either to exploit the riches contained in the seas or, more dangerously, to assist in regional rebellions. As Michael Leifer argued,

> Despite the striking differences between the foreign policy of Sukarno and Suharto, the experiences of the periods of national revolution and of outer-island dissidence have institutionalized a common apprehension among Indonesians of differing political persuasions of the intentions of all extraregional powers....This concern has been articulated in the official maxim of the Archipelago Principle—which represents the seas and straits surrounding and intersecting Indonesia as maritime bridges or interstices—and in opposition to regionally located foreign bases. (Leifer 1974: 418)

The Wawasan Nusantara doctrine has been reinforced by an acute sense of military weakness.

The Indonesian government has shown its determination to enforce control over its inland straits. On November 16, 1971, in response to a Japanese initiative within the Subcommittee on Safety of Navigation of the Intergovernmental Maritime Consultative Organization proposing that safety of navigation in the Straits of Malacca and Singapore be subject to supervision by an international board of management, the governments of Indonesia, Malaysia, and Singapore announced that safety of navigation in the straits was the responsibility of the coastal states concerned (Djiwandono 1986; Leifer 1983b). In September 1988 Indonesia closed Sunda and Lombok Straits at alternate times, ostensibly because of naval exercises in those waters. The act was generally interpreted by observers as a further indication of "Indonesia's long-term goal to have its sovereignty over the straits accepted, including its interpretation of rights of passage" (Lowry 1989). The closure of the straits was seen as "related to U.S. ratification of the protocol acknowledging the Archipelagic Outlook and the beginning of measures to incorporate the provisions of the LOSC into national law" (Lowry 1989).

Conventional Defense

Under the New Order, Indonesia's conventional defense capability has remained modest, even though the military has been the most dominant political force in the country. In relation to its population size and gross domestic product, Indonesia's defense spending has been the lowest among the ASEAN countries. The absence of clear and urgent external threats and the pressing needs of economic development underlie the low priority attached to the purely military aspects of national security.

Indonesia's defense spending rose from U.S.$1.3 billion in 1975 to $2.8 billion in 1983. In 1983, military spending, which also includes the budget for the police, was 4.2 percent of the GDP. (Under the New Order government the police force is organized as the fourth branch of the armed forces after the army, the navy, and the air force.) Since 1983, however, Indonesia's defense expenditure has consistently declined. In 1990 it fell to U.S.$1.7 billion (1.5 percent of the GDP), despite 7 percent growth in GDP. The decline in Indonesia's defense spending stands in contrast to the pattern of most other ASEAN countries. Singapore's defense spending rose from U.S.$251 million in 1972 to $1.081 billion in 1983 and to $1.640 billion in 1990. Thailand's defense spending rose from $367 million in 1975 to $1.562 billion in 1983 and to $2.040 billion in 1990. Like Indonesia, Malaysia reached a peak in defense spending in 1983, when its defense budget totaled $2.361 billion, but by 1990 the amount had declined to $1.560 billion in 1990. Interestingly, Indonesia's budget allocation for defense in 1990 did not differ much from the 1975 figures, whereas all of the other ASEAN countries' defense budgets had grown many times over: a sevenfold increase in the case of Singapore and Thailand, and a threefold increase for Malaysia. Even the Philippines, which had suffered a major economic decline, registered a twofold increase between 1975 and 1990, from $511 million to $1.052 billion (Dermawan 1992). Although Indonesia's total defense budget is probably much higher than the official figures, because of the frequency of off-budget funding, it does not really affect Indonesia's real defense capability. Off-budget funds are used mostly to improve the living standard of the troops and their families and as a source of graft for officers, rather than to buy arms.

With its limited defense budget, Indonesia has kept a relatively small military, stressing its mobility and efficiency. Currently the armed forces, minus the police, have a total of 278,000 active members. Of these, 212,000 are in the army, 42,000 in the navy, and 24,000 in the air force. The police force has 180,000 members. The army is by far the largest and most important branch of the armed forces, reflecting its dual function in society. Both the navy and the air force are relatively undeveloped.

In the past few years, however, Indonesia's defense expenditure has gone up. Most of the money has been used to modernize the weapons systems, such as by acquiring 31 frigates from former East Germany and two squadrons of Hawk fighter aircrafts from Britain. In 1994 Indonesia's military expenditure was $2.4 billion and in 1995, $2.8 billion. Nevertheless, because of the economic growth, the 1994 and 1995 military expenditures were only 1.5% and 1.6%, respectively, of the annual GDP (International Institute for Strategic Studies 1996: 182). The recent military purchases, intended to strengthen the navy and air force, are partly a response to the fluidity and uncertainty of the wider regional order in the post–Cold War era. The modest increases in Indonesia's defense spending and arms acquisitions does not follow the general pattern among Northeast and Southeast Asian countries, where the increases have been much higher.

Bilateral Cooperation with Neighboring Countries

To ensure its security from potential subversive threats coming from external sources, the New Order government has relied primarily on fostering friendly relations with neighboring countries. It has used a variety of means to this end, such as strengthening bilateral ties, engaging in bilateral military exercises, participating in regional cooperation, and promoting multilateral security dialogues.

One of the first acts of the New Order government was to end the confrontation with Malaysia and then to cofound ASEAN with four other Southeast Asian countries, namely Malaysia, the Philippines, Singapore, and Thailand. To ensure the security of their mutual borders, Indonesia and Malaysia signed a Border Crossing Agreement in May 1967. Under the agreement the two countries undertook to set up border check-posts along their Kalimantan border. A total of 27 posts were set up, 15 located in Sarawak, 3 in Sabah, and 9 within Indonesian territory. The agreement was specifically aimed at suppressing communist and other left-wing insurgents on both sides of the border (Anwar 1994).

Indonesia and Malaysia have built very close bilateral defense cooperation, engaging in regular joint military exercises. Indonesia also developed similar arrangements with the other ASEAN countries. Although ASEAN is not a defense organization (it specifically excludes multinational defense cooperation from its agenda), there already exists a network of bilateral and trilateral military ties within the association. These military ties serve many purposes, the most important being to foster mutual understanding. Bilateral and trilateral military cooperation is also important for dealing with common problems in border areas, especially maritime problems such as piracy, smuggling, drug trafficking, and navigational safety.

Regional Cooperation and Strategies

In addition to building good bilateral relations, Indonesia and its noncommunist Southeast Asian neighbors have developed regional cooperation through ASEAN. For Indonesia, the primary function of ASEAN was initially to restore its credibility in the region in the wake of the confrontation against Malaysia, as well as its credibility in the international community as a whole. That credibility was very important for Indonesia, particularly for its efforts to attract foreign investment.

ASEAN also serves a very important security function for Indonesia. At the time of the regional rebellions, neighboring countries that were hostile to Jakarta actively assisted the regional rebels and even allowed their territories to be used by foreign military powers against Indonesia. For instance, the rebels received financial help, arms assistance, and political asylum from Malaya and Singapore. An American pilot from the U.S. base in the Philippines was shot down in Ambon while carrying out an air bombing raid against Indonesia in support of the rebel cause. By developing close relations with the neighboring countries, particularly within a regional association that forbids its members to interfere in each other's internal affairs, Indonesia helps create a peaceful and stable regional environment for itself. Similarly, countries that in the past had felt threatened by Indonesia also began to feel relatively secure, thus becoming less likely to adopt defense strategies that Jakarta would see as threatening.

The signing in 1976 of the Treaty of Amity and Cooperation in Southeast Asia, forbidding the threat or use of force so that members have to settle their disputes through peaceful means, has enhanced regional security. Although many bilateral disputes have remained unresolved, it is now becoming unthinkable that an ASEAN country would go to war against a fellow ASEAN member for any reason. This situation has led observers to conclude that ASEAN has developed into some kind of a security community. ASEAN was never intended as a vehicle for regional integration; rather, it was designed to enhance the members' respective national interests. Still, the association has developed its own dynamics and has become the focus for a regional identity. Largely because of its role in enhancing both national and regional security, ASEAN has become an indispensable regional institution. This reality has gradually transformed the members' perceptions of their national and regional identities and of the link between the two. The development of a pluralistic security community, in which force is no longer an option in resolving disputes, certainly supports the notion of the growth of a community among the original ASEAN members (Alagappa 1995c).

At the same time ASEAN can be regarded as serving a realist security function for Indonesia. The presence of a shield of friendship around Indonesia is regarded as a cordon sanitaire against possible threats emanating from outside the region. Not only has ASEAN prevented the outbreak of conflicts among the member countries, but also, and equally important, it has helped to contain extraregional threats. This fact has enabled the Indonesian government to devote most of its attention and resources to the country's internal problems and development and to maintain a relatively small and undeveloped defense force (Anwar 1994).

In addition to its role within ASEAN, Indonesia has sought to enhance its national security through the promotion of a more autonomous regional order, in which the role of foreign military powers would be significantly reduced if not removed entirely. At Indonesia's insistence the Bangkok Declaration of 1967 that established ASEAN specified that foreign military bases were only temporary in nature and would remain only at the specific request of the host countries. Of even greater importance to Indonesian security, those bases were not be used against other countries in the region.

Indonesia has been an enthusiastic supporter of the ZOPFAN concept, introduced by Malaysia in 1971. ZOPFAN's most important components are the principle of pacific settlement of disputes, a Southeast Asia Nuclear Weapons Free Zone (SEANWFZ), and freedom from foreign intervention. Indonesia's promotion of the regional resilience concept within the ASEAN circle is clearly aimed at increasing regional members' responsibility for their own regional security and reducing their need to depend on external military powers for protection. All these activities clearly reflect Indonesia's desire to exclude external military presence from the region, a goal shared by all the country's leaders from the early days of independence to the present day, regardless of political persuasion (Lemhanas 1985).

Indonesia at first tended to view the Five Power Defence Arrangements (FPDA) between Britain, Australia, New Zealand, Malaysia, and Singapore with suspicion, seeing it as aimed primarily at containing Indonesia. In recent years, however, Indonesia's attitude toward the FPDA and other military alliances in the region has probably changed. As noted earlier, in 1995 Indonesia signed a Framework of Security Agreement with Australia. As Ikrar Nusa Bhakti argued,

> Whether it is realized or not, by the signing of the agreement on maintaining security, Indonesia is indirectly, through Australia, connected with a pattern of treaties that Australia has established with all its immediate neighbors and external powers....FPDA, Joint Declaration Principles between Australia and Papua New Guinea, and Australia, New Zealand and the United States (ANZUS). It means that Indonesia has not only indirectly become part of Western alliances, but also has a part in Australia's new forward defense strategy. (Bhakti 1996: 9)

The signing of the agreement with Australia indicates a shift in Indonesia's "free and active" foreign policy, clearly as a response to the new realities in the region, in addition to its desire to put the volatile bilateral relations between Jakarta and Canberra on a more solid foundation.

Indonesia attaches considerable importance to the development of broader regional security dialogues, both through official channels (first track) and via more informal channels involving academics, government officials, and military officers in their private capacity (second track). It plays an active role in the ASEAN Regional Forum (ARF). The government regards the ARF as the first-track approach to Asia-Pacific multilateral security dialogue. To represent the second-track approach, the Council for Security Cooperation in the Asia-Pacific (CSCAP) was established. Through these multilateral security dialogues, all participants hope that they can ensure peace and stability in the wider Asia-Pacific region. Both ARF and CSCAP can be seen as the most recent examples of the liberal institutional processes that are currently gaining force in the Asia-Pacific region.

Finally, the Indonesian government maintains its security by playing an active role in regional conflict resolution and prevention. Because the present Indonesian government sees its security as inextricably tied to the security of the region as a whole, it has taken a proactive role in various regional initiatives aimed at resolving existing conflicts and preventing new ones. For example, Indonesia tried to resolve the Cambodian conflict by holding "informal meetings" in Jakarta of the four Cambodian factions. Since 1989 Indonesia has hosted six "workshops on the management of conflict in the South China Sea," bringing together representatives of all claimants. The workshops are informal in nature and are not designed to resolve the conflicting jurisdictional claims. Instead, they are mostly intended as confidence-building exercises. The hope is that identifying common grounds for cooperation will allow the participants to defuse and contain the South China Sea conflict.

Conclusion

Indonesia's conceptions of security are comprehensive and multi-dimensional, encompassing both the external and the internal dimensions. Indonesia's view of the outside world, though characterized by long-held suspicion of the major powers, docs not entirely fit the realist model. Because of Indonesia's geographical fragmentation and its basic military weakness, the strategy adopted to insulate the country from hostile external forces has relied mainly on diplomacy and regional cooperation.

In the past three decades the Indonesian government has not been greatly concerned with direct military threats coming from outside. Instead, the government in Jakarta has been preoccupied with various internal sources of insecurity. These internal threats and challenges cannot be met by straightforward military means; rather, they require a range of policies and strategies that judiciously combine persuasion, force, and development efforts.

Unlike in the more established societies in the West, where political, economic, and military issues are largely considered separate, Indonesia regards all these issues as inextricably linked. Economic development is not viewed simply as a means to improve welfare, but rather as the only way to guarantee political stability, regime security, and national security. In the same way there is no clear separation between internal and external security concerns. As the confrontation with Malaysia during President Sukarno's rule showed, internal political instability can lead directly to regional instability. Because it is the largest country in Southeast Asia, Indonesia recognizes that internal political upheaval would equally endanger the security of neighboring countries. Such a spillover of instability could take the form of an adventurous foreign policy on the part of the Indonesian government to divert attention from internal conflicts, or it could cause an influx of refugees from the archipelago into neighboring countries.

Putting one's own house in good order, as exemplified by the pursuit of national resilience, is an important national and regional security strategy. Another factor in ensuring regional security is the development of regional cooperation. Indonesia puts a lot of faith in the ability of ASEAN to prevent the outbreak of conflicts and to contain bilateral frictions so that they do not lead to open warfare. Within ASEAN the security of the subregion is no longer perceived in zero-sum terms, and the use of force as an instrument of foreign policy has been mutually renounced. It can therefore be argued that among the ASEAN members, realist approaches to security have been tempered by or have given way to liberal institutionalist ones.

Indonesia's preoccupation with its own internal affairs has clearly contributed to its commitment to ASEAN. Although that commitment has helped foster the stability of the region as a whole, it has not fully resolved Indonesia's internal contradictions. On the one hand, the government's emphasis on internal sources of insecurity has led it to pursue a development-oriented policy in all aspects of national life. That policy has improved overall social welfare and maintained national unity and political stability. On the other hand, the approach has also encouraged the government, and especially the military, to exaggerate the extent and nature of domestic threats as a way to keep political control over the country. Although this strategy may give the government a sense of security in the short term, it will undoubtedly lead to instability in the long term, because the people will not tolerate forever all the rules and limitations that govern their lives in the name of stability and development.

In fact, the economic crisis that has gripped the country since late 1997 has undone much of the development that had occurred over the last twenty years, causing severe hardship to the people and leading to protests and demonstrations in many parts of the country. The economic crisis has also been joined and aggravated by the issue of political succession and cronyism that came to a head in the lead-up to the election of Suharto in March 1998 to a seventh term. The president has been given wide powers to deal with internal security problems, and the military has warned it will not tolerate public protests and violence. These developments suggest that domestic concerns will continue to feature prominently in Indonesian security thinking and behavior for quite some time to come.

Malaysia
Reinventing the Nation

K. S. NATHAN

Malaysia's security practice reflects the struggle to build a nation out of a state inherited from British colonialism—an effort that is premised on a broad notion of security incorporating political, military, economic, social, cultural, and psychological dimensions. Malaysian conceptions of national security are therefore informed by factors of history, geography, Malay nationalism and ethnoreligious identity, the goal of national unity and integration, the vision of becoming an industrialized country, and a strategic interest in shaping the immediate regional as well as the international environment. The drive to modernize, industrialize, regionalize, and globalize has impelled the national leadership to redefine and reinvent the nation by infusing a new sense of purpose and direction intended to strengthen national security as well as regional peace and prosperity.

The conceptualization and formulation of national security in Malaysia evidences a pattern that is not dissimilar to that in other developing countries where state and national boundaries are products of Western colonialism. In Malaysia, the state has definitely come before the nation. A major task of postindependence policy makers has been to create a nation out of the pluralistic state inherited from British colonial rule. The concept of "Malaysia" and conceptions of national security, therefore, embody the interplay between "nation" and "state." Indeed, in Malaysia "authority and sovereignty have run ahead of self-conscious national identity and cultural integration" (Rejai and Enloe 1969: 140).

It is pertinent to note here the multiethnic makeup of Malaysia (55 percent Malay, 30 percent Chinese, and 10 percent Indians with Kadazans, Ibans, Dayaks, and others making up the remaining 5 percent) and the problems arising therefrom. The Malays, who barely constituted the majority at the time of independence in 1957, consider themselves (along with the other natives) to be indigenous peoples entitled to certain rights and privileges that are not available to the Chinese and Indians, who are considered immigrant races. Malay survival and political domination and the resentment of the same by the other ethnic groups are constant themes in Malaysian politics that influence security thinking and policy.

The Malaysian state, through its central decision makers, formulates national security policies that are rooted in its own unique historical experience, in the way the nation-state developed after the attainment of independence, and in the institutional, constitutional, political, and socioeconomic structures inherited by the nationalist elites. The pursuit of national security in the Malaysian context is governed not only by the emphasis on state survival—requiring such strategies as deterrence and balance of power—but also by ethnonational security doctrines that have evolved from long-term considerations of group survival and which inform the nation's mission in domestic and international relations (Sandler 1995: 263).

Indeed, Malaysian national security conceptions are inseparable from the country's experience with British colonialism. Malaysian history provides a permanent guide to national decision makers. It shapes their view of security, the significance they assign to it in executing their tasks, and the limits governing their formulation and implementation of security paradigms in the real world. The relevance of history in Malaysia's security formulations is evidenced by the constitutional, political, and economic structures that the ruling elite have developed to protect and promote the multifaceted interests of a multiethnic society. Security conceptions invariably incorporate historical, psychological, and cultural dimensions. The current prime minister, Dr. Mahathir Mohamad, who has been in office since 1981, has defined security as follows:

> When we talk about national security, the picture that usually comes to mind is that of armed soldiers manning border posts or fighting in the jungle....But security is not just a matter of military capability. National security is inseparable from political stability, economic success and social harmony. Without these all the guns in the world cannot prevent a country from being overcome by its enemies, whose ambition can be fulfilled without even firing a single shot. All they need really is to subvert the people and set up a puppet regime.

Clearly economic difficulties are serious threats to national security. Failure to understand this threat may result in a cycle of recession followed by political instability, security threats and even greater recession. The skillful management of the economy and clear thinking are therefore an integral part of the strategy for national security.[1]

This conceptualization of security comprises both domestic and external dimensions. The concern with domestic security is manifested in the continued emphasis on internal peace, law, and order, which is considered vital to the daily business of governing and fulfilling the needs and demands of a multiracial society. Internal tranquillity is a sine qua non for development and progress. Hence legal instruments, even if they are draconian, are deemed essential for legitimating the government's authority and its capacity to manage a plural society like Malaysia. Conceptions of external security, however, are based on an assessment of the immediate threats and of the operation of the regional and global balances of power. In this sense, national security connotes the idea of strategic survival internally as well as externally. This chapter focuses on the domestic, regional, and international foundations of Malaysia's national security practice.

Domestic Foundations

All societies are influenced by their own past record as they cope with internal and external challenges and formulate social, political, and economic structures and policies designed for self-survival. Indeed, some societies are more strongly influenced than others by their historical experience—especially when its psychological, ideological, and political impact has been so profound that it is impossible to divorce the past from present and future security conceptions.

For Malaysia, the strongest ideological compulsion driving its domestic and foreign policies derives from the bitter experience with the communist insurgency from 1948 until 1960. Defeating internal communism and containing international communism became a cardinal principle of strategy for Malaysian decision makers entrusted with the security of the nation. The success of the Maoist revolution in China in 1949 heightened fears of a Beijing-led Asian communism engulfing the entire Southeast Asian region. That apprehension was strengthened by the ethnic character of the Malaysian communists, nearly all of whom were Chinese. Furthermore, the presence of a sizable ethnic Chinese population in Malaysia fueled official concern about their potential role as fifth columnists in the service of the Communist Party of Malaya (CPM) and the Communist Party of China (CPC).

The essential nature of the Malayan communist political agenda—whose primary objective since its formation in 1930 was "to carry on the struggle for national liberation, formulate a military program for the overthrow of imperialism and feudal aristocracy and to establish the Soviet Republic of Malaya by the coordinated efforts of the proletariat and peasantry" (Hanrahan 1971: 43)—was anathema to the Malays, who generally viewed Chinese involvement in the anticolonial and communist terrorist activities as "assisting one form of Chinese domination to replace another" (Fisk and Osman-Rani 1982: 9). It is quite apparent, then, that ethnicity has combined with ideology to produce a particular security orientation since the early days of independence. Malaysia's postindependence security decision makers incorporated this historical, ideological, and ethnic security orientation into policies and strategies for molding the nation. The formation of the CPM in 1930, the rejection by the United Malays National Organization (UMNO) of the Malayan Union proposals put forward by the British, and UMNO's suspicions regarding the program of the Independence of Malaya Party (IMP)—both of which entailed broader political and citizenship rights for non-Malays—cumulatively bore testimony to rising Malay political consciousness and pressures for a Malay-led Malaya (later Malaysia) following independence in 1957. These events also portended increasing Malay insecurity stemming from political developments in the years preceding and succeeding World War II. The Japanese occupation of Malaya from 1942 to 1945 only served as a catalyst to demands for Malay political leadership of the independence struggle and for an unchallenged Malay role in shaping the political economy of Malaysia in the postindependence era. Moreover, British colonial rule had encouraged the growth of "a Malay bureaucratic class which, after independence, continued to dominate the key organs of the state—the bureaucracy, judiciary, military and police—and provided the leadership of the United Malays National Organization or UMNO" (Crouch 1993: 136). Thus the referent units of Malaysian security were to be principally Malay in character and determined almost exclusively by the Malays, to whom power was transferred constitutionally by the British colonial masters on August 31, 1957.

The Constitutional Basis

Constitutions are essentially political-legal documents outlining the powers, functions, and limitations of the social groups and institutions that compose the body politic at a given time. They reflect the interests of prevailing power groups in society regardless of the manner in which they have been constituted. Politically dominant groups write into national constitutions their own interests, privileges, ideologies, aspirations, and goals—all of which establish a framework for a viable and orderly interaction among various groups in society. Constitutions as social documents evolve with time, as reflected by amendments. Nevertheless, certain provisions are regarded as sacrosanct despite radical changes taking place in society. Amendments affecting entrenched provisions threaten the security of those groups who have benefited from special provisions granting them political, economic, and social privileges vis-à-vis other communities and presumptive territorial rights to the land.

In short, a nation's constitution can serve as an important source of national security—even if that notion is selectively applied to legitimize the interests of a particular ethnic group. Article 153 of the Federal Constitution—providing for special rights and privileges for Malays and other natives with respect to public-service jobs, education, scholarships and training, and business licenses—remains an entrenched provision after 40 years of Malaysian independence even though the political dominance of the Malays remains assured and their economic position vis-à-vis the non-Malays has significantly improved.[2] Moreover, the concept of *Bumiputera* (literally, sons of the soil) that gained currency after the 1969 racial riots, as well as the initiation of the New Economic Policy (NEP), represent further political attempts to preserve this entrenched provision even if the economic position of the Malays has overtaken that of the non-Malays. Article 153 and Bumiputera must be viewed as two sides of the same coin, with the purpose of entrenching Malay dominance for as long as that is possible and thereby strengthening Malay feelings of security in relation to the other communities in Malaysia.

The citizenship provisions of the Federal Constitution shed additional light on Malay perceptions of national security. Stringent provisions under Articles 14 through 31 ensure tight controls over citizenship acquisition by non-Malays and foreigners, including foreign wives of Malaysian citizens (Article 15). And whereas it is difficult for foreign wives to gain citizenship, it is virtually impossible for foreign husbands (Sinnadurai 1978: 76). Such provisions are designed to preserve the Malay character of the Malaysian Federation—and hence the constitutional security of the politically dominant Malays.

Ethnicity and Security

Malaysian politics is communal politics. Unless the constitutional, political, and economic framework that entrenches Bumiputera rights is changed, it is reasonable to expect the present model of political development to continue. The prospects of a major shift in favor of de-ethnicization of politics must be measured against the strength of institutions that have become deeply rooted on an ethnic basis. Political mobilization and participation are officially encouraged along ethnic lines. The ruling Barisan Nasional (BN) coalition is itself a political and electoral arrangement along ethnic lines. Thus the whole notion of individual, group, and organizational security is closely tied to the communal character of the Malaysian political system. Attempts to form multiracial conceptions of political security through multiracial parties have either foundered because of the ethnic factor or been stifled by official intervention. The compulsion to protect ethnic security has also found expression in the suppression of the left in the post–World War II period, thereby virtually eliminating any prospect of nonethnic ideological discourse—that is, of removing ethnicity as the basis for approaching and resolving political, economic, and social issues in Malaysia. Since the late 1960s, and especially after the May 1969 racial riots, "ethnicity has increasingly dominated Malaysian political culture" (Sundaram 1989: 36). The Gerakan Rakyat Malaysia (Malaysian People's Movement), originally conceived as a multiracial party, has degenerated into essentially a party promoting Chinese interests. In Sabah, the multiracial Parti Bersatu Sabah (PBS; Sabah United Party) faced strong challenges from the federal government in Kuala Lumpur, especially under Mahathir's premiership, until it was finally ousted from power in 1995. Sabah is now ruled by a state government that is dominated by UMNO and resembles the ethnically oriented political model in peninsular Malaysia.

In Malaysia, as in virtually all multiethnic societies, ethnic politics is a means to an end: political stability, regime security, economic growth and development, and multiracial peace and harmony—all regarded as key values in the preservation and promotion of national security. Given the dominant role of the Malays in Malaysian political life, Malay security is invariably equated with Malaysian security. Malay feelings of insecurity are invariably translated into policies and strategies of coercion and accommodation designed to promote Malay ethnic interests. More recently, especially under the Mahathir administration, Malay interests have become more closely linked to the interests of UMNO (the ruling party).

The New Economic Policy from 1970 to 1990 was a key strategy through which the Malays attempted to overcome their insecurity in the aftermath of the 1969 general elections, which appeared to threaten their political dominance. Strategies of excessive state interventionism in the 1970s in support of Malay interests were gradually replaced in the 1980s and 1990s by economic policies that reduced the state's role in the economy but were motivated by the same objective of strengthening

Bumiputera control of the Malaysian economy. Such strategies for Malay ethnic survival and security included "Malaysia Incorporated," deregulation, suspension of NEP implementation (Sundaram 1989: 42), and establishment of the Heavy Industries Corporation of Malaysia (HICOM) for production of Malaysian-made cars. The government's privatization policy in the mid-1980s was clearly designed to "accelerate growth, improve efficiency and productivity, trim the public sector, reduce the government's financial and administrative role, and redistribute wealth to the Bumiputeras" (Sundaram 1995: 48).

Although the New Economic Policy has been replaced by the National Development Policy (NDP), the basic contours of Bumiputera supremacy in Malaysia's political economy remain intact. The new UMNO elite, created largely by the New Economic Policy, is loath to make any concessions that are seen as eroding the privileged position of the Malays in society, regardless of whether NEP targets have been achieved or even exceeded. Indeed, even the issue of whether or not the 1990 NEP targets had been achieved was deemed a matter of secrecy and "national security" (Means 1991: 189). In the wake of the 1986 elections, which confirmed UMNO's political dominance, certain party officials continued to tell non-Malays that they were "playing with fire" by questioning the special position of the Malays.[3] Because the NEP's prime objective was to reduce Malays' economic insecurity, or alternatively to enhance their economic security, foreign participation in the Malaysian economy was consciously encouraged in order to constrain the role of domestic capital, which was largely in the hands of the Chinese.

Economic nationalism in Malaysia strengthened the link between Malay ethnicity and Malay economic security (in contrast to a focus on *Malaysian* economic security) through the official preference for transnational capital over domestic Chinese capital, a preference strongly influenced by concerns about Chinese wealth accumulation in the nation (Sundaram 1993: 11). If Malaysian security equals Malay supremacy, then any perceived erosion of that supremacy must necessarily endanger Malay (and therefore national) security—regardless of how this equation affects the security of the non-Malays. A member of the Malay elite, Datuk Abdullah Ahmad, confirms the linkage between ethnic security and national security by his strong assertion that Malaysia's political system is premised on Malay supremacy and that "system breakdown" occurred in 1969 (the race riots of May 13) when this "sacrosanct social contract" between the Malays and non-Malays was violated (Ahmad 1988: 5).

Malaysia's political system has often been described as a consociational arrangement between the principal ethnic groups that constitute the nation's population of 20 million. Consociational political models are based on ethnic compromises arranged by the elites representing the various ethnic groups. To the extent that those compromises are seen by the general population as broadly safeguarding their interests, such a model is politically viable in the Malaysian case. The focus on Malay ethnic dominance in the Malaysian political system must, however, be balanced against the system's ability to deliver the goods to the non-Malays as well—a priority reflected in the Alliance/BN victories in all the general elections held to date, even in the face of UMNO's gerrymandering of electoral boundaries and its use of "siege legitimacy" to justify its dominance and tout its unique ability to "safeguard national security" (Brown 1985: 988–1008). Siege legitimacy, according to Brown, "implies the need not just to point to external threats, but also to particular internal cleavages which constitute potential sources of disunity and vulnerability" (Brown 1985: 998). In the case of the PBS-ruled Sabah, Mahathir appears to have successfully employed siege legitimacy in the run-up to the 1994 state elections by raising the issue of ethnic strife in Bosnia-Herzegovina "to evoke fears among Sabahans that Malaysian Muslims would be oppressed by a predominantly Christian leadership if PBS were to be reelected" (Gomez 1996: 94).

Nevertheless, the political record demonstrates the resilience of the present political framework and its ability to implement the doctrine of balance in addressing the multifaceted challenges posed by a multiethnic society. The viability of this framework requires substantial compromises by the non-Malay populace with regard to the Malay need for security through political domination. Younger generations of both Malays and non-Malays, however, might engender somewhat different notions of national security as the leveling process attains its goal of erasing differences between race and economic function—that is, governmental policies are designed to encourage economic participation by all ethnic groups and to discourage monopolization of economic activity by any one particular ethnic category. To what extent will younger generations of non-Malays continue to accept this Bumiputera–non-Bumiputera dichotomy based on Malay dominance? When will ethnicity become less consequential in deciding the basic political issue of who gets what, when, and how? Although these questions defy easy answers, one thing is clear: today the basic domestic structure of Malaysian security is built around Malay ethnic identity. As one Malaysian political activist notes: "The classification of Malaysians into Bumiputeras and non-Bumiputeras has long been an issue of contention in our political arena. Perhaps no other issue divides our people as much as this one" (Fan 1995: 175). Indeed, the ideology, policy, and practice of

"Bumiputeraism" has effectively intervened between Malay nationalism based on monoethnicity and the emergence of a truly Malaysian nationalism based on multiethnicity—even after 40 years of independence. It is therefore hardly surprising that virtually no serious reference has been made by Malaysian officials, scholars, and analysts to the existence of a Malaysian nationalism since the formation of Malaysia in 1963. After four decades of independence, the Malaysian state-nation is still in the process of building the Malaysian nation-state—and also a more pluralistic as well as inclusive conception of national security.

The Malay State, Islam, and Language

The concept of Malaya (later Malaysia) as comprising essentially the Malay state is embodied in the reference to the country as *tanah Melayu*, or Malay land. This basic Malayness was also preserved in the new name of "Malaysia" when Malaya was expanded to include Singapore (until 1965) and the North Borneo territories of Sabah and Sarawak. The identification of race with territory connotes an important element of security for the majority ethnic group in Malaysia, especially when that congruence also coincides with historical reality and political power. The security and sovereignty of the Malay state are preserved by constitutional provisions pertaining to the role of the nine Malay sultans, who also serve as heads of the Muslim religion in their states. The sultans therefore function as legitimizers of Malay sovereignty over Malaysia, a position that cannot be challenged under the constitution. In the years preceding Malayan independence, Malay rulers warned against the erosion of traditional Malay loyalties by stressing communalism—especially by pointing out the incompatibility of Islam (embraced by the Malays) and communism (largely a Chinese phenomenon) (Hua 1983: 98). Besides the institution of the Malay rulers, the Malay language or Bahasa Melayu (also known as Bahasa Malaysia) furnishes an additional tool of legitimacy for Malay dominance of Malaysia. The use of the national language as the main medium of instruction at all levels of education—primary, secondary, and tertiary—as well as the medium of official communication with government is yet another integral element of preserving Malay ethnic security and, by extension, Malay dominance in a multiethnic society in which other racial groups are individually as well as collectively weaker in the political domain. Their political weakness appears to be a requirement for Malay strength and Malay security. The Malaysian state, therefore, is only a political expression: its political fundamentals are Malay in origin and evolution. In short, the political basis of Malaysian security resides in Malay security.

Thus the Malay monarchy, the Muslim religion, and the Malay language constitute the major referent units of Malay and, by extension, Malaysian security. Nevertheless, these basic symbols of Malay security are subject to political manipulation in the interest of the rising Malay middle class. Many among that group have migrated from rural areas in the wake of industrialization, modernization, and urbanization—all of which are viewed by the ruling government, especially under Mahathir, as essential to both the transformation of Malay society and the promotion of Malay competitiveness vis-à-vis the non-Malays. The urbanization of the Malays, according to Mahathir, is an integral part of development and hence Malay security: "The whole process must be planned and executed with speed and thoroughness to produce a complete and radical change in the Malays. If this revolution is brought about they would be rehabilitated and their dilemma would be over" (Mahathir 1970: 114). The nation would be able to progress without the burden of a Malay problem.

The constitutional amendments of 1984 and 1993 relating to the powers of the Malay sovereigns indicate the degree to which established symbols of Malay sovereignty and security can be manipulated to achieve specific political agendas (Hari Singh 1995: 187–205). The role of Islam as the official religion of Malaysia is instructive. The Federal Constitution merely states that Islam is the "official religion" of the country; freedom of religion for all non-Muslims, who make up about 50 percent of the population, is also constitutionally enshrined. Islam's preeminent status is therefore a source of Malay/Muslim security, and it cannot be challenged under any circumstances. The Muslim-dominated leadership, however, practices a secular form of Islam to accommodate the multireligious sentiments of Malaysian society and, more important, to ensure that Islam does not become a tool reinforcing Malay backwardness but instead serves as a vehicle of progress so that the socioeconomic status of Muslims is at least on a par with non-Muslims. Mahathir was particularly concerned that the practice of Islam in Malaysia might produce the opposite effect of reinforcing Malay feelings of insecurity and inferiority in urban environments, which, at least until recently, have been dominated by the more sophisticated and better-educated non-Malays (Zainah Anwar 1987: 79). Thus the UMNO-led government is wary of the Pan-Malaysian Islamic Party's (PAS) goal of establishing an Islamic state in Malaysia. PAS's superficial understanding of the role of modern science, technology, industrialization, education, and administration inspires little confidence among the broad Malay segment or among the non-Malays with regard to its ability to provide a viable alternative to the UMNO and Barisan Nasional style of governance (Muzaffar 1987: 59–64). The country's first prime minister's view of

Islam in a multireligious context is particularly instructive in conveying the secular, liberal, modernist, and rather universalistic approach of the Malaysian government with respect to religion: "Islam means peace, love, cooperation, honesty, punctuality, hard work, honor and abstinence from licentious behavior. Islam stands for complete understanding between all peoples and all races" (Tunku Abdul Rahman 1986: 142–43).

Thus Malay/Muslim security is closely tied to official and, more precisely, modernist interpretations of Islam that reinforce ethnic security by focusing on nationalism rather than religion. Modernists reject theocracy as being incompatible with development and modernity (Mehmet 1990: 99). Deviance in the form of sectarianism or contradictory interpretations of the Koran is strongly discouraged, if not penalized, to preserve the ultimate goal of Muslim unity. Official concerns that disunity among the Muslims would expose them to political exploitation by outsiders as well as weaken them as a group tend to find expression in strong pronouncements and threats of severe sanctions including the use of the Internal Security Act to enforce compliance. The activities of the Al-Arqam movement, headed by Ashaari Mohamed, were viewed as a threat to national security because the sect threatened the core of Muslim orthodoxy as practiced in Malaysia. The banning of Al-Arqam, the extraction of confessions from its leadership, the suppression of religious literature and publications by Muslim individuals and organizations that are deemed to subvert Malay/Muslim unity and security—all provide strong evidence of the link between race and religion as referent units of national security in a domestic context.

Under the Mahathir administration, concerted efforts have been made to adopt a more uniform approach to religious issues and to reduce the diversity in practice that results from local control over Islamic affairs. Federal control over publications, imports, police, and internal security has enabled the center to circumvent problems arising from the diversity of local actions (Means 1991: 103).[4] The Islamization of public policy under federal authority has enabled Mahathir to integrate the role of Islam as an instrument of national security. The federalization of Islam, however, must inevitably impinge on the traditional authority and role of the sultan as head of Islamic affairs in his own state—eroding to some extent the Malay potentate's significance as a referent unit of Malay security. Furthermore, the constitutional amendments, which were designed to "clip the wings of the rulers," led to an erosion of their stature and influence that in turn "diminished their constraining role in tempering the exercise of executive powers" (Hoong Phun Lee 1995: 119).

Federalism and National Security

Malaysian federalism is a means to an end: the preservation of the territorial integrity and unity of all its component parts made up of the nine Malay states (Perlis, Kedah, Kelantan, Terengganu, Perak, Selangor, Negeri Sembilan, Pahang, and Johor), two of the three former Straits Settlements (Penang and Malacca), and the two Borneo territories (Sabah and Sarawak). The fourteenth component, the Federal Territories comprising greater Kuala Lumpur and Labuan, completes the political structure of federal government in Malaysia. The security of the federation stems from centralized control of key spheres such as finance, internal security (control over police and armed forces), foreign policy, and education.

This federalist notion of national security does not tolerate any attempts by state governments that could rupture the political and territorial unity of the federation, including efforts that are deemed secessionist by the federal center. In 1965, the removal of Stephen Kalong Ningkan as chief minister of Sarawak was preceded by an official declaration of emergency in that state. In Kelantan, similar emergency powers were used to dismiss the PAS-led BN coalition in favor of a profederal state government (Crouch 1996: 104–6). In Sabah, concerted pressure by the central government under Mahathir to subvert the PBS state government of Sabah in the 1980s, and especially after the PBS left the BN coalition in 1990, cumulatively point to the conclusion that federal resources and authoritarian measures will be employed with total effect to support a state if it is pro–Kuala Lumpur or to frustrate its ability to rule if it is deemed antifederal. Moreover, the centralized control over the police, the armed forces, and national intelligence gives the federal government effective instruments to thwart perceived threats to internal security arising from state-based intransigence. Federal-state tensions following the handing over of Labuan to the federal government on April 16, 1984, by the Harris Salleh government required the PBS to expend much of its energy to fight federal accusations that it was attempting to pull Sabah out of the Malaysian federation. When Mahathir decided that the PBS under Joseph Pairin Kitingan—leader of the predominant ethnic Kadazan community—was inimical to federal interests, the state's leadership crumbled under the weight of federal opposition. From Mahathir's perspective, the removal of the Kadazan-led multiracial PBS and the installation of a profederal UMNO-based state government in Sabah since 1995 have considerably eased tensions that could have undermined the internal security of that "recalcitrant" state.

In the context of federal-state relations, the three notable cases of Sarawak, Kelantan, and Sabah illuminate the problem of state formation in a situation where the pursuit of security, in the form of a drive to homogenize and silence differences, has become a crucial aspect of nation-building (Pasha 1996: 288). The "national security" requirement is used to justify draconian measures such as the Internal Security Act— as well as other restrictive legislation including the Sedition Act, the Official Secrets Act, and the Printing Press Ordinance—for the declared objective of maintaining public order and interracial peace and harmony.

Singapore as a National Security Concern

If history, identity, and nationalism are important ideational variables in explaining the security disposition of Asian states, then the role of Singapore as a predominantly Chinese state and its geopolitical proximity to Malay-dominated Malaysia provide significant insights into ethnic-oriented perceptions of Malaysian national security. The then Malaysian Defense Minister, Najib Tun Razak, aptly remarked that one of the root problems in bilateral relations is the mutual tendency "to carve out our perceptions towards one another based on Malay-Chinese racial and ethnic preconceptions" (Razak 1995: 19). Malay fears of Chinese dominance after Singapore's merger with Malaysia in 1963 formed the basis of the decision to expel Singapore from the Malaysian Federation two years later. The city-state's membership in the Malaysian Federation had tipped the ethnic scales in favor of the Chinese, whose economic status and role then posed serious threats to Malay identity and self-confidence. Separation was therefore viewed as a strategy to restore ethnic balance in favor of the Malays while strengthening their feeling of political security. Although Singapore-Malaysia relations have been moderated somewhat by the ASEAN factor, bilateral frictions arise periodically from the weight of history, geographical proximity, and the political economy of the two neighbors.

In the context of the ethnic sensitivities on both sides of the quarter-mile-long causeway linking the two ASEAN states, both governments have attempted to enhance their relative national security through confidence-building measures including frequent high-level exchanges, visits, and agreements for mutual cooperation. Such measures include the SIJORI development project involving Singapore, the southern Malaysian state of Johor, and the Indonesian island of Riau—underscoring the notion of joint development as a vehicle for enhancing mutual security. Additionally, bilateral military cooperation between Malaysia and Singapore via the Five Power Defence Arrangements (FPDA) is a confidence-building measure aimed at neutralizing mutual threat perceptions affecting national security (Baginda 1995: 21). Nevertheless, intermittent frictions rooted in history, nationalism, ethnicity, the city-state's access to water supply from Johor, and growing economic competition stemming from Malaysia's rapid industrialization[5] continue to affect mutual perceptions of national security and well-being. Thus, geopolitical proximity requires a continuous commitment to mutual understanding of each other's problems, needs, and perceptions for the preservation of national security on both sides of the causeway.

Development as Security

Development is a vital theme in the Malaysian government's approach to national security. Indeed, security cannot be defined without development. The very notion of comprehensive security as the philosophical basis of national security and development is rooted in the strategy to defeat the communist threat to Malaysia. The comprehensive approach emphasizes not only military actions against the communist guerrillas, but also political, administrative, economic, social, and cultural measures to consolidate national security.

The philosophy of development permeates all the five-year plans, including the most recent, the Seventh Malaysia Plan (1996–2000). The First Malaysia Plan (1966–70) approached national security through its objectives of promoting the economic and social integration of the peoples and states of Malaysia, raising income levels, employment opportunities, and education and training facilities, and diversifying the economy to reduce dependence on traditional commodities like rubber and tin, which at that time were the mainstays of the Malaysian economy.[6] The Seventh Malaysia Plan, however, has considerably broadened the economic foundations of Malaysian national security with its emphasis on a holistic approach to development. These are the plan's objectives:

1. Convert industries and production processes from labor intensive to capital, technology, and knowledge intensive.

2. Ensure sustained growth and balanced development.

3. Adopt a global approach to industrialization.

4. Reduce poverty and income disparities between ethnic and income groups and regions.

5. Develop a viable Bumiputera Commercial and Industrial Community (BCIC).

6. Accelerate privatization to improve efficiency and productivity and reduce the burden of the public sector, while at the same time strengthening Bumiputera participation in the economy through greater equity in ownership and management control.

7. Radically transform the Malaysian economy from input-driven (primarily through investments) to productivity-driven by enhancing the contribution of "total factor productivity" (TFP)—that is, additional output generated by upgrading skills, education, and organizational, production, and management technologies.

8. Place greater emphasis on human resource development, research and development, science and technology, and the critical role of information technology—all of which would drive Malaysia's national development and international competitiveness in the context of globalization.

9. Integrate the economic, social, and environmental aspects into the development process.

10. Protect the environment while improving the quality of life in its social, cultural, and psychological aspects.

11. Pursue all these goals via strategies marked by flexibility and pragmatism as well as creativity and innovation.[7]

The role of the state as an agent of development, and therefore of security, is viewed as crucial by ruling elites in the developing world. Rapid advances in science and technology must be directly addressed by the state in terms of its capability for innovation. Thus, strengthening of the state virtually coincides with the development of national resilience in the political, economic, and sociocultural dimensions (Alagappa 1987a: 20). And with the launching of the Multimedia Super Corridor (MSC) on August 1, 1996, Prime Minister Mahathir has now directly linked national security with technological progress. The Malaysian government sees multimedia as the strategic sector to achieve Vision 2020, that is, the attainment of developed-country status through productivity-led growth.[8] Malaysia intends to play a key role in the globalizing and harmonizing forces of the information age, thereby contributing to a convergence rather than a clash of civilizations. Indeed, economic and technological security are increasingly informing, redefining, and even supplanting traditional political-military conceptions of national security.

Vision 2020

The role of leadership in reinventing conceptions of security that reflect a dynamic balance between domestic capacity and external performance has never been more evident than under the premiership of Mahathir bin Mohamad. In 1991, Mahathir articulated his vision of

Malaysia in the next 30 years in a speech entitled "Malaysia: The Way Forward"—a conceptualization of national security combining elements of idealism and realism. Vision 2020, as both conception and strategy of national security, espouses the following agenda: to create a united Malaysian nation; to promote an outward-looking Malaysian society; to infuse society with strong moral and ethical values; to ensure that the state is democratic, liberal and tolerant, caring, economically just and equitable, progressive, and prosperous; and to develop an economy that is competitive, dynamic, robust, and resilient.[9]

The externalization of Malaysia's internal capacity has several dimensions:

- Political: a stable Malaysia geared toward resolving political, economic, social, religious, and ethnic issues within a broad framework of consensus and compromise

- Ideological: a growing national confidence in Malaysian values, general acceptance if not tolerance of democracy Malaysian-style, commitment to the basic values of a free enterprise economy, and a legacy of success in overcoming the communist threat to the nation

- Economic: a country that has by and large achieved the redistributive targets of the twenty-year New Economic Policy resulting in an economically confident Malay (Bumiputera) community that is presumably more sensitive to the needs of other Malaysians

- Social: a strengthened feeling among all Malaysians that the causes leading to the May 13, 1969, racial riots have been addressed and that a similar recurrence can be averted by good political management, mutual tolerance, and the promotion of interracial goodwill and harmony

- Regional: the development of political, economic, and security mechanisms for expanding cooperation and reducing regional tension—that is, the creation of an atmosphere that is conducive to Malaysian national interests

- International: a growing capacity to articulate issues that affect a wider spectrum of humanity in line with changing global interests and priorities (Nathan 1995: 220–37).

Five key political and economic indicators have motivated Vision 2020 and served as the domestic impetus for reinventing the "Malaysian Nation" and reconceptualizing national security. The first element is continuing political stability under a Barisan Nasional coalition government that has basically been ruling the country ever since independence. This 40-year record of stability, economic development, and social harmony remains unmatched. Although opportunities for the emergence of alternatives have certainly been limited, previous election results indicate that the BN enjoys a clear mandate to govern on behalf of all Malaysians. That mandate, in turn, has introduced a high degree of stability in planning for growth and development—indeed, Malaysia is now developing a master plan to enable it to achieve the status of a fully developed country. Such a visionary formulation would be virtually impossible in a politically unstable context rife with multiethnic tension and conflict with all the attendant consequences for economic progress. A rising confidence in Malaysia's political stability and economic prosperity is apparently driving the new conception of national security.

The second element is the country's creditable record of economic performance, which has inspired local and foreign investors' confidence in the Malaysian economy. The overall success of "Malaysia Incorporated"—that is, the privatization policy the government introduced in 1983—has boosted the confidence of Malaysians (especially Malays) in their ability to manage the national economy within the framework of broad national interests. Moreover, the creation of a narrow industrial base with heavy external inputs during the first Outline Perspective Plan (OPP1, 1971–90, also known as the NEP) stimulated indigenous interest in further Malaysianizing the progress toward industrialization under the Sixth Malaysia Plan (SMP, 1991–95) and the second Outline Perspective Plan (OPP2, 1991–2000). A notable feature of the National Development Policy, which replaced the NEP in 1990, is that it emphasizes growth, puts no time limits on redistribution, and does not specify numerical targets.[10]

The third element is the significant measure of national pride arising from decisions taken under Mahathir's leadership to develop heavy industry and to produce Malaysia's own national car, the Proton Saga, whose credibility and international marketability are now beyond dispute. The initial success in car manufacturing has encouraged newer designs and models for the domestic and external markets. This achievement, combined with the rapid growth of the manufacturing sector, is the major contributor to Malaysia's impressive GNP growth rates, averaging 8 to 10 percent in the last eight years. The fourth element, industrial progress and a general improvement in economic welfare, has been accompanied by labor discipline—that is, a sharp reduction in strikes by unionized labor during Mahathir's tenure since 1981, due either to wage increases or to fear of reprimand from the government. The fifth element is the government's readiness to use the Internal Security Act—as it did in October 1987 under "Operation Lalang" and in connection with the arrest in September 1994 and again in 1996 of leaders of the banned Al-Arqam movement—combined with the virtual absence of a unified voice to protest government excesses. All these factors have led to political stability. Vision 2020 draws upon these internal dimensions of national strength to build the external aspirations of the Malaysian nation.

In essence, Mahathir's "new thinking" in foreign policy rests firmly on the assumption of a stable, Malay-led, multiethnic Malaysia that is capable of satisfying national aspirations across a wide spectrum of competing demands and interests. Essentially, this new approach—indeed, assertiveness—in foreign affairs is directly linked to a strengthened feeling of national security. Furthermore, the concept of planned development—the attainment of rational targets based on competition and free enterprise as envisaged under Vision 2020—will eventually reduce NEP-based racial discontent (on the part of non-Malays) and presumably erase the prevailing Bumiputera–non-Bumiputera dichotomy in Malaysia's political economy.[11] Vision 2020 rests on an internal foundation composed of three key elements: first, national integration based on multiethnic cooperation and partnership as well the trend toward deracialization; second, the effective management of all forms of extremism, actual and potential, along the dimensions of race, religion, ideology, or even political and economic doctrine; and third, the creation of a climate that will propel Malaysia toward economic excellence in the next 30 years through wise management of the nation's financial, industrial, natural, and human resources, increased cooperation between the public sector and private sector, and a significant role for foreign investment in the nation's industrial transformation.[12] This internal foundation, built upon past and present achievements, is bound to affect the external dimensions of national security as Mahathir pursues his desire for a more activist role in international relations.

Regional Foundations

Malaysia's strategic survival during the Cold War required a keen appreciation of linkage dynamics operating at the domestic, regional, and international levels. At the time of independence it was patently clear to Malaysian policy makers—especially the prime minister, Tunku Abdul Rahman, who was for all practical purposes the manager of foreign policy—that strategies for national survival must be aligned with regional and global strategic trends. The Tunku opted for a two-pronged approach: a firm stand against international communism and a strong pro-Western ideological, economic, political, and military orientation.

Anticommunism and Regional Security

The Tunku's foreign policy itself was largely conditioned by Malaysia's own historical experience in fighting communist subversion within the country during the Malayan Emergency from 1948 to 1960. The Malaysian leader's keen understanding of communist strategy strongly influenced his conception of national security at the time of Malayan independence. At the domestic level, the Tunku had to ensure a stable, peaceful, harmonious, and prosperous multiethnic nation that would in turn provide a strong foundation on which to build the external dimensions of Malaysia's national security. Political compromise and accommodation became the hallmarks of the prime minister's domestic survival strategy—values that proved relevant to Malaysian stability for the better part of the Tunku's tenure from 1957 until 1970. In the external sphere, the young state required protection from internal subversion and external threat, so it concluded a bilateral security treaty with its former colonial master. The Anglo-Malaysian Defense Agreement (AMDA) proved critical to Malaysia's survival during the short period of confrontation with Indonesia (1963–66).

In terms of resisting the international communist threat in the 1950s, Malaysia was a clear beneficiary of the U.S.–sponsored network of global military alliances aimed against the Soviet Union and Communist China. Essentially, Malaysia's security needs were well provided for within the broad framework of Anglo-American defense cooperation in the first two decades of the Cold War and, after the Vietnam War, through the Five Power Defence Arrangements (FPDA) formed in 1971 to replace AMDA and comprising Malaysia, Singapore, Australia, New Zealand, and Britain.

Because regional security was defined mainly in ideological terms, the requirements of national survival made it imperative that Malaysia fit into externally devised security structures in the early years following independence. Given the dictates of Cold War politics, neutralism as a platform of foreign policy was not an option. Malaysia's foreign policy based on anticommunism was realistic to the extent that it maximized the benefits and opportunities while minimizing the costs and risks of national survival. Within this framework of possibilities, Malaysia pursued two foreign policy strategies at the regional level: one was conflict resolution through appeals to common ethnocultural and historical characteristics; the other was regional cooperation based on common economic and sociocultural foundations. Malaysia's attempt at conflict resolution via regional nonmilitary mechanisms would have achieved greater success had it not been for the sharply divergent ideological perspective held by Indonesia's President Sukarno regarding the formation of Malaysia. Sukarno's weltanschauung was determined by the ideological struggle between the New Emerging Forces, or NEFOS, and the Old Established Forces, or OLDEFOS (Nathan 1983: 28–47). In opposing the idea of a larger federation incorporating Malaya, Singapore, Sabah (North Borneo), Sarawak, and Brunei, Sukarno claimed leadership of NEFOS while condemning Malaysian Prime Minister Tunku Abdul Rahman as a collaborator with the old colonial order (OLDEFOS) in Southeast Asia. Thus, when in June 1963 the Philippines president, Diasdado Macapagal, proposed the formation of MAPHILINDO—a loose ethnocultural association based on Malay fraternity comprising the three states of Malaya, Indonesia, and the Philippines—the political foundation for such a relationship soon collapsed in the wake of conflicting ideological perspectives and territorial claims originating respectively in Jakarta and Manila. The failure of conflict resolution along pacifist lines culminated in Indonesia's three-year confrontation with Malaysia and the still unresolved Philippine claim to Sabah. The Tunku's successors, in line with the altered strategic scenario following the American exit from Indochina and the dictates of Malaysian national survival, pursued a policy of internal anticommunism and international nonalignment.

Commitment to ASEAN Regionalism

Malaysia's approach to regionalism is a response to the character of its own domestic national structure and that of the regional power structure. State-directed nationalism and state-directed growth, coupled with the growing necessity of pooling resources in the drive for modernization, have produced the related phenomenon of regionalism, which has evolved in the form of the Association of Southeast Asian Nations (ASEAN), inaugurated in 1967.

ASEAN regionalism is also reflected in the increased bilateralism that is a necessary by-product of the nation-building process in Southeast Asia. In Malaysia and Singapore the nation-building process is particularly instructive with respect to the role of ethnicity in mutual perceptions and the need to sensitize the foreign policy process to the realities of ethnicity: Chinese-dominated Singapore interacts with Malay-dominated Malaysia, and neither questions the basis of ethnic supremacy that governs both societies. Ethnicity is clearly an unstated factor in the national security perceptions that influence interstate relations within the framework of ASEAN regionalism. Hence the nation-building process in developing societies such as Malaysia and Singapore links national survival to regional stability and prosperity.

Regional stability reinforces regime security in every member state. Regional cooperation therefore achieves the simultaneous goals of promoting a regime's survival and satisfying the drive for modernization and development as integral components of postindependence nationalism. In this context, Prime Minister Mahathir asserts:

> So far as Malaysia is concerned, ASEAN remains in the forefront of our foreign policy priorities. The rationale behind this Government's thinking is the vital role of ASEAN as a stabilizing influence and as a catalyst in developing the economic resilience of the region.
>
> ASEAN has become an important platform for the development of closer relations with advanced countries as well as with international organizations. ASEAN, therefore, has an important role to play in national, regional and international affairs.[13]

In Malaysia's external security conceptions, a general ordering of foreign policy priorities reflects the relative weight given to each component. ASEAN ranks as the first priority in view of its influential role and direct impact on national and regional security. The Islamic countries are ranked second for their obvious role in forging an Islamic identity of which Malay/Muslim-led Malaysia desires to be an integral part. The Nonaligned Movement ranks third for its potential power in restructuring international relations in the future. The Commonwealth is ranked fourth, and all other countries not included in the first four categories occupy the fifth rank (Khoo 1995: 74–75). Through regionalism, central decision makers in Malaysia, like their other ASEAN partners, hope to reduce if not eliminate threats to national sovereignty. They believe that threats to regime survival "emanate largely from within their regions, if not from within these states themselves," stemming from geographic proximity, weak state structures, and "narrowly based regimes lacking unconditional legitimacy" (Ayoob 1989: 70–71). New challenges to nation-state legitimacy created by modernization, growth, and development—as manifested by transnational economic phenomena such as the growth triangles—provide additional impetus for the reassertion of that legitimacy through state attempts to control the pace and scope of economic regionalism in Southeast Asia.

ASEAN strategies of regional survival reflect formal and informal efforts at forging national and regional security. The formal efforts include periodic ASEAN summit meetings, annual ASEAN ministerial meetings, and numerous bilateral and multilateral meetings and agreements on a wide spectrum of political, military, economic, technical, and diplomatic matters. A key document outlining the ASEAN approach to regional security is the Treaty of Amity and Cooperation in Southeast Asia (TAC) signed at the first Bali Summit in Indonesia in February 1976. TAC represents ASEAN's strategy of conflict management whereby all member states agree to refrain from the use of force and resort to consultation to settle their disputes.

Informal regionalism, by contrast, incorporates personal diplomacy, academic meetings, and joint ventures between governments and the private sector in member states with respect to the development of growth triangles such as Singapore–Johor–Riau (SIJORI), the East ASEAN Growth Area (EAGA) covering the southern Philippines, Brunei, and the East Malaysian states of Sabah and Sarawak, and the Northern Growth Triangle involving Indonesia, Malaysia, and Thailand. The basic convergence of interests inherent in economic subregionalism may have several positive implications for regime security and officially sponsored regional cooperation (Thambipillai 1991: 313). However, because the state is still the primary actor managing as well as spurring economic growth in Southeast Asia, national governments tend to be apprehensive of subregional (microregional) activities that might conflict with broader (macroregional) efforts. For instance, ASEAN-wide projects such as the ASEAN Free Trade Area (AFTA), to be established by 2003, must not be seen to be failing while subregional activities are succeeding. Such a development would invariably imply that the state is losing control of its sovereignty to transnational forces beyond its control—with all the attendant consequences for national security. Thus while microregional activities are a reflection of the growing economic dynamism of Southeast Asia and the Asia-Pacific region, they also tend to increase the pressure on governments to perform, to be accountable, and to deliver the goods to their constituencies (Nathan 1994).

In the final analysis, the search for greater autonomy through regionalism—and therefore increased collective strength—by Third World states like Malaysia could well be governed by the desire of ruling elites to change the status of their countries from being mere "objects" of international relations to becoming "subjects" as well (Ayoob 1985: 29–45). In this regard, ASEAN's record is impressive in terms of gaining widespread recognition as a regional force in international relations. Malaysia's commitment to regionalism within the ASEAN framework is aimed at strengthening national and regional cohesion, which in turn enhances a sense of national and regional security.

Defense Capability for National and Regional Security

As national security conceptions are redefined to accommodate changing threat scenarios resulting from the demise of the internal communist threat and the collapse of international communism, the role of the Malaysian Armed Forces is being reconfigured. It is being transformed from a counterinsurgency force into a conventional force. Force modernization and the expansion of defense capability are designed primarily to augment national security in the era after the Cold War. Nevertheless, Malaysia's commitment to the notion of comprehensive security places emphasis on striking a balance between strengthening military capability *and* strengthening the socioeconomic and political basis of national security. Malaysia's post–Cold War national security strategy therefore comprises the following eight elements: (1) comprehensive security through domestic social cohesion and a stable regional environment; (2) diplomacy as a first line of defense; (3) commitment to the United Nations and its instruments for promoting peace, security, and development; (4) encouragement of regional security dialogues with the aim of promoting cooperative security; (5) promotion of confidence-building measures especially in the area of crisis management; (6) emphasis on military diplomacy through contacts, exchanges, training, and joint exercises; (7) promotion of bilateral and multilateral cooperation such as the FPDA; and (8) modernization of the Malaysian Armed Forces to defend national sovereignty and enhance national security (Razak 1995: 32–40).

The FPDA, which was formed in 1971 to replace the Anglo-Malaysian Defense Agreement (AMDA, 1957–1971) is viewed by Malaysia as augmenting national and regional security, and serves as a defense mechanism in the event of any external aggression, even though the Cold War and the communist threat have terminated. More significantly, the framework of training, weaponry, and joint exercises provided by the FPDA has the beneficial effect of enhancing the technological sophistication of the Malaysian Armed Forces by promoting greater interoperability and more advanced communications, command, and control systems.[14] Undoubtedly, Malaysia and Singapore are comfortable with a continued British military presence via the FPDA as a deterrent to the threat of regional hegemony posed by rising Asian powers such as China in the post–Cold War era. Additionally, the continuation of the FPDA can produce a positive impact on the final resolution of the Spratly Islands disputes through diplomacy rather than the threat or use of force.

The adoption of a holistic approach to national defense and regional security, especially with the demise of bipolarity in international relations, has inevitably meant a reduction in defense expenditure relative to other sectors of the national economy. The allocation of an average of only 2% to 3% of total GNP for defense (Razak 1995: 38) is strongly indicative of Malaysia's approach to national security: military power is but one dimension of the total equation, while other components such as political, social, and economic security are assigned greater significance in terms of contributing to peace, stability, harmony, and prosperity. For Malaysia, the integration of national defense capability with regional defense through existing mechanisms of bilateral and multilateral security cooperation is viewed as the best guarantee of regional security. The concept of regional defense precludes the notion of securing the regional strategic environment through traditional methods of alliance formation, which can be counterproductive, especially in a depolarized global environment.

Nonalignment, Neutrality, and Regional Security

Systemic changes in international relations affect a nation's security behavior in a variety of ways. Above all, dramatic changes in global strategic trends alter national perceptions and capabilities vis-à-vis the world order inasmuch as they have an impact on domestic policies and priorities. Malaysia reached such a juncture in the late 1960s, particularly after the announcement of the Nixon Doctrine in July 1969. A change of leadership in Washington was accompanied by a similar development in Kuala Lumpur. The Tunku gave way to his deputy, Tun Abdul Razak, who served as Malaysia's second prime minister from September 1970 until his death in January 1976. Indeed, it was Tun Razak who presided over fundamental policy formulations affecting internal and external security. Tun Razak was even more conscious than his predecessor of the need for strategic management of national and regional security in the wake of the American military withdrawal from Vietnam.

Malaysia proposed the creation of a neutralized Southeast Asia with a view to filling the regional power vacuum with greater indigenous regional content. Kuala Lumpur's initiative giving regional expression to the post-Vietnam balance of power came in the form of the Zone of Peace, Freedom, and Neutrality (ZOPFAN) Declaration, which was endorsed in principle by the ASEAN foreign ministers at their annual meeting in Kuala Lumpur on November 27, 1971. Malaysia's regional strategic perspective, underscored by the ZOPFAN idea, was being realigned to the new power configurations emerging at the regional and global levels. In post-Vietnam Southeast Asia, Malaysia now had to reckon with a new strategic scenario characterized by

- The birth of a communist or socialist Indochina

- The growing power and influence of the People's Republic of China following the end of the U.S. containment of China and the accompanying Sino-American détente

- The expanding economic role of Japan as major investor, trader, and creditor in Southeast Asia

- Reduced prospects for the involvement of American military power to stave off the collapse of pro-American or anticommunist regimes

- The growing political maturity, economic strength, and national and regional resilience of the ASEAN states, making them less dependent on external powers for managing regional security and stability

- The emergence by the late 1960s of a semblance of political and economic multipolarity (United States, USSR/Russia, Japan, China, EEC) coupled with rising polycentrism within the communist world as exemplified by the Sino-Soviet conflict—thus allowing regional actors to assert more control over their own regional environment.

Tun Razak regarded ZOPFAN as a noncontroversial concept that could be implemented gradually to fill the power vacuum created by the U.S. disengagement from the region. In proposing ZOPFAN while continuing to adhere to Malaysia's basic pro-Western strategic orientation, Tun Razak was in effect experimenting with a new technique of regional strategic management—that is, forging new directions for Malaysian foreign policy. The basic pro-Western stance of the ASEAN states, however, limited the full impact of the concept of zonal neutrality. As Charles Morrison and Astri Suhrke have observed: "Although Malaysia became the foremost advocate of regional neutrality after 1970, it was unwilling in the interim before neutrality could be achieved to give up completely its own defense commitments from Britain, Australia, and New Zealand" (Morrison and Suhrke 1978: 142). The Vietnamese reacted by proposing their own version of a neutralized Southeast Asia: the Zone of Genuine Independence, Peace, and Neutrality (ZOGIPAN). Moreover, ZOPFAN was premised on, and therefore flawed by, the requirement of great-power guarantees from the United States, Russia, and China. The track record of big-power interests in Southeast Asia—a record of conflict and collision—tends to nullify rather than reinforce any external guarantees for the neutralization of Southeast Asia. Nevertheless, as expressions of indigenous regional interests, ASEAN and ZOPFAN boosted regional confidence in forging more equitable partnerships with external powers in order to strengthen regional stability and promote economic development.

The Cambodian Conflict: Regional Containment

Regional conflict brings opportunities as well as constraints with respect to the pursuit of national security. During the ten-year period of Vietnam's military occupation of Cambodia (1979–89), the concept of ZOPFAN proved to be unworkable. The region was once again sucked into the politics of the revived Cold War, forcing regional states to exercise their survival options only within the framework of superpower relations.

In the scenario following the Vietnamese invasion of Cambodia in December 1978 (preceded by the forging of close security ties between Hanoi and Moscow only a month earlier), Malaysian security objectives and survival strategies may be summarized as follows: contain Soviet-Vietnamese expansion in Southeast Asia because it directly threatens the viability and coherence of ASEAN regionalism; use the Soviet-Vietnamese threat to engage American involvement to promote Malaysian/ASEAN interests; contain the problem of Indochinese refugees before they undermine the social and political stability of affected states; intervene in the Cambodian conflict with a view to managing it in favor of Malaysian national interests; and capitalize on the Sino-Soviet and Sino-Vietnamese rivalries with a view to neutralizing the influence of all three communist powers in Southeast Asia.

Malaysia's fears concerning excessive outside intervention in regional affairs found expression in the Kuantan Principle of March 1980. The Kuantan Principle stressed the need for superpower restraint in the Cambodian conflict in light of the earlier experience of the Vietnam War (1954–75) when large-scale intervention polarized regional politics for more than two decades. Nevertheless, Malaysia in concert with ASEAN, Japan, the United States, China, and the European Community confronted the Soviet-Vietnamese alliance, thereby exerting strong political, economic, military, and diplomatic pressure to compel Hanoi's withdrawal from the war-ravaged Khmer nation. Malaysia intervened directly in the Cambodian conflict by sponsoring the formation of the anti-Vietnamese Coalition Government of Democratic Kampuchea (CGDK) in Kuala Lumpur on June 22, 1982. By helping to establish the CGDK, Malaysia aspired to provide a noncommunist alternative government as an option to be considered by the Cambodian people.

Malaysia's stand on Cambodia evidenced respect for Khmer territorial integrity and political sovereignty and firm commitment to the principle of resolving international disputes by peaceful means. In any event, the CGDK formula as Malaysia's answer to regional conflict was a by-product of Cold War politics. It was an effective survival strategy to the extent that it was premised on superpower competition and external involvement. With the demise of the Cold War, however, national security strategies would have to be revised to give new direction and dynamic expression to the nation's pursuit of its vital interests.

The South China Sea Claims and Regional Security

The demise of the Cold War in Southeast Asia has raised the strategic profile of overlapping territorial claims in the South China Sea, posing security concerns for regional claimants vis-à-vis China. The resource-rich Spratly Islands have become an important issue for regional security because of the conflicting claims to sovereignty. Indeed, according to an ASEAN-ISIS report, "the Spratlys disputes represents the single most important potential threat to regional stability."[15] Malaysia staked its claim to Terumbu Layang-Layang (Amboyna Cay and Swallow Reef) in 1979 on the basis that the islet fell within its proclaimed 200-nautical-mile exclusive economic zone. Besides the economic stakes involved in the South China Sea claim, regional states like Malaysia are clearly wary of China's growing power projection capabilities since the Dengist Reformation of the late 1970s. The decision to build a major naval base in Sandakan on the northern coast of Sabah to "cope with increased foreign naval activities in the region"[16] was clearly based on national security considerations, including the ability to participate in the resolution of these territorial claims and to preclude China from dominating the outcome. In this regard, Malaysian defense capabilities have been enhanced by the FPDA, which in June 1983 conducted a naval exercise (coded Starfish) in the South China Sea, following which Malaysian marines established a permanent military presence on Terumbu Layang-Layang. In view of China's historic claim to sovereignty over the Spratlys (Ji Guoshing 1992: 2), combined with its enhanced military capability to enforce that claim, Malaysia has supported an ASEAN approach to dispute management based on negotiations. The 1992 ASEAN Declaration on the South China Sea, issued in Manila, urged all six claimants to renounce the use of force, to exercise restraint, and to create a positive climate for the final resolution of the overlapping claims.

Malaysia has also altered its perception of China. Although looked upon with caution, Beijing is not depicted as an enemy but as a friend and partner in the economic development and prosperity of the Asia-Pacific region. This revised approach to national security is strongly influenced by political pragmatism (recognition of China as a major power) and economic necessity (the prospect of economic cooperation with the world's largest single market of nearly 1.3 billion people).

Additionally, Malaysia's comprehensive security approach deemphasizes the need to identify enemies in a changing balance-of-power situation, both regionally and globally. Comprehensive security at the domestic level must be complemented by cooperative security at the regional level, pursued on the basis of mutual and equal security, respect for sovereignty, commitment to peace, restraint in the use of force, and rejection of hegemonism.[17]

Malaysia's commitment to ASEAN has substantially reduced intraregional threats to the country's national security—notwithstanding the Philippine claim to Sabah, which the two countries have agreed to put aside in favor of forging closer bilateral economic and defense cooperation.[18] The challenge for Malaysia, therefore, is to prove its capacity to be more responsible, equitable, and innovative in formulating and executing national objectives with a view to giving the country the competitive edge in international transactions.

International Foundations

In the realm of international security, Vision 2020 envisages the onset of certain strategic trends that will define the policy-making environment for Malaysia. These trends constitute the external foundation for Malaysia's security conceptions and foreign policy agenda: the demise of international communism; the strategic role of the United States after the Cold War; the rise of political multipolarity and economic regionalism; prospects for South-South cooperation; and future patterns of international trade.

The Collapse of International Communism

The rapid decline of communist ideology culminating in the collapse first of the Soviet empire (1989) and then the Soviet Union itself (1991) is a major development with important policy implications. The domestic impact of the collapse of world communism was revealed in the decision by the Communist Party of Malaya (CPM) to abort its armed insurgency against the Malaysian government in December 1989. Communism as a viable ideological and social system has been discredited in Southeast Asia by Vietnamese imperialism and Khmer atrocities in Indochina. The end of the CPM's armed struggle presents both an opportunity and a challenge: the prospect of positive development to achieve growth targets rather than the negative action of containing the threat of internal subversion (Nathan 1990: 210–20). The regional threat scenario has become more manageable now that China no longer poses an ideological threat, but China does present a political and economic threat to indigenous Southeast Asian societies with sizable ethnic Chinese minorities, such as Malaysia. Moreover, China's recent assertiveness over the South China Sea, especially its promulgation of a domestic law classifying most of the South China Sea as territorial waters, is worrisome (*Asia Yearbook 1995*: 24).[19] Nevertheless, the strategic success of Vision 2020 depends on the existence of a regional security environment that deemphasizes the Chinese threat while simultaneously asserting the need to contain, if not moderate, Chinese foreign policy.

Strategic Unipolarity

With the disintegration of the Soviet Union and a weak Russia, the United States, by all calculations of national power, is unrivaled by any other power center in the world—a situation that is likely to continue into the twenty-first century. In Southeast Asia the closure of the Clark air base and the Subic Bay naval base has been effected in the context of a thinner but geographically wider military presence of American power in terms of aircraft and warships. Malaysia too has offered repair and replenishment facilities at Lumut to encourage the continued deployment of U.S. strategic and conventional power in the region.[20] The U.S. strategic presence has thus far guaranteed the security of sea-lanes of communication while reducing the prospect of intraregional conflict over issues such as the contending claims to the Spratly Islands.[21] Malaysia expects the prevailing trend of U.S. strategic dominance in the Asia-Pacific region to continue beyond the twentieth century. Nevertheless Malaysia, like several other Asian states including China, India, and Indonesia, is uneasy over the U.S. capacity to extract unilateral advantage—such as by linking trade to democracy, human rights, and environmental issues, thus throttling certain legitimate national and regional aspirations.[22] Moreover, American security assurances for the Asia-Pacific region after the Cold War have done little to alleviate Malaysian and other Asian concerns regarding the "essential uncertainty and unpredictability of the regional security environment" (Ball and Kerr 1996: 40).

It is precisely those concerns that underlay the initiation of the ASEAN Regional Forum, which held its first meeting in Bangkok in July 1994. Malaysia, like its ASEAN partners, would prefer to decide the security agenda through dialogue with external powers. Such an approach provides the best insurance against the negative intervention of big powers in regional affairs; it also ensures their constructive engagement in support of regional stability, security, development, and prosperity. In the absence of a multilateral security structure, the ASEAN Regional Forum is Malaysia's best multilateral guarantee of national,

542   K. S. NATHAN

regional, and international security following the dramatic strategic transformations after the Cold War.

Economic Regionalism and the East Asian Economic Caucus Initiative

The primacy of economics in the post–Cold War world warrants the placement of a higher premium on economic performance and less emphasis on military-oriented security. And the ability to sustain, expand, and modernize a nation's military capability is dependent on economic growth. The link between economics and military power is nowhere more evident than in Russia, whose military capability has declined significantly due to the economic morass confronting it. Internal chaos and secessionist rebellions have further undermined national authority to the point where Russian power is no longer taken seriously in Asia, particularly in Southeast Asia. In contrast, Southeast Asia's buoyant economies have been able to augment military power.

The creation of regional economic associations, as well as greater economic integration, is merely a reflection of the congruence of national interests. Malaysia's proposal to set up an East Asian Economic Grouping (EAEG), first announced by Mahathir in December 1990, was a response to the unsatisfactory progress of the now concluded Uruguay Round of multilateral trade negotiations (Nathan 1995: 231). Moreover, Malaysia harbors genuine fears over "the emergence of an economic cold war, a vastly more complicated global struggle for economic influence where the powerful seek to dominate, even exploit, the weak. The emergence of powerful trading blocs like the U.S.–Canada Free Trade Area, and the European Community (EC), with a propensity for protectionism is particularly worrying for small countries like Malaysia."[23]

The concept of EAEG (later renamed EAEC, East Asian Economic Caucus) aims to build up negotiating strength vis-à-vis other economic groupings. In an important sense, EAEC can be regarded as the externalization of Malaysia's security conception via Vision 2020. Mahathir sees a natural geographical, cultural, ethnic, and historical affinity with other East Asian partners—the emergence, that is, of an East Asian consciousness—that lends viability to EAEC-style economic regionalism. Further, Mahathir's strategy of downplaying the Chinese threat to Southeast Asia has earned the anticipated dividend: China's "explicit and unwavering support" for the EAEC.[24] The conspicuous removal of China as a threat in Mahathir's foreign policy is also designed to strengthen local Sino-Malay business cooperation to capitalize on the "economic opening of China" and thereby boost Malaysia's economic performance.

Nevertheless, the EAEC concept has run into serious opposition from the United States. Moreover, Japan—a key player—has been ambivalent. Although Mahathir's idea may be sound, it must contend with competing ideas of regional and world order such as Asia-Pacific Economic Cooperation (APEC), inaugurated in Canberra in November 1989, which enjoys full participation by the United States and all major Asia-Pacific actors including ASEAN. The success of the Fourth APEC Summit in Manila (November 1996) means that EAEC will remain a secondary forum in the eyes of East Asian members for whom APEC has become the established process and instrument of economic regionalism.[25]

The United Nations, South–South Cooperation, and Islamic Solidarity

Malaysia accords high priority to the role of the United Nations—the only world forum where small and large countries alike can speak with an equal voice. Malaysia's confidence in the United Nations for the management of international security is evidenced by an early commitment to send troops to support U.N. peacekeeping operations in the Congo in the early 1960s. That effort was followed by participation in peacekeeping operations along the Iran-Iraq border, in Namibia, Somalia, and Cambodia, and more recently in Bosnia. During Mahathir's tenure since 1981, Malaysia has assumed several leadership roles in line with its positive contribution to U.N. activities for peace, security, and development: leadership of G-77, president of the 25th UNESCO General Conference, alternating U.N. Security Council member from 1988 to 1990, chairman of the International Conference on Drug Abuse and Illicit Trafficking, and chairman of the International Conference on Refugees. In 1996, Malaysia's representative, Datuk Razali Ismail, was elected president of the U.N. General Assembly. Malaysia's attitude toward the United Nations reveals a security conception that is based on the collective will of the international community. With the end of the Cold War, the role of the United Nations in security affairs has grown enormously, not only in scope but also in terms of the type and complexity of activity (Roberts 1993: 230). The Malaysian conception of international security corresponds closely to the expanded and multidimensional role of the United Nations in promoting a peaceful, just, and equitable world order.

In other spheres of international leadership, Malaysia has been in the forefront in forging South-South cooperation based on the conviction that development is the best source of security for nations of the South. Organizing high-level international meetings in Malaysia is but one strategy to enlist the cooperation of the North and South to promote socioeconomic development. Mahathir was instrumental in proposing three specific projects to augment South-South cooperation: the Bilateral Payments Arrangements (BPA) at the first G-15 summit, the multilateral Developing Countries Payments Arrangements (DCPA), and the South Investment, Trade, and Technology Data Exchange Center (SITTDEC) at the second G-15 summit in Caracas, Venezuela (November 27–29, 1991)—all of which are making reasonable progress. In 1993 Malaysia hosted the first expert group meeting on Exchange of Information on National Economic Policies (EINEP), relating to such issues as sustainable development, fiscal and monetary policies, trade and investment, and privatization.[26] Since the 1980s Malaysia has continued "to give priority to the enhancement of political, economic, trade, technological, and business investment cooperation among the countries of the South."[27] All these activities underscore Malaysia's security conceptions of the Third World in particular and world politics in general while charting new directions for Malaysian foreign policy and indeed for the developing world.

Given that most of the Muslim world was subjected to Western colonial domination, South-South cooperation and Islamic solidarity are complementary strategies for promoting national security and advancement. In this regard, the establishment of the "Development Eight" in Istanbul, Turkey, represents yet another Malaysian strategy to publicize the compatibility of Islam with modernization and development, thereby promoting Malaysian conceptions of national security and economic progress.[28] In much the same way as Third World countries have developed common interests vis-à-vis the West as part of the decolonization process, the Muslim world developed strong feelings of Islamic solidarity vis-à-vis their ex-colonial masters. For the Muslim world, "the idea of Islamic solidarity gave them a framework for increased cooperation among themselves in social, political, and economic fields" (Noor Ahmad Baba 1993: 42). Malaysia has taken the initiative in building Muslim solidarity since the early 1950s. Its efforts culminated in the Rabat Summit Conference (September 22–25, 1969), which formalized the establishment of the Organization of the Islamic Conference (OIC). Although the achievements of the OIC as a forum for international Muslim solidarity might be negligible in terms of restructuring the world order in favor of Muslim interests, its existence as a symbol of Muslim identity and security and its potential role as a political and economic force cannot be ignored.

For a Malay/Muslim-dominant multiethnic and multireligious Malaysia, the search for identity and security in the Muslim world represents the external dimension of the internal quest for ethnoreligious identity in a plural setting. Since Mahathir's accession to premiership, he has attempted to broaden Malaysia's Islamic credentials by creating the Islamic Bank and the International Islamic University in 1983, accelerating the government's mosque-building program, and strengthening ties with other Islamic countries—efforts designed to strengthen Malay ethnoreligious identity while "reinforcing UMNO's Islamic legitimacy among the Malays without kindling a degree of unease in the other ethnic communities" (Camroux 1994: 20).

International Trade and International Security

Economic foreign policy is strongly emphasized by the Mahathir administration. As the industrialization process accelerates and Malaysia becomes more integrated into the world economy through expansion of its competitive basis, international trade is becoming a vital strategy of national security and survival. Vision 2020 envisages the necessity for Malaysia to continue expanding its export base, both geographically and in terms of product diversification, in order to strengthen its competitive capacity in overseas markets (Zulliger 1993: 391). The country's rapidly expanding capacity for international trade is reflected in the numerous trade agreements signed in conjunction with the Malaysian premier's visits to Africa, South America, the South Pacific, the former Soviet republics in Central Asia, and the Caribbean—in addition to Malaysia's traditional trade partnerships with the ASEAN countries plus Japan, the United States, the European Community, Canada, Australia, New Zealand, and, of late, South Korea. Vision 2020 envisages the full development of Malaysia's export potential and the penetration of new markets for Malaysian merchandise, capital, and investments. The building of new economic links with the South is one of Malaysia's foreign policy strategies for reducing overreliance on Western markets. In recent years, the prime minister's annual visits to Central Asia, South Asia, Northeast Asia, Africa, and Latin America indicate the increased emphasis being given to the economic dimensions of international security. This perspective is based on official forecasts of a 4 percent expansion of the world economy in 1996 "supported principally by the strong growth of the developing countries, in particular the countries of East Asia."[29]

Challenges and Prospects

Malaysia's security goals, as expressed in its domestic and foreign policies, can be stated as follows: protection of national sovereignty with emphasis on political integrity and territorial unity; economic development and social justice in the context of a multiracial society; preservation of constitutional monarchy, Islam, and the special rights of the Malays; a firm commitment to ASEAN and promotion of other forms of economic regionalism that advance national interests; promotion of regional stability and security via ZOPFAN; and a commitment to promote South-South cooperation aimed at enhancing the economic welfare of the less developed world and supporting human rights and social justice worldwide.

Such conceptions of national security invariably call for adroit diplomacy to bridge the gap between national aspirations and international realities—in other words, the gap between desirability and possibility. In this context, the Malaysian leadership has evidenced a high degree of pragmatism in managing relations at all three levels: bilateral, regional, and global. Strategic management of domestic and foreign security policies has informed the present success enjoyed by Malaysians in terms of political stability, economic growth, social peace, and national prosperity. Malaysia's ability to manage structural constraints (such as multiracialism and a limited resource base) and convert them into positive forces for development and prosperity has, in the main, contributed to an expanded regional capacity to sustain and promote microlevel and macrolevel regionalism. The current scenario would undoubtedly be different without a strategic vision and the ability to manage difficulties while promoting possibilities. Indeed, such a strategic vision was already in place as early as 1967 when ASEAN was formed. Succeeding years merely witnessed the consolidation of that vision in the form of national and regional resilience. Thus ASEAN has enabled Malaysia and its ASEAN partners to manage bilateral relations on the basis of tolerance and mutual respect. This approach to national security at the regional level has in turn strengthened the foundations of regional cooperation and prosperity. It lends credence, as well, to the success of nascent regional economic and security agendas for the post–Cold War era such as EAEC and ARF.

The critical link between regionalism and nation-building lies in the fact that the former cannot succeed without the latter. Internal stability in each of the regional partners determines their individual as well as collective capacity to cooperate and advance at the regional level. In this regard, Mahathir's remarks are noteworthy: there is a strong correlation between rapid economic growth and strong, stable governments in East Asia, for together they provide the stability and consistency so essential to long-term investment and economic progress.[30] The ASEAN experience has confirmed this fundamental political condition of healthy regionalism. Moreover, a strong ASEAN can be helpful to individual member states in times of internal difficulties: the Third ASEAN Summit was held in Manila in December 1987 specifically to demonstrate ASEAN's support of the beleaguered Aquino administration following the collapse of the Marcos regime.

Nation-building is an ongoing process for many developing countries that were colonies of the European powers. The management of interethnic relations has been one of the most challenging tasks for multiracial states such as Malaysia after independence. Finding the right formula requires political maturity, economic wisdom, and even the occasional use of repression to promote the government's legitimacy and the regime's security. At a recent Vision 2020 conference, Mahathir justified governmental policies curbing political liberties as serving the national interest: "If the Government seems to be unduly strict and unwilling to accede to various demands made by various quarters, it is because we want to serve the best interest of the people and the nation."[31] Indeed, national security becomes a convenient device for regime legitimation and continuation of ethnic-based discrimination as a "temporary evil" in order to achieve the presumably greater good of national unity and the professed vision of a united Malaysian nation.

Meanwhile, the concept and practice of national security might well perpetuate Malaysia's status as a state-nation, strengthened as it is by a record of good governance, political stability, and economic prosperity, without its having to confront the real challenges posed by a genuinely constructed nation-state. Indeed, as long as the Malaysian state-nation can provide political stability, economic growth, domestic peace, social harmony, and sustainable development—the basic pillars of the comprehensive approach to national security—the transition to a full-fledged nation-state will not be viewed by decision makers as a major problematic of the Malaysian political economy.

In Southeast Asia, with the possible exception of Thailand, which was never colonized, the state came before the nation. The task of the independent state, therefore, was to create a nation—that is, to commence the nation-building process while at the same time maintaining racial harmony, social security, political stability, and economic development, all vital elements of national security. The Malaysian record of dealing with the multifold challenges of postindependence nationalism and regionalism is a record of strong state intervention and management of the political and economic dimensions of national security. The historic Gas and Water Accord (June 1988) and the Intergovernmental Agreement on the Second Crossing (March 1994) between Malaysia and Singapore represent not only major milestones in bilateralism but also major successes in ASEAN-style regionalism characterized by the spirit of tolerance and compromise.[32] This political ability to manage the nation-building process has produced the spillover effects of economic development and prosperity, both nationally and regionally. The resulting impact on the nation and the region tends to reinforce the hypothesis that postindependence national elites in Malaysia and ASEAN are managing the nation-building process through modernization, regime legitimation, resource mobilization, allegiance mobilization, and regionalism in Southeast Asia. The convergence of national and regional interests via ASEAN is but another manifestation of the same activity.

In sum, then, Malaysia's conception of security is a corporate aggregate of its own historical experience, its multiethnicity, its ethnonational vision, and its desire to seek recognition for its changed status from "object" to "subject" of international relations. The principal architects of the nation's survival strategies have been the prime ministers. Indeed, the role of Mahathir Mohamad in injecting a personal vision into national security formulation has been singularly instrumental to Malaysia's present high profile in world forums. Mahathir's conception of Malaysian security emphasizes the notion that leaders of multiethnic societies must continuously reinvent the nation to strengthen national security and promote regional stability.

Malaysia's national security managers now have to deal with an unexpected turn of events wrought by the financial crisis that has engulfed Southeast Asia beginning in July 1997 with the dramatic depreciation in the value of the Thai baht. In Malaysia, the financial crisis has compelled the political leadership to slow GNP growth from 7 percent to 4 percent in 1998 and to cancel several prestigious megaprojects. More than two million jobs are expected to be lost in 1998, and recovery is expected to take two to five years. This unanticipated economic crisis could have serious social and political consequences and could undermine the effort of the incumbent political leadership to forge a national community that transcends ethnic divides. Further, the credibility and survivability of Malaysia's current political leadership hinges strongly on the success of the economic strategies formulated to restore national and international confidence in the Malaysian economy. The financial crisis and its possible consequences underscore the strong nexus between economic and political dimensions of security in multiethnic Malaysia.

The Philippines
State Versus Society?

NOEL M. MORADA and CHRISTOPHER COLLIER

> *To meet the threats to the security of the state, the national government set as its paramount goal the immediate immobilization and dismantling of the unconstitutional opposition, which included the advocates and perpetrators of rebellion, the conspirators, the separatists, and the various lawless elements, which, although not politically motivated, undermined the authority of the government.*
>
> PRESIDENT FERDINAND E. MARCOS, 1978

> *National security, in the traditional view, was synonymous with national defense, with public safety, with the preservation and reimposition of order. The February Revolution has enriched that traditional view to include as the first order of priority the preservation of the rights and liberties [of] our people. National security [is] not a matter of keeping the people at arms length—or erecting higher walls or denser barbed wires between government and people, but bringing the people in....Security forces do not protect operations or establishment from the people, but for and in behalf of the people. And better still, with the people.*
>
> PRESIDENT CORAZON C. AQUINO, 1986

> *A country's need for security never changes....What changes are the ways in which the State tries to arrange this guarantee. The Ramos Administration now defines national security in non-military terms. It regards national security as founded ultimately on our country's economic strength, its political unity, and its social cohesion.*
>
> NATIONAL SECURITY ADVISER JOSE T. ALMONTE, 1994

The discourse on national security in the Philippines is rooted in conflicts over the identity of the nation-state, over regime legitimacy, and over socioeconomic inequality, which continue to create tensions between state and society. Unlike more established states (and those that more clearly reflect the realist model), the Philippine state has not achieved an effective monopoly of the means of coercion within its boundaries and is still engaged in a process of nation-building. The limited coercive and administrative reach of the Philippine state is manifest in the continued prevalence of private armed forces, particularly in the countryside, including rebel guerrillas, the armed retainers of oligarchic politicians, and paramilitary groups. Internal security has remained the priority down to the 1990s, and it is precisely because the "enemy" has been within, rather than an external "other," that conflict has arisen between the security needs of state and populace. Although the tensions between state and society reached a climax in the final years of the Marcos regime, they have not been resolved by the restoration of formal electoral democracy under Presidents Aquino and Ramos. If the U.S. military presence at Subic Bay and Clark Field provided an umbrella against external threats until 1992, it also had the potential of drawing the Philippines into superpower conflict. Although the immediate danger of global nuclear confrontation has receded, the American withdrawal has exposed an unprepared Philippine military to new regional security threats.[1]

This chapter traces the evolution of conceptions of national security under the administrations of Ferdinand Marcos (1965–86), Corazon Aquino (1986–92), and Fidel Ramos (1992–98). In shaping our account around successive presidential regimes we are not exaggerating the degree of executive agency with respect to wider social forces but bringing into clear relief the changing conceptualization of the referents, scope, and approach to Philippine security. Prominent here are swings between military repression and political settlement, between centralization and devolution of authority, and, especially pertinent in the post– Cold War, post–U.S. bases context, between concern with internal and external security. Underlying these dialectic themes is the ongoing tension between the security requirements of the state and those of the people. Our consideration of the national security policies of these three administrations leads us to argue that both state and society are most secure when they become mutually reinforcing through processes of institutionalized participation. The state becomes strong not when it privileges its own security over that of the people, but when its security becomes synonymous with theirs.

State, Oligarchy, and Social Revolution

The conceptualization of national security in the Philippines since the time of Marcos has evolved from a highly state-centered notion to a more society-oriented approach. At the heart of the debate over national security and democracy in the country is the proper role and extent of state power in promoting and protecting the national interest as well as the basic rights of individuals in society. Yet the boundaries of the state as an entity are themselves problematic. Before the arrival of the Spanish colonists, the most extensive political units in the archipelago were loose groupings of villages (*barangay*) and several Muslim sultanates. Under the Spanish, feudal land grants (*encomienda*) established a pattern of decentralized power, and the state came to be viewed as a source of patronage and an instrument for plundering society. The intensification of export agriculture in the nineteenth century gave rise to a landed oligarchy whose position depended on access to state power, and the interests of state and oligarchy became intimately intertwined. After independence from the United States in 1946, "national" security came essentially to mean the security of landed interests. This virtual identity was demonstrated by the state's response to the Huk peasant rebellion of the 1940s and 1950s. Rather than undertaking substantive land reform, as occurred in Japan, Taiwan, and South Korea, the state combined repression with token reforms, and peasants were encouraged to resettle from overcrowded northern islands to the sparsely populated Mindanao frontier. As indigenous Muslims were displaced by this historic migration, a new threat—this time to the territorial integrity of the young republic—emerged in the 1970s in the shape of the Moro National Liberation Front (MNLF).

Although formal electoral democracy was established early on in the period of American colonial rule (1898–1946), the franchise was initially restricted and democratic institutions served mainly to ensure the regular rotation in office of opposing factions among the landed elite. Formally structured around a loose two-party system, these factions actually rested upon chains of patron-client ties extending down into the rural power bases of landed politicians. As has been ably demonstrated in recent work on Philippine "bossism" (McCoy 1993; Sidel 1995; Lacaba 1995), these patronage ties were reinforced by local-level political violence, often exercised through powerful private armies. As the commercialization of agriculture accelerated with growing integration into global markets, patronage ties weakened and coercion intensified. Because local landed elites and provincial officeholders were typically one and the same, the distinction between private political muscle and the local armed forces of the state was frequently unclear. A constitution on the American model proclaimed the supremacy of civilian authority over the military, as well as the separation of powers among the three branches of government, but in the rural areas where most Filipinos lived these abstractions must often have seemed more formal than real.

In an avowed attempt to break the stranglehold of the landed elite, much of which had acquired diversified interests in industry by the 1960s, Ferdinand Marcos overthrew the 1935 constitution, declaring martial law in 1972. Militarization, centralization, and cronyism over the ensuing thirteen years undermined the security of both state and society, profoundly influencing the reconceptualizations of national security that followed the dictator's ouster in 1986. The legacies of martial law include continuing communist and Muslim insurgencies, an impoverished economy, a politicized military establishment that came to threaten the regime itself but is incapable of defending the national territory, and an enduring mistrust of the "strong" state. But the experience also gave rise to an invigorated civil society more capable of checking and balancing the state and of reinforcing it where it is weakest. Tensions between state and society persist. As the referent unit and scope of security evolve to embrace society, however, more comprehensive approaches may follow. Marcos's predominantly military strategy has been tempered by greater emphasis on political and diplomatic approaches under Aquino and Ramos. And changing conceptions of what the Philippine state is to be secured *against*—external aggression rather than internal subversion— suggest that military force is increasingly something to be projected outward, rather than inward against the citizenry.

Attempts to deepen the incumbent's legitimacy and security through the discursive conflation of state, regime, and government have been common to all three administrations surveyed here, with varying degrees of success. In their efforts to minimize the identity between state and oligarchy and to maximize that between state and society, all three have portrayed themselves, in differing senses, as both revolutionary and democratic. Marcos embarked upon a "revolution from the center" in 1972; Aquino rode a wave of "People Power" to the presidential palace in 1986; both Marcos and Aquino represented themselves as embattled democrats struggling to save the state from left and right alike. The Ramos government represented the full consolidation of Aquino's democratic restoration, which he defended against several failed coups, and embodied the nation's hopes for economic transformation to "newly industrialized" status.

The persistence of these efforts to appropriate populist appeal reflects the equally persistent ideological challenge from the Communist Party of the Philippines (CPP), which has struck deep roots in society. In its own attempts to reframe the referent units of Philippine politics, the organized left led by the CPP has stubbornly insisted on the essential identity of the Marcos, Aquino, and Ramos administrations as U.S. puppet regimes equally in thrall to the unaltering reality of "imperialism, feudalism, and bureaucrat capitalism," the three basic problems of Philippine society in the communist canon. This ideological threat gained its greatest force from the fusion of state and regime under Marcos, whose personal interests took priority as the referent unit of "national" security, along with crony capitalism. By identifying Marcos, the man, as the Philippines' basic problem, the Aquino revolution diffused the left's ideological potency somewhat, as have socialism's global reversals and the winding down of the "special relationship" with the United States. The urgency of combating internal social revolution has left the state ill equipped to confront external threats without the support of that relationship, and at the same time the passing of Cold War bipolarity has unleashed regional power rivalries that pose more of a danger than ever before.

Security Under Marcos

Ferdinand Marcos justified the declaration of martial law in 1972 by citing "the threat posed by the growth of rebellion and subversion" from both left and right, as well as the secessionist movement in the south.[2] Martial law was the necessary instrument of a beleaguered state that had the will to resist these rebellions in order to "save the Republic and form a New Society." Though the immediate threat came from the CPP—reconstituted in 1968–69 alongside a New People's Army (NPA) to take up the lost peasant struggle of the Huks—and from the MNLF, those groups could not be decisively defeated without uprooting the oligarchic "old society" that nourished them. The old society was ruled by "social and political elites manipulating a precarious democracy of patronage, privilege, and personal aggrandizement." In Marcos's view, "the old society had to go; it was no longer workable and could not be made workable ever again. Meanwhile, this very same society's affliction was devouring the state itself. If the political authority did not act and exercise its emergency powers, the death of that society would come about in a fratricidal clash of arms, a bloody social revolution" (Marcos

1979: 133). In his critique of old-society democracy, Marcos pointed out that "it existed in a political culture which was populist, personalist, and individualist in orientation." This kind of political culture, "destructive of human freedom," needed fundamental alteration, not just modification. Thus, when he launched his "September 21 Movement" in 1972, Marcos argued the necessity of a "revolution from the center" whereby the state would initiate a radical transformation of society.

Ideally, the kind of social change Marcos envisaged would narrow the gap between rich and poor, "if only for the sake of social stability." The stability of Philippine society was seen to rest on "the effectiveness of government as a patron of the poor." The social mission of government, amid widespread poverty, was to "turn wards into free men" (Marcos 1979: 82–83). In practice, however, the Marcos regime failed to achieve its stated goals because political order and stability were given priority at the expense of basic individual rights and freedoms. As centralized state power increased, the security interests of the state and those of the individuals in society came into conflict. In the absence of effective checks on executive power—Congress had been abolished and the Supreme Court emasculated—the state's predatory tendencies were amplified and "state" interests came to signify those of the Marcos family and their cronies. Corruption and lack of accountability led to steady economic decline (Hill and Jayasurya 1984; Boyce 1993). Wage earners' average monthly income fell some 20 percent between 1972 and 1980; agriculture suffered a drop of 30 percent and commerce 40 percent (Schirmer and Shalom 1987: 176). Whereas the poor's share of national income decreased during the same period, the rich increased their share. By 1981, the top 10 percent of families received twice the income of the bottom 60 percent: this was clearly not the New Society envisioned in 1972. Growth of gross national product declined steadily, from an average of 6.3 percent (1975–79) to 1.3 percent (1980–84) (De Dios 1993–94: 20). By the time the Marcoses were forced into exile in February 1986, the Philippines' foreign debt had surged close to $30 billion, much of it "behest loans" that benefited Marcos's family and his cronies.[3]

Although the legitimacy of the authoritarian regime was challenged both by moderate opposition groups and by growing communist and Muslim insurgent movements, Marcos sustained his hold on power by manipulating the security concerns generated by his own misrule. The prevailing Cold War environment was especially helpful in guaranteeing the continued flow of U.S. military assistance, given the strategic location of American bases at Subic Bay and Clark Field and the communist forward movement in Indochina. Marcos portrayed himself as a staunch American ally who needed sustained U.S. support in the battle against insurgency (Bonner 1988; Karnow 1989).[4] Increased military assistance after 1972 bolstered a defense budget that grew nearly tenfold from 608 million pesos that year to 5.3 billion in 1977. Military expenditures as a percentage of the national budget nearly doubled to 22.6 percent in 1977. The Armed Forces of the Philippines (AFP) increased in number to more than 113,000 in 1976 from just 35,000 in the early 1960s. The paramilitary Philippine Constabulary also carried out counterinsurgency operations alongside expanded "home defense units" and an Integrated National Police force brought under centralized control. (Local police had previously been under the charge of municipal mayors.)

Ironically, the growth of the military was accompanied by an increase in the strength of both the CPP/NPA and the MNLF.[5] According to the Philippine Department of National Defense, the number of NPA regular forces grew from 1,320 in 1972 to 4,900 at the end of the 1970s, then increased rapidly to 7,750 in 1982 and to 14,360 in 1984. In 1985 the CPP/NPA registered a dramatic 57 percent growth rate to reach a strength of 22,500 (Department of National Defense 1990: 7). Unlike the earlier Huk rebellion, which was concentrated in central Luzon, the NPA established a presence throughout the country (excepting only strongholds of the MNLF), stretching AFP resources thinly. The CPP's regular armed units, moreover, represented only the tip of a submerged political iceberg that by 1985 posed a realistic threat of eventually sinking the Marcos regime. An American congressional study released in November 1985 indicated that "the insurgency operates at various levels in nearly every one of the Philippines' 73 provinces" with CPP political organizations established in one-third of the country's 41,400 barangays, and in control of an estimated 12 percent of the provinces (U.S. Senate 1985: 2).

There was increasing concern in Washington about the absence of any "coordinated civilian-political doctrine to combat the insurgency." Although Marcos regarded the NPA as "a terrorist problem requiring, in the first instance, a military response," he was "more interested in his personal security and power" than in the military's effectiveness (Kessler 1989: 119). In an effort to maximize his own control he promoted loyalists such as his former chauffeur, fellow Ilocano, and relative Fabian Ver, who became Armed Forces chief of staff in 1981, and implemented a centralized system of Regional Unified Commands, which reported directly to Ver. At the same time, however, he allowed the growth of local paramilitaries whose chain of command and source of authority were often left deliberately obscure. The Civilian Home Defense Forces

(CHDF), established in 1976, provided a legal umbrella for a wide range of quasi-religious anticommunist cults, private plantation "landguards," and exercisers of provincial political muscle, which were now invested with state authority in the name of counterinsurgency. On the turbulent land frontier of Mindanao, in particular, the CHDF was at the forefront of widespread human rights violations as peasants were evicted by corporate-controlled paramilitaries and resistance was indiscriminately crushed. The most infamous groups included the "Lost Command" of Colonel Carlos "Charlie" Lademora, most active in and around the Guthrie palm-oil plantation in Agusan del Sur, and the "Philippine Liberation Organization" (PLO) led by a certain "Kapitan Inggo," which terrorized Davao City in the mid-1980s.[6] Many of these groups drew upon a syncretic, animistic folk Christianity that fueled visceral anticommunism, and evolved into the "vigilante" movements of the Aquino era. Widespread human rights violations generated broad opposition, and the military's ineffectiveness in containing insurgency created resentment within the ranks against unprofessional leadership, leading to the formation of a Reform the Armed Forces Movement (RAM). RAM recast the military's fundamental security referent in terms that transcended the Marcos regime, and indeed played a key role in his overthrow.

The military approach to the insurgency problem was accompanied by political and social efforts to undercut support for the insurgents. Marcos attempted to institute reforms: administrative purges in the civilian bureaucracy and the military were meant to rid them of corrupt officials; a land reform decree was supposed to redistribute land to poor farmers in the countryside; agricultural credit programs were extended to small farmers. Initially land reform enhanced Marcos's legitimacy in the countryside, blunted foreign criticism of his government, and put the landed elite on the defensive. Land reform created expectations about Marcos's New Society that deterred, albeit temporarily, recruitment of communist insurgents in the rural areas (Wurfel 1988: 166, 227). In the urban areas, Marcos tried to contain the influence of the CPP/NPA in the labor sector by underwriting the creation of the Trade Union Congress of the Philippines, a labor union whose leaders, known to be sympathetic to the Soviet Union, were co-opted by Marcos. In the youth sector, the Kabataang Barangay was set up to politically socialize young people into the regime's "New Society Movement."

Diplomatic efforts helped to preclude the possibility of external support for the CPP/NPA, which was in any case negligible. Relations were established with China (1975) and subsequently with Vietnam, and a pledge of mutual noninterference was signed with Vietnam in 1978

(Wurfel 1988: 182). Diplomacy was more significant in supplementing the military approach in the case of the Muslim secessionist problem. Initially Marcos adopted a "total war" policy against the MNLF and related groups, deploying more than half of the AFP in Mindanao and Sulu. Later, in the mid-1970s, the military approach was complemented by social and economic instruments in an effort to win some of the MNLF supporters to the government side. Arabic instruction was permitted in some public schools in predominantly Muslim provinces; university scholarships for Muslims were expanded; a Code of Philippine Muslim Personal Law was promulgated; the Philippine Amanah Bank provided financial assistance to Muslim entrepreneurs on generous terms; Muslim title to ancestral land was recognized in law. Marcos also increased appointments of Muslims to government positions (Wurfel 1988: 159).

What pushed Marcos into considering a negotiated settlement of the Muslim insurgency problem was pressure from the oil-rich Arab countries. The world oil crisis of 1973 did not spare the Philippines, and Marcos had to make concessions to those countries with regard to the Muslim problem in Mindanao. In September of that year, he allowed several high-ranking representatives from member states of the Organization of the Islamic Conference (OIC) to visit the Philippines on a fact-finding mission to Muslim provinces. The team concluded that only a political solution—not the military and socioeconomic approaches pursued by the Marcos regime—could bring an end to the conflict in the southern Philippines. Subsequently, at its foreign ministers' conference held in Kuala Lumpur in 1974, the OIC recommended that the Philippine government hold direct negotiations with MNLF chief Nur Misuari to begin the political process of ending the Muslim insurgency. The OIC, at the same time, refused to give the MNLF a belligerent status (similar to that of the Palestine Liberation Organization), a decision that clearly represented a victory for Marcos (Wurfel 1988: 159–60).

Nonetheless, the MNLF enjoyed extensive external support. Three countries provided both moral and material assistance to the MNLF: Malaysia, Libya, and Saudi Arabia. Malaysia was reported to have provided logistic support to the Moro fighters not so much because of Kuala Lumpur's commitment to religious fraternity, but as a reaction to the Philippines' secret military plan to invade the disputed territory of Sabah in the late 1960s. At the federal level, the government of Malaysia supported the MNLF struggle as a means of pressuring Manila to drop its claim to Sabah; at the state level, Tun Datu Mustapha Harun, the chief minister of Sabah, reportedly allowed the MNLF sanctuary for training, supply, and communications purposes (Che Man 1990: 138–39).

Libya's support was primarily motivated by its commitment to Islamic brotherhood and the Koranic obligation to relieve the persecution of the *ummah* (Islamic community). Libya reportedly provided about $1 million to cover the expenses of some 300 Muslim recruits who were undergoing training in Sabah in the early 1970s. After martial law was declared Libya began to deliver funds, weapons, and other equipment to the MNLF under the leadership of Nur Misuari. An estimated $35 million was contributed to the MNLF by Libya and the other OIC countries between 1972 and 1975. Libya also attempted to persuade member states of the OIC to impose sanctions against the Marcos regime, though without much success, and Muammar Qaddafi's full support for the MNLF was later moderated under pressure from the other OIC countries. Libya then played a mediating role between Manila and the MNLF. The Tripoli agreement, signed in December 1976, provided for an autonomous government in the predominantly Muslim provinces of the southern Philippines (Che Man 1990: 140–41).

Saudi Arabia also played a mediating role in the Mindanao conflict, providing both funds and sanctuary to other Muslim secessionist factions such as the Moro Islamic Liberation Front (MILF) and the Bangsa Moro Islamic Liberation Organization (BMILO). Through agencies such as the Muslim World League and Darul Ifta, Saudi Arabia also provided assistance to a number of projects in the Muslim areas of the southern Philippines. In 1980, when the Marcos regime failed to implement the 1976 Tripoli agreement in good faith, Saudi Arabia stopped its oil shipments to the Philippines—an effective instrument for pressuring Manila to abide by the agreement because about 40 percent of the country's oil supply came from Saudi Arabia (Che Man 1990: 141–42).

In an effort to improve his regime's image throughout the Muslim world, Marcos decided to strengthen the Philippines' diplomatic relations with Islamic states in the Middle East and Africa. This campaign took on many forms, such as the exchange of special high-level missions, intensified information programs, and, most significant, the realignment of Philippine foreign policy toward the Middle East. During the Arab-Israeli conflict in 1973, the Philippines condemned Israel's occupation of Arab territories as an act of aggression, sided with the Arab call for Israeli withdrawal, and recognized the Palestine Liberation Organization as the legitimate representative of the Palestinian people. First Lady Imelda Marcos was sent as a special envoy on a diplomatic offensive in the Middle East, highlighted by a meeting with Qaddafi that led to the signing of the Tripoli agreement (Che Man 1990: 145–46).

In April 1977 a referendum on autonomy was held as called for by the agreement, but it was boycotted by a majority of Muslims, who doubted Manila's good faith in implementing its terms. Moreover, the socioeconomic instruments of the state were seen largely as a means to assimilate the Muslims into the "Christian nation" they had resisted for centuries for fear of losing their identity as the Muslim *ummah* (Bauzon 1991; Che Man 1990). The involvement of outside powers in the conflict also contributed to the failure of the political settlement. Not only did the OIC's moral and material support for the MNLF and other groups strengthen their intransigent stance, but Marcos did not seek to find a political solution to the conflict so much as to bolster his administration's image in the Muslim world. The war resumed, though at a lower level of intensity than in 1972–76, and negotiations were not revived until the accession of Corazon Aquino to power in 1986.

Security Under Aquino

The historic "People Power" uprising of February 22–25, 1986, which ended the authoritarian regime, was sparked by an attempted RAM coup and joined by a diverse coalition of anti-Marcos forces including the church, the disenfranchised oligarchy, the middle class, and spontaneous masses, as well as some segments of the organized left. The focal point was Corazon Aquino, widow of slain opposition leader Benigno Aquino, who embodied the coalition's contradictory security interests. Her government was likewise a living contradiction, contested from within and from without by several opposed elements in the February coalition: military, oligarchy, and some left-leaning groups in civil society. The February "revolution" was first and foremost a restoration of the pre–martial law status quo, and Aquino's priority was the reestablishment of traditional democratic institutions (Thompson 1995). Under the 1987 Constitution the presidential form of government, upholding the separation of powers among the three coequal branches of government, was restored along with the system of checks and balances. Civilian supremacy over the military was also enshrined in the constitution.[7] An elaborate set of provisions was written to prevent the recurrence of the abuses committed under Marcos. A search warrant or warrant of arrest can be issued only by a civilian judge, for example, whereas under Marcos's 1973 Constitution, any "responsible officer" was allowed to issue such a warrant, including any military officer. In many instances in the past, the Marcos regime issued military orders that included the authority to detain suspected persons. The new constitution further states that the privilege of the writ of habeas corpus may be suspended only in case of invasion or rebellion (Nolledo 1990: 114, 116).

The powers of the executive were likewise limited under the 1987 charter. The salient provisions pertain to limiting the term of the president to a single six-year term; the public's right to know the state of the president's health; the prerogative of the legislature to revoke the president's decision to declare martial law; the authority of the Supreme Court to review the basis for proclamation of martial law; and the provision that a state of martial law does not suspend the operation of the country's constitution, nor does it supplant the functioning of the civil courts or legislative assemblies or authorize the conferment of jurisdiction on military courts or agencies over civilians where civil courts are able to function (Nolledo 1990: 596).

Under the Aquino government the informal sectors of society also gained the opportunity to play a role in strengthening democratic institutions. Aquino launched the Kabisig program, a partnership between government and various people's organizations and nongovernmental organizations (NGOs) to deliver basic goods and services at the grassroots level. A number of former communists resurfaced to work in the burgeoning NGO and cooperative community, whose phenomenal growth provided new structures and potential mechanisms for political change at both the national and local levels.[8]

During the first year of the Aquino administration, the approach taken in dealing with the communist insurgency differed dramatically from that of Marcos. In pursuit of a political settlement and as part of her election promise, Aquino released a number of prominent prisoners, including CPP leader Jose Maria Sison and NPA commander Bernabe Buscayno (Porter, 1987: 56–57). Aquino believed that most insurgents were not hard-core Marxists but were forced to bear arms against the government because of injustices under the Marcos regime. Out of this conviction, two strands developed in her government's policy toward the insurgents: first, the offer of general amnesty to those who would lay down their arms; second, talks with the rebel leadership to negotiate a cease-fire, ostensibly to enable her government to address their legitimate grievances. Although many more liberal members of the Aquino administration distrusted the CPP and doubted its commitment to democratic values, they were nevertheless aware that the Communist Party leadership was divided following its mistake in calling for a boycott of the 1986 presidential elections that in fact led to Marcos's fall. They also recognized that the party was not totally in agreement on continuing the strategy of "protracted people's war." The government hoped for a fundamental shift in CPP strategy that would reduce the importance of armed struggle and put more emphasis on political struggle, including participation in elections. If a cease-fire could be negotiated between the CPP/NPA and the Aquino government, a political settlement of the communist insurgency problem might also be possible. The human rights lawyers in the Aquino administration were all too aware of the counterproductive results of the military approach during the Marcos period, such as human rights violations by the AFP. In their view, suppressing the insurgency by force had contributed to the growth of the CPP/NPA in the past. It was only by restraining the military that the insurgents' growth could be contained (Porter 1987: 57–58).

The military establishment, however, was not convinced of the merits of the political settlement approach. It did not appeal to the mind-set of the AFP, its professional role, or its institutional interests. Chief of Staff General Fidel Ramos and Defense Minister Juan Ponce Enrile proposed a counterinsurgency strategy aimed at defeating the CPP/NPA through coordinated military and civilian programs. The Ramos plan did not include negotiation with the communist leadership. Instead it called for a combined civilian-military structure at various levels (regional, provincial, municipal) that was adapted from the design of U.S. counterinsurgency operations in Vietnam. It also called for greater civilian, government, and private-sector involvement in intelligence gathering, propaganda, and paramilitary support for the AFP. It appears that the key objective of the military behind the Ramos plan was to obtain a greater share of the national budget for counterinsurgency operations, a share that might have been significantly reduced under the negotiations strategy of Aquino. Likewise, the plan was designed to ensure that local officials who had been appointed by the Aquino government would cooperate with the AFP in its counterinsurgency efforts. Many local government officials appointed by Aquino were reportedly reluctant to get involved in the military's counterinsurgency operations (Porter 1987: 59).

Despite the military's lobbying efforts for the adoption of the Ramos plan, Aquino refused to accept the proposal on the grounds that it would prejudice the prospects for a peace agreement with the communists. Thereafter, the military leadership pressed her government to consult more with the defense establishment on the insurgency problem, including the details of the cease-fire agreement being negotiated at the time. The conflict between Aquino and the military was later exacerbated by Aquino's decision not to include any military representative in the peace talks—perceived by the military as a concession to the CPP, which had insisted on the AFP's exclusion (Porter 1987: 60). Subsequently, Enrile criticized the Aquino government's plan to limit the AFP to a defensive position while she pursued peace talks with the communist insurgents. Enrile also increased pressure on her to spell out the details of the cease-fire agreement with the CPP/NPA.

In the face of mounting criticisms from the military, Aquino withdrew her earlier order of restrictions on AFP operations against the insurgents but continued her administration's peace negotiations with the communist leadership. Enrile, claiming to speak on behalf of the entire military establishment, set out conditions for a cease-fire that were actually aimed at scuttling any peace agreement with the communists: no cease-fire agreement with the communists would be recognized if it involved the surrender of sovereignty by the government over any part of the national territory, the recognition of any areas as being controlled by the CPP/NPA, or the acknowledgment that any area or community was "defended" by any armed force other than the AFP or the national police forces of the government. These conditions were essentially aimed at precluding all avenues for compromise that might have been contemplated by Aquino's negotiators. They were also designed to prevent local government units from entering into separate cease-fire agreements with local communist units (Porter 1987: 65–66).

The rift between Aquino and the military on the insurgency issue widened as Aquino refused to act on the AFP's counterinsurgency proposals. Negotiations with the communist leadership met a number of setbacks as the military continued its operations against the insurgents. In September 1986 the military arrested Rodolfo Salas, identified as one of the top leaders of the CPP. Then rightist elements in the AFP reportedly staged several ambush operations against leaders of leftist organizations, such as labor leader Rolando Olalia. These were clearly efforts on the part of the military to derail the peace negotiations between the Aquino government and the National Democratic Front (NDF), which was representing the CPP/NPA.

Military pressure on the Aquino government later took the form of aborted coups even as Enrile's RAM supporters openly talked about the idea of changing the government while criticizing Aquino's policy toward the communist insurgents. The initial aborted coup, called "God Save the Queen," was aimed at eliminating the so-called leftist sympathizers in the Aquino cabinet who were considered to be primarily responsible for resisting the AFP's counterinsurgency proposals. The rightist military rebels, however, failed in their attempts to overthrow the government of Aquino because Chief of Staff General Ramos, a known believer in civilian supremacy over the military, threw his support behind Aquino. A cabinet revamp ensued wherein Enrile, along with suspected left-leaning cabinet members, was sacked by Aquino in a compromise deal with the military.

A 60-day cease-fire agreement with the CPP/NPA was finally signed in November 1986 after more than six months of negotiations that had begun in May. The negotiation process had to hurdle a number of fundamental disagreements over the extent of the cease-fire, the definition of what would constitute a violation of the agreement, and the issue of recognizing NPA-controlled areas. When the cease-fire agreement expired, negotiations at the national level were suspended following the "Mendiola massacre" of peasant demonstrators by government marines in Manila in January 1987. The peace negotiations were overshadowed by the ratification in February 1987 of the new constitution that formally legitimized the Aquino government under a democratic regime. By enhancing the legitimacy of the Aquino administration, the new constitution enabled it to gain the upper hand in dealing with the rebels. In a gesture of magnanimity following the ratification of the constitution, Aquino announced in late February an amnesty program designed to attract rebel surrenders (including those from the Muslim secessionist groups) by offering financial rewards for returned weapons, livelihood training programs, and the creation of rehabilitation centers for rebels throughout the country (Coronel-Ferrer and Raquiza 1993: 10–11; Villanueva 1992; Timberman 1991; Thompson 1992).

In a major shift of policy, Aquino rejected the NDF's offer in March 1987 to resume national-level peace talks with the communist rebels. Instead her government opted to hold peace talks with regional and local NPA commanders, taking advantage of the apparent rift within the ranks of the CPP/NPA on the issue. In an apparent reversal of her original stance in dealing with the insurgency problem, Aquino announced before a graduating class of the Philippine Military Academy on March 18 that her government was adopting a "total war" policy vis-à-vis the communist insurgents. With the rightist military becoming more restive and with more coup threats by RAM rebels, Aquino's government gave in to pressure from the defense establishment. The AFP undertook several military offensives against the communists and arrested top-ranking CPP/NPA leaders following Aquino's call for the AFP to "unsheathe the sword of war" against them. For its part, the CPP/NPA countered Aquino's "total war" policy with increased attacks in the urban centers against military soldiers and policemen, politicians, and even American military personnel. The NPA claimed responsibility for the assassination of three U.S. servicemen near Clark Air Base in 1987. About fifty soldiers and policemen were attacked by the Alex Boncayao Brigade, an urban guerrilla unit in metropolitan Manila, including

Aquino's former local government secretary (Jaime Ferrer), who was known to have advocated the formation of armed civilian vigilante groups to help the AFP in its counterinsurgency operations (Coronel-Ferrer and Raquiza 1993: 12–13). For the remainder of her term, which was punctuated by major RAM-led coup attempts in August 1987 and December 1989, Aquino's government prosecuted a war even more violent and "total" than that of its predecessor.

Two trends were especially conspicuous in AFP's "total war" under the Aquino government from March 1987: increasing reliance upon civilian vigilante and paramilitary groups such as Davao City's "Alsa Masa" ("Rising of the Masses"), a concept that rapidly spread nationwide and was portrayed as a spontaneous manifestation of anticommunist "People Power," and a marked escalation in the scale of mechanical violence deployed by the government. "Low-intensity conflict," as counter-guerrilla warfare was fashionably dubbed, went hand in hand with higher-intensity artillery and aerial bombardment such as had been characteristic of Marcos-era ground sweeps. This activity was reflected in a growing number of internal refugees, numbering some 33,600 families in Mindanao alone by 1990, more than ten times the figure in 1985 (Citizens' Disaster Rehabilitation Center 1991: 18; HALAD Foundation 1989).[9] The NPA also made increasing use of heavier weaponry such as mortars, grenade launchers, and recoilless rifles as these were captured from the military. According to AFP statistics, CPP/NPA forces continued to grow during the first two years of the Aquino government, reaching 25,200 by the end of 1987 (Department of National Defense 1990: 7).

Although the new constitution mandated the dismantling of "private armies and other armed groups" outside "regular" AFP forces, Aquino's presidential directive ordering the abolition of the hated CHDF was reportedly returned by Brigadier General Jose Magno unacted upon "for revisions," a telling indicator of the imbalance between formal civilian and informal military authority (Van der Kroef 1988: 632–33). In July 1987 the CHDF was replaced by the virtually indistinguishable Citizens' Armed Forces Geographical Units (CAFGUs), composed of former CHDF participants as well as members of vigilante groups such as the Tadtad ("hackers"), Pulahan ("red ones"), and Ituman ("black ones"). By 1992 there were almost twice as many CAFGUs deployed across the country as the 45,000 CHDFs of 1987. As was extensively documented by domestic and international human rights organizations, they continued to be implicated in the torture, death and disappearance of legal political activists and ordinary peasants as well as suspected insurgents.[10]

With regard to the Muslim secessionist problem, efforts to find a political settlement during the Aquino period suffered the same fate. An agreement was signed with the MNLF in September 1986 following a meeting between Aquino and Misuari wherein both parties agreed to respect a tentative truce entered into a month earlier and to hold substantive talks later under the auspices of the OIC. For their part, the MILF under Hashim Salamat and the reformist faction of the MNLF led by Dimas Pundato concurred with autonomy as the basis of negotiations with the Aquino government. Talks with the MNLF collapsed in July 1987, however, following Aquino's call for "total war" against the insurgents. Misuari ordered his troops to take on a defensive position vis-à-vis the AFP even as the Philippine Congress started to draft autonomy bills for Mindanao and the Cordilleras (Coronel-Ferrer and Raquiza 1993: 6, 12). The autonomy law passed by Congress needed the ratification of both Christian and Muslim residents in the affected provinces in Mindanao, but less than 50 percent participated in the referendum held on November 19, 1989. The anemic showing was widely attributed to a vigorous MNLF boycott campaign, and those living in predominantly Christian areas overwhelmingly rejected the autonomy law. Misuari criticized the autonomy law passed by Congress and argued that the 1976 Tripoli agreement promised a fuller degree of autonomy for the Muslims. Aquino later refused to entertain MNLF proposals for the resumption of peace talks.

Overall, the failure of the political settlement approach to resolve the insurgency problem may be attributed to the nature of civil-military relations during the Aquino period. As an unstable coalition of antagonistic forces under a weakened executive, the administration was vulnerable to Enrile's restive RAM supporters, who were able to scuttle Aquino's peace talks formula by intimidating her government with coup threats. At the same time, Aquino's inability to control the military gave the communist insurgents a reason to abandon the peace negotiations and resume hostilities against government forces, especially after Aquino announced her government's "total war" policy against both the CPP/NPA and the Muslim secessionist rebels. The restoration of traditional oligarchic democracy led to a Congress unwilling to pass the substantive reforms needed to address the root causes of social unrest.

Aquino's economic programs were scuttled by political instability and by the failure of the legislature to pass meaningful economic reform laws. Although Congress passed the Comprehensive Agrarian Reform Law during Aquino's time, most of its provisions protected the interests of the landowners. And despite the passage of the Foreign Investments Act, her government also failed to attract substantial new foreign investment because of its perceived instability. The investment law itself contained a significant number of exclusion lists that specified sectors where foreigners were not allowed to invest in the Philippines. The problem of monopolies in strategic sectors of the economy (banking, telecommunications, transport) was not dealt with squarely by the administration, whose efforts were focused more on the privatization of government enterprises and the recovery of "ill-gotten wealth" from the Marcoses and their cronies.[11] In the final analysis, the Aquino administration was a transitional period, a holding operation against restored martial rule. Its supporters felt vindicated enough by the peaceful transfer of power to her anointed successor, Fidel Ramos.

Security Under Ramos

As a matter of stated policy, national security under the Ramos administration was broadly defined as "a condition wherein the people's way of life and institutions, their territorial integrity and sovereignty, as well as their welfare and well-being are protected and enhanced" (National Security Council 1993: 1). This basic definition attempts to strike a balance between the security interests of the state and those of the people.

The broad conception of national security under the Ramos government takes into consideration the interrelationship of social, economic, and political factors and how all those factors affect the overall security of the nation. Upon assuming office in June 1992, Ramos vowed to continue with the process of democratic consolidation in the country that had begun under the Aquino government. The democratic order, however, was seen not as an end in itself but as a means to attain national political unity. In a society that has long been torn by internal strife and rebellion, Ramos recognized early on that the persistence of the insurgency problem would deny the country the political stability prerequisite to achieving economic growth and development.

In the short term, the Ramos government adopted as an immediate goal the attainment of a relatively peaceful political environment in the country. Unlike the Marcos regime, however, which saw the need to rely solely on the state's martial forces to bring about internal peace and order, Ramos did not believe that such an approach would be effective in dealing with the insurgency problem. His government opted for a comprehensive settlement of the armed rebellions, but it reserved the right to use military force if necessary. Rapid economic growth and development became a priority concern for this president who was elected with less than a quarter of the vote. Economic growth, however, would serve as a means to a higher end: the attainment of social equity and increased economic opportunities for the majority of Filipinos. Both the Aquino and Ramos administrations recognized at the outset the direct linkage between massive poverty and the persistence of armed rebellion in the country; the latter, however, was more candid in its identification of the oligarchic structure of society as the root cause of the insurgency problem. As Ramos's influential national security adviser, the retired general Jose T. Almonte, had put it,

> They talk about the need for national identity, of what the country should be in the year 2020. They don't say, however, who we'd have to be up against to achieve that. It's only the Communist Party and its New People's Army who have defined that the struggle has to be against the feudalists, the oligarchs. The oligarchs condemn the communists' anti-democratic means, but they just keep quiet about the communists' target. Why? Because they'll have to identify themselves as the problem (Tiglao 1995: 28).

As expected, the traditional oligarchic families attempted to resist the Ramos government's efforts to undertake meaningful economic reforms, as had been the case during the Aquino period (Hutchcroft 1994). Nevertheless, Ramos made it the cornerstone of his government's program to liberalize the economy of the Philippines in an effort to spur economic growth. His administration pursued full deregulation of the economy by dismantling protectionist barriers and providing proper incentives and support to make the nation's industries more efficient and competitive in the world market (Ramos 1992, 1993, 1993–94, 1995). The prime targets were the big monopolies in the banking, shipping, telecommunications, and insurance industries that had long been protected during the Marcos and Aquino periods. Opening these sectors of the economy to foreign competition forced the local industries to become more efficient and provide better service (Alburo 1993; Habito 1993–94; De Dios 1993–94, 1995; National Economic and Development Authority 1993–94).

External security was another high-priority concern for the Ramos administration in light of the country's vulnerable position following the withdrawal of American military facilities at Subic Bay and Clark Field in late 1992. For a long time, the U.S. bases in the country enabled the government to allocate its limited resources to internal security concerns. But when the Philippine Senate rejected the extension of the 1947 Military Bases Agreement in September 1991, the government had to start thinking of building the Philippines' external defense capability. The full realization of the country's vulnerability to external threats came in February 1995, when the AFP discovered a Chinese military buildup on Mischief Reef (Panganiban Reef), one of the islands claimed by the Philippines in the disputed Spratlys in the South China Sea.

Historically the Spratlys had served as a staging point for the Japanese invasion of the Philippines in World War II, and that experience reinforced the perception of a threat posed by the Chinese buildup on Mischief Reef. The presence of Chinese troops in the area impinges on both the territorial integrity of the Philippines and its exclusive economic zone. It is also seen as undermining the collective efforts of other small claimant states in the region to pursue a peaceful settlement of the South China Sea dispute. There is a perception among some Filipino policy makers that the incident on Mischief Reef is part of Beijing's long-term goal of enhancing its territorial claims in the area. If the Chinese buildup in the area goes on unopposed, the security of the sea-lanes of communication in the South China Sea could be undermined. That possibility cannot be discounted in the face of a widely held belief in the region that China is currently building its blue-water naval capabilities, which could be used to defend its maritime claims. Moreover, a number of Chinese policy statements and actions have done nothing to dispel the perception of a "China threat" in the region, a perception shared by some Filipino policy makers. In 1992, for example, the passage of China's Law of the Sea essentially reasserted its claim of sovereignty over the entire South China Sea.

In dealing with the country's insurgency problem, the Ramos administration essentially adopted the strategy of combining the political settlement approach with military force. In his speech before the Philippine Congress in July 1992, a month after his inauguration as president, Ramos announced four initiatives to promote "peace and security" under his government: the repeal of the antisubversion law, which effectively legalized the CPP and similar organizations; the grant of amnesty to insurgents and military rebels; the creation of a National Unification Commission (NUC); and the review of all cases of rebels under detention or serving sentence. These political initiatives were aimed primarily at projecting his government's sincere desire to achieve political unity and to end the insurgency problem, but not at the expense of the security of the state. The antisubversion law was repealed by Congress in September, and the NUC was created in the same month. As an advisory body to the president, the NUC was charged with making recommendations, within 90 days, pertaining to a comprehensive amnesty program and the government's peace agenda. Thereafter Ramos appointed key government emissaries to begin exploratory talks with the NDF, the MNLF and other Muslim secessionist groups, and leaders of the rightist military rebels led by RAM, on the political settlement of the insurgency problem.

Even as the framework for a political settlement of the insurgency problem was being laid down by the government, military operations by the AFP against the rebels were sustained amid continued attacks by communist insurgents and the Muslim secessionists. The NDF initially rejected Ramos's offer of amnesty, which was conditional on the rebels' laying down of arms. At the same time, the NDF sent feelers to the government on the resumption of peace talks on a limited agenda. In an effort to improve the atmosphere for peace negotiations with the rebels, Ramos ordered a series of high-ranking communist leaders and RAM rebel soldiers released from detention. These initiatives appear to have encouraged the insurgents to take up Ramos's offer of talks. Following exploratory exchanges in The Hague, a communiqué was issued by a joint panel of government emissaries and Jose Maria Sison and Luis Jalandoni, CPP founder and NDF vice chairperson, respectively. Gregorio "Gringo" Honasan, leader of the renegade RAM, along with rebel Marcos-loyalist troops, also indicated their willingness to participate in formal peace negotiations with the government through the NUC. In October 1992, MNLF leader Nur Misuari returned to the Philippines from self-exile in Libya to negotiate with the government following exploratory talks in Tripoli. Misuari agreed to negotiations without preconditions, and Ramos granted observer status to the OIC in the peace negotiations with the MNLF.

In initial talks with communist leaders in The Hague, the government agreed to hold formal negotiations without preconditions, based on mutually acceptable principles, to resolve the armed conflict. On the substantive agenda were the issues of human rights and international humanitarian law, socioeconomic reform, political and constitutional reform, an end to armed hostilities, and the disposition of forces. Subsequently the NUC refined The Hague joint declaration signed by representatives of the Philippine government and the NDF to include, among other points, the dismantling of all private armies, strict implementation of relevant laws, improvements in the administration of law, protection of the environment, provision for victims of armed conflict, and emphasis on the economic components of national unification. The negotiations with the NDF failed to prosper, however, because of major stumbling blocks: the refusal of the communist insurgents to lay down their arms and recognize the legitimacy of the Ramos government; the NDF's insistence that the government grant it belligerency status in the negotiations; and disagreements on the venue of the talks. The NDF also resented the Ramos government's policy of pursuing dialogues with regional party committees while ignoring calls for resumption of peace negotiations at the national level. The open split within the ranks of the CPP/NPA between hard-line "reaffirmists" of protracted people's war and opposition "rejectionists," a split that emerged fully at the end of 1992, has ensured the government's upper hand in dealing with the communist insurgents, both in political and military terms (Solidum 1994: 237).[12]

Substantial progress has been achieved in negotiations with the MNLF. Because of factional divisions within the MNLF and other secessionist groups, however, hostilities have continued—not only between government forces and rebels but also among the warring factions. The AFP has conducted a series of military offensives against a "lost command" of the MNLF, called the Abu Sayyaf, which reportedly has been responsible for a number of terrorist activities in Mindanao since 1992 (Turner 1995). Another faction, the MILF, was involved in a series of attacks against a government irrigation project in North Cotabato. Notwithstanding these military encounters, the Ramos government persisted in its negotiations with the MNLF, which threatened to withdraw on several occasions if the military offensives continued.

Following a series of talks held in Jakarta, the government and the MNLF agreed to a political settlement in June 1996 and signed a final peace agreement on September 2. The agreement resulted in the installation of MNLF leader Nur Misuari as governor of fourteen autonomous provinces in Mindanao following elections held a week after the signing of the peace pact. The agreement provided for the setting up of the Southern Philippine Council for Peace and Development (SPCPD), a transitional body to be headed by Misuari. The SPCPD will be guided by a consultative assembly composed of local officials and representatives from NGOs. The MNLF will supervise economic development projects in provinces covered by the council, but it was not allowed to oversee peacekeeping operations in the autonomous area of fourteen provinces and nine cities. Two key issues were left unresolved, however, that could serve as stumbling blocks to the SPCPD's viability: the MNLF's demand to set up its own regional police force of 20,000 former guerrillas and the integration of Muslim insurgents in the national armed forces (AOL Reuters [Internet], June 23, 1996). Moreover, the apprehensions of the Christian community in Mindanao (mainly on the part of big landowners and political clans in the area), manifested in sizable demonstrations following the signing of the agreement, could become a potential source of conflict and undermine its full implementation. The relative success of the negotiations can be attributed to the MNLF's change of position on the goal of an independent nation-state, abandoned under pressure from OIC member states. As host to the government–MNLF talks, Indonesia too had apparently influenced the rebel leadership to moderate its position.

The Ramos government has also entered into peace talks with the Moro Islamic Liberation Front (MILF), a breakaway faction of the MNLF that had been fighting the government in order to establish an Islamic state in Mindanao. A peace agreement that may be concluded with the MILF could enhance further the prospects for a lasting peace in the southern Philippines and enable the government's economic development projects in the area to finally take off. In April 1997, the Ramos administration announced an allocation of $1.6 billion for Mindanao to develop infrastructure, power, housing, irrigation, and livelihood projects in the region. Likewise, Ramos gave priority to the Muslim autonomous areas in Mindanao in his efforts to attract foreign investors into the country. A number of business projects in the area involving Malaysia, Arab countries, and some member countries of the European Union have been negotiated since the signing of the peace agreement between the government and the MNLF.

Negotiations with the RAM rebels—who had greater confidence in Ramos, their former military chief, than in Aquino—did not meet serious obstacles.[13] Even so, the issues raised by the rebel soldiers became more comprehensive, including social, economic, and political reform. Many of these concerns have been addressed by the Ramos administration, especially those pertaining to specific reforms within the AFP. Gregorio Honasan's victory in the senatorial elections held in May 1995 gives the RAM leadership a chance to be heard in the legislature, at least for the next six years, which augurs well for the political settlement of military rebellion against the state.

In the economic sphere, a key element of the Ramos agenda is the pursuit of liberalization. As noted earlier, economic reform is seen as closely linked to the solution of the insurgency problem, given its root causes in economic and social inequality. The framework for economic recovery and growth is embodied in a strategy termed "Philippines 2000." This program envisages the achievement, by the year 2000, of a per capita income of at least $1,000; economic growth of at least 6 percent; and a decline in the incidence of poverty from 50 percent to 30 percent (Ramos 1993–94: 120). In order to push his economic reform agenda, Ramos had to work closely with Congress, which provides the legal infrastructure for his reform policies. Ramos has recognized from the outset that he needs legislative cooperation if his reform efforts are to succeed. Aquino did not enjoy smooth working relations with the legislature: her appointments to important cabinet positions were rejected by members of the bicameral Commission on Appointments, legislation on reforms was delayed, and budget negotiations with the legislature were difficult (Parreñas 1993: 277–78) Notwithstanding the gains so far achieved by the Ramos administration, it too faces a number of constraints on reform. The predominance of the traditional oligarchy in the legislature may prove to be a major impediment to a faster pace of structural adjustment in the economy. Reform initiatives may be watered down by escape clauses—as was clearly the case with Aquino's Comprehensive Agrarian Reform Law, which effectively exempted much of the land owned by the oligarchy. Political bargaining may continue to impede the implementation of projects in the transport and telecommunications industries and regional economic programs such as the ASEAN Free Trade Area (Riedinger 1994: 139–46, 1995: 209–16; Gochoco-Bautista and Faustino 1994).

The political dominance of traditional oligarchs, however, may have started to wane, as suggested by the changing composition of Congress. In May 1995 a number of legislators from outside the traditional political clans were elected on the basis of reform credentials or cabinet performance in the Aquino and Ramos administrations. This trend may be partly attributed to the changing attitude of the voting public, whose preference for a new breed of politicians has been increasing since 1986. Change is also occurring in politics at the local level as NGOs and people's organizations exert increasing influence to unseat traditional politicians ("*trapos*") in the countryside.

The principal constraints on Ramos's economic reform program derive, of course, from the nature of the country's political system itself. Elected as a minority president, Ramos must rely on building coalitions in the legislature to ensure that his policy initiatives will be supported by law. Political bargaining can hardly be avoided, especially under a presidential form of government that is often considered a gridlock system. This reality partially explains persistent calls, mostly from Ramos supporters, for a shift in the country's political system from a presidential to a parliamentary form. But so long as political parties lack discipline and politics dwells more on personalities than on issues, the problem of political bargaining will remain.[14]

External Security: The South China Sea and Growing Regionalism

The Philippine Senate's decision on September 16, 1991, not to extend the 1947 Military Bases Agreement with the United States fundamentally altered the external defense posture of the country. The presence of U.S. military bases had long served as an effective deterrent to external threats, but their withdrawal in late 1992 rendered the Philippines' external defense capability weak.[15] The AFP was thus forced to undertake a modernization plan designed to reorient the military toward external defense.

Ramos signed the AFP Modernization Act into law in February 1995. Its passage came at a most opportune time—close upon the discovery of a Chinese military buildup on Mischief Reef, one of the islands claimed by the Philippines in the Kalayaan Group of the Spratlys. The principal thrusts of the military modernization program under the law are, essentially, (1) development of a self-reliant and strategically credible "Citizens Armed Force," the reconfiguration of the AFP structure, and the professionalization of the military; (2) reforms in the recruitment, training, employment, and management of AFP personnel; (3) development, validation, or modification of AFP doctrines; (4) acquisition and upgrading of appropriate technology and equipment; and (5) relocation, improvement, and construction of bases and other facilities. The law's provisions on doctrine clearly recognize the need to reorient the AFP from an internally to an externally directed force. The law called for the implementation of the AFP modernization program over a period of fifteen years and provided for a ceiling of 50 billion pesos (or U.S.$2 billion) for the first five years, beginning in 1996. Its provisions indicate the order of priority in terms of developing the capabilities of the AFP—namely, naval, air, and ground defense. The need to improve naval defense was highlighted by the Mischief Reef incident.[16] Although the Philippine navy was obviously no match for China's maritime capabilities, that did not deter the AFP from conducting limited strikes on nearby islands in an effort to destroy markers reportedly installed by the Chinese.

Given the country's weak external defense, the Ramos government had to rely primarily on diplomatic pressure against China on the issue. The main strategy was to undertake a series of diplomatic offensives, bringing international opinion to bear against Chinese actions in the Spratlys. Both bilateral and multilateral approaches (the latter primarily through ASEAN) were pursued. The Ramos government strongly protested China's continued occupation of Mischief Reef and denounced its buildup in the area as clearly undermining the spirit of ASEAN's 1992 Manila Declaration on the South China Sea. To sustain the pressure on China, the Philippine navy ferried a group of local and international journalists close to Mischief Reef, in an act the Chinese government labeled "provocative." As a form of diplomatic leverage,

Ramos refused to give in to demands that Chinese fishermen apprehended by the Philippine coast guard within the country's exclusive
economic zone in March be repatriated. Charged with illegal fishing and
smuggling, they were released only when China agreed to bilateral talks
on the South China Sea. Those talks resulted in a joint statement in
August 1995 indicating Beijing's commitment to abide by a "code of
conduct" in the South China Sea signed by the two countries. Among
other things, the agreement stipulated that the parties would refrain
from any destabilizing activities in the area and would adhere to the
spirit of ASEAN's 1992 Manila Declaration. A similar agreement was
signed by the Philippines and Vietnam in November.

China had been put on the defensive when senior ASEAN officials
collectively raised the Mischief Reef issue at the first ASEAN–China
dialogue in Hangzhou in April 1995. ASEAN's support for the Philippines sent a clear message that the group would not tolerate any destabilizing unilateral actions by the Chinese in the South China Sea. At the
height of the diplomatic tussle with China over Mischief Reef, the
Ramos government was careful not to allow Vietnam to enter the
picture, because that would only strengthen China's perception that
ASEAN was emerging as an anti-China bloc following Vietnam's entry
into the organization. Within the Philippine bureaucracy, there is
apparently no consensus on whether China should be considered an
immediate external threat to the Philippines in light of the Mischief Reef
incident.[17] Nevertheless, playing the Vietnam card vis-à-vis China
remains an option for some foreign policy bureaucrats as far as the South
China Sea dispute is concerned.

The Mischief Reef incident concretized the threat posed to the
Philippines by the unresolved territorial disputes in the Spratlys. During
his trip to Vietnam in March 1994, Ramos proposed to his Vietnamese
counterpart the establishment of a joint commission on the South China
Sea to undertake wide-ranging studies on the Spratlys issue. The
resulting commission may explore such ideas as demilitarization of the
area, maintenance of the status quo, and cooperative ventures among the
countries concerned (Ramos 1995: 236–37). This proposal became the
basis for the Ramos government's pursuit of a multilateral approach to
joint development of the South China Sea—a strategy that does not sit
well with Beijing, which prefers to limit joint development of the area to
bilateral agreements with other claimant states.

The Philippines may be expected to pursue its limited claim in the
Spratlys through a concerted diplomatic approach with the rest of the
ASEAN claimant states as well as by seeking support from the United
States and Japan.[18] Given the AFP's inability to engage the Chinese

military in defense of the Philippines' territorial interests in the Spratlys, this appears to be the most pragmatic approach. Although the Philippines might wish to invoke the provisions of its mutual defense treaty with the United States, that option remains foreclosed. The United States does not recognize any claims in the Spratlys dispute. Nor does it consider islands in the area claimed by Manila to be part of the Philippines' "metropolitan territory" covered under the treaty. Ultimately the Philippines would have to rely on self-help in the event of a military confrontation with China or any other claimant state over the Spratlys.

Overall, the diplomatic instruments used by the Philippine government in dealing with the threat posed by China in the Spratlys dispute appear to have had some limited success, if only in the short term. But to lend credibility to its diplomatic strategy, the Philippines will have to build up and modernize its external defense capability. Financing the modernization of the AFP will depend on sustained economic growth, however, which itself depends on the achievement of long-term internal political stability.

The Philippines' diplomatic strategy vis-à-vis China on the Spratlys conflict was put to a test in late April 1997 when the AFP discovered four armed Chinese naval vessels in the area claimed by Manila. Although China withdrew its ships following diplomatic protests made by the Ramos government, the Chinese embassy in Manila defended China's right to conduct marine surveys in the area as China asserted its sovereignty over the Spratlys and adjacent waters. That incident, along with China's continuing dispute with Vietnam over oil-drilling activities in the Spratlys, indicates that although Beijing may show much flexibility in dealing with other claimants in the South China Sea at the diplomatic level, it would not hesitate to commit what may be termed as "soft aggression" in the area. Undoubtedly, such behavior may be seen as part of China's overall strategy to further enhance its claim in the South China Sea.

Challenges to the Democratic Order

The foregoing discussion of conceptions of national security in the Philippines indicates that although it is a comprehensive and evolving concept covering a range of domestic and external security concerns, it has revolved mostly around internal problems related to nation- and state-building. Further, the Philippine state still exhibits several characteristics of a traditional state.[19] It has yet to demonstrate many of the hallmarks of a modern state, such as a clear distinction between the internal and the external or the public and the private, or a high degree of internal pacification and administrative reach. Both authoritarian and democratic regimes have faced major internal security threats focused on identity, legitimacy, and socioeconomic grievances since the late 1960s, primarily from the CPP/NPA and the MNLF. These threats have waxed and waned in relative importance during the period under consideration. Whereas the MNLF threat predominated during the 1970s, the CPP was the more prominent concern in the 1980s. The nature of the threats is also distinct: the communists sought to overthrow the entire political system, whereas Muslim rebels sought merely to displace the state in the south or to seek autonomy within it. To the extent that the MNLF has represented a threat to the nation's territorial integrity, it is similar in nature to an external threat—and that similarity is extended by foreign support for the Muslim rebels and by Manila's concomitant foreign diplomacy. Although Jakarta's brokering of the September 2, 1996, peace treaty is indicative of the Philippines' increasing reliance on regional ties in the post–Cold War era, growing ethnonationalist and Islamic consciousness since the collapse of communism could yet contribute to an unraveling of the agreement. Nor does the gradual disintegration of the CPP/NPA, any more than the defeat of the Huks before them, signify a definitive end to the problem of social unrest. There is a very real danger that complacency over short-term economic growth—growth without equity—will lead to a failure of resolve in addressing deep-seated structural problems; that danger is all the greater because the constant pressure of a powerful, organized left led by the CPP has begun to wane. This situation could result in another cycle of violent social unrest in the future.[20]

Indeed, the country's insurgent movements are primarily symptoms of insecurity rather than causes in themselves. Those who have joined them have often done so to seek the security that the state has failed to provide: participation represents an attempt at individual or community "self-help" in a situation of internal social anarchy. By addressing the symptom rather than the cause, by contributing to the anarchy, counterinsurgency policy has long aggravated the problem of insecurity. The fundamental questions of referent and scope (*who* and *what* is to be secured), which determine approaches to national security (the question of *how*), are themselves dependent in turn on identification of the threat itself: what is to be secured *against*? In a classic case of *quis custodiet ipsos custodes*, the Philippine military, which Marcos had expanded to "save the republic," first became a threat to civil society and then, during the Aquino period, undermined the very state it was pledged to defend. Today, the same military is no match for its potential rivals in an increasingly dangerous South China Sea.

The authoritarian experience has strongly conditioned conceptions of security in the Philippines. The result was a much weakened executive during the Aquino period just as the traditional oligarchy was resurgent and the military was at the peak of its influence—forces that could be counterbalanced only by an invigorated civil society. Aquino's legacy is the reestablishment of the prerequisite framework of formal liberties. However, the task of further empowering the Filipino people was left to her successors and the expanding community of NGOs and people's organizations. That community had its origins in resistance to the Marcos regime, however, and remains mistrustful of a "strong" state. Their mistrust can only be overcome when the state becomes sufficiently representative of, and accountable to, civil society and gives the people as much stake in state security as their rulers have.

For a long time, the most powerful stakeholder in the security of the Philippine state has been its American patron. When the state became endangered by Marcos's predations, the security goal of the U.S. State Department shifted from the defense of his administration to the preservation of an anticommunist regime. Marcos was abandoned and the United States joined his opponents in the uneasy coalition under Cory Aquino. Long-term American patronage, however, has left the AFP as underdeveloped as the state it is charged with defending—a condition that has suddenly become obvious with the withdrawal of the U.S. bases from the country. In the post–Cold War environment the Ramos government is seeking external security through improved regional ties, a project closely linked to the president's vision for economic development, "Philippines 2000." The southern Philippines, long considered a vulnerable "back door" to Muslim subversion, is now reconceptualized as a "front door" to trade with ASEAN. The Brunei–Indonesia–Malaysia–Philippines East ASEAN Growth Area (BIMP-EAGA), centered on Mindanao, is one of several trade polygons in the emerging AFTA (Ramos 1995). The reawakening of these regional trading links, long overshadowed by bilateral trade between metropole and colonial entrepôt, marks the beginning of a new postcolonial era in Southeast Asia. Since the days of the galleon trade, the Philippines' primary ties with the outside world have extended eastward to the American continent, and the country has often been regarded as peripheral to Southeast Asia. Today the Philippines increasingly seeks investment from, as well as trade with, its immediate Asian neighbors. It is promoting regional economic cooperation too, and is participating more fully in important regional organizations that are becoming central to local conceptions of security. The transformation of Subic Bay from American naval base to free trade zone and site of the November

NOEL M. MORADA and CHRISTOPHER COLLIER

1996 Asia-Pacific Economic Cooperation (APEC) summit is symbolic of that shift.

Another challenge to the democratic order is the traditional oligarchy. Although Ramos and his advisers recognize the obstacle that class presents to the goals of successful development and long-term security, their efforts to overcome it are constrained by the authoritarian experience. If anything is to be learned from changing conceptions of security in the Philippines over the past decades, it is that the state should join forces with society in pursuit of security goals, rather than taking up arms against its own people.

Singapore
Realist cum Trading State

NARAYANAN GANESAN

> *The meek may not have inherited the earth, but neither have the strong.*
> *Small animals survive and thrive in the jungles, as do small states in the*
> *international order. The price of their survival is eternal vigilance.*
>
> HSIEN LOONG LEE, 1984

> *No economy can afford to ignore the rest of the world, but for Singapore*
> *trade is the essence of our existence. Our imports and exports amount to*
> *three times the value of our GDP. Two thirds of our output of goods and*
> *services go to meet external demand. No other economy in the world is as*
> *open as ours. Few others therefore watch developments in the world trading*
> *system with as close concern and as much alarm.*
>
> HSIEN LOONG LEE, 1986

Singapore's conception of security is very much in the realist tradition. Its primary security concern is its political and economic survival in an uncertain and hostile environment. Self-help (through the development of national means) and power balancing (by engaging the major powers in Southeast Asia) are critical elements in Singapore's strategy to preserve and enhance its security. This realist behavior issues from Singapore's many vulnerabilities—its tiny physical size, its consequent lack of strategic depth and lack of natural resources, its location in a Malay world that until recently was hostile to it, its recent construction as a state—and the manner in which it became independent. Its realist behavior, however, is increasingly tempered by the growing economic interdependence and stability that characterize Southeast Asia. Singapore, together with its neighboring countries, has made a concerted and quite successful effort to render the immediate environment more benign through the development of regional norms and institutions as well as through subregional and regional economic cooperation. But regional institutions and growing economic interdependence have not, at least thus far, altered the importance of national self-help. Indeed, self-help continues to be at the core of Singapore's security thinking and behavior.

Singapore's conception of security has an internal dimension as well. Internal security relates to national unity, regime survival, and political stability. The concern with national unity stems from Singapore's short history as a separate political entity, as well as its multiethnic character. More than many other countries, Singapore, it is argued, cannot take its status as a nation-state for granted. Further, Singapore's leaders currently argue that the one-party system is the only viable system for Singapore. Communalism and communism have been cited as key threats to internal security. *Communalism* refers to ethnic chauvinism, which is perceived as having the potential to disrupt Singapore's interracial harmony. The communist threat to the state has taken the form of challenges to the dominant party system as well as labor and student unrest coordinated through front organizations for the outlawed Communist Party of Malaya. Because internal and international security are viewed as interconnected, Singapore's approach to security, it is argued, must be "total." That is, it must encompass the internal and international levels and must embrace political, economic, military, and psychological dimensions:

> In the contemporary world, warfare is seldom waged on the military front alone. The Vietnam War is a classic example of how even a superpower like the U.S. may be forced to swallow humble pie because of waning public support and a weakening military will. Part of Singapore's stratagem for security is embodied in deterrence through Total Defense. The latter is predicated on the assumption that an adversary always wages other forms of warfare in addition to military actions, be it political, social, economic or psychological. In the face of total war, total defense is therefore the logical answer. (Bey 1994: 3)

Conflation of Nation-State, Regime, and Government

The security discourse in Singapore is monopolized by a small group of political leaders and the bureaucratic elite. Their definition of national security is generally not contested. With only 2 opposition members out of a total of 83 members of parliament in the unicameral legislature, there is little challenge to the People's Action Party (PAP) government in parliament. Moreover, opposition parties have, at least until now, dealt with bread-and-butter issues to broaden their support base rather than esoteric matters like security. In any event, internal and external security issues are generally taboo subjects in parliament and are often cloaked by a veil of secrecy.

The government's conception of security is not contested by society at large or by any special interest groups. The vigor with which the PAP has pursued the goal of internal cohesiveness and its virtual monopoly over government and all its enforcement agencies leaves little enthu-siasm for political participation. In this regard, the PAP's push for a depoliticized citizenry has yielded tangible benefits. Moreover, the spontaneous emergence of a civic culture with its attendant interest associations and pressure groups—associated with liberal democracy—has not occurred in Singapore. Indeed, it has even been argued that the Singapore experience nullifies the generally accepted proposition that the middle classes in developing countries are the engine for participatory democracy (Brown and Jones 1994).

Against this general backdrop, only a few groups have attempted to negotiate with the government to secure greater public space as opposed to a totally corporatized society (Rodan 1993). The first and perhaps most serious attempt to negotiate with the government came from the local Malay community. A segment within the community, somewhat displeased over the essentially PAP-controlled Council for the Devel-opment of the Singapore Muslim Community (MENDAKI) for communal self-help, inaugurated the Association of Muslim Profes-sionals (AMP) in 1990. Although the government's initial response was somewhat ambiguous, it subsequently welcomed the move and noted that it was the equivalent of MENDAKI Swasta (private-sector MENDAKI). As a gesture of support, the PAP government offered the AMP a dollar-for-dollar matching grant of up to a million dollars. The condition for the grant was that the AMP work closely with MENDAKI and promote Malay unity. AMP's relative independence from the government was short-lived, however, for leadership squabbles led to the ouster of its chairman in 1994.[1] The current chairman, who works for a major local newspaper, has generally had a more conciliatory approach toward MENDAKI, and the two groups now coexist with greater accommodation.

The second attempt to negotiate with the government was led by the Association of Women for Action and Research (AWARE), a vocal women's rights group that has long argued for gender equality in Singapore. The organization has made significant contributions by counseling and supporting local women subjected to criminal and domestic violence. It has also lobbied for equal provisions in medical coverage for men and women, prodding the public sector to take the lead.[2] The PAP government—which has long been charged with paternalism, and sometimes with chauvinism—simply refused to yield to the pressure and stated plainly that because Asian males were expected to lead the family, the benefits they derived from gainful employment should reflect that basic value. The final attempt to negotiate with the government was articulated by the Nature Society of Singapore (NSS). The society, armed with 25,000 signatures, lobbied the government to reconsider development plans for an area close to the Pierce Reservoir in 1993. Because the area was a bird sanctuary, the NSS argued there was a need to protect it. The government dismissed the petition, however, arguing that development plans for humans had to take priority over birds in land-scarce Singapore. The Ministry for National Development subsequently challenged the NSS to offer alternative plans for future housing needs.

Such efforts to negotiate with the government should be viewed as attempts to create space for the emergence of public discourse on a number of issues—perhaps a civic culture of sorts in the making—rather than as political contestation. These illustrations clearly suggest that the policies of the state, especially those relating to security, are firmly in place and that challenges to state policies are unlikely to yield substantive change. Given the general acceptance in Singapore that security is the preserve of the state, the Singapore government has generally had a free hand in matters of security.

Among the governing elite the referent of security is incontrovertibly the city-state of Singapore. But increasingly the city-state is fused with the present political system, the government, and the PAP. Through constant references to the narrow range of policy options available and to the time and resources wasted by competitive politics, the PAP government has sent clear signals to the electorate that a dominant party system best suits Singapore's political and economic interests. In light of its own successful track record in maintaining social cohesiveness and promoting economic development, the obvious implication is that the PAP government best serves the interest of Singapore. More important, there has been a concerted attempt to make the state virtually indistinguishable from the government. Given the PAP's overwhelming control of the executive and legislative branches of government and the extensive links and personal relationships between the PAP and the bureaucracy, such a fusion is tantamount to narrowing the definition of the state, and by extension its interests, to those of the PAP as a political party. Consequently, conceptions of national security can conveniently take into account the interests of the PAP. This collapsing of referents poses little problem in Southeast Asia, because Singapore's immediate neighbors (Malaysia and Indonesia) have dominant political parties and employ similar strategies. The importance of strong government and the desirability of achieving regional stability through national resilience have become part of the conventional wisdom in the region. And the Association of Southeast Asian Nations (ASEAN), which now embraces nine and will soon include all ten Southeast Asian countries, has a deeply cherished policy of noninterference in the domestic politics of member states.

The national identity of Singapore, however, is problematic. Despite Singapore's overwhelmingly Chinese population, the government avoided propounding an ethnic identity for many years, embracing instead the notion of "ethnic neutrality." There were very good reasons, both external and domestic, for this policy. As the sole "Chinese" state in Southeast Asia, Singapore has long been viewed with suspicion by its Malay neighbors. Any attempt to equate Singaporean identity with Chinese ethnicity would also be vigorously resisted by the almost one-quarter of the country's citizens who belong to other ethnic groups. While pursuing a policy of ethnic neutrality, however, the government, has encouraged Chinese cultural identity insofar as it supports political and societal structures and facilitates economic activity and investment in East Asia. The use of Mandarin has been officially encouraged among Chinese since 1979 and continues to be promoted through annual campaigns. But whenever such an identity has the potential to disrupt Singapore's multiethnic character or to provoke Malay nationalist sentiment in the region, it is suppressed. Singapore's multiethnic political parties contrast dramatically with Malaysia's communal groupings; the PAP represents itself as transcending not only race but also class, and thus as the embodiment of the nation's collective corporate interests.

It is those collective interests that lie at the core of Singaporean national identity—an identity that has been skillfully constructed by leading PAP politicians and administrators and apparently internalized by much of the population. This identity is in turn routinely reproduced as "common sense" in everyday discourse and practices (Chua 1995). Although PAP leaders present this manufactured identity as "pragmatic" and nonideological, much effort has been invested in the creation and continuous reshaping of what amounts, in fact, to a national ideology. Its starting point is the idea of "survival" in a hostile environment; the means to that survival is economic growth. Growth necessitates a strictly meritocratic state that ensures stability by suppressing primordial ethnic and class rivalries—that is, by transforming politics into administration. By contrasting its own rational management of the collective good and its effective delivery of material prosperity with the selfish squabbling of sectoral or racial interests, the PAP state equates itself, and the values it propagates, with Singaporean identity.

In the early years of industrialization, individualism was upheld as a Singaporean virtue in order to promote entrepreneurial values, but with growing consumerism in the early 1980s came a shift in emphasis to "moral education" through religion. Great weight was placed on Confucianism, not only as an explanation for the economic success of Singapore and its East Asian neighbors but also as a means of avoiding the apparent cultural decadence and perceived decline of the West. A national identity based on Confucian values failed to distinguish Singapore from its neighbors, however, and conflicted with the multicultural imperative. Since the late 1980s, therefore, Confucian ethics have given way to a reframed discourse of "shared" Asian values and communitarianism explicitly conceived as a "national ideology." A government white paper on "Shared Values," tabled in 1991, stated that to institutionalize a national ideology was to "evolve and anchor a Singaporean identity, incorporating the relevant parts of our varied cultural heritages, and the attitudes and values which have helped us to survive and succeed as a nation." Most important among these are "placing society above the self, upholding the family as the basic building block of society, resolving major issues through consensus instead of contentions, and stressing racial and religious tolerance and harmony." Although "shared values" carry no legally binding status, they do enable the PAP, through its control over the state's ideological apparatus, to propagate the conflation of regime, government, and national identity in Singapore.

Core Values

Territorial sovereignty, domestic political order, and sustained high economic growth are the three core values that Singapore's decision makers seek to protect under the label of security. Of the three, territorial sovereignty is clearly an international security concern. Although domestic political order is an internal concern, it is rationalized on the basis of international security (and is linked to the legitimation of the government although for obvious reasons it is not articulated as such). Economic growth is an international concern, but it too can serve a domestic legitimation function.

Territorial Sovereignty

Singapore's concern with territorial sovereignty is rooted in historical and geopolitical considerations. The most important such consideration is the manner in which independence was unexpectedly thrust upon the city-state (Lau 1969; Milne 1966; Ganesan 1991). Singapore, which was granted home rule by the British colonial authorities in 1959, initially achieved its independence as part of the Malaysian Federation in September 1963. Tensions at the leadership and popular levels, ethno-religious considerations, and electoral challenges led to its bitter separation from the federation in 1965. Although Singapore was ejected from Malaysia, many political leaders in Malaysia did not accept Singapore as a sovereign state. There was much residual hostility.

Tensions between Malaysia and Singapore continued well beyond political separation. Especially contentious were the dissolution of joint-stock companies like Malaysia-Singapore Airlines, the introduction of a new currency for Singapore, and the establishment of an indigenous defense force, the Singapore Armed Forces (SAF), in 1967. Singapore's postindependence relations with Indonesia, too, were turbulent. Indonesia, under the political leadership of President Sukarno, embarked on a policy of military confrontation against the Malaysian Federation from 1963 to 1966 (Leifer 1983a; Hindley 1964; Mackie 1974). Whereas most of the military skirmishes occurred in the East Malaysian states of Sabah and Sarawak, Singapore too was subjected to Indonesian hostilities. Following the trial and hanging in Singapore of two Indonesian marines in 1968 for detonating a bomb that led to the loss of civilian lives, relations between Indonesia and Singapore became even more tense. Only after the 1973 visit of Singapore's prime minister Lee Kuan Yew to Indonesia did the tensions ease (Khoon Choy Lee 1993).

The collective experiences of the PAP government in the immediate postindependence period led to a sharp sense of vulnerability underscoring Singapore's preoccupation with survival, often cynically referred to as a siege mentality. The PAP government was acutely aware of the dim prospects of eking out an independent future without an adjacent hinterland. It impressed upon the Singapore population that, given the changed circumstances, survival was truly an issue. Accordingly, "survival was adopted as a one-word political slogan as well as a main theme underlying all analyses of problems and statement of policies and intent" (Chan 1971: 48).

The PAP government's understanding of vulnerability was exaggerated by historical precedents regarding the viability of city-states. All precedents pointed toward a union with the city-state's adjacent hinterland to create a wider community. The manner of separation from the Malaysian Federation, however, made reunion an impossibility. Hence, with no preparation for independence and no possibility of remaining a part of the federation, Singapore had to fend for itself. The outcome was a city-state that did not take its sovereignty for granted and constantly emphasized survival as the first priority of both domestic and foreign policy (Buszynski 1985; Rajaratnam 1965, 1988).

The twin themes of survival and vulnerability have always loomed large in the minds of policy makers. There may be times when both themes are latent, but they are never forgotten. In articulating Singapore's foreign policy, especially in international forums such as the United Nations, politicians and diplomats emphasize the inviolable nature of sovereignty. Singapore's leaders have gone to great lengths to point out that violation of a country's territorial integrity, especially that of a small country by a larger one, is inexcusable in the conduct of international relations. The reason is clear: if such violations are condoned in the international arena, there are no guarantees to Singapore's sovereignty. In other words, the fate that befell smaller countries elsewhere could, some day, befall Singapore. It is for this reason that Singapore led ASEAN's attack on the diplomatic front in the United Nations condemning the Vietnamese occupation of Cambodia. The Vietnamese action constituted a flagrant violation of Cambodia's territorial sovereignty, a precedent that, if left unchecked, had the potential to reorder interstate relations in Southeast Asia.

Singapore's ex–foreign minister Wong Kan Seng articulated the sovereignty principle thus: "The vulnerability of a small state is a fact of life. Singapore's independent existence is today widely recognized. But to answer our basic security, we can never allow tests to our sovereignty and internal affairs, even when well intentioned, to go unchallenged. Even today we have had to occasionally remind other countries to leave us alone to be ourselves" (Wong 1988: 3). The sovereignty principle is so deeply cherished that Singapore diplomats are known to disagree with the closest of allies in international forums. An example is the invasion of Grenada by the United States, which Singapore condemned in the U.N. General Assembly, even though Singapore's foreign policy has traditionally been pro-American and vital economic interests were at stake. The difficulty involved in managing such a situation is graphically illustrated in the address of Singapore's permanent representative to the United Nations before the U.N. Security Council:

> Mr. President, it is easy enough to demonstrate our adherence to principle when to do so is convenient and advantageous and costs us nothing. The test of a country's adherence to a principle is when it is incon-

venient to do so. I find myself in such a situation today. Barbados, Jamaica, the U.S., and the members of the O.E.C.S. (Organization of Eastern Caribbean States) are friends of my country. It is extremely convenient for me to acquiesce in what they have done or to remain silent. To do so, however, will, in the long run, undermine the moral and legal significance of the principles which my country regards as a shield. That is why we must put our adherence to principle above friendship. That is why we cannot condone the actions of our friends in Grenada. The stand which my country has taken in this case is consistent with the stand which we have taken in other cases where the principle of non-interference in the internal affairs of states was also violated. (Koh 1987: 10)

In the case of Indonesia's invasion of East Timor in 1975, however, Singapore's immediate self-interest appears to have won out over principles of sovereignty, noninterference, and peaceful resolution of disputes. Although Singapore initially abstained from voting on the issue at the United Nations, it subsequently supported Indonesia's position as a fellow member of ASEAN whose "internal affairs" are not to be "interfered" with.

Domestic Political Order

It is useful at this juncture to note that the concern with survival is not exclusively international. There is a domestic component that can be traced to the electoral challenges and the labor unrest that confronted the PAP in the 1950s and 1960s. Whereas the PAP government's initial suppression of opposition political parties and organized labor was inspired by security threats arising from the terms of the sensitive merger with the Malaysian Federation, the suppression itself would lead in time to popular disinterest and abandonment of opposition politics. That disinterest combined with strong economic performance, an efficient and incorruptible bureaucracy, and a monopoly on political recruitment, left the PAP unchallenged in its dominant position throughout the 1970s. Political opposition reemerged, however, in 1981 when the Worker's Party candidate, J. B. Jeyaratnam, secured a by-election victory in Anson constituency. In 1984 the number of opposition members in parliament increased to 2; in 1991, the PAP suffered its worst setback since the 1960s with a loss of 4 out of 81 seats to the political opposition. Its popular support was eroding as well. The PAP secured only 62 percent of the total votes cast in 1991, compared with more than 80 percent in the 1960s. However, in the most recent election, held in January 1997, the PAP managed to reverse the trend by obtaining some 65 percent of the popular vote. It remains to be seen whether this reversal is sustainable. Additionally, it should be noted that the PAP's decision to peg upgrading programs for public housing projects to voter support in individual constituencies has received mixed responses. Such linkage has been viewed as unethical because the budget for such programs derives from public coffers. Critics contend that the linkage is an attempt by the PAP to utilize public funds to reward its supporters.

The earlier decline in electoral support for the PAP government led to an emphasis on domestic political order. Domestic order, which is deemed to be synonymous with political survival, is equated with the continuation of the one-party system in Singapore. PAP leaders have gone to great lengths to emphasize that Singapore's political survival and prosperity are intricately intertwined with the dominant-party system. Consequently, the present political system is articulated as being in the national interest and ensuring the political stability of Singapore.

Domestic political order also relies on internal sociopolitical cohesion. Because of the multiethnic and multireligious composition of Singapore's population and the memory of racial riots in 1950 and 1964 (as well as the 1969 race riot in Malaysia), the PAP government has been acutely concerned with national unity. Together with communism, communalism was for a long time identified as Singapore's major internal security threat. Whereas the threat of communism has ended, communalism remains. The situation is exacerbated by transnational communal links with Malaysia and Indonesia and the anti-Chinese attitude prevalent in both these countries. Ethnic Chinese communities in Malaysia and Indonesia are in the minority but have done astoundingly well economically, making them targets for antigovernment and nationalist outbursts. Overseas Chinese communities have also been viewed as a fifth column for China. Apprehensions about these minority Chinese communities also contributed to hostility toward Singapore, viewed as a Chinese island in a Malay sea.

These considerations caused the PAP government to deal with the issue of ethnicity rather carefully. Singapore has traditionally downplayed ethnicity and projected itself as an ethnically neutral technocratic state. Nonetheless, given the political baggage that Chinese ethnicity carries with it in maritime Southeast Asia, Singapore's very existence invites scrutiny from its neighbors that has implications for its security.

Economic Growth and Development

The final core value, economic growth and development, is anchored in another domestic constraint: the absence of natural resources. Unlike its neighbors, Singapore is totally bereft of natural resources save for its strategic location at the heart of international air traffic and shipping lanes. Unable to provide for even its own basic needs such as food and water, Singapore is heavily reliant on its neighbors, particularly Malaysia, as well as on participation in the international economy for economic survival. To diversify its sole reliance on Malaysia for potable water, the Singapore government concluded a memorandum of understanding with Indonesia to purchase water from Bintan Island in Riau province at a 40 percent premium in cost over the Malaysian price of treated water. Its lack of natural resources, its small market, and its potentially hostile neighbors also imply that Singapore's economic survival depends on its effective participation in regional and global economic arrangements. This situation has led the country to depend heavily on foreign markets, investments, and labor.[3] Singapore's leaders are quick to point out the vulnerabilities associated with its heavy reliance on external markets:

> As a country which is highly dependent on international trade, it is of the utmost importance to be aware of the trends and developments taking place in the global economy. The growth of protectionist trends in the major Western markets, the tendency to abandon free trade principles and the refusal of some countries to open their markets to foreign imports are some of these trends and developments which can adversely affect Singapore's growth and therefore need to be closely monitored. Economic diplomacy is diplomacy in pursuit of our economic interests, and has been used to counter the problems caused by these trends and developments. (Chan 1987: 4–5)

Economic growth and development are central, too, to the legitimation of the PAP government. In the context of the economic and political crises of the late 1950s and early 1960s, the PAP government cut its links with the radical populist mass base that helped bring it to power and crush the opposition. These measures could be made acceptable only by the promise of performance, which in turn required efficient administration. In place of a mass base, Lee Kuan Yew forged an alliance with the civil service, whose technocrats "had little sympathy for political conflict and viewed the bargaining and competition of the earlier democratic process as irrelevant distractions, potentially destabilizing for the process of economic growth" (Khong 1995: 112). By presenting itself as the embodiment of society's common interests but as independent of its conflicting factions, the government is able to justify the exclusion of popular participation in policy making. But that justification is contingent on the continued success of government policy. Should economic growth falter, demands for greater participation will multiply.

In sum, then, territoriality and sovereignty are clearly the most important core values for Singapore. But given Singapore's lack of resources and its extensive reliance on international trade, economic security is critical to the state's survival as well. Historically Singapore's international vulnerability legitimated the PAP's monopoly on political power. Consequently, a strong government with virtually no electoral challenges was projected as a necessary condition for achieving external security. With time, however, the nature of the linkage has become blurred, and the survival of the current dominant-party system is now promoted as a necessary condition for achieving international security. In other words, whereas external security considerations were once deployed to justify the political system, the PAP government now projects internal political survival as a necessary condition for external security.

With regard to scope, Singapore's security policy initially emphasized international security. That focus was born out of the state's vulnerability in the immediate postindependence period, particularly due to the strained relations with Malaysia and Indonesia. The implementation of an externally oriented security policy, however, required internal cohesion. Consequently, the scope of security was broadened to include the domestic level. The links between the various levels and dimensions are far from coincidental. Rather, through a policy of state corporatism, the various domains have been brought together. The PAP government, with its emphasis on enlightened leadership, brings to bear its collective weight to ensure that the overarching goal of preserving internal and external security is attained. Such unity of direction is indeed enviable. Economic growth nourishes the resources and consequently the instruments of policy available to the government. The Singapore government, unlike its counterparts in some countries, is faced with practically no opposition to its formulation and implementation of policies pertaining to security matters.

Threats to Core Values

The threats to Singapore's core values combine internal and external elements. Threats to territoriality clearly derive from the immediate regional environment in maritime Southeast Asia. Until the end of the Cold War and up to the time of the Vietnamese troop withdrawal from Cambodia in 1989, Singapore also perceived an ideological threat from communism. Communism, however, is no longer viewed as a serious concern. The most recent concerns with ideological threats derive from values broadly associated with Western liberal democracy such as human rights, press freedom, and political contestation. Such values are viewed as challenges to the PAP government's sociopolitical hegemony. Threats to sustained economic growth arise from challenges to the international trading regime and to Singapore's economic competitiveness.

Geopolitical Threats

Although much of the trauma of the postindependence period has been overcome, the concern with survival is kept alive by a number of factors. Foremost among them is the structural condition arising from Singapore's geographic proximity to its immediate neighbors, Malaysia and Indonesia, and the huge disparity between its endowments and theirs. Singapore's primary security concern is firmly anchored in the Malay Archipelago (Alagappa 1991a). Within this security complex, Indonesia is the dominant power and Malaysia the medium power. The microstates of Singapore and Brunei have traditionally been concerned with threats from their larger neighbors. The Indonesian confrontation and the bitter separation from the Malaysian Federation serve as stark historical reminders for Singapore. The imperatives of geography and history are extremely compelling for Singapore's policy formulators, even though the first-generation political leadership that experienced the trauma of strained external relations has, for the most part, retired from political office. The acrimonious row between Malaysia and Singapore in March 1997 over Senior Minister Lee Kuan Yew's statement in an affidavit that the Malaysian state of Johor was "notorious for shootings, muggings and carjackings" demonstrates that although the two countries have extensive and mutually beneficial linkages, there are still latent undercurrents of tension that can be expected to surface from time to time.

Further, Singapore's predominantly ethnic Chinese population (78 percent) sets it apart from its regional neighbors. Chinese ethnicity in the Malay Archipelago has a long history of association with communist insurgencies and economic domination. Political elites in Malaysia and especially Indonesia have viewed the ethnic Chinese communities as a security concern at various times (Von Vorys 1976; Suryadinata 1985, 1990). Their astounding economic success has also attracted the envy of indigenous majority populations. Although the establishment of mutually beneficial links between successful Chinese businessmen and the political establishment and enforcement agencies have deflected some of the criticisms, both Malay and Indonesian nationalism have a long history of being expressed in anti-Chinese terms.

Despite its neighbors' identification of ethnic Chinese with "the communist threat," Singapore was itself fearful of communist expansion for many years, particularly with regard to the military capabilities of Vietnam, China, and the Soviet Union. Singapore was a staunch supporter of American "containment" policy in the Indochinese peninsula and was shaken by the North Vietnamese victory of 1975, which led to the establishment for the first time of a forward Soviet naval base in the region at Cam Ranh Bay. The Soviets' enhanced ability to project naval power into the South China Sea, which meant the potential to interdict the vital shipping lanes upon which Singaporean trade and prosperity depend, represented a significant geostrategic setback. That setback was closely followed by the Vietnamese invasion of Cambodia, seen by many as a step toward the formation of a Soviet-aligned "Indochinese federation." Singapore accordingly took the lead in the protracted war of diplomatic attrition over Cambodia between ASEAN and Vietnam. The collapse of the Soviet bloc after 1989 has replaced old fears with new uncertainties: Will the United States continue to play a significant military role in the region? What are China's political and territorial ambitions now that it is freed from the Soviet threat and experiencing rapid economic growth? And how will Indonesia's emergence as a newly industrializing power affect the balance of forces in Southeast Asia?

The opportunities and uncertainties that will be created by China's development in the next decade or two are especially important and warrant discussion. Linkages with China were problematic for Singapore in the past because of the PAP government's promotion of multiethnicity domestically and because of the perceived threat deriving from Chinese support for the outlawed Communist Party of Malaya. Malaysian and Indonesian anxieties and suspicions regarding Chinese ethnicity were an added consideration. As a result, Singapore was the last country in Southeast Asia to establish formal diplomatic ties with China, doing so in November 1990.

Yet, ironically, many observers have noted Singapore's recent enthusiasm for cultural identification with East Asia and its large economic portfolio in China. Although future regional stability is clearly predicated on China's behavior on a number of issues, particularly those involving overlapping territorial claims with Singapore's ASEAN neighbors, Singapore has no leverage whatsoever with respect to how China develops. In the event that China attempts regional hegemony, Singapore will be forced to demonstrate solidarity with ASEAN and the United States to reaffirm its location in Southeast Asia as well as to continue its security linkages with the United States.

Ideological Threats

Singapore was concerned with the ideological threat posed by revolutionary communism in the 1960s and the 1970s. The communist threat was critical in the 1960s when front organizations of the CPM infiltrated the labor movement and the Chinese high schools in Singapore. Through a two-pronged policy of legislation and suppression, coupled with pursuit of the domestic policy goal of providing economic and social security, the government was able to diminish the allure of communism as an alternative ideology. By the 1980s, communist ideology had become much less attractive. In 1989 the CPM disbanded, ending one of Singapore's most serious security threats.

The government has in recent years been concerned about the ideological threat posed by Western "universal" values. In the government's eyes, those values threaten to displace traditional Asian values like filial piety and ethnic consciousness—values that the government insists have helped Singapore to achieve social stability and economic prosperity. In an effort to counter this so-called threat, as well as to bolster its domestic and international position, the government has promoted Asian (Confucian) values and emphasized the role of ethnicity in the fulfillment of social obligations. This policy, which is sometimes incongruent with the ethnic neutrality policy, is carefully managed so that it does not threaten national identity and cohesiveness, which are critical to the preservation of national unity in the multiethnic state.

Apart from the threat to ethnic consciousness and filial piety, Singapore has expressed alarm over Western advocacy of democracy, press freedom, and human rights, as well as the link between labor issues and free trade. The Western dislike for dominant-party systems, which are often interpreted as gravitation toward totalitarianism and fascism, threatens the legitimacy of the PAP government. Consequently, broad-based political participation is acknowledged as a cardinal feature of Singapore's democracy but political contestation is frowned upon. Press freedom is problematic to the extent that it challenges the government's corporate monopoly over all the news and print media through the Straits Times Press Holdings and the Television Corporation of Singapore. Notwithstanding recent efforts to liberalize the media and telecommunications industry, the government retains firm control through statutory authority. Liberal conceptions of human rights challenge the legitimacy of the Internal Security Act, which allows for detention without trial—a legacy of the Malayan Emergency (1948–60) that facilitated the suppression of the CPM. In recent times, the act has been used against secret societies and drug traffickers. Even though labor issues do not present a significant threat in Singapore, the government has lent support to countries seeking to decouple the issues of international trade and domestic labor policy. It should also be noted that the free association of labor is incompatible with the PAP-managed monopolistic organization embodied in the National Trades Union Congress (NTUC).

Communalism

Communalism, another major internal security concern, relates to the politicization and mobilization of ethnic communities. Given Singapore's multiracial makeup and its relatively short tenure of 30 years as an independent state, the problems associated with the politicization of ethnicity are very real. The problem is compounded by the anxieties in Malaysia and Indonesia over their domestic Chinese communities. Two episodes in Singapore's recent political history demonstrate the threat of ethnic chauvinism. The first of these, the Maria Hertogh riots, occurred in 1950. In that instance, the Malay foster parents of a Dutch girl abandoned during World War II contested the return of the girl, Maria, to her natural parents after the war. The English judge presiding over the case sent Maria to a Christian convent while the case was being heard in court. The Malay press, which published photographs of Maria kneeling before the Virgin Mary, stoked Malay/Muslim religious sentiment—leading to the outbreak of riots that left 18 dead and 173 injured in two days.

The second incident, referred to as the Prophet Muhammad Birthday Riots, occurred in 1964 when Malays and Chinese fought street battles against each other in the predominantly Malay area of Geylang following a religious procession held to honor the prophet. Communalist Malay agitators as well as Chinese secret societies exacerbated the conflict, which resulted in 33 deaths and more than 600 injuries. Because of the fusion of Malay ethnic identity with religion, religiously inspired conflicts often deteriorate into communal clashes. Consequently, the Singapore government has been especially diligent in its efforts to maintain interethnic and interreligious harmony.

Economic Threats

For Singapore, economic threats are as significant as political threats. Their significance is due to Singapore's vulnerabilities. As noted earlier, Singapore has no natural resources, its domestic food production is minimal, and it relies on Malaysia and Indonesia for potable water. Further, the total revenue derived from trade-related activities is three times the value of domestically generated revenue. Given such heavy reliance on international arrangements for both its survival and prosperity, any disruption to a regular flow of water, food, and trade would constitute an economic threat. It is for this reason that Singapore is especially anxious to preserve security and maintain friendly ties with Indonesia and Malaysia, the source of most of the food and water consumed in Singapore.

Disruptions to domestic production and economic challenges from the regional environment are also seen as threats. During the process of economic restructuring undertaken following the 1985 recession, the Singapore government clearly committed itself to deepening its manufacturing base. This was to be done in relation to specific sectors or niches that involved a high value-added component. Consequently, the microelectronics industry was targeted for its optimal use of land and technology in creating value-added gains. In more recent times, the silicon wafer fabrication industry has been targeted as a niche market. Any regional development that challenges Singapore's preeminent status in sector-specific industries and its overall competitiveness in high-end manufacturing is viewed as a threat.

Challenges to the current global trading arrangements—which can take a variety of forms from the abrogation of preferential tariffs to economic protectionism—are also viewed as a threat. As in the other newly industrialized countries, the political leadership in Singapore is acutely aware that domestic prosperity is largely a function of the liberal international trading system. As such, the long-stalled GATT talks caused disquiet in Singapore. Singapore's strong lobby to host the World Trade Organization's inaugural meeting in 1996, apart from generating local revenue, was also meant to demonstrate to the international community the importance of international trading regimes to the country.

Nexus of Internal and External Threats

Two of Singapore's external security threats are directly linked to domestic security concerns. International threats from Malaysia and Indonesia, with an overlay of ethnic and religious sensitivities, aggravate the domestic concern over communalism. Because the majority Malayo-Indonesian/Muslim community is the minority community in Singapore, accounting for some 15 percent of Singapore's population, there is a tendency for ethnoreligious developments in Malaysia and Indonesia to have a spillover effect on Singapore. The external threat posed by economic protectionism can also undermine domestic security if it leads to lower levels of growth and employment—undermining the legitimacy of a government that increasingly relies on performance criteria rather than ideology. Domestic insecurity is seen as providing fertile ground for external interference, particularly in situations like a breakdown in intercommunal relations. According to Kuan Yew Lee:

> The most straightforward way to destabilize Singapore is to foment racial and religious discord. In a fragile, vulnerable multi-racial society, we can never complacently assume that a free-for-all in the marketplace of ideas will magically lead to truth and enlightenment. More than once in Singapore's experience it has led to riots and mayhem....Because the Singapore government has been unwavering in pursuing multi-racial policies, and firm in taking action against chauvinist agitators, since 1969 all the races have lived together in peace and harmony. But that does not mean that we can now afford to ignore racial sensitivities. In race we must come up against deep, atavistic human instincts which will take generations to overcome. Racial emotions can still be whipped up and passions inflamed by irresponsible rabble rousing. Once blood has been shed, many years of nation building and patient strengthening of inter-racial trust and understanding will come to naught. (Lee Kuan Yew 1988: 10–11)

For the Singapore government, domestic security is a vital precondition for the achievement of external security. Consequently, challenges to domestic security have traditionally been dealt with rather harshly. National unity and domestic order are perceived to be threatened, not only by communalism, but by class formation and labor unrest as well. Class formation has the potential to rupture social cohesion and threaten the broad-based support of the PAP government; labor unrest has the potential to disrupt domestic economic production and challenge the government's monopolistic labor organizations.

The relationship between internal and external security is complex. From 1965 to 1967 a high level of external insecurity during Singapore's struggle for survival legitimated the PAP's aggressive policies to restore domestic calm. In this case a negative external security environment conferred positive benefits for the management of internal security. Similarly, the successful deflection of external security threats allows for optimal deployment of resources to ensure domestic security. Hence the manner in which a stable or unstable security environment is used to enhance internal security is a function of leadership rather than circumstance.

Thus, despite the interactive nature of the internal and external security environments, the PAP government maintains an exclusive monopoly on the choice of policy instruments to deflect external threats. Although policy planning deals with both environments simultaneously, internal security concerns are not allowed to spill over into the external security environment. Tight controls over the print and electronic media allow for this divorce to the extent that the population at large generally perceives external security concerns as the government's exclusive realm. Unless there is an urgent need to sensitize the population to an external threat, public pronouncements on such matters are carefully controlled.

Approaches to Security

Singapore's approach to its international security has several layers and embraces both competitive and cooperative policies and instruments. At the core is a policy of deterrence and defense based on power—primarily national power and secondarily that of friends and allies. Concurrently, efforts are made to resolve disputes through negotiation as well as to improve the international environment. In this connection, bilateral dialogue and political and economic cooperation with Malaysia and Indonesia have a high priority. Singapore also views multilateral organizations—subregional, regional, and global—as useful instruments to enhance its security by making the international environment more benign and promoting economic growth.

Deterrence and Defense

Singapore relies on a large citizen army of some 250,000 soldiers with an Israeli doctrine of forward defense to create the strategic depth necessary for defense. Since 1967 when the Singapore Armed Forces was first formed, Israeli military doctrine, military organization, and training procedures have had a definitive impact on Singapore's policy planners. The Israeli connection is less obtrusive now, and Singapore prefers to project the Swiss conception of a citizen army because the Israeli doctrine presupposes a hostile environment and because the predominantly Islamic neighboring countries of Malaysia and Indonesia have yet to reach diplomatic accommodation with Zionism and its physical expression in Israel. It is no secret that Singapore's sophisticated weapons systems are second to none in Southeast Asia (Acharya 1994). But the army's high profile and its sophisticated weapon acquisitions are meant to serve as a deterrent. War is a policy option only when all diplomatic avenues have been exhausted:

> Contrary to the image that some people have, the role of the Singapore Armed Forces is not just to fight and win wars, but to preserve the peace. "To fight and win all your battles is not supreme excellence" so Sun Tzu told us some 2,500 years ago. "Supreme excellence consists in achieving your objectives without fighting." The SAF must strive for this supreme excellence because Mindef's mission is to preserve Singapore's peace and security without fighting, through deterrence and

diplomacy. However, should deterrence and diplomacy fail, we must win all our battles, and secure a swift and decisive victory over our aggressors. Deterrence and a swift victory both require a fighting fit armed force operationally ready at all times. (Yeo 1994: 1)

An effective deterrent must be a credible one. In the unlikely event that the military option is utilized, the doctrine of deterrence requires the ability to deliver a swift and decisive victory. To this end, Singapore's military strategy of forward defense has undergone some doctrinal changes. In the 1970s and 1980s, the defense establishment used the metaphor of "poison shrimp" to describe Singapore's strategy: a predator fish would be subjected to a bad stomachache if it ate the shrimp. More recently, in the 1990s, the doctrine is one of surviving and winning a war. In other words, whereas military planners were once content with the prospect of losing a war and inflicting costly damage on its opponent, the new doctrine emphasizes a "swift and decisive" victory for Singapore.

The deterrence strategy of the SAF, though substantive, is subjected to budgetary constraints and the lack of training space in Singapore. Defense expenditure in Singapore is currently capped at 6 percent of gross domestic product (approximately 28 percent of total government expenditure for fiscal year 1995). To compensate for shortages in training space, the SAF uses training facilities in a number of friendly countries, including Indonesia, Thailand, and Brunei in Southeast Asia. The most recent such agreement was made with Australia for the location of ten A-4 Skyhawks in Amberley, Queensland. Another serious problem is manpower: the number of males reaching the age of eligibility for national service has declined substantially from a peak of 22,000 to about 18,000 annually. The Singapore government has sought to compensate for these limitations in manpower with technology and has also engaged in balancing through alliances and alignments.

Alliances and Alignments

After achieving political independence in 1965, Singapore continued to be a member of the Anglo-Malayan Defense Agreement (AMDA) (Chin 1974), a legacy of negotiated independence from Britain. The alliance was meant to ward off joint external threats to Malaysia and Singapore and was useful in countering the Indonesian confrontation. With the phasing out of AMDA and the British withdrawal from areas east of the Suez in 1971, a successor organization, the Five Power Defence Arrangements (FPDA), was born. The FPDA, which also included Australia and New Zealand, and is still in effect. Although the FPDA is only a consultative arrangement, it enhances Singapore's security in several ways: it knits Singapore into the Western security system, provides for air training arrangements with Malaysia, and constitutes a basis for developing a defense relationship with Australia.

Beyond membership in the FPDA, Singapore has increasingly sought to align itself with the United States. Singapore's almost militant anticommunist position and its strong diplomatic support for the United States, particularly during the Vietnam War, allowed for the evolution of a special bilateral relationship. Senior Minister Lee Kuan Yew has repeatedly stated that the United States is a benign superpower that can protect the interests of vulnerable states from the hegemonic ambitions of extraregional as well as regional powers. The Singapore government is firm in its belief that without American intervention in the Indochinese peninsula to prevent the spread of communism, maritime Southeast Asia would not have had the breathing space to secure internal cohesion and extensive economic development in the immediate postindependence period. Consequently a debt of gratitude of sorts is owed to the United States, and Singapore has not been hesitant to indicate its willingness to continue this special relationship.

An American military presence is also in Singapore's national interest. During the Cold War it counterbalanced Soviet influence; in the future it can counterbalance the growing assertiveness of China and possibly Japan. It is also a check against Indonesia and Malaysia. Hence when it became apparent that the U.S. military would vacate its bases in the Philippines, Singapore signed a memorandum of understanding in July 1989 with the United States. Under the terms of the understanding, which was formalized in November 1990, Singapore would host the Logistics Command of the U.S. Seventh Fleet (Lim 1992). Together with some 200 personnel and dependents to staff the command, the United States would deploy four F-16 fighter aircraft in Singapore on a rotational basis. Apart from embedding American security interests in Singapore, this arrangement also serves as a warning to aspiring regional hegemons. And because the Seventh Fleet performs the vital function of keeping commercial sea-lanes open between the Indian and Pacific oceans, it is in Singapore's trading interest.

Singapore's alignment with the United States has not, however, been immune to the difficulties that accompany any close relationship. In recent times, a number of issues have been brought to the fore: the debates over Western versus Asian values, press freedom, human rights, and political participation, to name a few. Notwithstanding such seemingly regular hostile exchanges involving topical issues or values, the security relationship between the two countries is strong and is likely to endure. Singapore's assessment of the United States as a benign power and its attempts to engage it within a regional balance of power imply a realist approach to the management of security. Indeed, Singapore's lack of enthusiasm in supporting the ASEAN-sponsored declaration to make Southeast Asia a Zone of Peace, Freedom, and Neutrality (ZOPFAN) in 1971 was due primarily to its realist orientation.

Improving Bilateral Relations

Singapore has sought to nurture extensive bilateral relations with Malaysia and Indonesia, the two neighboring countries that can threaten it. Since the early 1980s many contentious issues have been dealt with at the bilateral level. Such issues include the supply of potable water to Singapore, overlapping territorial claims, control of the Flight Information Regent, and arrangements to jointly develop land parcels owned by the Malayan Railway company. An important recent development is the decision by Malaysia and Singapore to refer their overlapping territorial claims to the rocky shoal where Horsburgh Lighthouse is located to the International Court of Justice for arbitration. Bilateral channels are important, too, because ASEAN does not include contentious bilateral issues on its agenda. Quiet bilateral diplomacy has instead been the instrument of choice. In the absence of ASEAN-wide multilateral consultations it is perhaps only natural that bilateral approaches have predominated.

Bilateral links include regular exchanges between politicians and senior bureaucrats as well as a number of less formal activities ranging from golf to sports meets. More important, perhaps, are the regular military exercises that Singapore holds with Malaysia and Indonesia as part of a series of confidence-building measures (Acharya 1990). Moreover, senior regional military officers are regularly invited to attend courses at Singapore's Command and Staff College at the SAFTI Military Institute.

Although bilateral interaction has increased Singapore's confidence in its relations with Malaysia and Indonesia, the legacy of separation and confrontation is difficult to shrug off entirely. The residual brittleness is evident in the tension between Malaysian and Singaporean leaders over the "remerger" issue. In June 1996, Singapore's first prime minister (and current senior minister), Lee Kuan Yew, mentioned the possibility of Singapore's reabsorption into the Malaysian Federation if Singapore's independent existence as a state should go awry. Lee's comment provoked a sustained outcry among the Malaysian political elite, who felt that his remarks were meant as a warning to Singaporeans that their future might be dark indeed if the PAP government were not reelected to power in the forthcoming national elections. Consequently, Lee's comments were construed in Malaysia as condemnation of a Malaysian political system that emphasized communalism instead of ethnic neutrality. Similarly, in March 1997, shortly after the conclusion of the Singapore general election, a defeated political candidate from the Worker's Party, alleging political harassment by Singapore's PAP government, fled to the Malaysian state of Johor. Lee Kuan Yew, who challenged the defeated candidate's (Tang Liang Hong) interpretation of political developments in Singapore, went on to identify Johor in an affidavit that was subsequently made public as a place "notorious for shootings, muggings and carjackings." Almost immediately there was a sustained and publicly orchestrated outpouring in Malaysia of grievances against Singapore. This outpouring ranged from scathing criticisms of Lee by UMNO Youth, whose leader called Lee "uncouth and senile," to widely publicized demonstrations and mass media reports calling for a review of all bilateral dealings with Singapore. In fact, it was initially reported that Malaysian Deputy Prime Minister Anwar Ibrahim, chairing a cabinet meeting on March 26 in Prime Minister Mahathir's absence, endorsed a freeze in bilateral relations with Singapore.

Regional Cooperation

Singapore regards its membership in the Association of Southeast Asian Nations as a key element of its international security policy. In the context of Southeast Asia's political history and its division in the 1970s and 1980s into a communist Indochina and a noncommunist Southeast Asia, Singapore's membership in ASEAN was helpful in deflecting the communist threat (Van der Kroef 1976). ASEAN's security policies were aimed at Indochina in general and at Vietnam in particular (Leifer 1989). Singapore's aggressive and high-profile foreign policy in ASEAN, particularly against the Vietnamese occupation of Cambodia, is well documented (Alagappa 1993).

More significant is that ASEAN provides an institutional framework within which Singapore can manage relations with its two Malay neighbors. It is conventional wisdom in Southeast Asia that Indonesia is primus inter pares in ASEAN. Less noticed is the restraining effect of ASEAN on Jakarta's hegemonic ambitions. Singapore has been perhaps the greatest beneficiary of ASEAN over the last 30 years. Further, almost three decades of interaction has led to a fair measure of ease among member states that allows multilateral problems like piracy, smuggling, illegal immigrants, and pollution to be addressed cooperatively. In this regard, multilateral forums like ASEAN have a strong normative component in institutionalizing cordial relations among geographically proximate states. This institutional approach is not antithetical to

Singapore's deterrence strategy; rather, it is meant to perform a complementary function. Singapore's reliance on ASEAN and on cordial bilateral relations with Malaysia and Indonesia is vividly illustrated in a ministerial speech:

> The uncertainties underscore the need to forge personal and institutional links at all levels with the ASEAN countries, building on the foundations that have already been established. In an uncertain world, ASEAN is the rock on which we must anchor our national survival and progress. Malaysia and Indonesia are of special significance to Singapore. The younger leaders in Singapore have consciously worked towards maintaining the pragmatic working relationships with their counterparts enjoyed by older leaders and eventually developing their own close personal ties based on confidence and trust. (Wong 1988: 6)

In more recent times, especially from the late 1980s onward, Singapore apparently has attached increasing weight to a cooperative institutional approach in the pursuit of its security. This approach emphasizes mutual gain and the observance of principles and norms in the conduct of international relations. The change is no doubt a function of the demise of the Cold War as well as the strengthening of ties with regional countries. When a country's core values, internal and external, are secure, a cooperative approach becomes more feasible.

Economic Security

Given Singapore's reliance on export-led growth and the premium it places on the liberal international trading regime, which in turn nourishes its manufacturing sector, the maintenance of economic security is extremely important. At the same time as a sustainable manufacturing sector requires cost competitiveness, it is necessary to protect the local workforce from foreign competition. These twin objectives are not entirely reconcilable. Moreover, the PAP government's emphasis on performance criteria inevitably implies high growth rates and full employment. To deflect the burden brought on by high land and labor costs, Singapore has devised a strategy of investing its hefty savings and surpluses abroad in order to gain higher returns on investment. This policy of regionalizing the domestic economy is meant to allow for sustainable high growth on the basis of repatriated profits.

The creation of the Economic Development Board to coordinate Singapore's industrialization policy was the precursor to the creation of a large number of statutory boards to attract foreign investment and remain economically competitive: the Development Bank of Singapore, the Jurong Town Corporation, the National Productivity Board, and the

International Trading Company (INTRACO) in 1968. A year later, the Singapore Institute of Standards and Industrial Research (SISIR) was established. This state-coordinated preemptive economic policy paid off handsomely over the next two decades. Between 1965 and 1989 Singapore's GNP grew by 7 percent annually while its real GDP grew by 9 percent annually from 1971 to 1980 and a further 6.3 percent annually from 1981 to 1990 (*Key Indicators* 1990; *World Development Report* 1991). Monopoly control over the provision of a number of utilities and services, as well as the proliferation of state-controlled and partially state-funded Government-Linked Companies (GLCs), have further entrenched the state in the domestic economy. A recent survey revealed that the Singapore public service, together with an array of statutory bodies and GLCs, is currently the largest employer in the country.[4]

Economic security has an external dimension, as well, because approximately three-quarters of the country's GNP is derived from trade. Consequently, since the late 1980s Singapore has been pursuing external economic opportunities in order to sprout "a second wing"— typically through the creation and deployment of joint-venture capital funds with other countries and through direct investment in other countries by way of subnational and subregional cooperation. Economic security is also sought through regional economic cooperation and membership in multilateral trade regimes. Of the regional economic ventures, perhaps the most ambitious is the creation of a growth triangle involving Singapore, the southernmost peninsular Malaysian state of Johor, and the Indonesian province of Riau (Low and Toh 1993). The scheme involves uniting three geographically proximate areas to derive economic benefits through complementarity. The former common trading area of the Johore-Riau Empire was severed in 1824 by the demarcation of Dutch and British possessions and, subsequently, the three independent successor states. Differential development under colonial rule bequeathed distinct factor endowments in the three nodes of the triangle, and those endowments are now being reintegrated on the basis of comparative advantage. Land and labor costs in Riau are as little as one-half to one-quarter of the Singapore level, for instance, whereas Singapore offers efficient financial and business services already fully integrated into global markets. The triangle is viewed as a core area for growth that can be extended and replicated throughout the region and will contribute to the crystallization of an ASEAN Free Trade Area (AFTA) (Tsao Yuan Lee 1991). As part of its policy to nurture a second economic wing abroad, the Singapore government has also pursued investment opportunities abroad by setting up industrial parks in Suzhou

(China), Madras and Bangalore (India), and Vietnam. Spearheaded by political elites, such investments typically involve statutory boards, GLCs, and local multinationals.

Demonstrating its support for multilateral trade regimes, Singapore lobbied hard for the realization of AFTA, which was initiated in January 1993. Through a scheme of Common Effective Preferential Tariffs (CEPT), ASEAN hopes to achieve AFTA by 2003. Moreover, the headquarters of the Asia-Pacific Economic Cooperation (APEC) council is located in Singapore. Despite serious reservations from ASEAN members like Malaysia, Singapore has steadfastly moved in the direction of greater institutionalization of APEC. Recently Singapore has referred bilateral trade disputes with Malaysia to the GATT Council for resolution; finally, after intense lobbying, Singapore secured the privilege of hosting the inaugural meeting of the newly formed World Trade Organization (WTO) in December 1996. Collectively these efforts reflect the importance Singapore places on external economic security (Acharya and Ramesh 1993).

Threats to domestic economic security are deflected through a high domestic savings rate. The compulsory Central Provident Fund (CPF) requires that some 40 percent of all wage earners' income be saved and pooled into a national fund to provide for the purchase of public housing that is subjected to income ceilings. A high rate of domestic saving, especially when it is held in trust by the state, allows for fiscal stimulation of the economy during a recession. The PAP government has traditionally had high regard for liberal economic theory, which emphasizes the crucial role of savings and investment in order to stimulate and sustain economic growth. Beyond the CPF, the Singapore government has accumulated surpluses that currently stand in excess of 100 billion Singapore dollars. A large portion of that amount is invested in ventures abroad through the Government of Singapore Investment Corporation (GSIC), which coordinates its investment portfolio with the GLCs.

The shortage of skilled and semiskilled workers for sector-specific industries is another economic problem. Especially vulnerable are the shipbuilding and marine industry, civil construction, and the high-technology value-added electronics industry. The problem is carefully managed through labor legislation that allows for the importation of foreign labor from traditional sources like Malaysia and Indonesia and from new sources like Bangladesh, China, and Thailand. The PAP government is mindful of the need to control the intake of foreign workers to avoid displacing locals. To achieve this goal, a foreign worker levy for entrepreneurs is carefully coordinated with a ratio of foreign to local workers. Similarly, Singapore has recruited domestic helpers from a number of countries in the region, especially the Philippines and Sri Lanka. Foreign workers presently account for approximately 10 percent of Singapore's total population of about 3 million.

Internal Political Security

The need for measures aimed at strengthening internal security is much less pressing now than in the immediate postindependence period. Thirty years of independence has allowed Singapore to achieve a relatively cohesive national identity. The corporatized control of labor through NTUC, the projection of the state as ethnically neutral and secular, the consistent application of meritocratic principles and universal criteria for the public service and GLCs—such policies are generally well received and rarely challenged. Beginning in 1984, however, the PAP government embarked on a policy of "total defense" to reinvoke national identity and sensitize the population to the link between the state's ability to respond speedily to domestic crises and the positive impact of that ability in deterring would-be aggressors (B. H. Lee 1989).

The security of the political system and the PAP is maintained in a number of ways. Beginning in the 1960s, the PAP government has depoliticized its citizenry and relied increasingly on economic performance to enhance its own legitimacy. Using the language of meritocracy and a paternalistic governing style, the government has successfully marginalized the political opposition. And by co-opting the civil service, the PAP government has achieved an identity of interests with the bureaucratic elite on which it has increasingly drawn for its pool of parliamentarians. In this regard, it would be more accurate to speak of a ruling administration in the Singapore case (Khong 1995). Moreover, the nonideological and technocratic character of the government has allowed for a proliferation of statutory boards and GLCs to tap economic opportunities and provide for the dispensation of patronage and largesse to the ruling administration. Collectively these developments have not only allowed for the survival of the political system but, more important, blurred the distinction between the interests of the state and those of the PAP.

A paternalistic ruling style couched in the idiom of meritocracy offers little latitude for political challenge and contestation. There are effectively no strategic interactions between social groups. Such groups have traditionally had no access to state power. Their interests and activities are often preempted or co-opted by government agencies or initiatives—the manner in which the AMP was gradually made to reach accommodation with MENDAKI is a classic illustration. Often, though, the sensible recommendations of social groups like AWARE are ultimately adopted by the government without due acknowledgment to the social group—as was the case with a number of policies dealing with domestic and criminal violence against women. In a worst-case scenario, a social group may be entirely bypassed in its efforts to influence policy output—as was the case with the NSS.

Problems associated with drugs have traditionally been dealt with by the legal system. Harsh penalties are imposed on drug addicts, including prison terms and lengthy stays in reformative training centers, and drug traffickers face a mandatory death sentence. Beyond these legal measures, community self-help groups such as MENDAKI run halfway houses to help addicts reintegrate into the mainstream of society. Other nonconventional threats to security do not pose a problem per se and are generally dealt with efficiently by state enforcement agencies. Land and air pollution is strictly monitored by the Ministry of the Environment, for example, and sea pollution by the Maritime and Port Authority. Illegal immigrants are dealt with by the Police Coast Guard and the Immigration Department. Smuggling is monitored by the Customs and Excise Department. Singapore's extraordinarily efficient bureaucracy has generally been very successful in deflecting nonconventional threats to internal security.

Looking Ahead

Singapore's conception of security is primarily in the realist tradition. This is partly a function of perceived vulnerabilities due to its size, domestic constraints, and strained bilateral relations with the significantly larger neighboring states of Malaysia and Indonesia. The high premium placed on external security is instructive and certainly not unique in Southeast Asia. The entire region is made up of newly independent states that jealously guard their sovereignty. Although interdependence among Southeast Asian states is encouraged, such interdependence must not challenge state sovereignty. Where opportunities can be pursued without challenging the political status quo, there is likely to be progress. Where such opportunities directly challenge state sovereignty, there is likely to be stalemate.

The dominance of realist thinking in Singapore's security conception is facilitated by an exaggerated sense of vulnerability that is constantly reinforced through policy pronouncements. This realist outlook informs policy formulation only in relation to maritime Southeast Asia, however, which is Singapore's immediate security environment. Values associated with neoliberalism, values that derive from an idealist noncompetitive worldview, are increasingly informing Singapore's security policies outside maritime Southeast Asia, especially those pertaining to economic security. Yet even those attempts can be located within a realist worldview: Singapore is preoccupied with creating strategic depth in order to compensate for its vulnerabilities.

A competitive zero-sum worldview sufficed for Singapore in the immediate postindependence period and throughout much of the 1970s and 1980s. Recent changes in global systemic structures, however, have softened the idiom of archrealism for Singapore's policy makers. Dissipation of the communist threat, both internally and externally, has led to a growing emphasis on the observation of norms and rules in the conduct of international affairs. Moreover, a competitive worldview no longer fits the requirements of a trading state whose survival and prosperity depend on an open regional and international trading system. As the country matures and as regional efforts at economic and political cooperation gather momentum in Southeast Asia and the Asia-Pacific, Singapore's conception of external security is likely to become less realist and competitive. The demands of the regional environment will require no less. Little progress can be made in trade and investment opportunities with countries that sense they are being co-opted to fulfill the security needs of a trading state. Mutual gain, rather than mutual fear, provides a better foundation for economic interdependence and growth.

The future is also likely to hold a number of domestic challenges for Singapore's security—above all the reconciliation of a national identity that emphasizes, on the one hand, ethnic neutrality, and on the other, recent public policies such as promotion of communal self-help groups that utilize ethnicity as an organizing principle. Another challenge can be seen in the PAP government's attempts to deal with declining electoral support. Such a decline may be interpreted to mean that the PAP, despite its attempts to blur the differences between the ruling administration's interests and the state's interests, has not succeeded in convincing the population at large of its indispensability for the political survival of Singapore. Finally, industrial relocation outside Singapore by multinational corporations for the sake of greater economic efficiency may undermine the compact achieved with foreign multinationals to entrench Singapore's economic security. Such a development would also undermine the PAP government's ability to fulfill the performance criteria on which it has increasingly relied to secure its legitimacy.

PART III

Conclusion

Asian Practice of Security
Key Features and Explanations

MUTHIAH ALAGAPPA

The preceding chapters investigated and explained the security thinking and behavior of central decision makers in individual Asian states. Drawing on the empirical data and the insights from these chapters as well as other published works, this penultimate chapter seeks to ascertain and explain the key common features that characterize the practice of security in Asia. It is divided into two parts. The first discusses the five key features that characterize the practice of security in most if not all Asian countries. The five features are as follows: (1) the state is the primary security referent but it is also problematic; (2) security concerns of Asian states span domestic, regional, and global levels; (3) the core security concern is political survival, which is articulated by Asian central decision makers in a broad or "comprehensive" manner; (4) self-help is the dominant strategy but increasingly cooperation and community-building also characterize the Asian approach to security; and (5) Asian practices of security have been dynamic, and more change can be expected. Taken together these five features effectively capture and represent security practice in Asia, but they are by no means exhaustive. They are also not unique to Asia: several of them characterize the practice of security in other parts of the world as well.

The second part of the chapter endeavors to explain security practice in Asia. Two propositions are advanced. First, explanations of Asian security practice must incorporate and, where necessary, integrate intrastate, unit-level, and systemic factors. In this context the history and nature of Asian political units are crucial. Without them we cannot explain the contested nature and multiplicity of security referents, the concern with internal security, certain aspects of international security, and the broad scope and changing nature of security. Yet unit-level factors alone cannot explain all security behavior. Systemic constraints and opportunities are crucial as well. Undue emphasis on any one level—as in weak-state analysis that privileges the intrastate level, for example, or in structural realism that privileges the material structure of the international system—will miss certain key aspects and distort analysis. The second proposition argues that only a combination of material and ideational factors can explain the full range of security concerns and behavior of Asian governments as well as the variations among them. Ideational factors facilitate explanation in at least three ways: first, along with material factors, they determine social reality and influence both the definition and urgency of the security problem as well as the approaches deployed to preserve and enhance security. Second, by providing key insights into the construction of actor identity and interests, ideational factors extend the causal chain, and thus afford a deeper understanding and more complete explanation of the causes and nature of conflicts. Finally, they help explain variations in security behavior across states as well as changes in the security practice of individual states over time.

Because no existing theory can capture and explain every aspect of the practice of security in Asia, the concluding section of the chapter argues for the acceptance of multiple theories—in the fields of both international relations and comparative politics—and their selective deployment to address the puzzle in question. It also argues that teaching and research on Asian security must be broad-based, integrating history, culture, economics, domestic politics, and international politics.

PART ONE: BASIC FEATURES

One of the striking aspects of Asia is its great diversity. Asian countries vary widely in terms of size, political systems, level of economic development, sociocultural values, and military capabilities. These variations, which also affect security practice, undoubtedly make it difficult to generalize about all of Asia. Despite the diversity, it is possible to cite five common features that characterize the practice of security in most if not all Asian states.

The State: Primary but Problematic Security Referent

The first and most basic feature is that the state is the primary security referent for the central decision makers and in most cases for the *staatsvolk* as well. This characteristic stems from the fact that the nation-state is the most valued form of political organization in Asia. Indeed, the idea of nation as the basis for political community and the related construct of the nation-state are viewed by the elite and the lay public as normative ideals to be achieved.[1] The existence of secessionist movements is indicative of dissatisfaction with the specific construction of states, not with the idea of the nation-state. The goal of these movements is to create new nation-states in which the fit between the new state and their ethnic or religious nation will be closer, and in which they will become the dominant group that controls state power. Relatively recent liberation from colonial rule or semicolonial status, concern that others—especially the Western powers—may seek to subvert their independence, sensitivity to the arbitrariness or incompleteness of their nation-states, and the lack of significant competing ideas or actors at the regional level that can rival the nation-state for political allegiance are among the reasons for the strong attachment to the state in Asia. Unlike in Europe, there is little cause to argue that the state is in decline in Asia. The goal of the "national" political elites is to create strong modern nation-states. There is little interest in building larger political communities. In fact supranationalism is specifically guarded against. The exception is the economic realm, where international specialization is accepted and even promoted. In some cases specialization has led to the contemplation of larger economic communities. Such economic initiatives, however, have been undertaken in the belief that they will aid in industrialization and modernization and thus strengthen the state, not weaken it.

The problem, however, is that very few Asian states, among them Japan, Vietnam, Bangladesh, Cambodia, are nation-states in the strict sense of the term. The vast majority, including the postcolonial states as well as China and Thailand, are multinational states, and a few—North and South Korea, China, and Taiwan—are divided nations. Nearly all the multinational states are engaged in the process of building nations on the basis of inherited territorial boundaries. These nation-building projects along with other factors have alienated sections of the population—the Tibetans and Uigurs in China, the Malay-Muslims in southern Thailand, the Muslim Kashmiris and until recently the Sikhs in India, the Tamils in Sri Lanka, the Chakmas in Bangladesh, and until recently the Moros in southern Philippines and the many minority groups in Burma—that have come to view the existing state and the incumbent government not as providers of but as threats to security. In these cases, most certainly the state is not the security referent for the disaffected peoples. Their allegiance may lie with alternative religious or ethnonational entities. For the people caught in between, there may be no security referent other than their own immediate kin.

In the divided nations (Korea, China, Vietnam until 1975) the immediate security referent is the state. But there also exists concern with the security of the nation that extends beyond the present territorial boundary. South and North Korea, for example, view each other as bitter enemies, but neither would condone and in fact each would be very concerned about an attack on the other by a third country. And, although the two governments are hostile to each other, neither would deliberately pursue a policy specifically designed to cause massive harm to the other's population (see Chapter 6). As pointed out by Chung-In Moon (Chapter 7), the security of the Korean nation has begun to figure in South Korean security thinking. Similarly, China is concerned about the security of the Chinese nation, which is deemed to include not only Hong Kong, Macao, and Taiwan but, in some ways, also the Chinese populations in other states. Beijing's criticism of the Indonesian government for its failure to protect ethnic Chinese during the Medan riots in 1994 is illustrative of this concern with the security of the broader Chinese nation. It must be stressed, however, that although the two Koreas and the PRC take an interest in the security of the segments of their nations that are presently not part of the current state, the security of the state is the immediate concern and it takes priority when there is a conflict of interest between the two.

Even in countries where the nation and state coincide, the state need not always be the security referent for all peoples. In the post–World War II period, there was considerable distrust of the Japanese state as an agent and provider of security on the part of left-leaning groups (see Chapter 5). Over time that distrust has abated but not disappeared. The genocidal Khmer Rouge–dominated state was not the security referent for the bulk of the Cambodian people. Similarly, in the postunification period, the Democratic Republic of Vietnam (DRV) was not the security referent for a substantial segment of population in southern Vietnam, hundreds of thousands of whom fled the country.

Further, there is a tendency among governments, especially in communist and authoritarian states, to conflate their own security with that of the state. Survival of the incumbent government is often articulated as vital for the survival of the nation-state and for the people's well-being. The Chinese Communist Party, the Vietnamese Communist Party, the Suharto government, the State Law and Order Restoration Council in Myanmar—each sees its own survival as critical for the country's political and economic survival. Any challenge to their hold on power or to the political system they represent is therefore addressed, implicitly or explicitly, as a threat to national security. This was also the case during the era of authoritarian governments in Taiwan, South Korea, and Thailand: the Kuomintang (KMT) in Taiwan; the Syngman Rhee, Park Chung Hee, and Chun Doo Hwan military dictatorships in South Korea; the Sarit and Thanom-Praphat military governments in Thailand all defined national security to include the security of their own governments. As Panitan Wattanayagorn (Chapter 13) points out, the preservation and enhancement of the monarchy vis-à-vis other competing elite groups was a crucial part of the security conceptions of the Thai kings from Rama V through Rama VIII. In all these cases, the regime has become a crucial security referent for the central decision makers but not for the groups that contest the legitimacy of the current political system.

The point is that although the state is the primary security referent from the perspective of the central decision makers, this is not necessarily so with respect to other sections of the elite and the body politic. There are many situations in which segments of the elite or population may feel alienated from the state and may identify with other ideas and entities, some of which may compete with the existing state as the basis for political community. In these situations often there are multiple and competing security referents. The arbitrariness or incompleteness of Asian states qua nation-states, and dissatisfaction with the status quo on the part of some segments of the population or the central decision makers themselves, also underlie the security concerns of Asian leaders.

Security Concerns: Domestic and International

The second feature is that both the domestic and international arenas may be sources of insecurity for Asian states. Often the security concerns in these two arenas are interconnected, and the interface is particularly important for understanding the security behavior of certain countries. Internal security concerns frequently affect the international behavior of Asian states. That, however, does not imply that all their international security concerns can be reduced to this consideration. Similarly, it would be wrong to locate all internal conflicts in the international situation—a common mistake made by outsiders during the Cold War. The key point is that Asian security concerns span both the internal and international levels. The relative salience of the levels and their interconnections vary by country, issue, and circumstances.

The Concern with Internal Security

Internal conflicts have been a prominent feature of the Asian political landscape. Since 1945 Asia has witnessed numerous civil wars, armed insurgencies, coups d'état, regional rebellions, and revolutions, and innumerable racial, ethnic, and religious riots and unrests. Many of them have been protracted; several have had far-reaching political and territorial consequences. The civil war in Pakistan led to the breakup of that country in 1971; separatist struggles threaten the territorial integrity of Sri Lanka, India, China, Indonesia, Burma, the Philippines, and Thailand; political uprisings in Thailand (1973 and 1991) and the Philippines (1986) resulted in dramatic political change in those countries; political uprisings in Burma (1988) and China (1989) posed fundamental challenges to the legitimacy of their political systems and incumbent governments. In all, tens of millions of people have been killed in these conflicts. Most of the conflicts have been perceived and addressed by governments as threats to national security; some groups and peoples involved in the conflicts, however, have viewed the government and the state itself as a threat to security. Internal security concerns in Asia may be traced to conflict over two issues—national identity and political legitimacy. Socioeconomic grievances may also be a source of conflict, but often they feed into the conflicts over the ideational basis for delineating and organizing political community and over the normative framework for the acquisition and exercise of political power.

National Identity and Internal Conflict

One key consequence of the colonial period, as noted in Chapter 2, was the transformation of Asian political units into "multiethnic territorialisms" on the basis of which present-day states have been constructed. Colonial inheritance, especially the colonial boundary, is a crucial basis for the "national" imagination of Asian political elites (Anderson 1991). It has therefore been vested with a sacred quality. In the case of China, its political imagination is influenced by its historical position and possessions and by the humiliation and losses it suffered in its encounter with the colonial powers. Any infringement of present territorial boundaries is viewed by these states as a challenge to the legitimacy of their nation-states with the potential to fragment their countries. The political meaning attached to territory explains the deep attachment to the norm of territorial integrity and the present-day rejection of the very principle of national self-determination that the Asian political elites once deployed to good advantage against colonial authorities. In the postindependence period, national leaders have argued strongly for national unity and integration. Asian political elites are committed to building nations on the basis of their existing boundaries and peoples. Regardless of the model adopted, nation-building in multiethnic Asian societies has inevitably created tension and conflict because nation-building, as noted by Walker Connor (1972: 336), is inevitably nation-destroying. In Asia, as elsewhere, nation-building has privileged certain groups and values while subordinating, marginalizing, or even seeking to eliminate others. The process has generated two interrelated types of conflict.

In the first type, the contention is over the essence and character of the nation: what does it mean, for example, to be a Malaysian, an Indian, or an Indonesian? This kind of contestation occurs in the political heartland itself and has consequences for the entire country. Tensions between the ideas of Malaysian Malaysia and Malay Malaysia, between secular India and Hindu India, between Muslim Indonesia and *Pancasila* Indonesia, fall into this category. The inclusion of an additional two million Chinese under the Malaysia project—along with the demand by the People's Action Party (PAP) under the leadership of Lee Kuan Yew for a "Malaysian Malaysia" in which all citizens regardless of race will have equal rights and opportunities—was perceived by the Malay leadership as undermining the Malayness of the nation as well as threatening the dominant political position of the Malay community. This conflict over the identity of the Malaysian nation eventually led to the separation of Singapore from Malaysia in 1965.[2] Such concerns also featured prominently in the prologue to the May 1969 racial riots in Malaysia.

In India, secular nationalists and Hindu nationalists have conflicting ideas about what it means to be an Indian (Varshney 1993: 227–61). The secularist project, which has been the official doctrine of India's national identity since independence, embraces the cultural and economic security of all ethnic and religious groups and seeks to forge an Indian identity based on the goal of a modern future, based on modernization and economic development, and on common destiny. For Hindu nationalists, Hinduism is the source of India's national identity. Muslims, who form some 12 percent of India's population, are thus the adversaries of Hindu nationalists. The tension between the secular and religious ideas of the Indian nation has been present for decades: it led initially to the partitioning of India in 1947 and resurfaced with vigor in the 1980s.[3] Similarly, a major issue among the Indonesian nationalist elite in 1945 was whether Indonesia should be an Islamic nation. Although that contest was formally resolved through a compromise formulation, some Islamic groups continued to harbor the goal of an Islamic nation.[4] The Darul Islam movements and the PRRI rebellions in the 1950s were informed by this goal among others. The tension continued into the 1980s, when Islamic groups resisted the New Order's proposition that *Pancasila* should be the sole basis for political organization. Since 1965, the New Order government, particularly the military establishment, has continued to view political Islam, along with communism, as a key threat to the unity of the Indonesian nation and state (see Chapter 15).[5]

The second type of conflict is more explicitly between the *staatsvolk* who constitute the political center and indigenous minority communities in the periphery that have a historic attachment to specific territory and who frequently constitute the majority in those areas. Some of these minority communities have historic claims to statehood as well. Nation-building, which invariably is carried out in the image of the majority community, is viewed by certain minority groups as "internal colonialism" designed to undermine their political, sociocultural, and economic identities and interests, perhaps even survival. This outlook has contributed to a rise in ethnic, racial, linguistic, and religious consciousness and disenchantment with the existing nation-state and has led, ultimately, to violent minority demands for autonomy or separate statehood. Governments and the *staatsvolk* perceive the national consciousness of minority groups and their demands as a threat to national security.

Such a conflict between the politically dominant Punjabi community and the numerically larger Bengali community over identity of the Pakistani nation led to bloody civil war, India's military intervention, and the breakup of Pakistan, resulting in the emergence of Bangladesh as an independent state in 1971 (Qureshi 1993; Jahan 1972).[6] Conflict over identity informs the armed separatist struggles being waged by Muslim Kashmiris, by several insurgent groups in the northeastern states, and until recently by Sikh independence movements in India. In Sri Lanka, the attempt by the Sinhala majority to construct Sri Lanka as a Sinhala-Buddhist nation-state (Obeyesekere 1995) has alienated the Tamil minority, who deny the Sinhala claim for exclusive nationhood.[7] From their perspective, not only is the Sinhala-Buddhist construction materially disadvantageous, but their exclusion from the definition of what it means to be Sri Lankan raises basic questions about their identity as well as fears about the survival of Tamil culture and language (Pfaffenberger 1990).

Similar considerations inform the demands for autonomy or separation by the Chakma minority in Bangladesh (see Chapter 9), the Muslims in southern Thailand (Dulyakasem 1984; Farouk 1984), the West Irianese and East Timorese in Indonesia (Hastings 1984), the Moros in the Philippines (Mercado 1984; Madale 1984),[8] and until recently the twelve minority communities (Shans, Kachins, Kayah, Rakhine, Karen, Lahu, Naga, Mon, Palaung, Pa-O, Wa, and Chin) in Burma (Steinberg 1984).[9]

In Northeast Asia, only China has been prone to majority-minority conflict over identity. The conflict is due in large measure to Beijing's attempt to incorporate and integrate the former vassal states of Tibet and Inner Mongolia, as well as the Muslim provinces in northwestern China, as part of China proper. For several reasons, ethnonationalism is on the rise among the Muslim community in Xinjiang province (Gladney 1996), and the Tibetans have been engaged in a struggle for autonomy and independence since the Chinese invasion and occupation of their country in 1951. Beijing recognizes 55 minorities as nationalities, but only as part of China. It has denied the Tibetan claim for independence and has harshly suppressed ethnonational movements in Tibet and Xinjiang.

Political Legitimacy and Internal Conflict

In all but a few states (Brunei, Thailand, and Nepal), colonial rule destroyed or marginalized traditional political systems that were almost exclusively monarchical.[10] In any case, traditional systems and structures were not acceptable to most of the elite who waged the struggle for independence. They espoused new (and largely Western) ideas for political organization: democracy, variants of socialism, communism, and, later, indigenous versions of universal ideologies, among them Pancasila Democracy, Barangay Democracy, Burmese Way to Socialism, and socialism with a Chinese face or with Vietnamese characteristics. Thus after independence, the ideological basis for the structure of political domination and the associated normative framework for the acquisition and exercise of political power had to be constructed anew. Differences in ideology divided Asian political elites during the struggle for independence and after. Ideological competition at the national level was exacerbated by the global ideological conflict during the Cold War. In several cases the competition became violent as groups that did not succeed to power resorted to armed struggle to redefine the political (and economic) identities of their states.

In the first few decades of independence, the primary struggle in Asia was between communism and an assortment of noncommunist ideological beliefs. Communist parties or movements in China, Vietnam, Laos, Cambodia, Thailand, Malaya (later Malaysia), the Philippines, Thailand, and Burma, with support in many cases from the Soviet bloc, were engaged in prolonged armed struggles to capture political power and establish communist rule in their respective countries. The communists were successful in China in 1949, in North Vietnam in 1954, and later in 1975 in South Vietnam, Laos, and Cambodia. Although the armed communist struggles in the other states gradually lost momentum, at their height they posed serious threats to incumbent governments and the political systems they advocated. All these communist struggles, except that in the Philippines, have now terminated.

That, however, has not meant the end of ideological contestation in Asia. Since the 1970s authoritarian and communist systems have been challenged by groups advocating democracy or demanding increased political participation. These challenges have not taken the form of armed struggle; instead, mass mobilization and protests designed to undermine and bankrupt the legitimacy of the incumbent political systems and governments have become common. Mass rallies and demonstrations in the name of democracy resulted in the overthrow of Marcos and the authoritarian system in the Philippines in 1986, and they contributed significantly to the democratic transitions in Thailand, South Korea, and Taiwan. Although the democracy protests in Burma (1987–88) and China (1989) did not bring about change in the political systems of those countries, they discredited the government in Burma and caused much consternation to the CCP.

Political systems are still weak or in a state of flux in many Asian countries—especially in the socialist states of China and Vietnam, in the authoritarian states of Indonesia and Burma, and in Pakistan and Bangladesh. The political systems in these and several other Asian countries are likely to continue to be problematic and subject to contestation for some time to come. Moreover, the integration of national economies into the global economy, the rapid pace of economic growth or the lack of it and accompanying socioeconomic changes, and the growing force of the principle of popular sovereignty are likely to create or exacerbate ideological conflicts, especially in socialist and authoritarian countries. The structure of political domination may also be challenged by religious forces, particularly in countries that have Muslim majorities.

In the course of the last four decades, some of the internal conflicts over identity and legitimacy have reduced in intensity or "ended," while others have arisen anew. The construction of national identity and legitimate political systems and their consolidation are long-term processes that may take decades if not centuries. There is no necessary end. Nations and systems that appear consolidated at one point in time may weaken, and the reverse can also occur. There can be "progress," but also "regress." Turbulence and change is especially likely in Asia, where a large number of states are in the midst of fundamental economic transitions. This situation, combined with possible ideational changes, has the potential to generate tension and change in social and political affairs that will also affect the international concerns and behavior of Asian states.

International Security Concerns

For almost two decades now Asia has enjoyed relative peace. There has not been a major international war since 1978–79, when Vietnam invaded Cambodia and China undertook a punitive attack on Vietnam. The end of the Cold War terminated the Soviet-American competition in Asia, ended the Sino-Soviet conflict, and brought about an international settlement (but not resolution) of the Cambodian conflict. It also localized the Korean and Indo-Pakistani conflicts and eased tensions in several bilateral relationships including those between China and India, China and Vietnam, and Russia and Japan. For the first time in five decades, no major power perceives an immediate threat from another. Compared to the Cold War era, the threat environment in Asia has been dramatically transformed. Asia, however, is not free of international tensions. Conflict continues between North and South Korea, between China and Taiwan, and between India and Pakistan. There are territorial disputes between Japan and Russia as well as China and India, and there are multiple conflicting territorial claims in the East and South China Seas. In addition there are numerous border disputes and conflicting claims over continental shelves and exclusive economic zones (EEZs). Virtually every country in Asia has such disputes with its neighbors. In addition to these specific conflicts, the ongoing power transition in Asia stemming from the collapse of the Soviet Union and, until recently, the dramatic economic growth of East Asia is a cause of apprehension among Asian countries. Much of that apprehension was initially focused on Japan; now the focus is shifting to China. Uncertainty over the future security role of the United States in the region adds to the apprehensions of some Asian countries. Thus, despite the relative peace and prosperity in the region, international security continues to be of concern to Asian governments.

Political survival, defined broadly, is still a security concern in many Asian states. It is not always precarious or urgent, however, and it takes several forms. In its most basic form, the very existence of the state as an independent political entity is under challenge. This is presently the case with Taiwan and the two Koreas: one of the two Koreas may well disappear from the political map in the next decade or two, and Taiwan too may cease to be a sovereign entity. Singapore's survival as an independent state was perceived to be precarious by its leaders in the 1960s and 1970s because of the hostility of its larger Malay-Muslim neighbors. More recently Cambodia, which has been progressively reduced from a mighty empire to a small state, feared that it would be annexed by Vietnam. But the survival of Singapore and, to a lesser degree, that of

Cambodia (and tiny Brunei) now appears assured at least for the foreseeable future. Only the existence of Taiwan and the two Koreas is threatened seriously. There is no similar international threat to the existence of the other Asian states. Contemporary international norms, as well as their own internal structures and capabilities, support their continued existence as sovereign states.

For these countries, political survival concerns fall into three categories—territorial integrity, international challenges to their political ideologies, and constraints on their autonomy. On the issue of territorial integrity, most of the concerns have to do with boundary demarcation or conflicting claims arising from the delimitation of territorial waters and exclusive economic zones. Some, like the territorial dispute between Japan and Russia, have a historical dimension. These disputes, by and large, do not affect the integrity of states in any significant manner. Nevertheless, because of the political meaning or economic value attached to them, some such disputes, like the conflicting claims in the South China Sea, may lead to limited military clashes. Only in rare cases are they likely to lead to full-fledged international wars. There are, however, a few territorial disputes—such as Pakistan's claim to Kashmir or the Philippine claim to Sabah—that, if realized, will have major consequences for the political and territorial integrity of the affected countries. Because the Philippine claim to Sabah is all but dead, presently the only grave conflict in this category is the Indo-Pakistani dispute over Kashmir. The Kashmir conflict, however, is not entirely or even primarily about territory; as I will argue later, it is very much a conflict over identity.

The second concern is with international challenges to the political ideology of some states. As noted earlier, the legitimacy of political systems is weak or problematic in many Asian states, especially in China, Vietnam, Myanmar, and Indonesia. Governments in these countries are extremely sensitive to international political-ideological threats. Such challenges deny international legitimacy to the incumbent power holders and sustain internal challenges by providing dissidents with moral, political, and in some cases material support. During the Cold War, noncommunist governments confronted by internal communist movements were gravely concerned with the threat from international communism. One tended to magnify the other, and often the two became fused. In a somewhat similar fashion, several Asian governments, especially the authoritarian and socialist ones, are now concerned with internal and international democratic challenges.

In China and Vietnam, the socialist systems are in a state of crisis and have been redefined both to permit market-oriented economic reforms and to legitimate the continued monopoly of political power by the respective communist parties. Because democracy is seen as a threat to both these purposes, the Chinese and Vietnamese governments have firmly suppressed internal democratic challenges and opposed international support for them. Western projections of democracy and human rights as universal values are perceived as a threat. The same has been the case in Burma. Following the suppression of the popular 1988 uprising and the military's refusal to transfer power to the National League for Democracy (NLD), which won a landslide victory in the May 1990 elections, many Western governments demanded that power be transferred to the NLD. In addition to imposing sanctions, they provided moral, political, and very limited economic support for the prodemocracy groups both inside and outside Burma. To symbolize the opposition of the (Western) international community, Aung San Suu Kyi was awarded the Nobel peace prize. These actions have been perceived by the State Law and Order Restoration Council (SLORC) as a threat to the sovereignty of Burma and to Burmese values, a threat driven by imperial and conspiratorial motives. At base, however, is the concern for its own survival. Although the problem of ideological challenges is less acute in the other Asian states, it is still an important issue in many of them. This concern, in part, informs the fear of globalization in South Asian states (see Chapters 4 and 11) and the negative response of the East Asian states to the West's projection of democracy and human rights as universal values and impels their own propagation and defense of Asian values (Alagappa 1994; Hitchcock 1994).

The third concern with regard to political survival is tied to the belief that sovereign states have a right to manage their international affairs independently. Threats to autonomy have been of particular concern to some small states located close to disproportionately large ones: Nepal, Bangladesh, and Sri Lanka vis-à-vis India; Burma vis-à-vis China and India; Vietnam and Mongolia vis-à-vis China; Korea vis-à-vis Russia, China, and Japan; Cambodia and Laos vis-à-vis Vietnam and Thailand; Singapore, Brunei, and Malaysia vis-à-vis Indonesia; and Brunei and Singapore vis-à-vis Malaysia. Autonomy has also been of concern to the larger countries: Indonesia vis-à-vis the larger powers; India vis-à-vis China and the United States; China vis-à-vis the United States and earlier the Soviet Union; and now Japan vis-à-vis China.

The ongoing power transition in Asia is another cause of concern to regional states. In the 1980s the focus of apprehension was a rising Japan. The possibility of its becoming a "normal" power is still worrisome, especially to the two Koreas and to China. More recently the regional

concern has shifted to China. There is considerable fear and uncertainty
as to the behavior of a rising China. Such apprehension, however, is not
uniform throughout the region. Economic modernization and the
expected increase in Indian power has increased the autonomy concerns
of the other South Asian states. More generally, the ongoing power
transition and the collapse or weakening of Cold War security mechanisms have created a sense of uncertainty and unpredictability in the
region. The concerns arising from considerations of autonomy and the
power transition are long-term in nature but they do inform the perception of the severity of the other, more immediate concerns.

Although the internal and international security concerns have been
discussed separately, several of them are interconnected. The conflict
over Kashmir is both internal and international; the international
ideological threats perceived by China, Vietnam, and Burma are connected to the domestic challenges they confront with regard to political
legitimacy; some of the tensions and hostilities in the bilateral relations
of the Malay archipelagic states are connected to ethnic tensions within
those countries. The interconnection of the concerns at the two levels is
crucial to the understanding of a substantial part of the security behavior
of Asian states and their "comprehensive" definition of security.

The Scope of Security: A Broad View

The third feature of Asian security practice is that Asian central decision
makers articulate security in broad terms. The phrase *comprehensive
security*, first coined by Japan in 1980 and used widely in the ASEAN
states, is now gaining currency in most other Asian states as well.
Though labels and interpretations vary, comprehensive security generally implies that security goes beyond (but does not exclude) the military
to embrace the political, economic, and sociocultural dimensions.
Comprehensive security in the Japanese interpretation implies that the
pursuit of security requires not only the deployment of military power
but also "political power, dynamic economic strength, creative culture,
and thoroughgoing diplomacy" (Prime Minister Ohira, quoted in Akao
1983: 10). *Ketahanan nasional*—the Indonesian security doctrine articulated by the Suharto government after it came to power in 1966—posits
that security has political, economic, sociocultural, and military aspects,
that threats to security can issue from the domestic as well as the
international environment, that these are frequently interconnected, and
that the approach to security must be multidimensional (Alagappa 1988;
see also Chapter 15). "Security," according to the Malaysian Prime
Minister Mahathir Mohamad, "is not just a matter of military capability.

National security is inseparable from political stability, economic success, and social harmony. Without these all the guns in the world cannot prevent a country from being overcome by its enemies, whose ambitions can sometimes be fulfilled without firing a single shot."[11]

Since the early 1980s, China too has articulated security in broad terms and accorded greater emphasis to economic development and technology in the belief that national security depends on the nation's overall strength, not just its military might (see Chapter 3). China's definition of comprehensive security includes social and political stability. Comprehensive security, along with common and cooperative security, appears to have become more significant in the Chinese articulation of security in the post–Cold War period. More recently Vietnamese and South Korean leaders have begun to articulate security in broad terms as well (see Chapters 14 and 7, respectively). Indeed, it is possible to argue that comprehensive security is emerging as a norm in Asia. The comprehensive view of security in Asian states is more than just rhetoric—it does affect policy and behavior—but it is not an operational concept. It is better viewed as an intellectual foundation for thinking about security at the highest levels of government, with consequences for the determination of national priorities, including budgetary allocation, and the strategies to be deployed in the pursuit of security.

Political Survival: The Core of Comprehensive Security

For most states, the core component of comprehensive security is still political survival. This problem, however, is seen in holistic terms, and the political rather than the military dimension receives top billing. Political survival is thus defined to include not only international autonomy and territorial integrity but also one or more of the following: national unity, political stability, social harmony, law and order, protection of the existing political system, and survival of the incumbent government. Threats to these values are perceived to issue not only from other states but also from within the state. Such threats may be political, sociocultural, economic, or military in nature. The approach to political survival must therefore combine political, sociocultural, economic, diplomatic, and military measures.

Underlying the notion of comprehensive security is the belief that survival and prosperity are better served by all-around strength than by reliance on military power alone, the utility of which is perceived to be limited and becoming more circumscribed. This does not imply that military power is unimportant. In fact, one purpose of Tokyo's comprehensive definition of security was to develop the hitherto neglected military dimension and facilitate military cooperation with the United States (see Chapter 5). And, as will become evident from later discussion, the development of national military capabilities is commanding greater attention among Asian states in the post–Cold War era. Rather, comprehensive definitions of security are in some ways reactive and meant to draw attention to other aspects that have often been omitted in traditional definitions of security, especially during the Cold War, and to locate the military dimension in proper perspective. The dissolution of the Soviet Union, commonly attributed to its political and economic weakness, has reinforced the belief that security must be viewed in broad terms. The view of national power in broad terms—military, economic, demographic, geographic, diplomatic, and so forth—is similar to the earlier political realist view of power.

Economic and Sociocultural Security: The Nonconventional Dimensions

The security concerns articulated by Asian states often include economic and sociocultural security. Environmental security, except in the case of Bangladesh, does not figure in the national security agendas of Asian states—and even in Bangladesh it is an offshoot of the conflict with India over the sharing of transnational water resources. Among the nonconventional dimensions, economic security has very high priority.

Economic Security

Though frequently used, the term *economic security* is seldom defined. Most commonly it refers to the promotion and safeguarding of national prosperity. In Japan, *economic security*, when the phrase gained currency in the early 1970s, denoted the concern with "safeguarding the economic prosperity that was attained in a period of low-cost energy and other resources." In China, economic security relates to the drive to modernize and expand the economy. In the Philippines, economic security in the Ramos administration refers to "recovery and growth." In South Korea, it pertains to enhancing international competitiveness. Notwithstanding the lack of definition, economic security as articulated by Asian states has two aspects. First, economic growth, development, and other such goals are viewed as national priorities in their own right. Second, they are also viewed as a means to address security concerns associated with political survival. "Security through development" is a commonly accepted principle in many Asian states. Thus economic security is seen in the following roles: as a key element in augmenting national power, prestige, and influence and as a prerequisite for the development and sustenance of diplomatic and military power; as enabling governments to discharge their welfare function; as a critical resource for political and social stability and for enhancing national resilience; as a critical legitimation resource; and finally, as having the potential to deepen international economic interaction and through it to ameliorate the security dilemma and mitigate traditional security concerns.

Perceived threats to economic security vary with the circumstances of each country. For Japan in the 1970s, in light of its resource dependence and the international oil shock, the worrisome issues were interruptions in the supply of oil and the steep rise in oil prices. Its goal then was to ensure a steady supply of reasonably priced resources. In the 1980s, the dramatic appreciation in the value of the yen and the increasing difficulty of gaining access to markets in the United States and Western Europe emerged as critical concerns. For the export-oriented developing ASEAN countries, access to capital, technology, and markets, a stable exchange rate system, and an open, stable international trading system are critical. Developments, intentional or otherwise, that disrupt those conditions tend to be perceived as threats to their economic security. The initial concerns in many Asian countries over NAFTA and Europe 1992, for example, were precipitated by a fear of trading blocs. Dumping, asymmetric interdependence, smuggling, and international economic espionage have also been described as factors that undermine economic security.

Sociocultural Security

Large-scale migration, drugs, and cultural imperialism are among the sociocultural issues that have been cited as threats to security. Large-scale migration—the estimated two to six million Bangladeshis in the northeastern states of India, for example, or the presence of some half a million Filipinos in Sabah (Malaysia)—is of concern because of its perceived negative impact on the cultural and political identity of the receiving peoples and by extension their control of political power (Weiner 1995; see also Chapter 4). Large-scale migration is also seen as a social and economic burden and contains the seeds of tension and conflict between the sending and receiving countries. The mass migrations of Bangladeshis and Filipino Muslims, for example, have been a source of political unrest in the Northeastern Indian states (especially Assam) and in Sabah, respectively, and tensions have grown between those states and their federal governments. At times they have also generated tensions between India and Bangladesh and between Malaysia and the Philippines.

Drug trafficking and addiction are major concerns of some states.

Indeed, Malaysia at one point identified the drug problem as the number-one threat to national security. Drug addiction is perceived as having the power to undermine national vitality and productivity and even to subject the country to foreign domination. Memory of the Opium Wars and their role in China's subjugation informs Beijing's concern with the drug-related threat. Revenues from the narcotics trade are also believed to support criminal and terrorist activities to the detriment of law and order and, at worst, to support insurrections, insurgencies, and warlordism. Such problems are especially serious in Pakistan, Burma, and Sri Lanka, but they are also present in many other states. Finally, many Asian states are concerned with cultural threats—especially from the West—because of their possible negative consequences for social and political stability, the social essence of the nation, or regime legitimacy. Because their effects are often diffuse and protracted, sociocultural security concerns often, though not always, rank below threats to political survival and economic security.

Strategies

The threat or use of force is not viewed as relevant to promoting economic growth or safeguarding prosperity. No Asian government envisages a military attack on another to gain access to resources or markets. The limited use of military force in pursuit of the conflicting territorial claims in the South China Sea does not invalidate this assertion. The issue of contention in the South China Sea is sovereignty and territorial claim. That the disputed islets may have oil and other resources as well as strategic value increases the stakes. But this situation is different from one in which one country engages in military conflict with another to gain access to markets or resources. Similarly, autarky is no longer an option. Although some Asian countries still seek to protect certain sectors, all except North Korea have opened up or are in the process of opening up their economies and are pursuing international strategies. There is a strong interest in maintaining a free and open global multilateral trading system. The forum for Asia-Pacific Economic Cooperation (APEC) was in the forefront of the push for a successful conclusion of the Uruguay Round. Despite opposition from certain domestic constituencies, all the major Asian economies except China and Taiwan, both of which are eager to join the WTO, have signed the resulting agreement. At the urging of the Asian countries, APEC has adopted the concept of open regionalism to guide economic cooperation in the region.

Military force is one way that states address certain sociocultural security concerns—as in border control to prevent illegal immigration, piracy, and smuggling, for example, and in combating warlordism and terrorism. But political, legal, sociocultural, and economic measures at the national, bilateral, and regional levels are far more significant in addressing sociocultural issues. To counter cultural threats, for example, Asian states have deployed the following measures: mobilization of nationalism; expounding the virtues of indigenous values while high lighting the shortcomings of "foreign" ideas; strict regulation of the media; defining the bounds of political and nonpolitical organizations; employing political, legal, and police coercion. Asian governments have also acted in concert in international forums such as the World Conference on Human Rights and have supported governments like those in China and Burma that have been the target of Western political and economic pressure and sanctions.

Unlike the problems associated with political survival, the nonconventional security concerns are frequently not zero-sum in nature. Often states have a common interest in resolving them though bilateral and regional cooperation. The fact that force is irrelevant in addressing economic security and certain sociocultural concerns does not, from the perspective of the Asian political elite, prevent those issues from being regarded as security concerns. In other words, differences in the nature of the problem, the mind-set, and instruments of policy are not of consequence in assessing an issue as a security concern. What matters is the impact on national well-being as judged by the incumbent government.

Approach to Security: Competition and Cooperation

The fourth feature of Asian security practice is that it is characterized by both competition and cooperation. In response to the multidimensional nature of the problems of identity, legitimacy, and socioeconomic grievances, Asia's central decision makers deploy a wide array of measures—political, legal, economic, sociocultural, and military—to cope with internal security challenges. Although the specific combination varies, a carrot (economic development, power sharing, limited autonomy) and stick (legal and military suppression) approach has been common. Secession is ruled out, and autonomy is offered only after much blood has been shed. These aspects have been discussed in earlier sections.[12]

The focus in this section is on the Asian approach to international security that is characterized by a mix of coercion, dialogue, and cooperation. Self-help, especially in the form of alliance or alignment with one of the two superpowers, was the prominent strategy during the Cold War period. Beginning in the early 1980s, greater emphasis was placed on national self-reliance. That policy has become more pronounced in the post–Cold War era, although alliances continue to be critical for countries like Japan, South Korea, and Taiwan.[13] The changed threat environment and the dissolution or weakening of Cold War security arrangements have fueled recent interest in subregional and regional security cooperation. Though still in a nascent phase, cooperative security—the idea that security need not always be zero-sum and can be achieved through cooperation—is becoming an important component of the national security strategies of Asian states. For the short term, however, cooperative security in Asia will be a strategy for conflict prevention through confidence- and security-building measures and for shaping the normative structure rather than for the containment or termination of conflict.

The Dominance of Self-Help Strategies

Alliance and alignment were the key security strategies during the Cold War (see Chapter 2). Most Asian states allied themselves with one of the two superpowers. Several reasons underlay the prominence of alliance strategies during the Cold War. Asia was a high-threat environment: most Asian governments perceived urgent political-military threats to their national security from neighboring states. Asian states were weak, however, and unable to counter such threats on their own. Because the two superpowers, particularly the United States, were ready allies, alliance became the dominant strategy. There was no real alternative. India, Indonesia, and Burma initially opted for a strategy of non-alignment, but that ceased to be a viable option in the face of serious threats. The crucial rationale behind the alliance strategies of China, India, Vietnam, Pakistan, South Korea, and North Korea was not the regional or global distribution of power but the presence of threats. Although the capabilities of conflicting states entered into the calculation of severity, the threat perception itself was informed by considerations of identity, history, and specific conflicts of interest. All these considerations shaped the states' perceptions of the intentions of adversaries.

After the Cold War: Greater Emphasis on National Self-Reliance

Beginning in the early 1980s there was greater emphasis on national self-reliance, a trend that has become more pronounced following the termination of the Cold War. Several factors account for this change: transformation of the regional threat environment; reassessment of national security threats; increased national capability, often accompanied by strong nationalism; and the nonavailability of allies.

Although Asia continues to experience conflict and tensions, they are localized, much less interconnected, and limited in escalation potential compared to the Cold War period. Whatever their long-range apprehensions, none of the major players perceives any immediate threat from each other. Moreover, the political survival of most Asian countries is not seriously challenged. Even in the Korean, Taiwan, and Indo-Pakistani conflicts there is stalemate. In short, there is relative peace and Asia has been transformed from a high-threat to a low-threat environment. Concurrently, the national power resources of most East and Southeast Asian countries have increased dramatically. This state of affairs contrasts sharply with the earlier period when most Asian states were weak and dependent on one of the two superpowers—making for asymmetrical or "patron-client" alliance relationships. Today there is much greater pride, more self-confidence, and a growing desire to be more self-reliant and avoid the vulnerability that results from reliance on another country for security. The strong wave of nationalism in Asian states also supports the development of independent national capabilities.

Another critical factor is the nonavailability or unreliability of allies in the post–Cold War era. With the collapse of the Soviet Union and the changed orientation of Russia, all Moscow-centered alliances in Asia have been terminated. The United States, no longer engaged in a global ideological-cum-military struggle and increasingly consumed by domestic matters, is much less willing to take on new commitments. In fact, it seeks to redefine some of the earlier arrangements such as the U.S.–Japan security treaty. For several reasons, many Asian leaders think that Washington will gradually reduce (but not withdraw) its security role in East and Southeast Asia, and that belief has engendered a credibility gap despite numerous public pronouncements to the contrary by American officials (Halloran 1995). At the same time no Asian state has presented itself as a firm and credible ally of other Asian states. It is not surprising, then, that self-reliance should command more attention than the strategy of alliance.

The Buildup of National Military Capabilities

This emphasis on self-reliance is reflected in the buildup of national military capabilities. As indicated in Table 11, considerable resources are devoted to the defense sector. However, contrary to some assertions (Klare 1993; Segal 1992), there is no arms race in the region. Only in a few cases where political survival concerns are acute—the two Koreas, Taiwan, and India-Pakistan—is arms acquisition directly driven by considerations of threats and relative capabilities. Otherwise arms acquisition in the region is driven by several considerations, most of which do

TABLE 11

Defense Expenditure and Military Manpower of Asian States

| | Defense expenditure (millions of U.S. dollars) | | | Percentage of GDP | | | Estimated number of persons | | | | |
| | | | | | | | Armed forces (thousands) | | Reservists (thousands) | Paramilitary (thousands) |
	1985	1994	1995	1985	1994	1995	1985	1995	1995	1995
China	$ 27,107	$ 28,945	$ 31,731	7.9%	5.6%	5.7%	3,900.0	2,930.0	1,200.0	1,200.0
India	8,553	7,638	8,289	3.0	2.5	2.5	1,260.0	1,145.0	950.0	1,004.5
Japan	29,350	46,639	50,219	1.0	1.0	1.1	243.0	239.5	47.9	12.0
North Korea	5,675	5,660	5,232	23.0	26.6	25.2	838.0	1,128.0	4,700.0	115.0
South Korea	8,592	12,764	14,359	5.1	3.3	3.4	598.0	633.0	4,500.0	8.0
Taiwan	8,793	11,457	13,136	7.0	4.7	5.0	444.0	376.0	1,657.5	26.7
Indonesia	3,197	2,486	2,751	2.8	1.6	1.6	278.1	274.5	400.0	174.0
Malaysia	2,409	3,142	3,514	5.6	4.4	4.5	110.0	114.5	58.3	25.8
Singapore	1,622	3,118	3,970	6.7	5.0	5.9	55.0	53.9	221.0	11.6
Philippines	647	1,117	1,151	1.4	1.7	1.6	114.8	106.5	131.0	42.5
Thailand	2,559	3,630	3,896	5.0	2.5	2.5	235.3	259.0	200.0	161.5
Vietnam	3,277	992	910	19.4	5.1	4.3	1,027.0	572.0	3,000.0	50.0
Brunei	280	263	268	6.0	6.0	6.0	4.1	4.9	0.7	4.1
Pakistan	2,835	3,585	3,642	6.9	6.9	6.5	482.8	587.0	513.0	259.0
Bangladesh	341	475	500	1.4	1.8	1.8	91.3	115.5	n.a.	55.0
Sri Lanka	311	526	624	3.8	4.4	4.9	21.6	125.3	4.2	110.2

NOTE: Expenditures are based on 1995 constant dollars.
SOURCE: *The Military Balance 1996–97*. Oxford University Press for The International Institute for Strategic Studies, 1996.

not relate to threat perceptions and power balancing (Ball 1996). Further, although military modernization is receiving greater attention, it is still subordinate to the goal of economic modernization. Military modernization is likely to be downgraded if economic growth slows or falters. And the military capabilities being acquired, when viewed in a broader context, are not substantial.

Among the reasons cited in support of the proposition that an arms race is under way in Asia, two are prominent: one is high defense spending (the double-digit increases in the Chinese defense budget; the defense budget of Japan, which in absolute terms is the second-highest in the world; and the increase in the defense spending of certain Southeast Asian states), and the other is the acquisition of sophisticated platforms and weapons systems (China's acquisition of SU-27s, SU-30s, and cruise missile platforms, its possible acquisition of aircraft carriers, the air and naval acquisitions of some of the ASEAN countries). A closer examination, however, reveals the weakness in these arguments. Although Japan's defense spending is high in absolute terms, as a proportion of gross domestic product it has dropped to less than 1 percent. Further, much of the allocation goes toward the cost of personnel and for support of the American military presence in Japan. And Japanese capabilities are designed for immediate self-defense and to complement American strategy in the region, not to support a national vision or to compete with a specific state. Similarly, although China's defense spending is increasing, it is starting from a small base, and the Chinese air and naval forces still have many daunting problems to overcome.[14] The air and naval capabilities being acquired by the Southeast Asian states, except those of Singapore, are not substantial, and they are not directed at addressing or balancing any specific threat. Some countries, such as India (despite its perception of threat from China and New Delhi's interest in competing with Beijing) and Vietnam, have actually slowed if not halted the increase in defense spending to divert resources to other priorities. My purpose here is not to downplay military spending and acquisitions, but to put them in proper perspective. National capabilities, though being built up, are still relatively weak and inadequate in many states.

The Continuing Relevance of Alliance Strategies

Although South Korea and Taiwan have become stronger, they cannot address their security threats on their own. Alliance with and, in the case of Taiwan, informal commitment from the United States continue to be critical to their security strategies. Moreover, the U.S. commitment to these countries is firm. Although the United States has no formal treaty commitment to defend Taiwan, it is opposed to a forceful takeover by the PRC. That policy was made clear by the deployment of two U.S. aircraft carriers in response to the 1996 Chinese missile test firings designed to intimidate Taiwan during its first presidential elections. Japan continues to attach great significance to its alliance with the United States. Although the bilateral alliance suffered some erosion in the 1980s and early 1990s, the U.S.–Japan security treaty has since been reaffirmed and strengthened. If the China threat to Japan becomes more substantial, the U.S.–Japan security treaty may become even stronger.

The strategy of alliance, however, is not a viable option for all states, at least not to the same degree as that available to South Korea, Japan, and Taiwan. Pakistan, for example, which seeks to counter the perceived Indian threat through external balancing, has found it difficult to maintain a strategic relationship with the United States in the post–Cold War era (see Chapter 10). Because India is a common concern in both countries, Islamabad has been relatively more successful in maintaining strategic relations with Beijing. But even here, China has sought to improve relations with India and has adopted a more balanced position in the Indo-Pakistani conflict. In general it seeks to avoid involvement in South Asian disputes. In Southeast Asia, Thailand and the Philippines continue to have formal bilateral security treaties with the United States, but the vitality of those treaties is much eroded when compared to earlier periods. In Southeast Asia, the United States suffers a credibility gap. Malaysia and Singapore, along with the United Kingdom, Australia, and New Zealand, continue to be members of the Five Power Defence Arrangements. But this is a consultative arrangement and not critical to the security of Malaysia or Singapore.

Among the major powers, except for Japan, the strategy of alliance is not an option. India is concerned with the growing power of China but it has no credible ally or strategic partner. It has attempted, not very successfully, to maintain strategic relations with Russia, and has also improved relations with the United States (though New Delhi remains wary of Washington). China, concerned with American hegemony in East Asia, has entered into a strategic partnership with Russia. But such partnerships are weak and cannot be termed as alliances or even alignments. There are also several tension points in the bilateral relations among these countries. Rather than enter into alliance arrangements, the major powers, by and large, have attempted to improve relations with one another including their perceived adversaries. The nonavailability or distrust of alliance arrangements combined with the relative weaknesses of national capabilities, the general apprehension in the region about uncertainty and unpredictability, and the ideational changed noted earlier have fueled Asian interest in cooperative security.

The Emergence of Cooperative Security

Regional security cooperation is new to Asia. As noted in Chapter 2, multilateral cooperation and international law were not features of the historic "interstate" systems in Asia. Regional security cooperation began in Southeast Asia, where it is most advanced, but such efforts are also under way in South Asia and indeed throughout the Asia-Pacific region.

Southeast Asia: The Broadening and Deepening of Cooperation

The initial purpose of cooperation in Southeast Asia was not to supplant the alliance arrangements of member countries but to supplement them.[15] Because of this and other considerations there has been no effort to develop collective security or collective self-defense schemes in Southeast Asia. Rather, cooperation has been directed toward building trust and confidence among member states, developing principles and norms to govern their interaction, preventing disputes from degenerating into open hostilities, developing mechanisms for pacific settlement of disputes, and bolstering the collective political and diplomatic weight of the ASEAN countries. ASEAN's success in some of these efforts has transformed it into a partial pluralistic security community. In the post–Cold War era ASEAN's membership has broadened to include Vietnam (1995), Myanmar (1997), and Laos (1997).[16] ASEAN has also committed itself to realizing the ASEAN Free Trade Area (AFTA) agreement by 2003. Although considerations of national interest were initially the driving force behind ASEAN, the collective interests of ASEAN have begun to figure significantly in the thinking of the member countries. ASEAN identity and ASEAN interests remain subservient to the national identity and interests of member states, however, and this is unlikely to change soon. Nevertheless, cooperation through ASEAN has become an important component of the security strategies of the ASEAN states. ASEAN's past successes have also enabled it to assume a lead role in the development of security cooperation at the broader regional level through the ASEAN Regional Forum.

Asia-Pacific: The Beginning of Multilateral Security Cooperation

With the termination of the Cold War, cooperative security has begun to command broader attention in the Asia-Pacific region. Interest in cooperative security is not uniform, however: the ASEAN states and Japan are more enthusiastic than the others. ASEAN's interest in regional security cooperation is driven by several considerations: the growing nexus between Northeast and Southeast Asia and a recognition that Southeast Asian security cannot be addressed in isolation; concern over the fluidity and uncertainty in the regional strategic environment produced by the ongoing power transition; a desire to constrain and constructively engage the major powers (especially China); the weakening and, in some cases, collapse of Cold War regional security arrangements; and a wish not only to be involved but to take a lead role in building a new regional security architecture. Tokyo's interest in Asia-Pacific security cooperation has several purposes: to ensure the continued engagement of the United States in Asia; to participate more actively in the management of regional security; to secure domestic and international legitimacy for a greater Japanese political and security role; to broaden the choice of policy platforms available to Japan; and to engage and constrain the behavior of China.

Beijing's initial reaction to the ASEAN-Japan initiative on regional security cooperation was lukewarm. Although eager to participate in multilateral economic institutions, which it views as beneficial, China is generally suspicious of multilateral security arrangements. Fearing institutional "taming" and "entrapment," Beijing prefers the bilateral approach: such a strategy favors China in relation to most Asian states and also prevents the other states from ganging up against it. Nevertheless, several considerations—the fear of being left out, the desire to prevent such a forum from developing into an anti-China organization, the prospect of regulating the pace and agenda of the forum from inside, and considerations relating to its international image, prestige, and legitimacy—eventually led to Chinese participation in regional security cooperation. Such participation, however, was characterized by caution. Over time, perceiving the benefits of such cooperation (constraining the United States, for example), China has become more supportive of Asia-Pacific security cooperation.

For several reasons, the United States under the Bush administration was opposed to regional security cooperation. Washington preferred the hub-and-spoke approach to security in Asia, with Washington, of course, as the hub (Baker 1991–92). Only under the Clinton administration did U.S. policy change. Not wishing to be seen as the sole opponent of an Asian initiative, and persuaded that regional cooperation can serve American national interests by setting the rules of the road in an environment where the United States is still the predominant power, and also wishing to satisfy Tokyo, Washington supported the ASEAN-Japan initiative that led to the formation of the ASEAN Regional Forum (ARF) in July 1994 (Lord 1993).

These mixed motives—largely rationalist—have shaped the purpose, scope, and pace of regional security cooperation, which are all very modest. According to the chairman's statement issued after the inaugural meeting, the ARF is characterized as a high-level consultative forum to "foster the habit of constructive dialogue and consultation on political and security issues of common interest" and to make significant contributions toward "confidence-building and preventive diplomacy in the Asia-Pacific region" (ASEAN Regional Forum 1994). The agenda of the ARF includes confidence-building (essentially transparency) measures, preventive diplomacy, nonproliferation and arms control, peacekeeping, and the prevention of maritime disaster. Even in these areas, the targets, guided by the lowest common denominator, are modest and to be achieved gradually over a period of five to ten years. There is no grand scheme such as a projected regional community, a concert of powers, a collective security umbrella, or collective self-defense arrangements. There is not even a mechanism to resolve outstanding disputes.

The Role of Cooperative Security

In the spectrum of conflict management strategies, cooperative security is assigned a significant role only in conflict prevention among participating states.[17] Conflict containment and conflict termination are to be handled outside the ARF by appropriate states and arrangements. The ARF may, however, legitimate certain initiatives by endorsing them—as, for example, the informal multilateral workshop on the conflicting claims in the South China Sea, organized by Indonesia. The primary purpose of the ARF, however, is to contribute to conflict prevention by facilitating communications, providing information, increasing transparency, and reducing uncertainty. Even in that realm, its immediate goal is not to institute far-reaching security regimes but to help create a normative context that can lead to the emergence of such regimes in the future.

For the present, at least, cooperative security will be just one component in the national security strategies of Asian states. It will supplement rather than supplant national capabilities and alliances. Certainly the major powers (the United States, China, and now increasingly Japan) view it as an adjunct to their national capabilities and alliance systems. This, however, does not mean it is unimportant. As noted in Chapter 2, analysts often highlight the weakness of Asian regional institutions in addressing regional security problems. Often these weaknesses are emphasized in comparison with European institutions. Such a comparison is misplaced. The comparison should be with the Asia of the past, not with Europe. On that basis there is a relative abundance of formal institutions and an even greater abundance of nongovernmental institutions in Asia today than even a decade or two ago. Asia has in fact come quite a long way in a short time. Gradually, the regional institutional context is likely to become more dense and more consequential for the international behavior of states.

The national security strategies of Asian states, then, are becoming broader and more complex. Although strategies of self-help are still important, the norm of cooperative security is gaining ground. In addition to bilateral and multilateral cooperation focused directly on security, increased economic interaction and cooperation are also being encouraged in the belief that growing economic interdependence will strengthen ties, improve the material welfare of people in the affected areas, and generally help to ameliorate historical animosities and reduce traditional security concerns. Examples of economic cooperation with a strategic purpose include the various growth-triangle initiatives in Southeast Asia, the nordpolitik of South Korea, and the economic policy of Taiwan toward China.[18] The possible downside of such cooperation—tension issuing from considerations of relative gain, vulnerability issuing from increased dependence—is recognized. But the hope, at least for now, is that the benefits will outweigh the costs.

The Dynamic Nature of Asian Security Practice

The final feature of Asian security practice is its dynamic nature. Security practice in Asian states has undergone substantial changes in the course of the last three or four decades. Changes have occurred in the referent, the scope, and the approach to security. In countries such as Indonesia, Thailand, Malaysia (less Sabah), Singapore, and Bangladesh, where the identity of the nation has become consolidated in comparison to the early postindependence period, the nation-state, notwithstanding the grievances on the peripheries, has become more acceptable as the security referent for the vast majority of people. In most of these states there has been a noticeable shift in their security concerns from the domestic to the international level. In other states like Sri Lanka, contestation over national identity has become more severe, and ethnonationalism is on the rise among the Tibetans and Uigurs in China. The Indian case is complex. The vast majority of people who reside within the national boundary have come to accept themselves as part of the Indian nation. A substantial segment of the Muslim Kashmiris, however, continue to resist integration, and their struggle has become more intense in the 1990s. For them, the Indian nation has progressively ceased to be the security referent. The identity of the Sikhs as part of the Indian nation, earlier taken for granted, became problematic in the 1980s. The rise of Hindu fundamentalism may undermine the allegiance of the minority Muslim community to the Indian nation. In these three states (Sri Lanka, India, and China), concern with internal security has become more prominent (see Chapters 11, 4, and 3, respectively).

The values to be protected under the label of security have also altered over time. Some of the changes have been due to changes in political and economic systems, as well as in national goals and priorities. In countries like South Korea and Taiwan whose democratic transitions are being consolidated, regime and government have become distinct. Although protection of the democratic regime remains a core concern in South Korea and Taiwan, the perceived threat to that objective no longer comes from within but from other states. Further, the survival of particular governments in these countries is no longer a national security concern. In other countries, such as China, Vietnam, Burma, and Indonesia, however, the legitimacy of political systems has weakened for several reasons: the collapse of communism as the basis for political and economic organization; generational changes in leadership; achievement of projected national goals (liberation and unification in Vietnam); poor economic performance (Burma and Vietnam); the growing salience of norms related to human rights and democracy; or the corruption, economic inequality, and abuse of power that is prevalent in several of these countries. Weakening of political legitimacy has been accompanied by a rising concern with regime and government security. In China and Vietnam, for example, regime and government security were not a major concern from the 1950s through the 1970s. Beginning in the 1980s, however, they became key security concerns for the central decision makers.

The security agenda of states has been affected by changes in national priorities. Many Asian leaders, for example, have articulated the goal of modernizing their states. In pursuit of that goal some, such as China, India, and Vietnam, have launched major reform programs whereas others have promoted economic growth and technological development through vision statements like "Malaysia 2020," or "Singapore 21." The net result has been an elevation of economic matters in the national agenda. Except for the few states that are confronted with acute external threats, there is now no strict hierarchy among issues. Even in a country like South Korea whose political survival is under challenge, the public has begun to identify other issues—social and political stability, trade conflicts, lack of international competitiveness, economic sovereignty—as key security concerns surpassing the threat posed by North Korea (see Chapter 7). Resource allocation for defense in South Korea as a percentage of GDP has also declined over the years.

Similarly, the Asian approach to international security has undergone major changes. As observed in the preceding section, the emphasis during the Cold War on alliance and alignment has given way to a greater reliance on national capabilities. Asia has no history of indigenous multilateral security cooperation. Nevertheless cooperative security has become a key component of the national security strategies of the ASEAN states. It is now also being explored in South Asia and the broader Asia-Pacific region. Security through economic cooperation is also emerging as a component of the Asian approach to international security. Generally the Asian approach to international security has become more complex and multilayered, deploying multiple strategies and instruments.

Because nearly all Asian states are relatively new as modern nation-states and are still in the midst of fundamental transitions—economic, political, and sociocultural—and because the material and normative structures affecting them are changing too, further shifts in their security practice can be anticipated.

Asian Security Practice: Not Culturally Unique

The preceding five features that characterize security practice in Asia are not unique to Asia. There are also significant differences in the security behavior of the various Asian states. As such there is no one distinct Asian security practice. The primacy of the state as the security referent, its contested nature, the multiplicity of security referents, and internal and international conflicts over identity, legitimacy, autonomy, and territorial integrity—all these features also characterize the practice of security in Central and Eastern Europe, Russia, the former Soviet Central Asian Republics, Africa, and Latin America. Compared to the emphasis in the North Atlantic and Soviet bloc countries on the military dimension during the Cold War, the broad definition of security in Asia may have been distinctive, but this is no longer the case. Now economic and sociocultural concerns also inform the security thinking and behavior of Western decision makers. And some Western academics argue the case for defining security even more broadly than the way it is articulated by Asian elites and scholars.

Moreover, the comprehensive definitions of security in Asia are not so much a product of Asian cultures as a result of the nature and circumstances of the political units. The comprehensive definitions of security in the ASEAN states have their origins in the contested and changing nature of the state in those countries as well as their aspirations for development. Because national identity and political legitimacy are contested issues, the problem of political survival in these states goes beyond political independence and territorial integrity to embrace protection of the ideas that underpin the political organization of the nation and state, survival of the incumbent power holders, preservation of national unity, and social and political stability. These values can be endangered by nonmilitary threats as well as military ones, and their safeguarding calls for political, legal, economic, sociocultural, and military measures. A broad interpretation of political survival, developmental goals, and recognition of the need for multidimensional coping strategies explain the comprehensive definitions of security in these states.

In the case of Japan, because of its lack of natural resources, economic security has always been a high priority in modern times. In the interwar period Japan sought to secure access to resources through military conquest and the creation of a Greater East Asia Co-prosperity sphere. In the 1970s, Japan's articulation of comprehensive security was a response to changes in the international economic environment— Nixon's unilateral abrogation of the gold standard, the steep oil price increases in 1973 and 1978—and to its perception of a decline in the power of its protector the United States, signaled by the 1969 Nixon Doctrine, Sino-American alignment, and Soviet-American détente. The response was also conditioned by its post–World War II culture of antimilitarism, which inhibits the development of independent national military capabilities.

A comprehensive definition of security also seems to be characteristic of countries (such as Japan and the initial ASEAN five) that are not confronted with urgent international military threats. The shift in Beijing's and later in Hanoi's articulation of security from a focus on the military dimension to a broader definition coincided with their reassessment of international threats and, more generally, with a view of the international situation as favorable. The broad articulation is also linked to a recognition of their economic weaknesses, the declining legitimacy of their socialist systems, and concern over government legitimacy. In states like North Korea, South Korea, Taiwan, Pakistan, and India that face major external threats, the military dimension continues to be critical in security thinking and behavior, although even in these countries other concerns are beginning to command a more prominent place on their national security agendas.

Finally, the broad definition of security in Asia may be explained, in part, as the outcome of a structural norm of comprehensive security. Elites have been socialized to think that security must be viewed broadly and that survival and prosperity requires all-around strength. One of the first tasks of the ASEAN Regional Forum, for example, was to affirm this belief and to initiate a study on the "comprehensive concept of security, including its economic and social aspects, as it pertains to the Asia-Pacific region" (ASEAN Regional Forum 1994).

It is evident then that the broad definition of security in Asia is due in large part to the nature of Asian political units and their internal and international circumstances. The same is true of the recent broader definitions of security in the United States and Western European states. A perception that the character and scale of economic change may undermine those countries' domination of the international political economy, among other concerns, underlies their broader definition of security with added emphasis on economic security. Sociocultural concerns (the impact of migration on identity, for example) and environmental concerns have also contributed to the broad definition of security in the West. Thus there is nothing intrinsically Asian about a broad definition of security, although there may be a distinctive content to such definitions in Asia.

Similarly, the Asian approach to international security is not far different from that practiced in other parts of the world. Self-help—that is, national capabilities and alliances—are a key component of the Asian approach. As noted earlier, national military capabilities are being built up, and force has been used in the contemporary international relations of Asian states, although it is possible to argue, as we do later, that the role of force in Asia is changing. Historically, there is a strong realpolitik tradition in Asia, in both the Sinic and Indic systems. Japan, when it was a great power, used brute force in the pursuit of its political and economic objectives. Though peace was not precluded in the historic Asian systems, claims, such as that of Michael Haas, that the traditional cultures of Asia—Buddhism, Confucianism, Hinduism and Islam—provide it with "a complex set of norms of international relations in which peace was considered more normal than war" (Haas 1989: 3), and that "war, by no means absent, was engaged less often by Asians than by Europeans until the advent of European imperialism" (1989: 1) appear to be not well founded if not to misrepresent history. The accuracy of such claims and counterclaims notwithstanding, it is difficult to refute the assertion that self-help is a crucial part of the contemporary Asian approach to security. Any formulation of the "Asian way" that omits this component is suspect.

It is, however, possible to argue that the content of cooperative security in Asia in terms of principles, purposes, and procedures is in some ways quite distinct from its content in the North Atlantic region, at least for the present. To begin with, Asian states do not envisage a role for regional security cooperation in domestic conflicts. This stance is a result of their strong emphasis on the principles of sovereignty and noninterference in domestic affairs. For the present they also do not envisage a role for regional security cooperation in containment and settlement of international conflicts, especially if it entails the collective application of force. The preference is for bilateral negotiations and informal multilateral discussions, and for more intractable problems, the deferment of conflict settlement to future generations. Multilateral security cooperation is seen as particularly useful in conflict prevention. Even then, the emphasis is not on formal rules and procedures to regulate state behavior, such as regulation of military competition through binding and verifiable arms control agreements, but rather on creating trust and shared political understandings and fostering mutually beneficial relationships (in the economic and other realms) that will gradually ease threat perceptions, reduce the urgency of the international security problem, and in the long term contribute to the settlement or resolution of specific conflicts.

The Asian approach is preeminently political, focused on building trust and shared understandings, and in the process, shaping the normative context or the metaregime, rather than on the immediate regulation of state behavior through specific regimes.[19] Success at the meta level in building an international society is expected over time to lead to the creation of specific regimes.[20] Though it recognizes the importance of power, the Asian approach eschews formal collective management of power. Thus, Asian states emphasize political agreements on long-range goals, diversity and equality, consensus-building and face-saving, informal networking and the fostering of interpersonal relations, unilateral and voluntary disclosures and concessions, incrementalism, negotiations, and focus on noncontroversial areas, at least to begin with. This "Asian" approach—commonly characterized as emphasizing process over substance—differs from that of the West, which places a high premium on concrete goals, immediate benefits, and binding agreements with provisions for verification of compliance and arbitration of disputes.

This difference in approach is noticeable in the ARF and in APEC, whose membership includes both Asian and Western states. Whereas Asian leaders and bureaucrats value the various meetings among heads of government, ministers, senior officials, and other bureaucrats, both civilian and military, for the purposes identified above, their American,

European, and Australian counterparts tend to decry them for not producing concrete outcomes, arguing that these processes cannot be sustained in the absence of specific binding agreements and tangible benefits.

Haas (1989: 20–21) sees the "Asian way" as "a new form of state-craft" that "goes beyond previous theories of international integration" and posits a "cultural theory of international cooperation." We would argue that the contemporary Asian approach to cooperation can be explained by the fact that Asian states are now in a formational phase of an international society; that is, they are engaged in a process of con-structing the normative basis or consensual knowledge (principles and norms) to govern the interaction of states in the region. Historically, international society in Asia, when it existed, was hierarchical. Such a form is not acceptable to the contemporary Asian states, except possibly to the would-be hegemons of such a society. Although they have embraced some Western principles, such as sovereignty and territorial integrity, the Asian states resist the adoption of the full range of Western norms and principles, especially the recent developments that would limit sovereignty and open the way for justified intervention.

In the absence of an acceptable historical basis to build on, mistrust-ful of and reacting to the West's attempt to project its principles and norms as universal, as well as the historically rooted distrust of each other, and their efforts to consolidate the identity and structure of political domination within their states, Asian governments are seeking a normative framework that will take due account of their domestic and international ideals and interests. Such a normative framework would eventually also have to take account of power realities and conflicts. Its construction will inevitably be a slow and incremental process. ASEAN has had a fair measure of success in this endeavor over the last 30 years. The process has just begun among the Asia-Pacific states. This is a much larger grouping comprising an even more diverse set of states in terms of histories, power differentials, political systems, level of economic development, and hence identities and interests. The process of forging a normative framework among such a group of states will indeed be challenging and is likely to be protracted.

Like the broad definition of security, several aspects of the Asian approach to cooperative security may be explained in terms of the nature of Asian political units, their histories, their current national preoccupa-tions, and their present international circumstances. The preclusion of domestic conflicts from regional security agendas and the emphasis on consensus-building, for example, can be explained in terms of the premium the Asian states place on sovereignty and noninterference in domestic affairs, which in turn is linked to the history and nature of the political units. Their preference for measures like voluntary and unilateral concessions and disclosures may also be explained by their determination to preserve autonomy. The emphasis on political dialogue, incrementalism, and the deferment of conflict resolution to future generations can be explained by the bitterness that characterizes the recent history of Asia, a recognition of the limits and dangers posed by that history, the absence of a tradition of multilateral cooperation among sovereign states in Asia, and the consequent need to develop a culture of cooperation that takes into account the sensitivities of a diverse group of states. This suggests that the present distinctiveness in the content of cooperative security in Asia is likely to alter over time with change in the nature of the units and their domestic and international situations.

PART TWO: EXPLAINING ASIAN SECURITY PRACTICE

In seeking to explain security practice in Asia we make two related assertions. First, explanations of Asian security practice must incorporate and where necessary integrate factors at the intrastate, unit, and systemic levels. Second, both material and ideational factors are necessary to explain the security concerns and behavior of Asian states. Only a combination of these levels and factors can explain the full range of the security practice of Asian states. The salience of each level and set of factors will vary by country. The two claims are strongly interrelated, but for the purpose of discussion they are dealt with separately here. We begin with the first claim.

The Need to Consider Domestic, Unit-level, and International Factors

The states in Asia, except for Japan, are at once premodern and modern, and some even incorporate elements of a postmodern state.[21] The type of state and the associated attributes have a crucial bearing on the security thinking and behavior of Asian leaders. The problematic construction as modern nation-states, for example, helps to explain the contested nature of many Asian states as security referents as well as the multiplicity of security referents in those states. It also sheds light on the deep commitment of Asian leaders to values like political independence, territorial integrity, national unity, and political stability—the causes of nearly all internal conflicts and of several international conflicts that focus on identity (China–Taiwan, North–South Korea, India–Pakistan) and accounts for the acuteness of some international threat perceptions (Chinese and Vietnamese concern with the ideological threat from the West, for example). The goals of economic modernization and industrialization, and the growing integration of national economies into the regional and global economies, by affecting the identities, interests, and capabilities of states as well as the pattern and density of their international interactions, help to explain changes in the scope of security, in the nature and urgency of the security problem, and in the approach to security.

Yet unit-level factors alone cannot fully explain the security practice of Asian governments. Systemic constraints and opportunities, both normative and material, are also important because they affect the prospects for survival and the achievement of other goals like economic prosperity and a safe and predictable international environment. The declining urgency of the political survival problem for most states including very small ones like Brunei, Singapore, Bhutan, and the Maldives, for example, cannot be explained without reference to the normative structure—mutual respect for political independence and territorial integrity, noninterference in internal affairs, and nonuse of force to resolve disputes—which is increasingly favorable to the survival and strengthening of existing states. These norms may be violated, but not with impunity, as demonstrated by the Vietnamese experience in Cambodia. Vietnamese military invasion and occupation was strongly resisted by the ASEAN states on the basis that Vietnam had violated cardinal principles of international relations. Though it was not the only consideration, Vietnam's blatant violation of accepted norms was a key factor in mobilizing and sustaining world interest and opinion over a prolonged period, and denying international legitimacy to the Vietnamese occupation. Eventually Vietnam was compelled to withdraw from Cambodia.[22]

Similarly, the material structure is crucial in explaining some security concerns. The general apprehension over regional security as well as some of the specific concerns of states, including major ones like China and Japan, cannot be explained without reference to recent changes in the distribution of power. In the absence of the Soviet balance, China is increasingly wary of American hegemony. This concern has become more acute following the deployment of two U.S. carrier battle groups in the vicinity of Taiwan in response to the PRC's military exercises and missile firings in March 1996, and the reaffirmation of the U.S.–Japan security treaty in the following month. Beijing has come to view the U.S.–Japan alliance as enhancing and entrenching American dominance in East Asia, and also as increasing the security profile of Japan and facilitating its transition to the status of a normal power. The rise of China is a cause of apprehension in Japan and several other Asian states. The acuteness of such concerns, however, as well as the responses, are not uniform. As explained later, they have been shaped by other material and social factors at the unit level.

Further, some of the security concerns of Asian states span more than one level. The Kashmir conflict, for example, is an internal conflict between the Indian political center and periphery, as well as an international conflict between India and Pakistan that at various times has involved external powers including the United States, China, and the Soviet Union. The acuteness of the Chinese perception of the "threat of peaceful evolution from the West" is connected to and has fluctuated with the intensity of the domestic challenge to the legitimacy of communist rule. In these and other cases, explanations of security practice must integrate intrastate, unit-level, and international structural factors. Undue emphasis on any one level—as for example in weak-state analysis and neorealism, which privilege the intrastate and international levels, respectively—will be limited in their ability to explain Asian security behavior and may also be misleading.

Limitations of the "Weak State" Analysis

According to Barry Buzan, whose influential *People, States and Fear* (1983) popularized the concept of weak states in the study of Third World security, the behavior of these states, whose primary security concerns are internal, "can be understood better in terms of individual and sub-group security than in terms of national security" (p. 69). According to Mohammed Ayoob (1995), although the security problematic of Third World states has domestic, regional, and global dimensions, the "primary layer that flavors the entire cake is the domestic one" (p. 189). Brian Job (1992a) goes further: he argues that the traditional international security dilemma does not apply to the typical Third World state (pp. 17–18). According to him, "internal threats to and from the regime in power, rather than externally motivated threats to existence of the nation-state unit," are the primary if not the exclusive security concern of Third World states (p. 18).

Although all three acknowledge that the Third World encompasses a wide variety of states, their analyses nevertheless proceed on the basis of the typical Third World state—which is closer to a failed state than the average Third World state, at least in Asia. Buzan, Ayoob, Job, and others classify Asian states (except Japan) as Third World or weak states. Although most of the Asian countries are weak on one or more attributes of modern statehood, they are far from the prototypical Third World state as described by these analysts. Even those states (Bangladesh, Cambodia, Burma, Laos) that may approximate the typical weak state are not weak on all attributes of modern statehood. Bangladesh and Cambodia, for example, are weak in terms of political institutions and state capabilities, but strong as ethnic nations. This raises more general questions: how to define a weak state without being tautological, what level of weakness is necessary to qualify a state as weak, and how to deal with states like China, India, and Vietnam that are weak on some counts and strong on others.

A second limitation of weak-state analysis in explaining Asian security practice is that Asian states are concerned not only with internal threats but also with international threats. The two are often connected, but international threats are not merely an extension of internal vulnerabilities. The international security concerns and the nuclear behavior of China, India, Pakistan, and North Korea, for example, cannot be explained solely or even primarily in terms of internal security issues. Perceptions of a Chinese threat in Vietnam, Taiwan, India, and the Philippines, or perceptions of a Vietnamese threat in Thailand and Cambodia, are not a consequence of their weakness as states (though such weakness may aggravate the intensity of threat perception). And although internal factors figure in the mutual threat perceptions of India and Pakistan, they are not the sole or even the primary source of conflict between the two countries. Conflict over Kashmir and historical enmity—intensified by the huge difference in capabilities—drive the external threat perceptions of those states. Contrary to Job's claim, the international security dilemma is in some cases even more relevant to Asian states than it is to the so-called strong states of the North Atlantic region.

A third limitation of the weak-state idea is its inability to accommodate change in one or more attributes of statehood. Consequently it obscures the substantial strengthening, over the last three or four decades, of the nation's identity, the capacities of state institutions, and the governmental monopoly of force in many Asian countries. By the definitions advanced by Buzan, Ayoob, and Job, the states in East and Southeast Asia would still be classified as weak states. Yet the present situation in these states, compared to the 1950s and early 1960s, is vastly different.

The idea of the weak state, though it may have some limited analytic value, does not capture the practice of security in most Asian states. Asian states do not approximate the typical weak state. Although internal contestations over identity and legitimacy affect their international security behavior, that behavior is driven by other considerations as well, including the traditional interests of sovereign states and the constraints and opportunities issuing from international structure. The analysis of Asian security must accord due weight to both internal and international imperatives as well as to their interaction. Care must be taken not to skew analysis in favor of internal dynamics, as has commonly been done by analysts of Third World security, or in favor of the international material structure, as in neorealist analysis.

Limitations of the Neorealist Analysis

A first read might suggest that the realist paradigm effectively captures the Asian practice of security. Sovereign nation-states populate Asia; their governments claim to be the principal and legitimate actors in domestic and international politics; suspicion and competition characterize the interaction of Asian governments; international institutions are in a nascent phase and in short supply; and national military power and alliances appear to form the bedrock of national and regional security policies. Acceptance of these features at face value has led many an analyst to favor the realist lens in analyzing Asian security (Friedberg 1996; Betts 1993–94; Dibb 1995; Waltz 1993; Buzan and Segal 1994; Roy 1996). Although it is certainly relevant, an exclusive reliance on international material structure to explain Asian security suffers several shortcomings.

A major limitation of neorealist analysis of Asian security is its neglect of the domestic level, which flows from neorealism's assumption of a cohesive and sovereign state. In Asia, as noted earlier, the state in most cases is deeply problematic. Similarly, although there is a deep attachment to the principle of sovereignty, many states do not have the capacity to enforce it both internally and internationally. The political constructions and actors that neorealism takes for granted are in fact contested in many cases and also in a state of flux. Instead of being assumed, therefore, they must be problematized and investigated. Moreover, structural realism cannot accommodate the historical dimension or the aspirations of actors, such as nation- and state-building and the development of international society, that are not immediately related to power. Such factors, however, are crucial to the security thinking and behavior of Asian governments and must therefore feature in their explanation. Because of these shortcomings, neorealist analyses of Asian security cannot explain the contested nature of security referents and internal security concerns; can only partly explain the international security concerns of governments; and are unable to explain the nonconforming behavior of a country like Japan, for example, except as an aberration or a lag.

Whereas some realists hold to the position that internal security is not a proper concern of security studies (Morgan 1992), others like Barry Posen (1993) have attempted to explain the internal security problem (i.e., ethnic conflict) in terms of the realist security dilemma. Although this effort addresses a neglected level in neorealist analysis, Posen's explanation still suffers at least two shortcomings. First, it does not explore and explain what leads to the collapse of the imperial regime that creates the situation of "anarchy" that is his starting point. Second, the struggle for power, though important, cannot by itself explain internal conflicts. The inclusion of ideational factors will help overcome these shortcomings and provide a more complete explanation of internal security problems. The salience of ideational factors in explaining Asian security is the subject of the next section, but for the sake of completeness we deal here with its importance in explaining internal conflicts.

As noted in earlier discussion, because of the deep or strong normative and material interests at stake, the construction of national identity in Asian societies, as elsewhere, has been intensely contested and has frequently led to civil strife and protracted armed conflict, as in Pakistan, India, Sri Lanka, Bangladesh, Burma, Thailand, Indonesia, the Philippines, and China. Such conflicts over identity often embody conflicts about material interests and struggles for power, but they cannot be reduced to these considerations alone. Often the interplay among the factors is a complex one, and their relative salience is subject to change over time.

In the case of Sri Lanka, for example, the 1956 Sinhala-only policy was meant to cancel the advantage of the Tamils and favor the non-English-educated Sinhalese in the competition for public service positions. But since then, the Sinhala majority has attempted to construct a Sri Lankan national identity that revolves around "Sinhalese greatness in antiquity, the Sinhala language, and the Buddhist religion" (Pfaffenberger 1990: 251–52). The Tamil political parties responded in the 1970s by demanding the formation of Tamil Eelam (Eelam is the historic Tamil name for Sri Lanka) through the union of the northern and eastern provinces. This was primarily a ploy to force further concessions from the government and also to appease Tamil youth organizations that were becoming impatient. Lack of success in this effort and the progressive construction of Sri Lanka as a Sinhala-Buddhist state were perceived to be not only materially disadvantageous but threatening to the identity of the Tamils as Sri Lankans and dangerous to the survival of Tamil language and culture. At some point, the Tamils (the Liberation Tigers of Tamil Eelam [LTTE]) reached the threshold where Tamil and Sri Lankan identity as defined by the Sinhala majority became incompatible, and secession seemed to be the only solution.

We do not represent the foregoing as the definitive account of the ethnic conflict in Sri Lanka, but it is illustrative of our contention with regard to the salience of identity and its complex interplay with material interests and struggle for power in explaining internal conflicts. In the Sri Lankan case, material considerations appear to have been significant to begin with, although even then ethnicity or racial group was the basis for government discrimination and minority response. Progressively, material interests appear to have been subsumed by considerations of group identity. The historical tracing of the interplay of the various factors also explains the emergence and development of the conflict, and provides a better analytic framework than does the assumption of anarchy. Further, the domestic context is qualitatively different from the international anarchy that produces the security dilemma. In Sri Lanka, for example, a government does exist but it is unacceptable to a segment of the population.

Although one might argue that identity has been mobilized to serve the material interests of specific groups or individuals, such mobilization has been possible only because "members of the society have already made a preliminary identification with the solidarity group through political socialization, internalizing the core beliefs, sentiments and symbols" (Dittmer and Kim 1993: 240). Moreover, material factors cannot explain why the contestants have been willing not only to sacrifice economic gain but to endure prolonged, severe hardship and loss of life for the sake of purely symbolic gains in the realm of identity. Material explanations assume a certain cost-benefit rationality that is not always evident in conflicts over the identity of the nation, at least not during all stages of the conflict. That assumption of material rationality also helps to account for the failure of policies that seek to resolve such conflicts by offering material, especially economic, incentives. Identity is not merely an epiphenomenon. It has autonomous explanatory power. Consequently, the issue of identity must be addressed in its own right by those seeking settlement of such conflicts.

Contestation over the political ideology of the state is a second key source of internal conflict in Asia. However, unlike the ethnic or religious identities that lie at the heart of conflicts over the identity of the nation, secular political ideologies (democracy, socialism) do not command the same degree of passion. Further, the appeal of political ideologies is often limited to the elite. The gravitation of masses of people to ideological movements is based on their material circumstances and self-interest. Rural support for the Communist Party of the

Philippines (CPP) and the Communist Party of Thailand (CPT) in the 1960s and 1970s, for example, was due to poor economic circumstances and the repressive rule of authoritarian governments in Manila and Bangkok, not to any commitment to communist ideology. Even among the elites, ideological belief cannot be dissociated from the struggle to control state power. Often, an ideology is deployed as a legitimating rationale. But not all behavior can be reduced to such considerations, and political beliefs are not unimportant, as demonstrated by the democracy uprisings in the Philippines, South Korea, Thailand, Burma, and China. The point, however, is that because the state is the repository of political power, the ideological definition of the state determines who controls state power and its material resources. Thus material considerations may be as important as, and in some cases even more salient than, ideology in explaining such conflicts.

Considerations of identity and legitimacy provide a deeper understanding and a more thorough explanation of the differing interests and the internal conflicts they generate. This leads to another major limitation of neorealist analysis and to my second claim, which is that both ideational and material factors are necessary to explain Asian security practice.

The Need to Combine Material and Ideational Factors

The argument here is not that material factors are irrelevant. Indeed, material interests and the international distribution of power are among the key considerations that drive the security behavior of Asian states and must therefore figure prominently in explanations of Asian security practice. But material factors by themselves have limited explanatory power. The shortcomings of the realist paradigm noted earlier may be overcome by the inclusion of ideational factors such as identity, sovereignty, history, political and strategic culture, and the normative context. The salience of ideational factors in explaining state behavior is an issue of contention between realists and constructivists. Political realists like Morgenthau argue that "interest defined as power," not ideas, drives the actions of statesmen, although he accepts that the content of national interest depends on the political-cultural context (Morgenthau 1978: 5). Neorealists argue that anarchy and the international distribution of power are the key determinants of state behavior (Waltz 1979). In both variants of realism, but especially in neorealism, ideational and institutional factors are epiphenomena of the distribution of power.[23] Constructivists, on the other hand, argue that ideas have greater autonomy in explaining a state's behavior (Jepperson, Wendt, and

Katzenstein 1996). They posit a normative component to international structure, defined in part by "shared understandings, expectations, or knowledge," that informs the content of state identities and interests and regulates behavior (Wendt 1995). Further, they argue that even the meaning of material resources is socially derived and that features of international politics like the security dilemma and self-help are social constructions.

My position is closer to that of constructivism. The assertion that a combination of material and ideational factors is necessary to explain Asian security practice rests on the premise that ideas, although not unrelated to power realities, are distinct and have greater autonomy and consequences than allowed for by realists. Ideational factors may, of course, be deployed to justify actions that are in fact motivated by material considerations.[24] But for ideas to serve such purposes they must have a "living presence." They must resonate with key groups as well as in the body politic. Further, although power does play a crucial role, in the final analysis the institutionalization of ideas rests on their acceptance through practice by significant actors. Successful hegemony—the production of a shared idea or norm—rests on a synthesis that fuses all elements of the society into a "collective will," forging ideological unity.[25] Once an idea becomes established, it is less amenable to exploitation at will. With greater autonomy, it will be consequential for political behavior. The force of an idea may also erode as material conditions change or other ideas emerge. The relationship between ideational and material factors is therefore better conceptualized as interactive and recursive: their relative salience is subject to change over time, though often gradually. Ideational factors, as noted earlier, are critical in explaining internal security practices in Asian states. In this section we focus on the need to combine material and ideational factors to explain the international security concerns and behavior of Asian states. We begin with a brief review of some neorealist analyses and predictions for Asian security behavior.

Neorealist Explanations

Neorealists have attempted to explain and predict the regional security situation as well as the specific concerns and behavior of Asian states primarily in terms of the distribution of power and the ongoing power transition in the region. Aaron Friedberg (1996), for example, argues that Asia is moving toward multipolarity and that the transition is likely to be destabilizing. He foresees an Asia in which alignments are "more fluid, complex, and less certain" and crises are more likely to escalate to wars (pp. 26–29). In the long run, he argues, Asia "seems far more likely to be the cockpit of great power conflict" (p. 5). According to Richard Betts (1993–94), the future distribution of power in Asia is uncertain, "up for grabs," potentially unstable, and likely to lead to instability. Denny Roy (1996) asserts that the rise of China poses a long-term danger to Asia-Pacific security because Beijing will seek hegemony by force. China's growing power, it is argued, will provoke a military buildup by Japan, "plunging Asia into a new cold war." In his view the power transition in East Asia is certain to lead to "serious political tensions between China and Japan...[and] military conflict is likely if China's economic power continues to grow relative to Japan's" (p. 129). Applying structural theory, Waltz (1993) argues that Japan—existing in a contentious part of the world where there are or will soon be several nuclear powers, with the American military guarantee no longer reliable, and increasingly cognizant of the vulnerabilities of its dependency—has to worry about China (and the United States), and that it will be "pressed to follow suit [acquire nuclear capabilities] and increase its conventional abilities to protects its interests abroad" (68–69). Waltz asserts that even if Japan may not choose to, it will be forced by systemic pressures to become a great power with all the associated attributes including military power.

While not without insight, these and other such assertions based on power transition and structural theories alone are suspect for a number of reasons. First, there is no consensus among realists on which distributions of power are stabilizing or destabilizing. Similarly there is no agreement on how ascending and descending powers will behave. There is also the question of whether the theory of hegemonic war applies in the nuclear era. Second, it is nearly impossible to ascertain with any degree of certainty the actual distribution of power at any given time during a transition such as that under way in Asia. There are many imponderables, including domestic uncertainties. Third, even if the distribution of power can be accurately ascertained, structure rarely dictates a fixed course of action. Often it indicates a range of options. The actual option chosen will be determined by factors at the unit level. Neorealists have often stated that structure can explain only patterns (that wars will recur in anarchy, for example) and that the cause of a specific occurrence must be sought in the first and second images (Waltz 1959). In practice, however, they appear not to heed their own formulations. Neorealists continue to make assertions about the security concerns and behavior of individual countries based on the material structure—predictions that often, as in the case of Japan, have been wrong. Fourth, neorealist analyses tend to conflate power with threat. Although power is a significant factor, threat construction is informed by other factors as well, and most of them are social. Stephen Walt's (1987) emphasis on the balance of threat rather than balance of power as the basis for alliance formation is a useful correction, but it represents a substantial departure from neorealism in that it shifts the basis of state behavior from capabilities to intentions and highlights the significance of social factors in threat construction. The balance of threat argument has not been prominent in neorealist analyses of Asian security. Finally, the focus on international structure and power transition obscures the other security concerns of Asian states.

I do not mean to argue that material capabilities are unimportant. Clearly they are important. The increasing concern with China, for example, is a function of its growing power. But that development alone cannot explain the differences in perceptions of and responses to the "China threat." Consideration of other factors—norms, history, identity, interests—that bear upon the construction of security threats will enable a more complete explanation of this and other such developments, and more generally of the international security situation in Asia. In this connection we advance three propositions. First, ideational factors together with material ones determine social reality, and as that reality changes so will the nature and urgency of the political survival problem. Here we argue that the realist nature of international politics in Asia, especially during the Cold War, has been a social construction and that it is undergoing significant change. That change in turn is altering the nature, intensity, and urgency of the political survival problem for most Asian states. The second proposition is that ideational factors, by extending the causal chain backward, provide a more complete explanation of the international security concerns of Asian states. We substantiate this claim through a discussion of the ideational basis of the three most acute conflicts in Asia—China versus Taiwan, North Korea versus South Korea, and India versus Pakistan—which, in realist accounts, are usually explained in terms of the security dilemma. Our final proposition is that along with material factors, ideational factors are critical in the explanation of variations in state behavior both across countries and over time. They also help explain state behavior that neorealism would consider an anomaly. We support this third claim through a discussion first of the differences among Asian states in their perception of and response to the rise of China, and then of the factors that underlay the reappraisals of security that occurred at different times in China, India, Japan, and Vietnam.

The Social Construction and Changing Nature
of Asian International Politics

International politics in Asia, especially during the Cold War, resembled that of the realist paradigm, and political survival was a key problem for many Asian states. The realist features, however, were not simply a consequence of anarchy or the distribution of power. They were informed by social factors as well.

First, the commitment of Asian political elites to the realist core values of political independence and territorial integrity is due in substantial measure to their long experience, in some cases through centuries, of colonial and imperial domination and their relatively recent liberation from such domination. There is still considerable apprehension among Asian elites. Some fear that the United States and more generally the West seek to dominate Asia through other means—such as forward military deployment, advocacy of justified intervention, promotion of democracy and human rights as universal values, promotion of environmental protection and universal labor standards, insistence on international trading rules that may undermine the comparative advantage of Asian countries—and wish to deny the Asian states their rightful place in the region and the world. Asian governments, individually and collectively, they argue, must therefore be vigilant and must resolve to preserve their independence, as well as their power, prestige, and influence in the international system. The commitment to realist values is also informed by the weakness of Asian states as modern nation-states. Sovereignty is a key device for national political consolidation—to ensure autonomy, territorial integrity, and noninterference in internal affairs—and for some leaders to consolidate their hold on state power.

Second, many of the suspicions, tensions, and conflicts that characterize contemporary Asian international politics are informed by historical animosities such as those between China and Japan; China and Vietnam; China and Russia; Japan and Russia; Japan and Korea; Vietnam and Thailand; Vietnam and Cambodia; Thailand and Cambodia; Thailand and Burma; and India (the Tamil kingdoms) and Sri Lanka (the Sinhalese kingdoms). With the removal of the Cold War strategic overlay, some of the traditional lines of amity and enmity are resurfacing. The contemporary resonance of these traditional animosities may be traced to their long duration and bitterness, their contemporary deployment by governments to generate support for certain policies or consolidate their control of state power, or the existence of territorial and other disputes between traditional adversaries. Distrust among Asian countries also stems from a lack of knowledge about each other. Only with the end of Cold War has there been much autonomous interaction among Asian states. To reach a certain level of understanding will take time. Finally, as observed in Chapter 2, there is a strong realpolitik tradition in Asia. Power played a crucial role in the relations among kingdoms in the historic Sinic, Indic, and Southeast Asian systems. This strategic cultural tradition, reinforced by their experiences during the Cold War, continues to inform security thinking and behavior especially in China, India, Korea, Vietnam, and Thailand. The realist nature of international politics in Asia is thus not merely a product of anarchy or of the material structure. It is in considerable part an outcome of past and present ideas and interactions.

A realist might argue that even if this claim is correct, it is of no consequence because the outcome is still the same. It does matter, however, for it implies that the nature of international politics in the region can be altered. And Asian international politics is indeed changing, though only gradually. It is becoming less Hobbesian; principled and rule-governed behavior is on the increase; political survival, though always important, is not precarious for most countries; force, though still valued, is declining in utility; and finally, although national self-help and alliances continue to be vital elements of national security strategies, cooperation is becoming important. These changes are most marked in Southeast Asia. They are less marked in Northeast Asia and weakest in South Asia.

The Association of Southeast Asian Nations (ASEAN) member states have accepted, and in large measure abide by, certain key principles in the conduct of their international relations. These principles include mutual respect for political independence, territorial integrity, and national identity; noninterference in the internal affairs of one another; peaceful settlement of disputes; renunciation of the threat or use of force; and effective cooperation.[26] Unlike the early postindependence period—when Indonesia challenged the very existence of Malaysia, when the Philippines claimed the state of Sabah in Malaysia, when Singapore's survival was precarious because of Malaysia and Indonesia's hostility, and when Brunei feared absorption by Malaysia—ASEAN member states now recognize each other's claim to independence. They have a vested interest in the survival and stability of fellow members. The concerns of other ASEAN states and their consequences for the region now figure in the formulation of national interests.

Although the provision in the 1976 Treaty of Amity and Cooperation for pacific settlement of dispute remains unused, member states have found other peaceful means to settle disputes—or at least to prevent their escalation to open hostilities—and to ease tensions among themselves. Agreement has recently been reached, for example, to refer the disputes between Malaysia and Singapore over Pedra Branca Island, and between Malaysia and Indonesia over Simpadan and Ligitan Islands, to the International Court of Justice. Such action would have been unthinkable even a decade ago. Other border disputes and conflicting EEZ claims among the ASEAN states are the subject of bilateral and multilateral negotiations. The use of force to resolve disputes is declining as an option. Indeed, there has been no recourse to force to resolve political disputes since the 1960s.

Southeast Asia, long characterized as a region of "turmoil, rebellion, and conflict," the Balkans of Asia, and so forth, has since been transformed into a region of peace, stability, and prosperity. Indeed in recent times it has become fashionable for scholars to characterize ASEAN as a partial pluralistic security community. This transformation exemplifies my claim that international politics in Asia is socially constructed and, moreover, is being altered. This is not to say that competition and conflict have disappeared from the international politics of Southeast Asia; only that a strong international society, less prone to the arbitrary use of force, is developing in the subregion. This accounts for the simultaneous engagement of the Southeast Asian states in regional cooperation, the development of national military capabilities, and continued participation in alliance arrangements.

Though it is much less prominent, such change is not absent in the region at large. Asia has enjoyed relative peace now for well over a decade. There has been a considerable reduction in tensions among the major powers. Apart from the two Koreas and Taiwan, the existence of Asian countries as independent states is not internationally contested. Their claims to independence are accepted and recognized by other Asian countries and by the international community. The numerous disputes among these countries do not threaten their existence as independent political entities. Although there have been infringements, Asian states have by and large accepted the international norms of political independence, territorial integrity, and nonintervention in domestic affairs. Indeed, these norms have become key principles in the conduct of their international relations.

The role of force is also changing in Asia. Despite the persistence of flash points like the Korean, Taiwan, and Indo-Pakistani conflicts and the associated military buildup, there has not been an international war since 1979. Force might still be used to resolve these and other disputes, but its role in Asia seems to be shifting from physical use to deterrence, even in the case of those three volatile conflicts. Not only is the physical, diplomatic, and moral cost of using force increasing, but force has little utility for the attainment of the other high-priority goals of economic modernization and industrialization. Asian countries have a common interest in maintaining a peaceful environment in which to achieve these goals.

Although there is no history of multilateral cooperation in Asia, such cooperation is gradually emerging—as witnessed by the formation of the forum for Asia-Pacific Economic Cooperation (APEC), the ASEAN Regional Forum (ARF), and a multitude of informal intergovernmental and nongovernmental organizations. In addition to these multilateral endeavors, most Asian countries have instituted regular bilateral exchanges (such as those between China and Japan, China and Russia, China and India, and China and Vietnam) at senior levels to discuss and even settle outstanding issues. Many of these efforts are still in an early stage and their impact is difficult to assess. Nevertheless, the efforts at dialogue and cooperation are beginning to affect the normative context in the region in terms of the principles governing international behavior, including the legitimacy of force.

Finally, the economic dynamism of East and Southeast Asia is having a dramatic impact on the agenda of international politics in Asia, which has broadened to include economic and sociocultural concerns in addition to traditional political and military security matters. Economic modernization and political stability figure high on national agendas. Indeed, several Asians now argue that geoeconomics has replaced geopolitics as the primary substance of Asian and indeed global international politics. Even if one does not subscribe to this view, it is impossible to deny the prominence of economic, political, and sociocultural concerns for Asian governments. Apart from the few cases where political survival in its most basic form is an urgent concern, there is no fixed hierarchy among political, economic, and military-security issues.

The economic dynamism of East and Southeast Asia has also dramatically altered the pattern and increased the density of political, economic, and social interaction in the region. Since 1985, economic interaction among East and Southeast Asian states has become much more diverse and multilateralized, intra-Asian trade and investment have grown dramatically, and a deep commitment to open economic regionalism and global trading arrangements has emerged. The convergence of economic identities, goals, and strategies is creating a common basis for discourse among Asian states that in some cases is healing a long history of antagonistic relations. Not only is economic interdependence increasing the cost of using force, but institution-building in the economic domain has modified the regional context. Although the economic dynamism of East and Southeast Asia cuts both ways and may have destabilizing consequences as well (Alagappa 1997), the point is not that it will eliminate conflict altogether but that it is contributing to a more complex pattern of international politics. International politics in Asia is now characterized not only by competition and conflict but also by cooperation and interdependence. As the international politics of Asia becomes more multidimensional and complex, the realist paradigm will be increasingly inadequate, though not irrelevant, to explain the international interactions of Asian states.

From the foregoing discussion it is evident that determination of the nature and scope of the security problem derives from the collective understanding among the Asian states, an understanding that is shaped not only by the distribution of power but also by principles, norms, and history. Collectively these factors inform the prospects for survival and the construction of national interests and threats. During the Cold War, Asian international politics and the collective understanding of Asian political elites closely paralleled the realist paradigm. Today, however, both are in the midst of change: international politics in Asia is becoming less Hobbesian; principles and rules are gradually gaining in significance; state interaction is increasingly characterized by conflict as well as cooperation. Cooperation and learning, particularly in Southeast Asia, have contributed to a reconstitution of interests. The changing nature of international politics is in turn altering the nature, content, and urgency of the national security problem. With very few exceptions basic political survival has ceased to be a pressing concern for most states. Thus their international security concerns are more limited: dispute over the demarcation of territorial boundaries and conflicting territorial claims in the maritime space; ideological threats; and long-range concerns about constraints upon autonomy. Even such seemingly materialistic concerns, as we shall see, can be more fully explained through the incorporation of ideational factors.

Ideational Factors and Explanation of International Conflicts

In this section we develop the proposition that ideational factors, specifically considerations of identity and historical legacies, by extending the causal chain backward, can complement realist explanations and provide a deeper understanding of the international conflicts and security concerns of Asian states. The three most acute conflicts in Asia—between Taiwan and China, between North and South Korea, and between India and Pakistan—are outcomes of conflicting political imaginations that have become sharpened and entrenched by military competition, both local and global. Admittedly such competitions have created their own fears, mistrust, and dynamics. But it is important to note that although local power differentials and the international material structure have sharpened the survival concerns of these states and sustained the associated conflicts, they did not produce them in the first place. Threat construction is a product of the interplay of capabilities and intentions. As will become evident from the discussion that follows, the perception of intentions is strongly influenced by ideational factors. We begin with the survival conflicts confronting divided nation-states.

Conflict Between Divided Nation-States

Identity is the underlying cause of the conflict between China and Taiwan, which had its genesis in the civil war between the Chinese Communist Party (CCP) and the Chinese Nationalists (KMT). In the post–civil war period, both the CCP and the KMT were committed to the idea of "one China." Their dispute was over the ideological identity of the Chinese state as well as the title to rule China. The conflict was intensified and perpetuated by the global ideological and geopolitical competition, especially the U.S. support of Taiwan. In time the conflict evolved from a question of state ideology and regime security to one of Taiwan's national identity: does Taiwan have a national identity distinct from that of China, and does it have the right to exist as a separate state? For Beijing, Taiwan is a province of China. Its recovery (along with the recovery of Hong Kong in 1997 and Macao in 1999) is viewed by the CCP as vital for the restoration of Chinese unity, strength, and dignity, which were severely damaged by the imperial ambitions of the West and Japan. Taipei, no longer claiming to represent all of China but still identifying Taiwan as part of the Chinese nation, now seeks separate statehood for Taiwan.[27] Unification with the mainland remains the declared policy, but it is posited as a long-term goal to be achieved in phases through mutual agreement. At the popular level, however, there is substantial support for the ideas of a distinct Taiwanese identity and an independent Taiwan. Democratization in Taiwan has further sharpened the identity dimension of the conflict as well as the mutual threat perceptions of Taipei and Beijing. For Taipei, the Chinese goal of national unity challenges its very existence as an independent democratic state. For Beijing, democratization and Taiwan's drive for international recognition challenge the unity of the Chinese nation and recovery of national pride—key goals of the CCP as well as key pillars of its legitimacy claim. These threat perceptions, as observed by Roger Cliff (Chapter 8), cannot be explained in realist terms. Conflicting ideas about identity, not the realities of power, underlie the threat constructions of both these countries. Chinese power and U.S. support for Taiwan, however, sharpen the conflict.

The origins of the Korean conflict are a matter of debate. Some trace it to the geopolitical competition between the Soviet Union and the United States. Although the Soviet role in the origin of the conflict is not clear, there is little doubt that the United States acted on the basis of its containment policy, which was extended to Asia following North Korea's attack on South Korea (Gaddis 1982: 89–126). Others have suggested that the origins of the Korean conflict should be traced to internal developments in North and South Korea as well as the strong nationalism of Koreans and their desire for unification (Lach and Wehrle 1975: 89–92). Notwithstanding the competing accounts of its origins, the intra-Korean dynamic focused on unification and the political identity of the Korean nation-state now constitute the mainstay of the conflict. Imbued with strong nationalism and rejecting the perpetual division of the Korean nation, both North and South Korea are committed to the idea of a single Korean nation-state.[28] They differ, however, on when and how unification should be achieved as well as on the political identity of such a unified nation-state. From the outset, the survival of their respective political systems and incumbent governments was defined as essential to national security in both North and South Korea. Cold War alignments and military competition between North and South entrenched the conflict, breeding mistrust and antagonism between the two Koreas. Democratization in South Korea and the success of its capitalist model of development have further sharpened the ideological differences between the two Koreas. The dramatic increase in South Korea's political, economic, and military power and the concurrent weakening of North Korea on all three counts have also skewed the power differentials in favor of South Korea, isolating the North, increasing its insecurity, and pushing it to consider a nuclear option. The military competition between North and South Korea continues to be a symptom of the ideological conflict, not its cause. The military dimension does, however, sharpen the conflict and increase its urgency.

Realists explain the survival concerns of Taipei, Pyongyang, and Seoul and the associated conflicts in terms of the security dilemma, differences in material capabilities, military competition, and threats. These factors are certainly not irrelevant, but such explanations often miss the underlying causes of the conflicts and the social factors that inform threat constructions. As we have seen, at base the security concerns of these countries are driven by identity considerations: Must the entire Chinese nation be unified under one sovereign authority or can two sovereign Chinese states coexist? When and on whose terms should the Korean nation be unified? And, what should be the ideological basis for political organization of a unified Korean nation-state?

Further, internal political considerations often conjoin these factors. The effect of power realities, both local and international, has often been to increase the intensity and urgency of the security concerns, entrench them, and perpetuate the related conflicts. Ideational factors not only offer a deeper understanding of the causes of such conflicts, they also draw attention to the issues that must be addressed in negotiating political settlements.

Conflict Between Post-Partition States

Like North and South Korea, India and Pakistan are caught in an unending spiral of mistrust and conflict. At base the conflict is driven by conflicting ideas about the identity of their nation-states, rival national self-conceptions, and the vested interests of the power elite in Pakistan (especially the military establishment). The dispute over Kashmir is both symptom and cause of the Indo-Pakistani conflict. Pakistan was imagined and constructed on the basis of the two-nation theory—one for the majority Hindus and another for the minority Muslims. But the rejection of that theory by most Hindu and some Muslim leaders, the secular construction of India, and the predictions of certain Indian leaders that Pakistan would disintegrate all created insecurity in Pakistan. From the outset Pakistani leaders suspected that India harbored ambitions of reintegrating Pakistan into India as soon as the opportunity presented itself. Pakistan's concern for survival became even more acute after its 1971 breakup, in which Indian military intervention played a key role. The Kashmir problem is a remnant of the partition of British India and is rooted in the conflicting political imaginations of Pakistan and India. Based on the two-nation theory, Islamabad claims that Kashmir should be part of Pakistan. But the fact that Kashmir has a Muslim majority is of no consequence for secular India, which, excluding Kashmir, is home to more than 100 million Muslims. New Delhi fears that allowing Kashmir to secede will set a dangerous precedent that may undermine the idea of a secular, multiethnic, and multireligious India and stimulate other secessionist demands (Ganguly and Bajpai 1994).

The Indo-Pakistani conflict is also driven by competing national self-conceptions. India sees itself as the successor to the earlier Indian empires (both Hindu and Muslim) as well as the British Raj. Moreover, Indian leaders subscribe to the ideas of cultural and geopolitical unity— the basis for New Delhi's claim to regional leadership and its conception of Indian national security in subcontinental terms. This national self-conception is challenged by Pakistan, which sees itself as an equal of India. Pakistan's claim is not based on the distribution of power, of course, which has become even more skewed in India's favor since 1971.

Rather, it is based on the idea of cosuccession of the British Raj as well as Pakistan's desire for the mantle of greatness worn by the earlier Muslim empires in India and beyond. Whereas India seeks to marginalize the cultural differences between the two countries, Pakistan seeks to marginalize the similarities, amplify the differences, and attach itself to the Muslim world. Finally, insecurity resulting from internal strife over identity and control of state power in Pakistan, as well as the vested interests of the Pakistani military establishment, sustain the conflict (see Chapter 10). India is a good villain in the domestic politics of Pakistan (Khattak 1996).

One can see, then, that the conflict over Kashmir and more generally the Indo-Pakistani conflict is not just a product of anarchy or a dispute about territory. Jammu and Kashmir account for only 4 percent of India's national territory and less than 1 percent of its population. The crux of the conflict is over the political meaning of the territory for national identity, the national self-conceptions of the two countries, and the legitimacy of the Pakistani government. The military competition between the two countries is a reflection of all these considerations. Altered power realities that now strongly favor India have increased the acuteness of Pakistan's security concerns, escalating mistrust and tension and pushing Islamabad to develop a nuclear capability.

From the foregoing discussion it is evident that ideational factors are critical to the explanation of the three most acute conflicts in Asia, all of which are embedded in conflicting notions about the identity of nations and states. Social factors can similarly help to explain the intensity associated with threat perceptions among several other Asian states. Historical legacy, for example, is a critical factor in explaining the deep-seated distrust and suspicions among Vietnam, Cambodia, Thailand, and Laos; among China, Japan, and the two Koreas; between China and Vietnam; and among India and its neighbors. Historical memories arouse intense nationalism that magnifies the significance of power differentials or the material (economic and strategic) worth of the territories in question. In all such cases material explanations must be supplemented by ideational ones.

Ideational Factors and the Explanation of Variations in State Behavior

In this section we argue two points: first, although changes in the material capabilities of a major state may precipitate reaction from other states, the actual reaction will be conditioned by the specific interests at stake, the normative considerations at the unit level, and the histori-cally derived intersubjective understandings among the affected states.

Second, consideration of material and ideational factors at the unit level can explain behavior that structural theory would label as anomalous. In other words, what looks like abnormal behavior through the lens of neorealism may be shown to be normal by the constructivist approach. We develop these arguments first through a discussion of the variations in the perceptions and responses of the Asian states with respect to the rise of China and then by examining the changes that have occurred in the security assessments of selected states.

The "China Threat": Variations in Perception and Response

Conflating power and threat, neorealist analyses have presented the rise of China as a threat to regional peace and security and have claimed that other major powers like Japan will seek to develop counterweights to a rising power such as China and that it will constitute a structural anomaly if Japan does not behave in this manner. Though China's growing power is certainly a key factor, it cannot by itself explain the differences among the Asian states in terms of their estimations of the consequences of the rise of China and their responses to that event.

Japan's perception of China is a complex one. Many among the Japanese elite recognize the enormous cultural debt owed by Japan to China as well as the act of Japanese colonialism in China and the atrocities committed by Japanese troops in the early part of the twentieth century. Along with the cultural debt and imperial guilt, consideration of the potential for profit underlay the Japanese policy of dialogue and engagement, which was designed to encourage Beijing to become a constructive force for the peace and prosperity of the East Asia region. In line with this policy, Tokyo allocated a substantial part of its official development assistance for China and, in the post-Tiananmen period, adopted a softer line (compared to its G-7 partners) toward China. Japan was not unduly concerned about the rapid growth of the Chinese economy for the first decade of that expansion. Instead, a major concern was the possibility of internal turmoil in China and the perceived negative consequences for Japan.

The Japanese perception of China, however, has begun to change in the course of the last few years. The change is due not to the rise of Chinese power per se but to the perceived undesirable behavior of that country, specifically in relation to the Senkakus and the disputed Paracels and Spratlys in the South China Sea, Chinese missile firings in 1996 to intimidate Taiwan, and the continuation of Chinese nuclear testing, despite censures and appeals from the world community including Japan, until the formal signing of the Comprehensive Test Ban Treaty. Some in Japan now believe that China is behaving in the classic realist mode. This changing perception may be interpreted by realists as supporting their claim that the dramatic surge in China's power has provoked security concerns in Japan. However, it is not the growth in power by itself but the purposes for which that power has and may be deployed that informs the changing perception. In any case, Japan still does not perceive any direct military threat from a rising China. Apart from the Senkaku Islands, Japan has no specific dispute with China. Its apprehension, rather, is that in the long term China may seek to dominate East Asia and thereby constrain Japanese freedom of action in the region.

Although the changing Japanese perception of China may lend some weight to realist analyses, Japan's international security behavior is still far from conformance with realist predictions. Despite its possession of the necessary demographic, economic, and technological capabilities for more than two decades now, and the experience of intense friction in its bilateral economic relations with the United States in the 1980s, Tokyo has not developed the necessary attributes of a stand-alone great power in the realist tradition as had been predicted by realists. Instead of building up its military capability, with the end of the Cold War Japan is in fact scaling back its defense expenditure and personnel. The *New Taiko* adopted in November 1995 and the new guidelines for U.S.–Japan defense cooperation unveiled in 1997 do seek to dramatically expand Japan's security role. That role is still limited and remains within the scope of the peace constitution. Further, instead of developing a counterweight to the United States through internal and external balancing as predicted by Waltz, Japan has sought to provide for its traditional security concerns through the continuation and strengthening of its bilateral security treaty with that country. The bilateral treaty still serves the mutual interests of both the United States and Japan. The economic conflicts that bedeviled the bilateral relationship in the 1980s have largely abated. A reinvigorated United States is much less concerned about Japanese economic competition, while Japan, suffering a deep recession for the last five years, is engaged in reviving its economy through deregulation and steps to increase domestic demand. For several reasons, both countries have a vested interest in the continuation of the alliance, and it was reaffirmed in April 1997.[29]

With respect to China, Tokyo does not seek to engage in geopolitical competition or to counter Beijing through internal balancing. To the extent that it has security concerns focused on China, Tokyo seeks to address them through persuasion and dialogue, as well as through the U.S.–Japan security treaty, which may further strengthen if Beijing behaves aggressively. Tokyo also seeks to influence Chinese behavior by engaging the latter in Asia-Pacific multilateral institutions. Despite its enormous power potential, Tokyo appears to prefer bandwagoning, a practice associated with small powers, rather than balancing, which neorealists believe is encouraged by the system and is the proper behavior for a state like Japan. This anomalous behavior on the part of Japan can be explained only if due consideration is given to unit-level normative factors that Waltz (1993) slights in his analysis. Although he states that foreign policy behavior can be explained only by a conjunction of external and internal conditions, in predicting the future position and role of Japan Waltz privileges the former. In his view, "when a country receives less attention and respect and gets its way less often," then the internal inhibitions are likely to disappear because "pride knows no nationality." The internal inhibitions that Waltz treats lightly appear to be still strong in Japan. Moreover, although Tokyo does desire greater international status and a larger international role, it seeks to achieve them in the context of the U.S.–Japan security treaty and through such means as higher-level participation in the United Nations and regional multilateral forums, as well as by focusing on nontraditional security areas. Tokyo does not want to replay its earlier great-power role, at least not in terms of content and style. Thus, instead of creating insecurity and pushing Japan to become more like the United States or China, as structural theory would have it, the internal and international inhibitions and Japan's dependency and vulnerabilities appear to make continuation of the alliance with the United states an attractive proposition. The attraction between unlike poles appears to be greater than the pressure to become a like but separate pole.

In contrast to Japan's, India's perception of and response to the rise of China are more amenable to a realist explanation. India's concern with China can be traced to its defeat in the 1962 war, their continuing border dispute, New Delhi's national self-conception of India as the preeminent power in South Asia, and Beijing's support for Islamabad, which is perceived as designed to curtail New Delhi's subregional and regional entitlements. The dramatic growth experienced by China coupled with India's low growth rate have heightened India's long-range concerns. More immediately, however, India has attempted to improve relations with China, shelve the border dispute, and conclude confidence- and security-building measures with China to reduce the possibility of renewed border conflict. The purpose of those efforts seems to be to reach some kind of accommodation with China while buying time, as well as to limit Chinese support for Pakistan, with which it has a serious and probably irreconcilable dispute. At the same time India continues to maintain a credible defense, build up its missile capability, preserve its nuclear option, build up its economy, improve relations with other neighbors, reinvigorate strategic relations with Russia, and improve relations with the United States but without seriously compromising its autonomy.

Among the smaller states, perceptions and responses span a wide spectrum, and threat perception is the critical criterion. Of the continental states, Taiwan and Vietnam strongly perceive a Chinese threat. Taipei's perception of the China threat is the most acute, and it bears upon Taiwan's survival as a separate sovereign state. Apart from Taiwan, Vietnam is perhaps the most concerned with the China threat. Hanoi's fear of Beijing is rooted in history as well as its recent experiences, including the 1979 punitive Chinese attack and the current territorial disputes with that country along its northern border and in the South China Sea. North Korea, South Korea, and Thailand, while cautious of China as a big power, do not perceive it as a threat. In fact, they view China as a useful countervailing power: Thailand vis-à-vis Vietnam; the two Koreas vis-à-vis Japan and Russia. Burma and Pakistan view China, despite its growing power, as a friend and ally: Rangoon because of Beijing's support for SLORC; Islamabad because Chinese support is invaluable in dealing with the India threat. Among the island states, Indonesia and Malaysia do perceive a China threat but much less directly and intensely than do Taiwan and Vietnam. Their perceptions are rooted in their internal circumstances (the presence of economically powerful Chinese communities in both countries), in a territorial dispute with China in the South China Sea in the case of Malaysia, and in a historical reading of China as a country ready to intervene in the domestic affairs of other countries and to use force in international politics. These two countries had a much greater fear of China from the 1950s through the 1970s, when China was much weaker, than they do now, in a time when Chinese power is increasing dramatically. This difference can be explained only by the growing "resilience" of the two states and the altered orientation of China, as well as the changed national priorities and outlook of their leadership, particularly in the case of Malaysia. China is now viewed as an economic opportunity and a force to be harnessed for stability and prosperity in the region. In contrast, the Philippines did not view China as a threat until the Chinese military action on the island of Mischief Reef, which the former claims to be its own. Since then, Manila has articulated a Chinese security threat both to the Philippines and to the region (see Chapter 17).

Apart from the differing threat perceptions, the essentially geopolitical construction of the China threat is moderated in several cases by the benefits, actual and potential, of economic interaction with that country as well as the common ground most Asian states share with China vis-à-vis the West on principles like noninterference in domestic affairs and on norms relating to human rights and democratic governance. When one considers the specific interests at stake, each country's geopolitical position and level of development, and the relevant ideational factors, a more complex picture of the China threat in the region emerges than when one considers only the changes in relative material capabilities.

As for their responses, the behavior of those states that perceive a threat from China cannot be explained simply in terms of balancing or bandwagoning. Taiwan and Vietnam do not seek to bandwagon with China. Taiwan seeks to balance the threat from China by developing its own capabilities as well as cultivating the commitment of the United States. Vietnam is gradually beginning to develop its national capabilities but it has no way to counter China through external balancing. Consequently Hanoi has attempted to improve relations with Beijing and to settle disputes through bilateral negotiations. It also seeks to constrain China through participation in ASEAN and other regional and global forums. Malaysia, Indonesia, the Philippines, North Korea, South Korea, and Thailand have not sought to balance China in any significant way. Their military efforts have been devoted to developing general denial capabilities of their own. Several of them have taken measures to facilitate continued United States engagement in the region. But they have been unwilling to join any effort that smacks of an "anti-China alliance."

Apart from the lack of a common threat perception, the necessary power resources to balance China are in fact virtually absent in East and Southeast Asia. Many in East and Southeast Asia believe that China cannot be balanced. The United States is the only power that can balance China, but there is considerable reluctance to follow the American lead with respect to China. Aside from the incoherence of the U.S. China policy, there is doubt as to whether the United States will be a reliable partner, pursuing regional interests as opposed to American national interests. Further, many disagree with certain aspects of U.S. policy toward China, especially with respect to human rights and democracy. The general belief is that Washington will pursue its own agenda, which may at times be disadvantageous to Asian states. Such doubts help to explain the ambivalent attitude of the Asian states toward the United States: whereas they support American engagement in Asia in general, they do not want to be closely tied to the United States. This attitude has been a source of frustration to American policy makers and analysts. Japan is the only Asian country that now has the power to balance China, but it suffers many constraints including dependence on

the United States for its security. Because the smaller countries do not
have the wherewithal to do so, they recognize that it is better for them
not to antagonize China. Thus they are unwilling to join any kind of
anti-China grouping.

At the same time no Asian country wants to appease China or to become its satellite. The ASEAN members, for example, have collectively
confronted China on its use of force in the South China Sea. They also
seek to improve bilateral relations with China and to engage China in
multilateral institutions in the hope of regulating that country's behavior
through regionally accepted norms and collective diplomatic action.
More generally they are engaged in constructing a normative order that
inhibits the use of force and encourages pacific settlement of disputes.
The reluctance of these states to join an anti-China effort could well
diminish if the China threat becomes more substantial. But China
would have to behave aggressively toward most of its neighbors—
especially Japan, India, Vietnam, and Indonesia—to engender a common
threat perception in the region. Meanwhile, Asian states will continue to
develop their own national capabilities while pursuing bilateral and
multilateral engagement of China to make it a responsible player. Most
will also continue to support American engagement in the region, but
without becoming tied to the United States. Thus the response of the
Asian states to the rise of China is a complex one that includes elements
of engagement, balancing, and bandwagoning.

Explaining the Reappraisal of Security in Individual States

As is true of the explanation of the different perceptions and responses to the rise of China, only a combination of material and ideational factors at the unit and systemic levels can explain the changes in
the security assessments of individual states over time. We elaborate this
claim through a discussion of the factors that have contributed to the
changes that have occurred in the security orientations of China, India,
Japan, and Vietnam in the post–World War II period.

Chinese security has been reappraised and reconfigured on at least
three occasions: in the late 1960s through early 1970s, in the early 1980s,
and again after the termination of the Cold War. Because the international material structure remained bipolar during the first two reappraisals, changes in security policy on those occasions cannot be explained as
structural in origin. The driving factors in the first reappraisal were the
ideological conflict with the Soviet Union and the need to balance the
Soviet threat by aligning with the United States. The subsequent
reappraisal in the early 1980s was due primarily to differences in the
national priorities and worldviews of Mao Zedong and his successor,

Deng Xiaoping. Deng's emphasis on economic and scientific modernization, and his assessment of the international environment as relatively
stable and benign, led to the discarding of Mao's theory about the
inevitability of war and to a broader definition of security that emphasized economic, scientific, and technological modernization and lowered
the priority of military modernization. The latest reassessment, which
began in 1989–90, was stimulated by the collapse of bipolarity and the
termination of the Cold War. But the current security concerns and
approaches cannot be explained without reference to certain domestic
considerations as well, such as the concern with regime security that
became even more acute after the Tiananmen incident and the collapse
of communism in the Soviet Union and Eastern Europe; the increased
prominence of the People's Liberation Army in Chinese domestic
politics; the growing force of nationalism; and the continuing high
priority accorded to economic modernization. Despite its predominant
position, the United States was initially not labeled by China as a
hegemonic power. But since the deployment of the two American
aircraft carriers in the vicinity of the Taiwan Straits in March 1996 and
the subsequent reaffirmation of the U.S.–Japan security treaty, Beijing
has begun to view the United States as a hegemonic power, and has
sought to elevate its relations with Russia to the level of strategic
partnership as well as to strengthen its good neighbor policy and become
more active in multilateral forums like the ARF to advance its policies.

In India, national security has been reappraised and reconfigured on
two occasions—after 1962 and again in the early 1990s. In the first
instance there was no shift in the international or regional material
structure. The trigger was the devastating defeat in the border war with
China. The China threat—the gravity of which was further reinforced
during the second Indo-Pakistani war in 1965 when Beijing threatened
India with war on a second front—contributed to a compromise and to
subordination of the idealist elements in Indian foreign policy, which
were basically rooted in Nehru's worldview and his belief that power
politics would inevitably lead to war. In the post-1962 period, Indian
security policy became more realist, especially under Indira and Rajiv
Gandhi, whose geopolitical vision included Indian predominance in
South Asia. Termination of bipolarity and the Cold War has not affected
India's threat perceptions or its policy framework for dealing with its
South Asian neighbors, although there has been a tentative effort under
the Gowda and Gujral governments to reach agreements on several
bilateral disputes with neighboring countries. The loss of Soviet support
has weakened New Delhi's material capabilities in relation to the major
powers, particularly China. That weakening has stimulated India's

efforts to forge better relations with the United States and China. But this redirection as well as the reduction in defense spending were also due to India's dire economic circumstances that came to a head in 1991, to the gradual liberalization of the economy that followed, and to the different worldview of Narasimha Rao. Unlike Nehru and Indira Gandhi, who had a clear vision of the world and the region and of India's place in them, Rao was more pragmatic and business-oriented. Recognizing the weakness of the highly regulated Indian economy and the dynamism of the East Asian countries, he laid the groundwork for India's cooperative engagement with East and Southeast Asian states in economic and political matters.

The stimulants for Japan's first reassessment of its postwar security policy in the early 1970s were its own economic vulnerability to international economic developments and the perceived decline in power of the United States. The comprehensive definition of security that resulted from that reappraisal and the continued reliance on the security treaty with the United States were due to the strong pacifism in Japan. A second reappraisal was undertaken after the end of the Cold War. Despite the dramatic change in the structure and dynamics of the international system, despite the generational change in Japanese political leadership, and despite a public mood that is generally supportive of a greater international role, Japanese security policy has continued on its path of incremental change. The *New Taiko* emphasizes the continued importance of the U.S.–Japan security treaty and the need to strengthen it. The focus of the U.S.–Japan treaty, according to some analysts, will shift from the defense of Japan to regional security. Tokyo has also begun to explore multilateral security cooperation as well as bilateral dialogue with Russia, China, the two Koreas, and the Southeast Asian states. It also seeks to link economic assistance to activities that are deemed to promote security and stability in the region. All these departures, however, remain subordinate to the treaty with the United States. This and the persistence of incrementalism in Japanese policy, as noted earlier, can be explained only by the continuing public, legal, and institutional pressures in Japan against articulating and operationalizing a security policy based on a strong national military.

Vietnam too has reoriented its security policy. Although the concern over China remains, Vietnam's view of the international environment is now more favorable. Internal security, particularly the "defense of the socialist fatherland," has emerged as the primary concern (see Chapter 14). In contrast to the earlier emphasis on the military dimension, security is now defined more broadly to include the political-ideological, economic, and social dimensions. And the approach to security has shifted from one of pure struggle to "struggle and cooperation." Several reasons, all interconnected, account for these changes: the weakening of socialism as the basis for political and economic organization and the related concern with regime security that can be traced to the post-1975 period; the heavy political, diplomatic, economic, and military cost of trying to dominate all that was French Indochina; the reduction and eventual termination of Soviet political, economic, and military assistance; and the socializing effect of the regional system, principally the success of the ASEAN states in comparison to its own dire circumstances. Subsequent membership in ASEAN has also affected Vietnam's approach to security.

In many cases the reappraisals we have identified were stimulated by the interaction of changes: in the worldviews of political leaders; in national priorities; in the material structure and dynamics of the international political system; and in the global and regional political, cultural, and institutional context. Even where material structure has been a significant factor in stimulating change, the actual response has varied from country to country and has been conditioned by unit-level factors. In fact, change in material structure and its consequences are not always evident. Despite the dramatic changes of the late 1980s and early 1990s, Chinese leaders whose favorable view of the international situation was based on the continuation of the Sino–Soviet–American strategic triangle did not, at least initially, comprehend the gravity of those changes. They were therefore slow in reacting to them. It took the rapidity and severity of the Western economic sanctions against China in the wake of the Tiananmen incident for Beijing to realize the consequences of the changes and then to adjust its policy accordingly.

We recognize that the foregoing discussion is suggestive, rather than providing a substantive explanation of the various security reappraisals. The number and breadth of the issues discussed as well as space and time constraints prevent a more detailed account and fuller explanation. Nevertheless, it is illustrative of the thrust of our argument in this chapter that description and explanation of the full range of the security concerns and behavior of Asian states requires the combination of material and ideational factors at the intrastate, unit, and systemic levels.

Conclusion

Asian security practice is highly complex, contested, and dynamic. Central decision makers define security broadly; they are concerned with internal and international threats; they deploy self-help and cooperative strategies to protect the values they deem essential for the survival and prosperity of the nation-state, which is their central but problematic referent of security.

Each of the international relations paradigms has the power to explain certain aspects of Asian security practice. But none of them—neither those focused on the structure nor those rooted in unit-level attributes—can explain all the aspects. Realism, for example, which has been widely deployed in analyzing Asian security practice, has certain strengths but it also suffers several clear limitations. It draws attention to international security concerns arising from conflicts of material interests and changes in relative material capabilities. But as we noted in discussing the political survival concerns of Asian states, many of these conflicts and threat constructions are informed by competing ideas about national identity and political legitimacy, as well as by intersubjective understandings derived from state interactions over decades if not hundreds or thousands of years. More significant is that realism is unable to explain variations between countries (the differences in the security behavior of contemporary China and Japan, for example), changes in the security behavior of a single country (the differences between prewar and postwar Japan or between Indonesia under Sukarno and under Suharto), or the change in the behavior of a group of countries like the ASEAN states, whose approach to security has shifted from reliance on competition and self-help to embody elements of cooperative and community security. Moreover, the realist model, especially the neorealist variant, will be even less useful in the future. Asian international politics is in the midst of change and is becoming more complex. Political survival is an acute concern for only a few states today. The national agendas of the other states are becoming broader and more diverse. There is no strict hierarchy among issues as assumed in the realist paradigm. Competition and self-help as well as interdependence and cooperation characterize Asian international politics. Though still important, the role of force is changing and its utility declining.

Realism, one must conclude, is unable to capture the growing complexity of Asian international politics and the changing normative context. These limitations, however, can be substantially overcome by a consideration of ideational factors. The inclusion of such factors does not necessarily invalidate realism. As noted earlier, they can help fill out realist explanations by exploring the knowledge base that shapes the actors' understanding of reality and illuminating the derivation and ordering of their interests. Apart from enabling deeper understanding, social factors also make it possible to explain the differences in behavior across states and over time. The different political-cultural legacies of China and Japan, for example, explain the differences in their contemporary behavior. A strong realpolitik tradition, the desire to erase past shame and humiliation, and the goal of reclaiming China's rightful place in the region and the world explain the strong presence of realist elements in the security behavior of China. The strong post–World War II antimilitaristic legacy of Japan, on the other hand, inhibits the development of independent national military capabilities and the resort to force to settle international disputes. It explains in large part the "abnormal" behavior of postwar Japan. Constructivism is also useful in drawing attention to the changing nature of international politics in Asia and its implications for the security problematic. It explains not only the emergence of cooperative security but also the subsequent changes in beliefs and interests, as well as the transformation of the security problem from a sharply competitive zero-sum game into a mixed-motive game (competition and cooperation) such as has occurred with the ASEAN states.

The key point is that Asian security practice cannot be explained solely on the basis of material interests and power realities without reference to social factors. The international security concerns and behavior of Asian states are often a product of the interplay of ideas, interests, and power. To explain them properly one must draw upon, and where appropriate, combine the insights of the related paradigms and theories, especially those of realism and constructivism. Paradigms and theories may also have to be deployed selectively to suit the circumstances. Such synthesis and contextualization may not be acceptable to theorists who present these paradigms as incompatible because of their conflicting premises. Nevertheless, as pointed out by Peter Katzenstein (1996: 500–505), a certain amount of convergence has taken place, and recent developments have made for nuanced articulations of "realist and liberal positions that seek to integrate culture and identity into their analyses." Hasenclever, Mayer, and Rittberger (1996) point out that some synthesis is in fact possible between rationalism (neorealism and neoliberalism) and what they call weak cognitivism. They also call for a dialogue between rationalists and strong cognitivists.

One of the central claims borne out by this chapter is that the nature of the political unit itself is critical to our understanding of Asian security behavior. Thus it is necessary to move beyond these system-level approaches to examine the state and its internal dynamics. The few international relations theories that do link unit-level variables to international behavior have focused on decision making, institutional structure, regime type, and more recently nationalism. Though not explicitly investigated in the country chapters, some of these variables may help to explain certain aspects of Asian security behavior. But it is the state's internal dynamics, especially the contestations of national identity and political legitimacy, that lie at the heart of the internal security concerns that figure prominently on the security agendas of Asian central decision makers. Mainstream paradigms of international relations, however, cannot explain internal security because they are constructed on the assumption of cohesive, sovereign political units and legitimate actors. This is a major limitation. It is imperative that explanations of Asian security pay particular attention to the interaction of state and society. This chapter has limited itself to highlighting the significance of intrastate variables. Future work must go further to posit and then investigate hypotheses that link the domestic variables to the security problems and behavior of Asian states.

The understanding of Asian security practice requires the deployment not only of the insights provided by competing paradigms of international politics, but also of those derived from comparative politics. This is a demanding requirement. Few can develop expertise in so many different areas. And then there is the professional requirement to specialize and the pressure to compartmentalize political science into international relations and comparative politics. But these difficulties do not obviate the need for greater fertilization across these divides. Teaching and research programs on Asian security must begin to integrate the history, culture, domestic politics, and international relations of Asian states.

Conceptualizing Security
Hierarchy and Conceptual Traveling

Muthiah Alagappa

Discussion in the previous chapter of the key features of Asian security practice supports the observation in Chapter 1 that security must be conceptualized to go beyond the concern with international military threat to the political survival of the state. Because the nature of states and their internal and international circumstances vary widely, conceptualization of security must be capable of accommodating a multiplicity of referents; both internal and international challenges to political survival; a more comprehensive interpretation of political survival; a range of other related values; and an array of approaches that includes competition and conflict as well as cooperation and community-building. The need to conceptualize security to allow for variations in the referent, nature, and scope of the security problem, as well as in approach, and simultaneously to preserve the analytical utility of the concept, however, presents a formidable challenge. Because of that complexity and the lack of a coherent alternative basis, even some of those who are otherwise sympathetic to a conceptualization that goes beyond the concern with military force have become more cautious about, if not skeptical of, redefining security. Some, like Richard Ullman, have retreated from their earlier advocacy for a broader definition of security. Ullman (1995: 3, 12) now states:

If national security encompasses all serious and urgent threats to a nation-state and its citizens, we will eventually find ourselves using a different term when we wish to make clear that our subject is the threats that might be posed by the military force of other states. The "war problem" is conceptually distinct from, say, problems like environmental degradation or urban violence, which are better characterized as threats to well-being....Labeling a set of circumstances as a problem of national security when it has no likelihood of involving as part of the solution a state's organs of violence accomplishes nothing except obfuscation.

This belief that security cannot be conceptualized apart from state organized violence is a complete reversal of his earlier position that "defining national security merely (or even primarily) in military terms conveys a profoundly false image of reality [which] is doubly misleading and therefore doubly dangerous" (Ullman 1983: 129). Although we share the concern of Ullman and others with regard to the difficulties of redefining security, we do not infer that this must inevitably lead us back to the acceptance of a force-based definition. Our discussions in Chapters 1 and 19 strongly suggest that the conceptualization of security must not be limited to or even proceed on the basis of the means by which values are threatened or are to be protected, i.e., the "how" component. Further, although military force and war are important instruments, they do not exhaust the means to threaten or protect and enhance political survival. "Who" (referent) and "what" (values) are to be protected are critical elements in the structure of security. They determine the nature of security problems and how they are to be addressed. Those elements rather than the "how" component must be given priority in the conceptualization of security.

Based on the observations and findings in earlier chapters as well as other published works, this final chapter seeks to advance a conceptualization of security that incorporates but goes beyond the traditional force-based definitions; one that is externally relevant, that is, can be contextualized to accommodate diversity in referents, threats, and approaches, but that is also internally coherent and analytically useful. Given the enormity and complexity of this challenge, we are under no illusion that the formulation advanced here resolves all the associated problems, if indeed there can be a resolution of such problems. Our goal is more modest—to move the debate further along through a conceptualization that bridges the competing definitions, whose proponents often appear to be talking past each other.

Rather than begin afresh, as advocated by some (especially those of the postmodernist persuasion), the conceptualization advanced in this chapter modifies and builds on earlier definitions of security. The concept of security, as observed by Ole Waever (1995), Daniel Deudney (1990), and others, has a history, has certain critical characteristics (we disagree with Deudney on what these are), and operates in a certain context. Although it should not be limited by these considerations, if it is to be more than just an intellectual exercise, and if it is to resonate in a wider circle both in the intellectual and policy communities, then our conceptualization must incorporate and begin with some of the same key considerations but then must suitably modify, extend, or supplement them. This building-from-within approach is also in accord with our effort to find common ground to foster dialogue and a shared understanding of security.

In line with this thinking, the articulation of security in this chapter builds on two key features of the realist security problematic. First, the political community—presently the nation-state—is the primary security referent. Second, the concern with political survival constitutes the core of security. These two features, however, must be deepened and broadened to accommodate (1) the problematic nature of states and the existence of competing referents for political community within states, as well as the emergence of supranational entities like the European Union; (2) internal challenges to political survival; and (3) a more comprehensive view of political survival in terms of its content, threats, and coping strategies. The case for deepening and broadening the content of political survival is the focus of the first section of this chapter. The claim that a comprehensive notion is warranted even in this core area of security is a critical one. It is more difficult for realists to dismiss the claim to a deeper and broader notion of security that is rooted in a consideration of political survival—the central concern of their problematic—than to dismiss those claims advanced on the basis of alternative conceptions that seek to replace the state with "new" referents or broaden the security agenda to include nonconventional issues and problems.

The second section argues that although the problem of political survival is prototypical and constitutes the core of security, it does not necessarily preclude the broadening of the security agenda to include economic, sociocultural, environmental, and such other concerns. However, on this point, especially where such concerns are not linked to political survival, the case is less clear and less compelling. We are convinced that nonconventional concerns that affect political survival, even though they may not involve the use of force, can be viewed as security concerns. We are much less certain of the value of attaching the security label to nonconventional concerns that have only marginal or no connection to political survival. Nevertheless, we believe the conceptualization of security must not arbitrarily exclude them. If considered necessary, however, their inclusion must be undertaken cautiously and deliberately and must satisfy certain criteria. We argue that for an issue or problem to be labeled as a security concern, it must be vital to the political survival or well-being of a community, and it must be of such gravity and urgency that it requires the mobilization of a substantial part and ultimately, if the need arises, of all the resources of the community. The determination of relevance, gravity, and urgency is to be made by the community in concern.

The third and final section argues that instead of being limited to one specific definition that inevitably cannot bear the burden of internal coherence, external relevance, and parsimony, security is better conceptualized in a hierarchic manner with different levels of abstraction. At the highest generic level, we define security as *the protection and enhancement of values that the authoritative decision makers deem vital for the survival and well-being of a community*. This declarative definition, to be fleshed out later, is an inclusive one with the minimum necessary "intension" properties to indicate the critical essence of the concept and articulate the basis for inclusion and exclusion of an issue as a security concern.[1] It, however, does not specify membership, and its analytical utility is limited. Membership and analytically relevant concepts, however, can be derived from this generic definition by conceptual traveling, that is, descending the ladder of generality or abstraction by adding "intension" properties. This approach enables a conceptualization of security that can accommodate complexity, diversity, and change, as well as address concerns relating to analytical relevance. It also provides a basis for mapping, organizing, and finding conceptual order among the many neologisms—*security* with adjectives—that have entered the security literature. We begin with the claim that a comprehensive notion of security is warranted even in relation to political survival, the central concern of the realist security problematic.

Political Survival: The Need for a Broad Interpretation

Concerns relating to political survival constitute the core of the security definitions and practices of Asian states. This does not imply that political survival of all Asian states is precarious or that it is the highest priority that dominates and informs all other concerns as depicted in the realist paradigm. In fact, as pointed out in Chapter 19, political survival in its most basic form is a concern only to North and South Korea and Taiwan. For the others, political survival concerns are more limited and less urgent. They do not always override other goals and interests. Nevertheless, insofar as the domain of security is concerned, its core is composed of matters relating to political survival.

Realist features and the definitions of security rooted in them, such as those of Patrick Morgan (1992) and Stephen Walt (1991) are not inapplicable to Asian states. The nation-state is the most valued political unit in Asia. Asian central decision makers claim and act on the basis of sovereignty. They are concerned with threats to autonomy and territorial integrity from other states. And they devote substantial resources to the development of military capability, which they view as essential to protect and enhance national security. Asian security practice, however, is not confined to these elements. The notion of political survival as understood and practiced by Asian decision makers is deeper and broader in several ways. First, although the nation-state is a highly valued norm, the specific political construction of nation and state, and the basis for political domination, are contested issues in a large number of Asian countries. The existing nation-state is not necessarily the security referent for all peoples residing within "national" boundaries. From the perspective of governments, in addition to the nation-state, the security referent often includes a certain ethnic or religious group, a specific political system, or the power elite. Governments frequently fuse the security of these various entities. Thus a conception of security that is relevant to Asia and many other parts of the world must take account of the problematic nature of the state and of the presence of other security referents, some of which may compete with the existing state.

Asian security practice, however, does not support alternate conceptions that seek to replace the nation-state with other security referents such as the individual, society, the regional or global community, or humanity.[2] Admittedly there are human rights organizations in Asian countries that argue for individual security and environmental NGOs that argue for environmental security. Their aim, however, is not to do away with the state. In the case of human rights organizations their goal is to limit the reach of the state and to increase the political freedom and space for the individual. The goal of environmental organizations is to increase environmental awareness and to infuse such considerations into state policy. These and other such organizations do not view the state as inherently evil or ineffective. As noted in the last chapter, the nation-state is still the most appealing form of political organization, and there is no acceptable alternative to it in Asia. That Asian practices do not support the case for other referents, however, does not imply that this is the case in all other regions. In Europe, for example, it has been argued that in light of the ongoing changes in the nature of the Western

European nation-states, society in those states and the European Union itself are emerging as security referents (Waever 1995). Conceptualization of security must be flexible enough to accommodate these and other similar entities as referents.

Second, the international political survival concerns of Asian states are not only a product of conflicting material interests, the struggle for power, international anarchy, or the distribution of capabilities; they are also rooted in the collective understandings of states, derived from historical and contemporary interactions as well as their political and strategic cultural legacies. Considerations of identity, national self-conception, and historical legacies, for example, underpin conflicts between China and Taiwan, North and South Korea, and India and Pakistan that on the surface appear to be driven by material considerations and the realist logic of anarchy. Moreover, for some states, internal challenges rooted in the problematic nature of the political units—especially those challenges related to the construction of national identity and to the normative frameworks and institutions associated with the acquisition and exercise of state power—are as consequential if not more so than international ones. Often, concerns about political survival span several levels, and frequently they are interconnected. The sources of insecurity are multiple and will vary: for some states the primary problem may issue from their problematic construction; for others it may lie in the international material structure; and for yet others, the normative context may be more significant.

Third, in many cases what is to be secured is not only physical interests—life, territory, resources, or other material interests—but also ideas that form the political, cultural, and religious basis of the nation, and principles and norms on the basis of which institutions for political domination have been constituted. The range of values associated with political survival thus transcends autonomy and territorial integrity to include, among others, the following: consolidation of the ideational basis that underpins the construction of nation and state and constitutes the basis for political domination; preservation of internal order and political stability; promotion of economic growth, development, and distributive justice; preservation of the sociocultural essence of the nation; and the preservation and enhancement of an international context, both normative and material, that is conducive to the attainment of these and other values, interests, and goals.

Fourth, political survival is threatened not only by military force but also by competing political ideas and sociocultural values. Such factors can pose substantial challenges to the ideational components of political survival, and frequently they are as important if not even more consequential than military challenges. Ideational challenges underlay or contributed to the partitioning of British India in 1947, the ejection of Singapore from Malaysia in 1963, the breakup of Pakistan in 1971, the dramatic political changes that occurred in Thailand (1973, 1991) and the Philippines (1986), and the political challenges that confronted China in 1989 and that continue to confront Myanmar since 1988. Political ideas such as democracy and human rights are presently viewed by several Asian governments as threats to survival because of the perceived adverse consequences for political stability and economic development, and because of the challenges they pose to the political legitimacy of the incumbent elite. Migration is perceived as a threat because of its potential to challenge the identity of a nation-state or a subnational unit, in some cases with consequences for control of political power. Asian political elites are hypersensitive to such ideational threats to political survival and respond to them with as much vigor as the military challenges evince.

Finally, in addressing the multifaceted challenges to political survival, the coping strategies of Asian states traverse and integrate the political, diplomatic, legal, sociocultural, economic, and military realms. Some of the specific measures deployed in addressing internal security concerns, for example, include devolution of power and authority; political, constitutional, and legal provisions for majority and minority rights; strict regulation of political organization and the media; national education and cultural policies; emphasis on economic development; and political, legal, and military suppression. Military force is one among many policy instruments. It is not always the most important, and frequently it plays a supporting role. Excessive emphasis on this instrument can also be counterproductive. At the international level, national military capabilities, alliances, and alignments are critical components of the approach to national security. But, in addition to self-help, Asian states employ cooperation and community-building strategies at the bilateral, subregional, and regional levels to prevent, contain, and terminate conflicts; build confidence, trust, and shared understandings; and develop a normative context that is supportive of the consolidation of the existing nation-states, promotes economic growth and development, and more generally facilitates peaceful international interaction.

It is evident from the foregoing discussion that conceptualization of security even as it relates to the core value of political survival has to be deeper and broader than that articulated in realist definitions of security. It must be capable of accommodating contested and multiple referents and a broad range of values, threats, and coping strategies, and must include both the internal and international levels. Conceptualization of security must also embody the material and ideational dimensions of security problems. The incorporation of the ideational dimension into security analysis must go beyond simply plugging additional variables like ethnicity and nationalism into structural realist analysis (Krause and Williams 1996: 239–42). This is the shortcoming, for example, of Barry Posen's (1993) attempt to explain ethnic conflict in terms of an internal security dilemma and Steven Van Evera's (1994) attempt to develop hypotheses linking nationalism and international conflict. Group identities and nationalism are not always given, and they are salient in some situations and not in others. Security analysis must explore the processes identified in Chapters 1 and 19, because they can provide insights into the causes and effects of these and other variables, and elucidate their interconnection with political survival.

However attractive it may be in terms of analytical utility and theo-retical coherence, the limitation of security to an international structural problem, with the focus on state autonomy and territorial integrity and the military threats to these values, falls well short on the criterion of external relevance. Asian experiences, and those in many other parts of the world, do not support such a restrictive interpretation of political survival or the accompanying definitions of security. A comprehensive view of political survival is not novel. Governments in Asia and many other parts of the world have long interpreted political survival along such lines and have addressed related concerns as security issues. Further, this holistic view of political survival cannot be dismissed as applicable only to inconsequential states in the periphery. It is critical to the analysis of the security practice of even major states like China, Russia, and India, which have been identified by realists as having the potential soon to affect global and regional structures. Although it may not apply to them or may apply only in a marginal way, for such power-ful states as the United States a comprehensive view of political survival will facilitate better understanding of the security problems of most other states and will contribute to the development of appropriate and effective foreign and security policies around the globe. Incorrect understanding of such problems can be costly. Failure to understand the nationalist underpinnings and aspirations of the Vietnamese Communist Party and the consequent interpretation of the conflict as part of the global ideological struggle and as affecting vital American national interests, for example, cost the United States dearly in terms of blood, treasure, and domestic support, leading eventually to its defeat in the Vietnam War.

The deepening and broadening of the concern with political survival does not alter the focus of security, although its extension to include the intrastate level and ideational challenges implies that the theoretical underpinnings of security cannot be limited to the realist paradigm alone. It must also draw on other relevant theories and paradigms, especially those that deal with the interaction of state and society. It should be observed here that not every aspect of this broad notion must apply to each state. Rather, the inclusive view ensures that related issues are not excluded by definition, and that definitions and concepts appropriate to the circumstances of a state or to the inquiry in concern can be derived from it through further delimitation.

Nonconventional Dimensions and Security: The Connections

Although political survival, broadly defined, lies at the heart of Asian security practice, it does not exhaust the security agenda of Asian states. As noted in Chapter 19, Asian articulations of security often include economic, sociocultural, and, less commonly, environmental dimensions. There are two aspects to the nexus posited between nonconventional concerns and security.

The Connection to Political Survival

The first and the more common linkage has to do with expanding the list of concerns and strategies associated with the problem of political survival. Here, the inclusion of nonconventional dimensions takes one or more of the following forms: they are included as material interests to be protected or augmented in connection with political survival; as threats to national identity, political legitimacy, political stability, autonomy, or territorial integrity; as sources of internal and international disputes and conflicts; as affecting the capability of states and thus their international power, prestige, and influence; and finally as an instrument of policy in pursuit of the concerns associated with political survival. This linkage between nonconventional dimensions and political survival is best illustrated with reference to economic security, which has been defined by many Asian governments as a vital component of national security.

Economic growth and development are viewed as critical in addressing internal and international challenges to political survival. Internally, economic growth is valued because of the resources it makes available to address social and economic problems, and for the contribution it can thereby make to social and political stability and more generally to the management of internal conflict and thus to the development of national resilience. It is also viewed as a critical resource for political legitimation.

Many Asian governments claim their right to rule on the basis of economic performance and political stability (Alagappa 1995b: chaps. 2 and 11). Internationally, economic strength is viewed as a crucial element of national power, prestige, and influence, and a key prerequisite for the development and sustenance of military power. This is a key consideration in the Chinese articulation of economic security. Others like Japan view economic strength as a means to compensate for their weakness in the military instruments of power. Yet others like Taiwan, South Korea, and Singapore seek to deploy economic power in a strategic manner to enhance their prospects for political survival. More generally economic strength is viewed as vital to protect and enhance national interests and autonomy. Consequently, threats to economic growth and development are viewed as threats to national security.

This linkage between nonconventional concerns and political survival is a key component of the comprehensive definitions of security in Asian states. It does not require a fundamental redefinition of security. Its effect is to expand the range of interests, threats, and coping strategies that bear upon political survival. Such concerns as economic and energy security have always been viewed as connected to security, although their salience may have been overshadowed by the excessive focus on the military dimension during the Cold War. Therefore, this aspect of the linkage between nonconventional dimensions and security has not drawn much criticism from realists. Many accept such a limited broadening because of the belief that it can be accommodated by realist articulations of security. There is, however, one major difficulty that is not always appreciated. Although accommodating additional threats to political survival or viewing nonconventional issues as possible sources of interstate conflict may not be problematic for the realist paradigm, their resolution is. Resolution of these nonconventional threats does not rest only or even primarily on military force. Nonmilitary measures may be much more significant in resolving such threats to political survival.

For example, military force is only one of many options for the management of energy security. Most recently it was deployed to protect access to oil in the 1991 Gulf War. But in the long term, nonmilitary measures like finding alternative sources and reducing energy consumption and dependence may be more critical in the management of energy security (Romm 1993: 37–50). Similarly, although migration and environmental issues may threaten identity and control of state power or may produce domestic and interstate tensions and conflicts, military force and war are not central or even necessary to their resolution. Because of this consideration, some realists reject even the limited broadening or seek to limit it to aspects that involve the threat and use of force. From the perspective of the Asian central decision makers, however, the fact that force may be irrelevant to managing such concerns, and that the expertise required to manage them may be radically different, does not disqualify them from being labeled as security concerns. What matters is their impact on the political survival and well-being of their respective communities.

The Connection to the Well-Being of the Community

Such an interpretation leads to the second and more far-reaching linkage, which seeks to make concerns like economic well-being, sustainable development, a healthy environment, and a drug-free society security issues in their own right, not because of their consequences for political survival but because of their impact on the well-being of the community. This connection has been especially controversial and has been resisted by realists and others. Ullman's objection, cited earlier, to the inclusion of threats to well-being as security concerns is an example of such resistance. The case for and arguments against this linkage have been rehearsed in Chapter 1. As noted there, the case against the inclusion of "new" concerns has considerable merit but it is also flawed in several respects. The differences between the nonconventional and the so-called traditional concerns of security, though significant, are frequently exaggerated; it is fallacious to argue that concerns that do not involve the threat or use of force are not security issues; the nation-state is not the only referent of security; the meaning and content of security are not fixed, they vary across countries and regions and over time; and expertise cannot be the basis for defining what is and is not a security issue.

Notwithstanding these rebuttals, there is still the difficult problem of how to define and delimit the scope of security. In the absence of set criteria, all manner of things can be labeled as security concerns. The concept and the subfield will not have coherence. Further, one must consider whether attaching the security label to various concerns adds value in terms of analysis and policy making. Our view is that the added value arising from the second linkage is rather marginal. Although it may, at the highest levels in government, provide a framework for viewing the many and competing demands on the scarce resources of the state in a more integrated manner and facilitate prioritization among them, that can be done even without labeling them as security concerns. The case for the second linkage, i.e., making nonconventional issues security concerns in their own right, is thus less clear, and Asian practices do not provide strong support for it. Many of the nonconventional security concerns of Asian states in fact relate to political survival.

Nevertheless, the second linkage should not be excluded by definitional fiat. The inclusion or exclusion of nontraditional security concerns must be based on criteria that are independent of specific worldviews, and this must be specified as part of the generic definition of security.

Security: A Hierarchic Conceptualization

It is clear from the discussion in this book that the realist conception of security, particularly the neorealist variant, is inadequate but not irrelevant. It has certain validity at the international level for a large number of countries, but it does not encompass all of the legitimate security problems likely to confront them. The advocates for alternative conceptions of security do a valuable service in pointing out the shortcomings of the realist conception, especially the need to view the political survival problem in a broader perspective and the importance of including nonconventional concerns that affect political survival. However, as noted in Chapter 1, they too are not without limitations. The different conceptions have usually been presented by their proponents as contending and incompatible. The investigations in this book do not support such sharp divisions. On the contrary, they suggest a more inclusive view that incorporates elements from the various conceptions of security.

Rather than engage in an intellectual debate that is basically unresolvable because of the different worldviews in which the various conceptions are rooted, a more satisfactory approach would be to conceptualize security at a higher level of abstraction so that the concept can accommodate diversity and change. At the highest level, security would be cast as a generic concept; its essence and boundaries would be defined but not the actual referent, the specific values to be protected, the nature and types of threats to them, or how security is to be achieved. These aspects will feature in the more concrete concepts at the species and subspecies levels that can be derived by descending the "ladder of generality or abstraction," that is, by increasing the intension properties to make the concept discrete enough to suit the issue and task at hand.[3]

By freeing security from association with any particular referent, core value, or approach, a more abstract definition of security would permit inquiry at any level and into any issue or any combination of them that merits consideration under this label. The "conceptual traveling" that is enabled by this approach also permits the researcher to address the issue of specific concern by specifying or deriving subtypes from the generic definition of security without committing the error of "conceptual stretching."[4] Theories and concepts appropriate to each level and domain can then be deployed to facilitate inquiry. This is in keeping with our conclusion in Chapter 19 that more than one theory is required to explain the security concerns of Asian states. This approach also addresses several, though not all, of the concerns of both the realists and the advocates of alternative conceptions of security.

In particular, the generic definition permits a more inclusive view of security, and the concrete concepts derived from it address the concern relating to analytical utility. In this conceptualization, those desiring to limit their inquiry to the political-military dimension at the international level can do so by specifying the appropriate intension characteristics. Others can investigate the referents and values related to their concerns, again by an appropriate delimitation of the concept. This is not simply a schema to permit unrelated inquiries. The various concerns must still share a conceptual thread and satisfy certain criteria in order to be considered as part of the domain of security. A generic definition of security must fulfill these requirements.

The Essence of Security and Membership Criteria

Our generic definition of security—*the protection and enhancement of values that the authoritative decision makers deem vital for the survival and well-being of a community*—limits the referent of security to community on the basis that security is for and about people, who normally provide for their individual and group security by organizing themselves into communities. Usually, such communities have or aspire to political expression in the form of a nation-state. This definition, however, does not exclude other forms of expression such as the supranational European Union, which is developing some aspects of a political community. Nor does it preclude subnational or transnational communities that may or may not aspire to independent political community status but are nevertheless concerned with the survival of their communities as distinct sociocultural entities. This is the case with many minority communities in the multiethnic states of Asia and in other parts of the world. The definition does, however, exclude nonhuman entities like the international economic system or the ecological system as security referents in their own right.

The core concern of security in our generic definition is the survival and well-being of the community. It does not specify the vital values they seek to protect or the challenges against which those values have to be protected. It does, however, provide three criteria for determining membership, that is, for deciding whether an issue or problem warrants the security label. First, the value must be *vital* to the survival and well-being of a community. In other words, it must be a critical feature that defines the community—such as sovereignty, territorial integrity, and national identity in the case of a state, or certain sociocultural features like ethnicity, religion, or language in the case of minority communities in multiethnic states—and without which its very existence would be severely compromised. Such features may be physical or ideational, and they may include possession and milieu goals. Second, the threat or challenge to these vital values must be *urgent*, with grave consequences for the community. Although the threat and use of military force is a useful criterion in determining the urgency and gravity of threat, it is not the only criterion and may not always be critical. Relying on the threat or use of state organized force as the sole or even a necessary criterion can obscure other challenges that ultimately can have dramatic social and political consequences. A more appropriate criterion for determining gravity and urgency would be the perception of the community as well as the mobilization and allocation of its resources. If a substantial part—and ultimately all—of a community's intellectual and material resources will be mobilized to confront a challenge, then it could be labeled as a security concern.

The composition of defining features and the determination of what constitutes a serious threat, however, will vary by the history and nature of the community—premodern, modern, or postmodern, for example—as well as the material and normative contexts in which the community resides. National identity, for example, is problematic and a critical concern in most Asian states but not in most Western states. Even in those states where national identity is a concern, the tolerance level and what constitutes a threat to national identity can vary quite widely and can change over time. That the determination of vital values as well as the threshold for construction of threats will vary by community and circumstances may be illustrated with reference to the impact of migration on identity: some states have labeled migration as a security concern and others have not, or at least not to the same degree. Some countries like the United States and India (because of their histories, size, and the ideas that underpin their national identities, among other considerations) have a much higher tolerance level than, for example, Japan or South Korea, which define national identity strictly along ethnic lines. Thus even a few hundred thousand migrants are perceived as polluting and threatening Japanese and Korean national identity, whereas the six million or so Bangladeshi illegal immigrants in India and the substantial increase in the Hispanic population in the United States are viewed with less alarm, at least at the national level.

Because of its delicate demographic structure and the idea of a Malay-based Malaysia with the accompanying goal of Malay political domination, Malaysia is more tolerant of Malay-Muslim migrants, especially from Indonesia and the Philippines, but less tolerant of Chinese and Indian migrants. The inflow in the 1970s and early 1980s of a few hundred thousand Vietnamese boat people, predominantly of Chinese ancestry, was labeled a security threat, but the inflow of an even larger number of Muslim Filipinos and Indonesians was viewed with much less concern and even seen as a plus among some segments of the Malay elite. Similarly, Singapore's tolerance level with regard to migration is influenced by its physical location in a Malay world, the desire to maintain the dominant political position of the Chinese community, and the consideration of political and social stability. Tolerance levels also vary with time and changing circumstances. In Western Europe, for example, migration and its economic and identity consequences have only recently become, at least in some representations, a key social, political, and security problem. Consequently the determination of vital values, and of what constitutes urgent and grave threats to them, cannot be fixed across communities or over time. This leads to the third criterion: The vital values of a community and the threats against which they are to be protected must be determined by the community in question, that is, by its authoritative decision makers.

Our generic definition may be objected to at least on three interconnected counts: its openness to abuse; its subjectivity; and the problems it poses for theory-building. That this definition, particularly its provision for broadening the scope of security and leaving the judgment of what is and is not a threat to the authoritative decision makers of the community, is open to abuse cannot be disputed. However, because of its emotive content and the high priority and sacrifice it commands, the concept of security has always been open to abuse. Issues have been "securitized" or "desecuritized" by leaders and officials to serve their vested interests, to justify resource allocation, to justify their hold on power, to suppress political opposition, and so forth. Hence, the charge of openness to abuse cannot be the basis for rejecting the definition advanced here. In any case, such abuse can and must be discerned from the context of the norms, rules, and practices of the society in question. The analyst does not have to accept the views and actions of incumbent power holders. Those views can and must be compared to and evaluated in the context of articulations and practices of others in society, both in and out of government, who are competent to engage in the practice of security. There are several ways of discerning abuse. A crucial task of the analyst is to detect abuse and to factor that into his or her analysis.

The objection based on subjectivity has greater merit. Political survival of the community and its well-being, and the criteria for determining what is grave and urgent, are open to widely differing interpretations. They can be defined in less or more inclusive ways, and assessment of what threatens them cannot be objectively determined. However, as noted in Chapter 19, threat construction, even in the case of conventional threats, has a strong subjective component. It is informed not only by material factors but also by ideational ones including the collective understanding of actors derived from historical and contemporary interaction. A comprehensive view of security such as that advanced by our conception increases the subjective component. This, however, is the nature of the beast and has to be accepted. Any attempt to restrict the concept to give it greater certitude and rigor would distance analysis from reality and may be misleading. Ultimately, the determination of what constitutes a threat to survival or well-being will have to be made by persons holding responsible positions. As noted earlier, this does not imply that the analyst must necessarily accept the threat perception, say, of a government; only that it must be framed and validated in the context of the society's collective understanding. It cannot be imposed from the outside.

Finally, the claims that security is situational and must be explained based on the mutual knowledge of the society in question, and that the conceptualization of security must allow for diversity and change, may be interpreted as inhibiting to theory-building. It is difficult to refute the contention that the context-sensitive approach is less conducive to the development of universal generalizations. But that does not imply that no generalization is possible; only that generalizations will be bound by context, both spatial and temporal. Such generalizations are not without explanatory power. It should be observed here that even concepts and theories, such as those constructed on neorealist foundations, that purport to be scientific and universal have not lived up to their claims (Krause and Williams 1996: 235–42). For several reasons, theory-building in social science as envisaged in positivism has not fared well (Giddens 1979: 234–60). Consequently, shortcomings on this score cannot be the basis for rejecting alternative conceptions of security. Moreover, the purpose of the generic definition is to indicate essence and boundary. It must be judged by these criteria and not by analytical usefulness. The hierarchic conception, however, makes it possible to derive more concrete and discrete concepts through conceptual traveling. Such concepts will be analytically more useful and also facilitate theory-building. Because the concrete concepts are less subjective and less amenable to abuse, they may also minimize some of the shortcomings noted above, which of course are not unique to the more inclusive view of security articulated here.

Derivation of More Concrete Concepts

The generic definition is a bare-bones, declarative definition and is meant to be inclusive. Context-sensitive and analytically useful concepts may be derived from it through the creation of subtypes by moving down or up the ladder of generality, that is, by increasing or decreasing the attributes to specify the desired membership. For example, the security referent in the generic definition is community, which encompasses a broad range of human collectivities in the world. If the requirement is to investigate the security of the political community expressed in the form of nation-state, then the more distinct and relevant concept of national security may be derived by adding the attributes of sovereignty and territorial integrity to the minimal attributes of community. Through further delimitation, one can move further down the ladder to derive the additional subtypes of regime security, societal security, and communal security to investigate the security of regimes, society, and communal (ethnoreligious) groups, respectively. One may also move up the ladder to investigate the security of a regional community like the European Union.

Similarly, the scope of security may be specified by moving up or down the ladder of generality. In this regard several subtypes may be noted. High on the ladder are those that seek to indicate the full range of security concerns both in terms of values and threats. These maximalist security subtypes include concepts like comprehensive security, total security, and national resilience. They are essentially descriptive, not analytical, concepts. These maximalist subtypes subdivide into concerns with political survival and well-being. The former is concerned with the essential core of security whereas the latter relates to the conditions of existence. Political survival further subdivides into traditional or conventional security and nonconventional security. Political survival, defined in terms of autonomy and territorial integrity and international military threats to these values, forms the core of what some have termed traditional security. Nonconventional security comprises ideational, economic, and technological components that relate to political survival. Economic security can be further disaggregated into resource security, energy security, food security, market security, distributive justice, and so forth. Similar disaggregation is possible with the other components of nonconventional security. As with the referent and scope, subtypes may also be derived with respect to how security is to be achieved.

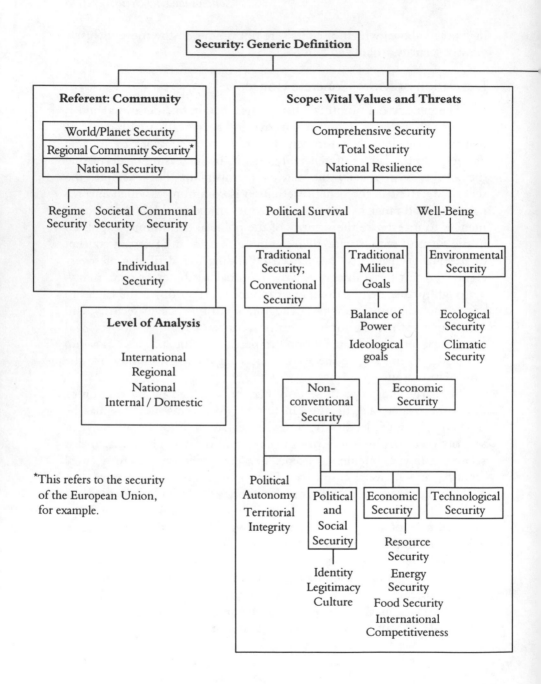

*This refers to the security
of the European Union,
for example.

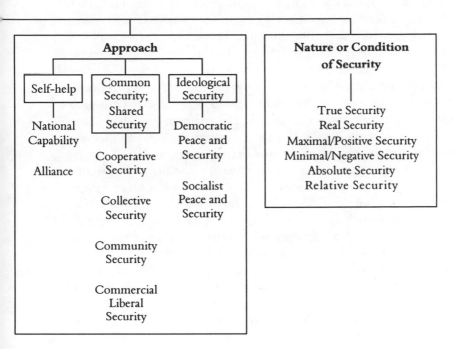

FIGURE 3
Security with Adjectives: Mapping and Organization

By enabling the derivation of discrete concepts to specify referents, to delimit the scope, and to identify approaches to security, this hierarchic conceptualization facilitates comparative analysis and prevents conceptual stretching and obfuscation. If the concern, for example, is to investigate how governments seek to protect and enhance the security of power holders, then the relevant concept is regime security, not national security although decision makers may deploy the latter concept to obscure the actual concern. Similarly, although the generic definition of security may define the scope in a broad manner, the derivation of subtypes enables investigation to focus on selected values and threats. An investigation of political survival, for example, can be broad, covering internal and international challenges traversing the physical, ideational, and nonconventional dimensions, or it can be targeted to investigate a specific concern such as ideological security or international military threats to sovereignty. If the objective is to investigate the security of energy supply, then the appropriate concept is energy security rather than resource or economic security, which are more general concepts.

This contention may appear obvious, but it warrants emphasis because it gets to the heart of the objection that a more inclusive definition of security is not compatible with analytical usefulness. It does, however, mean that specific terminology must be deployed for each referent, specific value or threat, or approach. But as illustrated by such terms as national security, international security, regional security, conventional security, nuclear security, low-intensity conflicts, self-help, collective self-defense, balance of power, collective security, and so forth, a degree of lexical specificity was already the practice even within the domain of the so-called traditional security. The same is true of the nonconventional aspects of security, as evidenced by concepts like societal security, communal security, individual security, ideological security, environmental security, economic security, cooperative security, and community security. Many of the discrete concepts, as illustrated in Figure 3, are already in use. Thus the "unsettling costs" of the proposed conceptualization of security should be minimal.[5]

In addition to facilitating focused inquiry and comparative analysis, this conceptualization based on different levels of abstraction, in conjunction with the structure of security elaborated in the Introduction, enables mapping and organization and the finding of conceptual order among the many terms—*security* with adjectives—that have become common in the discourse on security. Most of these terms can be grouped under the key elements of security: referent, level, scope, and approach. Some terms that do not fit under the constituent elements of security may be organized in a group that relates to the state or condition of security. Within each group the terms may be organized from the top down in terms of their generality. An exercise of this nature, as mapped in Figure 3, brings a certain order to the field and may also encourage greater discipline in the coining of new terms.

Conclusion

Security must be conceptualized with survival of the political community as its core. Political survival, however, may be threatened not only by other states but also from within a state. And challenges to political survival go beyond military force to include ideational, sociocultural, and economic ones. Although political survival constitutes the nucleus, conceptions of security must also be able to accommodate serious challenges to the well-being of a community, which may be viewed as forming the outer ring. The inclusion of well-being is not as novel as it may appear. The American goal of making the world safe for democracy, for example, has more to do with ensuring favorable conditions of existence than ensuring survival in the minimal sense. The extension of well-being to include nonconventional, especially environmental, dimensions may be viewed in a similar manner, although it is not clear what the added value will be from attaching the security label to such concerns. Nevertheless a conception of security that can embrace the aspects we have identified must necessarily be an inclusive one. A single all-embracing definition of security, however, is limited in analytical value. The conceptualization of security advanced in this chapter seeks to overcome that difficulty by articulating an inclusive generic definition, but one from which analytically useful discrete concepts can be derived.

All conceptualizations and definitions of security, including that advanced here, will have shortcomings. The conceptualization in this chapter, however, has several merits. It indicates the core concern of security and the basis for membership; it is abstract and inclusive, and it can accommodate different worldviews; it permits deepening and broadening but not indiscriminately; it enables the derivation of more specific and analytically useful concepts; and it can capture the complexity, diversity, contestation, and change that characterize the social practice of security. Further, it seeks to distill, preserve, and build on the essential meaning and practice of security. Among the advantages of the proposed conceptualization are its inclusiveness and its facility to engender more concrete and discrete concepts through "conceptual traveling," thus facilitating comparative analysis and helping us to find conceptual order among the many neologisms that have now entered the security vocabulary.

Reference Matter

Notes

Introduction

1. For an elaboration of the argument that the idea of Asia is an illusion, that culturally there are at least three Asias, and that "Asian" is not a counterpart of "European," see Steadman 1969.

2. For a discussion of the several uses of *Asia*, see Cohen, n.d., "Rashoman in South Asia."

3. This project initially conceptualized Asia to include Central Asia as well. Papers were commissioned to investigate security practice in the Central Asian states of Uzbekistan and Kazakstan. For a number of reasons, those two papers had to be dropped from the volume.

4. On subordinate systems, see the introduction in Cantori and Spiegel 1970.

5. "Back to the Future" is the title of an article by Mearsheimer (1990), which argues that post–Cold War Europe will be characterized by instability.

6. Most of the pessimists on this issue are from the West. Asians, for the most part, though concerned about uncertainties and possible setbacks, are less pessimistic. This divide between Westerners and Asians is obviously a crude one and should not be stretched. Some Western analysts, for example, share the optimistic outlook of Asian scholars.

7. At the first meeting of the ASEAN Regional Forum in 1994, it was agreed to entrust the incoming chair with, among other things, the responsibility to "study the comprehensive concept of security, including its economic and social aspects, as it pertains to the Asia-Pacific region." On comprehensive security in the ASEAN countries, see Alagappa 1988.

8. On international society, see Bull and Watson 1984 and Buzan 1993a.

9. Calculated on the basis of statistics contained in United Nations Conference on Trade and Development 1995: 337, 340.

10. For a dissenting view, see Krugman 1994.

11. Calculated from year-on-year growth rates (World Bank 1996: 22–23).

12. Calculated on the basis of data in World Trade Organization 1996: tables A3, A4, A5, and A6, pp. 138, 140, 143–44, 146–47, 149; and International Monetary Fund 1995: 70–71.

13. The allocation for defense in the East Asian countries, for example, is generally assumed to have increased sharply in the course of the last decade, although a detailed study of actual expenditures and how they are utilized has yet to be done. Some authors, Klare (1993) and Segal (1992), for example, have argued that an arms race is under way in Asia, but these remain superficial accounts. More work has been done on the reasons for defense spending. See, for example, Desmond Ball (1993–94), who argues that defense spending in Asia appears to be correlated with economic circumstances.

14. For a statement of this position, see Kausikan 1993. For a balanced discussion of the debate over human rights, see Ghai 1994 and Yasuaki 1996.

15. On the question of the existence of uniquely Asian values, see Emmerson 1996.

16. The phrase "West versus the rest," first used by Kishore Mahbubani (1992), has since been used by some officials and analysts in the West to depict an Asian threat to Western values and interests. See, for example, Huntington 1993.

17. Quoted in Mahbubani 1993: 13–14.

18. For an argument to the contrary (why Japan will not become a superpower), see May 1993–94.

19. For a survey of Asia-Pacific security studies, see Paul Evans 1994.

20. According to Haq 1995, the peace dividend has materialized primarily in the industrialized countries and to a lesser degree in selected developing countries in the Middle East and Latin America.

21. On rethinking U.S. security, see, for example, Allison and Treverton 1992. Several contributors to this volume argue that with the demise of communism and the collapse of the Soviet Union, the traditional security of the United States–defined as its protection as a free nation with its fundamental values and institutions intact–has seldom been so certain. But they argue that new concerns, particularly "threats" to cherished values from within, demand a redefinition of America's security. On rethinking Soviet security, see Gorbachev 1987.

22. See, for example, Buzan 1983, 1991; Booth 1991a, 1991b; Haftendorn 1991; Dalby 1992; Kolodziej 1992a, 1992b; Sorenson 1990; Allison and Treverton 1992; Ullman 1983; Mathews 1989; Westing 1989; Romm 1993. See also Palme Commission 1982.

23. On conceptual stretching, see Collier and Mahon 1993.

24. *Cooperative security* has been defined and used in different ways. See, for example, Carter, Perry, and Steinbruner 1992; Dewitt 1994; Gareth Evans 1994; and Nolan 1994.

25. On the role of concepts, see Sartori 1984; Collier and Mahon 1993.

26. The term *central decision maker* was coined by Stephen Krasner (1978).

27. This discussion of the logical-deductive and empirical-inductive approaches draws upon Krasner 1978: 35–45.

28. On milieu goals and their distinction from possession goals, see Wolfers 1962b: 73–75. Milieu goals seek to shape the international environment in which a state operates to make it more peaceful or conducive to the pursuit of national

goals. Possession goals, in contrast, include those values that are in limited supply and can only be held to the exclusion of others.

29. On the role of normative contexts in explaining the differences in the internal security behavior of Japan and Germany, see Katzenstein 1993. On the role of state structure and normative context in explaining Japanese security policy, see Katzenstein and Okawara 1993. On the "never again" resolves resulting from the bitter experience of the Pacific War and their effect on Japanese security behavior, see Bobrow 1993: 419–21.

30. It should be noted here that the empirical-inductive approach also has its limitations, including the interpretation of evidence, which is likely to be conditioned by one's theoretical persuasion.

31. The term *judgmental dopes* was coined by Harold Garfinkel in referring to analysts' treatment of the actors' understanding and reasoning in concrete situations as irrelevant to an analytical approach to social action. See Heritage 1987: 229.

32. Mutual knowledge is "a knowledge that is shared by all who are competent to engage in or recognize the appropriate performance of a social practice or range of practices" (Ira Cohen 1987: 287).

33. Market failure refers to a situation "in which the outcomes of market mediated interactions are suboptimal, given the utility functions of actors and resources at their disposal." The structure, rather than the actors, is viewed as inadequate, and this defect may be overcome through innovative institution building (Keohane 1984: 82–83). For a discussion of the distinction between distributional issues and market failure, see Krasner 1991.

34. The concern that discussions of security tend inevitably to be narrow underscores David Baldwin's (1995) call for the abolition of security studies as a subfield and its reintegration into international politics.

35. Comments by Oran Young in the chapter "Environment and Security" in Shultz, Godson, and Greenwood 1993: 351.

36. Buzan (1993b) argues that Waltz confuses structure and system.

37. For a discussion of the impact of revolutions on the international behavior of states, see Walt 1992. Although Walt is a strong proponent of neorealism, several analysts have noted that his balance-of-threat argument, as well as his argument of the impact of revolutions on the international behavior of states, come close to constructivism.

Chapter 1: Rethinking Security

1. These two versions have many common features, such as state-centricity, rational behavior, the central role of power (particularly military power), and self-help. The key difference is that neorealism claims to be scientific and seeks to explain international politics on the basis of an anarchic international structure, while political realism, or realpolitik, emphasizes national interest and power politics, which are attributed primarily to human nature. Although it has drawn much criticism and is deeply flawed in several respects (see Keohane 1986a), neorealism claims disciplinary authority (Krause and Williams 1996) and continues to be the most influential paradigm for the study of international politics (Kapstein 1995).

2. Buzan, for example, while arguing for a broad conception of security, also asserts the centrality of neorealist insights to understanding international politics. "The anarchic context sets the elemental political conditions in which all meanings of national and international security have to be constructed" (Buzan 1991: 21–22). See also Buzan, Jones, and Little 1993.

3. "The people" is one of several features in Buzan's analysis of the state. See Buzan 1983: chap. 2.

4. Ruggie's primary contention is that the state-centric model is not useful in detecting incremental systemic changes that may eventually overwhelm the state. See Ruggie 1993b, 1993c.

5. Paul Taylor argues that regional integration and the state have been and continue to be mutually supportive, each living off the other. See Taylor 1991; also Hoffmann 1991: 204–6.

6. This classification of capabilities is that of Joel S. Migdal (1988). Migdal's argument, however, is that developing states are weak in terms of these capabilities. This is still the case in most African countries but less so in Asia and Latin America. There is the possibility that in a post–Cold War setting the state in many African countries may further weaken or even disintegrate.

7. This has led Waever et al. (1993) to argue the case for treating society as a security referent.

8. On nationalism and international conflict, see Van Evera (1994); on revolution and international behavior, see Walt (1992).

9. An early work on internal war is that of Eckstein (1964).

10. On the various components of national identity, see Smith, 1991: 15.

11. The terms *nation* and *state* have been defined and used in many ways, often making for confusion and difficulty, and posing considerable obstacles to theorizing (Benjamin and Duvall 1985; Ferguson and Mansbach 1988: 111–42). *Nation* here refers to a unit of population that possesses a common heritage, a desire to live together in a community, and a will to preserve the inheritance that has been handed down (Renan 1970: 408–9). The identity of a nation may be constructed along the lines of a civic-territorial model or an ethnoreligious one (Smith 1991, Ra'anan 1990). *State* refers to a "structure of domination and coordination including a coercive apparatus and the means to administer society and to extract resources from it" (Fishman 1990: 428). This definition of *state* is concerned with organization and process of governance, as well as the principles that underlie them, not the units of action, decision, or policy. The latter is more accurately captured by *government* which is a key actor in domestic and international politics (Benjamin and Duvall 1985: 27).

12. Scheff (1994) and Brown (1996) are useful here.

13. On anarchy as the ordering principle, see Waltz 1979: 88–93. On the meanings of anarchy, see Milner 1993.

14. Wolfers (1962c: 154, 157) also suggests that security may be treated as an intermediate rather than an ultimate goal and as a means to ultimate ends, such as the promotion of human values (e.g., liberty). In this formulation, security need not always be the highest goal; it may at times be compromised in the pursuit of some other equally or more important value.

15. Neoliberalism accepts that states are the principal actors; they act rationally on the basis of self-interest; relative capabilities remain important;

and states must rely on themselves to realize gains from cooperation (Keohane 1993: 271).

16. Hedley Bull and Adam Watson (1984: 1) define international society as "a group of states (or, more generally, a group of independent political communities) which not merely form a system, in the sense that the behavior of each is a necessary factor in the calculations of others, but also have established by dialogue and consent common rules and institutions for the conduct of their relations, and recognize their common interest in maintaining these arrangements."

17. For a relatively recent version of commercial liberalism, see Rosecrance 1986.

18. A similar argument is made in Goldgeier and McFaul 1992.

19. The thesis of democratic peace has been contested by the realist school (Farber and Gowa 1995; Layne 1994; Oren 1996; Spiro 1996). The challenge has focused on the lack of causal logic of the democratic peace argument, the war-proneness of democracies, the claim that democratic peace is myth, alternative explanations as to why war has not broken out among democracies, and the assertion that there is no assurance that states will become or remain democracies. For responses to this critique, see the contributions by Bruce Russett and Michael Doyle in Brown, Lynn-Jones, and Miller 1996.

20. For a good discussion of economic security, see Buzan 1991: chap. 6.

21. See, for example, Neville Brown 1989, 1992; Buzan 1991: 19–20, 131–34, 256–61; Gleick 1990, 1991, 1993; MacNeill, Winsemius, and Yakushiji 1991: 52–73; Mathews 1989: 162–77; Myers 1986, 1989: 23–41; Renner 1989.

22. Drawing on the analogy of atomic energy and how nuclear fission became the dominant military, geopolitical, and even psychological and social force, Mathews (1989: 177) asserts that "in the same vein, the driving force of the coming decade may well be environmental change."

23. Senator Sam Nunn's justification of the environment as a key national security objective in which the Department of Defense has an important role could be viewed as an example of this. See Butts 1993: iii.

24. For the uses of economic power to achieve foreign policy goals, see Knorr 1975: chap. 6, 134–65.

25. This is part of Buzan's definition of economic security. See Buzan 1991: 19.

26. On the security dilemma, see Hertz 1950: 157–80; Jervis 1976: 72–76.

27. Institutionalists and constructivists, however, would argue that even if power and egotistic reasons are important at the outset, the process of cooperation may reconstitute identities and interests in such a way as to create new intersubjective understandings and commitments, which may make the institution endure even in the absence of the original rationale (Wendt 1992: 417). Thus, the disappearance of the Soviet threat does not necessarily lead to the end of NATO. If the process of cooperation has contributed to the creation of a European identity, and national interests are now defined in terms of this collective identity, then NATO may continue to exist. Although ASEAN is not an alliance like NATO, a similar explanation can be advanced with respect to its vitality after the Cambodian conflict. Many argued that with the termination of the Cambodian conflict, the association would come apart. Others set about to find new rationales, such as economic cooperation. However, the process of

cooperation over a twenty-year period contributed to a new intersubjective understanding among the ASEAN countries and the creation of an ASEAN identity that has become a factor in the formulation of the national interests of member states. This may, in part, explain the continued existence and in some ways the strengthening of the association in the post-Cambodia phase.

28. Collective security is a case of multilateralism as defined by John Ruggie (1993a).

29. Charles L. Glaser (1994) argues that, contrary to the conventional wisdom, realism is not pessimistic regarding cooperation. He holds that under a wide range of conditions adversaries can best achieve their security goals through cooperative policies, not competitive ones.

30. Joseph Grieco, however, is less dismissive of institutions. While still claiming the superiority of neorealism, he accepts that neoliberalism may help explain some concerns of states, such as cheating, and believes that realism needs to develop a theory of international institutions (Grieco 1993).

31. John C. Matthews (1996) argues against the distinction between security and economic realms. According to him, it is not the sector that determines the propensity to cooperate, but the anticipated cumulative effects on future advantages and state behavior.

32. On the conditions for security regimes, see Jervis 1983. On security cooperation between the United States and the Soviet Union, see George, Farley, and Dallin 1988.

33. On reciprocity, see Keohane 1986b: 1–27.

34. The following discussion draws from and builds upon Wendt 1992: 399–401.

35. The distinction between defense and offense is a problematic but still useful one.

36. On mature anarchy, see Buzan 1983.

37. On complex interdependence, see Keohane and Nye 1977: chap. 2.

38. The term *deep structure* relates to the ordering principle of the international system and was coined by Ruggie. The term *distributional structure* relates to the distribution of capabilities among states and was coined by Buzan. See Ruggie 1986: 135; Buzan 1993b: 54.

39. Although realists assume that states will act rationally on the basis of cost-benefit calculus in choosing strategies, they disagree on how states will behave. Robert Gilpin (1981) argues that states will seek to expand their power until marginal costs exceed marginal benefits. He holds that the contemporary international system has been witness to a succession of hegemonic powers that seek to organize international relations in terms of their respective security and economic interests. Waltz, as noted here, contends that the anarchic system encourages balancing (Waltz 1979: 126–27, chap. 8). His contention is based on the belief that power is not an end in itself but a means to the primary concern of states, which is to ensure survival and maintain their position. The difference between Gilpin and Waltz stems largely from their different assumptions about power. According to Gilpin, as well as the earlier realists, maximization of power is a key goal of the state; Waltz views power essentially as a means to ensure the survival and position of the state in the international system. Despite this difference, power is central to both theses.

40. Constructivism is one of the family of critical theories that also includes postmodernism, poststructuralism, neo-Marxism, and feminism. The term *constructivism* was coined by Nicholas Onuf (1989). Constructivism has also been termed *reflectivism* by Robert O. Keohane (1988). The discussion of constructivism in this chapter draws mainly upon the work of Alexander Wendt (1987, 1992, 1995).

41. These are Giddens's phrases (1994: 69).

42. One such debate has focused on predicting the future of Europe, with the neorealists forecasting an unstable multipolar Europe and the liberal institutionalists forecasting a more stable Europe rooted in a web of institutions. See, for example, Hoffmann, Keohane, and Mearsheimer 1990; Mearsheimer 1990; Russett, Risse-Kappen, and Mearsheimer 1991. See also Keohane 1993: 284–91. For another set of exchanges, see *International Security* 20, no. 1 (1995).

43. On pluralistic security community, see Deutsch 1957.

44. For a realist critique of constructivism, see Mearsheimer 1995a: 34–47, 1995b: 90–92. For a liberal institutionalist critique, see Keohane 1988.

45. A similar point is made by Nye 1988; Baldwin 1993:22–24; and Keohane 1993. For a comprehensive attempt to modify and supplement neorealism, see Buzan, Jones, and Little 1993.

Chapter 2: International Politics in Asia

1. This discussion of continental and maritime Southeast Asia draws extensively from Tate 1971.

2. The conference confirmed the "sovereignty, the independence and the territorial and administrative integrity of China" (Fairbank, Reischauer, and Craig 1978: 694) with intent to prevent the further dismemberment of China.

3. For text of the Yalta agreement, see Daniels 1984: 134.

4. The specific issues of contention included the use of bases on Japanese soil for military operations in other countries, the unrestricted freedom for the United States to introduce any weapon system (including nuclear weapons) into Japan, the provision that allowed the United States to intervene in large-scale domestic disturbances, lack of a firm U.S. commitment to the defense of Japan, U.S. veto over Japanese security arrangements with other countries, and lack of provision for termination of the treaty (Sneider 1982: 26–27).

5. Japanese defense efforts during the 1952–70 period were grounded in a series of reinterpretations of the peace constitution, as well as a series of statements of principles, such as the 1967 "three nonnuclear principles" articulated by Premier Sato.

6. The PRC initially turned to the United States, despite American support for the Nationalist government during the civil war (Lach and Wehrle 1975: 48). The American response, however, was at first uncertain and then negative, so the PRC–again despite the Soviet dealings with the Nationalist government during the civil war–reached an understanding and alliance with the Soviet Union.

7. Some Indians have argued that such assistance was more rhetoric than real, and that the United States and the United Kingdom exploited India's vulnerability and brought pressure to bear on India to negotiate on Kashmir while overlooking the improvement in Sino-Pakistan relations.

8. These premises were the junior-partner status of Japan, its security dependence on the United States, and the one-way U.S. commitment to the security of Japan without reciprocity.

9. India was a lone partial exception. It played significant diplomatic roles in the Korean and Indochina conflicts, supported decolonization (particularly the anticolonial struggle in Indonesia), and recognized the PRC very early on, arguing for its inclusion in the United Nations. But this did not significantly affect the course of developments in Asia and in any case was short-lived.

10. The hope was that if the Soviet Union and China could persuade the DPRK to give up its militant policy, then the ROK would be willing to discuss the North Korean demands for withdrawal of U.S. troops from South Korea as well as disarmament, thereby breaking the vicious circle.

11. These include the 1972 Simla agreement, the 1988 agreement on the prohibition of attack against nuclear installations and facilities, the 1991 agreement on advance notification of military exercises, and the 1992 declaration on the complete prohibition of chemical weapons.

12. Vietnam is required to comply with the provisions of AFTA by 2006; Burma and Laos have until 2008.

13. The first meeting among the foreign secretaries of the seven South Asian states was held in 1981. However, it was the 1983 foreign ministers' meeting that adopted the Declaration on South Asian Regional Cooperation. The charter for SAARC was adopted in the first summit meeting held in 1985.

Chapter 3: China

1. Theoretically, the developed socialist states in Eastern Europe should also be included in the second world. Given their close ties with Moscow, however, Mao seldom counted on them as a potential ally against the Soviet hegemon.

2. John Garver identified five categories, not three: (1) deterring superpower attack against China, (2) defending Chinese territory against encroachment, (3) bringing "lost" territory under Chinese control, (4) enhancing regional influence, and (5) enhancing China's global stature (Garver 1993: 253–54).

3. The border clash with the Soviet Union, for example, is an extension of the domestic policy of opposing "Soviet revisionism." In addition, Mao expected to restore domestic order and build up his personal prestige, which had suffered from the nationwide chaos caused by Cultural Revolution.

4. The "one superpower," of course, refers to the United States; the "several major powers" include China, Japan, Russia, and the European Union.

5. With the normalization of relations with Hanoi in late 1991, Beijing held between 1992 and 1994 that China's security environment was in the best shape since 1949. As of 1995, however, due to adjustments in the East Asian security strategy of the United States, rising tensions in Sino-Japanese relations, and growing momentum for independence on Taiwan, Beijing's concern over its security environment had increased considerably.

6. The term *peaceful evolution* was coined by former U.S. secretary of state (1953–59) John F. Dulles when he envisioned the communist states gradually deviating from the socialist path and integrating into the capitalist system. Beijing

uses this term to refer to a Western approach that employs nonmilitary means to secure the subversion of the socialist system.

7. Between 1955 and 1979, Taiwan was a security ally of the United States under the U.S.–Taiwan Defense Treaty. The Treaty was terminated on January 1, 1979, when Beijing and Washington normalized their relations, and the U.S. military personnel stationed in Taiwan pulled out three months thereafter.

8. Here *bourgeois liberalism* refers to a political tendency that rejects the guidance of the official ideology and negates the leadership of the CCP.

9. Since 1995 a discussion has been carried on among China's strategic analysts and the international studies community over the nature of U.S. policy toward China. Opinions include engagement, soft containment, or selective containment; the mainstream tends to identify a dual strategy of engagement plus containment.

10. This point is taken from an internally circulated research report.

11. The revised criminal law adopted in 1997 changed the name of "counterrevolutionary guilt" to "guilt of endangering national security."

12. This law stipulates (article 2) that "the land territory of the People's Republic of China consists of the mainland and its offshore islands, Taiwan and various affiliated islands including Diaoyu Island, the Penhu Islands, the Dongsha Islands, the Xisha Islands, the Zhongsha Islands, the Nansha Islands and other islands that belong to the PRC."

13. The PRC's national defense budget in 1979 and 1989 was 22.266 billion RMB yuan and 25.147 billion RMB yuan, respectively—a net increase of 2.881 billion RMB yuan, or 12.9 percent. However, given the high inflation rate brought about by the rapid economic growth in the 1980s, the actual military spending in 1989 was 25 percent less than in 1979. See U.S. Arms Control and Disarmament Agency 1995: Table 1.

Since 1989 the annual defense budget and inflation rate have been as follows:

Year	Budget (billion RMB)	Percent Increase	Inflation Rate
1989	25.15	15.4	18.0%
1990	29.03	15.4	3.1
1991	33.03	13.8	3.4
1992	37.79	14.4	6.4
1993	42.58	12.7	14.7
1994	52.04	22.2	23.0
1995	63.97	22.9	15.0
1996	71.50	11.8	6.1
1997	80.57	12.7	6.0 (predicted)

SOURCES: *China Statistical Yearbook*, 1990–96; relevant reports in *People's Daily* in corresponding years.

14. For instance, China's official figure for its defense budget in 1993 was $7.4 billion. According to the London-based International Institute for Strategic Studies (IISS), however, the figure could be as high as $21.76 billion, while the Stockholm International Peace Research Institute's (SIPRI) estimate is $37 billion, and the U.S. Arms Control and Disarmament Agency's figure is $56.2

billion. For further information, see IISS 1993; SIPRI 1994; and U.S. Arms Control and Disarmament Agency 1995.

15. Logically, bilateralism also prevents China—not just the United States—from mobilizing its international resources. However, given the reality that the United States possesses more international resources than China does and that multilateralism would only serve to widen the gap in the power balance, bilateral dealings are more preferable to China.

16. PRC leaders have suggested on various occasions that China is likely to use force against Taiwan in two scenarios: Taiwan formally declares independence, and foreign countries intervene.

17. Concerned over the island's increasing economic dependence on the mainland, Taipei in recent years has been trying to tighten its policy on investment in the mainland (Tamura 1996).

Chapter 4: India

1. G. S. Bajpai, India's first secretary general of external affairs, argued that nonalignment is vital and that in a world of power politics armed force is essential (Kavic 1967: 39–40). As early as June 1946, Nehru noted that if India were attacked it would defend itself by all the means available to it. Kavic (1967: 27) notes that this statement contains "the clear implication that such means did not exclude atomic bombs."

2. The *Panchashila* or Five Principles of Peaceful Coexistence between India and China (1954) are mutual respect for territorial integrity and sovereignty, mutual nonaggression, mutual noninterference in internal affairs, equality and mutual benefit, and peaceful coexistence.

3. Nehru had come up with something like the idea of nonalignment before the Cold War. See Damodaran 1995.

4. This issue is cited in virtually every annual report of the Ministry of Defense since 1990–91.

5. See, for instance, the reference to Nehru's dismissal of a swap in Kavic 1967: 68.

6. The migration issue is referred to in the Ministry of External Affairs annual reports. See, for instance, *Annual Report 1992–93*, p. 17, *Annual Report 1992–93* (Hindi version), p. 2, and *Annual Report 1994–95*, p. 3. See also brief remarks of K. P. S. Gill (1994: 125). Gill is the police officer widely credited with ending the Sikh militancy. In addition, see Narayanan 1994: 43–45. Narayanan was director of the Intelligence Bureau, Government of India, from 1987 to 1992.

7. Narayanan (1994) estimates "several millions" of Bangladeshi migrants. The "decadal growth [in migration] in many border districts was nearly 6 to 7% higher than that of the rest of the country" (p. 44).

8. For details see Heimsath and Mansingh 1971 and Brown 1963: 188–203.

9. The best dissection of this episode is Mansingh and Levine 1989: 41–44. See also Mohanty 1988: 77–78. On China's reactions to the 1986–87 episodes, see Klintworth 1992: 103–4. Klintworth claims that China calculated it could not take on the modernized Indian army.

10. Mohanty (1988: 78) suggests that China brought its strength in Tibet up to twenty divisions during this period.

11. See "Text of India-China Agreements," *Times of India*, Sept. 9, 1993.

12. There is a growing literature on the Indian Ocean Rim and the possibility of cooperation. See, among others, K. R. Singh 1995 and Ramamurthi 1994.

13. Over several decades these concessions, according to a close observer of the scene, have included "creating new ethno-political territories..., giving tribes the legal rights to mineral resources and offering protection, such as requiring inner-line entry permits and prohibiting outsiders from buying properties in tribal regions." Weapons were not "surrendered" but "handed over" to be stored in safe houses, often under the eye of peace councils led by tribal elders. In striking a deal the government generally "avoided claims of victory" and the militants "did not have to admit defeat." See Gupta 1995: 27.

14. See Dixit 1994: 932 for a recent foreign secretary's views along these lines.

15. Once again, this view is well illustrated by Dixit (1994: 933–36).

16. Ministry of Defense 1995, p. 2.

17. For opposition to multinationals see Kurien 1994: 116–18 and Initiative for National Renewal 1995: 27–36.

18. For explication of the term "hiding," see Schroeder 1986.

19. The United States, as an infant republic, also pursued a strategy of nonalignment in effect; see Damodaran 1995. For the terms "international society" and "society of states" see Bull 1977. For an Indian view of nonalignment and its past and present contribution to international society, see Damodaran 1995 and Rajan 1995.

20. Interviews with Indian diplomats in New Delhi.

21. The Iran–China–India triangle has been widely speculated upon. Narasimha Rao's visit to Teheran in January 1995 apparently "coincided" with the presence of the Chinese foreign minister, Qian Qichen. See Katyal 1995.

22. On the India–Russia–China triangle see Kurien 1994: 126. This would be a giant trading bloc. On an Israel–Southeast Asia–India front see Karnad 1994: 53–58. This is proposed as an anti-China, anti-(Islamic) fundamentalist configuration. On the Asian trinity see Wilson 1994.

23. Prime Minister Narasimha Rao on several occasions since the middle of 1995 has repeated that India will continue with R and D and production of key military items—the Arjun Main Battle Tank, the Light Combat Aircraft, the Prithvi missile. He has also stressed that India will keep the nuclear option open. See, most recently, "India Will Keep Its N-Option Open: PM," *The Pioneer*, Jan. 26, 1996. The report explains that Narasimha Rao made the remarks "in the context of the increasing American pressure on India not to deploy the indigenously developed missile Prithvi and sign the non-proliferation treaty on nuclear weapons." U.S. arms aid to Pakistan under the Hank Brown Amendment was also mentioned in Narasimha Rao's statement. The successor United Front government has reaffirmed Narasimha Rao's posture.

24. The treaty with Bangladesh comes up for renewal in 1997. Indications are that it will not be renewed.

25. The term "India Doctrine" comes from an article by Bhabani Sen Gupta, an influential analyst and columnist. See Gupta 1983: 20.

26. On India's involvement with regionalism see Sisir Gupta 1964 and Muni

and Muni 1984. Muni and Muni take the story from the 1960s to the beginnings of SAARC in the early 1980s.

27. Thus Nehru said: "India is going to be and is bound to be a country that counts for something in world affairs, not I hope in the military sense, but in many other senses which are more important and effective in the end." See Nehru 1983a: 47.

28. The public statements of the four initiatives as well as the Rajiv Gandhi Action Plan are reproduced in the Rajiv Gandhi Memorial Initiative (1993).

29. On the Sri Lanka episode see Chari 1994 and Muni 1993.

30. On the 1987 exercise that escalated into an India-Pakistan crisis see Bajpai et al. 1995.

31. General K. Sundarji, India's best-known "thinking" general, has noted that India should be in a position to deter a U.S.–led coalition of the type Iraq faced in 1991. This requires that India have a nuclear capability. In Sundarji 1993 (68–73) he sets forth the need for both a conventional and a nuclear capability to deter the United States.

32. Dr. A. P. J. Abdul Kalam, the head of the missile program, is widely credited with the success of the various projects under his charge.

33. Joshi (1992: 83–4) provides details on the kinds of items India will need over the next 10 to 15 years.

34. Sidhu (1996: 185) argues that in the missile program India has anticipated problems and will not be affected by international sanctions. There is a hawkish view in India that sanctions, denials, and a growing feeling of international isolation after the CTBT could, or should, push India to test. See, for instance, the story filed by Asha Chawla (1996), which quotes Indian strategic commentators to this effect.

35. A revealing story was filed by Krishna Prasad (1995) in which Dr. Gopalakrishnan of AERB is quoted as saying: "Unless the viewpoints of the Planning Commission and the Finance Ministry change considerably, NPC will find it tough to survive comfortably in the near future and come out with a viable business enterprise in the long run." While the nuclear program requires Rs. 5,000 crores during the Eighth Plan (1992–97), the government sanctioned only Rs. 400 crores.

36. Joshi (1992: 85) reports that R and D increased from 2.3 percent of total defense outlays in 1982–83 to 4.9 percent in 1990–91. J. Singh (1992: 59) reports a high figure of 4.6 percent between 1983–84 and 1992–93.

37. See Perkovich 1993 for a useful statement about the plausibility of the Indian and Pakistani nuclear postures and how they could be made more stable. Burns (1995) takes off from Perkovich and shows how various technologies and other measures might be used to give operational significance to a non-weaponized posture.

38. For the opposite argument see Sahni 1996: 98.

39. Sahni (1996: 99–100) argues that, overall, the cost of nuclearization is much greater than is usually conceded by nuclear advocates. K. Subrahmanyam estimates a minimal deterrent at $3 billion (in 1994 prices) and Vijai Nair comes up with $2.2 billion for a triad capability.

40. Sahni (1996: 102) notes that moral costs must be reckoned.

41. Narayanan (1994: 46) notes that the pressure to liberalize the Indian

economy "came from a technocratic elite and was not the result of a widespread public demand, not even of the political parties." See also Initiative for National Renewal 1995: 31.

42. See, for instance, Narasimha Rao, "World Summit for Social Development: Speech of Prime Minister of India, Copenhagen, Denmark, 11th March 1995," mimeo, p. 4, and Narasimha Rao, *Prime Minister Narasimha Rao Visits USA*, p. 4.

43. Both communities harbor a minority sensibility, a sense of siege. Although Hindus recognize that they are numerically superior, they see the demographic balance as changing in favor of Muslims. Moreover, they see "Hindu" India as being surrounded by Muslims—from the Middle East and North Africa at one end to Southeast Asia at the other. Gupta (1995: 15–17) too makes this point. Muslims, by contrast, are a numerical minority and look with apprehension at the consolidation of Hindus under the Rashtriya Swayamsevak Sangh (RSS), the Vishwa Hindu Parishad (VHP), the Bharatiya Janata Party (BJP), and the Shiv Sena.

44. These forces include the National Security Guard (NSG), the Rashtriya Rifles, the Border Security Force (BSF), the Central Reserve Police Force (CRPF), the Assam Rifles, the Indo-Tibetan Border Police (ITBP), and the Nagaland Hill Police. See Gupta 1995: 35–36.

45. In 1986–87, an Indian military exercise near Pakistan's borders led to a confrontation in January 1987. Indian moves appeared deliberately ambiguous and were seen as a warning to Pakistan regarding its interference in Punjab. In early 1990, Indian troop reinforcements in Punjab, Rajasthan, and Kashmir led to another dangerous standoff. This had been preceded by a number of state ments warning Pakistan about its role in Kashmir. On the events of 1987 see Bajpai et al. 1995.

Chapter 5: Japan

1. For a recent example of such a study see Katzenstein and Okawara 1993.

2. Article 9 states: "Aspiring sincerely to an international peace based on justice and order, the Japanese people forever renounce war as a sovereign right of the nation and the threat or use of force as means of settling international disputes. In order to accomplish the aim of the preceding paragraph [of Article 9], land, sea, and air forces, as well as other war potential, will never be maintained. The right of belligerency of the state will not be recognized." Although most Japanese constitutional experts read Article 9 as prohibiting all armaments including the Self-Defense Forces (SDF), the government's interpretation has been that the stipulation does not deny the right of self-defense, which is innate in any independent country, and therefore does not prohibit armaments if they are maintained for purposes of defending Japanese territory and not as a means of settling international disputes.

3. *Asahi Shinbun*, Oct. 27, 1995 (evening edition).

4. Since then Japan has decided to transfer to the United States those technologies relevant for portable surface-to-air missiles (SAMs), for the construction and remodeling of U.S. naval vessels, for the next-generation support fighter, for the digital flight control system to be installed on P-3C

antisubmarine patrol aircraft, and for joint research on ducted rocket engines (Defense Agency 1995a: 74).

5. The summary that follows owes much to an excellent review in Eto and Yamamoto 1991.

6. The following information is based on unpublished papers provided by the Japanese government.

7. The preparatory meeting of the forum was held in December 1993 in Tokyo, where the forum's theme was summarized in three points: transnational projects; projects with implications spreading across national boundaries; and projects that address issues common to at least two of the three countries. Its first ministerial meeting, held in Tokyo in February 1995, was attended by representatives from 25 countries and 8 international institutions.

8. Government pronouncements in the National Diet in March 1969, October 1972, and September 1985 (*Boei Handbook* 1995: 389–90).

9. Article 6 of the Treaty of Mutual Cooperation and Security Between Japan and the United States (June 23, 1960).

10. Government pronouncements in the National Diet in December 1969 and October 1981 (*Boei Handbook* 1995: 399).

11. In the general elections in 1993, the LDP gained 223 seats, losing the majority for the first time out of the 511 seats in the Lower House, whereas the SDP lost almost half its seats, dropping from 134 to 70.

12. *Yomiuri Shinbun*, Nov. 3, 1994; the English translation is from *Yomiuri Shinbun*.

13. "Yomiuri Poll," *This Is Yomiuri*, June 1995, p. 149.

Chapter 6: North Korea

1. See also the spirited exchange of views by Donald Gregg and Kathleen Bailey before the House of Representatives in "The Security Situation on the Korean Peninsula," Joint Hearing Before the Subcommittee on International Security, International Organizations, and Human Rights and the Subcommittee on Asia and the Pacific of the Committee on Foreign Affairs (Washington, D.C.: Government Printing Office, 1994).

2. For a good review of this literature see Roy 1994.

3. The consequences of this conflict apply to South Korea as well. Because of the North, politics in the South remains restricted to a right-center spectrum, because any labor party or leftist party is immediately branded as "pro-North." Thus politics in the South remains truncated and election contests are almost like primaries, in which the eventual Southern leader goes against the true leftist party, that in the North. This division has economic as well as political implications. Much of South Korea's tremendous economic development can be traced to decisions taken for the purpose of winning the contest with the North.

4. From 1985 to 1989 North Korea's GDP expanded by an estimated 2 percent a year compared to 10.4 percent for South Korea; see *Asia Yearbook 1991*: 6.

5. There is no shortage of rumors about Kim Jong Il: that in the late 1950s he sneaked into Osaka to receive mental treatment; that he went in disguise to East Germany to study; that he has never left the country, except to visit China, because of his terrible foreign language skills. His brother, Kim Pyong Il, is said

to be much more worldly and competent. Thus rumors abound that there is "palace intrigue" within the Kim clan.

6. House Subcommittee of Committee on Appropriations, "DOD Appropriations 1993" (Washington, D.C.: Government Printing Office, 1992), p. 679.

7. "Investigation of Korean-American Relations," (part 4, 1978), p. 37. Cited in C.-J. Lee and Sato 1982: 44.

8. Many nations, including the United States, have attempted to dethrone a leader as a cheap means of effecting a coup. Examples include the Bay of Pigs invasion in Cuba and the 1986 bombing of Muammar Qaddafi's residence in Libya. In both instances the United States disliked the leader but considered the costs of a total war too high.

9. There are exceptions to my argument, and I should note them here. The most obvious exception was the bombing of KAL flight 007 in 1987, which certainly constituted violence against the people of South Korea. However, in general North Korea has not used this type of terrorism against the South.

10. Painted on the top of the Yongbyon facilities in huge letters is the slogan *charyok kaengsaeng* ("independence" or "self-reliance").

Chapter 7: South Korea

1. See Wendt (1992, 1995) for the identity dimension of security. Alagappa (Chapter 1, this volume) neatly summarizes the constructivist perspective, which sees security issues in terms of intersubjectivity involving identity and structuration.

2. *Buguk gangbyong* can be seen as a Japanese colonial legacy. Since the Meiji Restoration, the idea of "rich nation, strong army" (*fukoku kyohei*, the Japanese pronunciation of the same Chinese characters) served as the ideology of national governance in Japan. See Samuels (1994).

3. In the semantics of the Korean language, state security (*kukga anbo*) is the equivalent of national security in the ordinary use of the term, whereas national security (*minjok anbo*) is a more comprehensive concept that encompasses the security of the entire Korean nation including the North, the South, and overseas Koreans. The semantic complexity arises from the fact that one nation is divided into two sovereign states.

4. It is estimated that about 30 percent of North Korea's people are classified as beneficiaries of the Kim Jong Il regime. Reunification by absorption would make them ultimate losers. Thus they might seek to resist the takeover rather than yield to the South Korean government.

5. The Ministry of National Defense has undertaken an active campaign to inform the general public of the new sources of insecurity. The campaign aims at achieving two objectives. One is to alert the general public; the other is to use the threats as an excuse to demand an increased share of the defense budget. Since the late 1980s, its annual *Defense White Paper* as well as other publications have consistently emphasized the new dimension of regional threats. Its portrayal of Japan as a potentially dangerous regional actor once elicited an official protest from the Japanese government.

6. Han's resignation was just the tip of the iceberg. Conservative and progressive forces have engaged in intense ideological and political debates since the

democratic opening in 1987. The debates have been greatly influenced by the nature of inter-Korean relations. A series of imprudent policy measures taken by the North have increasingly isolated the progressive forces and precipitated the revival of a conservative ideological trend in the South. Mass media have also played a significant role in crafting this social mood (see Moon 1996a: chap. 5).

7. A most telling instance can be found in the general election in 1996. A series of political scandals put the ruling New Korea Party in a difficult position in the election campaign. However, North Korea's provocative behavior along the DMZ immediately before the election turned voters conservative and helped the ruling party win the election against all odds. Seoul's mass media said that a *bukpung* (wind from the north) had saved the ruling party from an electoral disaster.

8. Several salient issues have demonstrated the severity of interagency rivalry: linkage versus delinkage of the nuclear issue and inter-Korean economic cooperation (NUB and the Ministry of Finance and Economy [MOFE] vs. ANSP, MOFA, and MND), shipments of rice to the North for humanitarian reasons (the Blue House, NUB, and MOFE vs. ANSP), a feud over the initiative within the Korea Energy Development Organization (MOFA vs. NUB), and soft landing versus crash landing (NUB and MOFA vs. ANSP and MND). The fact that deputy prime ministers were reshuffled six times under the Kim government underscores the intensity of the rivalry (see Moon 1996a: chap. 5).

9. In its dealings with North Korea the United States has been deeply divided. While the State Department has advocated a soft-line posture, the Department of Defense and the Central Intelligence Agency have favored a hard-line approach. But the Clinton administration has sided with the State Department, making the soft-line posture the official policy of the United States.

10. The South Korean government has supported the Conference on Security Cooperation in the Asia-Pacific (CSCAP), a civilian forum for security cooperation. Its Korean steering committee is presently housed at the Institute for Foreign and National Security Affairs, an official think tank of the Ministry of Foreign Affairs. It has also been sending its delegates to another regular nongovernmental forum on security cooperation organized by the Institute of Global Conflict and Cooperation of the University of California.

11. The incursion of the North Korean submarine into South Korean waters on September 18, 1996, and subsequent unrest underscore this point. After almost two months of intensive search involving 80,000 regular troops and tens of thousands of home reserve and civil defense forces, 13 of the reported 26 North Korean infiltrators were killed in gunfights, 11 committed suicide, and one was captured. Fifteen South Korean civilians and servicemen were killed in the pursuit. Economic losses in the operation are estimated to be more than 300 billion won (approximately $360 million). Mass media reporting of such incidents further heightens the sensationalism of military threats (*Munwha Ilbo*, Nov. 6, 1996).

Chapter 8: Taiwan

1. Later the constitution was amended so that the president was elected by popular vote, not by the National Assembly.

2. The Republic of China also officially claims Outer Mongolia as part of its territory.

3. The disposition of the offshore islands controlled by the ROC has been a source of controversy because they were not among the areas occupied by Japan from 1895 to 1945 and are considered by both the mainland and the Taiwanese governments to be part of Fujian province. In its most recent campaign platform, however, the opposition Democratic Progressive Party (DPP) affirmed that these islands were included in its conception of an independent Taiwan. See DPP Central Headquarters Election Strategy Committee 1995: 35.

4. The latter group does not include the small numbers of recent arrivals from mainland China. An additional ethnic group consists of the aboriginal peoples who make up about 1.7 percent of Taiwan's population.

5. Hakka are another Chinese ethnic group distinguished by dialect and other customs. Originally from north China, they are now found scattered throughout south and southwest China. Most Hakka in Taiwan (including the current president, Lee Teng-hui) are descended from ancestors who emigrated from Guangdong province prior to the twentieth century and are thus, along with immigrants from southern Fujian, included in the category *benshengren*.

6. The only exception is with regard to territorial disputes between the PRC and other countries, such as those over the Senkaku Islands or the islands of the South China Sea, where the ROC's claim that the territories have traditionally been part of China has tended to support that of the PRC (although Taipei argues that they belong to the ROC, not the PRC). See "Chinese First" 1996: 13.

7. The KMT argued that these policies were necessary for national security because political instability in Taiwan made it vulnerable to the PRC. Though this may have been true, there is little doubt that the same policies would have been pursued whether or not national security was truly affected. As argued earlier, it was only when these policies began to work to the detriment of the regime's security that they were changed.

8. With the growth of commercial ties since 1987, the PRC is also believed to be exploiting the economic interests of Taiwanese businesspeople to influence Taiwan's policy toward the mainland, and there is speculation about how many votes in Taiwan's elective bodies are "owned" by the PRC. See Chen 1992: 2; Yang 1994: 4.

9. The mainland took just 2 percent of Taiwan's exports in 1986, and there was no significant Taiwanese investment on the mainland prior to 1987 (*Liang'an jingji tongji yuebao* 1995: 24, 28, 57; Council for Economic Planning and Development 1995: 192).

10. There also has been suspicion that the mainland government is involved in encouraging illegal immigration to Taiwan (Central News Agency 1990: 44).

11. Private conversation with an agent of the ROC Ministry of Justice Investigation Bureau.

12. The existence of serious ethnic conflict, however, would mean that the value of the state as currently constituted was questioned by at least one significant domestic group.

13. In East Asia, only North Korea and Singapore spend a higher proportion of GDP on defense (Stockholm International Peace Research Institute 1994:

560). In dollar terms, this make Taiwan's defense expenditure nominally higher than the PRC's, although mainland China's actual defense expenditure is widely believed to be several times the official figure (International Institute for Strategic Studies 1995: 173).

14. Private conversation with a U.S. military official.

15. Taiwan was the seventh-largest trading partner of the United States in 1994 (U.S. Bureau of the Census 1995: 819–22).

16. Thus Taiwan's dependence on the United States for its military security against the PRC has ironically contributed to Taiwan's becoming more vulnerable to the PRC economically.

17. It should be noted, however, that democratization has complicated other areas of Taiwan's relations with the United States by giving the public a voice in matters, such as economic security, that affect them more immediately. As a result, Taiwan's leaders have become more resistant to U.S. pressure in bilateral disputes over nonmilitary issues.

18. Those efforts succeeded, for example, in 1992, when France agreed to sell Taiwan 60 Mirage 2000 fighter aircraft.

19. Taiwan is the most important source of direct foreign investment for several Southeast Asian countries. Total Taiwanese investment in Southeast Asia exceeds $15 billion (NDREG 1994: 65).

20. Hong Kong is also a member of all three organizations. Taiwan and China currently hold observer status in the WTO.

21. The ban on direct links also gives Taiwan a bargaining chip in its efforts to persuade the PRC to renounce the use of force against Taiwan (*China Times* 1991: 2).

22. Taiwanese individuals in their personal capacities have been allowed to participate in the working groups of CSCAP.

23. Similarly, it was Taiwan's linguistic and cultural relationships with the mainland that made the mainland such an attractive investment destination.

24. The one exception is the disputed Senkaku Islands, held by Japan but claimed by the ROC (as well as the PRC).

Chapter 9: Bangladesh

1. This should be understood in the sense that a threat to security is not merely a conventional military concept. For discussion on the subject see Kolodziej 1992b; Iftekharuzzaman 1992; Buzan 1991; Walt 1991; Sayigh 1990; Sorenson 1990; Alagappa 1987a; McNamara 1986; and Krasner 1983a.

2. Government of Bangladesh, Ministry of Law and Parliamentary Affairs, *The Constitution of the People's Republic of Bangladesh* (Dhaka, 1979).

3. *Constitution of the People's Republic of Bangladesh*, as revised by Proclamation Order 1 of 1977, p. 8.

4. One of the electoral strategies of the Awami League in the June 1996 parliamentary polls was to appease the military by pledging to build up a strong and well-trained national army. It also welcomed for the first time a good number of retired military officers, who were encouraged to compete in the election on the Awami League ticket. Apparently to "keep the army in good humor," the new annual budget for 1996–97 presented by the Awami League government pro-

vided for a 7 percent increase in defense expenditure. For a party that has returned to power after two decades in the political wilderness—following the military coup that ousted it from power because of grievances that included low defense spending—this budget increase indicates its continued vulnerability vis-à-vis the military.

5. For a detailed discussion on the subject see Ahamed 1985.

6. For further details see Hossain 1995.

7. *Asiaweek*, May 19, 1995.

8. This was one of the findings of the task force constituted in 1991 by the Interim Government that replaced autocratic rule in Bangladesh. The task force was composed of several hundred Bangladeshi experts who quickly produced a substantive report in four volumes dealing with various dimensions of the developmental challenges facing the country. See Task Forces 1991.

9. Task Forces 1991, 26–27.

10. For the same year, the proportions of urban and rural populations living below the poverty line were, respectively, 38 and 49 percent in India, 20 and 31 percent in Pakistan, 19 and 43 percent in Nepal, and 15 and 36 percent in Sri Lanka (United Nations Development Program [UNDP] 1995: 178–79).

11. UNDP 1995: 168–69.

12. UNDP 1995: 156–57.

13. When, immediately after the partition, Pakistan wanted to impose Urdu as the national language, the people of East Pakistan viewed the measure as an instrument of cultural suppression and protested. That reaction led to the historical language movement of 1952, which is widely viewed as the root of the urge for independent nationhood.

14. Recently the federal interior minister of Pakistan announced that his country would expel these people. He went on to announce that Pakistan would not accept stranded Pakistanis in Bangladesh, who have been awaiting repatriation since 1971. See *Bangladesh News Fortnightly*, Nov. 1–15, 1995.

15. Ministry of Information and Publications, Government of India, *India 90* (New Delhi, 1990), quoted in Swain 1993: 8.

16. This part draws heavily from Iftekharuzzaman 1994.

17. *Bangladesh Observer*, Jan. 26, 1996.

18. *Bangladesh Observer*, May 26, 1992.

19. The chairperson of the Awami League, Sheikh Hasina Wajed, blasted the government of Khaleda Zia for its failure to reach agreement with India over the country's legitimate share in the waters of the Ganges despite making much ado about the issue before coming to power. See the *Daily Star*, Jan. 8, 1994, and *Ittefaq* (in Bangla), July 30, 1994. On the other hand, its opponents continue to blame the Awami League for consenting to the commissioning of the barrage in the first place. Khaleda Zia, the present prime minister, led the "Farakka March" on several occasions as an instrument to mobilize public opinion in favor of her party on the platform of anti-Indianism. She has described Farakka as an Indian conspiracy that the people of Bangladesh will not accept.

20. During the 1991 elections Khaleda Zia and her Bangladesh Nationalist Party (BNP) leaders were reported to have pledged to bring more Ganges water if elected to power. See *Ajker Kagoj* (Dhaka), June 6 and 8, 1992. See also Baxter and Rahman 1991: 686–91. Prior to the national election of June 12, 1996, the

BNP portrayed the Farakka problem as part of India's well-planned "expansionist design." See *Financial Express* (Dhaka), May 17, 1996.

21. For details on the two proposals and each other's arguments see Abbas 1984: 124–29; Swain 1993; and *Keesings Contemporary Archives*, Sept. 18, 1981, pp. 31090-91.

22. For more on issues in Bangladesh-India relations see Hassan 1989; Iftekharuzzaman 1989; Huq 1993; Ghosh 1989.

23. According to one source, India has constructed barrages at the headwaters of 21 out of 54 common rivers. For details see *Financial Express* (Dhaka), May 17, 1996.

24. For a detailed analysis of the treaty see Hassan 1987: 101–38.

25. China waited until the fall of the Mujib government; the Muslim countries recognized Bangladesh following Mujib's participation in the summit meeting of the Organization of the Islamic Conference held in Lahore.

26. For details see Siddiqui 1987: 426–30. Hassan (1987: 93–94), provides a detailed analysis of the issue based on interviews with senior officials of the Indian army involved in the 1971 operation. See also Ghosh 1989: 66.

27. Sheikh Mujibur Rahman, quoted in Hassan 1987: 74.

28. For reasons why Bangladesh was frustrated at that early stage of cordial relations see Kuldip Nayar, "An Opportunity in Bangladesh," *Island* (Colombo), July 29, 1996.

29. *Keesings Contemporary Archives*, Sept. 1981, p. 27381.

30. Whether the 1977 agreement was the result of Bangladesh's move at the United Nations or the change of regime in India earlier that year remains to be examined. As a result of Bangladesh's move at the Special Political Committee of the U.N. General Assembly, a consensus was worked out by a group of non-aligned countries who urged Bangladesh and India to "meet urgently in Dhaka at the ministerial level for negotiation with a view to arriving at a fair and expeditious settlement." Before these talks could produce any result, the Congress government of Indira Gandhi was replaced by the Janata government headed by Morarji Desai. It was during the tenure of the latter, considered to be the warmest interlude in post-1975 relations between Bangladesh and India, that the agreement was signed.

31. India's share under the new agreement rose from 11,000–16,000 cubic feet per second to 20,500–26,500 cubic feet per second. It was, however, agreed that in the case of exceptionally low flows in the dry season, Bangladesh would be guaranteed a minimum of 80 percent of the volume earmarked for it in the schedule of allocation.

32. For details on the provisions of the agreement see, *RCSS Newsletter* (Colombo) 3, no. 1, Apr. 1997.

33. According to the SAARC charter, no "bilateral and contentious" issue may be raised as an official agendum. But the high-level meetings of the association provide opportunities for the political leaders to discuss matters of dispute informally.

34. Despite its limitations, the association has emerged as a forum where member states hold informal consultations on problems of regional security and stability. On the sidelines of the discussion of official agenda items, matters of bilateral and regional concern can be discussed practically without restriction.

Sharing of water resources between Bangladesh and India, the Indo-Pakistan controversy over the nuclear question, and the ethnic conflict in Sri Lanka are among such issues that have been discussed on several occasions in SAARC. For details see Iftekharuzzaman 1996.

Chapter 10: Pakistan

1. See Lodhi, 1994b: 301–2; see also Hanif 1989a: 15–16.

2. The Aid-to-Pakistan Consortium commits around $2 billion in credits to Pakistan; short and medium-term loans are provided by the IMF.

3. Official estimates put the current inflation rate at 13 percent, but independent economists put it at 22–25 percent. See Rashid 1996; see also Adil 1993: 61.

4. According to President Leghari, "cooperation with China in the defense and strategic fields has acquired even greater significance in the context of the virtual rupture of our defense relationship with the U.S."; see *News*, July 4, 1996.

5. According to annual police reports, 80 percent of crime in Baluchistan province, bordering on Afghanistan, is committed by Afghan nationals. See Zulfikar 1994a: 62; see also Yusufzai 1989: 25–26 and Hussain 1993: 4–5.

6. The ten-year-old Karachi conflict has resulted in more than 15,000 deaths. See Sultan Ahmed, "Karachi Killings: No Move for a Breakthrough," *Muslim*, Jan. 29, 1996; see also *Dawn*, Jan. 1 and Jan. 21, 1996.

7. In October 1994, the national census, postponed since 1991 because of ethnic tensions in Sindh, was indefinitely postponed by the central government in response to a united demand by Baluchistan's ruling and governing parties that the census be held following the repatriation of all Afghan refugees.

8. Pakistan's formation had been demanded by the Muslim League on the ground that the Indian Muslims were a separate nation, politically, socially, and culturally, from the Hindu majority.

9. In Baluchistan, for example, the center's refusal to respect aspirations for autonomy resulted in a prolonged armed conflict between dissident Baluch and the security forces of the state. See Harrison 1981: 34–40.

10. See Rubin 1995; see also Hussain 1992a: 21–22.

11. President Zia-ul-Haq's speech on May 22, 1988, cited in Hussain and Hussain 1993: 93.

12. Gen. Mirza Aslam Beg's address to the Pakistan Ordinance Factory seminar, Sept. 19, 1987. See *Defence Journal* 14, no. 11 (1986): 6.

13. Keynote address of Admiral Saeed M. Khan at a three-day international conference (Apr. 18–20) under the joint auspices of the Pakistan Navy and the Institute of Strategic Studies. See *Defence Journal* 20, nos. 5–6 (1994): 5.

14. Sardar Assef Ali's interview. See *Newsline*, Aug. 1994, p. 32.

15. See Brig. S. K. Malik 1991: 13.

16. President Ghulam Ishaq Khan's address to the National Defense College's Thirteenth Annual Convocation, May 1989. See *Dawn*, June 1, 1989.

17. These measures include ordinances, acts of parliament, and constitutional amendments that have increased the power of the executive and its law enforcement agencies. See Ahmed 1991: 46–47.

18. Prime Minister Benazir Bhutto's interview in *Newsline*, Nov.–Dec. 1993, pp. 46a–50.

19. *News*, Mar. 7, 1997.

20. President Leghari stresses, for example, that although the Kashmir dispute has "retarded peace and development in the region for almost half a decade, so long as the dispute remains unresolved, "we simply cannot lower our guard and our armed forces must remain alert and fully prepared to meet any challenges to our national security." See *Dawn*, Jan. 2, 1996.

21. *Dawn*, Nov. 18, 1986.

22. See Hussain 1995a: 38.

23. Rashid 1988; see also Richter 1989: 451.

24. Admiral Saeed M. Khan's keynote address, 1994. *Defence Journal* 20, nos. 5-6: 5.

25. See Maj. Gen. Rahat Latif 1993: 329.

26. According to one analyst, "Since outlays in defense have consistently been higher than the capacity of the economy to pay, the government has been forced to accumulate debts" (Naqvi 1996: 38). According to the state minister for finance at the time, Makdoom Shahabuddin, it was now official policy to use a percentage of the proceeds from privatization for debt retirement. See *Muslim*, July 19, 1996.

27. *News*, June 14 and 15, 1996.

28. Military spokesman quoted in Hussain 1992b: 24.

29. According to a Sindhi ethnonationalist leader: "We've had martial law for more than half the country's history. The imposition of martial law is based on violence [but even] short periods of civil rule have also been predominantly violent. We have seen the deployment of armed forces in Baluchistan, the killing of people, and the frequent use of detention laws to keep people in jail....Today Sindh is a totally occupied territory." See Mumtaz Ali Bhutto's interview in *Newsline*, Oct. 1991, pp. 26–27.

30. These concerns are articulated in the annual reports of the HRCP and periodic resolutions passed by WAF chapters in Karachi, Lahore, and Islamabad.

31. Pakistan was the seventh-largest borrower of World Bank loans in fiscal year 1995: its commitments totaled $705 million.

32. More than 39 million people live below the poverty line in Pakistan today; 77.5 million (55 percent of the population) lack access to safe water; 52 percent of the children under five are malnourished and 16 percent die. Meanwhile 279 rupees are spent on the military for every rupee spent on health and education. See Lodhi 1992: 29.

33. The nuclear issue has consistently come to the fore in Pakistan's attempts to improve its political and economic relations with Japan. During former prime minister Bhutto's visit to Japan in January 1996, for example, the Japanese prime minister and foreign minister placed special emphasis on Pakistan's signing the NPT and the CTBT. See *Muslim*, Jan. 18, 1996, and *News*, Jan. 19, 1996.

34. According to a senior Pakistani diplomat, for example, "India's greater size, population, strategic depth etc. are given factors which cannot be altered; but their effect is aggravated by the constant rise in India's military strength....As relations between the two countries are never free of tensions, due to the unresolved Kashmir dispute and a persistent Indian hostility to partition, Pakistan is obliged at all times to look to its defenses" (Akhund 1988: 14).

35. See Commodore Salimi (1988: 21). See also Lt. Col. Saleem (1993: 25).

36. See Lt. Col. Qazi 1964: 19 and Col. Ahmad 1965: 59.

37. See Vice Admiral Quadir 1988: 18 and Lt. Gen. Matinuddin 1993–94: 31–32.

38. Lt. Col. Syed Ali Hamid 1990–91: 28 and Commodore Salimi 1988: 21.

39. General Zia-ul-Haq; cited in Hussain 1988: 1.

40. According to former Foreign Minister Sardar Assef Ali, Pakistan is "now amongst the eight world players who are being consulted and given weight as far as nuclear non-proliferation is concerned." See *Dawn*, Apr. 4, 1996.

41. Former Prime Minister Moeen Qureshi's statement at a press conference in July 1993; cited in Lodhi 1994a: 227–28. Zia, for his part, declared that "Pakistan will never make a weapon and if it does, it will not explode it" (Ali 1984: 62).

42. Prime Minister Moeen Qureshi, cited in Lodhi 1994a: 227–28. See also *Defence Journal* 20, nos. 3–4 (1994): 60. Addressing a seminar in April 1994, Defense Minister Aftab Shaban Mirani clearly linked the two issues by stating that Pakistan wanted an equitable and nondiscriminatory nonproliferation regime in South Asia—adding that the "core issue" of Jammu and Kashmir "has bedeviled relations between Pakistan and India for almost half a century." See *Defence Journal* 20, nos. 3–4 (1994): 58.

43. Statement by Foreign Minister Sardar Assef Ali; see *News*, July 5, 1996.

44. President Leghari's address to the National Defense College; see *News*, July 4, 1996.

45. U.S. military and economic assistance played a major part in enabling Zia's military regime to retain power for eleven years.

46. U.S. economic assistance to Pakistan had been terminated in April 1979 on the ground that Pakistan had acquired a nuclear capability, but aid was renewed following the Soviet military intervention in Afghanistan.

47. According to Prime Minister Bhutto, Pakistan supports "regional non-proliferation on a regional basis." See Prime Minister Bhutto's address to a press conference in Karachi reported in *Defence Journal* 20, nos. 3–4 (1994): 57.

48. *Frontier Post*, June 8, 1989.

49. *Defence Journal* 20, nos. 3–4 (1994): 60.

50. The United States has been assured repeatedly by Pakistan that its nuclear program has been capped since July 1990 but that a rollback is impossible so long as an Indian security threat remains. See, for example, Pakistan Foreign Secretary Shahryar Khan's statement during a visit to the United States in February 1992, cited in McDonald 1992, and see Prime Minister Bhutto's press conference, Nov. 20, 1993, cited in *Defence Journal* 20, nos. 3–4 (1994): 57.

51. The United States is already India's largest trading partner, and there is large-scale U.S. private investment in India.

52. The M-11 ballistic missiles have a range of 300–600 kilometers.

53. *Economist*, Feb. 12, 1994.

54. According to General Chishti, a key member of Zia's initial martial law administration, during the cabinet discussion on the PDPA takeover in April 1978 he recommended that "we should install a favorable government in Kabul, using friendly Pushtun tribes" (Chishti 1989: 205). This appears to have been the strategy adopted by the Zia regime. According to Prime Minister Benazir Bhutto:

"There were crazy plans that since we lost Dacca, we'll take over Kabul and impose a regime of our own kind." See the prime minister's interview in *Newsline*, July 1989, p. 22.

55. The anti-Taliban alliance consists of the exiled government of President Rabbani; Commander Ahmed Shah Masood's Shura-i-Nazra, the Shiite Hizb-e-Wahdat of Karim Khalili, and General Rashid Dostum's Junbush-e-Milli.

56. Baluchistan's irrigation minister, Abdul Hameed Achakzai, declared in parliament that it was "impossible for untrained talibs who are not familiar with tanks, anti-aircraft guns and cannons to defeat well-trained and well-equipped Afghan commanders. It was Frontier Corps men who fought and helped pro-Pakistan forces entrench themselves." Cited in Zulfikar 1994b: 54. For the role of the Inter-Services Intelligence (ISI) in Afghan affairs see Askari 1989.

57. According to Army Chief of Staff General Beg, thousands of Kashmiris, trained by Pakistan's ISI, had fought in Afghanistan and subsequently returned to Kashmir, along with other ISI-funded guerrillas. See Harrison 1992: 97.

58. *Country Report Pakistan Afghanistan*, fourth quarter 1994, p. 14.

59. Politically contentious issues have been deliberately excluded from SAARC's ambit. See Charter of the South Asian Association for Regional Cooperation, Dhaka, Dec. 8, 1985.

60. For the most intensive study of Brasstacks see Bajpai et al. 1995.

61. Cited in Lodhi and Hussain 1990a: 20–21.

62. HRCP's annual report for 1995, for example, strongly condemns state torture, inhuman treatment, and deaths in custody. See Human Rights Commission of Pakistan, *State of Human Rights in 1995* (Lahore, n.d.).

63. Organizations such as the Citizens-Police Liaison Committee have been set up specifically to empower citizens confronted by violence and crime (Khan 1991). See also Abdus Sattar Edhi's interview in *Newsline*, Mar. 1995, p. 22.

64. Zaidi and Khan 1994: 44; see also Rahman 1994: 37–38, 43.

65. These measures include the second amendment to the constitution declaring the Ahmediyas a non-Muslim minority; Zia's system of separate communal electorates; the eighth amendment to the constitution providing constitutional protection to Islamic legislation; the establishment of Shariat courts; and promulgation of the blasphemy law.

66. See Hussain 1995b: 35–36; see also Hanif 1994: 26–28.

67. By recent estimates, 60 to 65 percent of Pakistani army officers are of Punjabi origin, rising to over 70 percent in the high command, whereas the Pakhtun component of the officer corps is between 30 and 33 percent. There are less than 2 or 3 percent Baluch personnel in the army; Sindhis represent less than 1 percent of the army's total strength although they constitute almost 25 percent of the total population. See Kennedy 1991: 946; see also Ahmed 1985: 241 and Zaidi 1989: 308.

68. It is claimed, for example, by senior military officials that because "political instability" is "endemic" in Pakistan, "we must suppress our extreme individual parochial concerns in favor of mutually agreed national projects and goals which can lift us morally, economically, militarily and socially"—goals that would, of course, be determined by the military, the most nationalistic of Pakistani institutions. See Maj. Gen. Latif 1993: 332–33.

69. Hussain 1992b: 23–24; see also Hanif 1992: 30–32.

70. Justifying MQM casualties in "police encounters," interior minister Major General (retired) Nasrullah Babar stated: "After all they had murdered more than 200 jawans [rank-and-file] of the police and Rangers. And they killed many poor people from upcountry [the NWFP and the Punjab], who were trying to make a living in Karachi." See *News*, Jan. 28, 1996.

71. Cited in Hussain 1995a: 38.

72. Sardar Assef Ali's interview in *Newsline*, Aug. 1994, p. 32.

73. A Foreign Office spokesman stated: "India has employed its intelligence agencies to destabilize Pakistan, particularly in the province of Sindh"; see *Dawn*, Jan. 5, 1996. Former Sindh chief minister Abdullah Shah claimed that the Afghan president, Burhanuddin Rabbani, had extended political and military support to the MQM's terrorist wing: "It's the three K issue—Karachi, Kabul and Kashmir." See *Dawn*, Jan. 22, 1996, and *Muslim*, Jan. 22, 1996.

74. *Dawn*, Apr. 11, 1997.

75. An alleged Indian rocket attack across the Line of Actual Control on January 26, 1996, which resulted in eighteen deaths and was followed by an exchange of heavy fire between Indian and Pakistani troops, demonstrated the dangers that exist due to the heightened state of Indo-Pakistan tensions over Kashmir. See *News*, Jan. 27, 1996, and *Muslim*, Jan. 28, 1996.

76. In 1992 and early 1993, Pakistan itself narrowly avoided being declared a terrorist state by the United States for its support of Kashmiri militants. See *Far Eastern Economic Review*, June 18, 1992; see also Ali 1993.

77. During the Gulf War, even while pro-Saddam sentiments were expressed by the former army chief, General Beg, it was under his command that the Pakistan army sent a contingent of troops to Saudi Arabia; see Hussain 1991: vii. Moreover, a number of Pakistani drug traffickers have been extradited to the United States, as has a World Trade Center bombing suspect, Ramzi Yousaf. Citing Ramzi Yousaf's arrest as a demonstration of Pakistan's resolve to act as "a frontline state against international terrorism," Prime Minister Bhutto called on the United States to help Pakistan in its fight against "radical Islamists and terrorist gangs" posing serious threats to Pakistan's security. A decision has also been taken by Pakistani authorities to extradite Arab extremists involved in the Afghan war to their home countries to address U.S. concerns that they were conducting terrorist activities from Pakistani soil. See Lodhi 1994a: 68–69; see also *Country Report Pakistan Afghanistan*, second quarter 1995, pp. 21–22.

78. *Country Report Pakistan Afghanistan*, fourth quarter 1995, pp. 16–17; see also *News*, Jan. 28, 1996.

79. *Country Report Pakistan Afghanistan*, fourth quarter 1995, p. 17.

80. *News*, Jan. 21, 1996.

81. Ilyas Khan, "Endless Battle," *Newsline*, Nov. 1996, p. 61.

82. These talks include Prime Minister Bhutto's visit to Teheran in November 1995, where she declared that "those who spread baseless rumors about differences between Iran and Pakistan [in the context of Afghanistan] seek to create division. Both the countries cannot dream of such a rivalry between the two brotherly nations"; see *Muslim*, Nov. 8, 1995. In January 1996, Iranian foreign minister Ali Akbar Velayati visited Islamabad and held discussions with the Pakistani prime minister and foreign minister on Afghanistan; see *Muslim*, Jan. 10, 1996.

83. *News,* Nov. 17, 1995.

84. As Pakistan's gas resources dry up, plans are under way to construct oil and gas pipelines from Turkmenistan via Afghanistan's western provinces. See *News,* Jan. 17, 1996.

85. *Dawn,* May 26, 1997.

86. In his speech at the Economic Cooperation Organization's summit in Ashkabad, Karimov accused Pakistan of prolonging the Afghan civil war by aiding the Taliban militia, while General Dostum, who took refuge in Turkey after the Taliban entry into Mazar-i-Sharif, alleged that Pakistan had bribed defecting General Abdul Malik (*Dawn,* May 16, 1997; *News,* May 26, 1997).

87. The Russian foreign minister, Primakov, also warned the Taliban that the collective security pact of the CIS would be invoked should the security of the Central Asian Republics be threatened by the Taliban.

88. *Dawn,* May 30, 1997.

89. *Dawn,* May 30, 1997.

90. Despite the 1971 experience (or perhaps because of it), within the Pakistan military there is still a deep belief that "it is the Army which is keeping this country intact. The day the fibre of this Army breaks, India will overrun Pakistan" (Chishti 1989: 56).

Chapter 11: Sri Lanka

1. Most works on security in Sri Lanka focus exclusively on the foreign policy and strategic role of Sri Lanka in South Asia. See, for instance, Kodikara 1990 and Muni 1993.

2. This survey on perceptions of security is based on a sample of 100 people and was carried out in December 1995. It was not done according to strict sociological methods of surveying, because its purpose was mainly to get a qualitative assessment of perceptions of security.

3. *Daily News,* Mar. 6–7, 1971.

4. See, for instance, Wilson 1979, Gunaratna 1990, and Chandraprema 1991.

5. *Ceylon Daily News,* Jan. 9, 1956.

6. *Ceylon Daily News,* May 26, 1958; *Silumina,* May 25, 1958.

7. *Hindu,* Mar. 11, 1994.

8. *Island,* Apr. 23, 1995.

9. See, for instance, the Report of the Working Group on Enforced or Involuntary Disappearances (Oct. 7–18, 1991), Commission on Human Rights, 48th session, Jan. 8, 1992.

10. UNP Manifesto, *Island,* Aug. 8, 1994; ICES Election Literature Collection.

11. From a survey on conceptions of security: interviews of a sample of 35 Sinhalese males and 35 Sinhalese females.

12. From a survey on perceptions of security: interviews of 10 Tamil males and 9 Tamil females, December 1995.

13. Election Manifesto of the People's Alliance, 1994; ICES Election Literature Collection.

14. Christian Bay has argued in an absorbing article that security is the poor person's freedom. He goes on to say: "For people who are heavily oppressed,

whether by political design or economic circumstances, or both, their measure of individual security determines the size of their limited space for freedom of choice" (Bay 1987: 129).

15. *Daily News*, Mar. 27, 1997.

16. This section draws on Bastian 1988.

17. Jayadeva Uyangoda, a university lecturer, and Victor Ivan, the editor of the Sinhala tabloid *Ravaya*, were among her closest advisers. Both were leaders in the 1971 JVP rebellion.

18. *Tamil Times*, Jan. 15, 1995.

19. Election Manifesto of the People's Alliance, 1994, p. 12.

20. Election Manifesto of the People's Alliance, 1994, p. 12.

21. *Sunday Times*, June 2, 1996.

22. *Island*, Mar. 6, 1996.

Chapter 12: Myanmar

1. The ruling State Law and Order Restoration Council (SLORC) stipulated in June 1989 that the name of Burma be changed to Myanmar Naing Ngan or Union of Myanmar. The new nomenclature also requires the use of *Bamar* instead of *Burman*, and the citizens and language of the country are now officially Myanmar (Burmese previously). These changes are not accepted by opponents of the regime, who still use the old names. Thus, the usage has political connotations. The use of the new terms in this chapter, however, simply reflects the fact that the change has been officially stipulated and is used by a substantial segment of the international community.

2. On November 15, 1997, the name of the military junta was changed from SLORC to the State Peace and Development Council (SPDC). The name change appears to be the consequence of a power shift within the military regime and is also intended to convey to the international community that the military regime has consolidated itself and its focus is now on development as opposed to restoring law and order. The significance of this name change for Myanmar's conception of security and the nature of domestic politics remains unclear, although drastic change appears rather unlikely.

3. Those who challenged the government's hegemony were considered a security risk to the state.

4. Here *Bamar* refers to the majority race (*Burman* in most Western literature), whereas *Myanmar* is used interchangeably for the state (Burma) and for its citizens (Burmese).

5. Pyus belonged to an ancient civilization that flourished in central and lower Myanmar for several centuries before the advent of Bamar nationhood in the form of the Bagan dynasty, founded in A.D. 956 (Thwin 1985: 17–21).

6. The term *paukphaw* represents the spirit of affection and goodwill between the people of China and Myanmar that ostensibly has existed since time immemorial. An example of mutual accommodation was the January 1960 settlement of the territorial boundary between China and Myanmar. In the Sino-Burmese Boundary Agreement, Myanmar ceded two frontier tracts of approximately 100 square kilometers each to China in exchange for a 130-square kilometer "assigned tract" inside Myanmar (see Nu 1960).

7. According to the 1983 census, the proportions of minority ethnic groups were: Shan, 8.5 percent; Kayin, 6.2 percent; Rakhine, 4.5 percent; Mon, 2.4 percent; Chin, 2.2 percent; Kachin, 1.4 percent; and Kayah, 0.4 percent (Government of Burma 1986: 21, table A-6). The census classification identified eight broad ethnic categories constituting 135 national groups: Kachin (12); Kayah (9); Kayin (11); Chin (53); Bamar (9); Mon; Rakhine (7); and Shan (33)— see the Myanmar-language daily *Loketha Pyithu Neizin*, Sept. 26, 1990.

8. Real per capita national income surpassed the 1985–86 value in 1995–96, and the economy grew by 33 percent in the period from 1992–93 to 1995–96 (*Myanview* 2, no. 3 [1996]: 1).

9. See, for example, "Declaration No. 1/90" dated July 27, 1990, clarifying SLORC's view on the transfer of power and the democratization process (Weller 1993: 194–96).

10. All were based at Manerplaw on the Thai-Myanmar border, the head-quarters of Kayin insurgent group under Bo Mya. The DAB was formed in November 1988; the 8-member NCGUB in December 1990; and the 47-member NCUB in August 1992.

11. For accounts sympathetic to "activists, targets and victims," see Amnesty International 1994 and Lombard 1992.

12. Address delivered on March 24, 1995, by Patron of the Union Solidarity and Development Association (USDA) Senior General Than Shwe on the occasion of the opening of the management course for USDA executives (*NLM*, Mar. 25, 1995).

13. Examples of SLORC-imposed limits are Myanmar's refusal to allow the continuation of the construction of the "Friendship" bridge spanning the border at Myawaddy in one of the busiest border trading towns (*Bangkok Post*, June 14, 1995); the travel restrictions placed on foreign nationals residing in Myanmar; and the requirement that civil servants obtain permission from their respective ministries before meeting foreigners.

14. The tribal minorities such as the Kayins, Kachins, Chins, and Kayahs, as well the more developed Shans, were never incorporated into the Bamar kingdom. The monarchs of central Myanmar opted for suzerainty rather than direct rule. Thus, the British probably found such an arrangement extremely convenient in terms of conserving administrative and military resources; they continued the practice with some modifications (see Taylor 1982: 13–14).

15. Compare Taylor's argument that "the idea of ethnic conflict as conceived in Western ascriptive terms" influenced both the Bamar nationalist elites and ethnic leaders and that the imposition of a modern nation-state system created an alien context for ethnic relations (Taylor 1982: 10).

16. For an account sympathetic to the "democratic forces," see Lintner 1990a. The official explanation may be found in Government of Myanmar 1989a and 1989b.

17. See, for example, the statement "Tatmadaw adopts strategy of saving the Union through tactic of preventing itself from disintegration," which was given as the rationale for the military intervention in 1988. Citation from the 33d press conference conducted by the Information Committee of SLORC on March 31, 1989 (*WPD*, Apr. 1, 1989); and SLORC secretary-1 major general Khin Nyunt's clarification at the 100th press conference on July 13, 1990, and his statements at

the 104th press conference on September 11, 1990 (Government of Myanmar 1990: 100, 248–50).

18. According to the SLORC chairman, General Saw Maung, the upheaval was "just like having an armed insurrection" in the country's heartland (interview with *Asiaweek* correspondents, *Asiaweek*, Feb. 3, 1989). For the ruling junta's view, see Government of Myanmar (1990: 222) and Tatmadaw Thar (1990: 126–34, 147–203, 237–55).

19. Speech delivered by SLORC chairman and the armed forces commander-in-chief Senior General Than Shwe at the military parade commemorating the fiftieth anniversary of Armed Forces Day (*New Light of Myanmar* [daily; hereafter *NLM*], Mar. 28, 1995).

20. Myanmar has entered into cooperative agreements with all the bordering states, and on June 11, 1991, it deposited the instrument of accession to the 1988 U.N. Convention against Illicit Traffic in Narcotic Drugs and Psychotropic Substances. A new and tougher antidrug law to replace those enacted since 1974 was promulgated in January 1993 in accordance with the convention. See, for example, "Perspectives," *NLM*, June 27, 1994, as well as the Feb. 10, 1994, and Mar. 4, 1995, issues of *NLM*. For the opposite view, see Lintner 1995c.

21. See, for example, the home minister's speech to the personnel of the Immigration and Manpower Department, in which he reminded them of the motto "The earth will not swallow up a people, but another [aliens] will"—see *NLM*, Feb. 8, 1994, and Maung 1994. The establishment of the new Ministry of Immigration and Population was announced on June 15, 1995. The portfolio was given to SLORC member Lt. Gen. Maung Hla, the military appointments general, commander of Special Operations Bureau No. 2, and ninth in the military hierarchy (*NLM*, June 16, 1995).

22. Khun Sa claimed to be fighting for an independent Shan state, but most observers saw it as a ploy to counter his drug warlord image (Lintner 1995b). The latter was borne out by his swift capitulation in January 1996.

23. Down from about 60,000 in early 1989. Estimated on the basis of data supplied in *Burma Alert* 5, no. 12 (1994), p. 3.

24. There had been considerable tension at the border before the exodus as the Myanmar side reportedly beefed up its troop deployments apparently to counter rebel activities. Both sides played down the incidents of shooting and confrontation that occurred, and the tension was quickly diffused (see *Asiaweek*, Feb. 21, 1992, pp. 22–25). The exodus involved some 250,000 Muslims of Bangladeshi origin who fled the Rakhine state, claiming to have been victims of religious and racial persecution. They were regarded as illegal economic migrants by SLORC. In April 1992 the two governments signed an agreement to repatriate them under the auspices of the U.N. High Commissioner for Refugees. The repatriation process is almost complete; more than 229,000 had been returned by April 1997 (AFP news [Internet], Apr. 30, 1997).

25. See, for example, statement attributed to Lt. Gen. Khin Nyunt with reference to Thai allegations of cross-border intrusion by Myanmar forces: "The problem had not grown big due to the existing good relations and mutual understanding between the two armed forces." (*Nation*, May 29, 1995).

26. See, for example, the editorial "From Appeasement to Encouragement," *Nation*, May 8, 1995.

27. However, the visit of U.S. congressman Stephen Solarz on September 4, 1988, along with the presence of a U.S. Navy battle group on the morning of September 12 in the Andaman Sea, some 190 nautical miles south of Yangon, seem to have been regarded by the Myanmar military as a direct intervention (Tatmadaw Thar 1990: 198–99, 239–41).

28. Aung San Suu Kyi was awarded the Nobel Peace Prize for 1991 and had received at least 30 international honors and awards as of mid-1995. She has been idolized by the Western media, NGOs, and anti-SLORC groups.

29. This statement by the military also may be interpreted as an attempt to denigrate the opposition groups by portraying them as "foreign stooges" and "axe-handles for neo-colonialists." The link between domestic and external threats then becomes a heuristic device to serve the regime's purpose.

30. There are altogether six objectives serving as the principal guidelines for the national convention. The other five are nondisintegration of the state, non-disintegration of national solidarity, perpetuation of sovereignty, the flourishing of a "genuine multiparty democracy," and the "further burgeoning" of "justice, liberty and equality."

31. Announced at the press conference convened by the SLORC Information Committee on July 21, 1989. Suu Kyi was released on July 10, 1995.

32. All the materials refuting allegations by the regime's opponents and critics as well as promoting SLORC's views and actions are directed mainly at the country's citizens. In particular, they are meant to neutralize the impact of foreign radio broadcasts in the Myanmar language by the Voice of America (U.S.), the British Broadcasting Corporation (U.K.), and All India Radio (India), which are believed to be widely received by the public at large.

33. For state perspectives on these issues, see "Perspectives" *NLM*, June 29, 1994; Lt. Gen. Khin Nyunt's speech at the second meeting of the Central Committee for Revitalization and Preservation of Myanmar Cultural Heritage on July 8, 1994 (*NLM*, July 9, 1994); and Sein 1995. Despite such attempts there have been resistance and defiance by some sections of the monkhood. The anti-Muslim rioting led by monks in Mandalay and other cities that broke out in March 1997 attested to the fact that religious dissent does exist.

34. Excerpts from the speech given by SLORC Secretary-1 Lt. Gen. Khin Nyunt at the prize distribution ceremony of the 1994 Independence Day Essay and Poetry Competitions and TV Quiz on January 5, 1994 (*NLM*, Jan. 6, 1994).

35. However, Western human rights groups and other critics maintained that there were still hundreds of additional political prisoners (*Bangkok Post*, Mar. 10, 1996; United Nations 1996: 2).

36. Since then, the government's tactic has been to tolerate Aung San Suu Kyi while dealing harshly with her supporters whenever they transgress existing laws and martial law provisions (*Asiaweek*, June 7, 1996, pp. 28–30).

37. A vivid example is the reported annulment of the cease-fire agreement by the Karenni National Progressive Party (KNPP), which accused the government of breaking the agreement by sending troops into the areas designated as the former's exclusive territory and engaging KNPP troops. This has led to renewed fighting between government troops and the rebels (statement dated Dec. 20, 1995, and posted on the Internet via "Burmanet" on Dec. 26, 1995).

38. The five principles are mutual respect for sovereignty and territorial

integrity, nonaggression, noninterference in each other's internal affairs, equality and mutual benefit, and peaceful coexistence.

39. See, for example, Myanmar foreign minister Ohn Gyaw's address to the 49th session of the U.N. General Assembly (*NLM*, Oct. 12, 1994).

40. One regional expert stated that the eventual target is 500,000 (Selth 1996: 19).

41. The weapons are mainly Eastern bloc designs of the 1970s. Possible substantial suppliers are the People's Republic of China, Pakistan, Poland, and Serbia/Yugoslavia (Selth 1996: 186–89; *Jane's Defence Weekly*, Dec. 3, 1994, p. 1).

Chapter 13: Thailand

1. On the Thai elite's involvement in national security issues see Tong-dhamachart et al. 1983: 9–11.

2. This is a view also shared by a faction of the elite itself. See the remarks made by Boonchu Rojnastein, the deputy prime minister in 1980–81, quoted in Alagappa 1987a: 32.

3. On King Rama V's reforms see Bunnag 1977.

4. When King Rama V was a minor (1868–73), the Bunnag noble family controlled the revenue flow to the state through major ministries that they controlled. Particularly during Chuang Bunnag's regency, royal annual revenue was reported to have declined from 4.8 million to 1.6 million baht. The young king was reported to have said that his revenue was barely enough to cover his monthly expenses. In 1871, the king ended up borrowing 8 million baht from the powerful Bunnag and their clan; see Phongpaichit and Baker 1995: 217.

5. For a historical discussion of Thailand's territory see Winichakul 1994.

6. Quoted by Winichakul in Phongpaichit and Baker 1995: 233.

7. Quoted by Barmé in Phongpaichit and Baker 1995: 235.

8. For an account of the 1932 revolution see Mektrairat 1992.

9. Some observers have characterized the domination of the bureaucracy in Thailand as "bureaucratic polity." See Wilson 1962; Siffin 1966; and Riggs 1966.

10. Described by Chai-anan Samudavanija; see Samudavanija 1990: 83–84.

11. For an account on the military's measures, see Tamsuk Numnonda, *Nation Building of Field Marshal Phibul Songkhram during WWII* in a series of speeches at Thailand Association of Social Sciences 2520-2521. Cited in Samudavanija 1990: 84.

12. On the military's thinking about development see Buntrigswat (n.d.) and Kullavanit (1989).

13. For an account of the army and its activities in domestic affairs see Bunbongkarn and Sukapanich-Kantaprab 1987: 27–59; and Bunbongkarn 1987: 49–67.

14. The military's development projects are known as the "development for security" programs; see Bunbongkarn 1987: 49–76.

15. Strong advocates include Jit Poumisak, who wrote about the monarchy as the crux of the country's political problems; see Poumisak 1979.

16. The official death toll for students was reported at 26, but others believe the real figure is higher; see Phongpaichit and Baker 1995: 311.

17. The policy seeking international support was called the "omni-direction" policy; see, for example, Chinwanno 1993; Bumrongsuk 1993.

18. For a detailed account see Alagappa 1987a: 39–77.

19. For an account of the conflict see "Top Advisor Questions Army's Concept," *Bangkok Post Weekly Review*, June 25, 1989.

20. The same message was used by two different supreme Commanders recently. See the "Message from the Supreme Commander" in *Defence of Thailand 1994* and in *Defence of Thailand 1996*.

21. There are different interpretations on the third pillar; see Phiu-nual 1990: 21; Phongpaichit and Baker 1995: 250.

22. On the origin of the conflict with the CPT see Tanham 1974 and Kerdphol 1986. On the Thai Muslim problems see Pitsuwan 1985 and Bunnag 1991.

23. For a brief discussion of the May incident see, for example, Bunbongkarn 1992: 131–33.

24. For a full account, see the report of the Fact Finding Committee (1992).

25. This is the estimate of the Central Bank of Thailand, cited in Theeravit 1993: 104.

26. In the 1995 Senate, 37 percent of the 265 members are active-duty military officers, 27 percent are retired military and bureaucrats, 17 percent are businessmen, 11 percent are active bureaucrats, and the remaining 8 percent are from various professional groups. See *Senate Members Registry* 1993: 166.

27. From a survey on leaders' perceptions on security issues conducted by the National Defense Research Institute; see *The National Security Strategy of Thailand in the Next Decade* (1993). Perceptions are drawn also from interviews with 33 senior leaders; see *Strategic Thinking* (1996).

28. Based on a series of seminar conclusions leading to publication of Thailand's defense white paper; see *The National Security Strategy of Thailand in the Next Decade* (1993); *Thailand 1997: Opportunity and Choices* (1994); *Thai Armed Forces in the Future* (1994).

29. According to one estimate, Thailand lost about 400 troops in the battle at Ban Romklao, a village on the northeastern border; see Chinwanno (n.d.).

30. As outlined in *The Defence of Thailand* (1994: 16).

31. According to the Ministry of Commerce; see *Document on Submarine Procurement Program* 1995: 1.

32. Using the Thai Buddhist Era (B.E.) dating system. The equivalent Christian era dates are in parentheses.

33. For a detailed account, see Mak 1993: chap. 6; Narayanan 1993: 43; Brooke 1995: 99–106.

34. For a brief discussion, see Napasinthuwong 1996: 15–37; the *Newsbrief*, Royal United Service Institute 1995: 6.

35. Some observers argued that the RTN's goal of a blue-water navy is not realistic, while others disagreed; see Mak 1993: chap. 6; Brooke 1995: 5; and Captain Napasinthuwong 1996: 15–37.

36. The RTN's proposal was debated in public for the first time and its white paper, entitled *Document for the Proposed Submarine Procurement Program* (1995), was discussed in newspapers, interviews, and academic forums and on televised programs. See *Bangkok Post* 1995a and 1995b.

37. For a report on official plan, see Nanuam 1995: A1; and "Air Force

Sees Need for F18 Jets to Meet National Security Needs," *Bangkok Post*, Sept. 18, 1995.

Chapter 14: Vietnam

1. The emphasis on organization, therefore, had a rather desperate note to it, as if organization alone would compensate for the weakness of the spirit or, indeed, replace the weak spirit itself while containing the chaos of social and political life. This was the essence of the state. The Vietnamese Communists' excessive focus on organization in all matters has been much discussed. The longtime general secretary Le Duan was one of the primary architects of this line, and although he believed in the importance of man, the organization factor was key in providing the structure that would ensure correct behavior and action (Elliott 1980: 210).

2. For a detailed discussion of the party's cultural policy and its effort to construct a new national culture during this early period, see Ninh 1996.

3. For a discussion of this period of intellectual questioning, commonly referred to as the Nhan Van Giai Pham period, see Boudarel (1991).

4. While party members were earnestly discussing in the pages of the party's organ, *Communist Review*, throughout 1988 and 1989 whether they, as exemplars of society, could engage in private commercial activities or even hire anyone, because that would be exploitation of labor, others were emphasizing that for *doi moi* to work, a fundamental reorientation of the national security view long predicated on a hostile environment was in order:

> Renovation is prompted by the objective demands of life. First and foremost it starts from the need to renovate internal thinking (*tu duy doi noi*). Foreign relations policy is the continuation of domestic policy. We cannot renovate internal thinking without renovating external thinking (*tu duy doi ngoai*). For example, if we want to implement well the current movement of "things that must be done immediately" in the country then it is clear that the outdated thoughts on external relations like "open the shirt to reveal one's back" and "the fear of enemies' exploitation" must change. (Phan Doan Nam 1988: 50)

5. This is one such assessment:

> After becoming ruling parties, these communist parties had, in their process of leadership, become subjective and willful, and had seriously violated objective law, thus affecting the development of the superiority of socialism, deforming socialism, and causing society to develop sluggishly and slowly. Even worse, they had become bureaucratic, alienated themselves from the masses, failed to keep themselves informed of and meeting the people's aspirations, violated the principles governing party activities, and breached the democratic principles within the parties and among the people. A segment of the party leadership had grown increasingly arbitrary and despotic. There is also the bitter lesson of the danger faced by a ruling party, against which Lenin warned long ago. (Phan Hai Nam 1990: 66)

6. There is a growing trend toward establishing Ho Chi Minh as a god in many villages in the north, particularly those that had seen many sons dead in the struggle against the French and in the Vietnam War. Professor Nguyen Duy

Hinh of the Center for the Scientific Study of Religion has noted this development with a measure of disbelief, calling it the "buddha-ization of Uncle Ho." See Nguyen Duy Hinh (1993: 351).

7. There is no doubt that the party attached great importance to fashioning a full body of Ho Chi Minh Thought. In 1992 it was reported that the state had established a national research project on Ho Chi Minh Thought, covering some eleven subjects, under the guidance of the Institute of Marxism-Leninism. The institute was to "bring together the country's scientists in order to achieve scientific projects of value, befitting the leadership stature and responding to the demands within and outside of the country." The list of the kinds of questions to be explored exemplified the newness of the venture as well as the expectations of Ho Chi Minh Thought. According to the director of the Ho Chi Minh Institute, which is under the Institute of Marxism-Leninism, they are as follows:

> What is Ho Chi Minh Thought? How did HCM Thought originate and develop, and through how many periods? What were the historical sources that helped form Ho Chi Minh the thinker as an eastern Marxist? (explain what made Ho Chi Minh different from other communist ideologists). HCM Thought comprises how many parts, and what is the structure of each part? Try to establish Ho Chi Minh's political ideological system: what fundamental ideologies does it include? HCM Thought does not have mistakes, but what about drawbacks? What are those inadequacies? How do we inherit and develop HCM Thought in the new historical context? (Song Thanh 1992: 9–10)

8. See, for example, the work of the scholar Phan Ngoc (1994) who explores components of Vietnamese culture that originated from the various ethnic minority groups, breaking away from the traditional heavy emphasis on the Chinese character of Vietnamese cultural borrowing.

9. See, for example, the collection on ASEAN edited by the head of the Institute of Research on Southeast Asia, Pham Duc Thanh (1996).

10. There were indications that the army also would like its role to be more specific and delinked from foreign policy. In the army's grassroots discussions of the party's draft congress documents in the days leading to the Seventh Party Congress in 1991, the comments often converged on the lack of clarity that existed about what it means and what it would take to turn the people's army into a regular modern army. Another point of convergence was the expressed desire to separate the discussion of national defense and security from that of foreign policy because they represented two different approaches (Thayer 1994a: 59).

11. In the words of the head of the Foreign Ministry's Department of International Organizations at the Asian Conference on Human Rights in Bangkok in 1993, "History has taught us that there can be no unique existing socioeconomic model that can squarely fit into every nation's unique and diversified reality. Therefore, there [cannot be] any single formula of human rights that can be imported, or worse, imposed from the outside" (Vietnam News Agency 1993: 57).

12. A significant number of top diplomats have become members of the Central Committee in recent years, including four deputy foreign ministers. It is worth noting that at the Midterm Party Conference in January 1994, Foreign Minister Nguyen Manh Cam was elevated to the Politburo (Vietnam News

Agency 1993: 57). Furthermore, the research institutes under the Foreign Ministry are among the most sophisticated in the country. Career diplomats are well educated, with wide-ranging experiences in the former Soviet Union, Latin America, Europe, and the United States. The Ford Foundation is one prominent international organization that is banking on the rising stars in the Foreign Ministry to take important leadership roles in the future. It has funded the participation of many younger men and women from the ministry in training and graduate programs in the United States, particularly at Harvard.

13. During my one-and-a-half-year stay in Vietnam, mainly in Hanoi, between 1991 and 1993, the rush of certain Vietnamese products to the northern border to meet Chinese demands was increasingly interpreted by the city's population as a Chinese plan to undermine Vietnam's effort to get on its own two feet. The demands changed rapidly during the time I lived in Hanoi, from copper (leading to the theft of telephone wires) to dogs, cats, and snakes (causing many problems for agriculture in some areas, apparently because of the explosion of the rat population) to specific agricultural products such as the silk of young corn, apparently for medicinal purposes (reportedly having devastating effects on the maturity of the corn crop). Such claims of a state-organized Chinese plan of economic destruction undoubtedly are exaggerated. Nevertheless, the mix of real and exaggerated incidents points to a deep-seated fear of China's intentions in all sectors of Vietnamese society.

14. See, for example, the interview with the chairman of the Committee for Overseas Vietnamese (Voice of Vietnam 1994: 73–74).

15. In 1993 the head of Hanoi's commercial crime office and the leader of Hanoi's drug unit were both arrested and charged with altering and falsifying police documents in a 1992 car-smuggling case on the border with China. Also in 1993 the director of the Housing Office of Ho Chi Minh City and four customs officers at the city's airport were arrested for receiving bribes (Agence France Presse 1993; Voice of Vietnam 1993: 67).

16. The Vietnamese government estimates that out of a population of some 70 million, 6 million follow Catholicism; 30,000, Protestantism; 10 million, Buddhism; 2.5 million, the Cao Dai religious sect; 1.5 million, the Hoa Hao religious sect; and 50,000, Islam. See Le Minh (1993: 71).

17. The government seems to have won the upper hand in March 1994 when the Vatican resolved Vietnamese objections to the appointments of top posts and agreed to future consultations with the authorities over such appointments. It seems that the Vatican would rather not have the Vietnamese Catholic Church's growth hindered any further by the already extensive shortage of top priests. Vietnam, therefore, finally had a new cardinal in November 1994, Father Pham Dinh Tung, who had been elevated to the position of archbishop of the Hanoi Diocese earlier in the year. He is 75 years old, however, and there is little doubt that conflict between the Vatican and Hanoi will erupt again when the time comes to decide on his successor, as well as on other posts and other issues such as the training of more priests and nuns. See Agence France Presse (1994a: 51).

18. The category of "absolute poor," defined as a person who is "incapable of satisfying his own minimum needs to sustain life" or more specifically, having an income of less than 15 kilograms of rice per month, encompasses 35.61 percent

of the rural population and 8.11 percent of the urban population. There are two other categories of poverty, however: "destitute," with an income of less than 12 kilograms of rice per month, encompassing 20.5 percent in the countryside and 4.26 percent in the cities; and "utterly destitute," with an income of less than 8 kilograms of rice per month, encompassing 7.96 percent in the countryside and 4.42 percent in the cities. See Do Nguyen Phuong (1994: 89).

19. Between November 22, 1988, and November 12, 1993, in the space of five years that constitutes the true takeoff of *doi moi*, a total of 120 "hot spots" appeared in Thanh Hoa, with 83 cases occurring in 1993. Se Nhi Le (1994: 71).

Hai Hung Province is another area reported to have suffered a high number of hot spots; 28 hot spots were recorded out of a total of 51 villages in Tu Loc District alone in the early 1990s. See Pham Van Tho (1994: 52).

20. The study of the hot spots in Thanh Hoa notes that "there have even been cases in which the militia and self-defense forces have been mobilized to attack people, which has had serious consequences and had a bad effect on hamlet and village order and security and internal security among the people" (Nhi Le 1994: 71).

21. As one study puts it, "There are hot spots that have arisen because some of the leading and managerial cadres at the primary level are corrupt and have violated the ownership rights of the people" (Nhi Le 1994: 71).

The situation in Hai Hung province was similar, involving land disputes and the inadequacies of the state structure: "Many incidents led to land and market disputes, and there were many conflicts that had been smoldering for a long time and that had not been resolved satisfactorily" (Pham Van Tho 1994: 52).

Chapter 15: Indonesia

1. *Pancasila*, or the Five Principles, was introduced as the ideological basis of the Indonesian republic shortly before the proclamation of independence on August 17, 1945. The five principles are Belief in One God; Humanitarianism; Indonesian Unity; Democracy, and Social Justice. *Pancasila* was introduced to block the Muslim parties' demand for an Islamic state, which was totally opposed by the non-Muslim minorities. *Pancasila* was intended to ensure that Indonesian society would not become secular, something that was abhorrent to the Muslim parties, and yet guarantee equal rights to all the recognized religions in the country.

2. The Republic of Indonesia inherits the territories controlled by the Netherlands East Indies (NEI). The NEI did not succeed in uniting the archipelago, with its many kingdoms and principalities, in the early twentieth century. Unity was achieved both peacefully, through treaties, and militarily, through long, drawn-out wars. Indonesian nationalism, however, has stressed the importance of the early empires of Sriwijaya (tenth to thirteenth centuries) and Majapahit (thirteenth to sixteenth centuries) as the historical antecedents for the new republic.

3. For a more detailed analysis of the regional rebellions see Leirissa (1991), who argues that they were not separatist movements but were really attempts by the regional commanders to develop the regions and save the nation from the increasing influence of the communists.

4. The "free and active" foreign policy doctrine was first enunciated by Vice President Mohammad Hatta in 1948. It was initially intended as a rebuttal to calls from the communist group that Indonesia join the socialist camp in the worldwide struggle against colonialism. Hatta argued that to protect its sovereignty Indonesia must not become directly involved in the Cold War. Instead, Indonesia should chart an independent course in international politics, always using its own national interests as the bases for action. See Mohammad Hatta, "Indonesian Foreign Policy," *Foreign Affairs* (Apr. 1953).

5. President Suharto's decision to refuse any further economic aid from the Netherlands probably also reflected his unwillingness to tolerate criticisms from Indonesia's former colonial master and the fact that the Dutch share in the overall IGGI assistance to Indonesia was insignificant.

6. The most prominent targets of socioeconomic jealousies are the ethnic Chinese, who control about 73 percent of listed firms by market capitalization, though they only make up 3.5 percent of the population (East Asia Political Unit 1995).

7. In recent years the government has sounded warnings about the proliferation of *Organisasi Tanpa Bentuk* (OTB) or "unformed organizations," which refers to the infiltration of existing social and political organizations by followers of the banned PKI, taking advantage of dissatisfaction with government policy.

8. The D-8 countries are Indonesia, Malaysia, Bangladesh, Pakistan, Turkey, Egypt, Iran, and Nigeria. The idea was put forward by Turkey's pro-Islamic prime minister, Necmetin Erbakan, in October 1996 (*Observer* 1997: 1).

9. Fretilin stands for Frente Revolucionaria de Timor Leste Independente, or the Revolutionary Front for the Independence of East Timor, whose key members include Ramos Horta. UDT is short for Uniao Democratica Timorese, or the Timorese Democratic Union. One of the UDT's founders, Mario Carrascalao, later became a governor of East Timor under Indonesian administration. Apodeti stands for Associacao Popular Democratica Timorense, or Timorese Popular Democratic Association.

10. The United States Congress has opposed the continuation of IMET (International Military Education and Training) for Indonesian military officers and the sale of several F-16 aircrafts to Indonesia because of alleged Indonesian human rights abuses in East Timor. In retaliation the Indonesian government announced in early June 1997 that it will pull out of IMET and is no longer interested in buying the F-16s, which were formerly intended for Pakistan. The Massachusetts legislature is proposing to ban business links between the state and Indonesia. The European Union has also issued various declarations condemning Indonesia's policy in East Timor. The cooperation treaty between ASEAN and EU, first signed in 1980, has not been renewed because of Portugal's veto, so that cooperation between the two regional organizations is still limited to the old agreement. These examples show how the East Timor issue is beginning to affect Indonesia's external economic and strategic interests.

11. Suryohadiprojo (1987) argues that although the role of wars in international relations has greatly diminished and wars largely replaced by political and economic interactions, wars can still occur, particularly among the smaller countries. Suryohadiprojo suggests that Indonesia should pay close attention to the attitudes of countries in the Asia-Pacific region, particularly those possessing

relatively large military capability. According to Suryohadiprojo the countries that must be watched are the People's Republic of China, Japan, Vietnam, India, and Australia.

12. The *Wawasan Nusantara* concept, introduced to the military at the 1966 and 1967 defense and security seminars initiated by the army, addressed both the fragmented security outlook and an equally fragmented command structure. The army had *Wawasan Benua* (Continental Outlook), the navy had *Wawasan Bahari* (Maritime Outlook), and the air force had *Wawasan Dirgant ra* (Aerospace Outlook). Each of the armed force branches had its own minister who reported directly to President Sukarno. Sukarno had maintained these fragmented outlooks and command structures to prevent the armed forces from becoming unified and too powerful, which could threaten his political control.

Chapter 16: Malaysia

1. Speech by Malaysian Prime Minister Mahathir Mohamad at the First National Security Conference, organized by the Institute of Strategic and International Studies (ISIS) Malaysia in Kuala Lumpur, July 15–17, 1986. *ISIS Focus* 17 (Aug. 1986): 16–18.

2. *Federal Constitution, Malaysia* (Kuala Lumpur: MDC, 1993), pp. 148–51.

3. *Far Eastern Economic Review*, Oct. 2, 1986, pp. 46–47.

4. Means 1991: 103.

5. See *Far Eastern Economic Review* 160, no. 23, (June 5, 1997): 24.

6. *Malaysia Official Yearbook 1967* (Kuala Lumpur: Government Press, 1968), p. 93.

7. *Seventh Malaysia Plan 1996–2000* (Kuala Lumpur: Malaysian National Press, 1996), pp. 3–31.

8. See speech by Dr. Mahathir at a conference on the multimedia supercorridor in Los Angeles on January 14, 1997. Cited in *ISIS FOCUS* 142 (Apr. 1997): 9–17.

9. "Vision 2020: Towards a Developed and Industrialised Society" (speech delivered by the deputy prime minister, Encik Ghafar Baba, at the National Seminar on Vision 2020, held in Genting Highlands on December 5, 1991); published by Socio-Economic Research Unit (SERU), Prime Minister's Department, Kuala Lumpur, 1991, p. 4.

10. *Malaysian Business*, July 1–15, 1991, p. 7.

11. See, for instance, Mahathir's speech, "The Second Outline Perspective Plan, 1991–2000," in Hamid 1993: 436.

12. For details see *Asia Yearbook 1995*: 168.

13. Speech by Dr. Mahathir Mohamad on Jan. 14, 1982; cited in Murugesu Pathmanathan and David Lazarus, eds., *Winds of Change: The Mahathir Impact on Malaysia's Foreign Policy* (Kuala Lumpur: Eastview, 1984), pp. 103–4.

14. *New Straits Times*, Apr. 16, 1997, p. 16.

15. "The South China Sea Dispute: Renewal of a Commitment for Peace," ASEAN-ISIS Memorandum no. 6, May 1995, p. 5.

16. *New Straits Times*, Aug. 10, 1988, p. 20.

17. *Towards a New Asia*, A Report of the Commission for a New Asia (Kuala Lumpur: ISIS Malaysia, 1994), pp. 13–14.

18. Malaysia's endorsement of the East ASEAN Growth Area following Dr. Mahathir's visit to Manila in February 1994 bears testimony to complementary strategic views held by both sides in the post–Cold War era; *New Straits Times*, Feb. 5, 1994, p. 10.

19. B. A. Hamzah, director-general of the Malaysian Institute of Maritime Affairs, has described the Chinese action as part of Beijing's ultimate objective "to convert the entire South China Sea into a Chinese lake." See *Asia 1995 Yearbook*, p. 24.

20. *Far Eastern Economic Review*, Nov. 7, 1991, p. 35.

21. For instance, Philippine Defense Secretary Renato de Villa expressed fears that a U.S. military withdrawal from the Philippines could trigger armed conflict over control of the oil-rich Spratlys in the South China Sea, claimed by the Philippines, China, Taiwan, Vietnam, and Malaysia. See the *Star*, Sept. 4, 1991, p. 18.

22. See, for instance, the report of the Carnegie Endowment Study Group, which states that Asians fear that the United States "will use new regional structures to pressure them on human rights and market access, although they differ among themselves on those issues"; *Defining a Pacific Community* (Washington, D.C.: Carnegie Endowment for World Peace, 1994), p. 10.

23. "Malaysian Foreign Policy in the 1990s" (address by Foreign Affairs Minister Datuk Abu Hassan Omar to the Malaysian International Affairs Forum on May 3, 1990); *Foreign Affairs Malaysia* 23, no. 2 (June 1990): 7.

24. *New Straits Times*, July 14, 1993, p. 14. See also Deputy Prime Minister Anwar Ibrahim's statement during his August 1994 visit to China; *New Straits Times*, Aug. 27, 1994, p. 1.

25. APEC members agreed to eliminate tariffs on computers and information technologies by 2000—an accord that provided the foundation for a far-reaching agreement at the meeting of the 123-member World Trade Organization in Singapore in December 1996; *Sydney Morning Herald*, Nov. 27, 1996, p. 14.

26. *Seventh Malaysia Plan* (Kuala Lumpur: Malaysian National Press, 1996), p. 667.

27. Statement by Malaysian Foreign Minister Datuk Abdullah Ahmad Badawi; *Malaysian Digest* 23, no. 5 (May 1996): 8.

28. Established on June 15, 1997, at the end of a four-day summit in Istanbul, the D-8 group of nations is composed of Bangladesh, Egypt, Indonesia, Iran, Malaysia, Nigeria, Pakistan, and Turkey; it has the declared aim of strengthening development cooperation among members. See *New Straits Times*, June 13, 1997, p. 2.

29. *The 1996 Budget* (Kuala Lumpur: Ministry of Information, 1996), p. 44.

30. *New Straits Times*, Dec. 6, 1993, pp. 1–2.

31. "Vision 2020: The Way Forward," keynote address by Malaysian Prime Minister Mahathir Mohamad at the Kongres Kebangsaan Wawasan 2020 (National Congress on Vision 2020), Petaling Jaya, Malaysia, Apr. 29–30, 1997, p. 9.

32. See the speech by Lim Hng Kiang, acting minister for national development, in *Speeches: A Bimonthly Selection of Ministerial Speeches* (Singapore: Ministry of Information and the Arts, Mar.–Apr. 1994), pp. 102–6.

Chapter 17: The Philippines

1. For a concise discussion of national security in the post-Marcos Philippines see Timberman 1989. Timberman specifically examined problems related to Western conceptions of national security as applied to the Philippines.

2. For a comprehensive background on martial law in the Philippines during the Marcos period see Brillantes 1987, Hawes 1986, Rosenberg 1979, and Wurfel 1988.

3. For details related to the Marcos family's plunder of the Philippine economy see Aquino 1987a and Manapat 1991.

4. For a comprehensive analysis of the communist insurgency in the Philippines see Jones 1989, Chapman 1987, Sison 1989, Medianski 1986, and Kessler 1989. For works on the Muslim secessionist movement in the Philippines see Bauzon 1991, Che Man 1990, George 1980, Gowing 1979, Majul 1985, May 1990, Tan 1977, Turner, May, and Turner 1992, and Turner 1995.

5. By the time Marcos was overthrown in 1986, the National Democratic Front was said to have been in control of about 20 percent of the country's villages, and the NPA guerrilla force was estimated at 7,000 full-time fighters and some 20,000 part-time guerrillas (Rivera 1994a: 253).

6. On the "Lost Command," see especially Catholic Institute for International Relations (1982), and on the PLO, see Collier (1997). See also Amnesty International (1982).

7. For a comprehensive discussion of transitional politics in the Philippines see Aquino 1987b, Bresnan 1986, Timberman 1991, and Wurfel 1988. For the role of the Catholic Church in the Marcos and Aquino periods see Youngblood 1990 and Huntington 1991.

8. The phenomenal growth of NGOs in the Philippines is part of the redemocratization process in the country. They are seen essentially as institutions of mass mobilization and as alternative venues for generating and utilizing socioeconomic development funds. They also have several advantages vis-à-vis the government in that they have better access to sectors of civil society (or the grass roots) than do formal government agencies and they function as a conduit of complementary resources between the state and the public and between the grass roots and funding agencies, both local and foreign (Tigno and Velasco 1992: D-3). In early 1992, there were a total of 17,000 NGOs registered with the Securities and Exchange Commission (SEC) of the Philippines (*Philippine Daily Inquirer*, Feb. 10, 1992, p. 12), whereas the Department of Interior and Local Government placed the number of NGOs throughout the country at 65,000. Their major concerns are education and training, community organization and leadership, cooperative credit, research, and health and nutrition (Tigno and Velasco 1992 and Clarke 1995). Many of these NGOs had in fact participated in the peace negotiations between the government and insurgent groups.

9. Mindanao's 33,600 documented displaced families in 1990 represented 82 percent of the national total.

10. See Task Force Detainees of the Philippines 1993. For more on the vigilante phenomenon see also R. J. May 1992. For a discussion of problems related to the emergence of anticommunist vigilante groups in the Philippines see Aquino 1988 and Lawyers Committee for Human Rights 1988.

11. For various analyses of economic problems in the Philippines during the Aquino period see Canlas 1993, Ilano 1989, Lopez 1989, Sanchez 1987, Tan 1988, and Villegas 1991.

12. For an elaborate discussion of the split within the CPP/NPA see Rocamora 1994 and "The Philippine Left" (1992), a special issue of *Kasarinlan*.

13. Ramos was the AFP chief of staff and defense minister under Aquino prior to being elected president in 1992.

14. See Rivera 1994b. Rivera argues in favor of institutional reform in the Philippines, which includes a shift to proportional representation and a unicameral parliamentary system. For a discussion of problems confronting the Ramos leadership from both the structural and systemic perspectives see Villacorta 1994.

15. For a discussion of the issues involving the Philippine Senate's rejection of a new military base treaty with the United States, see Kraft 1993 and Salonga 1995.

16. For background on the development and problems of the Philippine military see Kessler 1989, Thompson 1992, and Mak 1993.

17. Based on interviews with key informants from the Department of Foreign Affairs and Department of National Defense in Manila, May 1996. Apparently, some key foreign affairs officials perceive China as a benign regional power, whereas others have taken on a wary position. Within the defense establishment too there are differences in terms of how officials perceive China. One high-ranking defense department official even downplayed the strategic importance of the Spratlys, while some military officers in the AFP were wary of China's intentions in the region.

18. National Security Adviser Jose Almonte had expressed on several occasions the desirability of America's continued presence in the region as an effective deterrent to external threats to the Philippines ("Almonte: U.S. Presence Assures RP of Protection from Threats," *Manila Bulletin*, Jan. 8, 1996, p. 2).

19. On the distinction between modern and traditional states, see Giddens 1987: 3–4.

20. Note that for the first time since 1987, the Department of National Defense reported an increase in the number of NPA regulars during 1996, a rise of 4.6 percent to 6,300 (*Manila Times*, Dec. 31, 1996, p. 1). On the prospects for the Philippine left, see Kerkvliet 1996.

Chapter 18: Singapore

1. The first chairman, Dr. Hussin Mutalib, is a political science lecturer from the National University of Singapore. The incumbent chairman, Yang Razali Kassim, is a senior journalist with the *Business Times*.

2. Presently a female public servant in Singapore, unlike her male counterpart, is not entitled to medical coverage for her children.

3. The most recent census indicates that Singapore has a total population of 3.1 million persons. Included in this figure are a total of 300,000 foreign workers, approximately 10 percent of the population. Most foreign workers are employed either as blue-collar workers in construction and shipbuilding or as domestic helpers and caregivers.

4. Whereas the strength of the public service has been capped at 60,000 employees, total government-related employment stands at 170,000 persons, far ahead of Seagate Technology, Singapore's largest private-sector employer, which has a workforce of 18,000 employees.

Chapter 19: Asian Practice of Security

1. Benedict Anderson (1991) notes how national consciousness has become an integral part of Asian thinking.

2. For a good discussion of the different explanations for the separation of Singapore from Malaysia, see Sopiee (1974).

3. On the reasons for the recent resurgence of Hindu nationalism see Varshney (1993).

4. The compromise formula of "belief in almighty god" is one of the five key principles (*Pancasila*) that forms the basis for the Indonesian nation.

5. Suharto has in recent times become more supportive of Islamic groups, in part to strengthen his position and title to rule. Islam, however, is still not acceptable as an organizing ideology.

6. The case of Pakistan is an anomalous one in which the majority community felt persecuted. The Bengalis, accounting for some 56 percent of the population, were in the majority, but nonetheless they felt disadvantaged because of political domination by the Punjabi community.

7. The purpose of the Sinhala construction is both ideational and material—to elevate the psychological worth of the Sinhalese and enhance their material position, as well as to legitimate Sinhala domination of Sri Lanka's politics (Horowitz 1985; Pfaffenberger 1990) while marginalizing the position of the Tamils by depicting them as intruders and inferior (Krishna 1996: 307–9). Construction of Sri Lanka as a Sinhala-Buddhist nation also has the purpose of countering the perceived danger of Westernization.

8. The Muslim insurgency in the Philippines has been resolved (at least temporarily) by an agreement in September 1996 that provides a measure of autonomy for the Muslim provinces. Disaffected groups of the Moro National Liberation Front (MNLF), however, have joined the Moro Islamic Liberation Front (MILF), which has since stepped up its guerrilla war against Manila.

9. The insurgencies in Myanmar have been brought to a halt, at least temporarily, by the recent agreements between SLORC and the minority communities (see Chapter 12).

10. The traditional bases for political domination in Thailand and Nepal have since given way to quasi-democratic political systems.

11. Speech by Mahathir Mohamad at the First ISIS National Conference on National Security, July 15, 1986, at ISIS (Malaysia), Kuala Lumpur. For the text see *ISIS Focus* 17 (Aug. 1986): 16–20.

12. For a discussion of the strategies for addressing internal security concerns, see Alagappa, *National Security of Developing States* (1987a). On strategies for dealing with ethnic conflicts, see Horowitz (1985) and Montville (1990).

13. Taiwan has no formal alliance with the United States, but there is an implicit understanding that should the PRC use force in pursuit of its unification goal, the United States will intervene in support of Taiwan.

14. On the daunting challenges confronting the modernization of the People's Liberation Army Air Force (PLAAF), see Allen, Krumel, and Pollack 1995.

15. Indonesia did want regional states to terminate their alliances with external powers, but this proposal was not acceptable to the other members of ASEAN—Malaysia, Singapore, Thailand, and the Philippines. As a concession to Indonesia, the preamble of the 1967 ASEAN Declaration states that "all foreign bases are temporary and remain only with the express concurrence of the countries concerned and are not intended for use directly or indirectly to subvert the national independence and freedom of states in the area."

16. Cambodia's membership in ASEAN has been delayed because of the coup d'état by Hun Sen's forces in 1997.

17. On the spectrum of conflict management, see Alagappa 1995c.

18. For Taiwan, although attractive at the outset, over time this strategy increased its dependence on China, making for vulnerability. Taipei now seeks to limit Taiwanese investment in the mainland—but not very successfully. See Chapter 8.

19. On metaregime and its differentiation from regime, see Aggarwal 1985: 18–19.

20. In seeking to link the British theories of international society and the American theories of regime, Buzan (1993a) makes the case that an international society is a precondition for the development of regimes.

21. On premodern, modern, and postmodern states see Giddens (1987) and Sorenson (forthcoming).

22. The Indonesian annexation of Timor-Timor, on the other hand, has not met with the same degree of resistance within the region, although Singapore did in the early years abstain in the vote in the Trusteeship Council of the United Nations. Timor-Timor, however, was not an independent state, and Indonesia has had to justify the annexation on the basis that it has been consented to by the elected representative of the Timorese people. The annexation has still not been accepted by the broader international community.

23. Schweller and Priess (1997: 23) argue that traditional realism accepts that "institutions can, and sometimes do, matter."

24. Krasner (1993: 257) advances the argument that ideas initially are just hooks to justify actions that are motivated by considerations of wealth and power. He argues that material factors, not ideology, were responsible for the decision to select sovereignty from the rich variety of ideas in Europe. Sovereignty, according to Krasner, was not chosen for the form of order it represented but because it was a device to legitimate existing political practices. He does, however, accept that once an idea like sovereignty becomes institutionalized it has consequences for political behavior.

25. For a good discussion of the meaning of and conditions for successful hegemony in the Gramscian sense see Mouffe 1979: 168–204.

26. These principles were first articulated in the 1967 ASEAN Declaration and reiterated in subsequent concords, agreements, and treaties of the association. For the text of the ASEAN Declaration see *ASEAN Documents Series 1967–1986*, issued by the ASEAN Secretariat in Jakarta.

27. Taipei claims that mainland China and Taiwan are already two separate

political entities and that all it is seeking is international recognition of that fact until the time is propitious for reunification.

28. The German experience, and the prospect of the enormous political, economic, and social cost of absorbing North Korea have in recent times sobered the South Korean elite and tempered the attraction of the goal of unification. Their preference now is for a "soft landing" rather than a sudden collapse or "crash landing," although they may have little control over developments in North Korea.

29. The new guidelines have yet to be formally adopted. The Socialist party, although it has come to accept the U.S.–Japan security treaty, sees the new guidelines as a departure from existing laws and requiring new legislation.

Chapter 20: Conceptualizing Security

1. *Intension* refers to a set of meanings or attributes that define a concept or category and determines membership. See Sartori (1984: 22–28).

2. This may be due in part to the fact that this study is focused on the perceptions and behavior of central decision makers.

3. On genus, specie, and subspecie definitions and the "ladder of abstraction," see Sartori (1984: 44–46).

4. On conceptual traveling and conceptual stretching see Collier and Mahon (1993: 845–55).

5. On "unsettling costs" associated with the introduction of new concepts, see Sartori (1984: 52–54).

Bibliography

Abbas, B. M. 1984. *The Ganges Water Dispute*. Dhaka: University Press.

Abeysekera, Charles. 1992. "The Limits of Space: Human Rights and Foreign Aid." *Index on Censorship* 21, no. 7: 28.

Acharya, Amitav. 1990. *A Survey of Military Cooperation Among the ASEAN States: Bilateralism or Alliance?* Toronto: Center for International and Strategic Studies, York University.

———. 1992a. "Regionalism and Regime Security in the Third World: Comparing the Origins of ASEAN and the GCC." In Brian Job, ed., *The Insecurity Dilemma: The National Security Dilemma of Third World States*. Boulder, Colo.: Lynne Rienner.

———. 1992b. "Singapore's Foreign Policy in the Post–Cold War Era: Continuity and Change." Paper presented at a conference on Southeast Asian Foreign Policy, University of Windsor, Ontario.

———. 1994. *An Arms Race in Post–Cold War Southeast Asia?* Singapore: Institute of Southeast Asian Studies.

Acharya, Amitav, and M. Ramesh. 1993. "Economic Foundations of Singapore's National Security: From Globalism to Regionalism?" In Garry Rodan, ed., *Singapore Changes Guard*. Melbourne: Longman Cheshire.

Acheson, Dean. 1969. *Present at the Creation: My Years in the State Department*. New York: Norton.

Adil, Adnan. 1993. "The Price Bite." *Newsline*, Jan.

Agence France Presse. 1993. Hanoi, 27 Sept. In Foreign Broadcast Information Service, East Asian Service, FBIS-EAS-93-197.

———. 1994a. Hanoi, 17 Mar. In Foreign Broadcast Information Service, East Asian Service, FBIS-EAS-94-053.

———. 1994b. Hanoi, 16 Aug. In Foreign Broadcast Information Service, East Asian Service, FBIS-EAS-94-158.

————. 1994c. Hanoi, 7 Dec. In Foreign Broadcast Information Service, East Asian Service, FBIS-EAS-94-235.

————. 1995. Hanoi, 25 Jan. In Foreign Broadcast Information Service, East Asian Service, FBIS-EAS-95-017.

Aggarwal, Vinod. 1985. *Liberal Protectionism*. Berkeley: University of California Press.

Ahamed, Emajuddin. 1985. "Problems of Democracy in Bangladesh." In Salimullah Khan, ed., *Political Instability in Bangladesh: Problems and Prospects*. Dhaka: Dana.

Ahmad, Abdullah. 1988. *Issues in Malaysian Politics*. Singapore: Singapore Institute of International Affairs.

Ahmad, Col. Bashir. 1965. "Trends in Pakistan's Foreign Policy." *Pakistan Army Journal* 7, no. 1: 50–64.

Ahmad, Q. K., B. G. Verghese, R. Ayer, B. B. Pradhan, and S. K. Malla, eds. 1994. *Converting Water into Wealth: Regional Cooperation in Harnessing Eastern Himalayan Rivers*. Dhaka: Academic.

Ahmed, Feroz. 1985. "Pakistan's Problems of National Integration." In Mohammed Asghar Khan, ed., *Islam, Politics and the State: The Pakistan Experience*. London: Zed Books.

————. 1988. "Ethnicity and Politics: The Rise of Muhajir Separatism." *South Asia Bulletin* 8, nos. 1–2: 33–45.

Ahmed, Imtiaz. 1996. "Refugees and Security: The Experience of Bangladesh." In S. D. Muni and Lok Raj Baral, eds., *Refugees and Regional Security in South Asia*. New Delhi: RCSS/Konark.

Ahmed, Moudud. 1983. *Bangladesh: Era of Sheikh Mujibar Rahman*. Dhaka: University Press.

Ahmed, Sabihuddin. 1991. "Old Bottles, New Wine." *Newsline*, Aug.

Ahmed, Samina. 1995. "The Military and Ethnic Politics in Sindh." In Charles H. Kennedy and Rasul B. Rais, eds., *Pakistan 1995*. Boulder, Colo.: Westview.

Akao, Nobutoshi. 1983. Introduction to Nobutoshi Akao, ed., *Japan's Economic Security*. New York: St. Martin's.

Akhund, Iqbal. 1988. "Weapon-for-Weapon Approach." *Defence Journal* 14, no. 3: 14–15.

Alagappa, Muthiah. 1987a. *The National Security of Developing States: Lessons from Thailand*. Dover, Mass.: Auburn House.

————. 1987b. "A Nuclear Weapons–Free Zone in Southeast Asia: Problems and Prospects." *Australian Outlook* 41, no. 3: 173–80.

————. 1988. "Comprehensive Security: Interpretations in ASEAN Countries." In Robert A. Scalapino, Seizaburo Sato, Jusuf Wanandi, and Sung-Joo Han, eds., *Asian Security Issues: Regional and Global*. Research Papers and Policy Studies 26. Berkeley: Institute of East Asian Studies, University of California.

———. 1990a. "The Cambodian Conflict: Changing Interests." *Pacific Review* 3, no. 3: 266–71.

———. 1990b. "Soviet Policy in Southeast Asia: Toward Constructive Engagement." *Pacific Affairs* 63, no. 3: 321–50.

———. 1991a. "The Dynamics of International Security in Southeast Asia: Change and Continuity." *Australian Journal of International Affairs* 45, no. 1: 1–37.

———. 1991b. "The Political-Security Environment in the Asia-Pacific: Evolutionary Change." Manuscript.

———. 1991c. "Regional Arrangements and International Security: An Evaluation of ZOPFAN." In Miles Kahler, ed., *Beyond the Cold War in the Pacific*. Institute on Global Conflict and Cooperation Studies 2. San Diego: Institute on Global Conflict and Cooperation, University of California.

———. 1991d. "Regional Arrangements and International Security in Southeast Asia: Going Beyond ZOPFAN." *Contemporary Southeast Asia* 12, no. 4: 269–305.

———. 1993. "Regionalism and the Quest for Security: ASEAN and the Cambodian Conflict." *Journal of International Affairs* 46, no. 2: 439–57.

———. 1994. *Democratic Transition in Asia: The Role of the International Community*. East-West Center Special Report 3 (Oct.). Honolulu: East-West Center.

———. 1995a. "The Bases of Legitimacy." In Muthiah Alagappa, ed., *Political Legitimacy in Southeast Asia: The Quest for Moral Authority*. Stanford: Stanford University Press.

———, ed. 1995b. *Political Legitimacy in Southeast Asia: The Quest for Moral Authority*. Stanford: Stanford University Press.

———. 1995c. "Regionalism and Conflict Management: A Framework for Analysis." *Review of International Studies* 21: 359–87.

———. 1997. "Systemic Change, Security and Governance in the Asia-Pacific Region." In Chan Heng Chee, ed., *The New Asia-Pacific Order*. Singapore: Institute of Southeast Asian Studies.

Alburo, Florian A. 1993. "The Political Economy of Liberalizing Foreign Trade: Philippine Experiences." *Philippine Review of Economics and Business* 30, no. 1: 122–40.

Ali, Akhtar. 1984. *Pakistan's Nuclear Dilemma: Energy and Security Dimensions*. Karachi: Economist Research Unit, Pakistan and Gulf Economist.

Ali, Salamat. 1993. "Mortal Blow." *Far Eastern Economic Review*, 21 Jan., p. 19.

Allan, J., T. Wolseley Haig, and H. H. Dodwell. 1934. *The Cambridge Shorter History of India*. Cambridge, Eng.: Cambridge University Press.

Allen, Kenneth W., Glenn Krumel, and Jonathan D. Pollack. 1995. *China's Air Force Enters the Twenty-first Century*. Santa Monica, Calif.: Rand.

Alles, A. C. 1990. *The JVP 1969–1989*. Colombo: Lake House.

Allison, Graham. 1971. *Essence of Decision*. Boston: Little, Brown.

Allison, Graham, and Gregory F. Treverton, eds. 1992. *Rethinking America's Security*. New York: Norton.

Allot, Anna J. 1993. "Censorship in Burma." In Anna J. Allot, comp., *Inked Over, Ripped Out: Burmese Storytellers and the Censors*. Pen American Center Freedom-to-Write Report. New York: Pen American Center.

Almonte, Jose. 1986. "Towards Reshaping Philippine Martial Tradition." In M. Rajaretnam, ed., *The Aquino Alternative*. Singapore: Institute for Southeast Asian Studies.

————. 1994. Lecture before the National Security Training Center, Cagayan de Oro City, 15 Sept.

Amnesty International. 1982. *Report of an Amnesty International Mission to the Republic of the Philippines, 11–28 November 1981*. London: Amnesty International Publications.

————. 1990. Viet Nam: "Renovation" (Doi Moi), the Law and Human Rights in the 1980s. New York: Amnesty International, Feb.

————. 1992. "Myanmar, 'No Law at All': Human Rights Violations Under Military Rule." London: Amnesty International, Oct.

————. 1994. "Myanmar—Human Rights Still Denied." London: Amnesty International, Nov.

Amsden, Alice. 1989. *Asia's Next Giant*. New York: Oxford University Press.

Anderson, Benedict. 1991. *Imagined Communities: Reflection on the Origin and Spread of Nationalism*. 2d ed., revised and extended. London: Verso.

————. 1995. "Chinese Bases in Burma: Fact or Fiction?" *Jane's Intelligence Review*, Feb., pp. 84–87.

Andreski, Stanislav. 1980. "On the Peaceful Disposition of Military Dictatorship." *Journal of Strategic Studies* 3 (Dec.): 3–10.

Anwar, Dewi Fortuna. 1992. *Indonesia and the Security of Southeast Asia*. Jakarta: CSIS.

————. 1993. "Changes and Continuity in Indonesia's Regional Outlook." In Chandran Jeshurun, ed., *China, India, Japan and the Security of Southeast Asia*. Singapore: Institute of Southeast Asian Studies.

————. 1994. *Indonesia in ASEAN: Foreign Policy and Regionalism*. Singapore: Institute of Southeast Asian Studies.

Aquino, Belinda. 1987a. *The Politics of Plunder*. Quezon City: Great Books.

————. 1987b. Review of *Crisis in the Philippines: The Marcos Era and Beyond*, edited by John C. Bresnan. *Contemporary Southeast Asia* 9, no. 1: 54–58.

————. 1988. "The Philippines in 1987: Beating Back the Challenge of August." In Mohammed Ayoob and Ng Chee Ye, eds., *Southeast Asian Affairs 1988*. Singapore: Institute of Southeast Asian Studies.

Aquino, Corazon C. 1986. "A Strategy for the Future Waging of Peace" (Speech before the National Defense College Graduation, July 3). *Speeches of President Corazon C. Aquino, March 22–August 5, 1986*. Manila: Republic of the Philippines.

ASEAN Regional Forum. 1994. Chairman's statement.

ASEAN Secretariat. 1986. *ASEAN Document Series 1967–86*. Jakarta: ASEAN Secretariat.

Asia Yearbook 1991. Hong Kong: Far Eastern Economic Review.

Asia Yearbook 1995. Hong Kong: Far Eastern Economic Review.

Askari, M. H. 1989. "The Change in the ISI and Its Implications." *Defence Journal* 14, no. 8: 10–16.

Ayoob, Mohammed. 1985. "The Quest for Autonomy: Ideologies in the Indian Ocean Region." In W. L. Dowdy and Russel B. Trood, eds., *The Indian Ocean Region: Perspectives on a Strategic Arena*. Durham, N.C.: Duke University Press.

———. 1989. "The Third World in the System of States: Acute Schizophrenia or Growing Pains?" *International Studies Quarterly* 33, no. 1: 67–79.

———. 1991. "The Security Problematic of the Third World." *World Politics* 43, no. 2: 257–83.

———. 1992. "The Security Predicament of Third World States: Reflections on State Making in Comparative Perspective." In Brian Job, ed., *The Insecurity Dilemma: National Security of Third World States*. Boulder, Colo.: Lynne Rienner.

———. 1993. "State-Making and Third World Security." In Jasjit Singh and Thomas Bernauer, eds., *Security of Third World Countries*. Aldershot, Eng.: Dartmouth/UNIDIR.

———. 1995. *The Third World Security Predicament: State Making, Regional Conflict, and the International System*. Boulder, Colo.: Lynne Rienner.

Azar, Edward E. 1990. *The Management of Protracted Social Conflict: Theory and Cases*. Hampshire, Eng.: Dartmouth.

Azar, Edward E., and Chung-In Moon, eds. 1988. *National Security in the Third World: The Management of Internal and External Threats*. Aldershot, Eng.: Edward Elgar.

Baek, Jong-Chun. 1985. *Kukga Banguiron* (Thesis on national defense). Seoul: Bakyoungsa.

Baginda, Abdul Razak, ed. 1995. *Malaysian Defence and Foreign Policies*. Petaling Jaya: Pelanduk.

Bailey, Kathleen C. 1994. "North Korea: Enough Carrots, Time for the Stick." *Comparative Strategy* 13 (July–Sept.): 277–82.

Bajpai, Kanti P. 1996. "Abstaining: The Nonnuclear Option." In David Cortright and Amitabh Mattoo, eds., *India and the Bomb: Public Opinion and Nuclear Options*. Notre Dame, Ind.: University of Notre Dame Press.

Bajpai, Kanti P., P. R. Chari, P. I. Cheema, Stephen P. Cohen, and S. Ganguly. 1995. *Brasstacks and Beyond: Perception and Management of Crisis in South Asia*. New Delhi: Manohar, under auspices of the Program in Arms Control, Disarmament, and International Security, University of Illinois, Urbana-Champaign.

Bajpai, U. S., ed. 1983. *India's Security*. New Delhi: Lancers.

Baker, James. 1991–92. "America in Asia." *Foreign Affairs* 70, no. 5: 1–18.

Baldwin, David A. 1993. "Neoliberalism, Neorealism and World Politics." In *Neorealism and Neoliberalism: The Contemporary Debate*. New York: Columbia University Press.

———. 1995. "Security Studies and the End of the Cold War." *World Politics* 48, no. 1: 117–41.

Ball, Desmond. 1993–94. "Arms and Affluence: Military Acquisitions in the Asia-Pacific Region." *International Security* 18, no. 3: 78–112.

———. 1995. "Arms Acquisition in the Asia-Pacific." Paper presented at the Ninth Asia-Pacific Roundtable, Kuala Lumpur, June.

———. 1996. "Arms and Affluence: Military Acquisitions in the Asia-Pacific Region." In Michael E. Brown, Sean M. Lynn-Jones, and Steven E. Miller, eds., *East Asian Security*. Cambridge, Mass.: MIT Press.

Ball, Desmond, and Pauline Kerr. 1996. *Presumptive Engagement: Australia's Asia-Pacific Security Policy in the 1990s*. St. Leonards, New South Wales: Allen and Unwin.

Bangkok Post. 1994. 31 Mar. In Foreign Broadcast Information Service, East Asian Service, FBIS-EAS-94-062.

———. 1995a. "ASEAN Facing Weapons Crisis, Says Researcher." 24 Jan.

———. 1995b. "Military Urged to Clarify Its Arms Purchases." 6 Feb.

Barnds, William J. 1972. *India, Pakistan and the Great Powers*. New York: Praeger.

Barnett, Doak A. 1977. *China and the Major Powers in East Asia*. Washington, D.C.: Brookings Institution.

Basham, Arthur L. 1954. *The Wonder That Was India*. London: Sidgwick and Jackson.

Bastian, Sunil. 1988. "NGOs in Development." *Thatched Patio* 18 (Apr.): 12–18.

Basu, Baidya Bikash. 1996. "The Private Sector's Participation in Indian Defence Industry." M. Phil. diss., Jawaharlal Nehru University, New Delhi.

Baum, Richard. 1992. "Political Stability in Post-Deng China: Problems and Prospects." *Asian Survey* 32, no. 6: 491–505.

Bauzon, Kenneth E. 1991. *Liberalism and the Quest for Islamic Identity in the Philippines*. Manila: Ateneo de Manila University Press.

Baxi, Upendra. 1992. "Globalization: A World Without Alternatives?" International Centre for Ethnic Studies Annual Lecture, University of Colombo, 24 Nov.

Baxter, Craig, and Sayedur Rahman. 1991. "Bangladesh Votes 1991: Building Democratic Institutions." *Asian Survey* 31, no. 8: 683–93.

Bay, Christian. 1987. "Conceptions of Security: Individual, National and Global." In Bhikku Parekh and Thomas Pantham, eds., *Political Discourse: Explorations in Indian and Western Political Thought*. New Delhi: Sage.

Bayer, James A. 1995. "The North Korean Nuclear Crisis and the Agreed Framework: How Not to Negotiate with the North Koreans." *Asian Perspective* 16, no. 2: 191–222.

Begum, Khurshida. 1987. *Tension over the Farakka Barrage: A Techno-Political Tangle in South Asia*. Dhaka: University Press.

Beijing Review. 1982. "China, U.S. Issue Joint Communique." Vol. 25, no. 34: 14–15.

———. 1992. "China Knocks Heads on Drug Trafficking." Vol. 35, no. 15: 9.

———. 1994a. "China Set to Curb Organized Crimes." Vol. 37, no. 49: 5.

———. 1994b. "Policy on Dalai Lama Remains Unchanged." Vol. 37, no. 20: 13.

———. 1995a. "China: Human Rights Not in Politics Arena." Vol. 38, no. 9: 4.

———. 1995b. "China Significant for World Economy." Vol. 38, no. 18: 7.

———. 1995c. "President Urges Cross-Strait Summit." Vol. 38, no. 7: 13.

Bekaert, Jacques. 1993. "Vietnam and China: Towards Peaceful Co-existence." *Bangkok Post*, 21 Jan. In Foreign Broadcast Information Service, East Asian Service, FBIS-EAS-93-013.

Benjamin, Roger, and Raymond Duvall. 1985. "The Capitalist State in Context." In Roger Benjamin and Stephen L. Elkin, eds., *The Democratic State*. Lawrence: University of Kansas Press.

Berger, Thomas U. 1993. "From Sword to Chrysanthemum: Japan's Culture of Anti-Militarism." *International Security* 17, no. 4: 119–50.

Betts, Richard K. 1993–94. "Wealth, Power, and Instability: East Asia and the United States After the Cold War." *International Security* 18, no. 3: 34–77.

Bey, Soo Khiang. 1994. "Security and the SAF." Text of a speech delivered at the Temasek Seminar, Singapore.

Bhakti, Ikrar Nusa. 1996. "Security Cooperation Between Indonesia and Australia." Paper presented at the second Indonesian students' conference (Indonesia-Australia Relationship: Towards Greater Understanding and Cooperation), Canberra, 21–22 Aug.

Bhutto, Zulfikar Ali. 1964. *Foreign Policy of Pakistan: A Compendium of Speeches Made in the National Assembly, 1962–1964*. Karachi: Pakistan Institute of International Affairs.

Bialer, Seweryn. 1982. "The Sino-Soviet Conflict: The Soviet Dimension." In Donald S. Zagoria, ed., *Soviet Policy in East Asia*. New Haven: Yale University Press.

Bobrow, Davis B. 1993. "Military Security Policy." In R. Kent Weaver and Bert A. Rockman, eds., *Do Institutions Matter? Government Capabilities in the United States and Abroad*. Washington, D.C.: Brookings Institution.

Bobrow, Davis B., and Steve Chan. 1986. "Asset, Liability, and Strategic Conduct: Status Management by Japan, Taiwan, and South Korea." *Pacific Focus* 1, no. 1: 23–56.

Boei Handbook Heisei 7-nen Ban (Defense handbook 1995). 1995. Tokyo: Asagumo Shinbun-sha.

Bonner, Raymond. 1988. *Waltzing with a Dictator: The Marcoses and the Making of American Foreign Policy.* New York: Vintage.

Booth, Ken. 1979. *Strategy and Ethnocentrism.* London: Croom Helm.

———. 1991a. "Security and Emancipation." *Review of International Studies* 17: 316–26.

———. 1991b. "Security in Anarchy: Utopian Realism in Theory and Practice." *International Affairs* 67, no. 3: 527–45.

Booth, Ken, and Peter Vale. 1995. "Security in Southern Africa: After Apartheid, Beyond Realism." *International Affairs* 71, no. 2: 285–304.

Bose, Shikha. 1996. "Victims of a Security Dilemma: Chakmas and Refugees from Bangladesh." In S. D. Muni and Lok Raj Baral, eds., *Refugees and Regional Security in South Asia.* New Delhi: RCSS/Konark.

Bose, Sugata, ed. 1990. *South Asia and World Capitalism.* New Delhi: Oxford University Press.

Boudarel, Georges. 1991. *Cent Fleurs Ecloses dans la Nuit du Vietnam: Communisme et Dissidence 1954–1956* (A hundred flowers bloom in the Vietnamese night: Communism and dissidence 1954–1956). Paris: Jacques Bertoin.

Boyce, James. 1993. *The Philippines: The Political Economy of Growth and Impoverishment in the Marcos Era.* London: Macmillan.

Boyle, Kevin. 1995. "Stock-taking on Human Rights: The World Conference on Human Rights, Vienna, 1993." In David Beetham, ed., *Politics and Human Rights.* Oxford: Blackwell.

Bozeman, Adda B. 1993. "Introduction: War and the Clash of Ideas." In Stephen J. Blank, Lawrence E. Grinter, Karl P. Magyar, Lewis B. Waree, and Bynum E. Weathers, *Conflict, Culture and History: Regional Dimensions.* Maxwell Air Force Base: Air University Press.

Bracken, Paul. 1993. "North Korea's Nuclear Program as a Problem of State Survival." In Andrew Mack, ed., *Asian Flashpoint: Security and the Korean Peninsula.* Canberra: Allen and Unwin.

Bresnan, John, ed. 1986. *Crisis in the Philippines: The Marcos Era and Beyond.* Princeton: Princeton University Press.

Brillantes, Alex B., Jr. 1987. *Dictatorship and Martial Law: Philippine Authoritarianism in 1972.* Quezon City: Great Books.

———. 1993. "The Philippines in 1992: Ready for Take Off?" *Asian Survey* 33, no. 2: 224–30.

Brooke, Micool. 1995. "Helicopter-Carrier Marks Transition to Blue-Water Navy." *Bangkok Post,* 12 Dec.

Brown, David. 1985. "Crisis and Ethnicity: Legitimation in Plural Societies." *Third World Quarterly* 7, no. 4: 988–1008.

———. 1989. "Ethnic Revival: Perspectives on State and Society." *Third World Quarterly* 11, no. 4: 1–17.

————. 1993. "The Corporatist Management of Ethnicity in Contemporary Singapore." In Garry Rodan, ed., *Singapore Changes Guard*. Melbourne: Longman Cheshire.

————. 1994. *The State and Ethnic Politics in Southeast Asia*. London: Routledge.

Brown, David, and David M. Jones. 1994. "Political Development in Singapore and the Myth of the Liberalising Middle Class." *Pacific Review* 7, no. 1: 79–87.

Brown, Lester. 1977. *Redefining National Security*. Washington, D.C.: Worldwatch Institute.

Brown, Mackenzie D. 1965. "Hindu and Western Realism: A Study of Contrasts." In Joel Larus, ed., *Comparative World Politics*. Belmont, Calif.: Wadsworth.

Brown, Michael E. 1996. Introduction to Michael E. Brown, ed., *The International Dimension of Internal Conflict*. Cambridge, Mass.: MIT Press.

Brown, Michael E., Sean M. Lynn-Jones, and Steven E. Miller, eds. 1996a. *Debating the Democratic Peace*. Cambridge, Mass.: MIT Press.

————, eds. 1996b. *East Asian Security*. Cambridge, Mass.: MIT Press.

Brown, Neville. 1989. "Climate, Ecology, and International Security." *Survival* 31, no. 6: 519–32.

————. 1992. "Ecology and World Security." *World Today* 48, no. 3: 51–54.

Brown, Norman. 1963. *The United States and India and Pakistan*. Cambridge, Mass.: Harvard University Press.

Bui Thien Ngo. 1992. "Bao Ve An Ninh Quoc Gia Trong Tinh Hinh Moi" (Protecting national security in the new situation). *Tap Chi Cong San*, Sept.

Bull, Hedley. 1977. *The Anarchical Society: A Study of Order in World Politics*. New York: Columbia University Press.

Bull, Hedley, and Adam Watson, eds. 1984. *The Expansion of International Society*. New York: Clarendon.

Bumrongsuk, Surachart. 1993. "Thai and Cambodia's Problem: Impact on Thai's Security and Foreign Policies." In Chaichok Julsiriwongse, ed., *Five Decades of Thai's Foreign Affairs: From Conflict to Cooperation*. Bangkok: Faculty of Political Science, Chulalongkorn University.

Bunbongkarn, Suchit. 1987. *The Military in Thai Politics 1981–86*. Singapore: Institute of Southeast Asian Studies.

————. 1992. "Thailand in 1991." *Asian Survey* 32, no. 2: 131–39.

Bunbongkarn, Suchit, and Kannale Sukapanich-Kantaprab. 1987. "Civil Service Works of the Thai Army." In Surachart Bamrungsuk, ed., *The Thai Military System: A Study of the Army in the Context of Social and Politics* (in Thai). Bangkok: Institute of Security and International Studies.

Bunnag, Piyanart. 1991. "The Administrative Policy of the Thai Government Toward the Thai Muslims in Southern Provinces, 1932–1973" (in Thai). Research Report Series, no. 26. Bangkok: Chulalongkorn University.

Bunnag, Tej. 1977. *The Provincial Administration of Siam, 1892–1915.* Kuala Lumpur: Oxford University Press.

Bunnell, Frederick P. 1966. "Guided Democracy Foreign Policy 1960–1965." In *Indonesia*, no. 2. Ithaca, N.Y.: Cornell Modern Indonesia Project, Cornell University Press.

Buntrigswat, Sanchai. N.d. *Thailand: The Dual Threats to Stability in a Study of Communist Insurgency and Problems of Political Development.* Bangkok: Borpit.

Burma Socialist Programme Party. 1985. *Fourth Party Congress 1981: Party Chairman's Speech and Political Report of the Central Committee.* Rangoon: Burma Socialist Programme Party.

Burns, Susan M. 1995. *Stabilizing the Option: Deterrence, Confidence Building, and Arms Control in South Asia.* ACDIS occasional paper. Urbana-Champaign: Research Program in Arms Control, Disarmament, and International Security, University of Illinois.

Buszynski, Leszek. 1985. "Singapore: A Foreign Policy of Survival." *Asian Thought and Society* 10, no. 29: 128–36.

Butts, Kent Hughes. 1993. *Environmental Security: What is DOD's Role?* Carlisle, Pa.: U.S. Army War College, Strategic Studies Institute.

Buzan, Barry. 1983. *People, States and Fear: The National Security Problem in International Relations.* Chapel Hill: University of North Carolina Press.

———. 1988. "The Southeast Asian Security Complex." *Contemporary Southeast Asia* 10, no. 1: 1–16.

———. 1991. *People, States and Fear: An Agenda for International Security Studies in the Post–Cold War Era.* Boulder, Colo.: Lynne Rienner.

———. 1993a. "From International System to International Society: Structural Realism and Regime Theory Meet the English School." *International Organization* 47, no. 3: 327–52.

———. 1993b. "Waltz, His Critics, and the Prospects for a Structural Realism." In Barry Buzan, Charles Jones, and Richard Little, eds., *The Logic of Anarchy: Neorealism to Structural Realism.* New York: Columbia University Press.

———. 1995. "The Post–Cold War Asia-Pacific Security Order: Conflict or Cooperation." In Andrew Mack and John Ravenhill, eds., *Pacific Cooperation: Building Economic and Security Regimes in the Asia-Pacific Region.* Boulder, Colo.: Westview.

Buzan, Barry, Charles Jones, and Richard Little, eds. 1993. *The Logic of Anarchy: Neorealism to Structural Realism.* New York: Columbia University Press.

Buzan, Barry, and Gerald Segal. 1994. "Rethinking East Asian Security." *Survival* 36, no. 2: 3–21.

Cady, John F. 1965. *A History of Modern Burma.* Ithaca, N.Y.: Cornell University Press.

Calhoun, Craig. 1994. "Nationalism and Civil Society: Democracy, Diversity and Self-Determination." In Craig Calhoun, ed., *Social Theory and the Politics of Identity*. Cambridge, Mass.: Blackwell.

Camroux, David. 1994. *Looking East and Inwards: Internal Factors in Malaysia's Foreign Relations During the Mahathir Era, 1981–1994*. Australia-Asia Paper 72. Queensland: Griffith University.

Canlas, Dante. 1993. "The Philippine Economy in 1992." In Daljit Singh, ed., *Southeast Asian Affairs 1993*. Singapore: Institute for Southeast Asian Studies.

Cantori, Louis J., and Steven L. Spiegel, eds. 1970. *The International Politics of Regions: A Comparative Approach*. Englewood Cliffs, N.J.: Prentice-Hall.

Caparaso, James A. 1993. "International Relations Theory and Multilateralism: The Search for Foundations." In John G. Ruggie, ed., *Multilateralism Matters: The Theory and Praxis of an Institutional Form*. New York: Columbia University Press.

Carr, Edward Hallet. 1964. *The Twenty Years' Crisis, 1919–1939*. New York: Harper and Row.

Carter, Ashton B., William J. Perry, and John D. Steinbruner. 1992. *A New Concept of Cooperative Security*. Washington, D.C.: Brookings Institution.

Catholic Institute for International Relations. 1982. *British Investment and the Use of Paramilitary Terrorism in Plantation Agriculture in Agusan del Sur, Philippines*. London: CIIR.

Central News Agency (Taipei). 1987. "'Separatism' Not Linked to Barring Mainlanders." In *FBIS Daily Report: China*, 14 July, p. V1.

———. 1990. "Deporting Mainlanders Necessary for Security." In *FBIS Daily Report: China*, 10 Aug., p. 44.

———. 1992. "Li Appeals for U.S. Aid in Asian Security Plan." In *FBIS Daily Report: China*, 18 Sept., p. 56.

———. 1993. "President Urges 'Collective Security System.'" In *FBIS Daily Report: China*, 29 Mar., p. 75.

———. 1997. "Zui Xin Liangan Maoyi Qingshi Fenxi" (An analysis of the latest cross-strait trade situation). Feb. 28.

Chai, Sunki. 1993. "An Organizational Economics Theory of Antigovernment Violence." *Comparative Politics* 26, no. 1: 99–110.

Chaloemtiarana, Thak. 1979. *Thailand: The Politics of Despotic Paternalism*. Bangkok: Social Science Association of Thailand, Thai Khadi Institute, Thammasat University.

Chan, Heng Chee. 1971. *Singapore: The Politics of Survival, 1965–67*. Singapore: Oxford University Press.

———. 1985. "Political Parties." In Jon Quah, Seah Chee Meow, and Chan Heng Chee, eds., *Government and Politics of Singapore*. Singapore: Oxford University Press.

Chan, Joseph. 1995. "The Asian Challenge to Universal Human Rights: A Philosophical Appraisal." In James T. H. Tang, ed., *Human Rights and International Relations in the Asia-Pacific Region*. New York: St. Martin's.

Chan, Peter. 1987. "Singapore's Foreign Policy: Objectives and Achievements." Text of a talk delivered to White House Fellows, Singapore.

Chanda, Nayan. 1995. "Fear of the Dragon." *Far Eastern Economic Review*, 13 Apr., pp. 24–28.

Chanda, Nayan, and Kari Huus. 1995. "The New Nationalism." *Far Eastern Economic Review*, 9 Nov., pp. 20–26.

Chanda, Nayan, Rigoberto Tiglao, and John McBeth. 1995. "Territorial Imperative." *Far Eastern Economic Review*, 23 Feb., pp. 14–16.

Chandraprema, C. A. 1991. *Sri Lanka, the Years of Terror: The JVP Insurrection 1987–1989*. Colombo: Lake House.

Chapman, William. 1987. *Inside the Philippine Revolution: The New People's Army and Its Struggle for Power*. London: I. B. Tauris.

Chapon, Jean-Claude. 1991. Agence France Presse (Hanoi), 3 Mar. In Foreign Broadcast Information Service, East Asian Service, FBIS-EAS-91-042.

Chari, P. R. 1987. "Security Aspects of Indian Foreign Policy." In Stephen P. Cohen, ed., *The Security of South Asia: American and Asian Perspectives*. Urbana: University of Illinois Press.

———. 1994. *The IPKF Experience in Sri Lanka*. ACDIS occasional paper. Urbana-Champaign: Research Program in Arms Control, Disarmament, and International Security, University of Illinois.

Chawla, Asha. 1996. "India Stands by Its Decision on Test Ban Treaty." *Asia Observer* (New York), 6 Sept.

Cheema, Pervaiz Iqbal, and Zafar Iqbal Cheema. 1994. "Nuclear Arms Control in the Indian Ocean." *Defence Journal* 20, nos. 5–6: 13–30.

Che Man, W. K. 1990. *Muslim Separatism: The Moros of Southern Philippines and the Malays of Southern Thailand*. Singapore: Oxford University Press.

Chen Wei-pin. 1992. "Zhonggong shifou jieru xuanju lingren guanqie" (Whether Communists are intervening in elections causes concern). *Independence Morning Post (Zili zaobao)*, 9 Dec., p. 2.

Chin, Kin Wah. 1974. *Five Power Defence Arrangements and AMDA*. Singapore: Institute of Southeast Asian Studies.

China Daily. 1995. "National Statement on Security Assurances Issued." 6 Apr., p. 1.

China Times (Zhongguo shibao). 1988. "Haixia liang'an minjian guanxi ni yu guifan, kaolu kaifang jiaoliu juban guoji huo dong" (Nongovernmental cross-straits relations to be regulated, considering opening exchanges and hosting international activities). 25 Feb., p. 2.

———. 1991. "Guojia tongyi gangling quanwen" (Complete text of national unification guidelines). 24 Feb., p. 2.

"Chinese First." 1996. *Far Eastern Economic Review*, 1 Aug., p. 13.

Chinwanno, Chulacheeb. 1993. *Thailand's Foreign Policy in the 1980s* (in Thai). Bangkok: Center of Foreign Affairs Studies.

———. N.d. *Thai-Laos Relations: Conflict or Cooperation?* Forthcoming.

Chishti, Lt. Gen. Faiz Ali. 1989. *Betrayals of Another Kind: Islam, Democracy and the Army in Pakistan*. Delhi: Tricolour Books.

Cho, Han-seok, and Young-myong Kim. 1989. "Hankukui Banjon, Banhaek Pyongwha Undong" (Antiwar, antinuclear peace movement in Korea). In National Unification Board, ed., *Hanbandoui Gunchukgwa Pyongwha* (Arms control and peace on the Korean peninsula). Seoul: NUB.

Cho, Kap-je. 1995. "Taehan Minguk-un chonjaeng-ul kyolshim halsu itnun nara inga?" (Is Korea a country where war could break out?) *Wolgan Choson*, Mar., p. 243.

Cho, Soon Sung. 1969. "North and South Korea: Stepped-Up Aggression and the Search for New Security." *Asian Survey* 9, no. 1: 24–31.

Choi, Jang-jip, and Hyun-jin Lim, eds. 1993. *Siminsahoiui Dojun* (Challenge of civil society). Seoul: Nanam.

Choi, Jong-cheol. 1996. "Hankukui Kukgaanbo Junryak Gyuljung Chaegye" (Decision-making system of national security and strategy in Korea). Paper presented at a conference organized by the National Institute of National Intelligence, Seoul, Dec.

Chowdhury, Iftekhar A. 1990. "Bangladesh's External Relations: The Strategy of a Small Power in a Subsystem." Ph.D. diss., Australian National University.

Chu Shulong. 1994. "The PRC Girds for Limited, High-tech War." *Orbis* 38, no. 2: 177–91.

Chua, Beng-Huat. 1995. *Communitarian Ideology and Democracy in Singapore*. London: Routledge.

Chun, Hae-jong. 1968. "Sino-Korea Tributary Relations in the Chi'ing Period." In John K. Fairbank, ed., *The Chinese World Order: Traditional China's Foreign Relations*. Cambridge, Mass.: Harvard University Press.

Chun, Kyungman. 1996. "Hanbando Jubyon Anbohwangyunui Banhwa" (Changes in the security environment of the Korean peninsula). Paper presented at a conference organized by the National Institute of National Intelligence, Seoul, Dec.

Chun, Kyungman, and Chul-il Chung. 1994. *Shinanbo Jungchaek Gyuljung Chaegye Jungrip Bangan* (A study of the new security policy-making system). Seoul: Korean Institute of Defense Analysis.

Citizens' Disaster Rehabilitation Center. 1991. *1990 Annual Report*. Manila: Citizens' Disaster Rehabilitation Center.

Clarke, Gerard. 1995. "Non-government organisations and the Philippine state: 1986–93." *Southeast Asia Research* 3, no. 1: 67–91.

Claude, Richard Pierre, and Burns H. Weston, eds. 1992. *Human Rights in the World Community: Issues and Action*. 2d ed. Philadelphia: University of Pennsylvania Press.

Clough, Ralph. 1991. "Taiwan Under Nationalist Rule, 1949–1982." In Roderick MacFarquhar and John K. Fairbank, eds., *The Cambridge History of China*. Vol. 15, part 2. Cambridge, Eng.: Cambridge University Press.

Coedes, G. 1971. *The Indianized States of Southeast Asia*. Honolulu: University of Hawaii Press.

Cohen, Ira J. 1987. "Structuration Theory and Social Praxis." In Anthony Giddens and Jonathan Turner, eds., *Social Theory Today*. Stanford: Stanford University Press.

Cohen, Raymond. 1994. "Pacific Unions: A Reappraisal of the Theory That Democracies Do Not Go to War with Each Other." *Review of International Studies* 20: 207–23.

Cohen, Stephen. P. N.d. "Rashoman in South Asia." Manuscript.

———. 1984. *The Pakistan Army*. Berkeley: University of California Press.

———. 1987. *The Security of South Asia: American and Asian Perspectives*. Urbana: University of Illinois Press.

———. 1989. "Leadership and the Management of National Security." In Mohammed Ayoob and Chai-Anan Samudavanija, eds., *Leadership Perceptions and National Security: The Southeast Asian Experience*. Singapore: Institute of Southeast Asian Studies.

Collier, Christopher J. 1997. "The Politics of Insurrection in Davao, Philippines." Ph.D. diss., University of Hawaii.

Collier, David, and James E. Mahon, Jr. 1993. "Conceptual 'Stretching' Revisited: Adapting Categories in Comparative Analysis." *American Political Science Review* 87, no. 4: 845–55.

Commission for a New Asia. 1994. *Towards a New Asia*. Kuala Lumpur: ISIS Malaysia.

Commission on Global Governance. 1995. *Our Global Neighborhood: The Report of the Commission on Global Governance*. New York: Oxford University Press.

Connor, Walker. 1972. "Nation Building or Destroying?" *World Politics* 24: 319–55.

Copper, John F. 1990. *Taiwan: Nation-State or Province?* Boulder, Colo.: Westview.

Coronel-Ferrer, Miriam. 1994. *Peace-Building and Mediation in the Philippines*. Quezon City: Center for Integrative and Development Studies, University of the Philippines Press.

Coronel-Ferrer, Miriam, and Antoinette Raquiza, eds. 1993. *Motions for Peace: A Summary of Events Related to Negotiating the Communist Insurgency in the Philippines, 1986–1992*. Manila: Coalition for Peace.

Cortright, David, and Amitabh Mattoo. 1996. "Indian Public Opinion and Nuclear Weapons Policy." In David Cortright and Amitabh Mattoo, eds., *India and the Bomb: Public Opinion and Nuclear Options*. Notre Dame, Ind.: University of Notre Dame Press.

Cotton, James. 1992. "Understanding the State in South Korea: Bureaucratic Authoritarian or State Autonomy Theory." *Comparative Political Studies* 24, no. 4: 512–31.

————. 1995. "The North Korea–U.S. Nuclear Accord: Background and Consequences." *Korean Observer* 26, no. 3: 321–44.

Council for Economic Planning and Development. 1995. *Taiwan Statistical Data Book 1995*. Taipei: Council for Economic Planning and Development.

Country Report Pakistan Afghanistan. 1994. Fourth quarter. London: Economist Intelligence Unit.

————. 1995. Second quarter. London: Economist Intelligence Unit.

————. 1995. Fourth quarter. London: Economist Intelligence Unit.

Critchley, W. Harriet, and Terry Terriff. 1993. "Environment and Security." In Richard Shultz, Roy Godson, and Ted Greenwood, eds., *Security Studies for the 1990s*. Washington, D.C.: Brassey's.

Crouch, Harold. 1978. *The Army and Politics in Indonesia*. Ithaca, N.Y.: Cornell University Press.

————. 1993. "Malaysia: Neither Authoritarian nor Democratic." In Kevin Hewison, Richard Robison, and Garry Rodan, eds., *Southeast Asia in the 1990s: Authoritarianism, Democracy and Capitalism*. St. Leonards, New South Wales: Allen and Unwin.

————. 1996. *Government and Society in Malaysia*. Ithaca, N.Y.: Cornell University Press.

Cumings, Bruce. 1990. *The Origins of the Korean War*. 2 vols. Princeton: Princeton University Press.

————. 1992. "Spring Thaw for Korea's Cold War." *Bulletin of the Atomic Scientists* 48, no. 3: 14–23.

————. 1993. "Japan's Position in the World System." In Andrew Gordon, ed., *Postwar Japan as History*. Berkeley: University of California Press.

Dalby, Simon. 1992. "Security, Modernity, Ecology: The Dilemmas of Post–Cold War Security Discourse." *Alternatives* 17: 95–134.

Damodaran, A. K. 1995. "Before Non-alignment." In Kanti P. Bajpai and Harish C. Shukul, eds., *Interpreting World Politics*. New Delhi: Sage.

Daniels, Robert V. 1984. *A Documentary History of Communism*. Hanover, N.H.: University Press of New England.

Das, Veena, ed. 1990. *Mirrors of Violence*. New Delhi: Oxford University Press.

Datta, P. S. 1995. *Ethnic Peace Accords in India*. New Delhi: Vikas.

David, Steven R. 1991. "Explaining Third World Alignment." *World Politics* 43, no. 2: 233–56.

Davis, Zachary S., and Benjamin Frankel, eds. 1993. *The Proliferation Puzzle: Why Nuclear Weapons Spread*. London: Frank Cass.

De Dios, Emmanuel. 1993–94. "Notes on Philippine Growth and the Government's Medium-Term Development Plan." *Kasarinlan* 9, nos. 2–3: 15–20.

————. 1995. "The Philippine Economy: What's Right, What's Wrong?" In Daljit Singh, ed., *Southeast Asian Affairs 1995*. Singapore: Institute of Southeast Asian Studies.

Defence Bulletin. 1986. 10 Dec. Tokyo: Public Information Division, Defense Agency.

Defence of Thailand 1994. Bangkok: Ministry of Defense.

Defence of Thailand 1996. Bangkok: Ministry of Defense.

Defense Agency. 1995a. *Defense of Japan 1994*. Tokyo: Japan Times.

————. 1995b. "On the Theater Missile Defense." Mimeographed.

Defense Intelligence Agency. 1991. *North Korea: The Foundations for Military Strength*. Washington, D.C.: Government Printing Office.

DeNardo, James. 1985. *Power in Numbers*. Princeton: Princeton University Press.

Deng Xiaoping. 1986. "Deng Xiaoping On 'One Country, Two Systems.'" *Beijing Review* 29, no. 5: 25–26.

————. 1993. *Deng Xiaoping Wenxuan* (Selected works of Deng Xiaoping). Vol. 3. Beijing: People's Press.

————. 1994. *Deng Xiaoping Wenxuan* (Selected works of Deng Xiaoping). Vol. 2. Beijing: People's Press.

Department of Defense (DOD), United States Office of International Security Affairs. 1995. *United States Security Strategy for the East Asian-Pacific Region*. Washington, D.C.: DOD.

Department of National Defense, Republic of the Philippines. 1990. "Update on the Communist Insurgency Situation in the Philippines (as of March 31, 1990)."

Departemen Pertahanan Republik Indonesia. 1991. *Doktrin Pertahanan Keamanan Negara Republik Indonesia* (Defense and security doctrines of the Republic of Indonesia). Jakarta: Departemen Pertahanan Republik Indonesia.

Dermawan, Ninok Leksono. 1992. "Akuisisi Senjata RI dan Anggota ASEAN lain, 1975–1990." Ph.D diss., Program Pasca Sarjana, Universitas Indonesia, Jakarta.

Deudney, Daniel. 1990. "The Case Against Linking Environmental Degradation and National Security." *Millennium* 19, no. 3: 461–76.

Deutsch, Karl. 1957. *Political Community and the North Atlantic Area*. Westport, Conn.: Greenwood.

Dewitt, David. 1994. "Common, Comprehensive and Cooperative Security." *Pacific Review* 7, no. 1: 1–15.

Dhiravegin, Likhit. 1986. "The Postwar Thai Politics." Monograph Series, no. 11. Bangkok: Faculty of Political Science Research Center, Thammasat University.

————. 1996. *Thai Government and Politics* (in Thai). Bangkok: Thammasat University Press.

Dibb, Paul. 1995. *Toward a New Balance of Power in Asia*. Adelphi Paper 295. London: International Institute for Strategic Studies.

Diller, Janelle M. 1996. *The National Convention in (Burma) Myanmar: An Impediment to the Restoration of Democracy*. Occasional paper. New York: International League for Human Rights, 2 Apr.

Dinh Nho Liem. 1994. "Combining Foreign Relations with National Defense to Defend the Fatherland." *Tap Chi Quoc Phong Toan Dan*, Apr. Translation in Foreign Broadcast Information Service, East Asian Service, FBIS-EAS-94-134 (13 July 1994).

Diokno, Maria Serena I. 1994. *The 1986–1987 Peace Talks: A Reportage of Contention*. Quezon City: Center for Integrative and Development Studies, University of the Philippines Press.

Dittmer, Lowell, and Samuel S. Kim. 1993. *China's Quest for National Identity*. Ithaca, N.Y.: Cornell University Press.

Dixit, J. N. 1994. "Changing International Environment and Indian Security." *Strategic Analysis* 17: 929–42.

———. 1995. *Anatomy of a Flawed Inheritance: Indo-Pak Relations, 1970–94*. Delhi: Konark.

Djalal, Dino Patti. 1996. *The Geopolitics of Indonesia's Maritime Territorial Policy*. Jakarta: CSIS.

Djalal, Hasjim. 1995. *Indonesia and the Law of the Sea*. Jakarta: CSIS.

Djelani, Koen. 1993. "Aktualisasi Peran Pertahanan Sipil Dalam Pembinaan dan Pengembangan Ketahanan Nasional Khususnya Wilayah Pesisir Garis pantai Nusantara (Proyeksi Masa Depan)." Paper presented at a panel discussion organized by Lembaga Arthesis Studi Pengkajian dan Eksplorasi Kelautan, Jakarta, 12 Oct.

Djiwandono, Soedjati. 1986. "The Security of Sea Lanes in the Asia Pacific Region: The Prospect for Regional Cooperation." *Indonesian Quarterly* 14: 46–54.

Do Nguyen Phuong. 1994. "On the Phenomenon of Social Stratification in Our Country at Present." *Tap Chi Cong San*, May. Translation in Foreign Broadcast Information Service, East Asian Service, FBIS-EAS-94-115 (5 Aug. 1994).

Document on Submarine Procurement Program (in Thai). 1995. Bangkok: Royal Thai Navy.

Donnelly, Michael W. 1993. "Japan's Nuclear Energy Quest." In Gerald L. Curtis, ed., *Japan's Foreign Policy After the Cold War: Coping with Change*. Armonk, N.Y.: M. E. Sharpe.

Dorff, Robert H. 1994. "A Commentary on Security Studies for the 1990s as a Model Curriculum Core." *International Studies Notes* 19, no. 3: 23–31.

Doyle, Michael W. 1983. "Kant, Liberalism, and Foreign Affairs." *Philosophy and Public Affairs* 12, no. 3: 205–35; 12, no. 4: 323–53.

———. 1989. "Kant, Liberal Legacies, and Foreign Affairs." *Philosophy and Public Affairs* 12, no. 3: 3–35.

————. 1995. "Liberalism and the End of the Cold War." In Richard Ned Lebow and Thomas Risse-Kappen, eds., *International Relations Theory and the End of the Cold War.* New York: Columbia University Press.

DPP Central Headquarters Election Strategy Committee. 1995. *Gei Taiwan yige jihui* (Give Taiwan a chance). Taipei: Qianwei chubanshe.

Dubey, Muchkund. 1994. "Indo-Bangladesh Economic Relations." In S. R. Chakravarty, ed., *Foreign Policy of Bangladesh.* New Delhi: Har-Anand.

Dulyakasem, Uthai. 1984. "Muslim-Malay Separatism in Southern Thailand: Factors Underlying the Political Revolt." In Lim Joo-Jock and S. Vani, eds., *Armed Separatism in Southeast Asia.* Singapore: Institute of Southeast Asian Studies.

Dumont, Louis. 1970. *Religion, Politics and History in India.* The Hague: Mouton.

Dunigan, James F. 1983. *How to Make War.* New York: Quill.

Dunn, Lewis A. 1982. *Controlling the Bomb: Nuclear Proliferation in the 1980s.* New Haven: Yale University Press.

Dupont, Alan. 1996. "Indonesian Defense Strategy and Security: Time for a Rethink?" *Contemporary Southeast Asia* 18, no. 3: 275–97.

East Asia Political Unit. 1995. *Overseas Chinese Business Networks in Asia.* Canberra: Australian Department of Foreign Affairs and Trade.

Eberstadt, Nicholas. 1995. *Korea Approaches Unification.* London: M. E. Sharpe.

Eberstadt, Nicholas, and Judith Bannister. 1991. "Military Buildup in the DPRK: Some New Indications from North Korean Data." *Asian Survey* 31, no. 11: 1095–1124.

Eckstein, Harry. 1964. "Introduction: Toward the Theoretical Study of Internal War." In Harry Eckstein, ed., *Internal War: Problems and Approaches.* New York: Free Press.

Economic Daily News. 1988. "Zhonggong ruo yi wuli fan Tai, Riben hui yu jingji zhicai" (If the Chinese Communists invaded Taiwan, Japan would impose economic sanctions). *Economic Daily News (Jingji Ribao),* Taipei, 26 Oct., p. 1.

Economic Planning Board (EPB). 1991. *Yesan Gyeyo* (Budget outlines). Seoul: EPB.

Eiland, Michael. 1983. "Rivalry for Cambodia: An Old Affair." *Far Eastern Economic Review,* 10 Nov., pp. 50–52.

Ek, Ragnhild, and Ahmed Karadawi. 1991. "Implications of Refugee Flows on Political Stability in the Sudan." *Ambio* 20, no. 5: 196–203.

Elliott, David W. P. 1980. "Institutionalizing the Revolution: Vietnam's Search for a Model of Development." In William S. Turley, ed., *Vietnamese Communism in Comparative Perspective.* Boulder, Colo.: Westview.

————. 1993. "Dilemmas of Reform in Vietnam." In William S. Turley and Mark Selden, eds., *Reinventing Vietnamese Socialism: Doi Moi in Comparative Perspective.* Boulder, Colo.: Westview.

Elman, Colin, and Miriam Fendius Elman. 1995. "History vs. Neo-realism: A Second Look." *International Security* 20, no. 1: 182–93.

Emmerson, Donald K. 1996. "Do 'Asian Values' Exist?" Paper presented at a workshop on "The Cultural Sources of Human Rights in East Asia," cosponsored by the Carnegie Council on Ethics and International Affairs, Chulalongkorn University and the Japan Institute for International Affairs, Bangkok, Thailand, 23–28 Mar.

Environmental Protection Agency. 1996. *Environmental White Paper.* Seoul: Environmental Protection Agency.

Eto, Shinkichi, and Yoshinobu Yamamoto. 1991. *Sogo-anpo to Mirai no Sentaku* (Comprehensive security and the future choice). Tokyo: Kodansha.

Evans, Gareth. 1994. *Cooperating for Peace: The Global Agenda for the 1990s.* St. Leonards, New South Wales: Allen and Unwin.

Evans, Paul M., ed. 1994. *Studying Asia-Pacific Security.* Toronto: University of Toronto–York University Joint Center for Asia-Pacific Studies.

Evans, Peter. 1995. *Embedded Autonomy.* Princeton: Princeton University Press.

Fact-Finding Committee. 1992. "Report on Investigation Results Involving Violation and Survey of Damages from Demonstration Between 17 and 20 May 1992" (in Thai). Bangkok: Government House.

Fairbank, John K. 1968a. "The Early Treaty System in the Chinese World Order." In John K. Fairbank, ed., *The Chinese World Order: Traditional China's Foreign Relations.* Cambridge, Mass.: Harvard University Press.

———. 1968b. "A Preliminary Framework." In John K. Fairbank, ed., *The Chinese World Order: Traditional China's Foreign Relations.* Cambridge, Mass.: Harvard University Press.

Fairbank, John K., Edwin O. Reischauer, and Albert M. Craig. 1978. *East Asia: Transition and Transformation.* Boston: Houghton Mifflin.

Fan Yew Teng. 1995. "Class, Race, and Ethnicity." In Murugesu Pathmanathan and Robert Haas, eds., *Political Culture: The Challenge of Modernization.* Petaling Jaya: Center for Policy Sciences.

Fang Zhen. 1993. "Baomi 'Luka,' Buneng Quan Chediao" (Secrecy 'pass' cannot be abandoned). *Outlook Weekly* (Beijing), 22 Feb., pp. 17–19.

Fange, Anders. 1995. "Afghanistan After April 1992: A Struggle for State and Ethnicity." *Central Asian Survey* 14, no. 1: 22–30.

Farber, H. S., and J. Gowa. 1995. "Polities and Peace." *International Security* 20, no. 2: 123–46.

Farouk, Omar. 1984. "The Historical and Transnational Dimensions of Malay-Muslim Separatism in Southern Thailand." In Lim Joo-Jock and S. Vani, eds., *Armed Separatism in Southeast Asia.* Singapore: Institute of Southeast Asian Studies.

Fearon, James. 1991. "Counterfactuals and Hypothesis Testing." *World Politics* 43, no. 2: 1–45.

Feith, Herbert. 1962. *The Decline of Constitutional Democracy in Indonesia.* Ithaca, N.Y.: Cornell University Press.

———. 1963. "Dynamics of Guided Democracy." In Ruth T. MacVey, ed., *Indonesia.* New Haven: Human Relations Area File Press.

Ferguson, Yale, and Richard Mansbach. 1988. *The Elusive Quest: Theory and International Politics.* Columbia: University of South Carolina Press.

Fforde, Adam, and Stefan de Vylder. 1996. *From Plan to Market: The Economic Transition in Vietnam.* Boulder, Colo.: Westview.

Final Report of the Fact-Finding Commission. 1990. Pursuant to Republic Act 6832. Manila: Bookmark.

Fishman, Robert. 1990. "Rethinking State and Regime: Southern Europe's Transition to Democracy." *World Politics* 42, no. 3: 422–40.

Fisk, E. K., and H. Osman-Rani, eds. 1982. *The Political Economy of Malaysia.* Kuala Lumpur: Oxford University Press.

Foot, Rosemary. 1985. *The Wrong War: American Policy and the Dimensions of the Korean Conflict, 1950–1953.* Ithaca, N.Y.: Cornell University Press.

Ford, Franklin. 1985. *Political Murder.* Cambridge, Mass.: Harvard University Press.

"Forum: 'What Is Security and Security Studies?' Revisited." 1992. *Arms Control* 13, no. 3: 463–544.

Foundation for International and Strategic Studies. 1993. *Huan Qiu Tong Ci Liang Re: Yidai Lingxiu Men De Guoji Zhanlue Sixiang* (Climate is the same all over the world: the international strategic thoughts of a generation's leaders). Beijing: Central Document Press.

Friedberg, Aaron L. 1993–94. "Ripe for Rivalry: Prospects for Peace in a Multipolar Asia." *International Security* 18, no. 3: 5–33.

———. 1996. "Ripe for Rivalry: Prospects for Peace in a Multipolar Asia." In Michael E. Brown, Sean M. Lynn-Jones, and Steven E. Miller, eds., *East Asian Security.* Cambridge, Mass.: MIT Press.

Funabashi, Yoichi. 1991–92. "Japan and the New World Order." *Foreign Affairs* 70, no. 5: 58–74.

———. 1994. "Introduction: Japan's International Agenda for the 1990s." In Yoichi Funabashi, ed., *Japan's International Agenda.* New York: New York University Press.

Funabashi, Yoichi, Michel Oksenberg, and Heinrich Weiss. 1994. *An Emerging China in World Politics.* New York: Trilateral Commission.

Gaddis, John Lewis. 1982. *Strategies of Containment.* Oxford: Oxford University Press.

Ganesan, A. V. 1994. *The GATT Uruguay Round Agreement: Opportunities and Challenges.* RGICS Paper 8. New Delhi: Rajiv Gandhi Institute for Contemporary Studies, Rajiv Gandhi Foundation.

Ganesan, N. 1991. "Factors Affecting Singapore's Foreign Policy Towards Malaysia." *Australian Journal of International Affairs* 45, no. 2: 182–95.

―――. 1994. "Taking Stock of Post–Cold War Developments in ASEAN." *Security Dialogue* 26, no. 4: 457–68.

Ganguly, Sumit. 1989. "The Sino-Indian Border Talks, 1981–1989." *Asian Survey* 29, no. 12: 1123–35.

―――. 1993. "U.S.–Indian Relations During the Lyndon Johnson Era." In Harold A. Gould and Sumit Ganguly, eds., *The Hope and the Reality: U.S.–Indian Relations from Roosevelt to Reagan*. New Delhi: Oxford/IBH.

Ganguly, Sumit, and Kanti Bajpai. 1994. "India and the Crisis in Kashmir." *Asian Survey* 34, no. 5: 401–16.

Ganguly, Sumit, and Ted Greenwood, eds. 1996. *Mending Fences: Confidence- and Security-Building Measures in South Asia*. Boulder, Colo.: Westview.

Gao Anmin. 1992. "Navy to Participate in Economic Reform Drive." *China Daily*, 6 Apr., p. 4.

Gao Shangquan. 1995. "China's Economy Vital for Asia-Pacific." *Beijing Review* 38, no. 3: 17–19.

Garver, John W. 1993. *Foreign Relations of the People's Republic of China*. Englewood Cliffs, N.J.: Prentice-Hall.

Geertz, Clifford. 1973. *The Interpretation of Cultures*. New York: Basic Books.

Geiger, Wilhelm, trans. 1950. *The Mahavamsa*. Colombo: Government Information Department.

Genshiryoku Iinkai. 1995. *Genshiryoku Hakusho Heisei 6-nen Ban* (Atomic power white paper 1994). Tokyo: Okurasho Insatsu-kyoku.

George, Alexander, Philip J. Farley, and Alexander Dallin, eds. 1988. *U.S.– Soviet Security Cooperation: Achievements, Failures, Lessons*. New York: Oxford University Press.

George, T. J. S. 1980. *Revolt in Mindanao: The Rise of Islam in Philippine Politics*. Kuala Lumpur: Oxford University Press.

Ghai, Yash. 1994. *Human Rights and Governance: The Asia Debate*. Asia Foundation occasional paper 4. San Francisco: Asia Foundation.

Ghosh, Partha S. 1989. *Conflict and Cooperation in South Asia*. Dhaka: University Press.

Giddens, Anthony. 1979. *Central Problems in Social Theory: Action, Structure and Contradiction in Social Analysis*. Berkeley: University of California Press.

―――. 1985. *A Contemporary Critique of Historical Materialism*. Vol. 2, *The Nation State and Violence*. Cambridge, Mass.: Polity Press.

―――. 1987. *The Nation State and Violence*. Berkeley: University of California Press.

―――. 1994. *Central Problems in Social Theory: Action, Structure and Contra- diction in Social Analysis*. Berkeley: University of California Press.

Gill, K. P. S. 1994. "The Dangers Within: Internal Security Threats." In Bharat Karnad, ed., *Future Imperilled: India's Security in the 1990s and Beyond*. New Delhi: Viking/Penguin India.

Gillette, R. 1978. "U.S. Squelched Apparent S. Korea A-Bomb Drive." *Los Angeles Times*, 4 Nov., p. 1.

Gilpin, Robert. 1981. *War and Change in World Politics*. Cambridge, Eng.: Cambridge University Press.

————. 1987. *The Political Economy of International Relations*. Princeton: Princeton University Press.

Gizewski, Peter, and Thomas Homer-Dixon. 1995. *Urban Growth and Violence: Will the Future Resemble the Past?* Toronto: University of Toronto Press.

Gladney, Dru C. 1996. *Muslim Chinese: Ethnic Nationalism in the People's Republic*. Harvard East Asian Monograph 149. Cambridge, Mass.: Council on East Asian Studies, Harvard University.

Glaser, Charles L. 1994. "Realists as Optimists: Cooperation as Self-Help." *International Security* 19, no. 3: 50–90.

Gleick, Peter H. 1989. "The Implications of Global Climatic Changes for International Security." *Climatic Change* 15, nos. 1–2: 309–25.

————. 1990. "Environment, Resources and International Security and Politics." In E. Arnett, ed., *Science and International Security: Responding to a Changing World*. Washington, D.C.: American Association for the Advancement of Science.

————. 1991. "Environment and Security: The Clear Connections." *Bulletin of the Atomic Scientists* 47, no. 3: 17–21.

————. 1993. "Water and Conflict: Fresh Water Resources and International Security." *International Security* 18, no. 1: 79–112.

Gochoco-Bautista, Maria Socorro, and Jaime M. Faustino. 1994. *AFTA and the Philippines: National Economic Policy-Making and Regional Economic Cooperation*. Quezon City: Institute for Strategic and Development Studies.

Goldgeier, James M., and Michael McFaul. 1992. "A Tale of Two Worlds: Core and Periphery in the Post–Cold War Era." *International Organization* 46, no. 2: 467–91.

Goldstein, Judith, and Robert O. Keohane, eds. 1993. *Ideas and Foreign Policy*. Ithaca, N.Y.: Cornell University Press.

Gomez, Edmund Terence. 1994. *Political Business: Corporate Involvement of Malaysian Political Parties*. Townsville, Australia: James Cook University.

————. 1996. "Electoral Funding of General, State, and Party Elections in Malaysia." *Journal of Contemporary Asia* 26, no. 1: 81–99.

Goncharov, Sergei, John W. Lewis, and Xue Litai. 1993. *Uncertain Partners: Stalin, Mao, and the Korean War*. Stanford: Stanford University Press.

Goonesekere, R. K. W. 1988. *Fundamental Rights and the Constitution: A Case Book*. Colombo: Law and Society Trust / Open University.

Gorbachev, Mikhail. 1987. *Perestroika: New Thinking for Our Country and the World*. New York: Harper and Row.

Gordon, Sandy. 1992. "Domestic Foundations of India's Security Policy." In Ross Babbage and Sandy Gordon, eds., *India's Strategic Future*. London: Macmillan.

————. 1995. *India's Rise to Power in the Twentieth Century and Beyond.* New York: St. Martin's.

Gore, Al. 1990. "SEI: A Strategic Environment Initiative." *SAIS Review* 10, no. 1: 59–71.

Gosh, Jayati. 1990. "The Impact of Integration: India and the World Economy in the 1980s." In Sugata Bose, ed., *South Asia and World Capitalism.* New Delhi: Oxford University Press.

Government of Burma. 1949a. *Burma and the Insurrections.* Rangoon: Ministry of Information.

————. 1949b. *KNDO Insurrection.* Rangoon: Government Printing and Stationery.

————. 1952. *Is It a People's Liberation? A Short Survey of Communist Insurrection in Burma.* Rangoon: Ministry of Information.

————. 1986. *Burma 1983 Population Census.* Rangoon: Immigration and Manpower Department.

Government of Myanmar. 1989a. *Burma Communist Party's Conspiracy to Take Over State Power.* Yangon: News and Periodicals Enterprise.

————. 1989b. *The Conspiracy of Treasonous Minions Within the Myanmar Naing-Ngan and Traitorous Cohorts Abroad.* Yangon: News and Periodicals Enterprise.

————. 1990. *State Law and Order Restoration Council's Stand Clarified Regarding Myanmar Naing-Ngan's National Objectives.* Yangon: News and Periodicals Enterprise.

————. 1991. *State Law and Order Restoration Council Chairman, Commander-in-Chief of the Defence Services Senior General Saw Maung's Addresses.* Vol. 3. Yangon: News and Periodicals Enterprise.

Government Information Office. 1993. *A Brief Introduction to the Republic of China.* 3d ed. Taipei: Government Information Office.

Gowing, P. G. 1979. *Muslim Filipinos: Heritage and Horizon.* Quezon City: New Day.

Green, Michael J., and Benjamin L. Self. 1996. "Japan's Changing China Policy." *Survival* 38, no. 2: 35–58.

Grieco, Joseph M. 1988. "Anarchy and Cooperation." *International Organization* 42, no. 3: 485–508.

————. 1993. "Anarchy and the Limits of Cooperation: A Realist Critique of the Newest Liberal Institutionalism." In David A. Baldwin, ed., *Neorealism and Neoliberalism: The Contemporary Debate.* New York: Columbia University Press.

Gunaratna, Rohan. 1990. *Sri Lanka: A Lost Revolution: The Inside Story of the JVP.* Kandy: Institute of Fundamental Studies.

Gupta, Bhabani Sen. 1983. "Regional Security: The Indian Doctrine." *India Today,* 31 Aug., p. 20.

Gupta, Shekhar. 1995. *India Redefines Its Role: An Analysis of India's Changing Internal Dynamics and Their Impact on Foreign Relations.* Adelphi Paper 293.

London: International Institute for Strategic Studies / Oxford University Press.

Gupta, Sisir. 1964. *India and Regional Integration in Asia*. Bombay: Asia Publishing House.

Gurr, Ted. 1970. *Why Men Rebel*. Princeton: Princeton University Press.

——. 1994. *Minorities at Risk*. Washington, D.C.: United States Institute of Peace.

Ha, Young-sun. 1989. "The Korean Military Balance: Myth and Reality." In William J. Taylor, Jr., Young Koo Cha, John Q. Blodgett, and Michael Mazarr, eds., *The Future of the South Korea–U.S. Security Relationship*. Boulder, Colo.: Westview.

Haas, E. B. 1968. *The Uniting of Europe*. 2d ed. Stanford: Stanford University Press.

Haas, Michael. 1989. *The Asian Way to Peace: A Story of Regional Cooperation*. New York: Praeger.

Habib, Hasnan. 1987. "Politik Militer 13 Tahun Pertama Orde Baru." *Teknologi dan Strategi Militer* 3: 11–17.

Habito, Cielito F. 1993–94. "The 1993–1998 Medium-Term Development Plan of the Philippines: Paving the Way for Philippines 2000." *Kasarinlan* 9, nos. 2–3: 5–10.

Haftendorn, Helga. 1991. "The Security Puzzle: Theory-Building and Discipline-Building in International Security." *International Studies Quarterly* 35, no. 1: 3–17.

Haggard, S., and Chung-in Moon. 1990. "Institutions and Economic Policy: Theory and a Korean Case." *World Politics* 38, no. 1: 210–37.

Hahm, Taekyung, ed. 1992. *Nambukhan Gunbi Gyungjaenggwa Gunchuk* (North-South Korean arms race and arms reduction). Seoul: Kyungnam University Press.

HALAD Foundation. 1989. "Monthly Presentation of the Number of Internal Refugees in Mindanao for the Period 1984–1988." Davao City: HALAD Foundation.

Halloran, Richard. 1995. "Great Difficulty in Convincing Skeptical Asians." Trends 57 in *Business Times* (Singapore), May 27–28.

Hameed, A. C. Shahul. 1988. *Foreign Policy Perspectives of Sri Lanka: Selected Speeches 1977–1987*. Colombo: Lake House.

Hamid, Ahmad Sarji Abdul, ed. 1993. *Malaysia's Vision 2020: Understanding the Concept, Implications, and Challenges*. Petaling Jaya: Pelanduk.

Hamid, Syed Ali. 1990–91. "India's Strategic Designs in the Year 2000." *National Defence College Journal*.

Han, Daw Than. 1988. *Common Vision: Burma's Regional Outlook*. Occasional paper. Washington, D.C.: Institute for the Study of Diplomacy.

Han, Sung-joo. 1995. *Segyehwa Sidaeui Hankuk Oigyo* (Korean diplomacy in the age of globalization). Seoul: Jisik Sanupsa.

Han, Yong-sup. 1996. "Bumunbyol Kukgajonryakui Sangwan Gwangyewa

Usonsunwiui Byonhwa" (State strategy by sector and changing priorities). *Kukga Jonryak* (National strategy) 2, no. 1: 5–38.

Hanif, Mohammad. 1989a. "The Anatomy of Violence." *Newsline*, Oct.

———. 1989b. "Gun-runners of Karachi." *Newsline*, Oct.

———. 1992. "The MQM: The Hour of Reckoning." *Newsline*, July.

———. 1994. "In the Name of Religion." *Newsline*, Aug.

———. 1995. "Karachi's Killing Fields." *Newsline*, Mar.

Hanrahan, Gene Z. 1971. *The Communist Struggle in Malaya*. Kuala Lumpur: University of Malaya Press.

Hanum, Hurst. 1990. *Autonomy, Sovereignty, and Self-Determination: The Accommodation of Conflicting Rights*. Philadelphia: University of Pennsylvania Press.

Haq, Mahbub ul. 1995. "Whatever Happened to the Peace Dividend?" *Our Planet* 7, no. 1: 8–10.

Harries-Jenkins, Gwyn, and Jacques van Doorn. 1976. Introduction to Gwyn Harries-Jenkins and Jacques van Doorn, eds., *The Military and the Problem of Legitimacy*. London: Sage.

Harrison, Reginald J. 1974. *Europe in Question: Theories of Regional Integration*. London: Allen and Unwin.

Harrison, Selig S. 1981. *In Afghanistan's Shadow: Baluch Nationalism and Soviet Temptations*. Washington D.C.: Carnegie Endowment for International Peace.

———. 1992. "South Asia and the United States: A Chance for a Fresh Start." *Current History* 91, no. 563: 97–105.

Hasenclever, Andreas, Peter Mayer, and Volker Rittberger. 1996. "Interests, Power, Knowledge: The Study of International Regimes." *Mershon International Studies Review* 40, no. 2: 177–228.

Hassan, Shaukat. 1987. "India-Bangladesh Political Relations During the Awami League Government, 1972–75." Ph.D. diss., Australian National University.

———. 1989. "India Factor in the Foreign Policy of Bangladesh." In Shaukat Hassan and M. G. Kabir, eds., *Issues and Challenges Facing Bangladesh Foreign Policy*. Dhaka: BSIS.

———. 1991. *Environmental Issues and Security in South Asia*. Adelphi Paper 262. London: Brassey's for IISS.

———. 1993. "Problems of Internal Stability in South Asia." In Shelton U. Kodikara, ed., *External Compulsions of South Asian Politics*. New Delhi: Sage.

Hassan, Shaukat, and A. Rob Khan. 1989. "Bangladesh Floods: The Political Debate." In Shaukat Hassan and M. G. Kabir, eds., *Issues and Challenges Facing Bangladesh Foreign Policy*. Dhaka: BSIS.

Hastings, Peter. 1984. "National Integration in Indonesia: The Case of Irian Jaya." In Lim Joo-Jock and S. Vani, eds., *Armed Separatism in Southeast Asia*. Singapore: Institute of Southeast Asian Studies.

Hatta, Mohammad. 1953. "Indonesia's Foreign Policy." *Foreign Affairs* 31, no. 3: 441–50.

Hawes, Gary. 1986. "United States Support for the Marcos Administration and the Pressures That Made Change." *Contemporary Southeast Asia* 8, no. 1: 18–36.

Hayes, Peter. 1991. *Pacific Powderkeg*. Lexington, Mass.: Lexington Books.

———. 1993. "The Republic of Korea and the Nuclear Issue." In Andrew Mack, ed., *Asian Flashpoint*. Canberra: Allen and Unwin.

Hechter, Michael. 1975. *Internal Colonialism: The Celtic Fringe in British National Development*. Berkeley: University of California Press.

Heimsath, Charles, and Surjit Mansingh. 1971. *A Diplomatic History of Modern India*. Bombay: Allied.

Heritage, John C. 1987. "Ethnomethodology." In Anthony Giddens and Jonathan Turner, eds., *Social Theory Today*. Stanford: Stanford University Press.

Hernandez, Carolina G., and Jorge V. Tigno. 1995. "ASEAN Labour Migration: Implications for Regional Stability." *Pacific Review* 8, no. 3: 544–57.

Hertz, John H. 1950. "Idealist Internationalism and the Security Dilemma." *World Politics* 1: 157–80.

Hiebert, Murray. 1993a. "Land of Hope." *Far Eastern Economic Review*, 29 July, p. 52.

———. 1993b. "Parading for Work." *Far Eastern Economic Review*, 27 May, p. 60.

———. 1993c. "Taking Aim." *Far Eastern Economic Review*, 23 Dec., p. 42.

———. 1994. "Stuck at Bottom." *Far Eastern Economic Review*, 13 Jan., pp. 70–71.

Hill, Hal, and Sisisra Jayasurya. 1984. "Philippine Economic Performance in Regional Perspective." *Contemporary Southeast Asia* 6, no. 2: 135–58.

Hindley, Donald. 1964. "Indonesia's Confrontation with Malaysia: A Search for Motives." *Asian Survey* 4, no. 6: 904–13.

Hirabayashi, Hiroshi. 1995. *Japan's ODA: Assuming Leadership in a New Era*. Booklet in English, translated from *Gaiko Forum*, Feb.

Hitchcock, David I. 1994. *Asian Values and the United States: How Much Conflict?* Washington, D.C.: Center for Strategic and International Studies.

Ho Fang. 1995. "Dangqian De Guoji Anquan Xingshi" (The current international security situation). *Xiandai Guoji Guanxi* (*Contemporary International Relations*) 11 (Nov.): 2–6.

Ho, Peter. 1995. "The ASEAN Regional Forum: The Way Forward." In Sarasin Viraphol and Werner Pfennig, eds., *ASEAN–UN Cooperation in Preventive Diplomacy*. Bangkok: Ministry of Foreign Affairs.

Hoang Van Chi, ed. 1958. *The New Class in North Vietnam*. Saigon: Cong Dan.

Hodson, H. V. 1985. *The Great Divide: Britain-India-Pakistan*. Oxford: Oxford University Press.

Hoffman, Jeff. 1990. "Taiwan to End State of War with Mainland by May." *South China Morning Post*, 26 Dec., p. 1.

Hoffman, Steven A. 1990. *India and the China Crisis*. Delhi: Oxford University Press.

Hoffmann, Stanley. 1991. "Balance, Concert, Anarchy or None of the Above." In Gregory F. Treverton, ed., *The Shape of the New Europe*. New York: Council on Foreign Relations.

Hoffmann, Stanley, Robert O. Keohane, and John J. Mearsheimer. 1990. Comments by Hoffmann and Keohane and a rebuttal by Mearsheimer. *International Security* 15, no. 2: 191–99.

Holm, Hans-Henrik, and Georg Sorenson. 1995. "International Relations Theory in a World of Variation." In Hans-Henrik Holm and Georg Sorenson, eds., *Whose World Order? Uneven Globalization and the End of the Cold War*. Boulder, Colo.: Westview.

Homer-Dixon, Thomas F. 1991. "On the Threshold: Environmental Changes as Causes of Acute Conflict." *International Security* 61, no. 2: 76–116.

———. 1994. "Environmental Scarcities and Violent Conflict: Evidence from Cases." *International Security* 19, no. 1: 5–40.

Hong Ha. 1992. "Tinh Hinh The Gioi va Chinh Sach Doi Ngoai cua Ta" (The international situation and our foreign policy). *Tap Chi Cong San*, Dec.

Hong, Keun-soo. 1988. "Minju, Minjokgwa Jaju Tongili Joagyunginga?" (Is democracy, nation, and self-reliant unification left-wing?) *Shindonga*, Oct., pp. 200–209.

Hong Yang. 1995. "China Makes Progress in Drug Control." *Beijing Review* 38, no. 1: 15–19.

Horn, Robert. 1982. *Soviet-India Relations: Issues and Influence*. New York: Praeger.

Horowitz, Donald L. 1985. *Ethnic Groups in Conflict*. Berkeley: University of California Press.

Hossain, Ishtiaq. 1984. "Bangladesh-India Relations: Issues and Problems." In Emajuddin Ahamed, ed., *Foreign Policy of Bangladesh*. Dhaka: University Press.

———. 1991. "Management of Bangladesh's National Security Problems." *Round Table* (London), no. 317 (Jan.): 45–58.

———. 1995. "Bangladesh: A Nation Adrift." *Asian Journal of Political Science* (Singapore) 3, no. 1: 32–48.

House Subcommittee of Committee on Appropriations 1992. *DOD Appropriations 1993*. Washington, D.C.: Government Printing Office.

Hua Wu Yin. 1983. *Class and Communalism in Malaysia: Politics in a Dependent Capitalist State*. London: Zed Books.

Huang Hui-chen. 1987. "Dalu zhengce tiaozheng hou de 'Taiwanjie'" (The "Taiwan complex" after adjustment of the mainland policy). *China Times* (*Zhongguo shibao*), 15 Sept., p. 3.

Huang Linghua. 1993. "Zhengzhi yuanze youxian, jingji liyi cizhi" (Political principles the priority, economic interests secondary). *Liberty Times* (*Ziyou shibao*), Taipei, 17 May, p. 2.

Hunter, Helen-Louise. 1983. "North Korea and the Myth of Equidistance." In Tae-hwan Kwak, Wayne Patterson, and Edward A. Olsen, eds., *The Two Koreas in World Politics*. Seoul: Kyungnam University Press.

Huntington, Samuel. 1991. *The Third Wave: Democratization in the Late Twentieth Century*. Norman: University of Oklahoma Press.

———. 1993. "The Clash of Civilizations." *Foreign Affairs* 72, no. 3: 22–49.

———. 1994. "Balancing Power in Asia." *Japan Times*, 12 Nov.

Huq, M. Shamsul. 1993. *Bangladesh in International Politics: The Dilemmas of Weak States*. Dhaka: University Press.

Hussain, Akmal. 1993. "The Dynamics of Power: Military, Bureaucracy and the People." *Security and Economic Review* 1, no. 2.

Hussain, Mushahid. 1988. *Pakistan and the Changing Regional Scenario: Reflections of a Journalist*. Lahore: Progressive Publishers.

Hussain, Mushahid, and Akmal Hussain. 1993. *Pakistan: Problems of Governance*. New Delhi: Centre for Policy Research / Kornak.

Hussain, Zahid. 1991. "Pakistan's Gulf Dilemma." *Newsline*, Jan.

———. 1992a. "About Turn." *Newsline*, Feb.

———. 1992b. "The President vs. the Army." *Newsline*, July.

———. 1995a. "The Politics of Intelligence." *Newsline*, Mar.

———. 1995b. "Profile of a Terrorist." *Newsline*, Mar.

———. 1996. "Fall from Grace." *Newsline*, Nov.

———. 1997. "Democracy on a String." *Newsline*, Jan.

Hutchcroft, Paul. 1994. "Booty Capitalism: Business-Government Relations in the Philippines." In Andrew MacIntyre, ed., *Business and Government in Industrializing Asia*. Ithaca, N.Y.: Cornell University Press.

Hyder, Sajjad. 1987. *Foreign Policy of Pakistan: Reflections of an Ambassador*. Lahore: Progressive Publishers.

———. N.d. "Aspects of Foreign Policy: How Should Pakistan Negotiate?" Lahore: Group 83 Series.

Iftekharuzzaman. 1989. "The India Doctrine: Implications for Bangladesh." In Shaukat Hassan and M. G. Kabir, eds., *Issues and Challenges Facing Bangladesh Foreign Policy*. Dhaka: BSIS.

———. 1992. "Challenges to the Security of Bangladesh: Primacy of the Political and Socio-economic." *Arms Control* 13, no. 3: 518–30.

———. 1994. "The Ganges Water Sharing Issue: Diplomacy and Domestic Politics in Bangladesh." *BIISS Journal* (Dhaka) 15, no. 3: 215–35.

———. 1996. "Strategic Trends in South Asia in the Post–Cold War Context." Paper presented at the seminar on "New Approaches to

Security in South Asia," organized by Institute of International Studies, Colombo, 13 Jan.

Ikenberry, G. John, David A. Lake, and Michael Mastanduno. 1988. "Introduction: Approaches to Explaining American Foreign Economic Policy." In G. John Ikenberry, David A. Lake, and Michael Mastanduno, eds., *The State and American Foreign Economic Policy*. Ithaca, N.Y.: Cornell University Press.

Ilano, Alberto. 1989. "The Philippines in 1988: On a Hard Road to Recovery." In Ng Chee Yuen, ed., *Southeast Asian Affairs 1989*. Singapore: Institute of Southeast Asian Studies.

Ilke, Fred Charles. 1973. "Can Nuclear Deterrence Outlast the Century?" *Foreign Affairs* 51, no. 2: 269–71.

Independence Evening Post (Zili wanbao). 1987. "Taiwan kaifang zhengce de jiuge" (Disputes over Taiwan's open policy). 15 Oct., p. 2.

Information Office of the State Council of the PRC. 1995. "China: Arms Control and Disarmament." *Beijing Review* 38, no. 48: 10–25.

Initiative for National Renewal and Empowerment of People. 1995. *India Under Siege: Challenges Within and Without*. New Delhi: Wiley Eastern / New Age International.

Inoguchi, Takashi. 1988–89. "Four Japanese Scenarios for the Future." *International Affairs* 65, no. 1: 15–28.

———. 1991. "Japan's Response to the Gulf Crisis: An Analytic Overview." *Journal of Japanese Studies* 17, no. 2: 257–73.

Institute for National Strategic Studies, the U.S. National Defense University. 1997. *Strategic Assessment 1997*. Washington, D.C.: National Defense University Press.

International Institute for Strategic Studies (IISS). 1987. *The Military Balance 1987–88*. London: IISS.

———. 1993. *The Military Balance 1993–94*. London: Brassey's.

———. 1995. *The Military Balance 1995–96*. London: IISS.

———. 1996. *The Military Balance 1996–97*. London: IISS.

International Monetary Fund. 1988. "Burma: Recent Economic Developments." Washington, D.C.: International Monetary Fund, June 16.

———. 1995. *International Financial Statistics Yearbook*. Washington, D.C.: International Monetary Fund.

Iriye, Akira. 1967. "The Ideology of Japanese Imperialism: Imperial Japan and China." In Grant K. Goodman, comp., *Imperial Japan and Asia: A Reassessment*. Occasional paper. New York: East Asian Institute, Columbia University.

———. 1974. *The Cold War in Asia: An Historical Introduction*. Englewood Cliffs, N.J.: Prentice-Hall.

Ishii, Akira. 1995. "Shiren-ni Tatsu 'Sekai no nakano Nitchu-Kankei'" ('Japan-China relations in the world' at trial). *Kokusai Mondai* no. 418 (Jan.): 30–42.

Islam, Nahid. 1991. "Environmental Challenges to Bangladesh." *BIISS Papers* (Dhaka), no. 13.

Islam, Nurul Nazem, and Mohammad Humayun Kabir. 1986. "Indo-Bangladesh Common Rivers and Water Diplomacy." *BIISS Papers* (Dhaka), no. 5.

Iwanaga, Kenkichiro. 1985. *Sengo Nihon no Seito to Gaiko* (Political party and diplomacy in postwar Japan). Tokyo: University of Tokyo Press.

Jackson, Robert, and Carl G. Rosberg. 1982. "Why Africa's Weak States Persist: The Empirical and Juridical in Statehood." *World Politics* 35, no. 1: 1–24.

Jacobson, Jodi L. 1988. *Environmental Refugees: A Yardstick of Habitability*. Washington, D.C.: Worldwatch Institute.

Jahan, Rounaq. 1972. *Pakistan: Failure of National Integration*. New York: Columbia University Press.

Jain, Girilal. 1959. *India Meets China in Nepal*. Bombay: Asia Publishing House.

Jain, R. K., ed. 1984. *China and Southeast Asia Since 1949*. Vol. 1, *China and Thailand 1949–1983*. New Delhi: Radiant.

Jamieson, Neil L. 1993. *Understanding Vietnam*. Berkeley: University of California Press.

Jepperson, Ronald L., Alexander Wendt, and Peter J. Katzenstein. 1996. "Norms, Identity, and Culture in National Security." In Peter J. Katzenstein, ed., *The Culture of National Security: Norms and Identity in World Politics*. New York: Columbia University Press.

Jervis, Robert. 1976. *Perception and Misperception in International Politics*. Princeton: Princeton University Press.

———. 1978. "Cooperation Under the Security Dilemma." *World Politics* 30, no. 2: 168–214.

———. 1983. "Security Regimes." In Stephen Krasner, ed., *International Regimes*. Ithaca, N.Y.: Cornell University Press.

———. 1991–92. "The Future of World Politics: Will It Resemble the Past?" *International Security* 16, no. 3: 46–55.

Ji Guoshing. 1992. *The Spratly's Dispute and Prospects for Settlement*. Kuala Lumpur: ISIS Malaysia.

Jiang Zemin. 1992. "Accelerating Reform and Opening-Up." *Beijing Review* 35, no. 43: 9–32.

Job, Brian. 1992a. Introduction to Brian Job, ed., *The Insecurity Dilemma: National Security of Third World States*. Boulder, Colo.: Lynne Rienner.

———, ed. 1992b. *The Insecurity Dilemma: National Security of Third World States*. Boulder, Colo.: Lynne Rienner.

Joewono, Soetopo. 1981. "Mutual ASEAN-Japanese Interests in the Field of Regional Security." Paper presented at the fourth Japan-ASEAN symposium. Jakarta, 3–5 Sept.

Johnson, Chalmers. 1993. "The State and the Japanese Grand Strategy." In Richard Rosecrance and Arthur Stein, eds., *The Domestic Bases of Grand Strategy*. Ithaca, N.Y.: Cornell University Press.

Johnston, Alastair I. 1995. *Cultural Realism: Strategic Culture and Grand Strategy in Chinese History*. Princeton: Princeton University Press.

—. 1996. "China's New 'Old Thinking': The Concept of Limited Deterrence." *International Security* 20, no. 3: 5–42.

Jones, Gregg. 1989. *Red Revolution: Inside the Philippine Guerrilla Movement*. Boulder, Colo.: Westview.

Jones, L., and Il Sakong. 1980. *Government, Business and Entrepreneurship in Economic Development: The Korean Case*. Cambridge, Mass.: Harvard University Press.

Jorgensen-Dahl, Arnfinn. 1982. *Regional Organization and Order in Southeast Asia*. London: Macmillan.

Joshi, Manoj K. 1992. "Directions in India's Defence and Security Policies." In Ross Babbage and Sandy Gordon, eds., *India's Strategic Future: Regional State or Global Power?*. New York: St. Martin's.

Kahin, George McTurnan. 1970. *Nationalism and Revolution in Indonesia*. Ithaca, N.Y.: Cornell University Press.

Kanapatipillai, Valli. 1990. "July 1983: The Survivors' Experience." In Veena Das, ed., *Mirrors of Violence*. New Delhi: Oxford University Press.

Kapstein, Ethan B. 1995. "Is Realism Dead? The Domestic Sources of International Politics." *International Organization* 49, no. 4: 751–74.

Karnad, Bharat. 1994. "India's Weak Geopolitics and What to Do About It." In Bharat Karnad, ed., *Future Imperilled: India's Security in the 1990s and Beyond*. New Delhi: Viking/Penguin India.

Karnow, Stanley. 1989. *In Our Image: America's Empire in the Philippines*. New York: Random House.

Karp, Jonathan. 1995. "Filipino Migrant Workers: A New Kind of Heroes." *Far Eastern Economic Review*, 30 Mar., pp. 41–45.

Katyal, K. K. 1995. "India, Iran Make Headway." *Hindu*, 3 Jan.

Katzenstein, Peter J., ed. 1978. *Between Power and Plenty*. Madison: University of Wisconsin Press.

—. 1993. "Coping with Terrorism: Norms and Internal Security in Germany and Japan." In Judith Goldstein and Robert O. Keohane, eds., *Ideas and Foreign Policy*. Ithaca, N.Y.: Cornell University Press.

—. 1995. "Alternative Perspectives on National Security." *Items* (Social Science Research Council) 49, no. 4: 89–93.

—. 1996. "Conclusion: National Security in a Changing World." In Peter J. Katzenstein, ed., *The Culture of National Security: Norms and Identity in World Politics*. New York: Columbia University Press.

Katzenstein, Peter J., and Nobuo Okawara. 1993. "Japan's National Security: Structures, Norms and Policies." *International Security* 17, no. 4: 84–118.

Kaufman, Stuart. 1996. "A Net Assessment of American Military Forces in the Asia-Pacific Region." Paper presented at a conference organized by the Korean Institute of Strategic Studies, Seoul, Aug.

Kaung, Kyi May. 1995. "Theories, Paradigms, or Models in Burma Studies." *Asian Survey* 35, no. 11: 1030–41.

Kausikan, Bilahari. 1993. "Asia's Different Standard." *Foreign Policy*, no. 92 (Fall): 24–41.

Kavic, Lorne. 1967. *India's Quest for Security: Defence Policies, 1947–1965.* Berkeley: University of California Press.

Keerawella, Gamini B. 1990. "Peace and Security Perceptions of a Small State: Sri Lankan Responses to Superpower Naval Rivalry in the Indian Ocean, 1970–1977." In Shelton U. Kodikara, ed., *South Asian Strategic Issues: Sri Lanka Perspectives.* New Delhi: Sage.

Kennedy, Charles H. 1991. "The Politics of Ethnicity in Sindh." *Asian Survey* 31, no. 10: 938–55.

Kennedy, Paul. 1988. *The Rise and Fall of the Great Powers: Economic Change and Military Conflict from 1500 to 2000.* London: Fontana.

Keohane, Robert O. 1984. *After Hegemony: Cooperation and Discord in World Political Economy.* Princeton: Princeton University Press.

———, ed. 1986a. *Neorealism and Its Critics.* New York: Columbia University Press.

———. 1986b. "Reciprocity in International Relations." *International Organization* 40, no. 1: 1–27.

———. 1988. "International Institutions: Two Approaches." *International Studies Quarterly* 32, no. 4: 379–96.

———. 1989. *International Institutions and State Power: Essays in International Relations Theory.* Boulder, Colo.: Westview.

———. 1993. "Institutional Theory and the Realist Challenge after the Cold War." In David A. Baldwin, ed., *Neorealism and Neoliberalism: The Contemporary Debate.* New York: Columbia University Press.

Keohane, Robert O., and Joseph S. Nye. 1977. *Power and Interdependence: World Politics in Transition.* Boston: Little, Brown.

Keohane, Robert O., Joseph S. Nye, and Stanley Hoffmann, eds. 1993. *After the Cold War: International Institutions and State Strategies in Europe, 1989–1991.* Cambridge, Mass.: Harvard University Press.

Kerdphol, Saiyud. 1986. *The Struggle for Thailand: Counter-insurgency 1965–1985.* Bangkok: S. Research Center.

Kerkvliet, Benedict J. Tria. 1996. "Contemporary Philippine Leftist Politics in Historical Perspective." In Patricio N. Abinales, ed., *The Revolution Falters: The Left in Philippine Politics After 1986.* Ithaca, N.Y.: Southeast Asia Program, Cornell University.

Kerkvliet, Benedict J. Tria, and Doug J. Porter, eds. 1994. *Vietnam's Rural Transformation.* Boulder, Colo.: Westview.

Kessler, Richard J. 1989. *Rebellion and Repression in the Philippines.* New Haven: Yale University Press.

Key Indicators of Developing Asian and Pacific Countries. 1990. Manila: Asian Development Bank.

Khan, Amjad Hossain. 1994. "Development and Management of International River Basins: The Ganges Issue." In Bangladesh National Committee of the International Commission on Irrigation and Drainage (ICID), *Management of International River Basins and Environmental Challenges.* Dhaka: Academic Publishers.

Khan, Ilyas. 1996. "Endless Battle." *Newsline,* Nov.

Khan, Mohammed Ayub. 1964. "The Pakistan-American Alliance." *Foreign Affairs* 42, no. 2: 201–12.

Khan, Sairah Irshad. 1991. "Living with Crime." *Newsline,* Oct.

Khattak, Saba Gul. 1996. "Security Discourse and the State in Pakistan." *Alternatives* 21: 283–302.

Khera, S. S. 1968. *India's Defence Problem.* New Delhi: Orient Longman.

Khong, Cho Oon. 1991. "Leadership and National Security: The Search for Institutional Control." In Stephen Chee, ed., *Leadership and Security in Southeast Asia: Institutional Aspects.* Singapore: Institute of Southeast Asian Studies.

———. 1995. "Singapore: Political Legitimacy Through Managing Conformity." In Muthiah Alagappa, ed., *Political Legitimacy in Southeast Asia.* Stanford: Stanford University Press.

Khoo Boo Teik. 1995. *Paradoxes of Mahathirism: An Intellectual Biography of Mahathir Mohamad.* Kuala Lumpur: Oxford University Press.

Kim, Hak-joon. 1983. "The Rise of Kim Chong-il: Implications for North Korea's Internal and External Policies in the 1980s." *Journal of Northeast Asian Studies* 2, no. 2: 81–92.

———. 1995. "North Korea After Kim Il-Song." *Security Dialogue* 26, no. 1: 73–91.

Kim, Jongryom. 1992. *Kim Jongryom Hoigorok* (Memoir of Kim Jongryom). Seoul: Joongang Ilbo.

Kim, Samuel S. 1994. "Taiwan and the International System: The Challenge of Legitimation." In Robert G. Sutter and William R. Johnson, eds., *Taiwan in World Affairs.* Boulder, Colo.: Westview.

Kim, Yu-Nam. 1986. "Changing Relations between Moscow and Pyongyang: Odd Man Out." In Robert Scalapino and Hongkoo Lee, eds., *North Korea in a Regional and Global Context.* Berkeley: Center for Korean Studies.

Kimmit, Roger M. 1991. "Economics and National Security." *Dispatch* 2, no. 22: 398–401. Washington, D.C.: U.S. Department of State, Bureau of Public Affairs.

Klare, Michael T. 1993. "The Next Great Arms Race." *Foreign Affairs* 72, no. 3: 136–52.

Klintworth, Gary. 1992. "Chinese Perspectives on India as a Great Power." In Ross Babbage and Sandy Gordon, eds., *India's Strategic Future: Regional State or Global Power?.* New York: St. Martin's.

Knorr, Klaus. 1975. *The Power of Nations: The Political Economy of International Relations*. New York: Basic Books.

Knorr, Klaus, and F. T. Trager, eds. 1977. *Economic Issues and National Security*. Lawrence: University of Kansas Press.

Kodikara, Shelton U., ed. 1989. *Indo–Sri Lanka Agreement of July 1987*. Colombo: International Relations Program, University of Colombo.

———. 1990. *South Asian Strategic Issues: Sri Lanka Perspectives*. New Delhi: Sage.

———. 1993. *External Compulsions of South Asian Politics*. New Delhi: Sage.

Koh, B. C. 1984. *The Foreign Policy Systems of North and South Korea*. Berkeley: University of California Press.

———. 1988. "North Korea's Unification Policy After the Seoul Olympics." *Korean Observer* 19, no. 4: 384.

———. 1991. "The Effects of the Korean War on North Korea." In Chae-jin Lee, ed., *The Korean War: Forty-Year Perspectives*. Claremont, Calif.: Keck Center for International and Strategic Studies.

———, ed. 1992. *Hanguk Chonjaeng gwa Pukhan Sahoe Ju-ui Ch'ejae Konsol* (The Korean War and the development of North Korea's socialist structure). Seoul: Kyungnam University Press.

Koh, Tommy T. B. 1987. "Can Any Country Afford a Moral Foreign Policy?" Text of a speech delivered at the Georgetown University School of Foreign Service.

———. 1995. *The United States and East Asia: Conflict and Cooperation*. Singapore: Times Academic Press.

Kolodziej, Edward A. 1992a. "Renaissance in Security Studies? Caveat Lector!" *International Studies Quarterly* 36, no. 4: 421–38.

———. 1992b. "What Is Security and Security Studies? Lessons from the Cold War." *Arms Control* 13, no. 1: 1–31.

Komin, Suntaree. 1995. "National Decision-Making Behavior in Thailand." ISIS–SIPRI Workshop Paper. Bangkok: ISIS.

Kompas. 1992. "IGGI, Sebuah Kisah Balik" (IGGI, flashback). 27 Mar.

Kraft, Herman. 1993. *After the Bases Are Gone: A Philippine Perspective on the Future of Philippine–U.S. Security Relations*. Honolulu: Pacific Forum, Center for Strategic and International Studies.

Krasner, Stephen D. 1978. *Defending the National Interest: Raw Material Investments and U.S. Foreign Policy*. Princeton: Princeton University Press.

———. 1983a. "National Security and Economics." In Thomas Trout and James Harf, eds., *National Security Affairs*. New Brunswick: Transaction Books.

———. 1983b. "Structural Causes and Regime Consequences: Regimes as Intervening Variables." In Stephen D. Krasner, ed., *International Regimes*. Ithaca, N.Y.: Cornell University Press.

———. 1991. "Global Communications and National Power: Life on the Pareto Frontier." *World Politics* 43, no. 3: 336–67.

———. 1993. "Westphalia and All That." In Judith Goldstein and Robert O. Keohane, eds., *Ideas and Foreign Policy: Beliefs, Institutions and Political Change*. Ithaca, N.Y.: Cornell University Press.

———. 1995–96. "Compromising Westphalia." *International Security* 20, no. 3: 115–51.

Krause, Keith, and Michael C. Williams. 1996. "Broadening the Agenda of Security Studies: Politics and Methods." *Mershon International Studies Review* 40, no. 2: 229–54.

Kriengsak, Chareonwongsak. 1996. *Exploring the World of Ideas, Thai Politics: Research on People's Viewpoint Towards Thai Politics* (in Thai). Bangkok: Success Media.

Krishna, Sankaran. 1996. "Producing Sri Lanka: J. R. Jayawardene and Postcolonial Identity." *Alternatives* 21: 303–20.

Krugman, Paul. 1994. "The Myth of Asia's Miracle." *Foreign Affairs* 73, no. 6: 62–78.

Kullavanit, Pichit. 1989. *The Role of the Military in the Country's Development* (in Thai). Bangkok: National Defense College.

Kurien, C. T. 1994. *Global Capitalism and the Indian Economy*. New Delhi: Orient Longman.

Kux, Dennis. 1993. *Estranged Democracies: India and the United States 1941– 1991*. New Delhi: Sage.

Kyi, Khin Maung. 1994. "Myanmar: Will Forever Flow the Ayeyarwady?" In *Southeast Asian Affairs 1994*, pp. 209–30. Singapore: Institute of Southeast Asian Studies.

Kyodo (Hanoi). 1993. 21 Mar. In Foreign Broadcast Information Service, East Asian Service, FBIS-EAS-93-053.

Lacaba, Jose F., ed. 1995. *Boss: Five Case Studies of Local Politics in the Philippines*. Manila: Philippine Center for Investigative Journalism and Institute for Popular Democracy.

Lach, Donald F., and Edmund S. Wehrle. 1975. *International Politics in East Asia Since World War II*. New York: Praeger.

Lai Tse-han, Ramon Myers, and Wei Wou. 1991. *A Tragic Beginning: The Taiwan Uprising of February 28, 1947*. Stanford: Stanford University Press.

Lake, Anthony. 1993. "From Containment to Enlargement." *Dispatch* 4, no. 39: 658–64. Washington, D.C.: U.S. Department of State, Bureau of Public Affairs.

Lake, David A. 1996. "Anarchy, Hierarchy, and the Variety of International Relations." *International Organization* 50, no. 1: 1–34.

Lam, Truong Buu. 1968. "Intervention Versus Tribute in Sino-Vietnamese Relations, 1788–1790." in John K. Fairbank, ed, *The Chinese World Order: Traditional China's Foreign Relations*, pp. 165–79. Cambridge, Mass.: Harvard University Press.

Lam, Willy Wo-lap. 1991. "Taipei 'Peace' Declaration Recognizes Beijing Officials." *South China Morning Post*, 1 May, p. 1.

Lane, Max. 1991. "The Philippines 1990: Political Stalemate and Persisting Instability." In Sharon Siddique and Ng Chee Yuen, eds., *Southeast Asian Affairs 1991*. Singapore: Institute of Southeast Asian Studies.

Laothamatas, Anek. 1993. *Mobile Mob: Middle Classes and Businessmen with Democratic Development* (in Thai). Bangkok: Matichon Printing.

Larma, Manabendra Narayan. 1980. "Genocide in Chittagong Hill Tracts: An Appeal to World Conscience." *Amrita Bazar Patrika* (Calcutta), 19 Sept.

Larus, Joel. 1965. Introduction to Joel Larus, ed., *Comparative World Politics*. Belmont, Calif.: Wadsworth.

Lasswell, Harold D. 1950. *National Security and Individual Freedom*. New York: McGraw-Hill.

Latif, Maj. Gen. Rahat. 1993. *"...Plus Bhutto Episode": An Autobiography*. Lahore: Jang.

Lau, Teik Soon. 1969. "Malaysia-Singapore Relations: Crisis of Adjustment." *Journal of Southeast Asian History* 10 (Mar.): 155–76.

Lawyers Committee for Human Rights. 1988. *Vigilantes in the Philippines: A Threat to Democratic Rule*. New York: Lawyers Committee for Human Rights.

Layne, Christopher. 1993. "The Unipolar Illusion: Why New Great Powers Will Rise." *International Security* 17, no. 4: 5–51.

————. 1994. "Kant or Can't: The Myth of Democratic Peace." *International Security* 19, no. 2: 5–49.

Le Huu Nghia. 1994. "Firmly Maintain Political Stability and Renovate the Political System." *Tap Chi Cong San*, Feb. Translation in Foreign Broadcast Information Service, East Asian Service, FBIS-EAS-94-102 (26 May 1994).

Le Ke Lam. 1994. "Defense Strategy for Coastal Region Examined." *Tap Chi Quoc Phong Toan Dan*, Feb. Translation in Foreign Broadcast Information Service, East Asian Service, FBIS-EAS-94-083 (29 Apr. 1994).

Le Minh. 1993. "Firmly Grasp the Party's Concepts About Religious Affairs in the Current Situation." *Tap Chi Cong San*, Oct. Translation in Foreign Broadcast Information Service, East Asian Service, FBIS-EAS-93-216 (10 Nov. 1993).

Le Quang Thanh. 1994. "Maintaining Security in the Conditions of an Open Economy." *Tap Chi Cong San*, Feb. Translation in Foreign Broadcast Information Service, East Asian Service, FBIS-EAS-94-102 (26 May 1994).

Ledyard, Gari. 1983. "Yin and Yang in the China-Manchuria-Korea Triangle." In Morris Rossabi, ed., *China Among Equals: The Middle Kingdom and Its Neighbors, Tenth–Fourteenth Centuries*. Berkeley: University of California Press.

Lee, Boon Hiok. 1989. "Leadership and Security in Singapore: The

Prevailing Paradigm." In Mohammed Ayoob and Chai-Anan Samu-davanija, eds., *Leadership Perceptions and National Security: The Southeast Asian Experience*. Singapore: Institute of Southeast Asian Studies.

Lee, Chae-Jin, and Hideo Sato. 1982. *U.S. Policy Toward Japan and Korea: A Changing Influence Relationship*. New York: Praeger.

Lee, Chul-seung. 1988. "Jayoo Minjujuui Suhoga Wae Bandonginga?" (Why is preservation of liberal democracy reactionary?) *Shindonga*, Oct., pp. 210–21.

Lee, Hoong Phun. 1995. *Constitutional Conflicts in Contemporary Malaysia*. Kuala Lumpur: Oxford University Press.

Lee, Hsien Loong. 1984. "Security Options for Small States." Text of a talk delivered to the Singapore Institute for International Affairs, Singapore.

———. 1986. "Singapore's Economic Policy: Vision for the 1990s." Text of a talk delivered at the Commonwealth Institute, London.

Lee, Khoon Choy. 1993. *Diplomacy of a Tiny State*. Singapore: World Scientific.

Lee, Kuan Yew. 1988. Untitled speech delivered to the American Society of Newspaper Editors, Washington, D.C.

———. 1993. "Democracy and Human Rights for the World." *Media Asia* 20, no. 1: 33–38.

Lee, Lai To. 1988. "The PRC and Taiwan: Moving Toward a More Realistic Relationship." In Robert Scalapino, Seizaburo Sato, Jusuf Wanandi, and Sung-Joo Han, eds., *Asian Security Issues: Regional and Global*. Research Papers and Policy Studies 26. Berkeley: University of California, Institute of East Asian Studies.

———. 1991. *The Reunification of China*. New York: Praeger.

Lee, Manwoo, R. McLaurin, and Chung-in Moon. 1988. *Alliance Under Tension*. Boulder, Colo.: Westview.

Lee, Min-yong. 1996. *Hankuk Anbo Jungchaekron* (Thesis on Korean security policy). Seoul: Jinyoungsa.

Lee, Seok-Soo. 1993. "The Anatomy of the Korean Conflict." Ph.D. diss., University of Kentucky, Lexington.

Lee, Sook-jong. 1995. "Hankukinui Anbogwan" (The Korean view of security). *Kukga Jonryak* (National strategy) 1, no. 2: 212–34.

Lee, Tsao Yuan. 1991. *Growth Triangle: The Johor-Singapore-Riau Experience*. Singapore: Institute of Southeast Asian Studies.

Legge, John D. 1972. *Sukarno: A Political Biography*. London: Allen Lane / Penguin.

Leggett, Chris. 1993. "Singapore's Industrial Relations in the 1990s." In Gary Rodan, ed., *Singapore Changes Guard*. Melbourne: Longman Cheshire.

Leifer, Michael. 1964. "Communal Violence in Singapore." *Asian Survey* 4, no. 10: 1115–21.

———. 1974. "Indonesia's Regional Vision." *World Today* 30, no. 10: 418–25.

———. 1983a. *Indonesia's Foreign Policy*. London: Allen and Unwin.

————. 1983b. "The Security of Sea-Lanes in South East Asia." *Survival* 25, no. 1: 16–24.

————. 1989. *ASEAN and the Security of Southeast Asia*. London: Routledge.

Leirissa, R. Z. 1991. *PRRI-PERMESTA. Strategi Membangun Indonesia Tanpa Komunis*. Jakarta: Pustaka Utama Grafiti.

Lemhanas. 1982. *Telaah Strategi Nasional, 1982–1992*. Jakarta: Lemhanas.

————. 1985. "Upaya Pembentukan ZOPFAN/NWFZ di Asia Tenggara Bagi Ketahanan Nasional dan Ketahanan Regional." Paper presented at the Seminar on Southeast Asian ZOPFAN/NWFZ at the Indonesian Foreign Ministry, Jakarta, 14–15 Jan.

————. 1988. *National Resilience*. 2d ed. Jakarta: Lemhanas.

Levy, Jack. 1988. "Domestic Politics and War." *Journal of Interdisciplinary History* 18, no. 4: 653–73.

Levy, Marc A. 1995. "Is the Environment a National Security Issue?" *International Security* 20, no. 2: 35–62.

Lewis, John, Hua Di, and Litai Xue. 1991. "Beijing's Defense Establishment: Solving the Arms-Export Enigma." *International Security* 15, no. 4: 87–109.

Lho, Kyongsoo. 1988. "The Military Balance in the Korean Peninsula." *Asian Affairs* 19, no. 1: 36–44.

Li Ning. 1994. "China Adopts New Taxation System." *Beijing Review* 37, no. 11: 11–12.

Li Peng. 1992. "For an Effective International Cooperation." *Beijing Review* 35, no. 25: 7–9.

————. 1995. "Report on the Work of the Government." *Beijing Review* 38, no. 13: i–xv.

Liang'an jingji tongji yuebao (Cross-straits economics statistics monthly). 1995. Dec.

Liddle, R. William. 1978. "Participation and Political Parties." In Karl D. Jackson and Lucian Pye, eds., *Political Power and Communications in Indonesia*. Berkeley: University of California Press.

Lim, Hock Kwang Bernard. 1992. *ASEAN Security Cooperation: Singapore's Offer of Military Facilities to the United States*. Singapore: National University of Singapore.

Lim Joo-Jock. 1984. *Territorial Power Domains, Southeast Asia, and China: The Geo-strategy of an Overarching Massif*. Singapore: Institute of Southeast Asian Studies.

Lim Joo-Jock and S. Vani. 1984. *Armed Separatism in Southeast Asia*. Singapore: Institute of Southeast Asian Studies.

Lin Hung-lung. 1987. "Wenhua jiaoliu: Cong zujue dao kaifang" (Cultural exchanges: from obstruction to opening). *Independence Evening Post* (*Zili wanbao*), 7 Sept., p. 2.

Lin Tung-hsiung. 1987. "Guonei yali he Meiguo yali xia de waihui wenti"

(The foreign exchange problem under domestic and American pressure). *Journalist (Xin Xinwen)*, 23–29 Mar., pp. 57–58.

Lin Yinjia et al. 1991. *Deng Xiaoping Xinshiqi Junshi Zhexue Sixiang* (Deng Xiaoping's military philosophical thoughts in the new era). Beijing: Military Science Press.

Lindberg, Leon. 1967. *The Political Dynamics of European Integration*. Stanford: Stanford University Press.

Lintner, Bertil. 1990a. *Outrage: Burma's Struggle for Democracy*. 2d ed. London: White Lotus.

———. 1990b. *The Rise and Fall of the Communist Party of Burma (CPB)*. Ithaca, N.Y.: Cornell University Southeast Asia Program.

———. 1991. "Cross-Border Drug Trade in the Golden Triangle (S.E. Asia)." Territorial Briefing no. 1, International Boundary Research Unit (IBRU), Department of Geography, University of Durham.

———. 1995a. "Building New Bridges with a Former Foe." *Jane's Defence Weekly*, 9 Sept., 46–49.

———. 1995b. "Dangerous Prey." *Far Eastern Economic Review*, 9 Mar., p. 26.

———. 1995c. "Drugs, Insurgency, and Counterinsurgency in Burma." Paper presented at the Conference on Myanmar Towards the Twenty-first Century: Dynamics of Continuity and Change, Bangkok, June 1–3.

Lipset, S. M. 1960. *Political Man*. London: Heinemann.

Lipson, Charles. 1993. "International Cooperation in Economic and Security Affairs." In David A. Baldwin, ed., *Neorealism and Neoliberalism: The Contemporary Debate*. New York: Columbia University Press.

Liu Huaqing. 1993. "Jiandingbuyi De Yanzhuo Jianshe You Zhongguo Tese Xiandaihua Jundui De Daolu Qianjin" (Unswervingly advance along the road building a modern army with Chinese characteristics). *Jiefangjun Bao (Liberation Army Daily)*, 6 Aug., pp. 1–2.

Liyanagamage, A. 1993. *The Indian Factor in the Security Perspectives of Sri Lanka*. Sri Lanka: University of Kelaniya.

Lodhi, Maleeha. 1992. "Here Comes the Crunch." *Newsline*, Mar.–Apr.

———. 1993. "Bitter Harvest." *Newsline*, Apr.

———. 1994a. *The External Dimension*. Lahore: Jang.

———. 1994b. *Pakistan's Encounter with Democracy*. Lahore: Vanguard.

Lodhi, Maleeha, and Zahid Hussain. 1990a. "The Army's Long Shadow." *Newsline*, July.

———. 1990b. "General Elections?" *Newsline*, Oct.

Lombard, G. 1992. "The Burmese Refugees in Bangladesh: Causes and Prospects for Repatriation." *Thai-Yunnan Project Newsletter* no. 19 (Dec.).

Long, Simon. 1991. *Taiwan: China's Last Frontier*. London: Macmillan.

Lopez, Mario Antonio. 1989. "The Philippines: Managing Reform in a New Democracy." In Ng Chee Yuen, ed., *Southeast Asian Affairs 1989*. Singapore: Institute of Southeast Asian Studies.

Lord, Winston. 1993. "A New Pacific Community: Ten Goals of American Policy." Opening statement at conference hearings for Ambassador Winston Lord, assistant secretary of state designate, Bureau of East Asian Affairs, 31 Mar.

Low, Linda, and Toh Mun Heng, eds. 1993. *Regional Cooperation and Growth Triangles in ASEAN*. Singapore: Times Academic Press.

Lowry, Bob. 1989. "Why Indonesia Closed the Straits in September 1988." *Studies in Conflict and Terrorism* 16: 183.

————. 1993. *Indonesian Defence Policy and the Indonesian Armed Forces*. Canberra Papers on Strategy and Defence no. 99. Canberra: Strategic and Defence Studies Centre, Research School of Pacific Studies, Australia National University.

Lu Chao-lung. 1993. "Zhonggong qianfu zai Tai renyuan yu sanqian" (More than 3,000 mainland personnel hiding in Taiwan). *United Daily News*, 29 Oct., p. 2.

————. 1994. "Dui Tai yong wu keneng you ren xiang ying wang shi" (If force is used against Taiwan, there may be quislings). *United Daily News*, 27 July, p. 4.

Luhmann, Niklas. 1985. *Sociological Theory of Law*. Boston: Routledge.

Luo Tien-pin. 1993. "Zhonggong qianfu zai Tai jiandie hai you 3 qian duo ren" (More than 3,000 Communist spies still hiding in Taiwan). *Liberty Times* (*Ziyou shibao*), 29 Apr., p. 4.

Lynn-Jones, Sean M. 1991. "International Security Studies." *International Studies Notes* 16, no. 3: 53–64.

Lynn-Jones, Sean M., and Steven E. Miller. 1995. Introduction to Sean M. Lynn-Jones and Steven E. Miller, eds., *Global Dangers: Changing Dimensions of International Security*. Cambridge, Mass.: MIT Press.

MacFarquhar, Roderick. 1991. "Epilogue: The Onus of Unity." In Roderick MacFarquhar and John K. Fairbank, eds., *The Cambridge History of China*. Vol. 15, part 2. Cambridge: Cambridge University Press.

Mack, Andrew. 1991. "North Korea and the Bomb." *Foreign Policy*, no. 83 (Summer): 87–104.

Mackie, Jamie. 1974. *Konfrontasi: The Indonesian-Malaysian Dispute, 1963–1966*. Kuala Lumpur: Oxford University Press.

MacNeill, Jim, Pieter Winsemius, and Taizo Yakushiji. 1991. *Beyond Interdependence: The Meshing of the World's Economy and Earth's Ecology*. New York: Oxford University Press.

Madale, Nagasura T. 1984. "The Future of the MNLF as a Separatist Movement in Southern Philippines." In Lim Joo-Jock and S. Vani, eds., *Armed Separatism in Southeast Asia*. Singapore: Institute of Southeast Asian Studies.

Mahathir Mohamad. 1970. *The Malay Dilemma*. Kuala Lumpur: Federal Publications.

Mahbubani, Kishore. 1992. "The West Versus the Rest." *National Interest* 28 (Summer): 3–12.

———. 1993. "The Dangers of Decadence." *Foreign Affairs* 72, no. 4: 10–14.

———. 1995. "The Pacific Way." *Foreign Affairs* 74, no. 1: 100–111.

Mainland Affairs Council, Executive Yuan, ed. 1992a. *Dalu diqu touzi fagui huibian* (Compilation of mainland investment laws and regulations). Taipei: Mainland Affairs Council.

———. 1992b. *Dalu zhengce shuomingshu* (Mainland policy manual). Taipei: Mainland Affairs Council.

———. 1994. *Relations Across the Taiwan Straits*. Taipei: Mainland Affairs Council.

Majul, Cesar A. 1985. *The Contemporary Muslim Movement in the Philippines*. Berkeley: Mizan Press.

Mak, J. N. 1993. *ASEAN Defense Reorientation 1975–1992: The Dynamics of Modernization and Structural Change*. Canberra: Strategic and Defence Studies Centre, Research School of Pacific Studies, Australian National University.

Malik, Brig. S. K. 1991. "Pakistan: A Study in Threat Perception—I." *Pakistan Army Journal* 3, no. 4: 1–21.

Malik, J. Mohan. 1994. "Sino-Indian Rivalry in Myanmar: Implications for Regional Security." *Contemporary Southeast Asia* 16, no. 2: 137–56.

Manapat, Ricardo. 1991. *Some Are Smarter than Others: The History of Marcos' Crony Capitalism*. New York: Algeria.

Mandel, Robert. 1994. *The Changing Face of National Security: A Conceptual Analysis*. Westport, Conn.: Greenwood.

Mangold, Robert. 1991. "Security: New Ideas, Old Ambiguities." *World Today* 47, no. 2: 30–32.

Maniruzzaman, Talukder. 1982. "The Security of Small States in the Third World." *Canberra Papers*. Canberra: Strategic and Defence Studies Centre, Australian National University.

Manor, James, ed. 1991. *Rethinking Third World Politics*. New York: Longman.

Mansfield, Edward D., and Jack Snyder. 1995. "Democratization and the Danger of War." *International Security* 20, no. 1: 5–38.

Mansingh, Surjit. 1984. *India's Search for Power: Indira Gandhi's Foreign Policy, 1966–1982*. New Delhi: Sage.

Mansingh, Surjit, and Steven I. Levine. 1989. "China and India: Moving Beyond Confrontation." *Problems of Communism* 38: 30–49.

Mao Zedong. 1993. *Mao Zedong Junshi Wenji* (Collected military works of Mao Zedong). Vol. 6. Beijing: Military Science Press and Central Document Press.

———. 1994. *Mao Zedong Waijiao Wenxuan* (Selected diplomatic works of Mao Zedong). Beijing: Central Document Press and World Knowledge Press.

Marcos, Ferdinand E. 1978. *Five Years of the New Society*. Manila: Marcos Foundation.

———. 1979. *The Democratic Revolution in the Philippines*. Englewood Cliffs, N.J.: Prentice-Hall International.

Martin, Laurence W. 1962. *Neutralism and Nonalignment: The New States in World Affairs*. New York: Praeger.

Maruyama, Masao. 1963. *Thought and Behavior in Modern Japanese Politics*. Oxford: Oxford University Press.

Marwah, Onkar. 1987. "India's Strategic Perspectives on the Indian Ocean." In William L. Dowdy and Russell B. Trood, eds., *The Indian Ocean: Perspectives on a Strategic Arena*. New Delhi: Himalayan Books / Duke University Press.

Masaki, Stuart. 1995. "The Korean Question: Assessing the Military Balance." *Security Studies* 4, no. 2: 365–425.

Mathews, Jessica Tuchman. 1989. "Redefining Security." *Foreign Affairs* 68, no. 2: 162–77.

Matinuddin, Lt. Gen. Kamal. 1993–94. "Pakistan-India Relations: A Historical Perspective." *Regional Studies* 12, no. 1: 3–68.

Matthews, John C. 1996. "Current Gains and Future Outcomes: When Cumulative Relative Gains Matter." *International Security* 21, no. 1: 112–46.

Maull, Hanns W. 1990–91. "Germany and Japan: The New Civilian Powers." *Foreign Affairs* 69, no. 5: 91–106.

Maung, Mya. 1994. "On the Road to Mandalay: A Case Study of the Sinonization of Upper Burma." *Asian Survey* 34, no. 5: 447–59.

Maxwell, Nevil. 1970. *India's China War*. London: Jonathan Cape.

May, Ernst R. 1992. "National Security in American History." In Graham Allison and Gregory Treverton, eds., *Rethinking America's Security: Beyond the Cold War to New World Order*. New York: Norton.

May, Michael M. 1993–94. "Correspondence: Japan as a Superpower?" *International Security* 18, no. 3: 182–87.

May, R. J. 1990. "The Religious Factor in Three Minority Movements: The Moro of the Philippines, the Malays of Thailand, and Indonesia's West Papuans." *Contemporary Southeast Asia* 13, no. 4: 396–414.

———. 1992. *Vigilantes in the Philippines: From Fanatical Cults to Citizens' Organizations*. Philippine Studies occasional paper 12. Center for Philippine Studies, University of Hawaii at Manoa.

Mayo, Marlene. 1967. "Attitudes Toward Asia and the Beginning of Japanese Empire." In Grant K. Goodman, comp., *Imperial Japan and Asia: A Reassessment*. Occasional paper. New York: East Asian Institute, Columbia University.

McCloud, Donald G. 1995. *Southeast Asia: Tradition and Modernity in the Contemporary World*. Boulder, Colo.: Westview.

McCoy, Alfred W., ed., 1993. *An Anarchy of Families: State and Family in the Philippines*. Center for Southeast Asian Studies, University of Wisconsin.

McDonald, Hamish. 1992. "Destroyer of Worlds." *Far Eastern Economic Review*, 30 Apr., pp. 23–24.

McLane, Charles B. 1966. *Soviet Strategies in Southeast Asia: An Explanation of Eastern Policy Under Lenin and Stalin*. Princeton: Princeton University Press.

McLaurin, Ronald D., and Chung-in Moon. 1989. *The United States and the Defense of the Pacific*. Boulder, Colo.: Westview.

McNamara, Robert. 1986. *The Essence of Security*. New York: Harper and Row.

Means, Gordon. 1991. *Malaysian Politics: The Second Generation*. Singapore: Oxford University Press.

Mearsheimer, John J. 1990. "Back to the Future: Instability in Europe After the Cold War." *International Security* 15, no. 1: 5–56.

———. 1995a. "The False Promise of International Institutions." *International Security* 19, no. 3: 5–49.

———. 1995b. "A Realist Reply." *International Security* 20, no. 1: 82–93.

Media Group of the Committee for Propaganda and Agitation to Intensify Patriotism. 1994. *Cruel and Vicious Repression of Myanmar Peoples by Imperialists and Fascists and the True Story about the Plunder of the Royal Jewels*. Yangon: News and Periodical Enterprises.

Medianski, F. A. 1986. "The New People's Army: A Nationwide Insurgency in the Philippines." *Contemporary Southeast Asia* 8, no. 1: 1–17.

Mehdi, Tahir. 1994. "Malakand's Holy War." *Newsline*, Nov.

Mehmet, Ozay. 1990. *Islamic Identity and Development: Studies of the Islamic Periphery*. Kuala Lumpur: Forum.

Mektrairat, Nakarin. 1992. *The 1932 Revolution in Siam* (in Thai). Bangkok: Project on Social Sciences and Humanities Text Book Foundation.

Mercado, Eliseo. 1984. "Culture, Economics and Revolt in Mindanao: The Origins of the MNLF and the Politics of Moro Separatism." In Lim Joo-Jock and S. Vani, eds., *Armed Separatism in Southeast Asia*. Singapore: Institute of Southeast Asian Studies.

Mercado, Orlando S. N.d. "AFP Modernization: Towards Deterrence and Development." Speech before the Senate of the Philippines.

Meyer, Steven. 1978. *The Dynamics of Nuclear Proliferation*. Chicago: University of Chicago Press.

Mian, Zia. 1996. "Guns or Butter?" *Newsline*, June.

Migdal, Joel S. 1988. *Strong Societies and Weak States: State-Society Relations and State Capabilities in the Third World*. Princeton: Princeton University Press.

Milne, R. S. 1966. "Singapore's Exit from Malaysia: The Consequences of Ambiguity." *Asian Survey* 6, no. 3: 175–84.

Milner, Helen. 1993. "The Assumption of Anarchy in International Relations Theory: A Critique. In David A. Baldwin, ed., *Neorealism and Neoliberalism: The Contemporary Debate*. New York: Columbia University Press.

Min, Byung-Chun. 1973. *Hankuk Anboron* (Thesis on Korean security). Seoul: Daewangsa.

Ministry of Defense. 1993. *Annual Report, 1992–93.* New Delhi: Government of India.

———. 1994. *Annual Report, 1993–94.* New Delhi: Government of India.

———. 1995. *Annual Report, 1994–95.* New Delhi: Government of India.

Ministry of External Affairs. 1993a. *Annual Report, 1992–93.* New Delhi: Government of India.

———. 1993b. *Annual Report, 1992–93* (Hindi version). New Delhi: Government of India.

———. 1995. *Annual Report, 1994–95.* New Delhi: Government of India.

Ministry of Finance. N.d. *Economic Reforms: Two Years After and the Task Ahead.* Discussion paper. New Delhi: Government of India.

Ministry of Foreign Affairs (MOFA) of Japan. 1992. *Gaiko Seisho Heisei 3-nen-ban* (Diplomatic bluebook 1991). Tokyo: Okurasho Insatsu-kyoku.

———. 1994. *Gaiko Seisho 1993* (Diplomatic bluebook 1993). Tokyo: Okurasho Insatsu-kyoku.

———. 1995. *Diplomatic Bluebook 1995.* Internet version (www2.nttca.com:-8010/infomofa/index.html).

———. 1996. "Japan's Policy on the Russian Federation." Internet version (www2.nttca.com:8010/infomofa/index.html).

Ministry of Foreign Affairs (MOFA) of Korea. 1995. *Diplomacy White Paper.* Seoul: MOFA.

Ministry of Home Affairs. 1994. *Annual Report 1993–94.* New Delhi: Government of India.

Ministry of National Defense (MND). 1995. *21segirul hyanghan Hankukui Kukbang* (Korean defense in the twenty-first century). Seoul: MND.

———. 1995–96. *Defence White Paper.* Seoul: MND.

Mirchandani, G. G. 1968. *India's Nuclear Dilemma.* New Delhi: Popular.

Mirza, M. A. 1991. "PPP's Problem Child." *Newsline,* Aug.

Misra, K. P. 1980. "Paramilitary Forces in India." *Armed Forces and Society* 6: 371–88.

Mizan, Mizanur Rahman. 1989. *Bangabandhur Bhashan* (Speeches of Bangabandhu; in Bengali). Dhaka: Novel Publications.

Mohan, C. Raja. 1996. "CTBT: Pressure or Leverage?" *The Hindu* (New Delhi), 25 Feb.

Mohanty, Manoranjan. 1988. "India and China Relations on the Eve of the Asian Century." In Ramakant, ed., *China and South Asia.* New Delhi: South Asia Publishers.

Mok, Jinhyu. 1996. "Kukmin Anbouisik Byinwha" (Changes of people's security perception). Paper presented at a conference organized by the National Institute of National Intelligence, Seoul, Dec.

Montville, Joseph V., ed. 1990. *Conflict and Peacemaking in Multiethnic Societies.* Lexington, Mass.: Lexington Books.

Moon, Chung-in. 1989. "Democratization, National Security and Civil-Military Relations: Analytical Issues and the South Korean Case." *Pacific Focus* 5, no. 1: 5–22.

———. 1991. "The Political Economy of Defence Industrialization in South Korea: Constraints, Opportunities, and Prospects." *Journal of East Asian Affairs* 5, no. 2: 439–65.

———. 1995. "Segeyhwaui Wihyopkujowa Kukga Jonryak" (Threat structure of globalization and state strategy). *Quarterly Sasang* (Spring): 52–80.

———. 1996a. *Arms Control on the Korean Peninsula: International Penetration, Regional Dynamics, and Domestic Structure.* Seoul: Yonsei University Press.

———. 1996b. "Kukga Anbowa Kukga Jungbo" (National security and national intelligence). *Kukga Jonryak* (National strategy) 2, no. 1: 39–58.

———. 1996c. "Rethinking Arms Control and Peace on the Korean Peninsula: Search for Alternatives." *Economics of Korean Reunification* 1, no. 1: 50–67.

Moon, Chung-in, and Intaek Hyun. 1992. "Muddling Through Security, Growth, and Welfare: The Political Economy of Defence Spending in South Korea." In S. Chan and A. Mintz, eds., *Security, Growth, and Welfare.* New York: Unwin and Hyman.

Moon, Chung-in, and Mun-gu Kang. 1995. "Democratic Opening and Military Intervention in South Korea: Comparative Assessments and Implications." In J. Cotton, ed., *Korean Politics in Transition.* Sydney: Longman; New York: St. Martin's.

Moon, Chung-in, and Jung-hoon Lee. 1995. "Unraveling the Next East Asian Regional System: Historical Memory, Finite Deterrence, and Regional Cooperation." *Pacific Focus* 10, no. 2: 125–52.

Moon, Chung-in, and Seok-soo Lee. 1995. "The Post–Cold War Security Agenda of Korea: Inertia, New Thinking, and Assessments." *Pacific Review* 8, no. 1: 99–115.

Moon, Chung-in, and Sang-kyun Moon. 1995. "Mikukui Gunsaryok Gamchukgwa Asia-Taepyongyang Jiyokui Jaeraesik Kunsaryok: Chongpyongga" (American military reduction and conventional forces in Asia-Pacific: net assessments). *Jonryak Yonku* (Strategic studies) 2, no. 4: 8–59.

Moon, Chung-in, and Rashemi Prasad. 1994. "Beyond the Developmental State: Institutions, Networks, and Politics." *Governance* 7, no. 4: 360–86.

Moon, Chung-in, and Kil-jae Rhyoo. 1996. *Nambuk Gyonghyopui Junchijok Yeogun* (Political conditions for North-South Korean economic cooperation). Seoul: Institute for Unification Studies, Yonsei University.

Mooney, Paul. 1987. "Lure of the Mainland." *Far Eastern Economic Review*, 1 Oct., pp. 30–31.

Morgan, Patrick. 1992. "Safeguarding Security Studies." *Arms Control* 13, no. 3: 464–79.

Morgenthau, Hans J. 1952. "Another Great Debate: The National Interest of the United States." *American Political Science Review* 66 (Dec.): 961–88.

————. 1967. *Politics Among Nations: The Struggle for Power and Peace*. 4th ed. New York: Knopf.

————. 1978. *Politics Among Nations: The Struggle for Power and Peace*. 5th ed., rev. New York: Knopf.

————. 1985. *Politics Among Nations: The Struggle for Power and Peace*. 6th ed. New York: Knopf.

Morrison, Charles E., and Astri Suhrke. 1978. *Strategies of Survival: The Foreign Policy Dilemmas of Smaller Asian States*. New York: St. Martin's.

Morrow, James D. 1993. "Arms Versus Allies: Trade-offs in Search for Security." *International Organization* 47, no. 2: 207–33.

Mouffe, Chantal. 1979. "Hegemony and Ideology in Gramsci." In Chantal Mouffe, ed., *Gramsci and Marxist Theory*. London: Routledge.

Mueller, John. 1989. *Retreat from Doomsday: The Obsolescence of Major War*. New York: Basic Books.

Mujtaba, Hasan. 1991. "Night Without End." *Newsline*, Aug.

Muni, S. D. 1993. *Pangs of Proximity: India and Sri Lanka's Ethnic Conflict*. New Delhi: Sage.

Muni, S. D., and Anuradha Muni. 1984. *Regional Cooperation in South Asia*. New Delhi: National Publishing House.

Muscat, Robert J. 1990. *Thailand and the United States: Development, Security, and Foreign Aid*. New York: Columbia University Press.

Muzaffar, Chandra. 1987. *Islamic Resurgence in Malaysia*. Petaling Jaya: Penerbit Fajar Bakti.

Mydans, Seth. 1996. "In Peacetime, Vietnam's Army Turns to Business Ventures." *New York Times*, 21 July.

Myers, Norman. 1986. "The Environmental Dimension to Security Issues." *Environmentalist* 6, no. 4: 251–57.

————. 1989. "Environment and Security." *Foreign Policy*, no. 74 (Spring): 23–41.

Myint, Myo. 1994. "Pattern of Authority in Precolonial Myanmar." Report to the Institute of Southeast Asian Studies, Singapore.

Nanda, B. R. 1976a. Introduction to B. R. Nanda, ed., *Indian Foreign Policy: The Nehru Years*. Honolulu: University of Hawaii Press.

————, ed. 1976b. *Indian Foreign Policy: The Nehru Years*. Honolulu: University of Hawaii Press.

Nandy, Ashis. 1994. "Culture, Voice and Development: A Primer for the Unsuspecting." *Thesis Eleven* 39: 1–8.

Napasinthuwong, Paisan. 1996. "Strategic Doctrine for the Use of Small Aircraft Carrier." *Navikasart*, September 1996: 9–37.

Naqvi, M. B. 1994. "Afghanistan, What Afghanistan Are We Talking About?" *Defence Journal* 20, nos. 1–2: 13–16.

————. 1996. "Whose Budget Is It Anyway?" *Newsline*, June.

Narain, Govind. 1986. *Internal Threats and National Security*. USI National Security Lecture 7. New Delhi: United Service Institution of India.

Narasimha Rao, P. V. 1994. "India and the Asia Pacific: Forging a New Relationship." In *Prime Minister P. V. Narasimha Rao Visits Singapore, September 7–8, 1994*. New Delhi: Ministry of External Affairs, Government of India.

————. 1995. "World Summit for Social Development: Speech of Prime Minister of India, Copenhagen, Denmark, 11th March 1995." Ministry of External Affairs, Government of India, New Delhi. Mimeographed.

————. N.d. *Prime Minister Narasimha Rao Visits USA*. New Delhi: Ministry of External Affairs, Government of India.

Narayanan, Arujunan. 1993. "Thailand's Strategic and Defence Policy." *Military Technology* 17: 43.

Narayanan, M. K. 1994. *National Security: The Internal Dimension*. RGICS Paper 16. New Delhi: Rajiv Gandhi Institute for Contemporary Studies, Rajiv Gandhi Foundation.

Nasution, Adnan Buyung. 1992. *The Aspiration for Constitutional Government in Indonesia: A Sociological Study of the Indonesian Konstituante 1956–1959*. Den Haag: CIP-Gegevens Koninklijke Bibliotheek.

Nathan, Andrew J., and Helen V. S. Ho. 1993. "Chiang Ching-kuo's Decision for Political Reform." In Shao-chuan Leng, ed., *Chiang Ching-kuo's Leadership in the Development of the Republic of China on Taiwan*. Lantham, Md.: University Press of America.

Nathan, K. S. 1983. "Nationalism and Foreign Policy: A Case Study of Indonesia Under Sukarno." *NUSANTARA* (Journal of the Arts and Social Sciences of Southeast Asia) 10: 28–47.

————. 1990. "Malaysia in 1989: Communists End Armed Struggle." *Asian Survey* 30, no. 2: 210–20.

————. 1994. "The Role of Malaysia and Singapore in Nation-Building and Southeast Asian Regonalism." Seminar paper delivered at the Fourth Malaysia-Singapore Forum, Petaling Jaya, 8–11 Dec.

————. 1995. "Vision 2020: Strategic Evolution and the Mahathir Impact." In *Southeast Asian Affairs 1995*. Singapore: Institute of Southeast Asian Studies.

"National Defense Program Outline in and After FY 1996." 1995. Mimeographed.

National Defense Report Editorial Group (NDREG), Ministry of Defense. 1994. *Guofang baogaoshu* (National defense report). Taipei: Liming wenhua shiye.

National Defense University. 1989. *Kukmin Anbouisik Josa* (National survey of security perception). Seoul: National Defense University.

————. 1996. *Bomkukmin Anbouisik Josabunsok* (Survey and analysis of pan-national security perception). Seoul: National Defense University.

National Economic and Development Authority. 1993–94. "Highlights of the Medium-Term Development Plan, 1993–1998." *Kasarinlan* 9, no. 2–3: 125–35.

National Security Council (NSC). 1993. "Organization for National Security." NSC Secretariat, Quezon City. Unclassified and unpublished document.

National Security Strategy of Thailand in the Next Decade. 1993. Bangkok: Strategic Research Institute.

National Unification Board. 1988. *The Economies of South and North Korea.* Seoul: National Unification Board.

Nayar, Baldev Raj. 1976. *American Geopolitics and India.* New Delhi: Manohar.

Neher, Clark D., and Ross Marlay. 1995. *Democracy and Development in Southeast Asia: The Winds of Change.* Boulder, Colo.: Westview.

Nehru, Jawaharlal. 1981. *The Discovery of India.* New Delhi: Jawaharlal Nehru Memorial Fund / Oxford University Press.

————. 1983a. *India's Foreign Policy: Selected Speeches, September 1946–April 1961.* New Delhi: Ministry of Information and Broadcasting, Government of India.

————. 1983b. *Jawaharlal Nehru's Speeches.* Vol. 1, *September 1946–May 1949.* New Delhi: Ministry of Information and Broadcasting, Government of India.

————. 1994. *The Discovery of India.* New Delhi: Oxford University Press.

Nelson, Frederick M. 1965. "The World Outlook of the Chinese Empire." In Joel Larus, ed., *Comparative World Politics.* Belmont, Calif.: Wadsworth.

Nesadurai, Helen E. 1996. "APEC: A Tool for U.S. Regional Domination?" *Pacific Review* 9, no. 1: 31–57.

National Economic and Social Development Board (NESDB). 1995. *National Economic and Social Development Annual Report* (in Thai). Bangkok: NESDB.

Nguyen Duy Hinh. 1993. "Vai Nhan Thuc So Bo ve Phuong Phap Dieu Tra Ton Giao Hoc o Ha Noi" (Some preliminary perceptions on the census method concerning religion in Hanoi). In Bui Dinh Thanh, ed., *Chinh Sach Xa Hoi: Mot So Van De Ly Luan va Thuc Tien* (Social policy: some theoretical and practical issues). Hanoi: Nha Xuat Ban Vien Khoa Hoc Xa Hoi Viet Nam.

Nguyen Ngoc Truong. 1994. "Foreign Policy in the Period of Renovation." *Tuan Bao Quoc Te,* 6–12 Jan. Translation in Foreign Broadcast Information Service, East Asian Service, FBIS-EAS-94-062 (31 Mar. 1994).

Nguyen Thanh Lieng. 1990. "Be Ready to Fight and Defend the Fatherland's Islands and Archipelagoes." *Tap Chi Quoc Phong Toan Dan,* Aug.–Sept. Translation in Foreign Broadcast Information Service, East Asian Service, FBIS-EAS-90-206 (24 Oct. 1990).

Nhi Le. 1994. "The Problem and Reality of 'Hot Spots' in Thanh Hoa." *Tap Chi Cong San,* Mar. Translation in Foreign Broadcast Information Service, East Asian Service, FBIS-EAS-94-115 (15 June 1994).

Nihon Enerugi Keizai Kenkyu-jo. 1993. *Kokusai Sekiyu-josei no Chuchoki-teki Tenbo to Wagakuni no Sekiyu Antei-kyokyu Seisaku no Aritaka* (Mid- to long-term prospects of the international petroleum situation and Japan's policy for a stable petroleum supply). Tokyo: Okurasho Insatsu-kyoku.

Ninh, Kim. 1996. "Revolution, Politics, and Culture in Socialist Vietnam, 1945–1965." Ph.D. diss., Yale University.

Niou, Emerson M. S., and Peter C. Ordeshook. 1984. "Alliances Versus Federations: An Analysis with Military and Economic Capabilities Distinguished." Manuscript.

Nissan, Elisabeth. 1996. *Sri Lanka: A Bitter Harvest.* London: Minority Rights Group International.

Nolan, Janne E. 1994. "The Concept of Cooperative Security." In Janne E. Nolan, ed., *Global Engagement: Cooperation and Security in the Twenty-first Century.* Washington, D.C.: Brookings Institution.

Noland, Marcus. 1996. "The North Korean Economy." *Joint U.S.–Korea Academic Studies* 6: 127–72.

Nolledo, Jose N. 1990. *The New Constitution of the Philippines Annotated.* Manila: National Bookstore.

Noor Ahmad Baba. 1993. "Organization of the Islamic Conference: Conceptual Framework and Institutional Structure." *International Studies* 30, no. 1: 35–51.

North Korea: The Foundations of Military Strength. 1991. Washington, D.C.: Defense Intelligence Agency.

"North Korea: The Nuclear Card." 1990. *Far Eastern Economic Review,* 31 May, p. 24.

Nu, U. 1958. *Premier Reports to the People on Law and Order, National Solidarity, Social Welfare, National Economy, Foreign Affairs.* Speech delivered by the Prime Minister U Nu in the Chamber of Deputies, 27 Sept. 1957. Rangoon: Central Printing Office.

———. 1960. "Speech by the Hon'ble U Nu, Prime Minister of the Union of Burma, in the Chamber of Deputies on April 28, 1960." Directorate of Information, Rangoon.

Nye, Joseph S. 1988. "Neorealism and Neoliberalism." *World Politics* 40, no. 2: 235–51.

Obeyesekere, Gananath. 1995. "On Buddhist Identity in Sri Lanka." In Lola Romanucci-Ross and George DeVos, eds., *Ethnic Identity: Creation, Conflict, and Accommodation.* Walnut Creek, Calif.: Altamira.

Observer. 1997. "8 developing Islamic nations establish 'D-8.'" 15 June, p. 1.

Oerlemans, Johannes. 1989. "A Projection of Future Sea Level." *Climatic Change* 15, nos. 1–2: 151–74.

Oh, Kong Dan. 1991. *Leadership Change in North Korean Politics: The Succession to Kim Il Sung.* R-3697-RC. Santa Monica, Calif.: Rand.

Okabe, Tatsumi. 1996. "Chugoku Gaiko no Koten-teki Seikaku" (The classic nature of Chinese diplomacy). *Gaiko Forum* 88 (Jan.): 37–45.

Olsen, Edward A. 1986. "The Arms Race on the Korean Peninsula." *Asian Survey* 26, no. 8: 851–67.

Onuf, Nicholas. 1989. *World of Our Making*. Columbia: University of South Carolina Press.

Oren, Ido. 1996. "The Subjectivity of the 'Democratic' Peace: Changing U.S. Perceptions of Imperial Germany." In Michel E. Brown, Sean M. Lynn-Jones, and Steven E. Miller, eds., *Debating the Democratic Peace*. Cambridge, Mass.: MIT Press.

Organski, A. F. K. 1968. *World Politics*. New York: Knopf.

Orr, Robert M., Jr. 1990. *The Emergence of Japan's Foreign Aid Power*. New York: Columbia University Press.

———. 1993. "Japanese Foreign Aid: Over a Barrel in the Middle East." In Bruce M. Koppel and Robert M. Orr, Jr., eds., *Japan's Foreign Aid: Power and Policy in a New Era*. Boulder, Colo.: Westview.

Owada, Hisashi. 1996. *Gaiko towa Nani-ka* (What is diplomacy?) Tokyo: NHK Shuppan.

Owen, John M. 1996. "How Liberalism Produces Democratic Peace." In Michel E. Brown, Sean M. Lynn-Jones, and Steven E. Miller, eds., *Debating the Democratic Peace*. Cambridge, Mass.: MIT Press.

Ozawa, Ichiro. 1994. *Blueprint for a New Japan: The Rethinking of a Nation*. Tokyo: Kondansha International.

Pabottingi, Mochtar. 1995a. "Dilema Legitimasi Orde Baru: Bayangan Krisis Politik dan Arah Pemecahannya." In Syamsuddin Haris and Riza Sihbudi, eds., *Menelaah Kembali Format Politik Orde Baru*. Jakarta: Gramedia Pustaka Utama.

———. 1995b. "Indonesia: Historicizing the New Order's Legitimacy Dilemma." In Muthiah Alagappa, ed., *Political Legitimacy in Southeast Asia*. Stanford: Stanford University Press.

Pakistan National Report to the UNCED. 1992. Karachi: Government of Pakistan / JRC-IUCN.

Palme Commission. 1982. *Common Security: A Blueprint for Survival*. New York: Simon and Schuster.

Palmer, Norman. 1962. *The Indian Political System*. Boston: Houghton Mifflin.

Panikkar, K. M. 1960. *A Survey of Indian History*. Bombay: Asia Publishing House.

Pant, K. C. 1988. "Introductory Address." In Raja Ramanna, ed., *National Security and Modern Technology*. USI National Security Lecture Series. New Delhi: United Service Institution of India.

Parekh, Bhikku, and Thomas Pantham, eds. 1987. *Political Discourse: Explorations in Indian and Western Political Thought*. New Delhi: Sage.

Paribatra, Sukhumbhand. 1984. "Strategic Implications of the Indochina Conflict: Thai Perspectives." *Asian Affairs* 11, no. 3: 28–46.

———. 1988a. "The Security of the Sea Lanes: Perspective of Thailand." In Lau Teik Soon and Lee Lai To, eds., *The Security of the Sea Lanes in the Asia-Pacific Region*. Singapore: Heinemann.

———. 1988b. "Thailand: Defence Spending and Threat Perception." In Chin Kim Wah, ed., *Defence Spending in Southeast Asia*. Singapore: Institute of Southeast Asian Studies.

Park, Jae-kyu, ed. 1983. *Pukhan-ui Kunsa Chong-ch'aek* (The military policy of North Korea). Seoul: Kyungnam Institute for Far Eastern Studies.

Park, Kwon-sang. 1982. "North Korea Under Kim Chong-il." *Journal of Northeast Asian Studies* 1, no. 2: 45–61.

Park, Moon Young. 1994–95. "Lure North Korea." *Foreign Policy*, no. 97 (Winter): 97–105.

Park, Sang-Seek. 1993. "Northern Diplomacy and Inter-Korean Relations." In James Cotton, ed., *Korea Under Roh Tae-Woo: Democratization, Northern Policy and Inter-Korean Relations*. Canberra: Allen and Unwin.

Parreñas, Julius Ceasar. 1993. "Transition and Continuity in the Philippines, 1992." In Daljit Singh, ed., *Southeast Asian Affairs 1993*. Singapore: Institute of Southeast Asian Studies.

Pasha, Mustpha Kamal. 1996. "Security as Hegemony." *Alternatives* 21, no. 3: 283–302.

Paul, T. V. 1994. *Asymmetric Conflicts: War Initiation by Weaker Powers*. Cambridge, Eng.: Cambridge University Press.

People's Daily (*Renmin Ribao*). 1979. "Women jiang caiqu duozhong fangfa tong Taiwan dangju tebie shi tong Jiang Jingguo xiansheng shangtan zuguo tongyi" (We will use all means to discuss national reunification with Taiwan's authorities, especially with Mr. Chiang Ching-kuo). 6 Jan., p. 1.

Perkovich, George. 1993. "A Nuclear Third Way in South Asia." *Foreign Policy*, no. 91 (Summer): 85–104.

Perry, John Curtis. 1990. "Dateline North Korea: A Communist Holdout." *Foreign Policy*, no. 80 (Fall): 172–91.

Peterson, Peter G. 1992. "The Primacy of the Domestic Agenda." In Graham Allison and Gregory Treverton, eds., *Rethinking America's Security: Beyond the Cold War to New World Order*. New York: Norton.

Pfaffenberger, Bryan. 1990. "Ethnic Conflict and Youth Insurgency in Sri Lanka: The Social Origins of Tamil Separatism." In Joseph V. Montville, ed., *Conflict and Peacemaking in Multiethnic Societies*. Lexington, Mass.: Lexington Books.

Pham Duc Thanh, ed. 1996. *Vietnam–ASEAN*. Hanoi: Nha Xuat Ban Khoa Hoc Xa Hoi.

Pham Hung. 1982. *May Van De ve An Ninh Chinh Tri va Trat Tu An Toan Xa*

Hoi trong Tinh Hinh Moi (Some issues on political security and social order and safety in the new situation). Hanoi: Nha Xuat Ban Cong An Nhan Dan.

Pham Van Tho. 1994. "Hai Hung Renovates and Reorganizes the Party and Changes the Economic Structure." *Tap Chi Cong San*, Sept. Translation in Foreign Broadcast Information Service, East Asian Service, FBIS-EAS-94-231 (1 Dec. 1994).

Phan Doan Nam. 1988. "Mot Vai Suy Nghi ve Doi Moi Tu Duy Doi Ngoai" (Some thoughts on the renovation of external thinking). *Tap Chi Cong San*, Feb.

———. 1991. "The Problem of How to Coordinate Security, National Defense, and Foreign Affairs in the New Revolutionary Stage." *Tap Chi Cong San*, Mar. Translation in Foreign Broadcast Information Service, East Asian Service, FBIS-EAS-90-079 (24 Apr. 1991).

Phan Hai Nam. 1990. "East Europe: Some Reflections." *Quan Doi Nhan Dan*. Broadcast on Hanoi Domestic Service, 10 Apr. Translation in Foreign Broadcast Information Service, East Asian Service, FBIS-EAS-90-074 (17 Apr. 1990).

———. 1993. "Are They Prompted by Religious Aims?" *Quan Doi Nhan Dan*, 9 Aug. Translation in Foreign Broadcast Information Service, East Asian Service, FBIS-EAS-93-153 (11 Aug. 1993).

Phan Ngoc. 1994. *Van Hoa Viet Nam va Cach Tiep Can Moi* (Vietnamese culture and the new way to interface). Hanoi: Nha Xuat Ban Van Hoa-Thong Tin.

"Philippine Left" (special issue). 1992. *Kasarinlan* 8, no. 1.

Phiu-nual, Chalermkiet. 1990. *Thai Style Democracy: The Political Thought of the Thai Military 1976–1986*. Bangkok: Thai Khadi Institute, Thammasat University.

Phongpaichit, Pasuk, and Chris Baker. 1995. *Thailand: Economy and Politics*. New York: Oxford University Press.

Pike, Douglas. 1986. *PAVN: People's Army of Vietnam*. Novato, Calif.: Presidio.

———. 1987. *Vietnam and the Soviet Union: Anatomy of an Alliance*. Boulder, Colo.: Westview.

Pillay, K. K. 1963. *South India and Ceylon*. Madras: University of Madras.

Pirages, Dennis C. 1978. *Global Eco-politics*. North Scituate, Mass.: Duxbury.

Piriyarangsan, Sangsidh, and Pasuk Phongpaichit, eds. 1996. *Consciousness and Ideology: Political Parties and Democratic Movement in Thailand* (in Thai). Bangkok: Chulalongkorn University.

Pitsuwan, Surin. 1985. *Islam and Malay Nationalism: A Case Study of the Malay-Muslims of Southern Thailand*. Bangkok: Thammasat University.

Policy Affairs Research Council of the Liberal Democratic Party. 1995. "Kongo no Boei-ryoku no Arikata" (How the future defense capability should be). Mimeographed.

Popper, Karl R. 1966. *The Open Society and Its Enemies.* 2 vols. Princeton: Princeton University Press.

Porter, Gareth. 1987. *The Politics of Counterinsurgency in the Philippines: Military and Political Options.* Philippine Studies occasional paper 9. Honolulu: Center for Philippine Studies, Centers for Asian and Pacific Studies, University of Hawaii.

Posen, Barry R. 1993. "The Security Dilemma and Ethnic Conflict." In Michael E. Brown, ed. *Ethnic Conflict and International Security.* Princeton: Princeton University Press.

Poumisak, Jit. 1979. *The Face of Thai Feudalism.* Bangkok: Saengngoen.

Pour, Julius. 1993. *Benny Moerdani: Profile of a Soldier Statesman.* Translated by Tim Scott. Jakarta: Yayasan Kejuangan Panglima Besar Sudirma.

Powell, Robert. 1991. "Absolute and Relative Gains in International Relations Theory." *American Political Science Review* 85, no. 4: 1303–19.

———. 1996. "Stability and the Distribution of Power." *World Politics* 48, no. 2: 239–67.

Prasad, Krishna. 1995. "Nuclear Showdown." *Outlook* (New Delhi), 20 Dec., pp. 12–13.

Prawirasoebrata, Soebijakto. 1989. "Indonesia's Perception of Southeast Asia." Jakarta: Indonesian Executive Circle.

Purrington, Courtney. 1992. "Tokyo's Responses During the Gulf War and the Impact of the Iraq Shock on Japan." *Pacific Affairs* 65, no. 2: 161–81.

Qazi, Lt. Col. Shamsul Haq. 1964. "A Case for Citizen Army." *Pakistan Army Journal* 6, no. 1: 18–25.

Quadir, Vice Admiral Iqbal F. 1988. "Maritime Threats and Pakistan's Security." *Defence Journal* 14, no. 3: 18–20.

Quang Loi. 1990. "Beyond Containment: Washington's Quiet Crusade." *Quan Doi Nhan Dan,* 26 Apr. Translation in Foreign Broadcast Information Service, East Asian Service, FBIS-EAS-90-084 (1 May 1990).

Quinn-Judge, Sophie. 1997. "Building a Bulwark." *Far Eastern Economic Review,* 27 Mar., p. 24.

Qureshi, Saleem M. M. 1993. "Regionalism, Ethnic Conflict, and Islam in Pakistan." In Hafeez Malik, ed., *Dilemmas of National Security and Cooperation in India and Pakistan.* New York: St. Martin's.

Ra'anan, Uri. 1990. "The Nation-State Fallacy." In Joseph V. Montville, ed., *Conflict and Peacemaking in Multiethnic Societies.* Lexington, Mass.: Lexington Books.

Rabinow, Paul, ed. 1984. *The Foucault Reader.* New York: Pantheon.

Rahman, I. A. 1994. "The Lessons of Malakand." *Newsline,* Nov.

Rahman, M. Habibur. 1989. "Delimitation of Maritime Boundaries: Some Pertinent Issues for Bangladesh." In Shaukat Hassan and M. G. Kabir, ed., *Issues and Challenges Facing Bangladesh Foreign Policy.* Dhaka: BSIS.

Rahman, Tunku Abdul. 1986. *Challenging Times.* Edited by J. S. Solomon. Petaling Jaya: Pelanduk.

Rajah, Ananda. 1994. "Burma: Protracted Social Conflict and Displacement." Paper presented at the International Conference on Transnational Migration in the Asia-Pacific Region, Bangkok, 1–2 Dec.

Rajan, M. S. 1995. "Reforming the Sovereign State System: A Non-aligned Perspective." In Kanti P. Bajpai and Harish C. Shukul, eds., *Interpreting World Politics*. New Delhi: Sage.

Rajaratnam, S. 1965. Untitled speech delivered at the United Nations General Assembly.

———. 1988. "Evolving a Foreign Policy for Singapore." Text of a talk delivered at the Institute for Policy Studies, Singapore.

———. 1990. "Rocks, Faith and Miracles." Text of a talk delivered to the Alpha Society and Temasek Society, Singapore.

Rajgopal, P. R. 1988. *Violence and Response: A Critique of the Indian Criminal Justice System*. New Delhi: Uppal.

Rajiv Gandhi Memorial Initiative. 1993. *Rajiv Gandhi Memorial Initiative for the Advancement of Human Civilization*. Documents on Disarmament. New Delhi: Rajiv Gandhi Foundation.

Ramamurthi, T. G. 1994. "India, South Africa and the Indian Ocean." *Journal of Indian Ocean Studies* (New Delhi) 1: 8–14.

Ramos, Fidel V. 1992. "To Win the Future." Inaugural address of the President of the Republic of the Philippines, 30 June.

———. 1993. *To Win the Future: People Empowerment and National Development*. Manila: FOSE.

———. 1993–94. "Philippines 2000: Our Development Strategy." *Kasarinlan* 9, nos. 2–3: 120–24.

———. 1995. *From Growth to Modernization: Raising the Political Capacity and Strengthening the Social Commitments of the Philippine State*. Manila: FOSE.

Rana, A. P. 1976. *The Imperatives of Nonalignment*. Delhi: Macmillan.

Rangarajan, L. N., trans., ed. 1992. *The Arthashastra*, by Kautilya. New Delhi: Penguin.

Rashid, Abbas, and Farida Shaheed. 1993. *Pakistan: Ethno-Politics and Contending Elites*. Geneva: United Nations Research Institute for Social Development.

Rashid, Ahmed. 1988. "Keeping the Generals Happy." *Far Eastern Economic Review*, 8 Dec., pp. 13–14.

———. 1996. "Who Will Bell the Cat on Taxes?" *News*, 6 Jan.

———. 1997. "Power Grab." *Far Eastern Economic Review*, 23 Jan., p. 20.

Rawls, John. 1971. *A Theory of Justice*. Cambridge, Mass.: Harvard University Press.

Razak, Mohammad Najib Tun. 1995. *Asia-Pacific's Strategic Outlook: The Shifting of Paradigms*. Petaling Jaya: Pelanduk.

Reinhardt, Jon M. 1971. *Foreign Policy and National Integration: The Case of Indonesia*. New Haven: Southeast Asian Studies, Yale University.

Rejai, Mostafa, and Cynthia H. Enloe. 1969. "Nation-States and State-Nations." *International Studies Quarterly* 13, no. 2: 140–58.

Renan, Ernest. 1970. "What Is a Nation?" In Robert A. Goldwin, ed., *Readings in World Politics*. New York: Oxford University Press.

Renner, Michael. 1989. *National Security: The Economic and Environmental Dimensions*. Worldwatch Papers 89. Washington, D.C.: Worldwatch Institute.

Report on National Interests and Threats on the Border Areas (in Thai). 1995. Bangkok: National Security Council.

Reynolds, David. 1994. *The Origins of the Cold War in Europe: International Perspectives*. New Haven: Yale University Press.

Rhee, Kang Suk. 1987. "North Korea's Pragmatism a Turning Point?" *Asian Survey* 27, no. 8: 885–902.

Rhee, Sangwoo. 1986. *Hankukui Anbowhankyung* (Security environment of South Korea). Seoul: Sokang University Press.

Richardson, Michael. 1995. "China-Burma Ties Upset Neighbours." *International Herald Tribune*, 7 Apr.

Richter, William L. 1989. "Pakistan Under Benazir Bhutto." *Current History* 88, no. 542: 433–56.

Riedinger, Jeffrey. 1994. "The Philippines in 1993: Halting Steps Toward Liberalization." *Asian Survey* 34, no. 2: 139–46.

———. 1995. "The Philippines in 1994: Renewed Growth and Contested Reforms." *Asian Survey* 35, no. 2: 209–16.

Riggs, Fred W. 1966. *Thailand: The Modernization of a Bureaucratic Polity*. Honolulu: East-West Center.

Rivera, Temario C. 1994a. "Armed Challenges to the Philippine Government: Protracted War or Political Settlement?" In Daljit Singh, ed., *Southeast Asian Affairs 1994*. Singapore: Institute for Southeast Asian Studies.

———. 1994b. "The State, Civil Society, and Foreign Actors: The Politics of Philippine Industrialization." *Contemporary Southeast Asia* 16, no. 2: 157–77.

Rizvi, Gowher. 1993. *South Asia in a Changing International Order*. New Delhi: Sage.

Rizvi, Hasan-Askari. 1988. "National Security, Domestic Politics and the Military." *Defence Journal* 14, no. 12: 3–18.

———. 1991. "The Military and Politics in Pakistan." In Charles H. Kennedy and David J. Loucher, eds., *Civil-Military Intervention in Asia and Africa*. Leiden: Brill.

Roberts, Adam. 1993. "The United Nations and International Security." In Michael E. Brown ed., *Ethnic Conflict and International Society*. Princeton: Princeton University Press.

Robinson, Thomas, and David Shambaugh, eds. 1994. *Chinese Foreign Policy: Theory and Practice*. New York: Oxford University Press.

Rocamora, Joel. 1994. *Breaking Through: The Struggle Within the Communist Party of the Philippines.* Quezon City: Anvil Press.

Rockeman, R. Kent, and Bert A. Weaver. 1993. *Do Institutions Matter?* Washington, D.C.: Brookings Institution.

Rodan, Garry. 1993. "Preserving the One-Party State in Contemporary Singapore." In Kevin Hewison, Richard Robison, and Garry Rodan, eds., *Southeast Asia in the 1990s: Authoritarianism, Democracy and Capitalism.* Sydney: Allen and Unwin.

Romanucci-Ross, Lola, and Georg De Vos, eds. 1995. *Ethnic Identity: Creation, Conflict and Accommodation.* Walnut Creek, Calif.: Altamira.

Romm, Joseph J. 1993. *Defining National Security: The Nonmilitary Aspects.* New York: Council on Foreign Relations.

Rose, Leo E. 1987. "India's Regional Policy: Non-military Dimensions." In Stephen P. Cohen, ed., *The Security of South Asia: American and Asian Perspectives.* Urbana: University of Illinois Press.

Rosecrance, Richard. 1986. *The Rise of the Trading State: Commerce and Conquest in the Modern World.* New York: Basic Books.

Rosecrance, Richard, and Arthur Stein, eds. 1993. *The Domestic Bases of Grand Strategy.* Ithaca, N.Y.: Cornell University Press.

Rosen, Stephen Peter. 1995. "Military Effectiveness: Why Society Matters." *International Security* 19, no. 4: 5–31.

Rosen, Steven J. 1977. "A Stable System of Mutual Nuclear Deterrence in the Arab-Israeli Conflict." *American Political Science Review* 71, no. 4: 1367–83.

Rosenau, James N. 1989. "Global Changes and Theoretical Challenges." In Ernst-Otto Czempiel and James N. Rosenau, eds., *Global Changes and Theoretical Challenges: Approach to World Politics for the 1990s.* Lexington, Mass.: Lexington Books.

———. 1994. "New Dimensions of Security: The Interaction of Globalizing and Localizing Dynamics." *Security Dialogue* 25, no. 3: 255–81.

Rosenberg, David, ed. 1979. *Marcos and Martial Law in the Philippines.* Ithaca, N.Y.: Cornell University Press.

Rossabi, Morris. 1983. Introduction to Morris Rossabi, ed., *China Among Equals: The Middle Kingdom and Its Neighbors, Tenth–Fourteenth Centuries.* Berkeley: University of California Press.

Roy, Denny. 1994. "North Korea and the Madman Theory." *Security Dialogue* 25, no. 3: 307–16.

———. 1996. "Hegemon on the Horizon? China's Threat to East Asian Security." In Michael E. Brown, Sean M. Lynn-Jones, and Steven E. Miller, eds., *East Asian Security.* Cambridge, Mass.: MIT Press.

Rubin, Barnett R. 1989–90. "The Fragmentation of Afghanistan." *Foreign Affairs* 68, no. 5: 150–168.

———. 1995. *The Fragmentation of Afghanistan: State Formation and Collapse of the International System.* New Haven: Yale University Press.

Ruggie, John G. 1983. "Continuity and Transformation in the World Polity: Toward a Neorealist Synthesis." *World Politics* 35, no. 2: 261–85.

———. 1986. "Continuity and Transformation in the World Polity: Toward a Neorealist Synthesis." In Robert O. Keohane, ed., *Neorealism and Its Critics*. New York: Columbia University Press.

———. 1993a. "Multilateralism: The Anatomy of an Institution." In John G. Ruggie, ed., *Multilateralism Matters: The Theory and Praxis of an Institutional Form*. New York: Columbia University Press.

———. 1993b. Response to Ethan B. Kapstein. *International Organization* 47, no. 3: 503–5.

———. 1993c. "Territoriality and Beyond: Problematizing Modernity in International Relations." *International Organization* 47, no. 1: 139–74.

Rummel, R. J. 1983. "Libertarianism and International Violence." *Journal of Conflict Resolution* 27, no. 1: 27–71.

Russett, Bruce. 1993. *Grasping the Democratic Peace*. Princeton: Princeton University Press.

Russett, Bruce, Thomas Risse-Kappen, and John J. Mearsheimer. 1991. Comments by Russett and Risse-Kappen and rebuttal by Mearsheimer. *International Security* 15, no. 3: 216–22.

Sagan, Scott. 1994. "The Perils of Proliferation: Organization Theory, Deterrence Theory, and the Spread of Nuclear Weapons." *International Security* 18, no. 4: 66–107.

Sahni, Varun. 1996. "Going Nuclear: Establishing an Overt Nuclear Weapons Capability." In David Cortright and Amitabh Mattoo, eds., *India and the Bomb: Public Opinion and Nuclear Options*. Notre Dame, Ind.: University of Notre Dame Press.

Saldanha, Joao Mariano de Sousa. 1994. *The Political Economy of East Timor Development*. Jakarta: Pustaka Sinar Harapan.

Saleem, Lt. Col. Muhammad Ashraf. 1993. "Nuclear Deterrence: A Subcontinental Logic." *Defence Journal* 19, nos. 11–12: 23–28.

Salimi, Commodore S.B. 1988. "Maritime Defence of Pakistan." *Defence Journal* 14, no. 3: 21–23.

Salonga, Jovito. 1995. *The Senate That Said No*. Quezon City: University of the Philippines Press.

Samsung Economic Research Institute. 1996. *Nambukhan Tongil Sinario* (Scenarios for North-South Korean reunification). Seoul: Samsung Economic Research Institute.

Samudavanija, Chai-anan. 1982. *The Thai Young Turks*. Singapore: Institute of Southeast Asian Studies.

———. 1990. *State and Society: Thai's Three-Dimensional State in Siam Pluralistic Society* (in Thai). Bangkok: Chulalongkorn University Press.

———. 1993. *Economic Development and Conflict Resolution: The Case of Thailand* (in Thai). Bangkok: Chulalongkorn University Press.

———. 1994. *New Paradigm for the Study of State and Civil Society in Siam*

During the Globalization Era (in Thai). Bangkok: Institute of Public Policy Studies.

———. 1995. *A Century of Bureaucratic Restructure: An Evolution of State and Political Power* (in Thai). Bangkok: Institute of Public Policy Studies.

Samudavanija, Chai-anan, and Kusuma Snitwongse. 1992. *Environment and Security: Security of State and People's Insecurity* (in Thai). Bangkok: Institute of Security and International Studies.

Samudavanija, Chai-anan, Kusuma Snitwongse, and Suchit Bunbongkarn. 1990. *From Armed Suppression to Political Offensive.* Bangkok: Institute of Security and International Studies.

Samuels, Richard. 1994. *Rich Nation, Strong Army.* Ithaca, N.Y.: Cornell University Press.

Sanchez, Aurora. 1987. "The Philippine Economic Recovery: Some Issues." In Mohammed Ayoob, ed., *Southeast Asian Affairs 1987.* Singapore: Institute of Southeast Asian Studies.

Sandholtz, Wayne, Michael Borrus, John Zysman, Ken Conca, Jay Stowsky, Steven Vogel, and Steve Weber. 1992. *The Highest Stakes: The Economic Foundations of the New Security System.* New York: Oxford University Press.

Sandler, Shmuel. 1995. "Ethnonationalism and the Foreign Policy of Nation-States." *Nationalism and Ethnic Politics* 1, no. 2: 250–69.

Sanford, Dan C. 1990. *South Korea and the Socialist Countries: The Politics of Trade.* London: Macmillan.

Sanger, David E. 1992. "North Korea and the A-Bomb: Fear Is Fading." *New York Times*, 18 Sept., p. A4.

———. 1993. "North Korea Knew of West's Evidence on Atomic Program." *New York Times*, 13 Mar., p. A1.

Santasombat, Yos. 1989. "Leadership and Security in Modern Thai Politics." In Mohammed Ayoob and Chai-anan Samudavanija, eds., *Leadership Perceptions and National Security: The Southeast Asian Experience.* Singapore: Institute of Southeast Asian Studies.

Sarin, H. C. 1979. *Defence and Development.* USI National Security Lecture. New Delhi: United Service Institution of India.

Sarpay Beikman. 1992. *Zarti Man Sarpay Sardan Myar* (Patriotic literature). Proceedings of the Symposium on Patriotic Literature, Yangon, 27–29 Jan. 2 vols. Yangon: Sarpay Beikman.

Sartori, Giovanni. 1984. "Guidelines for Concept Analysis." In Giovanni Sartori, ed., *Social Science Concepts: A Systematic Analysis.* Beverly Hills: Sage.

Satha-Anan, Chaiwat. 1995. "Defense Budgeting." Paper presented at ISIS-SIPRI Workshop on Arms Procurement Decision Making in Thailand, Bangkok, 1 Mar.

Sayigh, Yezid. 1990. "Confronting the 1990s: Security of the Developing Countries." Adelphi Paper 251. London: IISS.

Scalapino, Robert A. 1988. Introduction to Robert A. Scalapino, Seizaburo

Sato, Jusuf Wanandi, and Sung-Joo Han, eds., *Asian Security Issues: Regional and Global*. Research Papers and Policy Studies 26. Berkeley: University of California, Institute of East Asian Studies.

Scharfe, Hartmut. 1989. *The State in Indian Tradition*. Leiden: E. J. Brill.

Scheff, Thomas. 1994. "Emotions and Identity: A Theory of National Security." In Craig Calhoun, ed., *Social Theory and the Politics of Identity*. Cambridge, Mass.: Blackwell.

Schirmer, Daniel B., and Stephen R. Shalom, eds. 1987. *The Philippines Reader: A History of Colonialism, Neocolonialism, Dictatorship, and Resistance*. Quezon City: Ken.

Schroeder, Paul W. 1986. "The Nineteenth-Century International System: Changes in the Structure." *World Politics* 39, no. 1: 1–26.

———. 1995. "The Author Replies." *International Security* 20, no. 1: 193–95.

Schultz, Richard, Roy Godson, and Ted Greenwood, eds. 1993. *Security Studies for the 1990s*. New York: Brassey's.

Schwartz, Benjamin I. 1968. "The Chinese Perception of World Order, Past and Present." In John K. Fairbank, ed., *The Chinese World Order: Traditional China's Foreign Relations*. Cambridge, Mass.: Harvard University Press.

Schwarz, Adam. 1996a. "Culture Shock." *Far Eastern Economic Review*, 22 Aug., p. 63.

———. 1996b. "Struggle or Smuggle." *Far Eastern Economic Review*, 22 Feb., p. 26–27.

Schwarz, Adam, and Matt Forney. 1996. "Oil on Troubled Waters." *Far Eastern Economic Review*, 25 Apr., p. 65.

Schweller, Randall L., and David Priess. 1997. "A Tale of Two Realisms: Expanding the Institutions Debate." *Mershon International Studies Review* 41, no. 1: 1–32.

Sciolino, Elaine. 1996. "Taiwan's Powerful Lobby Strives to Win Friends for 'Good' China." *New York Times*, 9 Apr.

"Security Situation on the Korean Peninsula." 1994. Joint hearing before the Subcommittee on International Security, International Organizations, and Human Rights and the Subcommittee on Asia and the Pacific of the Committee on Foreign Affairs. Washington, D.C.: Government Printing Office.

Segal, Gerald. 1992. "Managing New Arms Races in the Asia-Pacific." *Washington Quarterly* 15, no. 3: 83–101.

———. 1996. "East Asia and the Constrainment of China." In Michael E. Brown, Sean M. Lynn-Jones, and Steven E. Miller, eds., *East Asian Security*. Cambridge, Mass.: MIT Press.

Sein, Ba. 1995. "Welcome and Congratulate the Fourth Congregation of the Sangha of All Orders." *The New Light of Myanmar*, 14 Mar.

Selth, Andrew. 1986. "Race and Resistance in Burma, 1942–1945." *Modern Asian Studies* 20, no. 3: 483–507.

————. 1995. "Burma and the Strategic Competition Between China and India." Paper presented at the Conference on Myanmar Towards the Twenty-first Century: Dynamics of Continuity and Change, Bangkok, 1–3 June.

————. 1996. "Transforming the Tatmadaw: The Burmese Armed Forces Since 1988." Canberra Papers on Strategy and Defence 113. Canberra: Strategic and Defence Studies Centre, Australian National University.

Sen, Amartya. 1990. *On Ethics and Economics*. New Delhi: Oxford University Press.

Senate Committee on Armed Services. 1992. *DOD Authorization for Appropriations for Fiscal Year 1993 and Future Years of Defense Program*. Washington, D.C.: Government Printing Office.

Senate Members Registry (in Thai). 1993. Bangkok: Secretariat of the Senate.

Settabut, Noranit. 1987. "The Thai Armed Forces as a Political Institution" (in Thai). Monograph Series, no. 38. Bangkok: Faculty of Political Science Research Center, Thammasat University.

Shaw Yu-ming. 1989. "Zhonghua minguo zhi dalu zhengce" (The mainland policy of the Republic of China). *Ming Pao* (Hong Kong), 10 Oct., p. 5.

Shelley, Mizanur Rahman, ed. 1992. *The Chittagong Hill Tracts of Bangladesh: The Untold Story*. Dhaka: CDR.

Shultz, Richard, Roy Godson, and Ted Greenwood, eds. 1993. *Security Studies for the 1990s*. New York: Brassey's.

Siddiqi, Abdul Rahman. 1988. "Drugs and National Security." *Defence Journal* 14, no. 8: 1–7.

Siddiqui, Kamal. 1987. *The Political Economy of Rural Poverty in Bangladesh*. Dhaka: NILG.

Sidel, John T. 1995. "Coercion, Capital and the Post-Colonial State: Bossism in the Post-War Philippines." Ph.D. diss., Cornell University.

Sidhu, W. P. S. 1997. "Of Oral Traditions and Ethnocentric Judgements." In George K. Tanham, Kanti Bajpai, and Amitabh Mattoo, eds., *Securing India: Strategic Thought and Practice*. New Delhi: Manohar.

Siffin, William J. 1966. *The Thai Bureaucracy: Institutional Change and Development*. Honolulu: East-West Center.

Silverman, Jerry M. 1974. "Historic National Rivalries and Interstate Conflict in Mainland Southeast Asia." In Mark W. Zacher and R. Stephen Milne, eds., *Conflict and Stability in Southeast Asia*. New York: Anchor Books.

Silverstein, Josef. 1980. *Burmese Politics: The Dilemma of National Unity*. New Brunswick, N.J.: Rutgers University Press.

Singh, Bilveer. 1995. *East Timor, Indonesia and the World: Myths and Realities*. Singapore: Singapore Institute of International Affairs.

Singh, Dilbagh. N.d. "India's Defence Policy and Doctrine for the Eighties." In Gautam Sen, ed., *India's Security Considerations in the Nuclear Age*. New Delhi: Atlantic.

Singh, Hari. 1995. "UMNO Leaders and Malay Rulers: The Erosion of a Special Relationship." *Pacific Affairs* 68, no. 2: 187–205.

Singh, Jasjit. 1992. "Trends in Defence Expenditures." In Jasjit Singh, ed., *Asian Strategic Review 1991–92*. New Delhi: Institute for Defence Studies and Analyses.

Singh, K. R. 1995. *The Making of an Indian Ocean Community*. New Delhi: Jain Brothers.

Singh, S. Nihal. 1986. *Yogi and the Bear: The Story of Indo-Soviet Relations*. New Delhi: Allied.

Sinnadurai, Visu. 1978. "The Citizenship Laws of Malaysia." In Tun Mohamed Suffian, H. P. Lee, and F. A. Trindade, eds., *The Constitution of Malaysia: Its Development, 1957–1977*. Kuala Lumpur: Oxford University Press.

Sinsawasdi, Narong. 1986. "Power's Struggling Behavior in Thai Society" (in Thai). Monograph Series, no. 49. Bangkok: Faculty of Political Science Research Center, Thammasat University.

———. 1996. *Thai Politics: A Psychological Analysis* (in Thai). Bangkok: Oriental Scholar.

Sison, Jose Maria, with Rainer Werning. 1989. *The Philippine Revolution: The Leader's View*. New York: Cane Russak.

Six Decades of Democracy in S. Sivaraksa's Viewpoint (in Thai). 1994. Document from the television talk show "Different Perspectives" with Chermsak Pinthong and Chamlong Srimuang. Bangkok: Kred Thai.

SLORC Information Committee. 1990. *Press Conferences, Book Four*. Yangon: News and Periodicals Enterprise.

Smith, Anthony D. 1983. *State and the Nation in the Third World*. New York: St. Martin's.

———. 1986. *The Ethnic Origins of Nations*. Oxford: Blackwell.

———. 1991. *National Identity*. Las Vegas: University of Nevada Press.

Smith, Chris. 1994. *India's Ad Hoc Arsenal: Direction or Drift in Defence Policy?* Oxford: Oxford University Press.

Smith, Richard J. 1994. *China's Cultural Heritage: The Qing Dynasty, 1644–1912*. Boulder, Colo.: Westview.

Sneider, Richard L. 1982. *U.S.–Japanese Security Relations: A Historical Perspective*. Occasional paper. New York: East Asian Institute, Columbia University.

Snidal, Duncan. 1991. "Relative Gains and the Pattern of International Cooperation." *American Political Science Review* 85, no. 3: 701–26.

Snitwongse, Kusuma. 1994. "Thailand in 1993: Politics of Survival." *Asian Survey* 34, no. 2: 147–52.

Sobhan, Rehman, ed. 1991. *The Decade of Stagnation: The State of the Bangladesh Economy*. Dhaka: University Press.

———. 1993. *Bangladesh: Problems of Governance*. Dhaka: University Press.

Soenarso. 1970. "Indonesia and South East Asia." Speech presented at the

Foreign Correspondent Association of Southeast Asia Luncheon. Goodwood Park Hotel, Singapore, 3 Dec. Information Bulletin no. 027/Pen/-Ing/70, Indonesian Embassy, Singapore.

Soeya, Yoshihide. 1995. *Nihon-gaiko to Chugoku 1945–1972* (Japanese diplomacy and China 1945–1972). Tokyo: Keio University Press.

———. 1996. "The Japan–U.S. Alliance in a Changing Asia." *Japan Review of International Affairs* 10, no. 4: 265–75.

———. 1997. "Vietnam in Japan's Regional Policy." In James Morley and Masashi Nishihara, eds., *Vietnam Joins the World*. Armonk, N.Y.: M. E. Sharpe.

Sogo-anzenhosho Kenkyu-group (Comprehensive Security Study Group). 1980. *Sogo-anzenhosho Senryaku* (Comprehensive security strategy). Tokyo: Okurasho Insatsu-kyoku.

Sohn, Hakkyu. 1989. *Authoritarianism and Opposition in South Korea*. London: Routledge.

Sohn, Louis B. 1968. *Cases on United Nations Law*. Brooklyn: Foundation Press.

Solidum, Estrella D. 1994. "The Philippines: Moving the Country Forward." In Daljit Singh, ed., *Southeast Asian Affairs 1994*. Singapore: Institute of Southeast Asian Studies.

Solomon, Richard H., and Masataka Kosaka, eds. 1986. *The Soviet Far East Military Build-Up: Nuclear Dilemmas and Asian Security*. Dover, Mass.: Auburn House.

Song, Mun-hong. 1995. "Problematic Policy-Making on North Korea: Clumsy, Sensational, or Discordant?" *Shindonga*, Oct., pp. 259–61.

Song Thanh. 1992. "De Tu Tuong Ho Chi Minh Thuc Su Tro Thanh Kim Chi Nam cho Hanh Dong" (So that Ho Chi Minh thought will truly become the compass for action). *Tap Chi Cong San*, Mar.

Song, Young-dae. 1996. "Assessing Collapse Possibilities of the North Korean Regime." Paper presented at a conference organized by the National Institute of National Intelligence, Seoul, Dec.

Song, Young Sun. 1991. *The Korean Nuclear Issue*. Canberra: Department of International Relations, Australian National University.

Sopiee, Mohamed Noordin. 1974. *From Malayan Union to Singapore Separation: Political Unification in the Malaysia Region*. Kuala Lumpur: University of Malaya Press.

Sorenson, Georg. Forthcoming. *A State Is Not a State: Types of Statehood and Patterns of Conflict After the Cold War*.

Sorenson, Theodore C. 1990. "Rethinking National Security." *Foreign Affairs* 69, no. 3: 1–18.

South China Morning Post. 1988. "Red Carpet Treatment for Taiwanese Tourists." 1 June, p. 8.

Southerland, Daniel. 1987. "Taiwan to End 38-Year Ban on Travel to Mainland China." *Washington Post*, 20 Sept., p. A1.

————. 1988. "Taiwan Seen Expanding Unofficial Ties to China." *Washington Post*, 27 Feb., p. A19.

Spector, Leonard S. 1984. *Nuclear Proliferation Today: The Spread of Nuclear Weapons*. New York: Vintage.

Spector, Leonard S., and Jacqueline Smith. 1991. "North Korea: The Next Nuclear Nightmare?" *Arms Control Today* 21, no. 2: 9–21.

Spiro, David E. 1996. "The Insignificance of the Liberal Peace." In Michel E. Brown, Sean M. Lynn-Jones, and Steven E. Miller, eds., *Debating the Democratic Peace*. Cambridge, Mass.: MIT Press.

Steadman, John M. 1969. *The Myth of Asia: A Refutation of Western Stereotypes of Asian Religion, Philosophy, Art and Politics*. New York: Simon and Schuster.

Stein, Arthur. 1990. *Why Nations Cooperate*. Ithaca, N.Y.: Cornell University Press.

Steinberg, David I. 1982. *Burma: A Socialist Nation in Southeast Asia*. Boulder, Colo.: Westview.

————. 1984. "Constitutional and Political Bases of Minority Insurrections in Burma." In Lim Joo-Jock and S. Vani, eds., *Armed Separatism in Southeast Asia*. Singapore: Institute of Southeast Asian Studies.

————. 1992. "Myanmar in 1991: Military Intransigence." In *Southeast Asian Affairs 1992*. Singapore: Institute of Southeast Asian Studies.

————. 1993. "Liberalization in Myanmar: How Real Are the Changes? *Contemporary Southeast Asia* 15, no. 2: 161–78.

————. 1995. "The Republic of Korea: Pluralizing Politics." In Larry Diamond, ed., *Democracy in Asia*. Boulder, Colo.: Westview.

————. 1996. "Myanmar's Political Economy: Opportunities and Tensions." *Asean-ISIS Monitor* 13 (Mar.): 14–18.

Stockholm International Peace Research Institute. 1994. *SIPRI Yearbook 1994*. London: Oxford University Press.

Strang, David. 1991. "Anomaly and Commonplace in European Political Expansion: Realist and Institutionalist Accounts." *International Organization* 45, no. 2: 143–62.

Strategic Thinking. 1996. Bangkok: Strategic Research Institute.

Subrahmanyam, K. 1972. *Bangladesh and India's Security*. Dehra Dun: Palit and Dutt.

————. 1976. "Nehru and the India-China Conflict of 1962." In B. R. Nanda, ed., *Indian Foreign Policy: The Nehru Years*. Honolulu: University of Hawaii Press.

————. 1984. "Regional Conflicts and Nuclear Fears." *Bulletin of the Atomic Scientists* 40, no. 5: 16–19.

Suh, Dae-suk. 1968. *The Korean Communist Movement, 1918–1948*. Princeton: Princeton University Press.

————. 1988. *Kim Il Sung: The North Korean Leader*. New York: Columbia University Press.

Suharto. 1970. Speech at an official function in Kuala Lumpur, 18 Mar.

Information Bulletin no. 008/Pen/IND/70, Indonesian Embassy, Singapore.

Suhrke, Astri. 1992. "Pressure Points: Environmental Degradation, Migration and Conflict." Paper presented at a conference organized by the American Academy of Arts and Sciences and the University of Toronto, Washington, D.C., 11–12 May.

Sukarno. 1970. "Storming the Last Bulwarks of Imperialism." In Herbert Feith and Lance Castles, eds., *Indonesian Political Thinking: 1945–1965*. Ithaca, N.Y.: Cornell University Press.

Sukhumbhand Paribatra. 1996. "Regional and Global Implications of an Asean 10." *Asean-ISIS Monitor* 13 (Mar.): 4–8.

Suksamran, Somboon. 1982. *Buddhism and Politics in Thailand*. Singapore: Institute of Southeast Asian Studies.

Sundaram, Jomo Kwame. 1989. "Malaysia's New Economic Policy and National Unity." *Third World Quarterly* 11, no. 4: 36–53.

———, ed. 1993. *Industrializing Malaysia: Policy, Performance, Prospects*. London: Routledge.

———, ed. 1995. *Privatizing Malaysia: Rents, Rhetoric, Realities*. Boulder, Colo.: Westview.

Sundarji, K. 1993. *The World Power Structure in Transition from a Quasi Unipolar to a Quasi Multipolar State and the Options of a Middle Power in This Milieu*. USI National Security Lecture. New Delhi: United Service Institution of India.

Sundhaussen, Ulf. 1982. *The Road to Power: Indonesian Military Politics 1945–1967*. Kuala Lumpur: Oxford University Press.

———.. 1995. "Indonesia's New Order: A Model for Myanmar?" *Asian Survey* 35, no. 8: 768–80.

Sung, Dixson D. S., and Lawrence C. Ho, eds. 1986. *Republic of China: A Reference Book*. Taipei: Hilit.

Suryadinata, Leo. 1985. *China and the ASEAN States: The Ethnic Chinese Dimension*. Singapore: Singapore University Press.

———. 1990. "Indonesia-China Relations: A Recent Breakthrough." *Asian Survey* 30, no. 7: 439–67.

Suryohadiprojo, Sayidiman. 1987. "Agresi Militer ke Indonesia?" *Teknologi dan Strategi Militer* 1: 20–29.

———. 1989. "HANKAM Tahun 2000." *Teknologi dan Strategi Militer* 26: 11–20.

Sutter, Robert G., and Shirley Kan. 1994. *China as a Security Concern in Asia: Perceptions, Assessments, and U.S. Options*. CRS Report 95-46s. Washington, D.C.: Library of Congress.

Swain, Ashok. 1993. "Conflict over Water: A Case Study of the Ganges Water." *Security Dialogue* 24, no. 4: 7–17.

Swaine, Michael D. 1996. "China." In Zalmay Khalilzad, ed., *Strategic Appraisal 1996*. Santa Monica, Calif.: Rand.

Swaminathan, M. S. 1993. *Genetic Diversity and the Indian Seed Industry.* RGICS Paper 4. New Delhi: Rajiv Gandhi Institute for Contemporary Studies, Rajiv Gandhi Foundation.

Syed, Anwar H. 1974. *China and Pakistan: Diplomacy of an Entente Cordiale.* Amherst: University of Massachusetts Press.

Taiwan Research Fund. 1989. *Guofang baipishu* (National defense white paper). Taipei: Taiwan yanjiu jijinhui.

Tambiah, S. J. 1992. *Buddhism Betrayed? Religion, Politics and Violence in Sri Lanka.* Chicago: University of Chicago Press.

Tamura, Hideo. 1996. "Business Leaders Reach Out to Mainland." *Nikkei Weekly* (Tokyo), Sept. 2, p. 19.

Tan, Edita S. 1988. "The Philippine Economy: Recovery and Prospects for High, Sustained Growth." In Mohammed Ayoob and Ng Chee Yuen, eds., *Southeast Asian Affairs 1988.* Singapore: Institute for Southeast Asian Studies.

Tan, S. K. 1977. *The Filipino Muslim Struggle 1900–1972.* Manila: Filipinas Foundation.

Tanaka, Akihiko. 1996. "1970-nendai no Anzenhosho-seisaku no Tenkan" (Transformation of security policy in the 1970s). *Gaiko Forum* 9, no. 7 (special edition): 80–95.

Tanham, George K. 1974. *Trial in Thailand.* New York: Crane Russak.

———. 1992. "Indian Strategic Culture." *Washington Quarterly* 15, no. 1: 129–42.

Task Force Detainees of the Philippines (TFDP). 1993. *Pumipiglas 3: Torment and Struggle After Marcos: A Report on Human Rights Trends in the Philippines Under Aquino, March 1986–June 1992.* Quezon City: TFDP.

Task Forces on Bangladesh Development Strategies for the 1990s. 1991. *Report of the Task Forces on Bangladesh Development Strategies for the 1990s.* 4 vols. Dhaka: University Press.

Tasker, Rodney. 1995. "A Line in the Sand." *Far Eastern Economic Review*, 6 Apr., pp. 14–15.

Tate, D. J. M. 1971. *The Making of Modern Southeast Asia.* London: Oxford University Press.

Tatmadaw Thar Thutaythi Tit Oo. 1990. *1948 Khu Hnit Hma 1988 Khu Hnit Atwin Hpyat Than Lar Thaw Myanma Thamaing Akyin Hnint Tatmadaw Ghanda* (A concise history of Myanmar and the role of the armed forces from 1948 to 1988). Vol. 1. Rangoon: News and Periodicals Enterprise.

Taylor, Michael, ed. 1988. *Rationality and Revolution.* Cambridge, Eng.: Cambridge University Press.

Taylor, Paul. 1991. "The Political Community and the State: Assumptions, Theories, and Propositions." *Review of International Studies* 17: 109–25.

Taylor, Robert H. 1982. "Perception of Ethnicity in the Politics of Burma." *Southeast Asian Journal of Social Science* 10, no. 1: 7–22.

———. 1983. "Burma's Foreign Relations Since the Third Indochina

Conflict." In *Southeast Asian Affairs 1983*, pp. 102–12. Singapore: Institute of Southeast Asian Studies.

———. 1987. *The State in Burma*. London: C. Hurst.

Taylor, William J., and Michael J. Mazarr. 1992. "U.S.–Korean Security Relations: Post-Reunification." *Korean Journal of Defense Analysis* 4, no. 1: 152–78.

Tellis, Ashley. 1995. "South Asia." In Zalmay Khalidzad, ed., *Strategic Appraisal 1995*. Santa Monica, Calif.: Rand.

Tempo. 1990. 30 June, pp. 22–31.

Thai Armed Forces in the Future. 1994. Bangkok: Strategic Research Institute.

Thailand 1997: Opportunity and Choices. 1994. Bangkok: Strategic Research Institute.

Thambipillai, Pushpa. 1991. "The ASEAN Growth Triangle: The Convergence of National and Sub-National Interests." *Contemporary Southeast Asia* 13, no. 3: 269–314.

Than, Tin Maung Maung. 1989. "Burma's National Security and Defence Posture." *Contemporary Southeast Asia* 11, no. 1: 40–60.

———. 1992. "Myanmar: At Odds with the New World Order." *ISEAS Trends*, Mar.

———. 1993. "Neither Inheritance nor Legacy: Leading the Myanmar State since Independence." *Contemporary Southeast Asia* 15, no. 1: 24–63.

———. 1994. "ASEAN's Ties with Myanmar Set to Move into New Phase." *Business Times*, 4 May.

Thayer, Carlyle A. 1994a. *Vietnam People's Army Under Doi Moi*. Singapore: Regional Strategic Studies Programme, Institute of Southeast Asian Studies.

———. 1994b. *Vietnam's Developing Military Ties with the Region: The Case for Defence Cooperation*. Canberra: Australian Defence Studies Centre.

Theeravit, Khein. 1993. *Crisis in Thai Politics: A Case of May Bloodshed 2535* (in Thai). Bangkok: Matichon Press.

Thomas, Caroline. 1987. *In Search of Security: The Third World in International Relations*. Boulder, Colo.: Lynne Rienner.

Thompson, Janice E., and Stephen Krasner. 1989. "Global Transactions and the Consolidation of Sovereignty." In Ernst-Otto Czempiel and James N. Rosenau, eds. *Global Changes and Theoretical Challenges: Approaches to World Politics in the 1990s*. Lexington, Mass.: Lexington Books.

Thompson, Mark R. 1995. *The Anti-Marcos Struggle: Personalistic Rule and the Democratic Transition in the Philippines*. New Haven: Yale University Press.

Thompson, W. Scott. 1992. *The Philippines in Crisis: Development and Security in the Aquino Era, 1986–1992*. New York: St. Martin's.

Thwin, Michael Aung. 1985. *Pagan: The Origins of Modern Burma*. Honolulu: University of Hawaii Press.

Tien, Hung-mao. 1989. *The Great Transition: Political and Social Change in the Republic of China*. Stanford: Hoover Institution.

Tiglao, Rigoberto. 1995. "Right-Hand Man." *Far Eastern Economic Review*, 2 Nov., pp. 25–28.

Tigno, Jorge V., and Renato S. Velasco. 1992. "Problems and Prospects for Stabilization and Popular Empowerment in the Post-Aquino Philippines." In Felipe B. Miranda, Temario C. Rivera, Emmanuel Lallana, and Jorge V. Tigno, "The Post-Aquino Philippines: In Search of Political Stability." Manuscript, Social Weather Stations, Inc., Quezon City.

Timberman, David. 1989. "Leadership Change and National Security in the Philippines." *Contemporary Southeast Asia* 11, no. 2: 186–212.

———. 1991. *A Changeless Land: Continuity and Change in Philippine Politics.* New York: M. E. Sharpe.

Times of India. 1993. "Text of India–China Agreements." 9 Sept.

Tinker, Hugh. 1990. *South Asia: A Short History.* Honolulu: University of Hawaii Press.

Tiwari, Chitra K. 1989. *Security in South Asia: Internal and External Dimensions.* New York: University Press of America.

Tongdhamachart, Kramol et al. 1983. *Thai Elites' Viewpoint Toward the National Security: Implication to the Southeast Asian Region.* Bangkok: Chulalongkorn University.

Torode, Greg. 1994. "Military Wins Budget Boost." *South China Morning Post,* 22 Oct.

Tow, William. 1991. "Reassessing Deterrence on the Korean Peninsula." *Korean Journal of Defense Analysis* 3, no. 1: 179–218.

Toynbee, Arnold J. 1957. *A Study of History.* London: Oxford University Press.

Tran Dinh Huynh. 1993. *Tim Hieu Tu Tuong Ho Chi Minh ve Xay Dung Dang* (Understanding Ho Chi Minh thought on building the party). Hanoi: Nha Xuat Ban Chinh Tri Quoc Gia.

Tran Trong. 1990. "Imperialists' Strategic Offensive Against Socialism." *Tap Chi Quoc Phong Toan Dan,* Apr. Translation in Foreign Broadcast Information Service, East Asian Service, FBIS-EAS-90-107 (4 June 1990).

Truong Mau. 1995. "Moving Toward Socialism Is an Objective Necessity." *Tap Chi Cong San,* Nov. 1994. Translation in Foreign Broadcast Information Service, East Asian Service, FBIS-EAS-95-022 (2 Feb. 1995).

Tsai Huilin. 1993. "Minjindang guoda dangtuan chuni liang'an guanxi zhengce" (DPP National Assembly caucus drafts cross-straits relations policy). *Independence Morning Post,* 22 Mar., p. 1.

Tsuchiyama, Jitsuo. 1993. "Alliance Dilemma to Nihon no Domei Gaiko" (Alliance dilemma and Japan's alliance diplomacy). *Leviathan* 13 (Fall): 50–75.

Turley, William S. 1988. "The Military Construction of Socialism: Postwar Roles of the People's Army of Vietnam." In David G. Marr and Christine P. White, eds. *Postwar Vietnam: Dilemmas in Socialist Development.* Ithaca, N.Y.: Southeast Asia Program, Cornell University.

————. 1989. "Vietnam's Strategy for Indochina and Security in Southeast Asia." In Young Whan Kihl and Lawrence E. Grinter, eds., *Security, Strategy, and Policy Responses in the Pacific Rim.* Boulder, Colo.: Lynn Rienner.

————. 1993. "Political Renovation in Vietnam: Renewal and Adaptation." In Borje Ljunggren, ed. *The Challenge of Reform in Indochina.* Cambridge, Mass.: Harvard University Press.

————. 1996. "Vietnamese Security in Domestic and Regional Focus: The Political-Economic Nexus." In Richard J. Ellings and Seldon W. Simon, eds., *Southeast Asian Security in the New Millenium.* Armonk, N.Y.: M. E. Sharpe.

Turner, Mark, ed. 1987. *Regime Change in the Philippines: The Legitimation of the Aquino Government.* Canberra: Australian National University.

————. 1995. "Terrorism and Secession in the Southern Philippines: The Rise of the Abu Sayaff." *Contemporary Southeast Asia* 17, no. 1: 1–19.

Turner, Mark, R. J. May, and L. R. Turner, eds. 1992. *Mindanao: Land of Unfulfilled Promise.* Quezon City: New Day.

Ullman, Richard H. 1983. "Redefining Security." *International Security* 8, no. 1: 129–53.

————. 1995. "Threats to Global Security: New Views or Old?" Seminar on Global Security Beyond 2000 at the University of Pittsburgh, 2–3 Nov.

United Daily News (Lianhe bao). 1987. "Xinde dalu zhengce, xinde shehui dongli" (New mainland policy, new social forces). 6 Sept., p. 2.

————. 1988. "Zhengfu shenshen guihua xinde dalu zhengce" (Government carefully plans new mainland policy). *United Daily News,* 2 Mar.

————. 1989. "Dalu ke xiangwang Taiwan fuyu" (Mainland visitors drawn to Taiwan's wealth). *United Daily News,* 13 Mar., p. 3.

United Nations. 1993. *Report of the Regional Meeting of the World Conference for Asia on Human Rights.* United Nations General Assembly A/CONF.157/ASRM.8, 7 Apr. New York: United Nations.

————. 1996. "Commission on Human Rights." Fifty-second Session, Agenda Item 10. E/CN.4/1996/L.91, 22 Apr.

United Nations Conference on Trade and Development (UNCTAD). 1995. *Handbook of International Trade and Development Statistics 1994.* Geneva: UNCTAD.

United Nations Development Program (UNDP). 1995. *Human Development Report.* New York: Oxford University Press, for UNDP.

U.S. Arms Control and Disarmament Agency. 1995. *World Military Expenditures and Arms Transfers 1993–1994.* Washington, D.C.: Government Printing Office.

U.S. Bureau of the Census. 1995. *Statistical Abstract of the United States: 1995.* 115th ed. Washington, D.C.: Government Printing Office.

U.S. Public Law 96-8. 1979. 96th Cong., 1st sess. *Taiwan Relations Act.* In *United States Code: Congressional and Administrative News.* St. Paul: West.

U.S. Senate, Committee on Foreign Relations. 1985. *Insurgency and Counterinsurgency in the Philippines.* Washington, D.C.: Government Printing Office.

Uyangoda, Jayadeva. 1989. "The Indo-Lanka Accord of July 1987 and the State in Sri Lanka." In Shelton U. Kodikara, ed., *Indo-Sri Lanka Agreement of July 1987.* Colombo: International Relations Program, University of Colombo.

Valencia, Mark J. 1991. *Malaysia and the Law of the Sea: The Foreign Policy Issues, the Options, and Their Implications.* Kuala Lumpur: ISIS Malaysia.

Van den Veer, Peter. 1994. *Religious Nationalism: Hindus and Muslims in India.* Berkeley: University of California Press.

Van der Kroef, Justus M. 1976. "Hanoi and ASEAN: A New Confrontation in Southeast Asia?" *Asia Quarterly* 4: 245–69.

———. 1988. "Day of the Vigilantes." *Asian Survey* 28, no. 6: 630–49.

Van Evera, Stephen. 1994. "Hypothesis on Nationalism and War." *International Security* 18, no. 4: 5–39.

Varshney, Ashutosh. 1993. "Contested Meanings: India's National Identity, Hindu Nationalism, and the Politics of Anxiety." *Daedalus* 122, no. 3: 227–62.

Vasavakul, Thaveeporn. 1995. "Vietnam: The Changing Models of Legitimation." In Muthiah Alagappa, ed., *Political Legitimacy in Southeast Asia.* Stanford: Stanford University Press.

Vatikiotis, Michael. 1993. *Indonesian Politics Under Suharto: Order, Development and Pressure for Change.* London: Routledge.

Vatikiotis, Michael, Murray Hiebert, Nigel Holloway, and Matt Forney. 1997. "Drawn to the Fray." *Far Eastern Economic Review,* 3 Apr., pp. 14–16.

Vatikiotis, Michael, Michael Westlake, and Lincoln Kaye. 1994. "Gunboat Diplomacy." *Far Eastern Economic Review,* 16 June, pp. 22–23, 26.

Vellinga, Pier, and Stephen P. Leatherman. 1989. "Sea Level Rise, Consequences and Policies." *Climatic Change* 15, nos. 1–2: 175–90.

Verdery, Katherine. 1993. "Whither 'Nation' and 'Nationalism'?" *Daedalus* 122, no. 3: 37–46.

Verghese, B. G. 1990. *Waters of Hope: Himalaya Ganga Development and Cooperation for a Billion People.* New Delhi: Oxford University Press.

Vertzberger, Yaacov. 1990. *The World in Their Minds: Information Processing, Cognition, and Perception in Foreign Policy Making.* Stanford: Stanford University Press.

Vietnam News Agency. 1993. 5 Apr. Translation in Foreign Broadcast Information Service, East Asian Service, FBIS-EAS-93-074 (20 Apr. 1993).

Villacorta, Wilfrido V. 1994. "The Curse of the Weak State: Leadership Imperatives for the Ramos Government." *Contemporary Southeast Asia* 16, no. 1: 67–92.

Villanueva, A. B. 1992. "The State of Philippine Politics and Democracy During the Aquino Regime." *Contemporary Southeast Asia* 14, no. 2: 174–87.

Villegas, Bernardo M. 1991. "The Philippine Economy: 1992 and Beyond." In Sharon Siddique and Ng Chee Yuen, eds., *Southeast Asian Affairs 1991*. Singapore: Institute of Southeast Asian Studies.

Vo Nhan Tri. 1988. "Vietnam: The Combination of Economic Construction with National Defence." In J. Soedjati Djiwandono and Yong Mun Cheong, eds., *Soldiers and Stability in Southeast Asia*. Singapore: Regional Strategic Studies Programme, Institute of Southeast Asian Studies.

Voice of Free China (Taipei). 1991. "Premier Hao Says Stability Essential for Security." In *FBIS Daily Report: China*, 20 Nov., p. 71.

Voice of Vietnam. 1993. Translation in Foreign Broadcast Information Service, East Asian Service, FBIS-EAS-93-187 (29 Sept. 1993).

———. 1994. Translation in Foreign Broadcast Information Service, East Asian Service, FBIS-EAS-94-177 (13 Sept. 1994).

Von Hippel, David, and Peter Hayes. 1995. "DPRK Energy Efficiency Options: Preliminary Findings." Paper presented at the annual DPRK Economy Conference, University of California at San Diego, May.

Von Vorys, Karl. 1976. *Democracy Without Consensus*. Kuala Lumpur: Oxford University Press.

Vu Oanh. 1994. "Job Creation: A Fundamental and Urgent Task of Mass Mobilization Work." *Nhan Dan*, 9 May. Translation in Foreign Broadcast Information Service, East Asian Service, FBIS-EAS-94-097 (19 May 1994).

Wade, Robert. 1990. *Governed Market*. Princeton: Princeton University Press.

Waever, Ole. 1995. "Securitization and Desecuritization." In Ronnie D. Lipschultz, ed., *On Security*. New York: Columbia University Press.

Waever, Ole, Barry Buzan, Morten Kelstrup, and Pierre Lemaitre. 1993. *Identity, Migration, and the New Security Agenda in Europe*. New York: St. Martin's.

Walker, R. B. J. 1990. "Security, Sovereignty, and the Challenge of World Politics." *Alternatives* 15: 3–27.

Walt, Stephen M. 1985. "Alliance Formation and the Balance of World Power." *International Security* 9, no. 4: 3–43.

———. 1987. *The Origins of Alliances*. Ithaca, N.Y.: Cornell University Press.

———. 1991. "The Renaissance of Security Studies." *International Studies Quarterly* 35, no. 2: 211–39.

———. 1992. "Revolution and War." *World Politics* 44, no. 3: 321–68.

Waltz, Kenneth N. 1959. *Man, the State and War: A Theoretical Analysis*. New York: Columbia University Press.

———. 1979. *Theory of International Politics*. New York: Random House.

———. 1981. "The Central Balance and Security in Northeast Asia." Paper presented at the First Wharangdae International Symposium of the Korea Military Academy, Seoul, Sept.

———. 1986. "Reflections on *Theory of International Politics*: A Response to My Critics." In Robert Keohane, ed., *Neorealism and Its Critics*. New York: Columbia University Press.

———. 1990. "Nuclear Myths and Political Realities." *American Political Science Review* 84, no. 3: 731–45.

———. 1993. "The Emerging Structure of International Politics." *International Security* 18, no. 2: 44–79.

Wang Gungwu. 1968. "Early Ming Relations with Southeast Asia: A Background Essay." In John K. Fairbank, ed., *The Chinese World Order: Traditional China's Foreign Relations*. Cambridge, Mass.: Harvard University Press.

Warnapala, W. A. Wiswa. 1994. *Ethnic Strife and Politics in Sri Lanka: An Investigation into Demands and Responses*. New Delhi: Navrang.

Weinbaum, Marvin G. 1991. "Pakistan and Afghanistan: The Strategic Relationship." *Asian Survey* 31, no. 6: 496–511.

Weiner, Myron. 1995. "Security, Stability and International Migration." In Sean M. Lynn-Jones and Steven E. Miller, eds. *Global Dangers: Changing Dimensions of International Security*. Cambridge, Mass.: MIT Press.

Weller, Marc, ed. 1993. *Democracy and Politics in Burma: A Collection of Documents*. Manerplaw: National Coalition Government of the Union of Burma.

Wendt, Alexander. 1987. "The Agent-Structure Problem in International Relations Theory." *International Organization* 41, no. 3: 335–70.

———. 1992. "Anarchy Is What States Make of It: The Social Construction of Power Politics." *International Organization* 46, no. 2: 391–425.

———. 1995. "Constructing International Politics." *International Security* 20, no. 1: 71–81.

Wendt, Alexander, and Daniel Friedheim. 1995. "Hierarchy Under Anarchy: Informal Empire and the East German State." *International Organization* 49, no. 4: 689–722.

Werake, Mahinda, and P. V. J. Jayasekera. 1995. *Security Dilemma of a Small State*. Part 2, *Internal Crisis and External Intervention in Sri Lanka*. Kandy: Institute for International Studies.

Westing, Arthur H. 1989. "The Environmental Component of Comprehensive Security." *Bulletin of Peace Proposals* 20, no. 2: 129–34.

White House. 1995. *A National Security Strategy of Engagement and Enlargement*. Washington, D.C.: The White House.

Wiant, Jon. 1981. "Tradition in the Service of Revolution: The Political Symbolism of Taw-hlan-ye-khit." In F. K. Lehman, ed., *Military Rule in Burma Since 1962*. Singapore: Maruzen / Institute of Southeast Asian Studies.

Wickramasinghe, Nira. 1995. *Ethnic Politics in Colonial Sri Lanka*. New Delhi: Vikas.

Wight, Martin. 1991. *International Theory: The Three Traditions*. Leicester: Leicester University Press.

Wight, Martin. 1995. *Power Politics*. Leicester: Leicester University Press.

Wilcox, Wayne. 1972. "The U.S. and Asia." In Wayne Wilcox, Leo E. Rose, and Gavin Boyd, eds., *Asia and the International System*. Cambridge, Mass.: Winthrop.

Wilson, A. J. 1979. *Politics in Sri Lanka, 1947–1979*. 2d ed. London: Macmillan.

Wilson, David. 1962. "The Military in Thai Politics." In John Johnson, ed., *The Role of the Military in Underdeveloped Countries*. Princeton: Princeton University Press.

Wilson, Dick. 1994. *The Asian Security Management Challenge: A Future "Trinity" of China, Japan and India*. RGICS Paper 10. New Delhi: Rajiv Gandhi Institute for Contemporary Studies, Rajiv Gandhi Foundation.

Winichakul, Thongchai. 1994. *Siam Mapped: A History of the Geo-body of a Nation*. Honolulu: University of Hawaii Press.

Wolfers, Arnold. 1962a. *Discord and Collaboration*. Baltimore: Johns Hopkins University Press.

———. 1962b. "The Goals of Foreign Policy." In Arnold Wolfers, ed., *Discord and Collaboration*. Baltimore: Johns Hopkins University Press.

———. 1962c. "National Security as an Ambiguous Symbol." In Arnold Wolfers, ed., *Discord and Collaboration*. Baltimore: Johns Hopkins University Press.

Womack, Brantly. 1994. "Sino-Vietnamese Border Trade: The Edge of Normalization." *Asian Survey* 34, no. 6: 495–512.

Wong, Kan Seng. 1988. "Continuity and Change in Singapore's Foreign Policy." Text of a speech delivered to the Singapore Press Club, Singapore.

Wood, Perry L., and Jimmy W. Wheeler. 1990. *ASEAN in the 1990s: New Challenges, New Directions*. Indianapolis, Ind.: Hudson Institute.

Woodman, Dorothy. 1969. *Himalayan Frontiers: A Political Review of British, Chinese, Indian, and Russian Rivalries*. New York: Praeger.

Woodside, Alexander. 1976. *Community and Revolution in Modern Vietnam*. Boston: Houghton Mifflin.

World Bank. 1972. "The Economy of the Union of Burma." SA-34, South Asia Regional Office, Washington, D.C., Nov. 10.

———. 1989. *Sub-Saharan Africa: From Crisis to Sustainable Growth*. Washington, D.C.: World Bank.

———. 1996. *World Tables 1995*. Washington, D.C.: World Bank.

World Development Report 1991: The Challenge of Development. 1991. Oxford: Oxford University Press.

World Trade Organization (WTO). 1996. *International Trade: Trends and Statistics 1995*. Geneva: WTO Economic Research and Analysis Division and Statistics and Information Systems Division.

Worster, Donald. 1977. *Nature's Economy: A History of Ecological Ideas*. New York: Cambridge University Press.

Wright, Joseph J., Jr. 1991. *The Balancing Act: A History of Modern Thailand*. Oakland: Pacific Rim Press.

Wright, Quincy. 1964. *A Study of War*. Chicago: University of Chicago Press.

Wrong, Denis H. 1979. *Power: Its Form, Bases and Uses*. New York: Harper and Row.

Wurfel, David. 1988. *Filipino Politics: Development and Decay*. Quezon City: Ateneo de Manila University.

Xinhua News Agency. 1995. "Zai Jinian Kangzhan Shengli Zhujing Budui Laozhanshi Zuotanhui Shang Jiang Zemin Tongzhi De Jianghua" (Speech made by Comrade Jiang Zemin at the symposium commemorating the fiftieth anniversary of the triumph of the Anti-Japanese War), 25 Aug., Beijing.

Xu Yan. 1991. *Mao Zedong Junshi Sixiang Fazhan Shi* (A history of the development of Mao Zedong's military thoughts). Beijing: PLA Press.

Xuan Hai and Dang Ngoc Chien. 1994. "Strikes at a Number of Joint Ventures with Foreign Countries." *Tap Chi Cong San*, May. Translation in Foreign Broadcast Information Service, East Asian Service, FBIS-EAS-94-151 (5 Aug. 1994).

Xuan Yem. 1994. "Maintaining Secure Information Under the Situation of an Open-Door Economy." *Quan Doi Nhan Dan*, 25 Nov. Translation in Foreign Broadcast Information Service, East Asian Service, FBIS-EAS-94-244 (20 Dec. 1994).

Xue Mouhong and Pei Jianzhang, eds. 1988. *Dangdai Zhongguo Waijiao (Contemporary Chinese Diplomacy)*. Beijing: Chinese Social Science Publishing House.

Yan Xuetong. 1993. "China's Security After the Cold War." *Contemporary International Relations* 3, no. 5: 1–16.

Yang, Jae-in, ed. 1990. *Chuch'ae Sasang: Pukhan-ui Chongch'i Chu-ui* (Juche thoughts: the political ideology of North Korea). Seoul: Jyungam University Press.

Yang, Lien-Shang. 1968. "Historical Notes on the Chinese World Order." In John K. Fairbank, ed., *The Chinese World Order: Traditional China's Foreign Relations*. Cambridge, Mass.: Harvard University Press.

Yang Li-yu. 1987. "Minzhuhua yu bentuhua suo dailaide wenti" (Problems brought by democratization and nativization). *United Daily News (Lianhe bao)*, 30 Sept., p. 2.

———. 1990. "Liang'an guanxi de zhanwang" (The outlook for cross-straits relations). *United Daily News*, 22 June, p. 6.

Yang Sheng-ru. 1994. "Zhonggong shoumai Tai shang 'houshe'"

(Communists buying "voices" of Taiwanese businesspeople). *Liberty Times (Ziyou shibao)*, 12 Oct., p. 4.

Yang Wei-chieh. 1988. "Siyue, dao Manila; mingnian, dao Beijing ma?" (In April, to Manila; next year, to Beijing?) *Journalist*, 11–17 Apr., pp. 69–71.

Yasuaki, Onuma. 1996. *In Quest of Intercivilizational Human Rights*. Center for Asian Pacific Affairs occasional paper 2. San Francisco: Asia Foundation.

Yasutomo, Dennis T. 1986. *The Manner of Giving: Strategic Aid and Japanese Foreign Policy*. Lexington, Mass.: Lexington Books.

Yaungwe, Chao Tzang. 1987. *The Shan of Burma: Memoirs of a Shan Exile*. Singapore: Institute of Southeast Asian Studies.

————. 1990. "Ne Win's Tatmadaw Dictatorship." Master's thesis, University of British Columbia.

Yawnghwe, Chao-Tzang. 1995. "Burma: The Depoliticization of the Political." In Muthiah Alagappa, ed., *Political Legitimacy in Southeast Asia*. Stanford: Stanford University Press.

Ye Jianying. 1981. "Jianyi juxing liangdang duideng tanpan shixing disanci hezuo" (Propose holding negotiations on an equal footing between the two parties and implementing a third united front). *People's Daily (Renmin ribao)*, 1 Oct., p. 1.

Yearbook of International Organization 1986–87. 1986. 4th ed. Vol. 2. Brussels: Union of International Association.

Yeo, Ning Hong. 1994. "SAF Day Message 1994." Text of a speech delivered to the Singapore Armed Forces, Singapore.

Yin Nai-ching. 1990. "Ruguo zhonggong yao he wo you bangjiao guo jianjiao, wo jiang buhui caiqu tuichu huo duanjiao lichang" (If the Communists establish relations with a country having diplomatic relations with us, we will not adopt a stance of withdrawing or breaking off relations). *China Times (Zhongguo shibao)*, 22 Jan., p. 1.

Yomiuri Shinbun. 1994. "A Proposal for the Revision of the Text of the Constitution of Japan." 3 Nov.

Yoon, Dae-Kye. 1990. *Law and Political Authority in South Korea*. Boulder, Colo.: Westview.

Youngblood, Robert L. 1990. *Marcos Against the Church: Economic Development and Political Repression in the Philippines*. Ithaca, N.Y.: Cornell University Press.

Yu, Suk Ryul. 1982. "Political Succession in North Korea." *Korea and World Affairs* 6, no. 4: 34–57.

Yusufzai, Rahimullah. 1989. "The Frontier Connection." *Newsline*, Oct.

————. 1996. "Rise and Fall of the TNSM." *News*, 27 Jan.

Zagoria, Donald S. 1962. *The Sino-Soviet Conflict, 1956–1961*. Princeton: Princeton University Press.

————. 1988. "The Sino-Soviet Conflict." In Muthiah Alagappa, ed., *In Search of Peace: Confidence Building and Conflict Reduction in the Pacific*. Kuala Lumpur: ISIS Malaysia.

Zaidi, Mazhar, and Behroz Khan. 1994. "Holy Law." *Newsline*, May.

Zaidi, S. Akbar. 1989. "Regional Imbalances and National Questions in Pakistan." *Economic and Political Weekly*, 11 Feb.

Zainah Anwar. 1987. *Islamic Revivalism in Malaysia: Dakwah Among the Students*. Petaling Jaya: Pelanduk.

Zhou Enlai. 1990. *Zhou Enlai Waijiao Wenxuan* (Selected diplomatic works of Zhou Enlai). Beijing: Central Document Press.

Zhu, Hongqian. 1989. "China and the Triangular Relationship." In Yufan Hao and Guocang Huan, eds., *The Chinese View of the World*. New York: Pantheon.

Zhuang Jinfeng, ed. 1991. *Haixia liang'an minjian jiaoliu zhengce yu falu* (Nongovernmental cross-straits exchange policies and laws). Shanghai: Shanghai shehui kexue chubanshe.

Zia, Amir. 1996. "Crushing Burden." *Newsline*, June.

Ziring, Lawrence. 1988. "Public Policy Dilemmas and Pakistan's Nationality Problem: The Legacy of Zia." *Asian Survey* 28, no. 8: 795–812.

Zulfikar, Shahzada. 1993. "The Ethnic Factor." *Newsline*, Sept.

———. 1994a. "Contentious Count." *Newsline*, Oct.

———. 1994b. "Rout of the Warlords." *Newsline*, Nov.

Zulliger, Ernest. 1993. "The Malaysia Incorporated Concept: A Key Strategy in Achieving Vision 2020." In Ahmad Sarji Abdul Hamid, ed., *Malaysia's Vision 2020: Understanding the Concept, Implications, and Challenges*. Petaling Jaya: Pelanduk.

Zysman, John. 1991. "U.S. Power, Trade and Technology." *International Affairs* 67, no. 1: 81–106.

Index

In this index an "f" after a number indicates a separate reference on the next page, and an "ff" indicates separate references on the next two pages. A continuous discussion over two or more pages is indicated by a span of page numbers, e.g., "57–59."

Library of Congress Cataloging-in-Publication Data

Asian security practice : material and ideational influences / edited
   by Muthiah Alagappa.
       p. cm.
     ISBN 0-8047-3347-3 (cloth)
     ISBN 0-8047-3348-1 (paperback)
     1. National security--Asia.   I. Alagappa, Muthiah.
   UA830.A856 1998
   355'.03305--dc21   98-16563

⊗ This book is printed on acid-free paper.

Original printing 1998
Last figure below indicates year of this printing:

06   05   04   03   02   01   00   99   98